SHAPING THE POLITICAL ARENA

SHAPING THE POLITICAL ARENA

CRITICAL JUNCTURES, THE LABOR MOVEMENT, AND REGIME DYNAMICS IN LATIN AMERICA

Ruth Berins Collier and David Collier

PRINCETON UNIVERSITY PRESS   PRINCETON, NEW JERSEY

Library of Congress Cataloging-in-Publication Data

Collier, Ruth Berins.
Shaping the political arena : critical junctures, the labor
movement, and regime dynamics in Latin America / Ruth Berins Collier
and David Collier.
p.   cm.
Includes bibliographical references and index.
ISBN 0-691-07830-0 (cl)—ISBN 0-691-02313-1 (pb)
1. Labor movement—Latin America—History—20th century. 2. Latin
America—Politics and government—20th century. I. Collier, David,
1942– . II. Title.
HD8110.5.C65   1991
322'.2'098—dc20   90-21095
                                                              CIP

Publication of this book has been aided by a grant from
the Publications Program of the National Endowment
for the Humanities, an independent Federal agency

This book has been composed in Linotron Trump

Princeton University Press books are printed
on acid-free paper, and meet the guidelines
for permanence and durability of the Committee
on Production Guidelines for Book Longevity
of the Council on Library Resources

Printed in the United States of America by
Princeton University Press, Princeton, New Jersey

10 9 8 7 6 5 4 3 2 1
(Pbk.)
10 9 8 7 6 5 4 3 2 1

For Stephen, Jennifer, and Shep

Contents

Figures and Tables ————————————————————————

Figures

Tables

Acknowledgments

FIRST and foremost, we wish to give full recognition to the contribution of Ronald P. Archer and James W. McGuire. Their work on this project, which began with their role as research assistants, expanded to a form of collaboration that makes them coauthors of portions of the book. Specifically, Archer is coauthor of the analysis of Colombia and Uruguay in Chapters 5, 6, and 7, as well as portions of the analysis of Venezuela in Chapter 6. McGuire is coauthor of the analysis of Argentina in Chapters 5, 6, and 7. McGuire also provided invaluable assistance in the analysis of Uruguay. We deeply appreciate their analytic skill and hard work, and we greatly enjoyed collaborating with both of them.

A number of other Berkeley students worked as skilled research assistants or provided extensive comments on earlier drafts: Judith Biewener, Maxwell A. Cameron, Maria Lorena Cook, Peter Houtzager, Wendy Hunter, Ollie Johnson, Peter Kingstone, James Mahon, Carol Ann Medlin, Peter Molloy, Deborah L. Norden, Tony Pickering, Timothy R. Scully, Jeffrey Sluyter, Deborah J. Yashar, and Florence Zolin. Our Peruvian colleague Francisco Durand and also Cynthia Sanborn provided exceptionally skilled assistance.

This project was initiated under a grant from the National Science Foundation (SES 8017728), and the publication of the book has been supported by a grant to Princeton University Press from the National Endowment for the Humanities. Generous support for research assistance and other project expenses was provided by the Institute of Industrial Relations, the Institute of International Studies, the Department of Political Science, and the Center for Latin American Studies at Berkeley. Ruth Collier received support from a fellowship awarded by the Joint Committee on Latin American Studies of SSRC/ACLS, from the Berkeley Department of Political Science, and from the Berkeley Program in Mexican Studies. David Collier was supported by an award from the Latin American Committee of SSRC/ACLS, the Institute for the Study of World Politics, the National Fellows Program of the Hoover Institution, and the Faculty Fellows Program of the Kellogg Institute at the University of Notre Dame.

We acknowledge publishers' permission to draw material from the following two articles: Ruth Berins Collier and David Collier, "Inducements versus Constraints: Disaggregating 'Corporatism,' " *The American Political Science Review* 73, no. 4 (December 1979), pp. 967–86; and Ruth Berins Collier, "Popular Sector Incorporation and Political Supremacy: Regime Evolution in Brazil and Mexico," in Sylvia Ann Hewlett and Richard S. Weinert, eds., *Brazil and Mexico: Patterns in Late Development* (Philadelphia: Institute for the Study of Human Issues, 1982).

As we complete a project of this scope, we recognize with gratitude the role played by colleagues who provide that special combination of astute criticism, intellectual support, and sustained friendship. We especially single out John Coatsworth, Robert R. Kaufman, Guillermo O'Donnell, and John Wirth, who gave detailed and helpful comments on the manuscript. We also want to make special mention of Louis W. Goodman, Terry Karl, Philippe C. Schmitter, and Alfred Stepan. Alex M. Saragoza, in his role as Mexicanist, as chair of the Berkeley Center for Latin American Studies, and as friend, offered invaluable insight and encouragement.

Margaret Case, Sanford Thatcher, David Nelson Blair, and other colleagues associated with Princeton University Press provided outstanding assistance with the preparation of the manuscript. Greer and Sue Allen gave timely advice on such esoterica as ascenders and x-heights.

Institutional assistance, as well, occasionally goes far beyond the ordinary. Ruth Collier greatly appreciates the ongoing support of the Berkeley Institute of International Studies and of its staff, which provided an eminently hospitable setting for her work. She wishes especially to acknowledge the professional and personal generosity of the Institute's recent director, Carl G. Rosberg. David Collier's work was greatly aided by his opportunity to spend time in the remarkable environment for research and scholarly debate provided by the Helen Kellogg Institute for International Studies at the University of Notre Dame. The Institute's founding directors, Guillermo O'Donnell and Ernest Bartell deserve abundant credit for creating this outstanding research center.

Over a number of years, in response both to seminar presentations and written drafts, many other colleagues provided helpful suggestions that aided us in revising the book, and we can acknowledge only some of them here: Robert Alexander, Marcelo Cavarozzi, Marc Chernick, Julio Cotler, Tom Davis, Charles Davis, Henry Dietz, Albert Fishlow, John D. French, Gary Gereffi, Manuel Antonio Garretón, Paulette Higgins, Joel Horowitz, Friedrich Kratochwil, Eugenio Kvaternik, David Leonard, Jennifer McCoy, Michael McIntyre, Alejandro Portes, Juan Rial, Luis Salamanca, Peter H. Smith, J. Samuel Valenzuela, Aaron Wildavsky, Harold Wilensky, and Carlos Zubillaga.

We also recall the stimulating experience of writing this book at Berkeley while Gregory M. Luebbert was completing parallel research on Western Europe. We greatly valued our interaction with him over the two projects, along with the opportunity to work with graduate students who were intellectually engaged with the issues raised by both studies. His tragic death in a boating accident in May 1988 was an extraordinary loss.

Esther and Maurice Berins and Donald Collier were a source of encouragement throughout this project, and Malcolm Collier's insight and enthusiasm remain very much with us. Maurice Berins would have loved to see this book in print after the support he gave us in this endeavor, as in all aspects of our lives. Only our affectionate memories begin to ease our deep sense of loss.

Finally, our deepest gratitude goes to our children, Jennifer and Stephen, to whom this book is lovingly dedicated. They, unfortunately, had to live with the book as long as we did, and we regret that imposition. Their occasional prodding was as helpful and appreciated as their nearly constant patience.

SHAPING THE POLITICAL ARENA

Overview

IN THE COURSE of capitalist development in Latin America, one of the fundamental political transitions has been the emergence of worker protest and an organized labor movement, along with the varied responses of the state to this new actor within society. During a relatively well-defined period in most countries, a historic change took place in the relationship between the state and the working class. An earlier pattern—in which repression was generally a far more central feature of the state response to worker organization and protest—gave way to state policies that launched the "initial incorporation" of the labor movement. State control of the working class ceased to be principally the responsibility of the police or the army but rather was achieved at least in part through the legalization and institutionalization of a labor movement sanctioned and regulated by the state. In addition, actors within the state began to explore far more extensively the possibility of mobilizing workers as a major political constituency.

The terms on which the labor movement was initially incorporated differed greatly within Latin America. In some countries the policies of the incorporation period aimed primarily at establishing new mechanisms of state control. In other cases the concern with control was combined with a major effort to cultivate labor support, encompassing a central role of a political party—or a political movement that later became a party—and sometimes producing dramatic episodes of worker mobilization. The alternative strategies of control and mobilization produced contrasting reactions and counterreactions, generating different modes of conflict and accommodation that laid the foundation for contrasting political legacies.

The analysis of these distinct patterns of conflict and accommodation offers new insight into important contrasts among countries such as: whether a cohesive, integrative political center was formed or more polarized politics emerged; whether and how party systems came to channel social conflict; and, more specifically, why in some countries the electoral and trade-union arenas came to be dominated by parties of the center, whereas elsewhere parties of the left came to play a far greater role. The analysis sheds light on alternative patterns of sectoral and class coalitions, distinct modes of centrifugal and centripetal political competition, and contrasting patterns of stability and conflict. It also helps explain whether countries followed a democratic or authoritarian path through the period of new opposition movements and economic and political crisis of the 1960s and 1970s.

The emergence of different forms of control and mobilization during the initial incorporation periods, along with their varied legacies, is the focus of this book. The study is based on a comparative-historical analysis of the eight countries with the longest history of urban commercial and industrial development in the region: Argentina, Brazil, Chile, Colombia, Mexico, Peru, Uruguay, and Venezuela.

It bears emphasis that single-country monographs and historical studies focused on each of these eight countries have commonly asserted that the years we identify as the initial incorporation periods were historical watersheds that had a major impact on the subsequent evolution of politics.[1] Yet these analyses, focusing as they do on individual countries, not surprisingly have lacked consistent criteria for identifying and comparing the incorporation periods, as well as for carrying out a comparative assessment of their legacies. The goal of this book is to provide a framework for this comparison and to offer a methodological and analytic basis for assessing the causal impact of the incorporation periods on the national political regime.

In focusing on the state's role in shaping the labor movement and on the reactions and counterreactions at the level of national politics produced by these state initiatives, we do not intend to suggest that workers and labor leaders did not themselves play a major role in constituting labor movements. Their role has been amply documented,[2] and at various points it plays an important part in the present analysis.[3] However, our primary attention centers at a different level: the repercussions for the larger evolution of national politics of alternative state strategies for dealing with the labor movement. At this level of analysis, one can identify fundamentally contrasting trajectories of change that merit sustained attention in their own right.

In that the book seeks to trace out these contrasting trajectories of national political change, we see this study as part of the ongoing quest in the Latin American field over the past 30 years to explain the different paths of national development found within the region.[4] In this context, our analysis is

[1] For example, Argentina: Corradi 1985:58; Doyon 1975:153; Mallon and Sourrouille 1975:7; Horowitz 1990; Wynia 1978:43–44, 80; Luna 1969:15; Fayt, quoted in Ciría 1968:326; Waisman 1987; Torre 1989:530. Brazil: Schmitter 1971:127; Mericle 1977:304; Erickson 1977:11; Ianni 1970:89; Simão 1981:169. Chile: Morris 1966:2; Barría 1972:37–38; S. Valenzuela 1976:141; Bergquist 1981:45–46; 1986:75; Pike 1963:188. Colombia: Urrutia 1969a:109, 113; Dix 1967:91; Molina 1974:280; 1977:85, 101. Mexico: Hansen 1974:34, 98–101; Garrido 1982:11, 296; Córdova 1974; 1976:204, 211; 1979:9–11; Cornelius 1973:392–93. Peru: Sulmont 1977:82; Pareja 1980:115; Angell 1980:21; Adams 1984:36–37; and from a comparative perspective C. Anderson 1967:249. Uruguay: Finch 1981:9; Vanger 1963:272, 274; 1980:348; Caetano 1983a:5; Fitzgibbon 1954:122. Venezuela: Levine 1973:29; Alexander 1982:224; Martz 1966:62; Godio 1982:30, 85; and from a comparative perspective, C. Anderson 1967:283–84.

[2] At the level of a broad comparative-historical analysis, see Bergquist (1986). Many excellent monographic studies also adopt this perspective.

[3] Chapter 3 focuses on the early history of the labor movement from the perspective of worker organization and worker protest. In the analysis of the incorporation periods in Chapter 4, the discussion of the goals of actors within the state who initiate incorporation—the "project from above"—is juxtaposed with a discussion of the goals of the leading sectors of the labor movement, the "project from below."

[4] A partial list of relevant authors and citations dealing with the comparative analysis of South America and Mexico that address these themes might include J. Johnson (1958), Silvert and Germani (1961), Hirschman (1965, 1977, 1979), Di Tella (1965, 1968), C. Anderson (1967), Halperín Donghi (1969), Cardoso and Faletto (1969, 1979), Schmitter (1972),

both narrow and broad. It is narrow in that it focuses on critical transitions in the relationship between the state and one particular actor in society, the organized labor movement. Yet it is broad in that this focus serves as an optic through which a much larger spectrum of political relationships and patterns of change can be integrated into an explanatory framework. The analysis is likewise broad because it is framed by scholarly debates on democracy and authoritarianism, corporatism, patterns of state transformation in the face of new social forces, the formation of distinct types of party systems, and the relative autonomy of politics.

Obviously, the issues considered here are not unique to Latin America. They are, for instance, the focus of a broad spectrum of authors concerned with European development, from Karl Marx to T. H. Marshall and Reinhard Bendix, who have analyzed these themes within the context of what Bendix (1964:23) refers to as the "pervasive, structural transformations" of Western societies that encompassed in the economic sphere the spread of market relationships and in the political sphere the spread of individualistic authority relationships. Crucial to the latter was the extension of citizenship to the lower class, involving the right of "association" and "combination" and the diverse ways in which worker organization, worker protest, and state policy toward worker associations interacted to shape the evolution of national politics (Bendix 1964·chap. 3, esp. 80 87). The present study parallels the concerns of various analysts of Europe who have viewed the incorporation of the working class as a pivotal transition within this larger process of societal change.[5]

The method of this book is a type of comparative history designed to discover and assess explanations of change. The method has two components. The first is the generation and evaluation of hypotheses through the examination of similarities and contrasts among countries. The second is the procedure of "process tracing"[6] over time within countries, through which explanations are further probed. We thereby evaluate whether the dynamics of change within each country plausibly reflect the same causal pattern suggested by the comparison among countries. The result is an analysis centrally concerned with the elaboration of concepts and comparisons, but also shaped by the conviction that this elaboration must be anchored in a close, processual analysis of cases over long periods of time. The book thus presents an extended examination of each case over several decades, and we hope that for readers who lack a close knowledge of these countries, this historical presentation will make our argument clear. However, we do not intend this as

O'Donnell (1973, 1975), Bambirra (1974), R. Kaufman (1977a, 1977b, 1979, 1986), Stepan (1978b, 1988), D. Collier (1979), Therborn (1979), O'Donnell, Schmitter, and Whitehead (1986), and Bergquist (1986).

[5] Lipset and Rokkan 1967; Waisman 1982; Lipset 1983; Luebbert 1986, 1987; J. Stephens 1986.

[6] The procedure was proposed by George and McKeown (1985:34ff.). It is similar to the procedure of "discerning" earlier advocated by Barton and Lazarsfeld (1969) and of "pattern matching" advocated by Campbell (1975).

a general political history of these countries—nor even of the labor movement or of state-labor relations. Rather, the historical treatment is selective,
focused on probing arguments related to our principal thesis about the emergence and impact of the incorporation periods.

The Historical Argument

In the first decades of the 20th century, the relationship between the state
and the labor movement changed fundamentally. Prior to that time, state
policy commonly involved extensive repression of working class organization and protest, repression that on many occasions resulted in the death of
dozens or even hundreds of workers. This earlier era saw occasional ad hoc
state cooperation with labor groups in sectors too important economically or
politically to permit their continual repression, as well as occasional state
efforts to mobilize the support of workers. Nonetheless, the labor movement
was dealt with in important measure coercively—by the police or the army.

During a well-defined period in each country, this relationship was altered.
In general, some use of repression continued, but control was to a greater
degree accomplished through the legalization and institutionalization of certain types of labor organization. Unions became legitimate actors within
these societies. In conjunction with the unions' more legitimate role, political leaders also began to pursue far more extensively than before the option
of mobilizing workers as a base of political support.

This change to new modes of state-labor relations—from repression to institutionalization, from exclusion to incorporation—generally took place in
the context of a larger set of political transformations also occurring in the
early decades of this century. These included a decline in the political dominance of older oligarchic groups and the assumption of power by newer
elites drawn in part from the "middle sectors,"[7] whose social, economic, and
political importance was increasing rapidly with the sustained economic expansion and the growing importance of the urban commercial and manufacturing sector during this period. Reformist elements that emerged from the
more traditional elite also played a significant role in this period of change.
The new political leadership promoted a transition from a laissez-faire state
to a more interventionist state, a change signaled by the promulgation of new
"social constitutions." The state came increasingly to assume new social,
welfare, and economic responsibilities involving above all the modern sector
of the economy, but in a few cases also encompassing a restructuring of work
and property relations within the traditional rural sector.

The incorporation of the labor movement was typically high on this
agenda of change, though its timing varied among countries. In conjunction
with the new social and welfare responsibilities, the state introduced new
legislation regulating such things as working conditions, minimum wage,

[7] See discussion of this term in the glossary.

and social security. With the new economic responsibilities, the state began to establish a regularized system of labor relations, assuming a role as mediator of class conflict and arbiter of labor-management disputes. Actors within the state established regularized, legal channels of labor relations and made some concessions to correct the worst abuses of the working class, thereby seeking to take the labor question out of the streets and away from the police or army and bring it into the realm of law by providing mechanisms for the peaceful settlement of labor disputes. The goal, in the terms in which it was commonly conceived, was to "harmonize the interests of labor and capital." These changes were accompanied by the introduction of corporatism as a new set of structures for the vertical integration of society. Corporatism in Latin America thus involved the legalization and institutionalization of an organized labor movement, but one that was shaped and controlled by the state.

This, then, is the historical commonality of these countries. In the course of capitalist modernization, two broad new sectors produced by modernization, the working class and the middle sectors, began to be integrated into the polity in more subordinate and more dominant positions, respectively, within the framework of an important redefinition of the role of the state in society.

The argument of this book is that within the framework of this historical commonality, there were fundamental political differences in how this process of labor incorporation occurred. In most cases the result was ultimately the creation of an organized labor movement and system of industrial relations in important measure controlled and regulated by the state. Yet this occurred in very different ways. Correspondingly, the larger political legacy of these earlier periods differs fundamentally among countries. To introduce these differences, it is necessary to discuss further the incorporation periods themselves.

Types of Incorporation Periods.   We define the initial incorporation of the labor movement as the first sustained and at least partially successful attempt by the state to legitimate and shape an institutionalized labor movement. During the incorporation periods, institutionalized channels for resolving labor conflicts were created in order to supersede the ad hoc use of repression characteristic of earlier periods of state-labor relations, and the state came to assume a major role in institutionalizing a new system of class bargaining.

The analysis of initial incorporation revolves around two arguments. First, this fundamental change in state-labor relations occurred in relatively well-defined policy periods. These periods correspond to historical experiences as chronologically diverse as the Batlle era in the first decade and a half of the 20th century in Uruguay, the aftermath of the Mexican Revolution in the years following the 1917 constitution, the Vargas administration in Brazil beginning in 1930, and the Perón era in Argentina beginning in the 1940s. In most but not all cases, these incorporation periods coincided with the larger period of political reform and expansion of the role of the state discussed

above. Issues that arise in the identification and comparison of the incorporation periods are discussed in the glossary.

The second argument is that the different forms of control and support
mobilization that emerged, along with the distinct actors that led the incorporation projects, are a key to distinguishing among them. At the most general level, we identify two broad types of incorporation experiences: *state*
incorporation and *party* incorporation.

In the case of state incorporation, the principal agency through which the
incorporation period was initiated was the legal and bureaucratic apparatus
of the state, and the principal goal of the leaders who initiated incorporation
was the control and depoliticization of the labor movement. In the case of
party incorporation, a central agency of incorporation was a political party or
political movement that later became a party, and a fundamental goal of political leaders, in addition to control, was the mobilization of working class
support through this party or movement. This mobilization of labor contrasted sharply with the depoliticization characteristic of state incorporation.[8] In addition to distinguishing between state and party incorporation, we
also explore three subtypes of party incorporation, discussed below.

Legacy of Incorporation.   The distinct types of incorporation had a fundamental impact on the subsequent evolution of national politics. In all eight
countries the incorporation experience produced a strong political reaction,
and in most countries this reaction culminated in the breakdown of the national political regime under which the incorporation policies had been implemented. In the face of this reaction and of the counterreaction it often
produced, the ultimate legacy of incorporation commonly entailed outcomes
quite divergent from the goals of the leaders of the original incorporation
period. To understand these outcomes, one must examine closely these reactions and subsequent counterreactions. We will refer to the period of reactions and counterreactions as the "aftermath" of incorporation, and to the
longer-term consequences as the "heritage" of incorporation.

Two sequences of change may initially be identified. In cases of state incorporation, the incorporation project was principally concerned with state
control of the labor movement and was implemented under an authoritarian
regime. Correspondingly, the initial regime breakdown brought with it a process of democratization. In the cases of party incorporation, the incorporation period promoted progressive social policies and the political mobilization of the working class, and the regime under which incorporation
occurred was in most cases more democratic and competitive. Here the incorporation period triggered a strong conservative reaction, which in most
cases ultimately led to a coup and a period of authoritarian rule, followed

[8] Given the definition of incorporation periods presented above, the state by definition
played a role in both types of incorporation. The key question is whether, in addition, a
party or movement played a major role and whether a central goal was depoliticization, as
opposed to politicization in favor of this party or movement. For a further discussion of
these distinctions, see Chapter 5.

later by the institution of some form of more competitive, civilian electoral regime.

By tracing the movement of the countries through these different sequences of change, we gain new insights into the evolving role of the labor movement in sectoral and class alliances and hence into the character of these alliances, the articulation of these alliances with the party system and the character of the party system, and the way crucial issues concerning the legitimation of the state were resolved—or often, not resolved. Special attention focuses on whether a stable majority bloc emerged roughly at the center of the electoral arena, whether unions were linked to parties of the center or parties of the left, and, relatedly, whether the union movement was generally in the governing coalition or tended to be excluded. On the basis of these dimensions, four broad types of outcomes are identified: integrative party systems, multiparty polarizing systems, systems characterized by electoral stability and social conflict, and stalemated party systems.

The consequences of these distinct patterns were dramatically manifested in the period of social and economic crisis and new opposition movements during the 1960s and 1970s, a period that culminated in the emergence of "the new authoritarianism" in some, but not all, of the most modernized countries of Latin America. The problem of explaining this outcome, as well as the contrasting experience of other relatively modernized countries that retained civilian regimes, has received wide scholarly attention over more than a decade.[9] We argue that an important part of the explanation of these contrasting regime outcomes is the structure of contestation and cooperation in the national political arena, which was in important respects the legacy of incorporation and of the reaction to it.

For each country, the analysis extends either to the onset of these authoritarian periods or to approximately 1980. After this point, significant changes in the parameters of politics occurred. Nonetheless, contrasts among countries that are in part the legacy of incorporation remain fundamental to understanding the agenda of political issues faced both by military governments and by the leaders of later democratization efforts. A primary goal of the book is to explore this evolving legacy of incorporation.

Looking at the overall trajectory of the different countries through this sequence of change, one observes a complex relationship between the character of the incorporation period and its legacy. In the intermediate run, the control-oriented approach of state incorporation in some important respects created a greater opportunity for future polarization. This occurred for several reasons, among them that many of the legal controls of unions broke down with the competitive bidding for workers' votes under a subsequent democratic regime, and that state incorporation left unresolved the partisan affiliation of workers and unions, leaving them available for mobilization by other actors in later periods. By contrast the often radical mobilization of party incorporation created political ties and loyalties that in some cases

---

[9] O'Donnell 1973, 1975, 1982; Stepan 1973; Linz and Stepan 1978; D. Collier 1979.

later contributed to conservatization of the labor movement and its integration within a centrist political bloc. Thus one potential trajectory of change was from *control to polarization*, and a second from *mobilization to integration*. A major goal of the analysis is to probe the factors that led particular countries to follow either of these two trajectories.

A final observation is in order about the normative implications of alternative outcomes such as polarization and integration. Under some circumstances and from some normative perspectives, the "stability" or reduction of conflict that might be associated with the outcome of integration are preferable to instability and conflict. Under other circumstances and from other normative perspectives, stability and reduction of conflict may be seen as blocking needed change, whereas polarization may open new avenues for change. These alternative assessments were actively contested in the eight countries during the periods studied here, and they are explicitly debated by social scientists who study these countries. In this book, our goal is not primarily to evaluate these outcomes but rather to advance the understanding of the political context in which they were fought out.

Relative Autonomy of the Political and the Impact of Socioeconomic Change

The book thus explores the long-term impact of *political* differences among countries during the incorporation period. By contrast, much of the literature on political change in Latin America has focused on social and economic explanations. Although we do not claim to present a monocausal model—in that we do not pretend to explain all the observed variations or features of regimes on the basis of political factors—the political argument explored here nonetheless does raise the issue of the relative autonomy of the political.

In recent decades in the context of the larger debate—both Marxist and non-Marxist—on the state, much attention was paid to the issue of political autonomy, particularly on a theoretical level. Yet, during the period when dependency theory was ascendant in Latin American studies, political analysis at times seemed to lose its way and politics was often considered epiphenomenal. What really mattered was the underlying pact of domination, which came part and parcel with the economic base.[10]

Subsequently, concern with the political sphere was revived and reinforced. In part this was due to the particular conjuncture in Latin America. As the military regimes of the 1960s and 1970s left the scene, attention turned to the possibility of creating a political arena that safeguarded democratic values, even in a situation where the underlying economic parameters had not changed.[11] Thus, there was interest first in political values that were

[10] For a critique of this perspective, see Cardoso (1979).

[11] O'Donnell, Schmitter, and Whitehead (1986) and Goodman (forthcoming) are examples of this focus.

previously disparaged and secondly in institution-building in the political arena for the consolidation of democracy.

It seems clear that some facets of the political process act as powerful and fundamental causal variables in social life and provide the basis for an underlying "political logic" that animates change, which is in a sense analogous to the "capital logic" that is a central concern of the dependency perspective. One component of this political logic is the generation of political projects in order to form coalitions to gain or retain political power.[12] It consists of a potentially autonomous realm of conflict over political incumbency and entails a political dynamic that played a central role in shaping the incorporation projects. Another component is the pursuit of legitimation, which is a fundamental imperative of the state and one that may conflict with other imperatives such as the protection and promotion of capital accumulation (Habermas 1975; O'Connor 1973). In addition to the potentially autonomous dynamic of change that revolves around these imperatives of incumbency and legitimacy, other sources of political autonomy are found in vested interests, sunk costs, and institutional rigidities.

The argument is not that the socioeconomic context of politics is unimportant. Rather it is that the political arena is not simply fluid, constantly responding to socioeconomic change. Instead, because of an autonomous political logic and vested interests, it may be resistant to such change over significant periods of time. Socioeconomic change is important to political outcomes, but the political arena may to some degree follow its own pattern and pace of change, that at times takes a highly discontinuous form.

This pattern of discontinuity contrasts with many forms of economic and social change. Socioeconomic change, such as urbanization or economic growth, is often a continuous process that proceeds at a more-or-less even rate—or an evenly fluctuating rate. It commonly entails the aggregation of innumerable changes or decisions by individual actors over time. A model of this type of incremental change is so fundamental to neoclassical economics that on the title page of his seminal work *Principles of Economics*, Alfred Marshall (1916) placed the maxim *natura non facit saltum*—nature makes no leaps. Some political change—for instance, that in the "behavioral" or attitudinal realm—may also occur incrementally.

However, other aspects of political change, in the structural, institutional, and policy spheres, may be more discontinuous. This discontinuity consists of macro transformations, deriving from a process of decision making for the collectivity regarding the distribution of political and societal resources and associated issues of conflict and cooperation. This process leads to the founding of new legal orders, state structures, or other institutional arrangements.

[12] See Cavarozzi (1975:33–37). This focus is related to C. Anderson's widely noted discussion of the logic of "winning, consolidating, and maintaining power" that is part of his "prudence model" of developmental policy-making in Latin America (1967:87, Chaps. 3–4) and parallels both Anderson (1967:87) and Ames's (1987) concern with "political survival." The focus is obviously similar to the larger concern in political analysis with how the goal of gaining and retaining power shapes political action (Downs 1957).

Such episodes of macro change may be followed by periods of minimal change or by more incremental and perhaps more informal change. For instance, smaller incremental changes in policy may be made, laws may not be applied, their implementation may evolve, and institutions and structures may begin to operate or behave in different ways. But these involve relatively minor shifts within a framework in which changes on a large scale are relatively infrequent. Between such major changes, institutions and structural rigidities create a partially autonomous logic of the political arena.

It is within this framework that the uneven impact of social and economic change on politics, of the kind explored in this book, must be understood. This perspective is introduced further in Chapter 1.

Approach to Comparison

Selection of Cases.   The choice of the eight countries analyzed here is based on three criteria. First, along with vast differences in their social and economic makeup, these countries have the longest history of urban commercial and manufacturing development in Latin America. More than other Latin American countries, their modern sectors have for much of this century been sufficiently large to create an active arena of labor politics and state-labor relations. As a result, labor politics has long been a central issue on the national political agenda.[13]

Second, because these countries represent a "comparison set" that provides a useful basis for exploring hypotheses about industrial modernization, they have already received substantial attention in previous research on the political economy of industrialization and regime transformation. The present study therefore can build on an important body of analysis comparing the evolution of these cases. In particular, *The New Authoritarianism in Latin America* (D. Collier 1979), analyzed the same eight countries, focusing on the period of opposition movements, crises, and the rise of authoritarianism in the 1960s and 1970s. The present volume, by contrast, takes the analysis for these eight cases from roughly the beginning of the 20th century up to this period of opposition and crisis. It thus responds to the challenge posed

[13] In conjunction with this shared experience of economic and industrial growth and the related issue of country size, these eight countries loom large within the overall picture of demographic and economic expansion in Latin America. As of 1980 they contained 84 percent of the population of the 20 countries commonly defined as Latin America—i.e., with a "Latin" (Spanish, Portuguese, or French) colonial history—and as of 1979 they had 92 percent of the gross domestic product (not including Cuba). Although the major role of Cuba within the Latin American and international scene since the 1960s and the importance of the Central American crisis in the 1980s belies any argument that big countries are "more important," the demographic and economic preponderance of these eight countries merits note. Among the 20 countries, Brazil had 35 percent of the population, Mexico 20 percent, and the other six countries 29 percent. Among the 19 countries, Brazil had 32 percent of the GDP, Mexico 25 percent, and the other six countries 35 percent (Wilkie and Haber 1983:5, 280–81).

in the final chapter of *The New Authoritarianism*: that it is essential to view the rise and fall of authoritarianism in Latin America that occurred between the 1960s and the 1980s within the framework of longer cycles of regime change within the region (394–95).

Third, this set of countries is auspicious because for each of these cases there is an extensive body of historical and monographic literature on national politics and trade unions that constitutes an invaluable basis for the type of comparative analysis of secondary sources carried out here.

Differences and Commonalities among Cases. A principal challenge of comparative-historical research is to push the systematic comparison of cases as far as possible without pushing it to a point where it does violence to the distinctive attributes of each case. Scholarly debates on comparative research are enlivened by strong disagreements about where that point is located.

It is easy to enumerate prominent features of the national political evolution of each country that are of great relevance for this analysis and which appear conspicuously unique. For instance, in Mexico these would include the revolution and its very nonrevolutionary one-party heritage; in Uruguay the peculiar tradition of two-party politics, the reformist genius of Batlle, and the social welfare state, juxtaposed with the economic and political stagnation of recent decades. In Chile, they would include strong parties of the left located in a national political system also characterized by a strong right and deeply ingrained conservatism; and in Argentina the explosive mobilization of Peronism, its conservatization and fragmentation, and its troubled political legacy.

Any comparative analysis that did not address these distinctive attributes would fail to capture the reality of these countries. Yet it is equally obvious that a meaningful understanding of these cases cannot be gained only by dwelling on their unique traits, but must be achieved in part through a comparative assessment of the larger political issues that are fought out and the commonalities, as well as contrasts, in the political and institutional forms taken by the resolution of these issues.

Splitters and Lumpers. The problem of adequately assessing these similarities and contrasts suggests the relevance here of the distinction suggested by J. H. Hexter (1979:241–43) between two types of analysts: "splitters" and "lumpers."[14] Splitters are quick to see contrasts among cases and to focus on the distinctive attributes of each case. Their contribution is essential, since the close, contextually rich analysis they tend to produce is invaluable for understanding the cases under consideration, for bringing to light new information, for generating new hypotheses and theories, and for providing the basic data on which all comparative analysis depends. Lumpers, by contrast, have an eye for generalizations and commonalities, for fitting particular

---

[14] The following discussion parallels in important respects Skocpol and Somers's (1980) analysis of different approaches to comparison. Splitters generally follow their method of "contrast of contexts"; lumpers follow their method of "parallel demonstration of theory"; and the middle ground that we advocate corresponds to their "macro-causal analysis."

cases into broad categories. Their approach is likewise essential, since it plays an important role in synthesizing the details presented in case studies.

One major risk for the lumpers is the methodological problem identified by Eldon Kenworthy (1973) in his article entitled "The Function of the Little Known Case in Theory Formation or What Peronism Wasn't." Kenworthy, a specialist in Argentine politics, criticized the misuse of the case of Peronist Argentina, which at an earlier point was poorly understood by broad comparativists. These comparativists, according to Kenworthy, distorted the Argentine experience to fit it into their conceptual categories.

A variant of this problem, which has arisen in the comparative analysis of the historical periods of concern in this book, could be referred to as "the misuse of the best known case." In this instance, a general pattern for a whole region is derived from the best known case (or cases) writ large. For instance, in the analysis of state-labor relations and populism in Latin America, the experiences of two or possibly three leaders have often commanded the attention of analysts: Perón (a relatively well-known case among Latin Americanists), Vargas in Brazil, and perhaps Cárdenas in Mexico. Generalizations have too often presented a single picture for Latin America that combined elements of each of these experiences, forming a composite that ultimately corresponds neither to the original case or cases on which the generalization is based, nor to other cases to which it is applied (R. Collier 1982:98–100).

What is too often missing is an analytic middle ground between splitters and lumpers that encompasses simultaneously a concern with similarities *and* differences. In carrying out description, such an approach attempts to identify multiple patterns rather than necessarily to "lump" cases into a single type. In testing explanations, this approach employs the systematic examination of similarities *and* contrasts among cases as a means of assessing hypotheses about patterns of change.

An important concomitant of occupying this middle ground is the recognition of a crucial point: the claim that two countries are similar or different with regard to a particular attribute does not, and is not intended to, assign to them the overall status of being similar or different cases. It is relevant to underline this point because in the fields of comparative analysis and Latin American studies, when scholars engage in a carefully contextualized comparison of "whole countries,"[15] there can be a tendency to depict certain countries as "really" similar or different—to a degree that may paralyze comparative research. For instance, students of the Southern Cone commonly hold that Argentina, Chile, and Uruguay share an underlying socioeconomic structure that contrasts markedly with the rest of South America, giving a common "meaning" to the dynamics of their politics. Yet in terms of the structure of its party system, Uruguay has historically had much more in

---

[15] Obviously, no one really compares "whole countries," but only specific attributes of countries. This expression is used to refer to what Ragin (1987) has called the "case oriented," rather than "variable oriented," approach of comparative-historical analysis, which is strongly concerned with how each variable is embedded in its larger context within a given case.

common with Colombia than with its Southern Cone neighbors. Uruguay is not inherently more similar either to Colombia or to other Southern Cone countries. Rather, it shares with each important similarities *and* differences.

In sum, our methodological stance recognizes the contribution of both splitters and lumpers, but insists on the flexible application of a middle position that acknowledges a diversity of similarities and contrasts among any combination of cases.

Most Similar and Most Different Systems Designs.   In focusing on the analysis of similarities and differences, we employ two strategies of comparison, a combination of a "most similar" and a "most different" systems design (Przeworski and Teune 1970; Przeworski 1987).[16] These two designs are "ideal types," and the matching and contrasting of cases that they posit is never perfectly achieved in any real analysis. Yet they are invaluable points of reference in constructing comparisons.

First, the overall analysis of the eight countries can be considered a most similar systems design. These eight cases are broadly matched, in that among the countries of Latin America, they have overall the longest history of urban, commercial, and industrial development, and in conjunction with this development have experienced the broad transformations in the political sphere discussed above. Further, these changes have occurred within a common regional and cultural context. Against the backdrop of these similarities, this methodological design identifies four broad types of incorporation periods and seeks to discover whether corresponding contrasts emerge in the legacy of incorporation.

Second, the comparison of countries with similar types of incorporation constitutes a most different systems design. Countries with similar incorporation experiences typically exhibited major contrasts in the pattern of socioeconomic development, the characteristics of the labor movement, and other important political attributes. The comparison within these sets of cases therefore constitutes a most different systems strategy, which juxtaposes cases that are fundamentally different in a number of respects. Within the framework of these differences, if countries that had a similar incorporation experience were also similar in terms of longer-term outcomes, then one has a stronger basis for inferring that these outcomes were indeed a consequence of the type of incorporation. The profound differences in the background variables thus serve to place in sharp relief the conjunction of similar types of incorporation period and similar outcomes.

Types of Incorporation and Country Pairs

In addition to the distinction between state and party incorporation presented above, we identify three subtypes of party incorporation. The eight countries distributed themselves among the four resulting types of incorpo-

16 These correspond to J. S. Mill's (1974/1843) methods of difference and agreement, respectively.

ration periods in a way that placed two countries within each type. The book is thus organized around the analysis of four pairs of countries: Brazil and Chile, Mexico and Venezuela, Uruguay and Colombia, and Peru and Argentina. From the perspective of the most different systems design, it is essential to emphasize both the similarities and contrasts within each pair.

Similarities within Each Pair.   The core similarity in each pair derives from the analysis of the incorporation periods, presented in Chapter 5. The cases of state incorporation, where the state sought primarily to impose new methods of control, are Brazil (1930–45) and Chile (1920–31). Among the cases of party incorporation, where the concern with control was accompanied by a major effort at support mobilization, we distinguish three subtypes. First, in Colombia (1930–45) and Uruguay (1903–16), the mobilization of workers was carried out by traditional parties as an aspect of electoral competition within an established two-party system. Since these parties were founded in the 19th century and had strong ties to the economic elite, not surprisingly this type involved the most limited mobilization of the working class, being restricted largely to electoral mobilization. We refer to this category as *electoral mobilization by a traditional party*.

The other two types of party incorporation were led by new, explicitly anti-oligarchic parties, and both involved more comprehensive forms of mobilization. In Peru (1939–48) and Argentina (1943–55), the party or movement that led the incorporation period not only engaged in the electoral mobilization of workers, but also systematically and successfully built partisan ties to labor organizations and drove out of the labor movement elements affiliated with other parties, leading us to label these cases *labor populism*.

Finally, in Mexico (1917–40) and Venezuela (1935–48), the mobilization of the incorporation period took its most comprehensive form. In the other six countries the transformations of the incorporation period were almost entirely restricted to the labor movement in the modern sector of the economy and did not encompass peasants in the traditional rural sector.[17] However, in Mexico and Venezuela the incorporation project was extended to this part of the rural sector, accompanied by agrarian reform, and therefore represented the most comprehensive assault on rural property relations and on the existing oligarchy.[18] Given the comprehensive character of the transformations launched by these incorporation periods, we refer to them as *radical populism*.

---

[17] We treat workers in modernized rural enclaves as being in the modern sector. A discussion of these terms is found in the glossary.

[18] As is clear in Chapter 4 and 5, in the other four cases of party incorporation, the incorporation of the peasantry and the corresponding reorganization of rural property relations were not a central feature of this period for two very different reasons. In Peru and Colombia, the oligarchy was sufficiently strong to make this an unlikely outcome, whereas in Argentina and Uruguay and extensive traditional peasantry did not exist. Hence, although within both pairs of cases (Peru-Argentina and Uruguay-Colombia) this outcome had different *causes*, its *consequences* were partially similar, as we will see in Chapters 5 and 6. Although in Argentina important reforms occurred in the rural sector, they did not encompass a restructuring of rural property relations of the kind found in Mexico and Venezuela.

Two further observations may be made about this grouping of cases. First, although these pairs are derived from a comparison of the incorporation periods, this grouping of cases had deep roots in the periods prior to incorporation and extends well beyond them. Second, it is essential to think of these types of incorporation periods as analytic categories, not as perfect descriptions of each country. Obviously, the two countries within each category are not identical in terms of the defining dimensions, but they are far more similar to one another in terms of these dimensions than they are to the countries identified with the other categories.

Differences within Each Pair. In the framework of the most different systems design, we are centrally concerned with fundamental economic, social, and political differences within each pair. These differences represent the contrasting contexts within which the analysis focuses on the similarity in the incorporation period and on the hypothesized similarity in the legacy within each pair. In three of the four pairs (excluding Mexico and Venezuela), this most different systems design juxtaposes within each pair: (1) a more socially homogeneous, relatively urban, far more European society of the Southern Cone, which is relatively modernized in terms of per capita indicators of education, literacy, and urbanization—Chile, Uruguay, and Argentina—with (2) a more socially heterogeneous, less urban society, which has a substantial population of Indian or African extraction and which is considerably less modernized in per capita terms—Brazil, Colombia, and Peru (see Table 0.1).

Marked contrasts are also found between Mexico and Venezuela, though these contrasts have changed during the decades covered in this study. In the

TABLE 0.1
Pairs of Countries: Similarities and Differences

| | *Political Similarities during Incorporation Period* | | | |
| | | *Party Incorporation* | | |
Socioeconomic Differences	*State Incorporation*	*Electoral Mob. by Trad. Party*	*Labor Populism*	*Radical Populism*
More socially homogeneous, higher on per capita modernization indicators	Chile	Uruguay	Argentina	Venezuela[a]
Less socially homogeneous, lower on per capita modernization indicators	Brazil	Colombia	Peru	Mexico[a]

[a] This ordering of Venezuela and Mexico refers roughly to the period of the 1950s to the 1970s. In the late 19th century and the first part of the 20th century, the ordering of these two countries on several of these variables was the opposite from that reflected here (see Chapter 3), and in the 1970s and 1980s, they more nearly converged.

19th century and into the first decades of the 20th century, Venezuela was among the least developed of the eight countries. However, with the rise of the petroleum sector, by roughly the 1950s Venezuela corresponded more nearly to the first row in Table 0.1, with high levels of per capita income; whereas in important respects Mexico lagged behind. However, with Mexico's oil boom in the 1970s, it gained again on some indicators. Depending on the particular period under consideration, different contrasts therefore come into play in the comparison of Mexico and Venezuela.

Political differences within the pairs are also of great importance to the analysis. Some political differences vary consistently with the socioeconomic contrasts noted above, and others do not. For instance, given the link between patterns of socioeconomic development and the emergence of strong labor movements (see Chapter 3), the countries in the upper row of Table 0.1 generally have stronger labor movements, and those in the lower row, with greater surplus labor, generally have weaker labor movements. On the other hand, differences in type of party system are of great importance to the analysis, but do not vary consistently among the pairs. The strong parties of Chile and the weak parties of Brazil present a major contrast that is crucial for our analysis, though we will argue that in the 1960s these two countries were distinctive among the eight in the degree to which they were characterized by polarizing, multiparty politics. Similarly, it is important to distinguish the two-party system of Venezuela from the one-party dominant system of Mexico, though we label both integrative party systems.

Major parts of the book are organized around the discussion of these pairs. We juxtapose the two cases in each pair in order to explore their parallel (though certainly not identical) experiences with the incorporation periods and their legacies. At the same time, we explore contrasts within each pair.

Alternative Explanations

To assess the explanatory value of a focus on incorporation periods and their legacies, it is helpful to probe the relationship between this perspective and other explanatory approaches. Some of the most relevant of these approaches may be noted briefly here.

Many studies have explored the impact of social and economic change on the evolution of national politics in Latin America, focusing on such interrelated dimensions as differing levels of socioeconomic modernization, distinct patterns of economic development and social change, and contrasting modes of articulation with the international economy. Such explanations receive substantial attention in this book. Chapter 3 examines their impact on the initial emergence of different types of labor movements, and Chapter 4 assesses their role in the emergence of reform movements that challenged the "oligarchic state" and that in most cases launched the incorporation period. We address other aspects of the impact of socioeconomic change as well, though we hypothesize that once the incorporation periods occurred, distinctive political dynamics were set in motion that must be analyzed in their own right and not simply as a reflection of economic and social forces.

In addition to the impact of social and economic change, transnational political developments must be considered. For instance, the diffusion of ideologies and modes of political organization had an important impact. This includes the demonstration effect of the revolutionary ideologies and models derived from the Russian and Cuban revolutions, as well as the organizational and ideological alternatives presented to the labor movement in each country by the different types of trade unionism emerging in Europe and in other parts of Latin America. The policies of foreign governments were also of great importance, particularly those of the United States. Other international actors played a role as well, such as the international communist movement, whose evolving policy had a major impact on the coalitional position not only of national communist parties but also of national labor movements, thereby strongly influencing domestic coalitional patterns. Both world wars had major ramifications in Latin America.

Piecing together these various external influences, one can picture a kind of transnational historical "grid" through which these countries passed. The grid consisted of a series of historical episodes that occurred at the international level, and the episodes within the grid can collectively be thought of as phases in what is sometimes referred to as "world historical time." Considering these episodes in chronological order, and recognizing that some may overlap, they would include (1) the decline of anarchism and the rise of alternative approaches to worker organization, including socialism, communism, and national populism; (2) the Russian Revolution and its immediate aftermath, along with the internal wage-price squeeze triggered in part by the economic impact of World War I, which precipitated in most of Latin America and in much of the Western world a dramatic wave of worker protest; (3) the international depression of the 1930s; (4) the Comintern's coalitional strategy before and during World War II of "popular frontism" and class collaboration in support of the Allied war effort that was adopted as part of the struggle against fascism; (5) the onset of the cold war after 1945, which brought a dramatic change in coalitional patterns in a number of countries; (6) the internationalization of important sectors of the economy in these countries beginning as early as the 1950s in response to new external opportunities and pressures; (7) the Cuban Revolution and the broader international climate of social protest and radicalization of the 1960s and early 1970s; and (8) the international dimensions of the reaction that sought to limit the impact of this protest and radicalization, involving the very important role of the U.S. government.

One of the fascinating issues posed by this study is the uneven relationship between these phases of world historic time and the analytic phases that are the focus of this book—that is, the periods of the oligarchic state, initial incorporation, aftermath, and heritage. We thus confront the interaction between a *longitudinal* and a *cross-sectional* perspective: between the unfolding over time within each country of phases of political change, and a sequence of international developments that influenced all the countries at roughly the same chronological time, but often at a different point in relation to these internal political phases.

In this framework, timing is important. Depending on timing, an incorporation period may have been cut short by the impact of the depression; or, if it began later, its leaders may have had the "advantage" of appearing to offer a solution to the problems of the depression. Similarly, the conflicts of the aftermath period may have been worked out in the atmosphere of more conciliatory class relations of the later 1930s or early 1940s or in the more conflictual atmosphere of the late 1940s. Such differences had a significant impact on the patterns we analyze, and throughout the study we seek to be sensitive to this impact.

A final observation should be made about the problem of assessing rival explanations in a work of comparative-historical analysis such as this book. Research in this tradition draws great strength from its close focus on relatively few countries and from the rich treatment of cases often entailed in the construction of the complex categorical variables that are commonly employed. Yet this tradition is weaker in its capacity to address two issues that can be handled routinely with statistical analysis. Comparative-historical analysis lacks the capacity to state precisely the degree to which a given factor is a partial explanation of some important outcome, and it lacks a precise means of summarizing relationships in terms that are probabilistic rather than deterministic.

The practitioner of this approach must therefore rely on historical analysis and common sense both in weighing alternative explanations and in recognizing that the relationships under analysis are probabilistic and partial. It is in this spirit that we explore the impact of the incorporation periods: as explanatory factors that must be looked at in conjunction with other explanations and as important explanations that make certain outcomes more likely, but not inevitable.

The idea of partial explanation is crucial in the analysis of the pairs of countries. Simply because two countries had parallel experiences in the incorporation period, we would not expect that they will come out exactly the same on the relevant variables in the heritage period. Rather—as is particularly evident in the case of Chile and Brazil, where enormous differences might lead one to predict sharply contrasting trajectories of change—the hypothesized finding is that the two countries will prove to be *more similar than one might otherwise expect*. Our goal is to develop this kind of multivariate perspective in assessing our argument.

Organization of the Book

Following this Overview, Chapter 1 explicates the underlying analytic framework, drawing on Lipset and Rokkan's (1967) model of discontinuous political change that focuses on "critical junctures" and their legacies. The reader more concerned with the discussion of Latin America than with these generic issues of discontinuous change may wish to turn directly to Chapter 2, which examines the context within which the analysis is situated by exploring basic issues of state-labor relations within the region.

Chapter 3 begins the historical analysis, assessing the events that set our story into motion: the dramatic emergence of worker organization and protest at the end of the 19th century and in the first decades of the 20th century, during the era of what is commonly referred to in Latin America as the "oligarchic state." Chapter 4 then traces the emergence of the reformist challenges to oligarchic domination. This challenge was led by elements of the middle sectors and dissident members of the traditional elite, who in all eight countries eventually launched a reform period that inaugurated the transformation of the oligarchic state. To orient the reader, Figure 0.1 provides a chronological overview of these reform periods (R), as well as of the subsequent periods discussed below: incorporation, aftermath, and heritage. The definitions and assumptions that underlie the identification of these periods are presented in Chapters 1, 4 and 5, and in the glossary.

Chapter 5 analyzes the incorporation periods, exploring the distinctive dynamics of state incorporation and of the three types of party incorporation. As can be seen in Figure 0.1, in five of the countries, the onset of incorporation and the reform period discussed above coincided, whereas in three others there was a delay before the onset of incorporation (indicated by an arrow following the "R"). The circumstances of this delay are analyzed in Chapter 4.

Chapter 6 explores what we define as the aftermath period, constituted by the initial political reaction and counterreaction to the incorporation experience. Chapter 7 then analyzes the larger heritage, focusing on the institutional arrangements forged during the period of incorporation and its aftermath. The concluding chapter, in addition to synthesizing the argument, poses the question of whether the legacy of incorporation still persists or has been superseded in each of the eight countries. This question arises both in the countries that had military governments in the 1960s and 1970s and in those that experienced continuous civilian rule.

Following the concluding chapter, the glossary defines a number of terms used in this book and presents an extended discussion of the concept of the initial incorporation of the labor movement. Readers interested in the issues of method and comparison that arise in applying this concept should refer to the glossary, as well as to the analysis of critical junctures in Chapter 1.

Within each of the historical chapters—that is, Chapters 3 to 7—the order of presentation is intended to highlight the contrasts among the pairs of countries. Thus, each of these chapters begins with Brazil and Chile, thereby establishing one pole of comparison involving the traits associated with state incorporation (or its antecedents or legacy, according to the chapter). We then examine Mexico and Venezuela, the two cases that exhibited all the key traits of party incorporation and that thereby represent the other pole of the

Figure 0.1 Chronological Overview: Onset of Reform Period, Incorporation. Aftermath, and Heritage

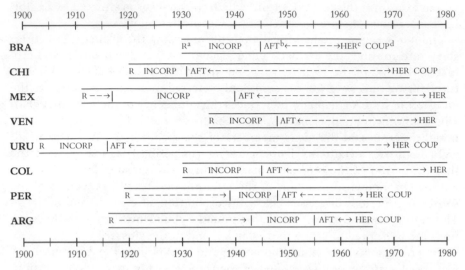

a R (reform period) followed by no dashes indicates that the incorporation period began immediately with the onset of the reform period. R with dashes and an arrow indicates a delay.

b AFT (aftermath period) refers to the immediate political dynamics following incorporation.

c HER (heritage period) refers to the longer-term legacy of incorporation. The heritage period encompasses most of the aftermath period, excluding only the episodes of conservative, authoritarian rule that followed incorporation in five of the cases of party incorporation. The complex issue of when each heritage period ends is explored in Chapter 8.

d COUP refers specifically to the major coups, which occurred in five of the countries in the 1960s or 1970s and which launched periods of military rule that interrupted the mode of party politics that characterized the heritage period. Chapter 8 asks whether the pattern of politics that reemerged after this period of military rule reflected a continuation of the heritage of incorporation.

comparison. Finally, we analyze the other two pairs, which in some important respects are intermediate cases.[19]

To encourage systematic comparison, we have presented the analysis of the eight countries in a standardized format that lends itself to the close examination of similarities and contrasts among cases. To this end, we have

[19] In the historical chapters, as a practical matter we faced the alternative of writing up the two members of each pair separately or weaving them into a single analysis. At different points we found the material lent itself more readily to one or the other mode of presentation, and we proceeded accordingly. The eight cases are presented separately in Chapter 3, which deals with the early history of the labor movement. In Chapter 4, both Brazil and Chile and also Uruguay and Colombia are presented together as pairs, and the same format is used for Brazil and Chile in the following chapters. In Chapters 4–7 all the remaining countries are presented separately, though with frequent comparison both within and between the pairs.

used a common set of headings within each chapter for most of the countries, introducing variations as needed to capture distinctive features of specific cases. These variations are particularly evident for Brazil and Chile, which, as cases of state incorporation, follow a contrasting trajectory of change.

The analysis proceeds in the following manner. In examining the emergence of working-class organization and protest in Chapter 3, we present for each country first an analysis of the socioeconomic context and then of the labor movement itself. The analysis of the reformist challenge in Chapter 4 focuses on the period of the oligarchic state, the emergence of the reform alliance, the initial transition and change of government, and the role of labor in the transition. The assessment of the incorporation periods in Chapter 5, for the cases of party incorporation, focuses on the "project from above"— that is, the goals and strategies of the leaders of the incorporation period; the "project from below"—that is, the goals and strategies of the labor movement, the political exchange on which the incorporation period was founded, the role of the party, and the emergence of opposition and polarization. For the cases of state incorporation, where there is little or no exchange, party role, or polarization, these latter three sections are replaced by a general analysis of labor policy. The analysis of the aftermath of incorporation in Chapter 6, in the cases of party incorporation, focuses on the conservative reaction, the formation of a new governing coalition in counterreaction to this conservative period, and the transformation of the party that accompanies the emergence of this new coalition. Finally, in analyzing the heritage of incorporation in Chapter 7, we first provide an overview of the party system and then systematically review for each country the reaction to the new opposition movements and crises of the late 1950s to the 1970s.[20]

The organization of the book is intended to facilitate different approaches to reading it. Readers who wish to focus on a particular analytic period in a number of countries can follow the headings for each country that correspond to the standardized subsections noted above. For readers interested in an overview of the analysis, each chapter begins with an introduction to the relevant step in the argument and provides a summary of the country patterns in that step. The write-up of each pair of countries in Chapters 5 to 7 begins with a further introduction to the pair, and Chapter 8 provides an overall summary of the argument. Finally, readers who wish to focus on a specific country should read the chapter introductions and the introductions to the relevant pair of countries as well as the appropriate country sections. For any of these approaches, readers will be aided by the Index of Countries by Analytic Period.

[20] For the countries where the heritage period as analyzed here is ended by a coup in the 1960s, this part of the analysis stops in the 1960s.

Part I

INTRODUCTION

1

Framework: Critical Junctures and Historical Legacies

Two roads diverged in a wood, and I—
I took the one less travelled by,
And that has made all the difference.
   —Robert Frost, "The Road Not Taken"

THE IDEA of crucial choices and their legacies, of which Robert Frost wrote, has long intrigued students of political change. Numerous scholars have focused on major watersheds in political life, arguing that these transitions establish certain directions of change and foreclose others in a way that shapes politics for years to come. Such transitions can, following Seymour Martin Lipset and Stein Rokkan, be called "critical junctures."[1]

The character of critical junctures and the perspective from which they are analyzed vary greatly. Some critical junctures, as in the choice of Robert Frost's wanderer, may entail considerable discretion, whereas with others the presumed choice appears deeply embedded in antecedent conditions. The critical juncture may involve a relatively brief period in which one direction or another is taken or an extended period of reorientation. Some analyses stress underlying societal cleavages or crises that lead up to the critical juncture, whereas others focus primarily on the critical juncture itself. Finally, some critical junctures may be seen as coming close to making "all the difference," as Frost boldly asserts in his poem. More commonly, the effect of the critical juncture is intertwined with other processes of change.

Yet underlying this diversity is a common understanding of change that is a cornerstone of comparative-historical research on development. It suggests what Paul A. David (1985:332) has called a "path dependent" pattern of change, in that outcomes during a crucial transition establish distinct trajectories within which, as he has engagingly put it, "one damn thing follows another." James Gleick (1987:8), in summarizing the version of this perspective known as "chaos" theory, captures a related feature of critical junctures in stressing the idea of "sensitive dependence on initial conditions."

To those who study revolutionary change, it comes as no surprise to suggest that political life exhibits the kind of discontinuities posited in analyses of critical junctures. What should be underlined is the extent to which this focus is widely employed in a diverse spectrum of research not concerned

[1] Lipset and Rokkan 1967:37ff.; Rokkan 1970:112ff.

exclusively, or even primarily, with revolutionary change. It plays a central role in Max Weber's analysis of the cyclical interplay between periods of continuity and sharp disjunctures—inspired by charismatic leadership—that reshape established social relations.[2] In major works of comparative-historical analysis of the 1960s, it is found in Barrington Moore's argument that within the process of modernization, different patterns of commercialization of agriculture were a historic watershed that set countries on different paths to the modern world; in Louis Hartz's comparisons of the founding of "fragment societies"; and in Alexander Gerschenkron's work on the "great spurt" in the industrialization process.[3] This perspective is central to research on the crises, sequence, and timing of development,[4] to recent studies of continuity and change in international and domestic political economy,[5] to older work on "institutionalization,"[6] to more recent work on the "new institutionalism,"[7] and to research on technological change.[8] Though the importance of this perspective is particularly evident in studies based on cross-national comparisons, it also plays a role in research on long-term patterns of change within individual countries and in studies of electoral realignment in the United States.[9] In rational-choice theory, a variant of this perspective is found in "threshold" models of collective behavior.[10]

Arguments about critical junctures have played an important role in research on labor politics. In their classic *Industrialism and Industrial Man*, Clark Kerr and his coauthors emphasize the long-term stability of the industrial relations system that was "crystallized by the leading elite at a relatively early stage" (1960:235). In Lipset and Rokkan's (1967) analysis, and to an even greater degree in the subsequent work of Carlos Waisman (1982, 1987), Gregory Luebbert (1986, 1987), and John Stephens (1986), the resolution of the working class cleavage has a profound effect in shaping national politics. Other studies have focused on critical junctures *within* the labor movement. Samuel Valenzuela (1979:esp. chap. 4) shows how the filling of "organizational space" during crucial phases of labor movement development "freezes" organizational alternatives within the labor sector; and Lipset (1983:1) analyzes how the "historic conditions under which the proletariat entered the political arena" shaped the subsequent emergence of reformist as opposed to revolutionary labor movements.

Following this tradition, the present study applies the idea of critical junctures and their legacies to the evolution of 20th century politics in Latin America, focusing on a period of fundamental change in the relationship be-

[2] E.g., Weber 1968:1111–1133.
[3] Moore 1966; Hartz 1964; and Gerschenkron 1962.
[4] Huntington 1968; Binder 1971; Grew 1978; Dahl 1971:chap. 3; Almond et al. 1973.
[5] See Krasner (1982, 1983, 1984, 1988); Katzenstein (1985); and Gourevitch 1986.
[6] Selznick 1957 and Huntington 1968.
[7] March and Olsen 1984, 1989.
[8] David 1985, 1987.
[9] Key 1955; Burnham 1965, 1970, 1974; Converse 1972, 1974; Rusk 1974; Brady 1988.
[10] See Schelling (1978:chaps. 3, 6), Granovetter (1978), and Przeworski (1986).

tween the state and the labor movement. This change responded to two sets of cleavages: that between workers and owners and that between workers and the state, expressed in the emergence of worker organization and protest beginning in the late 19th century; and that between the middle sectors and the oligarchy, expressed in the emergence of major reform movements in the first decades of the 20th century. Growing out of this new worker activation and these reform periods, there eventually emerged in each country the policy period we refer to as the "initial incorporation of the labor movement." This book argues that the incorporation periods constituted a critical juncture that occurred in distinct ways in different countries, and that these differences played a central role in shaping the national political arena in the following decades.

Historical studies of the eight countries analyzed in this book have routinely argued that the years corresponding to the incorporation periods were of great historical importance and had a major impact on the subsequent evolution of politics.[11] Yet this literature has lacked consistent criteria for identifying and comparing these periods, and the specific claims concerning their legacies vary greatly—since these studies obviously were not conducted within a common analytic framework. To date, no analysis has systematically compared these incorporation periods across a number of cases or pieced together the complex interactions among the characteristics of the antecedent political system, the incorporation period itself, and the legacy of incorporation.

This chapter establishes a common framework for analyzing critical junctures. The need for such a framework derives from the surprising lack of attention to the problems that arise in assessing arguments about critical junctures and their legacies, given how widely used this perspective is in the development literature.[12] It is easy to initially hypothesize that a set of countries passed through a crucial period of transition and that the transition occurred in distinct ways that had a profound impact on subsequent patterns of change. Yet many pitfalls are encountered in assessing the descriptive and explanatory claims contained in such an hypothesis. This chapter provides a framework for dealing with these pitfalls.

Building Blocks of the Critical Juncture Framework

A critical juncture may be defined as a period of significant change, which typically occurs in distinct ways in different countries (or in other units of analysis)[13] and which is hypothesized to produce distinct legacies.

[11] See note 1 in the Overview.

[12] Exceptions to the lack of attention to these methodological problems are found in the writing of Harsanyi (1960), Gerschenkron (1968), Verba (1971), and Krasner (1984).

[13] As noted above, this kind of framework is also used in the analysis of single countries, as in the literature on realigning elections in the United States. In single-country analyses, systematic comparisons are sometimes made; or less systematic (or implicit) comparisons

The elements in this definition may be illustrated with an example. In Barrington Moore's *Lord and Peasant*, the period of basic change is the commercialization of agriculture; the contrasts involve the varied role of different class and sectoral groups in this transition, particularly lord and peasant; and the legacy consists of different "routes to the modern world": bourgeois revolution and Western democracy, revolution from above, and fascism and peasant revolution and communism (1966:xvii, chaps. 7–9, e.g., pp. 413–14).

Thus, the concept of a critical juncture contains three components: the claim that a significant change occurred within each case, the claim that this change took place in distinct ways in different cases, and the explanatory hypothesis about its consequences. If the explanatory hypothesis proves to be false—that is, the hypothesized critical juncture did not produce the legacy—then one would assert that it was not, in fact, a critical juncture.

In addition to the three components contained in the definition, a number of further elements must be considered (see Figure 1.1).

1. The *antecedent conditions* that represent a "base line" against which the critical juncture and the legacy are assessed. In Figure 1.1, the arrow from the antecedent conditions to the legacy is intended to suggest the potential rival hypothesis that important attributes of the legacy may in fact involve considerable continuity and/or direct causal links with the preexisting system that are not mediated by the critical juncture.

2. The *cleavage* (or crisis)[14] that emerges out of the antecedent conditions and in turn triggers the critical juncture.

3. Three components of the *legacy*: a. *Mechanisms of production* of the

Figure 1.1 Building Blocks of the Critical Juncture Framework

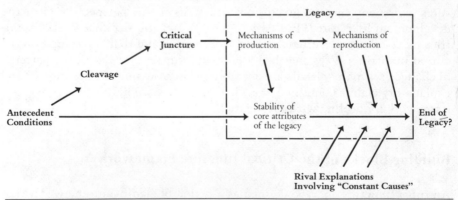

are made either with other countries, with earlier historical episodes in the same country, or with "counterfactual" alternative versions of how the critical juncture under study might have occurred.

[14] In general, a crisis occurs in a delimited period of time, whereas a cleavage may exist for a long time, simply to be exacerbated in a particular period in a way that produces a crisis and a critical juncture. However, in the present analysis the emergence of the crisis and the emergence of the cleavage more nearly coincide in that the crisis regarding the role of the working class accompanied the appearance of the worker-owner, worker-state cleavage that was produced by the initial appearance of a significant working class.

legacy. The legacy often does not crystallize immediately after the critical juncture, but rather is shaped through a series of intervening steps. b. *Mechanisms of reproduction* of the legacy. The stability of the legacy is not an automatic outcome, but rather is perpetuated through ongoing institutional and political processes. c. The *stability of the core attributes of the legacy*— that is, the basic attributes produced as an outcome of the critical juncture, such as the different constellations of union-party-regime relationships analyzed in the present book.

4. *Rival explanations involving "constant causes,"* which, as we argue below, represent one of several types of rival explanation that must be considered.

5. The eventual *end of the legacy*, which inevitably must occur at some point.

Issues in Analyzing Critical Junctures

Within the framework of these elements, we will now explore basic issues that arise in the analysis of critical junctures and their relevance to the present study.

1. *Identifying Hypothesized Critical Juncture and Variations in How It Occurs.* Because it is essential to the concept of a critical juncture that it occurs in different ways in different cases, issues of establishing analytic equivalence, that are standard problems in comparative-historical research, are abundantly present in this type of analysis. The differences in how it occurred have to be large enough to produce interesting "variance," yet this variance must not be so great as to undermine the idea that it really involves the *same* critical juncture.[15]

If the critical juncture is an immediate response to an external shock— such as the depression of the 1930s, the debt crisis of the 1980s, an international wave of social protest, or a war—it may occur more or less simultaneously across a number of countries and hence may be relatively easy to identify. However, the political response even to such well-defined external events may occur quickly in some cases and be long delayed in others. Further, when the critical juncture is triggered by external forces that impinge on different countries at different times, or by internal forces that may manifest themselves at different times, the result is again that the juncture occurs in different historical contexts, among which it may not be easy to establish analytic equivalence.

Yet such differences in timing are often crucial to the analysis, since they are one of the types of variations in critical junctures that are used to account for variations in the legacy, as in Alexander Gerschenkron's (1962) analysis

[15] Przeworski and Teune (1970, pt. 2) and Sartori (1970) remain the most incisive analyses of how variations in a phenomenon can become sufficiently large as to undermine the analytic equivalence of observations across a number of cases.

of the timing of industrialization. More broadly, the challenge is to establish a definition that effectively demonstrates that potentially major *differences* among cases in the critical juncture, in its timing or in other characteristics, in fact occurred in an analytically *equivalent* period—that is, that they represent *different* values on the *same* variable.

This dilemma arose in the research for this book, since some of the presumed incorporation periods were sufficiently different from one another that we were led to examine them carefully before concluding that they should all be viewed as analytically equivalent transitions. Relevant contrasts included the difference between the corporatist incorporation periods of most countries as opposed to the pluralistic incorporation period in Uruguay. We also encountered differences in the international and historical context of the incorporation periods due to major contrasts in timing, in that the onset of these periods varied over four decades, from 1904 to 1943. Our questioning led to the extended discussion of the definition of incorporation presented in the glossary and to the close attention in the analysis of individual countries to the issue of identifying the appropriate period.

2. *How Long Do Critical Junctures Last?* Critical junctures may range from relatively quick transitions—for example, "*moments* of significant structural change"[16]—to an extended period that might correspond to one or more presidential administrations, a long "policy period," or a prolonged "regime period."[17] Such variations in duration depend in part on the immediate causal mechanisms involved, which may produce a type of change that crystallizes rapidly or gradually. A dramatic political upheaval may produce rapid change. On the other hand, some changes may be the result of the sustained application of a government policy, involving an extended period of time.

The issue of wide variations in duration is important in the present analysis. Not surprisingly, in focusing on the historical episode in which a given set of public policies is actively applied for the first time, it turns out—due to the differing political dynamics of particular countries—that the government or a series of linked governments that first sustain these policies may in some cases be in power for only a few years and in others for much longer. In the countries considered here, the duration of the incorporation period ranges from nine years in Peru to 23 years in Mexico. As long as this policy period fits the definition of the particular critical juncture—in this case, the initial incorporation period—this poses no problem for the analysis, but the issue of this fit must be examined closely.

3. *Cleavage or Crisis.* An important part of the literature on critical junctures views them from the perspective of cleavages or crises, thereby placing particular emphasis on the tensions that lead up to the critical juncture. Since these cleavages are seen as producing or generating the critical junc-

---

[16] Cardoso and Faletto 1979:xiv.

[17] These variations in duration can raise the issue of appropriate labeling. With regard to the overall label, we retain the expression critical juncture as a reasonable compromise between alternatives such as founding moments or choice points, on the one hand, and period of transition, on the other.

ture, Valenzuela and Valenzuela (1981:15) refer to them as "generative" cleavages.[18] The argument of this book is that the working class mobilization and conflicts between the middle sectors and the oligarchy in the first decades of the 20th century represented generative cleavages.

If a cleavage is a central concern of the analysis, a careful examination of the cleavage itself is essential. Before testing hypotheses about the links among the cleavage, the critical juncture, and the legacy, it is useful to contextualize the analysis by exploring the meaning of the cleavage within the particular setting, raising the question of why it should be so important. In this spirit, Chapter 2 explores the social and political meaning of worker-owner and worker-state conflicts in Latin America, probing the question of why they tend to reverberate so deeply within the larger polity.

4. *Specifying the Historical Legacy.* The importance or lack of importance of a critical juncture cannot be established in general, but only with reference to a specific historical legacy. It is hardly novel to assert that one should not debate the importance of a hypothesized explanation without first identifying the outcome to be explained, yet it merits emphasis that inconsistencies in the identification of the outcome can lead to divergent assessments of the importance of the critical juncture.[19] In the present analysis, the incorporation periods are intended to explain the specific set of contrasts explored in Chapter 7 concerning party systems, associated constellations of political coalitions, and related issues of regime dynamics. In the framework of the discussion of similarities and differences among countries presented in the Overview, the fact that the countries with a similar heritage of incorporation in this specific sense differ profoundly on many other characteristics should not be taken as evidence that the incorporation periods were not highly consequential.

5. *Duration of the Legacy.* In analyzing the legacy of the critical juncture, it is important to recognize that no legacy lasts forever. One must have ex-

---

[18] Two alternative relationships between the cleavage and the critical juncture should be noted. First, the cleavage may be important because the activation or exacerbation of the cleavage creates new actors or groups and the critical juncture consists of their emergence. An example would be the emergence of the urban class and the organization of labor unions within the working class. Second, the cleavage may be important not because it leads to the emergence of new organized actors, but because it raises political issues so compelling as to trigger some kind of larger reorganization of political relationships. Both outcomes can, of course, occur, as in the analysis presented in this book, where the appearance of an organized working class played a central role in precipitating the critical juncture, but the critical juncture itself is identified with the state response, consisting of the initial incorporation of the labor movement.

[19] An example can be found in analyses of the critical juncture associated with the worker-owner cleavage in Europe in the first decades of the 20th century. Luebbert and Stephens place great emphasis on this cleavage, whereas Lipset and Rokkan deemphasize it and give greater causal importance to a series of prior cleavages. This discrepancy appears to be due in part to the fact that Lipset and Rokkan are explaining the emergence of modern party systems, whereas Luebbert and Stephens are concerned with explaining different trajectories of national regime evolution. The explanation of a somewhat distinct legacy leads to a contrasting assessment of this critical juncture.

plicit criteria for determining when it ends but must also be open to ambiguities about the end points. For instance, in assessing the heritage of incorporation in Brazil, Argentina, Peru, and Uruguay, we took as an end point for
the analysis their military coups of the 1960s and 1970s. These coups unquestionably represent a major discontinuity in national politics in all five
countries. Yet in the postmilitary periods in the 1980s, important elements
of the heritage of incorporation persisted. The choice about the end point is
best viewed as a matter for ongoing analysis, a theme which we address in
the final chapter.

The challenge of explaining the varied duration of the legacy is also a central concern. The legacies of some critical junctures are stable, institutionalized regimes, whereas others produce a political dynamic that prevents or
mitigates against stable patterns. In these cases, the "self-destruction" of the
legacy may be predictable from the critical juncture, though the length of
time before this occurs may vary greatly and is influenced by other factors as
well. The issues raised in the Overview concerning choices between control
and support mobilization in the incorporation periods, and their implications
for different patterns of radicalization or co-optation in the heritage periods
are basic to the stability of the legacy and represent a central concern of the
analysis.

6. *Comparing the Legacy with the Antecedent System: Assessing Continuity and Change.* In addition to carefully identifying the legacy, it is essential to compare it explicitly with the antecedent system. Even in revolutions,
political systems are never completely transformed, and in the study of revolution debates about continuity and change can be of great importance. The
discontinuities that accompany the less drastic critical junctures of concern
here are at least as ambiguous, and there is the risk that the enthusiast of the
critical juncture framework may be too readily disposed to find such discontinuities. The analysis of Uruguay and Colombia well illustrates the need to
consider these issues of continuity.

In some instances, one may be dealing with apparent continuities that conceal significant changes. For example, before the incorporation period Uruguay and Colombia were characterized by two-party systems with deep roots
in the 19th century, in which class divisions tended to be blurred and each
party had relatively stable patterns of regional and sectoral support. In the
legacy of incorporation, one finds the same party system with similar characteristics. The argument is obviously not that the incorporation period created this party system. Rather, it focuses on how the existence of this type
of party system shaped the incorporation period and on the specific ways in
which the incorporation experience in part perpetuated, and in part modified,
the party system.

Alternatively, one may find apparent differences that conceal continuities.
For instance, beginning in the 1940s the Argentine labor movement was
overwhelmingly Peronist, whereas previously it was predominantly socialist
and communist, a major change that was the immediate consequence of the
incorporation period. Yet for many decades after the 1940s, Peronism had an

ephemeral existence as a political party and consisted basically of a grouping of unions and federations that were perhaps the strongest in Latin America, but that were poorly articulated with the party system. Interestingly, this specific characterization of the post-1940s period could in fact also be applied to the pre-1940s period, when precisely these attributes were present. What is crucial about the latter period is that this outcome *followed* the incorporation period and hence reflected the failure, in contrast to the postincorporation experience of some other countries, to establish a stable political role for the labor movement.

These two examples underline the importance, throughout the analysis, of the careful assessment of continuity and change.

7. *Type of Explanation: Constant Causes versus Historical Causes.* The distinctive contribution of the critical juncture framework is its approach to explanation. It focuses on what, following Stinchcombe (1968:101–29), may be called "historical causes." Arthur Stinchcombe explains this approach by comparing two types of explanations of continuity or stability in social life: "constant causes" and "historical causes."

A constant cause operates year after year, with the result that one may observe relative continuity in the outcome produced by this cause. For instance, it has been observed that Latin American workers employed in isolated export "enclaves" commonly have a high propensity to strike, due to certain attributes of the enclave (Di Tella 1968). To the degree that there is continuity in this propensity to strike, it may be hypothesized that it is in important measure due to the *continuing* influence on workers' strike behavior of these same attributes. This is *not* the pattern of causation posited by the critical juncture framework.

By contrast, Stinchcombe's depiction of an historical cause corresponds to the intuitive understanding of critical junctures. In this case, a given set of causes shapes a particular outcome or legacy at one point or period, and subsequently the pattern that is established reproduces itself *without* the recurrence of the original cause.[20] Stinchcombe refers to the type of explanation that accounts for such a pattern of persistence as "historicist," and uses the expression "historical cause" to refer to the event or transition that sets this pattern into motion (1968:103, 118).

In addition to distinguishing between constant and historical causes, Stinchcombe emphasizes the importance of the processes that reproduce the legacy of the historical cause. These mechanisms of reproduction involve in part the fact that, once founded, a given set of institutions creates vested interests, and power holders within these institutions seek to perpetuate their own position (Stinchcombe 1968:108–18; Verba 1971:308). Stinchcombe also emphasizes the role of "sunk costs" that make the continuation of an established institutional pattern a less "expensive" option than creat-

---

[20] Stinchcombe (1968:102) uses the example of the emergence and persistence of Protestantism in Northern Europe. Once the events of the Reformation had occurred, Protestantism perpetuated itself and did not have to be created or caused all over again by subsequent reformations.

ing new patterns (1968:120–21). As Stephen Krasner puts it, "once a given set of institutional structures is in place, it embodies capital stock that cannot be recovered. This [capital] stock takes primarily the form of information trust and shared expectations" whose availability and familiarity reinforce the vested interests noted above (1984:235). In fact, these mechanisms of reproduction become a type of constant cause—but one that is distinctively a legacy of the critical juncture.[21]

For the purpose of our analysis, four issues concerning these mechanisms of reproduction should be underlined. First, to the extent that the outcome or legacy involves political institutions, this emphasis on mechanisms of reproduction raises issues central to current discussions of the "new institutionalism" (March and Olsen 1984, 1989) and to debates on the relative autonomy of politics. In fact, as Krasner emphasizes (1982, 1984), political autonomy is an important theme in the analysis of critical junctures.

Second, the existence of these mechanisms of reproduction and the possibility of the relative autonomy of politics—or of specific political institutions—underscores why it is appropriate to construct a critical juncture framework to begin with. This framework is concerned with a type of discontinuous political change in which critical junctures "dislodge" older institutional patterns. If these processes of reproduction and autonomy did not make institutions resistant to change, models of incremental change would be adequate. It is precisely because political structures often tenaciously resist change that we turn to the analysis of critical junctures.

[21] In addition to explicating the relationship between historical causes and constant causes, it is also appropriate to note the place of historical causes in broader typologies of different approaches to explanation, such as the distinction between deductive, probabilistic, functional, and historical or "genetic" explanation proposed by Nagel (1979:chap. 2).

An historical cause, in the sense intended here, is a particular type of genetic explanation that has a relatively "law-like" probabilistic character. Nagel defines a genetic explanation as one which "set[s] out the sequence of major events through which some earlier system has been transformed into a later one" (1979:25). In assessing genetic explanations, he rejects the idea of viewing them primarily as idiographic (concerned with unique events), as opposed to nomothetic (concerned with general laws) (25, 547–48). He observes that in genetic explanations, "not every past event in the career of the system will be mentioned," and that "those events that are mentioned are selected on the basis of assumptions . . . as to what sorts of events are causally relevant to the development of the system." At times these may be "tacit" assumptions, as in the more idiographic tradition of historical writing. Alternatively, in a more nomothetic tradition, they may involve "fairly precise developmental laws" (25). Genetic explanations may thus encompass a spectrum from more idiographic to more nomothetic approaches.

The models we are concerned with here often contain a fairly self-conscious and conceptually elaborate specification of the nature of the transition involved in the critical juncture that is open to extension to other countries or contexts. These models seek thereby to establish a pattern of explanation that, loosely speaking, may be called "law-like." Hence, the analysis of critical junctures involves a type of genetic explanation that falls more toward the nomothetic end of this spectrum. Since the laws or patterns they identify involve statements about the conditions under which given outcomes are more likely, rather than the conditions under which they are necessary consequences, this involves probabilistic explanation (26).

Third, in applying the critical juncture framework to a particular domain of analysis, it is useful to specify distinctive features of these mechanisms of reproduction in that domain. For instance, the traditional understanding of trade union politics and state-union relations suggests it is an area where a given constellation of political relationships, once institutionalized, has a strong tendency to persist. This tendency is directly discussed or strongly implied by a wide range of analyses. Familiar examples are Michels's (1959/ 1915) classic observations on the co-optation of labor-based socialist parties and the iron law of oligarchy; Olson's (1968) analysis of the collective action problems involved in union formation, which make coercion and state sanctions an important element in the creation and viability of trade unions; and the widely observed tendency of corporatist structures to perpetuate given patterns of union organization and of state-union relationships. These examples suggest how powerful, vested, self-perpetuating interests, embedded in sunk costs, can crystallize around prevailing patterns of union organization and state-union relations. The great importance of such elements suggests that a critical juncture framework is particularly appropriate in the analysis of trade-union politics.

Fourth, it is useful to distinguish between the mechanisms of the *reproduction* and the *production* of the legacy. There often occurs a significant interval between the critical juncture and the period of continuity that is explained by these mechanisms of reproduction. To the extent that the critical juncture is a polarizing event that produces intense political reactions and counterreactions, the crystallization of the legacy does not necessarily occur immediately, but rather may consist of a sequence of intervening steps that respond to these reactions and counterreactions. Because these intervening steps occur within the political sphere and because they follow the critical juncture, which is the point of differentiation among the cases, we consider them part of the legacy.

We therefore find it useful to refer to the dual processes of (1) the production of the legacy—involving its crystallization, often through such a sequence of reaction and counterreaction; and (2) the reproduction of the legacy, involving the process analyzed by Stinchcombe. This distinction corresponds to the contrast between the aftermath of incorporation discussed in Chapter 6 and the heritage of incorporation analyzed in Chapter 7.

8. *Rival Explanations: Constant Causes.* The core hypothesis is that critical junctures occur in different ways in different contexts and that these differences produce distinct legacies. Obviously, the assessment of this hypothesis must be attentive to rival explanations. One of the most important types of rival explanations consists of the "constant causes" discussed above, that is, attributes of the system that may contribute to the presumed stability of the legacy, but that are not the product of the critical juncture.[22] This issue arises in the present book in assessing the legacy of incorporation, an

---

[22] Thus, within the framework of the discussion of constant versus historical causes above, they do not include the constant causes that are part of the legacy itself.

important example being found in the explanation of the political stalemate in Argentina during the 1950s and 1960s. It is common to argue that this stalemate was a legacy of the convulsive rise of Peronism in the 1940s—that is, of the incorporation period. Alternatively, it may be due to underlying structural attributes of Argentine society and economy that both before and after the incorporation period were an ongoing, "constant cause" of the stalemate, and hence represented a rival explanation to the incorporation hypothesis. Thus, O'Donnell (1978) has argued that the particular type of primary products that Argentina exports are conducive to zero-sum policy conflicts between the rural and urban sectors, which in turn can contribute to political stalemate. Though it is difficult in any one study to evaluate a broad range of such rival explanations, this book attempts to address them when they seem particularly important.

9. *The Problem of Partial Explanations.* Some problems in the study of critical junctures are relatively standard issues in the field of comparative-historical analysis yet are of such importance in the present assessment of incorporation periods as to merit attention here. One of these concerns the issue of assessing partial explanations. This, indeed, is all that one normally expects to find in social research.

Compared to scholars who engage in multivariate analysis based on quantitative data, researchers who do multivariate analysis based on the systematic yet qualitative comparison of historical events face an interesting problem in assessing partial explanations and in making the assessment convincing. In quantitative analysis, there is no expectation that a given explanation will entirely account for a given set of outcomes, and quantitative techniques offer straightforward procedures for assessing what portion of the "variance" in the outcome is explained. Even if this is a quarter, or a fifth, or even a tenth, it is often considered a meaningful finding.

In comparative-historical analysis that deals with "whole countries,"[23] this kind of assessment runs into some of the same problems of assessing similarities and differences among cases discussed in the Overview. If two countries "look" similar in the incorporation period, the expectation in assessing the legacy of incorporation is that they should also "look" similar in the heritage period. Yet this expectation may pose an unrealistic standard that interferes with the adequate assessment of the hypothesis. If the incorporation period explains a quarter of the variation in the legacy—a substantial finding by many standards of analysis—the cases would in fact look quite different in the heritage period, and there could be risk of an erroneous rejection of the hypothesis. Thus, the criterion must be that they look sufficiently similar to suggest that the hypothesis has partial explanatory power. Employing this criterion is particularly important in the context of the most different systems design discussed in the Overview, which is based on the delib-

---

[23] For a comment on what it means to compare "whole countries," see footnote 15 in the Overview.

erate juxtaposition of pairs of cases that are different, such as Chile and Brazil, and Peru and Argentina.

10. *Other Rival Explanations: The Example of Suppressor Variables.* These problems of dealing with partial explanations in comparative-historical analysis also arise in addressing rival explanations. An example of particular importance to this study involves the potential role of "suppressor" variables (Rosenberg 1968) that conceal the relationship that one is assessing. For example, we hypothesize that the initial incorporation period in Brazil occurred in a way that weakened the role of parties in controlling and channeling the political participation of the labor movement, thus potentially leading to higher levels of worker politicization and radicalization. Yet Brazilian social and economic structure (e.g., the labor surplus economy and the minimal role of isolated, highly modernized export enclaves) was not conducive to a strong labor movement. Hence, it could be argued that the level of worker politicization was likely to be low, and the assessment of our hypothesis must focus on whether, given this low level, it was nonetheless *higher* than it would otherwise have been, due to the type of incorporation period. In multivariate quantitative analysis the effect of these different factors can be sorted out in a relatively straightforward manner. In comparative-historical analysis, a more subtle and subjective assessment is required, which includes the procedure of process tracing discussed in the Overview.

Conclusion

Our goal has been to identify issues commonly encountered in the analysis of critical junctures. Though it makes sense intuitively that societies go through periods of basic reorientation that shape their subsequent development, too little attention has been devoted to the problems that arise in assessing claims about the scope and nature of this impact. To make this assessment more adequate, one must devote careful attention to the identification of the critical juncture and the legacy, the comparison with the antecedent system, the distinction between constant and historical causes, the mechanisms of production and reproduction of the legacy, various kinds of rival explanations, and special problems of assessing the impact of critical junctures in the context of comparative-historical analysis.

Finally, a basic point should be reiterated. In an analytic framework that contains many elements, it is essential that these elements be examined with care. At the same time, it is also crucial that the main idea not slip from view. The goal of presenting these several criteria of assessment is to strengthen the test of the core hypothesis: that the critical juncture occurred in different ways and that these differences were highly consequential. In the present book, this hypothesis concerns the long-term impact of different types of incorporation periods. The goal of providing this framework for the analysis of critical junctures is to better assess this core argument about the transformation of Latin American politics.

2

Context: The Labor Movement and the State in Latin America

WE HAVE hypothesized that the emergence of the labor movement in Latin America, along with the forging of new patterns of state-union relations during the incorporation periods, had a major impact on the subsequent evolution of national politics. Why should this transition be so important? Why should the emergence of and response to working-class conflict have a major impact? Analysts of many different actors both in society and within the state are often adept at interpreting and explaining larger patterns of political change from the "angle" of the particular actor they study. Indeed, any larger picture of change can usefully be viewed from many different angles. Why, then, should the labor movement be of particular significance?

We argue that in crucial phases of Latin American development, labor politics has been a kind of coalitional "fulcrum." In different countries and different historical periods, organized labor has been a pivotal actor, and the choices made by other actors in positioning themselves vis-à-vis organized labor have had a crucial impact on national politics.

This idea is expressed subtly but pointedly in Alexander Wilde's analysis of the breakdown of Colombian democracy in the 1940s, an instance that nicely illustrates our argument as a kind of "crucial case" because it is one with a labor movement that was conspicuously weak. Wilde suggests that despite their weakness, the unions in Colombia contributed to democratic breakdown because their presence in coalition politics of this period was "constantly unsettling." They could force the political party with which they were then mainly identified, the Liberals, to "support or repudiate them," and in the process seriously strained the Liberals' commitment to the basic rules of the political game (Wilde 1978:45). Obviously, if the coalitional presence of unions can be constantly unsettling in a country where they are weak, they potentially play an even more central role in countries that have stronger labor movements.

Why should the coalitional presence of unions in crucial periods of change be "constantly unsettling"? Why should the labor movement be a coalitional fulcrum or a pivotal actor? What understanding do we have of labor politics in Latin America that allows us to build on the answers to these questions and to construct an argument about the larger political impact of the labor movement?

This chapter addresses these questions. We first examine general arguments about the political significance of the labor movement in Latin America, focusing on its strategic importance in the economic and political sphere and its potential role in legitimating or delegitimating the state. We then explore further the theme raised in the Overview concerning the choices of actors within the state regarding strategies of labor control and labor mobilization, along with the complementary choices on the side of actors within the labor movement regarding strategies of cooperation or noncooperation (the traditional anarchist position) with the state. In discussing these strategies, we introduce the idea of a "dual dilemma" that underlies the interaction between these two sets of choices. This interaction is explored further in the context of a discussion of corporatism, the concept commonly used to describe many of the principal institutions of state-labor relations in Latin America.

Political Importance of Labor Movement

The political importance of the labor movement may be looked at both from the perspective of its capacity for collective action and in terms of the special significance of this capacity in bestowing political support and mobilizing opposition.

Capacity for Collective Action. The location of many unionized workers in spatially concentrated, large scale centers of production and/or their strategic position at critical points in the economy or the polity gives them an unusual capacity to disrupt the economic and political system and hence provides incentives for sustained collective action. This capacity is fundamental to organized labor's political importance.

The contexts of work conducive to collective action are analyzed in the next chapter. They include: (1) isolated "enclaves" of export production, along with related networks of transportation and communication, that are crucial to the prosperity of the export sector in a number of countries and that can easily be paralyzed by strikes; (2) large-scale urban factory production located in close proximity to the centers of national political power in what are in many cases highly centralized polities, where strikes can have a dramatic impact on the political system; and (3) the most dynamic sectors of the urban industrial economy, which may employ fewer workers due to their more capital-intensive form of production, but where labor stability and rapid growth are commonly viewed by economic and political leaders as crucial to economic development. The paralysis of this latter sector through strikes is therefore an important economic and political event, and the use of repression to control strikes may be especially problematic because of its effect on the skilled labor force in this sector and the greater difficulty of replacing skilled workers. If the workplace is owned by a foreign enterprise, sentiments of nationalism can provide strong ideological support for collective worker action. In both foreign-owned and public sector enterprises, the potential negative political ramifications of the extensive use of repression may be greater than in nationally owned firms in the private sector. In sum, many workers are situated at points in the process of production that give them opportunities for collective action that may potentially have a considerable impact.

Political Significance of Worker Organization and Protest. Many authors argue that the collective action of workers has special political significance in the Latin American context. James L. Payne's (1965) widely noted thesis on "political bargaining" in Latin American labor relations suggests that in labor surplus economies such as those in many Latin American countries, unions' often weak position in the sphere of collective bargaining pushes them into the political arena. Further, in the relatively centralized political systems characteristic in much of Latin America, the national executive often quickly becomes involved in labor disputes, and key actors may commonly believe that the executive can and should "do something" about these disputes. Given this expectation, the failure to contain worker protest can threaten the stability of the national executive.

Other discussions view the political significance of workers' collective action in terms of its importance for the legitimation of the state (Waisman 1982:ix). The specific form of these arguments varies, but the recurring theme is the implicit or explicit comparative thesis that basic elements central to the legitimation of the state in some earlier-developing European countries are absent or incomplete in Latin America and that unions play a central role in efforts to compensate for this deficiency.

Part of the argument about incomplete legitimation revolves around the hypothesis that in the 20th-century world of nation states, the fundamental dependency of Latin American countries on the international economic system, the cycles of denationalization of their economies that occur as an aspect of this dependency, and the prominent role of foreign enterprises in economic development makes the legitimation of capitalism and of the capitalist state more problematic than in contexts where development is nationally controlled to a greater degree (Hirschman 1979:90–93). As Corradi (1978) put it, due to their external dependency, Latin American societies are chronically "decentered" in the economic sphere.

Alternative perspectives that provide a link between incomplete legitimation and issues of worker politics appear in O'Donnell's analysis of the "mediations" between state and society and Corradi's discussion of the political consequences of this decentering. O'Donnell (1977, 1979, 1982) suggests that given the uneven record of free elections and the problematic status of civil liberties in many Latin American countries, the mediation of citizenship has had a troubled history in the region, and two other mediations have played a larger role: nationalism and "populism."[1] Corradi makes a parallel argument

---

[1] O'Donnell refers to this third mediation in Spanish as the *pueblo* or *lo popular*. These terms are difficult to translate, since the most nearly equivalent terms in English—*people* and *popular*—have different connotations. Hence, we have used the term *populism*. In O'Donnell's analysis, these Spanish terms refer to a form of collective identity of previously marginalized sectors of the population "whose recognition as members of the nation came about through their demands for substantive justice, which they posed not as op-

in analyzing the consequences of economic "decentering." In reaction to this decentering, the political sphere is "the domain in which a society that has no control over its own destiny tries to repair the ravages of foreign domination." Thus, "culture and politics seek to integrate, from inside dependent societies, what economic power operating essentially from abroad, tends to disintegrate. This attempt at integration is what gives Latin American culture and politics their peculiar flavor. It is expressed most distinctively in 'populist' movements" (1978:41). Corradi also notes that in contrast to the postulated dependence of the economic sphere, these expressions of populism in the cultural and political sphere can exhibit an important degree of autonomy from economic forces. His argument about autonomy is consistent with the perspective we adopt in stressing the distinctive dynamic surrounding the political dilemmas of state-labor relations.

A further variant of this perspective on incomplete legitimation is found in the thesis that labor's importance is greater because Latin American development has not produced a strong national capitalist class. An early version of this argument was presented by Leon Trotsky in the late 1930s while he was living in exile in Mexico. Reflecting on the coalitional dilemmas of the political systems found in dependent, "semi-colonial" economies, Trotsky observed that "inasmuch as the chief role in backward countries is not played by national but by foreign capitalism, the national bourgeoisie occupies . . . a much more minor position." He argued that, as a consequence:

> The national proletariat soon begins playing the most important role in the life of the country. In these conditions the national government, to the extent that it tries to show resistance to foreign capital, is compelled to a greater or lesser degree to lean on the proletariat. On the other hand, the governments of those backward countries which consider it inescapable or more profitable for themselves to march shoulder to shoulder with foreign capital, destroy the labour organizations and institute a more or less totalitarian regime. (Trotsky 1968:10)

Though coalitional alternatives in Latin America are certainly more complex than this, Trotsky's observations usefully suggest that the tension in labor policy between a concern with the mobilization of labor support and with labor control can take a particularly acute, politically charged, form.

The crucial point for present purposes is that the organized working class is one of the most important "bearers" of the mediations and political symbols relevant to the problem of legitimacy. In O'Donnell's terms, the segment of the population that is by definition the bearer of the mediation of *lo popular* and also an important bearer of the mediation of nationalism is commonly referred to as the "popular sector."[2] With obvious variations across

---

pressed classes, but as victims of poverty and governmental indifference, who, moreover, embodied what was most authentically national" (1982, chap. 1).

[2] The popular sector may be defined as the urban and rural lower class and lower middle class. This is obviously not a traditional Marxist class category. For an exploration of some of these issues, see Laclau (1977).

countries and over time, the two most important actors within this sector are the organized labor movement—due to its special capacity for collective action discussed above—and, in some very important cases, an organized and politically mobilized peasantry. Populist appeals have of course been made to other segments of the popular sector, and beginning in the 1970s new forms of popular social movements based in the informal sector appeared to assume a larger role in Latin American politics. Yet over a number of decades in the 20th century, though obviously with major contrasts in their relative importance in different countries, these two principal segments of the urban and rural popular sectors—the labor movement and the peasantry—have produced the most important organized expressions of these mediations.

By securing the visible cooperation of the organized labor movement, the state can take an important step toward addressing problems of legitimacy. Alternatively, the labor movement can be a principal vehicle for protest against state policy and such protest can hurt the legitimacy of the state. With reference to the policies that raise issues of nationalism and antinationalism, unions can be either an invaluable resource for governments that wish to take nationalistic initiatives, or an important adversary of governments that reject such policies.

In sum, the collective action perspective calls attention to unions' concrete capacity to bestow support or generate opposition. The perspective that focuses on nationalism, populism, and legitimacy suggests why the collective action of workers becomes a potent force in Latin American politics, and why state responses to worker protest likewise become a pivotal domain of policy. These two perspectives offer a clearer basis for understanding why the coalitional role of labor can be "constantly unsettling," as Wilde put it. It can be constantly unsettling because labor not only has this substantial capacity for collective action, but because its collective action touches on larger, underlying issues of Latin American politics.

Putting State-Labor Relations in Perspective

At the same time that we emphasize political importance of the labor movement, we also wish to place labor politics in a realistic perspective by raising four points concerning the relation of the "formal" to the "informal" sector of the economy, the issue of the homogeneity versus heterogeneity of the labor force in the formal sector, the relationship between state-labor and capital-labor relations, and a recent challenge to arguments, such as that presented above, that focus on legitimacy.

Formal and Informal Sector.   Studies of the urban working class quite properly see the labor movement and unions as just one part of a complex world of work, and these studies at times express concern over an excessive focus on the organized labor movement. As one explores claims about the political importance of the labor movement, it is essential to be clear about what sector one is considering.

Spalding (1972:214) urges caution in not overstating the importance of organized labor in Latin America, noting that "despite the existence of huge
confederations, sometimes grouping more than a million members on paper,
only about 15% of the economically active population belongs to a
union. . . . The industrial sector, usually the focus of militant labor organization, represents only approximately 30% of the salaried population." Sofer
(1980:175) presents similar arguments, suggesting that "studies of political
parties and trade unions . . . focus attention on a minority of workers and
give short shrift to the unorganized."

Obviously, it is not productive to base an argument about the political importance of unions on a simplified notion that they include most of the labor
force or are in some sense "representative" of the larger urban working class,
encompassing unorganized workers and the informal as well as the formal
sector. It is also essential to recognize the large contribution of studies reflecting the concerns of the "new labor history" in shedding light on this
larger world of work in Latin America and its impact on societal change.

Far from maintaining that the labor movement represents this larger world
of work, we adopt the perspective of Portes and Walton (1975:103–4), who
differentiate sharply between the formal and informal sectors, treating them
as different classes with distinct interests and distinct relationships to other
classes within society. This "class differentiation" within the broader
"working class" resulted in important measure from the special capacity for
collective action of specific segments of the working population. The formal
sector emerged as the product of the political demands of these segments of
the working class and of state policies that responded to, or sought to preempt, these demands, leading to the creation of a formal, regulated, "high-
wage" sector of the labor force that became differentiated from the more
"traditional" informal sector (Portes 1983). Thus, the formal sector was created by politics and public policy, and its existence is in part an expression
of the political importance of the labor movement. In addition, one of the
major policy periods in which these policy initiatives occurred was, of
course, what we call the incorporation period. Thus, the present study can
be understood as an analysis of an important aspect of the genesis of the
formal sector of the economy and of the ramifications of this genesis for the
larger evolution of politics.

Homogeneity versus Heterogeneity. A second point of caution regarding
the political importance of the labor movement concerns the relationship
between the labor movement and the larger context of work within the formal sector. Jelin observes that studies of the working class that focus at the
level of unions and union politics tend to see the working class as a more
homogeneous actor,[3] whereas studies focused on the labor force within the
workplace tend to see the working class as more heterogeneous. In research

[3] This thesis was explored in depth in a public lecture given by Jelin at the Institute of
International Studies, University of California, Berkeley, in 1981.

on union politics, there is a risk of misrepresenting the diversity and complexity of the unionized sector of the work force.

This tension between homogeneity and heterogeneity raises issues that are both methodological and substantive. They are methodological in the sense that the level of analysis influences what is observed. A macro study of national trade union politics is indeed more likely to focus on the overall characteristics of the "forest," whereas a micro study of one or a few specific contexts of work tends to focus on the characteristics of individual "trees." From the first perspective, the forest looks more homogeneous; from the second, much less so. Both perspectives are needed to advance the understanding of Latin American labor, as they are in the analysis of any topic.

In addition, a substantive issue is involved, in that union formation and state-labor relations have an impact on these realities of homogeneity and heterogeneity. It is certainly the case that there is a high degree of heterogeneity within even the organized sector of the labor movement. However, it is worth noting that both in the course of initial union formation and subsequently, labor leaders and labor organizations seek to homogenize the labor movement as they attempt to bring it under their own leadership (S. Valenzuela 1983), trying to standardize conditions of work, units of collective bargaining, and often the political orientation of unionists. This homogenization is also pursued by actors within the state. Both the initial incorporation projects and subsequent state policy toward labor represent in part a systematic effort to standardize and homogenize the labor movement and relationships of work. Thus, a process of aggregation and homogenization is integral to the evolution of labor leadership, of union organization, and of state-union relations. At the same time, changes in the nature of work, changes in the labor movement, and many other factors may disaggregate, make more heterogeneous, or even destroy existing patterns of labor leadership, labor organization, and state-union relations.

In attempting to adopt an interactive approach to the relationship between the labor movement and political structures, we seek to be sensitive to both the methodological and substantive side of this issue. Thus, in analyzing union politics, we recognize that: (1) we are focusing only on one segment of the labor force, the formal sector; (2) this sector was created by politics and public policy in response to labor activation; (3) although there is always a risk that a focus on union politics can lead the analyst to see the labor movement as more homogeneous than it really is, such homogenization is inherent to the functioning of unions and state-labor relations and indeed is central to the topic of this book; and (4) at the same time that those who benefit from this homogenization will seek to defend the institutions that support it, others who benefit less may seek to modify or undermine these institutions. It is in part because of recurrent attempts to undermine these institutions that the legacy of episodes of labor policy such as the initial incorporation periods are often sharply contested.

State-Labor versus Capital-Labor Relations.   A third issue is the relative significance of state-labor relations, the central focus of this analysis, as opposed to capital-labor relations.[4] One perspective suggests that in Latin America state-labor relations may in fact be more important than employer-labor relations. This thesis is central to J. Payne's (1968) argument about political bargaining. Payne maintains that due to labor's weak position in the labor market and greater leverage in the political arena, a pattern of industrial relations emerges in which political bargaining is more important than collective bargaining as a means of pursuing labor gains. The implication is that to a greater degree than in the advanced industrial economies, state-labor relations are the crucial arena of interaction, rather than employer-labor relations. Goodman (1973:21) likewise underlined the paramount importance of the state in shaping labor relations in Latin America, though he stresses that in distinct historical periods and different countries, the form taken by state-labor-manager relations is diverse.

However, as Roxborough (1981:84–85) has pointed out, the degree to which the state plays a larger role in labor relations in Latin America than in the advanced industrial countries can easily be exaggerated. Further, with reference to Payne's argument about political bargaining, it is possible to suggest that instead of positing a tradeoff between the strength of labor organizations in the workplace and their strength in the political arena, one should think in terms of a complementarity between these two dimensions. By virtue of being a weak economic actor, labor may also be a weak political actor; or at the very least, a political actor deprived of the clout that comes from economic strength.[5]

The argument we wish to present does not depend on the thesis that state-labor relations are more important than state-capital relations. Rather, it makes more sense to argue that state-labor relations revolve in part around the distinctive political dynamics of support and legitimation discussed above, and that they therefore merit substantial attention in their own right. Bendix (1964:72–73) makes a parallel point in analyzing the earlier history of advanced industrial countries, suggesting that the initial emergence of labor movements and labor protest was fully as much a political issue as an economic issue. This political issue is our central concern.

Legitimacy.   Part of the argument about the political importance of the labor movement has focused on its role in contributing to, or undermining, legitimacy. Before embracing this perspective, it is appropriate to consider Przeworski's (1986:50–53) important challenge to analyses of regime change which focus on legitimacy. Przeworski argues that "the entire problem of legitimacy is . . . incorrectly posed. What matters for the stability of any regime is not the legitimacy of this particular system of domination but the presence or absence of preferable alternatives" (51–52).

---

[4] In countries and historical periods where a large public sector is unionized and the state is the owner of enterprises, these categories obviously overlap. But in many decades earlier in this century that are of central concern to this analysis, public ownership of enterprises was more limited and public sector unions were considerably less important within the labor movement.

[5] Albert Fishlow, personal communication, suggested this observation.

Przeworski has thus presented an invaluable challenge, which points to the need to analyze regime change at a more concrete level. The key question that must be addressed in responding to this challenge is the following: what are the attributes of given political "alternatives" that lead key actors to view them as "preferable"? It is evident that in the Latin American context, the identification (or conspicuous lack of identification) of the symbols of nationalism and populism with given regime alternatives can play a crucial role in defining these alternatives as desirable or undesirable. In addition, labor politics plays an important role in this process of definition. Therefore, even accepting Przeworski's framework, these symbolic dimensions of labor politics can be seen as closely linked to regime dynamics.

To conclude, arguments about the labor movement's political importance are complex and need to be made in light of the issues and challenges just discussed. However, within that framework there is substantial ground for viewing the labor movement as a powerful political actor in Latin America and for using the analysis of labor politics as a perspective from which to explore broader issues of political change.

Control, Support, and the Dual Dilemma

In light of the labor movement's political importance, it becomes clearer why, in distinguishing among types of initial incorporation, we have focused on the varying degree of emphasis on control and support mobilization. Having the capacity to control the labor movement is a major political asset, as is the capacity to mobilize labor's political support. Similarly, the lack of either of these capacities can be a major political liability.

In the analysis of such assets and liabilities, it must be recognized that the relationship between control and support mobilization is complex, even if the matter is looked at only from the side of the state. If one's perspective also encompasses the strategies adopted by the labor movement, the matter becomes even more complex.

This complexity may usefully be viewed in the framework of a "dual dilemma" in the relationship between the state and organized labor. From the standpoint of leaders who shape state policy, the dilemma concerns this choice between the option of controlling labor and seeking to mobilize labor support. On the side of the labor movement, the dilemma concerns the choice between cooperating with the state or resisting such cooperation, as well as the related choice between entering or not entering into the sphere of partisan politics.

Dilemma from the Standpoint of the State.   From the perspective of political leaders who shape state policy, the emergence of the working class raises explosive issues of how to control this powerful new force within society, but it also presents the opportunity to mobilize new bases of political support. Both of these options can be compelling.

The state in Latin America has been and continues to be centrally con-

cerned with controlling organized labor and limiting its political and economic strength. This control is a central issue in capitalist development and
ultimately involves what O'Donnell has referred to as the issue of maintaining "cellular domination" in society, that is, the basic capacity of capital and
the state to regulate the functioning of the economy in the workplace
(1982:chap. 1). Historically, the growth of the state's concern with the control of labor was closely connected with the long-term erosion of more traditional systems of private, clientelistic control of workers in the course of
modernization.[6] In the context of this erosion, the emergence of an organized
working class poses a basic challenge to the existing distribution of economic and political power, a challenge that we explore in some detail in the
next chapter.

At the same time, the option of cultivating labor support can be compelling. Political divisions even within a relatively narrow political elite may
encourage a more progressively oriented faction to increase its power
through building labor support, following a pattern of mobilization as an opposition strategy (Schattschneider 1960). Governments that adopt nationalistic economic policies commonly find labor support highly compatible with
this policy orientation.

However, such efforts at support mobilization characteristically involve
sharp disjunctures in political coalitions that may produce intense conflict,
making them potentially risky to initiate and difficult to sustain. To use
again Wilde's phrase, the constantly unsettling character of this dilemma is
reflected in the fact that the reaction to "pro-labor" policies and to the mobilization of workers as a support base has been a central issue triggering
many of the most dramatic regime changes in 20th century Latin America.
Dilemma from the Standpoint of Labor.   Labor's side of the dual dilemma
consists of the tension between a conception of the political sphere as an
essential arena for the defense of workers' interests and the concern that participation in politics will corrupt and co-opt unions and union leaders. The
dilemma centers around whether unions should play a broader political role,
either by establishing labor parties as political arms or by forming coalitions
with other sectors.

One aspect of the dilemma for labor is the issue of cooperation with the
state. From its early anarchist tradition, the labor movement has been aware
of the risk of co-optation and control that can result from such collaboration.
However, the failure to collaborate can leave labor without allies, influence,
and access to policymakers and public agencies. It entails foregoing the opportunity to establish an exchange relationship that can yield important benefits. The attraction of these benefits is particularly great in situations like
those in early 20th-century Latin America, when the conditions of work left
labor in a weak position and when the alternative was often repression.

[6] Obviously, clientelistic forms of control and other forms of clientelistic relationships
persist, yet they are supplemented by new forms of control and political articulation. See
Kaufman (1977a).

A variant of the dilemma concerns the link not just to the state, but to political activity and political parties more broadly—the issue of whether or not to enter the political arena and seek political office. Again, the dilemma derives from the influence that can be gained by winning public office—if only in a minority and opposition status—versus the risk of subordination of the union movement to the political logic of party politics and elections.

In fact, within Latin America the apolitical alternative has seldom been viable. This is due in part to labor's often weak position in the workplace, to the ability of the state to influence labor with both carrots and sticks, and to Comintern policy, which at important moments mandated cooperation with the state for the communist sector of the labor movement. Nevertheless, both in theory and in practice, the dilemma between autonomy and the advantages that can be gained through political participation, including at times state protection, is a real one.

Relative Impact of the State's Choices and Labor's Choices.   How important are the state's choices, as opposed to labor's choices, as they resolve their respective sides of this dual dilemma? The answer depends on what specific outcome is to be explained—that is, important for what?

If one wishes to explain why the incorporation periods occurred to begin with, it was obviously because a working class emerged, constituted itself as a labor movement, and often decided to challenge, rather than cooperate with, the state. On the other hand, if one wishes to explain why the incorporation periods took the specific form they did in each country, the answer will focus more centrally on the dynamics of intraelite politics and choices by actors within the state, although at various points choices made within the labor movement were also important.

In the countries identified in the Overview as cases of state incorporation, characterized by a sustained attempt to control and depoliticize the labor movement, the incorporation period was imposed on labor, with repression when necessary. Hence, the strategies of the labor movement toward cooperation or noncooperation with the state were of marginal relevance to the form of incorporation. On the other hand, labor's reaction became very important in the aftermath of incorporation.

In the cases of party incorporation, the political logic from the standpoint of leaders acting within the state was again crucial, but the strategy of labor was more central, and the incorporation period must be seen as the outcome of the interaction between the two sides of the dilemma. To address the labor movement's demands and overcome its reluctance to cooperate, actors in the state seeking to mobilize labor support at times had to pursue prolabor policies more aggressively than they otherwise would have, as the price of securing cooperation and support.

To capture this interaction in our analysis of the incorporation period in Chapter 5, we begin the discussion of each country by examining the goals of actors within the state (i.e., the project from above) and then explore the goals of leaders of the labor movement (i.e., the project from below). The discussion then proceeds to explore the interplay between these two projects.

An Interactive Perspective on Corporatism

Given the utility of an interactive perspective on state-labor relations, it is useful to go one step further and show how the social science concept—and the political practice—of corporatism can be understood from this perspective. State-labor relations in Latin America have been widely interpreted as corporative.[7] In most of the countries considered in this study, the dual dilemma unfolds within this corporative context, and the policy instruments employed by the state as it addresses the dual dilemma are in part the instruments of corporatism. This is especially true in the initial incorporation periods, one of the most important historical episodes in which corporative structures were introduced.[8]

Components of Corporatism.[9]   We have elsewhere defined state-group relations as corporative to the degree that there is (1) state structuring of groups that produces a system of officially sanctioned, noncompetitive, compulsory interest associations; (2) state subsidy of these groups; and (3) state-imposed constraints[10] on demand-making, leadership, and internal governance. Corporatism is thus a nonpluralist system of group representation. In contrast to the pattern of interest politics based on autonomous, competing groups, in the case of corporatism the state encourages the formation of a limited number of officially recognized, noncompeting, state-supervised groups.

Though at times it may be useful to view corporatism as a single syndrome of political relationships, to pursue these issues of control and support mobilization it is helpful to disaggregate the concept. The creation of corporative frameworks for shaping labor movements occurs in the context of very different relationships of economic and political power—as was already suggested in the typology of incorporation periods in the Overview—and this diversity suggests that there may be variations and subtypes of corporatism. In fact, some corporative provisions bestow advantages upon the labor organizations that receive them, whereas others do not. Important organizational benefits are bestowed both by provisions for the structuring of unions (such as official recognition, monopoly of representation, and compulsory membership) and also by the subsidy of unions. These provisions are quite distinct

---

[7] O'Donnell 1977; Kaufman 1977a; Collier and Collier 1977; Wiarda 1976; Erickson 1977; Harding 1973; Schmitter 1971, 1974; Mericle 1977; Córdova 1974; Reyna 1977; Corradi 1974; Petras 1969.

[8] This generalization does not apply to Uruguay, where the incorporation period was pluralistic rather than corporative. At the level of corporative labor legislation, it likewise does not apply to Peru. Due to the legislative paralysis at the height of the incorporation period in Peru, little labor legislation was passed. However, in other respects a corporative pattern was followed in Peru, and in both Peru and Uruguay the larger ideas about political exchange developed below are relevant (see Chapter 5).

[9] The following discussion draws on Collier and Collier (1979).

[10] We deliberately use the expression "constraints" to refer to these specific provisions, employing the term "control" more broadly, as in the above discussion.

from the constraints, which directly control labor organizations and labor leaders.

The idea that structuring and subsidy are benefits is supported by more general research on political organizations, which suggests that these provisions do in fact address basic organizational needs of labor unions.[11] These include the need to compete successfully with rival groups that seek to represent the same constituency; the need to be recognized as the legitimate representative of their constituency in dealings with other sectors of society; the need to recruit and retain members; and the need for stable sources of income. Because structuring and subsidy help meet these needs, they confer significant advantages to the unions that receive them.

Although these provisions may be of value to any interest association, two of them meet special organizational needs of unions. Provisions for compulsory membership have long been seen as crucial to the formation of unions, and their importance becomes clear in the problems of collective action that arise when strikes are conducted by individuals associated with two basic factors of production: capital and labor. Individual capitalists can protest the direction of economic or political change simply by failing to invest. They do not require collective organization to carry out what might be thought of as a "capital strike," and hence to have a major political and economic impact. Labor is far more dependent on collective action if it is to influence the economy and the polity. Further, whereas capitalists can consume rather than invest, the immediate economic hardship to individual workers who withdraw their labor is necessarily much greater, reducing the incentive to make such a decision on an individual basis and further increasing the need to aggregate individual decisions in order to undertake such a withdrawal (see Offe 1985). Hence, corporative provisions for compulsory membership that enforce participation in certain forms of collective behavior have a special value for unions.

Second, because unions bring together individuals of low income,[12] the problem of financial resources is far greater than it is for the interest associations of capitalists or many other groups. Hence, provisions for the subsidy and financing of unions are particularly important.

Inducements and Constraints.   Though structuring and subsidy thus provide important organizational benefits to unions, one must understand the political context in which these provisions appear in order to interpret their significance. As we have emphasized, corporative policies toward organized labor in Latin America have been introduced from above by political leaders acting through the state who have used these policies to help them pursue various goals, including the effort to control the behavior of the labor movement and/or to win its political support. It therefore seems appropriate, at least within the Latin American setting, to view structuring and subsidy not

[11] Bendix, 1964: 80–97; Olson, 1968:chap. 3; Wilson:1973:chap. 3.

[12] This is true especially in the early phase of the labor movement before the emergence of middle-class unions. Obviously, the working-class unions may include a "high wage" sector, but relative to capitalists, members' incomes are low.

simply as benefits but as inducements through which the state attempts to persuade organized labor to support the state, to cooperate with its goals, and to accept the constraints it imposes. In this context, corporatism may thus be viewed as an exchange based on an interplay between inducements and constraints.[13]

However, though one can distinguish between inducements and constraints, they are not diametrically opposed phenomena. This point brings us back to the theme raised above: the idea that state efforts at imposing control and mobilizing support can be, in their ultimate consequences, interconnected in complex ways. Analysts of power and influence such as Lasswell and Kaplan (1950:97–98) and Gamson (1968) distinguish between inducements and constraints but view both as mechanisms that serve to influence behavior. Constraints are seen as producing compliance by the application, or threat of application, of negative sanctions or "disadvantages." Inducements, by contrast, are offered to produce compliance by the application of "advantages" (Gamson 1968:74–77). In this literature, inducements are viewed as mechanisms of co-optation. As such, though they involve "advantages," they can also lead to social control.

The dual character of inducements is evident in the specific mechanisms of structuring and subsidy discussed above. These inducements may, like the constraints, ultimately lead to state penetration and domination of labor organizations, for at least three reasons. First, an inducement such as monopoly of representation by its nature is offered to some labor organizations and withheld from others. This provision has commonly been used in Latin America to undermine radical unions and promote those favored by the state. Second, unions receiving inducements must commonly meet various formal requirements to receive them. Finally, the granting of official recognition, monopoly of representation, compulsory membership, or subsidy by the state may make the leadership dependent on the state, rather than on union members, for the union's legitimacy and viability. This dependency may encourage the tendency for labor leadership to become an oligarchy less responsive to workers than to the concerns of state agencies or political lead-

[13] This conception of an interplay between inducements and constraints is consistent with standard discussions of the dialectical nature of state-labor relations in Latin America. Goodman (1972:232) has interpreted Latin American labor law, the most important formal expression of corporative frameworks for shaping trade unions, as containing both a "carrot and a stick" for labor. Spalding (1972:211) has analyzed the tendency of the state and elite groups in Latin America to "seduce and control" organized labor. The terminology employed in a standard manual of labor relations in the United States suggests that the inducement/constraint distinction is salient in that context as well. This manual contrasts provisions of labor law that involve "labor sweeteners" sought by unions with those involving "restrictions" on unions sought by employers. More broadly, in the analysis that played a crucial role in initiating the current debate on corporatism, Schmitter (1974:94) hinted at this distinction when he suggested, without elaboration, that corporative provisions that we have referred to as involving constraints may be accepted by groups "in exchange for" the types of provisions we have identified as involving the structuring of groups.

ers with which the leaders interact. The dual nature of the inducements explains why high levels of inducements, as well as of constraints, are often instituted by governments that are indifferent to cultivating labor support and whose goal is to produce a docile, controlled labor movement, as occurred in the cases of state incorporation analyzed in Chapter 5.

Labor Movement Responses. If both inducements and constraints can ultimately lead to control, it remains to be demonstrated that labor organizations really desire to receive the inducements—that these provisions in fact induce labor organizations to cooperate with the state and to accept the constraints. A preliminary examination of the evidence suggests this is often the case.

A useful opportunity to observe labor leaders' assessments of different corporative provisions is in the debate that often arises during the incorporation period, at the time of enactment of the first major legislation that provides a basis for legalizing unions and that commonly includes a number of inducements and constraints for the unions that become legally incorporated under the terms of the law. An important example is found in Argentina. The dominant sector of the Argentine labor movement initially rejected the labor policies of the military government that came to power in Argentina in June of 1943. Only when Perón began to adopt the program of this sector of the movement—that is, to support the organizational goals of labor as well as its substantive demands on bread and butter issues, in part through a labor law that placed heavy emphasis on inducements—did major sectors of the labor movement begin to accept his offer of cooperation (Silverman 1967:134–35).

In Mexico the reaction of the labor movement to the first national labor law in 1931 again reflected the dual nature of the law, encompassing both inducements and constraints. Labor leaders objected to certain constraints—the provisions for federal supervision of their records, finances, and membership lists—whereas they accepted the provisions for the recognition of unions, defined above as an inducement. Furthermore, they were dissatisfied over the absence of compulsory membership, a provision that we have identified as an inducement (Clark 1934:215; Harker 1937:95).

The debate within the labor movement over the passage of the 1924 labor law in Chile reflects this same pattern. The dominant Marxist sector of the movement generally accepted the new system, arguing that it had to "use all the social legislation of the capitalist state to fight capitalism itself" (quoted in Morris 1966:246). The debate within the labor movement showed that although this sector opposed the constraints contained in the law, it was attracted by the law's provisions that would help it extend its organization to new economic sectors and allow it to receive a state-administered financial subsidy derived from profit-sharing. The inducements contained in the law were thus initially sufficient to motivate the dominant sector of the labor movement to cooperate with the state.

The 1924 Chilean law illustrates another point as well. Though the inducements offered by the state have often been sufficient to win the cooperation of labor, this has not always been the case. Historically, the anarchists were acutely aware not only of the costs of the constraints that accompany the inducements, but also of the tendency of the inducements to lead to control. Thus, following the traditional anarchist position regarding the risks of co-optation arising from cooperation with the state, the anarchist sector of the Chilean labor movement rejected the 1924 law completely. Another example is the 1943 law in Argentina, which was widely opposed by organized labor. At that point the state was not willing to extend sufficient inducements to win the cooperation of the labor movement, which rejected the constraints. It is noteworthy that the Peronist law of 1945 provided the necessary level of inducements and was accepted by the labor movement, despite its similarly high level of constraints.

These examples suggest that although some labor groups will resist these inducements, the inducements have in fact served to win their cooperation and to persuade them to accept the constraints. Furthermore, the distinction between inducements and constraints is not merely an analytic point of concern to social scientists. It is, rather, a vital political issue in the history of state-union relations in Latin America, one which we will observe being played out at various points in the historical analysis below.

In conclusion, two observations may be underlined. First, this interaction among the components of corporatism, along with the closely related theme of the dual dilemma in state-labor relations, plays a central role in framing the analysis of both the incorporation periods and the legacy of incorporation. Second, the picture that emerges is not static, but highly dynamic. Thus, the introduction of corporative provisions of state-labor relations, often during the incorporation periods, should not be understood as producing structures or institutions that are unchanging. The literature on corporatism has repeatedly noted a major divergence between the goals of actors in the state who introduce corporatism, the initial reality of the corporative structures, and the ultimate consequences of these structures.[14] The question of how this divergence occurs is a central theme of this study.

[14] Hammergren 1977; Chalmers 1977:28–29; Ciría 1977; Stepan 1978b.

Part II

CLEAVAGE

Energone of
Labour market

Pattern of social
economic + social
growth
+
New

3

Labor: Emergence of Worker Organization and Protest

BEGINNING in the latter decades of the 19th century, older patterns of worker association oriented toward mutual aid societies began to give way to new forms of collective action. By the end of the second decade of the 20th century, most of the eight countries had seen the emergence of substantial labor movements and dramatic episodes of worker protest. Although the middle sectors would ultimately play a far more central role in initiating the change in government that brought the major challenge to oligarchic hegemony, it was the working class that was in a position at an earlier point to make its demands felt through the vehicle of mass protest and to pose what came to be known as the "social question."

The emergence of worker organization and protest grew out of the expansion of Latin American economies that occurred in response to a remarkable 25-fold increase in world trade between approximately the middle of the 19th century and the beginning of World War I (Furtado 1976:45). During this period, the primary product export sector within Latin America exhibited extraordinary growth. Though political factors played a role, the emergence of the labor movement cannot be understood without central reference to the economic, social, and demographic transformations of this era.

The character of these economic transformations varied greatly from country to country. According to their contrasting endowments of location, climate, and natural and human resources, these countries developed distinct combinations of extensive agriculture, intensive agriculture, and extraction of minerals and petroleum; contrasting patterns of urban-commercial development and incipient manufacturing for the domestic market; and vastly different degrees of reliance on European immigration to expand the modern labor force.

This chapter explores the impact of distinct constellations of growth on the emergence of national labor movements. The remainder of the book is, in effect, an analysis of the reactions and counterreactions to these initial developments. For each country, this chapter summarizes the contrasting patterns of economic and social change and then presents a brief account of the emerging labor movement. For all the countries, the account covers the period at least to 1920, thus providing a basis for comparing the rhythm of labor movement development in the last decade of the 19th century and in the first two decades of the 20th.

This part of the analysis has an important place in the larger design of the book. We argued in Chapter 1 that critical junctures such as the initial incorporation period can lay the foundation for political institutions that may come to have significant autonomy. By contrast, the present chapter explores a contrasting pattern in which the initial eruption of worker politicization appears to be strongly and directly linked to economic and social change.

A related goal of this chapter is to examine the evolution of the labor movement up to reform periods analyzed in the following chapter: that is, the periods inaugurated by the changes in government in 1920 in Chile, 1930 in Brazil, 1935 in Venezuela, 1911 in Mexico, 1903 in Uruguay, 1930 in Colombia, 1919 in Peru, and 1916 in Argentina. This analysis provides a "base line" against which the subsequent interaction between the labor movement and state initiatives toward labor can be assessed. For the countries where the beginning of the incorporation period was delayed beyond these changes in government, we briefly extend this assessment to the onset of incorporation.

To help orient the reader, Figure 3.1 provides a chronological overview of the emergence of labor protest and its timing in relation to the reform period and to major international events.

Grievances, Demonstration Effect, and Opportunity for Collective Action

The emergence of labor organizing and protest derived from an interaction among (1) the collective grievances created by dismal conditions of work typical of the early history of industrialization and commercial development in many countries; (2) the demonstration effect of European labor movements, especially the anarcho-syndicalist tradition of Spain and Italy and later the Russian Revolution and the international Communist movement; and (3) workers' opportunity to pursue new forms of collective action that was created by the rapid growth of the working class and by special forms of concentration of workers in new contexts of work, such as export enclaves.

With regard to grievances concerning conditions of employment, it is true that wages were sufficiently high in certain periods in some countries to attract large numbers of European immigrants into working-class employment, and indeed in various occupational categories, wages in Buenos Aires around 1914 were higher than those in Paris and Marseilles (Díaz-Alejandro 1970:41). However, wages were generally low, and even in the best of cases their purchasing power was subject to sharp fluctuations and tended to fall rapidly with inflation, as occurred during World War I in many countries. Workers' loss of purchasing power at this time was one of the factors contributing to the dramatic, continent-wide wave of worker protest in the late 1910s (Skidmore 1979:97).

Hours of employment were typically long, days of rest few. Employers had

Figure 3.1 Emergence of Labor Protest: Timing in Relation to Onset of Reform Period and Major International Events

Evolution of Labor Protest	Year	Onset of Reform Period and Major International Events
	1890 ---	
1890s: Major episodes of protest in Argentina, Chile, and Mexico. Some protest in Brazil. Modest in Uruguay and Peru.	1895 ---	
	1900 ---	
First decade of 20th century: Further growth of protest, reaching initial insurrectional proportions in Argentina, Chile, and Mexico. Major increase in Uruguay. Substantial increase in Peru.	1905 ---	Uruguay (Batlle—1903)
First half of 1910s: Substantial further increase in Uruguay. Intense urban protest in Peru linked to brief loss of oligarchic control of presidency.	1910 ...	Mexico (Resignation of Díaz—1911) [World War I—1914–18]
Late 1910s: Partly in response to model of Russian Revolution and wage-price squeeze triggered by economic impact of World War I, a major period of intense, often insurrectional protest in Argentina, Brazil, Chile, Uruguay, and Peru. Period of strong protest in Mexico. First major strikes in Colombia, some strikes in Venezuela.	1915 --- 1920 ---	Argentina (Yrigoyen—1916) [Russian Revolution—1917] Peru (Leguía—1919) Chile (Alessandri—1920)
	1925 ---	
Mid to late 1920s: Important strikes in Colombia and Venezuela.	1930 ---	[U.S. stock market crash of 1929 and onset of depression] Brazil (Vargas—1930) Colombia (Liberal Era—1930)
First half of 1930s: Little evidence of further worker protest prior to death of Gómez.	1935 ---	Venezuela (Death of Gómez—1935)

little concern with occupational safety; work injury tended to be the respon-sibility of the employee. Regulations concerning working conditions of women and children did not yet exist, and, more broadly, terms of employ-ment were defined with an informality that provided little protection for workers. Worker organizing, demands for collective bargaining, and strikes were commonly met with violence from the police, the army, private secu-rity forces, and strikebreakers. Correspondingly, early concerns of the labor movement included higher wages, the eight-hour day, days of rest, occupa-tional safety, indemnification for work injury, regulation of the working con-ditions of women and children, the right to collective organization and col-lective bargaining, and the right to strike.

Obviously, these conditions of work varied both over time and among countries, and at certain points such variations will be considered in the analysis. An example is the impact on worker protest of the wage-price squeeze during World War I. For the purpose of the analysis in this chapter, however, we will in general treat these conditions of work as a common problem of all the countries, rather than as a principal source of variation among them.

The second major factor shaping labor movements was the demonstration effect of developments in Europe. Especially prior to the emergence of dis-tinctively Latin American populist movements beginning in the 1930s, the basic political alternatives within the Latin American labor movement—an-archist, anarcho-syndicalist, socialist, and communist—as well as the timing of their emergence were all derived from the European experience. The dem-onstration effect of the Russian Revolution, which was seen as a model of successful seizure of power by a working-class movement, contributed to the dramatic surge of worker protest throughout the Western world after 1917, when workers "from Berlin to Turin, from Chicago to Lima, from São Paulo to Buenos Aires, rose in general strikes against their employers and the state" (Skidmore 1979a:97). The Russian Revolution and the emerging communist parties also presented a model of labor organization oriented toward strong links between unions and political parties, a model whose growing impor-tance contributed to the decline of anarchism (Spalding 1977:54). In subse-quent decades the changing policy of the Communist International toward class collaboration interacted in crucial ways with other features of each country's labor history. Finally, the United States government and the United States labor movement played a role during this period, particularly in Mexico, though their role would become even greater after the second World War.

These international influences contributed to a common rhythm of labor movement development shared by a number of countries. Within that frame-work, major variations among countries in the scope of worker organizing and protest can best be understood in light of internal economic, demo-graphic, and social dynamics within countries that created the opportunity for workers to organize and protest. The literature on the emergence of labor movements in Latin America[1] exhibits a broad consensus on the socioeconomic conditions of special relevance to creating this opportunity: (1) urban-commercial development, (2) industrial growth, (3) the emergence of isolated enclaves of export production, (4) conditions of labor shortage (or labor surplus), and (5) European immigration. Obviously, the comparative discussion of a limited set of factors such as these cannot possibly do justice to all the forces that create opportunities for labor movement formation. However, it can take an important step toward explaining the emergence of labor movements and can serve as a point of reference in the larger analysis of links between this socioeconomic context and the broader political transformations that are the focus of this book.[2]

Urban-Commercial Development. The growth of large cities and urban commerce created an important part of the demographic base for labor movements in Latin America, and the earliest instances of worker organization and protest were commonly found in the national capital—or, in the case of Brazil, also in São Paulo—among typographers, bakers, and workers in urban transportation and services. As a first approximation, one may compare countries on this dimension by assessing the overall growth of the largest city or cities. In comparing cities, it is useful to consider both the *absolute* size of the largest urban centers, which provides a measure of the magnitude of urban-commercial activity, and also their *relative* size that is, their proportional importance within the national context.[3] This latter variable captures such basic contrasts as that between a country where the largest city represented 2.5 percent of the national population (Mexico City in 1900) as opposed to nearly 27 percent (Montevideo in 1920; see Table 3.1 below). The sharply contrasting development of multiple urban centers in different countries also makes it appropriate to consider an indicator such as the proportion of national population in urban centers over 20,000, which, when juxtaposed

---

[1] See, for instance, Alexander (1965:3–5); Bergquist (1986:introduction); Di Tella (1965); Goodman (1972); J. Payne (1965:13–17); Poblete and Burnett (1960:20); Roxborough (1981:89–92); Sigal and Torre (1979:139–42); Spalding (1977:11–15); and Zapata (1979:196–97).

[2] In discussing arguments about links between socioeconomic conditions and the emergence of labor movements, it is important to note the risk of a reductionist view that sees labor movement development as arising directly out of socioeconomic change. We agree with the criticism made, for instance, by Katznelson and Zolberg (1986:introduction) of the analytic perspective from which working-class consciousness, activation, and organizing is conflated with the process of proletarianization itself. Indeed, the focus of this book, with its emphasis on the incorporation period, is precisely on how political factors mediate the relationship between the creation of a working class in the context of socioeconomic change and the emergence of its political role. Nevertheless, it is also useful to explore the direct links between socioeconomic change and the emergence of the labor movement, since these links obviously are also of substantial importance.

[3] For an insightful assessment of the use of per capita versus absolute indicators in research on Latin American development, see O'Donnell (1973:chap. 1).

with the proportion in the capital, permits an assessment of the importance of secondary urban centers (see Table 3.2 below).[4]

Industrial Growth. The growth of manufacturing and factory employment also created new contexts of work conducive to labor movements. The expansion of manufacturing in Latin America is often seen as associated with a later era of economic development, involving the period of "import-substituting industrialization" in the 1930s and after. Yet in many countries a manufacturing sector began to grow in the latter part of the 19th century, though the size of manufacturing establishments tended to be small during this earlier period. By the first decades of the 20th century, and in some cases earlier, workers in an incipient manufacturing sector, especially textile workers, played an important role in the labor movement. It is again useful to view this development both in terms of the absolute number of workers, which suggests the degree to which a critical mass of workers may have emerged; and the relative weight of these workers within the national labor force, which points to such marked contrasts by 1925 as that between countries where the factory work force was roughly 1 percent of the economically active population (Peru and Venezuela), and those where it was roughly 8 percent (Argentina and Uruguay; see Table 3.3 below).

Isolated Enclaves. Isolated enclaves of economic activity such as mining, petroleum extraction, and spatially concentrated, modernized agriculture created contexts of work in which class antagonisms and class conflict become sharply focused (Di Tella 1968:386–87), and strong labor organizations were commonly found in these settings. Where such forms of production were foreign owned and played a crucial role in the export economy, this effect is even more pronounced, since worker protest often fused with sentiments of nationalism directed against the foreign enterprise, and the economic and political impact of strikes was enhanced due to the importance of the exported product for national revenues. Transportation workers who brought the products of the enclaves to national markets and international ports were also likely to sustain strong labor organizations, in part for the same reasons.

Labor Shortages and Labor Surplus. Labor surplus economies are commonly seen as depressing wages, inhibiting labor organization, and in other ways weakening workers' bargaining position. Correspondingly, labor shortage economies are seen as conducive to the development of stronger labor movements. However, because the mechanisms through which these effects operate are complex[5] and measurement of the relevant variables is difficult, the

---

[4] This juxtaposition leads to an assessment quite similar to that found in the excellent comparative study of patterns of urbanization of Morse et al. (1971:esp. p. 7).

[5] The issue of a segmented labor market is an obvious example of this complexity. Another derives from Payne's (1965:13–17) widely cited thesis that it is precisely the presence of the labor surplus economy that makes collective bargaining ineffective and political bargaining essential from the standpoint of workers. In contexts of labor surplus, one might thus expect the interest of the labor movement in collective bargaining to be deflected to political action, so that there might be a stronger, rather than weaker, development of cer-

discussion will be limited to two aspects of this issue: the significance of a heavy inflow of European migrants into the urban labor market as an indicator of a labor shortage, and the onset of heavy internal rural-urban migration, which is commonly seen as increasing the urban labor surplus. In addition, labor shortages and labor surpluses associated with different phases of the business cycle and the resulting impact on the labor movement will at various points be noted.

European Immigration.   The massive influx of European immigrants around the turn of the century had a major impact on the emergence of national labor movements. These immigrants made up a large portion of the working class populations of Argentina, Uruguay, and southern Brazil in this early period, and the direct experience of many immigrants with labor movements in Europe played a central role in shaping labor movement development in these three countries. Through these immigrants, the demonstration effect of developments in European labor movements was conveyed in a far more direct fashion.

These five factors certainly do not exhaust the variables that account for different patterns of labor movement development. We do not pretend to compare other factors systematically, but one that will be noted below on an *ad hoc* basis—a distinctive dynamic of political leadership—appears so important for the development of the Peruvian labor movement that it seems essential to introduce it.

Approach to Comparison

In the discussion of each country, we sketch the economic and social context of labor movement development and the rise of the labor movement itself. Quantitative data available for these comparisons not surprisingly suffer from problems of reliability. In addition, appropriate comparative data are not always available for crucial time periods in certain countries. However, the goal of the present discussion is to establish a rough sense of orders of magnitude and an approximate ordering of the countries on the relevant variables. For this purpose, available comparative data are adequate. In fact, a close comparison of the data presented in Tables 3.1 to 3.3 with that in country monographs (see discussion of individual countries below) suggests that the comparative data are reasonably reliable.

Tables 3.1 to 3.3 present data, principally for the period around 1920–25, for some of the variables discussed above: the size of the national capitals plus São Paulo, presented in both absolute and per capita terms; the propor-

tain political forms of labor mobilization, the opposite of what might otherwise be hypothesized. However, in this particular period various currents in the labor movement rejected the cooperation with the state needed to make this tactic effective, so that this thesis may be less relevant during the earlier period being considered here.

TABLE 3.1
Population of National Capitals Plus São Paulo

	Year	City Population	City Pop. as Percent of Nat. Pop.	Source
Santiago	1920	507,000 (4)	13.4 (3)	B
(Chile)	1930	713,000	16.3	B
Rio de Janeiro	1906	811,443	4.0	A
(Brazil)	1920	1,157,843 (2)	4.2 (6)	A
São Paulo	1900	239,820	1.3	A
(Brazil)	1920	579,033	2.1	A
Mexico City	1900	344,721	2.5	A
(Mexico)	1910	471,066	3.1	A
	1920	615,000 (3)	4.3 (5)	B
Caracas	1920	92,000 (8)	3.3 (7)	B
(Venezuela)	1936	259,000	7.7	B
Montevideo	1920	393,000 (5)	26.9 (1)	B
(Uruguay)	1930	482,000	27.8	B
Bogotá	1918	144,000 (7)	2.5 (8)	B
(Colombia)	1930	260,000	3.5	B
Lima-Callao	1903	170,417	5.2	A, B
(Peru)	1920	255,000 (6)	5.3 (4)	B
Buenos Aires	1895	663,854	16.8	A
(Argentina)	1914	1,575,814 (1)	20.0 (2)	A

Notes: Order of countries corresponds to order of presentation in text and thereby juxtaposes the pairs of cases analyzed in later chapters. Numbers in parentheses reflect rankings of the eight capitals as of 1920, except for Buenos Aires (1914) and Bogotá (1918). Source A: Boyer and Davies 1973. Source B: Eakin 1978:400. Figure for Lima-Callao for 1903 combines data for Lima for 1903 from source A and data for Callao for 1905 from source B. All national population data are from Wilkie (1974: chap. 8) except for the 1895 figure for Argentina, which is from source A.

TABLE 3.2
Population in Urban Centers over 20,000 in 1920 as a Percent
of National Population

Chi 27.6 (3)	Mex 12.6 (5)	Uru 27.8 (2)	Per 5.0 (8)
Bra 13.0 (4)	Ven 11.7 (6)	Col 8.9 (7)	Arg 37.0 (1)

Notes: Numbers in parentheses reflect ranking among the eight countries. Data are from Wilkie and Haber 1983:86. Slight discrepancies vis-à-vis Table 3.1—such as that concerning the urban population of Peru in 1920—result from the use of different primary data sources.

tion of population in urban centers over 20,000; and factory employment, also presented in both absolute terms and as a percentage of the economically active population. Apart from one pair of variables (size of factory work force and population in urban centers over 20,000, both as a proportion of national population), these figures produce quite different rankings of countries. The goal of the following discussion is to sort out how these contrast-

TABLE 3.3
Factory Employment in 1925

	Factory Employment	As a Percentage of Economically Active Population
Chile	82,000 (4)	6.1 (3)
Brazil	380,000 (1)	3.7 (4)
Mexico	160,000 (3)	3.2 (5)
Venezuela	12,000 (8)	1.5 (7)
Uruguay	39,000 (6)	7.0 (2)
Colombia	47,000 (5)	1.8 (6)
Peru	21,000 (7)	1.2 (8)
Argentina	340,000 (2)	8.3 (1)

Notes: Numbers in parentheses reflect rank among the eight countries. Data are from ECLA 1966:13,17. Data on the economically active population for Uruguay were not available in the ECLA source and were estimated by extrapolating from data on factory employment as a percent of national population, based on the ECLA factory employment data combined with Wilkie's data on the national population (1974:chap. 8). For the other seven countries, the indicators of factory employment as a percent of EAP and of the national population were almost perfectly correlated.

Factory employment does not include mining and construction, and only industrial establishments operated by more than five persons are considered factories (see ECLA 1965:170). It should be emphasized that complete data permitting the application of this size criterion on the basis of anything other than rough estimates are not available. For the limited purposes of the present analysis, in which the principal concern is with the approximate ranking of countries, it is therefore helpful to note that the data from the same ECLA sources (Table I-16) for total manufacturing employment, including establishments operated by five or fewer persons, produce a similar ordering among countries. A comparison of this latter measure with the measure that includes factory employment reveals that countries that had larger populations and were less economically developed gained relative to smaller countries that were more developed. However, in terms of the ranking, these gains led to only two reversals: Chile and Colombia reverse between fourth and fifth (a finding consistent with the discussion below of the heavily artisanal character of the Colombian labor force and labor movement through the 1920s), and Uruguay and Peru reverse between sixth and seventh. Reversals in ranking of this type would not change the overall interpretation of the cases presented in this chapter. Further assessments of the reliability of these data are presented in the text below in comparisons of these data with those presented in monographic studies of individual countries.

ing rankings, along with the other factors for which such data are less readily available, combine to shape the labor movements. They are the explanatory factors of concern in this chapter.

The outcome to be explained is the rhythm and scope of worker organizing and protest, which may roughly be referred to as the initial "strength" of the labor movement, encompassing organizational strength both within and outside the workplace (S. Valenzuela 1983) and the capacity to use this organization in pursuit of collective goals. One important indicator of this capacity is the extent of collective protest.

Of the many conceptual issues that arise in the study of labor movements, two of particular relevance to this analysis may be noted here. First, especially in *later* historical periods, when institutionalized labor movements develop stable relationships with governments and are able to extract policy concessions in exchange for limiting the scope of protest, protest by itself is a poor indicator of labor strength.[6] However, in this earlier period, such relationships were far less common. Hence, scope of collective protest may be a more direct and useful indicator of labor movement strength.

Second, we can distinguish between an overall conception of the scope and strength of the labor movement and the particular form that the action of the labor movement may assume. Many hypotheses in the literature cited above are concerned with understanding this overall dimension, though some are concerned with explaining particular facets of labor movement development. An example of the latter is the hypothesis that the decline of anarchism and the growing concern in the labor movement with institutionalizing work relationships and developing stable ties with the national political system was in part a product of new concerns of workers that resulted from the decline of artisan production and the growing predominance of larger scale factory production (Alexander 1983). Another example is Bergquist's (1986) analysis of the conditions under which workers in the export sector contribute specifically to revolutionary forms of labor action. In the following discussion, attention will focus principally on the overall scope of organization and protest, at the same time that, as appropriate, distinct forms of worker activation such as these will be explored.

Brazil

Economic and Social Context.   Brazil was and is by a wide margin the largest country in the region, with many big cities, early commercial and industrial development on a large scale, and a major experience of European immigration—though little development of export enclaves. In part simply as a consequence of size, Brazilian development provided conditions hypothesized to be favorable for the emergence of a significant early labor movement.

In the mid-19th century, Brazil surpassed Mexico in having the largest national population among the eight countries (Boyer and Davies 1973), and in 1920 its population was roughly twice that of Mexico and three times that of Argentina (Morse et al. 1971). Along with Argentina, Brazil developed the largest urban sector in the region. The population of Rio de Janeiro passed the million mark in the 1910s, ranking behind only Buenos Aires, and São Paulo passed the half million mark in the same decade (Table 3.1). As of 1920 six Brazilian cities had populations greater than either Bogotá or Caracas (Table 3.1; Conniff et al. 1971:37), and as of 1925 the national factory work

---

[6] It is essential to assess whether the concessions involve narrow benefits for a co-opted leadership, in which case they would not reflect strength of the labor movement but, in part, manipulation by the state.

force was the largest among the eight countries, at nearly 400,000 (Table 3.3),[7] increasing by one third to over 500,000 by 1930 and remaining thereafter the largest in Latin America (ECLA 1966:Table I-17). According to Simão (1981:38), 15 percent of Brazil's industrial workers were in the state of São Paulo as of 1907, 30 percent in 1920, and 35 percent in 1940.

European immigrants played a central role in this demographic growth and correspondingly in the labor movement. The rapid expansion of São Paulo was based largely on massive European immigration, most importantly from Italy, and around the turn of the century its population was well over half foreign (Harding 1973:32; Fausto 1977:30). Native-born Brazilians played little role in the city's growth, and different sources place the proportion of foreigners among industrial workers in the range of 70 to 90 percent (Maram 1972:6). Although 43 percent of the labor force in Rio was foreign born as early as 1872, these foreigners were principally an older wave of Portuguese immigrants, and in the following decades the importance of foreigners declined, with native-born Brazilian workers, including a large number of former slaves, playing a more important role in the city's growth (Merrick and Graham 1979:106–07; Fausto 1977:25). However, though the contrasting composition of the population of the two cities was a major factor contributing to the development of an important labor movement in the much smaller city of São Paulo (Maram 1977:191), immigrant workers also played a central role in the labor movement in Rio. Between 1890 and 1920, 46 percent of labor leaders in Rio were foreign born (though the figure came to a remarkable 82 percent in São Paulo), and among the workers arrested in the general strike in 1920 in Rio, the large majority was foreign-born (Maram 1977:182–85).

In contrast to European immigration, substantial internal rural-urban migration did not begin until much later. For São Paulo, though not for Rio, such internal migration did not become important until the 1930s (Merrick and Graham 1979:123). It was noted above that migration from rural to urban areas may flood urban labor markets and create conditions less favorable for labor movement development, whereas the period prior to the onset of migration may be more favorable for the labor movement. This would suggest

[7] This level is roughly congruent, in the sense of placing Brazil approximately at the top within the comparison of eight countries, with the level suggested by the careful discussion of Merrick and Graham (1979:149–59). Taking their data for manufacturing in 1920 (Table VII-1), which excludes two occupational categories ("clothing manufacturing" and "other poorly defined") which they interpret as reflecting artisan employment, and subtracting employment in mining and construction (see their Table VII-3), one arrives at a figure of 475,000. While this excludes major sectors of artisan employment, it does not systematically employ the cutoff for size of establishment employed in the ECLA data and refers to a point five years earlier. Within the framework of the inevitably rough approximations involved in these data, the fact that it is higher than the ECLA figure by 25 percent therefore seems reasonable. Simão's (1981:38) tabulation of the 1920 data shows 275,512 in the category of industrial workers, a smaller number but again one referring to a point in time five years earlier than the data in Table 3.3. In any case, in comparison to the other seven countries, the number of industrial workers in Brazil was large.

another reason why, prior to the 1930s, one might expect a stronger labor movement in São Paulo.

Though many factors favored a strong labor movement, others did not. The export enclaves that in some other countries produced isolated concentrations of workers prone to labor protest played little role in Brazilian development (Leff 1982:79, 84–91). Similarly, the *relative* size of the urban/industrial sector was less favorable. As of 1920, the population of Rio as a proportion of national population ranked sixth among the eight countries (Table 3.1). Although in that year São Paulo's population as a proportion of total population ranked it below even Caracas, the eighth-ranked capital, the presence within Brazil of both these cities, along with the other large urban centers noted above, did nonetheless constitute a substantial degree of urban development, though a type of urban development that was far more disbursed than in most other countries. Brazil ranked fourth in the size of the factory work force as a percentage of the economically active population (Table 3.3).

Labor Movement. Since 1930, organized labor in Brazil has commonly been seen as weak, owing to a number of factors, including widespread poverty, a labor-surplus economy, and tight state control of unions. Yet in this earlier period, Brazil had an important labor movement. Labor organizing and strikes began to increase toward the end of the 19th century, and after the turn of the century mutual aid societies were superseded by more modern unions. European immigrants brought the anarchist traditions of the working class of their home countries, and anarchism quickly became the dominant force in the labor movement (Harding 1973:32–33). Early strike data for the state of São Paulo show 24 strikes for the period 1888 to 1900, including a general strike in the port of Santos in 1891 of at least 2,000 workers (Simão 1981:105, 124). Maram (1972:237) reports a similar rhythm of strikes at this time in Rio.

By 1903 the first regional labor federation was founded in Rio, and in 1906 the first national labor congress was held, forming the basis two years later of the Brazilian Workers' Confederation (COB). Increasing worker protest accompanied this organizational activity. Nineteen strikes occurred in the state of São Paulo in 1901–2 and somewhat fewer in the following three years, with the annual totals rising again to 9, 17, and 23 in 1906–8 (Simão 1981:127). Starting in 1906 multisector strikes became frequent (Harding 1973:38). In that year a railway strike in São Paulo spread to other sectors, becoming a general strike in the city, and also spread to railroad and textile workers in nearby Jundíai (Fausto 1977:138; Dulles 1973:20–21). At its height, this strike involved 15,000 workers (Simão 1981:105), and when it threatened to spread to other regions, the state police crushed the movement (Dulles 1973:20–21; Maram 1972:28–29). These same years also saw many strikes in Rio, including an extended work stoppage in the textile sector that probably represented the most important strike in Brazil up to that date (Dulles 1973:17; Maram 1972:159–62). In 1908 the COB organized a large demonstration involving 200 labor organizations from Rio, as well as participants from several other states (Schmitter 1971:140).

The government reacted to this strike wave with decrees requiring unions to register membership lists with a state agency and excluding foreigners from membership, as well as making them more liable to expulsion from the country for disturbing the peace. This campaign against foreigners and the continued repression of unions, combined with increasing unemployment, brought a lull in labor militancy until the latter part of the 1910s (Dulles 1973:24; Maram 1972:162, 167–68).

During World War I inflation eroded real wages, sparking food riots, mass protests, and strikes (Harding 1973:41) and inaugurating the period of major labor protest found in many countries during these years. In 1917 a general strike was called in São Paulo, paralyzing not only the city but also much of the state. At its height 45,000 strikers participated (Harding 1973:43; Fausto 1977:196). By the following year, the model of the Russian Revolution had contributed to a marked increase in the politicization of the labor movement, and the anarchist leadership of the labor movement in Rio became involved in plotting to overthrow the government (Dulles 1973:70–76). The strike wave between 1919 and 1920 was the most extensive that Brazil had ever experienced (Maram 1972:180), with 64 strikes in the city of São Paulo and 14 elsewhere in São Paulo state (Fausto 1977:161).[8] Though São Paulo was the center of worker mobilization, Rio also had a number of strikes, including a work stoppage in the textile sector that was the longest in the city's history. During this period of intense conflict, the unions initiating the strikes were far better organized and the level of organizational coordination between the labor movements of São Paulo and Rio much greater than in the past (Maram 1972:180). States such as Bahía, Pernambuco, and Rio Grande do Sul, where earlier labor actions were probably not fully reflected in the data, also experienced general strikes at this time (Dulles 1973:92).

In the 1920s, worker militance and protest declined and leadership began to pass from anarchists to communists. In 1922 the Brazilian Communist Party (PCB) was founded and its influence within the labor movement spread. As in Chile, the labor movement was weakened by the split between communists and anarchists, and the latter withdrew from the Workers Federation of Rio de Janeiro (Dulles 1973:207–12). Though banned by a state of siege between 1922 and 1927, the PCB worked to establish its own parallel unions in São Paulo and some other cities and in 1929 attempted to form a national organization, the General Confederation of Labor (CGT) (Schmitter 1971:141). In 1928 and 1929 the communists led a number of strikes, and by the 1930 transition they had become the dominant force in the labor movement (Harding 1973:50).

Thus, whereas the Brazilian labor movement during the first two decades of the 20th century did not achieve the scope of protest found in some other countries, the extensive strikes and worker organization in two principal cit-

---

[8] Simão (1981:128–29) gives somewhat lower figures: 31 for the city and 19 for the state.

ies suggest a substantial degree of development. Nonetheless, by the time of Vargas's rise to power in 1930, the movement was divided and in the weak position that characterized the situation of the working class in many countries during the 1920s.

Chile

Economic and Social Context.   During this early period, Chile saw substantial urban-commercial growth and the emergence of a large enclave sector, though the country was relatively isolated from major currents of European immigration. While Chile did not rank at the top among the eight countries on either the absolute size or the per capita importance of its urban and factory populations, it was one of the few countries to exhibit substantial development on both dimensions. Conditions were thus present that are hypothesized to be quite favorable for the development of the labor movement.

Chilean urban growth was substantial. The population of Santiago in 1920 exceeded half a million, thereby ranking fourth among the eight countries, and in per capita terms it ranked third, far ahead of the fourth-ranked capital, Lima, and behind only Buenos Aires and Montevideo (Table 3.1). Chile exhibited both marked demographic predominance of the capital and significant development of secondary urban centers, and it was one of the only countries whose ranking in terms of the proportional importance of the population in urban centers in 1920 was the same as the ranking for the proportional importance of the capital (Table 3.2). In 1925, a year for which comparative data are available, Chile's estimated factory work force of slightly over 80,000 (Table 3.3)[9] ranked fourth in absolute terms and third in per capita terms, on the latter variable falling somewhat behind Uruguay and more substantially behind Argentina.

Chile's urban, commercial, and manufacturing development was accompanied by the emergence of a major enclave sector that had levels of employment second only to those in Mexico. The number of nitrate workers, located in the northern provinces taken from Peru and Bolivia in the War of the Pacific, rose from approximately 5,000 in 1884 to roughly 50,000 in 1912 (Angell 1972:17), never falling below 43,000 between 1910 and 1920 (Mamalakis 1976:38). The organization of copper production into large, concentrated enclaves occurred in important measure during the second decade of the 20th century, and as of 1913, when the process of establishing the large mines had only just begun, total copper sector employment was 18,000 (Reynolds 1965:215–18). By 1911–12 ownership in the nitrate sector was approximately one third Chilean, with the British being the most important among the foreign owners (Jobet 1955:149). With the rise of large-scale copper extraction, Chilean ownership in that sector was further eclipsed, and by

---

[9] A nearly identical figure for the work force for that year, using a roughly similar cutoff point for factory size, is presented in DeShazo (1983:14).

World War I ownership was almost exclusively in the hands of U.S. firms (Reynolds 1965:221). Between 1900 and 1930, over 50 percent of foreign exchange was derived from nitrate exports, whereas copper still represented a small fraction of that amount as of 1913 (Mamalakis 1976:38; Reynolds 1965:215). Coal production was also important, though that sector had neither foreign ownership nor a significant role in the export economy.

European immigrants did not play the same role in Chile as in the countries on the Atlantic side of the continent (Skidmore 1979a:104). However, Spalding (1977:8) reports that between 1895 and 1912 approximately 30,000 skilled workers came to Chile from Europe, and Angell (1972:25) suggests that Europeans did play a role in the development of Chilean anarchism, although DeShazo (1983:xxvi) deemphasizes their importance.

Labor Movement. A strong labor movement developed early in Chile. Workers' organizational efforts shifted from mutual benefit societies to unions more explicitly concerned with wages and working conditions in the 1890s (Morris 1966:94), and the first major period of worker militance occurred between 1890 and 1907. During this period worker protest was met with heavy repression.

The first important strike was in 1890 in the newly expanding nitrate sector, starting among the port workers of Iquique and spreading rapidly throughout the nitrate region. According to Morris (1966:97–98), "By the time the military brought the situation under control, an estimated ten to fifteen nitrate workers had been killed and about a hundred wounded. The strike wave spread south from Tarapacá, reached as far as the coal fields of Lota and Coronel, and touched all the major industrial and port centers in between," eventually involving as many as 10,000 workers. Overall, the decade of the 1890s saw roughly 300 labor conflicts (Morris 1966:98).

The period 1903–7 brought unprecedented union growth. Unionization increased in the northern ports and nitrate zone, in the southern ports and coalmining areas, and in the urban industrial areas of Santiago and Valparaíso. In a revisionist interpretation, DeShazo (1983:112, 116) argues that it was in these urban areas in the center, where anarcho-syndicalism became particularly influential, that organized labor was strongest and had the greatest success, rather than in the north as is usually asserted. The number of strikes between 1902 and 1907 was 200 for the entire country, with 80 in 1907 alone (DeShazo 1983:103). The strike wave during these years, which culminated in the 1907 general strike in Santiago, was on a scale unmatched by previous labor actions. These figures place Chile behind the total in Argentina for these years, but well above Mexico, one of the other countries that by this time had already developed a particularly active labor movement.

In these opening years of the 20th century, the violent repression of strikes continued. A recitation of key events would include the 1903 dock strike in Valparaíso, in which some 40 workers were killed; the "red week" in Santiago in 1905, during which protesters virtually seized control of Santiago for several days and which left 200 to 400 dead or wounded; the 1906 railway workers' strike in Antofagasta in which 150 workers may have been killed;

and the Iquique massacre of 1907 in which 1,000 to 3,000 workers were killed as the army brutally put down a strike among nitrate workers (Morris 1966:98–99; Barría 1971:19; Angell 1972:13).

Following these defeats of the newly emerging labor movement and the economic downturn of 1907, collective protest declined in the next decade, though labor organization proceeded and the political orientation of the movement began to change. Following this heavy repression, the Democratic Party, which had been the dominant political force among the mutual aid societies, began to look elsewhere for support and moved away from a working-class program as it sought to broaden its base (S. Valenzuela 1979:433). Anarcho-syndicalism, the other major tendency within organized labor at the time, also felt the brunt of the repression: the number of unions, or "resistance societies," in which this tendency was influential was reduced from 57 to 11 in the period following the 1907 strikes, and the anarcho-syndicalist Workers Federation of Chile did not survive (S. Valenzuela 1979:432).

When the economy began to recover after 1909, the anarcho-syndicalists had considerable success in rebuilding resistance unions, particularly between 1912 and 1914 (DeShazo 1983:132), and in 1913 founded the Chilean Regional Workers Federation (FORCh). At the same time, Luis Emilio Recabarren, a labor leader of the left wing of the Democratic Party, split from that party and founded the Socialist Workers Party (POS), which later became the Chilean Communist Party (PCCh). Mutualist organizations continued to exist during this period, and another labor central, the FOCh (Federation of Chilean Workers), was formed in 1909 as a national mutualist federation of railroad metal workers. However, this mutualist tendency did not prevail. Over the next few years the FOCh opened its membership to all political tendencies within the labor movement and in 1921 became the labor arm of the Communist Party under the leadership of Recabarren.

Toward the end of World War I, favorable economic conditions and nearly full employment, combined with inflation and declining real wages, set the stage for recovery, growth, and greater militance within organized labor. On the one hand, then, the situation of labor on the eve of the Chilean reform period, which began in 1920, seemed to be one of resurgence. Ideologically, a process of radicalization occurred and communist and anarcho-syndicalist currents came to predominate within the movement. The period 1917–20 saw substantial growth of unions and union membership, and the FOCh demonstrated the ability to mobilize upwards of 100,000 people for demonstrations, such as those protesting high food prices in 1918–19.

A new strike wave was initiated in 1919 on a scale that would not again be matched in Chile until the 1950s (DeShazo 1983:164). In August 1919, 100,000 people demonstrated at the presidential palace (Skidmore 1979:105), and in September general strikes shut down Santiago, Iquique, Antofagasta, and Chuquicamata (Monteón 1982:139). As a result of increased worker militancy, collective bargaining became more widespread, more industry-wide contracts were signed, and there was greater recognition of unions by employers (DeShazo 1983:146). Alternative estimates of the number of strikes from 1917 to 1919 place them in the area of 110 to 120, and according to Government Labor Office data, 105 strikes occurred in 1920 alone (DeShazo 1983:165).

On the other hand, the labor movement suffered from a number of weaknesses. Internal conflicts, which would culminate in 1921 in the anarchist-communist split (which occurred elsewhere at this same time), were already growing as the communists began to consolidate their position within the FOCh, and these conflicts weakened the movement considerably. Furthermore, though the FOCh could mount impressive protests, actual membership in FOCh unions was modest. Accurate figures are not available, but S. Valenzuela (1979:454) estimates that in the peak year of 1925, the FOCh had at most 25,000 to 30,000 dues paying members, and DeShazo suggests a similar, but slightly lower, figure (1983:196).

Finally, the labor movement was also hurt by the massive repression triggered by the strikes and protests of 1919 and by the daily rallies and demonstrations mounted in support of Alessandri at the time of the 1920 electoral crisis. Working-class publications were closed, unions were raided by the police, labor leaders were arrested, and meetings were broken up. In this way, as Alessandri came to power, the strike wave was brought to a halt, and the 1917–20 resurgence of labor militance was reversed. (DeShazo 1983:184–85).

Mexico

Economic and Social Context. Because in recent decades analyses of the Mexican labor movement have tended to concentrate on its relative quiescence and the control exercised over it by the state, it is especially important to recognize the special characteristics of Mexican economic development up to the turn of the century and the substantial strength of the labor movement that emerged. Several factors were exceptionally favorable for the emergence of an important labor movement, and none were strongly unfavorable.

Until around 1840, when it was surpassed by Brazil, Mexico had the largest national population of any Latin American country. Likewise, until the mid-19th century, when it was passed by Buenos Aires, the Mexican capital was the largest city in Latin America, having reached a population of 200,000 as early as the late 1830s. Indeed, prior to that decade, the population of Buenos Aires was less than that of such secondary cities in Mexico as Guadalajara and Puebla, the two other largest urban centers at the time, and Rio's population did not pass that of Mexico City until the 1860s (Boyer and Davies 1973). Though the disastrous loss of territory to the United States at mid-century was a great setback to Mexican development, in both 1900 and 1920 Mexico City was still one of the largest cities in the region (Table 3.1).

A large industrial work force was created earlier in Mexico than any of the other countries. Alba (1968:217, 300–301), citing figures that should probably be taken only to suggest rough orders of magnitude, reports nearly 3,000 workers in textile mills alone in the mid-1820s, 12,000 in the mid-1850s, and 32,000 in the mid-1870s. By contrast, for Argentina he reports only 1,500 workers in all factories and workshops in the mid-1850s. Though other sources[10] provide somewhat contrasting figures for subsequent growth, their data present a consistent picture in terms of the remarkable levels of employment for the turn of the century and in the following decades. Keesing (1969: 726) places total manufacturing employment at over 500,000 in 1895, with over 90,000 in textiles alone, and these sources show it as remaining at roughly the same level through 1930, with small declines at various points during that period (Keesing 1969:724), due in part to the disruption of the Mexican Revolution.[11]

In absolute terms, Mexico ranks third in Table 3.3 in the size of its factory work force in 1925, and this comparison suggests that, unlike most of the other countries, which experienced rapid growth between 1900 and 1925, Mexico was much closer to its 1925 level of factory employment by 1900.[12] Mexico had a remarkably large industrial work force at an early point.

In per capita terms, on the other hand, Mexico lagged somewhat further behind. In 1920 the population of the capital as a percent of the national population ranked fifth (Table 3.1). Mexico, like Chile, had both a substantial predominance of the capital and a substantial development of secondary cities, and in per capita terms the urban population in 1920, like the proportional importance of the capital, ranked fifth (Table 3.2). Whereas Mexico's rank in 1925 in terms of the size of the factory work force was third, its ranking in relation to the economically active population and national population was fifth (Table 3.3).

In addition to urban and manufacturing development, Mexico had a major mining sector, with even higher employment levels than those noted above for Chile. Alba (1968:300) reports over 40,000 workers in mines in the 1820s and 70,000 in the 1880s, and Keesing reports over 80,000 mine workers in 1895, nearly 97,000 in 1900, and nearly 86,000 in 1910 (1969:730; 1977:14). Mining production earlier had involved primarily silver and gold, but toward the end of the century lead, zinc, and copper were increasingly mined as well (Bernstein 1964:51). Precious metals represented 79 percent of exports in 1877–78, declining to 58 percent in 1900–1901 and 46 percent in 1910–11, while nondurable producers' goods, principally raw materials for industrial production, rose from 15 percent, to 31 percent, to 43 percent at these respec-

[10] Colegio de México 1965; Rosenzweig 1965; and Keesing 1969, 1977.

[11] If one takes the Mexican figure for factory workers in 1925 in Table 3.3, which is from an ECLA source, and adds to it the corresponding ECLA figure for artisan workers in that year (ECLA 1966:Table I-18), the resulting total for manufacturing employment, 540,000, is similar to these other series.

[12] It is likely that factory employment as defined by ECLA (see Table 3.3) as a proportion of total manufacturing employment did increase between 1900 and 1925. However, it may be noted that between 1900 and 1925 industrial production expanded only 86 percent in Mexico, whereas it expanded 308 percent in Argentina (ECLA 1966:Table I-1). In this context of far less rapid growth, the shift to larger production units was probably advancing at a considerably slower pace in Mexico.

tive dates (Hansen 1974:15). Foreign and particularly U.S. ownership became important as early as the 1860s and began to play a major role by the 1880s. By 1911 Mexican ownership had been eclipsed in this sector (Bernstein 1964:19–20, 36–37, 75). The railroads—built in important measure to transport minerals—were principally constructed with U.S. capital (Hansen 1974:14).

With regard to the role of outside influences on the labor movement and the issue of labor surplus, conditions in Mexico may be seen as moderately favorable for the development of a strong movement. While Mexico did not receive the flood of European workers who immigrated to some South American countries, between 1887 and 1900 over 6,000 Spaniards came to Mexico, many being exiled leaders and intellectuals from the large Spanish anarchist movement. Their arrival appeared to coincide with a revival of anarchist organizing, and Spaniards played a visible role in labor leadership during this period (Hart 1978:17–18). Around this time anarchists from the U.S. Knights of Labor aided organizing efforts among textile and railroad workers (Hart 1978:80, 84), and in the first decade of the century the American Federation of Labor under Samuel Gompers supported worker organizing for instance, in the Cananea copper mines—and became linked to the opposition to Díaz (Clark 1934:278–79). Later, toward the end of the 1910s, the IWW played an important role among oil workers in Tampico (Hart 1978:80–81).

Mexico was not one of the countries whose many job opportunities attracted a large European work force during this period, and during the Porfiriato an excess labor supply played a role in weakening the labor movement (Rosenzweig 1965:423). However, Keesing (1977:7) suggests that more serious unemployment did not begin until 1900 to 1910, and Pontones (1976:135–37) finds that heavy internal migration, later such an important aspect of Mexico's labor surplus economy, did not really begin until the Revolution of 1910. Thus for Mexico, as for Brazil, there are grounds for suggesting that the impact of labor surplus on the worker movement, which is an important theme in analyses of later periods of labor history, was probably less pronounced during this earlier period.

Labor Movement. Mexico developed the earliest and one of the stronger labor movements in the region in the years prior to what we refer to as the reform period, which is particularly noteworthy since this period began so early in Mexico. Though workers' organizations in the 1860s and 1870s were typically mutual benefit societies, a number of organizations took on more explicitly trade union functions and initiated a number of strikes oriented toward demands related to working conditions. Of the 12 strikes between 1865 and 1874, eight were in the textile sector and four in mines.[13] Labor organizing accelerated during the 1870s, and the first national labor central was created with the founding of the Gran Círculo de Obreros de México under anarchist leadership. Within a couple of years, a moderate faction, which brought the Círculo closer to the government and did not advocate

---

[13] Díaz Ramírez 1974:13, 81; R. Anderson 1976:79–80, 331.

the strike as a weapon, took over the leadership. Nevertheless, strikes continued, with 13 strikes reported between 1875 and 1879 (R. Anderson 1976:331). In 1876, the Círculo organized a congress to unite workers, but the unity of anarchist and moderate elements could not survive the political divisions brought about by the presidential politics of the time.

During the Porfiriato, and particularly after 1880 with the boom in railroads and manufacturing, the government repressed the more militant elements of the labor movement, sending the anarchist and independent sectors of the movement into serious decline. Despite the repression, some serious strikes continued to occur, often involving the issue of salary reductions. However, the end of the century saw a dramatic resurgence of labor militance, stemming from a number of factors. Economic expansion under the Porfiriato had led to spectacular urban growth: the population of Mexico City doubled, and the industrial cities of Monterrey and Veracruz increased by 461 and 490 percent, respectively. Rapid growth of the urban labor force was accompanied by rising wages until 1897, when price increases brought deterioration in real wages at the same time that unemployment grew due to the contraction in industry, land evictions that led to some initial rural-urban migration, and a labor-saving shift from artisanal to factory production. A total of 55 strikes occurred in the 1880s, 45 in the 1890s, and 14 in 1900–1901 alone.[14]

In addition to these economic factors, new political dynamics emerged. Labor emissaries from the United States, particularly from the Knights of Labor and the IWW, helped to organize Mexican textile and railway workers and miners, and the Flores Magón brothers founded the anarchist Liberal Party and began intensive organizing efforts throughout the country. When anarchism thus gained new vitality in Mexico, it was an anarchism that had evolved away from mutualist and cooperativist models of organization toward anarcho-syndicalist tactics of the general strike, sabotage, and worker control of factories (Hart 1978:84, 87). The literature presents contrasting interpretations of the relative importance of mutualism and anarchism in the labor movement on the eve of the revolution, but anarchism was evidently a growing force.[15]

After a lull in activity during 1902–5, when a total of 15 strikes occurred, new labor organizations were formed and a new wave of labor protest began in 1906. The Cananea copper strike, which some analysts consider to represent the initial outbreak of the Mexican Revolution, was the first of the "landmark" strikes of this period, affecting the country's leading mining complex at a time when Mexico was the world's third largest producer of copper (Ruiz 1976:19). Under the influence of the Flores Magón brothers of the Mexican Liberal Party, the Gran Círculo de Obreros Libres was organized among textile workers in that year. When mill owners tried to fire the workers for organizing, a general strike of textile workers was held that affected

---

[14] Knight 1986 Vol. I:128; Hart 1978:85; R. Anderson 1976:330–31.
[15] Hart 1978:178–79; Carr 1972:45; Clark 1934:5, 14–17.

all textile mills in the country and closed 93 of them. In 1907 the Gran Liga de Empleados de Ferrocarril was organized, embracing 15,000 railroad workers, and a major railroad strike was called in 1908. Both the copper and textile strikes evolved into workers' armed rebellions, and both strikes were violently repressed by the army, which killed close to 300 workers (Ruiz 1976:23; Hart 1978:92, 98).

The roughly five-and-a-half year period from 1906 to the month of Díaz's resignation in 1911 saw a total of 119 strikes (R. Anderson 1976:332–33),[16] and this worker protest was an important part of the larger setting out of which the Mexican Revolution emerged. However, as noted above, the workers' movement did not play a direct role in the revolution. It may further be noted that from a comparative perspective, the number of strikes in this decade in Argentina and Chile was greater. Uruguay, with a far smaller population, was reported to have had roughly the same number of strikes around this time.

Venezuela

Economic and Social Context. Venezuela was one of the latest developing and smallest of the countries considered, and the reform period occurred the latest, following the death of Gómez in 1935. At the turn of the century, only Uruguay had a smaller national population (Wilkie 1974:chap. 8), and as of 1920 Caracas, with under 100,000 inhabitants, had the smallest population among the eight capitals. As a proportion of the national population, the population of the capital ranked seventh (Table 3.1), though because of Venezuela's relatively more dispersed urban population, the urban portion of the national population ranked sixth (Table 3.2). Similarly, as of 1925 there were only 12,000 factory workers, the smallest figure for the eight countries in absolute terms and the seventh ranked as a percentage of economically active population (Table 3.3). Limited available evidence suggests that until the 1940s the population of Venezuela included relatively few immigrants, and while some European workers were present in the labor movement, anarcho-syndicalism correspondingly was never an important force (Schuyler 1976:61–62; Ellner 1979:43–44).[17]

During the first decades of the century, this small, undeveloped economy did not favor the emergence of a labor movement. However, in the 1920s the oil boom began. Oil was first exported in 1918, and by 1929 production had expanded to the point that Venezuela was the world's largest exporter (Tugwell 1975:38), spurring both overall development and the growth of major

[16] It may be noted that in the series of strike data compiled by R. Anderson (1976:330–31), covering nearly 50 years, by far the largest number of strikes was in textiles (146), with railroads being a distant second (36), mines third (25), and tobacco fourth (19).

[17] However, in the 1920s and 1930s there were foreigners, particularly from the United States, among the skilled workers in the oil fields (Lieuwen 1967:51; Bergquist 1986:220–21).

enclaves of working-class employment. The population of Caracas grew rapidly to over a quarter of a million by the mid-1930s (Table 3.1), and the number of factory workers also increased rapidly, rising to 33,000 by 1935, 53,000 by 1940, and 70,000 by 1945 (ECLA 1966:Table I-17).[18] However, these data also show that well after this last date, the number of factory workers remained the smallest among the eight countries.

In the oil sector itself, employment also grew at an impressive rate, from 3,463 in 1922, to 16,175 in 1926, to 27,221 in 1929, fluctuating substantially after that time (Bergquist 1986:207, fig. 4.1).[19] This sector had two other attributes noted earlier as conducive to labor militancy: it was foreign owned, with 98 percent of the sector being controlled by U.S. and British interests in 1929 (Lieuwen 1967:44); and it quickly came to play a dominant role in exports, representing 1.9 percent of exports in 1920, 41.6 percent in 1925, 83.2 percent in 1930, and 91.2 percent in 1935 (Tugwell 1975:182).

However, in one respect the expansion of the oil economy may have created conditions less favorable for the labor movement. With rapid change in both the rural and urban sectors and the high rates of urbanization stimulated by the oil boom, by the 1930s a shortage of jobs had emerged in urban areas, potentially having a depressing effect on labor markets and union formation (Donnelly 1975:5, 59; Schuyler 1976:75–77).

Labor Movement.   The Venezuelan labor movement emerged latest among the eight countries. Partly as a result of the late timing of Venezuela's economic development and partly as a result of the repressive control exercised by the Gómez regime, it was still very small by the time of the onset of the reform period in 1935.

In the three decades from the 1890s through the 1910s, when many countries were profoundly shaken by the scope of labor protest, relatively little protest occurred in Venezuela. The year 1895 saw some protest by workers and artisans in Caracas, but the demonstrations did not reflect any real worker organization, and efforts to form organizations in the following year left no lasting legacy (Godio 1980:21, 28–29; Pla et al. 1982:18). A port strike and a trolley workers' strike are reported in 1908, a cigarette workers' strike in 1911, and the first national strike that linked workers in several urban areas in 1914, when telegraph operators achieved a coordinated work stoppage. What Godio refers to as the first "industrial" strike occurred in 1918 among approximately 1,500 skilled workers employed by the Bolivar Railway Company in the state of Yaracuy, but this strike, like the others, appears to have had little broad impact and was soon broken (Godio 1980:38–39, 44–46; Pla et al. 1982:19). Thus, compared to what occurred in other countries

[18] Though lack of precise definitions of categories makes comparison of levels of employment difficult, Donnelly's (1975:61) data also show a substantial, though lower, rate of increase, with the level of industrial employment for 1936 being 2.55 times that of 1920. In the ECLA data, the level for 1935 is 2.75 times that of 1925.

[19] The precise numbers on which Figure 4.1 was based were taken from p. 339 of a 1984 draft of this book that was kindly supplied by Charles Bergquist. Lieuwen (1967:51) presents figures for the late 1920s that are lower by a few thousand.

during these years, the scope of these "national" and "industrial" strikes was limited. An association of workers and artisans founded in 1909 in Caracas was the first genuine workers' organization in the country, and scattered organizing occurred during the following decade (Donnelly 1975:1–2). Nevertheless, the labor movement continued to have an ephemeral existence in terms of the level of organization and protest.

In 1919 to 1920, with the rising cost of living and the regional experience of massive labor protest, the Venezuelan labor movement experienced its greatest activity of the entire period up to 1935, including a number of strikes and further organizing efforts. However, worker demands were moderate. The strikes brought some economic benefits to workers, but the jailing of strike leaders combined with the growing repression by the Gómez regime brought an end to urban labor protest for some time.[20]

In 1922, to preempt further organizing and protest, Gómez established the Confederation of Workers and Artisans of the Federal District, an entity sponsored and directed by the government and used to organize support for Gómez. By the late 1920s it claimed a membership of over 20,000 (Donnelly 1975:85). However, the extent to which this grouping neither represented workers nor even served to fill "syndical space" among potentially organizable workers is suggested by a contemporary observer who noted that it was "composed of drivers of the carts owned by General Gómez used on public works, the masons employed by the government, the stonebreakers on the national highways, and the hucksters in the city market" (Donnelly 1975:82). Apart from the events of 1928 and the period of worker protest in the oil sector, both discussed below, the absence of further serious worker protest from the beginning of the 1920s until after the death of Gómez should probably be attributed less to the role of this organization and more to the comprehensive system of political control of the dictatorship, including systematic press censorship, an extensive spy network, close scrutiny of the mails, and harsh repression when needed to control opposition, combined with a few policy initiatives and some political rhetoric favorable to workers (Donnelly 1975:36–40, 85–87).[21]

In the newly emerging oil sector, the first strike occurred in July 1925 when 2,500 oil workers struck over wages and work rules. Two weeks later another oil strike by more than 2,000 workers encompassed workers in other forms of economic activity in neighboring areas. In part because these strikes caught the company and the government by surprise, compromises were achieved that included some benefits for workers. However, the strikes reflected neither prior worker organization nor a radical or revolutionary orientation among workers, and through a combination of systematic control and some improvement in the conditions of workers, employers and the government succeeded in preventing the emergence of an independent labor

[20] Donnelly 1975:9, 76–78; Godio 1980:48; Pla et al. 1982:20.
[21] Since initial concessions to workers noted in some other countries can hardly be said to have had the effect of limiting the expansion of the labor movement, the importance of these latter initiatives should not be overemphasized.

movement in the oil sector until the end of the Gómez dictatorship (Donnelly 1975:117–28, 150–62). Compared even to enclave mobilization in Colombia in the 1920s, labor action in the oil sector was thus limited under Gómez.

The other important episode of worker protest under Gómez occurred in conjunction with the student demonstrations of 1928 and was apparently the only major outbreak of labor protest between the oil strikes of 1925 and the death of Gómez in 1935. According to Alexander, "a strike was officially declared by the trolleycar workers of Caracas, and it was supported by almost all the other important labor groups in the city, even though the only kind of labor organizations in Caracas at the time were a few mutual benefit societies. The rebellious workers went out in the streets to demonstrate in favor of the students and against the Gómez regime." Protests included street demonstrations in Caracas, Valenzia, Maracaibo, and other cities; strikes in a variety of different factories and workshops; and other kinds of protests as well (1982:40).

In response to these protests, Gómez undertook new public works programs and other initiatives that provided direct or indirect benefits to workers, but he also introduced legislation that gave the government a legal basis for destroying existing unions. These controls contributed to the eclipse of important strikes until after the death of Gómez. However, the events of 1928—like those of 1918–19 in Peru discussed below—established a precedent for collaboration among students, intellectuals, and workers. This experience suggested the possibility of a new kind of populist alliance to leaders of what came to be known as the "Generation of 1928," a group of students, including Rómulo Betancourt, active in the protests of that year (Fagan 1974:40–42; Donnelly 1975:111–14). These students would become major political actors in the formation and leadership of Venezuela's modern political parties in the following decades.

By the onset of the reform period, then, the labor movement in Venezuela was the weakest of the eight under consideration. This weakness was due to the limited socioeconomic development of Venezuela, especially prior to the emergence of the oil sector, and the repressive control of unions, mixed with occasional government paternalism toward workers under the Gómez dictatorship. Only a few small unions existed as of 1935 (Fagan 1974:41), and Venezuela had experienced at most an intermittent history of labor protest up to that year. However, given the rapid emergence of an important enclave sector and Venezuela's increasingly important urban development in the 1920s and 1930s, it is not surprising that there was a marked increase in militance after the death of Gómez and the collapse of his system of political control.

Uruguay

Economic and Social Context. The development of Uruguay encompassed factors hypothesized to be both unfavorable and favorable for the emergence of a strong labor movement. Size was obviously unfavorable. Uruguay was and is a small country with a small economy. The population of Montevideo in 1920 was still under 400,000, ranking fifth among the eight capitals (Table 3.1). Barrán and Nahum (1979:167–68) found that the number of employees in industrial plants in Montevideo increased from just over 22,000 in 1889 to slightly over 30,000 in 1908 and provide a rough estimate of about 40,000 as of 1913. Given the context of continuing growth, these figures appear roughly consistent with the figure of 39,000 from the comparative data for 1925, which ranked Uruguay sixth among the eight countries (Table 3.3).[22] The Uruguayan export economy was not organized around isolated enclaves of economic activity of the kind particularly conducive to strong labor organization.

Uruguayan development had other attributes hypothesized to be more favorable to the development of the labor movement. The relative weight of the urban/factory population within this small but relatively modernized country was impressive. In 1920 Montevideo contained slightly over a quarter of the national population, a remarkable figure for this period that placed Uruguay first among the eight countries and well above the second-ranked country, Argentina (Table 3.1). This ranking was a result both of Uruguay's overall degree of urban development and of its pronounced primate-city pattern. Thus, if one considers the proportion of the population in urban centers as of 1920, which encompasses the more dispersed urban populations of countries with multiple urban centers, Uruguay drops from first place by a wide margin to being well behind Argentina and nearly tied with Chile, which lagged far behind it on the other measure (Table 3.2). Uruguay's population was concentrated in Montevideo to an unusual degree. The factory work force as a percent of total population was likewise large, ranking second only to Argentina and well ahead of that in Chile, the third ranked country (Table 3.3). Given Uruguay's pattern of urban growth, this work force was also concentrated in the capital to an unusual degree.

Other factors were also favorable for worker mobilization. Despite the decline in the relative proportion of foreigners in Uruguay after the mid-19th century, they remained an important part of the urban work force, constituting 62 percent of the workers in industrial production in Montevideo as of 1889. Given the proximity of Montevideo and Buenos Aires, Uruguay was also influenced by the evolution of Argentina's large and early-developing labor movement, as on occasions such as in 1904 when the expulsion of anarchist leaders from Argentina assumed an important role in the Uruguayan workers' movement. Unemployment was apparently not widespread around

---

[22] Though Barrán and Nahum apparently employ no cutoff for the minimum size of work place, the marked increase in average size of workplace that they report even over this earlier interval suggests a growing preponderance of larger workplaces. The overestimation that may result from counting smaller workplaces may well be compensated by the underestimation resulting from counting only the capital (the data in Table 3.3 refer to the national work force), which even in Uruguay obviously does not contain the entire factory population.

the turn of the century and thereafter, perhaps in part because workers lacking jobs were readily attracted to employment opportunities in Buenos Aires.[23]

Labor Movement. The period of reform led by Batlle, beginning in 1903, came early in relation not only to Uruguayan development but also to the development of all eight countries, so it is not surprising that the Uruguayan labor movement was still in an early stage of evolution at the beginning of Batlle's first government. However, in comparison not with the rise of Batlle, but with the experience of the other countries, Uruguay developed—relative to its size—a significant early labor movement.

The initial spread of European ideas about union organizing and the initial organizing efforts began in the 1870s, and the first important strikes occurred in the 1880s. The same decade saw the first strike of workers throughout an entire trade and the first effort to form a central labor organization. These activities subsided from 1888 to 1895, after which the recovery from the world depression brought renewed labor activity and the onset of the two-decade period that Finch (1981:53) identifies as the "formative" years of the Uruguayan union movement. In 1895 printers in the capital successfully struck for the eight-hour day, and the first strike to threaten the economy of the country occurred in 1896 among transportation workers. It lasted 26 days and was finally broken by the police. Though other strikes occurred in that year, strikes declined until the renewal of a more open political climate at the turn of the century (Rodríguez 1965:9–11; Finch 1981:53–54; Pintos 1960:43–49). The years 1901–2 saw a resurgence of union organizing around demands for wage increases and a shorter work day, and Rodríguez (1965:12) claims that by 1905, just after the onset of the Batlle period, "all" industries in the capital and several other urban centers had been organized.

From this starting point, subsequent labor movement development occurred after the initial assumption of the presidency by Batlle and must be understood within the framework of his active support for unions. Between 1900 and 1905 the number of worker associations grew from 16 to 69, and in 1905 anarchist unions, the dominant force within the labor movement, formed the FORU (Uruguayan Regional Workers Federation) following the pattern of the Argentine organization with a parallel name that had been founded in 1901 and renamed the FORA in 1904.[24] The socialists also founded a short-lived federation in 1905 (Alfonso 1970:33). While estimates place FORU's membership at the beginning of the second decade of the century at only 7,000, Finch argues that the federation held effective control over the approximately 90,000 industrial workers (Finch 1981:54), and the International Labor Office (1930:230) placed its membership in 1919 at 25,000. It remained the dominant force in the labor movement until the early 1920s.

[23] Barrán and Nahum 1979:97; Pintos 1960:76; Finch 1981:44–47.

[24] The word *Regional* referred to the international—i.e., the Latin American "region"— rather than national orientation of the federation.

Available data beginning in 1908 reflect the scope of labor protest at this time. Finch (1981:54–55) reports 100 strikes from 1908 to 1912, with a cumulative total of half a million working days lost. In 1913 he estimates that 50,000 workers went on strike in solidarity with a dispute involving tramway workers. Like most other countries, Uruguay also experienced a steep increase in strikes during and after the world war, with working days lost in strikes rising from about 67,000 in 1916 to approximately 140,000 in both 1917 and 1918, almost 600,000 in 1919, and over 645,000 in 1920 (Errandonea and Costabile 1969:135).

In sum, while there was some development of the labor movement prior to the onset of the Batlle period, this was not one of the countries that experienced a major growth of the labor movement in the last decades of the 19th century. This situation had only begun to change by the start of the Batlle period.

Colombia

Economic and Social Context. Colombian development exhibited several features hypothesized to produce a relatively weak labor movement. Around 1920 Bogotá had the smallest population, under 150,000, of any capital among the eight countries except Caracas, and Bogotá's importance as a percent of national population also ranked last (Table 3.1). Interestingly, while this low ranking might be seen as due in part to Colombia's pattern of development of multiple urban centers in which the national capital had less relative importance within the urban sector, in terms of the per capita importance of the urban population in 1920, Colombia's ranking only rises to seventh (Table 3.2), pointing to the relatively undeveloped character of Colombia's urban sector in general. Though the number of factory workers in 1925 placed Colombia fifth among the eight countries, these workers were dispersed among more urban centers,[25] so that the degree of industrial concentration, like the degree of urban-commercial concentration, was limited. This pattern of multiple urban centers occurred in conjunction with, and was reinforced by, pronounced regionalism that at times isolated developments in one area from other parts of the country.

Colombia experienced some enclave development, most notably oil exploitation in Barrancabermeja and the banana sector in Santa Marta. As in Venezuela, oil became important only in the latter part of the time period we are considering. The Tropical Oil Company employed 2,838 workers by 1924, and foreign and national banana growers employed about 20,000 as of 1928. However, while in both cases enclave production was foreign owned— the Tropical Oil Company was a subsidiary of Standard Oil, and the dominant employer in the banana sector was United Fruit—in the case of oil this

[25] For instance, as of 1918 McGreevey (1971:99) reports 6,000 workers in industrial employment in Medellín.

development came much later than enclave modernization in Peru, Chile, and Mexico, and these exports did not have the same preponderance in the export economy that the enclave sector had in the other countries. The production of Colombian oil for export did not begin until after 1925, rising to 17 percent of total exports by the late 1920s. At their peak in the late 1910s, bananas represented only 9 percent of exports and only 6 percent throughout the 1920s. While gold had earlier represented an important export, its extraction was decentralized and declined steadily in relative importance, representing about 5 percent of exports by the later 1920s. European migrants did not play a significant role in the Colombian work force, though foreign labor leaders occasionally did play a role, and while the dramatic loss of Panama in 1903 in the context of U.S. interference in Colombian politics led to important new concern with reform and national autonomy, it probably did not have the same impact as the War of the Pacific in Peru (see below).[26]

Labor Movement.   In this context, the emergence of the Colombian labor movement occurred late. Urrutia finds the first evidence of union-formation beginning in 1909. Under a government procedure for recognizing unions, 27 had been recognized by 1917. However, many of the early associations were mutual benefit societies rather than trade unions, organized in part at the initiative of the Church. There is little evidence of anarchist influence during this period. Many of these early unions were relatively short-lived, and some may not even have been workers associations at all. On the other hand, because recognition did not bestow any advantages prior to the passage of the labor law of 1931, additional unions may have failed to register (Urrutia 1969a:53–55).

More extensive organizing occurred in 1918, and the Social Action Confederation was formed in that year. This confederation was led by middle-class intellectuals not directly affiliated with either political party but having indirect links with the Liberal Party. The fact that "the stated purposes of the confederation were compatible with the Colombian president's conservative and Catholic ideology" (Urrutia 1969a:59) and that he was made honorary president of the group suggests the different character of these developments compared to those in most of the other countries.

Related currents in the labor movement emerged at this time with links to the newly formed party that called itself socialist. Given the moderate program of the party and the heavily artisanal character of the workers involved, this new sector was again more oriented toward the concerns characteristic of mutual benefit societies and also toward a concern with securing political representation than toward an economic and political agenda one might associate with socialism, or even toward collective bargaining. However, by 1924, in conjunction with a series of splits in the first national labor congress held by elements of this same group, new tendencies came to the fore, including one of a more genuinely socialist orientation. Individuals as-

[26] Urrutia 1969a:55, 57, 93, 100–2n; Bergquist 1986:298; McGreevey 1971:207; Sharpless 1978:24.

sociated with this tendency would later found the Socialist Revolutionary Party in 1926, which by 1930 became the Colombian Communist Party (PCC), and some of them assumed an increasingly important place in the labor movement, playing a critical leadership role in major strikes later in the 1920s (Urrutia 1969a:59–62, 82–83; F. González 1975:12–13). However, it does not appear that any national labor central had a particularly stable existence during this period.

The kinds of detailed studies of early strikes cited for several other countries are not presently available for Colombia. Torres Giraldo (1973a:327) mentions three isolated strikes in the last decades of the 19th century, but suggests that they were not associated with any systematic development of worker organizations. According to Caicedo (1971:64), the first important labor action was a strike in 1910 among several categories of transportation and construction workers on the Atlantic Coast that lasted five days. Caicedo mentions no other strikes until the end of the decade. These later strikes are the earliest mentioned by Pécaut (1973) and Urrutia (1969a), a source relied upon by many other analysts of Colombia. The first strikes reported by Urrutia were among the port workers of Cartagena, Barranquilla, and Santa Marta in early 1918, culminating in a mass demonstration by over 1,000 workers that evolved into a destructive riot, led to a state of siege, and produced substantial national shock at this appearance of overt class conflict. F. González (1975:9–10) similarly refers to this as the first "series" of strikes in the nation's history.

During the following year, in November 1919, a railroad strike spread in Bogotá to encompass a wide range of occupational groups, becoming the nation's first general strike (Caicedo 1971:65). In the 1920s, an important wave of strikes occurred. Strikes in Bogotá in 1924, along with major strikes among the workers of the Tropical Oil Company in 1924 and 1927, were met with substantial repression. The banana workers' strike against the United Fruit Company in late 1928 saw the participation of more than 20,000 workers. This strike triggered heavy state repression, leaving as many as 100 dead, followed in 1929 by mass arrests of communists and other leftists in different parts of the country due to a failed insurrectionary movement led by the Communist Party.[27] F. González (1975:13–14) mentions scattered additional strikes in the 1920s. Urrutia (1969a:53) indicates that between 1918 and prior to 1930, 68 additional unions were recognized, but the same uncertainties noted above apply to the significance of this figure, and F. González (1975:12) suggests that these were mainly artisan associations in the tradition of the 19th century. As of 1930 total union membership was estimated to be 11,000 (ILO 1930:216).

To summarize, the Colombian labor movement remained small in comparative terms and was not well institutionalized in terms of the existence of sustained labor organizations. Yet by the end of the 1920s, several major strikes had dramatically raised the social question from the point of view of

[27] Urrutia 1969a:91–108; Torres Giraldo 1973b:154–59; G. Sánchez 1976:79–99.

the elite. Given the late timing, it was one of the few cases in which elements of communist leadership had come to play an important role by the onset of the reform period (in 1930).

Peru

Economic and Social Context.   The relatively small scale and slow pace of Peruvian development did not seem to favor a strong labor movement. As of 1920 the population of Lima and its port city of Callao, which can be treated as a single urban area (Herbold 1971:109), was a quarter of a million, ranking above that of only Caracas and Bogotá (Table 3.1). Blanchard (1982:12) reports slightly over 16,000 factory workers in the province of Lima in 1920,[28] and the comparative data for 1925 show 21,000 nationally, ranking Peru above only Venezuela among the eight countries (Table 3.3).

On the other hand, Peru's population and economic activity were concentrated to an unusual degree in Lima. Whereas Peru ranked last among the eight countries in the proportion of urban population in 1920, it ranked fourth in the proportion of the population in the capital, the largest contrast between these two rankings found in any of the countries (Tables 3.1 and 3.2).[29] While Peru ranked last in the importance of the factory work force in relation to the economically active population (Table 3.3), this work force was concentrated to a greater degree in Lima, thereby making a slightly greater contribution to the creation of a critical mass of population available for worker mobilization.

Though from a comparative perspective the limited development of the urban/industrial sector did not by itself create conditions hypothesized to be favorable to the development of the labor movement, other factors were more favorable. Among the most important was the emergence of three substantial sectors of the export economy organized around enclave production. The sugar sector on the north coast employed 19,945 field workers in 1912, and 20,637 field workers and 3,796 refinery workers in 1915. By 1920 these figures rose to 24,020 and 4,840 (Sulmont 1975:255). Employment in the mines in the central highlands and in the oil sector on the north coast was 9,651 in 1905, 16,500 in 1910, and 22,500 in 1920. Data for subsequent years suggest that these figures, in which blue-collar and white-collar workers are not distinguished, refer almost entirely to blue-collar workers, and by 1929 the number of blue-collar workers in mining had risen to 29,457 (Blanchard

[28] While his figure includes "artisan shops," his discussion (pp. 11–12) makes it clear that it does not include artisan workers in general. As for the Barrán and Nahum figures for Uruguay discussed above, it also appears here that the lack of a specific exclusion of small workplaces may make this figure high in relation to the ECLA data, but the restriction of the data to the province of Lima may make it low. Taking these considerations together, it may be argued that there is reasonable consistency between the Blanchard data and the ECLA data in Table 3.3.

[29] The significance of this shift should be viewed with some caution, since the fifth through eighth ranked countries in terms of the proportion of population in the capital cluster fairly closely together, whereas the first three stand far above them (see Table 3.1).

1982:13 and Sulmont 1975:252–55). Blanchard (1982:142) reports that of these workers, 884 in 1905 and 2,678 in 1919 were in the oil sector.

These sectors had substantial weight in the overall export economy, with sugar and copper representing 46 percent of exports in 1900 and—together with oil, which began to emerge as an important export by the mid-1910s— 65 percent in 1915 and 59 percent in 1920. Foreign ownership played some role in the sugar sector and a major role in the oil and copper sectors, and one third of the miners during the 1920s worked for the U.S.-owned Cerro de Pasco Corporation alone. By 1913 U.S. capital was dominant in the oil sector.[30]

Outside influences on the labor movement and their interaction with political leadership within the country had a special dynamic in Peru. It is noteworthy that in all of Latin America in the first decades of the century, three of the most important intellectual/political leaders concerned with the working class were Peruvians: Manuel González Prada, José Carlos Mariátegui, and Víctor Raúl Haya de la Torre.[31] All had major formative experiences in Europe and played a central role both in transmitting and reinterpreting European radical thought in Peru and Latin America. González Prada was the "recognized ideological figurehead" (Blanchard 1982:62) of Peruvian anarchism (see also Werlich 1978:145). He had a profound influence on the other two leaders, and Klarén (1973:93) has called him the "patriarch of Peruvian radicals." Mariátegui and Haya in turn had major influence on the evolution of the Peruvian labor movement beginning in the late 1910s (see below).

The emergence of these leaders was rooted in part in events and transformations deriving from the impact of external forces on Peruvian development. Though Haya's political career took place primarily in Lima and abroad, it had roots in the experience of the social and economic displacement and political radicalization that accompanied the creation of the sugar enclave sector in the north of Peru. In the case of González Prada, the trauma of Peru's loss of the War of the Pacific, with the humiliating military occupation of Lima by Chile and the loss of valuable territory, played a central role in the development of his radical thought.[32]

Labor Movement.   In many ways Peru might not seem to be a favorable setting for a major labor movement. Yet the combination of the impact of enclave development, the interaction among the dislocation produced by the enclaves, the experience of the War of the Pacific, the intellectual and polit-

[30] Burga and Flores Galindo 1979:77; Sulmont 1975:253; Blanchard 1982:142.

[31] For a discussion of the role of intellectuals in shaping Latin American development and of the special role of these three Peruvians in the development of radical thought in Latin America earlier in this century, see Stabb (1967).

[32] Klarén 1973:chap. 5; Werlich 1978:143. The War of the Pacific had another, indirect, influence on the Peruvian labor movement. Peruvians had earlier been migrant workers in the nitrate fields that were appropriated by Chile after the war. They had been exposed to anarchist ideas brought to the nitrate areas by European exiles who came through Chile, and they later returned from Tarapacá to the southern Peruvian city of Arequipa and played an important role in the early development of anarchism in the south (information based on interviews by Francisco Durand in Arequipa and conveyed to the authors in a personal communication).

ical dynamics that emerged from these experiences, and possibly also the slightly greater relative concentration of population in Lima, provided the basis for a substantial labor movement, though one obviously on a smaller scale than in some of the other countries, and one in which vigorous labor protest ran well ahead of the systematic organization of unions.

In the urban sector, Blanchard (1982:68, 75–76) reports a growing rhythm of early strikes in the Lima-Callao area, with 107 strikes between 1895 and early 1912, 20 of which occurred before 1900. In Peru's first general strike in 1911, 6,000 workers marched to the plaza in front of the presidential palace waving red flags, having rejected the idea of carrying the Peruvian flag. The general strike of 25–26 May 1912 deliberately and successfully disrupted voting in the presidential election both in the capital and in other urban centers, leading so few people to vote that the election was invalidated and the choice of the president sent to the congress. The 1913 general strike, which began among the port workers of Callao, led to parallel strikes in many economic sectors and created a revolutionary atmosphere in Callao and Lima that resulted in the declaration of a state of siege. In the course of the strike, the port workers won the eight-hour day (Blanchard 1982:82; Sulmont 1975:82).

In 1913, following the model of the FORA in Argentina, the Peruvian Regional Workers Federation was formed by anarchists who had played a central role in the general strikes. Later in the 1910s, the anarchist tendency began to give way to anarcho-sindicalists, who rejected the anarchist tactic of direct action and promoted the organization of unions. Textile workers led this political current within the labor movement, and in 1915 they formed a central textile workers' organization that brought together unions from most of the large textile factories. In 1918 a broader group of 20 federations and unions covering many economic sectors both within and outside of Lima-Callao formed the Local Workers Federation of Lima, setting the stage for the dramatic labor protest and organizing efforts of 1918 and 1919 (Sulmont 1975:82–84).

The first of these protests began with a series of labor stoppages in Lima in December 1918, most prominently among textile workers, demanding the eight-hour day. The protest culminated in a general strike in January that paralyzed Lima for two days, spreading to Callao and other urban areas and to the mining and oil enclaves. The international context of dramatic worker protest in Buenos Aires and the model of the Bolshevik Revolution stimulated high expectations on the part of workers and fears on the part of propertied classes, to whom the rapidly spreading strikes "suggested that a nationwide attack on capitalism was about to occur" (Blanchard 1982:152). The main strike finally ended when President Pardo issued a supreme decree granting the eight-hour day, though scattered strikes continued in various parts of the country demanding immediate implementation of the decree (Blanchard 1982:151–59).

Haya de la Torre had been one of the delegates from the Federation of Peruvian Students (of which he became president in 1919) who were involved in aiding the strikers and assisting in the negotiations with President Pardo, and the strike committee used the offices of the federation as its headquarters. In the new organizing efforts after the strike succeeded, Haya chaired the meeting at which the important new Federation of Textile Workers of Peru was formed, and the close relationship he established with the textile workers at this time played an important role in the later development of APRA. Mariátegui's close ties with the working class also developed in this period of workers' struggles during and immediately after the world war.[33]

Several months after the eight-hour day strike, the Committee for Price Controls on Basic Consumer Items, which led a movement that represented 30,000 workers, called another general strike beginning on 27 May. Lima and Callao were again paralyzed. Yet the protest failed, due to the declaration of martial law, heavy use of repression, and the prompt arrest of the strike leaders, combined with the fact that widespread looting which occurred in conjunction with the strike alienated many workers (Blanchard 1982:159–66). However, the events connected with the strike represented an important step in the process through which the Pardo government was discredited, setting the stage for the rise of Leguía.

In the 1910s the enclave sectors also produced important episodes of worker militancy. Extensive protest in the sugar sector beginning in 1910, and in 1912 a massive outbreak of worker violence occurred in the Chicama Valley, spilling into other areas as well. Thousands of workers took part in the burning of sugar estates in a protest that amounted to "the most serious outbreak of labor violence in the history of the country" (Klarén 1973:33) and that produced "widespread fears of an imminent social revolution" (Blanchard 1982:128). In the repression that followed the strike, 150 workers were killed and worker organizations were suppressed. Through the mid- to late-1910s, with some involvement and encouragement by anarchists from Lima, a series of strikes was called in the oil sector, including particularly violent strikes in three major oil centers in 1917 that resulted in the death of eleven workers. Four strikes are reported in the Cerro de Pasco mining region in 1908–9, with scattered worker actions in the decade of the 1910s, culminating in major strikes in 1919. Yet in the face of continuing repression, little systematic organization of unions and worker protest took place in any of the enclave sectors during this period.[34]

Thus, while the enclave sector was a crucial arena of early labor protest and also played an important role in the early experiences of such leaders as Haya, in terms of the organizational—and intellectual—development of the labor movement, the focus was much more in Lima.

Argentina

Economic and Social Context. Argentina's rapidly growing economy provided conditions hypothesized to offer fertile ground for a strong labor movement. At the turn of the century and beyond, Buenos Aires was the largest

[33] Blanchard 1982:153, 155, 171; Sulmont 1975:86, 103.
[34] Klarén 1973:32–35; Sulmont 1975:60, 84; Blanchard 1982:138–44.

city in Latin America, growing by 137 percent between 1895 and 1914 to over 1.5 million. The capital's population as a percent of the national population ranked second only to Montevideo, and given the substantial development of secondary cities combined with the high overall level of urbanization, Argentina ranked first by a wide margin in the proportion of its population in urban centers (Tables 3.1 and 3.2).

Within this highly developed urban setting, the number of workers involved in nonhandicraft manufacturing rose from over 100,000 in 1894 to nearly 400,000 by 1914 (Merkx 1969:83). The comparative data on factory employment in Table 3.3, which exclude very small workplaces that appear to be included in Merkx's data and therefore give a lower figure for 1925 than he does for 1914, rank the absolute size of the work force in factories only slightly behind Brazil, the highest in the region. As a percent of the economically active population, the relative importance of factory workers was the greatest by a substantial margin among the eight countries. Sixty-two percent of men employed in industry and crafts, though a far lower percent of women, were foreign born as of 1914 (Tornquist 1919:11–13), bringing into the Argentine labor force large numbers of workers with direct experience with labor movements, and particularly with anarchism, in Europe. While unemployment data for this period are imprecise for all of the countries, this period in Argentina is generally one of high demand for labor, a principal cause of the heavy migration from Europe.

Among the factors seen as contributing to worker militancy, the only one lacking in Argentina was a major role in the economy of export enclaves. The most important parts of the Argentine export sector were not concentrated in isolated enclaves of economic activity and most were nationally owned. Mineral exports played little role (Díaz Alejandro 1970:5, 18).

Labor Movement.   Given this pattern of national evolution, Argentina not surprisingly developed what comparative analysts (Alexander 1965:35; Spalding 1977:2, 52) have seen as an exceptionally strong labor movement. Argentina's first trade union appeared among printers in Buenos Aires in the 1870s and held its first strike in 1878 (Iscaro 1973:46–47). Spalding (1977:23, 25) reports 48 strikes in the 1880s and 58 between 1891 and 1896, and by the mid-1890s at least 25 labor unions existed in the capital and more had appeared in other cities and towns as well. He also notes that the unions in Argentina were larger than in other countries, with an average of 100 members. After unsuccessful attempts to form a central federation in the 1890s, the Federación Obrera Argentina was founded in 1901 by anarchists and socialists. The latter broke away in 1902 when the anarchists consolidated their position as the dominant force in the labor movement, and FOA changed its name to FORA in 1904 to emphasize its internationalism.[35] In 1903 the anarchist federation had 42 member associations encompassing 15,212 workers, about twice as many as the socialists (Iscaro 1973:95–116).

Argentina's first general strike occurred in 1902, involving 20,000 workers.

---

[35] As noted in the discussion of Uruguay above, the addition of the word *Regional* to the name meant regional in the sense of *international*.

According to one analyst, rumors had spread throughout the capital that 30,000 armed workers had taken to the streets, and "the fear of social revolution hung in the air" (Oved 1978:260). The army was called in, police authorized strikebreakers to be armed, and numerous gun battles occurred between strikers and strikebreakers (258–60). Other events in the first decade of the century included a general strike in 1909, following the harsh repression of a May Day demonstration in which as many as 220,000 workers participated (Iscaro 1973:146); the assassination of the police chief of Buenos Aires in the same year by an anarchist in retaliation for the police role in the May Day repression, an act which was followed by the fourth state of siege since 1900 (Walter 1977:51); and a threat to call a general strike during the celebration of the centennial of Argentine independence, a threat that expressed the "internationalist" orientation of anarchism that rejected nationalist attachments—and hence this national holiday—as an obstacle to their cause.

This threatened strike brought the first major episode of the remarkable kind of conservative mobilization against the labor movement that would recur a decade later, in which mobs made up largely of upper class youths went on a rampage, destroying the offices of unions and of leftist newspapers and attacking "Jewish" neighborhoods. A short time later a bomb was set off in the Buenos Aires opera house. Though there were apparently no serious casualties, the event served as a justification for stringent new controls on union activity.[36]

In all, during the first decade of the century a total of 10 general strikes, involving the working population of at least one city, occurred either in Buenos Aires or in other urban centers. Between 1907 and 1910 alone, a remarkable total of 785 strikes occurred in Buenos Aires, by far the greatest number at this time in any of the eight countries, with nearly 1.4 million work days lost. In 1911, despite the reduced number of strikes, the number of work days lost was over 1.4 million (Spalding 1970:28,88).

During the half decade prior to the Yrigoyen presidency that began in 1916, the number of strikes remained under 100 per year. Anarchism began to decline, and syndicalists came to play a growing role in the movement, while socialist influence remained modest.[37] Finally, for the purpose of the comparison presented below it may be noted that in the period toward the end of the 1910s, after the rise of Yrigoyen, Argentina experienced an eruption of worker protest of greater magnitude than in any of the other countries (see Chapter 4).

Conclusion

The emergence of labor movements, which sets our story into motion, had roots in the rapid economic growth that took place beginning in the second

[36] Marotta 1961, vol. 2:71–77; Oddone 1949:231; Dorfman 1970:262.
[37] Di Tella and Zymelman 1967:537–38; Walter 1977:126; Baily 1967:26–29.

half of the 19th century in much of Latin America. The region saw the massive expansion of primary product exports, which in some cases occurred in conjunction with enclave development and which in general stimulated urban, commercial, and industrial growth. Part and parcel of this economic expansion was the emergence of a working class in the export, transportation, commercial, and manufacturing sectors. In reaction to poor conditions of work and to European models of labor movement development, workers began to organize and protest, thereby opening up a new political agenda centered on the social question. They posed the issue of how the state and economic elites should respond to worker protest and new working-class demands. These demands appeared to many as a major assault on established order, even when they focused on such relatively modest issues as the eight-hour day or the regulation of worker safety. When they took the form of the revolutionary program of anarchism or communism, they were indeed threatening.

The strength of the labor movement and the scope of protest varied with a number of factors: the size of the emerging working class (in absolute and relative terms), its degree of concentration in urban and enclave areas, the conditions of labor shortage or surplus in the labor market, and the ideological and organizational models and experiences brought with European immigrants. This chapter has explored these factors and the resulting characteristics of labor organization and protest for each of the countries. At this point, it is appropriate to provide a more explicitly comparative summary that focuses on three dimensions: (1) a comparison of the economic and social contexts out of which labor movements emerged; (2) cross-sectional comparisons of labor movements during the roughly three decades covered in this chapter; and (3) a comparison of labor movement development by the onset of the reform period.

Economic and Social Context.   Table 3.4 summarizes the socioeconomic development of the eight countries in terms of the factors conducive to the development of a strong labor movement. As can be seen in the table, while there is broad variation among countries, no country has a favorable score on all the variables, nor does any country have an unfavorable score on all of them. Thus, although Colombia probably had the conditions least favorable to a strong labor movement, it had at least some enclave production, was not at the very bottom on some of the socioeconomic indicators, and had at least some evidence of influence of European migrants. At the other end of the spectrum, Argentina probably had the most favorable conditions, yet lacked enclaves and did not have as pronounced a primate city pattern of development as some countries.

It is possible to sum the scores on the different variables,[38] though doing so obviously involves arbitrary assumptions about relative weighting. Pro-

[38] The results of summing the scores in Table 3.4 are as follows (two numbers with a slash reflect the change over time presented in the earlier table): Argentina 17; Chile 16; Uruguay 15; Mexico 15/14; Brazil 12/11; Peru 10; Colombia 7; Venezuela 6/10.

TABLE 3.4
Conditions Supportive of Early Labor Movement Development

	Chi	Bra	Ven	Mex	Uru	Col	Per	Arg
High on Absolute Size	2	4	0	3	1	1	0	4
High on Per Capita Indicators	3	2	0	2	3	1	0	4
Primate City Pattern	3	0	3	1	4	1	4	3
Enclaves	4	0	0/4	4	0	2	4	0
European Immigrants	2	4	1	3	4	1	1	4
Labor Surplus Economy	2	2/1	2	2/1	3	1	1	3

Notes: 4-Very Favorable; 3-Favorable; 2-Neutral; 1-Unfavorable; 0-Very Unfavorable. A slash indicates change within this early period. The last variable, labor surplus economy, is the only one for which *more* of the variable is *less* supportive of labor movement development. Hence, *more* labor surplus receives a *lower* score in this table.

ceeding either with such an arithmetic sum or on a more impressionistic basis, a more-or-less clear ranking of countries emerges. Argentina appears to have had the most favorable conditions for labor movement development, followed by Chile and then Uruguay. For the earlier part of this period, Uruguay was tied with Mexico, if we presume that heavy rural-urban migration had not yet had a major impact on the urban labor market in Mexico, but was one position ahead of Mexico once this situation of Mexico changed in the first decades of the 20th century. The next ranked case would be Brazil, followed by Peru. In last place were Colombia and Venezuela, with the latter moving somewhat ahead after the development of the oil enclaves.

Cross-Sectional Comparisons of Labor Movement Development. An examination of the scope of the labor movement in a series of specific periods— the 1890s, the first decade of the 20th century, the first half of the 1910s, and the latter half of the 1910s—reveals a relatively clear ordering of countries (see Figure 3.1). Major episodes of labor protest occurred during the decade of the 1890s in Argentina, Chile, and Mexico. In Mexico, in contrast to the other two countries, significant protest had begun a decade or so earlier. Some protest occurred in the 1890s in Brazil, and also in Uruguay and Peru, though on an even more limited scale. There is little or no evidence of an emerging labor movement either at this time or in the following decade in Colombia and Venezuela.

Roughly the same picture continues in the first decade of the 20th century. By this time the scope of protest in Argentina, Chile, and Mexico, in that order of decreasing magnitude, had reached even greater proportions, including important worker insurrections, and Brazil likewise experienced major labor protest during this period. Uruguay and Peru also had a number of strikes, though in Uruguay most of this decade came after the onset of the reform period. The effect of the early reform period on labor activation may help to explain why Uruguay was ahead of Peru at this time in terms of sustained labor organization.

The first half of the 1910s—*prior* to the major, continent-wide increase in labor protest during and after World War I—saw a relative lull in militancy in Argentina, Chile, and Brazil. On the other hand, at this point the scope of strikes in Uruguay was substantial, though again this may be accounted for in part by the government's support of strikes under the second Batlle administration. During these years Peru began to experience widespread strikes both in the urban and enclave sectors, though in part because of the far more repressive atmosphere in Peru the emergence of sustained labor organizations continued to be less common. At this point Venezuela and Colombia had at most sporadic labor protest and limited worker organization.

Finally, the years 1916–20 saw a major crescendo of labor protest, which took its more dramatic form in Argentina and then Chile, followed by Mexico, Uruguay, Peru, and Brazil. In Argentina and Uruguay, again, this protest must be seen in light of the fact that it came after the onset of the reform period. This was the period of the first strikes in Colombia, which had a substantial impact on national consciousness, and in Venezuela it was still a period of limited, incipient protest.

On the basis of these cross-sectional comparisons, one might thus view Argentina, Chile, and Mexico, in that order, as having the most extensive early labor movements. Uruguay, Peru, and Brazil constitute an intermediate group of countries that had labor movements that were quite substantial, but significantly behind those in the first group. Colombia and finally Venezuela had the least developed labor movements.

Given the qualitative nature of the comparisons made here and the small number of cases, it is impossible to provide a strong test of individual hypotheses about the impact of the economic and social context presented at the beginning of the chapter, much less about their relative weight in explaining the emergence of the labor movements. However, juxtaposing the comparison of labor movement development just presented with the summary of the socioeconomic factors presented above, it is evident that the two orderings are similar. Further, the qualitative description of individual country patterns presented in the main body of this chapter is supportive of the general thrust of these hypotheses. Hence, though our evidence is not precise, the picture that emerges is one of strong links between socioeconomic change and the scope of labor organizing and protest.

Labor Movement Development at Onset of Reform Period.   An important concern of this study is with the evolution of the labor movement up to the change in government that marks the onset of the reform period analyzed in the next chapter. It is therefore useful to compare the labor movements at the *analytically* equivalent point that corresponds to the onset of that period, in addition to comparing them in *chronologically* equivalent decades, as has just been done (Table 3.5). In the three countries where the incorporation period was delayed beyond the onset of the reform period (Mexico, Peru, and

Argentina), the character of the labor movement at that subsequent point will also be noted.

Two clusters of factors appear to account for the scope of labor organizing and protest at these specific points in time. First, within the framework of the analysis presented above, the scope of labor movement development is in part the result of the level and pattern of socioeconomic development that had been achieved by that time in each country. Second, it also depended on the timing in relation to certain international developments in labor movements that cut across a number of countries: two major international episodes of strikes (the strike waves of 1906–10 and of the immediate post-World War I period); and the regional evolution from anarchist, to syndicalist, and then to communist and in some cases socialist predominance in the labor movement.

In Argentina, Brazil, Chile, and Mexico by the onset of the reform period, substantial evolution of the labor movement had already occurred in the context of extensive urban-manufacturing development. However, in other ways these countries differed considerably. At the onset of the reform period in 1916 in Argentina, the Argentine labor movement was certainly the strongest in the region. This movement had important anarcho-syndicalist and syndicalist currents, with socialists, as we shall see, coming to play a significant electoral role vis-à-vis workers. The continent-wide eruption of worker protest at the end of the 1910s came shortly after Yrigoyen's rise to power in Argentina, posing a major challenge to his initial labor policies. By 1930 in Brazil, by contrast, the labor movement had a substantial measure of com-

TABLE 3.5
Labor Movement Development at Onset of Reform and Incorporation Periods

	Reform Period	Incorporation Period (if different)
Brazil	Substantial (1930)	
Chile	Extensive (1920)	
Mexico	Substantial (1911)	Substantial (1917)
Venezuela	Very limited (1935)	
Uruguay	Very limited (1903)	
Colombia	Limited (1930)	
Peru	Substantial (1919)	Extensive (1939)
Argentina	Extensive (1916)	Very extensive (1943)

munist dominance and had gone through a decade of relative quiescence, with the major protests of the late 1910s well in the past. By 1920 the Chilean movement was about to shift from anarchist to communist dominance and was entering a period of more limited protest after 1920—a decline that was hastened by vigorous repression in the first year of the new government. On the other hand, the Mexican labor movement was still substantially mutualist and anarchist by 1911, and the major wave of strikes of 1906–10 preceded the revolution and represented part of the context out of which it emerged. Though the Mexican Casa del Obrero Mundial cooperated with the Constitutionalists briefly during the revolution, this alliance quickly fell apart once the fighting was over and the dominant part of the labor movement returned to its prior anarchist orientation of the pre-1911 period.

By 1919 the Peruvian labor movement had already undergone substantial development, though the erosion of anarcho-syndical dominance had just begun, to be superseded shortly by two currents of leadership, one evolving from a socialist to communist orientation, the other ultimately emerging as APRA. The major eruption of strikes in the immediate postwar period was an important part of the context in which the reform government of Leguía came to power, though as we shall see the continuation of the strikes and protests in the following years, obviously with the support of these new elements of leadership, posed serious difficulties for Leguía's initially more favorable labor policies.

In Colombia, although the onset of the reform period came late, the prior development of the labor movement was less impressive. Colombia not only ranked far behind Argentina, Brazil, Chile, and Mexico, but also behind Peru. The labor protest of the late 1910s and the 1920s in Colombia, though substantial compared with its minimal level during previous years in that country, was on a smaller scale than that in Peru in the first half of the 1910s.[39] The scope of labor movement development in Colombia in the 1920s was probably more extensive than in Uruguay prior to 1903 in terms of episodes of worker protest that had a major national impact, though possibly more limited in terms of the development of sustained worker organization. Given the late timing in Colombia, a significant feature of labor politics in the

---

[39] Because this interpretation of Colombia's ranking plays an important role in the analysis in the next chapter, this particular paired comparison may be briefly elaborated. The 1928 banana workers' strike in Colombia, which as we shall see played an important role in bringing the Liberals to power, might be thought of as the rough equivalent of the upheaval in Peru in the sugar sector in 1912, which was just one of a number of protests in that sector in Peru. The 1924 and 1927 oil workers' strikes in Colombia, while important, were clearly less extensive than the long series of protests in the copper and oil sectors in Peru during the 1910s. While there were significant urban strikes in Colombia in 1910, 1918–19, and 1924, and apparently others in the 1920s, these appear to have been far more limited than the long history of strikes in Lima beginning in the 1890s and culminating in the dramatic labor upheavals of 1911–13 and 1918–19. Finally, efforts to sustain labor organizations appear to have been even more limited in Colombia in the 1920s than in Peru in the prior decade, and particularly toward the end of that decade.

1920s was a substantial current of communist orientation, which would later play an important role during the Liberal period in the 1930s.

Finally, the countries with the least developed labor movements by the reform period were Uruguay and Venezuela. Because Batlle's rise to power came exceptionally early, the labor movement by that time was just entering a period of rapid expansion. At that early point, the movement that did exist was anarchist and to a lesser degree socialist. In Venezuela, by 1935 the labor movement was even less developed. However, in the context of rapid urban growth and the consolidation of major export enclaves, the potential for a more important movement was growing and was quickly realized once Gómez's system of tight control of worker organizing collapsed.

Since our analysis is concerned with a comparison of labor movements at the onset both of the reform period and of the incorporation period, we should briefly note the experience of the three countries where the onset of incorporation was delayed beyond the beginning of the reform period (see Table 3.5). In Mexico the labor movement did not significantly change over the short interval between 1911 and 1917. On the other hand, in Peru the interval between 1919 and 1939 brought substantial growth of the labor movement and the emergence of APRA and the communists as the dominant currents. Yet the scope of the movement remained far more modest than in several other countries. In Argentina the long interval between 1916 and 1943 saw extensive growth of the labor movement and a shift toward the political predominance of socialist and communist unions. In the context of this growth, the Argentine union movement certainly remained one of the largest and strongest in the region.

Hence, although these delays brought substantial growth in the union movements in Argentina and Peru, they probably did not significantly change the relative ranking of the countries as of the onset of incorporation.

4

State: Reformist Challenge to Oligarchic Domination

IN RESPONSE to the growing strength of labor organization and the dramatic scope of worker protest in the first decades of the 20th century, political leaders became increasingly concerned about the "social question." They debated the appropriate role of the newly emerging working classes within the economic and political system and the problem of mitigating the exploitative conditions of work that appeared to encourage this new social protest. The debate on the social question was intertwined with a broader debate on social and political reform, and by the 1930s an important period of reform had emerged in all eight countries. In conjunction with these reforms, the state ultimately initiated what we refer to as the *initial incorporation* of the labor movement.

The evolution of this period of reform occurred at a different rhythm and in a different way in each country. Important contrasts include the nature of the reform project itself, the scope of opposition to reform from elements of the established political order, the timing of the incorporation period, the degree to which reformers were able to carry out their programs, and the degree to which they cultivated the support of the labor movement in conjunction with their challenge to the oligarchy.

This chapter first introduces the historical setting of this period of reform. The eight cases are then analyzed, with a focus on (1) the political system prior to the reforms, (2) the emergence of the reform alliances, (3) the immediate political transition and change of government that brought the reformers to power, and (4) the role of the labor movement in this transition.

In five of the countries—Brazil, Chile, Colombia, Uruguay, and Venezuela—the incorporation period, which is analyzed in the next chapter, began with this change in government. However, in Mexico, Peru, and Argentina, a substantial delay occurred between this change of government and the onset of incorporation. For these three countries, the present chapter explores the causes of this delay and brings the analysis up to the eve of the incorporation period, thereby covering the period from 1910 to 1917 in Mexico, from 1919 to 1939 in Peru, and from 1916 to 1943 in Argentina.

Historical Setting

The national political framework within which labor movements initially emerged in these countries is commonly referred to in Latin American political analysis as the period of the "oligarchic state" or of "oligarchic domination."[1] With the rapid economic expansion that began in most of these countries in the later 19th century (Venezuela lagged far behind), new elites whose economic power was based in the dynamic export sectors came to share political power with landed elites based in more traditional, nonexport sectors of the economy. These new elites came to achieve substantial sway in the political arena, contributing to the construction of states that provided political stability and encouraged the creation of basic infrastructure, often with a substantial role of foreign private capital, that helped promote this economic expansion. At the same time, the state remained laissez-faire in most areas of economic and social policy.

These different sectors of the economic and political elite, frequently referred to as the oligarchy, dominated politics, most commonly through the vehicle of restricted democracies often based on widespread electoral fraud or through dictatorial rule. Hence, the expression *oligarchic* usefully describes both the character of the state and the national political regime.

Beginning at the end of the 19th century, important reform movements began to emerge in opposition to these oligarchic states. Demands for reform came in part from sectors of the traditional elite left behind by the new prosperity, but even more importantly from new sectors created by the dramatic economic and demographic expansion of this period. This expansion included rapid urban growth and the development within the urban sector of a broad range of new economic activity in commerce and increasingly in manufacturing, as well as the growth of export enclaves. The emergence of the new middle sectors and working class, and the political movements and new forms of social protest in which they engaged, raised basic issues about the scope of the political system and the role of these groups within it. Debate on these issues focused on such themes as broadening the suffrage, the honesty and openness of elections, the social question, and the incorporation of the labor movement. In countries where worker protest in the modern sector had been accompanied by peasant rebellion and protest and/or by the widespread displacement of peasants from their land in the traditional rural sector, issues of peasant incorporation, land reform, and in some cases of the reform of policy toward Indians was also raised.

Though the evolution of these various issues of reform had a distinct character that responded in part to internal processes of change within each country, their evolution also responded to external influences. Such influences included the diffusion of new ideologies and techniques of organization from labor movements in Europe; a broad tradition of European Catholic and non-Catholic social thought, including the Papal Encyclical *Rerum Novarum*, known as the workingman's encyclical (Wiarda 1975:5–7), in which the Church addressed the social question; and subsequently the powerful demonstration effect of the Mexican Revolution, the Russian Revolution, and for

[1] See, for instance, Ianni (1975:chap. 8) and O'Donnell (1977:66), respectively.

some South American countries the exceptional scope of urban labor protest toward the end of the 1910s in Argentina.

In most of the countries these reform movements emerged and evolved in a gradual fashion. Yet in all eight cases a well-defined change in government serves as a benchmark in the inauguration of this period of reform and of the transformation of the oligarchic state: in Chile the election of Arturo Alessandri in 1920; in Brazil the Revolution of 1930 and the assumption of power by Getulio Vargas; in Uruguay the election of José Batlle y Ordóñez in 1903; in Colombia the beginning of the Liberal period and the election of Enrique Olaya Herrera in 1930; in Venezuela the death of Juan Vicente Gómez in 1935; in Mexico the 1910 Revolution and the fall of Porfirio Díaz in 1911; in Peru the second presidency of Augusto Leguía, beginning in 1919; and in Argentina the beginning of the Radical period with the election of Hipólito Yrigoyen in 1916.

To provide an overview of these transitions, Table 4.1 presents these dates, along with (1) the date of the new constitution associated with each reform period; (2) the date that the initial incorporation period was launched; and (3) the degree of labor movement development on the eve of the incorporation period.

These events spanned four decades of Latin American history and involved

TABLE 4.1
Regime Transition and Labor Movement Development

	Change of Government that Inaugurated Reform Period	New Constitution	Onset of Incorporation Period[a]	Labor Movement Development at the Onset of Incorporation Period[b]
Brazil	1930 (Vargas)	1934	1930	Substantial
Chile	1920 (Alessandri)	1925	1920	Extensive
Mexico	1911 (Madero)	1917	1917	Substantial
Venezuela	1935 (López Contreras)	1936, 1947	1935	Very limited
Uruguay	1903 (Batlle)	1917	1903	Very limited
Colombia	1930 (Olaya)	1936 (Const. revision)	1930	Limited
Peru	1919 (Leguía)	1920	1939	Extensive
Argentina	1916 (Yrigoyen)	1949	1943	Very extensive

[a] See definition in glossary and analysis in Chapter 5.
[b] Based on the analysis presented in Chapter 3.

very different kinds of transitions: the death of one dictator (Venezuela) and the collapse of the rule of another (Mexico); disputes surrounding a presidential succession resolved on the battlefield (Brazil, Uruguay, and again Mexico) or resolved under the pressure of intense urban social protest (Chile and Peru); and also conventional elections (Colombia and Argentina). These transitions also differed in the degree to which they led to a fundamental reorientation in political coalitions and to broad political and economic reform, as opposed to mild reform within the framework of the continuing dominance of established oligarchies. Even in the cases of drastic political disjunctures, the intermixing of continuity and change was complex. As Rodney Anderson (1976:299) has said for revolutionary Mexico: "The resignation of Porfirio Díaz . . . does not mark the death of one era and the birth of another; . . . the old regime lived on in institutions and ways with roots too deep and influences too pervasive to fall with the old *Caudillo* who had so long kept them secure. . . . Yet the events of the years that follow the *maderista*[2] triumph belong to another history."

These reform periods all mark an important step in a broader transition from the laissez-faire state, more characteristic of the earlier oligarchic period, to a conception of a more activist state. This new conception still asserted liberal notions of the primacy of property rights and at most a moderate role of the state in the ownership of productive enterprises. Yet it assigned to the state new social, welfare, and economic responsibilities that prominently embraced a changed relationship between the state and the new urban sectors, including the working class. This conception of the state's role was commonly spelled out in constitutions promulgated in the period following the initial change of government (Table 4.1). Mexico's 1917 constitution was the world's first example of "social constitutionalism," predating both the Russian and the Weimar constitutions, and along with them it became an important international model. New constitutions also appeared in Uruguay in 1917, in Peru in 1920, in Chile in 1925, and in Brazil in 1934. A constitutional revision was adopted in Colombia in 1936, and in Venezuela, following a modest revision in 1936, a fundamentally new constitution was adopted in 1947. Argentina's "social constitution" was adopted in 1949, only two years after the new constitution in Venezuela but extremely late in relation to the earlier reform period of Yrigoyen. This long delay will emerge as an important feature of the Argentine case.

Focus of Analysis

This chapter explores the development of this period of reform, and hence the political context out of which the incorporation period emerged. Four themes are highlighted.

Political Position of the Oligarchy. The initial reform period did not deci-

---

[2] I.e., the victory of the Madero forces in 1911.

sively bring to power the opponents of the old order. Indeed, in a number of countries a major political crisis accompanied the immediate succession to the presidency of the leader of the reform movement. Once this succession had occurred, to varying degrees the reformers faced opposition from groups identified with the old order. Differences in the degree and form of subordination of the reformers to the oligarchy are crucial to the interpretation of these periods.

These differences depended in important measure on what we will refer to as the political "strength" of the oligarchy and the way its position was articulated through the political system. Oligarchic strength is obviously a complex, multidimensional phenomenon (Payne 1968) not easy to compare across countries. Yet the literature (cited below) on these countries points to differences so profound that some discussion of contrasts among cases is possible. To help guide the reader through the analysis, certain preliminary observations about the position of the oligarchy in different countries are made in Table 4.2.

In Brazil and Chile the oligarchy is commonly seen as having had an unusual capacity for the direct exercise of power in the political sphere. During periods of electoral politics, it had significant capacity to sustain its position due to the electoral support it maintained through the clientelistic control of major portions of the rural sector. In Uruguay and Colombia, the political position of the oligarchy was likewise strong, in that these oligarchies also enjoyed electoral support in the rural sector, rooted in traditional systems of

TABLE 4.2
Political Position of Oligarchy at Onset of Reform Period

	Political Position of Oligarchy	Articulation through Political System	
		Position in Electoral Arena	Other Observations
Brazil	Very strong	Viable	
Chile	Very strong	Viable	
Venezuela	Weak	Weak	
Mexico	Weak	Weak	
Uruguay	Strong	Viable	Mediated through traditional two-party system
Colombia	Strong	Viable	Mediated through traditional two-party system
Peru	Moderate	Viable	Serious problem of political divisions within oligarchy
Argentina	Often viewed as unusually strong	Weak	

clientelistic control. However, Uruguay and Colombia had the distinctive attribute that the oligarchy's political position was mediated through both parties in well-institutionalized two-party systems.[3] Mexico and Venezuela, by contrast, fall at the opposite end of the spectrum. Here the period of the oligarchic state saw an erosion of the oligarchy's economic, social, and political position, which had no counterpart in the other cases.

Finally, Peru and Argentina in many respects differed greatly in the position of their oligarchies, both from one another and in relation to the other six countries. Peru might be seen as having an oligarchy that was in many respects strong but whose power was flawed due to extreme heterogeneity within the elite, a factor that contributed to severe political divisions and important political crises. Argentina is commonly seen as having an unusually strong, unified oligarchy, yet in periods of electoral politics this strength was flawed by the lack of a substantial peasant electoral base. These contrasting patterns of power, combined with these important flaws and certain conjunctural issues of timing, contributed to interesting parallels in the evolution of Peru and Argentina.

Worker Mobilization in Support of Reform Movement. In the face of oligarchic resistance to the reform movements, new political leaders adopted distinct approaches to attaining and consolidating power. Some leaders viewed the working class as a political resource that could be mobilized in the struggles among sectors of the elite, whereas elsewhere this form of mobilization was not employed, and leaders' concern focused more on the control of the working class. Though these differences are of particular concern during the incorporation periods considered in the next chapter, important contrasts among cases already emerge in the period considered here.

Drawing together the issues addressed under this and the previous heading, we may anticipate the distinction between two alternative coalitions that will be important throughout the analysis: a *populist alliance*, in which working class mobilization and in some instances peasant mobilization become an element in the struggles between the reformers and more traditional groups; and an *accommodationist alliance*, in which the reformers maintain at least the acquiescence, if not the support, of major elements of the oligarchy.

Timing of Incorporation in Relation to Change of Government that Inaugurated Reform Period. These contrasting relationships among the reformers, the labor movement, and the oligarchy contributed to important differences among countries in the timing of the initial incorporation period in relation to the onset of the reform period (see Table 4.1), with a significant delay in Mexico and long delays in Peru and Argentina. In Mexico the onset of the incorporation period was delayed in part by the civil war. In Peru and

---

[3] In discussing the Colombian oligarchy, Pécaut (1987:106, 108) underlines its strength in the sphere of social domination, but the fragmentation of the power it exercised through the state. However, the indirect control of the state provided by the dynamics of the two-party system probably gave the oligarchy more power within the state than was found in several other countries.

Argentina during the 1910s, the government launched what could have become an incorporation period; however, this initiative was aborted and incorporation was postponed for two decades.

This pattern of false starts and delays in the incorporation period in Peru and Argentina reflects the difficulty of initiating this major change in labor policy. The transition was difficult because of potential opposition from both the oligarchy and the labor movement. Important sectors of the oligarchy often strongly opposed policies that suggested any form of state-sanctioned institutionalization of the labor movement, as well as other policies favorable to the labor movement or to workers. A shift to such policies therefore commonly involved a sharp disjuncture in political coalitions that was difficult to initiate and to sustain. In addition, it was often difficult to secure labor's cooperation with these state initiatives, even when the initiatives included provisions "favorable" to labor. In some countries the labor movement had by this time achieved considerable strength and autonomy, giving it considerable capacity to resist cooperation with the state. Important sectors of the movement were anarchist and revolutionary and strongly opposed such cooperation.

Timing of Incorporation in Relation to Emergence of Labor Movement. A fourth theme is the timing of the onset of incorporation in relation to the emergence of the labor movement (Table 4.1). Though the debate on the social question and the initiation of incorporation were in part intertwined with a larger set of reform issues, the incorporation periods were obviously also a direct response to the emergence of the labor movement. However, this response varied greatly in the degree to which it was preemptive, in the sense of occurring at an early point in relation to the emergence of the labor movement; as opposed to emerging long after the initial emergence of labor organizing. An examination of this aspect of timing provides another perspective for analyzing how these political systems responded to this period of dramatic economic and social change.

Brazil and Chile

Period of the Oligarchic State. In both Brazil and Chile, the oligarchic states took the form of civilian, decentralized republics, characterized by a corrupt and limited democracy dominated by the oligarchies of a few strong regions. In Brazil, three states—São Paulo, Minas Gerais, and Rio Grande do Sul— dominated national political power, and an alliance between the first two frequently kept the third out of the pinnacles of federal government. Coffee interests, cattle ranchers, and sugar plantation owners played a prominent role in the politics of this period (Love 1970:9–13; Skidmore 1977). In Chile national government was dominated by the central part of the country, with owners of large agricultural holdings playing a predominant role within a framework in which this cohesive elite increasingly absorbed the elites of the urban commercial and incipient manufacturing sector. Bauer (1975:206;

see also 46) reports the observation that "the small group of influential families was so concentrated in downtown Santiago that the entire country was controlled by four square blocks in the city."

In comparative terms, the political position of the traditional oligarchy in Brazil and Chile was relatively strong due to a number of factors embedded in 19th-century history. Both countries had seen a relatively long period of civilian rule and oligarchic domination of the state. North (1966:13) has singled out Chile and Brazil as particularly clear cases of direct rule by the upper class during this period. In both countries, oligarchic hegemony was strongly supported by the Church.

Perhaps most importantly for present purposes, relatively stable rule in Brazil and Chile was accompanied by the early consolidation of large land holdings and the institutionalization of clientelistic ties in the countryside. The Brazilian and Chilean oligarchies were able to establish an entrenched system of clientelism on the large holdings in rural areas and had acquired experience in utilizing and manipulating these clientelistic relationships in the electoral arena. The bulk of the peasantry was not, of course, enfranchised or otherwise politically mobilized, but the machinery for clientelistic control was in place, as seen in the subsequent success of the oligarchy in controlling a significant proportion of the rural vote in subsequent decades in both countries.

In the context of this comparatively firm control of social relations in the countryside, the oligarchies ruled through relatively weak republics that emerged in the last decade of the nineteenth century with the change away from a centralized, autocratic regime. The weakness derived from somewhat different power configurations in the two countries. The First Republic of Brazil was weak at the federal level as power was decentralized and resided primarily at the regional level. This period of decentralized oligarchic rule has been referred to as the "politics of the governors." During the First Republic, "the President . . . would take as valid and would employ the weight of the Presidency to implement only those agreements reached by the state governments" (Lamounier and Meneguello 1985:5). By contrast, in Chile, the Parliamentary Republic's weakness derived from the national strength of the oligarchy and the power it exerted in the parliament. This strength led to a period of congressional supremacy that immobilized policy and was reflected in a level of ministerial instability that counted 121 different cabinets and 530 different ministers in the 33-year span of the republic following 1891. "From then until 1920, presidential authority was to disappear almost entirely; political parties were to multiply rapidly, and the oligarchs in Congress were to wield unrestricted power" (F. Gil 1966:48).

These patterns in the distribution of power were reflected in the nature of the political parties which, with the introduction of direct elections in the new republics for the first time, gave parties an important role. Before this time, Chilean parties were largely parliamentary groupings with little or no existence outside the legislature (Remmer 1977:207). By contrast, Brazilian parties were personalistic, local organizations with an ephemeral existence at the level of national politics and the national legislature. In Brazil, the Liberal and Conservative parties were too closely identified with the empire to survive its fall in 1889. The dominant party during the republic, which was established in that year, was the Republican Party, which embraced not only those groups that had originally opposed the empire but also the old oligarchies and political bosses from the old Liberal and Conservative parties. These local oligarchies controlled local and state politics through their control of the party. No national Republican party existed, because party organizations at the level of the state remained independent (Peterson 1962:14–16, 26). Thus the Brazilian political system was largely dominated by a nonideological, personalistic "party," one that was organized primarily at the local and state level.

The Chilean party system after the introduction of the Parliamentary Republic in 1891 was quite different. Having originated on the national level, these parties came to play a major role in Chilean national politics through their positions in the legislature during this period of parliamentary supremacy. These parties were more programmatically oriented than the Brazilian parties, though Remmer (1977:222–23) cautions that the degree to which this was so was quite limited and should not be overstated. In contrast to Brazil, then, the Chilean party system was competitive, and parties were more programmatically oriented and well organized on the national level.

Significantly, with the emergence of the reform period discussed below, these weak national political regimes proved unable to survive the economic, social, and political changes that were taking place. The oligarchic republics were not only challenged and opposed by new middle sector groups, but they fell of their own weight as support for the prior equilibrium of power was withdrawn on all sides in the case of Brazil and as the pattern of parliamentary instability culminated in complete immobilism in the case of Chile. Yet the traditional elite maintained a strong position for two reasons: first, because of the well established system of social control in the countryside, and second because of its continued strong presence in the political system, to the extent that the reformers in both countries experienced great initial difficulty in consolidating their power.

Emergence of Reform Alliance.   In both countries, dissident elites from politically marginal regions of the country—from Rio Grande do Sul in Brazil and from the north and south of Chile—combined with new urban middle sector and dissident military groups to form a cluster of discontented, opposition groups pressing for change and for political and social reforms. In both countries, the growing working class was an additional source of opposition and pressure for change, but it was not in alliance with the new coalition that eventually came to power. Quite the contrary, fear of the growth and radicalization of the working class was one of the concerns shared by the groups pushing for reform, and this fear contributed to their perception of the need for change.

In both Brazil and Chile, the old regime was disintegrating from within,[4]

---

[4] Schneider 1971:44; Baretta and Markoff 1981:17; F. Gil 1966:48ff.; Pike 1963:87ff.

and in both cases a civilian electoral alliance, called the Liberal Alliance, was formed as an opposition movement and was joined by military opposition centered among junior officers. These Liberal Alliances brought together a combination of newer urban groups and dissident regional oligarchies who challenged the power of the traditionally dominant groups. In Brazil, this co-alition consisted of middle sector groups, especially those centered in the Democratic Party of São Paulo and the dissident oligarchies of Rio Grande do Sul as well as of Minas Gerais, who were chafing over the choice of a Paulista[5] candidate to succeed the Paulista Washington Luiz, thus upsetting the established alternation of power between Minas Gerais and São Paulo.

Whereas the Liberal Alliance in Brazil was formed in 1928, just prior to the 1930 elections, various Liberal Alliances appeared throughout the Parliamentary Republic in Chile. These alliances were formed around newer middle sector parties, particularly the Radical and Democratic parties, as well as around factions of the older Liberal Party. The Liberal Alliance was the political expression of the new groups that began to emerge in the late 19th-century with the expansion of commerce and industry and the opening of new mining areas, particularly in the north, following the Chilean victory in 1884 against Peru in the War of the Pacific. As these groups gained social and economic importance, they began to emerge as a political force, and the Liberal Alliance began to win political victories in parliamentary elections during the course of the Republic.

In both countries, young officers in the military were the other essential ingredient in the new opposition coalitions. These officers opposed the corrupt, ineffective, decentralized parliamentary governments dominated by the oligarchies, and their goal was to establish a new order that would be centralized, modernizing, and nationalistic, and in which the armed forces would have a role as agents of "regeneration." Though in both cases there were specific institutional grievances and aspirations on the part of these young officers, the movement did not stop there but was generalized to these wider, societal goals. This development among the officers was paralleled and influenced by similar developments in the prefascist, antiparliamentary, nationalistic orientation of the military in Germany, Italy, and Spain (Nunn 1970:18).

In Brazil, *tenentismo*, as the military movement was known, grew out of the issues of the centralization and reorganization of the armed forces that arose in the civilian-military struggles between 1910 and 1924 and out of the military revolts of the 1920s (Wirth 1964:164). In Chile, the military movement grew out of army discontent over the perceived favoritism toward the navy during the Parliamentary Republic, stemming from the navy's role in the 1891 civil war. As in Brazil, the decade before the onset of the reform period saw a number of aborted military revolts. In 1907 the Liga Militar was formed, but its plans for a military coup in 1912 were aborted. Coups were also aborted in 1915 and 1919. That of 1919 was a double conspiracy comprising one group of senior army officers and the navy, which offered to sup-

---

[5] I.e., from São Paulo.

port the government in the face of a feared Communist uprising (Nunn 1970:11); the other, a dissident group of middle grade army officers called the Junta Militar.

Both the *tenentes* of Brazil and the army officers of the Liga Militar and the Junta Militar of Chile called for political, social, and administrative reforms. As noted above, two sources of their reformism were found in the corporate, institutional interests of the armed forces—or that segment of the armed forces they represented—and in their identification with the agenda of modernization and reform of the expanding middle sectors of which they were a part. A third source of their reformism, particularly relevant for present purposes, was their reaction to the growing proletariat and its radicalization. This was particularly explicit in the case of the Chilean army, which was called upon many times in the course of the Parliamentary Republic to suppress strikes violently. The young officers opposed the radicalization of the proletariat, but felt that such strikebreaking was an inappropriate way to deal with class conflict. Accordingly, both the Liga and the Junta were critical of the government's (and Liberalism's) inability to deal with the social question and included in their program social and labor legislation as well as electoral, judicial, and fiscal reform. While *tenentismo* was perhaps more oriented toward change in the rural latifundia system, it was in general inspired by the backwardness of the country and the poverty of much of the population, and it articulated a broad program of modernization and reform (Wirth 1964:164–66). It was likewise clearly part of a worldwide, anticommunist trend oriented toward an authoritarian, paternalistic treatment of the social question.

Initial Transition and Change of Government.   The termination of the old republic occurred in conjunction with the presidential elections of 1930 in Brazil and 1920 in Chile. Vargas and Alessandri, candidates for the Liberal Alliance in their respective countries, challenged candidates representing the hegemony of the traditional oligarchies and the liberal, decentralized republic. Both Vargas and Alessandri rose rapidly within the framework of traditional politics but took equivocal positions on the issue of maintaining the traditional political framework. Both addressed the social question in the electoral campaign and both made some attempt to attract working class support, though this appeal to workers was probably more extensive in the case of Alessandri. In both countries some members of the working class responded to these appeals. Nevertheless, the participation of the working class in the election and in the events surrounding it was slight. First of all, labor organizations and parties did not support the Liberal Alliance. Second, the number of workers eligible to vote was insignificant.

When the votes were tallied in Brazil, the official returns showed that Vargas had lost. The opposition immediately declared the elections fraudulent. However, Vargas initially accepted the electoral outcome, until a political assassination brought him over to the side of other dissidents, who in the interim had been unsuccessfully plotting an armed rebellion. The "Revolution" succeeded as both civilian and military groups withdrew their support from the government in the face of the armed campaign that ensued.

In Chile, the vote in the 1920 election, in which over 50 percent of the registered voters abstained, was extremely close. Recent analyses of this election indicate that Alessandri lost the popular vote with 49.4 percent, as opposed to 50.0 percent for his major opponent (Drake 1978:52; Alexander 1977:197). However, it was an indirect election, and the initial results suggested that Alessandri would win 179 to 174 in the electoral college. The Congress had the power to annul the victory of an elector after considering claims of electoral fraud and corruption, which, as always in Chile, were widespread on both sides. Since disqualified electors were not replaced, Congress had the power to decide the election itself, and the way seemed cleared to deprive Alessandri of the presidency. Government maneuvers pointed in this direction: government repression of student and working class supporters of Alessandri and a diversionary mobilization of the armed forces against a manufactured Peruvian threat in the north. However, this last backfired and made the loyalty of the armed forces even more uncertain than it had been, and at the same time the working class seemed increasingly amenable to revolutionary mobilization should the election be manipulated against Alessandri. The matter was finally settled when a group of non-Alessandri Liberals came out in favor of abiding by the election results and proposed a special tribunal to determine what the outcome had in fact been. The final decision was that Alessandri had won in the electoral college 177 to 176 (Alexander 1977:206). Most analyses agree that the decision could have gone either way but was influenced by the fear of social upheavals that would result if Alessandri were not inaugurated, on the one hand, and on the other by the confidence on the part of the oligarchy that Alessandri would present no fundamental challenge or threat to them, particularly as they still dominated the Senate.

Role of Labor in the Transition.   The role of the Brazilian working class in the events of 1930 was minor. In the northeast workers joined the fighting on the side of the rebel forces, but union organizations remained aloof. In general, mutual suspicion kept the two groups apart. The *tenentes* and civilian members of the Liberal Alliance feared the working class and the Communist Party, which was influential in the labor movement; they refused to accept any labor program proposed by labor leaders; and in several instances they refused to arm workers so that they might join the fighting (Harding 1973:58–65). The Communists, in turn, considered the dissident movement to be a narrow, largely regionalist one that did not offer any genuinely revolutionary possibilities, and they refused to join it. The victorious coalition thus owed the labor movement nothing, and upon achieving power it immediately proceeded to break a number of strikes mounted by workers in the face of the deteriorating situation following the world crash.

The role of labor in the 1920 election in Chile was only slightly greater than that in the Brazilian Revolution of 1930. This difference owes, perhaps, to the greater strength of the working class and the different timing of the two events. Though the election in Chile did not coincide with the world depression as it did in Brazil, it was nevertheless a time of serious recession and tremendous economic and social dislocation. Furthermore, it coincided with the heightened working class confidence and militance of the late 1910s and was manifested in the Marxist program adopted by the FOCh (Workers Federation of Chile) in 1919. Both of these factors led to an intense period of strike activity which continued into 1920.

The widespread reaction on the part of middle and upper classes in Chile was the espousal of reforms. As Pike (1963:172) has stated: "There were unmistakable indications that unless the ruling sectors made at least a few conciliatory gestures to the masses a wave of violence might sweep the land." On this point, the Liberal Alliance was not very different from the National Union, which it opposed. The two platforms were "nearly indistinguishable . . . in promises of educational, economic, and labor reform" (Drake 1978:48; see also Pike 1963:171). Furthermore, the platform of the Liberal Alliance, despite the campaign rhetoric, was supportive of the old order. The middle sectors, which were heavily represented in the Liberal Alliance, sought integration into the old order and made no "long-range commitment to reforms for the lower classes or to a protracted battle against entrenched privileges" (Drake 1978:49). Thus, both major electoral groups regarded social reforms as necessary palliatives.

Nevertheless, Alessandri and the Liberal Alliance, even more than Vargas, did appeal to and make an attempt to mobilize the support of the working class. As in Brazil, neither the labor confederations nor the Socialist Workers Party (POS, which became the Communist Party in 1922) supported the Liberal Alliance, seeing in Alessandri "a new oligarchy deceiving the working masses with false promises of a false evolutionism that tries to obtain the support of the working classes in order to become their masters tomorrow" (quoted in Drake 1978:50). Like the Brazilian Communist Party, the Chilean POS ran its own candidate in the elections. The potential contribution of the working class to Alessandri's victory, however, was not in electoral support—few workers had the right to vote. Rather, it came as the election moved into its second phase of the electoral college and then the tribunal. At this point the contribution of the working class consisted of the threat of popular revolution or civil war it seemed to pose. With the economic depression that followed the end of World War I, Pike (1963:171–72) has suggested that Chile seemed close to civil war, as labor militance and violence increased and a state of siege was declared in the mining areas. Furthermore, during this second stage, under the leadership of Recabarren, who had opposed Alessandri in the election, the POS and the FOCh supported the recognition of Alessandri's victory in the electoral college and threatened revolution should this be subverted. There is general agreement, as noted above, that the tribunal's decision owed a great deal to the threat of social protest posed by the working class, combined with the uncertain loyalty of the army.[6]

[6] Pike 1963:172; Drake 1978:54; Alexander 1977:201.

Though in Chile the trade union movement played a greater role and though there was active support mobilization, the dominant attitude remained one of palliatives, and Alessandri felt he owed the working class little, as subsequent events showed. Similarly, Alessandri's proposals for labor policy did not go much further than those of the National Union, and no bargain or exchange relations were entered into with labor leaders, who did not initially throw the weight of the relatively well-developed labor movement behind his election and did not—even when they later supported his inauguration—cast their lot with him.

Conclusion.   A series of factors set the parameters within which the evolution of state-labor relations occurred. The oligarchies in Brazil and Chile were strong, both in the sense of enjoying stable clientelistic control of social relations in the countryside and in the sense of having a strong presence in national political life, even after the initial transition in which they lost control of the national executive. This continuing strength of the oligarchy helps to explain the conservative cast to many aspects of policy-making and ensured that in conjunction with labor incorporation policies, social relations in the countryside would not be altered and agrarian reform would not be pursued.

This conservative cast of the political system was consistent with and reinforced by the marginal role of labor support in the rise to power of the reformers. In both cases widespread labor protest had become a prominent issue in national life at least two decades before the onset of the periods of reform and incorporation. However, to the extent that the debate within the respective Liberal Alliances dealt with labor issues, it was from a conservative, paternalistic perspective. In both cases a crisis over the presidential succession brought the reformers to power. In Chile labor support did play some role in the resolution of the crisis, but primarily by invoking fear among elites of the labor upheavals that might ensue if Alessandri was denied victory. Out of this comparatively conservative political context, there emerged in these two countries the most control-oriented incorporation periods of any of the cases considered in this study, implemented by governments whose rise to power had not been dependent on labor support, and which imposed elaborate structures of legal restrictions on the trade union movement.

Mexico and Venezuela

Period of the Oligarchic State.   In contrast to the relatively long period of civilian rule and oligarchic domination of the state found in Brazil and Chile, in Mexico and Venezuela one finds high levels of instability, long periods of military conflict, and a persistence of caudillo politics, which prevented any institutionalized pattern of civilian rule and precluded the formation of durable political parties. Throughout the 19th century, Mexico and Venezuela witnessed an incredible parade of military caudillos; internal wars; insurrections; and in the case of Mexico foreign invasions, wars, and occupations—

all of which added up to a history of extreme instability in which hardly a single president finished the allotted term of office. "In the first fifty years as an independent nation Mexico had over thirty presidents, more than fifty governments, two or even three governments claiming jurisdiction simultaneously, and one man, Santa Anna, as president nine times, not to mention one empire, five constitutions and two foreign wars" (Russell 1977:15). In Venezuela, the 19th century was marked by anarchy, civil war, and internecine caudillo conflict, punctuated by periods of longer-term caudillo rule. In neither country was the traditional oligarchy able to consolidate its rule through the establishment of stable civilian political institutions.

In this context of instability and with this failure to found stable institutions of political rule, the political position of the traditional oligarchy was substantially weaker than in the other six countries. Three other factors are also crucial to understanding the oligarchy's relative weakness. The first was the position of the traditional ally of the oligarchy elsewhere in Latin America, the Church. Under Guzmán Blanco in Venezuela and Juárez in Mexico, governments in both countries moved against the Church, and in Mexico in particular the Church was subject to the most extensive anticlerical movement anywhere in the region. Second, the years preceding the transformation of the oligarchic state constituted a period of land consolidation and concentration, the result of which was not clientelistic control of the peasantry by the landed elite, but quite the opposite. The consolidation of large landholdings caused tremendous dislocation, uprooting, and expulsion from the land for a large portion of the peasantry, thereby depriving the oligarchy of a base of political support that was important to its ongoing strength in all of the other countries except Argentina.

While this history of land consolidation is well known for Mexico, it is perhaps less well known in the case of Venezuela. The political instability throughout the 19th century prevented the consolidation of an oligarchy based on large landholdings throughout most of the country. With the frequent fighting, armies were often recruited with the promise of land, and, in addition to the looting, haciendas of enemy owners were usually distributed to the winning side (Powell 1971:15–16; see also D. Levine 1978:85–86). "By the end of the 19th century . . . owners of haciendas [were] growing in number but, owing to the vicissitudes of the struggle for national power, [were] limited in the land and rural populace under their control and in the degree of effectiveness of that control" (Powell 1971:17). In the Gómez era from 1908 to 1935, however, political order was achieved, and a process of land consolidation occurred. Gómez ruled, in part, by distributing vast tracts of land to his political cronies, and he himself increased his landholdings to an almost unimaginable extent. In addition, the oil boom that Venezuela experienced with the new exploitation of those reserves in the 1920s further increased the consolidation of land as the oil companies bought up vast estates. "There is overwhelming agreement among writers on the agrarian question in Venezuela that land concentration reached its most extreme degree during the reign of Gómez" (Powell 1971:21).

A third source of weakness of landed interests was the economic decline the agrarian sector experienced as oil quickly became the leading sector. With the growth of the oil economy (by 1926 oil became the country's largest export) came overvalued exchange rates, which made agricultural exports, particularly cocoa and coffee, noncompetitive; a loss of workers to the oil fields; and an abandonment of agricultural production in favor of the sale of land to oil companies and more profitable urban, commercial undertakings (Karl 1981:83).

The oligarchic states preceding the events we are about to explore were characterized neither by a weak parliamentary republic, as in Chile and Brazil, nor by the presence of deeply rooted parties, as in Colombia and Uruguay, but by a strong dictatorship that, coming at the end of a century of upheaval and instability, imposed order and stability over a period of several decades. The rule of both Porfirio Díaz (1876–80, 1884–1911) of Mexico and Juan Vicente Gómez (1908–35) of Venezuela was characterized by centralization, stability, state-building, consolidation of the latifundia, and modernization and construction of economic infrastructure. The two dictators were similar in these respects, though modernization went further in Mexico, given the country's higher level of industrialization (even though the Porfiriato long preceded the Gómez period). As Powell has stated: "One can read the career of Juan Vicente Gómez as a minor-key echo of a similar Latin American state-builder, Mexico's Porfirio Díaz."[7]

Emergence of Reform Alliance. The Pax Porfiriana and the "peace" established under Cipriano Castro and consolidated under Gómez were achieved at enormous cost to the national populations, creating hardships that stimulated the emergence of opposition groups. With the consolidation of latifundia during these periods, large numbers of campesinos were driven from their land in both countries. The 1937 census of Venezuela indicated that 89.4 percent of the campesinos did not own land. Furthermore, during this period commercial agriculture in Venezuela stagnated, thereby squeezing tenant farmers, who generally had not been replaced by wage laborers. The result was an eruption of peasant protest (Powell 1971:23, 26–27). In Mexico, a new aggressive land policy oversaw the expropriation of villages and their appropriation by *hacendados* and foreign land companies, and by 1910 a similar percent of the rural population was landless (Cockroft 1974:31; Katz 1974:1). In Mexico also, peasant protest resulted. The peasantry in these two countries therefore comprised an actual or potential opposition group that had no parallel in the other cases.

By contrast, the position of the newly emerging middle sectors was more similar to at least some of the other countries. In Mexico, according to Rodney Anderson (1976:243), the opposition to Díaz emerged among "a loosely organized group of state governors and their supporters, most of whom were also well-known landholders and businessmen." They came to be in increas-

---

[7] Powell 1971:19. Powell goes on, however, to stress Díaz's greater identification with commerce and industry, compared with Gómez's identification with the rural latifundio.

ingly open conflict with the *cientificos*, the group of technocratic advisers who surrounded Díaz, and this dispute loomed large as Díaz grew old and the question of an heir to his rule came to revolve around the selection of a vice president, which became a central issue in the 1910 elections. "Yet such factional disputes were part of the system, and business as usual might have continued had there not existed widespread discontent among . . . commercial farmers, medium-size domestic businessmen and merchants, and the significantly enlarged professional and intellectual classes—as well as among more marginal elements such as shopkeepers, retail merchants, and the group generally called the petite bourgeoisie" (R. Anderson 1976:243). Many were hurt by economic recession and opposed certain economic policies, especially Díaz's opening to and dependence on foreign capital and foreign markets.

Similar sources of opposition emerged under Gómez in Venezuela. Particularly after 1910 and the disruption of oil exports from Mexico, the petroleum industry began to change the face of Venezuela. The increased oil exports beginning in the 1920s were accompanied by the rapid growth of middle sector groups that serviced the oil economy. In the fifteen year period from 1920 to 1935, the number of both propertied and salaried artisans and white-collar workers in the service sector and state bureaucracy grew from 13,500 to 56,100 (Karl 1981:85). The oil boom, then, led to a "general rearrangement of the economy and of the residential pattern of the population" with employment in manufacturing growing rather slowly but steadily and that in commerce and service expanding rapidly. What began to appear in the 1920s was an urban, service-oriented economy not headed for an industrial take-off but which relied on "imports (ultimately paid for by oil) to fill its needs, and on semi-skilled service, commerce, and construction jobs to employ its people" (D. Levine 1985:29–30).

As in Mexico, these new sectors were largely excluded from participation in politics under Gómez and became an important potential source of opposition. The new commercial, financial, and middle sectors foresaw a more modernizing state and a more open political regime (Powell 1971:27–28). Also as in Mexico, the opening to foreign capital and foreign concessions became a major issue as well. Under the dictatorship, however, there was little opportunity for the expression of political grievances or opposition.

The opposition that did exist crystallized around a series of student demonstrations and strikes. After the first of these in 1912, Gómez closed the university until 1922 and disbanded the student federation until it was reorganized in 1927. In February 1928, the antigovernment speeches given during Student Week resulted in the jailing of over 200 students. Spontaneous mass demonstrations throughout Caracas and other cities persuaded the government to release the students. In April students joined junior army officers in an abortive coup. It was from among the student leaders of the "Generation of '28," who then went into exile, that the founders of the major opposition movements and Venezuela's modern political parties emerged. However, their emergence did not take place under the oligarchic state, but had to await the death of Gómez in the mid-1930s.

In the context of this growing opposition there emerged—for the first time in Venezuela and with roots going back to the middle of the 19th century in Mexico—a political reform movement that focused on the issue of democratic elections and to some extent social reform. This segment of the opposition movement, then, was quite parallel to that in Brazil and Chile, though in the case of Mexico and Venezuela the relevance of democratic elections was greater since they comprised a political arena in which the middle sectors had, if not an advantage, at least no handicap. In Brazil and Chile, by contrast, liberalism and electoral politics had been the political institutions of oligarchic domination and would for many decades continue to serve the oligarchy well, given the clientelistic relations that persisted in the countryside.

The role of important factions within the army was perhaps somewhat less pronounced in the opposition movement in Mexico and Venezuela than it was in Brazil and Chile, though oppositional elements were present. In Mexico, in the course of the second half of the 19th century, there were a series of reformist army officers, some of whom even participated in peasant rebellions and promulgated quite sweeping reformist declarations. However, these did not seem to represent a faction within the military so much as individual caudillos. In any event, there was no major military role in the 1910 Revolution, except in the negative sense that the very weakness of the army as a counterforce contributed to the erosion of support for Díaz and to many desertions from the military to the side of the rebels. In Venezuela, a cleavage opened within the army between the older traditional caudillos and a new generation of younger professionals that emerged in the context of Gómez's efforts to modernize the army. These junior officers and cadets of the military academy joined university students in the aborted coup of April 1928, presaging the coalition that would seize power in 1945.

As in Brazil and Chile, labor groups were also in opposition in Mexico and Venezuela. However, unlike the situation in the first two countries, middle sector opposition groups in Mexico and Venezuela were not preoccupied with the threat the proletariat seemed to pose, despite the high level of worker militance in Mexico after 1906 and because of the lack of development of a labor movement in Venezuela. Instead, these groups would prove more amenable to entering into a coalition with the working class as well as with the peasantry.

Initial Transition and Change of Government.   As both dictatorships wore on, discontent rose. In Mexico, three types of opposition movements appeared simultaneously: a movement for political reform led by Francisco Madero, whose goals were well summarized by the slogan "effective suffrage and no reelection;" a number of peasant movements arising among those who had been pushed off the land in the process of the consolidation of latifundia under Porfirio Díaz; and movements originating in or oriented toward the urban working class that were manifest both in the increasingly anar-

chist Mexican Liberal Party (PLM) and in the series of strikes and rebellions
that took place among various sectors of the working class between 1906 and
1910. It was the first of these that became dominant in the 1910 Revolution,
as many members of the PLM and the agrarian movements cooperated with
the Madero movement—sometimes, as in the case of the Zapatistas, exchanging support for the promise of reform.

Initially, Madero was timid in his proposals for political reform, having
accepted, in a book he published in 1908, the reelection of Díaz and urging
only that the vice presidency be left open to free, competitive election. However, following the famous Creelman interview in which Díaz indicated that
he might step down in 1910 and that he would welcome the formation of
opposition parties, Madero became a candidate for the presidency. After the
controlled election of 1910 officially produced an overwhelming victory for
Porfirio Díaz, Madero issued a call to arms, and the armed revolution began,
triggering the resignation of Díaz in May 1911.

In Venezuela, the transition came with the death of Gómez in 1935 (by
natural causes). The new government was led in the following decade by López Contreras (1935–41), a former Gomecista[8] general and minister of war,
and General Medina (1941–45), who in turn had been López's minister of
war. Despite this apparent continuity, the year 1935 can be used to signal the
end of the oligarchic state, since the social changes and political pressures
that had been building up under Gómez assured that the oligarchic state
would not survive him, but rather that significant changes would begin.
Though no coalition successfully confronted the Gómez regime and brought
about its downfall, important sources of opposition were growing, and these
would have a major impact on the future course of Venezuelan politics.

Role of Labor in the Transition. In Venezuela, Gómez died of natural
causes and labor obviously played no role in the immediate change of government. In Mexico, on the other hand, workers did participate in the movement that led to the fall of Díaz, though the role of the labor movement was
quite limited. As in some of the other countries, this change in government
came upon the heels of a great surge in worker militance, and some degree
of more general politicization and revolutionary potential of workers has
been inferred from the way in which some of the strikes evolved into antigovernment demonstrations and from the instances of workers rising in antigovernment rebellions (R. Anderson 1974:110–11). Two major strikes in particular, the Cananea mining strike and the Rio Blanco strike in 1906–7, are
often cited as evidence of revolutionary working class activity. Yet Knight
(1986, vol.1:126–29, 145–50) argues convincingly that these were not examples of proto-revolutionary mobilization but rather must be understood primarily in terms of local, economist issues with little revolutionary intention
or overtones. The PLM, he argues, had some influence among workers, but
this was limited; indeed most workers found liberalism more attractive than

---

[8] I.e., identified with Gómez.

anarchism, and of the various opposition factions, it was the Madero movement that was able to make the strongest appeal to workers.

The Maderista cause, then, found substantial receptivity and enthusiasm among workers, many of whom were active in antireelectionist clubs. Given the worker militance of the period, there were many rumors of possible workers' uprisings following the 1910 election. Yet the anticipated rebellion of company towns did not materialize, with the exception of an unsuccessful insurrection in Orizaba in November 1910 (R. Anderson 1976:27, 257–78). Many individual workers undoubtedly joined the rebels in answer to Madero's call to arms in November 1910, and there were some incidents of workers' rebellions, particularly at certain textile mills. In general, however, workers as a group stayed on the job and did not participate in the overthrow of Díaz, though there were incidents of noncooperation with the government—when, for example, railroad workers refused to operate trains transporting men and materiel as part of the government's war effort.

From Initial Change of Government to Incorporation Period. In Venezuela, the initial phase of the incorporation period emerged in a hesitant and uncertain manner in 1935 upon the death of Gómez. In Mexico, on the other hand, the onset of this period can be said to have been postponed during six years of false starts, crises, and changes of government and civil war that accompanied the Mexican Revolution.

This interim period in Mexico began with the Madero government, which followed Porfirio Díaz's resignation. The new government ushered in a period of unprecedented freedom of labor organizing and activities, and Knight (1986, vol. 2:442) argues that as a result workers felt they had a stake in the system and were willing to defend it, even though the victories and concessions they won were decidedly limited. Worker support was particularly apparent in March 1912 at the time of Orozco rebellion, to which workers responded with demonstrations of support for the government in various cities throughout the country. Workers also cooperated with the government and lent their services in ways that helped to pacify the country (Knight 1986, vol. 2:429).

Yet, on another level, the marginal role that labor played in Mexico in the Maderista movement and the lack of any real labor-Madero alliance in the 1910 Revolution was reflected in the relationship between labor and the Madero government. On the side of labor, there was a resurgence of revolutionary anarchism and strike activity that rejected alliance with or reliance on the state as a means of fulfilling working-class aspirations. In 1911 and 1912 the pace of strike activity picked up sharply, as workers demanded higher wages, better working conditions, and the recognition of unions. At the same time the greater freedom under the new regime ushered in a period of intense organizational activity. In 1911 the printers formed an anarchist-led union, which became very influential and encouraged the formation of still other unions. In 1912 anarchists founded the Casa del Obrero Mundial as a workers' study center and initiated a national effort to organize anarcho-syndicalist unions. The Casa achieved substantial unity among Mexican workers and became the dominant labor organization (Hart 1978:109; Ashby 1967:10).

On the side of the government, the apolitical, noncollaborationist position of the dominant anarchist labor movement was paralleled by Madero's emphasis on political rather than social reform, his basic acceptance of Porfirian economic policy, and his political naïveté, which left him with little interest in building a base of political support among the workers. As a result, Madero offered labor little in the way of reform. He was dedicated to decentralized administration and left the question of reforms primarily to the state governors—some of whom, including Carranza, were more aware of the necessity of mobilizing support, and instituted various labor reform measures (Beezley 1979:16–17). On the national level, Madero's sympathy to reform was tempered by his commitment to a free labor market untrammeled by government or structural distortions, such as union power. The result was a conservative labor policy in which armed force was employed to put down strikes, which established a department of labor and envisioned it as much to control labor and prevent strikes as to carry out reforms, and which distrusted and ultimately shut down the Casa del Obrero Mundial and unsuccessfully attempted to sponsor a more conservative labor federation to supplant it.

Despite a paternalistic attitude and reformist predisposition, which was motivated by a sympathy for the plight of the working class, Madero failed to put through any significant reforms. His fear and distrust of independent labor organizations, his commitment to business, and his free-market orientation prevented him from any reformist program and led to labor's disillusionment with the Maderista political movement.

Madero thus did little to mobilize popular support for his government. Instead of mobilization, he pursued a combined policy of repression and paternalism. However, Mexico's revolution was not over, and in the next few years this pattern changed substantially. In many of the countries, the new governing coalition had difficulty in initially consolidating its position, and in Mexico these difficulties were particularly great. In contrast to most of the other cases, the country was politically mobilized. The 1910 Revolution had encompassed a number of separate and largely autonomous movements and uprisings, including agrarian revolts, various regional rebellions, and episodes of worker protest. Furthermore, the army proved extremely weak in the fighting of 1910–11.

In this context, Madero's failure to build a support base proved fatal. His opposition was both greater and broader than that encountered in cases such as Brazil and Chile, including not only the Porfiristas, but the groups involved in the autonomous mobilization and subsequent dissolution of the Maderista coalition, including a genuine, popularly based social revolutionary movement. Thus, the Zapatistas moved into opposition almost immediately when Madero seemed to be backstepping on his commitment to agrarian reform, and a series of armed rebellions were carried out by rival antireelectionist leaders as well as by former Porfiristas whom Madero had failed to replace in the army and administration. One of these rebellions was successful and ended with the overthrow and death of Madero.

The death of Madero and the assumption of the presidency by Victoriano Huerta in 1913 brought a temporary restoration of forces closely identified with the oligarchic state. However, this restoration occurred in what was now a completely new situation. The continuing armed mobilization by many groups created a setting where the importance of the working class as a base of support for the rival political factions became critical. With each new stage and escalation in the fighting, the mobilization of labor as a support group became even more significant. Huerta, who was responsible for the ouster and death of Madero, recognized the political necessity of building such a support base; and though his government is often described as counterrevolutionary, he nonetheless went further than Madero in his policies of labor reform. He enlarged the size and more than doubled the budget of the Department of Labor (Ruíz 1976:40–41), helped unions win recognition from employers, urged legislation on industrial accidents, and favored the broadening to other sectors of Madero's agreement on wage benefits in and government regulation of the textile industry. While much of this activity was targeted at the non–Casa-affiliated sector of the labor movement, Huerta, with a notable exception following the 1913 May Day demonstrations, more or less tolerated the Casa despite its growing and increasingly overt hostility to his presidency (Hart 1978:118–125). Under Huerta, the Casa continued to grow and develop a clearer anarcho-syndicalist ideology, until it was suppressed by the government in May 1914, two months before Huerta was forced to resign.

The Constitutionalists, the group which opposed Huerta, also realized the necessity of mobilizing popular support. The top leadership of the Constitutionalist opposition was comprised of governors and political leaders of the three northern states that had been among the most reformist during the Madero presidency: Carranza of Cuahuila, Pancho Villa of Chihuahua, and Obregón of Sonora. During the anti-Huerta fight, Carranza, as First Chief of the Constitutionalists, decreed a number of reforms (Richmond 1979:51). The most important event in terms of labor mobilization, however, occurred after the Constitutionalists succeeded in forcing the resignation of Huerta and entered Mexico City. Despite this military success, the fighting continued to escalate as the anti-Huerta forces divided and turned against one another in a more clear-cut class cleavage, principally around the agrarian question. Even before Obregón entered Mexico City, the alliance with Villa had dissolved; and although Zapata had also fought against Huerta, he had never coordinated his movement with the Constitutionalists. With Huerta gone, the main battle was fought between the Carrancistas, on the one hand, and on the other the armies of Villa and Zapata, which were formally but ineffectively allied with one another. At this point, with an unprecedented escalation in violence and destruction and with Carranza at an initial disadvantage and forced from Mexico City, labor mobilization became even more important and was pursued more vigorously.

From the point of view of labor, the anarchist Casa retained its apolitical position in the beginning of the Huerta presidency, but began to move into open opposition as the year wore on. This change to advocacy and Huerta's suppression of the Casa prepared the way for the Casa's celebration of Carranza's arrival in Mexico City and its receptivity to the overtures made by Obregón on behalf of the Constitutionalists. The Carranza government was sympathetic to the Casa, which immediately reopened and was offered a new building by the government.

The Constitutionalists were divided into two factions. The liberals, represented by Carranza himself, advocated liberal political reforms, whereas the "Jacobins," represented by Obregón and other Sonorans, included social reforms in their programs and were more sensitive to the demands of the popular sectors and to their usefulness in building a base of popular support. The pressure exerted and initiatives undertaken by the Jacobins were responsible for the prolabor policies pursued by the Constitutionalists starting in 1914 and culminating in the constitution of 1917, one of the most progressive such documents of its time.

In the few months during which Carranza occupied Mexico City during the second half of 1914, the Constitutionalists made many overtures to the Casa. The Casa enjoyed the freedom to carry out rapid unionization, establish regional Casas, reorganize its national structure, and develop programs of ideological education, which, interestingly, began to advocate cooperation with the government and the discouragement of strikes. In addition to a building, the Constitutionalists gave the Casa a school and printing presses, and many state governors associated with the Constitutionalists instituted progressive labor codes. In addition, the Constitutionalists sought to relieve the poverty of the working class and supported a number of important strikes in a way that resulted in concessions to workers.[9]

Though the Casa accepted the Constitutionalists' offerings such as the building, it initially maintained its distance and declined to make political alliances. Furthermore, many members supported Zapata rather than Carranza and even collaborated with the Zapata-Villa forces when they occupied Mexico City from November 1914 to January 1915. In February, the Convention (the Zapata and Villa alliance) issued a Program of Political and Social Reform, which was the "most complete project of labor reform prior to the 1917 Constitution" (Carr 1976:82–83). This program, however, came too late, after Mexico City had once again been taken by the Constitutionalists, who sought in an even more determined manner to court Casa support.

Indeed, it has been argued that by November 1914, when the Constitutionalists left Mexico City in the face of the advancing armies of Villa and Zapata, the Casa was already deeply indebted to the Constitutionalists, who seemed to sympathize with labor and understand its needs. During the period when the Convention controlled Mexico City, from December 1914 to the following February, Villa and Zapata failed to win the overall support of

---

[9] Hart 1978:129; Carr 1976:80–81; Richmond 1979:53–54.

the Casa. In contrast to the apparent sympathy engendered by the Carrancistas, Villa was distrusted personally by most Casa members, and Zapata was distrusted for his religiosity. Both these latter were regarded as "reactionaries" (Hart 1978:133). This distrust was skillfully exploited by the Carranza camp. Also important was the limited, even "local" project of the Convention and its failure to enunciate a national political project and make a credible bid for state power.[10] By contrast, the Constitutionalists were able to project a revolutionary, prolabor position.

The commitment of the Casa to the Constitutionalists was consummated the following February in the famous pact by which the Casa agreed to form six "Red Battalions" of workers to fight for the Constitutionalist cause in exchange for the right to organize the working class throughout the country. "The Casa's final commitment of the urban working-class movement . . . came about because of a convergence of interests on the part of the Casa, which wanted to advance working-class organizing, and Obregón, who needed troops" (Hart 1978:132). The Casa's "explanation for this commitment went far beyond the mere condemnation of the forces of Villa and Zapata as 'the reaction' because of their alleged 'Church and banker' support. They reasoned that the agreement ushered in a new era of anarchosyndicalist working-class organizing and working-class consciousness" (Hart 1978:133). It has also been suggested that the Casa leaders threw their weight behind the Constitutionalists for tactical reasons because the Villa and Zapata movements were too marginal and weak to guarantee any real social change (Córdova 1972:31). In the following months the Casa did indeed carry out extensive organizational activities and the Constitutionalists won important victories, though the exact contribution of the Red Battalions to the course of the fighting has not been adequately assessed.

The pact with the Casa immediately brought to the fore the usual dilemma: the Constitutionalists needed labor support but were most uncomfortable with the way in which the Casa went about recruiting, propagandizing, and establishing an independent base. As long as the war lasted, the Constitutionalists continued to be solicitous of the Casa and to offer concessions and benefits to labor. By early 1916, however, when the Carranza victory seemed assured and when economic crisis and working-class hardship led to a new wave of strikes, the Carranza-Casa alliance began to come apart and was replaced by an increasingly militant pattern of confrontation, ending in August 1916 with the final closing and suppression of the Mexico City Casa (Knight 1986, vol. 2:425–26, 432–35). Nevertheless, as we shall see, this pattern of political mobilization of labor as a support group became a permanent feature of the Mexican political system, and in 1916 was renewed immediately by those union leaders, most notably Luis Morones, who, unlike the anarchists, thought the most advantageous course for the labor movement was found in alliance with the government.

Conclusion. The larger social context of the transformation of the oligar-

[10] Hart 1978:130–31; Carr 1976:91; Córdova 1973:25, 154, 167–68; Knight 1986 II:318.

chic state in Mexico and Venezuela contrasts markedly with the other six cases. In a setting of agrarian change and the relatively weak position of traditional elites, a broader range of coalitional options were open in two senses. First, the conservative alliance, that elsewhere blocked reform and made the strategy of labor mobilization in the modern sector a far more difficult option, was much weaker. Second, changing patterns of social relations in the countryside meant that peasant protest was occurring by the time of the initial change of government and, given the relative weakness of the landed oligarchy, agrarian reform was a plausible option.

In both countries the policies of the initial reform governments were moderate and the option of mobilizing labor was at first not seriously developed. In Mexico there was a considerable delay before the onset of the incorporation period. During this delay, a series of experiments in more mobilizational approaches to labor were explored, though these were not undertaken by anything that could properly be called a government, but by one side in the unfolding Mexican Revolution. These experiments nevertheless culminated in the onset of the initial incorporation period at the end of the war. In Venezuela during the decade after 1935, more cautious and intermittent experiments by the government took place. At the same time, however, bolder and more successful attempts at mobilization were undertaken by political movements in the opposition. These culminated in 1945, when, with the assistance of a coup by reform-minded officers, Acción Democrática came to power with the overwhelming support of both workers and peasants. These evolving experiments in support mobilization would have been far more difficult to carry out had it not been for the weakness of traditional elites, who in other countries succeeded in blocking political movements of this kind. Mexico and Venezuela are thus the two cases in which at the onset of the incorporation period a populist, as opposed to an accommodationist, alliance was most clearly a viable alternative.

Uruguay and Colombia

Period of the Oligarchic State.   The 19th century histories of Uruguay and Colombia saw long periods of civil war and violence that contrasted markedly with the relative political stability of Brazil and Chile and resembled more the experiences of Mexico and Venezuela. In contrast to these latter two countries, however, Uruguay and Colombia's well-institutionalized two-party systems grew out of conflicts among rival *caudillos* in the first half of the 19th century. In both countries segments of the elite were represented in both parties, which consisted of complex multiclass, multisectoral coalitions (Graillot 1973b; Gilhodes 1973).

Five attributes of the history of these parties are especially relevant here. The first is the long history of violence between adherents of the two parties, involving major civil wars, more localized military confrontations, and in Colombia intense episodes of communal violence. Personal physical security became intertwined with attachment to one or the other party, giving party loyalty an unusual intensity. This loyalty was felt not only by members of the economic elites who were the more obvious beneficiaries of the policies promoted by the parties, but very importantly by elements of the middle and lower classes in both urban and rural areas who were also intensely involved in the episodes of violence. Vanger (1963:10) notes that in the mid-19th century "during the Great Siege of Montevideo an Uruguayan was a Colorado or a Blanco, and neither he nor his children ever forgot it. . . . Fellow party members called each other 'co-religionaries.' " With reference to Colombia, Solaún (1980:5) refers to the "ingrained partisan hostility" and "hereditary hatreds" that were the legacy of violence between the two parties, and Kline (1980:61–62, quoting Santa) invokes the image that Colombians were "born with a party carnet attached to the umbilical cord."

Second, neither side was able to fully defeat the other in the periods of civil war, creating the need for some form of accommodation that resulted in a long history of party pacts, coparticipation, and interparty coalitions that set an ultimate limit on fratricidal violence (Vanger 1963:13–14; Solaún 1980:4–5). Such pacts would reappear in the accords later constructed between the two parties to deal with new forms of cleavage and violence in the mid-20th century.

Third, given the rigidity of underlying identifications with the two traditional parties, much of the give-and-take of politics revolved around intense fractionalization within parties, and conflicts surrounding presidential succession and policy-making commonly involved the evolution of cleavages among well-established factions within parties. This tradition of fractionalization, combined with the tradition of pacts, led Luis González (1984:3) to observe that one may alternatively view Uruguay as having a two-party system, a multiparty system, or a one-party system. This observation also fits Colombia. Whichever designation one prefers, the constellation of party traits that makes these alternative labels relevant is unquestionably distinctive in relation to the other countries.

Fourth, in each country one of the parties—the Colorados in Uruguay and Liberals in Colombia—had more strength in the urban sector. The other party—the Blancos in Uruguay, officially called the National Party as of the late 19th century, and the Conservatives in Colombia—had more strength in the rural sector.

Fifth, it would nonetheless be a mistake to identify the parties as merely reflecting a urban-rural cleavage. Each party was organized around complex clientelistic relationships that bound it to a multiclass, multisectoral coalition, and both parties in both countries included elements of rural landowning elites. Conservative rural interests were thus represented in both parties in both countries. The bases of this support grew out of the loyalties created in the earlier periods of conflict noted above and were maintained by elaborate patron-client networks that were an ongoing feature of both party systems in the twentieth century.[11]

[11] Dix 1967:222, 241, 245; Whitaker 1976:50; Nahum 1975:115–16.

Thus, in both countries the more conservative portion of the political spectrum during this period of change had a strong political and electoral base—an attribute that Uruguay and Colombia shared with Brazil, Chile, and Peru, but which contrasted markedly with the situation in Mexico, Venezuela, and, in a different way, Argentina. As we shall see below, the incorporation periods initiated by these traditional, multiclass, multisectoral parties had distinctive attributes in relation to the other countries.

Emergence of Reform Alliance.   Though there is some debate on the social and political origins of "Batllismo" in Uruguay—the movement and ideas of the Colorado leader Batlle, who was elected president in 1903—there is substantial agreement[12] that the rise of Batlle occurred in a context of substantial autonomy of politics from social classes and was not the expression of fundamental new movements within Uruguayan society. As suggested in the previous chapter, at the time of Batlle's rise to power, the urban working class was just beginning to be an important force in Uruguayan political life. Though the Colorado Party was certainly identified in a general way with the new middle sectors of Montevideo, and though Batlle had taken a conspicuously prolabor position in editorials in his newspaper in the 1890s, his rise was not the expression of a well-defined middle-class or working-class movement. At that time Uruguayan presidents were selected by the legislature, rather than through direct election, and Batlle came to power within the framework of a relatively autonomous political class as the result of elaborate bargaining and maneuvering within and between the two parties in the framework of a presidential election that occurred entirely within the Congress, rather than on the basis of a popular vote (Vanger 1963:Chaps. 2–4).

Thus, the rise of Batlle must be understood in terms of the emergence of an unusually creative leader, located within a political system that had significant autonomy from immediate economic and social forces and aided by a broad vision of the direction of societal change. Batlle was able to move ahead of his time, create a new political coalition around new urban social forces, and fundamentally shift the balance of power between the two parties for decades to come.

In Colombia, by contrast, the change in government in 1930 was the culmination of a much longer debate on political reform that had its origins in part in the movement of "Los Nuevos," a group of younger upper-class leaders who, in reaction to Colombia's loss of Panama in 1903 and the growing importance of foreign capital in the country, began to advocate a more active role of the state in guiding Colombian development. While some members of this group participated in founding the Colombian Socialist Party and later the Communist Party, many of them subsequently returned to the Liberal Party and provided it with important leadership (Sharpless 1978:23–24).

The reorientation of the Liberal Party also occurred in direct response to evolving issues of labor politics, central among which was the concern of the Liberal Party with losing its traditional strength in urban areas in the face of

[12] Barrán and Nahum 1979:213–68; Vanger 1980:101, 353; Finch 1981:9–11.

the increasing electoral importance of the Socialist Party, which had been founded in 1919 among urban workers. In 1921 the Socialists made important gains in both congressional and municipal elections, and electoral losses of the Liberals were attributed in part to this growing Socialist strength. In the 1920s the Liberals increasingly shifted away from their traditional laissez-faire posture toward a greater preoccupation with the social question and social welfare issues, as reflected in the platforms adopted at the party conventions in late 1921 and 1924.[13]

Another important step in the movement toward the electoral victory of the Liberal coalition in the 1930 election was the repression of the strike of United Fruit Company banana workers in Santa Marta in 1928. In comparison with the spectacular earlier histories of labor militancy in countries such as Argentina and Chile, this strike and the repression it evoked appear as a relatively isolated incident. Yet given the much later and weaker development of the labor movement in Colombia, the strike was perceived as a major event that discredited the Conservative government and the repressive labor policies with which it became identified. Jorge Eliécer Gaitán, a principal figure in the more progressive wing of the Liberal Party, played a central role in calling national attention to the crisis of Conservative labor policy reflected in the strike through a series of dramatic speeches in the national House of Representatives (Sharpless 1978:56–60).

Initial Transition and Change of Government. In Uruguay, the succession of Batlle to the presidency grew out of intricate coalition-building both within and between the two main political parties. Though other political leaders were doubtless aware of Batlle's progressive social philosophy, it may have been as much a liability as an asset in the context of this partisan maneuvering. Batlle's rise to the presidency was aided by an opportunistic switch from a strongly anti-National posture in 1901 of rejecting the tradition of party pacts, to a far more conciliatory posture toward the Nationals in 1903, which allowed him to take advantage of divisions in the National Party as he sought to gain the presidency. Once in office, Batlle triggered a National military revolt in 1903–4 by appointments to regional political offices intended to consolidate the position of the National faction with which he was in alliance. Following the Colorado military victory in 1904, Batlle switched again to a more strongly anti-National posture, abandoning the practice of the partisan sharing of regional political appointments and for the time being ending the tradition of coparticipation between the two parties.

In Colombia, the crucial initial shift in government came with the victory in the 1930 presidential election of Enrique Olaya Herrera as head of the National Concentration coalition, based on a relatively unified Liberal Party and some elements of the Conservative Party. The events surrounding the Santa Marta strike of 1928 and the larger, related issue of how to deal with the emerging labor movement played a central role in this electoral victory. Urrutia refers to this strike as "probably one of the turning points in Co-

---

[13] Molina 1974:129–36; Urrutia 1969a:73–75; Canak 1981:315–16.

lombian history" and suggests that the Conservative government's reaction to the strike "determined its downfall."[14] Other factors included the impact of the world economic crisis and additional scandals (apart from the handling of the strike) surrounding the Conservative government, as well as a split in the Conservative Party prior to the 1930 presidential election and caused in part by disagreements over the draconian antisubversive laws passed to deal with labor unrest.[15]

Role of Labor in the Transition.   The role of labor in these two cases contrasts markedly. Important differences in the interpretation of the rise of Batlle notwithstanding, there is no evidence of a direct role of the urban labor movement in his coming to power in 1903. In Colombia, by contrast, both the larger concern of the Liberal Party with sustaining its urban base in the face of the changing composition of the urban population and the events surrounding the major strike and repression of 1928 played a direct role in the sequence of events that led to the 1930 electoral victory.

Conclusion.   In drawing conclusions about Uruguay and Colombia, it is useful first to assess in comparative terms the degree of persistence of oligarchic power. In both countries, rural elite interests were strongly represented in both parties, so that these sectors of the elite sustained a presence in the political system. These rural elite interests maintained a strong system of clientelistic organization of support in rural areas, providing them with an electoral base in some ways comparable to that of the oligarchy in Brazil and Chile.

Given this persistence of oligarchic power, it is interesting to consider the timing of the reform movement and the incorporation period. This transition occurred chronologically very early in Uruguay, and in both cases was the earliest among the eight countries (along with Venezuela) in relation to the development of the labor movement.

These early incorporation periods raise the question of whether this transition was less threatening than in other countries and hence could be undertaken more easily. On the one hand, it would seem that this was not the case. Intensified party competition could, and in the past had, led to civil war in both countries, and in Colombia seriously contested presidential elections generally brought the threat of extensive violence (Solaún 1980:2). Opening new arenas of competition could be very threatening. On the other hand, it was also dangerous for either party to lose a potential political constituency. Such a loss could likewise disrupt the equilibrium between the two parties, and episodes of violence had also been triggered when one of the parties suffered a serious setback. Hence, there could be strong pressure for the more urban-oriented party in each country to move energetically to capture this new urban constituency.

In fact, what was operating was a combination of concern on the part of the Liberals and the Colorados with losing their electoral advantage in urban

---

[14] Urrutia 1969a:99, 108. See also Molina (1974:234).
[15] Urrutia 1969a:108–9; Solaún 1980:15; Canak 1981:323; Molina 1974:234–36.

areas, along with the attraction of gaining the support of new social sectors, within the context of well-institutionalized, two-party competition. One is, in a rough analogy, reminded of the classic analysis of two-party versus one-party dominant politics in the United States, which suggested that greater party competition tended to make incorporation of new groups a far easier transition (Schattschneider 1960:98–101).

Peru and Argentina

Peru and Argentina exhibit interesting commonalities during this period of political reorientation, notwithstanding profound differences in their economic and social development and prior political evolution. Both countries saw an important period of reform in the 1910s and 1920s. Both moved toward initiating an incorporation period in conjunction with these reforms, but in both cases these initiatives failed. Both countries experienced what is commonly interpreted as the restoration of a substantial degree of oligarchic dominance in the 1930s. They also experienced a long postponement, until the late 1930s or early 1940s, of the initial incorporation period.

These commonalities emerged out of contexts of national development in many ways quite distinct. In Argentina the degree of dominance of the oligarchy within the economic, social, and political system was exceptional. In Peru, the system of civilian, oligarchic rule established in 1895 was stable in comparison to the previous period. Yet sharp divisions within the oligarchy and crises over the control of the national executive began to emerge little over a decade after the creation of this system.[16] Further, the subsequent crisis of oligarchic control in 1918–19 on the eve of the reform period presents a picture strikingly different from that in Argentina at the time of Yrigoyen's assumption of power in 1916.

The reform periods that ensued were likewise marked by important differences, along with the similarities noted above. In Peru this period began with one of the most dramatic immediate attacks against the political leadership of the oligarchy found among the eight countries. This attack was accompanied by major innovations in the state and in public policy. At the same time, the regime in Peru moved in a strongly antidemocratic direction. In Argentina, by contrast, the Radical government began its rule in 1916 in a position of political subordination to the oligarchy, only gradually overcoming this subordination over the following 14 years—to a point that by the late 1920s the oligarchy, which still had a strong social and economic position, had lost political leverage with the government to such a degree that this loss itself became one of the issues behind the overthrow of Yrigoyen. While the Radicals introduced fewer innovations in public policy than did

[16] These crises include the attempted conservative coup against President Leguía in 1909 in the context of the split in the leading oligarchic party over his progressive policies, and the threat to oligarchic control posed by the intense popular mobilization and the brief presidency of Billinghurst from 1912 to 1914.

Leguía, their rise was linked to strong innovation in the character of the regime, in that it coincided with a new era of unprecedented honesty and openness in Argentine elections.

The analysis of these two countries in this chapter is necessarily more extensive than for the other six cases, since the interval between the onset of the reform period and the onset of the incorporation period is so long. In addition to covering the emergence of the new reform governments, this section provides an overview of the reform governments themselves, the evolution and crisis of labor policy under these governments in the late 1910s and early 1920s, the restoration of more conservative rule in the 1930s, and the evolution of state-labor relations in the 1930s and early 1940s. The presentation thus brings the story of these two cases up to the onset of their incorporation periods.

Period of the Oligarchic State.   Peru and Argentina differed greatly during this period in the composition and heterogeneity of their social structures, as well as in the stability of oligarchic rule. These contrasts are sufficiently important to our analysis that these social structures will be discussed here in somewhat greater detail than they were above for the other countries.

In Peru, the economic elite was heterogeneous in terms of the types of production on which its prosperity was based, the geographic location of this production, the work relationships involved in production, and patterns of ownership. Exports were diverse and included copper, sugar, cotton, oil, wool, and rubber. Mineral extraction occurred principally in the central highlands, sugar production and oil extraction on the north coast, cotton production throughout the north and central coast, wool production in the southern highlands, and rubber production in the Amazon basin. In the highlands the traditional agricultural sector produced foodstuffs for domestic consumption. These different sectors combined wage labor, systems of debt peonage, and semifeudal work relations in the highlands where Peru's large indigenous population was concentrated. The Indians constituted a large sedentary peasantry that stood in marked contrast to the absence of a peasantry in Argentina, a contrast that would play an important role in the subsequent political evolution of the two countries. Ownership of production was increasingly foreign in the copper and oil sectors. The sugar sector combined foreign ownership and national ownership both by internationally oriented immigrant families and older Peruvian families. Other sectors were nationally owned (Thorp and Bertram 1978:chaps. 4–5). Though one can identify a core elite consisting of the coastal sector of the oligarchy tied to the more modern parts of the export sector (especially sugar) and to urban commerce and finance, this core elite exercised its leadership within this heterogeneous context.

Despite this economic and social heterogeneity, Peru experienced beginning in 1895, in the aftermath of the defeat in the War of the Pacific with Chile (1879–84), a period of greater political stability known as the Aristocratic Republic. This period is usually dated as lasting until 1919.[17] During

---

[17] Burga and Flores Galindo (1979:7)—following Basadre (1963:3229, 3925, 3943–44).

this time electoral politics occurred within the framework of a narrow, manipulated suffrage and was dominated by members of the economic elite. As was common in Latin America during this period, the most important party, the Civilistas, was little more than an expression of the networks of influence of the economic elite, most importantly the core elite of the coast. Other parties, which were generally characterized more by their regional orientation than by any consistent ideological differences with the Civilistas, included the Democrats, the Constitutionalists, and the Liberals, though the Liberals were clearly identified with a more anticlerical position.[18]

In Argentina, by contrast, the economic elite was unusually homogeneous and cohesive. Its wealth derived from the extraordinary prosperity generated in the latter part of the 19th century and afterward by rapidly expanding exports of agricultural and pastoral products, principally wheat, corn, linseed, wool, meat, and leather (Tornquist 1919:167–71; Díaz-Alejandro 1970:18). The growth of these exports occurred within a far more homogeneous society, predominantly of European extraction, that lacked the large peasantry found in many other countries. The absence of a significant peasant population, combined with the impact of the Indian wars of the later 19th century and technological innovations such as the introduction of the barbed-wire fence, provided the opportunity to utilize major portions of the country for modern agriculture and grazing.

A number of factors contributed to the cohesiveness and prestige of the Argentine elite. First, in contrast to Peru, where the core elite of the coast produced a smaller portion of the nation's total exports, the products of the great farms and ranches of Buenos Aires province represented a large portion of exports within a far more prosperous and rapidly expanding economy. Second, it would appear that to a greater degree than in Uruguay, a country with which Argentina shared many economic and social traits, intra-elite struggles in the 19th century had tended to result in a clearer victory for one of the contenders, as occurred with Rosas and later with Roca and the Generation of 1880 (McGuire 1984:6). This pattern, in which a victorious political faction appeared to overwhelmingly defeat its opponents, foreshadowed the succession of majoritarian movements that would emerge in Argentine politics during the 20th century (Cavarozzi 1983:2). Third, in contrast to Peru, the dominance of national ownership in the exceptionally prosperous export sector (though not in associated transport and international marketing—see O'Donnell 1978:4) provided an internal base of capital accumulation that reinforced the elite's economic and social power. Another factor that contributed to the cohesiveness of the oligarchy was the spatial concentration of export production in the pampean region, which contained 90 percent of Argentina's cultivated land (Flichman 1977:101). The unity of the elite was also both reflected in and reinforced by the cohesiveness of its cultural institutions and the strength of the Argentine Rural Society, the interest association of the elite (Imaz 1970:92–111, 129–31, 247–48).

[18] Burga and Flores Galindo 1979:88; E. Yepes 1980:152; Werlich 1978:127–32.

The political system through which this elite dominated Argentine politics was based on a preponderance of the executive over other branches of government and a virtual monopoly of the electoral arena by what was known at the federal level as the Partido Autonomista Nacional (the National Party, also referred to as the Conservative Party), a loose coalition of regional parties and alliances organized around close personal relationships among leading members of the elite, which sustained itself in power through the use of electoral fraud (Spalding 1965:79–84; P. Smith 1978a:21).

Emergence of Reform Alliance.   In both Peru and Argentina, the emergence of a concern with reform extended over a number of years. In Peru this process may be dated from the first presidential administration of José Pardo, from 1904 to 1908, who represented the progressive wing of the Civilista Party. In response to the relatively early emergence of labor protest in Peru and a growing concern about the social question within the elite, Congressman Matías Manzanilla proposed to the Congress in 1905, with the support of the President Pardo, a labor law that included provisions for job security, working conditions for women and children, accident insurance, collective bargaining, strikes, and conciliation and arbitration procedures, encompassing all workers in the modern sector, including the sugar estates. In contrast to the response to a similar legislative proposal in Argentina to be described below, there was popular sector support for the Peruvian initiative. However, the more conservative elements of the Peruvian elite, along with foreign interests, blocked the measure in the Congress (Cotler 1978:164–65).

Pardo was followed by President Augusto B. Leguía (1908–12), a business leader with broad experience in international finance who had been Pardo's finance minister and who, like Pardo, represented the more progressive wing of the Civilista Party. Leguía continued Pardo's initiatives to modernize Peru and, in limited ways, to broaden the authority of the state.

Leguía's reforms triggered one of the important political crises that punctuated the two-and-a-half decades of Civilista rule. In 1909 the antireformist opposition to Leguía organized a coup in which he was kidnapped, later to be rescued by loyal troops. In response, Leguía turned to increasingly authoritarian methods to control the opposition, further worsening his relations with the more conservative Civilistas in the Congress, known as "El Bloque." This means of dealing with the opposition foreshadowed his style of rule during his second presidential term after 1919. Despite this congressional opposition, Leguía was more successful than Pardo in promoting labor legislation. In 1911 Peru's first general strike and two serious mine accidents in which many workers were killed increased concern with labor issues to the point were Leguía was able to push through Latin America's first work injury law (Cotler 1978:168–70; Werlich 1978:133).

A second important crisis occurred in 1912 when the Civilista candidate for the presidency, Antero Aspíllaga, was challenged by the leader of the opposition Democratic Party, Guillermo Billinghurst. Widespread labor protest continued in Lima in 1912, and Billinghurst actively courted labor support, promising further labor legislation, electoral reform, a reduction in the state's close identification with the economic elite, and food price subsidies for the poor that won him the name "Big Bread" Billinghurst. His campaign was accompanied by rallies that were exceptionally large for that time, and election day was greeted with a general strike to protest potential electoral fraud that might block his election. Because of a dispute over the outcome of the popular vote, the president was selected in the Congress, which, intimidated by the popular mobilization, chose Billinghurst in a compromise in which President Leguía's brother became vice president.[19]

As president, Billinghurst intervened in labor disputes in favor of workers and took other prolabor initiatives that for the time were progressive, though in fact they were less comprehensive than the unsuccessful labor law Pardo had earlier supported. This period also saw the use of popular mobilization to attack the growing conservative opposition to his government, including an attack on Leguía's residence in which Leguía nearly lost his life. In early 1914 Billinghurst was overthrown after 17 months in office in a military coup led by Colonel Oscar Benavides, who for decades thereafter would play a central role in Peruvian politics. Seeking to restore elite dominance of politics, Benavides governed for a year and then ceded power to Pardo (Werlich 1978:134–35; Cotler 1978:176–77).

The second Pardo administration from 1915 to 1919 saw the unfolding of the third major political crisis of the Civilista period. These years brought a heightened concern for reform, stimulated by a further increase in labor protest and the growing political activism of university students. This new political mobilization emerged in response both to the severe wage-price squeeze that occurred during and after World War I and to the international climate of revolution, protest, and reform that characterized this period.

As a progressive member of the oligarchy, Pardo sought to respond to this new mobilization with reforms that would to some degree address the social problems that underlay the protest. Yet the reforms initiated by Pardo proved both too progressive for conservatives within his own party and inadequate to respond to the accelerated pace of protest. Pardo refused to meet student demands for a wide-ranging university reform. In December 1918 and January 1919, the labor movement, under anarcho-sindicalist leadership and with the collaboration of students and intellectuals such as Haya de la Torre and Mariátegui, conducted a series of strikes of unprecedented magnitude, demanding a law decreeing an eight-hour day. Other dimensions of the crisis included the fears expressed in the Congress that Peru was on the verge of a Bolshevik revolution, as well as opposition to this reform on the part of the president and other members of the economic elite. Finally, in the face of intense strike activity and widespread economic paralysis in Lima, in mid-January Pardo gave in and decreed an eight-hour day.[20] Further intense strikes in May were more successfully suppressed by the government (see Chapter 3), but the larger legacy of this period of protest was a serious discrediting of

[19] It appeared that Leguía had hoped to use the crisis over the election to retain power, and he had not interfered with Billinghurst's mobilization efforts and had not prevented the disruption of the election. The compromise involving his brother allowed him to retain at least some degree of indirect influence in the government (see Werlich 1978:134–35).

[20] Cotler 1978:180; Werlich 1978:149; Sulmont 1975:85–86.

Civilista dominance and an opening of the political system to new directions of change—though not in a democratic direction.

In Argentina the Radical Party (Unión Cívica Radical), which under the leadership of Yrigoyen would later win the presidency in 1916, had its origin in 1889 in the Civic Union of Youth, formed to promote "electoral freedom, political morality, and provincial autonomy" (Remmer 1984:32). The growing base of support for the movement included university students and some sectors of the elite, including prominent members who had not benefited from the favors of the government (e.g., Mitre); Catholic groups reacting to the civil marriage law and the spread of public education initiated by the government in the 1880s; and other sectors reacting to the severe economic downturn of 1890, with intermittent support from elements of the military. Worker support did not appear to play a significant role in the emergence of this new coalition, and the social question did not appear to be a particular focus of concern within the movement.[21] The Radical movement thus represented a complex combination of concern with reform, more narrow discontent with the existing political and economic order, and, given the role of Catholic elements, a conservative reaction to government policies.

In the first few years of their existence, the Radicals organized provincial rebellions, which were quickly suppressed. In the electoral arena they practiced "radical abstention" from voting, in part in protest against the corruption of the electoral system, threatening instead to take power through rebellion, a tactic that was again easily suppressed in 1905. During the period before the Radicals achieved power, their program was narrowly focused on institutional and administrative demands centrally concerned with middle class issues of political participation. Their leader, Hipólito Yrigoyen, rarely made public appearances until 1916, the year he was elected to the presidency. Yet through a system of local party committees that provided services and favors, the Radicals carefully built an electoral machine that would provide the basis for their remarkable electoral victory in that year.

Though labor issues did not play an important role in the program of the Radicals, perhaps in part because their movement initially appeared relatively early in relation to the posing of the social question, a concern with social reform was emerging in Argentina. The Argentine Socialist Party, founded in 1896, was probably the strongest socialist party in Latin America. It soon came to be dominated by moderate, reformist intellectuals with a university background. While initially active in organizing among the working class, after a split with the syndicalists in 1906 it became less oriented toward cultivating worker support. However, after the Radicals obtained power in 1916, the Socialists would provide important electoral competition among workers, and they later became an important force in the labor movement in the 1930s.[22]

[21] Rock (1975a:43); though see also Romero (1963:210).
[22] Rock 1975a:48; Gallo and Sigal 1963:179ff.; Rock 1975a:50–52; Snow 1965:9; Spalding 1977:20–21.

Stimulated by the growing visibility of social problems and social protest, and also by increased attention to these problems in the universities and in the popular arts in the first decade of the 20th century, the government also became concerned with the social question. Under the second administration of President Roca, whose earlier administration had seen such initiatives as the anticlerical reforms noted above, the president in 1904 proposed to the Congress a comprehensive labor code.[23] However, the code met opposition from all sides, reflecting a resistance to the institutionalization of labor relations that would persist for many decades. Anarchists and Socialists saw the code as too restrictive of unions and as intended simply to subdue the growing labor movement, whereas conservatives found it a dangerous step toward state interference in the private sector that would hurt profits. Despite such opposition, between 1905 and 1907 some legislation was adopted, including laws making Sunday a day of rest, regulating the employment of women and children, and establishing a weak National Labor Department (Walter 1977:83–87, 104; Spalding 1970:554).

An alternative reaction to the social question was manifested a few years later, a response which would likewise emerge as a recurring pattern in Argentina. In 1910, in the face of a period of active labor protest and the threat to call a general strike to disrupt the celebration of the 100th anniversary of Argentine independence, the government allowed mobs made up principally of upper class youths to attack the offices of several unions and of the socialist and anarchist press, reflecting a pattern of direct conflict between classes unmediated by the state. Following the planting of a bomb in the Buenos Aires opera house, the adoption of the Ley de Defensa Nacional created severe new restrictions on labor activities, and labor protest declined markedly until after the Radicals came to office in 1916 (Marotta 1961, vol. 2:71–77; Dorfman 1970:262).

In response to growing pressures for an opening of the political system there was, however, more progress in the area of electoral reform under the presidency of Roque Sáenz Peña (1910–13). The Sáenz Peña law of 1912 established a secret ballot and new voting registration procedures that laid the basis for the Radical Party victory in the 1916 presidential election.

Initial Transition and Change of Government. In both Peru and Argentina, the initial change of government was the result of an election. In Peru the outcome of the 1919 election was sharply disputed, whereas in Argentina this involved the smooth transition following the Radical Party's electoral victory in 1916.

In Peru, this final crisis of the second Pardo government and the ensuing return to power of Leguía marked a major turning point in Peruvian history and the beginning of an important new era of development of the Peruvian state (Cotler 1978:182). Among the eight countries, this transition also represented the most direct assault on the political leadership of the oligarchy,

---

[23] Roca's labor initiative was thus parallel to, and indeed nearly simultaneous with, the first labor initiatives of Pardo in Peru.

an assault led by Leguía with the support or acquiesence of many sectors, including elements of the middle class, the labor movement, students, the military, and foreign capital. Yet despite the sharp political disjuncture brought by his rise to power in 1919, Leguía in fact played the complex role of a leader with strong links both to the more modern forms of Peruvian and international capitalism and also to more traditional sectors in Peru.

On the one hand, Basadre (1963, vol. 8:3555) considers Leguía bourgeois in terms of his social origin, and Cotler (1978:183) suggests that by this point Leguía was "the most lucid representative of the Peruvian national bourgeoisie." Indeed, Leguía apparently referred to his own movement as marking "the advent of the bourgeoisie" to positions of power (Karno 1970:217). Following his first presidency, Leguía had been exiled by Billinghurst in 1913 and had spent the intervening years in Europe, living principally in London and acting as president of the Latin American Chamber of Commerce, thus enhancing his contacts with foreign economic interests and his ability to promote the rapid capitalist modernization of Peru with the support of foreign capital.

On the other hand, Leguía stood at the intersection between what may be thought of as a bourgeois and an oligarchic orientation. He had enjoyed an enormously successful earlier career as an international insurance executive, but also had worked as a manager of sugar estates belonging to the British Sugar Company, and had himself owned coastal plantations and served as president of the National Agrarian Society, the interest association of the coastal elite, as well as belonging to the elite clubs of Lima (Werlich 1978:152). According to Klarén,[24] Leguía maintained close personal relationships throughout the sugar sector even during his second term as president, at the same time that his government represented a major assault on political institutions that had previously represented this sector.

Leguía returned to Peru in February 1919. He sought to fill the political void left by the discrediting of the Pardo government in the context of growing crisis and polarization discussed above, and to oppose Antero Aspíllaga, once again the Civilista candidate, who represented the more conservative tradition within that party. The constituencies to which Leguía appealed were diverse: in October 1918 the increasingly radicalized students at San Marcos University in Lima bestowed upon him their annual honorary designation as a "Mentor of Youth," in the hope that he might emerge as an advocate of university reform; and his return from Europe included a stop in New York, where he consulted with North American investors. Evidence suggests that British and American investors provided financial support to aid Leguía in the presidential campaign. Leguía also won support from the military, who found themselves in conflict with the Civilistas on a number of issues, including dissatisfaction with the antidemocratic direction Pardo's government had taken and its insufficient responsiveness to popular demands. State employees and the middle sectors more broadly also supported

---

[24] Klarén (1973:86) citing Basadre.

him, looking forward to a period of growth of the state and state employ-ment, as did Haya de la Torre, possibly Mariátegui,[25] and anarcho-sindicalist leaders.[26]

Though Leguía appeared to have won the presidential election, which oc-curred in mid-May, Aspíllaga refused to concede defeat and there was grow-ing fear that the electoral tribunal would invalidate many votes for Leguía and nullify the election. A new round of worker-student protest now de-manded strict enforcement of the eight-hour law, price subsidies for basic consumer items, and university reform. After a general strike at the end of May, growing street battles between protesters and government troops, and the spread of the confrontation to nearby towns and other parts of the coun-try, Pardo responded with heavy repression, including the closing of San Mar-cos University and the suppression of worker protest that included thousands of arrests and the killing of perhaps hundreds of protesters (Cotler 1978:181; Werlich 1978:151).

Amid the growing crisis and collapse of support for the Pardo government, the military became a decisive actor. While they had earlier overthrown Bil-linghurst out of opposition to his populist policies, key military leaders now believed that the old Civilista system had lost legitimacy and therefore sup-ported new directions of political change (Cotler 1978:186; Werlich 1978:151–54). In the 1919 crisis, the military—acting in close coordination with Leguía—intervened on July 4, a month prior to the scheduled inaugu-ration of the new president, arrested Pardo, sent him into exile, and placed Leguía in the presidency.

In a first step toward the increasingly authoritarian direction assumed by his government, Leguía immediately dissolved the Congress, the most im-portant center of Civilista political power. He justified the coup and the clos-ing of Congress with claims of a Civilista conspiracy against his assumption of the presidency. However, Leguía's consolidation of authoritarian control may well have been a carefully planned strategy, adopted in light of conflicts with the Civilistas during his earlier government.[27]

The political circumstances of the change in government in Argentina were quite distinct. In the wake of the electoral reform of 1912 and the grow-ing recognition by the Argentine elite that the assumption of power by the Radical Party would probably not threaten its fundamental interests, the Radicals won a substantial electoral victory in the 1916 presidential election. While different sources provide somewhat contrasting assessments of the outcome of the vote because of the problem of aggregating the vote totals for different Conservative regional parties, overall the Radicals gained approxi-mately 46 percent of the national vote, as opposed to 25 percent for the Con-

[25] Cotler (1978:182) includes Mariátegui among the supporters, whereas Werlich (1978:178) says he was not one.

[26] Sulmont 1975:90; E. Yepes 1980:155; Cotler 1978:182; Werlich 1978:150–53; Garrett 1973:38–39.

[27] Cotler 1978:182; Werlich 1978:150–51; Sulmont 1975:84–90; Garrett 1973:51–52; Pike 1967:214–15.

servatives, 13 percent for the Progressive Democrats (a party established by a former leader within the Radical movement), and 9 percent for the Socialists (Cantón 1968a, vol. 1:86). The Socialist vote was far greater in Buenos Aires, making the capital an important domain of electoral competition between the Radicals and the Socialists.

However, despite the major electoral shift to these parties in the presidential vote, the Conservatives still controlled the national Senate and the Supreme Court, as well as 11 of the 14 provincial governorships. The lack of a sharp departure in the orientation of the government was further suggested by the fact that five of eight cabinet ministers appointed by Yrigoyen in 1918 were either large landowners in Buenos Aires province or were closely linked to the export sector.[28] According to Peter Smith's (1978a:14) careful analysis, between 1916 and 1918, 48 percent of the Radicals in the Chamber of Deputies were members of what he identifies as the "aristocracy," and overall, 56 percent of the deputies were in this category.

Role of Labor in the Transition.   The role of labor was far more overt and important in Peru. The major wave of strikes and social protest in 1918–19 were central to the crisis that discredited the Pardo government, encouraged Leguía's return from exile, and, in the context of the dispute about the outcome of the 1919 election, helped to justify the coup that brought Leguía to the presidency.

Labor support was of some importance in Yrigoyen's victory in Argentina but was far more marginal and less visible than in Peru. Social protest played no immediate role in the transition, and at this point only a small proportion of workers could vote because of their immigrant status. Nonetheless, 22 percent of the registered voters in the federal capital in 1916 were manual workers, and the Radicals won four of the six districts in which manual workers represented more than 25 percent of registered voters, the other two being won decisively by the Socialists. The Radicals unquestionably made an effort to attract workers' votes, selling large quantities of bread, meat, and milk at subsidized prizes in working-class areas and creating an organization that had the same initials as the main labor federation, FORA, as a vehicle for cultivating labor support. Though precise measures of the success of these efforts in terms of the results of the 1916 election are not available, the labor vote was sufficiently important for the usually well-informed *Review of the River Plate* to comment in 1917, in explaining the government's support for striking workers, that this support was "the not unnatural result of the policy of a government that has come into power on a popular vote of unprecedented magnitude."[29]

Orientation of New Government.   Calling the new era in Peru the *Patria Nueva* (New Fatherland), the Leguía administration introduced many of the reforms found in other countries at this time. These included a new constitution, modeled in part after that of Mexico, that delineated an extensive

[28] Rock 1975a:95; Cantón 1968a, vol. 1:37–41; Snow 1965:31–34.
[29] Rock 1975a:142. See also Baily (1967:40); Walter (1977:139, 237); Rock (1975a:121–24).

new role of the state in society, major new initiatives in Indian policy, university reform, and a substantial modernization and expansion of the state apparatus. State revenues increased nearly fourfold between 1919 and 1927, and the number of public employees increased over sixfold between 1920 and 1930 (Yepes 1980:159; Garrett 1973:97).

At the same time, to a greater degree than occurred in most of the other countries during the analytically comparable reform period, the Leguía administration ruled during a rapid expansion of U.S. investment in Peru. Leguía's government played a central role in promoting this investment, in developing close ties with the United States, and in using its contacts in the United States to secure new resources to support the modernization of Peru and of the Peruvian state. Foreign loans were crucial in financing Leguía's development efforts, with the proportion of state revenues deriving from loans rising from around 5 percent in 1919 to around 45 percent in 1926 to 1928. Between 1920 and 1930 the proportion of exports derived from foreign-owned sectors of the economy rose from 17 percent to 49 percent. Leguía's close relations with the United States were symbolized by the fact that July 4, the date of the coup that brought him to power, became an annual holiday for the celebration of ties between Peru and the United States.[30] In this sense, the Leguía period brought a complex combination of the social reformism found at this time in a number of other countries and a process of opening to foreign capital and economic modernization more comparable to the Porfiriato in Mexico.

In addition to the consolidation of authority of the national state, this was also a period of authoritarian consolidation of power in the hands of Leguía. As noted above, he had used the momentum of his initial rise to power to dissolve Congress. Leguía claimed that its Civilista members had plotted with Pardo to deprive him of the presidency, and he engineered the election of a new Congress more responsive to his wishes. In the following years, Leguía increasingly centralized power in his own hands and those of close associates. Leading Civilistas were exiled, and Congress was maintained in a subservient role through the use of political patronage and if necessary the threat of exile to deal with uncooperative members. Press censorship and effective use of the newly modernized police also played a central role in the system of control. Elections were carefully structured by the government, and Leguía ran unopposed for reelection in 1924 and 1929 (Garrett 1973:90–96; Werlich 1978:155).

At certain points the attacks on the Civilistas took on a mobilizational and populist, not to mention destructive, character. In September 1919 pro-government mobs were permitted to attack the offices of two Lima papers linked to the oligarchy—La Prensa and El Comercio—that had criticized the government. The same evening they also attacked the homes of the former Civilista presidential candidate, Aspíllaga, and the former Civilista president of the

[30] E. Yepes 1980:157–58; Thorp and Bertram 1974:31–32; Werlich 1978:167.

Senate, Antonio Miró Quesada, whose family owned *El Comercio*. Similar attacks occurred in other cities (Garrett 1973:56).

Another basic characteristic of Leguía's rule was personalism. It is true that he succeeded in enlarging and strengthening the institutions of the state. However, in terms of institutionalizing relationships within the political arena, his contribution was limited. Leguía built around himself a "vast political clientele network with which he established close ties of personal dependency" (Cotler 1978:183), and his "most conspicuous supporters were the circle of relatives, friends, high public officials, and government contractors," one of whose most important traits was their "sycophancy" (Herbold 1973:104). Pike (1967:218) likewise notes Leguía's failure to construct a political party to provide an institutionalized channel for the energies and talents of those in his administration, and the Democratic Reform Party that Leguía created appeared to be little more than an immediate extension of his system of personalistic rule (Garrett 1973:76ff.).

To what extent was Leguía's government antioligarchic? On the one hand, he exiled important leaders of the Civilista Party who were prominent members of the oligarchy, and leading Leguiistas tended to have a more middle-class, business background and predominantly belonged to a different social club in Lima than the more aristocratic sectors of the elite. In energetically promoting more modern forms of Peruvian capitalism with the support of heavy infusions of U.S. capital, Leguía created a new "plutocracy" that rose to affluence during this period. Within both the coastal oligarchy and the highland oligarchy, new individuals rose to prominent positions.[31]

On the other hand, though Leguía systematically undermined the prior political system of the oligarchy, we have already noted that he stood between this newer, more bourgeois class and the older oligarchy. Similarly, his social and economic policies were generally favorable to the oligarchy, with important exceptions early in his administration (discussed below).

Important contrasts between the situation in Peru and the policies of the Radical government in Argentina during this period can be understood in terms of two underlying differences in the immediate political context: first, the greater subordination of the Radicals to oligarchic interests, particularly at the beginning of the Radical period, and the continuing strength of the Conservatives in the Congress; and second, the continuing vitality of a highly competitive electoral arena in Argentina. In this setting, the Radicals did not carry out fundamental social and economic reforms. In a spectrum of policy areas—taxation, tariffs, monetary policy, the promotion of industrialization, and policy toward the prevailing system of land ownership—the government made at most modest innovations and maintained close relations with established agrarian and foreign interests (Rock 1985:199ff.; 1975a:110). During the presidency of the more conservative government of the Radical leader Marcelo T. de Alvear from 1922 to 1928, between Yrigoyen's first and second terms, relations with the oligarchy were even closer.

---

[31] Garrett 1973:77–78; Burga and Flores Galindo (1979:8, 139); Favre 1969:106–7.

The Radical period was marked, however, by some important policy innovation, much of which was closely linked to the party's effort to build its electoral base. This in turn reflected the most fundamental innovation of the period, the creation of a competitive electoral arena. Among the most significant policy changes was the increase in the size of the state and of middle-class employment in the state, through which the Radicals sought to consolidate their base of middle-class electoral support. In 1921 and 1922 in the federal capital alone, on the eve of the presidential election between 10,000 and 20,000 new positions were created in the national government (Rock 1975a:223–24). The Radical-supported university reform of 1918 initiated a continent-wide process of democratization of universities and may also be seen as an aspect of the Radicals' effort to cultivate middle-class support, since students of middle class origin were becoming increasingly important in the universities (Rock 1985:200). Labor policy, discussed below, was another area in which the government sought to build its electoral base, thereby responding to electoral competition in urban areas from the Socialists.

Labor Policy under Leguía and Yrigoyen. The fate of labor policy under Leguía and Yrigoyen is an important commonality of these two cases. Both governments made significant early overtures toward labor, at various points supporting workers in collective disputes and in other ways aiding the labor movement and taking initiatives favorable to workers. However, neither government sustained these policies in the face of the intense urban and rural worker protest of the late 1910s and early 1920s, protest that was part of the international wave of worker militancy discussed in Chapter 3. In this period, as at a crucial subsequent transition point in the 1940s, the parallel evolution of these two cases is thus to some degree the result of timing.

In Peru, worker protest had been central to the political crisis that discredited the Civilistas and brought Leguía to power. There was some evidence of direct support for Leguía from elements of the labor movement, and the day of the coup was celebrated with a new round of worker demonstrations. Once in the presidency, Leguía reciprocated with a series of measures favorable to labor. He freed the workers jailed in the May 1919 strike, a measure greeted with another supportive demonstration by workers. In the early period of his administration, Leguía broadened the application of the eight-hour day law and extended work-injury, health, and safety provisions for workers; workers' protection for women and minors; and price controls for food and housing. The new constitution of 1920 recognized the right of workers to form unions, and a series of decrees in 1919, 1920, and 1921 established an Office of Worker Affairs (Sección de Trabajo) authorized to recognize unions and to conciliate and arbitrate labor disputes.[32]

Though Leguía thus initially favored urban labor, his policies toward labor and toward the popular sector in general soon turned in a more harsh direction. These two phases of policy appear to correspond to the larger coalitional

[32] Sulmont 1975:90; Werlich 1978:164; ILO 1930:224–25.

logic of his government. At the height of Leguía's attack on the Civilistas at the beginning of his presidency, popular sector support was politically useful for him, and this phase produced a type of "populist alliance" that encompassed the urban working class, along with other popular sector groups. However, once he had largely defeated the Civilistas, this support became less important and he shifted to what we have called an "accommodationist alliance." At this point, to the extent that popular mobilization got out of control, he was in a better position to repress it energetically. As we will see below, this shift in alliances may be observed with regard not only to urban labor, but also to enclave workers, Indians in traditional areas of agriculture, and university students.

Leguía was challenged by the labor movement from the start of his administration. At the demonstration in July 1919 in which workers celebrated Leguía's freeing of imprisoned labor leaders, a prominent labor leader stressed in his speech the orientation of the labor movement toward class conflict rather than political collaboration. A new Peruvian Regional Workers Federation, the name taken throughout the continent for anarcho-syndicalist federations, was formed just after the demonstration, and the declaration of principles of the federation published that month had a strongly anarcho-syndicalist orientation. According to Garrett, in September and October "violent strikes erupted in Lima and Callao, souring the government's support for labor." However, "Leguía could ill afford a major crackdown on labor while facing a severe challenge from the *civilistas*," and for the time being the government maintained a conciliatory posture.[33]

In 1920 a wave of strikes and worker demands in Lima triggered harsh repression, the deportation of a number of labor leaders, and new restrictive regulations reflected a hardening of the government's position toward labor. Though 1921 and 1922 saw fewer strikes, the period beginning in May 1923 brought a new wave of strikes and popular opposition to the government that culminated in November of that year in a series of work stoppages that "brought commerce to a standstill." A further increase in government restrictions included a "decree authorizing the induction of workers in key industries into the armed forces" (Werlich 1978:166), making it possible to shoot striking workers for desertion (this decree was, in fact, not applied). Such initiatives effectively eliminated any threat the labor movement could pose to the government but cost Leguía the support of all but a few co-opted unions, which continued to cooperate with the administration.[34]

By 1921 Leguía's cooperative relationship with university students had ended, and an important aspect of the wave of protest in 1923 was a renewed coordination of worker and student mobilization, again under the leadership of Haya de la Torre (see Chapter 3). The immediate occasion for this coordination was their shared opposition to Leguía's initiative to formally consecrate the Peruvian nation to the Sacred Heart of Jesus, "an attempt to link

[33] Garrett 1973:64, 65. See also Sulmont (1975:91); Basadre 1968, vol. 13:28.
[34] Sulmont 1975:91; Santistevan 1980:57; Werlich 1978:166.

God to the dictatorship" (Werlich 1978:165). Police suppression of this protest was followed by a general strike that paralyzed the capital (Werlich 1978:165–66; Sulmont 1975:103).

In retrospect one of the most important aspects of the suppression of this protest was the arrest and exile of Haya. This step inaugurated an extended period of residence abroad that launched his career as an important international leader of national-populist movements in Latin America. These years provided him with ideas about party organization that shaped the future development of APRA (Hilliker 1971:21). Haya's expulsion also removed from the country the most important political rival of Mariátegui, giving Mariátegui and the Socialist (later Communist) Party an important opportunity to make major gains in the labor sector in the period up through the early 1930s.

These two phases of Leguía's policies toward urban labor—of mutual support and cooperation, followed by suppression in response to increased or ongoing protest—were also reflected in labor policy toward the enclave sector. Beginning in December 1920, extensive worker protest paralyzed the Chicama Valley on the north coast, the most important center of sugar production in the country (Klarén 1973:45). The dispute commenced in the midst of Leguía's conflicts with the Civilistas, and in conjunction with this dispute Leguía initially adopted a favorable position toward the strikers, thereby antagonizing the plantation owners. However, by late 1921, as intense labor conflict continued and "as the political basis of the new regime shifted" (Klarén 1973:47) toward the newly prosperous economic sectors that came to be the core of his support coalition, Leguía reverted to severe repression. A large number of government troops were sent to quell the protest in early 1922, and the labor movement in the area did not reemerge for the remainder of the decade (Klarén 1973:47–48; Sulmont 1975:295–96).

The same two phases appeared in initiatives toward the more traditional sectors of agriculture. At the start of his government, Leguía pursued a spectrum of policies favorable to Indians, in part seeking the support of radicalized sectors of the middle class and attacking part of the traditional clientele base of the Civilistas. These policies stimulated new forms of popular mobilization. In the southern highlands, in response to the encouragement provided by the new government policies, as well as to changes in regional social structure and short-term economic fluctuations within the region, a major wave of Indian rebellions and land seizures ensued, culminating in a generalized peasant insurrection in the southern region that began in 1920 and continued at least to 1927. Leguía was forced to abandon his initial Indian program and resorted to traditional policies of repression. In just one locality in the department of Puno, 2,000 Indians were killed in late 1923. Subsequently, the traditional sector of the oligarchy to some degree reestablished its position among the Leguiistas.[35]

On one level, Leguía's initial populist measures in these different policy

---

[35] Cotler 1978:189; Burga and Flores Galindo 1979:119–34; Basadre 1968, vol. 13:308.

areas can be seen as a brief, carefully calculated transitional phase that may have helped him consolidate power. The limits to these populist initiatives could be viewed as clearly defined, within the framework of his close ties to international capital and his responsiveness to its concerns.

At the same time, it is interesting to note parallels between these events in Peru and the different regional insurrections that accompanied the onset of the Mexican Revolution. Given the extensive worker protest in Lima, the paralysis of work relationships on the north coast—in the heart of one of the most prosperous areas of export agriculture—and the generalized insurrection in the south, one might speculate about what would have happened if Leguía's leadership and move to the right had been less decisive or if his populism had been more genuine. However, a basic contrast with Mexico lies in the fact that while the long-term expansion of the export economy in Peru had produced substantial disruption in the rural sector, this disruption appeared to be far less generalized than in Mexico. Hence, the basic economic and social institutions of the oligarchy were much stronger.

Apart from the issue of the two phases of Leguía's labor policy, another basic question concerning his policies involves his role in supporting and regulating unions. As noted above, at the beginning of his administration he established a legal framework for recognizing trade unions and conciliating and arbitrating labor disputes. If this framework had been applied on a sustained basis, the Leguía administration would obviously constitute the initial incorporation period in Peru.

Scattered available evidence suggests that the activity of the Office of Worker Affairs and the number of unions formed under government auspices was probably limited and that this does not constitute Peru's incorporation period. Werlich (1978:165) twice refers to "several" unions that appeared in this period that were "peaceful labor organizations" or that sought cooperation with the government, and North (1973:184) suggests that Leguía's government "was engaged in setting up docile unions." According to Basadre (1968, vol. 13:28), "in some cases labor leaders were corrupted by the government (corrompidos por el oficialismo)," presumably leading them to cooperate with the Leguía administration. The impression that emerges from the literature is that the government's involvement in attempting to shape the labor movement did not affect many unions. It appears more reminiscent of a more traditional pattern earlier followed by authoritarian and dictatorial governments in various countries of securing the cooperation of a small number of unions that were used periodically to demonstrate political support. This is quite distinct from an effort to impose a new organizational framework on major sectors of the labor movement.[36]

[36] More research is needed on the scope of Leguía's initiatives in forming unions. This is so particularly because of an occasional tendency in the literature to dismiss Leguía's policies because he was "antilabor." From the perspective of the present analysis, Vargas's initiatives in the 1930s in Brazil were also antilabor, yet his successful efforts to impose a new form of controlled labor organizations clearly constitute an incorporation period. While the literature on Peru seems to suggest that Leguía's efforts, by contrast, were too

Several reasons may be suggested for the apparently limited application of these initiatives. First, Leguía did not construct a legal framework appropriate to the task. Garrett speaks of a "carrot and a stick" in Leguía's approach to workers, using a framework parallel to the discussion of inducements and constraints presented in Chapter 2. However, Garrett (1973:193–94) argues that the carrot involved the more general measures benefiting workers of the type noted above, whereas the stick involved the measures for dealing with trade unions as organizations. Other authors also note that the provisions for dealing with unions principally involved highly restrictive controls that were widely rejected by labor organizations.[37] An examination of labor law under Leguía suggests that the provisions to induce unions to cooperate with the state were extremely limited. Even compared with restrictive incorporation experiences such as that of Vargas in Brazil in the 1930s, the pattern in Peru is exceptionally control-oriented (Collier and Collier, 1979:973).

The legal framework set up by Leguía was thus sufficiently antilabor that it provided little basis for inducing unions to cooperate. Beyond the first year or so of his government, the principal channel for securing such cooperation was presumably through extending ad hoc benefits to the limited number of unions referred to above, rather than through a larger set of initiatives directed at the labor movement more generally.

Secondly, the application of these initiatives was obviously made more difficult by the continued predominance in the first years of the Leguía administration of an anarchist orientation in the labor movement and hence strong opposition to cooperation with the state. Further, this was a period of intense social protest in a number of sectors. This protest in part reflected a continuation of the wave of protest of 1918–19, in part a response to Leguía's favorable initiatives toward the popular sector at the start of his administration, and in part a reaction to new economic and social conditions that arose in particular sectors of the economy. Thus, Leguía's extremely control-oriented approach to unions was matched with strong resistance on the part of many unions to cooperation with his policies.

To summarize, this combination of Leguía's approach to labor, along with labor's strong opposition to cooperation with the state, undermined the initiatives that could potentially have led to an incorporation period in Peru.

In Argentina under the first Yrigoyen government from 1916 to 1922, labor policy was also initially an important area of innovation. Yet Baily (1967:36) emphasizes that Yrigoyen "had no specific labor program and therefore dealt with organized workers on an *ad hoc* basis," rather than seeking "to institutionalize the rights of labor." As in Peru, within the framework employed in this study, these years do not represent an incorporating period, but clearly are an important experiment in prolabor policy.

Yrigoyen was sympathetic to the aspirations of workers, supported their

limited to constitute an incorporation period, more detailed research is needed to fully demonstrate this.

[37] Sulmont 1975:91; Santistevan 1980:57; Martínez de la Torre 1947, vol. 1:251–52.

right to organize and strike, and involved the government in labor disputes in order to support what he viewed as a fair outcome. During the first three years of Yrigoyen's administration, he was restrained in the use of the police and army in settling labor disputes, and particularly in maritime and railway strikes of this period supported settlements favorable to workers (Baily 1967:34–35; Rock 1975a:125–52).

A concern with gaining the electoral support of labor played a central role in shaping labor policy. For instance, the Maritime Workers' Federation was an inviting source of support for the Radicals to cultivate, located as it was in La Boca, where nearly half the registered voters were manual workers[38] and where the two wings of the Socialist Party together had won a majority in the elections of 1914, 1916, and 1918. By supporting syndicalist-led unions such as the maritime workers, the Radicals sought to win votes away from the Socialists, and the government reacted harshly against strikes by municipal workers in 1916 and 1918 after the Socialists supported the strikers (Walter 1977:115, 139, 148; Rock 1975a:131–34).

In the years following 1916 labor militancy increased dramatically. In Buenos Aires alone the number of strikes rose from 80 in 1916, to 196 in 1918, 367 in 1919, and 206 in 1920. The number of strikers rose from 24,000 in 1916, to 173,000 in 1918, and 309,000 in 1919, declining to the still relatively high level of 134,000 in 1920. The number of working days lost increased from 49,183 in 1915 and 233,878 in 1916 to over 2 million in 1918, over 3 million in 1919, and over 3.5 million in 1920 (Di Tella and Zymelman 1967:537–38). While the immediate context of these strikes appears to be the inflation and erosion of real wages that occurred during the war and in the immediate postwar period (Rock 1975a:126), these worker actions, as well as the conservative reaction to them, were also encouraged by Yrigoyen's pro-labor policies, the demonstration effect of the Russian Revolution, the dramatic political developments in the immediate postwar period in other parts of Europe, and the Mexican Revolution.

In reaction to worker protest, the conservative mobilization previously seen in 1910 was renewed. At a meeting held in the Buenos Aires stock exchange in May 1918, which was chaired by the president of the Rural Society and attended by representatives of different sectors of the economic elite, the National Labor Association was formed with the principal purpose of attacking the labor movement through the use of strikebreakers. In early 1919 members of the economic elite and military leaders, expressing in part a nationalistic reaction to the role of immigrants in the growing social protest, formed the Patriotic League, whose elaborate paramilitary organization conducted vigilante attacks against worker organizations and other suspected subversives. This group also represented an implied military threat against the government if it did not take a stronger role in controlling labor protest. The emergence of these two associations must be seen in the larger context

[38] A far higher proportion than in any other district of the Federal Capital (see Walter 1977:74, 237).

of the very strong solidarity within the economic elite in the face of labor mobilization (Rock 1975a:153–55, 180–81).

The stage was now set for the crisis of 1919 known as the "Semana Trágica" (Tragic Week), a landmark in the evolution of Radical labor policy. In the context of a decline in real wages since the mid-1910s, workers at the British-owned Vasena metal works in Buenos Aires, "notorious for its starvation wages and the police measures it frequently took against its employees" (Rock 1975a:163), went on strike in December 1918. In the escalating violence that followed, both workers and police were killed as workers from outside the striking factory and youths, inspired by conservative groups to attack the workers, became involved. A mass meeting of individuals of middle- and upper-class background was held on January 10 in the Plaza Congreso to organize the conservative reaction to the strike. By January 12 the strike appeared nearly settled, but the police announced they had discovered a plot to initiate a Bolshevik revolution. Though evidence of the plot was scant, the police, along with the Patriotic League and the Labor Association, carried out a violent search of working class areas for presumed subversives, increasing greatly the number of people killed, injured, or jailed. Much of the repression was not directed at striking workers, but at the Russian-Jewish community, which was seen by members of the elite as a major source of revolutionary conspiracy. In all, as many as 700 to 800 people were killed, thousands were injured, and thousands arrested.[39]

The months following the Semana Trágica saw a rapid growth in union membership, intense strike activity, and the continuing expansion of the Patriotic League. As the growing participation of army officers in this organization seemed to suggest the danger of a coup, Yrigoyen ceased to support strikes and assumed a more repressive posture toward workers' organizations. Yrigoyen's effort to regain middle-class support in the period after these strikes is reflected in part in the fact that nearly two-thirds of the major increase in state spending between 1916 and 1922, heavily oriented as it was toward middle-class political patronage, came after the Semana Trágica. Perhaps to compensate for the shift away from more favorable policies toward worker protest, Yrigoyen introduced legislation in May of 1919 to institutionalize collective bargaining and a ten-hour day, and two years later proposed a comprehensive labor code. However, both of these initiatives, like the earlier 1904 code, met with intense opposition both from the labor movement and from conservatives and were not passed (Rock 1975a:190–94, 212, 223–24; Walter 1977:160, 168).

The Patriotic League continued to play an important role. In 1919, after a group of taxi drivers released a statement criticizing the league, members of the league organized an armed assault on the taxi union headquarters. When the taxi drivers responded with a strike, thousands of private cars driven in many cases by members of distinguished families were provided to break the strike, and support for and membership in the league grew rapidly. The cul-

[39] Rock 1975a:168–69; Baily 1967:36–38; Oddone 1949:195; Iscaro 1973:184.

mination of the league's efforts was its central role in the repression of workers on the sheep ranches of Patagonia in 1921–22. While the overall military operation against these workers was carried out by government troops operating under the ultimate direction of Yrigoyen (who was probably unaware of the brutality of the repression), White Guards from the Patriotic League were centrally involved, and estimates of the number of workers killed ranged from 1,000 to 2,000. In the aftermath of this episode, Colonel Héctor Valera, who had led the government troops, was assassinated in early 1923 by an anarchist worker of German extraction, who was in turn imprisoned and later murdered by a prison guard acting on behalf of the Patriotic League. The counterpart for the rural sector of Semana Trágica thus came to be known as "La Patagonia Trágica." Argentina, like Peru, thus experienced major repression in the rural sector, as well as the urban sector, during these years.[40]

As in the first decade of the 20th century, which saw the defeat of the early labor code and the initial major period of vigilante action by the right, again in this period there was a failure to institutionalize mechanisms of class mediation within the state. Instead, these conflicts, which involved a collision between the strongest labor movement and probably the most extensive conservative mobilization to appear in this period in the region, were played out in part through the unmediated confrontation of opposing classes. This appears to represent an important step in the emergence of what O'Donnell (1984:19–23) has identified as a distinctive trait of Argentine politics that he labels "anarchic corporatism," involving direct confrontations among the associations of different class and sectoral groups in which the state and political parties played only a weak role in mediating and aggregating societal interests.[41] The historic failure of the Radical Party during this period can thus be seen as one step in the evolution of this more generic predicament of Argentine politics.

In the aftermath of this extensive labor repression in Argentina, the labor movement (with the notable exception of the railway workers) found itself in a considerably weaker position. In addition to the prior repression, factors that contributed to this outcome included renewed competition after the war from imported goods in the Argentine market, the competition for jobs provided by new immigrants, the conservative cast of the Alvear presidency (1922–28),[42] and the limited support of his government for the labor movement. However, with Yrigoyen's campaign to regain the presidency in the election of 1928, the Radicals made effective use of their system of party committees that campaigned directly among workers, distributing patronage among them. Radical campaign propaganda also recalled the Radical support

[40] Rock 1975a:202–3; Marotta 1970, vol. 3:101; Iscaro 1973:202; Walter 1977:169.

[41] It was, of course, precisely this role that national states characteristically sought to play when they initiated an incorporation period.

[42] Among Radical members of the Chamber of Deputies in 1922–24, Smith (1978:14) identifies 41 percent of those in the Alvear wing as aristocrats, as opposed to only 14 percent in the Yrigoyen wing.

for the labor movement under Yrigoyen's first government. Other factors favorable for the Radicals included their successful use of economic nationalism to cultivate popular support and the weakened position of the Socialist Party. In the election the Radicals for the first time won decisively over the Socialists in all districts of Buenos Aires, even those with the largest working class populations. Overall, Yrigoyen received 57 percent of the national vote (Baily 1967:46–47; Rock 1975a:232–34, 240; Walter 1977:215).

Following this electoral success, in 1929 the second Yrigoyen administration secured the adoption of a law providing for an eight-hour day and a 48-hour week for urban workers, an important legislative landmark (Rotondaro 1971:113). However, private right-wing groups continued to play an important role in harassing and killing workers and unionists, and the passage of this one initiative did not mark a transition to a new pattern of state-labor relations.

From 1930 to Incorporation Period.   The crisis of the depression, interacting with the political crises of the Leguía and Yrigoyen administrations, brought a change in government in both Peru and Argentina in 1930. In terms of regime change, the two countries went in opposite directions, however. In Peru the closed political system of Leguía was replaced by a period of intense popular mobilization and far more competitive politics, including a presidential election in 1931 that appeared to have been conducted with reasonable honesty. By contrast, the more competitive electoral politics of the Yrigoyen period in Argentina were replaced by a new era of electoral fraud and manipulation. In both countries this new period brought what was in important respects a restoration of oligarchic dominance in the political system, though in Argentina this occurred immediately in 1930, whereas in Peru it did not occur until after a period of intense social conflict between 1930 and 1933. Though the 1930s saw a restoration of oligarchic influence in both countries, this decade also saw substantial growth in the role of the state in the economy, in many ways paralleling that in other Latin American countries.

In Peru, the onset of the depression and resulting constriction of international credit was a severe blow to Leguía's government, whose patronage base derived so heavily from foreign resources. The government was also hurt by an unpopular treaty with Colombia, and the accommodation between Leguía and the oligarchy on matters of economic policy that had been established by the early 1920s was again undermined by the late 1920s. The popular sector was also hurt economically by the onset of the depression, and this economic hardship, along with the prospect of an erosion of the repressive controls of the Leguía years, brought renewed worker protest. Leguía was overthrown by Luis M. Sánchez Cerro in late August 1930.[43]

The collapse of the Leguía dictatorship brought an explosion of popular mobilization. Since the nature and outcome of this mobilization is an important part of the background of Peru's later incorporation experience, it

[43] Werlich 1978:173; Cotler 1978:227–28; Karno 1970:227–28.

merits attention here. Initially, the most visible role was played by Mariátegui's Socialist Party, founded in late 1928 after the definitive rupture between Mariátegui and Haya de la Torre. In May 1929 Socialist labor leaders formed the General Confederation of Peruvian Workers (CGTP), which was intended to replace the relatively weak and ephemeral labor federations earlier identified with the anarchist phase of the labor movement. Mariátegui had opposed full affiliation with the Third International, but soon after his death in 1929 the party became affiliated and was reconstituted in May 1930 as the Peruvian Communist Party (PCP) (Sulmont 1975:118–23).

Acting in what was believed to be a "prerevolutionary" situation, the PCP closely followed the line of the Third International by opposing all reformist alternatives and aggressively pursuing an insurrectional strategy, most conspicuously in the labor sector. The party sought to establish workers' "soviets," promote a workers' insurrection, seize state power, and establish a dictatorship of the proletariat. These initiatives failed dramatically, being met by energetic government repression and leading to the destruction of the CGTP and the eclipse of the PCP within the popular sector and the labor movement, in favor of APRA.[44]

The other important, and up to a point more successful, force on the left was APRA. Haya had founded APRA as an international movement in 1924 while an exile in Mexico (Hilliker 1971:15). Shortly thereafter he presented APRA's five-point Maximum Program, advocating: "1. Action against Yankee imperialism. 2. The political unification of Latin America. 3. Nationalization of land and industry. 4. Internationalization of the Panama Canal. 5. Solidarity with all the peoples and oppressed classes of the world" (Haya 1976, vol. 4:73–74).

APRA was organized as a political party in Peru in October 1930, a month after the overthrow of Leguía.[45] In anticipation of the 1931 presidential election, in which Haya was a candidate, the party now proposed a Minimum Program containing proposals for an enlarged state role in the economy, economic nationalism, and corporative structuring of economic planning that had much in common with other Latin American experiences with populism. In contrast to APRA's earlier Maximum Program, the Minimum Program did not propose a full assault on established property relationships in Peru, and party leaders sought to reassure foreign interests concerning APRA's desire to maintain strong relationships of cooperation (Cotler 1978:236–42). North (1973:247) suggests that if APRA had come to power at this point, its policy orientation would have had many elements in common with the Cárdenas experience in Mexico and the first Peronist administration in Argentina.

The electoral campaign of 1931 provided the first major evidence of APRA's extraordinary organizational capacity. APRA emerged as the "most

[44] Sulmont 1975:123, 127, 139, 144; Cotler 1978:232–33; Balbi 1980:e.g. 143–45.
[45] See Stein (1980:154). North (1973:32) dates the founding to organizational meetings held a few weeks before in September of that year.

important mass party Peru had ever seen," possessing a "powerful party organization at the national, departmental, and local level" (Sulmont 1975:126). With great skill the party set up associated organizations in many spheres—among workers, students, youths, and professionals, and including cultural groups and sports groups. Given this commitment to building organizational bases, it is obvious that had APRA come to power at this point, it would have initiated Peru's period of the initial incorporation of the labor movement.

APRA's organizational strength was matched by its extraordinary capacity to create a sense of community among its members. "The totalizing character of APRA's organization encouraged the creation of symbols, rituals and myths that created a high degree of integration among its members . . . [reminiscent] of a religious brotherhood" (Cotler 1978:235). The charismatic leadership of Haya played a central role in cultivating this sense of community.

The Peruvian elite had severe misgivings about APRA's program, notwithstanding the party's assurances noted above. However, the elite reaction focused perhaps even more on the scope of the popular mobilization and APRA's dramatic capacity to win the intense loyalty of its followers. This reaction brought elite support firmly behind the rival presidential candidate, Sánchez Cerro, and this reaction was an essential element behind the elite fears and the atmosphere of class confrontation that emerged in this period (North 1973:51–52; Cotler 1978:236).

In the presidential election of October 1931 Sánchez Cerro obtained 51 per cent of the vote and won 64 seats in the Constituent Assembly (which functioned as a unicameral legislature), whereas APRA won 35 percent and gained 23 seats. A careful analysis of the immediate circumstances of the election and long-term patterns of APRA support suggests that the election was probably conducted with reasonable fairness.[46]

Yet APRA, convinced of its historic mission to transform Peruvian society, claimed the outcome was fraudulent. The party maintained a defiant posture toward the new government and Haya claimed the "moral presidency" of Peru (Werlich 1978:196). The party systematically tried to undermine Sánchez Cerro and to bring Haya to the presidency through two courses of action: first, a further intensive effort to build the party and promote popular mobilization; and second, through military insurrection. The battle between APRA and the government brought Peru "close to a state of civil war" (North 1973:112), and beginning in February 1932 and for many years thereafter, APRA faced severe government repression. The party's experience with repression became a further bond among its members (North 1973:112–13).

APRA's decision to pursue military insurrection launched the party's tragic tradition of violence, a tradition that was built into the party through its paramilitary youth organizations. Examples of this violence included an attempt by a young Aprista to assassinate President Sánchez Cerro in March 1932, an aborted attempt to seize political power that occurred in the same

[46] Werlich 1979:195–96; North 1973:49; and Stein 1980:189–96.

month, a naval mutiny in Lima's port of Callao in May, and the assassination of Sánchez Cerro in April of the following year (North 1973:112–15, 147, appendix 5).

Among many other violent events, two stand out as playing an especially important role in consolidating intense antagonism toward APRA on the part of the armed forces and the economic elite, thereby creating a deep tradition of anti-Aprismo. In July 1932 APRA launched a major insurrection in the provincial city of Trujillo, the APRA stronghold on the north coast. The insurrection enjoyed wide popular support in the north but failed to spread to the rest of the country and was soon crushed militarily. Tragically, a small number of army officers being held by the rebels were killed and mutilated, and the army retaliated by killing large numbers of Apristas. This event, which for decades afterward was commemorated by the army with an annual ceremony, formed the cornerstone for an intense and long-standing enmity on the part of the armed forces toward APRA, an enmity continually reinforced by the threat to the institutional integrity of the armed forces posed by APRA's perpetual infiltration and conspiracies among soldiers and younger officers. The events of Trujillo forged a strong bond between the armed forces and the oligarchy, based on their shared antagonism toward APRA. On the other hand, the army repression against the rebels strengthened the bond between APRA and the popular masses (Cotler 1978:246–47).

The other act of violence was the killing by an Aprista in 1935 of the editor of *El Comercio*, Antonio Miró Quesada, and his wife as they walked to lunch at the main social club of the oligarchy in the heart of downtown Lima. This event further galvanized antagonism toward APRA on the part of the elite. *El Comercio* became an implacable enemy of APRA, and the slaying became a symbol of APRA's assault on Peruvian national institutions (Cotler 1978:249–50).

Acts of violence such as these helped to lay the foundations for intense anti-Aprismo, yet elite reaction to the substantive program of APRA and to the party's overall strategy of mass mobilization also played a central role. In addition, as Bourricaud stresses, Peru's deep cultural and racial divisions played a part. Though APRA's leadership was relatively white and middle class, from the point of view of the country's white and mestizo elite, APRA's intense mass mobilization within "a country whose population consists for the most part of illiterate Indians" (Bourricaud 1970:167) posed a specter of racial and cultural antagonism that doubtless reinforced elite fears and enmities.

Though the Peruvian elite would continue to struggle against APRA for many years, the killing of Sánchez Cerro brought General Benavides to the presidency and thereby firmly reestablished the oligarchy's influence in Peruvian national politics. Garrett (1973:212) observes that all the ministers in Benavides's cabinet in late 1933 were members of the National Club, "the bastion of the 'oligarchy,'" and Leguía's earlier purge of Civilistas was avenged as many Civilistas returned to power and former Leguía supporters were "politically ostracized." Many younger Leguía supporters apparently joined APRA.[47]

Yet, as in Argentina, this government that in many ways was closely identified with the oligarchy also significantly expanded state intervention in the economy and adopted a series of social reforms favorable to the workers, obviously out of a concern with preempting portions of APRA's program. Benavides introduced further regulations of hours of work, enlarged the state's role in promoting public health among the popular sectors, and established a social security system, public housing, and public cafeterias for workers. At the same time, severe restrictions on trade-union organizing continued during these years, and hence the basic problem of dealing systematically with the organizational incorporation of the labor movement remained to be addressed.[48]

At the same time that the Benavides period—and the interval from 1920s to the 1940s more broadly—saw the ongoing postponement of the incorporation period, these years brought the continuing expansion of Peru's manufacturing sector and manufacturing work force. Thus, the social sector whose organization would finally be legitimated by the incorporation period in the 1940s continued to grow substantially, though Peru obviously remained far less industrialized than its larger neighbors. The overall value of manufacturing production doubled between the eve of the second Leguía administration and the early 1940s. The more dynamic sectors of manufacturing grew at impressive rates, with the value of footwear production increasing nearly sevenfold between 1918 and 1939 and that of cement roughly fourfold between the eve of the depression and the early 1940s. This expansion was accompanied by strong growth in employment in manufacturing establishments with five or more workers, which more than doubled between 1925 and 1935 and doubled again between 1935 and 1945, yielding a total increase over the 20-year period of nearly 320 percent.[49]

As the 1930s came to a close, these very changes in the Peruvian economy, interacting with many other factors, helped to encourage the gradual emergence of the incorporation period. The year 1939 saw the end of the nondemocratic rule of Benavides and the transition to a somewhat more democratic regime under Prado; a larger role within the economic elite of sectors oriented toward urban commerce and manufacturing who desired a more stable solution to the problem of dealing with APRA; and an international setting strongly supportive of greater collaboration between established political sectors and reformist and leftist parties. In this climate, a new phase in state-trade union relationships would finally emerge.

In Argentina, as in Peru, the economic hardships of the depression were a serious blow for the incumbent government, which had likewise made heavy use of the resources of the public sector for political patronage. In the 1930

[47] Garrett 1973:213. See also Cotler (1978:249); Sulmont (1975:164).
[48] Caravedo 1976:129–31; Cotler 1978:252; Pareja 1980:115.
[49] ECLA 1966:17; Caravedo 1976:51; Thorp and Bertram 1978:192.

legislative elections six months before the coup that overthrew Yrigoyen, the vote for the Radicals was 25 percent lower than it had been two years earlier, and the party lost dramatically in the working class districts where it had done so well in 1928. Following this defeat, amid reports of Yrigoyen's senility, his longstanding opponents found an easy opportunity to undermine his government, and in September 1930 he was overthrown in a military coup (Rock 1985:212; Walter 1977:224).

While the fall of the Radicals was thus in an immediate sense due to the *failure* of the resource base that had sustained them, Smith suggests that the Radicals were also undermined in part by their own *success*—including the further increase in their electoral strength in the 1928 election, declining Conservative electoral strength, and the marked shift, between 1916 and 1928, toward individuals of middle-class origin among Radical leaders. Whereas at the beginning of the first Yrigoyen government 48 percent of the Radicals in the Chamber of Deputies were "aristocrats," by the late 1920s the figure had dropped to 20 percent (Smith 1978a:14). Such trends, combined with the Radical's unwillingness to compromise with their political opponents that was perhaps a legacy of their many years in opposition prior to 1916, may have made Conservative political forces all the more eager to seize the opportunity of the crisis of the depression, remove the Radicals from power, and close the competitive electoral arena in which they fared so poorly (Smith 1978:14, 21–22).

The "neo-Conservative" decade of the 1930s in Argentina is commonly interpreted as reflecting to a substantial degree a restoration of more direct oligarchic dominance in the political system, a dominance once again maintained through widespread electoral fraud. The Roca-Runciman pact of 1933 with Britain, which provided a guaranteed market for Argentine beef on terms very favorable to Britain, was perhaps the most important symbol of what, because of the conspicuous foreign dependency promoted during this period, came to be known as the "infamous decade" (Rock 1985:214, 217, 223ff.). This period was nonetheless accompanied by a substantial increase in the state's role in the economy.

While the increase in state intervention included important increments in the state's involvement in labor relations, the evolving state role did not reach a point where it might reasonably be considered to constitute an incorporation period. The first president during this period, José Félix Uriburu, had in fact been a leading opponent of Yrigoyen's earlier prolabor policies and a prominent figure in the Patriotic League (Rock 1985:311). Under the subsequent government of Augustín P. Justo (1932–38), ad hoc relations of cooperation were established with certain unions, for instance the telephone workers, but the government also periodically used the police to protect strikebreakers in other sectors. Even in the sectors marked by cooperation, both the government and the unions each "attempted to use the other without offering any long-range commitment" (Horowitz 1979:342–43; see also 203, 349–52; and 1990:chap. 7). While the unions actively sought greater participation in different government agencies, no form of real political alliance was created and the government did not receive the active political support of unions with which it had ad hoc cooperative relations (Matushita 1983:93–94). As Horowitz (1983:108) put it, throughout this period the labor movement was not "an important part of the political equation."

Gaudio and Pilone (1983, 1984) show that the later 1930s saw an important increase in state involvement in conciliating labor disputes. While a significant development, this does not appear comparable in scope to the cautious "first phase" of the incorporation period analyzed in a number of other countries. Gaudio and Pilone stress the relatively small scale and ad hoc character of this involvement, emphasizing that it was "provisional" and not "routinized." They suggest that the "institutionalization" of this state role did not occur until the Perón period—though Perón's policies should definitely be viewed as the product of a progressive "sedimentation" of these earlier informal practices (1984:249–50).

Along with incremental evolution of labor policy, this period saw important change in the labor movement. In 1930 Socialist and syndicalist sectors of the movement formed the General Confederation of Labor (CGT), which would later come to be the cornerstone of Peronism. By the mid-1930s the Socialists were the strongest force in the labor sector, and Communists had come to play an increasingly important role. Following the popular front approach established in many countries beginning in 1935, Communist unions also joined the CGT and in the second half of the decade were the most dynamic political current within the workers' movement. In 1942 the CGT split between the sector that preferred the creation of a workers' party apart from the confederation; and the sector, dominated by the Socialists, but with an important role of Communists, which thought that the CGT should itself be the labor wing of either the Socialist or Communist Party.

These years also saw substantial expansion of Argentine industry, the number of industrial workers, and the scope of unionization. Whereas in 1935 the value of Argentine industrial production lagged 40 percent behind that of agriculture, by 1943 it exceeded agricultural production. Employment in manufacturing establishments of five or more workers grew by only a quarter from 1925 to 1935, but more than doubled between 1935 and 1945, yielding an increase of over 160 percent for the two decades. Union membership, already at a high level by the mid-1930s, grew significantly during these years, from almost 370,000 in 1936 to nearly 450,000 in 1941 (Spalding 1977:158–59; Rock 1985:232, 255–56; ECLA 1966:Table I-17).

Thus, on the eve of the rise of Perón, Argentina had a strong industrial sector and an extensively developed labor movement, which had achieved a substantial degree of institutionalization with relatively little state support. The labor movement would soon undergo a further, dramatic transformation due to the new state policies initiated by Perón beginning in 1943.

Conclusion.   In Peru and Argentina, the relationship between oligarchic strength and degree of mobilization in the incorporation period is distinctive in relation to the other countries. The pattern followed does not correspond to that suggested by four-way comparison of Brazil and Chile with Mexico and Venezuela. In these four cases, we observed an inverse relation between oligarchic strength and the political "space" available for a populist—as opposed to accommodationist—alliance at the onset of the incorporation period. By contrast, Peru and Argentina, despite the persistence of oligarchic power in both countries, went on in the 1940s to experience intensely mobilizational incorporation periods built on populist alliances. Let us review the steps that led up to this outcome (Figure 4.1).

In the 1910s and early 1920s in Peru and Argentina, the collapse of what might have been incorporation periods in both countries resulted from a "collision" between a strong labor movement and what was in important respects a strong oligarchy. This collision was made more intense by its timing in relation to two other developments: the inflation and decline in wages that occurred toward the end of World War I, and the worldwide wave of labor militancy following the Russian Revolution. These developments encouraged both more intense worker mobilization and a stronger and more frightened reaction on the part of the economic elite. The timing of the onset of the Leguía and Yrigoyen governments was thus especially unfavorable for inaugurating an incorporation period.

Subsequently, the long delay of incorporation and the economic growth that occurred during the delay allowed time for a further expansion and strengthening of the labor movement, as well as for the accumulation of political frustrations over the delay. This delay also positioned the incorporation periods in a new conjuncture: the international climate of democratization and mobilization of the 1940s. These factors together contributed to a highly mobilizational incorporation experience—which, in contrast to the pattern observed in the other four countries discussed above, occurred *despite* the persistence of oligarchic strength. In fact, as suggested in the figure, oligarchic strength indirectly *contributed* to the chain of events that led up to this type of incorporation period.

Figure 4.1 Delayed Incorporation in Peru and Argentina: Interaction between Oligarchic Strength and Degree of Mobilization

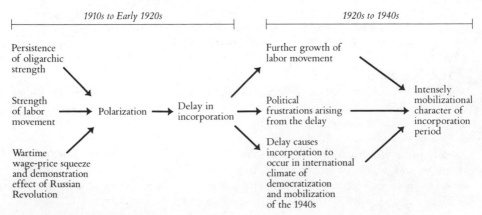

This juxtaposition of a highly mobilizational incorporation period and the persistence of oligarchic strength in the 1940s would again produce a major political collision that placed these two countries on a distinctive trajectory of change in the 1950s and beyond. The following two chapters explore how this occurred.

Part III

CRITICAL JUNCTURE

5

Incorporation: Recasting State-Labor Relations

THE PERIOD of initial incorporation of the labor movement is defined as the first sustained and at least partially successful attempt by the state to legitimate and shape an institutionalized labor movement. During this period, the state played an innovative role in constructing new institutions of state-labor and labor-capital relations and new approaches to articulating the labor movement with the party system.

The incorporation period emerged out of the experience of working class activation and elite debate on the social question discussed in the previous two chapters. This first major attempt to incorporate labor was important for a number of reasons: it addressed a fundamental crisis or potential crisis in these societies; it represented one of the most significant periods in Latin American history in which the state was challenged to address a fundamental reform agenda; and it constituted an opportunity to shape national political institutions for years to come, an opportunity that was seized—or in some instances aborted, initially postponed, and later reinitiated—in different ways in different countries.

Our basic thesis is that the incorporation periods were a crucial transition, in the course of which the eight countries followed different strategies of control and mobilization of the popular sectors. These differences had a long-term impact on the evolution of national politics. We do not intend to suggest that once the initial incorporation period had occurred, the patterns established remained unchanged. Quite the contrary, these periods set into motion a complex sequence of reactions and counterreactions, and the legacy of incorporation is to be found in the working out of this sequence. These reactions often led to consequences quite different from those intended either by the actors within the state who initiated incorporation or by the labor leaders who may have cooperated with them. Correspondingly, with regard to labels, when we assert that a country is an instance of a particular type of incorporation, we are referring to this earlier historical transition and not to the subsequent trajectory of change.

The analysis of incorporation is based on a number of choices concerning the appropriate identification of these periods and the treatment of subperiods within the overall incorporation experience. These issues may be of great interest to some readers and of little interest to others. We have therefore discussed them primarily in the glossary and have also treated them to some degree in Chapter 1. Questions concerning the beginning and end points of the incorporation periods are also addressed within the historical analysis in the present chapter, as well as in Chapter 4.

Figure 5.1 gives a chronological overview of the incorporation periods in the eight countries, identifying for each country both an initial, more cautious phase of incorporation, led by "conservative modernizers," and characterized to varying degrees by modernization, tentativeness, stalemate, and failure; and a second phase during which state initiatives generally assumed a more vigorous form.

Figure 5.1 Chronological Overview of Incorporation Periods

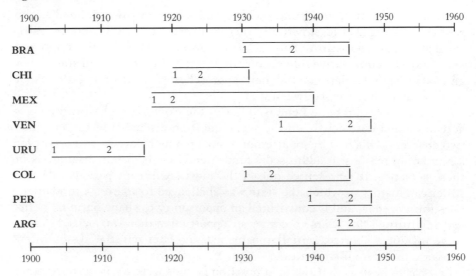

Notes: 1 = onset of first phase of "conservative modernizers"; 2 = onset of second phase of incorporation period.

Table 5.1 provides a more detailed overview of these two phases of incorporation, including the event (coup, assassination, election, or worker demonstration) that marked the transition between the phases. The table also shows the relation between the onset of the reform periods analyzed in the last chapter and the incorporation periods. In Mexico, Peru, and Argentina, the onset of reform brought an unsuccessful attempt to launch an incorporation project, followed by delays of varying lengths prior to the onset of the incorporation period.

Types of Incorporation Periods

The classification of these incorporation experiences is derived from the answers to a series of questions concerning the overall *goals* of the political leaders who initiated incorporation, the principal political *agency* involved in the incorporation period, two dimensions of the *mode* of incorporation,[1] and the *scope* of incorporation.

[1] If one were providing a generalized description of the incorporation periods, in contrast to the present concern with establishing a scheme for differentiating among them, a third

Goals: Control and Support. Was the major goal of the political leaders who initiated incorporation primarily to control the working class, with at most marginal concern with mobilizing its support, or was the mobilization of support part of a political strategy to gain and maintain power of at least equal importance?

Agency: State versus Party or Movement. Was the incorporation project principally concerned with linking the labor movement to the state, or was it, in addition, centrally concerned with linking labor to a political party or political movement that later became a party?

Mode: Electoral Mobilization. Did the leaders of the incorporation project seek the support of workers in the electoral arena?

Mode: Union-Party/Movement Linkage. Were strong organizational links established between labor organizations and the political party or movement through which support was organized?

Scope: Inclusion of Peasantry. In addition to encompassing modern sector workers in urban areas and modernized enclaves, was there a parallel mobilization and incorporation of peasants in the traditional rural sector?

These questions led us to distinguish four basic types of incorporation periods, delineated in Figure 5.2. We should reiterate that these are analytic types, not comprehensive descriptions of each case, and in fact not every country fits each category perfectly, as can be seen in the footnotes to the figure. However, the countries identified with each type are far more similar to one another in terms of the defining dimensions than they are to the other countries, and we believe this typology captures fundamental differences among the incorporation experiences.

State Incorporation. On the basis of the first two questions, we initially distinguish cases of state incorporation where the principal agency involved in the incorporation project was the state and the principal goal was to create a legalized and institutionalized labor movement that was depoliticized, controlled, and penetrated by the state. Among the countries considered here, the high point of state incorporation occurred under authoritarian rule, and the mobilization of the electoral support of workers was at most a marginal concern, though such mobilization did become important *after* these periods. Union-party links were prohibited, and preexisting political currents in the labor movement were repressed. A basic premise that helped sustain the governing coalition was that social relations in the traditional rural sector would remain unchanged. The two cases of state incorporation are Chile (1920–31) and Brazil (1930–45).

Party Incorporation. Given our definition of the incorporation period, the state played a role in all cases, and as can be seen in Figure 5.2 the control of

---

dimension of the *mode* of incorporation should also be emphasized: i.e., bureaucratic linkage, involving the systematic effort to establish bureaucratic ties between the state and the labor movement. This is obviously a basic feature of corporatism and is an important part of the incorporation experience in all of the countries except Uruguay. In Uruguay, in the pluralistic setting of the two presidential terms of José Batlle y Ordóñez at the beginning of the century, labor control tended to take the more "traditional" form of police surveillance of union activities rather than bureaucratic-corporative forms of control.

TABLE 5.1

Phases of Incorporation

	Onset of Reform Period	Aborted Incorporation Initiatives	First Phase: Conservative Modernizer	Second Phase: Full-Blown Incorporation Project
Brazil	1930		Vargas 1930–37	Coup of 1937; Estado Novo, 1937–45.
Chile	1920		Alessandri 1920–24[a]	Coup of 1927; presidency of Ibáñez, 1927–31.
Mexico	1911	Madero 1911–13	Carranza 1917–20	Assassination of Carranza in 1920; Sonoran Dynasty of 1920s, incorporation culminated in 1930s under Cárdenas.
Venezuela	1935		López Contreras and Medina, 1935–45	Coup of 1945; Trienio of 1945–48.
Uruguay	1903		Batlle 1903–7; Williman 1907–11	Batlle consolidated his position by onset of second term in 1911; Second Batlle presidency 1911–15, incorp. period extends to 1916.
Colombia	1930		Olaya 1930–34	López wins presidency in 1934; incorp. period extends to 1945.
Peru	1919	Leguía 1919–20	Prado 1939–45	In 1945, move beyond toleration of APRA to electoral alliance with APRA; Bustamante govt., 1945–48.
Argentina	1916	Yrigoyen 1916–20	Military leadership of June 1943 to Oct. 1945[b]	Worker demonstration of Oct. 1945 and election of Feb. 1946 consolidate Perón's power; Perón presidency of 1946–55.

[a] In Chile, the period 1924–27 saw crisis and instability as Ibáñez sought to consolidate his power.

[b] Immediately after the 1943 coup, these military leaders adopted highly restrictive policies toward the labor movement. The policy alternative represented by Perón's initiatives was already well-defined by late 1943, but Perón was strongly opposed by important sectors of military leadership until the second part of 1945. He formally became president in June 1946.

the labor movement was always a goal of the incorporation project. However, in six of the countries, a crucial additional agency was a political party or political movement that later became a party, and a central goal was the mobilization of labor support. These countries were distinguished as cases of party incorporation.[2]

The six cases of party incorporation had in common the fact that the incorporating elite sought to win the support of workers in the electoral arena. They differed in terms of whether strong union-party links were established and whether there was a parallel incorporation of the peasantry, thereby establishing the basis for identifying three subtypes of party incorporation.

1. **Electoral Mobilization by Traditional Party.** Colombia (1930–45) and Uruguay (1903–16) experienced active electoral mobilization of labor support, but the effort to link unions to the party was either limited or nonexistent, and the incorporation project did not encompass the peasantry. The political context was the expansion of the scope of electoral competition as an aspect of the competition between two traditional parties, both of which had existed since the 19th century. This was the most limited form of party mobilization, where new groups were added to the old party coalitions, where the addition of unions as a major element in these coalitions tended to be problematic, and where the economic elite maintained close ties to both parties.

2. **Labor Populism.** Peru (1939–48) and Argentina (1943–55) experienced active electoral mobilization of labor support and a major effort to link unions to a party or political movement, but the incorporation project did not encompass a peasantry.[3] Because the more extensive mobilization of this type remained restricted to labor in the modern sector, we refer to it as labor populism. The political context was the emergence or consolidation of a populist party or movement that displaced traditional parties and/or the traditional political class. The incorporation period was strongly antioligarchic, but not to the point of fundamentally altering property relations in the rural sector.

3. **Radical Populism.** Mexico (1917–40) and Venezuela (1935–48) experienced broad electoral mobilization of labor support, a major effort to link unions to the party, and, along with the modern sector working class, a parallel incorporation of the peasantry. Because the agrarian reform that accompanied peasant mobilization represented a more comprehensive assault on the oligarchy and on preexisting property relations, we refer to this as radical populism.

Two caveats may be introduced regarding the label party incorporation. First, we use this designation for the sake of convenience, yet as the definition makes clear, the category includes cases involving a "party or a political movement that later became a party." This is crucial because in Mexico and

---

[2] Since the state also played a central role in these cases, they could be called "party/state incorporation." However, this is a clumsy label, and we feel that in light of the above discussion the meaning of the label "party incorporation" is clear.

[3] Obviously, whereas in Peru this latter outcome was not plausible due to the strength of the oligarchy, in Argentina it was not plausible due to the lack of a major peasant population. It should be noted that both APRA and Perón did have rural electoral support, but not the support of an organized peasantry equivalent to that found in Venezuela and Mexico.

Figure 5.2 Types of Incorporation

	State versus Party Incorporation							
	State Incorporation		Party Incorporation					
Goals and Agency of Incorporation	Brazil (1930–45)	Chile (1920–31)	Uruguay (1903–16)	Colombia (1930–45)	Peru (1939–45)	Argentina (1943–55)	Mexico (1917–40)	Venezuela (1935–48)
Control of unions exercised by the state	Yes	Yes	Yes	Yes	Yes	Yes	Yes	Yes
Labor support mobilized by a party (or movement that becomes a party)	No[a]	No[b]	Yes	Yes	Yes	Yes	Yes	Yes
Mode and Scope of Incorporation			Types of Party Incorporation					
			Electoral Mobilization by Traditional Party		Labor Populism		Radical Populism	

Figure 5.2 (cont.)

Electoral mobilization	No	No	Yes[c]	Yes	Yes	Yes	Yes	Yes
Union linkage to party or movement	No	No	No	Weak[d]	Yes	Yes	Yes[e]	Yes
Peasantry included	No	No	No	No	No	No[f]	Yes	Yes

[a] Parties were introduced in Brazil shortly before the collapse of the Vargas government in 1945.

[b] A government-sponsored party played a marginal role under Ibáñez in Chile.

[c] Batlle's effort to mobilize workers' electoral support can best be thought of as a successful investment in future support, in that during the incorporation period itself, workers were still strongly anarchist and tended not to vote.

[d] The important role of the Communist Party within the main labor confederation and the ability of the Conservative Party to inhibit union formation by the Liberal labor confederation within certain regions seriously limited the development of links between the Liberal Party and the labor movement in comparison with the cases further to the right in the chart.

[e] The presence of the Communist Party within the main confederation initially diluted the tie between the PRM and the labor movement.

[f] Important benefits were extended to rural wage workers who could be considered part of the modern sector, as well as to some peasant groups. However, in the absence of a substantial peasantry, there was no project of peasant incorporation that was politically equivalent to those in Mexico and Venezuela.

Argentina the relevant organization at the onset of the incorporation period was a movement, not a party.[4]

Second, though the role of political parties is a crucial element in this classification, it must be emphasized that neither this typology nor the related typologies developed for subsequent analytic periods are intended as a substitute for more conventional classifications of parties. Indeed, such classifications may cut across the categories employed here. For instance, the two cases of state incorporation, Brazil and Chile, which both experienced an antiparty, depoliticizing incorporation period, had very different types of parties: those in Chile had deeper roots in society and were far better institutionalized, whereas those in Brazil were shallowly rooted in society and poorly institutionalized. In the two cases of labor populism, Peru and Argentina, the respective labor-based parties—that is, APRA and Peronism—likewise differed profoundly in their degree of institutionalization, both in the incorporation period and subsequently. These other patterns of variation among the parties are recognized in the present analysis and are occasionally introduced as factors that help account for differences between the cases within the country pairs. But it is important to insist that they are different dimensions of differentiation among the countries than those we seek to capture with the analysis of the incorporation periods and their legacies.

The analysis in this chapter is organized around the two well-defined poles evident in Figure 5.2. The cases of state incorporation—Brazil and Chile—exhibited none of the dimensions of mobilization, and the cases of radical populism—Mexico and Venezuela—exhibited all of them. As in the previous chapter, we first examine these two pairs of extreme cases and then turn to the two intermediate pairs.

In the treatment of each country, we first explore the "project from above" (i.e., the basic goals and strategies of the political leaders who initiated the incorporation period) and the "project from below" (i.e., the goals and strategies of the labor movement). For the cases of state incorporation, where labor policies were basically imposed on the labor movement, we then present an overview of the evolution of labor policy. For the cases of party incorporation, where labor policy was not simply imposed, but to a greater extent represented a bargain between the state and the organized labor, we present a more differentiated analysis that focuses on the political exchange with the labor movement, around which the mobilization of labor support was organized; the role of the political party or movement in mediating political support; and finally the conservative opposition that emerged in reaction to the mobilization and progressive policies of the incorporation period.

---

[4] As we emphasize in this and the following chapters, in Argentina Peronism continued to have an ephemeral existence as a party, yet by the definition of that term in the glossary, it unquestionably continued to function as a party.

BRAZIL AND CHILE: DEPOLITICIZATION AND CONTROL

Introduction

The fall of the oligarchic state in Brazil and Chile inaugurated a type of in- corporation that was distinct from those experienced by the other countries in this study. Unique among all the cases, this important historical transition occurred without the political mobilization from above of the working class. Underlying this form of incorporation was a particular coalition: state incorporation was based on a "hybrid" state or on a modus vivendi, imposed through authoritarian rule, between the traditional oligarchy and the newer reformist middle sectors. It was premised on the transformation to a new activist state along with the protection of the essential interests of the tra- ditional oligarchy, despite their loss of political control. Equally important, it avoided the expansion of the political arena and the mobilization of the popular sectors. Accordingly, there was no central role for a populist political party that could attract the loyalty and channel the political participation of the popular sectors. Furthermore—unlike party incorporation, in which unions were strengthened and in which the government often encouraged the spread of collective bargaining and, to some extent, union demand-mak- ing—in state incorporation the government severely constrained the newly legalized and legitimated unions in the sphere of labor-capital relations and conceived of unions more centrally as organizations through which the state could paternalistically grant social welfare benefits. In sum, state incorpora- tion oversaw the creation of a highly corporative system of state-labor inter- mediation. It did not share a basic feature of party incorporation, a kind of bargain, in effect, between the state and labor in which the terms of exchange between the actors reflected differential power relations. Rather than a bar- gain or exchange, the preeminent feature of state incorporation was the at- tempt to address the social question by repressing the preexisting unions and replacing them with highly constrained, state-penetrated labor organizations that would avoid class conflict and instead "harmonize" the interests of cap- ital and labor.

The incorporation period in these two countries must be delineated. In Brazil it is identified as the first presidency of Vargas, from 1930 to 1945; and in Chile, the Alessandri/Ibáñez period, from 1920 to 1931. In combining the Alessandri and Ibáñez presidencies into a single analytic period, it is worth noting that Ibáñez thought of himself as adopting the Alessandri agenda and pursuing the same goals and objectives that had been adopted but proved elusive in the Alessandri regime. This continuity is shown in the way the 1924 coup occurred: in the fact that it did not oust Alessandri from the pres- idency but rather forced the passage of his stalemated legislative program, par- ticularly a new labor law, and in the fact that following his resignation Ales- sandri was brought back to power by the Ibáñez forces. Alessandri himself recognized this continuity. In late 1932, when confronted with the suggestion that "President Ibáñez was in many respects the one who continued the work of your government, and, in large part, the one who realized many of the fundamental [but frustrated] aspirations of your program," Alessandri immediately replied, "Well, of course! It's true, and if we leave aside the arbitrary acts committed by Ibáñez, his program and achievements were nothing but the complement of mine" (Montero 1952:184).[5]

The incorporation period in these two countries is divided into two subperiods. At the outset, from 1930 in Brazil and from 1920 in Chile, the ongoing strength of the oligarchy led, as it did elsewhere, to a period of substantial stalemate and political immobilism of the new civilian government. In Chile, the deadlock was nearly complete, and even the issue of labor reform was not immune, despite the widespread agreement on the need for such reform on the part of the different sectors of the Chilean elite. In Brazil the situation was not so extreme. During the provisional government, Vargas was able to initiate changes and to proceed with a reform program in a number of areas, including new labor legislation. Nevertheless, the opposition remained strong, as was evident most dramatically in the São Paulo revolt of 1932 and in the influence of the liberal opposition on the 1934 constitution. In the following constitutional period, conflict and deadlock accelerated. The period 1930–37, then, was one of struggle and confrontation among the various elite sectors (Baretta and Markoff 1981:20).

That the initial period of attempted reform of the state was one of stalemate, of tentativeness, and largely of failure is not unique to these two countries. They differ, however, in the solution adopted to resolve the political impasse. In Mexico and Venezuela, where the oligarchy was comparatively weak, or in Colombia and Uruguay, where it was divided along long-standing partisan lines, the reform movement sought to pursue a mobilization strategy and enlist the support of the popular sectors to increase its political strength vis-à-vis the opposition. In Brazil and Chile, the strength of the oligarchy—due in part to its clientelistic control of the countryside and thus to the "unavailability" of the peasantry—meant that mobilization would not

[5] Further justification for treating these years as a single analytic period may be found in other quotations from both actors and observers. Referring specifically to labor policy, Olavarría, a family friend of Alessandri and close political associate of Ibáñez in the 1950s, said of the latter's presidency, "Finally making a reality the postulates advocated by don Arturo Alessandri, it had enacted the Labor Code and established the tribunals which must decide on conflicts of workers and employees with their employers" (Olavarría Bravo 1962, vol. 1:299). Also emphasizing the similarities between these two regimes, Alexander cites the comments of a number of observers who have called the Ibáñez regime "a bulwork of the social conquests of Alessandri's" or have pointed out that one "cannot fail to note that, for the most part, [the two regimes] were strikingly similar. . . . The general solutions that they both recommended for the economic and social problems are identical." Commenting on the change from the Alessandri to the Ibáñez regime, one remarked; "Alessandri has given way to Alessandrismo," and of Alessandri and Ibáñez another stated that these "two men . . . appear before history as perfectly complementary in a common and transcendental task" (1977:499–501).

be adequate to overcome oligarchic power. In these cases, the military became a more decisive actor. These military establishments included substantial reform elements that had constituted part of the core of the original "modernizing" opposition to oligarchic rule. Under the leadership of these groups, the military intervened to break the political impasse and to oversee the onset of the introduction of the new state. Thus, in the absence of mobilization as a strategy, the solution to the political stalemate in Brazil and Chile was found in the authoritarian regime backed by the military.

In Brazil, the authoritarian solution to impasse was imposed by Getulio Vargas in the coup of 1937, which initiated the Estado Novo. In Chile, the initiation of the authoritarian regime occurred more gradually through a less decisive process. It began with the 1924 military coup of Ibáñez, Grove, and other military officers, but authoritarian rule was not consolidated until 1927, when Ibáñez formally took over as head of state. The years that followed constituted the second subperiod in which the reform of the state was advanced and new institutions of labor incorporation were consolidated, although in both cases the new framework of state-labor relations had been initiated a few years earlier.

The result of these events in both countries, then, was a military-backed authoritarian regime and a coercively imposed modus vivendi among the dominant sectors. Despite the conflict that preceded and led to the authoritarian solution, no major sectoral cleavage emerged comparable to that which occurred elsewhere. Although the solution to the political impasse was coercive and authoritarian, the continuing power of the oligarchy made some sort of pact with it necessary. The modus vivendi imposed by the authoritarian regime was one in which the reformers, to whom the oligarchy had to cede control of the state, would protect the material interests of the oligarchy. The project of those who came to power was one of social, political, and administrative reform, which would change the nature of the state and displace the hegemony of the oligarchy, but would not attack the economic position of the oligarchy nor leave it without substantial political power. Significantly, in these two countries, there was virtually no popular sector mobilization and hence no populist alliance that would be the basis for such a cleavage. What emerged was a compromise state with a conservative-reformist or conservative-modernizing orientation based on a hybrid elite, which has been widely noted in analyses of both countries (Fausto 1970:113; Moisés 1978:2), and the political exclusion of the popular sectors.

Brazil and Chile, then, are distinctive in that the period of incorporation was characterized not by party-centered popular mobilization but by a politics of accommodation between the oligarchy and the reformers. This was based on at least three factors. The first was the ongoing political and economic importance of the oligarchy. The second was the social solidarity of the newer middle sectors and the oligarchy, a widely noted and important feature, though one that was not unique to Brazil and Chile. This was reflected in family ties and multiple economic activities of individuals that blurred the distinctions among sectors. It was also seen in the aspirations of the middle sectors to assimilate into the oligarchy (a phenomenon that led to the Chilean expression *siútico*, referring to one seeking such assimilation). The third was the overriding fear felt by both sectors of the danger of the rising working class, which, as we have seen, had never been part of the original reform coalition.

Project from Above

The project from above in Brazil and Chile had two broad components. The first was the consolidation of power of reformist groups once the transition from the traditional oligarchic state occurred in 1930 and 1920 respectively. The second was a set of substantive reforms, of which labor incorporation and the establishment of regularized and controlled channels of industrial relations as a response to the social question held a high priority.

Brazil. In Brazil, the period from 1930 to 1937 was one of stalemate and impasse. Vargas, however, began his presidency with substantial success despite important and growing opposition. The period before the new constitution of 1934, particularly before the 1933 elections to the constituent assembly, is one in which the modernizing project of the *tenentes* was begun. Several important innovations reflecting this orientation were made in the context of the impact of the world crash, in the face of which Vargas undertook new economic policies and in the process embarked on a centralization of political power. In 1930 Vargas issued a decree that lodged greater power in the federal government and paved the way for a series of moves that centralized the state and increased its role in economic modernization (Skidmore 1967:33). Notable among these was the transfer of responsibility for policy concerning the coffee sector from the states to the federal governments and the new policy of the federal government to regulate the supply of coffee through government purchases with the goal of promoting the recovery of the export sector (Dean 1969:196–206).

Another early emphasis of the Vargas government was social welfare legislation. Starting immediately in the first year of the new government, a number of decrees provided for retirement pensions for some categories of workers, industrial accident insurance, greater holiday benefits, regulation of working hours and of employment of minors, and benefits related to emergency treatment, and maternity benefits. Though Vargas had more success in promulgating these provisions than Alessandri, his Chilean counterpart, it should be noted that they were not implemented effectively in this earlier period (Flynn 1978:102).

Perhaps the most important measure undertaken by Vargas in this initial period was the establishment in 1930 of a Labor Ministry and the promulgation of a labor law in the next year. The law, which indicated the direction of labor policy during the Estado Novo, provided for the registration and legalization of unions. It also subjected the legalized unions to substantial state control, aimed particularly at eliminating politically oriented unions.

Quite clearly, it sought to replace the existing unions, which were under communist, anarchist, and socialist influence, with an apolitical labor movement made up of unions that would function as "consultative organs of government," substituting a model of class harmony and collaboration for one of class conflict (Harding 1973:71–73).

In the first years of the Vargas period, then, there was tenuous agreement on two issues—the elimination of state corruption and the necessity of addressing the social question by some sort of transformation of the "dangerous classes" organized in politically radical unions into a cooperative labor movement, even if the granting of some benefits were necessary. There was, however, substantial and growing conflict between the *tenentes*, who advocated authoritarian rule to advance their program of modernization, centralization, and structural change, and the liberal constitutionalists, who were strongly represented in Congress and whose power was lodged in the states. They thus resisted the centralizing measures and advocated a liberal democratic regime that would protect their political influence (Skidmore 1967:13; Baretta and Markoff 1981:5–25).

A major reason why Vargas was more successful than Alessandri in avoiding policy immobilism was the greater constitutional discontinuity with the Old Republic that occurred in 1930 in Brazil. In Chile, Alessandri tried to govern, at a comparable stage in 1920, within the framework of the preexisting Parliamentary Republic and confronted overwhelming congressional opposition. Vargas, by contrast, coming to power in the "Revolution of 1930," which constituted a more decisive break with the Old Republic, abolished the legislative bodies at the local, state, and national levels and assumed virtually dictatorial powers (R. Levine 1970:5).

Though congressional opposition was thus initially avoided, conflict erupted in other arenas. This conflict took the form of a series of confrontations, which were most explicit in the regional revolts of 1932 in São Paulo and Pernambuco, in which "Vargas narrowly prevented full-scale civil war" (R. Levine 1970:8). The conflict was also evident in 1934 in the Constituent Assembly over the issue of centralization and the degree of autonomy to be granted to the states. The 1934 constitution, though very much a hybrid document (Skidmore 1967:19), strengthened the hand of the liberal opposition. The general amnesty issued by the Constituent Assembly paved the way for the return of political exiles and strengthened the challenge of the liberal constitutionalists based in the states. The introduction of democratic procedures also weighted the balance in favor of the opposition since the rural oligarchy controlled local voting. Partisans of the *tenente* position, which was thus losing influence, "complained bitterly that Vargas was opening the door for the oligarchy to regain power in the states and thereby erase all revolutionary gains" (R. Levine 1970:11, 14–15).

By the middle of the decade, then, the conflict between Vargas and the opposition was out in the open. The deadlock intensified in 1934–35 as a series of clashes occurred between the minister of war and political figures in the state of Rio Grande do Sul. These battles ended in the resignation of the war minister, a key figure who was to become one of the chief architects of the Estado Novo (Baretta and Markoff 1981:20–21; Flynn 1978:84).

In 1934 the Constituent Assembly elected Vargas president until direct elections were to be called in 1938. From 1934 to 1937, then, Vargas ruled nominally within the framework of the 1934 constitution, frustrated by political immobilism and stalemate. During this period he maneuvered constantly to meet the opposition he faced. This maneuvering took at least two tacks. First, Vargas used the 1935 revolt led by the Communist Party and a manufactured Communist plot in 1937, the Cohen Plan, to get the Congress to grant him emergency powers under a state of siege and to win support for himself and for a repressive, authoritarian solution to the "Bolshevik threat." The second tack was the responsibility primarily of Vargas's allies in the army. The federal army did not have a military monopoly, as the states had armed forces which provided an independent power base to state politicians. In an effort to undercut the power of the opposition as well as to centralize the armed forces, federal army officers played a major role in making key appointments at the state level, isolating the opposition, and bringing the state armed forces under federal control (Flynn 1978:85; Skidmore 1967:26–27). This was a central aspect of the process of outmaneuvering the oligarchy and undermining the opposition to the 1937 coup, which provided the resolution to the political impasse.

The role of the army was critical in the events that led to the imposition of the authoritarian regime in 1937. Factions in the army had been planning an authoritarian solution since the 1935 Communist revolt (Skidmore 1967:29), and Vargas moved increasingly to their position as the conflicts unfolded during the next two years (see Flynn 1978:86). Finally, as the candidates for the 1938 elections seemed to offer the alternatives of either a return to oligarchic rule or mobilization of the lower classes, both of which were unacceptable to Vargas and his allies, the plans for a coup took shape. The coup occurred in November of 1937, and Vargas became president with authoritarian powers for a six-year term under the new Estado Novo constitution, modeled on European corporatism. The regime was the culmination of anti-liberal, corporative social thought that had both military and civilian currents (see Erickson 1977:16–18). Within the former, *tenente* tradition, General Góes Monteiro was a key player in the Estado Novo (Flynn 1978:84); within the latter, Francisco Campos and Oliveira Vianna were the principal authors of the 1937 constitution and some of the regime's major programs. The emphasis was clearly on political demobilization and social control.

An important feature of the Estado Novo was the further elaboration of labor legislation. Building on measures taken earlier in the Vargas presidency, the new Estado Novo legislation culminated in the Consolidation of Labor Laws of 1943. This highly corporative labor project will be discussed below. Beyond labor policy, the new programmatic departures were similar to those that were taken in the other countries as well. They included further centralization of the federal government and a reform of the civil service. In addition the state assumed a more active role in the economy, asserting control over exchange rates and imports, promoting industrialization, and more directly intervening in the economy through public works projects and public investment in such basic industries as railroads and steel. The reform of the state during this period has been called by one analyst "a major watershed" which constituted "the kernel of modern Brazil" (Flynn 1978:96).

In sum, the Revolution of 1930 constituted the end of oligarchic hegemony and the introduction of a new activist state. For present purposes, what is particularly interesting about Vargas's attempt to consolidate his power after 1930 and institute his reform program is the virtual absence of the mobilization of popular support. Some extraordinarily limited and tentative experiments with proto-populist politics were undertaken, but these were rejected in favor of more repressive approaches to social control. The hesitant and limited ventures to win popular support began at the very outset of Vargas's provisional presidency in 1930. In this particularly uncertain political context, Vargas made some effort to support popular policies in Rio de Janeiro as a way to build a political base, but the economic crisis and financial constraints inhibited their implementation. This approach soon gave way in mid-1931 to a period in which *tenente* influence reached its height and in which reforms were undertaken at the same time that popular support was dismissed in favor of the more authoritarian orientation of the now self-designated "dictatorship" (Conniff 1981:90–96).

A second experiment with the mobilization of popular support was undertaken in conjunction with the 1933 elections to the Constituent Assembly and the 1934 congressional elections. Much of this activity once again focused on Rio de Janeiro, where the government interventor, a loyal Vargas supporter and former president of the *tenente*'s Clube 3 de Outubro, sought to put together a multiclass coalition and form political parties that would appeal to the working class, in addition to other sectors (Conniff 1981:98–99, 109–11). Once this electoral period was over, however, support mobilization was not sustained as a political strategy. Indeed it is important to remember how limited it had been. Primarily a phenomenon in Rio de Janeiro, it had not even spread to São Paulo, the other major center of economic activity and working-class concentration. In 1930, Alberto, the newly appointed interventor of São Paulo, spoke out in favor of programs of social assistance and material benefits for workers as an answer to the social question. Yet, French (1985:108–12), who in his study searches for the roots and antecedents of populism in São Paulo, argues that Alberto clearly stopped far short of populist rhetoric or of an attempt to put together a populist coalition, despite the fact that he was trying to maneuver politically vis-à-vis the conservative Paulista establishment. In this, he followed the course of the Vargas government at the federal level and the new minister of labor, Collor. Nor did populism and working-class mobilization emerge as a feature of the 1936 municipal and 1937 presidential electoral campaigns in São Paulo (French 1985:205–9).

Thus, to the extent it existed at all, the strategy of working-class mobilization was an extraordinarily limited feature of state incorporation compared to party incorporation. Though initially Vargas had tentatively tolerated some experimentation with support mobilization, after 1934 repression was definitively chosen as government policy toward the working class (Conniff 1981:142). Vargas himself was not a candidate for the 1938 election, and the coup that aborted those elections also stamped out what popular electoral appeals may have been made in the course of the campaign[6] and ushered in the authoritarian Estado Novo. As we shall see in the next chapter, it was not until the early 1940s, when Vargas was anticipating a change in the structure of the regime, that he began to make a direct appeal to the working class, and in this he was able to refer to the paternalistic benefits that had been part of the Estado Novo's corporative social legislation. It was only at this point, in what can be viewed as a kind of transition to the following period of the aftermath of incorporation, that he began to identify himself as the "Father of the Poor," develop an "ideology" of *trabalhismo*, and finally establish a political party to attract the working-class vote. Nevertheless, as late as 1945, during his last ten months in office, Vargas "demonstrated a continuing lack of nerve and grasp of populist strategy" (Conniff 1981:169).

Chile. In Chile, the political impasse that characterized the parliamentary system and that blocked the reformist agenda was even greater than in Brazil. Not only did the Liberal Alliance, which had elected Alessandri, not have a majority in Congress, but its component parties were not united in their support of Alessandri's reform project. The Radicals, Liberals, and Democrats, which made up the Alliance, were all divided between those favoring the reforms and those who would vote against them (Pike 1963:174). Even after 1924, when congressional elections produced a majority for the parties in the Liberal Alliance, those parties remained sufficiently divided that the situation remained unchanged. As a result of congressional opposition, ministerial instability continued with the rise and fall of eighteen different cabinets in the years 1920–24 (Morris 1966:237), and virtually no legislation was reported out of that body as a result of the nearly total immobilism that ensued upon Alessandri's election.

As in Brazil, the army played a crucial part in providing the way out. In March 1924, Alessandri enlisted the support of the army in overseeing the congressional elections, producing charges by the Conservative opposition of intervention. When the new, pro-Alessandri congressional majority subsequently failed to act on Alessandri's legislative program, the army escalated its involvement (Nunn 1970:44). In September 1924, Majors Carlos Ibáñez and Marmaduke Grove and a number of other junior army officers sat conspicuously in the Senate galleries while that body, unable for four years to pass any significant legislation, debated a raise in its own pay. Apparently aware ahead of time of the officers' plan, Alessandri invited the officers, in effect, to propose a legislative program and promised, in case of further con-

---

[6] John Wirth, in a personal communication, has suggested that the Vargas forces engaged in some experimentation in support mobilization in the 1937 presidential electoral campaign by trucking workers who had been organized in government sponsored unions to political demonstrations.

gressional obstruction, "to close congress and convoke a constituent assembly to rewrite the constitution [and], with the army's support, . . . [to] 'make a new Chile.' "[7] Two days later, the officers, under Ibáñez's leadership, presented a list of demands to Alessandri that included a number of reforms, such as social security laws, income tax legislation, workers' health and accident insurance, and labor legislation. Under this pressure, which included the appointment of General Altamirano to head his cabinet, Alessandri was able to get immediate legislative action on these issues. Included in the new legislation was a labor law that formed the legal basis of unionization and union activity for the next several decades. However, the *junta militar*, which was set up as the political arm of the military, was not disbanded as originally arranged with Alessandri. Seeing this as a threat, Alessandri resigned the presidency. When Congress refused to accept the resignation, the junta closed the Congress.

In the following months, leadership of the junta was taken over by more conservative senior officers. Then, in January 1925, Ibáñez and Grove led a coup and brought back Alessandri to complete his term of office. Under the influence of Ibáñez, who became minister of war, the Congress was not reconvened (Loveman 1979:245). In the next months, Alessandri, backed by the army, was able to launch another period of substantial reform, including reform of the electoral system, the establishment of a central bank, and a new constitution, which strengthened the position of the president at the expense of Parliament.

Though Ibáñez had played a major role in all these events, his political ascendancy was not achieved for another two years. His plans to run for president in 1925 backfired, and for about a year and a half, until Ibáñez was able to get elected in May of 1927, Figueroa served as president of Chile. During that interim, the government took a turn to the right, in what has been called a "Bourbon restoration" in which the Conservatives favored a return to the old constitution and opposed the reforms that had finally been passed with the help of military intervention and pressure (Pike 1963:186). Under these conditions, the executive-legislative and reform-reaction battles were reopened, and a replay of the immobilism of the initial Alessandri period was again under way (Nunn 1970:106, 108). As the political situation deteriorated, Ibáñez managed to get control of the situation, having consolidated his leadership of the reformist group within the army. Thus, "as 1926 drew to a close, Chilean politics, turbulent since 1920 and under the watchful eye of the military since mid-1924, fell into the hands of a military man" (Nunn 1970:118). By the beginning of 1927, Ibáñez was in effective control of the government, appointing the cabinet, pursuing his reform program, and purging and arresting his opponents in the government (Nunn 1970:121–24). When Ibáñez attacked the judicial system, including the Supreme Court, Figueroa resigned. A special presidential election was hastily called for only two weeks later. It was marked by fraud, intimidation, and the imprisonment

[7] Nunn 1967:6. See also Morris (1966:235–36).

of opposition candidate Lafertte of the Communist Party, the only party that did not succumb to the pressure to support Ibáñez (Communist Party of Chile N.D.:46; Pinto Lagarrigue 1972:164–65; Nunn 1970:129). Under these circumstances, Ibáñez was elected with 98 percent of the vote.

As with the Estado Novo in Brazil, the Ibáñez presidency has been seen as laying the groundwork for the emergence of modern Chile. The introduction of the new activist state could be seen in a number of reforms similar to those in Brazil: the professionalization of the civil service and a reform of the educational system, an extensive public works program, and a new state role in the economy, including protective tariffs to promote industrialization and new state programs for extending both industrial and agricultural credit. The 1924 labor legislation was regulated primarily during the Ibáñez presidency, and in 1931 a new labor code consolidated and expanded the earlier legislation (Morris 1966:249–50). Pike (1963:188) has said of this modernizing period, "The institutional structure that has governed Chile down to the present day was fashioned by Ibáñez between 1927 and 1931;" similarly Bray (1964:86 n. 2), writing in the early 1960s, has commented, "The Ibáñez dictatorship (1927–1931) was the most creative administration of the 20th century from the standpoint of recasting government agencies and initiating government programs."

Project from Below

In contrast to party incorporation, which presented labor with a fundamental question of tactics as reformist political leaders sought an alliance with the working class, in the cases of state incorporation, in Brazil and Chile, the existing labor movement was given much less opportunity to cooperate or collaborate. Labor policy was much more a top-down affair designed to produce state-controlled unionism, and the repression of existing leadership and unionism was a central component of this policy. The main question confronting preexisting labor groups was how to react to the new government and the new labor law providing for union registration. On the one hand, registration implied submission to the state control embodied in the new law. On the other hand, registration also meant the extension of certain organizational benefits, and its rejection would tend to leave the old union movement sidelined and unable to compete in the face of active government efforts to organize the working class into "legal" unions. In the end in both countries, however this dilemma was resolved, preexisting unions did not have the power to withstand government repression.

As mentioned above, both Brazil and Chile experienced an initial period in which a reformist civilian government attempted to consolidate power before the military-backed authoritarian solution was worked out, that is, before the Vargas coup of 1937 that initiated the Estado Novo and before Ibáñez assumed power in 1927. It is during this initial period that the labor movement had to adopt some policy toward the new reformist governments, particularly as they were maneuvering to consolidate power. An important difference between the countries was that in Chile labor policy was immobilized in a way that was not the case in Brazil, so that the issue of what stance to take in the face of government attempts to establish a state-controlled and state-penetrated movement was posed immediately in Brazil, but not in Chile. The result was that in Brazil the existing labor movement took a somewhat more consistent oppositionist position during this phase. It did this despite the greater dominance of communist over anarchist influence and despite the initiation in 1935 of the popular front policy of international Communism, which of course represented a softening of the emphasis on class conflict in favor of greater collaboration. In Chile, by contrast, after heated debate the FOCh finally decided to work within the new legal framework. Whatever the differences, this phase ended in both countries with the imposition of authoritarian rule. The new phase saw a definitive defeat, through repression, of the dominant communist and anarcho-syndicalist influence, that is, of the most important of the existing labor organizations, and the stage was thus set for the policy of establishing a docile, controlled union movement.

Chile. In Chile the events of 1920–27 posed for labor the fundamental question of whether to support and cooperate with a government that might have the potential to be forthcoming with reforms and the degree to which it made sense to take advantage of political openings and to enter the political arena. During its combative period from 1917 to 1920, organized labor was able to present a united front, as seen in the formation of the AOAN, which organized the protests against the high cost of food. After 1920, however, and particularly as the FOCh became increasingly dominated by the POS and tied to international Communism, internal rivalries became more salient (DeShazo 1983:158). When Alessandri came to power, therefore, the labor movement was deeply divided and the different factions took distinct positions toward his government. The anarcho-syndicalists held their traditional position and rejected political participation and cooperation with the government. The POS and the FOCh were more open to cooperation with the government and followed a political strategy of coalition building.

The first half of 1921—the outset of Alessandri's presidency after the period of FOCh support when the electoral outcome had gone to the tribunal (see Chapter 4)—was a relatively favorable period for labor, despite the growing divisions within the movement. At this early phase, the Communist-aligned wing of labor cooperated with the new government. In many ways, labor was still at the peak of its strength, the FOCh had an impressive capacity for mobilization, and Alessandri, from a paternalistic perspective (DeShazo 1983:186–87), looked upon labor with more favor than any past president. In 1917, in reaction to the increase in strikes that began in that year, the government had established a procedure for mediating strikes; and in the first months of his presidency, Alessandri tended to use that procedure to intervene in labor disputes in a way that benefited labor (DeShazo 1983:186). During these initial months, the FOCh supported Alessandri, not only in exchange for his role in labor disputes but, DeShazo (1983:186) argues, more importantly in exchange for Alessandri's political support of the POS. More specifically, Morris has suggested that during these months there was a political understanding between Alessandri and the POS according to which the support of Recabarren (the leader of both the FOCh and the POS) was forthcoming in exchange for Alessandri's support of POS congressional candidates in the 1921 election (Morris 1966:107–8; Lafertte 1961:154). When those elections were held in March, Recabarren and Cruz were both elected to the Chamber of Deputies.

This rapprochement between Alessandri and the FOCh did not last long. By May 1921, in response to growing alarm at working-class mobilization, Alessandri began opposing workers when they struck and "by the end of 1921, his government began using the typical tools of repression, including police raids, searches, arrests, and violence, to subjugate a labor movement which refused to respect the will of its 'father.' " At the same time, newly organized employers began a "counteroffensive" to reverse the gains that labor had won in the previous three years (DeShazo 1983:188). They used lockouts and, in the context of deteriorating economic conditions, layoffs of union members to weaken unions, which no longer found a friend in the government. During the next two years, the unions were weakened and on the defensive, strikes declined, and, particularly following the FOCh's joining the Red International of Labor Unions, the labor movement was badly divided, failing in an attempt to achieve some unity in the face of this counteroffensive (DeShazo 1983:208).

In 1924, labor's position temporarily improved. Two factors contributed to this change. The first was an economic upturn that produced both increased employment and soaring prices, a combination favorable to worker militance. The result was a growth in the number of unions and in union membership and a new strike wave that was largely led by the anarcho-syndicalists in the urban areas of the central part of the country (DeShazo 1983:215). The second factor was political. The coup of 1924 presented labor with two new facts: the labor law that was passed as the first order of business and the overtures to the working class that the government once again seemed to be making. Labor's reaction mirrored that of 1921. The anarcho-syndicalists rejected both the labor law and the political overtures; the FOCh vacillated with respect to both. After much discussion and division, the FOCh finally took the controversial decision of accepting the labor law, arguing that it should "use all the social legislation of the capitalist state to fight capitalism itself" (cited in Morris 1966:246). The debate within the FOCh showed that while the constraints embodied in the law were evident, a number of inducements it contained were clearly attractive, as they would facilitate further organization and the unionization of new sectors and allow unions to receive a state-administered financial subsidy derived from the profit-sharing provision.

The experience of the FOCh over the next few years, however, did not immediately bear out this optimistic assessment, as important provisions of the law that offered protection to unions were not implemented until the end of the decade, and protection against discharge for union officers or candidates came only in the 1931 codification (Morris 1966:249–50). In the absence of regulation, the success of union activities was largely dependent on government support or opposition. In practice, FOCh's attempts to organize legal unions met with little success. With some exceptions, particularly in the south, the overall reaction of employers "was negative and was expressed in open warfare against union organizers, as in the nitrate *pampa*, or in more subtle moves to undercut organizing campaigns" (Morris 1966:249). In the nitrate area, where FOCh was particularly strong, its attempts to organize legal unions were thwarted by employers who fired union members and who could count on the cooperation of the police to arrest union leaders (Morris 1966:251).

With respect to the political overtures made by the government to the labor movement in 1924–25, the FOCh position vacillated. Initially somewhat receptive to the new junta that came to power in 1924, the FOCh gradually increased its distance from the government as the junta was taken over by senior officers and as the FOCh took on a less reformist coloration. By the turn of the new year, the FOCh had moved into a clearer oppositionist stance and sought to establish a united opposition front with the white collar workers union (UECh), which had recently been formed. However, within a week, the coup of January 1925 posed the question of political cooperation all over again, and both the FOCh and the UECh decided to support Ibáñez, in the context of a power vacuum in which the new junta looked to working-class support to help ward off a countercoup from the right (DeShazo 1983:222).

For a brief period, organized labor seemed to be in a position of substantial political strength. In many ways this represents a high point of labor activation, with many strikes and often favorable responses to labor demands from the junta. Indicative of the resurgence of labor activity was the dramatic increase in union membership—including both the FOCh, which doubled its dues-paying membership between 1923 and 1925, and the IWW—and a corresponding increase in strikes, from a low of 19 in 1922 to an unprecedented 114 in 1925 (DeShazo 1983:222; Bergquist 1986:64). The strike wave continued to gather momentum until May and June, provoking tremendous fear of social revolution within the elite. In late May, with Alessandri again in the presidency but with Ibáñez exercising growing influence from a ministerial post, the government renewed a policy of repression. The new policy was initiated in the nitrate fields of the north and included widespread arrests and the killing of 600 to 800 workers in La Coruña nitrate camps. The repression brought the strike wave to a halt.

During 1920–24, the FOCh, following the POS (which became the Communist Party in 1922), had emphasized coalition-building with other groups and parties at the expense of labor militance. DeShazo (1983:214, 218, 227–28) asserts that it played little role in the 1924–25 strike wave and that it had a muted reaction to the renewed repression in the middle of 1925 in order not to jeopardize its participation in the constitutional convention and electoral politics. In the presidential elections held in October, the Communist Party, UECh, and the mutualists formed a united front and chose Dr. José Santos Salas to run for president. Santos Salas did extremely well, winning almost 30 percent of the vote. The electoral front was renewed for the congressional elections the following month with the formation of an electoral pact by the Communist and Democratic parties and USRACh, a new organization of white collar groups and the railroad workers. In these elections the communists elected five deputies and, for the first time, a senator; and the USRACh elected four deputies. DeShazo (1983:233) suggests that the Communist Party's success was dependent upon USRACh support, and when this coalition fell apart, the problem of having neglected its working-class base in favor of coalition-building with white collar groups became clear.

Through all of the twists and turns, coups and countercoups, overtures and repression of the first half of the 1920s, organized labor was unable to pursue a strategy with which it could defend itself. By the end of 1925, the internal divisions within the labor movement, another economic downturn, and a weak political position once again meant that the labor movement could not prevent a renewed period of repression, which culminated in the policies of Ibáñez after he came to power in 1927, policies that effectively eliminated the existing independent labor movement for the period to 1931.

Brazil. On the eve of the Revolution of 1930, anarcho-syndicalist influence within the Brazilian labor movement had declined and was replaced by communist influence, though "yellow" or company unions continued to constitute a major segment. The response to the new government by the communists specifically and by labor more generally was apparently less ambivalent and less cooperative than that of the FOCh and the POS in Chile. The establishment of the new Labor Ministry and the new labor law were seen as instruments to control the labor movement and rid it of militant and communist leadership, and labor unions apparently did not accept the law or seek registration under its terms (Harding 1973:78, 90).

Perhaps the more clear-cut rejection and noncooperative attitude of Brazilian labor compared to its Chilean counterpart is due to the more immediate initiation of the new labor policy and the new labor law. In Chile the law was delayed for four years and its implementation even longer, while the political situation and the possible role of labor as a political resource was in flux. In Brazil, by contrast, the Labor Ministry was created in the same month Vargas came to power and the labor law followed within a few months. At a time comparable to that in which the Chilean Communist Party and the FOCh were debating the issue of the proper response, the result of the new policy in Brazil was an immediate attack by the government on the existing labor movement, including not only the repression of strikes, which occurred as well in Chile, but also a move against the unions and the existing leadership. Though before 1930 there was legislation that dealt specifically with unions as organizations, unions had been registered with the government according to provisions laid down in the civil code. This registration was canceled by the ministry, supposedly so that the unions could apply for registration under the terms of the new law the following year. In the meantime, however, the government carried out a campaign of harassment in which some Communist leaders were imprisoned or deported and, though not explicitly outlawed, Communist, Socialist, and anarchist groups were not "allowed to be active" (Harding 1973:81). The government harassed unions and purged their leadership by such tactics as splitting unions and manipulating elections. Furthermore, the new union law attempted to depoliticize the labor movement and would not recognize unions that were politically oriented or politically active, thus excluding from recognition the Communist, anarchist, and Socialist unions (Harding 1973:71). Finally, a new "Law of Two-Thirds," which limited the hiring of immigrants, clearly had implications for the composition of union membership, the nature of the leadership, and the political orientation of the unions.

The policy of noncooperation and of refusing union registration adopted by many unions and the Communist Party was ineffective in the face of this assault by the government and in the face of its move to create new, nonpolitical, cooperative, and government-controlled unions. As a result of the twin tactics of noncooperation on the part of the independent unions and of government harassment and nonrecognition, most of the communist and independent leaders lost control of their unions (Harding 1973:111).

The new constitution of 1934 ushered in a period of somewhat greater freedom in the labor movement with its provision for plural unionism, which allowed for the recognition of any union with a third of the workers. In the new, more open atmosphere, the Communist Party changed tactics and tried to win control of recognized unions, but though it had received substantial support among workers, it had not by 1935 won control of many important unions (Harding 1973:112). At the same time, in May 1935 the Communist Party moved to form the Confederação Sindical Unitária do Brasil with the aim of uniting unions independent of government control (Chilcote 1974:149).

The more tolerant period in union affairs quickly came to a halt. Brazilian politics seemed to be undergoing a process of radicalization and polarization as the communist-sponsored popular front organization, the National Liberation Alliance, grew substantially, uniting elements of the middle class with the more independent, militant workers on the left and as *Integralismo* grew as a fascist response to the effects of the world depression (Skidmore 1967:20–21). Under the terms of a new National Security Law, the Confederação was outlawed and shortly thereafter, the ANL was also closed and driven underground (Chilcote 1974:39–40). The following November, the Communist Party, under the influence of the faction that had rejected the popular front policy, carried out an armed revolt against the government (Skidmore 1967:22–23). Though labor was taken by surprise and played no role in the rebellion, which was easily put down by the government, the government used the opportunity to move openly against the left in the labor movement. Under the state of siege which ensued, the government closed many unions to eliminate the independent leadership (Carone 1973:220). The leaders of the remaining unions were by and large chosen by the Labor Ministry (Harding 1973:121).

Under the Estado Novo the system of state control through coercive, cooptive, and legal means was tightened and institutionalized in the imposition of a highly elaborated corporative structure. The reaction of labor was not completely passive, and there is evidence of some demonstrations, protests, and attempts to form labor organizations outside of governmental control (Carone 1973:124–26). However, given the coercive resources of the state through both the police and the legal system, these never amounted to much. As in Chile, then, the "high point" of the period of incorporation, the period of the Estado Novo in Brazil, was one in which independent unions within the labor movement were coercively eliminated and the question of labor's ultimate acceptance or rejection of the new labor policy and of the terms of incorporation was no longer relevant.

Labor Policy

The nature of labor incorporation reflected the accommodationist style of politics and was based on a fairly high degree of elite consensus, despite some opposition from employers. This consensus was seen most dramatically in the case of Chile, where the Conservative Party had proposed labor legislation prior to Alessandri's 1920 victory and where in fact many elements of the Conservative project, as well as the Liberal project, were largely incorporated into the 1924 labor law. In both countries the consensus about popular sector incorporation was based on three fundamental points. The first was that there would be a major effort on the part of the state to address the problem of the "dangerous classes" and to resolve the "social question" which working class militance had put on the agenda. This "question" was how to address the radicalization or potential radicalization of the working class—how to respond to the emergence of the working class as an economic and potentially a political actor. The second point of consensus was that there would be no parallel initiatives in the countryside. There would be no land reform or legalization of rural unions and the preexisting pattern of social relations—and hence the political base of the oligarchy—would remain untouched.

The third point of consensus was not to expand the arena of political conflict or to mobilize popular support. Neither Vargas nor Ibáñez depended on active popular support as did, for example, Cárdenas or Perón. In Brazil Vargas made no real attempt to mobilize the working class as a support group. On the contrary, a fundamental aim of his labor policy was to depoliticize the working class and divorce or isolate unions from political parties and from political activities. During the Estado Novo, Vargas did not organize a political party that would attract and channel worker support until the last year of his presidency. At that point, he was anticipating the change to a more open, democratic republic, and these events belong to another analytic period. Ibáñez did establish a party to organize blue and white collar workers. This party, however, was not a central part of the political dynamics of the period. Ibáñez did not, in fact, depend on popular support, he did not pay much attention to the party or give it much emphasis, and the party never succeeded in attracting much support. Thus, in both countries, the governments of the incorporation period left a political vacuum within the working class.

The style or type of labor incorporation that occurred in Brazil and Chile, then, is what we have labeled state incorporation. In contrast to party incorporation, it involved little or no political mobilization of the working class but rather emphasized its depoliticization. It was primarily a response to the social question posed by the challenge of a newly activated militant labor movement, in which the goal was to deradicalize the union movement by providing a legal framework and alternative union structures that would "harmonize" class relations, substituting class collaboration for class conflict (Harding 1973:73–74). This type of incorporation had perhaps three components: first, the repression of existing leftist-oriented unions; second, a paternalistic extension of certain benefits to workers to eliminate some of the underlying causes of worker protest; and third, the promotion of an alternative form of legalized state-controlled and state-sponsored unionism. Hence, during the course of the Vargas period in Brazil and rather more gradually in the Ibáñez and post-Ibáñez years in Chile, these two countries introduced highly constraining corporative laws. Legal provisions were elaborated that severely limited unions' right to strike and to pursue economic and political goals, placing more constraints on union organization, activity, and leadership than any other labor law in Latin America.

Brazil.   In Brazil, as we have seen, the years prior to the 1930 Revolution were characterized by a lull in working-class activity and protest. Nevertheless, there is no doubt that the social question was prominent in the minds of those who were responsible for labor policy during the Vargas years. The memory of the revolutionary general strikes led by the anarchists in the 1916–19 period lingered, and the decline of anarchist influence in the 1920s was hardly reassuring, as it was replaced by communist influence after the party was founded in 1922. Fearing revolution, political leaders sought to undertake a series of preemptive reforms. As the governor of Minas Gerais expressed it in 1930, "Let us make a revolution before the people do" (Harding 1973:48, 51). The response was quick in coming; one of the early acts of the new government was the labor law of 1931.

But the social question would be posed even more dramatically within a few years. In the brief period of political liberalism in 1934–35, a major strike wave occurred as workers protested soaring inflation, and work stoppages and social unrest occurred throughout the country, in rural areas as well as the major cities, particularly in the northeast (R. Levine 1980:61). Intense political polarization took place with the mobilization of right-wing Integralists on the one side and the communists and a series of new leftist groups and parties on the other (Carone 1973:408). Even foreign observers were alarmed and the U.S. military attache characterized the city of São Paulo as a powderkeg (R. Levine 1980:60). The culmination of this activity was the military revolt attempted by the Communist Party in 1935. At the onset of the Estado Novo in 1937, then, a solution to the social question seemed urgent.

The response of the Estado Novo was the most full-blown system of corporatism in Latin America. The orientation toward elitism and authoritarianism in the context of nationalist regeneration and modernization was clearly evident. It drew quite explicitly on Italian Fascism, sharing its disenchantment with the political squabbles and corruption of parliamentary democracy and substituting instead a corporate state on the Italian model. According to Erickson (1977:17):

> The founders of the Estado Novo believed that the liberal state could not function in modern industrial society and that the only way to prevent its degeneration into a Communist regime was to establish a corporative state. Francisco Campos, Vargas' minister of justice and author of the Constitution of 1937, stated that the advent of the masses into modern politics posed problems of such magnitude that the liberal states were forced to remove the most important issues from the realm of legitimate discussion.

The solution, then, was a system of preemptive, co-optive, "artificial" corporatism (Schmitter 1971:112) with heavy doses of state control of the labor movement combined with the extension of material and welfare benefits to workers. As Vargas said:

> Political discipline must be based on social justice supporting labor and the laborer so that he is not considered a negative value, an outcast from public life, hostile or indifferent to the society in which he lives. Only in this manner can a cohesive national nucleus be constituted, capable of resisting disorder and the seeds of disintegration. (cited in Ianni 1970:90)

The first element of labor policy of the Vargas government was repression of the existing, leftist unions and their leaders. The most intense phase of violent repression took place from 1930 to 1935. During this period, controls through the labor laws were supplemented by police raids of union headquarters and the jailing of union leaders. In the aftermath of the 1935 communist revolt, the independent labor movement was effectively eliminated.

With the onset of the Estado Novo, a new phase was begun in which labor policy to control the working class was centered in the further elaboration of labor law and the establishment of an organized labor movement subject to the control and direction of the Ministry of Labor. Perhaps because Brazil represents the purest form of corporatism in Latin America and because it borrowed most extensively and directly from European models, the characteristics of the system have been explored in detail in the literature.[8] Only the broad outlines need be presented here.

---

[8] See, for example, Erickson (1977), Mericle (1977), Harding (1973), Schmitter (1971), L. M. Rodrigues (1969), J. A. Rodrigues (1968), and M. Filho (1952).

Labor policy in the Estado Novo sought to establish a system in which the working class would be organized into a labor movement that replaced class conflict with industrial peace and the national interest. Unions were conceived primarily as social service organizations that would distribute benefits to workers and generally contribute to a collaborative social order. These goals were clearly spelled out in labor legislation, and the statutes of all unions were required to contain the "assurance that the association will act as an organ of collaboration with the public authorities and other associations with a view to furthering social solidarity and to the subordination of economic or professional interests to the national interest" (cited in Erickson 1977:35). In accordance with this view of unions, the provision of social welfare, initially begun in the earlier part of the decade, was extended under the Estado Novo, most importantly perhaps the program of social security.

By the end of the Estado Novo, labor law had established a detailed *enquadramento* (framing) of organized labor, that is, a state-defined structure setting out what unions could be formed and subjecting them to a number of rules and regulations. The provision for state recognition and registration of unions was accompanied by a series of requirements that afforded the state substantial control, including submission to the state of membership lists and by-laws. In addition, the laws contained a master plan that defined each union's jurisdiction. At the base level of the local union, these jurisdictions grouped together workers in similar crafts or industry in a local, usually municipal, geographical area. Only one union could be recognized within a single jurisdiction. Membership in that union was not compulsory, but strong inducements to join were present in the social welfare benefits distributed through unions and in the obligatory syndical tax, which was levied on all workers in the jurisdiction whether or not they were members.

In the state's organizational chart of the labor movement, no union could have direct links with others. Rather, any links had to be indirect, through the second organizational level, the federation. The federation was set up to embrace unions in the same craft or industry on a state-wide basis. At the highest level, federations were grouped by economic sector into seven different nonagricultural confederations at the national level. This system was not capped by a single confederation through which the Brazilian labor movement could achieve national unity.

In addition to defining in detail the structure of the labor movement, the state imposed a number of additional controls. The state was given the right to "intervene" a union, that is, to seize its headquarters, take charge of its funds, and install a new leadership. Even the threat of intervention became a powerful tool for achieving compliance with state goals (Mericle 1977:309). The state was also given the right to monitor union activity closely, as the law obliged each union to submit daily records of all union transactions and expenditures. The dependence of unions on the state for their finances was another area of state control. The syndical tax was established by which the state collected a union tax to be distributed among labor unions at the different organizational levels. Data from a later period suggest that this dependence was enormous—nearly total for the federations and confederations, and between a half and nearly three quarters for unions, which also were permitted to collect dues (Schmitter 1971:121). This financial mechanism of control was not limited to the subtle one of fear of withholding of funds: the law specified the activities for which this syndical tax could be spent. Expenditures for a whole set of social welfare activities were approved; use of the tax for strike benefits and other militant activities were not (Mericle 1977:316).

The law gave the Ministry of Labor substantial control over the leadership selection within the union movement. In addition to the more usual set of requirements concerning nationality, age, and occupational status, the law provided for an "ideological oath" by which leaders were required to provide "proof that they do not profess ideologies incompatible with the institutions and interest of the nation" (cited in Schmitter 1971:116). Furthermore, the law established election procedures that gave the Ministry of Labor great influence in the outcome. At the union level, the ministry was given the power to choose the union directorate, which in turn chose the union officers. The result, according to Dias (1962:196), was the imposition of a leadership most of which had no previous connection with the union. At the federation level, a different mechanism was put in place. Each union in a federation was granted one vote, regardless of size. Given the pattern of state-induced union formation, the ministry could easily muster the votes to overwhelm the larger or more radical unions. The means for the perpetuation of federation leadership acceptable to the state was found in the federation's leverage over member unions deriving from their dependence on federation funding. The same set of controls operated at the level of the confederation, which had more extensive and direct ties with the government. The reliability of the leadership at this level was particularly important precisely because of this special relationship with the state: "the confederations are essentially organs of the government's economic policy" (Oliveira Vianna, cited in Schmitter 1971:118). Through all of these means plus the use of extensive co-optation through the offer of jobs and material benefits, the government was so successful in installing a leadership that looked to the Labor Ministry and state, rather than to its grassroots, that a new term *pelego* was coined to refer to this new type of leader within the labor movement.

In emphasizing the role of unions as social welfare agencies, the law severely limited their activities with respect to wage-setting and collective bargaining and their right to strike, which, during the Estado Novo was abrogated altogether, and in subsequent years limited to use in conjunction with an employer's noncompliance with a collective agreement. A three-tiered labor court system was established to resolve grievances and collective disputes. During the Estado Novo, very few collective agreements were actually signed, and in 1943 a decree suspended collective bargaining for the duration of the war (Harding 1973:134). Instead, a pattern was established in which wage-setting was determined primarily by changes in the minimum wage, instituted in 1940, in which wages in different categories were set in terms of multiples of the minimum wages (Schmitter 1971:122–23). All contracts that were signed had to be submitted to the labor ministry or the labor courts for approval. All these provisions added to an extraordinarily high level of constraints on unions precisely in those areas that most basically concerned workers.

The orientation of the Vargas legislation, then, was to replace a potentially independent, radical, class-conscious, militant working class with a viable, co-opted organized labor movement that was dependent on and controlled by the state. Estimates of the size of the labor movement brought under government control vary. Emphasizing the shortcomings of available statistics, J. A. Rodrigues (1968:127–30) has done a careful study of the growth of the labor movement of the period. In terms of membership, he records a 2.6-fold increase between 1930 and 1945, from 180,000 to 475,000.[9]

This rise in membership represented an increase in the percent of industrial laborers who were unionized from about 20 percent in the 1930–34 period to about 25 percent in 1939, well before the end of the Vargas government. Finally, the government created many new unions among the previously nonunionized in the secondary cities of the country to counterbalance those in São Paulo and Rio de Janeiro, where the workers were more politicized and militant and had a longer tradition of trade-union struggle. This tactic of the government can be seen in the change in percentage of unions located in the São Paulo/Rio de Janeiro area. In 1934 these represented 44 percent of the unions, whereas by 1939 that percent was reduced by half.

Chile.   In Chile, fear of the threat posed by the working class was very high, and the salience of the social question was probably the greatest of the countries under consideration. The strike wave that began in 1917 was a convincing indication to both the traditional oligarchy and the middle sectors that something had to be done.

The response to working-class activation in Chile can be seen as a combination of two kinds of reaction that came together in the 1920s. The first was Conservative social thought, which in part drew its inspiration from the pronouncements of the Catholic Church, such as the papel encyclical Rerum Novarum. Indeed, it was the Conservative Party, not the Liberal Alliance, that was the first in Chile to formally advance a solution to the social question, and in 1919, before the election of Alessandri, the Conservatives introduced a labor project that was as comprehensive and "advanced" in terms of worker welfare and social thinking as the subsequent Liberal project. The approach was a paternalistic one that sought to preserve social order and patterns of stratification (Pike 1963:171, 175, 177). Alessandri shared much of the perspective of the Conservative project. Repression, he thought, would "sooner or later . . . turn [unions] into permanent conspirators against social and public order" (cited in S. Valenzuela 1976:141). His project sought "only a few

[9] Others, including even the Communists, report a lower union membership of 100,000 in 1930 (Pinheiro 1977:175–76; Dulles 1973:377). Assuming the same figure for 1945, this lower membership in 1930 would mean a larger increase over the period.

changes in order to preserve a society similar to the nineteenth-century model," some "mild palliatives" (Pike 1963:171, 177) that would be offered, in his words, "not only for reasons of humanity, but for considerations of economic expedience and for conserving the social order" (cited in Pike 1963:171). There was then, even before 1920, substantial consensus among the country's parties on the need for some sort of pre-emptive, paternalistic labor reform.

The second strand of labor policy sought a solution to the social question as part of a larger project of economic, political, and social modernization. Inspiration for this project on the part of many of its advocates came from the concurrent experiments of Spanish and Italian fascism. While Alessandri may be identified with the larger modernization project, there is no evidence that he identified with fascism. However, the reformist elements within the army, Ibáñez, Grove, and their colleagues, clearly did. Like the *tenentes* in Brazil they were impressed by its solution both to the social question and to the problem of parliamentary corruption and the ineffectiveness of liberal democracy (Nunn 1970:52; Loveman 1979:250).

The labor laws, which were finally passed under military pressure in 1924, were quite literally a combination of the Conservative and Liberal Alliance projects: with the inability of either one to garner a majority, the compromise worked out in the haste imposed by the military was essentially the establishment of a dualistic system of union structures that drew on both projects. The Conservative view was more oriented toward direct control. It proposed a union structure based on plant unions, which workers would be strongly encouraged to join. Such unions were favored because they were viewed as more amenable to state or employer control. It also proposed compulsory conciliation and arbitration as a further mechanism for control and the elimination of industrial conflict and worker protest (Morris 1966:130–31, 237, 269). The Liberal project advocated craft unions and voluntary conciliation, yet it too favored a high level of constraints and state regulation of union activities.

In the end, the package of laws that finally passed made the plant union compulsory, while the craft union was sanctioned but made voluntary, thus favoring the former but permitting dual membership. Though craft unions were granted the right to represent members, bargain, and sign collective contracts, in practice these unions were often largely ignored by employers in cases of dual membership (Alexander 1962a:288). The less favorable position of craft unions was also evident in their exclusion from the subsidy based on profit-sharing enjoyed by plant unions. The laws also regulated procedures concerning collective bargaining, making conciliation compulsory and regulating in detail the use of the strike. Both the formation of unions and the use of the strike among state employees was forbidden. The laws also regulated union expenditures and union leadership and required that Labor Ministry representatives attend union meetings concerning any change in statute or any leadership election and that they approve all expenditures of unions, which were required to submit both proposed budgets and annual reports (Alexander 1962a:272–73). In the end, the Conservative project was predominant in the final laws, and a system of industrial relations was established that clearly favored employers (Morris 1966:181, 269) and granted broad oversight powers to the government.

In addition to the laws that provided for union registration and regulation, for conciliation and arbitration machinery, and for regulation of the use of the strike, other laws addressed issues of social welfare. These included workman's compensation and the establishment of a system of compulsory social security, covering sickness, disability, and old age (Alexander 1950:74). Also included in the laws was a provision for profit-sharing, which was, as always, double-edged and was viewed explicitly by social thinkers of the day as a control mechanism that would increase incentive and productivity and make workers more compliant with decisions that they would otherwise be more likely to oppose (Morris 1966:139). Finally, the laws, in their treatment of unions, made a distinction between blue-collar and white-collar unions, clearly favoring the latter. This duality became a permanent and important component of labor politics in Chile.

The labor reform, then, was "not undertake[n] . . . out of benevolence or a desire to win the support of the labor movement. . . . [Rather it] was seen as a means to control the labor movement, to subordinate it to the state, and to cleanse it of leftists and Marxists" (Loveman 1979:250). We have seen how the law did not protect unions in the 1924–27 period. Quite the contrary, unions remained vulnerable to the opposition of employers, to the whims of political expediency, and to the coercive arm of the state. After Ibáñez became president in 1927, labor policy became a combination of heightened repression of Marxist and anarchist unions and an attempt to use the labor law to develop a docile, loyal union movement largely based on mutual aid societies. This later effort, however, was only just under way when Ibáñez was overthrown.

From the beginning of 1927, Ibáñez embarked on a reinvigorated antileft campaign. This intensified repression began in the months prior to his election, when he was minister of interior and vice president. Declaring that "there will be in Chile neither Communism nor Anarchism," he banned the Communist Party and unleashed a wave of raids on union headquarters. Within a short time, all major labor leaders as well as many party leaders and activists had "been arrested, gone into hiding, or fled the country" (DeShazo 1983:241–42).

With the elimination of free unions, labor policy turned to a second goal: the establishment of a state-sponsored, state-controlled labor movement. Though this effort never went as far as the parallel attempt in Brazil, it is worth noting that "Ibáñez was one of the first Latin American presidents to turn from opposing labor organizations to harnessing them through state sponsored unionization" (Drake 1978:59). Ibáñez established a legal foundation for this undertaking through the elaboration of additional labor law. A 1928 decree granted the government broad powers of control and supervision of unions, including the right of government officials to preside over union meetings. It set out restrictions on union membership and leadership, barring anyone whom the authorities considered "harmful to the social order." Limiting legal unions to those based on mutual collaboration of labor and capital, the law decreed that "all organizations whose procedures handicap discipline and order in work will be considered contrary to the spirit and standard of the law" (cited in Morris 1966:255). Finally, in 1931, the various labor laws were codified, and while the 1924 laws continued to form the basis of the industrial relations system, more corporative provisions were included in the codification, defining an even larger regulatory and overseer role for the state.

With the further elaboration of law enabling the government to be active in union affairs and with the decline of the FOCh through repression, Ibáñez took a series of initiatives to create his own union movement. A good history of this period is lacking, but what literature is available suggests that legal unions under cooperative leadership were established and a series of alternative labor confederations were founded as the Ibáñez government sought to embrace all tendencies within a state controlled labor movement. The state-sponsored union movement that Ibáñez sought to establish was based primarily on two kinds of unions. The first was the existing mutual aid societies. These associations, which were grouped in the Workers Social Congress, were favored by Ibáñez because of their moderate leadership and demands. Yet, they comprised a weak foundation, especially after the establishment of social security, which largely deprived the mutualist orientation of its raison d'etre. The second was white collar unions. These were federated in the Unión de Empleados de Chile.

In addition, the government sought to make inroads in areas of communist and anarchist strength. In 1927, the government sponsored the Vanguardia Nacional de Obreros y Empleados (National Vanguard of Blue- and White-Collar Workers) in an attempt "to go beyond repression and organize the workers into state-managed unions" (Monteón 1982:164). The Vanguardia was based on a group that split from the Communist Party (Barría 1972:61). The following year the Confederation of Plant and Craft Unions was founded and included sectors in which anarchists had been strong (Poblete 1945:32–33).

Finally, in 1929, the CRAC (Republican Confederation for Civic Action of Blue- and White-Collar Workers) was founded. Part workers' confederation, part political party, it was established as the vehicle to direct working-class activity into acceptable channels and to demonstrate working-class support for the government. In this last regard, the CRAC was "the closest thing to an Ibañista party that existed" (Nunn 1970:156). However, since the mobilization of labor support never became an important feature of the Ibáñez period, Ibáñez never saw the CRAC as a central institutional component of his government and was quite indifferent to it (Villalobos et al. 1976:923).

It is difficult to assess the extent to which Ibáñez actually succeeded in organizing the Chilean working class into legal, state-sponsored unions. Some analysts seem to think state-led unionization under Ibáñez was rather substantial; others, that it never amounted to much. Data available in stan-

dard sources are contradictory. The number of unions ranges in various estimates from 85 to 300, while the number of workers said to be members
ranges from 27,000 to 50,000.[10] It is interesting to compare these numbers
with the estimates of union membership before the Ibáñez presidency. FOCh
membership is perhaps equally difficult to estimate. After careful evaluation
S. Valenzuela (1979:454–55) estimates that the FOCh had at the most
25,000–30,000 members in February 1925, at a time when government support made membership seem very attractive. Recabarren reported a peak
membership of 60,000 in 1921—and a halving of that figure in the following
year due to government repression (S. Valenzuela 1979:454). The strength of
other tendencies in the union movement is perhaps even harder to estimate.
Somewhat arbitrarily, however, we may take FOCh membership as 30,000
and, for purposes of comparison, assume an equal number of non-FOCh affiliated unionists, bringing the total up to 60,000. If we compare this figure to
the 27,000–50,000 estimated for the legal movement sponsored by Ibáñez,
we may conclude that his movement encompassed a good proportion of the
existing labor movement, but, in contrast to Brazil, did not succeed in bringing the previously nonorganized working class into the new, state-controlled
union structure.

As in Brazil, then, the Chilean experience of incorporation had as its central characteristics the repression of radical and politically independent
unions and the establishment of a union structure controlled by the state,
within the framework of a highly constraining, corporative labor law. Yet,
Ibáñez never went so far as Vargas in this direction. Part of the explanation
for the more limited trajectory in Chile may have been the timing and duration of its incorporation period. In the first place, it occurred before and to
some extent was terminated by the 1929 crash and world depression, which
perhaps hit Chile harder than any other Latin American country and in the
face of which the Ibáñez government, like many others in Latin America,
was unable to stay in power. Secondly, given the greater political impasse at
the beginning of the Chilean incorporation period and the timing of the
coups that brought these periods to a close, the succession of Chilean governments had less time to implement these corporative policies. In Brazil fourteen years elapsed between the promulgation of the law that first legalized
labor unions and the end of the incorporation period, whereas the corresponding period in Chile was only half that long. There was another aspect
of the early timing of the period in Chile. The 1924 labor law was very innovative, as it was the first major labor law in Latin America and there were
not many models available anywhere to draw on. The Ibáñez period was concurrent with the formative stages of European fascism, so that the diffusion
of the latter, very direct in the case of Brazil, which copied whole sections of
the Italian Labor Charter of 1927, was less likely in the case of Chile.

Whatever the reasons, there are two ways in which the Chilean experience

[10] See, for example, Barría (1972:62), Jobet (1955:181), Montero (1952:129), Poblete
(1945:35), and Vitale (1962:68).

was more limited than the Brazilian. The first is that the labor law in Brazil under the Estado Novo was elaborated to the point of encompassing more traits of full-blown corporatism than that of Chile under Ibáñez. In making this comparison, however, it must be noted that the 1928 law pushed Chile to a slightly higher level of corporatism than the Estado Novo law of 1937, and the 1931 codification was higher yet. Vargas, however, elaborated his corporative system in 1939 and again in 1943, so that by the end of the incorporating periods Brazil had a substantially more corporative and constraining legal framework. Nevertheless, as we shall see below, over the next several years Chilean governments added provisions to the law, so that by the mid-1940s, both countries reached similar levels of corporatism at the level of labor law. These were the most highly corporative labor laws, with more provisions for structuring and constraining the union movement, of any countries in Latin America (Collier and Collier 1979:972–76). Finally, in making this comparison, it must be pointed out that though the *level* of corporatism in Brazil and Chile was similarly and uniquely high, the particular *way* in which the labor movement was structured in the two countries was not always similar. For instance, in Chile, the law emphasized small plant unions, whereas in Brazil the *enquadramento* provided for occupationally defined groupings across plants and fit them into a hierarchical union structure. In neither case, however, was a single, peak confederation permitted.

The second difference is the extent to which the two governments actually accomplished the creation of an "official," co-opted, in-house bureaucratized union movement whose leaders were more dependent on and responsive to the government than to the mass base of the workers. The Vargas government was very successful in this respect, creating a large number of such unions, which encompassed a greatly increased union membership. Though Ibáñez moved in this direction, he achieved much less.

In conclusion, it is important to remember that despite the differences, the Brazilian and Chilean patterns of state incorporation share a number of similarities, and these contrast with the pattern of party incorporation elsewhere. The first was the adoption of a very elaborate corporative legal framework, which had no parallel elsewhere in Latin America and through which the state structured the organized labor movement and controlled its activities, leadership, and forms of demand-making. The economic and organizational weakness of these two labor movements, owing to the way in which the state legally defined the system of industrial relations, has been widely noted by analysts of both countries.[11] The second was the pattern of accommodationist politics reflecting a modus vivendi among different sectors of the dominant classes, that is, a state alliance based on a hybrid elite. The third was the absence of a major attempt to mobilize popular sector political support and hence to establish a populist party. Vargas organized no political party during the Estado Novo until the very end (see next chapter). Ibáñez

[11] Bernardo 1982:199–200; Angell 1972; L. M. Rodrigues 1969:120–21; J. A. Rodrigues 1968:188; and Morris 1966:16.

did organize a party of blue and white collar workers, but it never amounted to much. Unlike the populist parties that appealed to the working class in the cases of party incorporation and that continued in the postincorporation period to attract labor support, albeit to different degrees, Ibáñez's CRAC completely collapsed with his fall from power. These similarities between Brazil and Chile were the point of departure for the subsequent trajectory of change followed by the two countries.

MEXICO AND VENEZUELA: RADICAL POPULISM

The onset of the incorporation period was marked in Mexico by the end of the civil war and the new constitution of 1917 and in Venezuela by the new government that followed the death of Gómez in 1935. As in Brazil and Chile, the challenge of this transition involved the political task of consolidating a new reformist coalition. In Mexico this task was undertaken against the backdrop of Madero's failure and the ensuing years of bloody civil war. In Venezuela it was undertaken in ambiguous circumstances. Following Gómez's death, government passed on not to the middle sector opposition but to Gómez's followers in the army, so there is little sense in which it could be said that the reformist opposition even came to power. Nevertheless, the death of Gómez marked the end of an era, and the coloration of the new government and its openness to reform was an issue to be explored and worked out. A crucial factor that distinguishes Mexico and Venezuela from Brazil and Chile was the strategy of the new political leadership vis-à-vis the popular sectors in their attempt to attain and/or consolidate power; that is, in Mexico and Venezuela political leaders viewed the popular sectors as crucial political resources that could be mobilized in the struggles among sectors of the dominant classes. This mobilization was a central feature of the incorporation pattern in these countries.

In Mexico and Venezuela, this support mobilization took the form of what we have labeled radical populism, in which both the working class and the peasantry were mobilized electorally and organized into functional associations, such as unions, linked to the reformist political movement or party. There was some difference between the two countries in this respect. In Venezuela both working-class and peasant organizations were united in the same national labor confederation and in the same sectoral structure within the populist party. In Mexico the two union structures remained organizationally separate—indeed during the 1920s the urban and rural popular sectors even tended to be affiliated with different parties, and from the 1930s on they formed parallel but separate sectors within the dominant, populist party.

The inclusion of the peasantry in the politics of support mobilization meant two things from the point of view of the present perspective. First, it made the politics of incorporation appear like a more radical challenge, since the appeal to the peasantry necessitated a call for land reform—an element not found in the other six incorporation projects considered here and one that seemed to constitute a more thorough-going attack on private property and capitalist (and precapitalist) relations of production. Second, the mobilization of the peasantry meant that the dependence of political leaders on the working class was somewhat diluted since an alternate base of popular support was available. Nevertheless, despite this greater coalitional flexibility, in both Mexico and Venezuela leaders' dependence on labor support was great and was reflected in strong prolabor policies and substantial state co-operation with existing labor organizations.

On the one hand, one must understand radical populism as an elite project to establish the political dominance of elements of the emerging urban middle sectors. To this end, populism was pursued as part of a political strategy in which the popular sectors were mobilized as a political support base, as a political resource to build a constituency in order to consolidate power. This mobilization did not take the form of the encouragement of autonomous mobilization from below, but of controlled mobilization from above. A central feature of this mobilization from above was the establishment of a reformist multiclass political party to channel popular sector political participation into support for the government.

On the other hand, what is crucial to understand is that the very process of support mobilization took on a dynamic of its own. In order to mobilize support successfully, an exchange was necessary in which real concessions were offered for the support sought, for the popular sectors were not so passive nor so easily duped that they would collaborate without extracting some benefits. This, then, is the source of the political dynamic contained within populism throughout Latin America. The exchange that is a fundamental feature of support mobilization, while not threatening the basic capitalist orientation of the state and while in fact doing much to co-opt the working class (and the peasantry where included, as in Mexico and Venezuela), nevertheless involved substantive concessions, the formation of a progressive alliance, and some degree of power-sharing with the working class. These alienated important sectors of society. The result was political polarization as the alienated groups defected from the coalition. Despite efforts of the political elite to maintain the multiclass alliance, it tended to break apart, so that increasingly there was a situation in which a progressive coalition in power was opposed by the dominant economic sectors, which formed a counterrevolutionary or counterreform alliance.

Genuine populism, then, was not a static or equilibrium condition but contained within it a political dynamic and contradiction that made it most unstable. It must be understood in terms of a central emphasis on this contradictory feature: though mobilization was undertaken largely from above, and though in many ways it is a co-optive mechanism, the dynamics of mobilization turned the incorporation project in a sufficiently progressive direction to result in political polarization, as important, economically dominant groups went into vehement opposition, a situation that was unsustainable in the context of capitalist development.

With respect to the role of the working class in Mexico and Venezuela, the contrast with Brazil and Chile may be emphasized. Unlike the attempt to depoliticize the labor movement that was characteristic of state incorporation, the mobilization strategy by its very nature involved as an essential aspect the politicization of the working class. In this way, incorporation involved as a first priority not only the integration of the labor movement as a functional group but also its integration as a political movement, organized in a multiclass political party that would reflect the populist alliance and that would channel working class political activity.

This difference meant that compared to state incorporation, radical populism involved more concessions and a more favorable political position for the labor movement. Leftist and independent unions were tolerated (though not necessarily favored) and in some cases even became part of the coalition. A corporative labor code was promulgated, but it had fewer constraints on unions and union activities. The same kind of officialist, state-penetrated union movement was not established, even though mobilization meant that the labor movement came to support the government and, in receiving benefits from it, became dependent on the state. These differences occurred within the framework of certain commonalities with state corporatism. In cases of state incorporation, some real benefits were paternalistically granted, and in cases of radical populism the political elite also recognized the importance of structuring a labor movement that it could control and of preventing the emergence of a strong, autonomous working class. Nevertheless, the adoption of a mobilization strategy implied a more advantageous power position for the working class, since the usefulness to the political leadership of popular sector support was dependent upon increasing the power of organized labor in order to enhance its weight as a political resource.

Compared to state incorporation, then, radical populism represents a contrasting model of labor incorporation, a different state response to the challenge of the emergence of an industrial working class. The different response corresponds to a distinct strategy for maintaining or consolidating the power of reformist political leadership. The two types of experiences differ with regard to the nature of conflict among contending factions of the dominant classes, the coalitions formed, the strategic political location of popular sectors, the degree to which they were mobilized, and the degree of class polarization that resulted.

Peasant Incorporation

Since in the following pages we will be primarily concerned with analyzing state-labor relations, which are the focus of this book, a few observations may be added here about a dictinctive feature of Mexico and Venezuela: the inclusion of the peasantry in the politics of incorporation. In their willingness to mobilize the peasants and, in the process, to adopt policies of agrarian reform, the leaders of the incorporation projects in these two countries thereby also demonstrated a willingness to risk the hostility of landowners and raise more basic questions about the sanctity of private property and about the scope of the new interventionist state.

In Mexico, the mobilization of peasant support began during the civil war that pitted Carranza against Villa and Zapata, whose main support was found among peasants, rural workers, and ranchers. Zapata in particular had a base in the peasantry and had promulgated the Plan de Ayala to promote peasant interests. In response the Constitutionalists backed agrarian reform, and after the war the new constitution championed issues of social justice and laid the legal basis for land expropriation. In the following years, mobilization of peasant support was undertaken by leaders at many levels, reflecting both the fluidity of the post-revolutionary period and the attempt to consolidate power in the face of it. On the federal level, the governments of the 1920s promoted centralized peasant organizations and parties and adopted agrarian reform programs to mobilize peasant support for multiple reasons: to prevent more radical, independent peasant movements; to confront pressures from counterrevolutionary groups, and to quash rebellions, the most important of which were the de la Huerta and Cristero rebellions (Hamilton 1982:68, 75).

Peasant support, like labor support, was also a basis of political power cultivated by governors. Perhaps the most dramatic, but certainly not the only, example occurred in the state of Veracruz, where the governor supported the agrarian leagues, organized by Communist-affiliated labor and tenant unions, in their fight against the landed elite. To gain peasant support the governor distributed land to peasants and allowed peasant leaders to occupy major political and administrative posts. In Michoacán, Governor Lázaro Cárdenas also carried out an agrarian reform program and armed women's leagues to defend the newly acquired land (Hamilton 1982:98–99).

During the six-year interim of more conservative government (1928–34), policy turned more hostile toward peasants. In an effort to eliminate independent bases of power, the central government moved to obstruct and forcibly defeat peasant mobilization by state governors. In addition, the land reform program was pronounced a failure, and an attempt was made to get the governors to call it off and provide guarantees to landowners. At the same time, many of the peasant leagues were destroyed or weakened (Hamilton 1982:99–100, 175).

The radical populist government of Cárdenas (1934–40) brought an abrupt change, as peasants were brought into the incorporation project in parallel fashion to the labor movement. During the Cárdenas presidency, nearly 18 million hectares of land were distributed to more than 800,000 peasants, surpassing in six years the accumulated totals up to that time (Hamilton 1982:177). In addition to the extent of the program, other aspects made it more radical than previous programs. First, previously exempted commercial estates became subject to expropriation, and many henequen, rice, wheat, livestock, and sugar estates were included in the program. Secondly, the government encouraged the organization and mobilization of rural workers, particularly over the issue of obtaining a labor contract, as a prerequisite for expropriation. Third, in part for ideological reasons and in part as a mechanism for maintaining the integrity of these large estates, communal production based on the *ejido* was encouraged and favored by the government. A new Ejidal Bank provided credit and in a host of other ways supported and oversaw the functioning of the *ejido*, promoting it over other kinds of rural ownership. All in all, the agrarian program of Cárdenas constituted a major assault on the power of landowners and provoked intense opposition (Hamilton 1982:164–78).

In exchange, of course, the government benefited from the political support that was forthcoming from the peasantry. To institutionalize the peasant-state alliance, agrarian leagues were constituted at the state level, and in 1938 these were brought together in the CNC (National Peasant Confederation). The CNC, representing about 3 million peasants and rural workers, was formally incorporated into the governing party, which Cárdenas reorganized in the same year.

In Venezuela, peasant mobilization and organization were closely integrated into the larger labor movement, which included both urban and rural sectors and which was regulated by the same labor law. To that extent, the longer discussion below applies equally to the incorporation of the peasantry. Nevertheless, a few additional details may be added at this point.

Between 1935 and 1945, the government itself had little interest in politically mobilizing the peasantry. With the 1936 labor law, a conservative incorporation project was initiated with the provision for legalized but highly constrained unions. During this period, however, groups in opposition to the government were vigorous in their efforts to organize a political movement (which eventually became the party Democratic Action—AD) and mobilize a support base. The peasantry as well as urban labor figured prominently in this strategy, and the agricultural sector received a great deal of attention in the development program of the new movement (Powell 1971:36, 56). The first peasant union was organized in 1937, and in the following years, as local peasant leaders joined the movement or were recruited by it, unionization spread, as did peasant protest and clashes with landlords. By 1945, 77 unions with a membership of over 6,000 were legally recognized, and Powell (1971:60) indicates that when not restricted to legally recognized unions, the effective peasant support base of AD when it came to power in 1945 consisted of "500 embryonic unions, with as many as 2,000 local peasant leaders in the villages and scattered hamlets, and an estimated 100,000 peasants within the orbit of influence of these local leaders."

Once in the power, AD continued to place high priority on the mobilization of peasant support, and agrarian policy became a central component of the new government's program. The agrarian reform law was promulgated in 1948, but even before that, indeed on the first day of the new government in 1945, agrarian policy began to take shape as guidelines to prevent peasant eviction were announced and a program of land distribution through leasing was begun. That program was expanded with more categories of public and private land made available for lease. The new constitution of July 1947 provided the legal basis for an agrarian reform law, which was promulgated in October 1948. However, it accomplished little since it was quickly superseded by the military coup, which ousted the government the following month.

Despite its abbreviated duration, the Trienio government, through its agrarian policy, was effective in mobilizing peasant support and consolidat-

ing a state-peasant alliance based on "an explicit quid pro quo: you help us
to achieve power with your votes . . . , and we will respond with an agrarian
reform through the channel of the Peasant Federation. . . . [The] mobilization
system . . . depended both on intermittent peasant contributions at the polls
and on a flow of agrarian goods and services in return" (Powell 1971:83).

After just the first year of the new government, land was distributed to
over 23,000 peasants. In addition, peasant organization increased dramatically. Over the three-year period of the Trienio, the number of unions grew
by a factor of almost ten and membership by a factor of almost 11 (Powell
1971:79). These peasant organizations were promoted as the vehicles
through which land and credit were distributed. Powell (1971:75, 80) suggests that the new policy led to a basic redistribution of power in the countryside, as these unions and their leaders were empowered by the terms of
the program to influence not only land distribution but also the location of
public works projects. To oversee the process, a commission was established
on which a sole representative of landowners could be outvoted by the other
four members—three government representatives and a representative of the
peasant unions. Furthermore, the formal role of unions in the policy process
had a partisan impact since most of these unions were linked to AD, the
government party.

The agrarian policy, taken as a whole, provoked much opposition. This
opposition came not only from landowners, who were no longer free to dis-
pose of their land without constraints, but also from opposition parties,
which did not establish the same links to peasant unions and stood to loose
politically from AD's mobilization strategy.

In both Mexico and Venezuela, then, the inclusion of the peasantry in the
incorporation project generated substantial opposition. However, by the end
of the incorporation period, the traditional landed oligarchy had been further
undermined. Hence, though this opposition was part of the pressure for the
subsequent move to the right (which will be explored in the next chapter),
this sector did not persist in subsequent decades as a powerful pole of antagonism to the populist party as it did in Peru and Argentina.

MEXICO

In Mexico the incorporation period was more drawn out than in any other country under consideration. Following a first cautious phase from 1917 to 1920, it consisted of three periods: two that can be characterized as populist, separated by a more conservative phase when a federal labor law was passed within a considerably less prolabor framework.

The incorporation period was launched in 1917 with the famous labor clauses of Article 123 of the path-breaking constitution. This provision was—and has remained—so important symbolically that in the Museum of Mexican History in Mexico City the chronological presentation of exhibits culminates in a display of a dramatically illuminated constitution, opened to that article. We can date the onset of the incorporation period to the new constitution, in which the state provided for a number of labor guarantees, including the right to form unions and to strike. Nevertheless, despite the signals clearly provided by the constitution and the concern with labor mobilization that underlay the adoption of the labor provisions, other aspects of party incorporation emerged somewhat more gradually after the conclusion of the civil war. Indeed, there was a division in the revolutionary family between the accommodationist faction, represented by the supporters of Madero and Carranza, on the one hand, and the populists, on the other. Starting in 1920 with the onset of the "Sonoran dynasty,"[12] the populists became dominant. A clearer populist orientation began to take shape under the presidency of Obregón from 1920 to 1924 and reached its climax in the following presidency of Calles from 1924 to 1928. Crucially, however, this period lacked one feature that was central to the populism of the 1930s in Mexico: though the organized labor movement played an important role in the populist coalition, working-class political participation had not been institutionalized through incorporation into a unified multiclass party that could perpetuate the state-labor alliance. During the conservative hiatus from 1928 to 1934, known as the Maximato, in which populism was largely abandoned, this failure contributed to the break up of the alliance. As of 1934 the establishment of channels for the political participation of the working class was still on the agenda and was addressed by government leaders during a second period of radical populism, which was instituted under Cárdenas.

The Cárdenas presidency represented a "complete" instance of radical populism, displaying all the features outlined above. By the time Cárdenas left the presidency in 1940, he had formed an alliance with the working class through its predominant confederation, the CTM (Mexican Labor Confederation), instituted a series of reforms, granted a number of prolabor concessions and benefits, and succeeded in incorporating the popular sectors into a multiclass integrative party. Taken as a whole, then, the incorporation pe-

[12] This refers to three Mexican leaders who dominated Mexican politics in the 1920s— Obregón, de la Huerta, and Calles—all of whom were from the northern state of Sonora.

riod to 1940 can be seen as the gradual and halting emergence of populism, culminating in the Cárdenas presidency.

Project from Above: The 1920s

At the end of the armed conflict in Mexico, which had been bitterly fought over so many years and had taken such a toll in human life and economic and social disruption, the victorious Constitutionalists faced the enormous task of reconstituting the state and consolidating their power. This task became the dominant feature of the incorporation period in Mexico. In this setting of the lack of well-established central control and fluid power relations that were attendant upon the upheavals of the revolution, the creation of new political resources in the form of an organized popular sector—both urban labor and the peasantry—proved decisive. It will be argued that the postrevolutionary decade was a period of gradual movement toward populism characterized by a narrowing of the support base of the state and increasing state dependence on urban labor. Carranza, the first postrevolutionary president, opened this period echoing the orientation of Madero, who emphasized the importance of a broad coalition, rejecting popular sector mobilization and alliance with the popular sectors. The Sonorans (most notably Obregón and Calles) opposed this orientation and insisted on mass mobilization of urban and rural sectors as the only way to consolidate the revolution. Obregón, who followed Carranza in the presidency, made a tentative beginning in this direction of the mobilization of mass support generally and labor support in particular. Yet he basically played a conservative game (partly dictated by the priority he gave to attaining U.S. recognition of the Mexican government) in which he played off all groups and parties against one another and refused to become dependent on any one of them. While his presidency opened with what looked like a firm alliance with the dominant part of the labor movement, it closed with his greater reliance on the rural sector, leaving labor very disappointed, and with substantial enmity and distrust between Obregón and the national labor leadership. Calles then assumed the presidency much more clearly identified with urban labor than rural groups and became more dependent on labor as his base of support narrowed. It is with Calles that the populism of the 1920s reached its height, though it remained incomplete in the sense noted above.

From the point of view of the state elite, the primary task of the postrevolutionary decade, then, was the consolidation of power. The challenge was a multiple one. On the one hand were the representatives of the Porfirian order and the counterrevolutionary elements. As Cline (1969:194–95) has said:

> The elements around which a general counterrevolution could form had by no means been eliminated during the epic years of civil strife. Though reduced somewhat in size and power, the old antirevolutionary factions—the Church, the large landholders, the established large merchant families, the Porfirian industrialists, and the regional political machines of the West and parts of the

South—could, when combined, exert considerable influence and pressure, especially if they were aided from abroad. Others might join. Disappointed revolutionaries were constantly drifting to their ranks. A new class of landlords and industrialists, formed from opportunistic revolutionary leaders, whose political ardor had cooled after they had obtained a sizable personal stake, might now support an antirevolutionary struggle.

On the other hand were the mobilized popular sectors, who were potentially the purveyors of social revolution. While representatives of the old order were a common challenge to the reformers throughout Latin America, the popular mobilization of both the peasantry and the organized working class that had been part of the revolutionary process was unique to Mexico. To some extent the mobilization of the popular sectors during the revolution was an autonomous movement from below. The insurrectionist tendencies of the working class, their participation in the Madero cause, and the mobilization of the peasantry primarily under Zapata demonstrated the social revolutionary potential of the popular sectors.

Given the need to consolidate power, the mobilization of the popular sectors from above as part of a strategy of political entrepreneurship was extensive. As noted in Chapter 4, such mobilization had become an important pattern during the revolution. During the course of the fighting, both rural and urban popular sectors had become an important political power and political resource, which had been mobilized by all factions. Initially, this mobilization from above was quite limited, particularly under Madero. There was some attempt to mobilize labor support in the Madero movement against Porfirio Díaz, but the role of labor in those events was not significant. As president, Madero did little to mobilize the popular sectors as a support group; however, some governors of that period, who were more reformist than Madero, went much further in granting concessions to labor and eliciting working-class support. Córdova has argued that it was the failure of Madero to engage in mass politics—to adopt a reformist program with which he could have mobilized mass support and thus could have made a more decisive break with the Porfiristas—that led to his failure to consolidate power and his vulnerability to Huerta's counterrevolutionary coup (Córdova 1972:30–31; 1973:21–24, 33).

As the intra-elite rivalry heated up, with the call to arms against the Huerta government, the attempt to attract labor support became more central. As mentioned in Chapter 4, even Huerta was cognizant of the need for some reforms to at least neutralize, if not attract, the labor movement as a political resource. On the other side, Carranza adopted a program of reforms to attract popular sector support both to recruit a peasant army and to attempt to forge a coalition with Zapata and Pancho Villa.

After Huerta was driven from the presidency in 1914 and the anti-Huerta factions turned against each other, the mobilization of the popular sectors by the reformist faction took a new counterrevolutionary turn, as it became part of a strategy directed not now against rival factions of the dominant class, but against the autonomous mobilization of the peasantry. In this context the Constitutionalists under Carranza mobilized the support of the Casa del Obrero Mundial, which formed the Red Batallions in exchange for a number of concessions. This was the first major episode of labor mobilization from above in Mexico, and it was the first time that a deal was struck with the working class as an organized, corporate group.

By the end of the fighting in 1916, the question of the strategy of mobilization caused a deep division within the elements of the winning Constitutionalists, since mobilization involved concessions which some—most notably Carranza himself—were unwilling to grant. The Casa-Carranza alliance had fallen apart, and Carranza seemed increasingly unwilling to pursue a reformist policy toward labor and grant concessions in exchange for support. The division between the liberals and the more reformist Jacobins headed by Obregón came to light clearly during the Constitutional Convention of 1917. Despite the opposition of Carranza, the convention produced a remarkably progressive document that established wide-ranging labor rights and laid the foundations for land reform, thereby providing the legal framework for and signaling an apparent national commitment to a new kind of politics based on mass support.

Yet, following his election in the same year, Carranza further turned his back on his own reformist past as governor of Coahuila and as revolutionary general and became increasingly conservative, moving further and further away from his commitment to land reform and support for the working class and becoming increasingly identified with the urban middle class and established landlords in the countryside (Richmond 1979). Opposing Carranza were the reformists, led by Obregón and his fellow Sonorans, Calles and de la Huerta, who drew the lesson from Madero's failure that consolidation of the middle sector revolution, represented by Madero and the Constitutionalists, was dependent upon a restructuring of the social bases of the state and the destruction of the Porfirian system of privilege. That is, they recognized the necessity of replacing the Porfirian dominant class with the ascendancy of small entrepreneurs and of grounding the transformation of the state in a *política de masas* in which the state championed the interests and demands of the urban and rural popular sectors, thereby strengthening the state with their support (Córdova 1973:23, 26). The mobilization of both the peasantry and the working class as support groups would address the challenges to the consolidation of power presented by both counterrevolutionary and social revolutionary groups. It would give the new leadership both electoral and military support against the former, and it would provide the mechanism for diffusing the impact of the latter by incorporating the popular sectors into the political system as a support group and establishing control over them. Furthermore, popular sector mobilization could create a crucial political and military counterweight to the army, still politicized from the revolution, and to politically ambitious revolutionary generals. It was Carranza's increasing rejection of mass politics, his policy of ignoring the social provisions of the 1917 constitution, and his tendency to follow Madero's path of an accommodationist alliance with the old dominant classes, rather than a populist alliance with the popular sectors, that began to divide the ranks of the former revolutionaries. The outcome in 1920, when Carranza attempted to impose a conservative successor over the more popular candidate Obregón, was the latter's rebellion, resulting in the overthrow and assassination of Carranza and the ascendancy of the populist alliance under the leadership of the "Sonoran dynasty."

It was over this last issue, the succession to Carranza, that the second major episode of labor mobilization occurred. In 1918 the CROM (Regional Confederation of Mexican Workers) was founded and quickly became the most important labor organization in the country. The CROM represented a combination of anarcho-syndicalist influence and a new approach that, in recognition of the weakness of the labor movement, replaced direct action with political alliances (Carr 1976, vol. 1:121, 127, 129). Despite this latter current and the fact that it was founded initially with state sponsorship, the relationship between CROM and the Carranza government was one of mutual suspicion, and it deteriorated further during the strike wave of 1919 (vol. 1:134). When Carranza began to prepare the way for a successor whom the CROM opposed, it embarked on a path of political action to support an alternative. For his part, Obregón needed the CROM to build support for his presidential ambitions. This convergence of strategy was consummated in 1919 in a written but secret pact between the CROM and Obregón, the candidate of the three contacted by the CROM who was willing to grant the most concessions in exchange for its support. As part of the bargain, the CROM organized a labor party, the PLM (Mexican Labor Party), to support Obregón's candidacy. Morones, head of the CROM, became an indispensable ally of Obregón during the whole period of presidential succession; and as Obregón's revolt took shape, the PLM withdrew its recognition of the Carranza government and organized both propaganda and armed groups to wage the dual political and military battle (Clark 1973:76).

Upon the success of the rebellion and following a brief period in which de la Huerta was interim president, Obregón was elected president. Though he was elected by a landslide, the problem of consolidating power remained an overwhelming one in view of the numerous challenges. Porfiristas and armed revolutionary generals continued to pose a threat, which seemed all the greater as long as the United States refused to recognize the new regime, thus keeping open the possibility of lending American support to a rebellion. In addition, the majority in Congress, which was becoming increasingly independent and powerful, was held by the PLC (Liberal Constitutionalist Party). Founded by Obregón and his supporters in 1917, the party supported the candidacy of Carranza. There is some disagreement about the nature of the party: Ruiz (1980:158) sees it as Carranza's political machine; whereas Garrido (1984:38) claims that the PLC was Obregón's personal vehicle. Whatever the case, the PLC supported Carranza's candidacy in 1917 and then the candidacy of Obregón in 1920, when he and Carranza parted ways. However, reflecting its original program of support for the limited Madero (and Carranza) program of reforms (Garrido 1984:38), the party was not willing to go as far in a reformist direction as Obregón. Once Obregón became president, the party became increasingly conservative and constituted an important source of opposition.

The challenge was not limited, however, to the "enemies" of the revolution in the form of the Porfiristas and armed generals, or even to the divisions between the Carranza faction and the Sonorans. It extended also to the rivalries within the "revolutionary family" or coalition being put together by the Sonorans and among the Sonorans themselves. Obregón came to power with the support of his two fellow Sonorans, de la Huerta and Calles, and with important backing from the more conservative middle classes (Garrido 1984:38), in the form of the PLC; the more progressive middle classes and students (Garrido 1984:39), in the form of the PNC (National Cooperativist Party); the working class, in the form of the PLM (Mexican Labor Party); and the peasants, in the form of the PNA (National Agrarian Party). Yet over the next four years the three Sonorans came to be identified with different parties and correspondingly with different social bases of support; de la Huerta went into overt opposition, while Calles increasingly differentiated himself from Obregón. Thus, there occurred a gradual splintering of the coalition due both to the personal ambitions of and rivalries among the Sonoran leaders themselves and also to conflicts among the different constituencies that formed their various bases of support. In these conflicts, the role of organized labor was central. The result was a narrowing of the support base for the presidency, culminating in a period of radical populism and state alliance with and dependency on labor during the presidency of Calles.

The first split in the coalition occurred when the PLC tried to dictate the political agenda of the government. De la Huerta and Calles, ministers of treasury and the interior respectively in the Obregón government, were outspoken critics of the PLC, which in turn accused the two of them of fomenting radical movements and advocating socialism. There was particular enmity between the PLC and Calles, who helped to strengthen the PLM in an effort to offset the PLC (Dulles 1961:128). The PLC opposed labor's growing strength and political clout, particularly that of the major labor confederation, the CROM, and its leaders. In 1921, the PLC was responsible for rejecting the proposal to set up a Ministry of Labor, which would give labor ministerial representation and which was a condition of the CROM-Obregón pact of 1919. The response of the CROM was dramatic, and in the ensuing rivalry the PNC and the PNA joined CROM's PLM in establishing a Social-Democratic Bloc to oppose the "reactionary" PLC. In this confrontation, Obregón refused to back the PLC, which, in the face of this united opposition and a campaign of intimidation directed by Calles, emerged from the 1922 election in a greatly weakened position, losing its congressional majority to the PNC.[13]

Once the conservative opposition was eliminated or controlled, the different factions of the Sonoran-led coalition began to split up. The support base

[13] Carr 1976, vol. 1:188–90; Dulles 1961:129–31; Brandenburg 1964:60.

of the three Sonoran leaders became increasingly differentiated and each of
them became associated with different parties: Obregón with the PNA, de la
Huerta with the PNC, and Calles with the PLM. Shortly after the 1922 elections, the electoral front formed by the Social-Democratic Bloc broke up in
the context of the maneuvering for presidential succession. Of his two fellow
Sonorans and heirs apparent, Obregón favored Calles over de la Huerta. Calles was supported by the CROM and its PLM, which went into battle against
the dominant PNC. The PNC in turn denounced what it saw as Obregón's
attempt to impose Calles as his successor. The stage was set for the first
split. When the Obregón government and the Laboristas supported the PNA
candidate in a disputed 1923 election in San Luis Potosí, most of the PNC
broke with Calles. De la Huerta seized the opportunity to resign from the
cabinet and declare his presidential candidacy for the PNC. His ambitions
were supported by diverse groups opposing Obregón. These included conservatives who thought Calles was a radical, nationalists who opposed the Bucareli Accords just signed with the United States, non-CROM labor leaders,
and army generals, who opposed the reduction of the federal army (Meyer
and Sherman 1979:579–80). In the rebellion which ensued, over half the federal army supported de la Huerta, while the government side was supported
by a peasant army organized by the PNA and by workers militias organized
by the PLM.

   The defeat of the de la Huerta rebellion, which resulted in the destruction
of the PNC, left a coalition of the PNA and the PLM dominant in Congress.
Increasingly, the two parties came into conflict and each came to be identified with one of the two remaining Sonorans, Obregón and Calles respectively. Despite the CROM-Obregón pact of 1919, the relationship between
the two had grown increasingly strained as Obregón's presidency wore on.
Obregón had tried to build a coalition that included all the political factions
of the revolutionary forces (Garrido 1984:44) and was careful not to get too
close to or dependent upon any one of them. Furthermore, in his effort to
consolidate power, Obregón sought good relations with more conservative
groups and felt compelled to do what was necessary to establish diplomatic
relations with the United States to prevent any American support for rebel
movements. "Efforts to consolidate his position and to insure the success of
his administration depended on his ability to placate powerful groups in society, especially businessmen, politicians of diverse interests, and military
men unenthusiastic about labor reform" (Ruiz 1976:76). As a result, while
unions during the Obregón presidency won many strikes and the CROM generally received official favor, Obregón was seen as an inconsistent and somewhat disappointing friend to CROM. He never allowed himself to become
identified with the PLM. Quite the contrary, Obregón had supported the formation of the PNA by PLM dissidents. The PNA became the PLM's main
rival and its growing importance prevented CROM and the PLM from establishing a dominant position in rural unionization. In addition, Obregón generally left the task of labor mediation to the state governments, preferring to
remain aloof and claim impartiality, while intervening on the side of capital

in conflicts in industries "that were foreign owned or that had an important impact on the nation's economy or whose hostility could undermine his political position" (D. Bailey 1979:86). Furthermore, there were specific disappointments. Contrary to the terms of the pact, CROM was not consulted about the ministers of agriculture and of industry, commerce, and labor, nor did it get a separate Labor Ministry or a national labor law. The government also failed to regulate the profit-sharing provision of the constitution, to promote and pass an acceptable social insurance provision, and to respond to CROM's demand for labor attachés in Mexican embassies (Clark 1973:104; Carr 1976, vol. 1:208).

Within this context of an uneasy alliance in which Obregón refused to bow to CROM's attempts to make labor the indispensable base of support, a number of incidents occurred that drove a deeper wedge between Obregón and the Laboristas. The first was the railroad strike of 1921, in which Obregón's conduct was such that the strike started with the threatened resignation of CROM leaders from the government and ended with the loss of CROM support among the railway workers. According to Clark (1973:99–100) this incident marked the beginning of coolness and suspicion between CROM and Obregón. The rift widened toward the end of Obregón's presidency as CROM took a number of "increasingly daring" (Carr 1976, vol. 1:208) political initiatives against the Co-operativistas and supporters of de la Huerta. Following the assassination of the Yucatán governor in late 1923 by supporters of de la Huerta, Morones challenged Obregón to expel all PNC representatives in Congress by threatening "direct action," and he finally made good upon this threat by blockading Co-operativista homes and kidnapping several Co-operativistas. Another incident occurred shortly thereafter in January 1924, in which CROM was implicated in the assassination of PNC Senator Jurado. Though the assassination was convenient for the president because of Jurado's political activities in opposition to the Bucareli Accords, Obregón issued a public statement accusing CROM in the murder, and Morones in turn accused Obregón of "using the murder as a weapon to kill the labor organizations" (Clark 1973:103).

With the gulf between Obregón and labor widening, Obregón looked increasingly to the peasants in the PNA as his base of support while labor and the PLM moved closer to Calles, who had been and continued to be sympathetic to labor. The alliance between Calles and labor was a long-standing one, which Calles had begun to forge as a minister in the governments of Carranza and Obregón. According to Dulles (1961:21), it was Calles who had originally been the emissary to form the CROM-Obregón alliance during the 1919–20 electoral campaign and who had done much to support and build up the PLM. His relationship with labor became even more important as the political maneuvering and factionalization among the Sonorans resulted in the fragmentation of the support base, leaving labor to assume the central role in the coalition supporting Calles. Calles was indebted to labor for its role in supporting his presidential ambitions against the de la Huerta rebellion, and this dependence on labor support was clearly seen during the campaign. He identified himself as a Laborista and as the candidate of the working class. He broadened his ties to Morones, accepted the PLM nomination, and was accompanied by Morones throughout the campaign. "Never had there been a candidate, nor has there been one since, who devoted so much energy to cultivating the support of the organized labor movement. Similarly, no candidate has received the hysterical adulation that CROM and its leaders bestowed upon Calles" (Carr 1976, vol. 1:209). Calles, then, came to power in 1924 with a narrower base of support and a greater dependence on labor than any previous president.

Though many sources of opposition had been eliminated during the Obregón years, as seen in the narrowing of the spectrum of parties, which formed the organizational representation of many of the politically active interests, the problem of consolidating power remained of key importance as Calles assumed the presidency. Specifically, the loyalty of two groups had to be ensured: that of the ambitious armed forces (though the de la Huerta rebellion had been defeated, the loyalty of the army and the actions of dissident generals remained a threat) and the Obregón forces, which remained a distinct faction within the political arena and had close ties to the army. In this context, labor played an important role. It formed an organized political counterweight to the Agraristas, who were the support base of Obregón, and a military counterweight to the army, recently demonstrated in its role in suppressing the de la Huerta rebellion (Carr 1976, vol. 1:203, 207–8; J. Meyer et al. 1977:84). Thus Calles had to play a balancing game among these three groups—a game that was particularly delicate given the antilabor position of both the Agraristas and the army, the former because of the competition between the PNA and the CROM over rural organizing activities and the latter because of fears that labor would be used to reduce the role of the army (J. Meyer et al. 1977:84).

Calles's initial cabinet reflected this need to balance groups. Two factions could be identified within the government. The first was a moderate developmentalist faction, represented by two important Obregonistas: Alberto Pani in the Ministry of Finance and Aarón Sáenz in the Ministry of Foreign Relations. This faction favored economic modernization and the regularization and promotion of economic ties to the United States. The second faction, more radical and nationalistic, was comprised of the Laboristas, led by Morones, who was appointed minister of industry, commerce, and labor.

It was this second faction that was initially dominant as Calles came to power, dependent on labor support to an unprecedented extent. Though Obregón and Calles were in some sense both populists, Calles went much further than Obregón: whereas Obregón deceived labor leaders with vain promises in exchange for mass support, Calles brought labor leaders into prominent roles in the political system (Córdova 1973:309). Of those in the new government, Morones was the closest to Calles, and Dulles (1961:273) and Carr (1976, vol. 2:29) both assert that Morones was the second most powerful man in the country, whose influence was comparable to only the president himself. In fact, other important ministers, including Pani, were forced to resign when they crossed swords with Morones. Thus, at least through 1926, which is generally regarded as the peak of its influence, organized labor, in the form of CROM and its PLM, rose to a position of preeminence within the governing coalition. The degree to which this was so can been seen in a book that is still considered authoritative in the field, in which an observer in the 1930s, looking back at the 1920s, used as a subheading for a section describing the Calles period "Labor in Power" (Clark 1973:106).

Project from Below: The 1920s

A strategy of mobilization from above is insufficient to explain the actual formation of a populist alliance. Also necessary is the emergence, in the face of these inducements, of a dominant sector within the labor movement willing to collaborate with the government. How did this come about in Mexico? How was the dilemma that pitted the attraction of the benefits of collaboration against its risks resolved in favor of cooperation with the government? The answer must be seen in terms of the past experience and history of the labor movement in Mexico and in terms of the weakness of groups proposing an alternative strategy.

The CROM alliance with the Sonoran presidents during the 1920s was not the first major episode of collaboration between the organized labor movement and political leaders in 20th-century Mexico. As we have seen, the first was the successful mobilization of the Casa del Obrero Mundial and its formation of the Red Battalions to fight on behalf of Carranza and his Constitutionalists. In exchange, the Constitutionalists supported a massive organizing campaign by the Casa. Though there was some opposition, the collaborationist faction was able to impose its will on the dissidents within the Casa. The organizational advantages that the pact brought the Casa gave a large impetus to those favoring collaboration, one of whom was Luis Morones, who during this earlier period developed "a close working relationship with the government . . . [and] subtly prepared the way for his future rise to power" (Hart 1978:128–29).

The formation of the Red Battalions constituted a precedent of collaboration that was particularly noteworthy since it was undertaken by an avowedly anarchist organization. Yet after the Constitutionalist victory, collaboration did not continue on either side. Carranza had never been very enthusiastic about a coalition with labor, and once installed in the presidency he found he no longer needed its support. The Casa, for its part, returned to a policy of autonomy and confrontation. The next significant event in establishing a collaborationist tradition in Mexico was the failure of the 1916 general strike and Carranza's subsequent repression of the Casa. This defeat represented the failure of the anarcho-syndicalist strategy of direct action in the industrial arena and led to a major questioning and rethinking of labor strategy.

The result of this rethinking was the formation in the following years "of

two currents within the working class—the 'reformist' trade unionism of the
CROM, founded in 1918, and the temporary merging of anarcho-syndicalist
and Marxist currents in the short-lived Gran Cuerpo Central de Trabajadores
and the Mexican Communist Party in late 1918 and 1919" (Carr 1981a:13).
For the "reformists," the failure of the Casa taught a lesson that consisted of
perhaps three parts. First, it showed clearly the ability and willingness of the
government to crush a weak labor movement. Second, in view of the very
real possibility of governmental repression and of the inability of a still small
and weak labor movement to achieve success through independent action, a
new strategy of working through political alliances and obtaining official protection rather than incurring official hostility was presented as an alternative. Finally, the turn to political activity would involve the formation of a
workers' party as labor's vehicle for entering the electoral arena. The organizational result of this reorientation was the formation of the Socialist
Workers Party in 1917, which unsuccessfully ran candidates in the 1917 congressional elections, and the founding in 1919 of the Labor Party as the political arm of the CROM, initially to provide support for the Obregón presidential candidacy. With the CROM-Obregón pact, which made explicit the
exchange of CROM support for concessions to labor, Morones and his Action
Group, which had quickly come to assume the leadership of the CROM,
seemed to have replaced repression of the labor movement with a policy of
official favor stemming from the ability of Morones to make the labor movement politically and militarily indispensable to Obregón and his attainment
of the presidency.

Many benefits followed from this position. Yet this reliance of Obregón on
CROM did not last long, as Obregón was careful to balance the role of
CROM and the Labor Party with support from the newly formed Agrarian
Party, which in fact came to occupy a more central role in his coalition. Nevertheless, with the end of the Obregón presidency and the events surrounding the contested candidacy of Calles and the de la Huerta rebellion, Morones
had another chance to once again make the Labor Party and the CROM politically and militarily indispensable and to trade this crucial support for concessions and an unprecedented position of political influence and power under Calles.

The second factor in terms of explaining the emergence of a dominant labor sector oriented toward collaboration is the weakness of groups associated
with an alternative strategy, both in terms of their "inherent" weakness and
in terms of the ability of the dominant collaborating sector of the labor
movement, that is the CROM, to weaken these rival groups by means of the
resources and leverage it gained through its participation in the governing
coalition. Substantial advantages in its competition for worker support accrued to the CROM: official favor in strikes, industrial disputes, and legal
recognition as well as harassment of labor dissidents.

The two major groups representing an alternative orientation were the
anarcho-synidicalists and the Communists. The weakness of the anarcho-
syndicalists—who founded the CGT as a rival labor confederation in 1921

and who had their strength primarily in textiles in the center of the country and in petroleum in the Gulf region—was based on a number of factors. First, the CGT's strategy of the general strike and the rejection of political action was widely interpreted in Mexico as having been a failure and was substantially discredited (Rivera Castro 1983:117; Roxborough 1984:12). In addition, many of the CGT's affiliated unions were geographically dispersed, even isolated, and thus it was administratively difficult, especially with limited resources, to maintain contact. In addition, divisions within the non-CROM labor movement, both the factionalism within the CGT and defection of the Communists, weakened the independent current in labor, as the factions competed for the same groups of workers (Rivera Castro 1983:133–35). Finally, the government, with the help of the CROM, broke CGT strikes and repressed CGT leaders, militants, and unions.[14] The initial result of these battles was a posture of open hostility to the government, and at the end of the Obregón presidency, the CGT found itself in the de la Huerta camp in opposition to the government (Trejo Delarbe 1976:136). During the next several years, however, unable to sustain its position, the CGT moved to a more collaborative stance: "The years of defensive struggle against the CROM had a high cost for the 'red' CGT. Its energies expended in a series of rearguard actions, the political practice of the CGT became increasingly divorced from its radical anarcho-syndicalist ideology. By the end of the decade the CGT was eager to curry government favour and had, de facto, abandoned its revolutionary pretensions in exchange for the feeble hope of government patronage" (Roxborough 1984:14).

The other source of independent unionism, the Communist Party, was also weak. The PCM had some strength in the more advanced industrial sectors and among *campesinos*, but in general it was not very important or influential, except for its role in the railroad strike of 1926–27 (Rivera Castro 1983:142, 185). As with the case of the CGT, its weakness in part derived from the small and dispersed nature of the industrial proletariat and from government repression (Rivera Castro 1983:149–50). In addition, however, the PCM had a difficult time devising a strategy with which it could maneuver between the CGT on the one hand and the CROM on the other. Many of the labor sectors in which the PCM was active were under the influence of anarcho-syndicalism and rejected partisan affiliation and political action. Yet, it could not attract the "reformist" sector of the movement, which in any case was under CROM control, because it failed to produce any benefits for its political stance. For instance, at the end of the Calles presidency, the PCM, arguing that it was too weak to consider other options, supported Obregón's candidacy for reelection without receiving any concessions in return (Rivera Castro 1983:150, 186). From this weak position, the PCM was left with the strategy of calling for the creation of a labor central that would unify labor, including the CGT and the CROM. These attempts, however, failed (Rivera Castro 1983:138–39, 146).

[14] See Rivera Castro (1983:133), Trejo Delarbe (1976:136), Roxborough (1984:13–14).

The Exchange: The 1920s

A populist alliance between labor and the state elite is founded on an exchange relationship, an implicit or explicit bargain in which each side seeks important benefits. Though labor is typically the subordinate member in such an alliance, it is nevertheless able to extract certain benefits for its cooperation, and these benefits tend to be greater the stronger labor is and the more dependent the state is on labor. This relationship can be seen over the course of the Obregón-Calles period.

As we have seen in the above discussion, Obregón benefited substantially from the alliance with labor. In the most general terms, labor lent crucial support to Obregón and constituted an important counterweight to the large, politically active army and to opposition groups in Congress. Unlike most political parties of the period, which were personalistic, ephemeral cadre parties (Garrido 1984:41), the PLM was able to play a decisive role because of its mass base. "The only permanent national organisations, centralised and highly disciplined, were *CROM* and the Labour Party, which alone proved capable of mobilising significant sections of the population across the Republic" (Carr 1972:15).

Obregón was able to count on labor support from the beginning of his candidacy. Both Obregón and labor opposed Carranza's policies and the candidate he put forth to succeed him. The Obregón-Morones pact, in which CROM pledged to organize a labor party to support Obregón politically, was signed shortly after Obregón announced his presidency, and CROM played a decisive role in his march to the presidency. Not only did CROM play a major role in directing Obregón's campaign and organizing support groups of workers and peasants, but labor was important in precipitating the final break between Carranza and the Sonorans. Amid considerable labor protest during the growing political crisis, the Sonoran rebellion took form when de la Huerta, as governor of Sonora, reacted to a strike by railroad workers, who clearly sympathized with Obregón in a way that constituted a rebellion of the state against the central government. Obregón issued a call to arms, and the three Sonorans promulgated the Plan de Agua Prieta, which called for a general uprising against Carranza. CROM responded by organizing groups of armed workers to fight in the insurrection (Carr 1976, vol. 1:149–52).

Once Obregón was in the presidency, CROM and the PLM continued to offer him important political support. As we have seen, labor was decisive in meeting congressional opposition and particularly in confronting the PLC efforts to control Obregón. In addition, Morones's ties to the AFL and Samuel Gompers in the United States was a valuable resource for the Obregón government, which was intent on gaining U.S. recognition and preventing U.S. support for any rebellion. Accordingly, Morones went to Washington as Obregón's representative, where he was successful in engaging the active support of Gompers, who waged an energetic campaign for U.S. recognition. Another source of political support was CROM's effective control of the national press through its organization of the printing departments of the newspapers in Mexico City. In this way, CROM was, in effect, able to exercise censorship and to prevent criticism of the government and cabinet members, as well as of CROM itself. This control of the press was to increase under Calles (Gruening 1928:373).

Finally, of course, the alliance with CROM afforded the state substantial control over labor. By repressing independent unions, supporting the CROM, and ensuring its dominance in the labor field, the government created a co-opted organized working class.

In exchange for this support of government, CROM got a number of concessions and benefits. In general, Obregón continued the new Sonoran pattern initiated by the transitional government of de la Huerta, a pattern which represented a radical departure in state-labor relations and which was accompanied by an alteration in capital-labor relations as well. Unions were not only free to organize and to strike without government opposition but often enjoyed government support, and for the first time the government was dependent on labor support and gained its own strength from the strength of organized labor (Carr 1976, vol. 1:153, 182).

As a result, CROM (and the PLM) gained a substantial voice and influence in government, and it received state support for expanding its organization, securing favorable settlements in labor disputes, and busting rival unions. Under Obregón, CROM leaders filled many important jobs in the government. The two most important were the appointment of Morones as director of the Federal Military Factories, from which position he controlled large appropriations, personnel, and munitions, and the appointment of a Cromista as governor of the federal district, giving CROM substantial influence in Mexico City. In addition, Cromistas filled many positions in the Department of Labor, including the chief of the Conciliation Section, which were used to the benefit of CROM in the settlement of industrial conflicts. The tendency for strike settlements to be favorable to workers was not the only way in which workers benefited in their disputes with employers; in fact the number of recognized, legal strikes declined over the course of the Obregón presidency after an initial, dramatic increase in 1921. In many other conflicts government pressured employers to agree to terms favorable to workers before the conflict came to a strike, and CROM was often able to appeal directly to Obregón to exert pressure in this manner (Carr 1976, vol. 1:183; Gruening 1928:343ff.).

In addition to favorable settlements in industrial disputes, CROM benefited organizationally from its alliance with the government. During the course of the Obregón presidency, membership in CROM grew dramatically. The increase indicated by CROM's figures from 50,000 to 1.2 million (including rural workers) is undoubtedly exaggerated, but it is clear that membership growth was "spectacular" between 1920 and 1924 (Carr 1976, vol. 1:178–79). Furthermore, CROM used its position in the government coalition to harass, even attack, and discriminate against rival Catholic, leftist, and independent unions. The CGT, founded in 1921 largely by dissidents from within the CROM, was particularly subject to attack in this way.

Finally, the state-labor alliance provided CROM with important financial subsidies from the government. Most importantly, CROM and the PLM were given the opportunity to raise money through supposedly voluntary contributions from government employees (Clark 1973:105). In addition the Ministry of Industry, Commerce, and Labor regularly supplied money to CROM unions to help finance their buildings, equipment, and annual conventions (Carr 1976, vol. 1:181–82), and CROM members were given railroad passes to attend these conventions (D. Bailey 1979:86).

Though the dominant CROM labor sector benefited in these ways, the confederation's overall assessment of Obregón was one of disappointment. In the most general terms, CROM leaders felt that Obregón had not given CROM the influence in government that it had bargained for and that had been agreed upon in the 1919 pact. Rather, as mentioned above, Obregón had tried to form a broad coalition without allowing his government to become too dependent upon any one sector and even sponsored the PNA, with which he became more closely identified and which represented an important rival organization to the CROM both in the political and the organizing arenas. In addition, a number of specific disappointments, failures to carry out the terms of the Morones-Obregón pact, and legislative defeats (see above) meant that by the end of the presidential term, Obregón and labor had gone their separate ways.

As we have seen, the state-labor alliance was renewed and strengthened under Calles, who was more dependent on labor support than Obregón had been. While Calles had been particularly close to labor and to CROM in particular, the 1923 de la Huerta rebellion, which challenged his succession to the presidency, was perhaps the event that cemented his reliance on labor, as CROM once again took up arms and formed workers' militias, apparently playing a fairly decisive role in the outcome of the armed conflict (Carr 1976, vol. 1:203).

As president from 1924 to 1928, Calles found CROM support crucial across a whole range of policies. Morones, both as a leader of CROM and as minister in the government, helped Calles pursue a nationalistic economic policy. When the Banco de Mexico was created, CROM led a publicity campaign for the bank and urged its affiliates to deposit funds there. As minister, Monores launched a campaign to favor national products and was a leading figure favoring the new petroleum law, which attempted to regulate foreign concessions. However, by 1927 when the ensuing conflict with the United States threatened to reach crisis proportions, Morones followed Calles's policy change and supported his solution to the conflict, involving a substantial backing off on the part of Mexico.

Another important contribution of labor and Morones was that of industrial peace. Morones preferred to negotiate wages and come to an arrangement with employers. The number of legal strikes continued to decline under Calles, from a peak of 310 in 1921 (or nearly 200 in 1920 and 1922) to 136 in 1924, and just seven in 1928 (Carr 1976, vol. 1:183; vol. 2:41). Further-more, of those strikes that did occur, the percentage of settlements favorable to employers increased (Clark 1973:119). "Strikes did undoubtedly decrease because Morones followed a definite program of collaboration with employ-ers even, at times, at the expense of the workers" (Clark 1973:120). Calles viewed social peace and the cooperation of the labor movement as essential to his efforts to achieve economic resurgence (Medín 1982:19).

In addition, CROM generally defended Calles against charges of bolshe-vism, which were quite widespread particularly among foreign businessmen, by adopting a strongly anticommunist stance and strengthening its ties to the AFL. Its effectiveness in this regard was enhanced by the newly created position of labor attaché in Mexican embassies throughout the world. To em-phasize its international alignment, CROM withdrew its labor attaché from Moscow (Carr 1976, vol. 2:50).

Finally, as in the preceding presidential term, CROM continued to exercise significant control over the press. This control was particularly important in a period when the government faced increasing hostility from conservative sectors, including owners of the major national papers (J. Meyer et al. 1977:105; Gruening 1928:372).

In the most general terms, then, the governments of the 1920s reaped the advantages typical of cases of party incorporation and the labor-state alliance at its core. These were both political and economic. Politically, labor pro vided legitimacy and support for the government. Economically, a poten-tially radical and oppositionist working class was converted into a cooperat-ing labor movement that supported capitalist reconstruction and modernization.

In exchange for its cooperation, the labor movement enjoyed unprece-dented levels of political influence within the state, extensive material ben-efits derived from state resources, and state support for CROM's effort to extend its dominance in the labor movement. CROM leaders came to occupy many important governmental posts. Most important among these was the appointment of Morones as minister of industry, commerce, and labor, and among the members of Calles's cabinet, he enjoyed a position of *primus inter pares.* That a labor leader should occupy such a position—in charge, after all, of not only a labor ministry but of a major economic ministry responsible for industry and commerce—was unique in the annals of Latin American his-tory. With Morones as minister, CROM unionists came to occupy important positions within the ministry. In addition, through the PLM, labor domi-nated the local government of Mexico City and increased its representation in the federal Congress, forming an important and unified minority.

This influence in government gave CROM tremendous financial and or-ganizational benefits as well as greatly increased leverage in collective bar-gaining. Through the continued "voluntary" contributions by government employees of one day's salary per month, as well as through increasing cor-ruption that came to permeate CROM unionism, CROM was able to amass substantial funds (Carr 1976, vol. 2:6–7). Further, Morones's position as minister gave him wide-ranging influence over labor matters, particularly over the conciliation and arbitration boards, on which CROM was able to control virtually two-thirds of the members—the labor representatives and most of the government representatives. Though good data are lacking, it seems clear that most decisions were handed down in favor of workers and that many workers were able to attain large wage increases (Carr 1976, vol. 2:26–27). Finally, the state-labor alliance gave CROM the opportunity to reinforce its hegemony over the labor movement. Through its ability to influence the decisions emanating from the Labor Department, including those of the conciliation and arbitration boards, CROM harassed and discriminated against the rival CGT and independent unions, and it employed tactics of intimidation and gangsterism to defeat non-CROM unions and to impose its domination of working-class organizations (Carr 1976, vol. 2:16ff.). Through these tactics and through the positive benefits CROM unions were able to reap as a result of their influence within the state, membership in CROM continued to grow dramatically, though the 2 million membership figure that CROM claimed for 1925–26 is undoubtedly inflated.

While the close relations between labor and the state yielded important advantages to CROM, there were also important limitations to CROM's power. Labor never achieved a strong enough position within Congress to pass the long awaited labor law, nor was CROM able to cut into the PNA base among the rural workers, despite the fact that the minister of agriculture was considered a CROM ally. Further, as dependent as Calles was on labor support, he was also constrained by the strength of the Obregón bloc and would not back CROM against powerful politicians identified with Obregón (J. Meyer et al. 1977:173–74). An important example was the case of Tamaulipas Governor Portes Gil, who opposed CROM and blocked its efforts to organize in his state.

In terms of the benefits to labor, then, the exchange revealed the way in which the power achieved by CROM was double-edged, and it reflected labor's classic dilemma. On the one hand, there is no doubt that organized labor received many benefits, and many workers were able to obtain wage gains as a result of the political power and state support labor attained as part of the bargain. Yet the other part of that bargain, support for the government, was a mechanism of control over and demobilization of the working class. On the most general level, this support took the form of backing the government and its project of capitalist modernization, thereby bringing the working class in line ideologically, so that it came to reject a class orientation in favor of a notion of class harmony and cooperative relations between labor and both foreign and national capital (Carr 1976, vol. 2:42; Krauze et al. 1977:84–86). Yet, control over the working class went much further.

In her discussion of the period, Clark (1973:106) quickly qualifies her notion of "labor in power" to explain that it really meant CROM in power. That, in turn, really meant a leadership clique in power, specifically the Action Group, headed by Morones. Echoing Michels's iron law of oligarchy, Gruening (1928:360) describes the situation: "The masses who ostensibly 'rule' are merely manipulated, sometimes for their benefit, but invariably for the leaders'." The corruption of these leaders became legendary and was readily visible in the ostentatious and flamboyant demeanor of, above all, Morones. Their behavior was often at the expense of the working class. Employers learned that industrial peace could be bought, that strikes could be called off for a price, and that more favorable collective agreements could likewise be arranged (Clark 1973:107; Ashby 1967:15). In addition, union funds—strike funds and funds for mutual benefit services and other purposes—were often diverted and found their way into the pockets of leaders. As Clark (1973:107) states, "Almost every labor organization—and not only in Mexico—has had much the same experience. The C.R.O.M. had more opportunity because it had more power."

Needless to say, the situation was particularly bleak for non-CROM workers. Some were recruited to the ranks of the CROM by use of substantial force. The confederation took particular aim at those who remained outside the fold, as CROM sought to eliminate the anarchist CGT and the independent unions. As mentioned above, Morones used harassment, intimidation, and gangsterism in this fight (Carr 1976, vol. 2:16). An example was the treatment of the railroad workers, who constituted the largest independent union. In 1926–27, the series of strikes they called were declared illegal by Minister Morones, who called in federal troops to put down the strikes. Pitched battles between CROM unionists and the railroad workers ensued, ending in the imprisonment of the leader of the railroad workers and the defeat of the union.

All in all, the state-labor alliance brought important benefits to both members of the coalition: to Obregón and Calles on the one hand, and, on the other, to labor, though this meant CROM and, especially, the CROM leadership. The dual dilemma is seen in the disadvantages. The result for labor was a corrupt labor movement that crushed independent unions and deradicalized the working class, subordinating labor's activity to the government line regarding the relationship between capital and labor (Córdova 1977:324–26). The disadvantage to the government was the opposition the state-labor alliance provoked, despite the state control exercised over the labor movement by virtue of the terms of exchange that underlay the coalition and state policies of promoting capitalist modernization.

Opposition to Populism: The 1920s

The present argument is that in the 1920s the incorporation period in Mexico, particularly the Calles presidency, was characterized by radical populism, displaying its classic features: a state-labor alliance, which, taking on its own political dynamic, created polarization and opposition to the prolabor stance of the government. The alliance and prolabor policies have already been described. Unfortunately, little research is available on the subsequent polarization and the formation of counterreformist groups. Nevertheless, references to the opposition engendered by the position of Morones in the government and to the prolabor policies of Calles, however vague, abound in the literature. For example, Medín (1982:17) refers to the "opposition to the enormous power concentrated in the hand of CROM and its leader Morones during the Calles presidency" as "one of the fundamental catalysts in unifying the different members of the Obregón camp." Enough fragments of information are available to suggest that polarization occurred around several issues involving different groups and interests: strong opposition to the government came from the United States, the national bourgeoisie, competing bases of popular support (for instance, the PNA), and the Church. In each of these conflicts Morones and the PLM/CROM played an important role.

The first conflict, then, involved the United States and those in Mexico who favored accommodation with the United States. In 1925, the Mexican government enacted new petroleum and land laws, which threatened to provoke a crisis in U.S.-Mexican relations. In this conflict, the role of labor is the least direct. Nevertheless, it is important to remember that Morones was the leading proponent for the nationalist position. Within the cabinet he lobbied for a strongly nationalistic petroleum policy. His triumph led to a crisis with the United States and with the government faction favoring conciliation, leading to the resignation of Alberto Pani as minister of hacienda. The role of the state-labor alliance in precipitating this crisis is suggested by a comment of U.S. Ambassador Dwight Morrow, who was ultimately instrumental in resolving the conflict. According to Morrow, Calles saw the petroleum law as "a gesture to satisfy the demands of the radical wing of the revolutionary group at a moment of serious internal tension" (cited in Carr 1976, vol. 2:48).

The second source of opposition generated by the role of labor in the governing alliance was the national bourgeoisie, which reacted strongly to the position of labor in the government and the shift in power that it represented. As we have seen, unionization increased, probably dramatically; wages tended to go up; and the arbitration and conciliation boards were apparently quite consistently prolabor. It is certainly the case that a number of factors blunted the impact of the political position of labor, the growth of the CROM, and the changing nature of industrial relations during this period. The state-labor alliance was decidedly double-edged in terms of the kind of organized labor movement it created. Though it dramatically increased the power of organized labor, the result of the alliance was, as we have seen, the creation of a co-opted union movement under an increasingly corrupt leadership that supported the government and its economic reconstruction and development projects, rejected a class orientation in favor of a collaborationist position, and became vehemently anti-Communist. Nevertheless, the creation of an officialist, moderate union movement may temper but rarely fundamentally overcomes the opposition of capital toward an expansion of unionization, the threat it feels to its control over the workplace, and the favored position of labor in the political arena.

The opposition of national capital during the Calles-Morones period is often mentioned in the literature, but details are vague (e.g., Clark 1973:257). Typical of these is the following: "From the first days of the new government, the principal leaders of CROM occupied important governmental posts and thus gave the government a radical character which created much opposition" (Garrido 1984:53). It also seems clear that in opposition to the power of labor, there was during this period substantial organizational activity on the part of capital to put pressure on the government (Durand Ponte 1979:167; Pozas Horcasitas 1981:278).

While there is little information about national capital in general, one valuable study emphasizes the primacy of the labor issue for the most important sector of Mexican capital, the elite of the northern city of Monterrey. Saragoza (1988:11) argues that for this group, "labor policy became the most visible point of contention." Furthermore, apprehension over labor policy and especially over the elevation of Morones to a position of such power and over the rising influence of the CROM was the most important factor in consolidating the Monterrey elite into an effective group that would defend its interests in the political arena (Saragoza 1988:126, 129). Though the Monterrey elite was regionally based, its concern about labor was cast in national terms. Given its power within Monterrey and its control of company unions there, the Monterrey elite had the labor situation under control at the local and state level. These industrialists, however, had begun to extend their business activities on a national scale and were concerned about "a strong national labor movement [that] menaced their ability to plan and to develop new markets without the harassment of dealing with unions and labor officials outside their control" (Saragoza 1988:134). With this concern in mind, they were motivated, as we shall see in greater detail below, to begin organizing national capital for political action.

During the Calles period, then, the labor issue was salient for national capital and turned capital against Calles.

> Businessmen despaired over Calles' unwillingness to curb Morones' excesses or to block the cabinet minister's encroachment into the nation's economic affairs. . . . In spite of the probusiness measures of the state, Morones cast a pall over the private sector. Moreover, [from the point of view of capital] Morones jeopardized progress, endangered the economic revival of the nation, and tarnished the mission of Mexican business, of Monterrey's industrialists in particular. (Saragoza 1988:134–35).

A third line of cleavage that intensified under Calles was that between labor and the competing agrarian base of popular support for the state. We have seen that already under Obregón there had been a substantial splintering of the revolutionary coalition and that two blocs were emerging: one led by Obregón, which looked to the PNA as the basis of popular support, and one led by Calles, which looked to labor and the PLM as the basis of popular support. During the campaign and election, the PNA as well as the PLM had supported Calles, and after the election the two parties even participated in a series of parliamentary blocs. Yet the splintering of the coalition continued once Calles came to power, and this cooperation did not last. To some extent, this conflict represented the personal ambitions of and rivalries between the two "strong men" of Mexico at that time (Clark 1973:123; Tannenbaum 1966:248). Yet it seems clear that the hostility and competition between their respective bases of support played an important and independent role in this conflict: agrarian sectors in the PNA and labor in the PLM were competing over the issue of organizing the peasantry and they were competing for political influence, an issue which took on a special dynamic given Obregón's presidential ambitions. Once installed as minister, Morones felt strong enough to attack the PNA; and as relations between the two deteriorated, the PNA withdrew from parliamentary cooperation with the PLM and declared its hostility to Calles (Clark 1973:124). As Clark (1973:122–23) has commented, though the general policies of Obregón and Calles were essentially the same, "their respective centers of strength lay in divergent and increasingly hostile groups." The presence of labor in the governing coalition, then, was once again clearly a central element in the opposition of the agrarian and Obregón factions.

The final conflict was with the Church. Church-state conflict in Mexico had a long history stretching back to the previous century and culminating in the religious articles of the 1917 constitution, which severely curtailed the role and rights of the Church in areas that were not strictly religious. On the defensive, the Church had assumed a number of stances that put it in opposition to the path of the revolution as defined in the constitution and as championed by the Sonorans. The Church conducted a campaign against state schools and secular education, and it opposed land reform as well as labor unions, which it forbade Catholics to join (Quirk 1973:119ff). Furthermore, it had supported the de la Huerta rebellion (Hamilton 1982:75).

Whereas Obregón had been a conciliator who avoided conflict with the Church by failing to implement the religious articles of the constitution, Calles, by contrast, came to the presidency with a history of initiatives taken against the Church, both as governor and as minister of interior. Unlike his more accommodating predecessor, he had a reputation as "an implacable enemy of the Church," as "a man of principle . . . determined to enforce the laws unrelentingly, to limit the powers of the Church," and as a man with a rumored readiness to move quickly in this regard (Quirk 1973:132–38).

This background seems sufficient to explain the anti-Church legislation that began when Calles assumed the presidency. Yet, though adequate primary research is not available to elaborate this argument, it might be suggested that the role of labor and the state-labor alliance may have been very great and indeed even decisive in the Church-state conflict. The history of Church opposition to secular unionism and its attacks on the CROM on the one hand, and, on the other, the leading role of the CROM and of Morones in launching and carrying out the state offensive against the Church are well known. From the early 1900s, the Church had begun to develop a program of social action to counter the menacing "socialist" movements among the workers, forming labor circles to preach Christian principles, social peace, and class harmony, and later denouncing secular unionism from the pulpit. It attacked CROM from the time it was founded, and finally, in 1921, moved to oppose secular unionism by creating a rival Catholic union movement. The stage was set for the violent fights between the Catholic and secular workers' organizations, which began to erupt in the early 1920s.[15]

It was against this background that Calles and CROM launched a major offensive against the Church, culminating in the 1926 decrees, which regulated and quite severely restricted Church activities (see Quirk 1973:167). Carr (1976, vol. 2:102ff.; see also Clark 1973:160) argues that CROM was the "principal author" of this offensive, playing the major role in provoking the Church-state crisis with its support of the schismatic movement of 1925 and directing and executing the offensive both from its position of power in the ministry and in the streets.

Though it might be going too far to suggest that the attack on the Church can be explained as a payoff to Morones and CROM that a politically indebted Calles owed following his election in the aftermath of the de la Huerta rebellion, it is nevertheless clear that labor's position in this conflict was central and that in an important way the offensive represented CROM's response to the inroads Catholic unions were making in organized labor and to this threat to CROM hegemony (Carr 1976, vol. 2:99).

After Calles became president, then, political opposition grew around several issues. In each case, different groups opposed the government over policies more or less directly related to the position of labor in the governing alliance and to the period of radical populism that ensued. By 1926 many of these conflicts reached crisis proportion. Relations with the United States seemed to be approaching a breaking point; the Morones-Pani conflict was heating up, with the latter threatening to resign; parliamentary conflicts and factionalism were so intense and alliances so ephemeral and fleeting that Calles governed by decree in the face of legislative immobilism (J. Meyer et al. 1977:114); the state offensive against the Church was met with the response of a religious and economic boycott on the part of the Church and with the Cristero Rebellion on the part of lay Catholics. In addition, the economy was stagnating, and the Yaqui Indians of Sonora rebelled, urged on by both the Church and de la Huerta, who was regrouping in the United States, where the government did nothing to stop various exiles from plotting against the Mexican government (Quirk 1973:190).

At the same time, another issue came to the fore that was to dominate and further polarize Mexican politics for the next couple of years: Obregón's candidacy for a second presidential term starting in 1928. The issue was a political lightening rod, raising as it did the very issue over which the 1910 Revolution itself had initially been fought: that of reelection. The change in the constitution that allowed Obregón to run a second time did not put an end to this political controversy. It dominated politics and in the end provoked another rebellion against the government.

---

[15] Clark 1973:90; Quirk 1973:129; Carr 1976, vol. 2:96.

In the issue of Obregón's candidacy, as well, labor in the form of the CROM/PLM was a central player for at least two reasons. First, Morones himself had presidential ambitions and in many ways seemed the likely successor to Calles.[16] Second, given the tension and suspicion that had grown between Obregón and CROM toward the end of the former's presidency, CROM was very hostile to the idea of a second Obregón term in which it would be politically marginalized and labor support would not count for much.

Given the tense, highly politicized situation and the certainty that the army would not accept a Morones presidency (J. Meyer et al. 1977:82), Calles decided to move to a more centrist position in an attempt to address the crisis and put an end to the polarization of Mexican politics. He not only supported Obregón, who was immensely popular, but more generally he moved away from labor, whose position was so central to all of the political cleavages and crises of that period. In the remaining years of his presidency, Calles came to an agreement with the United States, substantially compromising his position; he accommodated Obregón and thus his Agrarista support base; he made initial moves to achieve a modus vivendi with the Church; and he began to distance himself from Morones and CROM. "Calles was no longer finding it profitable or interesting to be known as the 'labor' and the 'bolshevik' president. [As a result] he was openly more conservative, and his government depended more and more upon the support of the right" (Clark 1973:127). The final coup de grâce came after the assassination of president-elect Obregón: when CROM was accused of being involved in the assassination, PLM members, including Morones, resigned their government posts and Calles named Portes Gil, an outspoken opponent of CROM, as provisional president.

The Calles presidency thus seems to represent a case of radical populism in which the populist dynamic or contradiction is evident. In the exchange through which the government offered the major labor confederation unprecedented benefits as it sought to mobilize labor support, the government gained the cooperation of a labor movement that pursued industrial peace, supported government economic policies, and undermined leftist and independent unions. Though a corrupt and co-opted union movement was the result of the state-labor alliance, the power of labor in the government and the concessions it won nevertheless led to the opposition and polarization that is characteristic of radical populism.

Crucially, however, this first period of populism lacked one feature that later emerged in the 1930s: the formation of a multiclass integrative party that would institutionalize the populist alliance. Though the organized labor movement played an important role in the populist coalition, the institutionalization of its political participation through its incorporation into a populist party did not occur.

---

[16] As J. Meyer et al. (1977:82) has said, "No había más pre-tapado que Morones" (roughly: No one seemed more likely to be elevated to the presidency than Morones).

The Maximato: 1928–1934

The next presidential term, known as the Maximato, constituted a more conservative phase of the incorporation period, with the government more concerned to establish its control over labor and less interested in mobilizing its support and maintaining a coalition with it. Obregón had won reelection, but had been assassinated before he took office. Following the political conflict that surrounded the issue of Obregón's second candidacy, the revolutionary principle of "no reelection" was reinstituted and the presidential term was extended to six years. During this term, three presidents held office: Emilio Portes Gil, whom Calles appointed as provisional president after Obregón's assassination; Pascual Ortiz Rubio, who ran for president when new elections were called; and Abelardo Rodríguez, who assumed office after Ortiz Rubio resigned. In each case, the presidency became an empty office, with real power being held by Calles, the acknowledged "jefe máximo," a position which gave the period its name.

The conservative trend evident toward the end of the Calles presidency was accelerated during the Maximato, and the progressive policies that had characterized most of the Calles presidency were reversed. Whereas "President Calles was anticlerical, prolabor, pro–public works, and nominally pro-agrarian . . . [the] governments of the callista period (1928–34) by and large dropped the anti-Church crusade, favored foreign capital, virtually abandoned progressive labor and agrarian programs, and sought a rapprochement with the United States" (Brandenburg 1964;66). The Maximato clearly represented a conservative, nonpopulist or even antipopulist interlude.

During the Maximato, a number of things occurred that are important for the present discussion. First, Calles formed a political party, the PNR (National Revolutionary Party), but coming as it did in a pause in the course of radical populism it failed to incorporate organized labor. Secondly, a federal labor law was passed, though this did not represent as major an incorporating event as it did elsewhere in Latin America since, under Article 123 of the 1917 constitution, the Mexican states rather than the federal government had already moved to establish labor laws. Finally, the labor movement underwent a major organizational transformation and the state-labor alliance was largely severed before being renewed under Cárdenas. With state support of the CROM mostly withdrawn, the labor movement underwent a process of disintegration as more and more groups withdrew from affiliation with the corrupt and now discredited Morones confederation. The other side of this disintegration was the beginning of the resurgence of a new labor movement that was more autonomous from the state and which, under the leadership of Lombardo Toledano, was committed to such autonomy.

The new party that Calles founded represented his solution to the political crisis at the end of his presidency. The consolidation of the state continued to be a major concern. No presidential succession had occurred peacefully and without violence since the revolution. The assassination of Obregón underscored the need for a mechanism to institutionalize executive succession. Furthermore, the Sonorans, who had been trying to impose their vision of the postrevolutionary state, were now left without an heir apparent. De la Huerta could not be considered after his 1924 revolt; Obregón was dead; and Calles was eliminated by the principle of no reelection. Not only had a political vacuum been left by the assassination of Obregón, but, in the midst of political polarization, political conflicts abounded and the social base of the state seemed to be slipping away. Supporters of Obregón rather than of Calles had become a majority in Congress (Garrido 1984:64), and they were, of course, particularly upset by the assassination and particularly hostile to the CROM. Always rivals of the Calles faction, their hostility increased after the assassination (Dulles 1961:372). Furtak (1974:28) has argued that the Escobar Rebellion of 1929 represented the opposition of the Obregón faction to the founding of the PNR and to other moves that they saw as intended to perpetuate the power of Calles at their expense. Opposing both the Obregón and the Calles factions were the Antireelectionists, who presented the major electoral challenge to Calles's candidate, Ortiz Rubio, in the 1929 elections. At the same time, various regional political and military caudillos continued to pose a challenge (Garrido 1984:64); and despite the change in policy at the end of Calles's presidency, the conflicts with the Church, capital, and the agrarians produced by the earlier populist policies were yet to be completely resolved and overcome. In addition, in this context, CROM was no longer an advantageous source of support.

Thus, at the end of 1928, Calles moved to found a political party, the PNR. The new party served as a mechanism to centralize power and unite the still dispersed foci of power into a single organization. Though in many ways the party was a confederation or coalition of regional caciques and revolutionary caudillos and their political parties and movements, it did represent the first step in the creation of central political control. The PNR also served as the personal vehicle for Calles, who was able to use the party to maintain political power without occupying the presidency. Indeed, the party became Calles's vehicle of control over the president (Medín 1982:40–41).

The hostility and opposition aroused by the Calles-CROM alliance prevented the incorporation of the labor central into the new Calles coalition and hence into the new party (Medín 1982:58), and the party failed to attract or incorporate popular support (Garrido 1984:173). Neither the PLM nor the PNA, the two major parties with popular support, participated in the organizing conference of the party (Garrido 1984:76). Quite the contrary, in 1930, those two parties joined other groups to form the National Revolutionary Alliance (ARN) in order to present opposition candidates in the congressional elections. Though a few labor groups did join the PNR, there was widespread hostility to the PNR on the part of both the CROM and the major independent labor groups which, during these years, broke from the CROM.[17] During the Maximato, then, the CROM and the PLM remained in clear opposition

[17] Garrido 1984:116, 155; Anguiano 1975:35; Dulles 1961:518–19.

to the PRN; the PNA, after it was brought to heel by the heavy hand of Calles's intervention in its leadership selection, subsequently joined the party.

The Maximato represents a hiatus in radical populism and a rupture in the state-labor alliance that characterized the Obregón and Calles presidencies. An abandonment of *la política de masas* (the politics of mass support mobilization) accompanied the turn toward conservative policies, a change of direction that held out little to attract popular support. Labor policy reflected declining state dependence on labor support. Neither the economic nor the political climate favored a prolabor policy. The 1929 crash and world depression sent unemployment skyrocketing and wages plummeting (Anguiano 1975:11–16). More concerned with restimulating the economy and increasing investment (including foreign investment), policy swung to a probusiness position that condemned most strikes. As a result, "a virtual moratorium on strikes was declared" (Cornelius 1973:405) at the same time that attempts to institute a minimum wage, as provided for in the constitution, were opposed by labor because the proposed wage was so low (Clark 1973:225–26). With the rapid rise in the cost of living that ensued in the early 1930s, real income fell.

In this conservative interlude, a policy of dividing and weakening the labor movement generally seemed to hold precedence over one of control and accommodation through an alliance with a unified and dominant confederation.[18] Though during most of this period Calles was hesitant to break completely with the CROM (Córdova 1981:134), under pressure from the anti-CROM Obregonistas the Maximato was more fundamentally characterized by a general process of *desmoronamiento* (de-Morones-ization) in which Morones and the CROM were discredited. The first Maximato president, Portes Gil, was known for his anti-CROM zeal and enthusiastically undertook to weaken the CROM and to purge its influence within the government. Portes Gil's attack on the CROM went much further than Calles had wanted and resulted in the drastic reduction of the confederation's syndical and political power (Medín 1982:54–55). Government tactics represented many of the same techniques of control, repression, and patronage that had been used by Morones. CROM unionists in the government and in official posts—including most importantly in the Department of Labor and on Conciliation and Arbitration Boards—were replaced by opponents of CROM; the federal army intervened in labor conflicts but against the CROM; and the government offered many incentives to union leaders to leave the CROM, including monetary rewards, government positions, and the promise of more favorable labor settlements. Moreover, CROM lost its income from state employees' "contributions" (Carr 1976, vol. 2:155; Clark 1973:134).

During the Maximato, there were some half-hearted moves to maintain some relationship with labor, but none met with much success. Initially Portes Gil, in seeking to develop alternatives to the CROM, offered support

---

[18] Clark 1973:263; Cornelius 1973:402, 405; Córdova 1981:56.

to the Communists and then encouraged efforts to form a United Syndical Front (Medina 1982:62,64). As part of his anti-CROM campaign Portes Gil sought to bolster the CGT. As a result, the CGT largely abandoned its anarcho-syndicalist line; and while it did attract a number of CROM dissidents, it remained small and suffered by ending up on the wrong side of the factional dispute between Ortiz Rubio and Calles (Córdova 1981:42; L. Meyer 1978:124–25). Finally in 1932, the government, perhaps with the 1934 election battle beginning to heat up and the utility of labor support once again apparent, became involved in sponsoring a Labor Chamber of the Federal District (Clark 1973:265, 270). Publicly promoted by the CGT, the chamber movement quickly spread to other states, and the following year the National Labor Chamber (CNT) was formed. Its program was one of supporting the government, opposing important strikes, and enforcing the new, controversial labor law that was opposed by most labor groups. Despite (or perhaps because of) its official support, however, it was a stillborn organization.[19] The CNT, founded at the end of the period and never embracing the dominant part of the labor movement, was the closest the Maximato governments ever came to renewing the state-labor alliance.

A key aspect of labor policy was passage of a federal labor law. Article 123 of the 1917 constitution had defined a number of labor rights and paved the way for the passage of federal legislation. It was regarded as a triumph for labor, and a federal law that would regulate the constitutional provision was high on the labor agenda. Nevertheless, during the period of labor's political ascendancy, no federal labor law had been passed. The inaction of Morones on this issue was due to his uncertain ability to control the drafting of the law or to guide it in a way that would favor labor. In addition, Morones was ambivalent about a law that would limit his discretionary power to favor the CROM over other labor federations. Discussions of a labor law were held in 1925, 1926, and 1928, but, reflecting a political stalemate, they accomplished little (Saragoza 1988:156). Finally, during the Maximato in 1929, the first labor bill was introduced.

Labor, capital, and the state all had specific interests in a new labor law. Labor, of course, wanted a federal law that was at least as favorable as those already adopted in the states where labor was strong and had substantial political power. Employers were particularly keen to have a federal labor law. The diversity and confusion of a plethora of labor laws on the state level did not serve them well, and they saw a federal law as a means of achieving greater institutionalization of control, predictability, and uniformity in labor relations on a national scale. At least equally important, however, a labor law was seen by conservative businessmen as a vehicle to curb the power of Morones (Saragoza 1988:135), that is, as an antipopulist device that would prevent a repetition of radical populism and the formation of a state-labor alliance.

Finally, for the Calles faction a labor law was an important element in the

---

[19] Clark 1934:271–74; L. Meyer 1978:129; Córdova 1981:138.

broader policy of centralizing political power. Many governors and local caudillos owed their power to the patronage relationships they had established with labor at the state or local level. The Calles faction saw the labor law as a means of achieving central control both over the labor movement and labor relations and over the political arena more generally by depriving those local and regional political leaders of their power base. These goals were to be accomplished by the way in which the law would extend federal government control over labor and make the federal government—more than the unions and their ability to strike bargains with local politicians—the source of labor benefits. President Portes Gil, in particular, the leader of the more progressive *rojo* faction within the new party, introduced the bill in an attempt to gain labor support for the state in the post-CROM era (Saragoza 1988:164; Medín 1982:65). With this bill he sought to crush Morones's power and to win the support of non-CROM labor. He saw in a new labor code the means to "outflank Morones, to undermine his support among workers, and to make the government—not the CROM—the key to labor's protection and welfare" (Saragoza 1988:157).

In the end, the bill failed to pass because all sectors opposed it. In order to fit into Portes Gil's strategy, the new code had to be prolabor, even if it were anti-CROM. The CROM was clearly aware of its intent, and independent labor was suspicious of the government's commitment (Saragoza 1988:158; L. Meyer 1978:151). Industrialists objected to the law as "overwhelmingly tilted in favor of workers" (Saragoza 1988:159) and as more radical than the constitution itself (Córdova 1981:52). The Monterrey industrial elite formed the national employers association COPARMEX as a new organization to unite Mexican capital in opposition to the bill. Opposition also came from foreign capital, as both Henry Ford and U.S. Ambassador Dwight Morrow came out strongly against it. Calles's failure to throw his weight behind the bill assured its defeat (Saragoza 1988:164).

In 1931, under President Ortiz Rubio, a new version of the labor code was introduced—one that made more concessions to capital. Though these were not sufficient to win the employers' support, Calles's strong commitment to this new version was enough to ensure passage. The result was a federal labor law opposed by both labor and capital. Employers continued to object to the law as too favorable to labor. It was, in fact, one of the least "corporative" of the Latin American labor laws and contained a mix of a relatively high level of inducements for labor and low level of constraints (see Collier and Collier 1979:973–76). This mix reflected the political importance of labor in the postrevolutionary Mexican state, even in the relatively nonpopulist, conservative period of the Maximato. Nevertheless, labor found many of the provisions of the law deeply disappointing and detrimental to its interests (see Clark 1973:215ff; Harker 1937:95). The law was more conservative than many of the existing state labor laws and accepted practices (Clark 1973:215; Córdova 1981:109). The adverse effects on labor were seen in the following months as a number of contracts were revised in favor of capital in accordance with the new law (Córdova 1981:113; Clark 1973:228). Despite the opposition of both labor and capital, the law was passed by Calles forces as a centralizing measure to consolidate political control.

With the decline of CROM from a position of power and with the new attitude of the state toward labor, the labor movement experienced a period of organizational disarray and dispersal during the Maximato. The very end of the period, however, saw the beginning of a renewal of a united national labor movement with the formation of the General Confederation of Mexican Workers and Peasants (CGOCM). This organization represented a new type of labor movement: one that was more independent from the state and closer to its mass base and that embraced a more distinctly class-oriented political ideology (Pozas Horcasitas 1981:274).

The political crisis at the end of the Calles presidency and the process of *desmoronamiento* that followed led not only to the abandonment of CROM as an alliance partner by prominent political actors within the state but also to the disaffiliation from the CROM of important sectors of labor. The corruption and authoritarian nature of the CROM had caused much discord and opposition, and by 1928 some unions were already beginning to withdraw from the confederation. The desertions from the CROM—and also from the PLM—accelerated dramatically after Obregón's assassination, and particularly under the barrage of government attack and repression that constituted the anti-CROM campaign of President Portes Gil.

In addition to the general process of disaffiliation from the CROM of individual unions, the internal discord within the confederation led to three important splits over the next few years. The first two represented the desertion of groups that abandoned the declining CROM but sought an alliance with the government, which the CROM was no longer in a position to effect. The third, however, was quite different in nature.

The first split, in the beginning of 1929, was led by Fidel Velázquez, Fernando Amilpa, and three other union leaders, known as the *cinco lobitos* (five little wolves), who, within a few years, emerged at the pinnacle of union leadership in Mexico and remained there for decades, Fidel Velázquez remaining as the octogenarian leader of the major labor confederation through the 1980s. These leaders represented small, weak unions in Mexico City, which they organized as the FSTDF and which were dependent on government support (Córdova 1981:64–65). They were important beneficiaries of Portes Gil's anti-CROM zeal and gained representation on the Conciliation and Arbitration Boards as Portes Gil moved to replace the CROM representatives (Roxborough 1984:16).

Though the FSTDF represented an important defection from the CROM, most Mexico City workers remained within the CROM. This changed in 1932 when, with government encouragement, Pérez Medina, who was the leader of the CROM's Mexico City affiliate and who was locked in a factional struggle within the CROM, led the withdrawal of most of the rest of the Mexico City unions (Clark 1973:265). It was at this point that the government showed a renewed interest in developing close ties with a collaborating labor organization, and it used the FSTDF, Pérez Medina's FSODF, and the

CGT as the basis for its initiative in establishing a government-sponsored movement in the form of the Labor Chambers, first with the founding of the Labor Chamber of the Federal District and culminating in the formation of the CNT (see above).

The third split from the CROM was the most important. It reflected the disaffection of a reformist faction under the leadership of Vicente Lombardo Toledano. Lombardo's differences with the CROM leadership had emerged by 1928, when he argued for the withdrawal by CROM from politics and the disbanding of the PLM. In the following years he underwent a process of radicalization, and by 1932, in a rather dramatic moment, his faction shouted down Morones at a CROM convention, thus preventing the erstwhile leader from speaking (Clark 1973:262). The final break came the following year, when Lombardo took many of the most important labor organizations out of the CROM (Córdova 1981:154), relegating the confederation to a minor force within Mexican labor (L. Meyer 1978:120).

Attracted to Marxism and close to the Comintern line and the Soviet Union (though not a member of the Communist Party), Lombardo became the major spokesman for a new kind of apolitical, noncollaborationist, class-conscious, and militant unionism. The CGT had abandoned its anarcho-syndicalist line and was collaborating with the government. The Communist unions—which, like the CGT, had initially received governmental favor in the anti-CROM campaign—were soon repressed once they were no longer needed, and the new Communist confederation, the CSUM founded in 1929, was forced underground (L. Meyer et al. 1978:126–28; Clark 1973:134). In this context, the momentum in the labor field rested with Lombardo, who soon founded a new labor central, the CGOCM. Within a year of its founding, it emerged as the strongest and most important labor confederation in Mexico, and one, furthermore, that took the most independent, combative, and class-conscious line (Córdova 1981:204–8). Nevertheless, it is interesting to note that, given the momentum of the CGOCM and the corresponding weakness of the alternative chamber movement being sponsored by the government, the CGOCM was founded with the participation of Fidel Velázquez's FSTDF. This change in affiliation of the FSTDF from the CNT to the CGOCM had important consequences for both groups: it meant the failure of the government's ability to sponsor the CNT as a strong central that would collaborate with it, and, in the following years, it would influence the nature of the labor movement under Lombardo's leadership.

During the Maximato, then, the strong state-labor alliance, which had prevailed during the 1920s, fell apart. From the point of view of major actors within the state, the logic of the political crisis at the end of the Calles presidency led to the dismantling of this alliance. In any case, with the decline of the CROM no alternative confederation had yet emerged with which the state could form an alliance even if it wanted one. Indeed, in reaction to the corruption of the CROM and its abuse of power associated with its alliance with the state, the new labor groups that were emerging adopted a policy of political autonomy and noncollaboration with the state. The Maximato thus saw, in addition to the disintegration of the labor movement attending the CROM's fall from power, the beginning of a parallel process of reconsolidating a new labor movement, one that had greater autonomy from the state and that was more class conscious and more combative. This new departure can be seen in the failure of the state-sponsored chamber movement and in the absence of major labor groups within the PNR, as well as in the growth of the CGOCM as a noncollaborative, class-oriented labor movement. The CGOCM remained critical of the more progressive platform that was written by the newly emerging reformist faction in the PNR in connection with the 1934 elections. Indeed, it declined to back Cárdenas, as the reformist candidate in those elections. From the point of view of the state, therefore, the *political* incorporation of labor—the question of the way in which it would participate in the political arena—was again on the agenda.

Project from Above: The Cárdenas Period

The height of Mexican incorporation period occurred during the *sexenio*[20] of Lázaro Cárdenas from 1934 to 1940, when the pattern of radical populism was resumed. This period displayed all the classical features of populism: popular sector mobilization and the formation of an alliance between the state and the popular sectors, concessions and reforms, political opposition and the consequent polarization largely along class lines, and the formation of a multiclass party to channel and institutionalize the political participation of the popular sectors.

What was the Cárdenas project and why did Cárdenas mobilize labor support? There have been perhaps two general interpretations of Cárdenas. In the first account, he is seen as a popular reformer putting the weight of the state behind the popular sectors and largely against capital—especially foreign but also national. In the second, Cárdenas is seen as a bourgeois reformer, putting the weight of the state behind the project of capitalist industrialization and against precapitalist structures that would inhibit capitalist development (Córdova 1972; 1973; Anguiano 1975:39–41). Thus, agrarian reform, for instance, can be seen alternatively as a collectivist, noncapitalist reform benefiting the peasantry or as a mechanism to achieve social peace in the countryside, eliminate traditional, "feudal" relations in the rural sector, increase agricultural production, and expand the domestic market for local industry (Hamilton 1982:139–40, 178–80), thereby facilitating capitalist industrialization. These two views correspond to two seemingly contradictory elements in Cárdenas's background. On the one hand, Cárdenas seemed to be a genuine reformer. He came to power representing the progressive wing of the PNR that criticized the turn against the popular sectors and the increasing role of foreign capital that occurred during the Maximato, and he

[20] The six-year presidential term.

had pursued popular reformist policies as governor of Michoacán. On the other hand, he had remained loyal to Calles.

How, then, are we to understand Cárdenas? Cárdenas was neither simply a progressive reformer nor simply a promoter of capitalist industrialization, though he clearly had an agenda beyond the reformist program. To some extent, reform may have been an end in itself, given the personal values of Cárdenas and of those who held power within his coalition, particularly the "radical agrarianists" and "radical labor" (Cornelius 1973:423–24). Beyond that, however, the reform program was clearly a means to other ends, as can be seen in the control that the government always tried to exercise over the working class and peasantry, at whom the reforms were largely aimed.

The reformist program, however, should not be seen primarily as a means to the end of capitalist industrialization and the pattern of development Mexico has subsequently pursued. First of all, the break with Calles and the disjuncture between Maximato policies and Cárdenas's reformist policies cannot be understood in terms of the promotion of capitalist industrialization, for the Calles policy also supported this goal. "After 1929, the Callistas approximated . . . the 'managerial modernizers' . . . firmly committed to expanding Mexico's economic infrastructure to improve the country's financial situation. . . . By the end of the Maximato investor confidence in the Mexican economy had been largely restored and various important steps had been taken toward putting the country's fiscal affairs in order" (Cornelius 1973:407).

Secondly, as Hamilton (1982:140–41) points out, the Cárdenas vision went beyond capitalist reformism to embrace a much more radical restructuring of society and an experimentation with "non-capitalist, quasi-socialist forms of ownership and control of the means of production." Third, though certain policies and the socioeconomic restructuring that the reforms involved may have facilitated subsequent industrial development (see Cornelius 1973:475–76), Mosk (1950:58–59) argues that "there has . . . been no continuity in government industrial policy between the Cárdenas administration and those which have followed." Under Cárdenas, economic policy focused on agriculture and decentralized development rather than large-scale industry in large urban centers, which predominated in subsequent policy (Mosk 1950:53, 57).

Finally, North and Raby have convincingly argued that although the Cárdenist reforms in many ways laid the foundations for capitalist industrialization in Mexico, it is incorrect to make a post facto or functionalist argument that Cárdenas was the far-sighted leader whose "radical programme and policies of mass mobilization simply constituted an alternative and more intelligent strategy to preserve the hegemony of the dominant classes." Such an argument "comes very close to presupposing an omniscient political leadership, with an all-encompassing plan and full knowledge of what would happen if certain *very risky steps* [the radical reforms] were taken. . . . Into the bargain, it credits the *cardenista* leadership with almost complete control of the historical process" (North and Raby 1977:26).

However functional for capitalist development the Cárdenas reforms may ultimately have been, their effects were not clear to the participants—either to Cárdenas, who thought capitalism could be pursued and promoted in the context of genuine reform, or the bourgeoisie, to whom the reforms seemed to contradict the requirements of capitalist accumulation rather than promote it. The reforms, in fact, had the immediate effect of polarizing politics and of alienating much of the capitalist class and large sectors of the middle classes. The current perception was certainly not one of the establishment of bourgeois hegemony. Whatever the long-term effects of the reforms and despite the reformist but procapitalist and even reformist *qua* capitalist stance of the political leadership, the perception at the time was one of a state that was allied with the subordinate classes at the expense of the bourgeoisie and the landowners; and this very perception is a kind of self-fulfilling prophecy. The opposition of the dominant classes indicates the extent to which such a reformist period and the alliance embodied in radical populism represents a contradiction within capitalist development. The extent of this opposition assured that a comparable period would never be attempted again.

In the context of the present analysis, the main Cárdenas project is seen as a political rather than an economic one: Cárdenas is seen first and foremost as a state-builder and a nation-builder. His primary commitment was to strengthening the state and its political institutions (Hamilton 1982:119), still fragile from the upheavals of the revolution. The Sonoran period had made only a start in the consolidation of the postrevolutionary state. The Calles presidency ended in crisis and the next six-year presidential term accomplished little in this regard. With respect to labor support, a conservative policy orientation combined with the effects of the world depression gave rise to a labor movement that, rather than forming an important element in the basis of support for the state, was increasingly alienated, expressing heightened levels of discontent and protest, and undergoing a process of reorganization, radicalization, and transformation into a politically autonomous labor movement. In addition, during the Maximato, the presidency was weakened by Calles's retention of power. In Cárdenas's strategy to strengthen the state and the presidency, his reformist instincts were similar to those of the Sonorans before the Maximato and the other Jacobins of the 1917 Constitutional Convention, and it was the same coalition of middle and popular sectors that he sought to reconstitute.

Though Calles is sometimes seen as an important postrevolutionary institutionalizer and state-builder (see Córdova 1977:chap. 6), establishing the party and overseeing the first peaceful presidential succession after the revolution, the order he imposed was largely a personal one that left political institutions weak. He used the party as a vehicle for his personal control, which he exercised to the detriment of the institutional power of the presidency. During the Maximato, Cárdenas opposed Calles's usurpation of presidential power and tried to bring about a reconciliation between Calles and Ortiz Rubio in order to strengthen the presidency. Once elected president, of course, Cárdenas had an immediate and personal interest in strengthening the presidency since he did not want to fall victim to the Maximato pattern and become another ineffectual puppet president while Calles pulled the strings. In terms of state-building, then, the Cárdenas project can be seen as one of strengthening civilian political institutions, particularly the presidency and the party, against civilian caudillos like Calles and against the army, whose power was still not clearly subordinated to the government.

The six-year plan, adopted by the party in 1933 over the opposition of Calles and used as a campaign platform by Cárdenas, made clear the goals of the ascending reformist faction and its objections to the conservative bent of the Maximato and to the implicit alliance it forged between the state, foreign capital, and the domestic bourgeoisie (Hamilton 1982:197–98). In a number of provisions, it called for state promotion of national rather than foreign control of the economy and committed the state to promoting industrialization. It also embraced a number of substantive reforms that provided a basis for the mobilization of popular sector support. Agrarian reform, which had been effectively halted during the Maximato, was once again assigned high priority since the political base of the governors at the core of the new political faction, including Cárdenas, was the peasantry and since agrarian reform had been the initial unifying issue among them. In addition, the six-year plan adopted the language of class struggle and asserted a state role in strengthening the organization of industrial labor. It also asserted a state role in expanding the educational system and in introducing a "socialist" curriculum while simultaneously excluding religious doctrine (I. Meyer et al. 1978:180). In general, then, the project of the Cárdenas faction reaffirmed the activist role of the state and the mobilization of a popular social base initially expressed in the 1917 constitution (Hamilton 1982:121) and sustained against the Carranza faction by the Sonorans. It sought to mobilize popular sector support to consolidate the power of Cárdenas and his faction, to strengthen state political institutions, and to promote domestic capital accumulation and the development of a mixed economy in which the state would play an autonomous role, controlling both capital and labor (Hamilton 1978:160).

A populist coalition, then, figured prominently in the goals of Cárdenas. Popular sector mobilization was the basis on which he could build support for himself and the presidency in order to win independence from Calles. As Cockroft (1974:265) put it: "If Cárdenas were to become . . . 'his own man' . . . then he would have to challenge the powerful Calles machine, with its control of the national political party and bureaucracy, its connections with big business and old-guard labor leadership (CROM), its friendliness with the foreign investment community, and its influence within the Army. . . . Where could Cárdenas turn? Historically, new leaders had turned to organized labor. . . . As it happened, a new labor movement was available to Cárdenas."

Cornelius's (1973:439–43) analysis has shown how few coalitional options Cárdenas had in confronting the Calles faction and how the populist coalition with radical labor and agrarians was the only rational strategy. This coalition also became a vehicle for building a counterweight to the army when Cárdenas armed the peasants and formed workers' militias. Finally, with this social base of support, the state was put in a position that facilitated its ability to establish autonomy from foreign and domestic capital and to carry out the substantive reforms for which the Cárdenas period is known.

The mobilization by Cárdenas of working-class support has been well documented and need not be belabored. During the months in which he campaigned for the presidency, Cárdenas established a new basis for state-labor relations and let it be known that his government would be sympathetic to labor both in its efforts to organize and in its confrontations with capital. The immediate result was a significant rise in strikes. What should be emphasized here is the political strength and position of relative autonomy of the labor movement that Cárdenas initially encountered. Unlike the peasantry, which joined the Cárdenas coalition and actively supported and promoted his presidency, organized labor maintained its autonomy and stayed aloof from the electoral battle, though the PCM, which was active in labor organizations, fielded an opposition candidate. Thus, despite his championing of labor issues, Cárdenas was not initially successful in mobilizing labor support behind his candidacy or his presidency.

The coalition with labor began to be put together only in June 1935 when Calles, reflecting the alarm of the business community at the increase in strikes and the prolabor decisions of the Federal Labor Board, used the occasion of the telephone and telegraph strike to criticize and threaten Cárdenas because of his prolabor position. In the Calles-Cárdenas power struggle that ensued during the following year, the labor-Cárdenas alliance began to take form. Cárdenas, for his part, became increasingly dependent on the mobilization of labor support in the face of the establishment of a new party by Calles and of Calles's attempt to perpetrate a coup. Labor, for its part, was induced to support Cárdenas since the primacy of the labor issue in the Cárdenas-Calles conflict meant that the defense of the working class became one and the same as the defense of Cárdenas and his presidency. Thus was the populist coalition of the Cárdenas government and labor constituted.

Project from Below: The Cárdenas Period

During the Cárdenas period, then, the labor movement resumed an active political role and renewed its willingness to collaborate with the government. Though the events of 1935 and the political dynamics of the Calles-Cárdenas conflict provided an enormous impetus to this reorientation of labor, the change must also be seen in terms of the presence of different factions within the labor movement, their particular orientations, and the politics of the move to weld these factions into a unified labor movement.

The reunification of labor began with the momentum and dynamism of Lombardo's UGOCM, as it engaged in a series of jurisdictional disputes and undertook an aggressive organizational campaign (L. Brown 1964:156). Despite impressive success, the labor movement remained divided until unity was for all intents and purposes achieved under the impetus of two events.

The first was the challenge contained in the Calles speech of June 1935, in which he denounced the recent strike wave and attacked Cárdenas for not controlling it. The Electricians' Union (SME) took the initiative in organizing a response by calling for the formation of a united front of the working class. The Committee of Proletarian Defense was formed, and only the CROM and the CGT, which supported Calles, remained outside. An important step toward achieving unity had been taken, and the following February the participating unions founded a new labor confederation, the CTM (Confederation of Mexican Workers), under the leadership of Lombardo (Hernández Chávez 1979:147). The second impetus for unity was the adoption of the new popular front policy by Comintern. In the preceding years, Communist influence in the unions had grown substantially. The change in policy set the stage for the willingness of unions under the influence of the Communist Party, which had been legalized by Cárdenas, to participate in a single workers' central.

The new CTM represented the reunification of labor into an organization whose dominant ideology was clearly Marxist. Yet within this framework of unity, two distinct tendencies, already apparent in the Maximato, persisted. The first was the "pragmatic" tendency led by Fidel Velázquez and the cinco lobitos and based on relatively small, weak unions that were more dependent on state support. The second consisted of the stronger, more independent, and often more combative unions, particularly a number of important national industrial unions and unions where the Communist Party had significant influence.

As secretary general of the CTM, it fell to Lombardo to mediate between these two tendencies. A Marxist, who was close to the international Communist line, he was above all a firm believer in the importance of labor unity. The high priority that he placed on labor unity led him to capitulate to the Velázquez faction in crucial instances (Fuentes Díaz 1959:338).

Such an instance occurred immediately, when conflict flared into the open over elections for leadership of the new CTM. When the candidate of the Communist tendency emerged victorious in the election for secretary of organization, the Velázquez bloc threatened to withdraw from the CTM. In the compromise worked out among the leadership, the position was given to Velázquez in the interest of maintaining unity. This was an important defeat for the Communist faction, for the secretary of organization controlled procedures for the formation of both labor federations at the state level and national industrial unions. With this power, Velázquez took the opportunity to build up a union movement loyal to him (Hamilton 1982:154–55). Thus, the "pragmatic" tendency grew in strength as the Communist tendency became increasingly isolated within the CTM (Hernández Chávez 1979:154).

The conflict between the two factions was again evident in the June 1936 decision of the miners and metallurgists to leave the CTM, and it culminated in the April 1937 confrontation leading to the withdrawal of the unions opposed to the Velázquez bloc. These represented a very large (but disputed) proportion of the unions, including some of the most important national industrial unions. Under intense pressure from the international Communist movement in accordance with the popular front line, these unions soon returned to the CTM, but did so on a weak footing, having lost most of their leadership positions within the confederation. Thus, during the Cárdenas period a unified labor movement was forged and maintained, but one that was under the increasing hegemony of the *cinco lobitos*.

Though the new united labor movement, which was emerging from the debris of the CROM experience during the 1920s, explicitly and self-consciously sought to maintain its autonomy from the state, it soon abandoned its apolitical stance. It did so as a result of various factors. The first was the weakness of labor, which left it particularly vulnerable to an attack like that launched by Calles. Such a threat seemed willy-nilly to thrust labor into an active political role. In fact, in many ways it was the labor movement, at least as much as Cárdenas himself, that took the crucial and initiating role in precipitating the break with Calles and in taking the lead in the power struggle as it shaped up during the final year, leading first to the temporary exile of Calles and then, in 1936, to the clear triumph of Cárdenas.

The weakness of the labor movement was in part a feature of the early stage of industrialization. The urban industrial work force was still small. Indeed, it has been suggested that it was smaller than it had been in the Porfirian era. Furthermore, perhaps half of the workers in manufacturing were artisans or employees of small shops (Hamilton 1982:109, 112). Because of this weakness, many union leaders saw the support of the state and political connections as crucial. It was this weaker sector of the unionized working class that belonged to the bloc led by the *cinco lobitos*, and it was this bloc, as we have seen, that became increasingly influential within the CTM. As a result, the CTM adopted a position that enabled it to reap the advantages of influence, access, and official support that came with being an important, even indispensable partner in the governing coalition. This logic must have seemed particularly compelling in a context in which the peasantry represented an alternative base of support. The political pitfalls in this had become explicit in the 1920s, when Obregón had played the two groups off one against the other, in a way that had perhaps contributed to the dramatic collapse of the CROM when that confederation was thus rendered dispensable. During the 1930s, the mobilization of both the peasantry and labor as support groups continued to limit the freedom of maneuver of labor. Furtak (1974:41), for instance, has argued that at the end of the Cárdenas presidency, the CTM supported the candidacy of Avila Camacho despite great initial opposition because of the threat of being left out of the coalition and losing its political clout after the *campesino* sector declared its support.

A second factor was the weakness of the apolitical alternative. The stronger sectors of the working class, consisting of skilled workers often organized in national industrial unions, were less dependent on state support and political connections. These unions, however, tended to be under the influence of the popular front policy, which emphasized political coalition-building for the fight against fascism, though this position was seen as temporary and dependent upon the existence of a progressive government.

Despite the anticollaborationist position spelled out explicitly in the statutes of the CTM, the move to a political position that supported the government took place immediately. At the CTM's founding congress, Lombardo adopted the position that the confederation should support the progressive policies of the Cárdenas government and avoid political strikes that could weaken it (Hamilton 1982:160–61). The support of the government became more unconditional after 1938 amid political polarization and the rise of conservative opposition to Cárdenas and his reform program (Hamilton 1982:263). The CTM also supported the institutionalization of this support. In October 1936 the confederation responded to the PNR's initiative and decided to participate in congressional elections under the party's banner. Again, in the national and international context of 1938, CTM support of an institutionalized collaboration was taken a step further, when both the CTM and the Communist Party supported the reorganization of the PNR as a coalition or popular front party with which the CTM would be formally affiliated (Alexander 1957:338). Thus, at a crucial moment, the apolitical, noncollaborative alternative was abandoned and, as we shall see, future attempts to revitalize it failed.

The Exchange: The Cárdenas Period

The change in labor's policy from one of autonomy to one of greater collaboration with the state can thus be seen as a result of several factors, including the dynamics of the Cárdenas-Calles struggle and the antilabor attack of Calles, factional rivalry within the labor movement, and the adoption of the popular front policy. Behind all of these reasons, however, stand the benefits offered by the Cárdenas state in exchange for labor's support. The relatively autonomous position of labor at the beginning of the period and Cárdenas's political dependence on its support meant that Cárdenas had to offer strong inducements to persuade labor to support and cooperate with the government. His radical populist program seemed to constitute a significant departure in the direction of capitalist development. In the factories he advocated the "socialization" of the means of production through worker control of firms unwilling to enter into fair collective bargains. In the countryside he stepped up the rate of land distribution to peasants to unprecedented levels and encouraged collective ownership. The degree to which he was finally successful in forging a populist alliance based on urban and rural popular sectors can be seen in his policy of arming workers and peasants and establishing militias among them.

Labor's gains and benefits from the coalition were ideological, political, organizational, and material. These concessions have been extensively covered in the literature and need only be mentioned here. On an ideological level, Cárdenas affirmed the centrality of class struggle. He championed socialism, and Marx, Lenin, and Stalin became important political symbols (Ashby 1967:36). Early in his presidency, Cárdenas legalized the Communist Party, which had support and influence within the labor movement, and appointed Communists to posts in the federal bureaucracy, especially in the Ministry of Education (Cornelius 1973:427). He introduced "socialist education" into the schools, and in his speeches he clearly aligned the state on the side of labor in its disputes with capital, arguing that in order to pursue social justice the state must intervene on the side of the weaker party. Ashby (1967:289) argues that the dignity thus imparted to the working class was an important achievement of the Cárdenas government.

Politically, the concessions to labor mirrored those of the Sonoran period of the 1920s. Though the CTM principles, reflecting anarchist influence, called for autonomy from government and rejected any collaboration, the CTM laid these aside and participated in party and electoral politics. In this way, labor came to hold seats in both houses of the national Congress, occupied governorships and other political posts at all levels of government, and played an important role in the nomination and election of national, state, and municipal officials, and in the political process more generally. In addition, labor often controlled the Labor Department and had controlling influence on conciliation and arbitration boards.

Organizationally and materially, the Cárdenas government strengthened working-class organizations and encouraged workers to strike and demand wage increases. To establish an independent social base for his government, Cárdenas needed a unified labor movement, a goal he defined early in his famous Monterrey speech. This goal, of course, paralleled and championed that being pursued concurrently within the labor movement itself. In the beginning of 1936, the Cárdenas government sponsored a unity labor congress (López Aparicio 1952:219), out of which emerged the CTM under the leadership of Lombardo. The CTM was the beneficiary of many state favors, including monetary subsidies, the recognition of CTM unions, and the persecution of CTM rivals, such that "the authority of the state was placed at the service of the labor central" (López Aparicio 1952:221). In this favorable context, membership in the CTM grew rapidly, and by the end of the Cárdenas presidency the confederation claimed about 1 million members.[21]

In addition, throughout the Cárdenas presidency, the state played an active role in the settlement of labor-capital conflict, oversaw the extension of collective agreements and supported the wage demands of labor. It supported and even encouraged strikes, adopting a policy which, especially in the first years, was "permissive, if not inflammatory" (Cornelius 1973:432). From an extremely low level of strike activity during the Maximato, the number of strikes rose dramatically from a nearly negligible number to between 650 and 675 in the peak year of 1936, falling off after the oil expropriation of 1938 (Cornelius 1973:432; Ashby 1967:297). In further support of wage demands, the Mexican courts and tripartite conciliation and arbitration boards tended

[21] See Ashby (1967:78–79), Cornelius (1973:431, 457), López Aparicio (1952:219).

to be quite consistently prolabor (Cornelius 1973:431–32). The government also implemented the constitutional provision for the mandatory payment of wages for the seventh day of the week, which raised wages by about 17 percent (Hamilton 1982:148). Guided by the principle of a "revolutionary" interpretation of the laws, the state took the position that wages should be based on the ability of companies to pay and set up commissions to determine this ability. These commissions, which reported to the Arbitration and Conciliation Boards, usually ruled in favor of labor (Hansen 1974:92). The government held the further position that if employers refused to grant wage increases that were economically feasible, they had to face the possibility of expropriation. The expropriated enterprises would be turned over to worker management and production cooperatives. Two of the most important cases of industrial conflict in which the state intervened were those of the National Railway Company and the foreign oil companies. Both these conflicts resulted in nationalizations and the introduction of some form of workers' management of the industry.

Despite the weight of the government in support of wage increases and the number of labor victories won during the Cárdenas period, the material benefits realized by most of the organized working class were limited. To a substantial extent the wage gains were canceled in real terms by inflation, particularly after 1938, in the wake of the oil expropriation and the reaction of foreign capital. Furthermore, expropriation and the introduction of worker self-management introduced contradictions that were not necessarily favorable to the workers. Again, particularly in the context of the growing economic and political crisis after 1938, the government withdrew its advocacy of strikes and even opposed several of them. Nevertheless, the state-labor alliance remained strong and was seen as affording the labor movement important benefits.

In sum, as Ashby (1967:287–88) observes: "The labor movement . . . was under the tutelage of the benevolent hand of government with regard to both organization and trade-union activities. At the same time, the segment of organized labor led by Lombardo Toledano (representing the vast majority of industrial workers), supported the government of General Cárdenas, and consequently achieved a position of influence over national economic policy never before realized." Ashby goes on to note, however, that as occurred elsewhere, ultimately "this arrangement . . . may have meant that organized labor came to depend too much on government patronage rather than upon its own economic power and, under succeeding administrations, not so favorably disposed toward labor, was to suffer a relative loss of influence."

From the point of view of the Cárdenas administration, the alliance with labor afforded the standard benefit of support. Most immediately, this support had been critical in enabling Cárdenas to come to power unencumbered by Calles's control. In addition, the alliance with labor allowed Cárdenas to strengthen the presidency by establishing a social base of support for the government that was increasingly autonomous from regional caudillos and regional political leaders; to create a counterweight, indeed an armed counterweight, to the power of the military; to strengthen the state in its conflict with international capital, most dramatically in the 1938 nationalization of petroleum; and to strengthen the state vis-à-vis domestic capital, including the important Monterrey capitalists. The alliance with labor was, of course, effected through the CTM, which, with state support, became the dominant force in the labor movement. As always, the establishment of a unified, centralized, and relatively powerful labor movement cut two ways. While it increased the power of labor, it created an organized entity with which the state could strike a bargain and hence, at least to some extent, control labor. The alliance with a centralized labor movement thus afforded the state the means to control labor dissent—both from the grassroots and from rival groups outside the CTM. As Hanson pointed out: "In bolstering the position of labor, the government had strengthened itself against the influence of foreign interests in the economy, projected a powerful instrumentality in the form of the trade union to offset the emerging strength of locally controlled industry, but at the same time it had maintained its control over the instrumentality. The union was another vehicle of growing central control of the economy" (quoted in Ashby 1967:273).

The Party: The Cárdenas Period

A key characteristic of radical populism is the incorporation of organized labor and the organized peasantry into a political party. We have seen how in the 1920s Calles failed to institutionalize his populist coalition in a party. The PNR, which Calles established in 1929, did not incorporate organized labor, and a reorganization of the party to incorporate and channel mass political participation was a goal Cárdenas stated as early as the first year of his presidency. The reorganization of the PNR into the PRM (Party of the Mexican Revolution) is the central event in the formal incorporation of the popular sectors into the party structure.

Though the reorganization of the party did not occur until 1938, it may be seen as the culmination of tendencies evident throughout the Cárdenas presidency. It had its roots in the early 1930s with the rise of a reformist faction that emerged in reaction to the conservative policies of the Maximato. Still reeling from the effects of the world crash, Mexico during the Maximato was the scene of economic downturn and labor protest. The PNR was associated with the propertied classes, and it lacked a base of popular support. Perhaps most importantly, the dual political system, in which Calles held effective power through his control of the party while the president remained weak, meant that government was ineffective, low in prestige, and unstable, as military plots to overthrow the government and political crises proliferated and as factionalization within the party became a serious concern (D. Smith 1974:55ff). By 1932, when President Ortiz Rubio resigned during one of the government crises, the secretary of President Rodríguez, his successor, observed: "The political panorama . . . could not have been more somber nor more discouraging. . . . There existed no government of sufficient strength and homogeneity to guarantee political stability and economic tranquility" (quoted in D. Smith 1974:69).

In this context, the Cárdenas faction emerged within the PNR and sought to revive the Sonoran orientation toward an alliance between the state and the popular sectors, premised on a reform program. That is, this faction sought to revitalize the political project of strengthening, institutionalizing, and legitimizing the state by means of securing popular support. The problem became one of changing the PNR from a personal vehicle of Calles to an institution that would support rather than oppose and weaken the state and the presidency. This required replacing the influence within the party of the Calles faction, caudillos, and caciques with that of the popular sectors.

The first victory of the reformist faction came in 1933 at the party convention, which accomplished three things: the nomination of Cárdenas as the party's presidential candidate for the 1934 elections; the adoption of the Cárdenas program as the party's "Six-Year Plan;" and a change in the party that facilitated the extension of PNR mobilization and organization to the local level by ending its coalitional nature through the requirement that all participant political organizations dissolve in favor of a unitary party organization (Garrido 1984:172–73).

This victory, however, was incomplete, and the PNR remained a weak vehicle for popular mobilization. The PNR, which had served as a means to centralize power within the revolutionary family, was still unable to extend its popular base, especially in view of the refusal of the independent trade unions to become involved in party and electoral politics or to collaborate with the state. Accordingly, once in the presidency, Cárdenas took further initiatives to incorporate popular sector political participation within the party. These became particularly important as the rivalry with Calles heated up. Cárdenas needed to strengthen his reform wing within the party by building a base of popular support, not only to do battle against Calles himself, but also, even after Calles was out of the country, to counter the influence of the Calles faction, which continued to be an important and powerful opposition force within the party and in politics more generally.

The institutionalization of mass support was pursued on two fronts simultaneously. First, there was an attempt to extend and strengthen working-class and peasant organizations. Cárdenas encouraged both urban and rural unionization and the unification of both worker and peasant unions into single national confederations. It must be emphasized, however, that unlike the case of Venezuela, worker and peasant unions as well as unions of state workers were, quite intentionally, all kept organizationally separate, rather than united in a single, potentially more powerful mass organization. In 1936 the CTM was founded as a united confederation of labor unions, and in 1938 the parallel CNC (National Peasant Confederation) was formed to unite peasant organizations. It is worth noting that the CTM embraced a broad ideological spectrum within the labor movement, including those unions under the influence of the Communist Party. Of the important working-class organizations, only the Morones factions of the CROM declined to join (although the CGT soon severed relations before later reorganizing). Thus, unlike the situation in many other countries, what was formed with state approval in Mexico was a unified labor movement that included the left, not one that isolated and persecuted it. Second, Cárdenas sought to institutionalize his alliance with these popular sector organizations through their formal incorporation into the party. Changes within the party took place in the beginning of 1936 with the adoption of the "open door" policy and the announcement of a "new PNR" that would increase worker and peasant participation in the party and change its base of support, transforming it into a mass organization.[22]

Despite the announcement of these policy innovations, real change was slow in coming, with the consequence that discontent among labor and the left rose. The internal dissidence led to a number of responses by the party. In June the party identified itself as an "organization of the left;" in August antilabor Portes Gil was replaced as head of the party; and in September a party manifesto broadened participation in the party by making membership in union or peasant organizations a requirement for party membership, thereby identifying the PNR as a class party associated with the policies of Cárdenas.

Thus, during the first three years of the Cárdenas presidency, the party changed substantially. It grew significantly in terms of numbers, incorporated workers and peasants as well as the middle sectors, and became a strong mass organization, such that "by the beginning of 1937, the PNR could claim it was a vast movement that included all the 'revolutionary' forces."

The changes taking place within the party—the broadening of its base, its radicalization on a rhetorical level, and its identification with the Cárdenas reform program—produced a major reaction by the right within the party and led to a period of intensified internal dissension. Within the party there began a process of polarization that mirrored that occurring outside of it and which was manifested in the June 1937 formation by the rightist faction of a Unión Fraternal Revolucionaria de la XXXVI Legislatura to oppose the "bloc" of "leftists" (Garrido 1984:224).

In this context, legislative elections were held that were notable not only for the violence that accompanied them, owing to the intensified polarization within the party, but also for the fact that for the first time union leaders were actually incorporated in the party, with a number of working-class and peasant leaders running as candidates.

In December 1937, Cárdenas announced his intention to reorganize the party to reflect the changes that had occurred and to give the popular sectors full representation. Three months later, at the 1938 party convention, the reorganization of the PNR into the PRM was formalized. The centerpiece of the change was the sectoral basis of party organization. Four sectors embody-

---

[22] This and the following discussions draw centrally on Garrido (1984:206–26).

ing the "revolutionary" alliance became the constituent components of the party: labor, the peasantry, the so-called popular sector (primarily state employees) and, for a few years until it was abolished, the military. Party membership was not individual but collective, being based on membership in labor unions or confederations that were formally affiliated with one of the sectors. The most important confederation in the labor sector was the CTM, while that in the peasant sector was the CNC. Each sector was to retain autonomy and to serve as a channel of political recruitment and candidate selection.

There are two plausible interpretations of the reorganization of the party. In the first, it is seen as part of the ongoing pattern of political mobilization of the popular sectors that was part of an effort to increase the power base of the Cárdenas faction in its struggle against other factions. In this view, the reorganization is seen as an attempt by Cárdenas to consolidate his power base into a kind of "popular front" of progressive forces or into a coalition party to unite political and class groups on the left (L. Brown 1964:281–90; Cornelius 1973:462–63).

This interpretation is consistent with the fact that the CTM (unlike the CNC, the peasant confederation) had considerable autonomy from the state and with the fact that in the beginning of 1937 it was the CTM that took the initiative in forming a popular front that included the PCM as well as the PNR. It is also consistent with the timing of the precursors of the 1938 reorganization: Cárdenas first spoke of reorganizing the party in 1935, at a time when he was unquestionably interested in continued mobilization, and he first experimented with the sectoral organization in elections in 1937 in three states and the federal district (Garrido 1984:220, 227), at a time when he was continuing his reform program of land distribution, nationalizations, prolabor industrial settlements, and support for the growth of peasant and labor organizations (Cornelius 1973:445–62). Finally, the reorganization occurred when opposition to Cárdenas's reformism was growing. Polarization was intensifying both within and outside the party: international fascism was growing influential within Mexico, groups on the right and extreme right were proliferating, and the right-wing movement *sinarquismo* was growing as a rival mass organization. In addition, days before the reorganization was formalized, the oil dispute came to a head with the nationalization of foreign oil companies, a move which produced intense international political and economic opposition. It might thus be argued that in order to defend and protect his program, Cárdenas was confronted with the need to consolidate and strengthen his base of support in the face of this growing opposition (Garrido 1984:233), and it is significant that in this same period Cárdenas was increasing the power resources of popular groups on other fronts, as in the formation of workers' militias (Cornelius 1973:463). In this interpretation, then, the reorganization of the PRM can be seen as an (ultimately unsuccessful) attempt by Cárdenas to further mobilize and strengthen the progressive forces against increasing opposition from the right and thus to safeguard his reforms.

In the second interpretation, the reorganization of the party is seen not as a part of the mobilization of the popular sectors but as precisely the opposite: as an about-face on the part of Cárdenas, which signaled the end of mobilization and an effort to exert a new control over the popular sectors. It can be argued that political mobilization as a strategy is viable only during economically favorable times and that more basically there is a fundamental contradiction in pursuing a radical reform program within the context of a capitalist state. By 1937, when the intention to proceed with the party reorganization was announced, the facts of economic life, in part a result of the reform program, had begun to turn against this strategy, and after 1938, amid the reaction to the oil expropriation, the economic situation was alarmingly bleak. Furthermore, at this time a new political offensive by the right was emerging and growing and placing substantial pressure on Cárdenas. In this situation, Cárdenas's relations with the popular sectors began to deteriorate. Concerned with the economy, Cárdenas called for industrial peace, emphasized class harmony, and sent in the army to put down strikes, at the same time that the rate of land distribution declined. The reorganization of the party in this context can be seen as an effort to eliminate the political autonomy of the popular sectors, to channel their activities into politically controllable organizations, and thus to deactivate them.

The general interpretation being advanced here is somewhat different from both of these. Cárdenas was not a social revolutionary but a reformer and, perhaps most importantly, a political entrepreneur. To mobilize the popular sectors as a political resource, he had to champion their cause and encourage a genuine increase in their political power. At the same time, Cárdenas wanted to be able to channel that political resource and was careful not to allow too much autonomous power to accrue to the popular sectors. Whether he was trying to call off political mobilization through the creation of a corporative party or strengthen the progressive forces through the formation of a coalition party, the important point is that radical populism involves a mobilization of the popular sectors into a political movement or party as part of a political strategy that necessitates both augmenting the real power of the popular sectors and controlling and channeling that mobilization.

Hence, the reorganization of the party was necessarily double-edged. On the one hand, it formally provided for labor representation and influence within the party. On the other hand, without a meaningful democratization of either the party or the unions, this system of labor representation was open to co-optation and control. A further limit on the power and influence of labor derived from the way in which the party's sectoral organization provided the state with a vehicle to structure the labor movement. By channeling their participation in different sectors, the party organizationally separated the working class, white collar government employees, and the peasantry. In this way, the party ensured the insulation of the various groups and allowed the state, through the party, to serve as the sole arbiter of intergroup relations, thus preventing a united, radical, and independent popular sector from emerging.[23] This said, however, the reorganization of the party and the incorporation of the labor movement into the PRM is insufficient to explain alone the pattern of Mexican state-labor relations that survived to the late 20th century. As we shall see, a crucial element in that explanation is the reaction to radical populism that took place in the following period.

Opposition and Polarization: The Cárdenas Period

It is in the nature of radical populism as a political strategy that it is effective only for relatively brief periods of time, for it provokes strong opposition and leads to political polarization along class lines. Cárdenas's alliance with the popular sectors entailed a political confrontation that "suggested that while the state continued to perform the functions of accumulation in the interests of the dominant class, it had abdicated its social control function and was in fact participating in the class struggle on behalf of the subordinate class" (Hamilton 1982:276–77). Strong opposition to the progressive policies of Cárdenas was mounted on all sides, including (1) the national bourgeoisie, largely led by but not limited to the powerful industrial elite of Monterrey, who opposed the state-labor alliance in the political sphere and the heightened level of class conflict in the sphere of industrial relations and who were "convinced that Cárdenas was the harbinger of a socialistic regime where capital would be slowly squeezed into submission by the state" (Saragoza 1988:188); (2) foreign capital, which most forcefully opposed the dramatic nationalization of the petroleum industry in 1938; (3) factions within the military, which felt challenged by the formation of worker and peasant militias as a counterweight to their coercive resources; (4) the middle classes, who turned increasingly hostile as they sought to defend their position against the rise of the proletariat (Michaels 1966:71); and (5) the Church, which particularly opposed socialist education and the espousal of models of class conflict.

This opposition had many expressions. These included capital flight abroad; attempts by the Church to mobilize opposition to government programs and to undermine peasant, labor, and student unions (North and Raby 1977:46); an economic and diplomatic offensive by foreign capital that included an international boycott of the nationalized petroleum industry; the emergence of a rival mass movement, the *sinarquistas*, promoting conservative, religious values and opposing agrarian reform; the appearance of fascist movements with connections to Nazi agents and members of the Spanish Falange (Hamilton 1982:261); the Cedillo military rebellion of 1938; and the formation of a plethora of right-wing opposition parties, many of which ultimately coalesced around the newly formed PAN and the promotion of the opposition presidential candidacy in 1940 of Juan Andreu Almazán.

The result of radical populism under Cárdenas, then, was an extraordi-

---

[23] Córdova 1976:225; Anguiano 1975:136; Garrido 1984:250.

narily high level of political polarization. Employing an index of polity polarization (Flanagan 1973:87) in a year-by-year analysis of the period, Cornelius (1973:440) concludes that the entire Cárdenas presidency was a period of intense polarization that should be characterized as crisis and confrontation. In this context, and with the contemporary example of Spain a vivid reminder, the threat of civil war seemed a real one.

Opposition and polarization occurred primarily around labor policy and agrarian policy. Of the two issue areas, however, labor policy was the more salient (Cornelius 1973:428, 440). It was clearly a central concern of the Calles opposition, for it was over this issue that the Calles-Cárdenas rupture broke into the open in 1935. Labor policy, particularly the formation of workers' militias, was also a key issue in the growing distrust of the military. Interestingly, though the generals were rather tolerant of the creation of rural militias among the peasantry, which they thought could be controlled, they saw the arming of urban workers as an unacceptable threat to their own power. The result was an "increasingly bitter polemic . . . between Lombardo Toledano and the generals, who accused him of seeking the destruction of the regular army and the establishment of a 'dictatorship of the proletariat' " (Cornelius 1973:459).

Labor policy was also a key issue in the relation between foreign capital and the Cardenist state. This was seen most dramatically in the 1938 expropriation of the foreign oil companies, though the petroleum industry was just one of many cases of expropriation of foreign capital. As in most of the other cases, the expropriation of the foreign oil companies was in fact the culmination of a labor dispute. It occurred in the middle of a period of growing political polarization. This period was characterized, on the one hand, by a series of government initiatives with respect to agrarian reform, mass mobilization and the strengthening of the state-popular sector alliance, expropriations in the commercial and industrial sectors stemming from unresolved labor disputes, and state intervention in other industrial disputes to secure major concessions to workers. On the other hand, the period witnessed the formation of political opposition movements and economic reprisals by the private sector (see Hamilton 1982:225–27; Cornelius 1973:455–62). The petroleum expropriation had the contradictory effect of creating enormous support for the government in response to a popular move that was viewed in terms of nationalism and anti-imperialism, and at the same time of accelerating and intensifying political polarization and opposition (Hamilton 1982:220, 229, 241). Hamilton, as well as many other analysts, sees the oil expropriation as the crucial event that caused the opposition to the Cárdenas reforms to crystallize in a way that began to put Cárdenas on the defensive— indeed that led him into retreat.

Finally, the labor issue was at the heart of the conflict between national capital and Cárdenas. Though important groups within the national bourgeoisie, particularly the Monterrey industrialists, opposed any assertion of state power in the private sector and wanted to curb the power of the state, the most salient issue and source of opposition to the activist Cardenist state was its prolabor policy and intervention in the labor market, in which capital did not want its dominance altered (Saragoza 1988:11–12). Thus, it was the political alliance with labor and state intervention in the labor market, rather than any state policies to control capital directly, that was the source of political polarization and confrontation between the national bourgeoisie and the state throughout the Cárdenas period and that accounts for the "apparent contradiction" that "a period of major confrontation between the government and owning groups was a period of growth and prosperity for the private sector" (Hamilton 1982:215, 184).

Playing a key role in the leadership of private sector opposition to the Cardenist state was the powerful industrial elite of Monterrey. In his study of this group, Saragoza (1988:11) has argued that in terms of the opposition of the Monterrey elite to the state, "labor policy became the most visible point of contention." The tension between these industrialists and the state that existed during the Maximato continued to grow from the very beginning of the Cárdenas candidacy, culminating, in some sense, in the 1936 strike at the glass factory of the powerful Garza-Sada family. This strike represented a major showdown between the Monterrey elite and the Cárdenas government. At this point, Cárdenas was still locked in conflict with Calles, who, after a brief self-imposed exile following his 1935 declaration and break with Cárdenas, had returned to the country and was in the process of organizing an opposition to the president. In the charged political context of the moment, the strike took on special meaning. The Monterrey elite initiated an economic shutdown of the city, and Cárdenas responded through his personal intervention in the dispute. It was on this occasion that Cárdenas, firmly aligning himself with the workers, issued the famous Fourteen Points that outlined the government's prolabor policy, and it was this confrontation, Saragoza (1988:chap. 8) argues, that was critical in increasing the resolve of the Monterrey elite to enter the political battle against Cárdenas, and in so doing, to enlist the opposition of entrepreneurial and other groups on a national level.

On the local level, the "Monterrey group" used a combination of tactics— spies, thugs, propaganda, the support of fascist groups, and a new organization, Acción Cívica—in a renewed attack on the CTM and Cárdenas's policies in Monterrey (Saragoza 1988:183, 186–89). This offensive was successful. "A year after Cárdenas' Fourteen Point speech . . . his labor supporters appeared on the run [in Monterrey]; Cetemista [CTM] strength had dwindled dramatically. . . . The elite's disruptive tactics, coupled with old animosities toward Lombardo Toledano, had rendered the Cetemista organization in Monterrey nearly impotent in its battle against the Garza-Sadas. . . . The American consul concluded that the 'glass company appears to have completely broken the radical syndicate' " (Saragoza 1988:189–90).

The Monterrey elite, however, did not view their local victory as sufficient. A direct political confrontation at a national level with the state seemed necessary, and the Monterrey elite attempted to unify domestic capital in opposition to Cárdenas. Though ultimately unsuccessful in unifying capital under its banner—largely because Cárdenas successfully responded with the Chambers law that structured and combined the commercial and industrial associations into peak confederations in which the state was powerful (Saragoza 1988:195)—the Monterrey elite played a crucially important leadership role in the rise of the opposition to Cárdenas.

> At the national level, the elite attempted to galvanize anti-Cárdenas forces through their support of various organizations and to mobilize capital against the Cárdenas regime. At both levels, the elite supported the rough tactics of the fascist *sinarquista* movement, funded a widespread campaign in print and radio to disseminate their propaganda, and promoted the formation of various anti-Cárdenas, conservative organizations among students, women and workers. . . . By taking such a visible position against Cárdenas, the *regiomontanos* became a pole of attraction to which anti-Cárdenas sentiment gravitated regardless of the motivation. (Saragoza 1988:182)

Finally, at the national level, the Monterrey elite played a key role in the anti-Cardenist opposition that resulted in its support of the popular Almazán challenge to the PRM in the 1940 presidential elections and in its support of the newly formed opposition party, the PAN.

In sum, as in the 1920s, labor policy figured prominently in the political polarization that grew out of radical populism in Mexico. The literature has singled out two major turning points with respect to the growth of opposition to Cárdenas, and these both involve the opposition of different sectors of capital to state intervention in the private sector, primarily with respect to state support of workers in the sphere of industrial relations. In the case of domestic capital, this event is the 1936 glass factory dispute; in the case of foreign capital, it is the 1937–38 petroleum conflict. The intensification of opposition to the Cardenist state led to the increasing strength and boldness of conservative sectors within the government and within the state coalition and to the weakening and retreat of the progressive Cardenist alliance. The beginning of this retreat from populism can be seen in the dramatic decline in 1938 of land distribution in the rural areas and of strikes in the urban areas, as well as in the choice of Avila Camacho, rather than of Cárdenas's progressive heir apparent, Francisco Mújica, as the official party's candidate to succeed Cárdenas in the presidency. This policy modification was insufficient to address the concerns of the opposition. Backed by the Monterrey elite, Juan Andreu Almazán mounted a popular challenge to the PRM in the 1940 elections and a new rightist opposition party, the PAN, was formed. Though the PRM retained control of the government, Mexican society reached a level of polarization that would dominate the vision of Avila Camacho as he succeeded to the presidency.

VENEZUELA

In Venezuela, the death of Gómez in 1935 signaled the end of the oligarchic state; yet how great the break would be remained an open question. The two presidents of the next decade, indirectly elected by Congress, were both identified with Gómez and his regional base in Táchira: López Contreras (1935–41) was the son-in-law of Gómez as well as his minister of war and Medina Angarita (1941–45), López's handpicked successor, had been the latter's close aide during the Gómez period and subsequently became his minister of war (Lieuwen 1961:56–59). Nevertheless, the spontaneous outpouring of anti-Gómez sentiment that erupted upon Gómez's death signaled the beginning of a new era that encompassed a sufficient number of labor reforms to mark this the cautious onset of the incorporation period.

The somewhat ambiguous nature of this transition meant that the following decade, from 1935 to 1945, was a period characterized by fluctuating policy on the part of both the government and the reformist opposition, as both vacillated between positions of accommodation and conflict. On the one side, the government alternated between political opening and repression. On the other, the new political organizations and parties that sprang up in the initial opening following the death of Gómez pursued a dual strategy of cooperation with and opposition to the government. The contrasting elements of this dual strategy were emphasized differentially at different times by the various political groups. However, as the success of an accommodationist strategy remained uncertain, political mobilization increasingly came to be a key tactic of the reformist groups and their attempt to come to power. As in Mexico, this mobilization occurred in urban and rural sectors, both as political parties organized labor and peasant unions and as workers and peasants themselves organized and affiliated with opposition parties in order to enter the political arena to press their demands.

Initially, then, the reformist opposition adopted a wait-and-see posture, exploring the possibility that the new government could be influenced to pursue the desired reforms. López Contreras, who assumed the presidency in 1935, tried to steer a middle course between the reformist opposition and the Gomecistas. The result was vacillation on the part of the government: a partial and temporary political opening, accompanied by some reforms including a labor law, followed by a period of renewed repression and a swing away from the reformists. In reaction, the reformists began to mobilize a popular base among the urban and rural popular sectors. Though Medina, who became president in 1941, was more open to reform, ultimately the course of reform and inclusionary politics was not sufficiently sure or fast to satisfy the reformist opposition. As it became clear during the course of the decade that cooperation with the government would not be successful in producing the demanded reforms, the opposition turned increasingly to mass mobilization as a strategy to achieve its aims. In 1945, with the tremendous popular support that had been mobilized during this period, the largest opposition group, organized as Acción Democrática (AD) joined a coup plot by military officers and overthrew Medina, thereby ushering in a full-fledged period of party incorporation based on radical populism. This period of AD rule, which came to an abrupt end three years later when a military coup overthrew the government, is known as the Trienio.

Initial Phase of Incorporation: Transition to Populism

Though the 1935–45 period was inconclusive in many ways, as was the first part of the incorporation period in other countries, it is considered here as the opening phase of working-class incorporation, for it clearly represented the beginning of a new era with a new agenda. In particular, during these years a new labor law was introduced, though in practice it remained a limited reform. Even more impressively, significant growth in unionization occurred and became the vehicle of substantial mobilization of labor's political support, though this mobilization was initiated by the opposition parties still struggling to achieve reforms and come to power, rather than by the government.

Upon the death of Gómez, violent demonstrations and riots against Gomecismo and the Gómez family broke out. It was in this context of opposition, protest, and political activation that López Contreras assumed the presidency and pursued a vacillating policy. Initially he instituted a cautious political relaxation, including a general amnesty for political exiles, but this opening was not to last long. Rightists demanded a return to repression, while reformist groups demanded an expansion of the political opening and of political participation. Following a bomb attack on the governor of the federal district in February 1936, the government once again clamped down on dissent and suspended constitutional guarantees. In reaction, a general strike was called in Caracas to protest this action and to issue a call for reform.

López responded with a further political opening, which included the removal from public office of a number of Gomecistas, including members of Gómez's immediate family (Schuyler 1976:99). His "February Program" outlined a broad agenda of reforms in health, education, fiscal, and commercial policy. In addition, it indicated that the government would look favorably upon the formation of labor unions (Pla 1982:50–51; Ellner 1979:2), and the López government began to prepare a new labor law.

In the political opening, a number of new organizations emerged. Unions were formed in the oil camps and in the manufacturing and service sectors in Caracas, and four new political groups or proto-parties were founded: the UNR, composed primarily of liberal entrepreneurs who supported López Contreras and his February Program; the PRP, composed of Communists affiliated with the Third International and many labor leaders; the BND, a regional organization in the Zulia oil camps; and the ORVE of Betancourt and other Communist and noncommunist activists of the "Generation of 1928."

However, this political opening was short-lived. In April 1936, the ORVE, PRP, and UNR formed the April Bloc to pressure the Congress for economic and political reforms. In response, the Gómez-selected Congress not only rejected these proposals, but passed the Lara Law, a repressive measure aimed at maintaining public order through restrictions on mass organizations and their activities and through the prohibition of communist, anarchist, and other doctrines that would discredit state institutions (Fagan 1974:50). A June general strike that spontaneously spread from Caracas throughout the country (Martz 1966:32) failed to prevent the passage of this law, though some alterations of the law were made. The new constitution of July also failed to address the reform agenda of the opposition. It restricted the suffrage to literate males, retained indirect national elections, and excluded Communists from legitimate political activity (Fagan 1974:51). Furthermore, with the support of the right, the government became increasingly repressive of unions and mass organizations. In addition, a cabinet reorganization resulted in the elimination of those ministers who had been closest to the opposition (Alexander 1977:198), and new right-wing organizations, which embarked on campaigns against the opposition, were encouraged by the government (Ellner 1979:31–32).

At the same time, the new labor law permitting and regulating both urban labor and peasant unions was passed. Coming when it did, there is no question that the law sought to respond to the rising social protest by providing an acceptable, state-regulated framework for labor organizing and union activity. In many ways the law represented a new departure in its recognition of the right of association and the right to bargain collectively and strike and in its social welfare and profit-sharing provisions. Nevertheless, though many analysts have regarded it as progressive—at least on paper—it was in many ways more akin to the early laws of the state corporatist pattern. Indeed, the Venezuelan law of 1936 had more constraints and fewer inducements than either the Brazilian law of 1931 or the Chilean law of 1924 (Collier and Collier 1979:975). From July to December 1936, the government recognized 109 new labor and peasant unions, with a membership of 56,000, under the provisions of the new law (Fagan 1974:49). This approach toward unions did not last long, however. The government failed to apply its own labor law and turned to an increasingly repressive antiunion position as unions developed ties with Communist and noncommunist opposition parties. It was less willing to recognize as legal either industrial conflicts or new unions. This antiunion orientation culminated in 1940 when the government withdrew legal recognition of more than one-third of the unions (Fagan 1974:56; Powell 1971:63).

The restriction of the political arena under López Contreras had important repercussions on the strategy of the reformist opposition. The ORVE, PRP, and BND shifted from a posture of conciliation, in which they were willing to explore the possibilities of implementing a reform agenda through cooperation with the government, to one of aggressive opposition to the government, which they now judged as an obstruction. The new strategy had two components: a move to achieve unity of the opposition groups and the initiation of a period of much more intense mobilization by these groups of a mass base of support. The result was the formation in October 1936 of the PDN (National Democratic Party) as a unity political party, encompassing most of the opposition groups and union leaders. Though the Communists within the newly consolidated opposition continued to emphasize the unique importance of the working class, the noncommunists looked to other classes as well, particularly turning their attention to the organization of peasant unions.

Popular mobilization by the reformist opposition continued to intensify during the remainder of the López Contreras government for two main reasons. The first was the continued repression that underlined the impossibility of an accommodationist alternative. The PDN was denied legalization. A December 1936 to January 1937 strike in the oil fields over the petroleum company's refusal to operate under the law was broken under the provisions of the new labor law, and in the following months government repression was stepped up in light of the wide support the strike had generated throughout Venezuelan society (Bergquist 1986:240–41). Also in January, the government annulled the victories of members of the opposition who had managed to win some local and congressional elections (Martz 1966:39–40). In the next month several opposition leaders were jailed, and the government canceled the legal recognition of the parties that made up the PDN, as well as that of the student federation and several labor groups.

The second impetus to the mobilization of a mass base was the break up of the PDN as a result of ideological differences. One issue was the multi-class orientation of the noncommunists, to which the Communists objected, given their commitment to working-class struggle. In addition, though both the ORVE and the PRP supported the Allies in World War II, ORVE took a more anti-imperialist stance, while the Communists took a more conciliatory position in accordance with popular front policy. As relations between the two deteriorated, the Communists withdrew from the PDN and revived the PCV. The resulting split led to intense rivalry and competition between the two groups, and in this competitive nexus, both sought to mobilize a support base among the working class by forming and supporting unions. By 1940, most union activists were PCV or PDN militants (Fagan 1974:58–59).

In the face of this mobilization, President Medina, who succeeded López Contreras in 1941, initiated a period that was more open and inclusionary politically, but once again, the cooperation or conciliation between the government and the reformist opposition ultimately broke down. Government policy toward the labor movement changed substantially when Medina came to power in 1941. He inaugurated a period of greater political freedom than had been known before in Venezuela, and a "marriage of convenience" (Betancourt 1979:72) was forged between Medina and the Communist Party, which, following the renewed popular front strategy of international communism, supported Medina as part of an antifascist political strategy. In return, the government encouraged the formation of unions and revised the labor law, providing job security for union leaders.

Unprecedented political freedom followed: the mass-based parties were recognized by the government and were allowed to function openly, political prisoners were released, exiles were permitted to return, and union formation was encouraged by the government. The ongoing rivalry between Acción Democrática, the legalized successor to the PDN, and the PCV led to a tremendous organizational drive as "each tried to extend its mass base principally through the organization of unions controlled by its militants." The result was a "deepening penetration by parties" (Fagan 1974:61–62) of the much enlarged union movement.

By 1944, both parties had mobilized extensive mass bases, with AD dominant among peasant unions and the PCV in urban labor unions. This last, PCV dominance among urban labor unions, changed abruptly in 1944, when, in an act that has not been adequately explained, the Medina government dissolved a labor congress and the Communist unions, which comprised over half the labor movement. Medina's actions seem perplexing in view of the cooperation between his government and the Communists: this cooperation was based on the need for the government to have some popular support in the new political opening and on the "unqualified public support" (Boeckh 1972:174) lent by the Communists to the Medina government in accordance with the renewed popular front policy of international Communism. By most accounts, Medina's hand was forced by the walkout of AD from the labor congress and its subsequent charges of sectarianism, at a time when the PCV was not legal and unions were prohibited from political activity. Whatever the explanation, the outcome of these events was extraordinarily favorable for AD, which was thus given a unique opportunity to extend its influence. By 1945, AD for the first time controlled a majority of labor unions (Fagan 1974:65–66).

At the same time that mobilization was pursued as an opposition strategy, AD cautiously explored one final avenue of accommodation surrounding the presidential succession in 1945. In a move to counter the possible candidacy of López Contreras, Medina nominated Diógenes Escalante, a moderate whom AD decided to support after Rómulo Betancourt, the prominent AD leader, interviewed him and was assured of his position on a broad series of reforms, including direct elections and universal suffrage. When ill health aborted Escalante's candidacy, Medina was unable to settle upon a substitute candidate agreeable to AD. As a result, with the tremendous popular support that had been assiduously mobilized during the decade, AD joined a conspiracy by military officers. The coup brought AD to power and ushered in a three-year period, known as the Trienio, characterized by party incorporation and radical populism.

Project from Above

The seven-man junta that assumed power in October 1945 included four AD leaders and only two military officers. AD dominance was underscored by the fact that Betancourt became head of the Revolutionary Government Council. Government policy quickly began to reflect the AD program of economic and social modernization. In response to opposition criticism and pressure, the Medina regime had instituted a number of reforms, but in the view of AD these had not gone far enough. Fundamentally, the AD program was one of modernization based on the opportunity to "sow the seeds of petroleum." Denouncing as inadequate the Medina law of 1943, the new government adopted an oil policy in which the government would share the profits of the oil industry equally with the foreign oil companies. It further determined to use government oil revenues to pursue a broadly based pattern of economic development that would diversify the economy and decrease dependence on oil. The AD program included measures to promote and stimulate agriculture and industry both through requirements that foreign oil companies invest in nonextractive sectors and through direct government initiatives, as in the formation of the Venezuelan Development Corporation and programs of agricultural and industrial credit and state investment in infrastructure, power, and steel. This modernization policy also meant a commitment to measures that would promote social welfare, particularly in the areas of health and education. Much of this basic orientation toward social welfare was reflected in the new constitution, which guaranteed housing, education, and health and provided for labor's right to work, organize, strike, share in profits, and receive retirement benefits, paid vacations, sick pay, and severance pay (Lieuwen 1965:74).

Perhaps most immediately on the AD agenda, however, was political and electoral reform, with the consequence that popular sector support remained at least as crucial a political resource to AD in power as it had in the previous decade when AD was in opposition. Though, or perhaps because, AD finally came to power by means of participation in a military coup rather than through some electoral or insurrectional show of popular support, there is no question that AD saw an alliance with the urban and rural popular sectors as a centerpiece of its political strategy. Because of the path it took to attain power, AD was dependent upon the military as the guarantor of its political power (Schuyler 1976:268–69). Hence, AD's attempt to establish some degree of political autonomy and lay its claim to legitimacy rested on the calling of elections and the institutionalization of an electoral regime. With the introduction of new reforms, all citizens over 18 were enfranchised, and direct elections were held at all levels. In the new open political climate, two new parties were immediately formed: the more conservative COPEI, which became the major opposition force, and the URD (Democratic Republican Union), a more progressive force centered around groups that had backed the Medina government. The Communists constituted the fourth electoral force.

In this atmosphere, AD needed popular support to consolidate its power as well as to carry out a nationalistic, modernizing reform program that, at the very least, would provoke the opposition of the old guard at home and of international capital abroad. In this regard, the party entered the Trienio well-prepared.

During the previous decade AD, playing a game of opposition politics, had forged an impressive coalition with the popular sectors. It had done this primarily by sponsoring and organizing popular sector unions among the peasantry and the urban working class. Powell (1971:64) has estimated that when AD came to power in 1945 it brought with it an organizational base of about 1,000 union locals under AD leadership, representing about 200,000 members or individuals under AD influence, divided about equally among the peasantry and the working class. Schuyler (1976:211) asserts that labor was AD's most important base of support, with the working class comprising 50 to 80 percent of its membership, despite its emphasis on organizing a multiclass movement and particularly on extensive organizing of the peasantry. After 1945, popular support remained a crucial political resource, and the AD program continued to champion measures that would attract worker and peasant support: the government committed itself to land reform and to a more prolabor policy, arguing that Medina had abused his wartime emergency powers to end strikes, that he had failed labor in his intervention in the 1944 industrial dispute with the newly formed petroleum unions, and that the 1945 revision of the labor law was inadequate (Lieuwen 1961:66–67).

Project from Below

Two factors distinguish the collaboration of the Venezuelan working class with AD leadership from the pattern of collaboration that took place in Mexico. First, as mentioned, for the first decade, this collaboration took place with a populist party in opposition rather than with one in power. Secondly, because of the very late pattern of modernization on which Venezuela was only just embarking in 1935 and because of the lack of opportunity to organize trade unions under Gómez, there was virtually no preexisting labor movement whose sympathies the middle-sector leadership could win over on the basis of a bargain or exchange involving the offer of concessions and reforms. Rather, the middle-sector political movement and the labor movement evolved or emerged more or less simultaneously, and to some extent the leadership of the two was fused: labor leaders were among the founders of AD and its precursors, while AD leaders, in mobilizing a support base, became important labor organizers. (The Communists, of course, were also important organizers of the labor movement; we will come to them below.) Despite these differences, the collaboration of the labor movement with AD can be analyzed in the terms employed in the analysis of Mexico: labor strategy, particularly in the face of repression, and the weakness of an alternative strategy.

Initially, in the brief political opening that characterized the onset of the López government, unions began to organize, particularly among skilled workers, quite independently of the opposition parties, which were also then taking organizational form (Fagan 1974:46). From July to December 1936, the government recognized 109 new unions with a membership of 56,000 under the provisions of the new labor law (Fagan 1974:49).

Though the PRP and the ORVE started to organize factions in the unions, union party linkages in 1936 were still very loose to the extent that they existed at all, and in general, unions were more oriented toward economic goals through collective bargaining than toward political action. Fagan argues that this orientation of labor changed as a result of the restriction of political liberties and the repression of unions that increasingly characterized the López government in the course of 1936: "In fact, it was an action taken by the government that pushed the unionists and party leaders into their first attempts at coordination" (1974:50, 59). On the heels of the rejection of the opposition-supported reform program in April, the Congress proposed the Lara Law. In response, the ORVE, PRP, BND, and the student federation joined five unions in carrying out a general strike around a number of political demands, including the rejection of the Lara Law (Ellner 1979:28–29).

It was both the successes and failures of this strike that seemed to demonstrate to unionists the apparent advantages of joining the larger political struggle and seeking political allies. Though the successes were indeed limited, the aftermath of the strike did witness the dismissal of pro-employer Gomecistas in the Labor Office and the promulgation of a new labor law, which, while giving the government a number of mechanisms of control over the labor movement, also included a number of improvements over the 1928 law (Ellner 1979:30). In this way, the initial foray of the unions into political action seemed to offer some benefits. This success, however, was outweighed by the failure of the strike both in achieving its other demands and in provoking an increasingly antiunion position by the government, starting with the imprisonment of the strike committee (Ellner 1979:31).

Another outcome of the strike was political polarization, as party and union opposition groups moved closer together and the right consolidated behind López, whose government took a turn toward greater repression of the opposition. With the further disappointment over the July constitution, the PDN was founded in October by labor groups as well as by opposition parties and the student federation. In the polarizing atmosphere, the government became increasingly hostile to unions as it began to see labor as part of a larger opposition movement. It was unwilling to enforce its own labor law in cases where it benefited workers, and it broke the December 1936 to January 1937 oil strike. Although the PDN supported the striking workers, it had little involvement in the strike itself, the main demand of which was union recognition. Nevertheless, "from this point the government began to deal with unions as part of what it perceived as a leftist mass-based political opposition" and "became increasingly unable or unwilling to distinguish between parties and unions" (Fagan 1974:54, 56). Thus, in the repression following the oil strike and the January elections, labor leaders were expelled from the country. "López began to virulently attack unions for engaging in politics . . . (and) the government . . . adopted anti-union positions in collective conflicts throughout the country" (Fagan 1974:55). After 1936 there was a sharp drop in the number of collective conflicts recognized as legal by the government, and fewer and fewer new unions were given recognition each year until 1940, when the legal recognition of over a third of the unions, representing nearly half of the membership, was canceled (Fagan 1974:56; Powell 1971:63).

Like the repression of the Casa in Mexico under Carranza, the events of 1936–37 in Venezuela suggested to many unionists the necessity of changing the government and thus favored the strategy of political action (Ellner 1979:48–49; Fagan 1974). As a result, the labor movement came to be affiliated with the political parties and was receptive to the organizational campaigns of both the PDN and the PCV.

The Venezuelan labor movement was thus, virtually from its inception, identified with political parties and larger political projects. This identification would culminate in the collaboration between the labor movement and the AD government during the Trienio. The collaboration during that period was certainly facilitated by the new preeminent position held by AD in the labor movement following Medina's 1944 move against Communist unions (see above). Yet this surprising and apparently circumstantial event is not sufficient to understand the development of a collaborationist orientation within the labor movement. Another important factor was the weakness of alternatives.

As mentioned, the anarchist tradition was very weak and thus a major source of an alternate, anticollaborationist posture present in other countries was lacking in Venezuela. An "antipolitical" tendency did begin to emerge within the labor movement at the time of the 1936 strike that was stimulated by the impending Lara Law. This was the setting in which the labor movement first became involved in political action and in collaboration with political parties. Yet during this period, the opposing antipolitical tendency became allied with conservative groups and adopted a progovernment position, thus failing to constitute an alternative, direct action, anticollaborationist orientation.

Though it became a major force within the labor movement and presented an important alternative to affiliation with AD, the Communist Party presented no real alternative to multiclass collaboration either. Most of the period was the time of the popular front policy of international Communism, and the Venezuelan Communist Party, like the Mexican party, came under the strong influence of Browderism, which emphasized a rather extreme form of collaboration in which social and political goals were forsaken in the cause of furthering the Allied war effort. In 1936 the Communists had joined the ORVE in forming the PDN; and when the coalition fell apart, the PCV turned to collaboration with the government, though a dissident communist faction did emerge over this issue.

Indeed, during this period, popular front collaborationism led somewhat paradoxically to an increasing divergence between the Communists and the Betancourt faction. Analyzing the defeats of 1936, the latter adopted a more intransigent position with respect to the possibility of any collaboration with government, while the Communists drew the lesson that defeat had resulted from the left's failure to support López's reform program sufficiently. Given these differences, PDN unity fell apart: the Communists withdrew from the PDN and reconstituted the PCV for a number of reasons, but among these was their assessment that the PDN represented too narrow a coalition (Ellner 1979:49–52). At an early point, then, the Communists abandoned the policy of opposition to the government in favor of one of support for López and "progressive" acts of his government.

PCV policy changed briefly during the years of the Hitler-Stalin pact, but with the German invasion of the Soviet Union in 1941 the party once again embraced popular frontism, and in a dramatic about-face it rallied to support the new president, Medina, whom it had considered a "veritable fascist" just a few months before (Ellner 1979:62–63). During the Medina period, at a time when AD continued to pursue a more anti-imperialist and oppositionist line, the Communists emphasized class harmony and political stability as part of an effort to support the war effort and to supply the Allies with an uninterrupted flow of oil. During this period of an even more extreme version of the popular front, the PCV opposed strikes and organized mass mobilizations in support of the Medina government, which responded by legalizing the party (Ellner 1979:5, 58–65).

In the decade between the death of Gómez and the onset of the Trienio, then, the labor movement was divided. Until 1944 the majority of unions in the urban sector were not allied to the middle sector movement as represented by AD but rather were affiliated with the PCV. Nevertheless, a major portion of the labor movement that emerged in the course of the intense organizational drive of AD and the Communists was politically oriented, largely subordinated to party political considerations, and in one form or another a part of a multiclass coalition. In the case of the PCV-affiliated faction, labor was allied with the government. In the case of the AD-affiliated faction, it remained in opposition to it, though this was soon to change.

The major exception to the political-collaborationist orientation was the dissident Communist faction, known as the Machamiques, which took open organizational form only at the end of the post-Gómez decade in 1945. This faction emerged initially in 1942 in opposition to the PCV's agreement to support Medina's candidates in the congressional elections in exchange for government recognition as a legal party. Not only were the Machamiques critical of a policy that they saw as unconditional collaboration with the government, but they also adopted a position of focusing attention on the class organizations of unions rather than on political parties (Ellner 1979:164). This more overt factionalism within Venezuelan Communism reflected the discussion and differences within the international Communist movement over formulating a new political strategy that accompanied the end of the war and of popular front policy (Ellner 1979:165).

It was at this time of Communist factionalism that AD came to power. Relations with the Communists got off to a bad start. For their part, the Communists opposed the coup and the new government, and they even prepared armed resistance to it. Both Communist factions adopted this position of opposition, the Fuenmayor leadership faction within the PCV, which had remained allied with the overthrown Medina government, and the Machamiques, who by then were grouped in the PCVU. AD, in turn, responded by jailing leading Communists. Betancourt belittled the importance of the PCV and saw no reason to seek its help or support.

The hostility between AD and the PCV soon subsided and relations between them improved. Once the nature of the new government became clear, the major decision confronting the Communists was what position to take vis-à-vis the AD government. That AD had maintained a more militant, anti-imperialist stance during the war and had in this sense outflanked the Communists, complicated Communist assessment of AD. On the one hand, AD's past record pointed to the more progressive components within AD. On the other, AD's victory combined with Medina's turn against the Communists demonstrated the fruitlessness of the policy the PCV had pursued of collaborating with the government. With the onset of the cold war and the international criticism of Browderism, the PCV moved to the left, renouncing its antistrike policy, and unity of the two Communist factions emerged as a possibility. In October 1946, the two groups put up a joint list of candidates for the Constituent Assembly and agreed on the position of conditionally supporting the progressive acts of the government. In July a unity congress brought most of the Machamiques back into a reconstituted PCV, which adopted a policy of qualified support of the government. While the Betancourt faction in AD, under the impact of the cold war and the overtures of the AFL's Serafino Romualdi, moved toward a harder anticommunist position, a left faction within the party, which generally encompassed the trade unionists, was more responsive to the PCV's support. During most of the Trienio, then, the PCV and AD worked out a modus vivendi and refrained from attacking each other.[24]

PCV support, though conditional, was important to the government during the Trienio in a number of ways. In the labor arena, the PCV emphasized the importance of labor unity and cooperated with AD in the formation of the CTV as a unified labor central, which PCV unions joined even though Communists were excluded from leadership positions. In the name of unity, the PCV even dissolved some of their own unions and joined AD-led unions (Ellner 1979:175–77). In the more political-electoral arena, PCV cooperation was also important. Ellner (1979:109) has suggested that the party played a role of "loyal opposition," as opposed to the other parties, whose commitment to democracy under AD could not be counted on. The PCV distinguished left and right wings within AD and adopted the policy of "working patiently to strengthen the progressive forces in AD" (cited in Ellner 1979:114). In so doing, the party avoided general criticism of the government. Anticipating a process of polarization, the PCV also sought to strengthen and unify "democratic" and progressive forces, proposing a united front of the left, which would include PCV, AD, and the URD. Though this united front was never

[24] Alexander 1957:259 and 1982:234; Ellner 1979:109, 112, 164.

established, the PCV did seek to support the AD government by running a presidential candidate in the December 1947 elections, in order to thwart the electoral boycott planned by the opposition parties to embarrass the government (Ellner 1979:113–16).

The only group active in the labor movement that refused to support the Trienio government was that composed of the remaining Machamiques, who had rejected the reunification of the Communist movement within the framework of the reconstituted PCV. Led by union leader Quintero, they formed the Proletarian Revolutionary Party (PRP) and came to be called the Black Communists, as distinct from members of the PCV, who became known as the Red Communists. The Black Communists declined to support AD or join the CTV, and thus represented the only alternative to collaborationist trade unionism.

Thus, most of the labor movement came to support or cooperate with the AD government during the Trienio. While the Communists in the labor movement (except for the PRP) maintained a certain coolness, the AD labor leadership, for the most part, fell behind the party's line, which to some extent reflected the impact of the onset of the cold war and to some extent reflected the perceptions about the requirements of power consolidation. Accordingly, retreating from the more militant stand they had previously taken, AD labor leaders turned during the Trienio to a cautious stance on the use of strikes and an emphasis on the "battle of production." This new orientation was reflected in a change in international affiliations. AD labor leaders severed relations with Lombardo's hemispheric labor confederation, the CTAL (Confederation of Latin American Workers), denouncing Lombardo as a "Russian spy," and in 1946 they developed close ties to Serafino Romualdi, who was employed by the U.S. State Department's Office of Inter-American Affairs to set up a rival international labor confederation sponsored by the AFL (Ellner 1979:102–3). In the end, however, a divided CTV did not join the CIT founded by Romualdi.

In sum, labor for the most part supported the AD government, but with varying degrees of enthusiasm. The Communists cooperated, but somewhat reluctantly. The AD labor leaders did so enthusiastically, but they were generally identified with the left wing of the party. With a more socialist orientation, they favored a rapid implementation of reforms and closer cooperation with the PCV, and many disagreed with the party's emphasis on social peace and class harmony. In the 1960s, many of these labor leaders would split from the party, as they did in the postincorporation period in Mexico. During the Trienio, however, with its greater commitment to a reformist program, their policy was to support and collaborate with the government.

The Exchange

As in all cases of party incorporation, the coalition with labor during the Trienio was effected through an exchange in which the government granted a number of important concessions to labor in return for its support and for a significant measure of control over the labor movement. Initially, AD asserted coercive control over labor: as one of its first acts, it suspended the right to strike and instituted a system of compulsory arbitration. These measures, however, were soon repealed, and AD was able to rely on less draconian measures of the labor law and more on the means of control derived from party ties and influence. Prominent among these last was the co-optation of union leaders who also occupied party and electoral posts. These co-opted union leaders "were generally considered the executors of the party's will in the union movement" (Boeckh 1972:189).

Perhaps the clearest benefit for AD was the massive electoral support it enjoyed. Given the need to legitimate its position and consolidate its power, the new government moved quickly to institute electoral reform. It decreed universal suffrage for free, open, and direct elections to a constituent assembly. In these elections, held in October 1946 and contested by four parties, AD won overwhelmingly, winning 137 out of 160 seats or 79 percent. This level of support was maintained in the frequent elections that took place throughout the Trienio. In the congressional and presidential elections of December 1947 as well as in the municipal elections of the following May, AD won over 70 percent of the vote (Martz 1966:75). In this competitive electoral context, AD continued to mobilize popular sector support successfully, and the coalition the party had forged with the peasantry and the working class in the previous decade was maintained and cemented during the Trienio.

The advantages that accrued to the AD government from the coalition with labor were not limited to electoral support. In 1945 AD's newly achieved dominance in the union movement was still substantially challenged by the Communists. By the end of the Trienio, the balance of power in the labor movement had changed substantially in AD's favor, and Communist support was largely limited to textiles, transport, and a minority of the unions among the petroleum workers. The change in the balance of influence within the union movement was advanced by the government's power, set forth in the labor law to recognize unions: new AD unions were generally recognized immediately, whereas the recognition of Communist-led unions was often delayed (Fagan 1974:69; Ellner 1979:100). Similarly, the government discriminated in favor of AD through its power to extend contracts negotiated by AD unions to all workers within the given industry and by the power, which could be used to the detriment of the PCV, to declare the legality or illegality of strikes, though it is not possible from existing data to determine the extent to which this power was used (Boeckh 1972:189).

Influence within the labor movement was beneficial to the government in at least two ways. First, it provided the basis for mass demonstrations in support of the government at moments of political crisis (Martz 1966:260), though the government rejected labor mobilization at the time of the 1948 coup. Second, government influence on labor was central in the establishment of regularized channels for industrial relations, the moderation of certain working-class demands, and the peaceful settlement of industrial disputes. In key sectors of the economy, the government opposed strikes, preferring to manage industrial disputes through a tight government-party-union linkage in which the party labor bureau decided on "acceptable" demands that it would then try to achieve through political intervention and the exertion of pressure on employers (Fagan 1974:72).

This new institutionalization of industrial conflict was increasingly important for the AD government as time went on during the Trienio. The onset of the cold war coincided with AD's assumption of power, and it had a conservatizing impact on the party as it moved to a more overtly anticommunist position, moderated its anti-imperialism, discouraged strikes, and emphasized the battle of production (Ellner 1979:102). The AD leadership argued in favor of the necessity to maintain "social peace" in order to avoid a conservative reaction. This strategy included the avoidance of strikes and the active role of the Ministry of Labor to intervene in labor disputes and of the government in general to win concessions from industry for labor. This policy and the measured pace of reform, which many AD leaders such as Betancourt espoused, were not widely accepted by the party unionists. Through their initiative and over the objections of Betancourt, the Constituent Assembly passed a reform of the labor law in 1947. Unionist opposition was also responsible for frequent outbreaks of wildcat strikes, which AD and the CTV, the new labor confederation, were unable to prevent (Ellner 1979:105–6). Nevertheless, an important degree of social peace was maintained and strikes were avoided in 89 percent of potential labor conflicts through the use of executive decrees and compulsory arbitration. Only 45 strikes were allowed to run their course (Ellner 1979:118).

In 1948, the mechanism to ensure social peace became even more central to government policy. As in Mexico, a crisis in the oil industry (though of quite a different nature) induced a retreat from the prolabor policy and a decline in the government's ability to extract material concessions from employers. During the Trienio, oil production grew spectacularly, its contribution to national income more than tripling (Ellner 1979:119–20). In 1948 changes in the world market brought this growth to a halt. To reorient the economy away from petroleum, the government turned away from a high-wage policy. Also like Mexico, a second factor prompted a change in labor policy: the growth of opposition and a proliferation of right-wing military plots against the government (Ellner 1979:121). In response, the government moved to a more explicit antistrike position and AD union leaders began to emphasize the importance of economic growth and accordingly to sign three-year contracts as part of what was recognized as a "truce between labor and capital" (Ellner 1979:122).

An additional benefit of close links to the labor movement was the access the Venezuelan government was afforded to the United States government through international labor ties. Just as the Calles government was able to use the Morones-AFL connection as a channel to the U.S. government, so was Betancourt able to benefit from the AFL's Romualdi's activities in Venezuela to advance the interests of the Venezuelan government. Romualdi, for instance, intervened to secure U.S. willingness to sell surplus farm machinery to Venezuela at a reduced price and generally to smooth relations between the two countries and counter Venezuela's "radical" image (Ellner 1979:107).

As part of the exchange, labor enjoyed a list of advantages that seem quite familiar from the Mexican case. The new government moved quickly to set up a Ministry of Labor, which oversaw the implementation of social legislation and took new initiatives in labor policy. In 1947 the labor law was revised. Broadening the use of the strike and setting up the mechanisms for the resolution of industrial disputes, the law "went far in the establishment of modern trade unionism in Venezuela" (Martz 1966:259). Under government encouragement, the number of unions and the rate of unionization increased quite dramatically. In just the one year of 1946, the number of unions more than tripled, as over 500 were formed and recognized by the government (Fagan 1974:69; Martz 1966:259–60). Among the new labor organizations, the most important were the petroleum workers union, formed in 1946, and a national labor federation, the CTV (Confederation of Venezuelan Workers), founded the following year. The CTV unified virtually all of organized labor, rural as well as urban, and was recognized as the legitimate voice of labor.

Like the Cárdenas government, the AD government encouraged unions to make demands and pressured capital to enter into collective negotiations and to sign collective contracts. The contours of labor policy began to come into focus at the end of 1945, a mere month and a half after the new government came to power, when Minister of Labor Leoni oversaw the renewal of the contract in the oil industry and obtained many concessions for workers. In 1946 the new oil workers union signed a contract in which important concessions to workers concerning wages, layoffs, medical and housing benefits, and other benefits were exchanged for longer term contracts. This pattern, which was repeated in the 1948 contract, was held up by Leoni as a model for industrial relations in Venezuela (Bergquist 1986:260–61, 266). A very active minister, Leoni often intervened in collective bargaining on the side of labor and was able to secure important gains for labor. As Martz (1966:260) has stated, "Government mediation resulted in a series of pro-labor decisions as consistent and unbroken as the anti-labor decisions of earlier regimes." The result was that whereas only a few collective agreements had even been signed before the Trienio, over a thousand were signed during it. These contracts often included an impressive expansion of fringe benefits; and, while good data are hard to find, it seems clear that real wages for unionized workers rose substantially (Fagan 1974:70–74; Ellner 1979:117). Other policies of benefit to workers included subsidized food and the reduction of rents and of many other basic consumer prices, such as those for electricity, gasoline, and kerosene; expansion of the social security system, education, public health, and workers' housing; and school lunch programs and nurseries for working mothers (Bergquist 1986:264).

Aside from Mexico, Venezuela was the only country of those considered here to include the peasantry in the initial incorporation project and consequently the only other one to undertake a land reform program at this time. From the beginning of the Trienio, Betancourt began a "de facto" agrarian reform, distributing both public and private land to peasants and instituting a rural credit program. In 1947, a decree dealing with rural land rental "radically changed the locus of control over private land in rural areas and formalized the functions of the peasant syndicate leaders in the distribution of land to peasant tenants. In other words, it consolidated political power in the hands of the peasant syndicate leaders" (Powell 1971:75). In 1948, an agrarian reform law was passed and a National Agrarian Institute was established to implement it, but the coup that put an end to radical populism followed within a month, and, as we shall see, the course of agrarian reform was reversed over the next decade. Nevertheless, during the Trienio, land and credit policy underwrote among the peasantry a parallel process of unionization and political mobilization to that in the urban labor sphere, with the number of peasant unions rising from 53 to 515 and the corresponding membership increasing from 4,000 to 43,000 (Powell 1971:79).

Finally, under the new government, labor and the organized peasantry achieved unprecedented political influence. Labor leaders linked to AD held important positions in the government. Several participated in the Constituent Assembly, where they introduced prolabor provisions into the constitution of 1947. These provisions were subsequently included in the revision of the labor code. Sixteen union leaders were elected to legislative bodies and three to the National Congress, and others were represented in autonomous public institutes (Fagan 1974:76).

Given the role of labor leaders in the development of AD and the role of party leaders in the formation of the union movement, there was a fusion between union and party roles that makes it particularly difficult to trace the pattern of influence between the two. There is no doubt that the party was to some degree an instrument of control over and restraint on labor. Yet, the influence clearly went in both directions. "The consensus . . . is that the influence of unionists in the party during the Trienio was great. Officials of labor federations sat on [all levels (from national to local) of] the party's labor bureau . . . which was the key link between the party and unions. While unions received the party line through the bureau, the bureau itself appeared to strongly represent labor interests in party councils" (Fagan 1974:75–76).

The pattern of influence varied according to the level of union organization. Party control was probably greatest at higher levels, where leadership co-optation was the strongest. It was weaker at the local level, which remained more closely tied to the grassroots despite the fact that at this level as well union leaders had dual roles as head of the labor bureau of the local AD branch. Despite the double-edged nature of union affiliation with AD, Boeckh (1972:193) concludes that during the Trienio labor "was closer to the seat of power and had easier access to it than ever before and probably . . . since."

The Party

As the preceding indicates, in Venezuela as in Mexico the mobilization of popular sector support was effected through a populist party that would channel political participation. The leaders of AD and its precursors had long recognized the importance of the party in this regard and had placed great emphasis on the permanent organization of a national party whose local branches would reach into the smallest villages (Martz 1966:147). As we have seen, they had accomplished a great deal in terms of organization and the mobilization of peasant and working-class support in the years preceding the advent of the AD government in 1945. During the Trienio, with the advantages of being in power, the party increased its influence and support tremendously.

Like the Mexican party, AD became an important vehicle for incorporating working-class political participation. Most obviously, it mobilized the electoral support of the vast majority of workers as individuals. In addition, however, it provided a channel for other, nonelectoral forms of working-class participation through its ties to the unions as organizations. It did this in two ways: first, through the fusion of leadership that existed between union and party organizations, and second through the partial sectoral organization of AD itself.

The fusion of party and labor leadership resulted from the simultaneous emergence of the trade union movement and party organization. AD as an organized political party and labor organization evolved together in the years following 1935 in substantial measure under the leadership of the same people, with leaders of the one helping to found or extend the organization of the other. This fusion and the identification of union leaders with AD was intensified after 1944, when Medina moved against the Communists, and then of course during the Trienio, when the AD government explicitly favored AD unions.

The fusion of leadership can be illustrated with a couple of key examples. Some of the most important founders of the early unions were involved in founding the PDN, out of which AD evolved. Pérez Salinas, founder of the linotypists union and subsequently the first secretary-general of the CTV, and Valmore Rodríguez, founder of the first petroleum workers union, were among the founders of the underground PDN (Martz 1966:256–57).

Like the PRM in Mexico, AD sought to institutionalize its coalition with labor through a kind of sectoral organization of the party, though the specific structures differed from those of the Mexican party. First of all, the labor sector of AD embraced both urban and peasant unions, which were united in the CTV. Secondly, unlike the Mexican case, where unions were affiliated with the party as corporate entities, Venezuelan law prohibited unions from having political affiliation (Martz 1966:264). Membership was thus individual rather than collective. However, the party was organized to include a formal position for workers and peasants. A labor bureau was set up within the party structure at all levels—national, regional, district, and municipal. These labor bureaus were elected by assemblies of workers and peasants, and the bureau heads were automatically members of the party executive committee at the same level. Thus party and union positions were intertwined with no separate career track for union leaders, since they were recruited from among party activists and party labor bureaus were composed of union leaders (Fagan 1974:145).

As we have seen, sectoral representation of labor in the party was double-edged, with influence going in both directions between party and union. The sectoral organization of the party provided for worker representation within the party through control of the composition of labor bureaus. An example of the power that the AD labor bureau could have was the 1947 reform of the labor law, which was passed over the objections of Betancourt at the bureau's insistence. Simultaneously, however, sectoral organization gave the party influence over the recruitment of labor leadership and more generally over labor policy. Leadership fusion and the sectoral incorporation of labor in the party thus became mechanisms for influencing labor demand making, channeling working-class political participation, and mobilizing working-class support for AD.

Opposition and Polarization

As in Mexico, radical populism provoked much opposition and political polarization. Though the reform policy was primarily one of national economic modernization that would benefit the national bourgeoisie, opposition mounted among virtually all groups, save the popular sectors. And, as in Mexico, labor policy and the alliance with the popular sectors was central in the growth of this opposition. Higher wages were primarily seen by the foreign and domestic bourgeoisie as higher labor costs. Collective bargaining was seen as a loss of control over the firm. Though the oil companies opposed much of the government's oil policy concerning taxation and the halting of new concessions, "it was the government's labor policies . . . that by 1948 constituted the gravest immediate threat to oil company profits" (Bergquist 1986:265).

Perhaps most importantly, prolabor government policy and the government-labor alliance were seen as an unacceptable change in the balance of political forces: labor was built up as a political force with easy access to government authorities in a way that meant a retreat for capital, which had by-and-large been favored by the Medina government. Labor policy, then, provoked a widespread, counterreformist reaction.

> The Venezuelan right, grouped around the exiled ex-President Lopez Contreras, generally was vituperative about the AD administrations, and took AD's labor policies and alleged leniency with unions as evidence that the dictatorship of the proletariat was imminent. . . . The indigenous business world, which widely had been considered the main pillars of the Medina administration, was

generally not opposed to the paternalistic approach [toward the working class] ... but it apparently did not want ... [it] to go so far as to make it into a political force and a serious match for business. The rapid unionization and the easy access of labor to government authorities was more than they were willing to tolerate. Employers complained constantly that union demands backed up by the government exceeded the capabilities of the economy (Boeckh 1972:191).

In general, then, the radical populism of the Trienio produced particularly intense conflict not only because it aroused opposition to the substantive concessions to labor, but also because it represented the introduction of a new political game with a new set of rules. The new game placed a premium on mass organization, a resource traditional interests did not enjoy. Thus, traditional groups—particularly business interests, landowners, and the Church—were left with a growing sense of powerlessness (D. Levine 1978:90).

The government-labor alliance and populist politics also alienated the other political parties that were active at the time. AD's tactics of mobilizing overwhelming popular support in urban and rural unions worked to deprive even the other parties of a base of mass support. As a result, the newly formed COPEI and URD, as well as AD's older rival, the Communist Party (PCV), took an increasingly active oppositionist position. Furthermore, the overwhelming support that the AD government enjoyed led it to adopt a monopolistic position from which compromise seemed unnecessary and the alienation of other groups seemed to pose no threat. Accordingly in a campaign against corruption, the AD regime attacked high officials in the former regimes of Gómez, López, and Medina (these last two presidents being themselves targets of the campaign). It eliminated the old guard in the federal bureaucracy. It alienated the Church by its reformist education policy, and, of course, it aroused the deep hostility of landowners with the agrarian reform. Both these latter groups gravitated to COPEI, which also found support in the Andean region, which had formed the political base of the pre-1935 governments, while URD attracted the urban middle sectors and those in the Medina political faction. Finally, the AD government provoked the enmity both of international capital by its petroleum policy and of the military.

Most analysts attribute the opposition of the military to its loss of political influence under the new civilian, electoral regime instituted by AD. Lieuwen's (1961) analysis suggests, however, that the military's perspective was less strictly corporate. Rather, it was more integrated with broader social issues and connected with the general pattern of opposition and polarization that was occurring. Military conspiracies, first by a López faction and then by a Medina faction, threatened AD rule, and in reaction AD became more vocally antimilitaristic and was allegedly planning to arm the popular sectors and set up a party militia (Lieuwen 1961:88; Martz 1966:307). Amid the mounting tension between the military and the government, "opposition political leaders ... made their complaints known to the military ... [which was] further egged on by industrialists and landholders horrified at the social upheaval AD seemed to be promoting" (Lieuwen 1961:88). The AD government, then, fell not because it alienated only the military, but because of the broad opposition radical populism provoked. As Daniel Levine (1978:92) has stated: "The overthrow of AD thus stemmed ultimately from the threat its continued rule had come to pose to a wide range of social interests." Similarly, Hellinger (1984:49) has suggested that the government fell because "the Venezuelan bourgeoisie was insufficiently mature to accept at that time the structural changes in the economy and society that the Trienio government was introducing in order to . . . make possible the reproduction of capitalist relations of production. . . . [It] was not prepared to accept the institution of labor unions, for example."

The result of radical populism in the Trienio, then, was "extreme polarization" (Fagan 1974:81) and the activation of an accelerating or spiraling populist dynamic in which the loss of support, occurring as an outcome of a populist alliance and reformist program, led to an increasing dependence of the government on a popular-sector support base. As opposition mounted, the government, "in order to strengthen its remaining base of legitimating support . . . succeeded in producing an ever more dependable, but ever narrower, support structure" (Powell 1971:84). "As a result, by 1948 [urban and rural] organized labor . . . was perhaps the only secure base of the government's support" (Fagan 1974:81), and it was insufficient to prevent the counterreformist coup, which reflected the widespread opposition to radical populism and attracted the passive—if not active—support of broad sectors of society.

URUGUAY AND COLOMBIA: ELECTORAL MOBILIZATION BY A TRADITIONAL PARTY

In contrast to other cases of party incorporation, in Uruguay and Colombia the parties that led the incorporation period—the Colorados and the Liberals—were traditional, multiclass, multisectoral parties founded in the 19th century. By contrast, in the other four countries the incorporating parties emerged in the 20th century in response to issues of social protest and social reform. Due to the deeply ingrained multiclass and multisectoral character of the Colorados and Liberals, issues of fractionalization arose quickly as soon as the progressive wing of the party initiated the more intensive phase of reform and tried to establish its dominance over the more traditional wing of the party. Hence, the conflicts and polarization of this period involved as much intraparty as interparty tensions.

The incorporation periods in Uruguay and Colombia were also distinctive, as noted in Chapter 4, in that they came early. The Batlle era in Uruguay was early in an absolute, chronological sense—being the first incorporation period in the region—and also came early in relation to the emergence of the Uruguayan labor movement. In Colombia, incorporation came considerably later in chronological terms, beginning in the 1930s, but was early in relation to the development of the Colombian labor movement. This early timing had important consequences for the dynamics of incorporation.

Uruguay and Colombia exhibit other commonalities as well. In both countries a tradition of power-sharing between the two main parties was abandoned during the incorporation period as the reform party sought to establish its dominance, forming a "party government" (*gobierno de partido*). Both parties introduced major labor reforms to cultivate the working class as a political constituency, with the goal of building a new electoral majority. However, due to the early timing and hence the limited electoral role of workers, especially in Uruguay, this appeal was more an investment in the future, rather than in current electoral support. Yet it appears to have been a successful investment, in that both parties emerged from this period commanding a majority in the electoral arena.

The construction of links between the incorporating party and unions was even more problematic than the electoral appeal to workers, in part due to party fractionalization. Efforts by the progressive wing of both parties to build such links tended to be particularly threatening to the established balance of forces within the party and sharply exacerbated intraparty tensions. For this and other reasons, the partisan mobilization of unions by the incorporating party, which was a central feature in other cases of party incorporation, either did not occur at all during this period (Uruguay) or was only partly successful (Colombia).

Though there was some rural reform in both countries, neither saw a major effort to extend the incorporation project to the rural sector. Both countries had previously experienced civil wars or major civil violence in rural areas, yet control over rural property relations on the part of the most powerful landed interests was strong, and these interests were well represented in both traditional parties in both countries. Correspondingly, policies that went beyond modest rural reform to a more fundamental restructuring of property and political relationships in the countryside were not adopted.

URUGUAY

During the Uruguayan incorporation period, José Batlle y Ordóñez launched his extraordinary program of social, economic, and political reform. This period is best understood in two phases. In the first, which began with Batlle's first administration (1903–7) and extended through that of Williman (1907–11), the primary focus was on extending Colorado dominance over the state and securing Batlle's control of the Colorado Party. The second, which saw the passage of important segments of Batlle's reform program, began during his second administration (1911–15) and lasted until mid-1916, during the Viera administration (1915–19). This active phase of reform brought growing division in the Colorado Party and came to an end with the defeat of the Batlle forces in the 1916 elections for the Constituent Assembly and the subsequent decision of President Viera to withdraw his support for extending Batlle's program. The famous "Alto de Viera" (Viera's Halt) ended the incorporation period.

Project from Above

When Batlle came to power in 1903, he faced two important challenges: a military revolt by elements of the National Party—also known as the Blancos—and division within his own Colorado Party. By the end of his first administration in 1907, he had successfully addressed both problems and had begun to present to the legislature his program for the political and economic transformation of Uruguay. Although prior to 1903 Batlle had strongly emphasized worker rights during his tenure as editor of the daily newspaper, *El Día*, upon achieving the presidency he first turned his attention to the threat to Colorado rule presented by the revolt of the National Party. Consequently, Batlle's labor and social program was delayed. Nevertheless, even during his first presidency Batlle used his position to support workers' right to strike and took a strong stand favoring workers' demands, thereby making this earlier phase part of the incorporation period.

Just months after Batlle's election, forces of the National Party led by Aparicio Saravia rose in revolt because Batlle had broken the terms of the 1897 agreement for coparticipation between the parties. This revolt ended in compromise, only to be followed by a full-fledged civil war that lasted until Saravia's death at the battle of Masoller in 1904 (Vanger 1963:160–61). Upon defeating the National Party's forces, Batlle ended the coparticipation agreement of 1897, as well as the partisan division of Uruguayan territory. Batlle was by now strongly opposed to coparticipation (Vanger 1963:33) and, like López during the incorporation period in Colombia in the 1930s, believed in the need for "government by the majority party" (*gobierno de partido*). The national state and the Colorado Party would rule all of Uruguay. If the Nationals wished to hold political offices, they would have to win them in elections, not through political insurrection and negotiation.

By defeating Saravia and the National Party's insurrection, Batlle also reunited the Colorado Party behind him, pushing the supporters of the 1897 agreement to the fringes of party power in the 1905 Chamber elections. As Vanger put it, after winning the 1905 election "Batlle was now undisputed leader of a Colorado Party united as never before" (Vanger 1963:187). Yet since Batlle was close to the end of his first presidential term, his main problem was to use this unity to ensure the selection of a successor compatible with his longer-term goals.

In late 1905 Batlle began the process of nominating Claudio Williman to succeed him. Though Williman was not a reformer, he was a staunch opponent of the Nationals and supported Batlle's hard-line partisan position. His selection both assured continuity in relation to the initiatives Batlle had taken up to that point and allowed Batlle to maintain sufficient political control to assure his own reelection four years later (Vanger 1963:215–17). Batlle next began organizing the 1906 Senatorial elections. His success in seeing five of six Colorado senators elected led him to present his Labor Project (Proyecto Laboral) in December, just three months before the end of his first term. In December of 1906 Batlle had observed that "we have had a senate composed of good patriots, but conservatives. The new senate, on the other hand, will be entirely liberal and will not put any obstacles in the way of reform" (quoted in Vanger 1963:255). Aware that this legislation was unlikely to pass during the Williman administration, Batlle nevertheless successfully included it in the 1906 party platform, which outlined his proposals for future legislation, thereby establishing the new directions in which he wished to take the Colorado Party. Yet Williman, although a strong partisan supporter of both Batlle and the Colorado Party, was also a social conservative. As a result, Batlle's reform legislation was set aside during Williman's administration and the active phase of the incorporation project did not begin until Batlle's second administration.

Although Batlle's first term served primarily to prepare the ground for his reforms, it appears that Batlle already had in mind the nature of his program (Vanger 1963:255–56, 274; Vanger 1980:101–2, 198). Batlle's vision of the future involved a hierarchy of goals. He wished to create strong political institutions that would prevent a return to the unstable, personalistic, and often dictatorial governments that characterized the late 19th century. Batlle had already successfully ended the tradition of the "two Uruguays," one National and the other Colorado, with his victory in the 1904 Civil War. But to consolidate his success a broader vision was necessary. First, the Colorado Party had to be unified and modernized. With Batlle's first administration unity had been achieved. In his second administration he would continue to develop local, popular, party organizations. Second, to achieve these goals and build on his past successes, Batlle felt that Uruguay's economy, polity, and society had to be redirected. It was to serve these ends that Batlle developed his project to make Uruguay what he referred to as a "model country" (Vanger 1980:vii).

Batlle's model country program was built around three interconnected visions of the future: an economically independent and industrialized Uruguayan economy; an educated, secular, economically secure, working class linked politically to the Colorado Party; and a fully democratic political system, ruled by a nonpresidential, nine-person council, the Colegiado. When we look at precisely how these goals were to be achieved, we can begin to get a full picture of the place of labor policy within Batlle's program.

In 1903 Uruguay's economy was dependent on its export of livestock and hides, as well as on the foreign-owned companies that dominated the transportation, power, finance, and commerce sectors of the economy. Given Uruguay's limited physical and demographic resources, Batlle believed that as long as this dependence continued, Uruguay's economy would remain small and backward. Batlle's economic policies had much in common with those adopted in other countries, but the policies were remarkable because they came so early. Batlle encouraged immigrant capitalists to enter the country to promote local industry and provide jobs. He argued that the foreign bond market with its fixed interest rates, rather than foreign-owned companies, was a better source of capital to promote growth (Vanger 1963:245–47). According to Batlle, Uruguayans should "aspire to administer [capital investment] ourselves and to create sufficient funds of our own for the development of our economic life" (Vanger 1963:246). But how could this be achieved given Uruguay's small internal market? Batlle's answer was legislation creating government-run enterprises to compete with or replace the foreign-owned companies and protecting Uruguay's nascent industrial sector (Vanger 1980:155).

Batlle's social legislation was closely tied to this vision of a diversified and expanding Uruguayan economy. Batlle's goals were an educated and financially secure popular sector that had the strength to organize and participate in the nation's political life. By establishing free primary and secondary education, an eight-hour work day, old-age pensions, as well as by ensuring worker freedom to organize, strike, and vote, Batlle hoped to create a new source of support for his model country project and for the Colorado Party (Barrán and Nahum 1982:132). Batlle presented his social program as an alternative to that of the anarchists, then his most powerful competitor for support from the working class. He believed class conflict was not inevitable but rather the result of errors in policy and social relations. He sought to correct those errors (Zubillaga 1983:42), and in the course of doing so pursued the social welfare policies that Finch (1981:40), who tends to summarize Batlle's achievements with caution, describes as a "program of extraordinary breadth and radicalism." It was these policies that "gave rise to Uruguay's reputation as a 'welfare state' " (Finch 1981:40).

During both his administrations, Batlle supported worker efforts to organize into unions and to strike for increased wages. During the 1911 general strike, in a speech to 1,000 cheering strikers, Batlle called on the workers to "organize yourselves, unite, and try to achieve the improvement of your economic conditions" (quoted in Vanger 1980:127). A day later, responding to criticism of his support for the strike, Batlle wrote that "the labor element is an important part of the nation and the nation cannot be said to be really well off as long as the worker's economic situation is not good. . . . The day when [the worker] organizes politically, goes to elections, makes up a considerable part of the legislature and makes his voice heard on all public questions, it will no longer seem so strange that a President speaks to him and treats him with respect" (quoted in Vanger 1980:129).

In 1906, and again in a stronger version in 1911, Batlle presented the Labor Project to the Uruguayan legislature. Finally passed in November 1915, this legislation included an eight-hour workday and a six-day week, as well as provisions for maternity leave and child labor protection. In 1916 the old-age pension and free public education proposals were also passed, further advancing Batlle's long-term goal to generate worker support for the Colorado Party and for his project.[25]

Recognizing that the positive effects of his economic program would take time to develop, as well as the possibility that future opposition to his project might place a president in power who would overturn his legislation, Batlle developed a third set of proposals to protect his project from a future reaction. He proposed the Colegiado, a nine-person executive council that would rule the country in place of a president. According to Vanger, Batlle advocated the Colegiado because it would prevent the emergence of a dictator capable of reversing the institutional changes Batlle himself had made or planned to make as he sought to turn Uruguay into a model country (Vanger 1980:162).

With this element of his program, Batlle's overall strategy emerges. His economic policies would create lower transportation, financial, and utility costs, expand employment, and increase wages. These, together with his social legislation, especially the eight-hour day and his support for worker organization, would "insure worker support for the Colorados—support that would counteract defections that likely would result from his pushing Uruguay in the direction he intended it to go" (Vanger 1980:132; see also Rama 1955:42–43). Batlle's "emphasis on the worker as citizen opened the campaign to expand the Colorado vote for the Colegiado by bringing workers to the polls" (Vanger 1980:211).

Though Batlle's program encompassed some innovations in the rural sector, these were less ambitious than those aimed at the urban population. He was strongly interested in the modernization of agriculture, particularly through promoting more intensive use of land. However, he put off the more ambitious initiatives aimed at this goal until after his second term—at which point he was in a poor position to promote them. During his second presidency, policies to encourage agricultural modernization were limited to such

---

[25] Vanger 1980:209; Fitzgibbon 1954:180–81; S. Hanson 1938:128; Nahum 1975:55–56, 91.

things as model agronomy stations to demonstrate new techniques and prizes for innovation in agro-ranching (Vanger 1980:137–39, 198–200).

Finch (1981:10) argues that "it was made clear during 1904 that the Colorados did not plan an attack on the principle of private landownership, nor an attempt to rescue public lands . . . which landowners had absorbed" (see also Fitzgibbon 1954:135), and that there was an implicit pact that property in the rural sector would be respected. Other measures enacted by Batlle that affected rural areas—such as "higher land taxes, taxes on inheritance and absentee ownership, minimum wage legislation, colonization schemes, credits to small producers—were easily evaded or had minimal impact" (Finch 1981:11, 92–96). However, even these initiatives, along with Batlle's interest in promoting agricultural modernization, were opposed by rural elites. The large landowners generally supported either the National Party or the conservative wing of the Colorados, and they also reacted strongly to their own lack of access to national political power during the years when the Batlle Colorados dominated politics. This reaction from the rural sector proved to be an important part of the conservative reaction to Batlle's reforms.[26]

Project from Below

Labor leaders maintained an ambivalent relationship with Batlle and his reform movement. The early timing of the incorporation period, as well as the significant number of immigrants from Southern Europe who entered Uruguay at the turn of the century, meant that the labor movement was still anarchist, and Batlle's attempt to develop worker support for the Colorado Party was strongly contested. The anarchist's widespread influence within the labor sector encouraged workers to avoid taking part in the political conflicts between Colorados and Nationals. In 1904 during the civil war, the anarchist-led labor movement remained neutral (Vanger 1963:167) and continued to argue for a nonpolitical, confrontational role for labor. In May 1911, just prior to the general strike of that year, a split developed within the FORU (Uruguayan Regional Workers' Federation) between anarchists who favored "revolutionary anarcho-communism," and Socialists who sought immediate economic gains for workers. The final statement of the FORU's third congress endorsed " 'anarcho-communism' as its final goal and proposed 'boycotts, sabotage, partial and general strikes' as 'revolutionary means of reaching the complete economic and social emancipation of the world proletariat' " (Vanger 1980:122).

Workers opposed to the anarchists had coalesced around Emilio Frugoni, a labor leader and former Colorado who founded the Uruguayan Socialist Party (PSU) in 1910. Aided by the abstention of the Nationals, and with discrete

[26] Finch 1981:11; Vanger 1980:133. Vanger (1980:199) cautions against underestimating the scope of Batlle's goals for rural change. Yet, as noted above, Vanger (1980:137) himself emphasizes that Batlle in fact postponed, and ultimately never implemented, his own most ambitious rural initiatives.

Colorado support, the Socialists formed an alliance with the Liberal Party for the Chamber elections in 1910 and won a position for Frugoni. The party endorsed Batlle in the presidential election of November 1910 and generally supported his reform program, while continuing their opposition to the anarchist role within the labor movement. Despite these early successes, by 1912 the Socialists still had fewer than 500 members.[27]

In 1913 the anarchist-led FORU temporarily collapsed when Montevideo workers refused to support its call for a second general strike, leaving the Socialists as the only organized advocate of worker rights entering the November 1913 elections. The Socialist program in 1913 was similar to Batlle's and encompassed such basic demands as women's suffrage and labor legislation, including the eight-hour day, increased worker housing and rent control, as well as protective legislation for rural workers (Vanger 1980:274). But with the Nationals once again voting, the Socialists polled less than 800 votes and Frugoni lost his seat. The party would not regain representation in the legislature until the 1920s.

During the incorporation period, worker demands were primarily expressed through strikes and focused on wage increases, a day of rest, the eight-hour day, rest breaks, rehiring of strikers and union organizers, worker pensions, as well as employer recognition of unions. These proposals were all actively supported by Batlle, either through legislation or through administrative directives.

This congruence between labor demands and Batlle's program did not immediately translate into working class electoral support for Batlle, however. During these years workers generally seem to have accepted the anarchist proscription on voting. The Socialists never gained more than a few hundred votes during the incorporation period, and many workers were either afraid to participate in a public vote, were foreigners and therefore ineligible, or were rural immigrants with strong traditional attachments to the National Party. With the collapse of FORU in 1913, anarchist strength within the labor movement seemed to be falling, and at least one union leader (probably an anarchist) called on workers to support Batlle during the 1916 elections (Vanger 1980:274; Barrán and Nahum 1982:130–31). Yet, though the evidence is unclear, workers do not appear to have become an important source of support for Batlle at the ballot box during the incorporation period.

The Exchange

The relationship between Batlle and the Uruguayan labor movement was thus a curious one. On the one hand, Batlle proposed a series of sweeping social reforms that greatly improved the lives of Uruguayan workers (Barrán and Nahum 1985:114–15). On the other hand, few labor union or federation

[27] Rial 1985; Vanger 1980:96, 144, 211; Barrán and Nahum 1981:468–69; Nahum 1975:27; Alba 1968:83.

leaders actively supported Batlle, either by suggesting to their members that they vote for him or by supporting his programs through channels such as the declarations of the various labor congresses.

Batlle's support for the labor movement was based on both philosophical and pragmatic grounds. Philosophically, Batlle supported a democratic Uruguay. He believed that a successful democracy required the integration of all social classes. If workers organized politically, their needs would be met through a functioning democracy. Therefore, Batlle believed that if electoral rights were extended to the working classes, many of the indignities that led to class conflict would be ameliorated through the normal operation of democratic institutions (Vanger 1963:256–58). But if workers were uneducated, unorganized, and lacked the time to pursue "the life of civilization" (quoted in Vanger 1963:256), then a stable democratic system would not be possible. Batlle therefore believed he must actively provide the working class with the time to pursue non-work-related goals.

But Batlle also had more pragmatic reasons for his support of labor. In 1910 few workers were registered to vote, and even fewer actually did so (Rama 1955:46, 52–54; see also Finch 1981:57–58). As a result, they remained perhaps the greatest untapped electoral resource in Uruguay. Given the relatively equal electoral strength of the Colorado and National parties, the party that could gain the support of the working class could ensure its majority status. Vanger suggests that Batlle supported the labor movement as an investment for the future (Vanger 1980:129–32, 350–51). As the labor movement grew in organizational and political strength, Batlle's record of continued, progressive labor legislation would make his Colorado Party an obvious recipient of workers' electoral support. While labor was currently weak and disorganized, when it did grow Batlle hoped it would find its place within the Colorado Party. As Finch (1981:58) put it, "The Colorados were winning the allegiance of the urban working class and in so doing they pre-empted the reformism of the socialists and restricted the influence of anarcho-syndicalism such that the unions—or at least their growing membership—became more concerned with conditions of employment than with social revolution."

Batlle demonstrated his support for the labor movement in a number of ways, one of the most important of which was his labor legislation, his Labor Project. Batlle's Labor Project got off to a slow start, mostly, as Batlle himself noted, due to the strength of conservatives within the Senate and to his concern with not antagonizing them in the interest of consolidating party strength and insuring his reelection in 1911. As a result, the 1906 Labor Project was presented primarily as a signpost for future policy (Vanger 1963:258).

The 1906 proposal included five basic reforms: (1) an eight-hour day for manual workers, ten-hour days for clerical workers, with one extra hour during the first year after the bill was to be implemented; (2) an abolition of night work; (3) one day of rest per week; (4) regulation of child labor; and (5) a one-month, unpaid, maternity leave for women (Vanger, 1963:258). The eight-hour day had been "one of the points demanded in practically every strike since 1900" (S. Hanson 1938:124).

Batlle's labor proposal was considered in the legislature during the Williman administration but was changed in committee to what was, in effect, a proposal for an eleven-hour day. Batlle asked friendly legislators to keep the bill off the floor until his second administration, when he could get a "real eight-hour day" bill enacted (Vanger 1980:18). In fact, just a few months after Batlle began his second administration, he sent a revamped and considerably stronger version of his labor proposal to the legislature, thus initiating the active phase of the incorporation period.

The June 1911 version of Batlle's labor project provided for an eight-hour day for all urban workers and permitted no overtime. It extended maternity leave to one-and-a-half months and insured state financial support of 20 pesos during the time off. Finally, it kept the child-labor law provisions as well as the six-day work week, while easing the abolition of night work for certain businesses.[28]

Reaction to the 1911 proposal was intensely negative from business elites, with the Uruguayan Industrial Union, as well as most other elite groups, coming out in strong opposition. This reaction, together with the Manini defection in 1911, prevented the legislation from becoming law until November 1915. It went into effect in February 1916. Once the legislation did go into effect, employers refused to comply with the new laws, and workers reacted by initiating a series of strikes. These strikes were strongly supported by the new, pro-Batlle, Viera government, and workers were victorious in each one. The government's commitment to strong enforcement was reflected in the fact that 25 inspectors, some of whom were anarchists and Socialists, were hired to insure the law's implementation.[29]

Besides this labor legislation, Batlle also presented other social legislation setting up old-age pensions and establishing free public and primary education, which became law during the Viera administration. Batlle's loss in the July 1916 Constituent Assembly elections ended his labor initiatives, except for a worker's compensation law passed in 1920. Attempts to buttress the eight-hour work day with a minimum wage law for urban workers failed in 1927, as did a 1923 proposal for worker profit sharing and a 1919 proposal to strengthen the old-age pension law.[30]

Batlle did not confine his support for Uruguayan workers to general social legislation. Throughout his two administrations he pursued an often active policy of supporting workers' right to organize and strike, "such that a strike ceased to be in itself an act of political opposition or confrontation" (Finch 1981:57). In 1904, through *El Día*, Batlle expressed as he had many times before his strong support for strike activity, a controversial position given the prevalent distaste for worker organizations. He argued that "incitement to

---

[28] Vanger 1980:209; Fitzgibbon 1954:129–30; S. Hanson 1938:128.
[29] Vanger 1980:209; Barrán and Nahum 1979:175; 1985:113–14, 133–35; Pintos 1960:96; S. Hanson 1938:131; C. Rama 1955:48–49.
[30] Nahum 1975:75, 91, 124; Hanson 1938:148–49, 152.

strike, the right to refuse to work, propaganda to establish and affirm the ties of solidarity among workers on strike, are all legitimate and acceptable rights" (quoted in Vanger 1963:106). As a result, the "Police Chief, instead of stamping strikes out—and it almost seemed that Montevideo was going through a strike wave—acted as strike mediator" (Vanger 1963:106). In 1904 striking workers paraded past Batlle's home cheering him for his support for them (Vanger 1963:106).

Batlle maintained this policy during his second administration, as did his successor, Colorado President Viera, during the crucial period of worker protest between February and July of 1916. In 1911 Batlle supported the general strike called by the anarchist-led FORU, despite bitter opposition and the loss of considerable political support from conservatives. Again, in 1916, Batlle's former police chief, Campognaro, now serving under President Viera, upheld the policy of police neutrality despite considerable anarchist provocation and fired a neighborhood police official for using excessive force against strikers (Vanger 1980:129; Barrán y Nahum 1985:138–39).

Though Vanger calls Batlle's strike policy one of "benevolent neutrality" (Vanger 1963.210), Batlle often went further to extend direct government support to striking workers. Batlle's support of labor was a continuing source of controversy during his administrations, yet because many of the companies involved in labor conflict were foreign-owned, it was easier for Batlle to maintain this posture. Batlle put considerable pressure on the British rail company during the 1905 strike, forcing it to accept worker demands in return for a hoped-for government subsidy. Batlle often sent government ministers to mediate between employers and strikers. During the 1911 general strike, Batlle's government hastened the trolley car company's capitulation by levying stiff fines on the company for every trolley car not in service during the strike. Finally, during the strikes in 1916 against employers flouting the new eight-hour day law, the Viera administration sided with the strikers in every case, putting pressure on the employers and providing food for strikers and their families, thus helping workers to extend the strike. Some of Batlle's supporters actually helped organize a union in the telephone company.[31]

But while Batlle unquestionably did make a sustained attempt to legitimate and shape an institutionalized labor movement, the incorporation project in Uruguay was fundamentally different in one respect from that in the other seven countries. Batlle did not attempt to bring trade unions as organizations under party or state protection and control, though he did attempt to shape the overall political orientation and immediate behavior of the labor movement. A discussion of this contrast is necessary to round out the picture of Batlle's relations with Uruguayan workers.

Through a continuous series of speeches, laws, and newspaper editorials, Batlle supported the right and the necessity of worker organizations and the strike. He made it clear that under his administrations labor unions were no

[31] Vanger 1963:206–7; 1980:122–25, 274.; Barrán and Nahum 1985:132, 134–36, 139.

longer to be viewed as "foreign-led revolutionary cells" (Vanger 1980:350), but as legitimate participants in Uruguay's economic and political life (Finch 1981:57). On numerous occasions, Batlle urged the working class to organize. While Viera later backed away from these policies, as did Baltasar Brum's successors after 1923, the legacy of Batlle's administrations was to be the general acceptance of workers' right to organize and strike.

Yet one legacy Batlle did not leave was one of close state or party relations with labor unions. Batlle did not "try to replace Anarchist union leaders with Colorados or to set up Colorado sponsored unions" (Vanger 1980:350–51). The reasons why Batlle did not take this initiative include the consequences such a move would have had for Colorado party unity, as well as the early timing of the Uruguayan incorporation period. Regarding the first, with the defection in 1911 of the anti-Colegiado faction led by Manini, Batlle decided to deemphasize his public support of labor. The reason was that "unions were too weak, hostility to them was too great. To set up Colorado unions would play into anti-Colegialist . . . hands" (Vanger 1980:351). In Uruguay, as in Colombia (see below), any attempt to build strong organizational ties between the labor movement and a traditional, multisectoral, multiclass party could easily produce sharp splits in the party. In the case of the Colorados, such initiatives raised the challenge from more traditional party sectors that was expressed by Batlle's opponents with the saying, "Are we Colorados or are we Socialists?" (Vanger 1980:351).

The challenge of balancing between his labor reforms and the requirements of party unity was not a new one for Batlle. His dependence on traditional party attachments was evident during his presidential campaigns in 1903 and 1910, when he toned down his more radical positions. In 1913 Batlle again deemphasized the worker vote and relied on a strategy of getting out the committed Colorado vote through traditional clientelistic means and by accusing Manini of working with the Nationals. Batlle was unwilling to alienate moderate Colorados by highlighting his support for workers, especially since they constituted on the whole a potential, future source of support.[32]

A second reason that Batlle did not attempt to establish state regulation of labor organizations involves timing. Uruguay's incorporation period came early in comparison with other countries in Latin America, and corporatist ideas and models had only a limited circulation in the pre–World War I period. This early timing also helps to account for the high proportion of anarchists in the Uruguayan labor movement. Relations between Batlle and the anarchists were never good: his newspaper attacked anarchists (Vanger 1980:234), and anarchists refused to support his administration. In 1910 the anarchist study center stated, "We do not combat a specific person or government, [but] we will always be against The Government, whatever its political color" (quoted in Vanger 1980:69). It is likely that if Batlle had attempted

[32] Vanger 1963:55, 63; 1980:57–96, 217, 275–76, 350.

to compete directly with the anarchists, his relation with the labor movement would have been more antagonistic.

The further reason for the antagonism between the anarchists and Batlle, other than the obvious ambivalence of the anarchists toward any government, was that while Batlle in general did not favor state control of the labor movement, he did oppose some kinds of strike activity. Thus, along with his general support for the labor movement, he also sought to control and channel it. In speech after speech, Batlle made it clear that while he supported workers' right to strike, he also supported their right to ignore the strike and cross the striker's picket lines, a position anarchist and Marxist unions bitterly condemned. During the Batlle and Viera administrations, police maintained informants within labor organizations to keep track of anarchist activities and plans, and the police arrested strikers who carried out violent attacks on strikebreakers or company property. But Batlle made no attempt to formalize these controls and never sponsored legislation to regulate unions.[33]

The anarchist orientation of the Uruguayan labor movement also helps explain why workers did not provide more electoral support for Batlle. Vanger, in discussing the 1910 elections, suggests that there were several reasons for this lack of support. "Workers did not vote massively for Batlle, because they were not citizens, were not motivated, feared that they would get into trouble with their employers or others if they voted wrong (voting was public by signed ballot), or followed the advice of their Anarchist leaders: 'The worker will not vote' " (Vanger 1980:100).[34]

Another explanation of the weak worker vote for Batlle may be that Batlle's challenge to workers, that they should "organize, vote, participate," was always deemphasized at election time (Vanger 1980:275). In 1903, 1910, and 1913, Batlle presented himself as the able politician, the "mature Batlle,"

[33] Vanger 1980:128, 350; Barrán and Nahum 1985:136–37. This is not to say that some attempts were not made to extend legal control over the labor movement during the Uruguayan incorporation period. In 1905 Herrera and Roxlo, two National deputies who had introduced labor legislation in 1903, reacted negatively to the railroad and port workers' strikes and presented a bill "which would require unions to register with the government" and regulate union membership (Vanger 1963:208). In 1915 two Colorado deputies proposed a general labor law that would have expanded worker representation within state industries and created mediation boards composed of worker, employer, and government representatives. Both Batlle and the labor unions opposed this type of legislation, and it was not passed (Barrán and Nahum 1985:98–99).

[34] On at least one occasion, however, Batlle did win worker support for his initiatives. Initially the anarchists, afraid workers would start voting for Batlle, attacked the passage of the labor project in November 1915 as government electoral propaganda (Barrán and Nahum 1985:104–5), while some newly arrived immigrants opposed the law because the abolition of overtime reduced their opportunity to gain extra income (115–16). S. Hanson reports that "many urban workers feared that their wages would be cut if the hours were reduced by law" (1938:130), and their fears were justified when employers promptly attempted to do so. However, in the end, it was the government's firm support of worker complaints of violations of the law that eventually won worker support for the legislation after its successful implementation (Barrán and Nahum 1985:113).

or the "party leader." Yet, Batlle's long-term program was based on the eventual development of strong worker support, first for the Colegiado, and then for the Colorado Party and its social policies. Batlle could not participate directly in building a strong labor movement or the Manini faction would use this activity to hurt him politically. At the same time, labor did not develop a strong, cohesive movement on its own, partly due to anarchist leadership, partly to the lack of industrial development and the economic slump caused by World War I. The economic dislocation caused by the war greatly reduced worker incentives to organize. With falling wages, increased food costs, and rapidly rising unemployment, few workers turned out to support Batlle's Colegiado proposal in the July 1916 elections (Barrán and Nahum 1985:70, 77–78). As a result, Batlle lost his electoral majority as a large sector of the Colorado Party defected to Manini, a defection that was not balanced by a comparable increase in worker support.

While Barrán and Nahum are correct when they point out that "it is clear that Batlle sought worker support, acted and legislated in order to achieve it, and, to a certain degree, obtained it" (1982:132), it was ultimately not enough to prevent Batlle's electoral defeat in 1916. While Batlle's project basically mirrored demands of working class organizations and was part of a concerted effort to create electoral ties between the labor movement and Batlle's wing of the Colorado Party, in the short run his would-be exchange relationship with labor did not provide the political support he needed. As we shall see below, in the longer run he was more successful.

The Party

Batlle as party leader had two fundamental goals: first, to end the period of "two Uruguays," characterized by weak national governments and partisan civil war; and second, to unify the Colorados and establish them as a dominant party. When Batlle came to power in 1903, the Colorados were badly split between supporters and opponents of the 1897 coparticipation agreement. With his victory over Saravia in the 1904 civil war, Batlle united the formerly divided Colorado Party just when the Nationals seemed on the verge of taking power (Vanger 1963:273). With the defeat of the Nationals, the politics of warfare was replaced by the politics of ballots. The complexion of Uruguayan politics had changed fundamentally.

The Colorados had dominated the state bureaucracy since the 1880s. Government workers became an important base of the Colorado Party, a trend that was strengthened when legislation was passed in the 1890s providing pensions for school teachers. More importantly, the central state and the party faction that controlled it had a remarkable degree of control over government positions throughout the country. Though this power of appointment was reduced by the 1897 coparticipation agreement, Batlle's success in defeating the Saravia forces in 1904 inaugurated a period of one-party dominance that gave him almost undisputed power over political patronage and party electoral lists. Batlle's coalition was thus based on the support of partisan Colorados who viewed Batlle as the victor of the 1904 civil war, as well as on government employees who depended on Batlle for their jobs. By manipulating the appointment of political chiefs in the interior and by controlling the Colorado Party directorate, Batlle was able to insure victories for his supporters.[35]

By the end of Batlle's first term, the National Party had been successfully excluded from virtually all positions of political power. With the defeat of the Nationals and their abstention from electoral politics between 1906 and 1913, Batlle was able to focus on securing his reelection for 1911 and began to launch his social reform program. With his successful reelection, and with his new image as the "mature Batlle," Batlle began his second administration with a united party. Yet as he pushed his reforms through the legislature and extended government support to striking workers, the party began to divide, and a more conservative wing emerged to oppose the ambitious reform effort.

With the growing rift between Manini and Batlle, first over Batlle's handling of labor protest in 1911 and later over Batlle's Colegiado proposal in 1913, Batlle was incapable of pushing his legislation through the divided Senate and had to wait until the 1913 Senate elections to restore his control. Despite the party division, Batlle was able to use his command of state patronage to gain the unanimous support of the Colorado Party at the 1913 party convention, in which the Manini group refused to participate, for his reform and Colegiado projects, as well as for his hand-picked Senate candidates (Vanger 1980:248–50). This success showed how control of the executive branch by party factions enhanced their power. In the 1913 senatorial elections, the Manini wing was forced to run as a separate party, and Batlle was able to paint them with the pro-National brush. They fared poorly, as Batlle's list won five of the six positions, the other going to the National Party, which once again was contesting elections. Batlle's ability to control the party lists was crucial to explaining his success in winning the first electoral battle between the factions.

The primary reason Batlle was able to maintain strict control over the electoral machinery and to keep National vote totals low was the public signed ballot. Government workers and party officials who failed to support Batlle faced the prospect of losing their jobs. This is why the 1915 electoral law, which established the secret ballot and greatly expanded the eligible electorate, was so important (Nahum 1975:75–76). No longer able to insure electoral obedience, and facing growing discontent with his Colegiado proposal and social reform legislation, Batlle went into the July 1916 elections at a serious disadvantage.[36] Since this election would determine the proportion of delegates each party and party faction would have at the Constitutional Convention called by Batlle to consider his Colegiado proposal, the outcome was

[35] Vanger 1963:176, 180, 221; Finch 1981:42; Vanger 1980:276.
[36] In other respects as well, the 1915 electoral reform reduced the ability of National Party elites to control votes.

crucial. Although Batlle attempted—through the eight-hour day legislation as well as his active strike support during the crucial pre-election period—to generate enough working-class support to offset Colorado defections to the Manini wing, he was unsuccessful.

Emboldened by the growing split within the Colorado Party, the Nationals made a major electoral effort in 1916. Though the Colorados won 52 percent of the vote to the Nationals 48 percent, 9 percent of the Colorado vote went to the Manini wing. Although Manini's wing was unwilling to help the Nationals take power, they were willing to ally with the Nationals to oppose Batlle's Colegiado proposal at the Constitutional Convention and end Batlle's reform program (Nahum 1975:79).

Thus, having entered the 1916 contest with an electoral majority and a president strongly supportive of both the Colegiado and social reform, Batlle lost both. His defeat convinced President Viera that to extend the Batlle program would only contribute to growing National strength and division within the Colorado Party. Viera's decision to call a "halt" to the reform project in 1916 (the "Alto de Viera") and to break with Batlle was extended in 1919 when he ran his own list in the elections. The party split again in 1926, and by the time of the 1930 elections, the Colorados would present four different lists. The party unity created by Batlle in 1904 had disappeared.

Opposition and Polarization

The opposition to Batlle first crystallized in the rift between Manini and Batlle, beginning with their disagreement over the handling of the 1911 general strike. Attempts by opponents of Batlle's reform program to encourage an actual split between the two initially failed. Nevertheless, the next two years left Manini increasingly disillusioned with Batlle's radicalism and his Colegiado proposal (Vanger 1980:128–29, 178–80). It was not until Batlle's public announcement of his constitutional reform project in March 1913 that Manini moved into open opposition, becoming a central figure in the growing opposition to Batlle. In Manini's view, "It was not just the Colegiado; fundamentally, Batlle's excessive radicalism, his converting Uruguay into an 'experiment station for exotic novelties,' must be stopped" (Vanger 1980:218–19). On May 24, in his "Are we Colorados or are we Socialists?" speech, Manini made clear his differences with Batlle over the reforms. Again, Batlle tried to defuse the growing tension but was unsuccessful as Manini formed the Anti-Colegialist Executive Committee in September to contest the November 1913 Senate elections.

Though Manini lost badly in his attempt to wrest the leadership of the Colorado Party from Batlle, his opposition made him leader of conservatives who rejected the Batlle program. Over the next two years Manini, with National Party leader Luis Herrera, began the process of forming a powerful rural interest group that was constituted in December 1915 as the Rural Federation. Representing the nation's wealthy cattle ranchers, the Rural

Federation was meant to restore the influence of the conservative sectors of Uruguayan society. Herrera argued that if workers, with no press or influence, could receive such attention from the government, then why should ranchers and farmers who owned the press and had such enormous economic influence not have a larger voice? This sentiment was echoed by another major actor within the new federation, who stated that a society in which everyone governs except for those who produce cannot be properly ruled (Caetano 1983a:17–19, 26). The cities, Herrera argued, are lost and the salvation of Uruguay will have to come from the countryside.

The growing influence of the Rural Federation was matched by new initiatives within the National Party. Batlle's Colegiado proposal convinced National Party leaders to contest the 1913 Senate elections and prepare a full mobilization for the 1916 assembly elections. Supported by the Catholic Church and the Rural Federation—as well as by two other major economic sectors, business (represented by the Liga de Defensa Comercial) and industry (represented by the Cámara de Industrias)—the conservative National and the Colorado anti-Batlle forces entered the 1916 elections hoping to end the Batlle era once and for all.

Batlle's loss in 1916 and Viera's "halt" to the reform movement were greeted with euphoria by the conservative sectors. Batlle, meanwhile, attempted to downplay Viera's declaration, arguing that the "halt" was only meant to be temporary as the Colorados reorganized to defeat the Nationals in the November 1916 legislative elections. Nevertheless, Viera was strongly supported by conservative groups and his policy began to veer further to the right. Whether the strong support received by Viera led him further down the anti-Batlle path than he had originally planned, or whether it simply convinced him to continue an already determined policy, the change in program occurred (Caetano 1983a:34, 41–44).

Batlle's response was to deemphasize the reformist aspects of his program and return to the traditional politics of elite bargaining. Over the next few months Batlle supporters in the legislature declared against the secret ballot and pushed through a postponement of the November elections until January 1917, in the hope that the party division could be healed. Intense negotiations between the Batlle and Manini wings failed. As the Constitutional Convention met, the Batlle forces boycotted the proceedings. Finally, Batlle negotiated with the Nationals the passage of a new electoral law that reapportioned and expanded the number of Chamber seats and ended the secret ballot, to the detriment of the Manini faction. All of these moves were geared toward giving the Batlle forces more room to maneuver and time to plan their comeback (Caetano 1983a:59).

The conservative groups, meanwhile, prepared for what they hoped would be a final blow to Batlle. On 26 December 1916 Manini, now head of an independent Partido Colorado General Rivera, joined with the Nationals and the Rural Federation to form the Popular Coalition to oppose Batlle in the January 1917 Chamber elections. The conservative coalition entered the elections with high hope that the end of the Batlle era had arrived. Nevertheless, Batlle won a solid victory. However, the Batlle-dominated legislature faced an antagonistic executive and an opposition-dominated Constituent Assembly. The result was deadlock, as neither Batlle nor the conservatives could muster the forces to defeat the other. This deadlock would continue for the next 16 years.

Thus, in 1916 to 1917, the era of active reform came to an end. Batlle and his wing of the Colorado Party remained a powerful force in Uruguayan politics, though he would not again be president. A few further reform measures were passed, and relatively few reforms were reversed or rescinded, though government support for unions and strikers was eroded. However, not until 1933 was there a regime change and a dramatic shift of power away from the Batlle wing of the Colorados.

COLOMBIA

The incorporation period in Colombia began when the Liberal Party won the presidency for the first time in half a century in 1930 and successfully constructed a new urban political constituency. An important reason for this success was the party's mobilization of popular sector electoral support through a series of social and labor reforms. A far more problematic aspect of this reform was the Liberals' effort to create a labor movement with organizational ties to the Liberal Party.

The rhythm of the incorporation period responded to the struggle between the two wings of the Liberal Party: the moderate wing, led by Enrique Olaya Herrera and Eduardo Santos, and the more radical, reformist wing, which had grown out of a younger sector of the Liberal Party known as Los Nuevos, led by Alfonso López Pumarejo. The shifts in power between these two wings led to four distinct phases: (1) the Olaya administration (1930–34), characterized by mild labor reforms and interparty pacts; (2) the first administration of López (1934–38) and, more specifically, the two years when his party faction controlled the legislature (1935–37) and launched the Revolución en Marcha (Revolution on the March), which included extensive labor reforms; (3) the period beginning with the administration of Eduardo Santos (1938–42), when labor issues were deemphasized as his government took a less supportive position toward labor; and (4) the final phase of the second López administration (1942–45). Reacting to a failed coup attempt in 1944, López passed a number of important labor laws and initiated a new period of active state support for labor organizing. With López's resignation in 1945 and the crackdown on unions immediately initiated by his successor, Alberto Lleras Camargo, the incorporation period ended.

Project from Above

The project from above must be looked at in terms of the dynamics of these successive phases of the incorporation period. In the 1930 presidential election, the Liberal Party and its candidate, Enrique Olaya Herrera, defeated a divided Conservative Party that appeared incapable of meeting the social and economic challenges of the Great Depression. Olaya believed the future of the Liberals lay in seeking common ground with the Conservatives to assure the reactivation of the Colombian economy. Olaya called his administration the "National Concentration" and moved quickly to include Conservative leaders in his cabinet. He opposed the mobilization of the popular sectors, but argued that the ruling elite and the parties would have to accept some reforms to reduce worker protest (Horgan 1983:286–89; Molina 1974:240–41, 247). Olaya's program, therefore, emphasized the creation of the conditions for political and social stability necessary for the improvement of Colombia's economy and its international image. He used state resources to prevent interparty conflict, to create the conditions necessary for renewed foreign investment, and to introduce relatively nonconflictual reforms. With the support of the important Antioquian Conservative and industrialist, Carlos Restrepo, the financial and latifundista Liberal elite, as well as the traditional Liberal party bosses eager to restore party hegemony, Olaya began his administration with a considerable base of support.

Yet Olaya's coalition was fragile. Given the cleavages within the Liberal party between his moderate wing and the more progressive wing identified with López, Olaya's program proved difficult to carry out. He had to walk a narrow path, avoiding interparty and intraparty conflict in order to convince foreign investors of Colombia's stability. During this first phase of the incorporation project, Olaya had, first of all, to deal with the growing economic crisis and the social and political forces it had created, including both urban and rural worker protest. Second, regional and local party bosses wished to use the state to establish the future dominance of the Liberal Party, which had been excluded from power for 50 years. Olaya had to find a way to defuse the growing violence in the countryside as Liberals began to remove Conservative rivals from positions of power and to mete out retribution for a half century of real or perceived oppression.

A central problem was how to initiate reform in such a way as to prevent a break between the moderate and progressive wings of the Liberal Party. The Olaya project, therefore, stressed the avoidance of conflict, but did include a number of modest labor and social reforms codified in Law 83 of 1931. This law for the first time recognized the right of workers to form unions and provided tangible benefits to legally recognized unions. More important, the Olaya administration directly supported, and sometimes even participated in, union formation and intervened in favor of workers in some strikes. Finally, by initiating a mild form of state economic intervention, as well as a generally protectionist economic policy, Olaya was able to create the conditions which, along with the general improvement of the world economy after 1932, contributed to a pronounced economic recovery (Urrutia 1969a:117, 119; Molina 1974:244–47) .

The problem of interparty conflict was less tractable. With the 1931 labor legislation, Olaya temporarily shored up his support with the López wing of the party. Olaya also attempted to win Conservative Party support, especially that of the Nationalist wing led by General Alfredo Vásquez, who likewise supported mild labor reforms. The Vásquez group was strongly opposed at the national level by the majority Conservative faction led by Laureano Gómez, who refused to collaborate with the Liberal government and opened a concerted offensive against it.[37] The Conservatives had reason to be bitter.

[37] The extreme tone of Gómez's opposition is reflected in his statement in 1931 that "in his rage against Conservatism, President Olaya did not limit himself to being a corrupter. He has been a bloody and unjust persecutor as well. His is a cruel, impious soul. He is literally soaked with the honest blood of his brothers. And he smiles" (quoted in Solaún 1980:22).

While Olaya had divided the country's fourteen regional governorships evenly between the two parties, partisan struggle at the regional level acquired its own dynamic. Local Liberal *caciques* sought to take advantage of the greater Liberal dominance in the national arena to quickly consolidate the party's power. In several regions, especially the northeast, partisan violence was intense as Conservatives resisted the Liberals. The transition might have ended in civil war had the Peruvians not invaded the Colombian border town of Leticia in 1933. The subsequent war with Peru created national unity and temporarily ended the strife as local Conservative and Liberal party bosses signed peace treaties so they could turn their attention to the invasion. While the partisan conflicts that led to local and regional violence remained basically unresolved, and would later return with renewed force, Olaya and the Liberal party had gained some breathing space to deal with the economic and social problems facing Colombia.[38]

As the 1934 election approached, social protest continued to grow as the urban and rural Liberal Party base failed to realize the expected gains from the Liberals' return to power. By the end of the Olaya administration, exports had recovered their predepression value and the industrial sector had returned to its pre-1929 growth rate. Yet the benefits of renewed growth had not yet been extended to the mass of urban and rural workers. In the face of considerable worker protest, Olaya issued a decree on May Day in 1934 establishing the eight-hour work day. At the same time, rural party bosses were frustrated by the lack of state support for their efforts to extend Liberal control over local and national patronage. This growing dissatisfaction, together with the fact that by late 1933 Lopez had emerged as the only national Liberal figure capable of leading the party into the 1934 elections, strengthened the reformist wing of the Liberals and brought López to power in an election uncontested by the Conservatives.[39]

As president from 1934 to 1938, López led the way in expanding the social role of the state through his implementation of the reform program called the Revolution on the March. The López program was in some ways an extension of Olaya's, but in other ways a radical departure. Like Olaya, López emphasized protectionist measures to end the "colonial" economy and create an independent, national economy (Molina 1977:16). While Olaya had introduced the idea of the interventionist state, López made it a centerpiece of his policy, arguing that the state's primary purpose was to guide and channel individual acts toward the public good (Molina 1977:14). Launching a major reform effort, López pushed through Congress such initiatives as (1) taxes on income and wealth; (2) a constitutional provision stating that workers and trade unions would receive special protection from the state which, in practice, meant state support for union formation; (3) an expanded state role in social welfare; and (4) a modest land reform.[40] Finally, and most at

[38] Oquist 1980:102–7; Maingot 1967:237–38; Guzmán 1968:15–39; Fluharty 1957:45.
[39] Fluharty 1957:44–45; Chu 1972:10–12; CIE/DAP 1973:55; Horgan 1983:613–16, 623.
[40] See Molina 1977:14–20, for a complete statement of the Liberal Party program during the first López administration.

odds with the moderate Olaya wing of the Liberal Party, López established what he called *"un gobierno de partido"* (party government). Rejecting the pact made by Olaya with the Conservatives, López stated that such an arrangement was alien to the desires and wishes of his supporters, who sought to use state power to establish Liberal dominance and to transform Colombian society (Molina 1977:20–21). Unlike the Olaya administration, which had sought partisan peace and a reduction in social conflict, the López government adopted a confrontational approach to both the Conservative Party[41] and the nation's economic elite. As a consequence, this phase was characterized by coup rumors, labor and popular sector demonstrations supporting López and the "Revolution," and a growing polarization within the Liberal Party and in Colombian society generally.

López's decision to actively mobilize labor, thus initiating the second phase of the incorporation period, involved two primary goals. First, López sought to provide the Liberal Party with an enlarged support base to promote Liberal hegemony over the state. Second, he wished to create a political ally to help ensure his control over the Liberal Party and thus restrain opposition to his program from moderate Liberals and to co-opt opposition from the left by Gaitán and his radical UNIR (Revolutionary Leftist National Union) and, later, by the Communists. López put his program into effect by initiating a variety of measures supportive of labor and by politicizing the state through a series of patronage-based political appointments. Labor responded to the López program by becoming a crucial part of López's support coalition, together with rural party bosses eager to extend Liberal Party control over the entire country.

López's rural mobilization must be understood in the framework of traditional partisan struggles characteristic of the Colombian rural sector. His rural program did not involve the kind of wide-ranging agrarian reform and peasant mobilization found in Mexico and Venezuela. Party leaders at the regional level tended to have close ties to regional elites and were therefore unsupportive of major efforts to organize and mobilize peasants. López did undertake some limited agrarian reform initiatives that served primarily to regularize the holdings of rural squatters in certain areas and to settle a relatively limited number of disputes in the coffee haciendas of Cundinamarca and Tolima. While to some extent these initiatives did strengthen the political and economic position of rural workers, the reforms served mainly to end ambiguities in the system of rural property relations, with the goal of strengthening most existing rural relationships. According to Dix (1967:90), "the position of the large estate which was already under cultivation was not really touched." Landowners were well represented in Congress. While they had been unable to block the limited reforms that were passed, which seriously displeased many of them, their strong political role meant there was

[41] At the beginning of his administration, López did offer a limited form of cooperation to the Conservatives, but the partisan character of his offer led the Conservatives to reject it (Tirado 1981:62).

little likelihood that agrarian reform initiatives would turn into a more general attack on rural property relations. Rather, the initiatives that did occur addressed limited challenges to existing rural relationships, "and, at the same time, kept intact the networks of patronage that maintained clientelist bipartisan control in the countryside."[42]

During the first two years of the López administration, the moderate wing of the Liberal Party became increasingly disenchanted with the López program, especially its use of the state to expand the role of labor. Beginning in 1936 this opposition led López to new reform initiatives, as he prepared for the 1937 legislative elections. López further amended the Constitution to strengthen the right of the state to intervene in the private sector of the economy as part of his attempt to increase the state's role in economic planning and in mediating worker-employer conflict (Gibson 1948:361). He also moved to separate church and state by establishing state control over education, thus challenging the dominance of the Church over Colombia's school system. These actions struck at the very base of the Conservative Party power structure and the laissez-faire economy. Fluharty wrote that "after López, the state as innovator, controller, and director was to be in constant struggle with the idea of the state as maintainer . . . of the oligarchy" (Fluharty 1957:46). Finally, from 1936 to 1937 López expanded his administration's relations with labor, and recognition of new unions reached a record high in 1937 (Urrutia 1969a:53).

The third, and most quiescent, phase of the incorporation project began with López's failure in 1937 to maintain control of the legislature and of the party. By 1937 Liberal rural bosses, who had entered the López coalition because they favored his partisan attacks on the Conservative Party, became increasingly disenchanted with his move to the left. While López's agrarian reform was limited in scope and had been successful in defusing Gaitán's more radical UNIR movement, his support of land redistribution did cost him support among Liberal latifundistas (Oquist 1980:109). The death of Olaya Herrera in 1937 and the ascension of Eduardo Santos to lead the moderate wing of the Liberals led to massive defections from the López camp. The Nuevo program was in place, but the dissension created within the Liberal Party by the scope and conflictual nature of the reforms spelled the end of further major reforms during López's first administration. By late 1937 Santos had captured the 1938 presidential nomination from Darío Echandía, the candidate of López and labor. The coalition that had supported the Revolution on the March had come unraveled.

After the Santos administration (1938–42), characterized more by benign neglect than by actual opposition to organized labor, López recaptured the presidency in 1942 over massive Liberal opposition. López was able to win, as in 1934, because the moderate wing did not have a candidate with comparable national stature. Nevertheless, a significant fraction of the Liberal Party ended up supporting the dissident candidacy of the moderate Liberal

---

[42] Zamosc 1986:13; see also Hirschman (1965:148–50); Dix (1967:90).

Carlos Arango, who received a remarkable 41 percent of the vote despite the support for López of most of the Liberal department committees (there was no Conservative candidate). While unable to prevent López's return to the presidency, the moderates did maintain control of the legislature, thus preventing any resumption of his reform program until 1944. From 1942 to 1944 López was forced to work through the bureaucracy, and the rate of union growth remained at the levels to which it had declined during the Santos administration.

The fourth, and final, phase of the incorporation period began in 1944, when an isolated group of officers took López prisoner in the southern city of Pasto and attempted an unsuccessful coup. One factor that inhibited the success of the coup was the concern of military leaders with López's popular support, especially from labor, and with the popular protest the coup might provoke (Maullin 1973:58; Caicedo 1971:89–90).[43]

López used the opportunity to declare a state of emergency and issued a decree that greatly increased the ability of unions to organize, although it also increased state control over the labor movement. López then refused to end the state of emergency and restore legislative power until Congress ratified his new decree. Union recognition reached its peak for the entire 1930–46 period in 1944 and 1945, as López attempted to create support for his government. Six-hundred thirty-three unions were recognized in these two years, two-and-a-half times as many as during 1937–38, the previous high point of union recognition.[44] During this period López faced growing opposition from the right by Liberal latifundistas due to his earlier rural reforms, and from the left by Gaitán and his growing support in the urban popular sector, with moderate Liberals receiving the support of important sectors of the industrial and financial elite. In this context, López became increasingly dependent on the support of organized labor.

López's need to use emergency powers to secure labor legislation during his second administration is a clear indicator of the growing weakness of the reform faction of the Liberal Party.[45] By ruling under a state of emergency,

[43] Maingot, in discussing the conditions that led to the attempted coup, points out that "Conservative propaganda, and especially the chaotic internal situation[,] finally provided the necessary stimulus to move, even if it was only after a rationalization process heavily tinged with Conservative loyalties" (Maingot 1967:281). In explaining the coup's failure, Maingot emphasizes the dependence of the Colombian military on civilian initiative and leadership and lack of support for the coup from Conservative politicians and the rest of the military (283, 286). Maullin, on the other hand, stresses military leaders' fear of López's popular support (Maullin 1973:58). In either case, the coup quickly failed and López was released.

[44] Bergquist 1986:355; Powers 1979:235–36; Urrutia 1969a:53.

[45] López had begun his second term in office with a demonstrably less reformist program. Yet the interpretation of Fluharty among others, of "The Reformer Reformed" (Fluharty 1957:66), of an increasingly conservative López, may be incomplete. Following this interpretation, many commentators, when discussing the Labor Decrees of 1944 and 1945, have deemphasized the benefits for labor they contained. If López had moved back to the center, why did he push these new reforms at considerable cost to his government? In fact, the evidence seems to indicate that López moved to the left in 1944 and 1945, partly in an

López was able to make use of the expanded powers of the president and thwart moderate Liberal and Conservative Party opposition within the legislature. At the same time, the Santos wing of the party used its control of newspapers identified with the Liberals to criticize López and launch intense personal attacks on members of his family, so as to discredit his administration. As the polemics increased, with the Conservative Party also doing what it could to heighten the tension, López was eventually driven to resign in late 1945.[46]

The resignation of López and the assumption of the presidency by his more moderate successor, Lleras Camargo, marked the end of the period of state mobilization of labor and the beginning of a period of intense intraparty and interparty polarization that would lead to a Conservative victory over a divided Liberal Party in the 1946 presidential elections and a decade of violent, partisan struggle. In an attempt to restore party unity, Lleras quickly broke the most important, militant and Communist-dominated unions (Oquist 1980:112–13). However, his efforts were ineffective, since his government faced growing opposition both from Santos's moderate wing and the increasingly radical wing led by Jorge Eliecer Gaitán, who actively continued and broadened the labor mobilization initiated by López. By 1946, the Liberals were unable to agree on a presidential candidate, and the split between the two Liberal factions was complete.

Project from Below

The leaders of the incorporation project in Colombia dealt with a labor movement, major sectors of which were disposed to cooperate with the state. Due to the relatively late emergence of Colombia's labor movement, to Colombia's relative isolation from major currents of European immigration, and to the timing of the incorporation period, anarchism had played little role in Colombian labor politics (Urrutia 1969a:55). Instead, during the incorporation period debates within the labor movement on cooperation with the state were more strongly linked to the evolving position of the Communist Party toward such cooperation.

Beginning in the 1920s the nascent labor movement's project focused on a set of demands then called "los tres ochos" (the three eights): eight-hour work days, eight hours of rest (i.e., one day off per week), and eight hours of

---

attempt to shore up his labor support, but also as a response to Gaitán's more radical campaign for the presidency, also initiated in 1944. After López's resignation in 1945, he did move to the center, attacking both the Turbay and Gaitán presidential candidacies. He supported his old nemesis, Eduardo Santos, because he "was convinced that unless the party settled on Santos as a compromise, 'the decision [of the voters] will be adverse' " (Braun 1985:107–8). As it turned out, he was correct.

[46] Another factor behind López's resignation was apparently his inability to secure official permission to leave the country to secure medical treatment for his wife, who was seriously ill.

daily education for workers' children (Archila 1984:64–85). With the Liberal victory in 1930, the labor movement found itself at a crucial decision point: would it cooperate with the Liberal government to achieve its goals, or would it maintain an independent, oppositional stance toward capital and the state?

Parties located to the left of the Liberals' progressive wing had important influence in the labor movement and advocated an independent stance. Thus, the Socialist Revolutionary Party (PSR), formed in 1926 with important links to the Communist movement,[47] supported this position, stating that "we are not naive enough to believe that the Liberal party . . . will accompany us in the battle we must wage alone to secure the triumph of justice and to change the miserable lot of the workers" (cited in Molina 1974:230). But the Communists and their supporters were apparently out of step with the majority of labor leaders. Shortly after the election of 1930, the PSR collapsed, as much of its leadership crossed back to the Liberal Party with the hope of securing government positions. However, the Communists continued their policy of denouncing cooperation with the state. As a result they lost considerable rank and file support to the Liberal Party in the early 1930s, as well as to Gaitán and his UNIR within the crucial transportation sector.[48]

Because the Liberal Party, through its control of the state, was able to offer concrete, immediate benefits to cooperative labor unions, it was difficult for the Communists and Gaitán's UNIR to convince labor leaders to follow an independent, confrontational strategy. The Labor Law of 1931 made possible the unionization of workers in a number of sectors, while at the same time the Liberal government's land reform initiative defused Communist and UNIR attempts to link the primarily urban labor movement with organizations of rural workers. A concrete example of the Communists' inability to prevent growing Liberal control over the labor movement was the Liberal administration's successful mediation of the 1934 banana zone strike. While workers did not achieve an end to the piece-rate system, they did receive substantial increases in wages and benefits. As a result, Communist control over the banana unions was undercut and the government's efforts to win the cooperation of workers received a significant boost (Bergquist 1986:335, fn 66, 342–48).

Although the strategy of political cooperation was being accepted by increasing numbers of labor leaders, it by no means extended to all urban and industrial areas in Colombia. Workers in Antioquia's rapidly growing industrial sector either remained unorganized, or were being organized by groups, linked to the Church and to employers, that more nearly resembled company unions (Medhurst 1984:59, 65–66, 75). This outcome was crucial since Antioquia was one of the regions where the Jesuit-sponsored UTC (Union of Colombian Workers), the labor confederation that later established a special

<hr/>

[47] The Colombian Communist Party (PCC) was not formally established until 1930.
[48] Powers 1979:199; Pécaut 1973:124; F. González 1975:24–25.

relationship with the Conservative government, would develop its greatest strength after 1946.[49]

A standard interpretation of the Liberals' failure to organize this sector is that these workers, mostly women, were unsupportive of the "political bargaining" strategy of the Liberal CTC (Confederation of Colombian Workers), as well as of its close connections with the Liberal and Communist parties.[50] The preferences of these workers, therefore, was presumably to avoid the highly politicized CTC and its tactics of political bargaining with the Liberal government. Yet the notion that women, as a group, were more conservative and less likely to support the CTC and its strategy of political bargaining ignores important evidence. It is certainly true that, except for a few unsuccessful attempts to organize some textile and coffee-shelling (trilladora) plants, and despite considerable growth in the industrial sector after 1934, few efforts were made to organize workers in Antioquia during the Liberal period. However, explanations based on gender or workers' strategies seem incomplete. Indeed, already in the 1920s, female workers were heavily involved in organizing and directing strikes in the textile and coffee-shelling factories (Molina 1974:115; Bergquist 1986:351–54).

An alternative explanation focuses on the role of regional political elites. Most of Colombia's industrial sector was located in the department of Antioquia, a coffee-rich region with a powerful entrepreneurial elite. This elite, mostly Conservative, maintained considerable local and regional power during the Liberal period after 1930. It is probable that this elite acted as a barrier to Liberal attempts to organize workers within the region. The importance of Conservative versus Liberal dominance at the level of departments is suggested by the large number of industrial workers unionized by the CTC in the 1930s in the Liberal department of Cundinamarca, as opposed to the considerable progress of the Conservative-supported UTC in organizing the Antioquian industrial sector during the later Conservative administrations of Ospina Pérez and Gómez (Urrutia 1969a:206–7).

As Medhurst (1984:73) notes, "Apart from small craft unions and peasant organizations, it is apparent that the UTC's early constituent unions came

[49] Urrutia argues that the real attraction of the UTC was that it avoided politics, and he rejects the argument that the UTC was a Conservative creation. He points to the role of Liberals in its founding as well as to the UTC's explicit decision in the late 1940s to reject any political commitments (Urrutia 1969a:206–11). Yet the direct and indirect links with the Conservatives seem clear. The UTC, while not founded by the Conservative Party, was organized by the Catholic Church, a staunch and highly partisan Conservative ally. The UTC's Catholic origins as well as its refusal to engage in political bargaining made it, as Oquist (1980:113) points out, "the favored labor instrument of the Conservative government. Organized by Jesuits [in 1946], backed by many industrialists, and with the support of the new government, the UTC prospered at the expense of the CTC." Therefore, while the Conservative Party did not create the UTC, its supportive policies made it a success and an important weapon in the partisan struggle of the late 1940s. See also Medhurst's discussion of this issue (Medhurst 1984:79–82).

[50] Urrutia 1969a:206–7, 211. See also the discussion of female industrial workers in Torres Giraldo (1973c:33–35); and Chu (1972:204).

chiefly from the manufacturing sector and, above all, from the manufacturing sector of Antioquia." The UTC's success in Antioquia was due to its willingness to work closely with highly paternalistic employers, mostly Conservative. In discussing the UTC union in one of Antioquia's most prominent textile firms, Medhurst found that the union, as of the 1950s, operated as little more that a "company" union. Management "accepted the union as a means of regulating and legitimizing its dealings with the work force and as a way of pre-empting alternatives. Its tolerance was initially dependent on the eschewing of overtly conflictual patterns of labor relations" (Medhurst 1984:75). The UTC's deferential attitude toward Antioquia's employers, and the support it received from the Conservative government, may well explain why it succeeded where the CTC failed.

It would seem, therefore, that while the CTC's failure to organize the industrial sector in Conservative Antioquia may have been due in part to worker opposition to its strategy or goals, another factor may have been the weak political position of the Liberal national government in a region dominated by the Conservative Party. This weakness must have been clear to labor organizers who would otherwise have been supportive of cooperation with the national state. Without the active collaboration of regional political elites with the Liberal government at the national level, worker organizations would remain weak and marginal; with this collaboration, some of their economic goals were being achieved.

The division within the labor movement over strategy vis-à-vis the Liberal government was clear at the first labor congress in 1935, which founded the CTC. Two executive committees were elected, one dominated by leaders supporting cooperation with the Liberal government, the other controlled by the Communists. This sometimes acerbic division left the newly formed CTC weak, divided, and little more than a political pressure group. Following the Communists' acceptance of the COMINTERN's "popular front" strategy, a second labor congress was held in 1936, which healed the earlier division within the movement. This congress was heavily subsidized by the López administration, which paid the way for union delegates and, in return, received the unconditional support of the new labor central (Urrutia 1969a:172–73).

The decision of union leaders to pursue a strategy of close collaboration with the Liberals was cemented at the 1938 CTC congress. A number of labor activists wanted the CTC to support López's candidate for the 1938 elections, Darío Echandía, against the party nominee, Eduardo Santos. The labor movement faced a crucial choice: would it back the wing of the Liberal Party most supportive of the labor movement, or would it extend its policy of cooperation with the state to any Liberal Party candidate, even one decidedly cool to labor? The labor congress, despite opposition from López's supporters, ratified labor's political approach and supported the Santos candidacy, notwithstanding his ambivalent position toward labor. The final declaration of the congress stated that "labor organizations should work tenaciously against the postulate of labor's political neutrality, *since it has been through politics that the workers have obtained the improved conditions that they enjoy today."*[51] From this point until the mid-1940s, labor leaders generally sought the support, both financial and organizational, of whichever Liberal faction controlled the government. In exchange, they accepted state mediation of strikes as well as a limitation of strike objectives to primarily economic concerns. Thus, by 1938 there was substantial coordination of policies and goals between the labor movement and the government.

The Exchange

During the incorporation period, the Liberal Party, through favorable legislation and a variety of prolabor initiatives, accomplished three interrelated goals. First, the Liberals developed a new approach to state-labor relations that contrasted markedly with the harsh treatment of labor organizations and demands by Conservative governments in the 1920s. With this new labor policy, the Liberal Party rewarded urban workers for their important support in the 1930 elections. Second, the new labor policies allowed the Liberals to reverse the earlier gains of the Socialist and Communist parties within the labor sector. In part as a consequence, the Liberals established themselves as the majority party. With control over the state, the Liberals were able to use state resources to woo a new urban constituency (of which labor was an important part), while at the same time restoring voting rights to many Liberal partisans in rural areas. Finally, the Liberals fashioned a number of formal and informal ties with the growing labor movement, exchanging responsiveness to worker concerns and support for the CTC for labor's support and cooperation.

Prior to the Liberal victory in 1930 and the 1931 Labor Law, labor legislation was primarily used by Conservative governments to suppress the organization of unions. While the Liberal Party gave some support to labor organizing prior to 1930, its lack of access to state power meant that its support was limited mostly to wide-ranging criticisms of the Conservative government's violent suppression of strike activity, as occurred during the 1928 banana-zone strike. Given the party bosses' tight control over the rural electoral machinery, the Liberals focused on urban areas in their search for an electoral majority, since urban electoral fraud was harder to hide. As a result, urban workers provided the edge in the cities that gave Olaya and the Liberal Party their victory in the 1930 presidential elections (Molina 1974:247–48).

Recognizing the importance of this new source of party strength, Olaya initiated a number of laws during his administration to maintain this urban support base. The most important was Law 83 of 1931, which extended safeguards for union organization and strikes. Throughout the Olaya administration these early efforts at developing a labor code were attacked by Conservatives and some Liberals as unconstitutional. The López administration

51 Urrutia (1969a:176), emphasis in original.

(1934–38) responded to these earlier challenges by providing the constitutional basis for the existing labor code and creating the groundwork for its later expansion through the constitutional reform of 1936. The 1936 reforms established, for the first time, that workers had a constitutional right to organize and strike and that the state would provide special protection to trade unions. State control over union activity was strengthened through decrees in 1937 and 1938, which regulated the organization of labor congresses as well as union elections and finances (Molina 1974:247–48; Urrutia 1969a:173n).

During the subsequent Santos administration, no new labor legislation was passed, in keeping with the view that "the union movement should be left to its own fate" (Molina 1977:93). Nonetheless, the rate of union recognition, while falling from the rates achieved under López in 1937 and 1938, remained above the levels of the Olaya administration. Later, the second López administration was responsible for perhaps the most significant labor legislation passed in Colombian history, providing important benefits and inducements for unions but also imposing important constraints. Under the state of emergency declared in 1944 after the military uprising, López issued Decree 2350 and later Decree 2414, which eventually became Law 6 of 1945. This legislation established the closed shop, but also required all new unions to incorporate as enterprise unions, thereby limiting the scope of union activity. It likewise created new regulations for strikes and provided job security for local, regional, and national labor leaders, as well as for workers engaged in union organizing. Finally, the law prevented employers from issuing new labor contracts during a strike, thus protecting unions from strikebreakers (Urrutia 1969a:155, 163–64).

The labor legislation of the Liberal period provided workers with strong inducements to organize. Prior to 1930 the state had recognized only 99 unions, often short-lived and limited to mutual aid activities, whereas from 1930 to 1945 the Liberal governments recognized more than 1,400 unions. There were three primary reasons for the growth in union organizations during this period: the increased legitimacy given to unions and the strike weapon by Law 83 of 1931 and the 1936 constitutional reforms; the provisions in the labor code providing security for union organizers and strikers; and, finally, direct government support under the Olaya and López administrations for union activities. This government support included Labor Ministry help in setting up new unions, as well as direct financial support for the CTC.[52]

In Colombia, as elsewhere, the benefits for unions were combined with constraints. Law 83 of 1931 included a "right to work," open shop clause, which almost certainly hindered union formation. It also required a two-thirds strike vote by union members, although this was reduced to a simple majority by Law 6 of 1945. The decrees of 1937 and 1938 placed recognized unions under strict state supervision, while the 1945 law prohibited the cre-

---

[52] Urrutia 1969a:53–54, 117, 119, 173, 185; Caicedo 1971:79–81; Molina 1977:92–93.

ation of industrial or craft unions. Also, provisions of the 1945 law requiring plant unions made it difficult to organize beyond that level, thus severely weakening national confederations (Medhurst 1984:72–73).

The response of labor to Liberal initiatives can be roughly divided into two periods. The first, between 1930 and 1936, is characterized by the opposition of the Communists and of Gaitán's UNIR to cooperation with the Liberal party and their increased marginalization, as the majority of labor movement leaders moved into a close relationship with the state. The Olaya administration, besides its passage of the 1931 labor law, provided considerable state support for union organization and strike mediation and met many of the demands of labor through subsequent legislation. The important railroad workers' union won state pensions for its workers in 1932. In 1934 worker protest led to the extension of key reform legislation that established two-week vacations, sick-leave and disability insurance, severance pay, and an eight-hour work day (Horgan 1983:623). By the end of the Olaya administration all three of los tres ochos demanded by labor had been granted. As a result, labor leaders advocating cooperation with the state could point to a number of concrete victories.

The second period of labor-state cooperation began in 1936 and continued, with some interruptions, through 1946. In 1935 Gaitán dissolved the UNIR and returned to the Liberal Party to serve in the López administration, and in 1936 the Communists initiated their "popular front" strategy. New unions were now recognized at an unprecedented rate. Between 1935 and 1939, 155 of 218 labor disputes were resolved through state mediation, including 70 after strikes had been initiated. In 1937 FEDENAL, the river and dock workers' confederation, was granted closed-shop status by the government, and the 1945 labor legislation granted this status to all enterprise unions that had majority support in the work place (Urrutia 1969b:179).

Labor's response to Liberal initiatives went well beyond cooperation in settling labor disputes. The vote of the urban working class was clearly important in the 1930 election of Olaya, while the CTC, subsidized by the state during the López administrations, provided support for Liberal presidential candidates, including the Santos candidacy of 1938 and again in the 1946 elections. In intraparty disputes the CTC campaigned hard for the nomination of López's 1938 candidate, Darío Echandía, and again in 1942 for López. Given that López received only 59 percent of the vote in 1942 (there was no Conservative Party candidate), it is possible that labor support gave him the edge over the moderate Liberal candidate, Arango.[53]

Finally, the labor movement as a whole was an important counterweight to the Conservative strength within the military and the Catholic Church. In 1936 rumors of a Conservative-led coup against López led to massive May Day demonstrations in his support, during which López appeared on the balcony of the presidential palace with leading members of the Communist Party. In July 1944, thousands of workers were again mobilized to respond to

[53] Molina 1974:247; Urrutia 1969a:174–77, 185–92; Sharpless 1978:120–29.

an attempted coup against López. The worker demonstrations of both 1936 and 1944 played an important role in the decision of the military to remain neutral to Conservative coup overtures in those years.[54]

To conclude this assessment of the exchange, it should be stressed that while labor received considerable support and inducements from Liberal governments, labor's importance to the incorporating party, as a whole, must not be overstated. As has been emphasized before, in all eight countries the incorporation project was just one part of a larger program of reform and state-building, and in the Colombian case it was a somewhat more subordinate part. It is true that the suppression of labor by the Conservative government in the 1928 banana strike provided the Liberal Party with an issue that was crucial in helping it achieve power in 1930 and that encouraged the Liberals to launch the incorporation period. Perhaps recognizing the importance of labor support, Olaya did respond to labor protest in 1934 by passing several further labor reforms. Yet neither his administration nor that of Santos were dependent on labor for electoral victories, once the Conservative Party chose to abstain from legislative and presidential elections after 1934. While the labor movement played an important role in intraparty politics, especially in its support of López, by its peak in 1945 it still had only about 150,000 members—though of course this limited size was in part due to the still relatively small overall size of the modern sector in Colombia.

Further, though this new exchange relationship of the incorporation period was an important innovation, it obviously took place within a political system dominated by two long-established, multiclass parties. As a consequence, labor was an important additional component, but within a multiclass, multisectoral party. Labor was not an economic or political sector of great political weight (in contrast, for instance, to Argentina) and its significance lay in its long-term effect in what had been a carefully balanced political system. Referring to the urban support mobilization of the Socialists in the 1920s, Urrutia notes, "As in other two-party systems . . . the importance of a third party in Colombia did not depend on the strength it achieved, but on the influence it had on the two great mass parties. When faced by the threat of losing some of its urban strength to the Socialists, the Liberal Party decided to reform" (1969a:71). With the removal of literacy and property requirements for voting brought by the 1936 electoral reforms, the rural vote increased, helping local and regional party bosses maintain their important place within the Liberal Party during the incorporation period and thus partially offsetting the potential influence of urban labor (Powers 1979:205–6).

The policies initiated by the López reform wing did cause considerable opposition from the Liberal moderates. Yet by undercutting the base of the independent left during the early incorporation period, the Liberals were, nonetheless, able to consolidate their hold on the urban areas and successfully prevent the emergence of a significant Socialist or Labor Party. As a conse-

[54] Pécaut 1973:152; Urrutia 1969a:124–25; Powers 1979:204–5; Maingot 1967:284; Maullin 1973:58.

quence, the Liberals emerged from the incorporation period as the majority party, as they had been earlier in the 19th century,[55] a position they continued to hold in the post-1958 period.

Though the support of the labor movement may not have been crucial to Liberal dominance during the incorporation period, especially given the Conservatives' abstention, it played a critical role in the party crisis between 1942 and 1946. As in 1938, in 1946 the CTC leadership again demonstrated its close ties to the Liberal government and the party leadership by supporting the "official" party candidate, Gabriel Turbay. Nevertheless, there were significant labor rank-and-file defections to Gaitán (Sharpless 1978:121–22). Although the Liberal Party had developed extensive ties with the leadership of the labor movement, it was apparently less able to exercise influence over the rank-and-file, especially in the face of Gaitán's strong electoral appeal in 1946. As a consequence, the party leadership did not develop the capacity to bring the rank-and-file with it when it moved to the right in 1945. The growing division within Liberal Party ranks encouraged the Conservatives to reenter electoral competition late in the presidential campaign. The Liberals tried to respond, but the split between the Turbay and Gaitán wings had become too wide to be bridged. As a result, the Liberals lost the executive in 1946, as well as any hope of reinitiating the Liberal reform program.

The Party

As in Uruguay, the evolution of the incorporation project in Colombia was directly connected to the dynamics of splits within the party that led the incorporation effort.[56] Two often-reinforcing cleavages divided the Liberals in 1930 and dominated intraparty and interparty politics for the next 20 years.

The first cleavage grew out of the decision in 1921 to attract Los Nuevos with their support for organized labor, back into the party. While their inclusion brought new life to the Liberals, it also created an increasingly strong

[55] Delpar notes that Liberals dominated the elections between 1863 and 1884. This dominance came to an end with Núñez's defection to the Conservatives after the 1884 Civil War (Delpar 1967:291–93). However, Dix notes that "Because of the influence which the incumbent government has customarily exercised over the ballot box, it is difficult to discern with any exactness the percentages of the electorate loyal to the parties at a given time. It may be that the Conservatives held a 'permanent' majority during the nineteenth century, taking into account the Church's influence in rural areas." However, property and literacy requirements excluded most rural voters and Liberals do seem to have had significant urban support, especially from artisan groups, since their founding. Dix goes on to note, "Since at least the 1930s indications are that, with a widened and more urbanized vote, the majority has been Liberal" (1967:221).

[56] The three presidents during the Liberal period had different relationships with, and attitudes towards, the labor movement. Therefore, in discussing the relationship between the Liberal Party and labor it is important to note that at any point during the 1930–46 period we may be discussing only one sector of the Liberal Party, usually that tied to the national directorate and to the faction controlling the presidency.

faction that demanded major social, and especially labor, reforms. Led first by López and later by Echandía and Gaitán, this reformist faction supported strong social reforms, mobilization of urban and rural workers, and an interventionist state. The mobilizational, often confrontational, style of this faction vis-à-vis the Conservatives would find considerable support among many traditional party bosses due to their interest in establishing Liberal hegemony over the national and local institutions of government and patronage.[57]

The second cleavage, closely related to the first, concerned how the Liberals would use the state in their partisan struggle with the Conservatives. The moderate wing of the Liberals, led by Olaya in 1930 and later by Santos and Turbay, felt that partisan conflict should be avoided as much as possible so as to restore political stability and create the conditions for increased foreign investment and a return to economic growth after the onset of the depression. This group, heir to the earlier Republican wing of the party, thus emphasized economic development and a gradualist program of mobilization and social reform. But the reformist sector of the party and traditional rural party bosses wished to use the power of the national state to actively reinforce the Liberals' position at the local level.[58]

During the years of Conservative dominance, these differences within the Liberal Party had been muted. In 1922 the Socialists and associated labor organizations decided to back the presidential campaign of the Liberal candidate Benjamin Herrera as the Liberals' ideological shift toward support of labor was initiated. Herrera, as chief of the Liberal Party, ordered local party directorates to include peasant and worker representatives within the party's electoral lists (Molina 1974:79). The Liberals' decision not to present a presidential candidate in 1926 led dissident party members to participate in forming the Revolutionary Socialist Party, which promptly collapsed with the election of a Liberal to the presidency in 1930.

By the late 1920s the Conservative Party had become increasingly divided over how to handle the growing social protest in the cities and countryside, as well as over the economic distress caused by the onset of the depression. With the Conservatives unable to unite behind one candidate for the 1930 election, the Liberal directorate chose to enter the electoral fray and nominated Luis Olaya, in part due to his close relations with U.S. bankers (Bergquist 1986:346–47), but also due to his friendly relations with important Conservative factions, especially Antioquian industrialists (Molina 1974:241–42). While achieving only an electoral plurality, Olaya defeated his two Conservative opponents and began the process of returning Colombia to international creditworthiness and political stability.

Olaya's goals as he assumed the presidency had contradictory implications for his posture toward the Conservatives. His goal of restoring economic growth in an economy ravaged by the depression required close cooperation

[57] Molina 1977:240; Horgan 1983:216–17; Guzmán 1968:38; Tirado 1981:35–48.
[58] Horgan 1983:211–15; Chu 1972:38; Molina 1977:20–21; Guzmán 1968:15–39.

between the Liberal government and the country's major producer groups, including the largely Conservative Antioquian industrialists and coffee growers. On the other hand, Liberal leaders hoped to build on the party's 1930 successes in urban areas to achieve an electoral majority. One obvious constituency was the growing working class. This partisan effort, however, would inevitably create interparty tensions that would have conflicted with Olaya's efforts to restore the Colombian economy and insure foreign investors of the country's political stability.

Olaya's initiatives toward the labor sector, while important, therefore remained modest. It was the victory of López in 1934, however, that led to a major Liberal attempt to organize and mobilize Colombia's urban workers. López, as leader of the reformist wing of the party, depended on the development of a strong urban sector to offset the growing rural support base of the party's moderate wing, especially after his agrarian reforms in 1936 and 1937. In 1935, López amended the statutes of the Liberal Party to require all national and department directorates to include at least one representative of the workers although the party had already begun to do so in 1934. Labor leaders were encouraged to run for office on Liberal lists, although this practice was interrupted during the Santos administration.[59] In the same year, with the support of the union president of a major Liberal daily, the Liberals were instrumental in forming the CTC, which was greatly expanded by the subsequent inclusion in 1936 of elements of the labor movement linked to the Communists (Urrutia 1969a:170-73,176-78).

The relationship between the Communists and the Liberals was stormy. The Communist Party had originally been founded by some of Los Nuevos, and the Communists' position with respect to the Liberals before 1936 was inconsistent. While attacking cooperation with the state, they entered into secret electoral alliances with the Liberals (for example, the Pact of Tunja). The Communists' attack against the Liberals rapidly alienated the urban popular sector, and by 1936 the Communists had lost most of their urban support. While the moderate Liberals consistently opposed Communist participation in the CTC, López continued to support their presence. Perhaps one reason was that the Communists' efforts at organizing rural workers against Liberal and Conservative landowners might contribute to weakening moderate Liberal caciques in the areas where the Communists were active. As it was, López passed land redistribution measures, which won him important support in areas where the Communists and UNIR had been strong. Another factor behind López's support for a Communist role may have been that Colombia's Liberal Party, like the Colorados in Uruguay, long antedated the Communists and thus did not initially develop in intense competition with the Communists, as had AD in Venezuela, APRA in Peru, or Peronism in Argentina. This may have made it easier for López to avoid a narrowly

[59] There is little evidence as to whether this policy was continued. However, given the electoral reforms of 1936, it seems likely that dissident López, Gaitán, and Chaux lists in 1942, 1946, 1947, and 1949 included representatives of the labor movement.

partisan approach to the labor movement and to cooperate in this way with the Communist Party. In any case, the Liberal moderates were unsuccessful in excluding the Communists from the CTC until the 12th CTC congress in 1960 (Pécaut 1973:124–25; Caicedo 1971:130–31).

In 1936 the CTC organized a second labor congress. Due to the Communists' acceptance of the Comintern's popular front strategy, the earlier division within the confederation was healed. By this point, the leaders of the trade-union movement were either Liberal, or allied with Liberals, as was their worker constituency. The CTC congress was financially supported by the Liberal Party, which in return received strong support from the labor confederation. The Liberals' financial support for the CTC continued, except for the Santos period, well into the 1970s. Also, both members of the López administration and Liberal leaders participated in the 1936 congress. The labor congress held in 1938 mirrored the growing division within the Liberal Party, especially between moderate Liberals and the left. Nevertheless, the congress ratified labor's basic political stance and voted to support the Santos candidacy.[60]

The sequence of labor congresses illustrates the failure of the López wing of the party to win labor support for its faction rather than for the Liberal Party as a whole. The Communists' support of López was extended to Santos when the moderate wing won the 1937 legislative elections (the Conservative Party abstained) and the presidential nomination, despite Santos's attempts to exclude or reduce Communist influence within the CTC's executive committee at the 1938 congress. The popular front strategy tied the Communists to the Liberal government, required little in return, and continued through late 1939 despite opposition from Santos and the moderate wing of the Liberal Party to the Communists' presence in the CTC. The German-Soviet pact of 1939 led to the first break between the Communists and the Liberals, which was subsequently healed shortly after Germany invaded the Soviet Union in 1940 (Urrutia 1969a: 179–82). But it is clear that labor-party relations during the Santos administration were primarily neutral or geared to reducing the Communists' role in the CTC.

With the reelection of López in 1942, labor representatives again took an important role in the Liberal party, primarily in the López wing. When a small group of Conservative officers attempted to overthrow the López government, workers organized mass demonstrations in protest. But strong opposition from moderate Liberals and the Conservative Party and the defection of Liberal rural bosses to the moderates in legislative elections prevented López from extending the reform movement begun in 1934. The presence of Liberal Party leaders at the 1943 CTC congress and their strong appeal at the congress for labor support suggests that they were trying to rally the labor movement behind them (Urrutia 1969a:185; Caicedo 1971:89). Yet these efforts were initially unsuccessful in overcoming moderate Liberal opposition within the legislature, and it was not until the 1944 coup attempt,

[60] Powers 1979:201; Caicedo 1971:130–32; Urrutia 1969a:173; Caicedo 1971:80.

and López's assumption of emergency power, that a new decree, protecting labor organizers from employer retribution and striking workers from strikebreakers, was issued. The result was a major increase in new labor organizations, but also a growing division within Liberal ranks, which led to the resignation of López in 1945 and the division of the Liberal party in 1946 between the moderate Turbay and the more radical Gaitán.

With López's resignation in 1945, the Liberals' use of state resources to cultivate labor as a key new support base for the Liberal Party came to an end, though Gaitán continued his wide-ranging effort at popular mobilization from outside the state. During the period of bipartisan cooperation from 1946–49, the CTC initially managed to maintain its position. Yet with the creation of the UTC by the Catholic Church in June 1946 and the competition that the UTC represented, along with the repression of the CTC at the end of the 1940s and the Liberals inability at that point to provide the confederation with political protection, the CTC soon declined. "By 1950, it was clear that the CTC could not be a threat to the Conservative government" (Urrutia 1969a:198), and in the post-1958 period the confederation never regained a strong position in the labor movement. While the analysis of this outcome must in part await the next chapter, this remarkably rapid erosion of the CTC, despite a decade of Liberal government support, merits some comment here.

Several factors contributed to the weakness of the CTC and to the Liberals' inability to sustain it more effectively. All these factors were related to the particular characteristics of the two-party system out of which the incorporation project emerged, including the crucial fact that, in contrast to most other cases of party incorporation, the party that led the reforms of the incorporation period was not created with the goal of initiating these reforms. The first factor involves the problem that López's efforts to build organizational ties with the labor movement immediately produced tensions within the Liberal Party, greatly complicating his efforts. Second, and relatedly, it seems likely that the Liberals' extensive initiatives in support of the labor movement were seen by workers in important measure as coming from López and Gaitán, and not from the Liberal Party as a whole. Thus, while the CTC leadership at times cooperated with other factions of the party, the loyalty felt by workers themselves was in important measure directed toward a faction of the Liberals, rather than to the party as a whole.[61] This contrasts greatly with the experience of other countries where the incorporating parties were created with the purpose of initiating the reforms of the incorporation period. Third, the fact that López did not a take a strictly partisan approach to the CTC, but rather cooperated with the Communists in the formation and maintenance of the confederation, greatly complicated partisan ties between the confederation and the Liberals. We noted above that this

---

[61] While the substantial labor vote for Gaitán in 1946 is consistent with this conclusion, we will note in the next chapter that indirect evidence suggests that urban labor did vote for the National Front after 1958.

decision of López may have been linked to a tradition of partisan relationships quite distinct from that in most other cases of party incorporation.

Fourth, given Colombia's deep tradition of two parties and of the strong hold of the Conservatives over a region and city—Antioquia and Medellín, where a crucial part of the manufacturing work force was located—an important part of the organizable labor movement was politically inaccessible to the Liberals. Fifth, the ground was further cut out from under the CTC because the initial antireformist reaction to incorporation was led by another political party—the Conservatives—that actively and successfully promoted an alternative labor confederation. By contrast, in some other cases of party incorporation, at the time of the conservative reaction the existing confederation was confronted with repression rather than a more-or-less viable organizational and political alternative. Whereas repression by itself may reinforce earlier loyalties, repression plus a viable organizational and political alternative may undercut them.

Since in Uruguay, as in Colombia, the legacy of incorporation did not include strong (or indeed, any) organizational ties between the party and the labor movement, it is interesting to explore the extent to which these five factors are relevant to the Uruguayan case, given the parallel two-party tradition. First, we noted in the analysis of Uruguay that if Batlle had made partisan overtures toward the unions, it would similarly have aggravated cleavages within the Colorado Party. Second, in Uruguay the reform initiatives also came from only one wing of the party, but in this case it was a wing that continued for decades to be strong and to be the "bearer" of the legacy of incorporation, rather than being undercut, as occurred after the 1958 accords in Colombia. Third, though the Uruguayan incorporation period occurred before the Russian Revolution and the issue of dealing with the Communist Party did not arise, there appears to be a parallel between the two cases in the lack of insistence on a partisan homogenization of the labor movement. Fourth, party traditions in Uruguay likewise divided the country into partisan blocks along regional and sectoral lines—yet with a crucial difference. Whereas Colombia had an unusual degree of development of multiple regional centers, one of which was Conservative, Uruguay had only one city, which was predominantly Colorado. Hence, while the political tradition was similar, the difference in urban structure meant that in Uruguay it was not the case that a portion of the urban labor movement was politically inaccessible to the Colorados because of the National loyalties of the city where it was located. The fifth factor is not relevant to Uruguay, since there was no effort under the Terra dictatorship to redirect the partisan loyalties of the working class.

To conclude, in both countries the legacy of weak ties between the incorporating party and the labor movement seems to derive in part from the distinctive contexts of these traditional two-party systems. Yet, while in the case of the first factor this tradition seems to have operated in a similar way, with regard to some of the other factors it functioned quite differently in the two countries.

Opposition and Polarization

In Colombia, the polarization and violence that grew out of the period of Liberal rule was more prolonged and destructive than that following any other incorporation period. As we have seen, the Liberals' effort to mobilize popular support, as well as their attempts to assert party dominance in the larger political system, produced a major counterreaction, both from within the Liberal Party and later from the Conservatives. The intraparty cleavage was muted between 1930 and 1935 as the Liberals consolidated their control over the government. But López's support of labor and his continued alliance with the Communists, as well as the "radical" constitutional amendments passed in 1936, greatly increased intraparty tensions. By 1942 these differences had become insurmountable and were later compounded by a mass mobilization initiated by Gaitán in 1944. The Liberal Party division of these years encouraged the Conservatives to return to the polls, first in the congressional election of 1939 and then in the presidential election of 1946. As a result, the locus of conflict shifted from the Liberal intraparty division to conflict between the two parties, as the Liberals and Conservatives struggled for control of the Colombian state at both the national and local level. The partisan conflict plunged Colombia into an increasingly violent, prolonged rural civil war, which by 1960 took the lives of over 200,000 people (Oquist 1980:6–7).

López's candidacy in 1942 was attacked from the moderate wing of the Liberal Party, as well as from the growing radical wing controlled by Gaitán, who felt it was time to effect a more thorough mobilization of the country's popular classes. This conflict within the party was heightened by López's use of the state of emergency to force through a number of labor decrees and was to lead to his resignation in 1945. The new Liberal president, moderate Lleras Camargo, quickly moved to limit the strength of the reform wing by suspending the most independent and radical unions in the CTC. A general strike was called by the CTC in late 1945 and was promptly declared illegal. FEDENAL, which had enjoyed close relations with the López wing of the party, went on strike in December and Lleras moved quickly, breaking the strike by using the military to protect strikebreakers.[62]

At this point polarization increased as the progressive wing of the Liberals moved toward a more populist, mobilizational posture. Gaitán's presidential candidacy in the 1946 election quickly drew strength from the popular and working class sectors, building upon the attack of the Liberals' moderate wing on the labor movement, as well as its growing conservatism. Abandoning the traditional party structure, Gaitán began to build his campaign by erecting an alternative party machine centered in urban areas, as well as in former UNIR strongholds. His strategy thus represented an extension, in a more radical form, of the mobilizational policies of López. The Liberals' moderate wing chose Gabriel Turbay as its presidential candidate, a former

[62] Sharpless 1978:99–100; Braun 1985:78–79; Oquist 1980:111; Pécaut 1973:204–5.

Nuevo now joining the Viejos, while the Conservative Party leader Laureano Gómez opportunistically provided financial support to the dissident Gaitán candidacy (Sharpless 1978:109, 111; Powers 1979:238).

As the campaign proceeded, the division within the Liberal Party grew deeper and increasingly bitter: López stated that he would not vote for either candidate. "My interests," he said, "would be more secure under an Ospina government" (Ospina was the Conservative candidate) (quoted in Guzmán 1968:41). It was at this time, just two months before the election, that Gómez backed the candidacy of the moderate Conservative, Ospina Pérez, whose entry in the presidential contest ended the 16 years of Conservative abstention from presidential elections. With this renewal of electoral competition, levels of participation went up sharply. While the Liberal Party maintained its majority status and thus its control of the legislature, Gaitán's insurgent candidacy won 45 percent of the Liberal vote (including an overwhelming vote in a number of urban areas), costing Turbay and the Liberals the presidency (Sharpless 1978:128–29). The end of the period of Liberal control of the government was thus the result of a split in the Liberal Party, just as the rise of the Liberals sixteen years before was facilitated by a split within the Conservative Party.

Though members of the moderate Liberal wing quickly moved to form a coalition government (La Unión Nacional) with the Conservative President Ospina and the Conservative Party, Gaitán began the push to consolidate his hold on the Liberal Party. His ability to win 45 percent of the vote in 1946 without help from the party machine indicated an enormous rank-and-file support that could not be overlooked by national and regional party leaders, especially after Turbay's death in late 1946. In 1947 Gaitán's faction won the legislative elections (55 percent of the Liberal vote) and increased the Liberal party's control over the legislature. "The election was Gaitán's final test within Liberalism. On October 24 the Liberal congressmen proclaimed him their presidential candidate for 1950. The Liberal departmental directorates did so a day later" (Sharpless 1978:154).

Gaitán found himself in a difficult position. If he kept the Liberal Party in the coalition with the Ospina administration, his supporters would begin to drop away. On the other hand, if he withdrew from the coalition, the Liberal Party would lose access to state patronage and face the potential of massive partisan violence, as well as the loss of control over the rural grass roots of the party (Sharpless 1978:166–67; Wilde 1978:38–39). Gaitán chose a difficult middle course that left him open to charges of ineptitude. "His lack of interest in formulating a firm policy toward the Ospina government—sometimes refusing collaboration, sometimes encouraging it—sowed confusion in Liberal ranks, even among his own followers" (Sharpless 1978:156).

By March 1948 the fragile coalition fell apart due to growing violence triggered when rural Conservative chiefs began to take back the political power they had lost in 1930. On 9 April, Gaitán was assassinated and partisan violence erupted throughout the country, particularly in Bogotá. The Bogotazo, or the "Nueve de Abril" (Ninth of April) as it came to be called in Colombia, caused over 2,000 deaths and destroyed the capital city's downtown area. "The bogotazo made politicians realize that the system itself was at stake" (Wilde 1978:47), and members of both parties moved quickly to suggest alternatives to the Ospina government. The Liberal leadership, headed by Darío Echandía, reacted by calling for the resignation of Ospina and the appointment of Santos to fill out his term. Gómez proposed a military government. When Ospina refused both suggestions, Echandía agreed, despite CTC opposition, to reestablish the National Union coalition. The new coalition "was instrumental in calming the nation. All but a few Liberals responded to Echandía's order for cooperation with the government, and in major cities, peace was restored."[63]

While the effort to contain the violence did restore the coalition government, it did not reunite the Liberal Party. Echandía's assumption of Gaitán's leadership position, while supported by Santos, López, and Lleras, was strongly opposed by large sectors of Gaitán's support base, led by Francisco Chaux. Both wings of the party were waiting for the June 1949 congressional elections to determine the Liberal Party presidential candidate for 1950. While Echandía's faction was expected to win, Gómez, now the Conservatives' presidential candidate, began to put increased pressure on Ospina to withdraw from the coalition and prepare the Conservative Party for a complete return to power. In May 1949 the coalition broke down when Ospina removed the Liberal governors and appointed radical Conservatives in their places. By October, on the eve of the presidential election, Gómez's supporters practically controlled the national government and violence in the countryside continued to grow as new Conservative governors began to remove Liberals from the electoral registry (Guzmán 1968:75). Faced with growing Conservative and Church attacks on the Liberal Party, certain that the election results would be fraudulent, and faced with a growing split within the party between those who wished to continue cooperating with the Conservative government (the "peace faction") and those who supported civil war (the "war faction"), Echandía announced the Liberals' withdrawal from the presidential elections.

Stung by this series of reverses, the increasingly disorganized Liberal Party sought to launch a counterattack from its remaining area of strength, the Congress. As the war faction began to create guerrilla command structures, the peace faction sought a new truce with Gómez. On 2 November 1949, Gómez refused any accord with the Liberal Party. On the ninth, the Liberal congressional delegation began to discuss impeachment proceedings against the Conservative president, Ospina.

Ospina, at the urging of Gómez, reacted strongly. He declared a nationwide state of siege, which greatly expanded his constitutional powers; dissolved all legislative bodies including local, state, and national assemblies; initiated heavy press censorship; and imprisoned important Liberal politicians. The Liberal response was at first incredulity and finally the complete dissolution

---

[63] Martz 1962:62. See also Guzmán (1968:41–54); Braun (1985); Wilde (1978:39, 47).

of the peace faction, as many of its leaders went into exile. The war faction began to prepare for civil war. On 27 November 1949, Gómez was elected president unopposed, and the Conservative Party was assured of complete dominance over the national state. With the exclusion of Liberals from all areas of government, both national and regional, the institutional breakdown was complete. Colombia's elite politics, based on a "conversation among gentlemen" within the traditional political class (Wilde 1978), had collapsed. In the following years, the civil war (La Violencia) rapidly escalated as the party elites lost control over their rural partisans. The violence became increasingly decentralized and spontaneous as peasants attacked rival villages and organized partisan guerrilla bands and self-defense leagues. By 1953 over 150,000 people had died (Oquist 1980:4–7, fn 4) and the country found itself under military rule.

How can one best summarize the causes of the breakdown? On one level, the assault against the Liberals launched by the Conservatives was a reaction to the Liberals' effort to become the dominant party in Colombia, of which their labor policy was just one element. At another level, it was the divisions within the Liberal Party over the type of popular mobilization employed in the effort to achieve this dominance and over whether an effort should be made to push the Liberals' dominance further that split the Liberals and undermined their position in the electoral arena. Here, labor policy was obviously a central issue.

Yet another way of looking at labor's role in the breakdown is in terms of its larger impact on coalitional dynamics. As Wilde (1978:45) put it, "The unions did contribute to the breakdown of oligarchical democracy. They did not do this by transforming the nature of politics, as they might have done. They did not decisively shift the cleavages of the system nor become the new base of the Liberal Party, for their organization was too weak. . . . Their presence, however, was constantly unsettling. . . . [They] could force the party leadership to choose to support or repudiate them, and could strain party commitment to oligarchical *convivencia* in a situation of obviously changed conditions."

Thus, the Liberals entered into a difficult period divided and incapable of successfully reasserting their majority. López's and Gaitán's mobilization of the popular sector, and their efforts to expand the role of labor within the Liberal Party, assured the division of the Liberals and left them helpless to oppose a united effort by the Conservatives to recapture the state. Beginning in 1946, with the collapse of the López government and a series of intensely contested elections, political participation increased sharply, and it was in part the sharp divergence in the approach to responding to this expansion of participation that widened the gap between Gaitán and the rest of the party leadership. Divided, the Liberals were unable to respond to Ospina's "strategy of conciliation and coalition," thus strengthening the position of their arch enemy, Laureano Gómez (Wilde 1978:56–58).

In the conclusion to his insightful analysis, Wilde raises the question of whether the breakdown should be understood as resulting from the class conflicts and ideological cleavages set loose during this period or whether it is better understood in more strictly political terms, as involving a collapse of traditional political rules of the game that had governed the relationship between the two parties (1978:62–67). He favors the latter explanation. However, from the perspective of our analysis of incorporation periods, these two explanations are closely interrelated. The incorporation period arose in response to issues of class conflict and the new ideological positions posed by the emergence of an organized working class, and as in many other countries this reform period in turn increased class conflict in certain respects. At the same time—and this is the crucial point—as occurred in other cases of party incorporation, the substantive reforms of the incorporation period were accompanied by an intense partisan effort at constituency building, an effort that broke the traditional rules of party competition. Thus, issues of class conflict and the breaking of political rules may be seen as interconnected features of a larger model of incorporation periods, features which jointly contributed to the breakdown.

PERU AND ARGENTINA: LABOR POPULISM

The experiences of Peru and Argentina with incorporation had many common traits. Regarding the antecedents, both countries had experienced failed attempts to initiate incorporation periods in the 1910s and 1920s, followed by a long postponement of incorporation. In the intervening years, both saw an incremental growth of the state role in the labor movement, yet without experiencing a policy period that fits the definition of incorporation.

In the incorporation period itself, Peru and Argentina saw intense popular activation in the urban sector, involving both the mobilization of electoral support of workers and the consolidation of strong ties between trade unions and the party or movement that led the incorporation project. Partly due to the long delay of initial incorporation in relation to the reform period of the 1910s and 1920s, the incorporation project in each country was built on top of an already strong popular movement—the APRA Party and its labor base in Peru and the CGT (General Labor Confederation) in Argentina.

Perón's reform program had a far greater impact in rural areas than did that of APRA, and Perón's policies went further in directly affecting the economic interests of the export elite. Yet in neither case was there a basic restructuring of property relations in the rural sector or widespread peasant mobilization, in marked contrast to Mexico and Venezuela. Correspondingly, the economic elites of the agrarian sector remained an important economic and political force in both Peru and Argentina and emerged as a powerful pole of opposition to the new political forces unleashed by the incorporation period.

With regard to the character of the populist party, there was a major contrast and a major similarity. A central feature of the Peruvian experience was the exceptionally strong, well-disciplined organization of APRA. By contrast, the party structure to which the CGT came to be linked in Argentina was not well institutionalized, either during the incorporation period or for many years thereafter, and for many purposes it is more appropriate to think of Peronism as a political movement rather than a party.[64] Despite this contrast in party organization, APRA and Peronism were similar in the degree to which they were overwhelmingly dominated by a single personality—Víctor Raul Haya de la Torre and Juan Domingo Perón. Subsequent antagonism toward the two parties was directed as much at these two individuals as toward the parties more broadly.

The coherence of policy during the incorporation period differed substantially. The incorporation project in Argentina was one of the most extensive in terms of the scope of new labor legislation, the growth in the number of unions and union membership, the coverage of social benefits, and the dramatic shift away from earlier patterns of state-labor relations to one in which, in symbolic and ideological terms, the government dramatically sided

---

[64] Recognizing this fact, for the sake of convenience we will generally refer to Peronism as a party.

with the working class. By contrast, the incorporation period in Peru emerged incrementally under the government of Prado between 1939 and 1945, and even during its more ambitious phase from 1945 to 1948 was marred by political stalemate, legislative paralysis, a failure to initiate many proposed reforms, and intense antagonism among the principal actors involved. These years were relatively unproductive in terms of new labor legislation.

These features of the Peruvian experience could lead one to question if this incorporation period was in fact an important transition in Peru. Such skepticism might be reinforced by the observation that prior to the 1940s APRA was already a major force in the labor movement. Hence, more than in most cases, the incorporation period could be seen as reinforcing an already existing political relationship between the labor movement and a populist party.

Yet despite political failures and policy paralysis in many spheres, APRA's remarkable organizational capabilities allowed it to make excellent use of its access to state resources. The result was a fundamental transformation in the sphere of labor relations, to the extent that this period is commonly interpreted as a crucial transition in the evolution of APRA's position in the labor movement.[65] However, it was not as dramatic a reorientation as occurred in several other countries.

[65] Sulmont (1977:82) considers the Bustamante period "a crucial moment in the political life of the country" which "permitted the worker movement and the popular sector more broadly to consolidate its trade-union and political organization." Pareja (1980:115) suggests that by using the resources secured through its role in the Bustamante administration, "APRA became the most important vehicle for the institutionalization of the labor movement. The relationship between the party and trade unionism expanded to the point of near identity." Parallel observations are made in Angell (1980:21) and Adams (1984:36–37), both of whom stress the importance of APRA's access to state resources in achieving this end. From a comparative perspective, Anderson (1967:249) makes the more general observation that "the die of Peruvian postwar politics was cast" in the 1945–48 period.

PERU

The incorporation period in Peru consisted of two phases: the tentative initiation of incorporation under President Manuel Prado from 1939 to 1945, who falls into our category of "conservative modernizers"; and a second, more extensive phase, when APRA shared power under the administration of José Luis Bustamante i Rivero from 1945 to 1948.

Initial Phase of Incorporation: The Prado Government

The presidential transition of 1939 and the Prado government of 1939–45 represented a modest step toward a more democratic form of politics. The electoral process of 1939 saw a more genuine competition for the presidency—though APRA remained illegal—as well as the return of the national executive to the hands of a civilian leader. Occurring as it did on the eve of the war in Europe, the election became sharply polarized around the issue of fascism. Prado sought to bring together in his electoral alliance all nonfascist and antifascist sectors, including industrialists and members of the oligarchy with links to industry. Prado enjoyed the tacit support of APRA and the Communists in the election, both of which supported his antifascist posture and viewed him as a representative of the more modern wing of national capital, which they had long hoped could play a constructive role in advancing progressive political goals. APRA was not allowed to present candidates for either president or Congress, but both presidential candidates approached APRA, seeking its votes. Though there was substantial confusion within the party about how to use its votes, Prado's overwhelming victory in the election suggests that many Apristas in fact voted for him (Caravedo 1976:135–37; Cotler 1980:167; Werlich 1978:219).

In the spirit of cooperating with the war effort, APRA ended its military plotting against the government and both APRA and the Communists sought to restrain popular mobilization. While APRA remained illegal until the end of Prado's term, repression of the party diminished. Many imprisoned Apristas were released, and APRA was permitted to carry out substantial organizing activity. The climate of greater tolerance also extended to unions, and under preexisting legislation[66] government recognition of unions became more extensive. Whereas under Benavides only a limited number of unions (33) had been recognized, principally in the areas of commerce, transportation, and communications, the Prado administration saw a substantial expansion of union recognition (118 unions), with many of these being in the

[66] The legal basis for government recognition of unions had existed since the second Leguía administration.

manufacturing sector.[67] Peru had thus entered the second of what Pareja views as three sequential phases in the evolution of government policy toward union formation. The Benavides period had seen sharp restrictions, and the Prado period brought an important opening, to be followed later by a period of "full development" under Bustamante.[68]

Just as the European conflict had influenced the dynamics of the 1939 presidential election, it also shaped subsequent thinking about issues of democracy and labor incorporation. As the end of the war came closer, the imminent defeat of fascism and the accompanying democratic spirit of the times influenced many Latin American countries, including Peru. Further, the military alliance between the United States and the Soviet Union led Latin American Communist parties to adopt new forms of political collaboration in support of the war effort.[69] This collaboration further increased the plausibility of undertaking a new political initiative that sought, in a more institutionalized way, to incorporate previously banned opposition movements into the political system. In the context both of New Deal labor policy and the World War, the U.S. government came to look favorably on efforts to establish an institutionalized role for labor movements in Latin America. The United States established friendly relations with APRA, and the U.S. Embassy in Lima encouraged Prado to relax restrictions against the party. Encouragement for new directions in labor policy came from other sides as well. Vicente Lombardo Toledano, the prominent Mexican labor leader and head of the international labor confederation CTAL (Confederation of Latin American Workers), also visited Prado and encouraged him to permit the formation of a new labor confederation (Cotler 1978:261; Werlich 1978:231; Sulmont 1975:181).

These changes at the international level both shaped internal dynamics in Peru and interacted with other processes of change within the country. With Peru's ongoing economic growth, further stimulated by the war, new sectors—including both the leaders of an emerging manufacturing sector and also middle-class groups—came increasingly to challenge the earlier dominance of agrarian elites and to support a democratic opening. These sectors played a prominent role in the formation in Arequipa of the FDN (National Democratic Front), the coalition that went on to win the presidential election of 1945 (Sulmont 1975:186; Caravedo 1978:58).

The opening of Prado's labor policies went further as his term advanced. In 1943 and 1944 the government supported the participation of a full delegation of labor representatives, including Apristas, in major international labor

---

[67] Here and below, available data on union recognition do not correspond precisely to presidential administrations. However, the data do give a reasonably clear idea of the contrasts among different periods.

[68] Pareja 1980:115. See also Werlich (1978:222); Cotler (1978:254); Sulmont (1975:275).

[69] While the Communist Party had not hesitated to collaborate with conservative governments such as that of Prado, they would now also cooperate with APRA, as in the formation of the Confederación de Trabajadores Peruanos in 1944 and the FDN in 1945 (see below).

congresses. In 1944 Prado tolerated the formation of the CTP (Confederation of Peruvian Workers) led by Communists and Apristas. The first general secretary of the CTP was Juan P. Luna of the Communist Party, and correspondingly the confederation was initially affiliated internationally with CTAL. However, the first occupant of the key position of secretary of organization was the Aprista Luis Negreiros Vega, and APRA took full control of the new confederation in 1945. An important step in the consolidation of APRA's position was the three-day general strike in late 1944, which was promoted far more actively by Aprista than by Communist labor leaders. This signaled a new phase of labor mobilization and greatly enhanced the credibility of Apristas vis-à-vis the Communists as the most dynamic leaders within the labor movement. Building on this momentum, as well as on the leverage gained from their association with the government, APRA won control of the CTP in new elections held in September 1945, and Luna was replaced as Secretary General by the APRA leader Arturo Sabroso Montoya. Under APRA leadership, the CTP withdrew from CTAL.[70]

As the presidential election of July 1945 approached, Benavides returned to Peru from his post as ambassador to Argentina, hoping to become the next president. However, the democratic spirit of the time doomed his initiative, leaving him instead in the role of a key broker in the process of selecting a consensus nominee for the presidency, and also as the guarantor, once a candidate had been agreed upon, of the acquiescence of the armed forces (Cotler 1978:261; Werlich 1978:229–30).

Arequipa had traditionally been a locus for the formation of political and military movements that have gained national power in Peru, and the formation of the FDN in that city by a broad, multiclass coalition of leaders concerned with ensuring an honest election and a genuine restoration of democracy proved to be a crucial step in the democratic opening. The FDN selected as its candidate José Luis Bustamante i Rivero, a distinguished legal scholar of middle-class background from Arequipa who was Peru's ambassador to Bolivia.

Bustamante wished to end Peru's history of alternation between oligarchic and military rule and allow APRA to gain access to power and carry out programs of social reform. Given the earlier history of violence associated with APRA, Bustamante strongly believed that the alternative could well be violent revolution. He made the legalization of APRA and APRA's participation in the FDN a condition of his acceptance of the nomination, a condition tolerated by Prado only as a result of the mediation of Benavides, who now supported the FDN and its candidate. The FDN thus came to include both APRA and the Communist Party. They ran as the Party of the People and the Socialist Vanguard, respectively, thereby altering their names to avoid identifying themselves as international parties, which were banned by the Peruvian constitution. The FDN adopted a Programa Mínimo, which drew heavily on APRA's program, favoring trade union autonomy and the promo-

[70] Pareja 1980:16–17, 22–26, 46–47; Sulmont 1975:181–82, 184–85, 189.

tion of more "just" relations between labor and capital, political and economic decentralization, tax and fiscal reform, industrial and export promotion, and expansion of public education (Werlich 1978:230–34; Sulmont 1975:185–87).

The FDN won an impressive two-thirds of the vote against a more conservative candidate, Ureta, who was supported by those, such as the intensely anti-Aprista daily *El Comercio*, unpersuaded of the merits of bringing APRA into the political system. APRA provided the bulk of the popular support for the winning coalition, and within APRA, the labor vote was an important component of this support, though its importance should not be overemphasized. The APRA coalition in fact encompassed a complex mix of middle class elements, which were of great electoral importance and provided virtually all of APRA's national leadership. In the northern departments the APRA coalition also included peasants and elements of the older provincial aristocracy (North 1973:109, 156).

Project from Above

The project from above that animated the Bustamante administration is best understood by examining the goals and initiatives both of Bustamante and of APRA. Though APRA was a popular movement that in one sense was bargaining with Bustamante "from below" as it sought to establish its position within the electoral (and later governing) coalition, it was nonetheless acting "from above" in relation to the labor movement.[71] APRA's goals are thus appropriately treated as part of the project from above.

At the most general level, Bustamante's project was the same as Prado's, involving an acceptance of the institutionalization of the labor movement and of APRA's role as a central actor in this process. They both accepted a "party incorporation" approach to the labor question, though they did not lead the party that carried out this approach.

However, in comparison with Prado, Bustamante's goals involved a far more ambitious effort to bring democracy to Peru, achieve social reform, and integrate APRA within the political system—as well as secure APRA's political support as part of the FDN coalition. Bustamante hoped to replace earlier patterns of elite domination of politics and military rule with a democratic government seriously concerned with achieving social justice. If this could not be achieved, he believed that Peru faced a serious danger of violent revolution. While he shared APRA's concern with injustice and supported parts of APRA's program, he opposed many goals of the party and "was apprehensive about the [party's] anticlerical origins, Marxist ideology, revolutionary élan, and authoritarian overtones." Along with these misgivings, Bustamante had, up to a point, a sophisticated understanding of the historical role of

---

[71] Though APRA was heavily engaged in worker mobilization, its national leadership was overwhelmingly middle class.

APRA. "Bustamante believed that APRA had provided a necessary vehicle for mass participation in politics and that it would triumph at the polls in the near future. He hoped to have a moderating influence on the party, so that it would act more responsibly when it gained power in its own right" (Werlich 1978:234). Bustamante thus intended the incorporation period both to build upon APRA's constructive contribution and in a tutelary manner to modify what he viewed as the destructive aspects of the party's program and political traditions.

Bustamante's new approach to APRA enjoyed substantial support from Peru's elite. Political leaders, such as Benavides and Prado, and prominent leaders of the agro-export elite, such as Beltrán and Gildemeister, were now willing to support an opening toward APRA in light of their perception of the growing moderation of the party's program (Werlich 1978:230; Thorp and Bertram 1978:189).[72] At the same time, Beltrán was greatly concerned that during the Bustamante administration the agro-export elite would lose control of national economic policy, and he sought to find new ways of increasing the elite's political leverage to protect its economic position. In response to his suggestion, a group of leading members of the agro-export sector purchased the daily newspaper *La Prensa* with the purpose of using it to influence public opinion during the Bustamante period (Cotler 1980:170–72).

Along with this specific initiative to incorporate APRA, Bustamante planned a range of complementary policies intended to permit greater freedom for the development of trade unions, promote more equitable relations between labor and capital, promote industrialization, expand public education, and encourage political decentralization through establishing elected municipal governments (Sulmont 1977:83).

In discussing Bustamante's political project, it is essential also to note what emerged as a fatal flaw in his approach to governance. Though Bustamante recognized in principle the necessity of accepting the existence of APRA and of an organized labor movement, he lacked the political "vocation" to deal with APRA within the framework of his administration. Indeed, Bustamante "proudly asserted that he was not a 'politician' " (Werlich 1978:234). This antipolitical posture extended specifically to the sphere of labor relations. In his book on his presidential administration, he asserted that in dealing with labor disputes, he had a special concern with determining in each case whether it involved a justified effort on the part of particular unions to rectify a situation of inequity, or whether it involved the political instigation or demagoguery of political parties. In the former cases just solutions were sought, whereas in the latter cases repression was applied (Bustamante 1949:155–56). Though under some circumstances an apolitical approach such as this might have been appropriate, in this context it left no room for coping with the give-and-take of politics. It made Bustamante a

---

[72] Thorp and Bertram (1978:391, fn. 34) note that figures such as Gildemeister, owner of the largest modern sugar estate on the north coast, expressed great amusement at APRA's more conservative posture.

poor leader of a coalition in which a group as politicized as APRA was a central actor.

Bustamante's apolitical stance, which recognized the need for greater social justice but abhorred "political" approaches to achieving this end, was in a sense similar to the "state incorporation" approach to labor relations explored in the analysis of Brazil and Chile. The profound difference in the case of Peru was that this apolitical posture was maintained by a leader who, ironically, had made a mobilizationally oriented party the political centerpiece of his own coalition and of the incorporation project. Bustamante's personal attitudes about politics notwithstanding, Peru was a case of party incorporation.

APRA's goals must be understood in terms of the marked changes in the party's ideology and rhetoric that had been occurring at least since the early 1940s. As Davies (1971:462–65) emphasizes, APRA had long maintained a more moderate line in private communications with the elite. However, the 1940s saw a marked change in the party's public posture.

Haya's attitudes toward the United States were strongly influenced by his favorable impression of the reforms of the New Deal, President Roosevelt's "good neighbor" policy toward Latin America, and the need to cooperate in the war effort against fascism. Haya's earlier rhetoric about "Yankee Imperialism" was replaced by a concern with maintaining a system of "democratic interamericanism without empire" (Cotler 1978:258). His conciliatory posture toward the Peruvian elite was dramatically reflected shortly after APRA was legalized in May of 1945, when he led a "reuniting of the leader with his people" in downtown Lima that was the largest mass rally Peru had ever seen. Gesturing toward the main social club of the oligarchy as he spoke, Haya declared that APRA "would not take wealth from those who had it, but would create it for those who did not have it." Referring to those who in the past had repressed APRA, he urged his followers to "forgive those who knew not what they did" (quoted in Sulmont 1975:187). Given the extraordinary potential for mass mobilization suggested by the size of the rally, many Apristas were greatly disillusioned by Haya's moderate tone.

Other changes involved a softening of the party's anticlerical posture and the abandonment of initiatives that would have fulfilled the longstanding commitment to addressing the plight of the Indian. No effort was made to expand the suffrage, which remained restricted to literate males. Agrarian reform was not pursued, and outside the modernized enclaves and their immediate hinterland, the party made little effort to promote peasant mobilization. To reassure its opponents that APRA had abandoned its tradition of violence, the position of secretary of defense within the party's National Executive Committee was not filled in 1944, and in 1948 the position was abolished. However, the "Defense Commands" of the party were maintained—and later in the Bustamante period were actively involved in conspiring against the government (Werlich 1978:233; Cotler 1978:264–65; Adams 1984:37)

At a more immediate level within the FDN coalition, an important concession was the fact that Haya was not the presidential candidate. However, it was commonly believed that he would be the candidate in the presidential election of 1951, so this appeared to be a short-term compromise that could soon be followed by a full APRA victory (Cotler 1978:261; Werlich 1978:233).

At the same time that one can speak of an overall reorientation of APRA's stated program, diverse political currents within the party must be recognized. The national leadership and parts of the mass following of the party were principally committed to a reformist posture focused on the modern sector. At the same time, some secondary leaders and important segments of the mass base saw cooperation with the FDN simply as a step toward a more sweeping transformation of Peruvian society, to be accomplished by violence if necessary.[73]

Project from Below

Because the incorporation period came so late, the agenda of labor movement demands was somewhat different than in several other countries. Much basic social legislation had been adopted some years before in Peru (see Chapter 4), and issues such as the eight-hour day that were a central concern of the labor movement at the onset of the incorporation period in some other cases had at least partially been addressed in Peru. Most political tendencies within the labor movement shared a concern with two basic goals that had not yet been achieved: the political and legal acceptance of trade unions as organizations, and institutionalized collective bargaining. Another major goal was the recovery of wages lost due to the inflation of the World War II period (Sulmont 1975:182–83, 195).

Within the framework of these common concerns, different political currents were found in the labor movement, the two most significant being identified with the two most important Aprista labor leaders, Sabroso and Negreiros. For Sabroso and the more moderate sector of the labor movement, state recognition and the opportunity to collaborate with state agencies were central goals of unionism. For Negreiros, who played a particularly active and successful role in organizing unions and promoting collective bargaining agreements during the Bustamante period, these initiatives served as means of initially consolidating the position of unions in order more effectively to pursue mass mobilization and insurrectional goals at a later point. In the interest of pursuing these longer-term goals, Negreiros organized "defense groups" within labor organizations, yet his ties within the party were more with the national APRA leadership than with the sectors that organized the 1948 APRA revolt in the Port of Callao. Hence, these defense groups within the labor movement played little role in the 1948 revolt. The Negreiros sec-

---

[73] Sulmont (1977:86–87) delineates two basic political currents within the party; Moya (1978:158–63) identifies four.

tor of organized labor did, however, have important ties with the small Trot-skyite wing of the labor movement (Sulmont 1975:191, 195; Moya 1978:163).

The Exchange

Though the Bustamante years saw many political and policy failures, key actors were moderately successful in using the exchange relationships of this period to achieve some of their goals. Bustamante succeeded in securing the initial electoral support of APRA as he ran for office, and the labor vote was certainly a component of that support, though not necessarily a large component. Some labor groups did play an active role in the electoral campaign (Pareja 1980:36–37). However, once Bustamante was in office, intense conflicts arose with the Apristas in Congress, so that the benefits Bustamante derived from this part of the exchange were short-lived.

The other benefit that Bustamante sought from his alliance with APRA, and through it with the labor movement, was the opportunity to shape and channel the future evolution of the party and associated labor sectors. During his administration, Bustamante's influence on the party was virtually non-existent. However, as will be argued in later chapters, in the longer term APRA's participation in the coalition had a strongly conservatizing effect on the party. Further, while the process of union-organizing was perceived by the elite during the 1945 to 1948 period as highly threatening, in fact it had the ultimate consequence of placing the control of much of the labor move ment in the hands of the more conservative, Sabroso wing of APRA. Hence, within a longer time-frame, Bustamante's goal was to a substantial degree achieved.

A principal goal of APRA was to strengthen its relationship to the labor movement, a relationship that played a central role in the party's strategy for dealing both with the Peruvian left and with the right. On the left, APRA's major opponent was the Communist Party, and the sphere of trade unions was the arena of APRA's most intense competition with the Communists.[74] Through the incorporation project, APRA gained access to state resources that gave it a great advantage in this partisan competition, aiding it in winning control of the CTP, which had initially been headed by a Communist labor leader, and in gaining an overwhelmingly predominant position in the labor movement in general (Pareja 1980:146).

APRA's relationship to the labor movement included an important dimension of control. Pareja (1980:111) stresses that trade union structures set up by APRA encouraged the "control and manipulation" of worker protest and served to isolate workers from the insurrectional currents planning the 1948 revolt. APRA used its control of unions for its own partisan advantage. "APRA's union leaders cooled down potential strikes in order to maneuver

[74] Bustamante (1949:153) bitterly observes how APRA and the Communists made trade unions a central arena of partisan struggle.

in and out of Congress and sometimes used strikes for political objectives quite removed from the workers' concrete claims" (North 1973:157). Thus, APRA could be judged as successful in using its relationship with the labor movement to advance its partisan goals.

APRA's relation with labor was, in turn, an important aspect of its strategy vis-à-vis conservative opponents. According to Adams, "the party's control over organized labor was its most effective means of placing pressure on [its opponents] and formed the most important part of the Aprista-inspired popular mobilization which the party hoped would offset [elite] opposition to the Aprista reform project" (1984:37). This aspect of APRA's strategy backfired. While the FDN and its effort to integrate APRA into the political system had initially been supported by important segments of the economic elite, elite opposition quickly emerged not only to the economic program but also specifically to the extensive popular mobilization promoted by APRA. In the political battle triggered in part by this mobilization, APRA lost.

From the standpoint of the labor movement, the two most important benefits were unprecedented levels of union recognition and major gains in purchasing power. In both areas, Sulmont identifies two phases: a successful workers' "offensive" in the period to 1947, followed by a "counter-offensive" on the part of capital in 1947–48 (1975:192).

The data on union recognition are impressive. Whereas the rate of recognition had been slightly under ten per year under Benavides and somewhat over 20 per year under Prado, it rose to nearly 90 per year in 1945–47. The peak year was 1946, the year of the "APRA cabinet," when 163 unions were recognized (Sulmont 1975:275–76). Seventy-eight unions were recognized in the manufacturing sector between 1945 and 1948, and for the first time government-recognized unions were established in the sugar sector on the north coast and in the mining enclaves in the central highlands. A major organizing effort was also carried out in the oil sector on the north coast. In addition to the total of 271 unions recognized between 1945 and 1948, many others were created or reorganized but did not reach the point of formal recognition. Subsequently, in the context of the collapse of APRA influence in Congress and in the government, only seven unions were recognized in 1948 (Sulmont 1975:190, 275).

The problem of low wages was recognized by Bustamante, and legislated wage increases were an important part of the economic program. Though available data are uneven in their coverage, they suggest a significant erosion of wages from the late 1930s to the mid-1940s in the context of war-time inflation. This erosion was followed during the Bustamante period by a sharp increase in wages, with real manufacturing wages in 1947 standing an impressive 67 percent above their 1944 level. Within the manufacturing sector, increases were greater in the more heavily unionized industries, suggesting the importance of union-party-state linkages in achieving wage increases. Apart from direct wage increases, the government also subsidized the prices of basic consumption items. As with union recognition, the final period of the Bustamante administration saw a shift in policy on wages and subsidies.

Between 1947 and 1948, with rising inflation and the loss of APRA influence in the government, some of these wage gains were eroded, and the subsidies were abandoned in 1947.[75]

In addition to extensive union recognition and wage gains, the numerous collective bargaining agreements consummated during this period brought many other improvements in working conditions. Finally, the working class also achieved unprecedented congressional representation under the Bustamante government. Within the APRA delegations, six deputies and one senator were workers. Four of the Communist deputies were workers (Cotler 1978:264; Pareja 1980:39–40; Sulmont 1975:188).

In sum, this was a period of substantial working class gains directly linked to labor's collaboration with APRA. At the same time, these gains were secured at the cost of submission to what was in fact a relatively conservative labor leadership, clearly reflecting labor's side of the dual dilemma.

The Party

Before assessing continuity and change in the evolution of APRA and its relation to the labor movement, it is essential to explore the role of the party's basic organizational characteristics and of party leadership in the Bustamante period. APRA's unusally strong organization greatly enhanced its ability to pursue its goals under what proved to be unfavorable circumstances. The nature of leadership, on the other hand, had a destructive effect on the party and tragic consequences for the evolution of Peruvian politics.

The APRA's unusually strong organization was important because it enabled the party to partially overcome its disadvantageous position within the FDN alliance. From the time of Haya's first meeting with Bustamante after the election, a strong personal antagonism emerged between the two leaders. Haya had expected to be prime minister. However, due to tensions and a failure of personal communication between Haya and Bustamante, not only was Haya not offered the position, but no Aprista ministers were included in the national cabinet during the first six months of the Bustamante administration. Even in the period of the "APRA cabinet" from January 1946 to January 1947, APRA held only three ministries, and the period after January 1947 saw the growing exclusion of APRA from power following the assassination of the prominent conservative newspaper publisher Francisco Graña Garland, apparently by an Aprista. The congressional strike by the conservative opposition to APRA that began in July 1947 paralyzed Congress for the remainder of Bustamante's presidency, seriously limiting the APRA's legislative initiatives after that date (Werlich 1978:235–40).

Nonetheless, due to APRA's remarkable organizational capacity, the party was able to take extensive advantage of its access to state resources, even

[75] Bustamante 1949:152–53, 156, 195; Thorp and Bertram 1978:188; J. Payne 1965:22–23; Sulmont 1975:192, 266.

under these unfavorable conditions. As a legacy of the repression of the 1930s, the party had developed a strong tradition of internal discipline, a "strictly hierarchical quasi-military organizational style" that was markedly authoritarian (Adams 1984:28). This tight organization was effectively employed in many spheres. "The party's rigid discipline gave APRA's 'parliamentary cell' a single, unified voice on all major issues" (Werlich 1978:236). While APRA's direct control of top executive positions was limited, the party accomplished a great deal through the Congress. APRA had an absolute majority of seats in the Senate and also a working majority in the Chamber of Deputies during the period of cooperation between APRA and other non-APRA members of the FDN (Werlich 1978:236). Upon entering the legislature, APRA established the right of Congress to override presidential vetoes with a simple majority vote (Pike 1967:284). As Werlich put it, "If APRA could not institute its program from the executive branch, it would do so from the chambers of parliament" (1978:236).

Though Apristas never occupied more than three ministerial positions in the cabinet, APRA "penetrated the public bureaucracy, establishing [party] 'cells' whose primary responsibility was to the party and its leader (Cotler 1978:267), thus undermining conventional lines of authority in the government. "This pattern of infiltration was extended to unions, schools, and universities, which became responsive to partisan directives. . . . APRA in effect established itself as a power parallel to that of the government" (Cotler 1978:267) and achieved substantial control over the functioning of the public sector. APRA also influenced the armed forces through the political use of military promotions initiated from the Congress (Cotler 1978:267; 1980:173).

The other feature of the party that strongly influenced the evolution of the Bustamante period involved Haya's leadership. Perhaps due to the long years of repression during which the party was never publicly accountable for its positions, Haya and other leaders developed the habit of maintaining very different political postures when dealing with different constituencies, allowing them to be "all things to all men" (Davies 1971:637). Although this vacillation may have helped to ensure a low rate of defection from the party prior to the Bustamante period (Davies 1971:637), it established a political practice that later had disastrous consequences. Under Bustamante this vacillation produced an erratic and indecisive style of leadership. "Disgruntled Apristas charged that Haya followed the last advice given to him by members of his intimate circle—the 'bureau of confusion,' as they called it" (Werlich 1978:243).

Haya's behavior could possibly be interpreted as a creative adaptation to an ambiguous and difficult political situation. Yet it is hard to apply such an interpretation to what was certainly the most unfortunate aspect of this behavior: Haya's alternation between encouraging the radical wing of APRA to prepare for armed insurrection and pursuing other agendas that involved the neglect or even suppression of these more radical tendencies. This vacillation had a "destabilizing" effect on the party and, in the context of the military conspiracies of the mid-1940s, tragically set into motion forces that Haya could not control (North 1973:145–46, 151–52).

Having now explored the basic functioning of the party and its leadership in this period, we may examine more specifically continuity and change in the party and its relationship to the labor movement during the Bustamante period. Before stressing the changes, four areas of continuity must be underlined. First, while APRA had been created with the goal of carrying out reforms like those initiated under Bustamante, APRA was not, as of the 1940s, a new party, and its basic characteristics of strong organization, tight internal discipline, and capacity for mass mobilization date from the 1930s. Second, any analysis of the ties between APRA and the labor movement must recognize that APRA previously had, and would continue to have, overwhelmingly middle-class leadership and a major middle-class component within its mass base (North 1973:36, 222). Third, even well before the formal founding of APRA as a political party, this middle-class leadership had as early as 1919 actively courted a working-class constituency and energetically supported worker organizations. Fourth, as of the early 1930s APRA had already gained a predominant position in the labor movement in relation to the Communists, a position it retained on the eve of the Bustamante period. Hence, neither APRA's interest in the labor movement nor its strong position in that sector was new.

Within the framework of these continuities, it is nonetheless clear that in the mid-1940s these party-union linkages were greatly strengthened. As Pareja (1980:8) put it, "Between 1945 and 1947, the relationship between APRA and the labor movement reached its fullest expression; the goals and mode of action of the organized labor movement converged to the point of becoming identical."

The relationship between the party and the labor movement was clearly one of mutual dependence. Pareja (1980:115) notes that "APRA became the most important vehicle for the institutionalization of the labor movement," and Villanueva (1977:72) likewise emphasizes the extreme dependence of the CTP on the party during this period. At the same time, as noted above, APRA's role in the labor movement was an essential element both in its political posture vis-à-vis the Communists and the left and in its strategy toward the right. The former strategy was successful, whereas the latter was not.

In addition to consolidating its position in the labor movement, the party also more sharply defined the limits of its mobilizational efforts. As noted above, despite a long history of rhetoric in favor of improving the conditions of the Indians and land reform, APRA engaged in little peasant mobilization outside the immediate vicinity of the export enclaves, did not promote agrarian reform, and made no effort to expand the narrow suffrage. APRA thus defined its posture as a party oriented toward popular sector mobilization within the modern sector—that is, in urban areas, modern export enclaves, and to some extent the immediate hinterland of the enclaves. The party did not challenge social relations more broadly in the highlands and hence did not threaten the base of power of the more traditional sector of the agrarian elite. While APRA promoted the unionization of the modern sector of agriculture, it did not challenge more fundamental property relations in that sector.

Opposition and Polarization

The polarization that emerged in Peru must be understood in light of the fragmented character of the FDN coalition. Even prior to Bustamante's inauguration as president, personal animosity emerged between Bustamante and Haya, and they soon found themselves in intense conflict. Indeed, in any account of the role of leadership in the fate of the Peruvian incorporation experience, the combination of the naive, apolitical posture of Bustamante and the political vacillation and unpredictability of Haya would stand out as major causes of the political failures of this period. The economic elite quickly abandoned its initial support of, or acquiesence in, the FDN and came to oppose not only APRA, but also Bustamante, due in part to what they viewed as his excessive tolerance of the Apristas.

Elite opposition to APRA focused both on the economic program with which APRA and to some degree Bustamante were identified, and also on the union organizing, popular mobilization, and ongoing violence promoted by the party. The offending economic policies included the major wage increases, expansion of public spending, state subsidies for basic consumer items, exchange and import controls, and an overvalued exchange rate. This typical package of populist policies (Cotler 1980:174) discouraged new investment and triggered what for that era were substantial levels of inflation: around 30 percent per year in 1947 and 1948, with a four-year total of 85 percent for the 1944–48 period (calculated from Sulmont 1975:262).

While APRA had hoped that popular mobilization would give it leverage against the elite, in fact the growing politicization of society and rapid unionization galvanized elite opposition. Changing authority relations in the workplace due to unionization, as well as APRA's rising power in schools and universities, appeared to pose a profound threat to established patterns of authority. Elite opposition was also intensified by the violence promoted by APRA, part of which revolved around the antagonistic relationship between APRA and the press already observed in the 1930s. In 1945 APRA pushed through a new press law intended to curb attacks on the party by leading newspapers. A protest rally opposing the law was countered by an even bigger demonstration of Apristas, some of whom attacked the offices of *El Comercio* and *La Prensa*. Later, a major turning point in the collapse of APRA influence in the government was the assassination of Graña, the publisher of *La Prensa*, following a period of particularly harsh attacks by *La Prensa* on APRA. This event echoed the killing of the editor of *El Comercio* in the 1930s. It triggered the replacement of the "APRA cabinet" by a "military cabinet" that included five military officers, among them General Manuel A. Odría, known for his intense anti-Aprismo, in the position of minister of interior (i.e., of police). Odría would lead the coup against the Bustamante government in 1948.[76]

The atmosphere of turmoil was further aggravated by a series of "political beatings, bombings, and murders," primarily directed against opponents of APRA (Werlich 1978:239); and by ongoing strikes, walkouts, marches protesting shortages and inflation, and riots, one of which led to the death of a provincial governor (Werlich 1978:241). APRA's continuing conspiracies with members of the military were understandably viewed as highly threatening to the institutional integrity of the armed forces.

The enemies of APRA coalesced in the National Alliance, and Pedro Beltrán emerged as a central leader of this group. The National Agrarian Society played a prominent role in sustaining the Alliance, which encompassed a broad spectrum of the economic elite, including that of coastal and highland agriculture, as well as the urban commercial and industrial sectors. The Alliance also received support from the Communists, who with the end of the world war and the coming of the cold war abandoned their collaboration with other progressive parties and once again acted on their traditional anti-Aprismo. Among its various initiatives, the conservative opposition arranged a boycott of the Congress, beginning in July 1947 and extending to the end of Bustamante's term, which paralyzed that body and drastically reduced APRA's influence in the government. Bustamante, in turn, was incapable of providing a viable alternative to this growing polarization between the "sect," as APRA was called by its opponents, and the "clan," as the economic elite or "oligarchy" was sometimes called.[77]

In the midst of these other conflicts, the revolutionary wing of APRA was preparing a military revolt to be coordinated with a mass insurrection. Haya encouraged these initiatives, at the same time that he conspired with military leaders in an attempt to arrange a coup that would oust Bustamante and permit new elections that would give APRA a stronger position in a new government (Cotler 1978:271). The revolutionary plotting culminated in the disastrous revolt in Lima's port of Callao on 3 October 1948. While pro-APRA forces did seize control of most of the fleet located in the port and some insurrectional activities were carried out in other parts of the city, the revolt failed and was soon crushed militarily. In the midst of this crisis Haya again vacillated, negotiating with both right and left and thereby contributing to the party's failure to stage the popular insurrection that was to have been coordinated with the military uprising.

At this point Bustamante outlawed APRA and "troops seized the party's headquarters, newspapers, and radio stations. Within a week more than 1,000 Aprista leaders had been arrested" (Werlich 1978:245). On 27 October 1948

---

[76] Werlich 1978:239; Sulmont 1975:196–99; Cotler 1978:269; Werlich 1978:236, 239; Bustamante 1949:361.

[77] Pike 1967:286; Sulmont 1975:196; Moya 1978:125; Werlich 1978:240–42; Cotler 1978:270.

Odría carried out the military coup that ended the Bustamante period and launched eight years of intense repression of APRA.

Conclusion

The circumstances that led to this final collapse of the Bustamante administration point again to a basic theme of this section: while many aspects of the period 1945–48 in part reflected continuity with the earlier experiences with APRA, the events of the 1940s decisively reinforced earlier patterns. APRA's violence had its origins in the 1930s, and intense anti-Aprismo also dated from that period. In the 1940s APRA had an opportunity to place these problems in the past, and it failed to do so. Hence, while many of the political and social antagonisms that would make it difficult for APRA to be fully readmitted to the political system in the 1950s and beyond had much deeper roots, the events and mistakes of the 1940s reinforced these problems for the party.

It is reasonable to ask whether APRA's presumed mistakes of the 1940s were perhaps an avoidable consequence of the profound political divisions within the party. The answer would appear to be no. As we will see later in the analysis of the aftermath of incorporation, APRA's leadership in fact had a remarkable capacity to persuade party members to accept a change of course in the 1950s, and the more radical wing of APRA might well have been dissuaded in the 1940s from attempting to seize power through violence. Thus, it might be more reasonable to argue that the top APRA leadership committed a major blunder under Bustamante. Alternatively, a slightly less critical argument might suggest that it was in fact difficult for the leadership to make a realistic assessment of the degree of mobilization and violence that was best suited to strengthening APRA's position within the Bustamante government. As it turned out, the assessment that they made was indeed a poor one.

ARGENTINA

Project from Above

In cases of party incorporation, the analysis of the project from above has been centrally concerned with how political leaders used the incorporation periods to build new constituencies in order to gain and consolidate power. This strategy emerged dramatically in Argentina, with the rise of Juan Domingo Perón from his position as a colonel involved in the 1943 coup to his inauguration three years later as president. As in Peru, this period in Argentina saw intense popular mobilization combined with the marked persistence of the power of agrarian elites—a juxtaposition that would have fateful consequences for the subsequent evolution of politics in these two countries. Yet Peru and Argentina also differed in many respects during this period, one of the most important being the limited institutionalization of Peronism as a political party, in comparison with APRA.

The immediate rise of Perón began with the military coup of 4 June 1943, which ended 13 years of "neo-conservative" rule in Argentina. The coup derived from several military concerns. One was the fear that electoral fraud, on which the prior civilian regime had based its power, was producing growing opposition and possibly paving the way for a radicalization of Argentine politics. The military also had serious misgivings about Robustiano Patrón Costas, the prior civilian government's likely presidential candidate in the election scheduled for 1944. Patrón Costas, a wealthy sugar plantation owner, was regarded by proneutrality officers as overly sympathetic to the Allies in World War II and by most members of the military as an exponent of an archaic social order. The military's actions were also motivated by a strong sense of nationalism and a commitment to promoting industrialization as a basis for military power and national strength. Although there was substantial military concern with the social question, this concern initially took an antiunion form with the restrictive labor legislation adopted within a month of the coup. More broadly, key officers were fundamentally opposed to basing the Argentine political order on principles of liberalism and the practice of party politics, and they saw the fascist regimes of contemporary Germany and Italy, and particularly the Franco regime in Spain, as "useful models for reorganizing Argentina."[78]

Within the military, perhaps the most influential force behind the coup was the United Officer's Group (GOU), an informal grouping of second-rank officers who were fervently anticommunist, but also strongly opposed to joining the Allied cause against the Axis. During the two months following the coup, the GOU jockeyed for power with pro-Allied military forces, receiving an initial boost when several GOU members, including Juan Perón,

---

[78] Potash 1969:184; see also Potash (1969:183, 197); Rouquié (1982, vol. 2:17–18, 22); Potash (1984:202); Panaia et al. (1973:115–54).

were named to important government posts. In October the GOU's position was strengthened when several pro-Allied officers were replaced by members of the GOU. Perón was named head of the National Labor Department, which two months later was elevated to cabinet level as the Secretariat of Labor and Social Security. Perón was able to use his new position, his skill in military politicking, and his friendship with General Edelmiro Farrell, who became president in February of 1944, to pave the way for his own ascension to power. Faced with a formidable rival from within the GOU, Colonel Enrique González, Perón worked skillfully behind the scenes to force his resignation, and Perón soon became General Farrell's closest adviser. Perón was named minister of war in June of 1944, vice president in July, and president of the National Council on the Postwar Era (Consejo Nacional de Postguerra) in August, and he amassed influence both within the military and among the country's political class and the elite.

As skillful as Perón was at maneuvering for power within the military and within the state elite, an additional driving force behind his rise to the presidency was his ability to attract worker support. Perón had been in contact with labor leaders since 7 June 1943, the day Pedro R. Ramírez was sworn in, and these early contacts laid the groundwork for Perón's later mobilization of the workers. Perón's policies toward workers and unions became the vehicle for pursuing a series of interrelated and mutually supportive goals. Though many of these goals coincided with those of the GOU and the Argentine military more broadly, it was Perón's distinctive contribution to bring these goals together in a project focused on labor mobilization (Potash 1969:209–10; Ciría 1972:1; Kenworthy 1970:155).

Perón's political agenda must be seen in the context of growing concern with the "social question" and with the issues linked to that concern: class conflict and the role of the state in mitigating such conflict, fear of revolution in the face of the growing influence of the Communist sector of the labor movement, and also, to some degree, a genuine concern for the poor. When speaking before business audiences, Perón continuously returned to the themes of revolution and the threat of communism, arguing that this threat should be averted by a systematic state effort to organize the labor movement and channel social conflict. These goals were linked with a commitment to promoting a particular type of economic development. To achieve class harmony, Perón redistributed national income and erected protectionist barriers to promote national industrialization, thereby creating jobs for the newly mobilized working class and ensuring Argentina's economic independence and security. The need for economic independence was strongly felt, due in part to growing preoccupation that the end of World War II could lead to the loss of markets in Europe and a new war between the Soviet Union and the United States (Wynia 1978:45–52; Waisman 1987:168, 171).

At the same time that this economic agenda benefited the urban working class and the urban industrial sector, it worked against the interest of rural export elites, whose profits were taxed heavily in order to subsidize urban industrial development (Waisman 1987:175, 184). This economic assault was accompanied by elaborate verbal attacks, in which Perón, as a complement to his effort to bestow new dignity upon the working class, inveighed frequently against Argentina's oligarchic social and political system, "preaching the destruction of 'oligarchy' " (Rock 1985:272). However, in terms of concrete policies, no agrarian reform was adopted as occurred in Mexico and Venezuela. Perón attacked the oligarchy but did not destroy it.

Though Perón was centrally concerned with mitigating class conflict and achieving economic growth, his search for a major new political constituency also played a central role in his labor and industrial policy. Perón had high political ambitions, and in contrast to the predominantly antilabor posture of the military government, he viewed labor as an important potential base of political support. Although the labor movement had grown significantly in the 1930s and early 1940s and labor militance was increasing, especially in the Communist unions, neither the Communists nor other labor leaders had achieved a major electoral or political mobilization of the working class during this earlier period. The labor movement had not established itself as a major political actor and remained available for political entrepreneurs in the 1940s. It was this opportunity that Perón seized to achieve power (Waisman 1987:192–93; Horowitz 1990:chap. 1).

There were important, though complex, connections between the overall Peronist project and the type of support coalition that Perón successfully constructed. A standard argument about Perón's policies for promoting industrialization and their relationship to his labor policy is that these initiatives came in a historical period—that of the easy phase of import substitution—when such policies could be in the interest of both industrial workers and industrialists. State support for the expansion of industry could thus be well received by both groups. Even policies favoring higher wages for workers might, at least in the long run, prove favorable for industrialists as well, since the higher wages of the workers would increase the demand for industrial goods.[79]

Nevertheless, Perón's relationship to industrialists was ambiguous. Although some authors argued that the industrialists who emerged out of this phase of industrialization, the so-called "new industrialists," were part of Perón's original support coalition, subsequent analysts have contested this view. They suggest that those industrialists who participated in Perón's government generally did so as individuals, while the most important Argentine business association, the Argentine Industrial Union (UIA) opposed the policies enacted while Perón was secretary of labor and only issued statements of support when it became clear that Perón would be in power for some time. Ultimately, the government took control of the UIA.[80]

The response to Perón's policies of other sectors of Argentina's economic

[79] Peralta Ramos 1972:96–98; O'Donnell 1973:55–59; D. Collier 1979:chap. 1.

[80] Merkx 1969:94; Di Tella 1965:71; Imaz 1970:32; Kenworthy 1970:chap. 6; Mainwaring 1975:76–197; Cúneo 1967:180–90; Waisman 1987:174–75, 185.

elite, especially rural exporters, was one of suppressed opposition. These exporters had considerable reason to oppose Perón, in that through the creation in 1946 of the state-controlled Argentine Institute for Trade Promotion (IAPI), Perón initiated a major redistribution of profits from rural producers to the urban sector. He also prevented rural landowners from raising rents charged to tenant farmers and enforced rural labor laws that gave some protection to agricultural workers. However, this sector of the economic elite did not engage in active opposition because it was counterproductive, indeed risky, to do so. The fate of the UIA noted above made it clear what could happen to a business association that actively opposed the government. Hence, the Argentine Rural Association (SRA) did not constitute an important source of opposition to Perón, limiting itself to occasional criticism. However, the underlying anti-Peronism of the export elite was given full rein after the coup of 1955; indeed, this was the very oligarchy that Perón constantly lambasted in speeches and in communications to the working class (Waisman 1987:186; Cúneo 1967:160–65, 216–21, 247–49).

Another important aspect of Perón's coalition was his evolving relationship with the armed forces and the Church. Although Perón's rapid rise in influence, especially under General Farrell, created some resentment among fellow members of the GOU, and although conservative military officers were disturbed by Perón's labor policies and his personal conduct (e.g., his relationship with Eva), until 1949 most of the military was not actively opposed to him. Nevertheless, the increasingly personalist tenor of Peronist rule, as well as growing questions about the role of Eva Perón, generated significant opposition within the military and remained a permanent concern for Perón during his last five years in power.[81]

Relations between the Church and Perón were originally much more positive. The Church of the 1930s and 1940s was generally antiliberal and feared the power of the left, making them responsive to Perón's basic appeal (Waisman 1987:182). But the Church reacted even more negatively than Perón's military colleagues to growing evidence of Perón's unorthodox personal lifestyle and moved into active opposition when Perón called into question the Church's role in society, hammered out during the 19th century Church-state conflicts. Thus, both the military and the Church were to move from relatively supportive or nonconflictual roles to become crucial elements of the opposition that would eventually drive Perón from power.

Two important segments of the Argentine population that do seem to have joined the urban working class in supporting the Peronist governments were the rural working class and the middle classes of both country and city (Llorente 1980:390–94). In contrast to what took place in the urban areas, however, the support of rural labor was not primarily mobilized through the unions. The Argentine Federation of Rural Workers and Stevedores (FATRE), founded in 1947, had jurisdiction over day workers in the key cattle and grain

---

[81] Rouquié 1982:60–61; Luna 1969:275–76; Potash 1969:88, 95–98, 102, 228.

industries of the Pampean region, but it organized only a minimal proportion of the total rural working population. Support from the rural working classes was generated through labor legislation (the Statute of the Peón); wage increases; enforcement of rural rent freezes, which greatly benefited tenant farmers; clientelist arrangements with rural electoral bosses tired of years of benign neglect from the central government; as well as support from some pro-Peronist members of the rural clergy. These policies won important electoral support from the rural working class.[82]

It must also be noted that nearly 1 million people moved from rural to urban settings between 1936 and 1947. Some studies initially suggested that this internal migrant population was socially and politically predisposed to support a populist movement like Peronism and in fact may have constituted a more important source of support for Perón than organized labor. However, subsequent scholarship has called this conclusion into question. First, scholars have found few significant differences in social characteristics between the migrants and the unionized population of Buenos Aires. Second, research on voting patterns in 1946 indicates it was the industrial work force, not migrants, that secured Perón's electoral victory. A balanced approach might suggest that both the migrants and organized workers were important in Perón's electoral coalition, though obviously at key points in Perón's rise to power it was the organizational capacity of the union movement that was crucial in massive demonstrations of support. This reinterpretation of the role of internal migrants and organized labor is important because it makes clear that Perón's incorporation project did indeed depend heavily upon, and indeed was built on top of, a preexisting labor movement.[83]

In conclusion, Perón's incorporation project sought to reduce the likelihood of revolution and communist influence in the labor movement by redistributing wealth from the rural exporting sector to the urban working class. In creating a support coalition to bring himself to power and carry out this project, Perón ended organized labor's marginal role in the country's political life by making it the central pillar of his movement. The economic elite played a more marginal role—either as supporters or opponents of Perón—than one might have expected, given the economic policies which dramatically redistributed wealth from the rural to the urban sector, and given Perón's symbolic attacks on the traditional elite. As for the other politically relevant sectors, the rural poor provided votes, while the armed forces were more a source of tacit consent than of active support. The Church supported Perón in the early stages of his presidency, but in late 1954 it became an important source of opposition.

[82] Luparia 1973:187–88, 200; Blanksten 1953:267; Sebreli 1984:26, 132; Llorente 1980:394; Wellhofer 1977:353.
[83] Germani 1965:230–31; Fillol 1961:83; Baily 1967:82; Butler 1969:429; Kenworthy:1975; Halperín Donghi:1975; Little 1975; Wellhofer:1974; 1977; P. Smith 1972; Murmis and Portantiero 1971.

Project from Below

To understand why a major portion of the Argentine labor movement supported Perón, it is necessary to examine the goals of the unions prior to the
1943 coup and to assess changes during the 1930s that led unions to reassess
their earlier caution about participating in partisan politics. The most important actor during this earlier period was the CGT, Argentina's major labor
confederation. Since its founding in 1930, the CGT had insisted on the need
to maintain independence from political parties but had, nevertheless, actively lobbied state agencies to encourage an expanded state role in providing
for the needs of the working class. The CGT presented demands for a minimum wage; a shorter work week; paid vacations; holidays; severance pay;
free public education; accident, maternity, and old age insurance; and CGT
participation in state agencies dealing with labor issues (Ciría 1968:305–10).
    Congressional approval of some social legislation in the 1930s, as well as
the growing state role in the economy during those years, increased this political involvement of the labor movement. Nevertheless, tension developed
within the labor movement between those who supported pursuing reform
measures through the legislature, primarily the Socialists, and those, like the
Syndicalists, who insisted the only way to ensure enforcement of the law
was direct worker participation within the state. These conflicts were
heightened by the expansion of the labor movement, occasioned by the
growth of Argentina's industrial sector during the late 1930s and early 1940s
and by the rapid growth of Communist-led industrial unions. While this division between Socialists, Syndicalists, and Communists was papered over
when World War II broke out, by 1942 these differences had become too great
and the CGT split, with the new industrial unions, primarily Communist,
forming the CGT-2, and the Syndicalist and Socialist unions, mostly concentrated in services and the transport sector, forming the CGT-1. The CGT-2,
given its leftist orientation and adherence to the Popular Front strategies of
that period, was more prone to support political activism; whereas the CGT-
1 took a relatively non-political and strongly anticommunist stance under
the personalist leadership of José Domenich. Despite the split, in 1943 both
factions of the CGT strongly protested the restrictions placed on unions by
the new military government (Tamarin 1985:162–163; Matsushita 1986:171,
245–46, 259).
    Thus, on the eve of the incorporation period, the leadership of the labor
movement was increasingly inclined to play an active role in politics,
whether through the legislature or by lobbying state agencies. At the same
time, the labor movement was, in relation to the other seven countries, probably the strongest and best organized, despite the division within the CGT.
Thus, conditions were ripe for forging new institutional relationships between labor and the state at the same time that a large number of labor's
demands were yet to be met. Even more than in Peru, the incorporation project in Argentina was therefore built on top of highly developed labor organi-

zations. Argentina's growing postwar economy, together with Perón's need
to build a secure support coalition, brought a period of rapid expansion in the
political importance of the labor movement and in worker benefits, as the
labor movement in turn helped propel Perón to the presidency.

The Exchange

Perón's rise to power was built on a highly visible exchange of new worker
and union benefits for political support. As typically occurs with the corporative structuring of labor movements, the benefits also constituted a new
basis for state control, which Perón used to impose a dramatic political transformation of the Argentine labor movement.

This exchange may be understood in terms of three phases. Before Perón's
election as president in 1946, he depended heavily on the support of a relatively independent labor movement, and his personal political power was
limited because he did not have formal control of the state and faced considerable opposition within the military and among the economic elite for reasons both personal and programmatic. From 1943 to 1946, Perón was thus
centrally concerned with winning the support and cooperation of a labor
movement that, given its size and strength, was ripe for incorporation. During Perón's first administration, from 1946 to 1952, he gradually brought the
labor movement under his control, while continuing to offer major benefits
to workers and unions. The third period, the final years of his presidency,
saw some erosion of the mechanisms by which Perón controlled the labor
movement. Nonetheless, Perón retained strong underlying support within
the working class. The following discussion focuses on these three phases,
noting in each the benefits extended, the controls imposed, and the popular
support bestowed.

Coming to Power, 1943–1946.   In the three years prior to the 1946 presidential elections, Perón moved swiftly both to generate labor support and to start
bringing the labor movement under his control. In the process, the unions
made significant gains, while giving up an important degree of autonomy.
However, labor got a great deal out of the exchange relationship during this
period, in important measure as a result of Perón's need to build the political
support that would carry him to power.

With the creation of the Labor Secretariat in late 1943, Perón began to do
more than simply listen to labor leaders' complaints and demands, a change
that was welcomed by key leaders of the CGT-1 and CGT-2. Perón now began acting on the various concerns brought to his attention by organized labor, formalizing his discussions with worker representatives, bringing its
leadership into the policy process, and providing state assistance to govern-
ment-sanctioned unions. One consequence was an immediate surge in
worker victories in labor disputes, as Perón forced employers to negotiate
with recognized unions.

Besides putting his clout as labor secretary behind the unions, Perón also began to enforce existing social legislation, while securing an increase in its scope and coverage through the passage of new laws. In this way, the long backlog of labor demands, extant since the 1930s, was met. New laws protected rural workers and tenant farmers, expanded the regulation of the workplace, provided accident insurance, extended or created paid holidays and vacations and severance pay to nearly the entire work force, and restricted the dismissal of workers. Labor courts were created, which handled worker grievances; a minimum wage was established; a year-end bonus amounting to one month's wage was granted; and a new Law of Professional Associations was passed, which ended many of the antilabor provisions of the law put in place during the first months of the military government

This flood of prolabor legislation initiated what many workers would later come to view as a "golden age" in the relationship between the labor movement and the state (Halperín Donghi 1983:105; Cavarozzi 1983:25–28). Of these changes, the most important was certainly the 1945 Law of Professional Associations. Perón rescinded an earlier law that imposed more restrictions on unions and provided fewer benefits, and he replaced it with this new law, whose terms were considerably more favorable.

Although such initiatives represented major changes in labor policy, they did not immediately translate into significant changes in worker income, in that real wages increased little between 1943 and 1946. Rather, the changes introduced by Perón had two immediate effects: first, the ground was laid for strengthening the internal cohesion of the labor movement, while reducing its autonomy; and second, and perhaps most important, Perón gave the labor movement a degree of recognition as a social and political actor previously unknown in Argentina. Perón sought to remake labor's image from that of a source of conflict and foreign ideologies to that of a respected political actor esteemed for its contribution to the country's economic, social, and political life. Perón's skill in making direct popular appeals, his defense of the *descamisados* (the shirtless ones),[84] and his frequent declarations about the dignity of labor, all served to increase worker self-esteem and to legitimize labor's new role.

This period was notable not only for these positive benefits to labor, but also for important steps to bring the labor movement under state control and, eventually, under Perón's personal control. The Law of Professional Associations gave the state the power to recognize or not recognize a union, thus allowing it to grant favored unions the right to strike and bargain collectively with employers. Perón skillfully used these and other powers to eliminate political opponents in the labor movement, especially in unions controlled by the Communist Party. He had initially made overtures to key Communist

[84] This term actually means "coatless" rather than "shirtless," but we follow Navarro's (1982:50–52 and note 15) carefully explained translation. The material in this paragraph is drawn from Doyan (1975:153); Silverman (1967:130, 140–41, 169–70, 307); Alexander (1962:177–79, 192–205; 1979:39); Little (1979:334–35); D'Abate (1983:59); Rotondaro (1971:174–75, 177–79); Matsushita (1983:267); Collier and Collier (1979:972); Díaz-Alejandro (1970:124); Ciría (1968:107).

labor leaders, releasing José Peter, head of the powerful meatpackers union (FOIC), from prison. When the FOIC subsequently refused to moderate its demands, Peter was returned to prison and union funds were transferred to dissidents previously expelled from the union. They in turn formed a new union, which received state recognition and benefits originally promised to the FOIC, and this union subsequently replaced the FOIC as the most important in the meatpacking industry. In May 1945, the FOIC was dissolved when the Communist Party decided to disband all its unions and try to win back the support of workers who had joined unions recognized under the Law of Professional Associations.

With differing nuances, a similar process took place in the footwear, textile, and metalworking unions. In each of these industries, the government created or encouraged "parallel" unions that undermined established organizations controlled by Communist labor leaders. The construction workers' union, Argentina's second largest, was also controlled by Communists prior to the 1943 coup, and though a parallel union did not replace it immediately, government persecution of its leaders and militants had caused it to disintegrate by 1945.[85]

By 1946 the Communists—as well as other leftist, Syndicalist, and independent union leaders who refused to give up their autonomy—had lost virtually all influence within the Argentine labor movement. The bold use of state power during this period to eliminate opposition from the labor movement foreshadowed the increasingly authoritarian nature of Peronism.

However, it must be noted that in many cases workers themselves deserted unions that did not shift quickly enough to accept a reduction in autonomy in exchange for the enormous benefits of government recognition. This base level support for Perón's policies became more organized and widespread as Perón converted the newly reunited CGT into a vehicle of personal support. Throughout 1944 and 1945 the CGT and other labor organizations helped organize massive pro-Perón and progovernment demonstrations that expressed support for Perón's social and labor policies. However, the most important expression of organized support came after 9 October 1945, when Perón was forced to resign by military officers who opposed both his policies and his unconventional relation with his future wife, Eva Duarte.

Perón's resignation and subsequent jailing by the military were followed by events that both reflected his success in capturing the support of the working class and also set the stage for a more thorough organization of this support. Perón, having been granted permission to make a farewell address, skillfully placed his military opponents in a quandary by announcing a new wage increase, which, he "hoped," the new government would implement (Kenworthy 1970:210–11). This move led his opponents to throw him in jail, but once Perón had been removed the military found itself divided and unable to organize a new government. Although Perón feared that his gamble

[85] Alexander 1962a:177–79; Bergquist 1986:160–62; Iscaro 1973:262; Del Campo 1983:182–86; Alexander 1982:178–79.

had failed, in fact the CGT organized on 17 October 1945 what was up to that time the largest mass demonstration in Argentine history. This demonstration emerged as a central event in what Luna (1969) in the title of his book on these events has labeled a "decisive" year in Argentine history. The military, fearful of social unrest and divided in its opposition to Perón, backed down, releasing him from prison after he promised to disperse the protesting crowds. Rather then reenter the government, Perón turned his attention to organizing an electoral coalition that would bring him to power in the presidential elections of early 1946.[86]

In the following months Perón completed his effort to convert worker support for his social policies into a personal vehicle to power. He organized his base into three party organizations, all of which supported his presidential candidacy and followed his lead selecting candidate lists. The first, and most important, was the newly created Labor Party. Founded by prominent labor leaders a week after the 17 October demonstration, the party's primary purpose was to restore Perón to power, defend the gains already made by the labor movement, and insure increased labor participation in policy-making (Pont 1984:38, 134–38; Reyes 1946:54). At the same time, Perón organized support within the Radical and Conservative Parties, enhancing his personal control by using more traditional politicians from those parties as a counterweight, within the Peronist lists, to Labor Party leaders whose power was increasing rapidly due to their capacity to mobilize mass support. Perón chose a member of the newly formed pro-Peronist Radical splinter group as his running mate, bypassing a popular Socialist leader who would have been a more plausible candidate. This choice of an individual from a less important part of his support constituency for a key leadership role reflected what would become a central feature of his approach to leadership: his tendency to manipulate followers within his movement, rather than develop a group of skilled and strong leaders.

The extent of Perón's victory in February 1946 surprised everyone, including the Peronists. Perón benefited from a well-organized campaign and from the United States' clumsy support for his opponent, winning an absolute majority with 52 percent of the vote. In the space of just four months, Perón had passed from his apparent defeat in the first half of October 1945 to winning the presidency, rising to power with the support of an organized working class that had responded to three years of vigorously prolabor social and economic policy (Kenworthy 1970:227).

Perón's First Administration, 1946–1952. The balance between inducements and constraints began to shift once Perón had won the backing of the vast majority of workers and was installed in the presidency. Yet this shift by no means brought a cessation of benefits to labor. Fewer and fewer strikes were approved by the government, but in cases where the strikers had Perón's backing, they stood a strong chance of success. In a meatpackers' strike

[86] Page 1983:124–26; Luna 1969:273–342; Kenworthy 1970:210–11; Potash 1969:262, 267–82; Reyes 1946:55.

in late 1946, the government implemented the workers' demands by decree, producing an exceptionally favorable settlement for the union (Doyon 1977:444–45).

Similarly, although relatively little ground was broken in terms of new social legislation, existing laws were extended and implemented. Between 1943 and 1946 the number of people covered by social security had tripled, and it would do so again by 1952, with over 5 million workers covered, approximately 70 percent of the work force. Health insurance was expanded; price controls on food and other basic items were instituted; housing credits were granted to workers; public employment expanded; and real wages increased nearly 60 percent between 1946 and 1949, falling somewhat after this, while labor's percentage of national income rose sharply between 1946 and 1950.[87]

Other important benefits accrued to labor unions and their leadership. Perón's industrial promotion policies, his shift of resources from rural production to the urban industrial and service sectors, and his policies of granting easy credit to labor-intensive industries greatly expanded the size of the urban labor force, bringing with it an increase in union membership. Organized labor had grown only slightly in the period immediately prior to 1945, when it passed the half-million mark. But it had reached nearly 900,000 members by 1946, over 1.5 million in 1948, roughly 2 million in 1950, and 2.5 million in 1954, almost five times the 1941 level (Doyon 1975:154, 158). Given the relatively high level of unionization in Argentina in 1941, this increase was remarkable. This numerical expansion was accompanied by a major increase in the strength of government-recognized unions, which were in effect government-protected monopolies that benefited from the automatic collection of members' dues. Labor leaders saw their personal prestige and salaries grow substantially, while many received public recognition through election to Congress or appointments to government posts, including membership in Perón's cabinet.[88]

Together with these significant gains, the constraints on labor also grew, the most important being limits on the right to strike and the practice of intervening in recalcitrant unions and removing labor leaders who showed signs of independence. When the Perón government presented the "Rights of the Worker" in February of 1947, a set of rights that became part of the constitution in 1949, the right to strike was not even included. The leadership of the CGT went along with this restriction, often accepting labor contracts that led its members to carry out wildcat strikes. The government would then suppress the strikes, only to grant most of the demands made by the workers (Baily 1967:111, 129).

One of Perón's most effective means of controlling unions was his power to declare strikes illegal. Given this power to determine the legality of a

[87] Silverman 1967:294, 307; Alexander 1962a:208; Baily 1967:77, 99; Rotondaro 1971:184; Rock 1985:263–66; Díaz-Alejandro 1970:124.

[88] Díaz-Alejandro 1970:124–25; Rotondaro 1971:220–21; Cantón 1966:56–57.

strike and the fact that employers had to pay back wages in those cases where the strike was declared to be legal, those unions that lacked Perón's blessing were at a major disadvantage. The use of the CGT to take over non-Peronist unions became increasingly common during Perón's first presidency, and by 1954 nearly all of Argentina's largest unions had been intervened. Since intervention meant that the unions, and their property, were placed under the control of CGT-nominated trustees until new elections were called, this meant that by the mid-1950s Perón had consolidated nearly total control over organized labor.

The CGT was formally separate from the government, but Perón and Eva effectively controlled it, in part through the continuous manipulation of its leadership. This practice contrasts dramatically with a case such as Mexico, another instance of highly mobilizational party incorporation, where during the incorporation period in the 1920s and 1930s such a degree of manipulation by the president did not occur. In Argentina this method of controlling unions was evident in January 1947, seven months after Perón assumed the presidency, when Perón had the CGT's newly elected secretary general and former president of the Labor Party removed on trumped-up charges and replaced by a little-known unionist beholden to Perón. Subsequent leaders were named at the whim of the Peróns, including José Espejo, a baking company truck driver who was previously unknown to the committee that named him, but was a personal friend of Eva Perón. By 1950 the CGT was completely under Perón's control, and its statutes were amended in that year to recognize its total allegiance to Perón (Page 1983:181; Rotondaro 1971:211).

The high level of constraints after 1946 had no apparent impact on labor's electoral support for Perón or on labor's participation in pro-government demonstrations. Labor organizations played a central role in Perón's reelection in 1951, and available evidence shows no working class defection from Perón's support coalition. After a constitutional amendment in 1949 allowed Perón to hold the presidency for a second term, the CGT began organizing the campaign to reelect him in 1951. A special congress was called in 1950 demanding a second term for Perón, and mass rallies were organized by the CGT, in one case mobilizing nearly 250,000 demonstrators (Alexander 1962:183). Local union affiliates were the primary mechanism for getting out the vote. After a failed coup attempt in September 1951, Perón again mobilized his supporters, beginning a pattern that would continue until 1955 of using large demonstrations to keep the armed forces at bay and to conduct electoral campaigns.

Yet the 1951 election was significantly different from that which first brought Perón to power. Whereas the 1946 election had been among the cleanest in Argentine history, the 1951 contest was marred by widespread electoral fraud, partisan manipulation of district boundaries, and serious constraints on non-Peronist candidates and parties, especially with respect to access to the media and right of assembly. Several important opposition leaders were jailed. In short, by 1951 the practices of manipulation applied to trade unions had been extended to electoral politics (Rock 1985:305; Blank-sten 1953:77–86; Little 1973a:278–89). These authoritarian tendencies of the Peronist government make it difficult to fully gauge the true extent of Pe-rón's support at this time, and they cast doubt on the final result, in which Perón's vote total grew to 62.5 percent of the vote, compared to 52 percent in 1946.

Final Years of Perón's Presidency.   Perón's close relationship with the labor movement remained a cornerstone of his political power between 1952 and 1955. Nevertheless, two significant events in 1952, the inauguration of an economic stabilization program and the death of Eva Perón, had an impor-tant influence on that relationship.

In 1952 Perón was faced with an incipient foreign exchange crisis and growing inflation. In response, Perón initiated what was up to that time the most ambitious stabilization program in Argentine history, based on a two-year wage freeze, a significant contraction of domestic consumption of meat products, intended to yield an increase in exports and a reduction in state spending. The relative acquiescence of the working class and of labor leaders to the stabilization program suggests the strength of the underlying support for Perón. Rather than blame Perón for the resulting decline in real wages, unionists took out their discontent on the leadership of the CGT and of their own unions.

The CGT, still headed by Espejo, had responded to Perón's stabilization program with a call for greater worker productivity, essentially falling into line behind Perón. This subservience to the government cost Espejo his job, and other union leaders who had lost touch with the basic concerns of their membership found themselves suddenly voted out of office or pushed out through base-level rebellions (Doyon 1978:582–86; Walsh 1985:135). Yet these incumbents were removed only to be replaced by other relatively sub-servient unionists. It is true that wildcat strikes became more common, the number of strikes and work days lost due to strikes increased, and union members became more active in union affairs, suggesting a strong base-level reaction against the leadership's collaboration with the government. How-ever, Perón was able to weather the negative reaction of workers, due to the major social and symbolic benefits he had previously granted to labor, his resulting ability to draw on the underlying loyalty of the working class, and the absence of a viable alternative to the Peronist government and to the CGT, which he continued to control effectively.

The illness and death of Eva Perón in 1952 also changed Perón's relation-ship with labor. By 1952 Eva Perón had become the most important person within the Peronist movement after Perón himself. She was Perón's principal link to the organized labor movement, president of the Women's Peronist Party, and directly responsible for a great part of the government's social wel-fare program. Her death provoked an extraordinary expression of mourning from the working class, with nearly 2 million people attending her funeral. The loss of such an important and loyal partner was a serious blow to Perón and the Peronist movement. And yet Eva's death, the affection so many of the poor felt for her, and Perón's own efforts to exalt her memory converted her into a kind of cult figure and symbol for the Peronist Movement, thus in some respects strengthening the ties between the working class and Peronism.[89]

The Party

A discussion of the Peronist Party must begin with the observation that even though Perón built a powerful political movement, he personalized his rule and chose not to build a strong party organization. In light of standard definitions of the term *party* (see glossary), it is still appropriate to refer to Peronism as a party, even though its form and name changed periodically. Yet whatever underlying continuity this evolving and often amorphous party exhibited must be understood in light of its roots in this powerful political movement.

Although the weak organization of Peronism as a party receives considerable attention in this and the following chapters, we will find that the framework of the Argentina-Peru comparison places this attribute of Argentine politics in an interesting perspective. In the context of the far stronger organization of the APRA party in Peru, Peruvian party politics faced many of the same crises and dilemmas in the aftermath and heritage periods that arose in Argentina. Our search for an explanation of these outcomes will focus in important measure on other traits that the two countries had in common, though the weakness of Peronism will remain an important theme as well.

During Perón's initial rise to power, he first turned to the Radicals in an effort to establish a party base. Perón sought their support as early as 1944, and though initially rebuffed, made a second effort by securing the nomination of three second-level Radical leaders to cabinet posts in August of 1945. Perón's overtures had some support within the party, but later in the year the pro-Perón fraction lost in internal elections and subsequently broke with the Radical Party, forming the UCR "Renewal Board" (UCR-Junta Renovadora). Although the UCR-JR supported Perón's candidacy in 1945 and provided him with a running mate, the party lacked the popular support necessary to serve as Perón's primary electoral organization. Small groups of Conservative Party politicians who formed "Independent Centers" also endorsed Perón's presidential candidacy, but they likewise represented a minor source of support.[90]

For his major electoral support, Perón turned instead to labor. In October 1945 union leaders formed the Labor Party (Partido Laborista), modeled in part after the British party of the same name (Page 1983:138; Del Campo

---

[89] Rock 1985:306–7; Fraser and Navarro 1980:164–65; Page 1983:263; Navarro 1983:15–23.

[90] Potash 1969:242, 245; Kenworthy 1970:234–39; Ciría 1983:50–52.

1983:226–29). The Labor Party had considerably more popular appeal than the UCR-JR or the Conservative "Independent Centers," and Perón, wary of letting this party acquire too much leverage, placed on his electoral lists many politicians from among his Radical and Conservative supporters. Perón subsequently dissolved all three of these party groupings after the elections, uniting all members in a new organization called the Sole Party of the Revolution (Partido Unico de la Revolución—PUR). Whereas the veteran politicians quickly deserted their old organizations to enter the PUR, Labor Party leaders were less eager and only after considerable persuasion did they join. Several leaders refused, and Perón directed the full resources of the state against them, imprisoning the Labor Party president, Cipriano Reyes.[91] The elimination of the Labor Party marked an important step in the evolution of Peronism and in the evolving weakness of the party branch of the movement.

Over the next seven years Perón continued to tinker with the organization of his support base. This process finally came to an end in 1954 with the formal constitution of the Peronist Movement. The movement was composed of three principal pillars: the Peronist Party; the Women's Peronist Party, created in 1949 and run by Eva Perón as her personal political machine; and the CGT. Both the Peronist Movement and its three components were organized along similar lines, with Perón the supreme leader of all the Peronist organizations and a Strategic Command closely supervised by Perón in charge of the day to day running of the movement. Under the Strategic Command were the executives of the three branches, also tightly controlled by Perón. Besides these organizational structures or *ramas* (branches), which concentrated power in Perón's hands, the movement and branch statutes gave Perón complete control over branch and movement decisions. Perón and his various executive councils chose all candidates for political and union office, limiting popular participation to the choice of leaders of the Basic Units (Unidades Básicas), into which the branches were divided. These Basic Units functioned as ward-type organizations located either in the work place, in the case of the CGT, or territorially, in the cases of the Peronist Party and the Women's Peronist Party (Ciría 1972:5–11).

The division of the Peronist Movement into three branches helped to dilute the power of any one of the branches. Nevertheless, the CGT quickly became Perón's preferred organization for purposes of getting out the vote. Many Peronist activists did not even belong to the Peronist Party or the Women's Peronist Party, and Perón continuously asserted that parties were anachronisms and that Peronism was a movement, not a political party (Palermo 1986:98). With electoral mobilization left to the unions and many of the welfare functions of the state run through the Eva Perón Foundation, the role of the Peronist parties was further reduced. Also, by keeping such tight rein over the parties' decisions, Perón prevented the emergence of a well-entrenched party bureaucracy and of experienced, popular political leaders. Thus, the party's primary function was reduced to dispensing public employ-

[91] Baily 1967:106–8; Rock 1985:282–83; Pont 1984:51–52; Ciría 1983:157–63.

ment to party members, a function that gave nonunion members an incentive to join (Palermo 1986:12).

Despite Perón's interest in building an "organized community," Perón's leadership style emphasized direct personal appeals and ideological indoctrination rather than building organizations. As noted above, Perón often stated that his purpose was to build a movement, rather than a party (Little 1973b:656, 657, 660; Carri 1967:35). This stress on direct mass appeals and ideological indoctrination at the expense of organization contrasts sharply with Haya de la Torre's leadership of APRA in Peru. At the same time, an underlying similarity with APRA must also be stressed. A central theme in analyses of APRA both for the 1945–48 period and for the 1950s and 1960s concerns Haya's extraordinary degree of personal domination of the party—to the point that it was "his" party. Despite APRA's high level of organization, like Peronism it was subject to a more traditional form of *caudillo* domination by its leader. As we shall see below, in both countries this personal domination later became an obstacle to leadership change that could have greatly facilitated accommodation between the party and other political forces. Hence, although it is essential to recognize the organizational weakness of Peronism, it is also necessary to understand that the presence of strong party organization, as in the case of APRA, does not necessarily preclude the kind of *caudillo* domination of the party that played such a disruptive role in both Peru and Argentina.

Although Perón's failure as a party-builder may have derived partly from his conviction that parties were obsolete vehicles to popular mobilization, other reasons for his inattention to institution-building may be found in his military background and in the context in which he governed. With reference to the first, in an analysis of a partially parallel situation in Peru in the 1970s, Stepan has argued that rulers of military origin find it difficult to institutionalize political participation. The hierarchical authority that is familiar to the military is profoundly different from the more ambiguous authority relations that must to some degree be tolerated if meaningful participation is institutionalized (1978:311–16). With reference to the second, Perón directed his appeal to a social class—the Argentine working class—which was already organized before a Peronist Party was formed. As noted above, by 1945 more than 500,000 workers were members of unions, a figure that was close to 1 million by the end of 1946. Hence, Perón had an organizational alternative to building a strong party.

Whatever the particular combination of causes, the outcome was a weak party. Not only was the Peronist Party limited in its functions, it had a limited role in getting out the vote and dispensing patronage. Perón's tight control over decision-making prevented the emergence of strong party cadres, especially at the upper and middle-level positions, posts generally held by politicians personally beholden to Perón and with little independent popular support. These weaknesses were compounded by Perón's populist appeal, which demanded personal rather than institutional loyalty. Parties, therefore, were meant to help the leader in his pedagogical role, inculcating the

Peronist Movement's ideology and "mystique" (Little 1973b:656, 657). With the fall of Perón, the very diffuseness and lack of institutionalization of the party made it an easy victim during the Aramburu government, whereas it proved impossible to eradicate Peronist influence within the labor movement.

Opposition and Polarization

The immediate crisis that led to the end of Perón's government in 1955 did not involve a confrontation over Perón's labor reforms. In fact, economic policy had already taken a more conservative turn by the early 1950s. This turn to the right did not convince industrial elites to support Perón, but tensions between the government and industrialists were definitely not among the factors that led most immediately to Perón's overthrow. Similarly, although the export elite intensely disliked Perón's verbal attacks on the "oligarchy" and his assault on traditional norms of deference and hierarchy of Argentine society, they were not inclined to translate this dislike into active opposition to the increasingly repressive government, especially after Perón's 1952 economic plan gave them new price incentives and easier credit. In fact, the Rural Society continuously expressed its acquiescence to Perón's government, even praising his economic policies.[92]

The polarization that led to the 1955 coup involved a distinctive political dynamic, though with strong economic undercurrents. Generalized disaffection with the government—resulting partly from the economic downswing and the abandonment of economic nationalism, but more significantly from the increasingly monolithic character of the regime and the deterioration of Perón's leadership—was transformed into active opposition by a conflict that began in late 1954 between the government and the Church. This disaffection was not manifested in the results of the 1954 vice presidential and congressional elections, but rather in more indirect signs that Perón's supporters were backing him less enthusiastically than before. The death of Eva Perón, the 1952 stabilization plan, the easing of restrictions on foreign investment in 1953, and the increasingly servile role of the CGT may have weakened the intensity of worker support and to some extent might help explain the relatively indifferent reaction of labor to the overthrow of Perón (Calello and Parcero 1984, vol. 1:29–30).

Other factors that generated opposition to Perón included increasingly visible political corruption and a growing perception that Perón was neglecting his presidential duties. The suspicious death of Eva Perón's brother, who was also Perón's private secretary, while his business activities were under investigation and Perón's dalliance with underage school girls spurred Church and military opposition. A primary factor was also the increasingly authoritarian character of his rule, which left little or no room for the normal functioning

[92] Mainwaring 1986:14–24; Wynia 1978:70–71; Cúneo 1967:216–21.

of an opposition. Government manipulation of elections and continued violations of civil liberties suggested that Perón would not permit elections that posed any threat to his power. Finally, the increasingly pervasive penetration of Peronist ideology into society, including required reading in public schools of Eva Perón's autobiography, brought growing opposition from the Church. When the Peronists began to organize youth branches, reaching directly into the family, the Church reacted sharply to this invasion into what had been its territory since the resolution of the Church-state question in the 19th century. When Perón learned, in late 1954, that Catholic priests were organizing rival youth groups, he confronted the Church directly for the first time.

Over the next few months, Perón attacked the Church with increasing virulence. Not only were state subsidies for Catholic schools rescinded, but legislation was drawn up to rewrite the agreement between Church and state and to make divorce and prostitution legal. The Church responded by organizing mass demonstrations against the government. In June 1955 one Church-organized demonstration drew over 100,000 marchers. The government responded harshly, exiling two Argentine priests who played an important role in the march. In the tit-for-tat conflict, the Church responded by excommunicating anyone who played a role in exiling the two priests, implicitly extending the punishment to Perón.

The increasingly bitter conflict provided the impetus for navy officers, in alliance with Radical, Conservative, and Socialist politicians, to attempt a coup against Perón on 16 June 1955. Though the revolt failed, hundreds of civilians died when navy pilots attempted to assassinate Perón by strafing and bombing the Plaza de Mayo. Perón survived, and in the immediate aftermath his enraged supporters went on a rampage, attacking priests and burning Catholic churches. Perón quickly moved to cool the conflict, seeking to conciliate the opposition by offering it access to the media and bringing acceptable compromise figures into his cabinet. The opposition, sensing the weakness in Perón's position, demanded greater concessions and Perón abruptly about-faced and reverted to confrontation.[93]

Seeking to reenact his remarkable political comeback in 1945, Perón announced his resignation on 31 August, and the CGT promptly orchestrated a mass demonstration to convince him to change his mind. Perón withdrew his resignation, called for retaliation against anti-Peronists in a fiery speech, and dared the military to act against him. At the same time that some CGT officials discussed the possibility of creating a worker militia—a strategy Perón rejected, although leaving it a future possibility—further coup plans were being laid by the military. The new uprising, this time with the army joining the navy, began just two weeks later, on 16 September. Perón refused to accede to the military demand that he resign, and three days later the navy raised the stakes by threatening to destroy the new and expensive Peronist-

[93] Halperín Donghi 1983:81; Rock 1985:315–16; Luna 1972:85; Potash 1980:182–88; Rouquié 1982:107–10; Page 1983:293–94, 305–10; Godio 1985:28–33.

built Eva Perón oil refinery in La Plata. Although Perón's immediate response to this new threat was ambiguous, the next day he quietly abandoned the country to begin an exile that would last nearly 18 years.

Conclusion

The suddenness and depth of the changes initiated by Perón must be seen in light of the long delay in the incorporation period in Argentina. Following the conservative reaction of the late 1910s and early 1920s that helped to derail Yrigoyen's tentative overtures to the workers, more than two decades passed before government leaders again made a broad effort to win the support of the labor movement. By the early 1940s, industrial expansion had greatly increased union membership, labor leaders had abandoned most of their earlier reluctance to participate in politics, and the unions, following the founding of the CGT in 1930, had acquired an unprecedented capacity for collective action. Labor's new orientations and resources, the Communist Party's successful union organizing during the 1930s, and the still embryonic character of union-state and union-party ties made workers and unions attractive allies for Perón—whose project of labor mobilization brought together his search for popular support, his concern with controlling the left and regulating class conflict, and a larger vision of industrial growth and economic expansion. Given labor's substantial strength and Perón's urgent need for popular support, Perón had to make real concessions to achieve this support. These concessions posed a major threat to the elite. At the same time, labor's long travail under antiworker governments, Perón's prolabor policies, and the sudden change in the working class's economic and social position left a powerful impression, which Peronism used to build intense loyalty to the movement and to Perón himself.

Two alternative visions of Argentina's history emerged out of this experience. For the elite, the Argentina of the pre-1930s appeared to be a golden age in which the oligarchy ruled over a hierarchical and harmonious society. To the working class, this era was one of repression, hunger, and low social status, all conditions that changed drastically during their golden age, the postwar years of rapid expansion of the labor movement, growing real wages, and rapidly increasing employment. With the fall of Perón, these contrasting visions created two distinct political subcultures (Cavarozzi et al., 1985:16–23). The problem was not simply one of two rival parties. Rather, "there were 'two countries': one whose inhabitants could only conceive of Argentina with Perón, and another that could only accept Argentina without Perón and, in terms of power, without Peronismo" (Floria, cited in O'Donnell 1973:129).

Perón's overthrow in 1955 eroded the internal cohesion of his movement, but it did not diminish the antagonism between his followers and opponents. The struggle between Peronists and anti-Peronists, despite complexities introduced by divisions within each group, was the central tension in Argentine politics from 1955 until at least 1970, when the axis of political conflict to some extent shifted to a left-right ideological spectrum. The depth of the antagonism between Peronism and anti-Peronism was due partly to the superimposition of this conflict on a major class cleavage in Argentine society. However, it also resulted from the long-delayed, highly mobilizational, and strongly confrontational mode of labor incorporation. This pattern of incorporation fostered strong opposition among urban elites. Furthermore, because it was not accompanied by fundamental changes in the rural sector that would permanently undermine the power of the rural elites, these rural elites remained as another major pole of opposition to Peronism. The result was a style of incorporation that generated very strong supporters *and* opponents.

Part IV

LEGACY

6

Aftermath: Reaction to Incorporation and Postincorporation Dynamics

IN ALL EIGHT COUNTRIES, the incorporation periods produced strong political reactions, and in most cases the regimes under which incorporation had been inaugurated eventually broke down in the face of rising opposition. This chapter analyzes the aftermath of incorporation, focusing on this regime change and the reshaping of state-union-party relations that accompanied and followed it.

The two broad types of incorporation periods—state and party incorporation—triggered distinct political reactions. In Brazil and Chile, state incorporation had been antidemocratic and antimobilizational. It had been carried out under authoritarian regimes, and this authoritarianism generated substantial opposition that culminated in the restoration of competitive, electoral regimes. Under these new regimes, the question of the political role of the working class, postponed rather than answered in the incorporation period, had to be addressed anew. The repoliticization of the working class, and of the parties and other channels through which labor would participate in the new competitive regime, emerged as major political issues.

The countries that experienced party incorporation followed a contrasting pattern. Party incorporation had been reformist and mobilizational and had occurred under regimes that were in most cases more democratic.[1] The opposition movements that emerged were conservative and oriented toward political demobilization. In Argentina, Peru, and Venezuela, the incorporation period was brought to an end by a military coup that ousted the reformist governments and inaugurated a period of counterreformist military rule. In Uruguay and Colombia, the incorporation period ended with a relatively mild conservative reaction under the existing civilian regime, followed later by a coup that pushed the conservative reaction even further. In Mexico alone the incorporating party managed to stay in power, and under its own leadership the reformism of the incorporation period was brought to a halt.

In sum, except for Mexico, the aftermath of party incorporation can be traced out in two steps: (1) a conservative reaction in which the party or leadership that led the incorporation period fell from power and (2) an initial

---

[1] As we saw in Chapter 5, in Mexico, Uruguay, and Colombia, the incorporation periods occurred under more-or-less competitive regimes. In Argentina, Venezuela, and Peru, the incorporation periods were initiated under authoritarian regimes or regimes whose electoral credentials were dubious. Yet the leaders of these incorporation projects later consolidated their power in relatively free elections. Among these latter three cases, only in Argentina did the regime subsequently become authoritarian during the incorporation period.

period of a restored, competitive regime, during which a number of measures were initiated to ensure that the polarization of the incorporation period would not recur. Though in Mexico the incorporating party remained in power, that country experienced the same political changes as the other countries in this last period.

The analysis of the aftermath period covers the following years (see Figure 6.1): in Brazil, from the fall of Vargas in 1945 to 1960; in Chile, from the fall of Ibáñez in 1931 to 1952; in Mexico, from 1940 to 1952, a period which saw a self-transformation of the governing party in a conservative direction; in Venezuela, from the 1948 coup, through the restoration of a competitive regime in 1958, to the early 1960s; in Uruguay, from the halt in the reform effort in 1916, through the coup of 1933, through the restoration of a competitive regime in 1942, to the mid-1940s; in Colombia, from the resignation of López in 1945, through the coup of 1953 and the restoration of a semicompetitive, civilian regime in 1958, to roughly 1960; in Peru, from the 1948 coup, through the restoration of a semicompetitive regime in 1956, to roughly 1960; and in Argentina, from the coup of 1955, through the restoration of a semicompetitive regime in 1958, to roughly 1960.

Aftermath of State Incorporation

For the cases of state incorporation, the analysis begins with this restoration of competitive regimes in 1945 in Brazil and 1931 in Chile. In these cases, a crucial item of "unfinished business" from the earlier incorporation period

Figure 6.1 Chronological Overview of Aftermath Periods

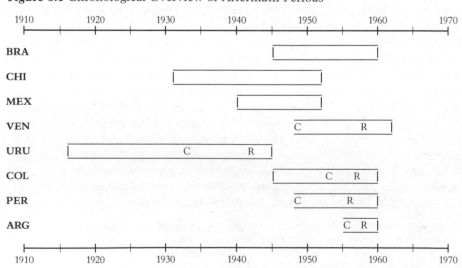

Notes: For countries that had coups after the incorporation period, C = coup, R = restoration of a more competitive regime.

was the *political* role of the working class. The depoliticization of the incorporation periods had provided only a temporary resolution of this issue. From the point of view of the labor movement, the political opening represented a new opportunity for political participation and influence, and in this new context the repoliticization of the working class occurred quickly. As a concomitant of the prior depoliticization of the incorporation period in Brazil and Chile, the incorporation experiences had not left a legacy of deeply ingrained political ties between the union movement and a multiclass party or party bloc that was capable of holding power. Hence, in the aftermath of state incorporation, workers' political affiliations were less well-defined, and in that specific sense the labor movement had a greater degree of political independence. In this context, the repoliticization and radicalization of the working class occurred quickly. In both countries during this period, the Communist Party achieved substantial success in attracting worker support, and a significant challenge to state-controlled unions was mounted, though the pace at which this took place and the degree of success were not as great in Brazil, at least in part because of the reimposition of state controls.

From the point of view of reformist elements within the political elite, one of the problems in the aftermath of state incorporation was the absence of the type of political party—commonly referred to as populist— that had been created or reinforced in many cases of party incorporation; a multiclass party with strong ties to the working class that could potentially be a vehicle to generate support for reform. To address this problem, reformers who had previously been leaders during the earlier periods of state incorporation—that is, Vargas in Brazil and Marmaduque Grove in Chile—now established such parties, which successfully gained influence within the working class. However, unlike most of the parties that had led party incorporation, these postincorporation parties in the cases of state incorporation—specifically the PTB in Brazil and the Socialist Party in Chile—never achieved a majority position. Rather, they became junior partners in political coalitions headed by other, center or center-right parties. Characteristically, during elections these coalitions had a populist character, but once the government was in power the actual practice of policy-making shifted toward the orientation of the accommodationist alliance that had been worked out during the incorporation period. Eventually, these experiments in "populism" failed with the discrediting of the coalitions and the radicalization of the populist parties. Here again, this process went further in Chile.

We define the aftermath period for Brazil and Chile as corresponding to this aborted experiment with coalitional populism, which ended in 1960 in Brazil and in 1952 in Chile. Two features mark this failure. First, the populist party (or important factions within it), and especially its working-class base, was insufficiently rewarded for its electoral support and began to reject the collaborative, coalitional strategy in favor of more radical orientations. Second, the center or center-right party that held the predominant position in these coalition governments could no longer hold on to power. With the collapse of these attempts, a process of polarization, set in motion during the aftermath period, subsequently became a central feature of political life.

Aftermath of Party Incorporation

For the cases of party incorporation, two issues were pivotal in the aftermath period. The first was the conservative reaction, with its counterreformist policies that in most cases included the marginalization or repression of the party and unions that had earlier played a key role in the incorporation period. The second was the terms under which these parties would subsequently be readmitted to the political game—or, in the case of Mexico, would be capable of continuing in power. The conservative reaction to incorporation made clear the limits to reformism and also the inability of the political system to deal with the opposition and polarization engendered by it. This situation gave rise to various attempts to avoid future polarization by constituting a broad centrist coalition that could consolidate civilian rule. Accordingly, party leaders oversaw a number of changes in the parties that had led the incorporation periods. We will focus on three dimensions of party evolution, which occurred to varying degrees among the cases: (1) a programmatic shift toward the center; (2) the expulsion or departure of the left; and (3) the success of the party, despite its conservatization and loss of leftist support, in retaining its mass constituencies, specifically its ties to the working class, and where relevant the peasantry, encompassing both electoral support and party-union organizational ties.

Another aspect of the attempts to ensure that a return to, or consolidation of, civilian rule would not lead to a repetition of polarization was the adoption of conflict-limiting mechanisms. One such mechanism, used by the military in Peru and Argentina, was the ongoing ban on the incorporating party, even after civilian rule was restored. Another, adopted by the political parties in Venezuela and Colombia, was a pact or accord through which they agreed to limit political conflict among themselves. A third, found only in Mexico, where alone the incorporating party remained in power, was the strengthening of a one-party dominant system. These differences among the countries point to another: the role of the party in overseeing the political transitions of the aftermath period. This was weakest in Argentina and Peru, strongest in Mexico, and intermediate in Venezuela, Uruguay, and Colombia.

The different experiences in the aftermath of party incorporation are summarized in Table 6.1. In Mexico and Venezuela, the party that had earlier led the incorporation period maintained at least a relatively dominant position in this transition. These parties gave up important parts of their earlier reform programs in exchange for retention of, or renewed access to, power, and they successfully used state resources to retain much of their mass worker and peasant base. A contrasting pattern is found in Peru and Argentina, where the incorporating party played a far more subordinate role in the transition, in the context of some form of ongoing ban of this party. Uruguay and

Colombia are in a sense intermediate cases, with the party that led the incorporation period playing a more nearly "coequal" role in the transition with the other traditional party in these two-party systems (or, in the case of Uruguay, a faction of that party).

An Antiunion Variant of Populism

In introducing the cases of party incorporation, we wish to call attention to an additional theme that emerged in the aftermath period. We have noted that the military presidents who led this period of conservative reaction in part carried out a "negative" political project, attempting to undo the reforms, popular mobilization, and populist coalition that derived from the incorporation period. In addition, in the late 1940s and early 1950s Rojas in Colombia, Pérez-Jiménez in Venezuela, and Odría in Peru had a "positive" political project, through which they sought to build their own base of working-class support.[2]

The nature of these three projects merits particular attention here because they were shaped by an important international conjuncture in a way that represents an interesting cross-fertilization between the incorporation period in Argentina and the aftermath period in the other three countries. In the 1940s and early 1950s, Peronism posed a dramatic model of the methods that could be used by a military leader to generate working-class support, and Peronism's salience for Pérez-Jiménez, Rojas Pinilla, and Odría was reinforced to some degree by Perón's deliberate efforts to export the model. However, what was absolutely essential to the original was missing in the copies: the underlying political logic and the method of achieving power in the first place.

Perón had come to power in Argentina on the basis of the vigorous mobilization of working-class and trade-union support in exchange for major policy concessions. By contrast, the military-leaders-turned-president who imitated Perón had come to power on the basis of precisely the opposite relationship to the popular sector: the demobilization of the organized working class and the systematic destruction of its trade-union organizations. Thus, within the framework of our larger study, Peronism enjoyed the historical advantage of constituting the initial incorporation period in Argentina. By contrast, these imitators adopted elements of Peronism in the context of the conservative reaction to incorporation, and by and large they failed. However, some variation appears among the three cases in the success of these efforts, with Odría in Peru being somewhat more successful.

[2] An even briefer experiment along these lines was undertaken in Chile by Carlos Ibáñez when he returned to power in 1952 (see Chapter 7).

TABLE 6.1
Aftermath of Party Incorporation: Transformation of Party that Led Incorporation Period

	Mexico	Venezuela	Uruguay	Colombia	Peru	Argentina
Party that led incorporation period	PRM/PRI	AD	Colorados	Liberals	APRA	Peronist
1. Role of party in transition to new regime	Dominant	Strong	Substantial[a]	Coequal[b]	Subordinate	None
2. Pact, accord, or other conflict-limiting mechanisms	Strengthening of one-party dominant system	Punto Fijo and other pacts	Effort to prevent loss of Colorado support to the left	Pact of Sitges and National Front, 1957–58	Partial electoral exclusion of APRA, Pact of Monterrico, and *convivencia*, 1956	Electoral exclusion of Peronism, aborted pact with Frondizi, 1957–58
3. Programmatic shift toward the center	Yes	Yes	No[c]	Yes	Yes[d]	Some[e]
4. Expulsion or departure of left	Yes	Yes	No	Yes	Yes[f]	No
5a. Retention of workers' electoral support	Yes	Yes	Substantial	Yes[g]	Yes[h]	Yes
5b. Retention of union-party link	Yes	Yes	No[i]	Greatly weakened	Yes[j]	Yes[k]
6. Retention of electoral support of peasants and links to peasant organizations	Yes	Yes	No[l]	Defections in some areas[o]	Minimal[m]	No[n]

[a] In collaboration with President Baldomir and the Independent Nationalists.

[b] In collaboration with Conservatives.

[c] Reform renewed in 1940s and 1950s.

[d] Move to center-right.

[e] Fact of being out of power reduced pressure for programmatic homogenization of Peronism and helps explain its relative heterogeneity.

[f] Occurred after failure of APRA insurrection in 1948, then subsequently in 1959.

[g] Transferred to National Front.

[h] With some erosion in the 1960s.

[i] Never existed.

[j] But with significant challenges beginning in the 1960s.

[k] Within framework of poorly institutionalized party. The main organizational locus of Peronism was the CGT.

[l] Rural workers voted mainly for Blancos.

[m] Mainly in vicinity of modern enclaves.

[n] Absence of large peasant sector. Perón had support of rural workers.

[o] Vote largely transferred to National Front.

BRAZIL AND CHILE: ABORTED POPULISM

Introduction

The immediate aftermath of incorporation in Brazil and Chile saw a dramatic change as the authoritarian regime gave way to a period of political opening, with the introduction of both competitive elections and greater trade-union freedom. The authoritarianism of the incorporating regime generated substantial opposition, which finally came to a head amid two different international developments. In Brazil, this was the worldwide onset of a "democratic" period, ushered in by the victory of the Western democracies and the defeat of fascism in World War II. In Chile, the change of government followed the onset of the Great Depression, which perhaps hit Chile harder than any other Latin American country and in the face of which existing regimes were discredited and dramatic regime changes occurred throughout the continent. Under this impetus, a decisive political change was brought about as both Vargas and Ibáñez were forced from power in 1945 and 1931 respectively, and competitive regimes were introduced.

In both Brazil and Chile, the political opening brought to the fore a major issue: the political reactivation of the working class and the question of its political role and participation, which had not been addressed earlier, given the goal of depoliticizing labor during the incorporation period. From the point of view of labor, the reactivation of the working class took place in a context defined by three features of state incorporation: (1) a very constraining, highly corporative, and, as A. Valenzuela (1978:32) said of Chile, an "anti-labor Labor Code"; (2) an official union movement set up and controlled by the government; and (3) the depoliticization of the working class owing to the repression of political parties that articulated working-class demands and to the absence of mobilization of labor support. These features defined the agenda of the working class in the postincorporation period: the attempt to alter the legal constraints under which the union movement operated, the attempt to replace official, state-controlled unionism with independent unions under democratically elected leadership, and the opportunity to repoliticize the labor movement and redefine its political role.

With the political opening and the change to a democratic project, working-class repoliticization occurred rapidly. This was seen first in the substantial electoral success of parties appealing to the working class. In both countries the Communist parties and newly formed populist parties (the PTB in Brazil and the Socialist Party in Chile) stepped into the political void left by state incorporation and made impressive electoral gains.

With the introduction of greater syndical freedom, these parties likewise rapidly gained positions of influence within the unions and among union leadership. Thus, with the liberalization of union elections official unionism began to break down. Because unions were not tied to a major populist party that held power over substantial periods, as had occurred in some cases of party incorporation, the labor movement retained a type of political independence which facilitated this process of change, compared to, for instance, that of Mexico and Venezuela. Though in both Brazil and Chile the challenge to official unionism was substantial and fast in coming, the countries differed with respect to the degree to which democratic unionism emerged. In Brazil, in the context of both greater continuity in the transition from the authoritarian period to a competitive regime and a stronger state role in suppressing labor reactivation, the breakdown of official unionism occurred only gradually and partially in the subsequent years, whereas in Chile the replacement of official unionism with democratic unionism occurred quickly and pervasively.

Finally, despite the repoliticization and reactivation of both labor movements in this period, neither had much success in changing the labor laws and hence the structuring of and constraints on the union movements and the industrial relations systems in their respective countries. As we shall see, this failure corresponds to labor's more general lack of success in this period in satisfying its demands in the political arena through participation in centrist coalitions pursuing moderate programs.

The repoliticization of the working class was of interest not only to the working class itself. From a comparative perspective this repoliticization represented "unfinished business" from the point of view of the middle sector reformers, since state incorporation, with its emphasis on political demobilization, had failed to address the issue of the political mobilization or participation of the popular sectors. The failure to establish a successful incorporating party meant that there was no official or acceptable channel for working-class electoral mobilization. Thus, the aftermath of incorporation was characterized by a "belated" attempt to establish populist parties to structure working-class participation. These were moderate, multiclass parties that would make a special appeal to the popular sectors, particularly the urban working class, since a basic tenet of the accommodationist modus vivendi was the exemption of the countryside from any mobilization.

Interestingly, this attempt was made by the original leaders of the middle sector reformers. In the case of Brazil, it was undertaken by Vargas himself in the last years of his presidency, when he anticipated the change to electoral politics and set up two parties as his vehicles for making the transition. The first was the PSD, the Social Democratic Party, based, not surprisingly, on the coalition he had put together and the sectors that had benefited under his presidency: bureaucrats and the political machines of the Estado Novo, as well as industrialists, bankers, and landowners. The second was the PTB, the Brazilian Labor Party, founded as the vehicle for labor representation. In Chile, Ibáñez's CRAC had been a failure. It was in existence for a mere year and a half before Ibáñez was forced from the presidency, and he never developed or used it as an important political instrument. In 1930, when Ibáñez formed a National Congress, the seats that were distributed by agreements made among the heads of the various political parties, the CRAC was allo-

cated only a very few positions.[3] Always weak, the CRAC did not survive
Ibáñez's presidency. In the aftermath period, the initiative to form new populist alliances combining reformist middle sector leadership with working-
class support was then left to the original middle-class reformers, including
Ibáñez's initial coconspirators. It first took the form of the Socialist Republic
of Marmaduque Grove, which lasted for twelve days. Upon its failure the populist thrust was then rechanneled into the formation of the Chilean Socialist
Party, which grew primarily out of the military, out of Alessandri's reformist
movement, and out of the ill-fated Socialist Republic of Grove, who himself
became the standard bearer of the new party (see Drake 1978:139).

In neither country were the middle sectors united around the new populist
party. Rather, they were also—even primarily—associated with other centrist or center-right parties that did not have a large working-class base of
support. In Brazil, these middle sector groups were attracted to both the PSD
and the liberal, anti-Vargas UDN, whereas in Chile they primarily supported
the Radical Party. Thus, the political center was not committed to a populist
alliance, but was pulled in two directions, toward both the right and the left.

The change from an authoritarian to an electoral regime, then, produced a
kind of competition between two alternative lines of political cleavage or
two alternative sets of political alliances. One was the accommodationist
alliance, inherited from the previous period, an alliance that united the dominant classes in opposition to the lower classes—or more precisely to the
urban lower classes, since the rural lower classes were to a significant degree
absorbed in a clientelistic relationship with the landed elite, a relationship
that was translated into political and electoral support. The alternative pattern of alliance and cleavage was more sectorally based. It consisted of the
populist alliance of the newer middle sectors and the urban working class
versus the traditional, oligarchic elite and its rural support base.[4] The middle
sectors, while not establishing a hegemonic position in this period, did
emerge in a pivotal position from which they could move in either direction,
toward either of these two alliances. The centrist middle sectors were thus
split between these two possibilities, and their leadership vacillated between
them.

Both alliances held out certain advantages to the middle sectors and their
political leadership. The preservation of the accommodationist alliance was
made attractive by the ongoing economic and political power of the oligarchy. The oligarchy's electoral strength and hence its strength in the national
Congress despite its loss of the presidency, its credible potential threat of
calling in the military,[5] and the dependence of the national economy on ex-

[3] Urzua (1979:37) gives the figure of 14 seats; Barría (1972:63) puts it at 19.

[4] This is, of course, the same pair of coalitional alternatives discussed in Chapter 4.

[5] The threat of military intervention, quite explicit and even activated during the 1946
Republic in Brazil, is less recognized by analysts in the case of Chile. Though it never
surfaced to the same degree in Chile, it was nevertheless an option held in the background
and presenting a credible threat. A strong and sustained anti-Communist or anti-Marxist
tendency existed within the military, which generally came to be sympathetic to fascism.

port earnings meant that the right could be isolated and thwarted only at great peril. The populist alliance also had certain advantages. Given the electoral strength and political power of the right, the populist alliance was the strongest basis from which the middle sectors could oppose the right and its orientation toward liberal, laissez-faire economic policies and build a constituency for a more nationalistic, protectionist economic policy that would assign to the state a significant role in promoting industrialization.

This question of the laissez-faire state versus greater state intervention in economic policy and more generally the question of the balance among the sectors of the dominant classes had in a sense been put on the back burner with the imposition of authoritarian rule during the incorporation period. In fact, the substantial reforms and redefinition of the state that had been carried out under the authoritarian regime were not to be reversed. These innovations had not only responded to the needs and demands of a growing constituency, but in turn had also created or accelerated the growth of such a constituency with the increase in the number of state employees and the development of industry dependent on an active state role in economic policy. Furthermore, the traditional elite, whose basic political and economic interests had been protected, had learned that they could accommodate themselves to the new state role. As a result of the creation of this modus vivendi worked out among sectors of the dominant classes, which safeguarded the interests of the traditional elite at the same time that it accomplished the reform of the state, the return to electoral politics was not a return to the status quo ante. Nevertheless, the basic issue of the orientation of economic policy remained a highly politicized question,[6] and the return to power of the traditional elite was a very real possibility, which Vargas sought to prevent precisely by mobilizing an urban working-class support base and engineering voting legislation to this end (French 1989:7). Given the ongoing strength of the traditional elite, which had been safeguarded in the previous period, laissez-faire interests were now, in an electoral period, in a position to exert greater pressure. These interests were in fact very influential in the subsequent governments in both countries and were a major factor in pulling the center to the right.

The postincorporation period, then, was one of tension or competition between two alternative alliance patterns and ultimately the defeat of one of them—the populist alliance. Despite the formation of populist parties, the PTB in Brazil and the Socialist Party in Chile, the ongoing power and influence of the right assured the dominance of the accommodationist alliance.

With the victory of the Popular Front of 1938, there was speculation about military intervention, and though it never occurred, unsuccessful plots throughout the aftermath period did. Some of these plots involved groups with ties to Ibáñez, who himself had ties to some of them (Nunn 1975:273–75; Joxe 1970:78–81; González Videla 1975: 223–25, 1015, 1021–30, 1044; Loveman 1979:275–76, 328, 344; Barría 1971:36, 39).

[6] In analyzing the politics of 1945, Vianna (1976:252) has emphasized the importance of the "national" question and the opposition of commercial, financial, and agricultural export sectors to the national industrial orientation of Vargas.

The period was characterized by the electoral predominance of the PSD in Brazil and the Radical Party in Chile. Yet both these parties were interested in attracting working-class electoral support and hence became attracted to the possibility of an electoral alliance with the new populist parties. Hence, the aftermath of state incorporation was characterized by experimentation with such alliances between the center and a repoliticized labor movement and working class attracted to both the Communist parties and the new populist parties.

The experiment with these alliances began cautiously following the transition from the authoritarian regimes to more open, competitive regimes. These transitions were problematic and uncertain in both countries. Nevertheless, Brazil underwent this transition with somewhat greater continuity, whereas Chile experienced greater discontinuity and a more difficult transition period before institutionalized patterns of civilian government were established. Vargas had been able to anticipate the kinds of changes demanded by the opposition. During the last years of his government, 1943–45, he moved to redemocratize the country, announced elections, and sponsored two political parties, the PSD and the PTB, which together embraced the forces that supported him and which became two of the most important actors on the political scene during the 18-year life of the republic established in 1946. Though in 1945 Vargas himself was forced from power, the transition to more open, competitive politics took place within the framework he had established and power passed formally to the two parties associated with him. As one of the political actors observing the transition noted, the coup that ousted Vargas was "*sui generis* because power was not handed over either to the military or to the opposition" (quoted in Nunes and Geddes 1987:108). Rather, this military intervention oversaw the reinstallation of the Vargas machine, this time in a democratic guise.

Despite the changes that did occur in the Brazilian transition—the forced resignation of Vargas and the atmosphere of crisis surrounding the succession—the transition in Chile was even more abrupt. Ibáñez too was forced to resign the presidency amid widespread agitation and demonstrations calling for his resignation and the withdrawal of military support for him. Unlike Vargas, he had done little to anticipate the end of authoritarian rule and to set up structures or vehicles for the transition to competitive politics. The established parties, which Ibáñez controlled and manipulated during his presidency, asserted their independence when his power was in decline, and his CRAC, "the closest thing to an Ibañista party," remained small and weak and collapsed with his fall from power (Nunn 1970:156). Without party continuity, the transition period in Chile was more complex and prolonged.

Following the transitional governments that replaced Vargas in 1945 and Ibáñez in 1931 and oversaw competitive elections, conservative governments representing the accommodationist alliance came to power in both countries. In Brazil, this was the government of Dutra, the PSD candidate, who represented the accommodationist coalition put together by Vargas: the local political bosses from the Old Republic, bureaucrats, landowners, bankers, and industrialists who favored the new, activist state (Roett 1978:74). In Chile, the 1931 elections produced a victory for Montero, Ibáñez's minister of interior, who was supported by all the major center and right parties, Radical and Democratic as well as Liberal and Conservative (Pike 1963:209). Thus, though no single party in Chile reflected the accommodationist alliance as the PSD did in Brazil, the accommodationist alliance nevertheless survived the return to competitive party politics with the decision of the traditional Liberal and Conservative parties to support a bland and nonthreatening Radical candidate.

The transition in Chile, however, was not so simple. In the face of the economic crisis produced by the world depression following the 1929 crash and Montero's inability to develop an effective program, there was a very brief hiatus in the ascendancy of the accommodationist alliance. With the growth of widespread opposition to Montero's ineffectiveness and rightward drift, conspiracies against his government were formed, and in June 1932, a military coup led by Marmaduque Grove overthrew Montero and established a junta that declared the "Socialist Republic." The Socialist Republic was populist in orientation, "a moderate, rather middle-class breed of socialism, more radical in appearance than actuality" (Drake 1978:76). Nevertheless, it threatened the upper class and after just 12 days was overthrown. The brief Socialist Republic was an important event in the development of Chilean populism. To build popular support, progovernment committees were formed at the local level and extensive mobilization, particularly of the working class, was undertaken (S. Valenzuela 1979:569). It was out of the coalescence of these groups that Grove formed the Socialist Party, a moderate rather than Marxist party, which, Drake (1978:11, 13–14, 74–80, 93–95) convincingly argues, was best characterized as populist.

The government that succeeded the Socialist Republic was headed by Dávila, the most moderate member of the original three-man junta, who "tried to revive Ibáñez's model of development" (Drake 1978:71, 82) and presumably the accommodationist alliance upon which it was based. Military government, however, had been discredited and the transition to a democratic regime was still on the agenda. Both Dávila and his military successor were turned out of the presidency, and new elections were held on 30 October 1932 to return the country to civilian rule. These elections brought back to power Alessandri, whose political base was located in the centrist Radical and Democratic parties (Drake 1978:92).

Both the Dutra and Alessandri governments were conservative ones that preserved the accommodationist alliance, rejecting the possibility of putting together a populist coalition. The exclusion of a populist base of support in the working class soon became clear even though in Brazil the PTB endorsed Dutra and may have been decisive in his victory (Harding 1973:177), and in Chile, Alessandri, known as the "Lion of Tarapacá" in 1920 for being the first presidential candidate in Chile to make an electoral appeal to the working class, claimed that he was "the same as in 1920" (cited in Drake 1978:91) and tried to repeat his earlier working-class appeal. The strength of the accommodationist alliance, however, precluded the emergence of the populist alliance that seemed to be inherent in these facts. In the event, the conservative orientation of both governments soon provoked widespread opposition from the working class.

Following these conservative governments, governments that appeared to be more reformist came to power: the second government of Vargas, who ran as a PTB candidate in 1950, and the Popular Front government of Aguirre Cerda of 1938. These governments were based more explicitly on the populist parties (and, in the case of Chile, the Communist Party as well). However, given the ongoing strength of the oligarchy, including its strength in Parliament, once these governments were in office the centrist parties were at least as oriented toward an accommodationist coalition as toward a coalition with the populists. Therefore, the populist party remained a very junior partner in the coalition. In subsequent governments the position of the populist parties was even weaker. As a consequence, they failed to extract enough for their collaboration to satisfy the working class, and during this period (the 1950s in Brazil and the 1940s in Chile) an increasingly radicalized, noncollaborationist tendency emerged within the party and the trade-union movement. In each country, this was reinforced by a relatively powerful Communist Party that competed for working-class loyalty and support, though in Brazil it had to do this from an underground position. Disappointed with coalition politics and influenced by the Marxism of the Communist parties, the populist parties developed important left wings. A process of polarization began, and the period ended with the abandonment of the discredited pattern of coalition politics.

It is thus useful to analyze developments in Brazil and Chile in terms of three phases experienced by both countries. These phases are presented in Table 6.2. Too much should not be made of the unfolding of these three stages, as they seem primarily to be conjunctural coincidences rather than systematic consequences of the model of incorporation. Nevertheless, we will use them to guide the following analysis.

What does seem to be a systematic outcome of incorporation, however, can be described in terms of two dynamics that occurred over the course of these three stages. The first is the political reactivation of the working class. The political opening led to the politicization of the labor movement as both

TABLE 6.2
Phases of the Aftermath in Brazil and Chile

	Brazil	Chile
Conservative governments	Dutra (1946–51)	Alessandri (1932–38)
Populist attempts	Vargas (1951–54)	Aguirre Cerda (1938–41)
Coalition governments	Kubitschek (1956–61)	Ríos (1942–46)
		González Videla (1946–52)

Communist parties and new populist parties entered the political void left by state incorporation, attracted electoral support among workers, and achieved substantial influence in the trade unions. The result was a disintegration of official unionism, though this went much further and occurred much more rapidly in Chile. On the other hand, as we shall see, the new democratic union leadership in Chile brought the labor movement into the framework of the labor code and broke the resistance within the labor movement to legalization under the terms of the code.

The second theme is the failure of populism. Populist parties were "belatedly" formed, and they entered populist alliances with center or center-right parties. However, unable to bring about a sufficiently reformist policy orientation, populism became discredited. The alliances began to come apart, and toward the end of these periods the populist parties began to rethink their orientation. In Chile, the discredited Socialist Party began to reorganize as a more clearly Marxist and class-oriented party. In Brazil, where the parties were more heterogeneous and less ideological, the reorientation to a more radical and less collaborationist position was taken by the PTB, particularly its left wing, which was closest to the working class. At the same time, other, more class-conscious groups were forming within the union movement. Thus, with the reactivation of the working class and the collapse of the populist alternative, the stage was set for increasing polarization.

Labor Reactivation under Conservative Governments

In both Brazil and Chile, the transition from the authoritarian period of incorporation to a civilian electoral regime saw a dramatic political reawakening of the working class and rapid growth of influence of both the Communist parties and the newly founded populist parties. In Brazil, this occurred at the end of the Estado Novo, when Vargas oversaw an important political opening and was instrumental in founding the populist PTB. It has been suggested that this opening, in which Vargas sought to mobilize a working-class support base, provoked the military coup that ousted him, and that although it cannot be understood apart from the diffusion of democratic norms and the international politics that attended the end of World War II, this change in regime may have been not only an antifascist, prodemocratic move, but also "an instinctive defensive reaction by the more conservative elements of Brazilian society against . . . the recent transformation of the Estado Novo" (Jaguaribe 1965:171). In Chile, as we have seen, the conservative government elected after the coup against Ibáñez fell in turn to a military coup, and the Socialist Republic was declared. Though the life of the Socialist Republic was counted in days and its orientation was more moderate and populist than radical and Marxist, it had the effect, like the opening overseen by Vargas, of alarming the right. Accordingly, the next governments elected in both countries were conservative, representing a reassertion of the accommodationist coalition in reaction to the uncertainties of the electoral and political opening and the unknown political potential of the working class, which, during the authoritarian period, had seen its functional associations legalized and, especially in Brazil, had seen a great increase in unionization. This was, of course, the perpetuation of the same alliance fashioned earlier during the period of state incorporation, but now the orientation was shifted to the right, as, in a more open political context, laissez-faire interests had more influence.

The Dutra government in Brazil (1946–51) and the Alessandri government in Chile (1932–38), then, were conservative ones that renewed the accommodationist coalition in a new electoral context. In Brazil, this orientation was so strong that in the 1945 election both the PSD and the UDN chose conservative military officers as their candidates, as the "urban middle sectors joined with landholders to form a phalanx against any radical change in the social or economic status quo" (J. Johnson 1958:172). Favoring economic liberalism and orthodox economic policies to combat inflation, Dutra represented the victory of conservative laissez-faire forces. His cabinet represented this conservative orientation and included UDN party members and well-known anticommunists (Skidmore 1967:65, 71).

In Chile, Alessandri ran in 1932 with the official backing of the centrist Radical and Democratic parties, but unofficially many conservatives, especially of the Liberal Party, supported him. He appealed to the right as a "reformist strongman" (Drake 1978:92) who could restore order after the upheavals and the quick succession of unsuccessful governments of 1931–32. He was opposed on the left by both the Socialists and the Communists. Once in power, the conservative nature of the government and the alliance with the right became clear, as he "kept conservative parties in the saddle" (Drake 1978:166) and gave the "best patronage positions to Conservatives and . . . Liberals" (Drake 1978:175). The orientation of the Alessandri government can be seen by the strength of and political offensive taken by the economic elite, whose interest associations became increasingly active and gained important access to the government. The peak associations of agricultural and industrial interests (SNA and SOFOFA) consolidated their efforts by joining in 1933 with the mining association and national Chamber of Commerce to form a single Confederation of Production and Commerce, and during the Alessandri presidency they participated in "a 'parceling out' of government authority relevant to their functional, occupational interests" (Drake 1978:190). Furthermore, under the influence of the economic elite, the "arch-conservative" (Loveman 1979:264) Gustavo Ross was appointed minister of treasury and oversaw an orthodox and conservative approach to national reconstruction of which the lower class bore the brunt.

These, then, were the conservative governments that were in power at the time of the political openings and repoliticization of the working class. As might be expected, they were not friendly to labor, though the degree to which they moved against the labor movement differed, with the Brazilian government reasserting much more of the earlier pattern of control than that in Chile. An important consequence was the emergence of a democratic union movement in Chile and, to a substantial extent, the reconsolidation of an officialist union movement in Brazil.

Brazil. The end of the Estado Novo as a distinct political period of incorporation actually came before the coup that ousted Vargas in October 1945. It began instead in 1943, when Vargas began to anticipate the transition to a more democratic era. In this context, he turned his attention to the development of a new popular political movement, in particular to the attempt to win the support of labor. With this in mind, he offered new benefits to labor in the form of expanded social welfare legislation, and he began developing a new doctrine of *trabalhismo*. Emphasizing a state-labor coalition based on the state-controlled unions and on Vargas's new identification with labor and working-class welfare, *trabalhismo* was used in speeches of Vargas and other government officials as a basis for mobilizing labor support (Skidmore 1967:39–40; Flynn 1978:109–12).

By the end of 1944, he began to make important concessions to the organized working class, a move that altered substantially several of the features of state incorporation that he had introduced in the previous years. First, in a departure from the pattern of union leadership characterized by appointed interventors, Vargas allowed union elections, in which dissidents were permitted to run and were even in some cases victorious. Secondly, in exchange for a commitment of political support, he released Luis Carlos Prestes and other Communist leaders from jail and legalized the Communist Party. Third, he began to tolerate strikes, which, under the labor law, were illegal. In addition, he permitted higher wage increases than were characteristic un der the Estado Novo. Finally, in April 1945, he recruited officials of the Labor Ministry and union bureaucrats to establish the PTB as a vehicle to mobilize labor support. Thus, in exchange for support from labor—and indeed to mobilize that support Vargas permitted substantially more freedom within the union movement. This attempt to mobilize political support, of course, involved the explicit encouragement of the politicization of workers, in contrast to their depoliticization during the Estado Novo.

Vargas was only partially successful in these attempts to mobilize political support. Not only the PTB, but also the Communists, still under the influence of the popular front policy, fell in line behind Vargas, joined the *queremista* movement of support for Vargas and his (never realized) candidacy in 1945, and organized a united labor front, the Workers Unification Movement (MUT), as a political vehicle for worker participation in the movement. They called for an end to strikes and organized mass rallies to support Vargas. In the end, however, as opposition to Vargas grew—and in fact became ever more urgent precisely because of his attempted mobilization of labor support—his backing from labor was insufficient to either prevent or oppose the coup that removed him from office in 1945.

The period of political opening, which Vargas inaugurated toward the end of his government, provided a new context for working-class politics. The next couple of years, particularly 1945–47, were characterized by an upsurge in working-class activation. It was a period of renewed politicization of the workers after the Estado Novo, which had as a goal their depoliticization, and it was a period of ferment and protest in the trade union arena. In both the electoral sphere and in the trade-union movement, the Communist and populist parties, the PCB and the new PTB, scored significant successes.

As soon as some political freedom was restored, the Brazilian Communist Party (PCB) emerged from the period of repression as the strongest Communist party in Latin America (Skidmore 1967:65), with its support base among the working class virtually intact. The December 1945 elections were held as scheduled, and the PCB declined to support Dutra. Fiuza, the PCB candidate, was in many ways not particularly appealing to workers: he was an unknown figure who was a technocratic businessman rather than a party activist. Nevertheless, he won about 10 percent of the vote (Schneider et al. 1965:57), a level of support that was repeated in the congressional elections in which the party elected 14 deputies and a senator (Chilcote 1974:53). Furthermore the party received a plurality of votes in a number of industrial cities and state capitals (French 1989:9; Alexander 1957:121). The year 1945, then, saw a huge increase in party members and supporters (see Chilcote 1974:117; Schneider et al. 1965:48). In the state and supplementary congressional elections of January 1947, it again did well, electing two additional deputies and 46 members in 15 state legislatures. In addition it won a plurality of 18 in the Municipal Assembly of the federal district, and in São Paulo it replaced the UDN as the third largest party (Chilcote 1974:53, 299n).

The PTB also did well in these two sets of elections. In 1945 it won just about the same percent of the congressional vote as the PCB, though it elected more deputies (22). In 1947, the PTB was the only party in addition to the PSP to improve its position significantly (Harding 1973:215). The active role of Vargas undoubtedly contributed to this outcome. Though elected senator as a PSD candidate, Vargas remained the leader of the PTB and devoted considerable energy to building up the PTB and campaigning for its congressional candidates in 1947. It is noteworthy that the PTB had quickly gone into opposition to Dutra under the leadership of Vargas, who by December 1946 had broken openly with the government (Skidmore 1967:65, 67, 74–75).

Though the electoral appeal to the working class of the PTB and the PCB was impressive, the program of these parties was quite moderate. The PTB, of course, was a party sponsored by Vargas, who after initial neutrality, briefly brought the PTB in line to support the PSD's Dutra in the presidential elections. Though the PTB was a populist party representing controlled mobilization of the working class from above, it is important to remember not only its quick change to a stance of opposition, but also the concessions that even this type of mobilization requires. On the eve of the 1947 elections, when Vargas was already beginning to identify his electoral fortunes with the PTB, he began to call for expanded benefits to workers, including an increase in the minimum wage, paid Sundays and holidays, and profit sharing. He even spoke of evolution toward socialism and of a democracy of workers (Harding 1973:213).

Similarly, the PCB was pursuing a moderate program of "peaceful development." Though the party put forth its own candidate rather than supporting Dutra, it adopted a rather moderate, reformist position emphasizing class collaboration, national bourgeois revolution, economic development, and increased productivity. Though many Latin American Communist parties adopted similar programs at this time, in the case of Brazil the PCB was not only following the international communist line but was also acting cautiously because of the fragility of its new legal status, hoping to demonstrate its credentials as a legal party—a consideration that continued to loom large throughout the postincorporation period. Nevertheless, the party quickly became Dutra's "most implacable opposition," criticizing government policy (Skidmore 1967:65–66). The party worked actively to expand its influence both in the electoral sphere and in union organization, where it was confronted with a labor movement increasingly prone to press for its interests. Given its position within unions, the PCB was in a particularly good position to respond to these pressures and assume the leadership of the outbreak of working-class protest that occurred in 1946, though, given the party's moderation, it did so somewhat hesitantly (Harding 1973:182).

Despite the moderate stance of the PCB and the PTB, then, a dramatic change was taking place. The new electoral law led to a sudden expansion of the electorate and the new provisions for voter registration were specifically designed by Vargas to favor the working class he had been courting. Thus, in 1945, the PCB and the PTB, those parties explicitly appealing to workers and workers' issues, won about 20 percent of the vote for the federal House. The dramatic and sudden success of these class-oriented parties can be seen in the electoral results in the major urban centers where together the two parties received an absolute majority of the total vote, winning nearly three-quarters in the industrial region of São Paulo (French 1989:7, 9). Two years later, in 1947, their influence was still growing.

In the trade-union arena, as well as the electoral arena, the post-1943 period was characterized by democratization, reawakening, and reactivation. With the introduction of greater trade-union freedom, the PCB and the PTB came to assume the leadership of many unions. In the new climate, the nature of state structuring of the labor movement was once again on the agenda of both union groups and state actors. Interestingly, the first attempt to change the corporative Estado Novo labor law was initiated not by unionists but by the government with the purpose of increasing the controls over the new labor movement and restricting PCB influence and worker activism. In reaction to the growing politicization of workers and independent unionism, José Linhares, the interim president appointed by the military following the coup against Vargas, introduced a new law providing for plural unionism. The Estado Novo labor code, which effectively called for compulsory, monopolistic, singular unions, had allowed the government, especially under an authoritarian regime in which interventors were installed in positions of union leadership, to establish official, state controlled unions and to remove any influence of dissident factions. However, under the changed conditions of the political opening when PCB and PTB supporters assumed the leadership of many unions, these features of the Estado Novo labor law became organizational advantages to the PCB and the PTB. In fact, in 1945 the PCB explicitly decided to try to gain influence within the official unions rather than establish parallel unions precisely because of these and other advantages bestowed on official unions (Alexander 1957:119). The Linhares move toward plural unionism, then, was an attempt to provide a new structure through which the government could deny the PCB and the PTB the advantages of monopoly and other organizational benefits and instead encourage the formation of unions free of PCB and PTB influence. The strength of opposition to this change, however, forced Dutra to repeal the law.

The issue of the legal framework of the labor movement again arose at the Constituent Assembly of 1946. Analyzing the debates at the Assembly, Vianna (1976:250ff) concludes that the PCB and the PTB opposed the corporatist legislation of the Vargas era as well as the pluralist position, which was again raised. Instead, these parties favored a legal framework that would promote a unitary and autonomous labor movement. Together, however, the PTB and the PCB represented only 19 percent of the votes in the Assembly and could not prevail against those favoring the status quo. As a result, the corporatist framework embodied in the Estado Novo labor legislation was readopted and continued in effect throughout the period to 1964 (and indeed throughout the following two decades of military rule). It was this context, then, that dominated state-labor relations during the Dutra government.

Throughout 1946, though the PCB was still taking a reformist line, it clearly provided an alternative to the left of *trabalhismo* (French 1989:13), and it actively opposed the conservative position of the Dutra government, advocating a more reformist program. At the same time, it directed much of its activity and energy to the union movement, where it continued to increase its influence. In addition, the PCB took another offensive in the labor field when the MUT called a labor congress in order to establish a labor central. During this period the PCB was also active in organizing peasants and agricultural workers, and it sponsored the first rural strikes since 1930.

The most important development following the fall of the Estado Novo was the upsurge in working-class militance and the wave of strikes in all the major cities of Brazil in the first months of 1946 (Harding 1973:180). The legal conditions surrounding these strikes seemed uncertain. Vargas had not applied the Estado Novo prohibition on strikes at the end of his government, and it was generally understood that the new constitution to be promulgated later that year would legalize the right to strike (Harding 1973:187). Yet these strikes provoked calls for a harsh response from employers.

The magnitude of this strike wave and what it represented merits emphasis. It was "unequalled in scope and intensity until the early 1960s, in the period of acute confrontation under Quadros and Goulart. . . . [The strikes call into question] interpretations of the Brazilian working class which ascribe to it a lack of capacity for organizing and expressing demands, interpretations usually associated with the idea of the relative 'backwardness' of Brazilian workers or their malleability resulting from rural, and later urban, patronage, both social and political" (Flynn 1978:137–38).

Analyzing the São Paulo working class, French (1989:5; 1985:565–66) also emphasizes the degree to which this "dramatic entry" of the working class constituted a "radical break" with the pattern of paternalistic/authoritarian control of the past. Like Flynn (see 1978:182, n. 9), he rejects the accepted line of analysis that emphasizes the passivity of the Brazilian working class and the ongoing manipulation and control of the labor movement from above based on (1) material benefits that may have been forthcoming under the "advanced labor legislation" of the Estado Novo; (2) a patronage network through which the Labor Ministry could entrench its control down to the union level through the PTB, assisted by the distribution of social welfare benefits; and/or (3) populist rhetoric and demagoguery. Instead, French emphasizes the importance of a new working-class consciousness that emerged in the political opening of 1945, the appearance of a new activist union leadership that came under PCB influence and that was responsive to the rank and file and opposed to government regulation and control, and pressures on the PTB to move to the left and to a more proworker position, especially given the competition from the PCB, which functioned as a more effective force on the left articulating working-class interests and mobilizing working-class support. The strikes represented a new level of working-class consciousness which, "to achieve their goals, both Getúlio Vargas and Luis Carlos Prestes would have to come to terms with . . . [and] which they had not created and did not control. . . . [Workers] were already demonstrating that they were far from being automatic followers simply manipulated from above" (French 1989:6–12).

The Dutra government responded to each of these offensives. To maintain or reestablish its control over the unions, which was slipping as communist influence increased, the government often intervened in union elections in order to install a loyal leadership faction. Further, in July 1946, a number of changes were made in the procedures for union elections. At the same time that the secret ballot was introduced, other changes were made which, Harding (1973:196–97) argues, "under the guise of increasing union democracy . . . actually increased . . . the control [of the ministry]." The government also hardened its position on strikes, often repressing them with the use of force. In addition, with the new constitution still pending, a new law allowed strikes in principle, but effectively outlawed them, as they were permitted only in "non-fundamental" or "accessory" activities, and then, only if the employer failed to implement a collective agreement, arrived at by compulsory and binding arbitration if necessary (Harding 1973:187–89). Finally, the government revived a number of Estado Novo provisions in order to increase its control over the union movement: a law limiting the right of association, which it used to ban the MUT; a national security law, which it used to repress labor activities and intervene in unions; and the ideological oath, which after a year of nonenforcement was once again used to eliminate radicals from labor union leadership (Harding 1973:194–95).

In response to the MUT call for a labor congress, the Labor Ministry issued its own call for a congress, which it hoped to control. However, the MUT, illegal but still functioning, decided to cooperate with the Ministry, and the resulting congress of September 1946 was deeply split. When the progovernment delegates walked out, reconvened, and called on the Ministry of Labor to dissolve the congress, the remaining PCB and PTB delegates (the PTB having moved into a position of greater opposition to the government because of its repressive policies toward labor) managed to establish the Workers Confederation of Brazil (CTB). The government wasted no time in declaring the CTB illegal and deposed the leadership of unions that joined.

In the last months of 1946, the PCB continued to increase its influence in the union movement. More experienced than the PTB in organizing and mobilizing workers, it became the principal force within labor in a number of cities and organized city-wide labor federations, though these were not allowed by the labor code (Harding 1973:210–12). Finally, after the January 1947 elections and with the onset of the cold war, Dutra moved to suppress the PCB completely. Having already dismissed all Communists from government employment, in May 1947 the government obtained a court ruling that allowed it to move even more directly against the PCB on both party and trade-union fronts. It banned the party; suppressed the still functioning confederation, the CTB, the peasant leagues, and the municipal inter-union federations; expelled the party's congressional representatives; intervened in 143 of 944 labor unions; and indefinitely postponed all union elections (Chilcote 1974:53–54; Harding 1973:223–24). In 1950, 234 unions remained under the direct control of the Ministry of Labor (Humphrey 1982:18).

With the political opening that followed the authoritarian Estado Novo, then, important changes took place in both the party/electoral and the trade-union arenas. Whereas the Estado Novo had aimed to depoliticize workers, Communist and populist parties now had substantial success in mobilizing worker support. Furthermore, whereas the Estado Novo had installed an official, compliant, heavily constrained union movement deprived of the right to strike, in the new context union elections were allowed, a democratic, dissident leadership began to emerge, and some strikes were tolerated. This opening, however, did not last long, and after a brief interlude, the Dutra government set about reviving officialist union leadership, or *peleguismo* (J. Rodrigues 1968:131), and reimposing much of the control that had characterized the Estado Novo. This reimposition of control was not total, however, and would once again be eroded in the more open political context.

Chile.   A similar pattern occurred in Chile, though with a major difference. In Chile too the overthrow of authoritarian rule and the political opening that followed produced a dramatic reawakening and repoliticization of the labor movement in which both Communist and populist parties made impressive gains. And in Chile too the democratically elected government that came to power after the transitional period moved against the renewed labor activism with repressive measures and continued reliance on a highly constraining labor law. However, during this period in Chile, the Communist

Party was allowed to function openly,[7] and the government did not reimpose official unionism. Rather, official unionism quickly passed into history to be replaced by democratic unionism, an issue that was once again on labor's agenda in Brazil.

With the fall of Ibáñez in 1931, the political structures he created disintegrated. His party, the CRAC, did not survive, and the leaders of the official union movement were quick to adopt independent positions, especially in the face of annual union elections. The reestablishment of a competitive regime led to a flurry of political activity on the left, as several fledgling socialist parties were formed and as the Trotkyists split from the Communist Party and tended to make common cause with the new socialists. In the 1931 elections, the socialists backed the candidacy of Alessandri, while the two Communist parties ran their own candidates, but made a poor showing (1.2 percent combined—Drake 1978:68). In the 1932 elections, the official Communist Party repeated that level of support, but Marmaduque Grove, the head of the Socialist Republic who ran as a presidential candidate from exile, attracted 17.7 percent of the vote, the second highest after Alessandri, who won with 54.7 percent.

In 1932, then, parties appealing to the working class, and particularly the Socialist Party, then in gestation and to be founded the following year, contributed a new element to Chilean electoral politics. Drake (1978:see esp. 2–13, 93–97, 108, 139–64) has convincingly argued that during this early phase of its development, a period that corresponds to what we have called the aftermath of incorporation, the Socialist Party is best understood as a populist party, being characterized by personalism, paternalism, a charismatic leader, a multiclass constituency, a reformist or welfare approach to rapid industrialization, and an ideological eclecticism that emphasizes national and mass rather than international and class orientations. As in Brazil in 1945, populist and Communist parties together attracted about a fifth of the vote, and thus the way was opened for new kinds of participation in the electoral arena.

Even more dramatically than in Brazil, the transition from authoritarian to democratic regimes was accompanied by the redemocratization and repoliticization of unions. The Ibáñez government had eliminated the radical labor leadership that was emerging throughout the union movement in the 1920s by means of both repression and the application of the labor law in a way that legalized a collaborationist labor movement based on white-collar workers and about 150 mutual aid societies, the remaining area of moderate labor leadership (S. Valenzuela 1979:566). With the greater union freedom after the fall of Ibáñez, leftists once again began to move into positions of influence and leadership. The process, however, was one of creating a union movement where one had nearly ceased to exist. The onslaught against labor

[7] This difference may be largely due to a difference in timing. At the comparable chronological time of the onset of the cold war, the Chilean Communist Party was outlawed as well.

had been a dual one, entailing both political and economic forces: the repression during the Ibáñez dictatorship and the effects of the world depression, which were particularly severe in Chile, reducing imports in 1932 to 12 percent of the 1929 value and mineral production to less than half and producing massive unemployment (Drake 1978:60–61).

Initially, the Communists rejected legal unionism, viewing the labor laws as instruments of control and repression. Under their leadership the FOCh was reconstituted, but it did not make a successful comeback. Its opposition to legal unionism did not win much support, and the FOCh, which had had 127 councils in 1927, could muster only 25 in August 1931 (S. Valenzuela 1979:567–68). The Communist rejection of the legal route thus initially left the legal unions, the largest component of organized labor, without party ties.

This picture changed, however, during the mobilization of support for the brief Socialist Republic. This experience produced new coalitions and organizations, out of which the Socialist Party emerged the following year and established strong links with the legal unions (S. Valenzuela 1979:568–73). Under these conditions, the remnants of the labor movement began to reorganize. In 1931 the legal unions of Santiago formed a new confederation, which some professional unions joined the following year. This body was important in leading strikes in 1933–34. In 1932 a national confederation was formed, and in 1934 it merged with the Santiago confederation to form the CNS. Identified with the Socialist Party, the CNS embraced "virtually all" the legal unions and thus a majority of the labor movement (Alexander 1977:711–12). Communist influence was clearly of secondary importance. During most of the Alessandri government, then, the strongest and dominant sector of the labor movement was that grouped around Grove and the Socialist Party. The Communists had split, with the Trotskyist (Hidalgo) faction giving "conditional support" to the Socialist Republic, and the Stalinist (Lafertte) line opposing it (Drake 1978:80). Many anarcho-syndicalist unions and even some former Communist-controlled unions aligned with the Socialist Party (Drake 1978:134). Thus, in short order after the downfall of Ibáñez, unions had reestablished their links to political parties, though the previously dominant Communist Party was losing the organizational battle to the more populist and personalistic Socialists.

The nature of the politicization of unions changed after 1935 when the Communist Party adopted the popular front policy, allowing it to reenter the union arena as a more serious contender. With the new policy came the acceptance of legal unionism. It also paved the way for the formation of a united labor central. In 1934, the FOCh had rejected unity overtures made by the CNS. After the adoption of the popular front line, the Communist Party began to court Socialist and Radical leaders, and in 1936 the CTCh, the Confederation of Chilean Workers, was formed, uniting the FOCh, the CNS, and the Unión de Empleados, which was affiliated with the Radical Party.[8] The

[8] Some sources also suggest that the anarcho-syndicalist CGT joined the CTCh (S. Valenzuela 1979:573).

CTCh adopted an explicitly political and electoral mission of mobilizing support for the Popular Front. In this context, and with the annual union elections provided for by the labor code, legal unionism in Chile ceased to be official unionism and was instead autonomous from the state and closely tied to the Socialist and Communist parties.

The Alessandri government was harsh and often quite repressive with respect to the labor movement, even though it promoted legal unionism. Through a grant of extraordinary presidential power and the suspension of civil liberties, Alessandri moved against unions (Peppe 1971:57). Many important strikes took place, and the relationship between the government and the labor movement was one of bitter struggle. In 1936 Alessandri tried to break a railroad workers' strike. Though he was unsuccessful, the experience was important in the set of events that led to the unification of leftist parties and unions in the Popular Front and the CTCh, the united labor organization (Alexander 1950:84 and 1977:732).

Although legal unionism grew substantially under Alessandri, he distrusted the CTCh, which, as an openly partisan organization, was active in promoting the Popular Front as an opposition force to the Conservative and Liberal Parties with which Alessandri was allied. A report to the CTCh's 1939 congress characterized Alessandri's attitude toward the legal labor organizations as one of "hostile tolerance." The report noted the barriers to organization, state interference in the activities and leadership selection of unions, the dissolution of unions for political activities, and the failure to lift the Labor Code's restrictions on federations. Furthermore, the application of the code was said to suffer from lack of inspection and employer subterfuge (Alexander 1977:645–46). All in all, however, government policy remained much less hostile to labor than that of the Dutra government in Brazil and did not present a major setback for the independent labor movement in terms of the reimposition of official unionism. Quite the contrary, this was a period of substantial disintegration of official unionism and growth of a politicized labor movement, autonomous from the state but with close ties to political parties, particularly the Socialist Party.

Populism Accommodationist Style

Though the first postincorporation governments were conservative and, to different extents in Brazil and Chile, maintained controls and constraints on the union movement, in both countries an open, competitive political regime was maintained. By the end of the Dutra and Alessandri governments, the working class had made substantial demonstrations of its electoral clout. The logic of a populist electoral coalition became even more compelling. The center or center-right, for its part, did not have the electoral popularity to stand on its own. This was true of both the PSD in Brazil, which during the 1950s could muster only about a third of the seats in the federal Chamber (Roett 1978:68), and the Radical Party in Chile, which in the Chamber elections between 1937 and 1949 won about a fifth of the seats, approaching only a third in the unusually good showing of 1941 (Urzua 1979:75–76).

For their parts, the parties attracting working-class support were also open to a coalition with the dominant PSD and Radical Party, respectively. Given the origins of the populist parties (the PTB and the Socialists), this was no surprise. In Brazil, the PTB had been founded as the institutional expression of a part of the Vargas coalition, which sought to attract working-class support through a populist appeal of *getulismo*. In Chile, the PS was founded as a populist party with middle-class leadership under the magnetic personality of Grove and appealing increasingly to a working-class support base (Drake 1978:139–64).

The Communist parties were also open to an electoral coalition. The 1938 election in Chile occurred shortly after the adoption of the popular front strategy of Comintern, and indeed it was the Chilean Communist Party (PCCh) that took the initiative in forming the coalition. In Brazil, the PCB did not become a formal member of the electoral coalition as did the PCCh in Chile, because it was still illegal, and in any case in 1950 it was under the influence of the "new leftist" line adopted as a result both of cold war antagonisms internationally and repression under Dutra. Nevertheless, the party soon turned to a reformist line of substantial moderation in its program and of collaboration with noncommunists both in the political arena and in the unions (Chilcote 1974:57ff.).

As a result of the political logic that made a populist electoral coalition attractive to parties oriented to both the political center and the working class, the conservative governments in both countries were followed by governments more explicitly oriented to and based on working-class support. Indeed, in formal coalitional terms, they included the populist parties oriented toward the working class. These were the governments of Vargas and Kubitschek in Brazil from 1951 to 1961 and of Aguirre Cerda, Ríos, and González Videla in Chile from 1938 to 1952. The governments that followed the postincorporation conservative governments, then, seemed to represent a replacement of the accommodationist alliance with a populist alliance.

In both countries, the initial experiment with a populist coalition was the most dramatic. In Brazil, this episode corresponded to the second presidency of Vargas. Vargas started preparing his presidential comeback by opposing the conservative and antilabor orientation of Dutra and formally aligning himself more closely with the PTB than the PSD. In 1950 he attempted to forge a populist alliance and ran on the PTB ticket, conducting a rather populist electoral campaign. In addition to the PTB, he was supported by the populist PSP (Social Progressive Party), and, with the Communist Party outlawed, was able to move into the vacuum and secure the support of labor (Harding 1973:235, 237). His victory thus seemed to bring a populist coalition to power. In Chile, this period began in 1938 with the Popular Front government, dominated by the Radical Party but including in the coalition the Communist and Socialist parties.

Though the election of Vargas in 1950 and Aguirre Cerda, the Popular

Front candidate, in 1938 seemed to signal a dramatic change in terms of the success of a reordered coalition, the reality was quite different. Even as an electoral alliance, the populist coalition was compromised by the inclusion of heterogeneous components: in Brazil Vargas received significant support from the PSD and occasionally even from the UDN, even though both parties were formally in the opposition. In fact, in the campaign Vargas had actively courted PSD support. In Chile Aguirre Cerda was supported not only by the Popular Front parties but also by the Ibañistas, the Nazis, and southern landowners. The very personalities of the new presidents also provided a clue to the nature of the government. Vargas was, after all, the founder of the Estado Novo and the person who had initially worked out the accommodationist modus vivendi in Brazil. In Chile, Aguirre Cerda had been recruited from the right wing of the Radical Party and had only reluctantly accepted the strategy of forming a popular front, having initially opposed it (Drake 1978:186). Indeed, the Radicals first explored the possibility of an electoral alliance with the parties of the right and turned to the Popular Front only when it became clear that the right (the Liberals and Conservatives in coalition) felt confident enough to run its own candidate. Both Vargas and the Chilean Radicals were clearly hesitant to initiate a sweeping change in political alliances.

In fact, what was occurring was the establishment of a populist alliance for electoral purposes, but not for governing purposes. The electoral arena contained within it incentives for the formation of a populist alliance, but in the governing arena, the accommodationist alliance, based on the strength and substantial veto power of the right, was not so easily overturned. The difference between the electoral coalition with the working class and the governing coalition with the right in Chile has been noted by Drake (1978:338): "The gap between rhetoric on the hustings and action in office grew as those dominating electoral resources and those dominating other levels of power became separate groups." A similar point may be made for Brazil.

The cabinets named by the two presidents give some indication of the governing alliance being formed or perpetuated, and the strength of the right in Congress gives some indication of the great difficulty in supplanting the accommodationist alliance with an alternative populist alliance. In Brazil in 1950 the victorious PTB was given only one cabinet ministry, as was the populist São Paulo-based PSP, which also supported Vargas. On the other hand, the PSD, which had formally opposed him, was awarded four ministries, and the UDN, which also formally opposed him, was given one, as many as the PTB and PSP, which supported him in the election. In the Federal Chamber, the PSD won 37 percent of the seats and the UDN won 27 percent. Together these parties thus had 64 percent of the seats, compared to 17 percent for the PTB or to 25 percent for the PTB plus the PSP, the populist alliance that supported Vargas's presidency.

In Chile in 1938, the Radicals dominated the cabinet, holding the seven most important ministries. The Socialists were given the three "least important" ministries and the Democratic Party got one, while the Communists, though having initiated the Popular Front, declined to participate in cabinet

positions. Though Liberals and Conservatives were not given any cabinet positions, they did receive some important posts in the government "and some
critical slots even went to holdovers from the Alessandri years" (Drake
1978:210). Furthermore, in Congress these last two parties did quite well.
Together they held 48 percent of the seats in the Chamber compared to 40
percent for the Popular Front parties (20 percent for the Radicals, 13 percent
for the Socialists, 4 percent for the Communists, and 3 percent for the Democratic Party—Urzua 1979:75). Drake (1978:211) sums up the position of the
Socialists and Communists in this way: "Following a slim electoral victory,
the Front entered office with shaky unity and only partial control of the government. . . . Aguirre Cerda was a right-wing Radical. The Marxists were underrepresented in the cabinet. A hostile majority in the Congress, the bureaucracy, and other state institutions was braced against radical change.
Without even considering domestic and foreign elite economic interest
groups or the military, the constraints on Marxist participation and plans
were formidable."

Despite these impediments to a substantially reformist turn, these governments did constitute the first in each country that included parties oriented
to the working class. This first experience with populist politics produced
great uncertainty and fears within the political right, and in both countries
there was talk of military intervention to prevent the assumption of power
of both Vargas and Aguirre Cerda. In the end, of course, such intervention
did not occur, but both governments were characterized by very conflictual
politics. As a result, the premature end of both presidencies, just three years
later, came amid failure, with the deaths of both presidents—the suicide of
one and the other "a broken man" (Loveman 1979:283) with no political options left.

In both countries, then, this period was one of very conflictual politics in
which the president had a difficult time mediating between the polarizing
sides and consequently of finding a firm base of support for policy-formation
and governing. Politics assumed a zero-sum quality, intensified by an alarmist rhetorical attack on the government from the rightist press. Given the
strength of the right and the ever-present threat of its call for military intervention (a coup attempt did in fact take place in Chile), both presidents made
a major attempt to conciliate the right and allay its fears, and both were reluctant or unwilling to rely on working-class support in a way that would
alienate the right. The zero-sum political context left the presidents nowhere
to go, and both presidencies ended in failure.

Brazil.   In Brazil as workers were increasingly disaffected from the Dutra
government, Vargas had seen his opportunity to prepare his reelection by mobilizing a working-class constituency. The contradiction between policies required to appeal for electoral support and the coercive Estado Novo controls
reimposed by Dutra again became evident. After coming to power in 1951,
Vargas quickly moved to follow his campaign promises and establish the
conditions for greater union freedom and autonomy from government control. Most importantly, he reinstituted union elections, which had been in-

definitely postponed under Dutra, and repealed the ideological test, which had effectively excluded Communists from leadership positions within the unions. Though the Communist Party was not legalized, these measures nonetheless allowed Communists (as well as younger PTB leaders and other radicals) to assume leadership posts and substantial influence within the unions. It became particularly important as the new leftist line—which reflected the cold war antagonisms emerging in the late 1940s and which was formally adopted by the PCB in 1950—was gradually abandoned in favor of a program of moderate social reform and short-term goals (Chilcote 1974:58). The Communist Party thus moved away from its policy of opposition to Vargas and noncollaboration with reformist parties and organizations toward a policy in which it began by 1952 to cooperate with unions and to develop an alliance with the PTB (Chilcote 1974:60–61). Weighing heavily in the PCB orientation was, in addition to the twists and turns of policy in international Communism, its continued illegality. This fact made cooperation with the PTB attractive since the PCB could use the PTB as a vehicle for political activity; and the PTB in turn was aided by the greater discipline and organizational capacity of the PCB (Harding 1973:326, 352–53). As a result of these changes, under Vargas a new democratic leadership emerged at the union level, though the bureaucratic, *pelego* leaders still controlled the federations and confederations.[9]

The result of Vargas's concessions toward the labor movement, combined with the erosion of real wages through a mounting inflation, was a new life, radicalization, and militance within the movement. During the second Vargas presidency, strikes and protest accelerated. In 1951 there were 173 strikes, and in 1952 this number rose to 264. In 1953, São Paulo workers staged a general strike, which affected 276 industrial enterprises and constituted "one of the most notable chapters in the economic and political struggle of the contemporary working class movement in Brazil" (Moisés 1978:5). This strike, which affected over 300,000 workers and was maintained for 27 days, resulted in some wage gains and, in addition, in the formation of the PUI, an inter-union organization in the state of São Paulo. While the total number of striking workers in 1953 reached 800,000, the following year, the last of the Vargas presidency, this number was again exceeded, as more than 1.2 million workers went out on strike, including about 1 million in a São Paulo general strike. This strike, the largest yet in Brazilian history, was called by the PUI to protest the high cost of living (Telles 1981:42–59).

Though the concessions granted the labor movement were consistent with Vargas's goal of creating a winning electoral coalition, the labor reactivation that followed complicated his attempt to put together a governing coalition. Like Aguirre Cerda in Chile, Vargas assumed the presidency amid great controversy and the alarm of the right. The anti-Vargas, antistatist UDN opposed his inauguration, arguing that he did not have the constitutionally required majority and warning that he would impose a new dictatorship

[9] L. M. Rodrigues 1969:105; J. A. Rodrigues 1968:133; Harding 1973:244–45.

(Skidmore 1967:101). To address this hostility, Vargas made many overtures to the UDN during the first half of his presidency and tried to bring it into the government. Such a strategy, however, was threatening to the PSD and alienated a substantial part of Vargas's PTB support, resulting in the resignation of the sole PTB cabinet member. The right, in turn, reacted sharply to Vargas's association with and concessions to the labor movement and to the perceived or potential victory of *trabalhismo*, which was identified with the unacceptable laborism of Perón, viewed with fear from across the border. The effort to attract UDN support collapsed in mid-1952, and Vargas had to turn elsewhere to establish a base of support.

That task, however, proved ultimately illusive. The problem of a governing coalition was made particularly difficult by a mounting inflation, so that at the same time that Vargas was making concessions to the working class, he was trying to address the economic situation by implementing a rather orthodox stabilization program—hardly a position from which to attract or retain working-class support. Vargas remained caught in a zero-sum situation. On the one hand, he wanted to reestablish control over the labor movement. The reactivation of the labor movement represented a major challenge to Vargas, particularly in view of his stabilization program and also of the clamor of the military and industrial groups who blamed Vargas for these developments and urged him to reinstitute the ideological oath and crack down on the workers (Harding 1973:261). On the other hand, with his overtures to the UDN rejected, Vargas had little choice but to look to the workers for support. In this, however, he vacillated and was never willing to take the risk of really mobilizing labor support by the kinds of concessions needed to make a realistic appeal or to take the risk of strengthening working-class political organizations necessary for building an effective support base. Even the PTB was neglected. "The fact was that Getúlio's strategy of relying on working class support rested on little more than a threat" (Skidmore 1967:137; see also 113).

The 1953 strike, which intensified the incipient polarization and the zero-sum character of politics, put Vargas in a difficult position from which he never found a way out. "He was under attack from many of the strikers for having failed to live up to his promises, from the UDN for instigating the strike, and from mainly PSD spokesmen for the Ministry of Labour for having been too liberal towards the unions and having removed, in particular, . . . the ideological test for candidates in union elections" (Flynn 1978:163).

Vargas's reaction was to agree to review the minimum wage and to reorganize his cabinet. The cabinet changes reveal Vargas's attempt to pursue the twin and contradictory goals of stabilization and austerity, combined with labor support. The former was to be the responsibility of his new minister of finance, Oswaldo Aranha, an old friend and finance minister of the 1930s. For the latter, João Goulart, who had close ties to labor, was recruited to the position of minister of labor, where he would be in a position both to attract working-class support and assert the ministry's control over the labor movement (Flynn 1978:166; Harding 1973:264–65). Goulart's pro-labor reputation, however, probably did more to alarm conservatives (who associated him with a "syndicalist" and "demagogic" regime like that of Perón—Skidmore 1967:114) than it did to convince a skeptical working class. The working class was increasingly suspicious as Vargas continued to procrastinate on a decision regarding the increase in the minimum wage, which had been badly eroded in real terms since the prior adjustment in 1951.

In February 1954, as Vargas delayed and strikes continued, the military finally sent a warning that Goulart must be replaced. The day of his resignation, Goulart finally came forth with a recommendation that the minimum wage be increased 100 percent. In the next several months Vargas lurched to the right and then to the left, unable to find or establish any base of support. In March and April the government reinstituted certain controls over unions and entertained a new recommendation for a 50 percent adjustment in the minimum wage. On May Day, however, following demonstrations and a bus strike in opposition to this recommendation, Vargas announced a 100 percent increase, thus marking his last zigzag in attempted alliance-building. Once again, however, workers saw this as too little too late and failed to be impressed (see Harding 1973:277–78) at the same time that virtually all other sectors were alarmed by Vargas's dramatic and rhetorical move. As the political situation deteriorated, Vargas was increasingly isolated. When the army called for his resignation in August, he took his own life.

Chile. In Chile the history of the presidency of Aguirre Cerda shows a similar, though perhaps less extreme, pattern of polarization and a vacillating president trying unsuccessfully not to alienate the right and unwilling to rely on the left. The attenuated character of the conflict may have been due in part to the historical period involved—the Popular Front itself was, of course, an outgrowth of Comintern policy, which subordinated class conflict to the formation of broad, antifascist coalitions with the "progressive" bourgeoisie. Thus, the Chilean Communist Party, which had played an initiating role in the formation of the Popular Front, also acted in a restrained manner in order to maintain it, despite Comintern's return to a hard line during the brief period of the Stalin-Nazi Pact. The heterogeneity of the coalition, however, like that in Brazil, was a contradictory one that produced stalemate and a failed presidency (Loveman 1979:276).

As in Brazil, this period saw a new climate of labor freedom. Unionization efforts were redoubled and the number of labor conflicts and strikes rose. A new feature on the scene was labor activity in the countryside. Aguirre Cerda responded by trying to reassure the jittery right. In March 1939, the planters' association, the SNA, appealed to the president, who responded by calling a halt to all rural unionization, thereby preserving the rural social structure and the oligarchy's base of political support. Interestingly, the Socialist and Communist parties and the CTCh, the labor central formed as a product of the Popular Front and as the political vehicle of the labor movement, acquiesced in this unconstitutional suspension of rural unionization. This understanding embodied the basic agreement or exchange of the Popular Front: labor moderation and social peace in the countryside in exchange for Socialist participation in government, for presidential rejection of the outlawing of the Communist Party, demanded by the right, and for the congressional passage of the president's industrial program in a compromised form (Loveman 1979:280).

Despite this bargain, distrust and conflict continued on a number of dimensions. The right continued to oppose the Popular Front, using a combination of obstructionism and confrontation as well as attempts to woo the government to its side. It relied particularly on its majority in Congress, a barrage of charges of "illegality, tyranny, anarchy, incompetence, and corruption," the threat of "incursions on freedom of the press and assembly," and "alarmist rumors of economic and political collapse" (Drake 1978:232–33). The Popular Front parties were quite weak in the face of this attack. The Socialist Party, itself faction ridden, was increasingly in conflict with the Communist Party; and the Radical Party was divided over allying with the rightist or the Popular Front parties. The result was political immobilism. By the end of 1939, only one major piece of legislation had been passed, in addition to the compromise industrial program (Loveman 1979:282).

Early the next year, Aguirre Cerda reorganized his cabinet, replacing designees of the Popular Front parties with wealthy appointees who were personally loyal to him. The rightward trend of Aguirre Cerda's presidency continued during 1940 as the government took further moves to appeal to the right and to curtail labor conflict in both rural and industrial areas, and as conflict within the Popular Front reached the breaking point with the withdrawal of the Socialist Party and the CTCh, where the Socialists held a majority.

The victory the following year of the Popular Front parties in the 1941 congressional elections seemed to set the stage for a change to a more reformist orientation. For the first time, the right lost control of both houses in the legislature. The left doubled its percentage of the vote over the 1937 congressional elections for a combined total of over 32 percent, with the Socialists winning 18 percent, the PST (a Socialist splinter) winning nearly 3 percent, and the Communists winning 12 percent (Drake 1978:260). Despite this impressive victory, such a move to the left was not possible. When Aguirre Cerda proved too independent from the Radical Party in matters of ministerial and patronage appointments, the party withdrew its support from the president and opposed his legislative programs. When he died later in the year, Aguirre Cerda was without a significant power base, and the Popular Front government passed with relatively few achievements (Loveman 1979:282–83).

Coalition Governments

In the subsequent presidential elections in both countries, the electoral logic of a populist coalition continued to be persuasive. Consequently similar electoral coalitions were formed, but this time in a more conservative guise, following the trauma of the conflictual politics of the preceding period. In Brazil in 1955, Kubitschek ran as the candidate of a PSD-PTB coalition, but then, unlike 1950, the presidential candidate clearly identified with the center-right PSD rather than the PTB. The populist component of the coalition came in the vice presidential candidate, the PTB's Goulart, who again aroused the opposition and alarm of the UDN and the anti-Vargas forces, both civilian and military. After initial opposition, the Communist Party, along with the MNPT, the electoral front it established to mobilize the labor vote, threw its support behind the coalition ticket (Harding 1973:291–97).

In Chile too the outcome of the next election—in fact of the next two elections—produced presidents more clearly identified with the centrist party. In 1938 Aguirre Cerda had been the candidate chosen by the Popular Front coalition. By the time of the 1942 elections, however, the Popular Front as a formal organization had fallen apart, and Ríos Morales, like González Videla in 1946, ran as the candidate chosen by the Radical Party acting alone. Nevertheless, both the Socialist and Communist parties decided to support Ríos. By 1946, the Socialists again dropped out of the coalition with the Radicals. The Communists, however, not only continued their participation, but for the first time in Chilean history joined the cabinet. Thus, in both countries, some form of coalition was maintained. Nevertheless, the presidents were more identified with the centrist party, and on a formal level the populist and/or Communist parties played a more subordinate coalitional role.

Corresponding to the closer identification of the presidents with the centrist parties, these periods in both countries were characterized by governments less oriented toward social reform and more oriented toward establishing the conditions for rapid economic growth. In Brazil, those who benefited most from the government's policies were "the larger financial and industrial interests, and the agrarian bourgeoisie linked to the production and export of coffee . . . precisely . . . those elements that Kubitschek could appeal [to] through the PSD, and from which he drew his continuing support" (Flynn 1978:198). Labor was not so favored. Kubitschek clashed several times with labor, particularly over his reluctant and tardy adjustment of the minimum wage in a period of rapid inflation. In Chile, Ríos, a member of the right-wing of the Radical Party, remained critical of Aguirre Cerda's cooperation with the Communists and has been described as a profascist Ibañista (Pike 1963:247) and a violent anticommunist (Gil 1966:71). He moved to reestablish firmer ties with the right and formed a conservative cabinet of "right-wing Radicals and aristocratic Liberals, including the president of the SNA" (Drake 1978:270–71). Though reaching the presidency with somewhat less conservative credentials, González Videla also oversaw a more conservative administration. From the beginning, conservatives, especially from the Liberal Party, were included in the cabinet, and as time went on the government moved further to the right and closer to the traditional elite (Drake 1978:285).

The more conservative coloration of these governments, the closer identification of the presidents with the centrist or center-right party, and the retreat of the Chilean Socialist Party from the governing coalition in 1946 provide a clue about the major feature of this subperiod in both countries: the discrediting of populism and the collapse of the populist attempt. The center or center-right proved itself unwilling or, in the face of the strength of the traditional elite, unable to govern through a populist alliance with parties attracting working-class votes, and those parties, in turn, did not derive sufficient benefit from their collaboration. Concentrating on their party/electoral projects of cooperation and coalition-formation, these parties provided leadership of the labor movement that was quite moderate and failed to extract much from the government for their cooperation. The result of this subordination of working-class issues led to a change among party and labor groups toward a position of advocating more radical and class-conscious alternatives. It led to the discrediting of the collaborative strategy, political polarization, and the failure of the populist attempt.

Brazil. In Brazil during this period the PTB remained a vehicle of the Vargas coalition, preserving an electoral coalition with the PSD. In many ways, the Communist Party was more oriented toward its party-political project—seeking legalization and alliances with moderate parties and groups through which it could carry on its political activity—than it was toward the rank-and-file interests of union members. Apparently in exchange for dropping charges against its veteran leader Prestes, the party supported the candidacy of Kubitschek. Interestingly, as more and more Communists assumed leadership roles in the unions, the party abandoned its opposition to the syndical tax, which continued to make the unions dependent upon the government but which the Communists were now in a position to take advantage of (Harding 1973:332). They also responded to Vice President Goulart's attempts to forge cooperation and a degree of unity within the labor movement, thus effecting to some degree a PTB-PCB-*pelego* alliance within organized labor. Because of this alliance, critics of the Communist union leaders began to refer to them as "pelegos vermelhos" (red *pelegos*), thus suggesting that they had become more tied to the PCB, the PTB, and Goulart than to their own grass roots and that they were dependent on the syndical tax (Harding 1973:341–42).

The result of this collaboration was disappointment for both parties. The PTB lost influence among the working class, and by 1960 it was no longer the dominant force in the labor movement. Labor leadership was mainly taken over by Communists, though many nominally joined the PTB and worked through that party (Harding 1973:450–51, 482). The PCB failed to win its legalization and, like its Chilean counterpart, ended the period in clandestinity. Both parties continued to support the government and its policy of developmentalism, and indeed they supported Lott, the PSD presidential candidate in 1960. His defeat further discredited this populist position (Chilcote 1974:74; Harding 1973:452, 457).

At the same time, the independent movement that had begun to emerge within organized labor under the second Vargas government in the first half of the 1950s became more vigorous under Kubitschek in the second half of the decade. In 1956 following the de-Stalinization campaign initiated in Moscow, new Marxist groups, some of which split from the PCB, began to operate within the labor movement. Partly from the ranks of these groups arose the MRS (Movement for Trade Union Renewal) and other *renovador* (renewal) groups, which promoted union autonomy and a reorganization of the union structure to increase worker participation. Specifically, they advocated the reorganization of unions from the bottom up, or a *sindicalismo de base*, in opposition to the control of labor from above, by the Labor Ministry working through the *pelegos* and other labor leaders.

New tendencies emerged from the ranks of the PTB as well. A left wing of the party began to take shape that broke with the developmentalism of Kubitschek. Instead it advocated a radical nationalist, anti-imperialist position that would define a new relationship between the party and the labor movement. The PTB had been established as a party based on Estado Novo political leaders and labor bureaucrats and their ability to channel labor support to Vargas and away from the PCB (Benevides 1976:63–64; Carone 1981:xvii). Over the next fifteen years it began to move away from that position as it collaborated closely with the PCB. This evolution of the PTB was given a large impetus by the populist content of Vargas's suicide note in 1954, in which he spoke in terms that conjured up the image of an international capitalist conspiracy that blocked gains of the working class and the national economy.[10] As 1960 approached, with the emergence of the radical wing, more independent leaders led the party in a more dynamic way, open to promoting the demands of the new leftist organizations and the more class-conscious workers (Carone 1981:xviii). Indeed, under Goulart many of the radical nationalists in the PTB were to move to the left of the PCB, which took a relatively cautious, moderate approach (Harding 1973:535).

In addition, two other important developments began in the radicalization process of the Brazilian labor movement. The first was the formation of horizontal interunion groupings which, although not legal, were tolerated in a political context of competitive bidding for popular support. These pointed "to a break in the whole structure of government-controlled unions" (Flynn 1978:202). Though they remained primarily at the regional level (J. Rodrigues 1968:163), they were important building blocks for the formation of a national central.

The second was the rise in worker protest and strike activity. Building on the minimum salary campaign of 1956 and the São Paulo general strike of 1957, worker activation and protest continued to grow, reaching new heights in 1958 with the rise in inflation and pressure on real wages and culminating in a wave of unrest and violence (Telles 1981:esp. 109–13; Harding 1973:408). At the end of 1958, Kubitschek adopted a stabilization plan, which the labor movement opposed in the absence of a promised adjustment in the minimum wage. Since the prior adjustment two years earlier, the value of the minimum wage had eroded substantially. A new adjustment was

---

[10] Benevides 1976:66; Flynn 1978:170; Skidmore 1967:142.

finally made at the end of 1958, but it was soon wiped out by the quickening rate of inflation, and strike activity and protest escalated. The outpouring of popular protest included incidents in which hundreds of people were injured or killed in clashes with police. By June 1959, in anticipation of the upcoming presidential election the following year, Kubitschek abandoned the stabilization plan in the face of this labor protest (Harding 1973:390–97; Telles 1981:84).

The cycle of inflation and worker protest and strikes to protect real wage levels continued through the end of the Kubitschek presidency. In 1959, the state of São Paulo experienced 954 strikes, and in December of that year a wave of unrest and violence spread to cities throughout Brazil (Harding 1973:408). Kubitschek responded to the rising tide of labor protest with charges of subversion and the attempt to crack down on the labor movement through the use of such tactics as the arrest of union leaders, police occupation of and intervention in unions, and the threat of breaking strikes. Efforts were made within the government both to reinstitute the ideological test for union leaders and to curtail the right to strike (Telles 1981:84). This response, however, was ineffectual and strikes accelerated in 1960 (Harding 1973:408–12, 417). The year ended on a note of serious labor conflict as some of the most important unions struck for higher wages. In November, railroad workers, port workers, and seamen called the "paridade" strike, which was soon followed by strikes by metal workers, printers, and textile workers, among others (Harding 1973:467–71).

By the end of the Kubitschek presidency, the organized labor movement had changed dramatically. Economic growth and industrialization had increased the number of unionized workers, and electoral competition and bidding for worker support afforded the labor movement new freedom of maneuver and an opening in which to organize and strike in pushing its demands. As we shall see below, a new, more radical labor leadership made inroads on *pelego* leadership, mobilization around strikes increased the weight of the rank and file (though this was still limited by the absence of a factory committee structure, that was to remain a serious weakness of the Brazilian labor movement), and strike activity also resulted in the creation of wider, interunion organizations to coordinate strikes.

In the new opening, the monolithic structuring of the Estado Novo began to break down, as Communists, Socialists, *renovadores*, Catholics, as well as *pelegos* and the Labor Ministry all competed for influence. The Vargas coalition could no longer count on its influence within the labor movement. Whereas the organized working class backed the presidential candidates of the PSD-PTB coalition in 1946, 1950, and 1955, by 1960 this coalitional form of populism had collapsed. The PTB and the PCB again endorsed Lott as the coalition candidate. The *renovadores*, however, supported Quadros in opposition to Lott, and even the *pelegos* declined to support Lott, following a split with Goulart. The final collapse of the form of populism attempted in the 1950s was seen in the support Quadros received among important segments of the working class and their rejection of the coalition candidates. Not only did Lott lose the election, but Goulart, the vice presidential candidate of the PSD-PTB coalition, lost in Rio Grande do Sul (his home state), São Paulo, and Guanabara, the most industrial states with the greatest concentration of workers (Harding 1973:481–83, 443–43, 451). By 1960, a process of ideological reorientation and polarization was clearly under way.

Chile. In Chile, the collaborative posture of the Socialist Party was initially sustained, despite the collapse of the Popular Front and the more conservative nature of the government that succeeded Aguirre Cerda in 1942. Under Ríos, the PS participated in a very conservative cabinet that included even the president of the National Agrarian Society (Drake 1978:270). Such collaboration produced great opposition within the party, and in 1943 dissidents elected Salvador Allende secretary-general, ousting from that position Marmaduque Grove, the personalistic caudillo of the party. Under the new leadership, the party withdrew from the Ríos government, while the defeated Grove took his faction out of the party and formed the Authentic Socialist Party (PSA). This division, in addition to the earlier defection of the group that constituted the PST, left the Socialist Party substantially weakened.

The reorientation of the party, however, came slowly. Allende's stewardship of the party passed to Bernardo Ibáñez, under whose leadership the party adopted a "Third Front" orientation. Emphasizing personal ties and ideological affinities with populist parties such as the PTB in Brazil, APRA in Peru, and AD in Venezuela (Drake 1978:278), the party seemed to be defining an independent reformist position. Nevertheless, it continued to follow a collaborationist path and once again participated in the cabinet of interim President Duhalde, who assumed power when Ríos fell ill.

The Duhalde government was even more hostile to labor, repressing strikes and demonstrations led by the PCCh. Despite this policy, the PS stayed in the cabinet that included members of the armed forces, with whom it sought to form a Third Front. This policy led to the further discrediting of the party. By 1946, therefore, the Socialists decided to go their own way and nominated Bernardo Ibáñez to oppose González Videla in the presidential elections. From a high point in 1941, however, the Socialists' electoral fortunes plummeted. In the 1945 congressional elections, the party's portion of the vote had fallen to 7 percent (or 13 percent for the PS and PSA combined), and in 1946 it mustered a mere 2.5 percent for its candidate, who failed to win a single *comuna* (Drake 1978:275, 282).

The Communist Party also continued to play a moderate, collaborationist role. Like the Socialist Party, it had supported Ríos as less objectionable than the candidate put forth by the Conservative and Liberal parties, the erstwhile Carlos Ibáñez, a man, as it turned out, of many guises. While the Communists did not trust either candidate, they thought that Ríos was more likely to support the Allied cause in the Second World War. The Communists thus subordinated an immediate concern with promoting the interests of workers and peasants to this larger international priority (Drake 1978:268). The PCCh's collaborationist policy went furthest with the 1946 election of González Videla. Gonazález Videla was a Radical, but unlike Ríos or even

Aguirre Cerda, he was identified with the left wing of the party. Despite the end of the war, the Communist Party continued to argue in favor of a popular front alliance and not only supported González Videla, but in a change of policy even joined his cabinet, though the price of participation was keeping a lid on labor militance. "Government repression and the weakness of the Marxist parties and unions kept worker activism down from 1946 to 1952. Union collaboration with the bureaucracy, especially the Ministry of Labor, served to restrain more than fulfill worker demands" (Drake 1978:285).

This collaborationist orientation of the populist and Communist parties was ultimately unsuccessful and generated disaffection and opposition within the working class. The consequence was the beginning of a process of radicalization among the working class and the adoption of a more class-based orientation. As we have seen, collaboration had led to splits and a weakening of the Socialist Party. Nor did the Communist Party fare any better for its collaboration. At first, the party was able to take advantage of its position in the González Videla government to extend its influence in governmental and state agencies. Furthermore, though it continued to collaborate in the government, in the new postwar atmosphere the Communist Party maintained a more combative posture and was less willing to compromise. Under its leadership, labor conflict reached a new height for the postincorporation period, and new offensives were undertaken in the rural areas, where in 1946 alone over 300 unions were formed and over 650 labor conflicts broke out among agricultural workers (Loveman 1979:283). The Communist Party also made impressive gains among the electorate, as was clearly seen in the 1947 municipal elections (Drake 1978:285).

This very success, combined with the new cold war atmosphere emerging at the time, prompted the right to take the offensive against the Communists and more generally against organized labor. Conforming to its agreement with the right, the government responded with new legislation that drastically restricted unionization among rural workers and outlawed agricultural strikes (Loveman 1979:283–84). Furthermore, González Videla came to view the Communist Party as subversive and saw strikes as Communist attempts, coordinated and directed from Moscow, to overthrow the government (González Videla 1975:629–41). As a result, the Communists were expelled from the cabinet in 1947. When the Communist Party responded with strikes and protests, the government in turn answered with military repression and in 1948 with the Law for the Defense of Democracy, which banned the Communist Party. "Mobilized in the 1930s and partially institutionalized by the start of the 1940s, the Marxist movement was nearly moribund by the 1950s" (Drake 1978:267). Thus, even more definitively in Chile than in Brazil, the populist alliance, based on a coalition of centrist and leftist parties, collapsed.

In reaction to its failing fortunes, the Socialist Party underwent a period of doctrinal redefinition as a younger generation, under the leadership of Raúl Ampuero Díaz and again including Allende, took control of the party. Though the party was moving away from populism and toward a more radical, class-based orientation, it did so gradually, looking first toward laborist models and remaining internally divided over the issue of alliances with both the Radicals and the Communists. Taking a more moderate approach, the Bernardo Ibáñez faction broke away, taking with it most of the unions and the party label. Allied to the AFL in the United States, the Bernardo Ibáñez party was ready to join the anticommunist campaign being waged by González Videla. Yet even the Ampuero faction, reorganized as the PSP, remained for the time being uncertain and hesitant about the extent of a doctrinal reorientation (Drake 1978:282, 290–302). Nevertheless, the course was begun and would continue.

In both Brazil and Chile, then, the end of this analytic period saw the collapse of the attempt to integrate the working class into party/electoral politics through a populist alliance of a center or center-right party with parties appealing to the working class. This attempt was premised on the political dominance of the PSD in Brazil and the Radical Party in Chile and on the ability of these parties to make coalitions and alliances and reach understandings with all the other major parties. By the end of this period, however, both these parties had lost their dominant positions. In Brazil, the majority of seats held by the PSD with the return to democracy in 1945 was reduced to about a third by the 1950s, and most of those seats were won on the basis of electoral coalitions. In 1960, of course, the PSD failed to retain the presidency. In Chile too the Radicals ended in defeat. Though they maintained about 18–20 percent of the vote in the four congressional elections between 1932 and 1945, by 1949 the party split into three. Though the split was temporary, it was indicative of the disillusionment with coalition politics and the general disintegration of the parties that had been part of it (Drake 1978:293). In 1952 the Radical Party lost the presidency.

The failure of the populist alliance could also be seen from the point of view of the junior partners in the coalition: those parties that were to contribute working-class support. The end of this period saw the beginnings of a new turn to the left and a more class-conscious orientation by the labor movement and parties appealing to the working class. In Brazil, *renovador* groups within the union movement grew in influence and radical factions emerged in both the PTB and the PCB. This challenge did not immediately precipitate a change of course by the PTB or PCB. Rather, they continued to pursue a collaborationist orientation and supported PSD and UDN, as well as PSP and PTB, candidates in the 1958 congressional and state elections, and also PSD presidential candidate Lott in 1960 (Harding 1973:351). Nevertheless, change was taking place, and a process was begun that would accelerate in the next period, particularly with Lott's defeat.

Likewise in Chile, the splits in the Socialist Party, which exposed the collapse of its populist policy, led to a rethinking of strategy that foreshadowed the more clear-cut turn to a more doctrinally Marxist position that would be adopted in the next period. Thus, the failed Popular Front politics of the 1940s would be replaced by a more class-based Workers Front politics in the 1950s (Drake 1978:300).

In Chile, the collapse of the populist alliance between the center and parties appealing to the working class was particularly striking. Except for a relatively brief period of participation by the PSP in the succeeding government, neither the Socialists nor the Communists again participated in coalitions with centrist parties. In Brazil, populism as an electoral coalition between the center-right and parties appealing to working-class support—that is, between the PSD and the PTB—also ended in failure, though the collapse was not as definitive as it was in Chile. Like the Chilean Socialist Party, the PTB was undergoing a process of radicalization. Yet it remained a more heterogeneous party and its agenda, along with that of the working class, remained more populist and reformist than class-oriented and socialist. Furthermore, it continued to collaborate with the PSD in the 1960 presidential elections. Nevertheless, the bankruptcy and ultimate break-up of this form of populism was signaled by the failure of the coalition to win those elections and its consequent loss of the presidency.

Distribution of Benefits

These periods, then, from 1950 to 1960 in Brazil and from 1938 to 1952 in Chile, saw the emergence of a populist electoral alliance in which populist and Communist parties supported middle sector parties and participated in the governments formed by them. On the governing level, however, this alliance did not destroy or replace the accommodationist alliance with a new one to the left. Rather, though the working–class-oriented parties and the union movement that formed their base now operated in a freer, more open, and less repressive climate and though some concessions and reforms were achieved, these were periods of political vacillation and continued and substantial influence of the political right. Though the working class was explicitly included in the coalition in a way that was unprecedented in these two countries, these experiences, which were part of the aftermath period, were quite different from the radical populism that had characterized Mexico and Venezuela in the analytically distinct period of incorporation. Rather than mobilization in a multiclass political movement, these periods were characterized by expedient electoral coalitions of mutually suspicious partners. In Brazil and Chile, though electoral support was sought, the political leadership was not willing to mobilize the working class by strengthening and politicizing the union movement and working-class parties along the lines that had occurred in Mexico and Venezuela. Nor were they willing to identify politically with the working class and work to achieve the ascendancy of the populist coalition. Instead of radical populism and the threat of a "syndicalist" or a "workers'" republic that would result in the alienation of the center-right, these periods saw the continued influence of the center-right and its participation in the governing, if not always the electoral, coalition. These periods were characterized by (1) a new, more active role of the state in promoting industrialization, (2) important middle-class gains, and (3) the preservation of the political strength and veto power of the traditional oligarchy in the countryside. The working class saw gains, but they were limited. The most important of these was the increase in unionization and the emergence—more quickly and thoroughly in Chile and with more false starts and setbacks in Brazil—of a free, democratic union movement. On other fronts, however, the record for labor was disappointing.

Industrial Promotion. Perhaps more than anything else, these periods in both countries are noted for new departures in state promotion of industrialization. The stage for such state initiatives had been set previously in two senses. First, as mentioned above, the Estado Novo and the Alessandri/Ibáñez period of the 1920s had introduced a new, more activist conception of the state, which began to define a new role and assume greater responsibility in the economic sphere. This was particularly evident in Brazil, where the Estado Novo saw the creation of a national steel company and a number of mixed corporations (Skidmore 1967:44). Secondly, particularly in response to the world depression of the 1930s, the state adopted a number of policies that had the effect of promoting industrialization, though at this earlier stage the intent of these policies was usually to address the problem of deficits in the balance of payments. In the postincorporation period, however, the role of the state in directing economic growth increased substantially, particularly after the conservative governments of Dutra and Alessandri, which to some extent represented a brief return to economic liberalism (Hewlett 1980:39; Loveman 1979:264–65). In this period, then, the state elaborated the earlier policies, most importantly tariffs and exchange rate controls, with the expressed purpose of protecting domestic industry and advancing import-substituting industrialization. Furthermore, a number of new measures were undertaken to promote industrialization.

In Brazil, under Vargas and Kubitschek, the state assumed a much more prominent role in the economy, with "deliberate attempts . . . to eliminate the structural bottlenecks (inadequate transportation, insufficient electricity), the sectoral lags (in chemicals and in metalworking industries), and regional disequilibriums (between the northeast and the center-south and between the hinterland and the coast) . . . by means of state control and public investment" (Hewlett 1980:39). In 1952 the Vargas government created the BNDE, a national bank for economic development, and in the following years the national petroleum and electric power companies were established. Under Kubitschek, there was a great increase in public investment and an increasingly dynamic government role in directing economic growth, including a role in attracting foreign investment.

Similarly in Chile, a new commitment by the state to actively oversee the industrialization process was undertaken by the new government in 1938. In 1939, the Aguirre Cerda government established CORFO, a national development corporation. With this agency, the government undertook the responsibility for economic planning and direction by identifying certain industrial sectors to support through various sorts of credits, subsidies, government investment, and the establishment of public and/or mixed enterprises. The development of a mixed economy can be seen in the share of public investment: by the early 1940s in Chile, "the public sector accounted for more than 50 percent of all internal investment capital" (Loveman 1979:259).

In general, then, the orientation of economic policy was toward industrialization and growth. With sufficient growth, an expanding economic pie could be distributed and issues of redistribution and social conflict could be avoided. This policy represented an effort to avoid hard choices—indeed to avoid a commitment to a particular political coalition. It was an effort to span both populist and accommodationist alliances and to avoid sectoral and class conflict. Foreign investment and financing were relied on to ease the pressure on the agricultural sector (Drake 1978:217–19; Loveman 1979:285–87), and inflation was tolerated as the price of social peace. In both countries, then, these were periods characterized by developmental nationalism and a something-for-everyone orientation (Skidmore 1967:167).

Middle-Sector Gains.   As might be expected from the support base of these governments and from the economic policy adopted by them, the middle classes did well under these governments. The size of the middle class expanded significantly not only as a result of economic growth in general, but also as a result of growing public employment as the state expanded. In fact, Jaguaribe has characterized Brazil during this period as the "cartorial" state, emphasizing the expansion of public employment to enhance the state's middle-class base of support (Schneider 1971:23). A similar expansion occurred in Chile, where between 1930 and 1940 public employment has been estimated as more than doubling (Loveman 1979:259).

Furthermore, the interests of the growing middle class were well attended to by these governments. In Brazil, public employees, the largest sector of the middle class, were not allowed to form unions or to strike under the terms of the labor law. Nevertheless, some interest associations were formed, and in 1952 the National Union of Public Servants (UNSP), the first national association of public employees, was founded and had immediate success in promoting a favorable Statute for Federal Public Employees (Schmitter 1971:204). Flynn (1978:196) has characterized Kubitschek as "essentially a politician of and for the middle class." Within the manufacturing sector, these middle sectors gained dramatically in comparison with the working class. According to the data of Mata and Bacha (1973:328–29), management salaries increased nearly three times those of the working class between 1949 and 1958. These income gains for management categories represented more than double the gain in manufacturing productivity, whereas workers' wages failed to keep up with productivity gains.

In Chile, the labor law clearly favored the middle sectors by the distinction it made between workers (*obreros*) and white-collar employees (*empleados*). Based on this legal classification, a minimum wage was established for white-collar employees in 1942 (though not until 1960 for blue-collar workers), and the former were also provided with automatic cost of living adjustments (Angell 1972:66). In addition, the government disproportionately rewarded the middle sectors in terms of state jobs, health care, housing, education, and social security benefits (Drake 1978:225). Real wages for the middle classes went up accordingly. One calculation suggests that from 1938 to 1950 white-collar wages increased 2.2 times relative to the price of a loaf of bread. According to another, between 1940 and 1953 white-collar real income rose 46 percent, even faster than the 40 percent increase in national income (Drake 1978:286, 229).

Traditional Oligarchy. In both countries, during the aftermath period the government tried very hard to assure the traditional oligarchy that there would be no fundamental assault upon their interests. The most basic element in the oligarchy's acquiescence, if not support, of the continuation in power of these governments was the clear unwillingness of the government to entertain any suggestion about land reform or change in the rural social structure. As Skidmore (1967:169) has said about Brazil, landowners "had little reason to fear significant changes in Brazil's archaic pattern of land tenure. On the contrary, Kubitschek, like Vargas before him, never raised the land question in a way other than to suggest politically innocuous measures such as the expansion of rural credit, or the improvement of food distribution through the construction of new storage facilities." In Chile the Radicals were equally adamant on this point. When the Communists began organizing rural syndicates in 1939, the Radicals acted decisively to defend rural interests rather than their coalition partners. When in the first months of the Aguirre Cerda government the Communists and Socialists led a rural unionization effort and substantial conflict broke out, the president suspended rural unionization, a supposedly temporary measure that remained in effect throughout the Ríos government as well (Loveman 1979:278–79). Interestingly, the Communist and Socialist partners of the Radicals acquiesced in this suspension as the price for continuing the coalition government and their participation in it. At the beginning of the González Videla government, the Communists again became active in organizing rural unions, and again, at the behest of the traditional elite, the government took a stand against its own coalition partner, not only suppressing such unionization but also this time finding the excuse to expel the Communists from the cabinet and then outlawing the party (Drake 1978:289).

This defense of the traditional rural sector against unionization appeared essential for the traditional elite because its clientelistic control in the rural sector formed the basis for its electoral power under competitive political regimes. In Brazil, it was the source of support of the oligarchy, which was concentrated within the PSD. The PSD continued to hold a plurality in Congress and retained a dominant position in the cabinet, even in the one presidency during this period in which its candidate was not elected. Likewise in Chile, the clientelism that was based in the land tenure system was the basis for the oligarchy's continued political strength. The traditional oligarchy found its political expression in the two traditional, right-wing parties that dated from the 19th century, the Liberal and Conservative parties. Though they maintained a separate identity during this period, they often acted in concert or in coalition. The right lost the presidency starting in 1938, but it retained substantial political clout and continued to constitute a major influence in the formation of national policy. In Congress, it retained a plurality of the seats (Urzua 1979:75) and was able to exercise a veto power on policies of greatest concern. Furthermore, these parties held ministerial positions in Aguirre Cerda's Popular Front government after 1941 and controlled "a large share of political positions" under Ríos and González Videla, including, under the latter, the minister of finance, who acted as "a virtual prime minister" (Cavarozzi and Petras 1974:525).

Labor Movement.   During the aftermath periods in both countries, the political support of the working class was important to the governments in power. For the first time in both countries political organizations representing the working class were part of the electoral coalition. As a result, a number of concessions were made by these governments.

Compared to the restrictive, authoritarian, repressive period of initial incorporation and to the more antilabor period of the previous Dutra and Alessandri governments, the following period saw much greater organizational freedom. Both countries registered substantial increases in the number of unions and union members. In percentage terms this growth was more dramatic in the case of Chile, given the difference in unionization during the incorporation period and hence the lower level from which it began the aftermath period. In Brazil during the 1950s, the number of unions increased by about 50 percent, while union membership grew about the same amount between 1952 and 1960 (J. Rodrigues 1968:125, 134). In Chile, the number of legal unions doubled under Alessandri (Loveman 1979:268) and continued to grow at least as rapidly under Aguirre Cerda,[11] reaching a peak in 1941, at which it more or less stabilized for the remainder of the period. At the same time, membership increased at a rate of 130 percent (or an average annual increase of nearly 12,000) under Alessandri, 66 percent (or an average increase of 16,560) under Aguirre Cerda through the peak year of 1941, and 47 percent (or an average annual increase of 9,000) under the coalition governments that followed the Popular Front.[12]

In Brazil, unionization among industrial workers increased from 25 percent in 1939 and 30 percent in 1950 to 33 percent in 1960 (Harding 1973:11). Starting from a lower level at the end of its incorporation period, Chile underwent a more rapid increase in unionization, reaching a comparable (somewhat higher) rate of unionization at the end of the aftermath period, and indeed a comparable level even for the same historical period. In 1952 the rate of unionization in Chile reached about 19.3 percent among the nonagricultural work force and 38.3 percent among industrial workers, a pre-1970 peak,

[11] Data from Morris and Oyaneder (1962:18) indicate about a doubling of unions under Aguirre Cerda, whereas Drake's (1978:229) data indicate a tripling.

[12] These figures are calculated from Morris and Oyaneder (1962:20). S. Valenzuela (1979:576) cautions, however, that such figures may reflect some double counting of those who, under the Chilean Labor Code, may have been members of both plant and craft unions.

with the possible exception of some additional improvement in the immediately following period to 1956. By 1960, the year the Brazilian aftermath period ended, the Chilean rate had dropped to 30 percent of industrial workers (somewhat lower than the Brazilian figure) and 14 percent of the nonagricultural work force (A. Valenzuela 1978:28).

In addition, the aftermath of state incorporation was a period of greater freedom in union politics. In Brazil, the Communist Party remained outlawed, but union elections were substantially freer, and a number of Communists and leftists assumed leadership positions within the unions. Non-*pelego* leaders made substantial inroads, and strikes were tolerated and rose in number. In Chile, the *pelego*-type of leader and state-controlled union did not outlast the Ibáñez government, and official unionism was quickly replaced by democratic unionism. In 1938, the Popular Front government brought a new atmosphere of union freedom that reflected the new political position of labor and its indispensable role as a source of political support. Government-labor relations were good, and labor representatives sat on important committees and agencies, including CORFO. Labor legislation was applied in ways favorable to workers, particularly during the early years of the Popular Front, a period when strikes actually declined (S. Valenzuela 1976:156; 1979:574). Generally, during the aftermath period, with encouragement from the government, legal unionization was legitimated, and collective bargaining spread and became institutionalized (Falabella 1980:329).

Another gain made by the working class during this period concerned wages. The data are scarce and to some extent contradictory. Nevertheless, it seems likely that over the period there were some gains, though in real terms they were not dramatic.

In Brazil under Dutra, wages were kept down. In the initial postincorporation period real wages fell, recouping their 1946 level only briefly in 1949 and then again in 1954 (Kahil 1973:65). Though data for this period are available only for Guanabara and somewhat less completely for São Paulo, Kahil in his analysis suggests that this pattern is broadly indicative of the situation in Brazil as a whole, if anything underestimating the deterioration of wages outside these two relatively industrialized regions with their concentration of workers, higher levels of unionization, and more educated, skilled, and politically conscious labor force (Kahil 1973:67–69). With no change in the minimum wage since 1943, and hence with a substantial erosion of real wages, Vargas seized this issue in his effort to win working-class support in his 1950 presidential bid. Accordingly, once in the beginning and, as we have seen, once again at the end of his presidency, he revised the minimum wage. These adjustments, however, were only slightly higher than the rate of inflation.

After 1954, real average wages continued to rise primarily in response to adjustments in the minimum wage, deteriorating between these adjustments (Kahil 1973:65–66, 70). This pattern of erratic real minimum wage levels produced small improvements through the period to 1960 (see Erickson 1977:100; Fishlow 1973:87). Calculations for the growth in average (rather than minimum) real wages show somewhat better performance, though given the fluctuations, the different end points yield rather different results: according to Oliveira (1977:80) an increase of 4.6 percent from 1949 to 1954 and 24.1 percent between 1954 and 1958, or what Bergsman (1970:59) calculates as an average rate of annual increase of 2.4 percent for the decade 1949–59, and what Kahil (1973:65–66) shows as an improvement of 9 percent by November 1959 over the 1946 level.

In Chile too there were wage gains for workers, but these were modest at best. Based on calculations using figures provided by the Radical Party (cited in Drake 1978:286), the average daily wage of a worker remained virtually unchanged relative to the price of a loaf of bread between 1928 and 1938, and then increased 28 percent between 1938 and 1950. On the other hand, while the nominal average daily wage of workers increased 456 percent in this latter period, the price of basic commodities rose 532 percent, though some miners (in coal and nitrate) and especially textile workers managed to stay ahead of this price rise by 15 percent to, in the case of the textile workers, nearly 40 percent.

These two gains—institutional growth and freedom and some material improvement—must be seen in terms of two other trends: growing income inequalities and the failure to change the legal constraints within which unions operated. In neither country did the growth of working-class income keep up with the gains of other sectors, nor did wages keep up with productivity.

In Brazil, workers did not share equally in this period of economic and industrial growth. According to one calculation, during the period 1949–58 real wages rose only 79 percent of the increase in productivity, while bureaucratic salary increases were more than twice the gains in productivity (Mata and Bacha cited in Oliveira 1977:80). Other estimates show even worse distributional trends. Bergsman (1970:59) finds that between 1949 and 1959 average real wages rose at an average annual rate of 2.4 percent, while the increase for productivity was almost three times as great, 6.6 percent. The high economic growth years under Kubitschek contributed their share to this pattern of growing inequality. For 1955–59, Harding's (1973:316) figures show an increase in wages of 15 percent, compared to a 37 percent increase in productivity and a 75 percent increase in profits, while Caudal (cited in Oliveira 1977:80) gives a figure of 12.3 percent growth in real wages in manufacturing, compared to a 72 percent growth in productivity between 1955 and 1962.

A similar picture may be drawn for Chile. Drake (1978:225) has suggested that "the widening gap between the middle classes, notably white-collar employees, and the workers was a hallmark of the Front administration and subsequent Radical governments of the 1940s." Cavarozzi's (1975:162) figures present a comparison of the increase in nominal wages during the Aguirre Cerda government: 99 percent for workers; 133 percent for white-collar workers in the private sector; 151 percent for administrators and functionaries in the private sector; and 198 percent for administrators and functionaries in the public sector. This pattern is not very different from that of the whole coalitional period. According to the figures of the Radical Party referred to above, from 1938 to 1950 nominal wages for a blue collar worker went up 4.6 times, compared to 8.5 times for a white collar worker. Relative to the price of a loaf of bread, blue collar workers' wages rose by 28 percent while that of white collar workers rose over four times as fast at 117 percent. Another estimate of the 1940–53 period suggests that while real national income rose 40 percent, workers' income rose only 7 percent, while that of white-collar employees rose 46 percent and that of "proprietors" rose 60 percent (Petras 1969:133).

The second disappointment for labor was that, despite the generally more favorable climate for unions, there was very little change in the legal framework in a direction that favored workers or that altered the basic, restrictive labor codes that had been adopted in both countries in the period of incorporation. In Brazil, there was a failure to accomplish any major overhaul of the highly constrained industrial relations system, including the repeal of the syndical tax, which became a major issue during this period. Nevertheless, some concessions on which Vargas campaigned and which he subsequently granted did have an impact. This was most importantly the repeal of the ideological test that had been a requisite for union leadership and which had effectively excluded Communists from leadership positions within the unions. The result of dropping this test and of freer elections was, as we have seen, the breakdown of official unionism and *pelego* control of the syndicates. The marked increase in Communist and radical influence within the union movement had profound importance in the direction of the movement throughout the decade and the beginning of the 1960s. Nevertheless, the basic structure of the labor movement and the industrial relations system, as well as the law on which they were based, were left in place (L. Rodrigues 1969:120–21; J. Rodrigues 1968:187). These continued to act as strong constraints on the labor movement and to limit its capacity for effective action.

In Chile there was an even more thorough failure of the labor movement and working-class spokesmen to extract any concessions with respect to the legal framework of organized labor and the industrial relations system. Though the Ibáñez labor code was the most elaborated, constraining law of the time in Latin America, by the end of the period of incorporation Brazil emerged with an even more elaborated, constraining law. In 1936 under Alessandri, additional constraints were added to the labor law and the subsequent Popular Front and Radical coalition governments failed to reform the law in a direction more favorable to labor. Rather, things took a turn in quite the opposite direction. In 1940–41 legal changes took place that prohibited strikes in public services and banned unions in public and quasi-public agencies (Cavarrozi 1975:159–60). Furthermore, in 1942, under Ríos, the president was given the power to declare emergency zones and break strikes. This provision was used frequently and extensively (Cavarrozi 1975:164–65). Finally in 1948, under González Videla, an additional change in the labor law added new constraints that brought Chile up to a position or level of constraints and "corporatism" comparable to that of Brazil and unique in Latin America (see Collier and Collier 1979:973). In terms of the Brazil-Chile comparison, then, this period saw in effect the completion of a highly constrained industrial relations system that was accomplished under the Estado Novo in Brazil but in a comparative sense was left unfinished during the earlier and shorter incorporation period under the Ibáñez government in Chile.

There was another sense in which the postincorporation period in Chile had the effect of "catching up" with what had been accomplished in Brazil during the period of incorporation—or completing the unfinished business of incorporation in Chile relative to Brazil: during this aftermath period in Chile the labor movement was brought within the legal framework. This was no insignificant matter since during the incorporation period itself a state-controlled, co-opted union movement never succeeded to the same extent or reached the same proportions it did in Brazil.

In the aftermath, substantial debate took place within labor over the legitimacy of the legal union movement, and a competing "free" trade union movement, which rejected the state's role in registering and regulating unions, had been an important current within labor. Unlike the anarchists, who had initially rejected the labor law of 1924, the Communists had initially accepted it, arguing the case for using "all the social legislation of the capitalist state to fight capitalism itself" (cited in Morris 1966:246). After the repression of the Ibáñez presidency, however, they changed their position. Until the 1935 popular front policy, the Communists opposed such a format for working-class organization.

The Socialists, however, decided to take advantage of the legal protections, inducements, and advantages offered (Angell 1972:104). The legal unions established under the Ibáñez government continued to comprise the largest bloc within the labor movement (S. Valenzuela 1979:568). In the context of the great discontinuity of regime during 1932 and the brief establishment of the Socialist Republic, these unions came under the influence of various groups on the left. Thus, democratic unions began to form that were politically autonomous from the government, though since they were formed under the law, they were highly constrained legally. The Socialists quickly consolidated a strong base in the unions, and the growth of legal unionism was rapid during the Alessandri government. Though the Socialists were anxious to establish unions under the law, the government also had a role in this growth. Alessandri encouraged the formation of legal unions—a commitment he made during his first presidency as a way of controlling the union movement. The ascendancy of a legal labor movement was given further impetus by the Popular Front coalition, which meant an additional inducement in the form of a friendlier government attitude toward unions, and by the conversion of the Communist Party to the legal route. Though free unions continued to exist,[13] this period in Chile essentially resulted in the legiti-

---

[13] Alexander (1962a:258) estimates that in 1948, nearly one-fourth to one-third remained free.

mation and working-class acceptance of legal unionism—that is to say, of the organization of the working class into unions registered by the state and controlled under the terms of a highly constraining labor code. Bringing the labor movement within the framework of the labor code was an important step in undermining its revolutionary orientation (S. Valenzuela 1976:157–58). Though this reorientation was a common result of legalization throughout Latin America, it is particularly important to remember this effect in the case of Chile, where, as various authors have noted,[14] close ties between the labor movement and Marxist parties has often led to the attribution of greater revolutionary consciousness on the part of the working class than was in fact the case. In this regard Drake (1978:285) reports, "One Socialist complained that the institutionalization of labor into cooperation with government in the 1940s had produced a union movement almost as tamed by the state as those paternalized by Vargas in Brazil and Perón in Argentina."

In sum, in Brazil and Chile during the aftermath period, populist parties were formed to address the issue of the political participation of the working class. Yet the accommodationist alliances of the middle sectors with the rural oligarchy against the popular sectors had already been set during the incorporation period, and these populist parties did not achieve any substantial success. In the postincorporation period they participated in a complex game of coalition politics in which they were willing to enter into electoral coalition with centrist parties that in turn courted their electoral support. It was a game at which they never won, however, since, despite the electoral coalition, the governing coalition forged following the election was more likely to reflect the underlying accommodationist pattern of politics and to involve a coalition of the center and the right, at the expense of the left and of the working-class support base of the populist parties. Neither the Brazilian PTB nor the Chilean Socialists during the period in which they participated in these coalitions achieved the influence necessary to propose and implement its political project. Despite the concessions granted to the working class during this period, the populist parties that had brought working-class support to the electoral coalitions became discredited for their failure to produce greater results in return for their collaboration.

A process of radicalization began in the labor movement and in the Socialist Party in Chile and the PTB in Brazil. In both countries politics started to become increasingly polarized. In Brazil the Vargas presidency ended with a populistic rallying cry in the form of Vargas's suicide note, which, far from setting a populist tone for the subsequent government, had the effect of mobilizing the right in opposition to populism and of encouraging polarization. The ensuing period under Kubitschek saw the early stirrings of a radical tendency within the labor movement and the PTB. In Chile, by the end of the coalition governments, the Communist Party was banned and the Socialist Party was extremely weak, having been largely discredited for its collaboration with a government which failed to produce significant reforms and con-

---

[14] S. Valenzuela 1976:158; Landsberger and McDaniel 1976.

cessions to the working class. By 1952 in Chile and by 1960 in Brazil, the labor movement and those parties, or tendencies, that attracted working-class support began to move away from a position of collaboration with centrist parties. Thus, the attempt to create a hegemonic multiclass populist party—or even a looser form of populist coalition—did not succeed in these two cases, due to the dynamics set in motion by the strategy followed in the incorporation period, that is, an accommodationist strategy rather than a mobilizational strategy.

MEXICO AND VENEZUELA: TRANSFORMATION OF THE MAJORITY COALITION

In Mexico and Venezuela, the radical populism that characterized the period of party incorporation provoked a strong conservative reaction from many quarters, and substantial political polarization ensued in both countries. With mounting counterreformist opposition, the incorporation period came to an end in Mexico with the election of a more conservative successor to Cárdenas in 1940 and in Venezuela with the military coup that ousted the AD government in 1948. The aftermath of party incorporation involved the working out of the conservative reaction and the effort to put a halt to the polarization that threatened political stability on a long-term basis. In Mexico and Venezuela this was done more successfully than in the other cases of party incorporation. About a decade after the end of the incorporation period, a transformed populist party, representing a broader, more conservative coalition, oversaw the institutionalization of civilian rule, fortified with the political resource of popular sector support that enabled it to stabilize the system by preventing or defeating challenges by the left. These political resources included most importantly the maintenance of a populist alliance between organized labor and the state, effected through the governing party (Mexico) or parties (Venezuela). During the aftermath period, however, the nature of the alliance changed significantly in the course of the working out of the conservative reaction.

In Mexico, the transition was characterized by greater continuity than in Venezuela, as Cárdenas himself responded to the kinds of demands being made by the opposition. Aware of the extent and depth of the reaction his government had generated, Cárdenas moved to appease his opponents and preserve the political order of the incorporating party-state that he had constructed by acquiescing in and legitimating the candidacy within the party of a more conservative successor over the more reformist heir apparent in the 1940 elections. In this way, and very probably with the aid of a fraudulent election, the transition away from radical populism to a more conservative government was accomplished within the same institutional framework.

Important changes and discontinuities did occur, of course, in the Mexican transition: the replacement in power of a progressive coalition by a conservative one and the atmosphere of crisis surrounding the succession are not to be belittled. Nevertheless, the transition in Venezuela was considerably more abrupt. As in Mexico, right-wing conspiracies against the populist government proliferated. In the face of this threat from the right and in response to the prospective decline in oil revenue and the consequent decision to adopt policies to help make Venezuelan manufacturing more competitive, the AD government revised its labor policy. It became concerned to hold down wages and moved more explicitly toward a position that opposed strikes and advocated a position of class-harmony (Ellner 1979:120–24). Unlike the situation in Mexico, however, these moves to call off radical populism and occupy the political center did not prevent a right-wing coup, which brought down the government in 1948. Thus, in Venezuela the conservative reaction resulted in the ouster of the AD government, the banning of the party, and the repression of labor unions, while in Mexico the conservative reaction was in a sense internalized by the party, which continued to hold power.

The conservative reaction arose in opposition both to the substantive reforms and also to the state-popular sector alliance that had been central to radical populism. Radical populism, as we have seen, did not involve an anticapitalist orientation, though in the case of Mexico collective ownership among the peasantry and, more occasionally, among workers was advocated. Rather it was an attempt by a reformist faction of the political elite to gain power and to attain the political resources to carry out its program by mobilizing popular support. Nevertheless, although the reforms took place within the context of state support for capitalist industrialization, the mobilization of the working class entailed more concessions than important sectors of the bourgeoisie were willing to grant. The concessions and reforms also alienated other groups whose interests were adversely affected, such as large landowners whose land was expropriated, and the Church, which opposed the educational reforms and other measures that sought to decrease its influence in society.

Opposition to the substantive program of reform was accompanied by the opposition of these groups to the emerging *form* of politics, that is, by the emergence of an ascendant state-popular sector alliance that was embodied in a dominant and exclusive political party. In Mexico, the PNR/PRM stood virtually alone during the incorporation period, with the exception of a few ephemeral groups, and monopolized official political life. In Venezuela, other parties were formed—parties that participated in elections during the Trienio and that would become institutionalized in Venezuelan politics. Nevertheless, with the overwhelming victories achieved by AD in the elections, it too moved toward a monopolization of political life. As Lieuwen (1961:87) stated, "AD was too strong, and as a consequence tended to become too dominant, too uncompromising. . . . The Government tended to become an exclusive AD preserve."

The opposition thus had the goal not only of terminating the reforms of radical populism but also of dismantling precisely that which was distinctive about this type of incorporation period—the alliance between the state and the popular sectors, as embodied in the populist party. This was particularly clear in the case of Venezuela, where AD was banned by the military government that took over in 1948. In Mexico, although the party retained power, the diverse sectors that supported the opposition candidate Almazán in the 1940 elections found common ground in their opposition to the state coalition that had been put together under Cárdenas and from which they had been excluded. These included the industrial bourgeoisie, particularly around Monterrey, which was not dependent on the state and had opposed the pro–working-class orientation of the Cárdenas regime; the professional and middle classes, who were liberal, favored parliamentary democracy, and opposed socialism; and independent trade unionists who resisted such close political collaboration on the part of labor and the organizational linking of their unions to the state party.

Despite the opposition to the populist alliance, in both countries the alliance was preserved or, in the case of Venezuela, reconstituted after the military interregnum. The dominant part of the labor movement continued to favor cooperation with the state and the maintenance of the multiclass coalition. Not all labor groups accepted the logic of collaboration. Dissenting views arose particularly as the cold war developed and intensified and as the party's commitment to reform receded. Nevertheless, with the political resources that accrued to the aftermath governments, derived from the earlier mobilization of working-class support and from the ties that had been established between labor and the populist party, the noncollaborationist faction of the labor movement was marginalized. The position of the peasantry in the populist alliance was also retained, and in both Mexico and Venezuela the peasantry became the most solid base of support for the PRI and AD respectively.

From the point of view of the labor movement, populism had done three important things that helped to preserve this alliance. First, it created the conditions that made collaboration look attractive to at least the dominant sector of labor. The dynamics of populism led to the offering of benefits and advantages that acted as inducements for labor to enter a political coalition with the middle sector political leadership and to view such collaboration as maximizing labor's influence within the state. In Mexico, this orientation toward collaboration with the state on the part of one faction of labor was initially reinforced by the popular front policy of the Communist faction. Second, during the incorporation period, steps were taken to institutionalize this multiclass coalition and the incorporation of labor in a political party that became the channel of popular sector political participation. Third, the very process of offering these benefits and forging this coalition led to the opposition of large sectors of the upper and middle classes, to the isolation of the state-popular sector alliance, and to conservatizing pressures. This conservative reaction may have enhanced the argument favoring the tactic of union support for the party, for such collaboration was seen in some labor quarters as necessary to oppose the counterreform movement in the case of Venezuela and as necessary to retain influence on government in an effort to prevent even more severe reverses in the case of Mexico.

From the point of view of the political leadership, the state-labor alliance also remained valuable as a source of both political support and political control over the labor movement. However, the form of the alliance and the balance of power within it was no longer considered appropriate. Thus, though the state-labor alliance was preserved, it was considerably transformed as a result of the reaction of political leaders to the conservative reaction. In this context, the narrower populist alliance was replaced by a broader one more nearly approaching a coalition of the whole. The conservative reaction showed the limits of radical populism and the contradiction of pursuing such reform within the context of a capitalist state. It pointed to the necessity, within this context of a capitalist state, of avoiding such polarization, of including the bourgeoisie and middle sectors in the dominant political coalition, and thus of forging a new multiclass coalition, this time displaced toward the right.

In these two countries, the effort of political leaders to combat the conservative reaction in order to either retain (Mexico) or first regain and then maintain (Venezuela) power included all four components outlined in the introduction to this chapter. The first was programmatic. The loyalty of the alienated dominant classes would be won with the adoption of many of their policy prescriptions, in short, with the substantial easing up on reforms and a policy turn to the right. The second was the exclusion of the left from the alliance. The third was the retention of the alliance with the popular sectors (urban and rural) and the continued incorporation of labor as a support group. The fourth was institutional: the establishment of conflict-limiting mechanisms that would help avoid the polarization that had resulted in the toppling of the AD regime in 1948 and that threatened PRM dominance in 1940. In Mexico, the mechanism employed was the strengthening of the one-party dominant system. In Venezuela, the mechanism was the functional equivalent, the party pact. Daniel Levine's (1978:94) description of the pattern of elite negotiation and compromise that was institutionalized in the Venezuelan regime is equally apt for the Mexican case; it was a pattern of conflict resolution in which "privacy, centralization, and control were the watchwords."

These changes occurred in Mexico during the next two presidencies of Avila Camacho (1940–46) and Alemán (1946–52). In Venezuela they occurred after the interim of authoritarian rule, when civilian government was restored and AD returned to power in 1958.

MEXICO

Mexico was the only case of party incorporation in which the conservative reaction did not ultimately culminate in a coup. Nevertheless, similar dynamics characterized the aftermath period in Mexico, since the political logic of retaining power in that country was very similar to the political logic elsewhere of returning to power on a more secure and durable basis. Accordingly, though the party remained in power, it underwent the same process of conservatization as the other incorporating parties that had been ousted from government. Furthermore, a similar consequence of the polarization in Mexico and elsewhere was the introduction of conflict-limiting mechanisms. In the other countries, these took the form either of the continued exclusion of the incorporating party from power (Argentina and Peru) or of a party pact by which the incorporating parties agreed to limit political conflict upon their resumption of power. In Mexico, perhaps because there alone the party remained in power, the structural response to prevent a recurrence of polarization was distinctive: it took the form of institutionalizing a one-party dominant regime.

Because in Mexico the PRM remained in power, it is not relevant to address separately the period of conservative reaction when the incorporating party fell from power. Instead the analysis will depart slightly from the outline followed in the other cases of party incorporation and proceed immediately to the formation of a new governing coalition and the four components of this change outlined above.

Programmatic Shift toward the Right

In Mexico, the programmatic shift to the right to recapture the loyalty of the alienated economic sectors began immediately in the post-Cárdenas years and indeed could already be detected in some of the policies adopted toward the end of the Cárdenas presidency itself. After 1938 and the economic downturn that resulted in part from the expropriation of oil (as well as the increasing political opposition to the social reforms and to the state alliance with the popular sectors), Cárdenas's relations with the popular sectors began to change. He began to call for industrial peace, struck notes of class harmony, and sent in the army to put down strikes. At the same time the rate of land distribution to *campesinos* began to fall off. Furthermore, Cárdenas acquiesced in the choice of, if he did not actually choose, Avila Camacho as his successor over more reformist alternatives. Nevertheless, the presidency of Avila Camacho beginning in 1940 constitutes a decisive break with the more reformist Cárdenas period.

On the most general level, the change in policy represented a shift in emphasis from social reform to industrial modernization. Industrialization became an increasingly explicit priority during the Avila Camacho administration, particularly as World War II established conditions that favored the development of Mexican manufacturing. The emphasis on industrialization implied more favorable policies toward capital at the expense of labor. Yet, in many ways it was the abandonment of social reform in the face of rightist opposition, rather than a decisive turn to industrialization, that was the initial thrust of the new policy orientation (Mosk 1950:60–61). Even before the new economic model was put in place, the commitment to social reform and to the state alliance with the popular sectors was abandoned in view of the new task of reincorporating the disaffected classes. Reassurances were given to the conservative opposition and much of the Almazán program was adopted, so that a short time after the election, the Almazán opposition, which had been talking of armed revolt a few months earlier, announced it would be "Avila's best ally" (Hayes 1951:101).

The displacement of the dominant political coalition to the right, begun by Avila Camacho, was accelerated and intensified under Alemán between 1946 and 1952. The commitment to rapid industrialization was pursued even more single-mindedly under Alemán, now with the added ingredient of the encouragement for foreign investment that became available after the war. Businessmen were recruited into the new cabinet. In the countryside, a change in the constitution once again permitted large holdings (González Casanova 1982:61), and in the cities the Alemán government opposed strikes and initiated a new crackdown on labor.

At the same time that the state became more involved in promoting industrialization and carrying out extensive public works and infrastructural projects, the share of social expenditure in the federal budget fell by over 20 percent to the lowest percent of the overall budget since the depression (Wilkie 1970:85). This change is charted by national budgetary tabulations, which show a shift away from social expenditure to economic expenditure under Avila Camacho, a shift that was accelerated under Alemán (Wilkie 1970:38). With the programmatic move to the right, the government coopted most of the opposition from the right and the private sector.

Exclusion of Left and Retention of State-Labor Alliance

The move to the right had a direct effect on labor policy and on state-labor relations. On the most fundamental level, the acceptance of class conflict and the need of the state to intervene on behalf of labor as the weaker combatant, enunciated and substantially implemented under Cárdenas through government support of strikes and labor demands, was replaced by an emphasis on the promotion of class harmony in which the policy of a special relationship or alliance between the state and labor was replaced by Avila Camacho's policy of "national unity."

With this new orientation, the government no longer promoted unionization, strikes, or material gains for workers. Under Avila Camacho and Ale-

mán, the index of the urban minimum wage plummeted from 103 in 1938–
39, near the end of the Cárdenas government, to 66, near the end of the Alemán government in 1950–51,[15] with a comparable drop in wages in the manufacturing sector (from 100 in 1939 to 50 in 1946, followed by a small rise
and fall back to 54 in 1952—Bortz 1977:157–58). In seeking an explanation
for what seems to be an anomalously sharp decline in the context of rapid
economic growth, economists have subjected this period to particularly critical analysis. While various hypotheses have been proposed to suggest that
the overall decline in wages was not so great as the data suggest, it does nevertheless seem to be the case—and this is most important for present purposes—that the fall in wages in the modern and organized sector of the economy was indeed tremendous once the prolabor policy of Cárdenas was
abandoned (Gregory 1986:219–25, 260). During this period of high economic
growth, industrialization, and falling real wages, the percent of national income going to wages declined from 30.5 percent to 18.6 percent while that
going to corporate profits increased from 26.2 percent to 36.9 percent, over
the years 1939–55 (Handelman 1976:272).

Accompanying the erosion of wages was a decline in strikes, despite the
tightening of the labor market and increased employment produced by rapid
economic growth (Wilkie 1970:185). The one exception to this pattern occurred with the sharp increase in strikes in 1943–44.[16] In addition, under
Avila Camacho unionization stagnated, though it began a secular trend up-
ward under Alemán (Middlebrook 1981h:409). Finally, changes in the labor
law made immediately after the Cárdenas presidency adversely affected labor. At the very outset of his administration, at the end of 1940 and the beginning of 1941, Avila Camacho called a number of extraordinary sessions of
Congress to change the federal labor law. These changes made the dismissal
of workers easier and further regulated and limited the right to strike. Furthermore, a law defining a new "crime of social dissolution" was used
against dissident union leaders (Trejo Delarbre 1976:144; Medina
1978b:288).

A central part of the new labor policy was the marginalization of the left
within the labor movement. Indeed, the exclusion of the left from the dominant coalition could be seen most dramatically within the labor movement.
From the very first, Avila Camacho put distance between himself and Lombardo, the Marxist leader of the CTM during the Cárdenas period. Ex-president Rodríguez, a close political ally of Avila Camacho, proposed a purge of
the labor movement, and in 1941, in a way that remains unclear (see Camacho 1980:52–53) but apparently with government support, Lombardo was
forced out of the position of secretary-general of the CTM, and with him, the
Marxist orientation that had become dominant within the confederation

[15] Wilkie 1970:187; see also Gregory 1986:220.

[16] Middlebrook (1981b:200, 206) has suggested that to some extent this exception in the
downward trend of strikes might be explained by the tactic of textile and mining workers
who struck separately rather than as a group, thus somewhat artificially increasing the
figures.

(Miller 1966:36). Fidel Velázquez, who replaced Lombardo as secretary-general, brought about a new orientation of the CTM, one that accepted private property, opposed communism and withdrew the CTM from communist-influenced international labor organizations, and favored moderation in labor activities and demands.

The new orientation was evident in two pacts entered into by labor. In 1942, the CTM renounced the use of the strike for the duration of the world war, and to implement this policy it sponsored a pact of national worker unity with other labor confederations and groups, which suspended inter-union conflict, strikes, and walkouts and agreed to cooperate with the government in the war effort. This *pacto obrero* was nearly a unilateral pledge on the part of labor: with no participation by capital, it represented an agreement between labor and the government in which labor would support the government policy of labor peace in exchange for the expectation that, in the face of strong counterreformist pressures, the government would recognize unions as collective bargaining agents and would persuade employers to adopt a cooperative stance.

Under the circumstances, labor did not fare well. The government made a number of moves that weakened its position vis-à-vis employers and the state, such as decrees giving the state greater power to decree wages and further restricting work stoppages. With rank-and-file sentiment turning against the debilitating policy of national unity and collaboration, especially in view of economic crisis and deteriorating real wages, the CTM began to turn away from the *pacto obrero*. The new line, developed by Lombardo, abandoned the policy of national unity and stressed an anti-imperialist position. In maintaining the antifascist position, however, Lombardo stressed unity with the national bourgeoisie in advocating a pattern of industrial development based on national economic independence and rising living standards for the working class (Fuentes Díaz 1959:343; Medina 1978b:327–30). The result was the renewal of the orientation toward class cooperation and worker moderation, now formalized in a labor-management agreement between the CTM and the National Chamber of Manufacturing Industries (CNIT), a newly founded group of nationally oriented industrialists, in which both groups agreed to submit disputes to a mediation board (Mosk 1950:28).

The reorientation of the CTM was not simply the result of government pressure and initiative. The political and economic context of the time was an important factor. On the most general level, the objective conditions for a still emerging working class in a newly industrializing country were not favorable. The working class was still relatively small, there was a large labor surplus, and many workers were artisans or employees of small workshops. Though some sectors of the working class were quite strong and fought for independent unions, many others were dependent on government support. This, of course, was the tradition of the *cinco lobitos*, who were now replacing the Lombardo faction as the leadership clique within the CTM. Juxtaposed to this weakness was the strength of the antilabor offensive taken by the right in the postpopulist period. Right-wing industrialists even opposed the 1942 pact: preferring to crush the union movement, they argued that it ceded too much to labor. Because of the opposition of commercial and industrial confederations, Avila Camacho abandoned his proposal, accepted by labor, to form a tripartite commission (Medina 1978b:308). In addition, as we shall see below, the right took a number of initiatives within the labor movement itself. In this context, the experience of the Cárdenas government seemed to show to many within the labor movement the advantage of allying with the government in order to advance the interests of organized labor.

Factors within the labor movement also contributed to the new orientation. Collaboration, of course, had been a feature of the Mexican labor movement since the days of CROM dominance and constituted the formative experience of the newly installed CTM leadership. The tradition was thus not only an institutional one, but also a long-standing personal one. Furthermore, in the competition among the factions within the CTM, alliance with the government may also have become an opportunistic tactic in interfactional leadership rivalries.

Another, perhaps underestimated, reason for this reorientation may have been the emerging competition to the CTM that came from the right. Right-wing Catholic organizations, the *sinarquistas* and the PAN, tried to attract labor away from the CTM, and in 1941 PAN formed a rival National Catholic Federation of Labor. In addition, the following year two new confederations were formed, the COCM and the CPN, and throughout this period Morones's CROM continued to exist as a more conservative confederation in opposition to what had been the Marxist orientation of the CTM during the Cárdenas period (Hayes 1951:117). These rival confederations adopted a collaborationist position and were willing to cooperate with the government. In 1944–45 these last three, the CROM, COCM, and the CPN, which along with the CTM participated in forming the CON to carry out the *pacto obrero*, lined up in opposition to the CTM and finally expelled it from the CON.

Finally, though there was competition within the labor movement from the right, there was little challenge from the left. A major factor in the reorientation of the CTM was the popular front policy of international Communism and hence of Marxist tendencies within the Mexican labor movement. Because of this policy, the Marxists provided little opposition to the turn taken within the CTM and in fact were enthusiastic backers of the 1942 pact and the formation of a broad antifascist coalition, extending their support to the Avila Camacho government. Even before the CTM endorsed the Avila Camacho candidacy in 1940, for instance, the PCM lent enthusiastic support and later announced its willingness to act as "the shock brigade of avilacamachismo" (quoted in North and Raby 1977:51). When the CTM, substantially weakened by growing opposition to the policy embodied in the 1942 pact, was forced to modify its position, it was Lombardo who forged a new labor-management accord.

Throughout the Avila Camacho presidency, then, the state-labor alliance was retained, despite the less favorable attitude of the state toward labor and the reconstitution of a broader, multiclass dominant coalition now displaced to the right. Labor continued to support and cooperate with Avila Camacho in part because of the popular front policy and in part because of the greater threat presented by the right, which made the president appear like a centrist compromiser. In his effort to pursue a policy of national unity to retain labor in the coalition and to steer a middle ground between labor and a vocal right that was calling for much harsher antilabor measures, Avila Camacho offered labor some inducements for cooperation with his program. Social security was adopted in 1941, though it took a few years before implementation was under way, and in 1943 a decree of emergency salaries gave the president the power to increase wages (López Aparicio 1952:231). Not only was this decree applied in various sectors, but the threat it represented stimulated employers to sign contracts that were perhaps somewhat more favorable to workers than might otherwise have been the case (Medina 1978b:314). Overall, however, the precipitous decline in real wages suggests that this measure was extraordinarily limited in its impact. Also, though many policies adversely affected labor, the transitional government of Avila Camacho essentially respected union rights (Fuentes Díaz 1959:345). This was to change in the next presidential term.

The end of the war, which coincided with the beginning of Miguel Alemán's presidency (1946–52), provided a new context in which the postpopulist direction of the Mexican state and the nature of the transformed state-labor alliance became more explicit. Whereas the new direction had been somewhat obscured or moderated by the wartime emergency and the collaborative wartime effort, the end of the war and the onset of the cold war dramatically changed the context in which the collaboration of state, labor, and capital had been pursued, and it accelerated the trends that began with Avila Camacho. The new ideological climate, combined with pressure from the United States, led the Mexican government to assume a stronger anticommunist position, which changed significantly the more cooperative, albeit increasingly uneasy, relations between the government and the left that had more or less continued under Avila Camacho. Of the contenders for the presidency in 1946, what distinguished Alemán were "his experiences as chief of political control during Manuel Avila Camacho's administration, [which] . . . had governed with [wartime] emergency powers [allowing] . . . Alemán to consolidate and modernize the mechanisms of control" (Newell and Rubio 1984:87). The next *sexenio* represented a change from an inclusionary regime aimed at cooperation among different forces and orientations to one that excluded orientations different from what was becoming the orthodox interpretation of the revolution (Medina 1979:93). Significantly, for instance, in 1949 the Mexican Communist Party lost its registration as a legal party with the right to present candidates for election.

From the perspective of many labor groups, particularly the left within the union movement, the end of the war and the onset of the cold war led to a change in strategy: to the abandonment of what was seen as a position of temporary, tactical, wartime cooperation and concessions and a "return" to a more militant, aggressive posture. Beneath the surface of the wartime collaborationist policy of "unity at any cost" had simmered substantial labor discontent. Many labor groups had opposed the 1942 pact, and as wages plummeted, a substantial strike wave had occurred in 1943–44 despite the pact. The political defections within the labor movement could be seen in the considerable opposition to Alemán's presidential candidacy within the CTM (though the confederation itself and the PCM both backed him) and in the withdrawal of national industrial unions from the CTM, starting with the miners in 1942.[17]

In the new postwar climate and in the context of a rapid rise in the cost of living, this labor discontent erupted more forcefully and the reaction of the new president was quick and decisive. Under Alemán, the left was definitively excluded from the dominant coalition. At the same time, despite the new harder line toward labor, the government moved to ensure the maintenance of the state-labor alliance, though in the new context this was accomplished by means that were considerably more coercive. In this way, the Alemán government was responsible for a new departure in the nature of the regime in Mexico.

The years 1947–48 were a watershed that signaled clearly these postwar changes in the exclusion of the left from the dominant coalition and the new pattern of state-labor relations. In that brief period, labor unity broke up. The dissident faction of the labor movement assumed a position of greater opposition and labor militance and broke from the CTM. The faction that remained in the CTM assumed a new orientation of a more asymmetrical form of collaboration with the state. The response of the government to the independent movement within labor was a new technique of coercive control over the labor movement which came to be called *charrismo*.

With the end of the war, then, labor unity collapsed as various union groups abandoned the policy of multiclass collaboration and sought to assert their independence from the state and return to a period of Cárdenas-type reforms. The first manifestation of a split among different factions of the labor movement occurred in the closing days of 1946, when the oil workers called a strike that was repressed by the government. This response split the oil workers union, with the more militant faction calling for independent unionism. The split was echoed within the CTM as a whole, with Lombardo—at this point still championing labor unity—opposing the dissidents and siding with the conservative leadership of the CTM. This division within the CTM intensified in the beginning of 1947 with the election of secretary-general of the CTM. In this election, Amilpa, one of the *cinco lobitos* (the conservative leadership clique then in power) was challenged by dissident leaders of the railroad workers unions, who espoused greater independence from the government. Lombardo again emerged in his accustomed role of arbiter and again sided with the *cinco lobitos*, implicitly supporting the illegal maneuvers of Amilpa's election (Medina 1979:126) in order to pre-

[17] Medina 1979:143; Basurto 1984:52–53; Roxborough 1986:15, 31–32.

serve labor unity. Unity was not maintained, however, and the dissident leadership left the CTM and founded the CUT as a rival confederation, based primarily on the railroad workers. In the beginning of 1948, the railroad workers were joined in a pact of solidarity by the independent miners and the oil workers, who the previous month had left the CTM.

The next step in the fractionalization of the labor movement and in the expulsion of the left from the CTM and the dominant coalition occurred three days later on 10 January 1948. With the end of the war, Lombardo advocated a change in tactics from one of collaboration within the official political family to one of greater distance and independence (Medina 1979:114). To this end he advocated the founding of a new progressive party that would be independent of the official PRM/PRI and the government. Proposing this idea originally in 1944, he acquiesced in Avila Camacho's request not to pursue it until after the presidential elections of 1946 (Medina 1979:118). In 1947, in the context of the leadership succession within the CTM, he apparently made a bargain with Amilpa: in exchange for Lombardo's support, Amilpa would support the new party (Medina 1979:126). With the intensification of the cold war during the summer months (in September the Rio Treaty of regional security was signed by countries of the Western Hemisphere), the agreement was broken: Lombardo took up a more militant anti-imperialist position, and Amilpa was all too eager to comply with Alemán's urging to reject CTM affiliation with Lombardo's new party, the Popular Party (the PP, which later became the PPS) (Hayes 1951:167–68). The result was another split in the CTM in the beginning of 1948 with the expulsion of Lombardo and three CTM secretaries who had supported the PP.

The CTM was thus purged of leftist influence. From the point of view of the government, however, the job remained incomplete for the labor movement as a whole: though the challenge within the CTM leadership had been defeated, the challenge from labor had grown, as a majority of the organized working class now escaped party discipline and influence. At this juncture, the party could count about 92,000 members in the CTM and an additional 31,000 in other PRI-affiliated confederations. These figures compare to an estimated CUT membership of nearly 150,000 and an additional 216,000 workers that included those in national industrial unions not affiliated with confederations (Leal 1985:40).[18]

This fragmentation of the labor movement posed a major challenge for the government politically and economically. Politically the government remained dependent on the state-labor alliance, which seemed to be in the process of dissolution. Economically, the Alemán project of industrialization sought to subsidize industry through low prices in certain key sectors, yet

---

[18] Membership figures must always be used with caution. Using different data that show nearly double the total unionized workers, Medina (1979:146–47) has presented a different balance of workers in collaborating versus independent confederations, of about 500,000 to 330,000. With a similar total figure for the CTM, the 400,000 indicated for the other PRI-affiliated confederations raises some question and differs very substantially from the 95,000 members given for the previous year, 1947, in Medina (1978b:287).

these sectors, especially oil and railroads, were precisely those in which the workers were prominent in the dissident movement (Medina 1979:152). Under these circumstances the government turned to a new method, foreshadowed in the 1946–47 oil strike, to bring the wayward unions back into the coalition and into the CTM: government intervention in internal union affairs, particularly in leadership struggles and rivalries within the unions. The first clear case, which gave the new form of state-controlled unionism its name, *charrismo*, occurred in the railroad workers' union in 1948. Similar interventions occurred in the oil workers' union in 1949 and in the mining and metal workers' union in 1950. With these interventions, the independent union movement collapsed: the proposed new labor confederation, the UGOCM (General Union of Mexican Workers and Peasants), was denied official recognition and in any case was debilitated, as was Lombardo's new political party, by the reaffiliation of the intervened unions with the CTM.

In this way, the CTM and state-labor relations acquired a number of characteristics that were to endure. The left was eliminated within the CTM, which withdrew from CTAL (the left-leaning hemisphere-wide union confederation founded by Lombardo) and assumed a strong anticommunist position. Symbolic of these changes was the change in the slogan of the CTM from "For a Classless Society" to "For the Emancipation of Mexico." The state-labor alliance, as embodied in the labor sector of the party, thereby also excluded the left.

The fragmentation of the union movement also marked a division between different types of labor organization—a division which, begun during the Cárdenas period and patched over in the context of the policy of "unity at all costs," now became much more explicit. The unions that left the CTM were national industrial unions and were often in the more important economic sectors of the economy. While the CTM continued to embrace some national industrial unions, the more typical form of organization within the CTM was the regional and state federation based on heterogeneous, small, enterprise unions. Thus, to the extent the state-labor alliance was effected through the CTM, that alliance excluded—or at least was substantially more problematic with respect to—the left within the labor movement and workers in the more important and dynamic economic sectors, in which the unions adopted a more independent stance.

Another characteristic that emerged clearly at this time—or reasserted itself in a more definitive and institutionalized form—was the consolidation of control of the CTM by a collaborationist, bureaucratized, entrenched, and self-perpetuating leadership clique. For a decade Lombardo had mediated between the two rival tendencies within the CTM: the more left-leaning tendency and the more "moderate" one, headed by the *cinco lobitos*, most prominently Fidel Velázquez. On several occasions, Lombardo, primarily to maintain labor unity, had sided with the moderates. His final support of Amilpa to replace Velázquez in 1947 made it clear that the rivalry between the moderates and the more independent leftists had been definitively won by the former. The result was the split of the opposing tendency from the

CTM to the point that even Lombardo was forced to leave, as the moderates consolidated their position. In 1950 Fidel Velázquez again became secretary-general of the CTM and, at the close of the 1980s, remained in the post. With the co-optive resources coming from the state, oligarchic control of unions by a leadership clique became well institutionalized. Government intervention was rarely needed to perpetuate the dominance of the *charros*, though the technique developed in the 1940s defined a new method of state action to control independent unionism, which was called upon when necessary (Medina 1979:137; Roxborough 1984:26).

Finally, the state-labor coalition became more assymetrical, with greater union dependence on and identification with the state. As Medina (1979:134) has said, the support labor gave to the government was no longer at arms length as under Cárdenas, nor was the support extended in the context of special circumstances—national and international—as under Avila Camacho. Now the support was unconditional and uncritical and was granted without extracting anything in return in the way of guarantees.

Conflict-Limiting Mechanisms

The final major change that occurred in the aftermath of incorporation was the establishment of new conflict-limiting mechanisms in order to overcome and, in the future, prevent the political conflict and polarization that characterized the period of radical populism. Changes within the party and in the electoral system were made to institutionalize an inclusionary multiclass coalition within the party and to strengthen the one-party dominant system.

The changes within the party reinforced the shifts in the governing coalition and were aimed at decreasing the role of the party and subordinating it to the state, imposing greater discipline within the party, and reducing the power of the sectors within the party, especially that of labor. Measures to limit the political role of the party and subordinate it to the state were undertaken at the beginning of Avila Camacho's presidency when the party newspaper was turned over to the Ministry of Interior and party radio stations were taken away (Garrido 1984:309; González Casanova 1982:57). Efforts were also made to impose greater discipline within the party. Though political opposition to the PRM was defeated in the 1940 elections, the political polarization continued to be expressed within the party. Factionalism reflecting the many divisions within the party (the right, the Calles faction, the Cárdenas left, and those identified with Avila Camacho) was expressed in the formation of congressional blocs that became obstacles to the reconstitution of a governing coalition that could consolidate support for the government (Garrido 1984:313; Medina 1978b:185). To impose greater discipline, the party first issued a declaration condemning the formation of such blocs and then moved to control them by institutionalizing a rotating leadership of the blocs in which a bloc "president" would be installed and charged with overseeing discipline. An additional attempt to control intraparty factionalism was the requirement that candidates presented by any one party sector have the approval of the other sectors. Consequently, in the 1943 legislative elections, the labor and peasant sectors were forced to accept many candidates who were unrelated to their organizations (Garrido 1984:336).

Other measures aimed at weakening the party sectors and subordinating them to the central administrative organs. An Avila Camacho loyalist was named to head the CNC and thus bring the peasant sector into line, and a leadership change within the CTM was in one way or another effected, in which Lombardo was replaced by Fidel Velázquez. In addition, the military sector, which embraced important factions identified with Cárdenas as well as with Almazán, was disbanded.

Finally, changes in the party were made to weaken the left and increase the strength of the center. Most important were the changes that increased the political weight of the so-called popular sector, which embraced white-collar and middle-class groups in order to counter the influence of the labor and peasant sectors. The membership in the popular sector was expanded beyond its major initial constituency of public sector unionists to include a larger number of the self-employed, such as artisans, professionals, and co-operative members, as well as small agriculturalists, merchants, and industrialists. In addition, the CNOP was formed as a new confederation of the popular sector organizations to help displace the CTM's role as mobilizing agent for the party.

Though the reinforcement of the popular sector was clearly intended to dilute the influence of labor on the left, it also addressed the challenge presented from the right, which in some sense was even greater, for being more powerful and less loyal. It was, after all, the right that had posed the major opposition to the party in 1940, while the left was loyally though reluctantly concurring in the moves of the party to the right. It was also the right, not the left, that in the first years of Avila Camacho's presidency opposed the moves toward class collaboration and national unity, as they were expressed, for instance, in the *pacto obrero* (Medina 1978b:308). The task set by Avila Camacho was thus to end the political polarization by creating a political force nearer the center that would strengthen the state and provide the foundation for a program based on class compromise. The strengthening of the popular sector of the party did provide the state with a source of popular support for a centrist program. Furthermore, it not only weakened the relative influence of labor and the peasants, but also preempted the efforts of the right to incorporate the middle class (which had voted in substantial numbers for Almazán) as an opposition group (Garrido 1984:320). It may be noted that the formation of the CNIT, a confederation of newer industrialists who were less politically powerful and more economically dependent on the state, was a parallel move to counterbalance both the labor opposition on the left and the intransigent Chambers of Industry and Commerce on the right. Similarly, it has been suggested that the state may have encouraged the formation of the PAN as a force in the center in an effort to control and weaken the more dangerous *sinarquistas* on the right (O'Shaughnessy 1977:77).

These changes, which both altered the balance of forces within the PRM to favor the popular sector over the labor and peasant sectors and also weakened the autonomy of these sectors, were in place by the time of the 1943 legislative elections. Despite these changes and a nonaggression "pact of honor" in which the CTM, the CNC, and CNOP pledged to respect each other's spheres of influence in the apportionment of party candidates among the sectors, the elections were marked by intense sectoral competition. The result was great disunity and tension. Nevertheless, the dominance of the popular sector was achieved and could be seen in the distribution of seats in the new legislature: of the 144 seats held by the PRM, over half, or 75, were from the popular sector (of which 56 were from the CNOP), compared to 46 from the peasant sector (of which 43 were from the CNC), and 23 from the labor sector (of which 21 were from the CTM) (Garrido 1984:338; Medina 1978b:193–98). The loss of influence of the labor sector could also be seen in the distribution of major posts: the presidency of the Electoral College and the presidency of the legislature both went to the CNOP, while the leadership of the majority bloc went to the CNC (Medina 1978b:205).

These changes culminated in the January 1946 reorganization of the party and the transformation of the PRM into the PRI. Many scholars point to the 1938 party reorganization and the establishment of a corporative party as the basis of the subsequent system of political domination in Mexico. Though that reorganization constitutes a crucial step, it is important to pay at least equal attention to these subsequent changes and the reorganization of the party as the PRI. "The PNR was a party of parties: the PRM was a party of sectors. If the former implied the de-organization of the [component] political parties, the latter accomplished the de-organization of political classes and their [re]organization as sectors. Starting with the entry of labor into the state party, the problem of the state was to control the labor sector and its organizations. . . . Thus a new process was initiated that would culminate in the founding of the PRI" (González Casanova 1982:55).

The change to the PRI was both ideological and structural. Ideologically, this transformation is well summed up by the change in party slogans from "For a Workers' Democracy" to "Democracy and Social Justice." Structurally the change consisted of weakening the power of the sectors and strengthening the central party apparatus, as power was concentrated in the central organs of the party and greater hierarchy was imposed. In accordance with the provisions of the new electoral law passed the previous month, the PRI was based on individual rather than collective membership. The electoral and party activities of the sectors were restricted and the system of nomination of party candidates was changed from one of sectoral designation by caucus or executive order to a system of nominating conventions and primaries.

The further subordination of the sectors and their organizations particularly affected labor, which had been the most autonomous of the sectors. Furthermore, labor depended on the power of sectoral organization to compensate for its relatively small numbers and geographical concentration (Scott 1964:141). Labor was particularly vociferous in its opposition to the changes, and it was in this context that Lombardo left the party. As noted, in the following years conflict and labor opposition escalated. Dissension took place both outside of and within the party. In the face of these objections, the old system of sectoral nominations was reinstituted at a party convention in 1950, but only after the left had been expelled from the CTM and hence from the labor sector. Furthermore, the more hierarchical organization of the party was maintained, and the sectors came to comprise a system of support for the government subordinated to the central organizations of the party (González Casanova 1982:62).

The changes, then, altered the balance of power within the party. They represented a change from a coalition party to a multiclass integrative party characterized by a more uneven partnership in which the labor movement became increasingly subordinate. Instead of referring to itself as a popular front organization or as a pact among the revolutionary sectors, as the PRM of Cárdenas had, the PRI began to make reference to a "political association of citizens" (González Casanova, 1982:59). "The change from the PRM to the PRI . . . was one from a party in which the weight of the proletariat and of the popular bases was considerable . . . to one in which the direct involvement of the workers' organizations was brought to an end, internal political debate in labor centrals disappeared, assemblies of the base were endangered, while the power of the central organs increased, characteristic of the new process of hierarchization of the state" (Gonzalez Casanova 1982:60). Garrido (1984:347) has argued that by the end of the Avila Camacho presidency, executive control over the legislature was accomplished with the elimination of internal debate within the party and correspondingly also in the Chamber of Deputies.

This limitation on debate and pluralism within the party was complemented by the other major conflict-limiting mechanism, the new electoral law of 1946, which strengthened the one-party dominant system in Mexico. Because the 1940 elections had taken place amid such polarization and had been marked by fraud and violence, the Avila Camacho government and the electoral system more generally lacked legitimacy (Medina 1978a:17). Many groups were calling for reform of the electoral system, and the government, for its part, not only wanted to establish greater legitimacy, but also needed an instrumentality for minimizing polarization and conflict and for ensuring Alemán a more decisive victory. ·

The new law moved to reinforce the one-party dominant system in three ways. First, it centralized the electoral machinery and strengthened the government's ability to control the electoral process. This assertion of central control was in part a response to charges of fraud at the local level, and to this extent it helped to address the problem of legitimacy. Simultaneously and not coincidentally, however, greater control was now lodged in central organs that were dominated by the PRI. Second, the law moved to eliminate regional and ephemeral parties and to institutionalize a party system based on permanent, national parties. It did this by establishing requirements for the formation and legal registration of political parties: a minimum national membership of 30,000, with at least 1,000 in each of two-thirds of the Mexican states. Furthermore, to participate in elections, parties had to be registered one year in advance.

Third, the law limited opposition parties and restricted electoral competition. The various requirements had the effect of limiting not only small and regional parties, but also religious parties and those of the "extreme" right and left, which tended to be small or regionally based. The new law also made registration much more difficult than the 1918 law, which it replaced. Further modifications of the law in 1949, 1951, and 1954 increased the membership requirements, making the formation of opposition parties even more difficult.

With these changes the PRI was able to dominate the electoral arena and institutionalize a one-party dominant regime. In subsequent decades it controlled all governorships and most municipal governments, and its overwhelming dominance of the national Congress became so complete that it posed an embarrassment to government claims that Mexico was a competitive democracy. On the bases of the changes that occurred in the aftermath of incorporation, essentially by 1950, both the PRI and the Mexican political system took the form that it would maintain during the subsequent decades (González Casanova 1982:62).

VENEZUELA

In Venezuela the dynamics of party incorporation led to polarization and opposition, culminating in a military coup. The 1948 coup ushered in a decade of military rule during which AD was outlawed, the labor movement was attacked and repressed, and state policy retreated from most of the substantive reforms of the AD government. Given the strength of the conservative reaction, AD leaders, like their counterparts in other cases of party incorporation, guided their party toward the political center in order to reestablish and consolidate civilian rule once the military regime was brought down in 1958. The result was quite a different coalition and a less reformist agenda than that which had characterized AD during the Trienio. As Petras (1970:100) has said, "In order to rule, Betancourt chose to come to terms with the major institutions of the old order, the foreign and domestic investors, the military, and the large landholders. Based on a highly bureaucratized party and a trade union apparatus closely linked to the government bureaucracy . . . Betancourt, Raul Leoni, and the extreme right wing of the AD were able to drive populists, nationalists, and moderate reformers outside of the party."

Conservative Reaction

In contrast to Mexico, the conservative reaction to radical populism in Venezuela culminated in the military overthrow, on 24 November 1948, of the AD government and the onset of a decade of authoritarian rule that completely excluded the populist party. Lombardi is most explicit in his interpretation of the government of Pérez Jiménez, who was in power for most of the decade, as a reactionary one, stating that this "anachronistic decade" represented a "throwback to earlier forms. Pérez Jiménez bears a closer kinship to Juan Vicente Gómez and Antonio Guzmán Blanco than to any modern military chieftain" (Lombardi 1982:226–27). However great the similarity to the pre-1936 period may or may not have been, what is clear is the anti-AD sentiment of the groups that supported the coup. In addition to the military, these included bourgeois and middle-sector groups, who were alarmed by the radical rhetoric of AD, as well as Lopecistas, Medinistas, and other political and sectoral groups, all of whom were united by the exclusivity of AD and its monopoly of power (Boeckh 1972:194).

Pérez Jiménez did not consolidate his power until the death, in November 1950, of Delgado Chalbaud. The original junta that assumed power in 1948 was composed of three military officers, Delgado, Pérez Jiménez, and Llovera Paez, among whom Delgado was the dominant figure (Martz 1966:89). Delgado had been minister of defense under the Gallegos government and, like the other two members of the 1948 junta, had earlier participated in the coup that brought AD to power in 1945. While the 1948–50 junta was in some ways less repressive than the subsequent government under Pérez Jiménez, the conservative reaction to the radical populism of the Trienio began in this initial period. More importantly, both the junta and later Pérez Jiménez moved energetically to eliminate AD and sought to dismantle the state-labor coalition it had built, as well as to demobilize the popular forces that had provided the AD regime with support. The specific targeting of the populist coalition of the Trienio can be seen in the immediate attack on AD party and union leaders and the banning of the party in December 1948, within days of the coup. Two months later the CTV and many AD-affiliated union locals were declared illegal. By contrast, the government was initially more tolerant of the Communists. At first the PCV operated semiclandestinely and was not declared illegal until May 1950. The dissident Black Communist faction (PRP), which unlike the PCV had not cooperated with AD and the CTV during the Trienio, escaped government repression, as did the unions in which the PRP was influential. The PRP lent support to the military regime until the two Communist factions were reunited in the mid-1950s.

Upon coming to power, then, the military junta moved quickly to destroy AD as a functioning political organization. Within days of the coup, AD's political leadership was either in prison, in exile, or in hiding. Given the close, often interlocking, relationship between party and union leaders, the AD union leadership was severely affected by this first wave of repression. During the initial few weeks of the new government, the army took over AD-controlled unions, placed their leaders in prison, confiscated their records, and froze their union bank accounts (Fagan 1974:83). Although these moves were aimed more at AD than at the labor movement per se, the more focused attack on unions was soon to come.

While much of AD's leadership was immediately sent into exile or prison following the coup, other AD leaders began to organize cautiously from hiding. By February 1949, party and labor leaders had a significant clandestine organization in place (Fagan 1974:83–84). In that month, the AD-dominated CTV issued a series of demands to the new junta. These included the release of imprisoned union leaders, a restoration of freedom of association, the end of government intervention in union activities, and the release of government-impounded union funds. When the original demands were met with arrests, the CTV initiated a newspaper strike that quickly spread to a number of other important Caracas trade unions (Fagan 1974:84). The stage was set for a confrontation between labor and the state.

With the CTV gearing up for a general strike, the junta reacted quickly by dissolving the labor confederation and its member organizations. In one stroke the junta eliminated all but four minor federations (Fagan 1974:84). While the 705 locals that had made up the CTV were still intact, the Labor Ministry quickly enforced a series of directives that made it increasingly difficult for those unions to continue functioning. Specifically, they could not operate legally until they held new elections, over which the government imposed stiff controls: government permission was required to hold the elections; former officers were declared ineligible; government inspectors had to be present to certify the elections; and the junta sometimes imposed its own lists or promptly arrested newly elected officers (Fagan 1974:86).

In addition to the high level of outright repression applied during the first year, the junta briefly pursued a parallel policy of allowing some AD union leaders to cooperate in forming a government-dominated petroleum workers union that would replace the former CTV-affiliated federation. However, after the oil workers strike of 1 May 1950, this experiment came to an end, and the government greatly increased its repression of the labor movement (Boeckh 1972:196). The May strike was organized by AD and the Communist Party (PCV) in the hope that a long strike in the oil industry would provoke a military coup led by more sympathetic officers (Godio 1982:96). Instead, the government responded harshly and the strike was undermined. On 8 May 1950 the PCV was outlawed, as were the 43 unions affiliated with it (Godio 1982:92–96). As a result of government pressure, by the end of 1950, only 387 of the former CTV unions still functioned, down 63 percent since the confederation was suspended (Fagan 1974:86). Most of the defunct unions were the relatively inexperienced and newly created rural unions, but even the stronger, more experienced urban unions soon lapsed into inactivity as well.

With the assassination of Delgado Chalbaud in November 1950, apparently by security officers connected to Pérez Jiménez, Pérez Jiménez himself took control of the junta, and the attacks on AD and the labor movement intensified. As Alexander noted, as long as Delgado headed the government, the dictatorship was a mild one that claimed to be moving toward elections "as soon as possible" (Alexander 1982:354). The 1951–58 period was to be substantially different, as Pérez Jiménez rejected free elections, heightened repression of political parties, and intensified his attack on independent labor unions. By the end of 1951, most of the CTV unions that had survived the 1950 crackdown had dissolved. In 1952, repression of the parties and the unions was stepped up. "By mid-1953 few unions of any type existed" except for a few PRP unions that collaborated with the government (Fagan 1974:88). Interestingly, this greater repression occurred in the context of a failed attempt to establish party and union structures that would provide Pérez Jiménez with a base of support and thereby legitimate his rule.

In 1952, Pérez Jiménez created a personalist political party, the Independent Electoral Front (FEI) and called general elections. Believing that with AD eliminated he would have little difficulty in defeating both COPEI and URD, he allowed the two parties to field candidates. As the election tally came in and it became increasingly clear that URD had won a landslide victory, Pérez Jiménez stopped the vote count and a week later announced that he had won. In the wake of the election, the URD joined AD and the PCV on the list of proscribed parties. While COPEI was not banned, its leaders were arrested or fled the country (Alexander 1982:341). By January 1953, virtually all opposition political activity in the country had come to a halt, and Pérez Jiménez put increased pressure on party leaders operating underground.

While AD had been able to maintain an extensive clandestine organization during the first year of the dictatorship, after 1952 the heightened persecution reduced its strength, although it continued as the strongest group within the underground.

At the same time, a new element in the regime's labor policy was introduced: the attempt to constitute a government-dominated trade union movement. While the original junta had attempted to form a government-controlled oil workers federation and had forced local unions to elect lists approved by the government, it did not attempt to organize a national confederation under government control. This step was taken by Pérez Jiménez. In 1952 Peronist labor leaders persuaded Pérez Jiménez to copy Perón's labor model (Godio 1982:92). The Workers Independent Union Movement (MOSIT, later the CNT) was founded that year, and in 1954 it joined Perón's Latin American labor confederation (ATLAS) (Alexander 1982:338).

As elsewhere, the attempt to emulate Perón was doomed to failure. Peronism represented a model of a labor movement that provided crucial support for a military leader, particularly one subsequently seeking legitimacy through electoral means, as Pérez Jiménez attempted to do in 1957. But Peronism was also inherently a model of populism, that is, of the active mobilization of working-class support through concessions, and it was precisely as a conservative reaction to populism that the 1948 coup and the Pérez Jiménez government must be understood. Thus, like the FEI in the party sphere, the MOSIT/CNT in the labor sphere failed to provide a vehicle for support mobilization, and Pérez Jiménez relied primarily on repression. With the failure of tactics such as intervention in union elections, the creation of parallel unions favored by the government, the determination of contract terms by the Ministry of Labor, and the removal of the strike as an instrument of demand making, the government resorted to police terror, arrests, torture, and concentration camps. In this context, the government's construction of union buildings and resort towns for workers did little to conceal its antilabor orientation (Boeckh 1972:197–99). Thus, the attempt to build a progovernment labor movement had little impact, and whatever unions were formed did not survive the January 1958 coup that overthrew Pérez Jiménez.

In addition to dismantling the state-labor coalition and the demobilization of popular forces, both of which had been an important part of radical populism, the Pérez Jiménez government also opposed the substantive reforms of the Trienio. Pérez Jiménez "entirely abandoned the reformist orientation of AD" (Tugwell 1975:47). This was particularly clear in the area of oil policy where he backtracked considerably, dropping the ideas of an anticyclical fund and a nationalized petroleum sector. Pérez Jiménez cooperated with and accommodated the foreign oil companies by extending new concessions, allowing generous profits, and abandoning attempts to extend government control over the foreign oil companies (Tugwell 1975:47–48). Unlike the thrust of the Trienio, which sought to capture state revenues from oil and use them to promote industry and agriculture and sought to employ an activist state policy to steer a course toward a more balanced pattern of development, policy under Pérez Jiménez turned almost exclusively to the export of oil. As a result, by the end of his government, Venezuela became "a petroleum factory" (Betancourt, quoted in Tugwell 1975:49).

Agricultural policy was also dramatically reversed. Not only was the distribution of land and credit to *campesinos* halted, but many peasants were evicted from land acquired under the Trienio's agrarian reform program. In addition, land the AD government had come to control was returned to private hands, and commercial farmers rather than the peasants became the beneficiaries of government agrarian policy. The "counter-revolution" in agrarian reform thus represented a "drastic reversal" of government policy. According to Powell's estimate, by 1958 "almost all the land that had been used for agrarian reform under AD from 1945–1948 had come under private control, and almost all of the peasants formerly settled thereon had been evicted," sometimes violently. In the decade of military rule, peasant organization suffered the same fate as the larger labor movement more generally: the number of peasant unions decreased from 515 with over 43,000 members to just 79 with about only 1,000 members (Powell 1971:90–94).

Given Pérez Jiménez's attempt "to refashion a centralized autocracy like that of his predecessor Gómez" (Tugwell 1975:20), the dictator failed to form a coalition with the national bourgeoisie, even though the private sector had opposed AD's reforms and had encouraged the military to overthrow the government in 1948 (Martz 1966:307). As a spinoff of both the tremendous expansion of oil revenues based on increased production from new concessions and the public works projects undertaken by Pérez Jiménez, industry grew rapidly during the 1950s, more than tripling in terms of nominal output (Fagan 1974:82), although it must be remembered that this is an increase from a low initial level of industrialization. Despite this growth, industrialists had few political ties to Pérez Jiménez and could not be considered part of his coalition (Story 1978:168). The Pérez Jiménez government represented a reversal of the previous commitment of the state to assume responsibility for the promotion of industry, retreating from the policies which were initiated and later resumed under the democratic governments that preceded and followed the dictatorship (Story 1978:280). Furthermore, Pérez Jiménez severely restricted the activities of FEDECAMARAS, the national private sector association, and of all other interest groups, reducing them to virtual inactivity (Story 1978:164, 167). As a result of these policies—as well as of an increasing level of corruption and economic mismanagement, both of which reached major proportions during the latter years of the dictatorship (Tugwell 1975:47)—the industrialists were firmly in opposition, as were most other organized sectors of Venezuelan society, by the time of the 1958 coup that ousted Pérez Jiménez.

Formation of New Governing Coalition

The coup of 1948 set the agenda for AD. The party's fortunes were dependent not only on the return of civilian party politics, but also, as Betancourt in particular saw it, on the adoption by the party of changes that would prevent a repetition of the political dynamics of the Trienio that had led to AD's military overthrow. Specifically what was needed, in this view, was the forging of cooperative relations among parties and social groups to prevent a recurrence of the earlier opposition and polarization. These "lessons" of the Trienio and of the conservative reaction to it played a key role in orienting AD's strategy in 1958 toward the creation of a kind of coalition of the whole which would be necessary to sustain civilian rule (D. Levine 1973:esp. 236–37; Arceneaux 1969:156, 257–59).

The specifics of this basic agenda to create a broad coalition differed from that in Mexico. Nevertheless, it had the same four basic components. Like the PRM in Mexico, the proscribed AD moved away from its radical populist program to gain the confidence of the rightist opposition as a prerequisite for the restoration and maintenance of a democratic regime and for AD's return to power. This move was initiated through a series of agreements among the exiled leaders of the major parties. The agreements were contained in the Pact of Punto Fijo and a number of other pacts, which in addition to defining the broad outlines of a moderate policy orientation to which the parties were committed, also established certain parameters for political competition and instituted a number of conflict-limiting mechanisms. Part and parcel of AD's shift to the right was the alienation of the left and its exclusion from the coalition. Finally, as in Mexico, despite the shift to the right and the exclusion and alienation of the left, AD was able to maintain its influence in the newly reconstituted labor movement, both urban and rural.

Programmatic Shift toward the Center.   AD's ability to return to power depended on the calling of elections by the new military junta. In the longer run, however, the Trienio taught Betancourt that staving off a military coup and retaining power once elected was dependent upon AD's ability to "gain the support or the tolerance of the institutions and groups in Venezuelan society which had effective power to overthrow such a regime, even though they might not have many votes. These groups include the military, the Catholic Church, and the nation's principal economic groups, the industrialists and the bankers" (Alexander 1982:388–89).

The first order of business for AD, then, was to win at least the passive if not the active support of groups it had alienated during the Trienio by alleviating their fears and deemphasizing the party's former radicalism (Blank 1973:138). It did this first by adopting a series of agreements, particularly with the representatives of the business community and of the other political parties, on a moderate social and economic program. These initiatives actually began during 1957 before the ouster of Pérez Jiménez and continued through the final Pact of Punto Fijo agreement in October 1958.

The development of cooperation among diverse groups was rooted in the nearly universal hostility to the Pérez Jiménez government. Virtually every organized sector of Venezuelan society found itself in common opposition to the dictatorship by late 1957. The dictator's harassment of the Catholic Church, as well as the arrest of several priests, had led the archbishop of Caracas to issue a severe criticism of the government in May 1957. The government's economic policy, especially its decisions to cut industrial credits to all sectors but construction and not to increase protectionist tariffs, alienated the growing industrial elite. The opposition included industrialists in the construction sector, previously Pérez Jiménez's "greatest allies," who moved against the government due to its failure to pay its bills. Finally, the financial sector grew increasingly dissatisfied with Pérez Jiménez's use of the previously small Banco de Tachira as the major conduit of state monies, while his creation of a parallel military organization (Seguridad Nacional) increased military discontent (Rangel 1966:43-44; Karl 1986:207–8).

During the last five years of the Pérez Jiménez dictatorship, the divisions and animosities among the political parties had begun to fade, partly due to the common experience of imprisonment and repression (Alexander 1982:390). AD had been joined in opposition by Villalba's URD after the elections of 1952 were annulled. While COPEI was not banned, as URD and AD had been, its leadership was harassed and often jailed. As early as 1956, AD leaders in exile were calling for the creation of a "united front of all opposition groups" to oppose the dictatorship (Alexander 1982:393). This gradual rapprochement between the parties was spurred by the meeting in mid-1957 between Betancourt and Villalba, both in exile at the time in New York. Adopting a broad set of shared principles, both party leaders agreed to support the candidacy of COPEI's Caldera in the 1957 elections (Alexander 1982:395). In August 1957 Caldera was arrested by the Pérez Jiménez government and jailed until December. On 19 January 1958 Caldera went into exile and was met at the New York airport by Betancourt and Villalba (Alexander 1982:395–96). Over the next week, the three party leaders agreed on the need for cooperation, and two days after the coup—Villalba having already left for Venezuela—Betancourt and Caldera reached a broad agreement on working together to institutionalize the future democratic regime (Alexander 1982:396–97).

The coordination and compromise among the party leaders in exile was paralleled within the country. In June 1957, the younger generation that came to form the leadership of the underground organizations of the four major parties, AD, COPEI, URD, and the PCV, united to establish the Junta Patriótica in order to rally civilian opposition to Pérez Jiménez (Alexander 1982:387). Led by the URD youth leader, Fabricio Ojeda, the Junta Patriótica moved quickly to organize an anti-Pérez Jiménez mobilization. When the Junta Patriótica called for a national general strike on 21 January 1958, AD-led trade unions were joined by the Catholic Church, the National Council of Bankers, the National Chamber of Commerce and Industry, and the Chamber of Construction Industries in support of the strike (Karl 1986:209). In the course of the strike, the police killed 300 and wounded 1,000 protesters (Martz 1966:95), but the military refused to suppress the protest. Pérez Jiménez left Venezuela on 23 January and a new military junta took control.

Though the Pérez Jiménez dictatorship had been overthrown, the future of democratic government in Venezuela was still not assured. AD emerged from the decade of dictatorship as it entered it, as the largest electoral force, albeit less dominant. Yet AD now had a new commitment to compromise with the major economic and social groups in the interest of stabilizing the democratic system. Betancourt had spent much of 1957 and 1958 establishing friendly relations with the business sector, often through face-to-face meetings (Alexander 1982:392, 416–17). Along with Villalba of the URD, he had assured business leaders that AD did not plan any changes in the structural basis of the Venezuelan economy (Rangel 1966:46).

The final compromises were formalized in a series of agreements during 1958: the Emergency Plan put in place after the coup in February, the Worker-Employer Accord of April, the Minimum Program of Government, and the Pact of Punto Fijo of October. These agreements were intended to allay the fears of groups that had opposed AD during the Trienio. They represented the establishment of cooperative relations with the aim of defending civilian rule.

The Emergency Plan developed by the exiled leaders of the major parties in consultation with business, consisted of worker wage subsidies, a large increase in public works expenditures, and other initiatives intended to placate both the popular forces organized by the Junta Patriótica and also the potentially hostile economic elite. Further, under the new regime, the government would pay the enormous debts Pérez Jiménez had run up with Venezuelan industrialists (Karl 1986:210).

In the Worker-Employer Accord, capital and labor agreed to avoid industrial conflict in favor of conciliation of differences (see below), and in the other agreements, the parties reached a broad consensus on the outlines of future labor and economic policy. AD backed away from its previous commitments to the nationalization of foreign corporations, especially the oil companies, and to a gradual transition to socialism, in favor of a form of state capitalism that guaranteed the right of private property. The major parties agreed on a national development model based on industrialization through foreign and national capital that would restore state credits and high protective barriers for local industry in exchange for business acceptance of a substantial increase in the role of the state in the national economy (Karl 1986:214).

Just as AD had softened its position on the role of foreign and national capital, it also shifted its policy toward landowners and the Roman Catholic Church. The parties agreed to compensation for land redistributed under the agrarian reform (Karl 1986:214) and placed more emphasis on colonizing state-owned land than breaking up inefficient large haciendas (D. Levine 1978:97; Kirby 1973:207). At the same time, they agreed to increase state subsidies for the Church (Church subsidies were tripled during the first year of the provisional government), while guaranteeing the Church increased independence from the government. As D. Levine noted, both AD and the Church softened their previous positions: AD moved away from its previously strident anticlericalism, while the Church was less resistant to changes in the public education system. The presence of COPEI in the government and its role as mediator between AD and the Church helped ease the tensions earlier created during the Trienio (D. Levine 1973:44–46).

An accommodation between AD and the military was worked out in the year following the 1958 coup. The original provisional junta included two supporters of Pérez Jiménez, and only strong protests, led by the Junta Patriótica, convinced the military to oust them (Karl 1986:210). At least one military faction was completely opposed to the participation of AD and the PCV in the coming democratic regime. Led by Castro León, this faction attempted to overthrow the provisional junta in July 1958. Unable to generate any support from the other parties, and with the Junta Patriótica mobilizing over 300,000 protesters, the coup failed (Martz and Myers 1977:365). Despite Castro León's failure, fears of a military coup continued and served as a major constraint on AD's actions in 1958. In the Punto Fijo accord, the parties agreed to modernize the military's hardware, to maintain the mandatory year of universal military service, to improve military salaries, and to forego trials of military officers involved in repression during the dictatorship (Karl 1986:212). In return, the military agreed to transfer power to the parties through elections scheduled for December 1958. Over the next few years military conspiracies continued, but none gathered enough support to prove successful.

Conflict-Limiting Mechanisms. In addition to a programmatic shift toward the center, AD moved to reassure formerly alienated groups, above all the other political parties, by allaying their fears of AD's monopolization of the political arena. Many analysts have referred to what AD's opponents had seen as the party's "arrogance" in the 1940s. Martz (1966:87), for instance, refers to "the rather brassy, even arrogant AD apparatus." During the Trienio, AD had used its overwhelming popularity to pursue reformist programs despite the opposition they aroused, opposition that culminated in the 1948 coup. To prevent a repetition of the failed experiment in democracy, AD now decided to forego its potential for hegemonic dominance or monopoly in the political and labor spheres. Instead, it sought to establish a broad-based, inclusionary regime that limited conflict—a regime in which all major parties would play an important participatory role so that they would have an interest in maintaining a democratic regime.

The first step was taken in late 1957 and early 1958, when the three major party leaders met informally in New York and agreed to the principle of power-sharing. This rather vague consensus was spelled out and elaborated over the next year and finally formalized in the Pact of Punto Fijo, signed by the AD, COPEI, and URD presidential candidates. "As Rómulo Betancourt noted, this pact reflected a belief that extreme partisanship and intense conflict during the Trienio had opened the doors to military intervention" (D. Levine 1978:93). The heart of the agreement was the guarantee that each party would participate in the government, regardless of who won the elections. While the pact did not establish specific quotas, the parties agreed to share power and state resources (Karl 1986:213).

Within the executive branch the agreement concerning a coalition government was implemented when Betancourt won the 1958 presidential election. He subsequently appointed only three AD ministers to the fifteen-member cabinet, splitting the remaining positions between the other two parties and independents sympathetic either to AD or to the new democratic government more broadly (Martz 1966:106–7). For the next two years, Venezuela's fledgling democracy would be ruled by this coalition of the three parties involved in the pact.

The power-sharing agreement was not limited to the formation of a government coalition, but was to extend throughout the electoral system and to nongovernmental organizations. The specific mechanism developed was proportional representation. In agreeing to proportional representation, rather than winner-take-all elections, AD demonstrated its willingness to "underutilize" its electoral strength (Karl 1986:217) and to provide the necessary incentives for the minority parties to support and defend the new regime.

In the trade union movement, AD followed the same set of agreements and accepted the use of proportional representation. Union elections at all levels were held on this basis, so that all political tendencies and currents that had influence within the labor movement were represented and included in the system. In this arena, however, the introduction of proportional representation did not contrast most immediately with a winner-take-all system. Rather, the contrast was with the precedent already set in the initial reconstitution of the labor movement: this consisted of equal representation of the major parties, a practice used on the Labor Unity Committee that evolved out of the strike committee organized to bring down the Pérez Jiménez government (Alexander 1982:409). In comparison, proportional representation meant increased representation for AD, more in line with its actual strength among organized workers. Nevertheless, AD did accept a dilution of its strength within the labor movement in order to cement its relations with URD and COPEI, but not with the Communist Party. Because of its decision to give nearly 25 percent of the top labor positions to the URD and COPEI, a percentage well beyond their relatively meager position within the CTV, AD was significantly underrepresented in the executive committees of the unions and federations (Alexander 1982:410–11; McCoy 1985:254 table 6.1).

During the aftermath period, the use of proportional representation, as well as the careful creation of areas of fundamental agreement between the parties and major interest groups, successfully limited interparty and social conflict. While conservative elites were not completely happy with the new regime, it had moved far enough to the right to keep them from actively supporting its overthrow. The same could not be said for the left.

Exclusion of the Left. As in Mexico, an integral part of the move to reconstitute a governing centrist coalition was, of course, the exclusion of the left. As AD moved to the center and sought greater accommodation with its former adversaries, it inevitably provoked the opposition of the left. Not only was AD's commitment to reform compromised as a result of accommodation with the right, but the price of military loyalty so crucial in the face of ongoing military plots against the democratic government included as well a free hand for the military in the conduct of the government response to left protest, or in the conduct of what the military saw as an anti-subversion campaign. Therefore, as AD moved to constitute a majority coalition in the political center, the outcome of AD policy and conservatization was a spiraling of left protest, answered with a hardening government reaction. The ensuing state of siege, suspension of constitutional rights, and abrogation of freedom of the press stimulated even greater protest, which in turn was met with ruthless suppression of protesters through arrest and torture.[19] The first years of the civilian regime, then, saw an escalation of protest and suppression in the context of AD's shift to the right. As the left moved toward greater opposition, AD did not adjust its program in an attempt to retain leftist support and prevent an open split. Rather it was more concerned with maintaining its newly constituted coalition with the right and took a hard line toward the left, which it now regarded as expendable.

AD's shift to the right created both internal and external contradictions. As in Mexico, both the Communist Party and the internal left within AD were affected. The former was the first to be excluded. Initially, the posture of AD was more inclusive and emphasized the participation of all political tendencies in a kind of social pact strategy that would achieve social and industrial peace. This strategy was represented in the Worker-Employer Accord (Avenimiento Obrero-Patronal) of April 1958. The accord was a response to the growing alarm with which AD and the other parties, recently cooperating in the Emergency Plan of February, viewed the mobilization of labor and its potential for disrupting the path to elections. This mobilization, which had first been expressed in the anti–Pérez Jiménez demonstrations, continued in the face of economic recession and unemployment that gripped Venezuela beginning in 1958. At the initiative of the parties, a united labor movement and the Venezuela employers association, FEDECAMARAS, signed the Worker-Employer Accord in which both sides agreed to improve social and economic conditions and to avoid labor conflict through a moderation of working-class demands and the establishment of bilateral commissions of conciliation of labor conflict (Salamanca 1988:136–44). The accord was an explicit compromise in which, in exchange for this moderation of labor demands and industrial peace, capitalists pledged to support the new democratic order (McCoy 1985:130).

This inclusionary approach in which all groups committed themselves to the social pact changed abruptly the following October. Despite PCV support for the new democratic regime, both within the Junta Patriótica and the labor movement, AD, COPEI, and URD leaders chose to exclude the PCV from the negotiations that led to the Pact of Punto Fijo and from future coalition governments. Betancourt believed that the PCV "had no place in a coalition of democratic parties seeking to establish and solidify a democratic party system" (Alexander 1982:419). The exclusion of the PCV drove a wedge in Venezuelan politics and in the labor movement. Whereas the inclusionary ap-

[19] Harding and Landau 1964:118–20; Ellner 1980:3–7.

proach of the Worker-Employer Accord had resulted in a commitment of virtually all to support both the democratic regime and the social pact policy, the exclusion of the PCV increasingly made the left less willing to accept the sacrifices and trade-offs that these commitments brought with them (Salamanca 1988:144). The PCV briefly continued to support the democratic regime, but in 1960 and 1961, when it was attacked and excluded the labor from—as well as the broader political—arena, it turned to armed rebellion.

The URD was the other major party to form part of the opposition in reaction to the rightward turn of the governing coalition. Whereas the PCV was excluded from the governing coalition, the URD, which had initially been included, defected from it. Moving toward the left, the URD withdrew from the government in November 1960 over its opposition to Betancourt's refusal to recognize the Castro government in Cuba (D. Levine 1973:52).

Within AD itself, a distinct left wing, with an identification quite separate from the wing under Betancourt's leadership, had begun to take shape underground during the Pérez Jiménez period, when the party leadership was in exile. Whereas the exiles became increasingly convinced that democracy was possible only through compromise, the experience of the younger underground militants, who had emerged to fill the leadership void, convinced them that only intense popular mobilization and socialist revolution would end the injustices in Venezuelan society (D. Levine 1973:42–43). This "generational-ideological" split between the exiled and underground party leaders was intensified by the 1959 Cuban Revolution, which convinced the AD left wing of the feasibility of armed struggle and socialist revolution (D. Levine 1973:47–48). Furthermore, the decision of the leaders of AD and the other parties to exclude the PCV from the Punto Fijo discussions and from the subsequent coalition government deeply angered AD activists who had worked closely with the PCV to bring down the dictatorship (Alexander 1982:446).

The first break with the left within AD occurred in April 1960, when the great majority of the party's Youth Federation, as well as many party leaders who had come of age during the Trienio, were expelled. Betancourt and the party leadership had become increasingly disenchanted with the party's left wing and its increasingly strident criticism of the AD coalition government. While the left called for a return to the mobilizational, populist approach of the past, Betancourt rejected older populist appeals, which had so often been justified by evoking and mobilizing "the people" (el pueblo). Betancourt argued that "the people in abstract does not exist. . . . The people are the political parties, the unions, the organized economic sectors, professional societies, (and) university groups" (D. Levine 1973:49). As the polarization within the party increased, the left moved toward direct confrontation with the party leadership as it began to organize strikes against the AD government (McCoy 1985:43; Blank 1973:157). Both Betancourt and the other major AD faction, the ARS, were eager to precipitate a split with the left (Alexander 1982:448–49) and used the latter's refusal to accede to party discipline as an excuse to expel the Youth Federation leadership from the party. As a result of the split, AD lost its majority in the Chamber of Deputies and was forced to rely more closely on the support of its coalition partners (Martz 1966:108). The former AD left reconstituted itself as the Movement of the Revolutionary Left (MIR).

AD suffered a second defection in 1962 when its ARS faction (named by its enemies after an advertising agency) joined the opposition. The ARS, which dated back to the Trienio, staked out a middle-ground position between the party leadership and the group that eventually formed the MIR (Ellner 1980:12–13). It had supported the expulsion of the Youth Federation in 1960 and then moved to take control of the party apparatus. In late 1961 the party leadership reacted and expelled the ARS in January 1962 (Martz 1966:183–88; Ellner 1980:15–16). While the ARS split has been ascribed to "personalistic factionalism" (Martz 1966:183; Lieuwen 1965:187), like the previous defection of the Youth Federation, it was also quite clearly a consequence of AD's programmatic shift toward the center. Specifically, the ARS objected to the retrenchment on the reform program in favor of alliances with the right and the coalition with COPEI, to repression of dissent, and to the abandonment of a neutral foreign policy, as seen most clearly in the approval of U.S.-instigated sanctions against Cuba (Ellner 1980:14, 16; Harding and Landau 1964:120).

The conflict between AD and the left escalated over the next two years. With the Cuban model fresh on their minds, MIR and the PCV both went into armed opposition between October and December of 1960, initiating a series of violent urban demonstrations against, and attacks on, the AD government. In 1961, they extended their campaign against the AD government into the Venezuelan countryside, organizing rural guerrilla groups that were formally constituted as the Armed Forces of National Liberation (FALN) in 1962. Once the PCV and MIR moved to armed insurrection, the government response was predictable. On 13 June 1963 it ordered the arrest of all known Communists and "pro-Castro extremists." In October, the legislature removed the congressional immunity of MIR and PCV senators and deputies and they were promptly arrested (Alexander 1982:484–86, 495–96; Kelley 1977:95).

The break with the left in the party arena was mirrored in the union sphere. At the onset of the democratic period, the PCV had impressive union strength. Second only to AD nationally, it was the dominant force in unions in the federal district. The events of 1960 and 1961 left the CTV deeply divided and ended the period of cooperation within the labor movement that had existed since the Trienio. Open conflict pitted the progovernment forces of AD and COPEI against the left opposition. Throughout 1961, AD, working with COPEI, took advantage of its majority status to squeeze out the left from union and federation councils by strictly applying the principle of proportional representation, rather than allowing the left somewhat greater representation in an effort to bring it within the labor establishment in which it would thereby have a stake. When the labor congress met in December

1961, AD and COPEI joined together to expel both the PCV and MIR from every level of the CTV organization.

Retention of Labor Support. Finally, as in Mexico, despite the shifts and reconstitution of its coalition, AD sought to retain the organized working class as an important part of its support base. This presented something of a challenge given the strength of the left within organized labor. In Mexico the PRI maintained its position within the labor movement through the mechanism of *charrismo*. The tactics used in Venezuela were not all that different.

During 1960, the split within the CTV widened, and by December in the meeting of the confederation's General Council, the PCV, leftist leaders within the CTV, and their brand of worker militance were attacked as undemocratic (Salamanca 1988:170). By then, the battle lines had already been drawn as the PCV, the MIR, and the URD had moved into the opposition. In unions in Caracas and the oil fields, in particular, the opposition had been poised to defeat AD. In the face of this challenge, AD unionists resorted to terrorism and violence that was tolerated and sanctioned by the police. AD goon squads attacked meetings, and there were many allegations that petroleum companies fired opposition workers at the behest of the Labor and Interior Ministries. "Increasingly the situation resembled a civil war and in November, 1960, the PCV-MIR-URD coalition called a general strike to bring the AD administration down" (Boeckh 1972:206–7). The strike never materialized, but the struggle within the labor movement between the left opposition on the one hand and AD and COPEI on the other intensified (Alexander 1964:241).

During the following year the process of polarization continued within the labor movement as "AD and COPEI labor militants, representing the government coalition, voted as one in the CTV on all major issues and were opposed by a PCV-URD-MIR coalition" (Fagan 1974:99). Local elections continued to be disruptive and involved clashes and even deaths as factions boycotted the elections, refused to recognize the results, and held parallel meetings. In these elections, AD and its coalitional partner COPEI managed to win 207 of the 243 local union elections held during the first ten months of that year (Alexander, 1982:489–90). With the outcome of the upcoming fourth congress of the CTV dependent on the results of local union elections, the government intervened to assure the election of union officers affiliated with the governing coalition (Fagan 1974:100).

At the end of 1961 the left opposition was formally purged from the CTV: AD and COPEI members of the CTV called an extraordinary congress during which the PCV, MIR, and URD were expelled from the confederation and the executive committee was restructured to include only AD and COPEI members. Not surprisingly, the opposition rejected this so-called fourth congress, continuing to recognize the members elected at the third congress of 1959 until the next regularly scheduled congress, due in November 1962 (Salamanca 1988:173).

The purge of the left within the labor movement had potentially significant repercussions for the government coalition's working-class support base. The PCV and MIR had a large following within the labor movement, and during 1962 protest and conflict escalated as the two groups led armed marches through the streets (Salamanca 1988:173). Nevertheless, the left was effectively outmaneuvered in its fight within the CTV, and in 1963, in recognition of its defeat, it formally constituted the CUTV. The CUTV, however, failed to become a major factor in the labor movement: unable to compete with the advantages of the CTV, it was unable to retain even its original support—including that of URD, which soon rejoined the CTV. With the left opposition initially controlling only a modest 10 percent of the labor movement in 1961, by 1964 the CUTV had little importance (Blank 1973:232).

This development within the CTV as a whole had its counterpart within the Peasant Federation (FCV). The most important challenge within the peasant movement was the attempt by veteran leader Ramón Quijada to lead the FCV into opposition. His failure, like that of dissidents in urban industrial unions, revealed the same pattern of government response and the use it made of both coercive and hegemonic resources.

In the mid-1960s, the familiar division over the pace of reform, appropriate tactics, and the dilemma presented by the twin goals of class defense and support for the democratic government once again rose to the surface, this time within AD itself. The struggle pitted FCV leader Quijada, a PDN-AD militant from the 1930s, against AD moderates. The former advanced a two year time frame for the distribution of land and credit to all who applied for it; the latter advocated a broader integrated reform program over four to ten years (Powell 1971:194). The dispute spilled over into the fourth congress of the CTV, which Quijada threatened to boycott. When the CTV in turn threatened to replace the entire FCV directorship, Quijada joined the opposition and affiliated with the ARS. The open split led to the formation of two rival peasant federations, which divided the peasant movement into two virtually equal halves. The rival organizations then fought it out at the level of the state federations, with the CTV intervening many of them. These bitter and often violent conflicts resulted in the ultimate victory of the progovernment faction, aided by government intervention that consisted of both carrots and sticks, both "persuasion" and "muscle." The moderates could count on the support of the Betancourt government: political resources, financial and manpower aid to unions, and strategic distribution of agricultural subsidies and land titles under the new agrarian reform law. The advantages of this support were ultimately overwhelming, and by mid-1962 the moderates had won decisively. The FCV was purged; a coalition of AD and COPEI partisans divvied up the leadership posts at national and state levels; and the further tactic of land invasions, which had been quite widespread and responsible for substantial land distribution in the beginning of the Betancourt government, was disavowed (Martz 1966:281–84; Powell 1971:104–10, 195–96).

In addition to the more coercive and repressive mechanisms sometimes employed, then, AD had a number of resources with which it was able to maintain the support of the urban and rural labor movement in the face of its conservatization and the challenge from the left. First, as in Mexico, divisions within the labor leadership were important, and AD could count on the cooperation of an important faction to insure its influence within the labor movement. Much of the labor leadership generally supported Betancourt and the "old guard" of the AD, and the move against the left benefited this major faction within the labor movement. In fact, the decision of AD to expel the left from the CTV was orchestrated, to a significant extent, by the union leadership itself (Alexander 1982:445). As had occurred during the Medina government, the expulsion of the left from the labor central greatly increased AD's strength within the labor movement.

Secondly, with the support of the Venezuelan government, hundreds of new unions were formed and legally recognized. In 1961–62, 1,017 new unions were formed, and by 1964 the number of regional and industrial federations had doubled. Many of the new unions were in the agricultural sector, where AD was traditionally very strong. These new unions diluted the left's support considerably in subsequent union elections. Furthermore, ties between the government and AD unions gave the latter's important advantages of access and government support in the collective bargaining process. These advantages were apparent to all and allowed AD to regain and retain its support. We will return to these themes in the next chapter. For now, it may simply be noted that by 1964, AD controlled over 70 percent of the labor movement (McCoy 1985:145, 149–50).

Third, coming on the heels of a decade of harsh repression, the new government had much to offer that was attractive to the labor movement. It offered the CTV and its unions protection and government support through the access available from AD affiliation. AD also maintained labor support through its program, which promised benefits to the working class, the provision for which had been explicitly included in the compromises of the pact. These benefits included a state commitment to full employment; subsidized food and housing programs; as well as health, education, and social security legislation. Finally, AD retained labor support because the rank and file of the organized labor movement was strongly supportive of the new democratic government, and the PCV and MIR's decision to undertake armed insurrection greatly reduced their influence within the labor movement and undercut their attempts to regain it.

During the Betancourt government, then, the CTV never seriously escaped the control of AD despite the threat posed by the opposition. Instead, the government was able to maintain both urban and rural labor as a support group. During the early 1960s the CTV dutifully supported the government in the boycott of Cuba, opposed the guerrilla movement, supported the Alliance for Progress and a generally pro-U.S. orientation, and even accepted a salary freeze in accordance with the government's economic policy. It collaborated in a policy that led to an increasing tendency away from the signing of short-term contracts, thus minimizing disruption and adversely affecting real wages by delaying cost-of-living adjustments as well as any possible negotiated increases. The CTV also accepted a 1961 wage cut of 10 percent in the public sector and, in the following year, the government's deferral of negotiations in that sector (McCoy 1985:140, 149).

Hence, during the aftermath period, the labor movement came to abandon an orientation toward class struggle and to accept an orientation toward a social pact, based on collaboration and compromise within a context of capitalist development and democratic reformism. With the expulsion of the left from the CTV, this "syndicalism of conciliation" became deeply entrenched (Salamanca 1988:146; McCoy 1985:188).

URUGUAY AND COLOMBIA: REINFORCING TRADITIONAL TWO-PARTY SYSTEMS

Whereas in three other cases of party incorporation (Venezuela, Peru, and Argentina) the incorporation period ended dramatically with a coup and a period of military rule, Uruguay and Colombia experienced a more gradual transition to the full conservative reaction. In both countries incorporation ended under a less progressive president of the same party that had led the incorporation project: in Uruguay in 1916 under President Viera of the Colorado Party, and in Colombia in 1945 with the presidency of Lleras Camargo of the Liberal Party.

Subsequently in Colombia, the growing strength of the populist Gaitán faction of the Liberals split the Liberal Party in the 1946 presidential election and gave the Conservatives the opportunity to win the presidency. The first three years under the new Conservative President Ospina saw an effort to sustain bipartisan cooperation, which basically maintained a situation of partisan impasse. It was not until 1949, the year after the explosion of violence that followed the assassination of Gaitán, that this cooperation collapsed. A period of vigorously anti-Liberal policies emerged, later followed by the coup of Rojas Pinilla in 1953.

Uruguay, following its incorporation period, experienced a far longer impasse between the Batlle forces and their conservative opponents, which lasted from the second half of the 1910s to the late 1920s. At that point, an unsuccessful attempt to renew the Batlle reform program deepened the conservative reaction, ultimately culminating in the coup of 1933.

The polarization and conservative reaction in the two countries differed greatly in their degree of partisanship. In Colombia this reaction had a major ideological and programmatic component, but also reflected the intense partisan response of the Conservatives to the Liberals' attempt to establish one-party dominance during the incorporation period. In this sense the Colombian experience paralleled that of Mexico and Venezuela, where the partisan monopolization of power by the incorporating party likewise played a large role in stimulating the conservative reaction. Thus, in Colombia, with the collapse of bipartisan cooperation in 1949, the Conservatives sought to eliminate any role of the Liberal Party within the state.

In Uruguay, by contrast, the reaction to incorporation was not so much along partisan lines as along ideological and programmatic lines, reflecting a bipartisan response that cut across the Colorados and the Nationals. Thus, the forces that brought an end to the incorporation period in 1916 and the coalition that took power with the coup of 1933 included elements from both parties, and after 1933 the opposition to the more conservative government of Terra included the progressive wing of both parties.

The level of violence during the aftermath period also differed greatly. Uruguay experienced virtually no violence, whereas Colombia experienced more than any other country, consisting of the extraordinary outbreak of conflict known as La Violencia. This outcome might seem surprising, because Colombia traditionally had a weak labor movement and the scope of labor mobilization during the incorporation period had been modest. The extreme violence associated with the aftermath in Colombia had roots that extended back before the incorporation period, and it must be understood in light of a deeply ingrained trait of Colombian politics: power shifts between the parties at the elite level tended to resonate at the mass level, particularly in rural areas, in the form of intense eruptions of partisan strife. At the same time that the violence had deep roots, issues of labor politics played an important direct and indirect role in triggering this specific episode. The partisan conflict of the 1940s grew out of the incorporation and reform period that began in 1930, which in turn had been launched in important measure over the social question. Further, the assassination in 1948 of Gaitán—who was closely identified with labor reform—played a role in triggering the strife of the late 1940s, as did the volatile relationship between the progressive wing of the labor movement and the Liberal Party in that period. Thus, both this longer tradition of conflict and labor issues are essential to understanding the violence that began in the late 1940s.

The transition at the point of the restoration of a more competitive regime, in 1942 in Uruguay and in 1958 in Colombia, also differed markedly between the two countries, given this contrast between ongoing bipartisan cooperation in Uruguay versus the collapse of bipartisan cooperation in Colombia, and also the contrast in the level of violence. In Colombia, following the intensely partisan civilian dictatorship of the Conservative president Laureano Gómez and the military dictatorship of Rojas Pinilla, both accompanied by extraordinary levels of rural violence, the challenge of ending partisan strife was particularly great. Correspondingly, an elaborate and highly formalized political compromise was engineered in the late 1950s, to the point that a specific pattern of future alternation of partisan control of the presidency was literally written into the constitution. In this compromise the Liberals committed themselves to a type of bipartisan cooperation that left little room for the party's earlier reform agenda or mobilization policies. This compromise also served to strongly reinforce the dominance of the two traditional parties.

Uruguay did not face an equivalent challenge of dealing with partisan antagonisms or widespread violence, and the adjustments and compromises accompanying the restoration of a democratic regime in 1942 were far more limited. The progressive wing of the Colorado Party did not have to give up its earlier reform agenda, and a new period of reform began soon after. The 1942 transition in Uruguay was parallel to that in Colombia, however, in that it reinforced the traditional party system.

In the context of this reinforcement of the established two-party pattern in both cases, important similarities also existed between the Colombian Liberals and the Uruguayan Colorados in their ongoing electoral and organizational relationships with urban political constituencies. Both parties retained the labor vote they had courted during the incorporation period, and both had weak organizational ties with the labor movement.

URUGUAY

Conservative Reaction

The Uruguayan incorporation period was over in 1916, with the end of Batlle's reform initiatives. Yet many years of political impasse followed before the prospect of a resurgence of Colorado Party reformism increased polarization in the late 1920s and early 1930s, culminating in the coup of 1933 that ushered in a more extensive conservative reaction.

Given that Batlle's reforms came so early in relation to the reform periods in other countries, their scope was remarkable. In light of that scope, the conservative reaction of the 1910s that culminated in 1916–17 was mild, having taken place within the established framework of competitive party politics. Following the long impasse, the further extension of the conservative reaction in the early 1930s was also mild in comparison with all other cases of party incorporation. Finally, the institutional and party transformation accompanying the return to democracy in 1942 was likewise limited. A central goal of the following discussion is to capture these distinctive dynamics, in the framework of the strongly democratic norms of the Uruguayan political system.

Impasse and Growing Political Tensions. The institutional context of Uruguayan politics from the late 1910s to the early 1930s was the collegiate system adopted in 1917. Under this arrangement Uruguay had a bicephalous executive with guaranteed representation of the minority party. The powers of the president were divided between a nine-member National Administrative Council, referred to as the Council, which controlled domestic and economic affairs; and a president, whose authority was limited to the Ministries of Defense, Interior, and Foreign Affairs, and to the National Police (Lindahl 1962:26–27, 34–35; Caetano 1983a:77, 106).

Roughly the first decade under the collegiate executive was a period of impasse. Batlle remained the most powerful figure on the Uruguayan political scene, and he continued to defend his earlier reforms and sought, generally unsuccessfully, to introduce further reform. It was not until the late 1920s that a series of new issues arose that pushed Uruguayan politics beyond the impasse of the 1920s to greater polarization. At this point important changes within both parties led to a controversial new pact among party factions that strengthened the position of a progressive coalition. The emergence of this coalition in turn triggered a more thorough-going conservative reaction.

The evolution of the Colorado Party that played a central role in these new developments was due in part to leadership change. By 1929 two of the conservative Colorado factions had fallen apart, in one case because of the death of Viera, and Batlle's death in 1929 led to a struggle for control within his faction. Among the Colorados, many of Batlle's supporters wished to continue his emphasis on open party leadership and the choice of neutral or independent candidates to maintain party unity against the Nationals. This group was opposed by Gabriel Terra, who had long been against the Council and had been unsympathetic to Batlle's social reforms. Batlle had never trusted Terra, but had found that he provided a useful balance against dissident Colorado factions.

By moderating his opposition, Terra was able to win the Batlle wing's nomination for president in 1930. The Batlle faction's decision to present a candidate of their own, rather than supporting an independent, was not accepted by the smaller Colorado factions. The Manini wing insisted it was Manini's turn to be the candidate and refused to support the Terra nomination. The solution that each faction should run its own candidate was not viable for Manini, given the Batlle faction's large numerical advantage. To avoid further conflict, the Batlle wing agreed to an unusual bargain: should Manini win 17.5 percent of the Colorado vote, they would give him the Presidency (Lindahl 1926:156–59).

The Nationals, meanwhile, were also suffering from growing division. Herrera had long lived in uneasy symbiosis with the traditional ("Principalist") leadership of the National Party. Opposed to Herrera's attack on the Council and his growing influence, and supportive of coparticipation between the two parties, the traditionalists knew, nonetheless, that Herrera was their only hope of winning the presidency in 1930. Consequently, they once again supported him, but the division was becoming increasingly apparent.

The flux within the parties was matched by a renewed mobilization of conservative sectors, which began to call for the formation of a peak association to represent the interests of the various producer groups. In April 1929 the Rural Federation proposed the creation of an umbrella organization, the Committee of Economic Vigilance, which played an important role in the political crisis of the early 1930s (Caetano 1983b:44–47). The renewed conservative reaction was later propelled in part by the deepening economic depression, but it was also very importantly a reaction to the resurgence of the reformist Batlle wing of the Colorados. Starting in 1928 the Batlle-controlled Chamber had begun to push new reform programs, and this " 'second impulse' of the reform process,"[20] like the conservative reaction, subsequently was further stimulated by the growing economic crisis. The conservatives, organized around the Committee of Economic Vigilance and the Rural Federation, counterattacked with a successful 48-hour producers' strike in October 1930 (Caetano 1983b:57). As the country moved toward the November 1930 election, tension grew.

In the 1930 election for president and the Council, the Colorados achieved their greatest victory since 1916. Manini failed to receive his required vote, making Terra the president. The increase in the Colorado vote probably occurred in part because the special electoral arrangement with Manini led to increased competition among the Colorados, and hence a higher vote (Lindahl 1962:162–63).

[20] Caetano 1985:149. See also Caetano (1983b:53); Jacob (1983:11, 14–17).

This defeat of the Nationals was the catalyst for a major division within that party. Over the next year the "Principalists," now known as the Independent Nationalists, began the struggle for party control. They did not wish to support Herrera again, since he had already lost three presidential elections. In January 1931 Herrera announced that his faction would abstain from Council elections, thus making his opposition to the Council clear. In July 1931 the Independents won control of the party convention and began to negotiate with the Batlle Colorados to break the administrative deadlock.

These negotiations led to an interparty agreement that played a central role in a loss of power of conservative forces, which in turn contributed to the events that led to the 1933 coup. In September 1931 the Independent Nationals and the Batlle Colorados reached an accord that came to be known as the *pacto de chinchulín* (pork-barrel pact), a derisory name provided by Herrera (Caetano 1983b:59). The pact, through which the two factions achieved strong control of state resources, marked a major departure for the Batlle wing because it both brought a renewal of coparticipation and marked a break between the Batllistas and the other Colorado factions, as well as between the Independent Nationals and the faction led by Herrera. The Batlle Colorados and the Independents had, between them, a majority on the Council, leaving them free to implement the agreement (Lindahl 1962:169). The pact both strengthened the position of the two participating party factions and held the promise of breaking the ongoing political immobilism. At the same time, the pact sharply diminished the power of Terra and Herrera, and thus of the conservative part of the political spectrum (Taylor 1952:306; Lindahl 1962:172).

The political opportunity presented by the new pact, combined with the demands on the government created by the effects of the depression, led the more progressive factions of the two parties to propose a series of new reforms, including the extension of retirement benefits to all workers, a comprehensive minimum wage, recovery of public rural lands that had fallen into private use, the reduction of the military budget, and the creation of a new state entity, the National Administration for Fuel, Alcohol, and Cement (ANCAP), which would oversee an important increase in the state role in the economy. Though most of these policies were not adopted during this period, these proposals strongly reinforced the idea that a new period of reform might be launched.

On the other side of the political spectrum, conservative groups advocated the elimination of the pork-barrel pact and began to promote a new constitution that would replace the collegiate executive. President Terra embraced this cause, arguing that in the depths of the depression, when Uruguay most needed leadership, no one could effectively govern. It was therefore necessary to return to a strong presidential system (Caetano 1983b:59; Lindahl 1962:178). Terra's campaign, which directly attacked the Batllista's basis of power, greatly strained his relations with them. This strain was further increased by Terra's "discovery" of a Communist "conspiracy" to overthrow his presidency, after which he initiated a crackdown on Communists and threw a Communist deputy into prison. This action, which was illegal and was perceived as a direct attack on the prerogatives of Chamber of Deputies, caused much consternation.

In the November 1932 Council elections, the Batlle Colorados won a decisive victory and increased their control of the Council, a development that the economic right found threatening. The Manini Colorados had joined the Herrera Nationals in abstaining from the election, and Terra and Herrera proceeded to step up demands for an end to the Council and a return to the presidential system. Leaders of the Batlle wing countered by demanding the elimination of the presidency altogether.

With tensions already high, Terra began a tour of the interior in which he continuously attacked the Council and the constitution. Conservative producer groups, especially ranchers in the interior, strongly supported him and encouraged the campaign. Coup rumors became common. Reacting to this direct criticism, senators of the Batlle Colorado and Independent National factions started a movement to censure Terra. Pointing to his handling of the Communist "conspiracy," as well as administrative scandals, they began to cross-examine several of Terra's ministers. In early February "Terra was quoted as saying that only an immediate plebiscite on constitutional reform could prevent civil war" (Taylor 1952:308). The crisis intensified with new signs of collaboration between Terra and Herrera, the presentation of a motion for Terra's impeachment in the Senate, the growing political impasse, and increasing public turmoil. The conservative press called for a "blow against the Constitution," and "immediate constitutional reform 'via the shortest path'" (Caetano 1983b:82), implying support for a coup by Terra.

Coup of 1933 and the New Regime. The situation came to a head when Batlle's newspaper, *El Día*, attacked Terra's coup intentions. Terra responded with a decree that newspapers "attributing dictatorial intentions to the President" would be censored (Taylor 1952:311). On 30 March, the Council condemned the decree and forwarded to the Assembly the recommendation that the decree be nullified. Early the next day, the Assembly, after an angry rejection of Terra's excessive use of presidential power, nullified the decree. Hours later, Terra, with Herrera's support, initiated a coup, arresting most members of the Council, closing the Assembly, and establishing a nine-member Junta de Gobierno to rule the country.[21]

With the electoral route closed to them, Terra and Herrera thus chose another path. Terra successfully neutralized the army and reorganized the police, making it an "obedient tool in his hands" (Lindahl 1962:183). Unable to win through the ballot box and with strong support from conservative groups organized through the Rural Federation and the Committee for Economic Vigilance (Caetano 1983b:86–87), Terra and Herrera resorted to force, thereby launching a new phase in the conservative reaction in Uruguay.

In carrying out the coup of 31 March 1933, Terra enjoyed the backing of a

[21] Caetano 1983b:73; Lindahl 1962:176–77, 181–84; Taylor 1952:309, 312–13; 1960:23, n. 4.

broad coalition which in the period before the coup had been weakly represented in the elected institutions of the state and which increased its influence under the new regime. This coalition included Terra's own wing of the
Colorado Party,[22] some other minority Colorado factions, the majority faction of the National Party, and the country's most important industrial and
agricultural interests. Terra's leadership during the postcoup period was in
important respects shared with Herrera, who was closely linked to elite
agrarian interests. He also had what later proved to be the major liability,
given the Uruguayan context, of important ties to European fascism (Rial
1984a:16; Taylor 1960a:29).

Bipartisan government was thus a crucial feature of this period. The two
major government leaders, Terra and Herrera, a Colorado and a National respectively, were backed by the conservative wings of the two main parties.
The opposition was also bipartisan. The core of the opposition was the Batlle
Colorados and the Independent Nationals, the more progressive wings of
these two parties. The relatively small Socialist and Communist parties, as
well as the organized labor movement, also played a role in the opposition.

Terra's goals at this point were twofold. First, he was opposed to the reforms of the incorporation period, as suggested by his earlier assertion in
1928 that "we have brought into practice a great part of the program that
Karl Marx formulated in his postulates of international Communism and that
he counseled to the proletariat of all countries" (quoted in Weinstein
1975:69). The new political conditions following the coup provided an opportunity, if not to undo Batlle's program, at least to block a new round of
Batllista reforms. Second, and relatedly, Terra wished to modify the 1918
constitution and eliminate the collegiate executive, which had posed such
an obstacle to his presidency in the years before the coup.

Compared to other countries that had coups in the aftermath period, Uruguay's experience with authoritarianism was mild. To the extent that armed
force was used in the coup and afterwards, it involved mainly the police. The
military remained marginal to the event, having been carefully neutralized
by Terra. Indeed, the coup was initiated by Terra, not by the police or armed
forces.[23] Though these years are often referred to as the Terra "dictatorship,"
the scope of repressive control was limited. Control was exercised instead
through elaborate changes in constitutional and electoral rules, much more
than through the suppression of the party system.

Very crucially from the standpoint of this analysis, in connection with this
use of electoral engineering, rather than other forms of repression, there was
no legal prohibition of any political party or party faction (Rial 1984a:105,
109). An attempt to eliminate or undermine the party that had led the incorporation project—which was familiar from the experiences during the aftermath period of Venezuela, Peru, Colombia, and Argentina—did not occur.

[22] Terra had belonged to the Batllista faction of the Colorado Party, but in the period after
the coup, his more conservative faction came to be the "Terra" wing of the party. See Rial
(1984a:153).

[23] Taylor 1960a:24; Rial 1984a:15–16; Jacob 1983:56; Frega et al. 1987:97.

Correspondingly, as we shall see, at the end of this authoritarian period the expectation that this party had to be transformed in order to be readmitted to the political arena did not arise. The result was that the Uruguayan party system passed through this period far less changed than in any other case of party incorporation.

Authoritarian rule may have been mild in part because the polarization before the coup did not encompass a major popular mobilization. More fundamentally, by the 1930s Uruguay already had relatively well-ingrained democratic norms, and conservative forces were cautious about violating these norms in pursuit of their objectives.[24]

In the coup itself, Terra arrested most members of the National Council, dissolved the legislative assembly, and blocked the roads entering the capital to discourage the mobilization of opposition. The nine-member *junta* that he established was drawn from the various groups that supported him, and jointly with Herrera he picked the 99 members of a new Deliberative Assembly intended to function as a legislature until the constitution was changed (Taylor 1960a:23 fn 4, 25; 1952:313 and fn 38).

In dealing with its opponents within the traditional parties, the Terra government made modest use of arrests, exile, and censorship. Terra's son was to note that "the government did not need to utilize any other forces than the police to maintain order. It detained 12 people, who four days after the coup had been freed, and exiled five politicians of the old regime" (quoted in Jacob 1983:67). Though the number of forced exiles rose to 75 by the end of 1935, not one of the major political figures of the two largest party groupings that opposed Terra—the Batllista Colorados and Independent Nationalists—was expelled. Under government censorship, opposition newspapers "began to appear with blank spaces where censored articles would have appeared" (Jacob 1983:67). Nevertheless, these restrictions did not prevent the opposition press from criticizing the regime and publicizing opposition events.

The deaths of two opponents of Terra provide both a sense of the drama of this period and also, given that these were signal events of the repression, of the limited scope of authoritarian control. Terra's police attempted to arrest ex-President Baltasar Brum on the day of the coup. Brum, certain that the coup would fail and that the people would rise up and prevent it, refused to accompany the police and waited for the uprising at the door of his house, revolver in hand. The police responded by cordoning off his house. When the realization sank in that he was alone in his defiance, Brum committed suicide. His funeral "became the first great political act of the silenced opposition" (Jacob 1983:66), and Brum's death was a blow to the legitimacy of Terra's government (Taylor 1952:313 fn 39). The killing of a Batllista activist, Julio César Grauert, provided the second martyr for the opposition. In Octo-

[24] Decades later in the 1970s, when polarization did include intense popular mobilization, such norms obviously did not prevent the emergence of a highly repressive regime in Uruguay. Yet in comparing Uruguay's earlier authoritarian experience of the 1930s with that of other countries in the analytically comparable aftermath period, it is hard not to conclude that very different norms were operating.

ber 1933, as part of the campaign against Terra, Grauert went to an outlying city to join other Batllista politicians in a public demand for the restoration of civil liberties. When police attempted to arrest them, Grauert and two other politicians refused to accept the arrest and drove toward Montevideo. On the way they were stopped by the police and Grauert was shot. Though he was seriously wounded, the police refused to allow him to see a doctor for 40 hours, and by the time he was taken to the military hospital in Montevideo, it was too late (Jacob 1983:68). These two deaths were, unquestionably, tragic. Yet they hardly added up to a picture of severe repression.

Terra's more extensive use of repression was directed not at the main leadership of the traditional parties, but at labor activists and a few members of the most left-wing factions of the Batllistas. Between March and September 1933, over 300 workers were arrested and charges were made that the regime used physical and mental torture against some of those detained. Strikes were often met with violence, worker locals and Communist newspapers were shut down, and worker meetings prohibited. Terra responded to a student strike in opposition to the coup with a law that greatly reduced the autonomy of the national university and gave to the executive the power to name the university's dean (Pintos 1960:255, 271; Jacob 1983:117). These acts, together with the 1934 constitutional provision prohibiting public sector strikes, greatly reduced the effectiveness of labor and student opposition.

In dealing with its opponents in the traditional party system, rather than making extensive use of repression, the Terra government depended more on constitutional changes and innovations in electoral rules. In June 1933 the government scheduled an election for a Constituent Assembly. Terra sought to use Uruguay's Electoral Court to supervise the vote, but the members refused. Terra dissolved the court, and his Deliberative Assembly selected a new one. The opposition had already planned to abstain in protest against the government and the tightly controlled process of constitution-making, and after the dissolution of the Electoral Court they suspected even more strongly that the elections would be fraudulent (Taylor 1952:316). With the opponents of the government abstaining, a Constituent Assembly favorable to Terra was easily elected and the Assembly subsequently approved a constitution prepared by Terra and Herrera. Again with the opposition abstaining, the constitution was overwhelmingly approved by voters in April 1934.

The constitutional provision of greatest immediate importance was that permitting the reelection of Terra, who was by then at the end of his original term of office. His reelection, illegal under the 1830 and 1917 constitutions, was, according to Terra himself, "the only way open to continue, with security, the renovating program of the revolution" (quoted by Jacob 1983:58). Conveniently, the vote through which Terra was reelected occurred the same day as the plebiscite that approved the new constitution, which provided the legal basis for his reelection (Jacob 1983:58).

Other changes in the 1934 constitution were designed to further consolidate the control of Terra and Herrera and of their respective party groupings. Executive power was centralized in the presidency, at the same time that the power of the Council of Ministers was increased. Membership of the Council was selected according to a complex electoral rule that assured Terra's and Herrera's dominance. Thus, the party faction receiving the most votes within the party receiving the most votes—that is, Terra's Colorados—had the right to appoint six of the nine ministers (four directly by the president). The faction receiving the most votes of the party receiving the next largest vote total—that is, Herrera's Nationals—had the right to appoint the other three.[25]

Another significant change concerned the composition of the Senate, which was expanded from one senator for each of 19 departments to a total of 30, all elected at-large. On the basis of the same electoral rule described above, half the Senate seats would be awarded to the Terra Colorados and half to Herrera Nationals, producing what was referred to as the "half and half" Senate. This arrangement assured Terra's and Herrera's control of the legislature. Herrera saw the goal of the Senate as being to "correct, amend and rectify the poorly thought-out or extreme ideas that come from the Chamber of Deputies" (quoted in Jacob 1983:60), in which opposition parties, including parties of the left, continued to be represented. The new constitution also strengthened executive authority by eliminating the legislature's role in dealing with the budget, public debt, and borrowing and by requiring an absolute majority to create new taxes. At the same time, the autonomy of the municipalities and departments was reduced, placing their administration under the supervision of the executive, which was dominated by Terra and Herrera.[26]

Terra and Herrera also consolidated their position through changes in electoral legislation. The major opposition factions of the two traditional parties had decided to abstain in the elections held under the 1934 constitution, yet there was no certainty that they would continue to do so. Given the way the constitution was written, either the Batllistas or the Independent Nationalists could return to power by winning a majority within their respective parties. To insure their continued control over the government, Terra and Herrera introduced legislation that gave authority over party names (the *lema*) and party symbols to the majority party factions as of the 1934 elections, thereby perpetuating Terra's and Herrera's control. Among other things, the Terra and Herrera factions could determine which factions would run as part of their respective parties.[27]

Though Terra effectively redesigned the constitution and electoral laws and marginalized the progressive factions from power, he was less effective in overturning the substantive reforms earlier introduced by Batlle. These reforms had become "too deeply embedded in the national fabric for any of them to be greatly altered, much less destroyed, without a structural revolution; and for that the country was obviously not prepared" (Whitaker

[25] Frega et al. 1987:14; Lindahl 1962:186; Weinstein 1975:72–73.
[26] Taylor 1960a:26; cf. Jacob 1983:59–60; Frega et al. 1987:14; Faraone 1965:83; Fitzgibbon 1954:146.
[27] Caetano and Rilla 1985:35–36; Taylor 1960a:29; Frega et al. 1987:14; Jacob 1983:61–62; Whitaker 1976:123.

1976:119). Terra's impact was not primarily to reverse earlier reforms as to block further reform, and in this sense his government did have policy consequences strongly favored by the economic elite. In addition, Terra also provided important new benefits for the agrarian elite, a key supporter within his coalition.[28]

In the aftermath of the coup, the appropriate strategy of the opposition initially remained in doubt. This was partly due to an internal struggle within Batllismo over the successor to José Batlle y Ordóñez. In addition, a considerable part of the Batllista wing, primarily the more conservative and clientelistically oriented sectors, had followed Terra and supported the coup in 1933. Uncertain as to their actual electoral strength and marginalized from state power, the Batllistas' first reaction, as noted above, was to deny the legitimacy of the new regime and, together with the Independent Nationalists, abstain from electoral participation. However, the success of Terra's April 1934 plebiscite convinced them of the need to pursue a more active strategy. In 1934 and 1935 efforts to launch a mass demonstration and an armed revolt failed, in part due to the government's skill in sewing discord within the opposition. After the failed revolt, the opposition pursued a peaceful strategy to overthrow Terra.[29]

In 1936, the Spanish Civil War presented a common cause around which Terra's opponents could mobilize. The Spanish Republicans enjoyed wide support in Montevideo, and rallies in favor of the Republicans took on an anti-Terra character. This led the government to impose new restrictions on "public acts" that concerned the political affairs of a foreign country. The entire opposition participated in the demonstrations, and the strong support for the Spanish Republicans created tensions between Terra and his pro-Franco Herrera allies.[30]

Political developments at that time in Europe also presented the Uruguayan opposition with the model of the popular front strategy, based on a coalition of reformist and left parties. However, certain characteristics of the Uruguayan opposition limited the appeal of this model. The electoral weakness of the Socialist and Communist parties and the disunity of the labor movement made them minor participants in such a front, giving the traditional parties little incentive to pursue such an option. In addition, many Colorados and Nationals within the opposition were more interested in a return to the precoup political system than in the political alternative suggested by a popular front, and they likewise did not want to give the left an opportunity to recruit new followers from their own mass base. Finally, they feared that such a coalition would simply strengthen the government's resistance to change (Frega et al. 1985:55).

Conflicts within the Governing Coalition.   Though the opposition played a significant role in the eventual return to democracy, divisions within the

[28] Finch 1981:16; Caetano 1983b:89; Jacob 1983:15–16, 27.
[29] D'Elia 1982:16; Taylor 1952:316; Weinstein 1975:74; Pintos 1960:261–64; Jacob 1983:69–70; Rial 1984a:106–7.
[30] Weinstein 1975:74; Rial 1984a:108; Pintos 1960:278.

governing coalition were also crucial. Various factors contributed to these divisions. One source was a series of disputes over the complex system of distribution of patronage within the coalition—along with other forms of political infighting. Significant initial defections occurred in 1934 and 1935, and in 1936 important members of the Herrera wing withdrew their support. The death in 1936 of a key member of the Colorado Party who had played a central role in Terra's rise to power was a setback for Terra, and personal tensions between Terra and Herrera also played a role.[31]

Conflicts between agrarian and industrial interests likewise weakened the coalition. The initial support of industrialists had been based on their opposition to further social legislation. However, in many respects the policy concerns of industrialists diverged from those of agrarian elites. Especially with the industrial expansion of the 1930s and the industrialists' growing importance in the economy, they increasingly objected to policies favoring the agrarian sector (Finch 1981:16; Frega et al. 1987:69).

Tensions that emerged in response to European fascism and the growing imminence of World War II also divided the coalition government. The evolving crisis in Europe exacerbated disagreements among different political sectors concerning their sympathy with or opposition to fascism, and also toward the related issue of Uruguay's participation in Inter-American meetings and agreements that came to be linked to Allied solidarity against the Axis. Within the governing coalition, the Herrera group was strongly identified with fascism and later with the Axis. Terra was far less committed to fascism, and the Colorado faction within the governing group likewise did not share these sentiments (Finch 1981:18; Whitaker 1976:131–32).

These splits would have posed a particular problem if the opposition had joined in a popular front for the 1938 elections, when both the presidency and the legislature were at stake. However, due to the factors noted above and to yet additional electoral rules intended to inhibit such a front, it was not formed. Thus, facing less pressure to maintain their unity, the Terra and Herrera factions presented opposing candidates in the 1938 elections (Rial 1984a:109–11).

Terra was greatly concerned in 1938 with insuring the continuation in power of his faction of the Colorado Party (Jacob 1983:64). To achieve this goal, Terra decided to insure his party's victory in the 1938 presidential election by presenting the voters with two Colorado candidates, both close relatives of his. Eduardo Acevedo, Terra's father-in-law, represented the more conservative, authoritarian wing of the government's Colorado support base, whereas Alfredo Baldomir, Terra's son-in-law, was generally perceived to represent the more progressive element. Uruguay used the system of the "double simultaneous vote," which combined the primary election with the final presidential election and which aggregated the separate votes for each faction of a party to produce an overall party vote, which then counted for the leading faction. As a result, having two major Colorado candidates gave the party

---

[31] Frega et al. 1987:15–16; Jacob 1983:63; Taylor 1960a:28.

a major advantage. Baldomir, apparently with the support of Batllista voters who ignored their leaders' order to abstain, defeated Acevedo by 121,000 to 98,000 votes and gave the Colorado Party one of its most lopsided electoral victories.[32]

Formation of New Governing Coalition

Following the election of Baldomir, the weakening of the Terra coalition and the strengthening of the opposition went even further. First, the ongoing industrial expansion continued to strengthen the urban sector with which Batllismo was identified (Finch 1981:17). Second, the growing European conflict and the predominance of a pro-Allied orientation in Uruguay discredited leaders such as Herrera who were strongly identified with fascism. Third, the overwhelming victory of the Colorado Party in the 1938 elections challenged the legitimacy of the equal division of government between the Colorados and the Herrera Nationalists. Fourth, and relatedly, the increased voter turnout suggested that the Batllistas could no longer enforce electoral abstention among their rank-and-file (Weinstein 1975:76). These considerations convinced Baldomir that a break with Herrera was possible, and perhaps even necessary, and helped initiate a rapprochement between Baldomir and the principal opposition to Terra—the Batllistas and the Independent Nationalists. The result was a negotiated transition that culminated in the 1942 coup, the new constitution of that year, and the restoration of democratic government with the election of Juan José de Amézaga in November of 1942.

Upon taking office, Baldomir indicated his interest in charting a new course and undertaking constitutional reform (Jacob 1983:64–65). In this commitment, as well as in his gradual move toward support for the allies when World War II began, he was strongly opposed by Herrera. By 1941 the break became complete when Herrera's faction made an alliance with the Acevedo Colorados—who represented the most conservative wing of the Terra Colorado support base—in order to oppose Baldomir's appointee as president of the Chamber of Deputies. Baldomir responded by demanding and accepting the resignations of the three ministers who belonged to the Herrera faction, which formally ended the ministerial coparticipation established by the 1934 constitution.[33]

As Herrera's position became more marginal, the relationship between Baldomir and the opposition grew closer. The opposition had quickly picked up on Baldomir's statements of June 1938 regarding the need for constitutional reform and staged a massive demonstration in July in support of a new constitution and democracy. Between 200,000 and 350,000 people turned out for the rally, suggesting the strength of the opposition at this point. This appar-

---

[32] D'Elia 1982:23; Rial 1984a:18–19, fn. 16, 111; Jacob 1983:64; Weinstein 1975:75; Fabregat 1948:394–95.

[33] Frega et al. 1987:112–13; Lindahl 1962:187; Faraone 1965:92; Taylor 1960a:29.

ent strength, together with the perception that the Batllistas had been crucial in Baldomir's electoral victory, pushed the Baldomir government further in its pursuit of democratization (Frega et al. 1987:100; Faraone 1965:87).

Major sectors of the opposition were well aware of the potential for a rapprochement with Baldomir and hastened to indicate that the 1938 demonstration did not reflect opposition to the Baldomir government. The Batllistas and the Independent Nationalists pointed to certain positive aspects of the Baldomir administration, such as its support for a neutral Electoral Court and a new constitution and its increasingly antifascist stance, as grounds for optimism about collaborating with him (Frega et al. 1987:100–101).

Following the 1938 demonstration and the opposition's decision to seek an accommodation with Baldomir, the discussions between the opposition and the government began in earnest. Very crucially, Baldomir was centrally concerned with ensuring that the splintering among the opposition that had occurred under Terra did not result in the defection to the left of followers of the traditional parties. Baldomir viewed any kind of popular front alternative as a grave threat to political stability that could erode the traditional party system. He therefore introduced new electoral legislation in 1939 that made it virtually impossible for the opposition to return to electoral competition from outside the traditional parties (Frega et al. 1987:104–6).

Because electoral rules again put a premium on being the majority faction within either of the traditional parties, the Batllista and Independent Nationalist leadership was in a quandary. If the Batllistas proved to be the majority faction of the Colorado Party, the law would allow them to win the presidency. If they were not, then their votes would contribute to a victory for the government faction in the 1942 elections, thus making them accomplices of the very system they were opposing. If they did form a completely new party, they could not identify their party with the traditional names, symbols, and colors of the Colorados. The debate, in the end, was won by the accommodationists who, encouraged by the prospects of cooperation with Baldomir, felt that the "conquest of power should be carried out in two steps: first, by reentering parliament, thus creating a counterweight to the Presidency and, in the second stage, winning control of the government" (Frega et al. 1987:109).

At the same time that Baldomir was encouraging the reunification of the Colorado Party, he also took concrete steps toward an accommodation with labor. Beginning in 1940, workers began to win a majority of the strikes they undertook, and the Baldomir government began to pursue a policy of concertation between labor and industry. Baldomir's new stance toward labor was backed by legislation, including the creation of a special legislative commission to study the living conditions of Uruguayan workers, and subsequent policies that grew out of the Commission's report included the extension of retirement benefits to all public employees and a new workplace safety and accident insurance plan. These initiatives, together with Baldomir's support for the allied cause in World War II, led the newly formed worker central, the

General Workers Union (UGT), to support Baldomir's efforts to carry out the transition to democracy in 1942.[34]

Baldomir also pursued policies more favorable to industrialists. During the Terra period there had been a clash between the economic projects of the cattle exporters and the industrialists. The Baldomir government abandoned the careful balance between the two groups maintained by Terra and moved decisively in the industrialists' favor. The industrial interest groups had taken a sharply critical stance toward Baldomir until 1940, when the government reorganized the exchange and import controls in favor of industry (Lamas and Piotti 1981:203–4). Though the industrialists continued to oppose Baldomir's social policies, their interest in expanding the internal market made them more tolerant of redistributive measures that would enlarge the consumption power of labor (Millot et al. 1973:119). At the same time, the increasing unification of the labor movement under the direction of the Communist Party and, as of 1942, the UGT, along with the Communists' policy of providing all possible support for the allied cause, led to a labor position that "supported the new industrial policies as well as agreements with management to help develop manufacturing" (Lamas and Piotti 1981:204). This union strategy created a climate of relative labor peace and made the industrialists more willing to accept new state intervention in capital-labor relations.

With the support of this coalition, Baldomir pushed ahead with a new constitution and a transition to democracy. In 1940 and 1941 he requested the preparation of drafts of the constitution, including opposition party leaders in the process. However, due to the composition of the Senate, Baldomir was unable to gain legislative support for the proposal. In addition to opposition within the Senate, led by Herrera and Acevedo, the Electoral Court also began to create problems for the transition process. While giving the Acevedo wing the right to run as a faction of the Colorado Party, the Court refused to grant the same right to the Batllistas and the Independent Nationals (Taylor 1960a:29; Frega et al. 1987:118). With the alternative of a legislative route to reform closed, an obvious alternative was that chosen by Terra in 1933: a coup d'etat.

On 21 February 1942, Baldomir dissolved both Congress and the Electoral Court and formed a Council of State to guide the transition process. In contrast to the 1933 coup, on this occasion there was no need to use even the police. The only group that overwhelmingly lost power was the Herrera Nationals. The UGT, all the traditional party factions except Herrera's, the Communist Party, and the major industrial groups supported the coup (Frega et al. 1987:123; Rial 1984a:19).

The Council of State moved quickly to report out the constitution (Taylor 1960a:30). Following a change in electoral laws that allowed the Independent Nationalists to run as a separate party under their old name, and with the

[34] Errandonea and Costabile 1969:58, 142; Frega et al. 1987:82; Lamas and Piotti 1981:203–4; Millot et al. 1973:118–19.

overwhelming approval of the new constitution by plebiscite in November, the final obstacles to the transition were overcome.

Absence of Pacts and Coparticipation

In contrast to the elaborate pacts that marked the end of the conservative reaction in Venezuela and Colombia, in Uruguay the transition had occurred through incremental negotiations between the Baldomir government and the opposition. What was negotiated was neither a complex set of new political structures nor an understanding about the economic policies of the future regime. Instead, they negotiated a set of modest changes in the political institutions established by Terra.

This outcome can be seen in the limited change in comparison with the 1934 Constitution. The 15-15 division of the Senate was abolished, as was coparticipation at the level of the cabinet and directorships of state corporations. The Senate continued to be selected through proportional representation, with the whole country treated as a single district. Mandatory minority party representation among the ministers was abandoned. Thus, the elements of coparticipation imposed by Terra and Herrera were dropped, and the basis was laid for bringing the Batlle Colorados and the Independent Nationalists back into the system (Weinstein 1975:77). The Electoral Court was restored, with the understanding that the majority of its members should be neutral figures. Ironically, many of the electoral rules of the Terra period, which had been opposed so forcefully by the Batllistas and Independent Nationalists when they were excluded from the system, were accepted now that the former opposition was once again included in the political game.

The final important agreement between Baldomir and the Batllistas concerned the Colorado Party's choice for president, a compromise "independent" candidate, Juan José de Amézaga. In the election, the Colorados outpolled the National Party 329,000 to 131,000, and the Amézaga's list won 234,000 votes, as opposed to only 129,000 for Herrera. The constitution won by a vote of 443,000 to 131,000, suggesting that opposition to the new constitution was largely limited to the Herrera wing of the National Party (Fabregat 1948:443–46).

Absence of Transformation of the Party

A prominent feature of the aftermath period in most cases of party incorporation was the conservatization of the party—and the associated labor unions—that had earlier led the incorporation project, as well as the institution of conflict-limiting mechanisms. Such compromise appeared necessary to permit this party to return to power or to retain power.[35]

---

[35] In Colombia and Venezuela it returned to power; in Peru it partially returned to power; and in Mexico it stayed in power.

SHAPING THE POLITICAL ARENA

In Uruguay no such compromise occurred. This outcome was manifested in several ways. First, a relatively reform-oriented Colorado Party regained a dominant position in the political system to a degree that it had not enjoyed since 1916. As the 1938 and 1942 electoral results demonstrated, the reunification of the Colorado Party marginalized the Nationals for some time, and the Batllista's overwhelming victory in the 1947 presidential elections only made this new dominance more evident, to the point that for a while Uruguayan politics became a "one-party show" (Taylor 1960a:32). Ironically, one reason for this new Colorado Party power was precisely the electoral laws supported by Herrera and Terra and passed under Terra. Under the double simultaneous vote, it was possible for the Colorados to win the country's highest office with lists that did not necessarily command a plurality of the votes.

Second, the Batlle Colorados did not expel or restrict their more progressive wing. In fact, quite the opposite occurred. Both Baldomir and the Batllista leadership wished to *prevent* the defection of progressive Colorados to left parties, in a setting where the popular front alternative appeared to pose the threat that this might occur.

Third, the conservatization of the unions encountered in some other countries did not occur. Though workers continued to vote for the Colorado party and the worker vote played an important role in giving the Colorados their electoral dominance, trade union organization was pluralistic and linked to parties of the left. During the World War, the UGT—formed in 1942 and dominated by the Communist Party—managed to unite the labor movement within the framework of the Communist policy of wartime collaboration. Yet the movement soon divided again, and by the mid-1940s a majority of the unions had abandoned the UGT. As a result, the union movement became fragmented, as it had been prior to 1933.[36]

Fourth, in some other countries this transition saw the emergence or renewal of mechanisms of power-sharing. By contrast, in Uruguay the provisions for coparticipation that were an important part of the pre-1933 system and of the Terra regime were abandoned in 1942, reflecting the extremely strong political position of the Colorados and their lack of need for compromise with the other parties.

Finally, and relatedly, in other cases of party incorporation, the conservative reaction of the aftermath period often brought a strong reassertion of the power of rural elites, and the transition back to some form of more competitive regime occurred in a way that assured the continuation of their stronger role. In Uruguay, by contrast, this transition saw a reduction of the power of the rural sector. This outcome was in part the result of changes in the legislature introduced in the 1934 and 1942 constitutions. Prior to the coup of 1933, the legislature had been chosen along regional lines in a way that overrepresented rural interests. The switch to proportional representation and at-large elections in both chambers greatly increased the representation of ur-

[36] Handelman 1981a:373–74; Errandonea and Costabile 1969:142, 145.

ban interests. What had previously been the more equal balance of power between city and countryside was dramatically altered by these changes, further increasing the representation of those seeking reform and a more activist state (Rial 1984a:99–100, fn 2).

Another political factor that contributed to the shift in the rural-urban balance was the discrediting of Herrera—a leading representative of rural interests—and his declining electoral fortunes. This outcome was due in part to his strong identification with European fascism, which ran against prevailing political preferences in Uruguay. However, by the early 1950s Herrera had substantially regained his earlier stature.

Yet another factor that contributed to the shift in the rural-urban balance was the expansion of industry during these years and the growing closeness between the goals of the Batllista Colorados and the industrial sector (Finch 1981:16–19). Though the Batllista program had always supported industrial development, prior to 1930 the industrialists were relatively weak and were apprehensive about the onslaught of social and labor reforms of the Batlle era. Starting in the 1940s, the state became more active in mediating labor-capital relations, and the industrialists, in turn, recognized that the continued growth of their sector depended on an expansion of internal demand and redistribution. Though never completely happy with the expansion of social and labor legislation, after 1940 the industrialists were more accepting of such initiatives and played a more conciliatory role than they had prior to 1933.[37]

To conclude, in some respects the Uruguayan aftermath experience differed from that in all other cases of party incorporation, above all in the limited degree of enforced conservatization of the party that had earlier led the incorporation project. The Colorados did not change their program or ideology to achieve the transition, and in fact went on to a new period of reform in the 1940s. Part of Baldomir's strategy was to channel electoral participation away from any kind of a popular front alternative and back into the traditional parties, and in that sense constraints were imposed on the parties. However, as noted above, this strategy served to prevent the *defection* of the left, as opposed to promoting the *expulsion* of the left, as occurred in this period in some other countries. Yet this outcome was not imposed on the established party leadership, which by and large was reluctant in any case to enter into coalitions in which it would have abandoned its traditional party affiliation.

The rules governing elections and parties exhibited both continuity and change. Some of the electoral rules carried over from the Terra period also reinforced the position of the traditional parties during and after the transition. On the other hand, the traditional form of interparty coparticipation

[37] Frega et al. 1987:86–89; Millot et al. 1973:119. It may be noted that in Uruguay, the labor-capital alliance in the industrial sector that might be hypothesized to be associated with the incorporation period in fact was more nearly achieved in the aftermath period.

was sharply reduced in 1942 and was not sought by the Colorados, given their strong position.

At the same time that the Uruguayan experience was distinctive in comparison with other cases of party incorporation, many similarities are evident with Colombia. In both countries the restoration of a more competitive regime following the conservative reaction brought back to power the two traditional parties under conditions that reinforced their dominance in the political system. In both countries, the party that had led the incorporation period—the Colorados and the Liberals—retained the majority electoral position they had earlier won, based in part on substantial support among workers. Finally, in both cases the labor movement had, or would soon come to have, substantial independence from the traditional parties. This outcome derived from several factors, including the difficulty during the incorporation period in both countries of strongly linking unions to a traditional, multiclass, multisectoral party. In Colombia, as we shall see in the next section, this outcome was reinforced by the way the National Front diffused the unions' partisan ties.

COLOMBIA

Conservative Reaction

In Colombia, the end of the incorporation period came with the resignation of López Pumarejo in 1945 in the midst of intense opposition and crisis. With his resignation, the reform project would no longer be carried out from the presidency. Yet the dramatic move to the right would not occur for several years. First of all, within the reformist wing of the Liberals, Gaitán continued to promote an energetic reform agenda. Second, the three years following the resignation of López in 1945 saw a coalition government of Liberals and Conservatives. From 1945–46, López's successor, the Liberal President Lleras Camargo, reversed López's earlier posture of maintaining a government based exclusively on the Liberal Party and initiated a coalition government called the National Union. With the victory of the Conservative Party in the 1946 presidential elections, President Ospina continued this bipartisan coalition. Gaitán, head of the reformist wing of the Liberals, took over the party leadership in 1947 and participated in the coalition government over the next year, as did Darío Echandía, who succeeded Gaitán as leader of the Liberals after Gaitán's assassination in 1948. Both of these party leaders wished to push the Liberals to begin a new period of mass mobilization and reform, but they were seriously constrained by the coalition government, whose purpose was to prevent the emergence of partisan violence.

Given the Liberal presence within the government, Ospina had to avoid any overt attack on the Liberals' base of urban and labor support. One consequence was that although the UTC, the trade union confederation identified with the Catholic Church and Conservative Party, was formed in 1946 and did receive some support from the Conservative government, Ospina was unable or unwilling to officially recognize it until late 1949, after the Liberals had definitively withdrawn from the National Union coalition. In the short run, the CTC maintained and even enhanced its position within the trade union movement, reaching its greatest strength in 1947 and 1948 with around 900 member unions and over 100,000 members (F. González 1975:43; Martz 1964:213).

The intense conservative reaction began in late 1949 as Laureano Gómez's influence within the Conservative Party grew and partisan violence in the countryside escalated. Gómez was strongly opposed to collaboration with the Liberals and pushed Ospina to close Congress. As president beginning in 1950, he initiated a Conservative civilian dictatorship and attempted to impose a "Hispanic counterrevolution."

In the analysis of this period in Colombia, two dimensions must be distinguished. First, the Gómez period was a reaction to the interrelated initiatives of the López years: the incorporation project, the mobilization policies of López more broadly, and his successful, partisan effort to turn the Liberals into the majority party in Colombia. In reaction to these developments, Gómez sought to take the political system far to the right and to reestablish Conservative Party hegemony.

Second, the effort to reestablish Conservative hegemony produced a violent response that had no counterpart in the analytically comparable period in the other countries, but had deep roots in Colombia's tradition of partisan conflict. This involved the virtual civil war, known as La Violencia (The Violence), that emerged between the Liberal and Conservative parties as a reaction and counterreaction to Gómez's efforts to reassert Conservative dominance. With the rapid growth of the state in the 1930s and 1940s and its growing role in the economy, access to the state and its patronage resources had become even more crucial to the ongoing functioning of the parties. Beginning in 1949, and accelerating under the Gómez government starting in 1950, Liberal access to the state was cut off and many Liberals, especially in rural areas, reacted by organizing insurgent armies and guerrilla organizations.

The Gómez government (1950–53) saw the use of state power to attack and marginalize Liberal bases of support. With the aid of intensely partisan Conservative governors, regional Conservative elites used repression and strong-arm tactics to take back political power lost between 1930 and 1946. In urban areas, repression of CTC labor unions was stepped up, while the law prohibiting parallel unions was repealed, giving the UTC the opportunity to establish government-supported trade unions in areas formerly dominated by the CTC. The CTC was correctly perceived by the Conservative government as a Liberal weapon in the growing partisan struggle, and the CTC leadership became the target of direct repression. Well-known Communists, active within the CTC, were murdered. The CTC, overestimating its strength, called for a national strike on the day of the 1949 presidential election, hoping to bring down the Conservative dictatorship. The strike was a complete failure, and CTC influence fell drastically. In 1951 the Gómez government passed new labor legislation that made strikes more difficult, required government permission for union meetings, and repealed the 1945 law that forbade firing union leaders. The result was that by 1952 the government-supported UTC had replaced the CTC in most major sectors of the economy, as well as making important progress in unionizing major industrial firms in Conservative Antioquia, which had not previously been organized by the CTC (Dix 1967:111–12; Caicedo 1971:106–7; F. González 1975:46).

Gómez's program was a mixture of social policies that harked back to the days of colonial Spain, along with economic policies supportive of foreign capital and fiscal austerity. Gómez wished to turn "the course of the nation away from popular republicanism toward the Hispanic state of Ferdinand and Isabel." Resurrecting the traditional Iberic "dogma of the Two Swords" (i.e., the fusion of political and religious authority—Martz 1962:87), Gómez proposed to end the separation of Church and state and remake the country's political institutions. In 1952, while partisan strife raged in the rural regions, Gómez announced the formation of a new Constituent Assembly to enact constitutional reforms. Presented to the nation in March 1953, the proposals generated a storm of controversy. First, the new constitution would greatly expand the powers of the president and the central state, while weakening the legislature, judiciary, and local government. The Congress, with virtually no independent power, would be composed of a directly elected lower house and a purely advisory upper house corporatively organized around functional representation. The UTC was to be the representative of labor within the upper chamber. The most widely criticized aspect of the new constitution was the restriction of the vote in municipal elections to heads of households. Finally, the new constitution would have abolished the separation of Church and state and would have made the Church an integral part of the new regime.[38]

By 1953, opposition to the Gómez dictatorship became widespread. In 1952 Ospina had announced his candidacy for the 1954 presidential election. Gómez opposed Ospina's candidacy and the division within the Conservative Party became apparent. Ospina and his Liberal supporters were dismayed by the growing partisan violence and the government policies that fueled it. While Gómez was pushing for a "Hispanic counterrevolution," the authority of the Colombian state over increasingly large areas of the country eroded. National party leaders, who had condoned, and in some cases initiated, the partisan violence, were no longer able to control the partisan struggle, which was becoming increasingly brutal and which caused nearly 150,000 deaths between 1948 and 1953. At the same time, the military was increasingly dissatisfied with its own role in the repression of Liberals and the failure of the "scorched earth" approach to ending La Violencia.[39] With both parties divided, it was increasingly clear that the traditional parties were incapable of ending the violence. The politicians finally turned to the military, and to General Gustavo Rojas Pinilla in particular, to end the political deadlock. When Gómez reacted by trying to remove Rojas from command of the armed forces, the military initiated its first successful coup in over a century. Supported by all but the Gómez wing of the Conservative Party, the new military government, headed by Rojas, came to power committed to ending the civil war and restoring civilian government.

The Rojas government, which originally was dominated by civilian politicians of the Ospina wing of the Conservative Party and supported by the Liberal Party, would in fact become a direct threat to the traditional parties. Rojas's original cabinet was made up primarily of Conservative politicians who opposed Gómez and who expected a quick return to power. But influenced by Juan Perón of Argentina, Rojas attempted to build a personal power base of his own. Rojas apparently imitated Perón in a number of ways in his attempt to mobilize popular support for his own rule, as can be seen in the parallels between the programs and organizations developed by Rojas and Pe-

[38] Melman 1978:75; Fluharty 1957:131–32; Martz 1964:87, 105, 114, 152.
[39] Oquist 1980:6; Ruhl 1980:185; Dix 1967:113; Hartlyn 1984a:40; 1981a:58.

rón. However, Rojas was much less successful (Szulc 1959:228–30; Melman 1978:93–94).

Rojas's initial popularity was boosted in July 1953 when he offered amnesty to the Liberal insurgents. His proposal was generally accepted, and by August much of the fighting had ended. Yet by 1954, as it became obvious that Rojas did not soon plan to allow a return to civilian rule, his support began to fade. In late 1953 and again in 1954 Rojas initiated a series of tax reforms that angered coffee growers and industrialists. When Rojas established three state-owned banks, the financial sector also began to move into opposition. Like Pérez Jiménez in Venezuela, Rojas initiated numerous public works projects which, with falling coffee prices and increasing graft and corruption, led to growing balance of payments difficulties, rising inflation, and capital flight. The country moved into a recession caused in important measure by economic mismanagement.[40]

With the political and economic elite in opposition, Rojas began a number of projects that pushed further his attempt to establish a personal base for his continuation in office. Rojas first tried to build support within the labor movement by revising the labor code to expand provisions for job security and other measures calculated to increase his labor support. Yet, with the bulk of the antilabor legislation introduced by Gómez still on the books, both the UTC and the CTC rejected Rojas's overtures. Unable to generate support within the established trade unions, Rojas attempted to build his own competing labor organization. In 1953 a group of Perón-oriented labor leaders established the CNT (National Confederation of Workers) and joined Perón's international confederation, ATLAS. In 1954 Rojas recognized the CNT in the hope of using it as a base of political support. The Catholic Church, seeing the new Peronist labor central as a threat to the UTC, bitterly opposed it. Rojas also organized the Greater Labor Council (GCO) in 1955 to coordinate his labor policy. But Rojas's attempt to emulate Perón in the organization of labor failed as, under intense Church and UTC pressure, he backed down and allowed the two new labor organizations to wither away. Though labor was able to maintain its independence from Rojas, the Rojas years were a difficult time for the established labor confederations. By the time of Rojas's fall from power in 1957, the Colombian labor movement was greatly weakened. Of the CTC's approximately 900 member unions, only 27 remained in 1957. The UTC also saw its strength reduced, falling from its earlier level of over 500 in the early 1950s to under 300 trade unions in 1957 (Melman 1978:99, 115–16; Caicedo 1971:115–16).

Yet Rojas did not give up. As elite opposition grew, his rhetoric became more strident as he attempted to generate support within urban and rural lower-class areas. Imitating the Eva Perón Foundation established in Argentina, Rojas created a welfare agency SENDAS (National Secretariat of Social Assistance) headed by his 21-year-old daughter, María Eugenia Rojas. While this organization never received the financial support of its Peronist counter-

[40] Martz 1964:177, 231, 233; 1978:100–101, 108–9; González 1975:49.

part, its initiatives, together with the growing employment generated by the public works program, apparently did win Rojas some support in lower-class neighborhoods (Melman 1978:103–5). It was precisely among these groups that Rojas would generate his strongest vote when he entered electoral politics in the late 1960s.

Rojas also attempted to form a political party, the Third Force, as an alternative to the traditional Liberal and Conservative parties (Melman 1978:116–19). Rojas did not put much effort into the party, possibly due to considerable Church and elite opposition, and it quickly faded away. Yet civilian political leaders became increasingly convinced that Rojas constituted a real danger to the power of both traditional parties.

In the face of this threat, and with partisan violence again on the rise, the López wing of the Liberal Party made an accord with the Ospina faction "binding them to a common effort in opposition to the [Rojas] government" (Fluharty 1957:291). By 1956 the Liberal Party, reunited, moved in opposition to Rojas, and Lleras Camargo was sent to Spain to discuss a new coalition government with Gómez. In mid-1956 Gómez agreed to support such a coalition and the Ospina faction joined the anti-Rojas coalition in March 1957 (Kline 1980:71; Melman 1978:132–33).

With the political, economic, and religious elite in opposition, the Rojas coalition shrank to certain sectors of the military and a few fringe groups like the Socialist Party. Veering to the left, Rojas supported a series of progressive reforms suggested by a socialist presidential adviser in 1957 in a last ditch effort to generate popular support. But by this point Rojas had even lost the support of the lower class as the recession and an austerity program prevented his government from fulfilling its promises. On 7 May 1957, political, business, and labor leaders staged a national strike against the Rojas government to protest his attacks on the traditional political and economic elite, his heavy censorship of the press, and growing rural violence.[41] Three days later, Rojas was deposed by a military junta.

Formation of New Governing Coalition

With Rojas out of power, the Liberals and Conservatives moved quickly to establish the basis for a new coalition government. In June 1957 Lleras, Gómez, and Ospina signed an initial agreement, and a final accord was hammered out in Sitges, Spain, in July. The agreement was incorporated into the constitution through a national plebiscite held on 1 December 1957. Receiving the nearly unanimous support of the Colombian electorate, the Pact of Sitges, paralleling the Venezuelan Pact of Punto Fijo, became the basis of a bipartisan coalition government, the National Front (Frente Nacional). The Front was inaugurated with the presidential election of May 1958 and the

---

[41] Medina 1984:85–122; Melman 1978:92, 125–28; González 1975:94; Urrutia 1969a:224.

installation as president in August of the Liberal leader Alberto Lleras Camargo.

The National Front was of course not the first coalition government established by the two traditional parties. Historically, they had engaged in power-sharing agreements, and after 1946 the parties attempted through a coalition government to restore party peace. The violence of the Gómez administration, Rojas's eventual failure to curb it, and the threat of Rojas's self-perpetuation in power convinced the major party leaders that only a far more elaborate, formalized agreement to limit conflict would suffice. The Liberals, with their new urban support developed in the 1930s and 1940s, were clearly the majority party. The Conservatives were unwilling to see a return to Liberal electoral dominance and had the means to prevent it, given their support within the military. A return to full party competition would only add fuel to the violence in the countryside, which was once again growing and which between 1953 and 1957 alone had resulted in nearly 25,000 additional deaths (over 135,000 deaths had occurred between 1948 and 1952—Oquist 1980:6–7). What was needed, therefore, was a formula to limit party conflict, yet allow the traditional political elite to remain in power. The Pact of Sitges was the result of this search for a new foundation for the political rule of the traditional party elites.

Conflict-Limiting Mechanisms. The 1957 plebiscite, which ratified the National Front as part of the constitution, was the first major step toward institutionalizing the party agreements. At the heart of the proposed constitutional reform was the concept of parity. The Liberals and Conservatives agreed to divide equally all legislative, judicial, and bureaucratic positions, from cabinet ministers, senators, and Supreme Court justices to municipal sanitation crews.[42] Parity ensured equal party access to the resources and prestige of national and local governments and removed one major source of the partisan violence that had arisen with the Conservative victory in 1946.

Unlike the more informal Venezuelan party pact, the Front established a tightly structured "consociational" regime (Dix 1980b) that was enshrined in the national constitution. Not only was parity between the parties formally established, but each major party was in effect given a legislative veto, as all legislation had to be passed by a two-third congressional majority.[43] Finally, the parties sought to prevent rebel party factions from organizing new parties by stipulating that no other political parties could run candidates during the 16-year period of the Front from 1958 to 1974. However, as we will note later, this did not prevent groups opposed to the Front from presenting themselves as Liberals or Conservatives and running under those names.

One position, however, could not be divided: the presidency. The original agreement, but not the plebiscite, called for a Conservative president in 1958, with the two parties alternating in the presidency until 1974. But the Gómez and Ospina wings of the Conservative Party were unable to agree on

---

[42] Hoskin 1980:105–6, 127; Dix 1967:133–34; Kline 1980:72.
[43] Dix 1980b:307–8; Hartlyn 1988; Kline 1980:72.

a mutually acceptable candidate. With the entire agreement in danger of collapsing, the Conservative factions finally supported the candidacy of the Liberal, Lleras Camargo. The agreement on alternation was added to the constitution by amendment in 1959, thus establishing, along with parity, the second major aspect of the pact.

The new electoral system obviously eliminated partisan competition in elections. The electoral struggle would not be *between* the parties, since their seats were guaranteed, but *within* the parties, as the various factions attempted to secure a majority of their party's seats. Without partisan competition, the elections, rather than becoming mechanisms for mobilizing partisans and emphasizing party differences, served to limit party competition, and electoral participation dropped from the exceptionally high levels of the late 1940s. In this, at least, the National Front was successful. Rural partisan violence also fell off quickly, though violence continued at low levels for several years.

Technocratic Orientation of the Front. The first priority of the Front was the restoration of peace and constitutional government. Other objectives, such as economic development and social reform, were initially secondary. But the Rojas government's mismanagement of the economy, as well as the fall in coffee prices, had left the Colombian economy in a serious recession As the threat of violence receded, the National Front increasingly focused on ways to promote economic development, while at the same time attempting to address social and economic inequalities. The subsequent governments, given the divided legislature and the resulting policy immobilism, came to depend on an increasingly technical, bureaucratic approach to economic development and on a "trickle-down" approach to social reform (Dix 1967:147, 150; Cepeda and Mitchell 1980).

As occurred in Venezuela, one consequence of the Front was the removal of potentially conflictual issues from the political agenda. The Front did undertake a number of well-publicized reforms, including an expansion of public housing and government expenditures on health, municipal services, community self-help programs, education, and land redistribution (Dix 1967:148–58). Yet as Dix (1967:147) noted, "Such changes were hardly to be revolutionary. On the whole they were to be confined within limits that would not damage the fundamental interests of the most influential adherents of the two traditional parties. . . . Moderate reforms were to be effected in order that more basic changes would not become necessary." As a consequence, a bureaucratic and technical approach to national problems, especially to issues of redistribution, became common. Cepeda and Mitchell (1980:253) point out: "Colombia's National Front coalitional system removed many issues of development policy from direct exposure to political debate. With sixteen years of national power virtually guaranteed to a fairly homogeneous group of traditional party leaders, the probabilities increased that questions of economic strategy would be defined as 'technical' and solved accordingly. There was a proliferation of functionally-specific public agencies, designed to operate with efficiency—rather than equity, mass involvement, or other values—as their major goal."

Programmatic Shift to the Center. As occurred in several other countries, the reformist wing of the incorporating party moved toward the political center in the aftermath period. While the circumstances of the move were somewhat different in Colombia, the result was much the same. By supporting the Front, the Liberals accepted a situation in which there was no possibility of continuing anything like the Revolución en Marcha. The left was either marginalized or chose to leave the party. At the same time, the Liberals moved to recapture their position within the resurgent CTC and in 1960 engineered a final and decisive expulsion of the left from the labor confederation. Yet while the Liberal Party was able to maintain, at least for a time, its position within the CTC, and while the working class seems to have transferred its support for the Liberal Party to the Front, the nature of the Front agreement greatly reduced the strategic importance of the CTC to the Liberal Party. The development of parallel labor confederations, the decision to end partisan competition and mobilization, as well as the necessity to work closely with Conservative Party factions all weakened the party-labor relationship.

The Liberals' programmatic shift obviously occurred in reaction to the violent partisan conflict of the 1940s and 1950s. In 1945 the break between the moderate and reformist wings of the Liberal Party seemed complete. But the subsequent period of escalating Conservative repression and party warfare made this division increasingly irrelevant. The new issue that divided the two wings was how to respond to the growing partisan violence. As Tirado (1977:151) notes, "the old fight was over reformism and moderation; the new issue was collaboration versus opposition." In the 1930s and early 1940s, López had been the major exponent of one-party government, while the Olaya moderates had supported coalitions with the Conservatives. By the mid-1950s López became increasingly convinced that the only way to end partisan violence was to restore a two-party, coalition government. But Gómez rejected his overtures and the Santos wing of the Liberal Party continued to oppose collaboration. By 1954, however, the Santos wing concluded that Lopez's policy was the only way to bridge the differences between the two parties and restore civilian rule (Tirado 1977:189–91). By 1958, therefore, the Liberal Party was reunited around its support for the Front.

The Front placed major constraints on the Liberal Party. The parity and two-thirds majority rule in Congress meant that to insure a successful governing coalition, the Liberals would have to work closely with at least one wing of the Conservatives. Not only did these conflict-limiting mechanisms create an institutionalized bias against progressive legislation, but the electoral system, and its encouragement of intraparty factionalism, insured that "legislative conflict did not revolve . . . around specific governmental policies related to economic and social matters" (Hoskin 1980:106). Instead, it principally involved legislative maneuvers designed to maintain the strength of divergent party factions.

But the Front agreement was not the only reason for the Liberal Party's change in orientation. The decade of party warfare had also affected the views of Liberal Party leaders. An active effort to restore the special relationship between the Liberal Party and the urban working class would clash directly with the policy of demobilizing the Colombian electorate. Political stability, not reform, became the central preoccupation of the Liberals. Kline (1980:66–67), analyzing the speeches of the first National Front president, Lleras Camargo, notes that "the theme clearly emerges that Colombia was not ready for a democracy with a loyal opposition. Democratic competition for power, Lleras thought, would lead to violence. The only way to avoid this was through a coalition government of both parties." Reform, especially of the incremental variety common during the Alliance for Progress period, while pursued, was secondary to the establishment of a stable political order.

There was little place within the new regime for the left and its strategy of popular mobilization. Some Liberal leftists turned to armed insurrection, while others joined together, around the son of López, Alfonzo López Michelsen, to oppose the National Front government. While the Liberals could and did exclude the left from the governing coalition, they were unable to exclude it from the electoral arena. Unlike the hierarchical organization of the parties in Venezuela and Peru that had earlier led the incorporation project, the Colombian Liberal Party leadership had little or no control over the use of the party name or over the regional party directorates and positions on regional Liberal lists. In 1958 the Communists gained some offices running on Liberal lists and, beginning in 1960, worked together with López Michelsen's MRL (Liberal Revolutionary Movement) (Dix 1967:273, 278–79). Given the proleft, pro-Castro rhetoric of the MRL, as well as its bitter attacks on the National Front, it is likely that the Liberal Party, had it enjoyed the internal party discipline of its Venezuelan or Peruvian counterpart, would have expelled the MRL faction.

López Michelsen and the MRL faced major disadvantages in running against the National Front. First, wide sectors of Colombian society saw the Front as the only means of ending the years of partisan strife. Second, the regime initiated a series of defensive reforms, which, while perhaps merely palliative, made it difficult to mobilize the urban working class. Third, anti-Front sentiment was strongest not in the cities, but in rural areas deeply affected by the violence. López Michelsen had considerable appeal among peasants and rural *caciques* angry over the Liberal "sell out" to the Conservatives. His support came primarily from rural areas, and the MRL never did attempt a mobilization of the urban electorate. Finally, the Liberal Party and the National Front governing coalition controlled sufficient resources to combat the MRL challenge between 1960 and 1966. Faced with these obstacles, López Michelsen began his own move to the right as early as the end of 1960, expelling some Communist members of the MRL and condemning Castro's "betrayal" of the Cuban Revolution (Dix 1967:147, 262–64, 289–90; Martz 1962:333–34).

Retention of Labor Vote.   Despite the Liberals' move to the right and their attempt to control and eliminate the influence of the left, they were apparently able to transfer the electoral support of the organized working class to the National Front. Both the UTC and CTC leadership supported the establishment of the Front in 1958 and reacted negatively to the Cuban Revolution. But it is more difficult to determine whether the rank-and-file did. The evidence, quite indirect, is that the working class did support the Front candidate even in the 1970 elections, when Rojas's ANAPO posed the greatest challenge to the Front, winning 39 percent of the national vote. In a 1970 survey, 48 percent of all respondents said they supported the National Front, while 38 percent said they did not. However, working-class respondents supported the governing coalition by a 58 to 29 percent margin. It is also noteworthy that support for the Front was especially strong among people with membership in voluntary associations, which included trade unions.[44] If the working class supported the Front even in 1970, the year of strongest opposition to the Front, it would not be unreasonable to infer that working-class support was even stronger in 1958. Thus, it would appear that the Liberals were able to transfer labor movement support to the Front.

With regard to the rural sector, this was of course the part of Colombia's electorate that had developed the strongest traditional identifications with the parties through a century of primarily rural civil war. Correspondingly, with some exceptions, the rural sector supported the Front. However, the Front brought changes in rural political relationships. The lack of party competition and growing electoral abstention under the Front greatly increased the importance of those party activists, or *caciques*, who could guarantee votes for Front candidates. With the demobilization of the urban electorate, rural party bosses became important, not only in providing blocks of captive votes, but also in determining party candidates. While the Conservatives were much more dependent on peasant support, the Liberal Party also received an important part of its votes from this sector. To maintain its position in the countryside, and to fight off challenges from the MRL and leftist guerrillas, the Front used a mix of defensive reforms like the highly technical and only moderately effective 1961 agrarian reform, along with military repression (especially against rural enclaves of Communist Party strength) to prevent the emergence of autonomous rural organizations that might threaten the Front. It was not until the late 1960s that the Front tried to directly organize the peasants, an attempt that had to be ended when the peasant movement nearly escaped government control.

[44] Martz 1964:324; Talbot Campos and McCamant 1971:120; Melman 1978:214. These percentages are quite suggestive if we keep in mind that the trade union movement had around 1 million members. Since no other organization or association had anywhere near this number of members, it is likely that a large proportion of all Colombians belonging to voluntary associations are members of trade unions. It should be noted that the survey on which this finding is based (Losada and Williams 1972) covers only Bogotá and may not be representative of Colombia as a whole. However, in 1970 Rojas received a large vote in Bogotá, suggesting that the survey should have identified major sources of opposition to the front.

The major defection from the Front in the rural sector during the early 1960s was the substantial rural vote for López Michelsen's MRL. López received considerable support from rural regions, especially those that had suffered violence during the 1940s and 1950s. As noted above, the main explanation is that these voters (overwhelmingly Liberal) supported López out of dissatisfaction with the Liberals' decision to enter into the Front with the Conservatives. These rural voters held the Conservative Party responsible for the violence they had previously suffered.

Therefore, López's rural support came from die-hard Liberals from violence-torn areas. His rural support was not initially due to any special appeals to rural interests as such, although he did begin to emphasize such interests after the first elections revealed his strength in rural areas. This support was surprising, given that his original program was geared to urban workers.[45]

Weakening of Party Ties with the Labor Movement. In contrast to the experience following several other cases of party incorporation, the Liberal Party maintained a much weaker institutional link with labor unions and the CTC. This may be attributed both to the nature of the governing coalition and the growth of the rival UTC confederation.

This is not to say that labor's role was unimportant in the creation of the National Front, and both the UTC and the CTC, as well as the Communist Party, provided crucial support for its formation. There may well have been a link between this support and the rise of real wages under the first Front government, though this outcome may have been due in part to the general improvement in the economy that occurred in the early years of the Front.[46]

In this period, the Liberals likewise did continue to have some important influence within the labor movement. Though the Liberals had considerable difficulty in controlling the left within the party, they were more successful in dealing with the left within the renascent CTC. In 1950 the CTC, already falling apart, had suffered a split between elements affiliated with the Liberals and with the Communists. But the break was never official and, with the fall of Rojas and the initiation of the National Front, Communist and Liberal labor activists began the process of rebuilding the CTC labor central. The Communists' interest in strengthening the CTC was primarily due to their concern with counteracting the dominance of the UTC within the labor movement. In just two years, the CTC went from an empty shell with only 27 member unions to once again in 1959 being an important confederation with more than 400 unions (Caicedo 1971:115–16, 122).

However, the growing presence of the Communists within the labor movement, as well as the wave of strikes initiated by the CTC between 1958 and 1960, led the Liberal government to press the CTC to expel the Communists. Liberal and Communist leaders had already skirmished at the 1958 labor congress, and the fears subsequently generated by the Cuban Revolution gal-

---

[45] Dix 1980a:135; Talbot and McCamant 1972:19.
[46] Hartlyn 1981a:352; 1981b:13; Urrutia 1969a:224.

vanized the Liberals' effort to push the Communist unions out, with government support, at the 1960 congress.[47]

Nonetheless, the close relationship between the CTC and Liberal Party during the earlier incorporation period was never fully restored. Although the CTC's leadership, especially after 1960, was mainly Liberal, and though some union members appeared, as individuals, on Liberal electoral lists, the two were not formally linked and the CTC occasionally acted contrary to the wishes of the Front governments. One reason for this loosening in the labor-party relationship was that the labor movement became less important as an electoral ally during the Front period. More importantly, however, the Liberal Party, by participating in a coalition government, could not afford to associate too closely with the CTC, for fear of alienating Conservative allies. Relations between the UTC and the Conservative Party were also eroded, and the type of relation that had earlier existed between the UTC and the Conservative governments of Ospina and Gómez was not revived. After the beginning of the National Front, the Church became increasingly less partisan, and the UTC followed suit. As a result, in comparison with several other countries, the Colombian trade union movement developed a relatively high degree of autonomy from political parties (Dix 1967:333–34, 337).

[47] F. González 1975:52–54; Caicedo 1971:129–33; Martz 1964:323; Dix 1967:273–74.

PERU AND ARGENTINA: "DIFFICULT" AND "IMPOSSIBLE" GAMES

In comparison with other cases of party incorporation, the conflict-limiting mechanisms of the aftermath period in Peru and Argentina took a distinctive form. Although a more competitive, civilian regime was restored following the military government that led the conservative reaction to incorporation, under this civilian regime severe restrictions were placed on the electoral role of the parties that had led the incorporation project—APRA and Peronism.

These restrictions were less harsh in Peru than in Argentina. In Peru, some Apristas were allowed to run on an independent list and were elected to the national Congress in 1956, and after 1956 APRA had a significant presence in the Congress. The party was legalized after the 1956 presidential election and was allowed full electoral participation in the 1960s, except that there was an ongoing veto of the assumption of the presidency by APRA, and particularly by Haya de la Torre, the party's founder and leader. Though partially proscribed in the electoral sphere, APRA was permitted to play an active role in the syndical arena. In Argentina, Peronism was subjected to more severe electoral restrictions, although it was likewise permitted to function in the syndical arena.

This shared pattern of ongoing electoral exclusion created distinctive dynamics. It produced in Argentina what O'Donnell (1973:chap.4) suggestively called an "impossible game" of politics, which revolved around the dilemma that the party that had previously held a majority position within the electorate was not allowed to win elections. By contrast, the situation in Peru might usefully be labeled a "difficult" game, which allowed more scope for the normal functioning of politics, but within limits that likewise produced recurring political crises. Along with these crises, for present purposes some of the most important consequences of these impossible and difficult games are seen in their implications for the internal dynamics of Peronism and APRA.

PERU

Conservative Reaction

Following General Manuel Odría's coup of 27 October 1948, which ended the Bustamante government, Odría initiated the energetic repression of APRA, seeking to eliminate the party from the Peruvian political scene. As many as 4,000 people were arrested in the eight months after the coup, and the government resorted to the torture and the assassination of Apristas. After two months in hiding, Haya de la Torre sought refuge in the Colombian embassy in Lima. Claiming that Haya was a common criminal, Odría refused to grant him permission to leave the country, thereby violating what was then the Latin American custom of permitting the exile of leading political opponents. Haya spent more than five years in the embassy building, which the government surrounded with trenches and barbed wire, covering the doors of the building with spotlights, tanks, and machine guns.

Along with this blatant symbol of repression, the general atmosphere of anti-Aprismo was reinforced by a variety of initiatives, such as the introduction of a more elaborate version of the annual ceremony honoring the army officers killed in Aprista uprising of 1932 in Trujillo. The Law of Internal Security of July 1949, possibly the most repressive in South America at that time, gave the government exceptionally wide powers of surveillance and control and restored the death penalty.[48] Thus, the fears triggered by APRA's policy initiatives and popular mobilization during the 1945–48 coalition government, along with the violence initiated by APRA and Apristas during that period, brought down upon the party a major new wave of repression.

The APRA-dominated labor confederation, the CTP, was outlawed and its top leadership jailed. Arturo Sabroso, the secretary general, was temporarily replaced by Luis Negreiros, a leading union organizer from the earlier incorporation period, who now headed the CTP in its underground phase. In 1950 Negreiros was captured and killed in the street by the police. The government made some effort to fill vacant leadership positions in APRA unions with cooperative leaders, and the former Communist labor leader Juan Luna (the first head of the CTP in 1944) played an important role in this effort. However, these initiatives were never successful. The continuing loyalty of workers to APRA in the face of the repression was expressed after the killing of Negreiros, when thousands of workers apparently defied government orders and went to pay their final respects as his body lay in police headquarters. The rate of recognition of new unions dropped to a low level in relation to the Bustamante period—from approximately 88 per year to just ten per year (Sulmont 1975:213, 218–19, 276).

Odría had come to power with strong support from the agro-export elite, and this support was quickly repaid with decree laws that revised Peru's for-

[48] Werlich 1978:248–49; Sulmont 1975:214; Pike 1967:290–91.

eign exchange controls, dramatically increasing the profits from exports (Bustamante i Rivero 1949:308ff.; Astiz 1969b:139). Odría launched a policy of promoting the export sector and foreign investment to such a degree that, beginning in 1948, Peru became "the example *par excellence* in Latin America of [the] dream of orthodox development economists" (Thorp and Bertram 1978:205). Foreign investment was encouraged through the Mining Code of 1950 and a new Petroleum Law in 1952, and following the recommendations of a U.S. consulting firm, "Peru became the first nation of Latin America and one of a few in the world to abolish all exchange controls" (Werlich 1978:250). In response to government policy and the increased demand for Peruvian products during the Korean War, Peru experienced an export boom (Thorp and Bertram 1978:208, 210, 222).

Odría's support coalition evolved significantly during his presidency. Though his government was initially close to the export elite, this relationship was not to last, and he developed an important degree of autonomy from this sector. Odría abandoned his original commitment to form only a short-term provisional government and instead held a rigged election in 1950 to legitimate a six year presidential term ending in 1956. Toward the end of his term, he threatened the freedom of the elite-owned press, adopted "gangster tactics" (Villanueva 1962:133) in forcing wealthy families to donate houses and other expensive gifts to government leaders, and took advantage of provisions of the Internal Security Law to harass members of the oligarchy with whom he was quarrelling (Villanueva 1962:133; Astiz 1969b:140).

Though Odría was anti-APRA, he made a strong appeal to the popular sector. In doing this, he sought both to broaden his own base of support and to construct an alternative to the kind of popular mobilization APRA had been promoting. It appears that in comparison with Rojas Pinilla in Colombia and Pérez Jiménez in Venezuela, Odría was far more successful in this effort to win popular support. He developed a particularly viable alternative to APRA's popular mobilization within the trade union sector, an alternative that he had already begun to explore before his coup, as we shall see below.

Payne argues that Odría "was antiunion but not antiworker. While on one hand he gave employers what amounted to complete liberty to destroy the unions in their shops, he would give startling wage and social benefits to the workers. He decreed, for example, seven blanket wage increases while in power. . . . [Odría left] power with many people convinced that he had done more for the worker than anyone in the history of Peru. Odría's labor policy was, in an elephantine manner, paternalistic" (J. Payne 1965:51).

Odría's aid to the popular sector took other forms as well. He sponsored public housing and many other public works projects, stimulating the construction industry and increasing working-class employment. The major increase in public spending associated in part with these projects was one of the areas in which his economic policy clearly departed from the laissez-faire tenets of the oligarchy. In establishing a more paternalistic relationship between the state and the poorer classes in Lima, Odría emphasized charity and gifts to the poor. He sought to provide an alternative to APRA's approach in which benefits from the government came in response to the mobilization and articulation of working class demands. Odría's wife, María Delgado de Odría, in imitation of Eva Perón, played an important role in this show of paternalism.[49] Her numerous charitable visits to the poor were extensively publicized on the front page of the government newspaper, *La Nación*. The María Delgado de Odría Center of Social Assistance, formed in imitation of Eva Perón's welfare organization, was a principal channel for her charitable activities (D. Collier 1976:58–59).

Among the most important aspects of Odría's effort to reestablish a more paternalistic form of politics was his extensive promotion of squatter settlements, the self-built, low-income communities that surround Lima and other Peruvian cities. Squatter settlement residents played a prominent role in efforts to demonstrate that Odría's government had wide popular support. Odría's special relationship with these settlements represented in part an attempt to shift the locus of worker solidarity and worker organization out of the place of work—the arena overwhelmingly dominated by APRA—to the place of residence. Correspondingly, it focused Odría's efforts at generating support in an important sphere of the informal sector, that of self-built housing, and away from the formal sector, which APRA had been energetically attempting to expand through its efforts at unionization.

Interestingly, Odría's political initiatives toward squatter settlements had already begun under the Bustamante government while Odría was minister of interior, suggesting that his subsequent strategies of support mobilization had already begun to take form before the coup. Once Odría was president, this strategy received its fullest expression in the largest and most important settlement whose formation he sponsored, the "Twenty-Seventh of October," named after the day of his coup. To move to this settlement, one had to join the neighborhood association, which was run by close associates of Odría. Though initially anyone could join, except for known Apristas, toward the end of Odría's term of office, when he was considering running for president again in 1956, members of the association were required to join Odría's party. The association played an active role in demonstrations of support for Odría. The headquarters was decorated with large pictures of Odría and his wife, as well as of Perón and Evita. Members of the association, as well as of other settlements, were periodically marched to the central plaza of Lima in demonstrations of support on such occasions as the anniversary of the coup, Odría's birthday, and his wife's birthday (D. Collier 1976:59–60).

Though Odría was initially successful in consolidating his government, beginning in 1953 a series of factors turned against him. With the end of the Korean War boom, export earnings dropped, reducing his latitude in public spending and in granting benefits to the popular sector. Those that he did grant drew criticism from the economic elite as fiscally unsound. The visible corruption of Odría's government and his sometimes arbitrary style of rule also became a political issue. The military became concerned that criticism

[49] Or, perhaps more properly, "maternalism."

of Odría's government would lead to criticism of the military itself, and in 1954 and early 1955 two military plots occurred against him. To preempt further plots, in early 1955 Odría announced a presidential election for June 1956 and promised to cede power to the winner.[50]

Formation of New Governing Coalition

The year 1955 witnessed intensive efforts to construct a new coalition to ensure that Odría would stand by his commitment to leave office. The prominent role of members of the economic elite in this process and the subordinate role of APRA is noteworthy. Pedro Beltrán, a leading supporter of the 1948 coup, played a central role in this effort to prevent Odría's continuation in office, a role in which Beltrán now had the tacit support of APRA. Beltrán was the owner of a small coastal cotton hacienda, a prominent member of the National Agrarian Society, former Peruvian Ambassador to the United States, director of La Prensa, and Peru's leading advocate of laissez-faire economic policies. Through La Prensa Beltrán campaigned for the abolition of the Internal Security Law so that APRA could participate in the election. Odría refused to rescind the law, but in late 1955 an amnesty allowed some leading Apristas to return to Peru, though Haya remained abroad. However, when Odría organized his own political party, fears were renewed that he intended to retain power, and another military revolt occurred in February 1956. At this point Odría jailed Beltrán, accusing him of involvement in the military plot, an action that further discredited the government.[51]

Interestingly, Beltrán fought Odría in part on Odría's strongest ground: squatter settlements. Beltrán launched a major campaign in the pages of La Prensa on the problem of housing and was involved in supporting what at the time was the largest squatter invasion to have occurred in Peru, that of the "City of God" settlement, formed on Christmas Eve 1954. In La Prensa's campaign against Odría on the issue of squatter settlements, the newspaper frequently illustrated its arguments with references to this new settlement. Beltrán maintained that a less paternalistic approach to settlements that encouraged self-help, within a laissez-faire framework more congenial to much of the economic elite, would more effectively address problems of housing and poverty (D. Collier 1976:69–72).

As of May 1956 the three contenders for the presidency were Hernando de Lavalle, Manuel Prado, and Fernando Belaúnde Terry. Lavalle was "a well-to-do member of the best society and a consulting barrister of high repute" (Bourricaud 1970:265), who until just before the election was supported by Odría, as well as by conservatives who were intensely anti-APRA. Prado had been president from 1939 to 1945, when he initiated the first phase of the

---

[50] Sulmont 1975:232–33; Caravedo 1978:127–28; Cotler 1978:293; Werlich 1978:255; Bourricaud 1970:264.
[51] Werlich 1978:255; Cotler 1978:294; Malpica 1968:72; Alexander 1962:104–5.

earlier opening toward APRA. He was the son of a Peruvian president, a prominent member of the urban financial-commercial elite with extensive involvement in urban real estate and manufacturing, and a member of one of the wealthiest families in the country. In social terms he was a leading member of the "oligarchy." Belaúnde was an architect and planner. He had been a member of the chamber of deputies as a non-Aprista participant in the FDN coalition in 1945–48, and also dean of the Faculty of Architecture in Lima. The movement that supported his candidacy was called the National Front of Democratic Youth, later to become the Acción Popular (Popular Action) party. His campaign stressed the theme of passing leadership to a younger generation and the need to mobilize the energies of the Peruvian population to address problems of development (Bourricaud 1970:231, 232, 249–54; Sulmont 1977:168).

Though Odría permitted APRA to hold a national party convention and though Apristas would be able to vote, he did not legalize APRA prior to the election. Yet APRA votes would determine the outcome, and the central issue became whom APRA would support. All three candidates were committed to legalizing APRA after the election. Among the three choices, Belaúnde was the alternative most compatible with APRA's reformism, yet APRA doubtless feared Belaúnde's movement precisely because it was APRA's most important reformist rival. In addition, it did not appear likely that Odría would allow Belaúnde to become president if he won the election, particularly if he won due to an informal coalition with APRA. Supporting Lavalle was also an alternative, but the *quid pro quo* he offered was modest compared to that ultimately proposed by Prado. Prado therefore emerged as APRA's most plausible coalition partner.[52]

Pact of Monterrico and the Convivencia.   The immediate compromise that determined the outcome of the 1956 election was the Pact of Monterrico, an electoral agreement reached in early June in a meeting among Odría, Prado, and APRA leaders in Odría's home in the Lima suburb of Monterrico. Odría "unofficially transferred his support from Lavalle to Prado, probably in return for a pledge that [Prado] would not vigorously investigate the corruption of the outgoing regime. APRA agreed to endorse Prado and instruct its partisans to vote for [Prado's] parliamentary slate. [Prado] promised to legalize [APRA] following his victory. To weaken Belaúnde, several Apristas were permitted to run for Congress as independents in four important departments" (Werlich 1978:257).

With APRA's support, Prado won the election with 43 percent of the vote and gained a majority in both houses of Congress. Belaúnde gained an impressive 35 percent of the presidential vote, thereby establishing himself as a major contender in the 1962 presidential election and also providing a first suggestion of the scope of the reformist movement emerging outside of APRA. Ironically, though under Prado APRA would indeed hold to its agreement to limit popular mobilization, one such act of mobilization did occur

---

[52] Alexander 1962b:104; Werlich 1978:257; Bourricaud 1970:267.

just after the election. In response to fears that Odría would not respect the electoral outcome, APRA held a general strike in late June in support of Prado, who was indeed inaugurated in late July of 1956 (Sulmont, 1977:168; Werlich 1978:257–28).

The cooperation between Prado and APRA also had a longer-term component, in that they entered an ongoing political alliance known as the *convivencia*. In a number of respects, APRA played a subordinate role in this alliance. Haya himself remained abroad for most of Prado's term to avoid a repetition of his earlier personal conflicts with Bustamante. APRA supported the general outlines of Prado's program—support that was actively reflected in the pages of the party's daily newspaper, *La Tribuna*. By following the more conservative line of Sabroso within the labor movement, APRA played a central role in controlling popular mobilization. Also, to project a more modest version of its political goals, the party abandoned its earlier aggressive slogan "only APRA will save Peru" (Cotler 1978:300). In exchange, APRA received significant payoffs, including access to state resources that helped to strengthen the party and leverage in the Labor Ministry that helped APRA consolidate its hold on the union movement.[53]

In certain respects the accord of 1956 was reminiscent of the FDN coalition with Bustamante in 1945, although the agreement of the 1950s placed APRA in a considerably more subordinate role.[54] In both of these elections, the support of the economic elite was divided between two presidential candidates, and APRA contributed decisive support to the more progressive of the two. Yet it must be recognized that supporting Bustamante, a middle-class lawyer and diplomat, was very different from cooperating with Prado, who was "the epitome of the oligarchy which the Apristas were pledged to remove from power" (Alexander 1962b:104). In addition, whereas in 1945 APRA openly ran candidates for Congress and established a powerful delegation in both chambers, the party was in a far more subordinate position in 1956. It was still outlawed at the time of the election, was only allowed to present a few congressional candidates on independent lists, and, in contrast to the Bustamante years, did not hold ministerial positions under Prado. Following the harsh repression of the Odría period, which represented a second major cycle of repression and persecution of the party (the first was in the 1930s), APRA approached the 1956 accord in a weak political position, which was reflected in the terms of the agreement.

APRA's compromise may be placed in perspective by looking at Peru from the comparative perspective of Venezuela. In Venezuela, a coalitional outcome that would have been partially equivalent to Haya's compromise with Prado would have occurred if in 1958 Betancourt had been denied the right to run in the presidential election and had accepted a role as a junior coali-

[53] Cotler 1978:295; Werlich 1978:258; A. Payne, 1968:33.

[54] 1956 was the third time that APRA had supported a non-Aprista presidential candidate. In 1936 APRA was not allowed to present its own candidate and Apristas voted for Eguiguren. President Benavides annulled Eguiguren's victory because it resulted from APRA's support, and Benavides continued in the presidency until 1939 (Cotler 1978:251).

tion partner under the presidency of a prominent business leader with whom he had been negotiating during the transition period. The contrast between the two cases is striking.

APRA's alliance with Prado was justified within the party on the ground that Prado was linked to a progressive sector of the economic elite that would ultimately come to oppose both the feudal economy of the highlands and also external economic domination.[55] The new alliance was also compatible with a major tactical shift within the party's leadership. Following the disaster of the 1948 Callao revolt, the leaders had abandoned the goal of armed insurrection and wished to discourage mobilization that might again get out of control. As of 1956 the leadership was firmly committed to a strategy of electoral politics (Cotler 1978:296; North 1973:165, 171).

In exchange for its support of Prado, APRA did not receive ministerial positions, but the party did achieve the congressional representation noted above and was also accorded special consideration in a variety of policy areas. As in the 1945–48 period, favorable policies concerning urban labor and the labor movement were crucial. APRA received state support for its effort to retain and consolidate its control of the CTP, and the CTP received favored treatment by public agencies. At the same time, these agencies actively hindered the organizing efforts of Communist labor leaders. APRA enjoyed important leverage in the Congress, and it was understood that Haya could later stand as a candidate in the 1962 presidential election.[56]

APRA's ongoing alliance with Prado came as a shock to many party members. Whereas the electoral pact of 1956 "surprised many rank and file Apristas, . . . even greater amazement attended the party's support for Prado after his inauguration" (Werlich 1978:267). Yet the *convivencia* usefully met important needs of both Prado and APRA and was stable throughout Prado's administration, even during the stabilization program of 1959–60, which introduced policies whose immediate impact was unfavorable to labor.

One view would suggest that, as Haya put it, the *convivencia* was a "convalescence, a period which enabled the party to recover and gain strength . . . before embarking on a fresh journey" (quoted in Bourricaud 1970:269). APRA's compromise was perhaps also a "carefully calculated risk." In 1956 "the essential thing was to keep a democratic government in power for the next six years so that the Aprista Party might win the 1962 elections and at least have a chance to carry out its program" (Alexander 1962:105). Another reason for the party's willingness to enter the accord with Prado was a concern with basic organizational maintenance. After the hardship of the Odría years, the immediate advantages of once again enjoying access to state resources and state protection may to some degree have outweighed the longer-term costs in terms of eroding APRA's coalition and program. Before 1956 the party had been illegal for all but four years of its 25-year existence, and

---

[55] As noted in the incorporation chapter, Cotler suggests that this was already a consideration in APRA's somewhat more cooperative relationship with Prado in 1939 (1980:167).
[56] Werlich 1978:258; Sulmont 1977:168, 177; Jaquette 1971:113.

the issues of legalization and the consolidation of party organization was understandably a basic concern (Adams 1984:46–47, 124).

This concern with organizational maintenance could be looked at from quite a different perspective, however. Werlich suggests that even by the mid-1940s, the maintenance of the party had already become an end in itself. The concerns of the party's top leadership became increasingly divorced from the earlier radical agenda, as APRA's "heroic leaders of the 1930s now seemed addicted to expensive food and drink, silk suits, comfortable homes, and chauffered limousines" (1978:243). By the 1950s this process of conservatization and cooptation may have gone considerably further and may have played a role in shaping the accord with Prado. Correspondingly, in the eyes of many Apristas, the *convivencia* completely betrayed the programmatic goals of the party.

A final observation may be made about the informality of the agreement with Prado, which in comparative terms was much less formalized than the agreements of 1957–58 in Colombia and Venezuela. Indeed, from APRA's point of view it was extremely important that this be the case. In the interest of protecting the party's political credibility, APRA leaders denied they had made a pact with Prado (Bourricaud 1970:268–69). This difference in part reflects the contrast with Colombia and Venezuela, where the accord was reached among political parties, functioning as more or less equal actors; as opposed to Peru, where APRA was not allowed to participate fully in politics and was forced to make what was in many respects a humiliating compromise. It was hardly a compromise that APRA wanted to have enshrined in the national constitution, as occurred with the National Front agreement in Colombia.

Programmatic Shift toward the Center/Right. As in other countries analyzed above, the aftermath period in Peru saw the conservatization of the political party that had led the incorporation project. Two features of the Peruvian situation were distinctive, however. First, while in some other countries it is appropriate to speak of a move toward the center, in Peru it was a move toward the center/right. Second, while the compromise of 1956 represented an important step in the conservatization of APRA, it obviously involved the continuation of a process of conservatization, discussed in Chapter 5, that had begun in the 1930s. Yet in the 1950s these changes went further.

This conservatization was unambiguously reflected in Haya's writings. In an article published in *Life* magazine the month after he was released from the Colombian embassy in 1954, Haya declared that "democracy and capitalism offer the surest road toward a solution of world problems" (*Life* 3 May 1954:164), a statement that was a far cry from APRA's original positions and that immediately produced a sharp reaction from the more progressive wing of the party (Cotler 1978:300–301). Haya's book *Treinta años del Aprismo* (*Thirty years of Aprismo*), published in 1956, dropped the Marxist perspective of earlier writings, "concentrating much more on the 'revolutionary' implications of scientific and technological advances, the need to utilize foreign capital and the irrelevance of Marxist doctrine in Latin America" (Adams 1984:46).[57] These themes are particularly noteworthy, appearing as they did at the beginning of a period of pronounced radicalization of Peruvian politics, and of Latin American politics in general. Haya, like other leaders of earlier populist movements, was moving in a different direction.

Specific policies that APRA supported under the Prado administration were consistent with these general themes, though in labor politics and agrarian reform the policies of the 1950s sustained a party position already evident in 1945 to 1948. In the labor sector, the party continued the Sabroso line established in the 1940s of opposing a highly mobilizational, class-conflict oriented approach to trade union politics. In his (1965:119) analysis of APRA's labor affairs bureau (buró sindical), James Payne goes so far as to assert that "in the period 1956–61 the buró was largely concerned with curtailing extremist activities in the labor movement." Already by the mid-1940s APRA had abandoned its original proposals for a sweeping agrarian reform. Hence, its support for the recommendations of a government commission on agrarian reform, which proposed no fundamental changes in the modern sector of agriculture (Adams 1984:50), likewise reflected continuity with APRA's earlier, more conservative position. APRA did not wish to disrupt property relations in the modern sugar estates of the north coast, an economic sector in which the party had an important part of its trade union base.

In terms of more general economic policy, on the other hand, APRA had introduced a broad package of populist measures in 1945–48. Hence, the party's support for Prado's economic policies did represent a sharp departure. This change was especially evident in APRA's response to the government's economic stabilization program of the late 1950s. In the face of rising inflation, budget deficits, and the impact of the recession in the United States, Pedro Beltrán became both prime minister and finance minister and introduced the kind of austerity policies that in this period in Latin America characteristically brought intense labor protest. APRA played an important role in restraining labor's response.[58]

Consequences for APRA: Short-Term Gains, Long-Term Erosion. The consequences of APRA's further conservatization may be considered at three levels: the reaction within the party itself; the party's relationship to its traditional bases of political support; and APRA's relationship to new political constituencies emerging in the 1950s.

Within APRA's own ranks, the most immediate issue was opposition to the compromise of 1956. Intense internal dissent had earlier been triggered by the leadership's failure to support the APRA revolt of 1948 in Callao, and many APRA radicals were expelled or left of their own accord in the late 1940s and early 1950s. Though the compromise of 1956 brought new dissent

[57] For a detailed analysis of contrasts between this book an Haya's earlier writings, see Valderrama 1980:67–72.

[58] Werlich 1978:259–60; Adams 1984:50. This episode is analyzed in the next chapter.

within the party, it was not until 1959, with the radicalization encouraged by the model of the Cuban Revolution, that APRA experienced major new defections. Given the extent to which the party compromised itself in the alliance with Prado, APRA retained a remarkable hold on its members, and many Apristas who emphatically disagreed with the direction of the party remained loyal to it. According to North, one member stated that " 'some Apristas cried when they voted for Prado' in 1956, but they voted for him because they were 'loyal' to the party."[59]

North argues that "the party's leadership was extremely capable" and played a central role in securing this loyalty. "A remarkably large number of the key leaders were extremely good public speakers—they presented their arguments cogently and with style." Many were prominent intellectuals and established authorities on Peruvian society and history, with many publications to their credit. "When they argued that 'the moment had not arrived' for the radicals' proposals, that 'the conditions were not ripe,' " their opinions carried great weight.[60]

The capacity of the leadership to retain the loyalty of dissidents was above all due to the extraordinary role of the *jefe máximo*, Haya himself. "APRA grew up around a single man, a hero" (Bourricaud 1970:175). "Haya's person had . . . become legendary" (North 1973:182), to the point that he had virtually become a "God figure" within the party (North 1973:178), a status doubtless reinforced by his five-year imprisonment in the Colombian embassy. His influence was such that, "despite his increasingly conservative political position, more than any other party leader [Haya] kept radicals inside Apra. He made them believe that he personally presented and even represented their views in party councils" (North 1973:185–86). Haya's qualities of vacillation that previously had disastrous consequences in the mid-1940s doubtless facilitated this role of persuasion.

These strong attachments to the party promoted by skilled leaders were reinforced by the shared experience of repression—the years in the "catacombs"—and also by the personal histories of many Apristas. For one Aprista whose experience probably reflected that of many members, "his friends were in the party, his family was in the party, his love affairs were in the party, and his most courageous political acts were performed for the party" (North 1973:182). These bonds tied many dissidents to APRA.

In the short run, APRA likewise appeared to retain its working-class electoral base, and as in the mid-1940s the party made effective use of its access to state resources to expand its role in the labor movement. Because APRA was not allowed to run in the 1956 election, it is hard to assess the party's electoral support in that year, though the APRA vote was obviously a major factor in Prado's electoral victory. However, North (1973:222) argues that despite the alliance with the right, APRA's electoral support was relatively stable—in terms both of the level of support, involving about a third of the vote,

---

[59] North 1973:182. See also North (1973:171) and Valderrama (1980:89).
[60] All quotations from North (1973:182).

and in many respects the regional distribution of support. She reaches this conclusion by comparing the two presidential elections of the early 1960s with the only other election in which there was an identifiable APRA vote, that of 1931. Obviously, this continuity must be viewed within the framework of a six-fold increase in the number of voters between 1931 and the early 1960s. However, despite this massive change in the scale of the electorate, APRA retained the basic distribution of its original constituency, with overwhelming support on the north coast, in the mining enclaves of the central highlands, and among the urban working class and sectors of the middle class in greater Lima (Werlich 1978:195, 280; Sulmont 1975:236).

As under the Bustamente government of 1945–48, some of the most important immediate benefits in terms of building the party that derived from APRA's compromise of 1956 were again in the trade-union sector. Indeed, while APRA continued to have a predominantly middle-class leadership, the labor sector exercised substantial leverage within the party. Evidence of this leverage is found in the bargaining that occurred over the formation of the congressional lists for the 1956 election. In the initial agreement concerning the role of Apristas on the independent electoral lists, the candidates for the Senate did not include a worker representative. The Textile Federation, long an Aprista stronghold, threatened to withdraw support for the coalition if it was not represented in the Senate. APRA rearranged the list, eliminating another candidate and replacing him with a representative from the textile sector, who was elected to the Senate and went on to play an important role in promoting legislative projects of importance to workers (Payne 1965:80–88).

This leverage produced important benefits for the labor sector. The dramatic further expansion of the trade union movement after 1956 was a product of APRA's alliance with Prado, and in this period "in the minds of the majority of organized workers, APRA's fate was tied to their own" (North 1973:229). During the Prado administration unions were recognized at the rate of 66 per year, close to the rate of the earlier Bustamante period, which had been 88 per year.[61] This was also a period of major partisan gains for APRA within the labor movement. The proportion of workers in unions not linked to APRA declined from roughly a quarter of the labor movement in 1957 to around 10 percent in 1961 (J. Payne 1965:97, 99–101).

The Prado period also saw important changes in the legal framework for union organizing. In part due to the legislative crisis and paralysis of the Bustamante years, between 1945 and 1948 this legal framework had remained relatively unfavorable, with substantial constraints and few inducements for unions. After 1956 a series of new legal provisions moved Peru to a far higher level of legal inducements for the labor movement (R. and D. Collier 1979:973).

The CTP was officially reestablished in 1956, once again under the leadership of Arturo Sabroso. As of the mid-1940s Sabroso's less mobilizational approach to trade unionism had already won out within the party over the

---

[61] Recalculated from Sulmont (1975:276).

more radical approach of Negreiros, and after 1956 Sabroso further consolidated this approach, maintaining a close identification with the perspective of "democratic trade unionism" (*sindicalismo libre*) promoted in Latin America by the United States' AFL-CIO, an approach that deemphasized class conflict and sought to strengthen unions in their dealings with the state and as actors in the sphere of collective bargaining. In promoting its approach, APRA and the CTP had a number of important advantages over their opponents: long experience in the labor sector, a leadership with excellent organizational skills, and great legitimacy that derived from their years of struggling underground during the Odría dictatorship. APRA union leaders skillfully presented the alliance with Prado as a tactic intended to achieve democracy and trade-union freedom. The secretary general of the CTP commanded high level attention within the Ministry of Labor, and the labor minister's decrees resolving collective bargaining disputes commonly ran strongly against the preferences of the employer. On occasion, other ministers were brought in to persuade employers to accept the agreements (Sulmont 1977:100, 171; Spalding 1977:256; J. Payne 1965:65, 169).

APRA's accomplishments within the labor sector included such important measures as a major new workers' pension program adopted in response to active lobbying by Aprista members of the two houses of Congress in 1960–61, a process in which the APRA representative from the textile sector who was a member of the Senate played a prominent role. APRA's influence in the Ministries of Labor and Education allowed the party to sponsor public works and development projects that both strengthened the patronage resources of APRA legislators and helped to consolidate APRA's position among school teachers. Within the labor movement, the textile sector—which beginning with the 1918–19 strikes had been the "cradle" of APRA unionism—was among the most conspicuous beneficiaries (J. Payne 1965:81–85; Pease 1977:30; Chaplin 1967:82).

APRA followed a dual strategy on strikes. The party and its labor leadership wished both to use its strength in the labor sector as a resource in dealing with employers and with the state, but at the same time did not wish to pose a major threat to the government. Hence, APRA made extensive use of the threat of strikes, usually without actually carrying them out in a way that seriously threatened the Prado administration. Thus, under Prado there was only one general strike. It occurred in May 1960, in response to the repression of workers following worker protest of the economic stabilization program. This one-day strike was fully successful, was joined by non-APRA unionists, and enhanced the prestige and effectiveness of APRA leaders within the labor movement (J. Payne 1965:122, 168–69).

Though APRA retained and further consolidated its traditional bases of support, the party failed to move beyond its original constituencies and respond to the rapid economic and demographic changes occurring in Peru, or to the new social sectors produced by these changes: new segments of the urban working and middle class, students, professionals, and major sectors of the peasantry in areas where traditional structures of control were disintegrating. Within the electoral sphere, the scope of change was reflected in the tripling of the electorate between 1945 and 1956, due in part to the introduction of women's suffrage. The electorate had further increased by roughly 50 percent as of 1963, yielding a total increase of nearly 330 percent over the 18-year period (Conniff 1982:19). As the electoral arena grew dramatically, APRA maintained its relative position, but lost an opportunity to expand its base to encompass a majority of the electorate.

Instead, the 1950s saw the emergence of a "new reformism" (Sulmont 1975:234–36), led particularly by Acción Popular, the Christian Democrats, and the Social Progressive Movement, which appealed to these new sectors. APRA failed to become part of this new reformism, tied as it was to its traditional constituencies and to its alliance with Prado, and stymied by the veto on its full electoral participation—a veto that would continue through the 1960s (Sulmont 1975:234–36). Thus, as of the 1962 presidential elections, Henry Pease (1977:27) identifies two clearly defined political "blocs" in Peru: one democratic-reformist, the other "oligarchic." APRA, ironically, belonged to the latter.

APRA's limitations as a reformist party were perhaps most dramatically reflected in its failure to become involved in the peasant sector—apart from the party's already well-established role in the immediate hinterland of the export enclaves. These years saw rapid social change and an erosion of traditional mechanisms of social control in broad sectors of the highlands, along with the beginning of a major new period of rural land seizures and peasant movements. Acción Popular, the Christian Democrats, the Communist Party, and other parties of the Marxist left all became actively engaged in the organization and political mobilization of peasants. APRA largely neglected this massive new constituency, even though it represented a major portion of Peru's national population, as well as having been a central concern of the party's early ideology.[62]

To the extent that APRA's 1956 pact with Prado led the party to give up the historic opportunity to play a central role in the new reformism, the pact would appear to have been a blunder. However, one interpretation would suggest APRA had little choice, assuming the party leaders wished to enter into a normal electoral role following their long experience of repression that had begun in the 1920s. Belaúnde, who played a central role in the reform movement, *was* allowed to run in the 1956 election, though at the last minute he had to stage a mass protest in order to avoid being removed from the ballot (Werlich 1978:256). APRA was *not* allowed in that year to run either a presidential candidate or official party candidates for the legislature, and probably no amount of last-minute protest would have changed this. APRA was thus denied normal electoral participation at precisely the time when the new reformism was being launched in the electoral arena, and it subsequently

[62] Adams 1984:52. APRA did establish an organization called FENCAP to organize and mobilize peasants. However, until the 1960s its role was minimal, and even then it had only a modest impact. See Chapter 7.

was allowed to take on a larger electoral role only because it avoided a strongly reformist stance. Though APRA may have blundered, its alternatives were severely constrained.

Thus, APRA was engaged in a political exchange, the terms of which it could not control. By modifying its reform agenda, APRA hoped to achieve electoral acceptance and to win "respectability in the eyes of the nation's elite and soften the antagonism of the armed forces" (Werlich 1978:267), with the hope that in 1962 the party would finally be allowed to become a full participant in the electoral system. Yet this effort to obtain respectability undermined the party. APRA was placed in a kind of "damned if you do, and damned if you don't" predicament.

An alternative interpretation, noted above, would focus on the conservatization and co-optation of the top party leadership. It could be argued that although APRA's coalitional choices were constrained, they may have responded to the preferences of party leaders, and perhaps especially those of Haya.

Whatever the interpretation of APRA's choices, they set into motion a pattern of change distinct from that analyzed in other countries, particularly Venezuela and Mexico. In those two countries, in conjunction with the effort during the aftermath period to limit future conflict, the party that earlier had led the incorporation project moved to the center, and yet retained a much greater capacity to respond to future directions of political change. In Peru, by contrast, the conflict-limiting mechanisms were imposed on APRA in the form of serious restrictions on electoral participation. Given these restrictions, and with far less adequate access to state resources, APRA lost the capacity to respond to new directions of change.

ARGENTINA

Conservative Reaction

The initial phase of the conservative reaction to incorporation in Argentina, under the brief government of General Eduardo Lonardi from September to November 1955, was restrained in its treatment of Peronism. The second phase, which began when General Pedro Aramburu replaced Lonardi as president, involved much harsher anti-Peronist repression and did much to cement the antagonism between the Peronist and anti-Peronist camps.

The post-Peronist era thus began with moderation, indeed on both sides. At the time of his overthrow, Perón did relatively little to mobilize support for a potential confrontation that could well have degenerated into civil war. President Lonardi, for his part, did not plan to deal harshly with Peronism as a whole. In the view of the new president and his immediate circle of supporters, the task was to purge the Peronist movement of its corrupt and authoritarian leadership, thus paving the way for a quick restoration of civilian rule and possibly even the return to power of a reorganized Peronist party. As a result, Lonardi made few moves against the leadership within the Peronist labor confederation, the CGT, and left completely intact Perón's legacy of prolabor and social legislation. As Lonardi stated toward the end of his brief presidency, his goal was to continue and even expand the social welfare functions of the state, while maintaining the unity of the working class.[63]

Unfortunately for Lonardi's policies of conciliation, he had few supporters among his military colleagues, who generally favored harsher treatment of Peronism. Outside of the state, a harsh approach also had broad support within the economic elite and the middle sectors. After complex maneuvering among different military factions, Lonardi was overthrown in November 1955 and replaced by General Pedro Aramburu. Aramburu promptly embarked on a campaign to eliminate Peronism, banning the party and severely restricting the political rights of former Peronist officials. The newspaper *La Prensa*, which Perón had transferred to the CGT, was returned to its prior owners, and pro-Peronist military officers were retired from the armed forces.[64] The labor movement was, not surprisingly, a central focus of Aramburu's anti-Peronist crusade. The government sought to eliminate Peronist labor leaders, and from the time of Aramburu's inauguration, when the CGT's general strike was repressed and mass imprisonments of labor leaders were carried out, a series of decrees sought to achieve this goal. The military took over the CGT, and an anti-Peronist was named head of the labor ministry. Though an attempt to ban all Peronist unionists from office was mod-

[63] Senén González and Torre 1969:14–15, 51, 103–4, 138–39; Ranis 1965:33; Rock 1985:333–34.
[64] Rock 1985:334; Guardo 1963:55; Rodríguez Lamas 1985:147; Rouquié 1983, vol. 2: 136; Potash 1980:231.

erated after just four months, this period saw the reemergence of many Socialist, Communist, and other non-Peronist labor leaders who, with the support of the military, began to take back control of unions in which these parties had played a prominent role prior to the incorporation period. On occasion they used force to regain physical control of union locals.

Although the military supported the reemergence of non-Peronist labor leaders, their posture toward the labor movement itself was more ambiguous. Decrees were issued that, if enforced, might have greatly weakened the labor movement as a whole. Such modifications included restrictions on the right to strike, right-to-work laws that weakened the hold of established Peronist unions on the workplace, restrictions on the political participation of unions, the end of union control over work conditions, and the removal of union monopolies within given economic sectors. However, these changes in labor law were only partially enforced under Aramburu or subsequent governments.[65]

Finally, in addition to attacking Peronist institutions, Aramburu attempted to erase reminders of the Peronist era. This effort included bulldozing Perón's downtown residence, destroying statues of Perón and of Eva, and renaming cities and provinces previously named after them. It became illegal to use Peronist symbols, including even pictures of the ex-president and his wife, either in public or in private (Page 1983:343; Guardo 1963:55).

These attacks on the institutions and symbols of Peronism were part of a wider strategy that guided the actions of the Aramburu government. Though Aramburu sought to reduce the power of unions in the labor market, he also sought to convince workers that a non-Peronist government was not necessarily hostile to labor. In fact, by the time Aramburu stepped down in May 1958, real wages had increased nearly 10 percent from their 1955 levels. This gain for workers was combined with price controls, new holidays, and laws that increased protection for some labor categories (Rouquié 1983, vol. 2:129; Alexander 1962a:213–214; Cavarozzi 1979a:31, 48).

Though Aramburu enjoyed strong support within the armed forces, in June 1956 a small group of military officers opposed to Aramburu's anti-Peronist policies initiated a revolt under the command of General Juan José Valle. The revolt had little chance of succeeding and was quickly suppressed, yet 27 people accused of participating were quickly executed. This harsh and dramatic departure from prevailing norms for dealing with military rebellions defined this as an exceptionally punitive response, and the leaders who had been killed quickly emerged as martyrs of the Peronist movement.

These executions marked a decisive turn for the worse in the relations between Peronists and the government, triggering a three-year campaign of bombings and sabotage by Perón's supporters that came to be known as the Peronist "resistance." The emerging generations of Peronist militants never

[65] Cavarozzi 1979a:19, 23–24, 40, 75–76; Gazzera 1970:67; Alexander 1962:213; James 1979:62; 1981:390–92; Ranis 1965:38; Ducatenzeiler 1980:57–58.

forgot these executions. Indeed, those who later kidnapped and murdered Aramburu in 1970 used them to justify their actions.[66]

It was apparent from the outset that the Aramburu government considered itself transitional, barring unforeseen setbacks. Aramburu did not seek to perpetuate himself in power through the formation of a political movement of the type created by other Latin American presidents who took office during the conservative reaction to incorporation, including Odría in Peru, Pérez Jiménez in Venezuela, and Rojas Pinilla in Colombia. In December 1955, top government officials, including Aramburu, signed a decree in which they committed themselves to a timely return to democracy and renounced aspirations to run for office when elections were called, and as early as July 1956 a timetable was set for the end of military rule. By March 1957, most military leaders, including Aramburu, had agreed that presidential elections would be held in February 1958, and in November 1957 the government issued a decree officially establishing that date. Aramburu's own preference for a swift return to civilian rule was decisive in keeping the country on a course toward elections when a choice emerged in mid-1957 between holding to the existing election timetable, as opposed to enacting a long-term stabilization plan whose regressive effects might well have encouraged the implantation of an extended military dictatorship. In October 1957, in the midst of rumors that Vice President Rojas was attempting to provoke worker protest to justify the abandonment of elections and the perpetuation of military rule, Aramburu reaffirmed his commitment to the electoral timetable.[67]

Attempt to Form New Governing Coalition

In all cases of party incorporation where the conservative reaction to incorporation brought periods of military rule, during the aftermath period the prospect of reopening the electoral arena and restoring civilian rule posed the challenge of forming a new governing coalition. We have already seen that in Peru, this process was greatly complicated by the ongoing ban on APRA. In Argentina, a partially similar ban also made the initial formation of such a coalition problematic, and sustaining this coalition proved even more difficult.

The Ban on Peronism. From a comparative standpoint, the political restrictions imposed on Peronism *during* the Aramburu government were similar to those in other countries in this phase of conservative reaction to incorporation. What was distinctive in Argentina, and in Peru, was that restrictions on party competition were later maintained *after* the electoral arena was reopened. The ban on Peronist candidacies for top political offices was sustained until the 1966 coup, when the rest of the country's political parties were also banned under the post-1966 military government.

---

[66] Rock 1985:336; Potash 1980:235; James 1988:85ff.; Page 1983:412.
[67] Potash 1980:227–28, 252, 258–61; Gallo 1983:69; Cavarozzi 1979a:61–62.

After the coup that brought it to power in late 1955, the Aramburu government moved quickly to ban the Peronist party, arresting and imprisoning many party leaders and justifying these measures by claiming that the party's totalitarian character placed it outside the law. In the next few months the government issued decrees forbidding the political participation of Peronist politicians and former Peronist officials, and in October 1956 the norms for assessing the legality or illegality of parties were institutionalized in the Statute of Political Parties. Because the judiciary, then anti-Peronist, would determine if a party was illegal, it became clear that the official Peronist party would not be allowed to participate in the upcoming 1958 elections.

After the 1958 election, the Frondizi government began to relax the ban on Peronism. Specifically, the restrictions on political participation of Peronist politicians and former Peronist officials were repealed, permitting the formation of neo-Peronist parties not directly under Perón's control. Nevertheless, the government sustained the military-directed dissolution of the Peronist party and, in 1959, the courts upheld the government's contention that legal recognition should not be given to the Justicialist Party, an organization set up in 1958 by Peronist politicians who took orders directly from Perón. This court decision dealt a severe blow to Peronist hopes of re-creating a unified political organization that could contest power in the newly reopened political arena.

The greatest relaxation of the electoral ban on Peronism came prior to the 1962 congressional and gubernatorial elections and on the eve of the 1965 congressional contest. In the months before each of these elections, the government did permit candidates nominated by the neo-Peronist Popular Union Party. But just as APRA's success in the 1962 elections precipitated a coup in Peru, so the Popular Union's victories in Argentina's 1962 gubernatorial elections triggered a coup, even though the Popular Union was obviously much more beholden to the leaders of the large industrial unions than to Perón himself (James 1988:175–76). It was not for another decade, until just before the May 1973 election, that legal recognition was given to a party overtly linked to Perón, and Perón himself was not allowed to run for president until September 1973.

The Impossible Game. The impact of the ban on Peronism in frustrating the formation of a new governing coalition is the focus of Guillermo O'Donnell's well-known analysis of the "impossible game" of politics in Argentina during this period (1973:chap. 4). O'Donnell's basic argument is that the proscription of Peronism set up a situation in which the vote-getting strategies of the main political parties led inexorably to unstable governments. Although the label "impossible" may overstate the degree to which alternative outcomes were foreclosed, O'Donnell's analysis and his vivid label deservedly remain a basic point of reference in the analysis of this period.

The central fact of the game was the prohibition of Peronism, which in O'Donnell's view could have won 35 to 40 percent of the vote, more than any other single political force in the country. Given the ban, voters who would otherwise have supported Peronist candidates were an attractive target for the non-Peronist parties competing against each other for political office. Non-Peronist candidates had two options: either promise concessions to the Peronists in exchange for electoral support or attempt to unify the anti-Peronist vote behind them. The former strategy was doomed, since if a non-Peronist candidate won an election with Peronist votes, the military—following one of the implicit rules of the game—would either veto the outcome or veto the promised concessions to Peronism. Meanwhile, competition among the anti-Peronist leaders made it difficult for any party to unify the anti-Peronist vote behind a single candidate. Once the Peronists realized that any attempt to forge an effective coalition with one of the non-Peronist parties would be vetoed by the military or would be followed by a veto of the promised concessions, they would be strongly tempted to undermine the game (O'Donnell 1973:166–99).

From the perspective of the comparative analysis of how new governing coalitions were formed during the aftermath period, the key point in O'Donnell's argument is that it was not possible to form a stable governing coalition. The rules of the game were so structured that rational action by each player (the pursuit of elective office) created a situation in which no player could win in the sense of achieving a meaningful electoral victory that would not be annulled by the military. Thus, the process of forming stable new governing coalitions, observed in other countries during this period, was blocked. In this chapter we will explore how the first iteration of this impossible game was played out in the 1958 presidential election and in the accompanying pact between Perón and Frondizi. Subsequent iterations are analyzed in the next chapter.

The Perón-Frondizi Pact.   Within the framework of this game and paralleling the experience of Peru, the ban on Peronism in Argentina posed an opportunity for a pact through which Peronist votes would be pledged to another party or candidate. But the Radical Party was sharply divided over whether it should enter into such a secret coalition. On the one hand, the wing led by Frondizi favored an accord and opposed the labor policies of the Aramburu government. On the other hand, a more conservative sector of the Radicals, organized around Ricardo Balbín, generally supported Aramburu's measures and was opposed to any agreement with Peronism, hoping instead to win voters back to the Radical Party (Cavarozzi 1979a:43–45; O'Donnell 1973:182; Gallo 1983:53). By the time of the party congress in December 1956, the division had been sharpened by personal conflicts and by disagreement over the rules for choosing a presidential candidate. In early 1957 the party split into the People's Radical Civic Union (UCRP), led by Balbín, and the Intransigent Radical Civic Union (UCRI), led by Frondizi.

Frondizi now began to develop a program geared to attracting Peronist voters, whereas the Aramburu government threw its resources behind the more anti-Peronist Balbín, handing over control of some provincial governments to the UCRP and naming UCRP members to important cabinet positions. With Balbín's allies making use of their positions in the government to introduce electoral rules designed to enhance the UCRP's chances, Aramburu set the date for elections to select delegates to a new constitutional convention. Thus, during the first crucial test of electoral strength between the two Radical factions, Frondizi found himself in the awkward position of supporting pro-Peronist policies in an election whose purpose was to legitimate the replacement of the Peronist constitution. Perón ordered his supporters to cast blank ballots, and in the July 1957 elections the number of blank ballots surpassed the votes of Balbín's UCRP and of Frondizi's UCRI: 24.3 percent, 24.2 percent, and 21.2 percent, respectively, with minor parties capturing the remaining vote (Potash 1980:225). Although Balbín was able to defeat Frondizi, the election results made it clear that even a slight shift of Peronist voters to the UCRI would allow it to win the 1958 presidential elections.

At the same time that Frondizi implicitly backed the ban on Peronism, he had also been trying to win the Peronist vote since shortly after Aramburu took office. Prior to the 1957 constituent assembly elections, Frondizi had hoped his endorsement of moderately prolabor policies would win Peronist support. After the elections, however, Frondizi recognized that Perón retained firm control over his supporters and that, consequently, prolabor policies would not be enough to capture the Peronist vote. Therefore, in January 1958 Frondizi reportedly agreed to an electoral pact with Perón, under which Perón received assurances that if Frondizi were elected, his government would call new presidential, legislative, and constituent assembly elections by 1960 and remove all limitations on Peronist political participation.

Two main factors appear to have induced Perón to make this agreement with Frondizi. On the one hand, he could not be certain that his supporters would continue to cast blank ballots in the future. On the other, the emergence of neo-Peronist parties, which to varying degrees evoked the tradition of Peronism but did not consider themselves subject to Perón's personal authority, apparently made Perón apprehensive about losing control of his movement. This apprehension was strengthened when Aramburu legalized the participation of several of these parties for the 1958 elections in an apparent attempt to drive a wedge between Perón and the neo-Peronist politicians.[68]

As an experienced tactician centrally concerned with controlling his own movement, Perón may have initially presumed that the neo-Peronist parties would be outlawed at the last minute and that Peronists could then be easily convinced to cast blank ballots. With the neo-Peronist parties unable to compete, the blank ballot strategy would have the advantage of preventing Frondizi from becoming a rival focus of Peronist allegiance. However, when the government decided to legalize the neo-Peronist parties, Perón may have concluded that a pact with Frondizi would be the lesser of two evils in terms of keeping control of his following. By supporting Frondizi, Perón could contain the potential challenge to his leadership from within his own movement. At the same time, the risk to Perón seemed limited because, in the immediate future, the military was unlikely to allow Frondizi to carry out

[68] Guardo 1963:109–11; Cavarozzi 1979a:42–45; Potash 1980:263–70; Page 1983:258; Potash 1980:262–63, 266.

the policies necessary to keep up his end of the pact or to lure Peronist voters into the UCRI. This left the future of the Peronist movement unresolved, an outcome that contributed to Perón's continued control.

Perón therefore threw his support behind the UCRI, giving Frondizi an easy victory in the 1958 elections with nearly 45 percent of the vote and giving the UCRI a large majority in the legislature and control of nearly all provincial governments (Potash 1980:270). Thus, in 1958 Frondizi began his presidency with an electoral mandate and legislative support similar to that enjoyed by Prado in Peru in 1956.

Initial Dynamics of Frondizi Government. During his election campaign, Frondizi had proposed a "national and popular" program similar to Perón's in its support for state-led industrialization, restrictions on foreign capital, and the preservation of labor's share of national income. However, Frondizi contemplated greater union autonomy from the state than had existed under Perón, and he planned to give more attention to increasing productivity in the agricultural export sector than Perón had done except toward the end of his administration. Increased exports were seen as a prerequisite to generating the foreign exchange necessary to finance the large infrastructure projects and capital goods industries integral to continued economic development. In addition, the UCRI's program contemplated the full reentry of Peronism into the electoral arena and the strengthening of the institutions of liberal democracy (Cavarozzi 1979b:11).

In the period immediately after his inauguration in May 1958, Frondizi took a number of initiatives that appeared to respond to his earlier agreement with Perón, though in other respects his policies were disappointing to Peronism. Peronist politicians received amnesty with respect to any charges brought against them by the Aramburu government, and the ban on Peronist symbols was removed. Frondizi also reestablished union monopolies in various sectors, thus opening the way for renewed Peronist dominance within the labor movement. On the other hand, Frondizi either refused to, or was unable to, lift the ban on the Peronist party. Nor were any steps taken to bring about Perón's return to Argentina. At an early point Perón apparently began to complain that Frondizi was not politically reliable. Conflict also started to emerge over Frondizi's economic policies. During the electoral campaign Frondizi had referred to his intention to make some use of foreign capital in promoting development, but he had given no details of his plans (Potash 1980:283). As it turned out, they were very ambitious indeed and became a major source of conflict with Peronism.

In July 1958 Frondizi stunned political observers when he announced that Argentina would sign contracts with foreign oil companies in an attempt to bolster known reserves, a significant reversal of his long-held nationalist stance toward foreign involvement in the exploitation of Argentina's natural resources. Apparently, during 1956 and 1957 Frondizi had become convinced that foreign participation in domestic oil production was the only way in the short run to make Argentina self-sufficient in this resource. The costs of barring this participation—which included an estimated U.S. $1 million per day expenditure of the country's scarce foreign exchange on imported oil—seemed to outweigh the benefits. Because Frondizi had implied during his election campaign that he still opposed contracts with foreign oil companies, many who had voted for him viewed his post-inaugural reversal as a blatant betrayal (Pandolfi 1968:78–84; Potash 1980:284).

The disintegration of the Frondizi-Perón accord was pushed further not long after Frondizi took office by the policy implications of an increasingly acute foreign exchange crisis. This crisis made it clear that a gradual rise in agricultural productivity would not be enough to generate the resources needed for an ambitious program of industrialization. In the short run, massive direct foreign investment was an obvious alternative means of gaining access to these resources. Such investment would be hard to secure given government hostility to big business and a statist approach to development, and an obvious way to attract investment was to abandon these basic postulates of the UCRI's campaign platform. Large domestic and international corporations soon emerged as a major source of investment, and an economic stabilization program was imposed at the end of 1958. It took more than a year before the fruits of the program began to be realized, and by this time the Peronists, and particularly their representatives in the unions, had become irrevocably alienated from the UCRI government, owing above all to the regressive effects of the stabilization program on labor's share of the national income (Wynia 1978:101–2).

Peronist opposition to the Frondizi government, although initially muted during the period when the legislature was working to restore the Peronist labor code, began to crystallize after Frondizi's agreement with foreign oil companies. It then grew rapidly as a result of the government's decision to couple the restoration of the Law of Professional Associations to a one-year wage freeze and limitations on the right to strike. Angered over these policies and over an increasingly assertive UCRI legislative block, an informal group of Peronist labor leaders known as the "62 Organizations" protested the government's policies in August 1958. When the government did not respond, the "62" called a general strike for October 1958, demanding an end both to the wage freeze and to limits on the right to strike. Meanwhile, oil workers initiated wild-cat strikes against the government's plans to promote foreign capital and the Frondizi government responded with a state of siege. This measure freed the military to carry out an energetic crackdown on labor protest, and the military also successfully demanded the resignation of Frondizi's principal adviser, Rogelio Frigerio (Cavarozzi 1979b:24, 28–32).

In January of 1959, amid the privatization of some sectors of the economy as part of the stabilization plan, thousands of workers seized a state-owned meatpacking plant to protest its transfer to the private sector. This event triggered a wave of sympathy strikes and led to a call by the "62" for a general strike. The government responded by unleashing the military, which retook the plant, arrested important labor leaders, and put some of the largest industrial unions under trusteeship.

The remainder of 1959 saw a sustained confrontation between the Frondizi government and the Peronist unions. The unions initiated a series of strikes, including three general strikes, which cost 11 million working days in the federal capital, and Peronists carried out a wave of bombings and other attacks against the government. The government—faced with rising inflation, falling real wages, massive labor protest, and intense pressure from the military to take decisive action—arrested thousands of unionists, placed others on an industry blacklist, kept major unions under state intervention, and removed government officials who were seen as not sufficiently anti-Peronist[69]

Peronist attacks on the Frondizi government culminated in Perón's decision in June 1959 to repudiate publicly his accord with Frondizi. Perón released what he claimed to be the text of the 1958 pact, which was purportedly signed by Frondizi, thereby causing acute embarrassment to the Frondizi government. According to Potash, the timing of Perón's initiative is understandable because by this time there was little to be gained for Perón in maintaining further informal contact with the president. Instead, Perón was now trying, "in paradoxical combination with his own enemies, to bring Frondizi to his knees" (Potash 1980:304–5).

Assessment. What had gone wrong? Several issues must be considered. Above all, Frondizi was caught in a situation in which he was under great pressure to pursue economic policies that would meet with strong opposition from Peronism and the labor movement—yet he was constrained from offering them other payoffs that might have helped to neutralize their opposition. In some other countries during roughly this period, such payoffs were successfully used to win the acquiescence of worker-based parties and the labor movement. In Argentina, two ingredients of the ban on Peronism blocked such payoffs. First, the continued proscription of the Peronist party and of Perón's return to Argentina meant that Perón could not receive the benefits that would plausibly win his cooperation. Second, up to a point Frondizi tried to gain union support for his overall program through policies favorable to unions, but he was always under extreme pressure from military opponents critical of initiatives favorable to the labor movement (Potash 1980:286–87). This pressure, and the continuing prohibition of Perón and Peronism, reflected one of the implicit "rules" of the impossible game: that politicians who won the presidency with Peronist support were not allowed to deliver the promised concessions in exchange for this support—or at least were seriously constrained in delivering them.

Thus, up to a point, the model of the impossible game seems to account for the collapse of this coalition. On the other hand, the role of other factors may also be noted. First, it appears that in the year or so before Frondizi became president, he became strongly committed to a development model that departed sharply from his own previous thinking and from his public positions during the electoral campaign. This new development model was far less compatible with his coalition with Peronism, and it can hardly have

[69] Wynia 1978:88–89; James 1979:169–71, 174; Cavarozzi 1979b:35; Ministerio de Trabajo 1961:24; Carri 1967:96.

helped his relations with the Peronists to make such an abrupt about-face once he came to office. Second, the timing was unfavorable. Peru was also pushed to a stabilization program in 1959, but this occurred three years after the onset of the Prado administration, perhaps giving more time for the Prado-APRA alliance to be cemented. In Argentina, by contrast, Frondizi had to deal with this economic crisis early in his administration, seriously limiting his opportunity to offer immediate payoffs to Peronism. Third, in comparing Peru and Argentina, one is also left with a sense of an enormous difference in the scale, power, and militance of the labor movement. Though Peru was beginning to move toward an opening to the left in the labor sector, the scope of protest was modest compared to Argentina. These factors may help explain why Frondizi in Argentina faced a far more intractable coalitional problem than did Prado in Peru.

Hence, although the dynamics of the impossible game seem central to explaining the coalitional failure in Argentina, these other factors probably aggravated an already difficult situation. The result was intense conflict between Peronism and a non-Peronist civilian government, a pattern of conflict that was to become endemic in Argentina between 1958 and 1966.

Initial Transformation of Peronism

From a comparative perspective, a central attribute of the Argentine case was that Peronism failed to return to power during the aftermath period. This outcome contrasted with all other cases of party incorporation, where the party that had earlier led the incorporation project did hold power or, in the case of Peru, at least shared power during part of that period. Correspondingly, important compromises that occurred in conjunction with returning to power, such as the expulsion of the left from the party and the move toward the center, did not occur in Argentina. This led to a distinctive dynamic of change, which will be explored at the level of the unions, the Peronist left, and the neo-Peronist parties.

The Unions.   After 1955, Peronist unions developed substantial independence from Perón and from what remained of the Peronist party. The origins of this independence are found in part in the opposition of younger Peronist unionists to Perón's more conservative policies in the last years of his presidential administration.

Later, Aramburu's law barring former Peronist labor leaders from union office further encouraged the emergence of a new generation of leadership, and these leaders played a central role in the opposition to Aramburu's government. The repression Aramburu directed against the Peronist labor movement during these years led to the creation of the Peronist resistance movement which, organized within the unions, carried out strikes, factory seizures, bombings, and sabotage, causing the loss of millions of work days in the federal capital and creating powerful solidarity among these young Peronist unionists. Many new union leaders made their reputations during the resistance. Voicing continued support for Perón, these leaders had to look after the day-to-day concerns of workers and developed increasingly independent views about the unions' role in Argentine society.[70]

Finally, on an ongoing basis, the independence of these new leaders from Perón was reinforced by Perón's lack of access to state resources, his absence from the country, and the banning of the Peronist party.

The union elections of 1956 and 1957 showed that the government was wrong in thinking that a ban on former Peronist union leaders and changes in union electoral rules would give non-Peronist unionists control of the major labor organizations. By 1957, the new cohort of Peronist labor leaders had gained control of most major industrial unions and was also well entrenched in white-collar and service sector unions controlled by non-Peronists. Many were elected during brief respites from being in hiding or in prison, and nearly all won in the face of government support for their adversaries.

If the first step in the growing independence from Perón of the Peronist labor movement was the emergence of a new generation of Peronist leaders, the next step came with the emergence of the "62 Organizations," the informal organization of prominent Peronist union leaders (McGuire 1989:99–101, 155). Although the "62" proclaimed unswerving loyalty to the exiled leader, it was only a matter of months before tension became visible. The leaders of the "62," traditionally suspicious of politicians and still steeped in the insurrectional mentality forged in the period of resistance to Aramburu, were taken aback by Perón's decision to order his followers to vote for Frondizi. After heated debates the "62" finally agreed to endorse Frondizi. Bowing to Perón's demands, the "62" used Perón's authority, as well as Frondizi's commitment to restoring the Peronist labor code and legalizing the CGT, to convince recalcitrant union activists to support the pact (James 1979:104–5). The growing difficulty in persuading labor activists to follow Perón's lead offered ample evidence of the increasing independence of the union sector of Peronism from Perón's leadership.

The Peronist Left.   In contrast to most other cases of party incorporation, Perón did not exclude the left from within the Peronist movement or seek to eliminate its influence during the aftermath period. This outcome must be understood in light of the ongoing ban on Peronism and the fact that the movement had no opportunity to make this programmatic compromise in order to regain power. Though the Peronist left was far from unified on questions of program and strategy, it included politicians and union leaders who advocated the expropriation of large landholdings and the nationalization of basic industry. Despite Perón's own opposition to such changes in property relations, he did not repudiate the Peronist left, but rather encouraged it. This encouragement must be seen as an aspect of Perón's tendency to cultivate elements within his movement with the goal of making them heavily dependent on his continued personal backing. Perón would use them as a counterweight against other sectors of Peronism that had independent bases

---

[70] James 1979:85–86; Cavarozzi 1979a:35–41; Ministerio de Trabajo 1966:table 25.

of power (Rock 1985:358). The Peronist left was such a group, and Perón played it off against sectors better equipped to challenge his leadership, such as the younger generation of union leaders and Peronist politicians in the interior of the country. Perón also felt no pressure to control the left because he was not in government and was not trying to maintain a governing coalition.

Perón's encouragement of the Peronist left began during the period of repression under the Aramburu government. By January 1956 Perón was actively supporting a policy of sabotage and armed insurrection that he believed would lead to a revival of his political fortunes. With the bloody military repression of the Valle uprising in June 1956, which ended the hope that significant support for Perón's return could be found within the military, many of the younger union activists, as noted above, were inspired to initiate the Perón-backed resistance against the Aramburu government. In November 1956, Perón gave John William Cooke, an imprisoned leader of the Peronist left, his mandate to command all organized Peronist forces in Argentina and to take full control of the movement in case of his death (Goldar 1985:40). However, Cooke was seen by most Peronist leaders as too radical, and with the formation of the "62" in September 1957, Perón created a counterbalance to Cooke's special role by establishing an umbrella organization, the Coordinating and Supervisory Council of Peronism, to oversee both the "62" and the sectors of the movement under Cooke. Nevertheless, Cooke retained an important position within Peronism.

Cooke's special relationship with Perón was controversial. After his escape from prison in mid-1957, Cooke established himself in Santiago and began to promote revolutionary goals and methods. In the months preceding the fall of Perón's government, he had promoted the creation of armed worker militias and after the coup "created a tendency within Peronism that defined itself as antibureaucratic, socialist, profoundly national, and sister to all the world's exploited [peoples]" (Goldar 1985:10). The Peronist left on important occasions refused to follow Perón's own dictates, and as the 1958 elections drew near and the details of the Perón-Frondizi pact became known, Cooke and his supporters refused to follow the "62" endorsement of the pact or Perón's direct orders, and they campaigned for the blank ballot.[71]

Perón's only move to demote the left during the aftermath period came in 1959, when pressure from more moderate sectors of his own movement led him to dismiss Cooke as his personal delegate. However, Cooke's demotion was not accompanied by a repudiation by Perón of the Peronist left within the union leadership, and Cooke—who spent much of the early 1960s in Cuba, where he fought in the Cuban militia at the Bay of Pigs—continued to communicate with Perón. Perón came out repeatedly in support of Andrés Framini, a union leader who allied himself with the Peronist left during his long battle with the more conservative Augusto Vandor for control over Peronist unionism. Nor did Perón repudiate the guerrilla *focos* or extremist ur-

[71] Potash 1959:521; Page 1983:354; Hodges 1976:34–36; James 1976:279.

ban groups who acted in his name during the early 1960s, thereby partly sustaining the image Cooke had crafted for Perón as a "leader of national liberation" (Goldar 1985:9–10; James 1976:279n; Rock 1985:359).

The year 1959 marked an important step in the growth of the Peronist left in the labor movement, especially in the smaller unions like the hospital workers, leather workers, pharmaceutical workers, and naval engineers. Many of these workers reacted negatively to the emergence both of more conciliatory Peronist leaders who maintained a dialogue with Frondizi and of neo-Peronist politicians who had stopped demanding Perón's return (James 1976:273–75). By the early 1960s, the main source of strength of the Peronist left was in the labor movement. The views of this union left were clearly laid out in the "Huerta Grande" meeting of 1962 organized by Andrés Framini with Perón's support as part of his campaign to thwart the then growing "Peronism without Perón" movement (Ducatenzeiler 1980:109–11). But Framini himself, an important leader of the textile workers' union, as well as Perón, had never previously supported many of the demands made at the meeting, and they were in fact more concerned with playing off the left against the increasingly independent mainstream of the Peronist union movement than they were in shifting Peronism toward the left. Nevertheless, although the left remained a relatively minor current during the late 1950s and early 1960s, it would emerge in the late 1960s and early 1970s as an increasingly important component of Peronism.

The Neo-Peronist Parties.   The dissolution of the official Peronist party and the ongoing ban on office-holding for former Peronist politicians gave rise to another distinctive feature of the Argentine experience: the emergence of neo-Peronist parties. Whereas APRA in Peru, the Liberals in Colombia, and AD in Venezuela experienced splits to the left during this period, these neo-Peronist parties might, by contrast, be thought of as splits toward the center or center right. While adhering to basic tenets of Peronism, they generally did not accept Perón's control. By rejecting his control, these new parties were able to qualify for political participation within the framework of the restrictions placed on Peronism by the Aramburu government. Needless to say, these parties had to reject explicitly the revolutionary or insurrectional tactics advocated by Cooke and the leaders of the resistance, and to commit themselves to electoral means of gaining power. Among these parties, the Popular Union was the most important and initially the most inclined to follow Perón's expressed desires. In 1957, for example, this party obeyed Perón's command to cast blank ballots for the constitutional convention, at the same time that several other neo-Peronist parties did participate. In 1958, however, the Popular Union ran its own candidates for presidential electors and national deputy seats. The Popular Union's movement toward independence from Perón accelerated after Frondizi's election, when its main branches in the federal capital and the province of Buenos Aires came increasingly under the sway of metalworkers' leader Augusto Vandor and his allies in the "62."

In comparison with the Popular Union, the other neo-Peronist parties, based largely in the interior of the country, were from the start more explicit in asserting their independence from Perón. Many participated not only in the 1958 elections, but also in the 1957 and 1960 contests, when Perón instructed his followers to cast blank ballots (Lewis 1973:408–14). Although Argentina was and is sparsely populated outside a few main metropolitan areas, the Peronist party organizations in the interior were important to the movement's overall political strength. This occurred in important measure because Argentina's electoral system overrepresented the less populated provinces, above all in the Senate. Though these neo-Peronist parties had only a minor role in the immediate aftermath period, in the following years analyzed in the next chapter they played a central, though unsuccessful, part in the search for a more stable coalitional role for Peronism.

7

Heritage: Between Hegemony and Crisis

THE INCORPORATION PERIOD and its aftermath helped shape the type of political coalitions that crystallized in the eight countries and the way these coalitions were institutionalized in different party systems. These outcomes in turn influenced the forms of regimes that would emerge, their internal dynamics, and the evolution of national politics in the following years. This chapter analyzes these outcomes as the heritage of incorporation.

The analysis proceeds in two parts. The first presents an overall assessment of the party system, and the second sets this party system in motion by exploring its dynamics when confronted by the period of new opposition movements and political crisis faced by countries throughout Latin America from the late 1950s to the 1970s. We argue that the varying scope of this opposition and crisis in each country can be explained in part by characteristics of the party system and its political or hegemonic resources. Some countries experienced severe polarization, whereas in others the polarization was more mild and to one degree or another was effectively contained by established political actors. In this part of the analysis we explore both the economic challenges reflected in the politics of stabilization policy and the political challenges that derived from the emergence of new opposition movements in the party arena and in labor and peasant organizations.

In some countries the polarization and crisis culminated in military coups, followed by extended periods of military rule, whereas elsewhere the civilian regimes had a greater capacity to deal with these conflicts. We argue that each country's prior experience in the incorporation and aftermath periods played an important role in shaping these alternative outcomes—though the explanatory power of this earlier experience must be looked at in a context in which many other causal factors also had an impact.

It is important to recognize the considerable overlap between the aftermath and heritage periods. Some traits we identify as features of the heritage were direct outcomes of the incorporation experience and hence can be observed during the aftermath period as soon as the incorporation experience was over. By contrast, other features of the heritage emerged only later, in the course of the aftermath. Given this dual genesis of heritage traits, in the sections that follow we will at various points have occasion to consider some of the same chronological periods we analyzed in the last chapter, but now from a somewhat different point of view. For most of the countries, however, the emphasis will be on the post-aftermath period, when all the traits of the heritage were in place.

The interval discussed in this chapter therefore begins with the civilian regimes of the aftermath period. That is, for the cases of party incorporation, we treat the heritage period as beginning immediately following the restoration of civilian rule, where it had been suspended.[1] For the cases of state incorporation, it begins with the restoration of a competitive regime within a year of the end of the incorporation period.

With regard to the end of the heritage period, we view the problem of identifying its erosion or termination as a complex issue, which we address in an exploratory manner in the final chapter. For five of the countries, within the present chapter, we extend the discussion up to the date of the military coup of the 1960s or 1970s that brought an abrupt end to the civilian regime and the existing party system. The earliest of these coups occurred in Brazil in 1964, the latest in Chile in 1973. These coups are seen not only as the endpoint of our study, but also as an *outcome* of the political dynamics that we attribute ultimately to the type of incorporation. In other countries, where no coup interrupted the political patterns we describe as the heritage of incorporation, the analysis is carried to the conclusion of the presidential term ending roughly around 1980.

We thus focus on the following intervals (see Figure 7.1): in Brazil, from 1946 to the coup of 1964; in Chile, from 1932 to the coup of 1973; in Mexico, from 1940 to 1982 (the end of the López Portillo presidency); in Venezuela, from 1958 to 1978 (the end of the first Carlos Andrés Pérez presidency); in Uruguay, from 1942 to the coup of 1973; in Colombia, from 1958 to 1986 (the end of the Betancur presidency); in Peru, from 1956 to the coup of 1968; and in Argentina, from 1957[2] to the coup of 1966.

Overview of the Party System

The period analyzed in this chapter is by and large one of civilian, electoral regimes in all eight countries. The only exceptions are the brief military interventions that occurred in Argentina, Peru, and Brazil, interventions of the "moderating" type that were limited both in duration and in that they did not introduce military rule, but rather oversaw the transfer of power among civilian groups (Stepan 1971:63).

The analysis of each country begins with an overview of the party system, focusing especially on three dimensions. The first is the degree to which the party system was characterized by cohesion or fragmentation; that is, the degree to which one or two parties dominated the electoral arena or, conversely, the degree to which electoral competition dispersed political power. The second is the presence of centrifugal or centripetal political dynamics. Some regimes were characterized by a strong polarizing dynamic whereas others were characterized by a strong, stable centrist coalition expressed or

[1] In Uruguay, where the authoritarian coup of 1933 was civilian rather than military, the heritage begins with the restoration not of civilian rule, but of a more competitive regime in 1942. In Mexico, there was no discontinuity in civilian rule or in the dominance of the revolutionary party, and the heritage period is treated as beginning in 1940.

[2] The date of the first semicompetitive election under Aramburu, involving the vote for the Constituent Assembly of that year.

Figure 7.1 Chronological Overview of Heritage Periods

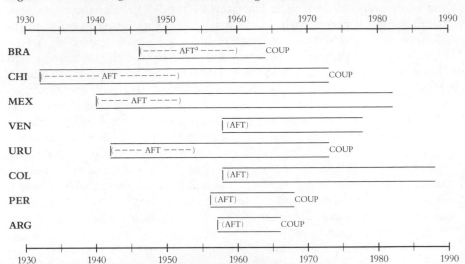

Notes: The complex question of when the heritage ends as an analytical period is addressed in Chapter 8. The analysis in this chapter brings the discussion up to the major coups of the 1960s and 1970s for Brazil, Chile, Uruguay, Peru, and Argentina; and for the other three countries to cutoff dates around 1980—1982 for Mexico, 1986 for Colombia, and 1978 for Venezuela.

[a] AFT in parentheses refers to the portion of the aftermath period covered in the previous chapter, which is also treated here as the first part of the heritage period. See explanation in footnote 1 in the accompanying text.

embodied in dominant parties or party alignments that inhibited political polarization. The third aspect of the party system is the nature of the linkage between organized labor and political parties. Of particular concern is whether the union movement was linked to a leftist or labor party or to a multiclass/centrist party, and whether the party to which labor had organizational ties was usually in the governing coalition, or rather excluded from it.

We view the contrasting outcomes on these three dimensions as deriving in part from the types of incorporation and aftermath periods experienced in each country. Specifically, they were shaped by the nature of links forged (or not forged) with the labor movement during the incorporation period, which presented a unique opportunity for establishing union-party ties; by the consequent formation (or lack thereof) of a multiclass centrist party with labor support; and by the types of conflict-limiting mechanisms worked out (or, as in the cases of state incorporation, not worked out) in the aftermath period.

Opposition and Crisis

In addition to providing an overview of different types of party systems, the goal of this chapter is to explore the reaction of each type to the regional experience of new opposition movements and political and economic crises of the late 1950s through the 1970s.[3] During this period, the eight countries exhibited very different patterns of change, some undergoing severe crises that culminated in military coups and others experiencing much greater regime continuity. While many factors contributed to these contrasting outcomes, our principal concern is to explore the argument that the different political structures that were a legacy of incorporation played a central role.

The economic and political factors that shaped this period of crisis may be sketched briefly. With regard to economic factors, this was a period of important change in the Latin American economies and their links with the international economic system. It is widely argued that this period saw a fundamental reorientation, beginning in the 1950s, toward the "internationalization" of Latin American economic development that brought major changes in the ownership and financing of key sectors of the economy. The rapid increase in foreign direct investment, especially following the Korean War, was widely perceived as a loss of national control of economic development that, within the framework explored in Chapter 2, posed important problems for the legitimation of the state. This was also a period of growing difficulties with balance of payments and inflation in a number of countries, and economic stabilization programs and the politics of stabilization became major issues. In the context of the denationalization and problems of legitimation just noted, the enforcement of conventional approaches to economic stabilization became considerably more difficult.

With regard to political factors, the period of the late 1950s to the 1970s saw the emergence of new international models of opposition politics that sharply redefined the spectrum of plausible political alternatives within Latin America. In this sense these years had much in common with the period of the late 1910s analyzed in Chapter 3. Beginning in the late 1950s, the Cuban Revolution dramatically posed the possibility that a socialist experiment could survive in the Western Hemisphere, producing an immediate impact on the political goals of the left in many Latin American countries. Perceptions of Cuba also had a strong impact on the right and the military within each country, as well as on the U.S. government and its support of counterinsurgency and of a spectrum of nonrevolutionary political alternatives within the region. Although the U.S. role receives little direct attention in the analysis below, it is an important feature of the larger context.

The combination of new political hopes on the left and new political fears in other parts of the political spectrum set the stage for a major polarization within the region. Amid these hopes and fears, political dynamics revolved in part around the "objective" potential for radicalization in each country, but also around the "perception of threat" (O'Donnell 1975) on the part of the military and other more conservative sectors within each country.

As the 1960s wore on, other developments in the international arena fur-

---

[3] Thus, whereas in the previous chapters we were concerned with analytically comparable—but chronologically often quite distinct—periods, the second section of this chapter explores how the different party systems that were the heritage of incorporation reacted to a set of challenges experienced more-or-less simultaneously in all eight countries.

ther contributed to this climate of radicalization and polarization: the intensification of the Vietnam War; the antiwar movement in the United States; the worldwide wave of urban social movements and social protest of the late 1960s that encompassed the First World, the Second World (Czechoslovakia), and the Third World; the Chinese Cultural Revolution; and later the growing imminence of the United States' defeat in Vietnam.

It may be argued that this period of new opposition movements and crisis can be divided at a point somewhat before the end of the late 1960s, when this further set of developments greatly intensified both the sense of opportunity, from the point of view of the left, and the sense of crisis, from the point of view of established political sectors within Latin America. Brazil and Peru had crises and coups before or around the time of this shift, whereas Chile and Uruguay had crises and coups after the shift. Argentina had coups in both phases, though the coup on which we focus was in the first of these, in 1966. Hence, in a sense we are looking at the experience of these countries in two somewhat different phases of a larger period of crisis. In comparing these cases, the characteristically greater severity of the crises in the later period must be kept in mind.

Party Heritage: A Typology

This analysis of opposition and crisis and the dimensions that underlie the comparison of party systems can be synthesized on the basis of a typology that provides an overall summary of the party heritage. The following discussion elaborates on the three dimensions on which the typology is based and suggests the specific types of outcomes that emerge from the interaction among the dimensions.

   1. *Presence of a majority bloc in the electoral arena located near the political center.*[4] Such a bloc might involve either the electoral dominance of a single party, as in Mexico; of two parties linked through stable ties of cooperation, as in Venezuela and Colombia in the initial phase of the heritage period; of two parties that compete actively in the electoral arena, but in a context of centripetal competition, as in Venezuela and Colombia later in the heritage period; or of two parties that compete in a setting in which the competition is mitigated both by intermittent cooperation and by special electoral rules, as in Uruguay. The other countries lacked such a bloc (in Peru and Argentina, due in part to an electoral ban), despite repeated efforts to form one. It is a crucial attribute of these countries that wherever such a majority bloc existed, the electoral support of workers played an important role in sustaining it. Whether such a bloc emerged depended on the early history of the party system (especially rel-

   [4] The term "center" is intended to be quite relative (see glossary) and also rather broad. Here we have in mind political alternatives that reflect neither the extreme conservative reaction to incorporation found in several countries nor a Marxist or leftist political alternative. The term would encompass both the more reformist post-1958 period in Venezuela and the considerably more conservative post-1956 government in Peru.

evant for Uruguay and Colombia), the scope of popular mobilization in the incorporation period, and the nature of the compromises and party transformations that occurred in some cases, following the conservative reaction to incorporation.[5]

2. *Organizational links between the union movement and a party or parties of the center.* As we have seen, the organizational ties of unions to political parties is quite a different issue from the electoral orientation of workers. Again dividing the countries into two broad groups, in Mexico, Venezuela, Peru, and Argentina, the union movement was linked to parties located broadly speaking at the center. By contrast, in Uruguay and Chile it was linked to parties unambiguously on the left, and in Colombia and Brazil the unions' ties with the left played an increasingly important role. The character of these organizational ties derived in part from the political links between parties and unions established (or not established) during the incorporation period and in part from subsequent processes of compromise and conservatization (following party incorporation) or opening and radicalization (following state incorporation) in the aftermath period.

3. *Presence of the union movement in the governing coalition.* Though this factor might seem to overlap with No. 2, it produces a contrasting differentiation of cases. Only in Mexico and Venezuela was the union movement consistently linked to the governing coalition through the heritage period. In all other countries it was in an oppositional role for much if not all of this period. These outcomes again derive from the patterns earlier forged in the incorporation and aftermath periods.

Figure 7.2 presents the cube defined by these three dimensions. The figure locates on the corners of the cube the four overall regime types that are the outcomes of the incorporation experience and its aftermath:

1. *Integrative Party System* (Mexico and Venezuela). These cases had a stable centrist majority bloc in the electoral arena, and the labor movement was organizationally tied to the political center and thus linked to the governing coalition. These regimes generally preempted or defeated leftist and opposition movements, contained social conflict and polarization, and were stable and hegemonic.

2. *Multiparty Polarizing System* (Brazil and Chile). Here, no centrist majority bloc existed, and the labor movement was tied to the center either ineffectively (Brazil) or marginally (Chile) and was generally in a role of opposition. The result was polarization, though this process went much further in Chile, and both cases experienced a coup that ushered in a long period of military rule.

3. *Electoral Stability and Social Conflict* (Uruguay and Colombia). These regimes had a stable centrist majority bloc in the electoral arena, but unions were not organizationally linked to it. In Uruguay the unions were consistently oriented to parties of the left and hence generally played an oppositional role, and in Colombia they were increasingly oriented in a similar way. The result

---

[5] Among the countries analyzed here, to the extent that such a majority bloc was formed, it was in all cases located roughly in the middle of the political spectrum, for reasons explored in the previous chapter. In other historical or geographic contexts, it is obviously possible that such a majority bloc might be located at a different place in the political spectrum.

Figure 7.2 Dimensions of the Party Heritage: Centrist Majority Bloc, Union-Party Links, and Coalitional Role of Unions

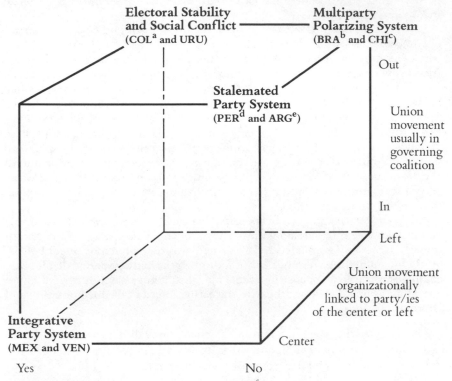

Electoral Stability
and Social Conflict
(COL[a] and URU)

Multiparty
Polarizing System
(BRA[b] and CHI[c])

Out

Stalemated
Party System
(PER[d] and ARG[e])

Union
movement
usually in
governing
coalition

In

Left

Union movement
organizationally
linked to party/ies
of the center or left

Integrative
Party System
(MEX and VEN)

Center

Yes   No

Stable centrist majority bloc in electoral arena[f]

Note: Party heritage refers to time periods indicated in Figure 7.1.

[a] Though unions maintained significant ties with the two traditional parties in Colombia, they were increasingly affiliated with the left or were politically independent.

[b] Briefly at the end of the heritage period, the Brazilian labor movement was more effectively linked to the governing coalition under Goulart from 1961 to 1964.

[c] Briefly at the end of the heritage period, the Chilean labor movement was more effectively linked to the governing coalition under Allende from 1970 to 1973.

[d] The Peruvian union movement was in the opposition for much of the 1960s, though not under the Prado administration from 1956 to 1962. Although a major move to the left within the labor movement was beginning just at the end of the heritage period, for most of this period the bulk of the union movement was at the center.

[e] Though there was a "Peronist left" within the Argentine labor movement, as will be clear in the analysis below this was hardly equivalent to the left orientation of the union movement in several other countries.

[f] Maintained either by one party or by two parties linked through ongoing ties of cooperation.

was relative continuity in the electoral sphere, combined with rising social conflict, including major episodes of labor protest and a gradual militarization of politics in order to confront a growing insurgency. This ultimately led to military rule in Uruguay but stopped short of it in Colombia.

4. *Stalemated Party System* (Peru and Argentina). Here the ban on APRA and Peronism often frustrated the formation of a centrist majority electoral bloc. The labor movement was largely at the center rather than on the left, yet the ongoing ban meant that the labor movement was not linked to the governing coalition during a major part of (Peru) or throughout (Argentina) the heritage period. This had the consequence of undermining the formation of a stable electoral majority bloc in both countries and of producing instead political stalemate, which ultimately culminated in military rule.

A Note on the Strength of the Labor Movement

Although the present argument focuses on the impact of parties and of party-union relations on the intensity of polarization and crisis, other factors are important as well. For the moment, we will underscore one additional explanation: the strength of the labor movement. We earlier noted that the concept of labor movement strength is complex, and overly facile comparisons among countries should be avoided. Nonetheless, certain contrasts within the pairs of cases are so great that they can be presented with reasonable confidence.

A ranking of the eight countries in terms of the scope of worker organization and protest in the first decades of the 20th century was presented in Chapter 3. As noted there, important shifts in factors that influence levels of worker protest took place in the following decades, calling for a reassessment of the ranking if it is to be applied to a later period. For instance, the onset of massive rural-urban migration in Brazil and Mexico in the intervening years was seen in the literature on those two countries as weakening their labor movements, and the emergence of export enclaves in Venezuela altered its initial position in the first two decades of the century as one of the countries with a particularly weak labor movement.

In light of the rankings for the earlier period and these subsequent changes, the following comparisons within the pairs of countries seem plausible. The Venezuelan labor movement had at least caught up with that in Mexico, so there was not a major contrast between them as of this later period. For the other pairs, by contrast, the differences were greater: Chile had a stronger labor movement than Brazil, Argentina a stronger labor movement than Peru, and Uruguay a stronger labor movement than Colombia. These contrasts in labor movement development played an important part in explaining key differences between the countries in each pair. For example, they help account for the higher level of polarization and social conflict in Chile compared to Brazil, and in Uruguay compared to Colombia. Also, with respect to this latter pair, this contrast in labor strength helps to explain the occurrence of a coup in Uruguay and the absence of one in Colombia. Finally, the vast difference in the scope of union organizing and protest between Argentina and Peru was central to the contrasting level and character of the perception of threat in the two countries in the 1960s.

BRAZIL AND CHILE: MULTIPARTY POLARIZING POLITICS

Introduction

The heritage of state incorporation in Brazil and Chile was a multiparty, polarizing regime. Within the framework of important contrasts between them,
these two countries emerged among the eight considered here as having the
most fractionalized party systems, the least cohesive political centers, sharp
episodes of polarization, and substantial policy immobilism in the heritage
period.

As we saw in the previous chapter, the mechanisms of conflict regulation
that were established in different degrees and forms in the aftermath of party
incorporation did not emerge in these two cases of state incorporation. Further, the popular sectors and the labor movement did not come to be tied
either to governing parties or to parties of the political center. In these conditions, though unions continued to be tightly controlled and severely constrained by highly corporative labor laws, the labor movement underwent a
process of politicization and radicalization, which began in the aftermath period and intensified after the failure of the attempted populist coalitions. As
in the other countries, these processes and the growth of a left opposition
accelerated in the late 1950s and 1960s. In Brazil and Chile, however, labor
was a central player in this development.

In the last chapter we saw a frequent pattern in the cases of party incorporation during the aftermath period. The parties that led the incorporation
period excluded the left within the party and moved toward the center at the
same time that they retained broad popular sector support. These parties provided the basis for a centrist majority bloc in the electoral arena. Furthermore, primarily with the goal of retaining power and/or preventing a future
loss of control of the presidency, party leaders took the initiative to create
this majority bloc through pacts or other conflict-limiting mechanisms. By
contrast, in the cases of state incorporation, the attempt to create a similar
majority bloc in the aftermath period failed, and no comparable structures of
conflict limitation were established. The populist parties that were formed
just at the end of or just after the incorporation periods—the PTB in Brazil
and the Socialist Party in Chile—did not have the capacity to form the basis
of a centrist majority bloc, take similar initiatives, or play an equivalent role.
This contrast, which reflects a shared attribute of Brazil and Chile, proved
crucial in the emergence of a polarizing dynamic and the pull to the left of
these "belatedly" formed populist parties. As a consequence, these two countries experienced patterns of conflict and polarization and an important degree of policy immobilism distinct from those found in the other six cases.
This pattern of an increasingly polarized multiparty system with a weak center was the heritage of incorporation in Brazil and Chile.

Despite some major differences, which will be emphasized below, it therefore becomes clear that Brazil and Chile were similar in a number of ways. Particularly when one looks comparatively, one sees that they shared traits that made them quite distinct from the other cases considered in this book. It is the present argument that these traits derive from the distinctive way these two countries experienced the critical transition that has been highlighted—the pattern of state incorporation, as opposed to party incorporation, and the consequent unfolding of a different trajectory of change.

The analysis of the heritage of incorporation in Brazil and Chile will point to the following similarities.

1. The two countries shared a highly constrained industrial relations system, in which unions were particularly weak and dependent on the state.

2. Both experienced a consequent displacement of the workers' struggle into the political arena.

3. At the same time, a legacy of state incorporation was a labor movement that was not tied to governing parties of the political center. It goes without saying that the political independence from the state that derives from this trait should be narrowly understood and should be seen in conjunction with the fact that the state, through labor law, constrained labor unions and their activities in the sphere of industrial relations. In other words, there is a crucial distinction being made between relative independence from the state in the party-political sphere and independence (or lack of it) in the sphere of formalized industrial relations. Further, this political independence became a more clear-cut feature in the postaftermath period. During the aftermath itself, would-be populist parties were founded in an attempt to establish a multiclass integrative political structure that could hold power. As we have seen, however, these experiments were not successful, and the populist attempt failed. By the end of the aftermath period (1960 in Brazil and 1952 in Chile) the nature of organized labor's participation in the political arena was quite different. It was associated with radicalizing opposition parties—either Communist parties or formerly populist parties that were moving to the left, and indeed labor had an important role in this process of radicalization.

4. The absence of a populist or multiclass integrative party that bound the labor movement to the government, then, led to a distinctive political dynamic, specifically a fragmented and polarizing party system, in which the labor movement played an important part. Throughout Latin America, there were left tendencies in the labor movement, particularly in the wake of the Cuban Revolution, which had a powerful demonstration effect. In Brazil and Chile (and also in Uruguay) these tendencies became dominant within labor organizations, at least on the level of national labor organizations. This is not to say that at the grassroots radicalization was widespread—indeed there is evidence that it may not have been in either Brazil or Chile, though it clearly went further in Chile. Nevertheless, national labor organizations in these two countries played a key role in a larger process of polarization. A part of this process was the radicalization of the labor movement and key sectors, even if not the majority, of the mass base, and the labor movement in turn played a central part in the development of the left in national politics. Brazilian and Chilean politics can only be understood in terms of the centrality of this dynamic of political polarization and the role of the organized labor movement

within it. Again, this pattern is very different from that which occurred in most other countries, and the contrast with the hegemonic parties in Mexico and Venezuela is particularly striking.

5. After the failure of the populist attempts in the aftermath period, new experiments to create a viable political center occurred. Such experimentation was rather extensive in Chile and took place over nearly two decades, from 1952 to 1970. By contrast, in Brazil it was extraordinarily brief and can be analyzed within the truncated presidency of Quadros in 1961. In both cases, the dynamic of polarization prevented success. The difference in the duration of these experiments is an important one, which has led analysts to see the politics of this period as "typical" of Chile and to discount it in the case of Brazil. Nevertheless, it may be instructive in understanding the political dynamics of these two countries to make explicit the similiarities here, without understating the differences.

6. Finally, uniquely in Brazil and Chile, the political center failed to retain its hold on the presidency and, with the election of Allende and the assumption of the presidency by Goulart, the government initiated or was seen as threatening to initiate a major move to the left. Such an event did not occur in the other six countries during this analytic period, and this development played a major role in the rising polarization in both cases. The accelerating polarization culminated in a military coup in 1964 in Brazil and 1973 in Chile. Though it is clear that in some "objective" sense the "left" as represented by Goulart was not equivalent to that represented by Allende, what is crucial is that the polarization went as far as it did, given the weak, nonideological nature of Brazilian parties and a labor movement so highly constrained by corporatist structures. It is also the case that relative to the political center of gravity in Brazil (i.e., substantially to the right of the reformist center in Chile) the move toward the left that did occur was significant to the point that Goulart was perceived as a Bolshevik threat who would establish a syndicalist state and unacceptably alter existing property relations.

This last point brings us back to the issue of the differences between these two countries. Chile was a much more urban, socially mobilized society. In contrast to Brazil, it had strong, "European-style" parties, some of which dated back to the last century and evolved in a way that also followed a "European" pattern of ideologically based parties of a liberal right, a Marxist left, and a moderate center, including a party based on the European-founded Christian Democratic movement. Chile's labor movement was based in export enclaves as well as in urban centers and did not have to face a labor surplus economy to the same extent as Brazil. Through some combination of these and other factors, Chilean society was much more highly politicized, with partisan identities being fundamental, running deep, and orienting political life, whereas in Brazil they counted for little, even among politicians.

Corresponding to these differences were contrasts in the ties between parties and unions. Partly as a result of the banning of the Communist Party in Brazil, though also due to the above sociopolitical differences, the Chilean labor movement had longer-standing and more deeply rooted ties to the left and specifically to Marxist parties. Given the differences in the aftermath period and the much greater duration of the postaftermath period considered here, the Chilean labor movement and the left parties with which it was associated had much more experience with participation in the political arena. These political and economic factors made the Chilean labor movement stronger than its Brazilian counterpart. The weaker position of Brazilian labor was also due to that country's much longer and more thorough-going incorporation period, which imposed a greater degree of state penetration, many aspects of which, as will be discussed below, the labor movement was able to overcome only more gradually and partially. Finally, as a culmination of all these differences, the political left in Chile was stronger and much more radical, polarization there went much further, and the "threat" to the right represented by Allende was much greater than that represented by Goulart.

Without denying these differences, a few caveats are in order. One should not underestimate the degree to which class antagonisms and cleavages came to characterize Brazilian politics. It will be argued that in periods when constraints were relaxed, the labor movement was more politicized than is often recognized. These cleavages were also expressed in the party system to a greater degree than is commonly realized. It is certainly true that in Brazil parties were weak, and even in the electoral arena, an ad hoc, opportunistic pattern of electoral alliances came to predominate. Yet, as we shall see, toward the end of the period considered here, intraparty cleavages more rooted in programmatic differences came to characterize all three of the major parties, and the resulting factions tended to regroup in interparty alliances and fronts that were ideologically more coherent. On the other hand, Valenzuela (1978:11) has argued that one should not overestimate the role of class politics based in ideologically self-conscious parties as the unique source of political cleavage in Chile. These ideologically oriented parties were in fact rather heterogeneous in terms of the interests and classes they aggregated. In addition, the parties of similar ideological tendencies were often likely to compete with one another rather than cooperate and to back candidates and join forces with parties across ideological lines.

Also, the Chilean labor movement was weaker than one might imagine from the facts that working-class parties did well in the electoral arena and that workers played such a major role in the politics of the Allende period. Indeed, the heavy hand of the state continued to limit severely the scope of union freedom and activity through both a highly constraining labor law and repression, and the CUT prior to 1970 was quite weak. Falabella (1980:344) has emphasized the dependence of unions on the state in bargaining over economic and political issues and the way in which the resulting pattern of state-centered bargaining both increased state control of unions and encouraged unions to focus their attention on the government and on parliament in advancing their economic and social goals. Arguing that the CUT began to achieve some influence and strength only at the end of the Frei period, Angell (1972:220) has declared, "for most of its life its weaknesses were more evident than its strengths." Similarly, in an analysis published in 1969, Petras (1969:237ff) described a working-class movement in almost total disarray and faced with government opposition. Until the victory of Allende, a pro-labor government never came to power—not even prolabor to the extent of populist governments elsewhere—no less a more clear-cut ideologically oriented leftist government with a working-class base.

On the other hand, in the early 1960s the Brazilian labor movement managed to carve out an area of much greater *political* independence from state control than one might expect, in light of the imposition of the most elaborate form of corporative labor relations introduced in Latin America and in light of the substantial continuity in the legal framework after the end of the Estado Novo. Though the Brazilian union movement was enormously weakened by the labor law, as was the Chilean labor movement, Brazilian labor in fact largely managed to escape from *pelego* control and pursue an important political role on the national scene that was quite independent of the government and governing political parties—in a way that was not possible for the labor movements of, for instance, Mexico or Venezuela.

The analysis of Brazil and Chile must reflect this interplay of similarities and differences. Though these caveats against an overdrawn, simplified characterization of Brazil and Chile are important, it is certainly the case that the two countries are different in the ways mentioned above. Yet, they also share a commonality that has not been recognized in most accounts of Latin American politics and which is being emphasized here. Despite important differences, both countries, stemming from a distinctive pattern of state incorporation, subsequently developed polarizing, multiparty systems that lacked the kind of conflict-limiting mechanisms found elsewhere. With a labor movement that was highly constrained in the sphere of industrial relations but more independent in the political arena, and with a strong political right, politics became increasingly polarized, and the center lost its hold on power, prompting, after a period of intensified crisis and deadlock, a military coup and in both countries the most extended periods of military rule in Latin America during the last two decades.

In sum, a few points are worth emphasizing in introducing this analysis of Brazil and Chile. First, it is necessary to be precise in specifying the similarities between the two countries—the claim is not that in some more general sense these two countries are "similar." Second, we assume a model of multiple causality in which we trace out the consequences of only one set of causal linkages. Therefore, we are in a position to account for some similarities, but we do not expect identical outcomes in the two cases, as other factors also come into play in shaping these outcomes. That is, similar incorporation periods are not expected to produce identical regimes, but rather legacies that are more similar than one might otherwise expect, given all the other differences that mark these two countries. Third, there is some risk of falling back on traditional images and underestimating the degree of mobilization and polarization in Brazil and perhaps also in some ways overstating it in Chile; clear and marked differences certainly exist, but it is important not to distort the comparison so that these differences nullify the similarities—similarities that become more apparent in the larger comparative framework of the eight countries.

Overview of the Party System

As mentioned, in many ways the Brazilian and Chilean party systems differed greatly. In describing the Chilean parties and party system, analysts have typically presented a "European account." To a substantial extent, the Chilean party system was based on parties that were deeply rooted in society, that were well-institutionalized, and that endured over time. The parties of the right and some of those in the center traced their origins to the last century, while the major parties on the left were founded in the first few decades of the present century. Of all the major parties, only the Christian Democratic Party was a relative newcomer, with origins in the Falange Nacional of 1936 and emerging as the PDC in 1957. Perhaps more importantly, these parties were strong—party identification was a pervasive and fundamental aspect of both individuals and groups throughout Chilean society, and party dynamics were an absolutely central part of Chilean politics (Garretón 1983:23–31). Finally, Chilean parties were notably ideological, with the left, center, and right tendencies all well represented.

The Brazilian party system seemed to be just the opposite. Instead of a European account, a typically Latin American account of the Brazilian party system has predominated. Brazilian parties were of recent, postwar origins: they did not predate by more than a year the 1946 Republic introduced in the aftermath of incorporation, and in fact the Republic and the parties were born of the same democratization process. Though the Brazilian Communist Party dates back to the 1920s, as does the Chilean Communist Party, the Brazilian party played a much more minor role than its Chilean counterpart, due in large part to its longer period of proscription. In other ways also, the Brazilian parties have not been considered well-institutionalized. The major parties were notoriously weak: party identification accounted for very little in Brazil and the parties themselves exercised no discipline over their members, who in fact tended to switch party affiliation with surprising frequency, particularly on the local level. The parties were loose groupings almost totally devoid of ideological commitment and identification. Emphasizing these weaknesses of the Brazilian parties, Peterson (1970:142) has characterized them as "empty vessels to be filled anew before each election."

Despite the importance of these differences, there are a number of ways in which the party systems of the two countries shared certain traits and functioned in a similar manner. Significantly, two prominent analysts of the Brazilian and Chilean party systems, Santos (1974) and A. Valenzuela (1978, 1985) respectively, have borrowed from Sartori's analysis to emphasize the central importance of a shared characteristic, one which is quite distinct from the party systems of the other six countries in this study. Specifically, Brazil and Chile were described as cases of "polarized pluralism" (Santos

1974:84; A. Valenzuela 1978:8). Both countries had highly fractionalized party systems displaying a pattern of fragile alliances and shifting coalitions among parties, which made consistent policy formation difficult. In addition, from the end of the incorporation period, both underwent a process of political polarization. Perhaps most importantly for present purposes, what needs to be added to this analysis is that these party systems lacked certain conflict-limiting mechanisms and hegemonic resources in the form of political ties between centrist parties and the popular sectors that could function to deliver political support to the government. In contrast to the hegemonic party systems of Mexico and Venezuela, the Brazilian and Chilean party systems were incapable of checking polarization and providing a consensual middle ground for policy formation. These features of the party system can in large measure be traced back to the pattern of state incorporation and its failure to mobilize the labor movement politically or establish an integrative populist party. Within this commonality, a difference between the two countries was that in Chile polarization was expressed largely *through* strong ideological parties; in Brazil polarization was expressed *despite* the nonideological and weak parties.

Party Fractionalization

These two party systems had conspicuously high levels of fractionalization. The extraordinary level of fractionalization in Chile is perhaps a better known phenomenon and has been analyzed in some detail by A. Valenzuela (1985). Before 1965, in the 33 years following the end of the incorporation period, no party won more than 24 percent of the votes in parliamentary elections. In 1965, the PDC won an unprecedented 42 percent, but in the remaining two parliamentary elections before the 1973 coup, its percentages slipped back to under 30 percent. Except for the 1965 and 1969 elections, the two largest parties were not able to account for half of the parliamentary seats. Corresponding to these low percentages is the large number of parties that attained representation in parliament.

Another measure of this same phenomenon is the party fractionalization index. A. Valenzuela (1985:table 3) presents two such indexes that, employing somewhat different measures, indicate the high degree of dispersion of parliamentary seats among many parties. On average, the level of party fractionalization in Chile was found to be the third highest among 27 democracies, ahead of such well-known cases as the Fourth Republic of France and Israel (Sartori 1976:313, cited in A. Valenzuela 1985:8). The Chilean case, then, is quite an extreme example of multipartyism.

Though the major Chilean parties are in many important respects highly institutionalized, it is worth noting certain aspects of instability in the party system. The first is the change in the array of parties. A chart of party splits, and occasionally mergers, would make a map of the most complicated highway interchange look simple. The second is the coalition behavior of parties.

Given the small size of the parties and the pattern of party splits, parties displayed a strong tendency to form electoral coalitions, often with parties of very different ideological commitments. Even after 1958 when joint lists were outlawed, electoral coalitions continued to be formed in which one party would support another party's candidates (A. Valenzuela 1985:17). The coalitional pattern observed in the aftermath period became an even more explicit and prominent feature of Chilean democracy: these electoral coalitions broke apart quickly after the election, usually within a few months. This pattern of shifting, fluid coalitions continued as deals, understandings, and arrangements were made and remade between the president and parliamentarians of different parties, among whom the president had to try to put together a governing coalition (A. Valenzuela 1978:7–8). The instability inherent in this situation is indicated by the tremendous number of cabinet changes throughout the period from 1932 to 1973. A. Valenzuela's data show that with the exception of two presidencies, "cabinets lasted for an average of less than one year and individual cabinet members held office for only a few months" (1985:15).

The high degree of fractionalization of the Brazilian party system is perhaps less obvious, since the 1946 Republic is often viewed as dominated by three major parties, the dominant PSD, along with the PTB and the UDN. Many analysts have even replaced the three-party image with something closer to a two-party image, seeing the period in terms of the dominance of the coalition between the two parties founded with Vargas's support, the PSD and the PTB. In this view, the pro-Vargas "ins," represented by a large, multiclass, integrative coalition of the PSD and PTB, are seen as opposed by the "outs," represented by the much smaller UDN.[6] This characterization does point to a major line of cleavage: the PSD and the PTB represented the social forces Vargas had attracted, while the UDN, actually the second largest party during most of the 1946–64 period, was publicly and often stridently anti-Vargas. Yet the coalitional pattern was more complex and less stable than this suggests, and in any case, the two parties together weighed less and less heavily over time: though the PTB increased in strength over the period, it did not offset the decline of PSD support in the face of an overall tendency in the party system toward increased fractionalization.

The best case for the existence of the PSD-PTB coalition can be made at the national level of presidential and vice presidential elections. Even here, however, the coalition was problematic. As we have seen, though the PTB supported Dutra's bid for the presidency as the PSD candidate in 1946, during his term of office a national pact was effected that included the UDN, which held cabinet posts, and that at the same time excluded the PTB, which had

[6] See, for instance, Benevides (1976); Schmitter (1971:382); and Skidmore (1967:55, 146, 189, 214). As Santos (1979:128), who strongly disagrees with this interpretation, has said, one of the most universally accepted assertions about Brazilian politics between 1946 and 1964 is that "a strong, if tense, coalition through the period between the rural-based Social Democratic Party and the urban-based Brazilian Labor Party lent stability to Brazil's constitutional regime."

no cabinet positions (Santos 1974:135). The exclusion, in fact, was such that Vargas, then a PSD senator, found it politically necessary to condemn the Dutra presidency and the conservative PSD-UDN coalition from early on and subsequently chose affiliation with the PTB as the more promising base from which to launch his presidential candidacy in 1950. Thus, in that election there was no formal PSD-PTB coalition candidate. Instead, Vargas won as head of a coalition of the PTB and the PSP (a populist party based in São Paulo and the fourth largest party nationally), and the PSD declined to support him, though many PSD supporters did vote for him. The weakness of a PSD-PTB governing coalition during the Vargas presidency has already been analyzed above.

The high point of the PSD-PTB coalition occurred in the next presidential election, with the victory of a coalition slate of Kubitschek of the PSD for president and Goulart of the PTB for vice president. Yet even here some caution is required in interpreting this as evidence of the importance of this coalition. Whereas Dutra had been elected with over half the vote (52 percent), and Vargas with nearly half (47 percent), Kubitschek won as a minority president, beating his two major opponents with slightly more than a third of the vote, which in percentage terms was divided 36-30-26 (Schneider et al. 1965:56). Furthermore, only after the 1958 congressional elections did the PSD and the PTB combined reach a majority of the seats in the federal Chamber. Even then, however, party discipline was weak, so that other alliances had to be sought to sustain a majority (Santos 1979:138).

In the 1960 presidential contest, the PSD and the PTB once again formed an electoral coalition, headed by a PSD candidate for president and including a PTB candidate for vice president. In these elections, the last before the 1964 coup, the weakness of the coalition was exposed most dramatically when the coalition candidate for president lost. The victory of Goulart once again in the vice presidential contest does not mitigate this coalitional failure. First of all, he won with fewer votes than Quadros of the UDN, the winning presidential candidate. Second, and more importantly, he was identified with the prolabor wing of the PTB, and his victory, alongside that of Quadros, represented the victory of a realigned populist coalition (the "Jan-Jan" movement, referring to the nicknames of Quadros and Goulart) and thus something quite different from the PSD-PTB coalition, which was clearly based on the supremacy of the PSD and the subordinate role of the PTB.

Even electorally, then, the PSD-PTB coalition was neither stable nor dominant. To the extent that an electoral coalition existed at all for presidential contests, it grew increasingly unable to attract the vote during the course of the 1946–64 period. Starting out by attracting a majority vote for its candidate, its support declined in every subsequent presidential election in which the coalition operated, proceeding to the election of a minority president and finally to the defeat of its candidate.

The inappropriateness of a two-party-like image of the PSD-PTB versus the UDN is even more evident in elections at other levels. It then becomes clear that the two parties formed neither a stable electoral nor a stable governing alliance. Instead, the period was characterized by fluid and shifting coalitions involving all the parties. In terms of an electoral alliance, there was no consistent pattern at the local level, and in fact the two Vargas parties were often in competition with each other. During the 1946 Republic, electoral alliances became increasingly important, and by 1962, 41 percent of the vote for congressional elections was cast for alliance candidates, as opposed to only 15.6 percent for the PSD, the largest vote-getter on its own (calculated from Schneider et al. 1965:60). Interestingly, in this context of increasing importance of electoral alliances, there was no tendency for the PSD and the PTB to combine forces. In fact, in the 1960 and 1962 elections, state governors and federal deputies were elected through PSD-PTB alliances in only two and three states, respectively (Schneider et al. 1965:59, 63). In terms of a governing alliance, it is clear that parliamentary coalitions were not fixed along stable lines, but were ad hoc and in constant flux (Santos 1974:128, 164).

If we reject the idea that the PSD-PTB coalition was a central feature of the Brazilian party system, then we would seem to be presented with a three-party model. However, this model also understates the degree of party fractionalization in the 1946 Republic. A three-party model is consistent with the existence of either a dominant party, along with two smaller parties, or a more or less even division of the electoral arena into thirds. The Brazilian system started out with a predominant party, but a rapid process of fractionalization set in so that very soon, as in Chile, no single party was large enough to attract a high percentage of the vote on its own. Within a short time, no party commanded the support of anywhere near a third of the electorate, as seen in the distribution of votes for the federal Chamber of Deputies. In the 1945 elections to the federal Chamber, the PSD, the largest party throughout the period, won 42 percent of the vote, but it was not able to sustain this performance in the following years. Quite the contrary, in the next elections its percentage was almost halved, and by the last election of the period, in 1962, while still the largest vote-getter on its own, the PSD managed a mere 16 percent (Schneider et al. 1965:60).

The distribution of congressional seats is another indicator of the same pattern of fractionalization. In the five elections to the federal Congress in the 1946–64 period, no fewer than nine parties won seats in 1945, and that number increased over the period: 12 in 1950 and 1958, and 13 in 1954 and 1962 (Santos 1974:98), producing an average almost identical to that for Chile. Indeed, indices of party fractionalization in Brazil were nearly as great as those for Chile. Whereas Chile's level of fractionalization ranked third on the list of 27 democracies in Sartori's analysis, Brazil, if it had been included, would have ranked seventh (Santos 1974:102). Whereas the level of fractionalization in Chile declined somewhat toward the end of the period, with the emergence of a strong Christian Democratic Party, the Brazilian fractionalization scores increased over the period, starting lower with the stronger showing by the PSD in 1945, but increasing steadily so that the last precoup legislatures in both countries reveal virtually identical scores.

Polarization

Chile. In addition to being highly fractionalized, the party systems of Brazil and Chile were polarizing, rather than integrative. This assessment of Chile is a common one. There is widespread agreement among students of Chile that political polarization and the "erosion of a centrist consensus" was a crucial feature of politics, and one that accelerated over time, especially with the single party strategy of the Christian Democratic period and then with the election of Allende (A. Valenzuela 1978:7). Valenzuela (xiii), for instance, has singled out political polarization as "the main characteristic of the Chilean system by mid-twentieth century;" it was increasingly pervasive as time went on (Stallings 1978:76).

Given how universal this characterization is, it is interesting that the indicators of polarization are not so clearly reflected in aggregate national electoral statistics such as a growth in the popularity for the parties of the right and left at the expense of centrist parties. In an examination of election results for the Chamber of Deputies for the entire period from 1932 to 1973, the following pattern emerges. First, there was a secular decline in the ability of the right to attract votes. In the most general terms, the right lost about 10 percent of the vote per decade: in elections in the 1940s, the modal vote received was in the fourth decile, in the 1950s it was in the third decile, in the 1960s it declined to the second decile, each decade containing one election in which the right slipped substantially below the modal level. It should be noted that over this period the suffrage was widened substantially, so that this decline in percentage represents more than a fourfold increase in the actual number of votes for the right. Second, the left increased its support from about 10 to 30 percent if just the postaftermath period following 1952 is considered. Compared to the success it had attained in the Popular Front, however, another interpretation is that it essentially managed to recover that earlier level after the disastrous decline it suffered in the late 1940s and 1950s. Again, it must be remembered that the number of actual voters who supported the left, as opposed to its percentage share, increased enormously—by a factor of twenty from 1937 to 1973 (calculated from A. Valenzuela 1985:table 1). Third, the data also reveal a steady growth of centrist parties through 1965, from about 30 percent in 1932 to 56 or 60 percent, depending on the assignment of parties to this center category.[7] The year 1965 is clearly exceptional in terms of center support, and in the following elections the percentage of votes returned to the level of the preceding election, at 43 to 44 percent, and it dipped again in the one parliamentary election held under Allende.

In terms of these data, then, discernible polarization occurred only after 1965. In that year, support for the right reached its nadir and subsequently recuperated, support for the left was growing after its decline in the 1950s, and support for the center reached its peak and subsequently declined.

[7] See A. Valenzuela (1978:6), as opposed to A. Valenzuela (1985:table 1).

Though electoral data reflect a *process* of polarization after 1965, they do not seem to reveal a high *level* of polarization in terms of a weak center and strong extremes. The party system does not look bifurcated; on the contrary, the center remained an important third force between right and left. Yet analysts such as A. Valenzuela (1978:6–7, 59) have argued, following Sartori's model, that it is precisely this structural situation of an "occupied center" that produces the centrifugal forces of polarization, in contrast to the two-party dynamic, which instead induces centripetal movement to the center.[8]

Other indicators in Chile make it clear that this process of polarization began well before 1965 and that it reached an impressively high level. Two other aspects of polarization are relevant here: the institutional consolidation of the right and left blocs combined with lack of concerted action by the parties in the center, and a process of ideological escalation.

Compared to the left, the institutional consolidation of the right in Chile was a longer-term process and ultimately took a stronger form. As mentioned above, the right developed a pattern of cooperation and concerted action throughout this period. Starting with the National Union, which was formed by the right to oppose the challenge posed by Alessandri in 1920, the Conservative and Liberal parties continued to cooperate in the electoral arena, particularly in presidential elections, occasionally supporting the center as a joint electoral tactic. They teamed up in support of Figueroa in 1925 and Montero in 1931, though in 1931 some of the Liberals supported Alessandri, who ran in opposition. In 1932, one of the few exceptions to this pattern of cooperation occurred, and the election resulted in the victory of Alessandri, the maverick Liberal, who in any case was moving rapidly toward the more traditional right. In 1938, in opposition to the Popular Front, the right formed the National Convention, and in 1942 the two major parties on the right decided to support Ibáñez in an act of desperate opposition to the center-left coalition. This cooperation on fielding a presidential candidate was renewed in 1952. In 1958, victory went to the bloc that was most united, even though it was, in the aggregate, the smallest, as the right was able to elect its own candidate to the presidency. In the next presidential election in 1964, the candidate supported by the right was again victorious, but this time it backed the centrist candidacy of Frei of the PDC. With this long history of cooperation behind them, in 1966 the parties on the right merged to form the National Party.

By the end of this period, the left also managed to achieve substantial institutional consolidation, though it did so out of a much more fractious back-

---

[8] This model has been challenged by analysts of Brazil, who have argued that polarization occurred not when the center was occupied but when it disintegrated or was evacuated (Hippolito, cited in Lamounier and Meneguello 1985:11). This apparent difference may be one of the identification of stages or sequences in the process of polarization. It may be, for instance, that whereas Valenzuela focused on the stage in which an occupied center produces polarization (which need not necessarily involve the disintegration of the center), Hippolito focused on the correlation between the simultaneous processes of polarization and the evacuation of the center, which may be an aspect of polarization.

ground and fell short of forming a single party. Throughout this period, the parties on the left were sharply divided along doctrinal lines. In the early part of the period, the Communists were split into Stalinist and Trotskyite factions, each of which ran opposition candidates in the 1931 presidential elections. The Socialists, once they appeared on the scene, were also divided, and during the Popular Front and coalition governments of the aftermath period, as we have seen, underwent a number of splits. In addition to these "internal" problems, of course, was the intense hostility between the Socialists and the Communists, both of whom ran separate opposition candidates in the 1932 presidential elections. Their rivalry was often debilitating for the left even during the Popular Front and following years when they both participated in the electoral coalition with the Radicals.

This picture of factionalization and hostility within the left began to change at the end of the aftermath period as the fortunes of the left parties plummeted. In 1952, with the Socialists split into the PS and the PSP, and with the Communists outlawed, the People's Front was formed as an electoral coalition of the PS and the Communists, and Allende ran as the Front's presidential candidate. With this beginning, further consolidation of the left took place. In 1956, the two Socialist parties joined the Communists in forming an enlarged electoral alliance, the FRAP. Ties within the left were further solidified in 1957 when the two Socialist parties reunited, and the new coalition was further strengthened the following year with the legalization of the Communist Party. In 1958, Allende again ran for president as the candidate of the united left, and did very well, coming in a close second behind the candidate of the right. It is a common interpretation that if it were not for the defection from the FRAP of a minor opposition candidate who won a mere 3 percent of the votes, Allende would have won the presidency, since the margin of victory was even smaller. The FRAP continued to hold together as an electoral alliance for presidential elections in 1964 and did very well indeed, increasing its percentage from 29 percent in 1958 to 39 percent. It was the anticipation of this formidable showing in 1964 that led the right at the last minute to make common cause with the Christian Democrats to defeat Allende.

This institutional consolidation in the form of a leftist electoral coalition for presidential elections took place, as we shall see, in the context of increasing radicalization. Accordingly, there were some defections to the left, particularly of the MIR in 1964–65 and the USP in 1967. Nevertheless, the main elements of the left maintained the coalition and even amplified it when it was reorganized into the Unidad Popular (UP) to include the Radical Party and a new left-wing splinter from the Christian Democratic Party. It was under the banner of this united coalition that Allende won the 1970 presidential election.

To this picture of institutional consolidation on the right and the left, we must add a very different history of institutional evolution in the center. First, while there was great party continuity on the right and the left, there was institutional change and experimentation in the center, as the Radicals, an antiparty Ibáñez movement, and a new Christian Democratic Party rose and fell from power in turn. In addition to institutional instability in the form of a succession of centrist parties and movements over time, the institutional weakness of the center was seen in its internal competitiveness and inability to achieve institutional consolidation. Following the aftermath period and with the decline of the Radical Party, the centrist parties were unable to collaborate in electoral alliances. In every presidential election from 1952 on, the centrist parties supported different candidates. As in the aftermath period, the largest centrist party tended to form alliances with parties of the right or left, rather than with other forces in the center, and with few exceptions, it is in this way that centrist presidents continued to be elected. Thus in 1952, Ibáñez put together a heterogenous coalition with elements of both right and left, through which he achieved victory despite Radical opposition. The Ibáñez presidency was one of tremendous coalitional instability, in which Ibáñez turned to nearly all groups in turn. Yet, while at different times he took both populists and rightists into his government, both the Radicals and Falangists under Frei rejected his overtures (see Cavarozzi 1975:256, 259). In 1964 the Christian Democrat Frei won with the support of the Liberal and Conservative parties, though again the Radicals remained in opposition.

Though a divided center was usually able to retain control of the presidency in one guise or another, this was not always the case. In 1958 the inability of the Christian Democrats and the Radicals to cooperate was decisive in the center's loss of the presidency: though, as mentioned, the left would have managed a slight margin of victory over the right if it had not suffered a minor defection, a coalition of the PDC and Radicals would have given a united center a more substantial plurality over both. In 1970, the center was again divided and the Radical Party joined the UP coalition that elected Allende.

Not only was there a lack of institutional consolidation by the centrist parties in the form of the failure to form coalitions, but as parties on the right and left were cooperating and merging in the 1970s, the parties in the center were fragmenting. Ibáñez's PAL suffered a series of splits and virtually disintegrated within the first two years of his presidency under the pressures of policy-making in a polarizing party system. The Radical and Christian Democratic parties also experienced defections. In the late 1960s and early 1970s, two left-wing factions broke from the PDC as the party moved to the right, and two right-wing factions broke from the Radical Party, as that party collaborated with the left.

This last point is related to the other aspect of polarization: the ideological escalation that took place over this period. Despite the political polarization that occurred particularly during the Aguirre Cerda presidency (1938–41), the aftermath period was generally one of compromise. The parties of the left were guided by the multiclass collaborative orientation of either populism or the popular front strategy. The right learned that it could cede its hold on the presidency and compromise in some areas in exchange for the protection of its basic interests. The Radical center was a pragmatic one, opportunistically willing to cooperate with both right and left and playing a brokerage role.

In the subsequent period, however, ideological lines hardened. On the left, the splits in the Socialist Party were the harbingers of this process. By 1952 the Popular Front strategy of collaboration with the bourgeoisie was replaced by the People's Front, in which the Communists and Socialists presented a joint candidate to compete in the presidential elections, and by 1955 the Socialist Party formally abandoned its populist orientation in favor of a commitment to a more radical Workers' Front, which represented the primacy of a working-class constituency and the affirmation of the socialist goals of nationalization and redistribution (Drake 1978:305). A comparable process of ideological definition occurred on the right, as a free-market, laissez-faire ideology became more explicit and influential, particularly as the economic problems of stagnation and inflation mounted. In many ways, its major spokesman and representative was Jorge Alessandri (son of Arturo), who was president of the most important interest association of Chilean capital, the Confederation of Production and Commerce, and who favored sanctions against firms that accepted money from CORFO, the state development agency. This ideology became particularly influential during Alessandri's tenure as minister of finance from 1947 to 1950, again at the end of the Ibáñez government, and most especially under the following government when Alessandri himself became president.[9]

The ideological lines hardened still further in the 1960s under the impact of two developments. The first was the Cuban Revolution, which had a big impact on the FRAP, as seen in its 1964 platform (Drake 1978:308) and in the consequent discussion within the left of the tactic of abandoning the electoral road in favor of a revolutionary path. It was a combination of the radicalization and increasing strength of the left that made the 1964 election such a polarized one, as the alarmed right decided to join the center in an anti-Marxist common cause and as rumors of a military coup in the event of an Allende victory were countered by threats of resistance and general strikes. The polarization on a rhetorical level and the anticommunist fervor reached such a pitch that many people stored up on canned goods in case of a FRAP victory, and airline reservations out of Chile were booked up for months before the election (Gil and Parish 1965:49).

The second change was the replacement of a pragmatic center with a new ideological center in the form of the Christian Democrats' commitment to a reformist Third Way. A. Valenzuela (1978) has usefully suggested the way in which this new ideological component in the center adversely affected the possibility of political compromise, bargaining, and coalition-formation, particularly once the Christian Democrats came to power in 1964.

These components of polarization intensified as the 1960s proceeded, with the split within the left of the MIR and USP, which rejected the electoral game, and the victory within the Socialist Party of its left wing, which ad-

[9] Stallings 1978:80–81; Cavarozzi 1975:315; Hirschman 1965:284n.

vocated a more radical, classist, noncollaborationist position that accepted the tactic of armed struggle (Drake 1978:309). The right in turn took an ever-more-strident anti-Marxist position and also moved toward withdrawal from the electoral arena, where it was losing ground under the impact of electoral and agrarian reforms and rural unionization. Instead of relying on "inside influence," it depended increasingly on "outside pressure" (Cusack 1970:414) based on its corporative economic institutions, especially the Confederation of Production and Commerce (Cusack 1970:401), on its influence on more technically oriented advisory committees and policy-making boards such as financial policy institutions (Stallings 1978:57), and on certain " 'more reliable' state institutions [such as] the *Contraloría General*, the Judiciary and the Armed Forces" (Cavarozzi 1975:351, 399). In this context of ideological polarization, the Third Way of the PDC lost ground as the party itself succumbed to the forces of polarization, with the main sector of the party tending increasingly to the right and the left wing finally splitting off and joining the FRAP.

Needless to say, the polarization accelerated sharply once Allende was elected in 1970. The 1971 municipal elections were widely interpreted as an indicator of increased polarization in which "the electorate perceived the contest to be between a Popular Unity coalition and a more status quo-oriented opposition" (A. Valenzuela 1978:54). In congressional elections, this perception became institutionalized: as foreseen in the 1964 elections, the center disappeared completely, and all post-1970 congressional by-elections as well as the 1973 congressional elections were fought on a two-way basis of the UP coalition against a united opposition (Stallings 1978:145). Despite the electoral alliances, party affiliations and the right-center-left distinction can still be analyzed, though some caution is necessary because of the politics and negotiations of coalitional agreements. If the Radicals are defined as centrists, as they are in A. Valenzuela's (1978, 1985) analyses, the 1973 congressional elections reveal a defection from the center to the left in comparison with the 1969 elections, with the right maintaining about a fifth of the vote for deputies and the center and left each ending up with about a third. Much of the decline in the center, however, is due to the waning appeal of the Radicals, whose vote in 1973 dwindled to 3.5 percent. If one considers the Radicals as part of the left, given that they joined the FRAP, the left, of course, comes out ahead of the center, rather than even with it. In any case, it is interesting that the Socialists and the Communists were the only ones to increase their support in the post-1969 period (from Stallings 1978:243, table A.1).

Thus, polarization was a central phenomenon of Chilean political life, even though there may have been more limited widespread popular radicalization than is sometimes assumed and the distribution of support for the major political tendencies did not change dramatically over time (A. Valenzuela 1978:39). Instead, polarization occurred through the growing importance of ideology and the hardening of ideological positions along with the particular dynamics of a fractionalized party system.

Brazil. Students of Brazil have also highlighted the crucial role of polarization in the pattern of political dynamics, particularly in the 1960s. It figures prominently in analyses of those who emphasize the causal importance of the economic contradictions of Brazilian development. They tend to see polarization as a kind of intervening variable in the course of political change generally and in the breakdown of civilian rule and military intervention in particular. It is an even more prominent part of the newer and growing literature that sees the dynamics of the party system itself as playing a more important and even an independent role in these political developments (Lamounier and Meneguello 1985:7–8).

Given the nature of the Brazilian parties—the fact that, especially compared to the Chilean parties, they were so much weaker, less ideological, and more heterogeneous—one might expect that polarization was not likely to be reflected in national electoral data, and in many ways this is the case. Nevertheless, if we assign right, center, and left ideological positions to the UDN, PSD, and PTB respectively (as leading Brazilian scholars such as Santos [1974:106, 114], Lamounier and Meneguello [1985:10–11], and Souza [1976:33] do), some interesting patterns emerge. The composition of the federal Chamber that resulted from the five elections from 1945 to 1962 saw a decline of PSD membership from over a half to under a third, while the UDN essentially held its own, particularly after its initial losses from 1945 to 1950, and the PTB increased dramatically, from 8 percent[10] to 30 percent, achieving virtual parity with the PSD (Fleisher 1981:62; Souza 1976:144). What one sees then is a pattern of a declining center and a growing left.

One must be careful about this interpretation: there are obvious problems with assigning clear left-right designations to parties that may have exhibited some ordering but that were basically nonideological and heterogenous. Additional complications arise from the fact that candidates' identification with a party in Brazil was often opportunistic and even short-lived, and many of these candidates ran on coalition tickets.[11] In any case, as in Chile, these data do not indicate a polarized bimodal distribution into right and left blocs, but they do indicate a *process* of polarization over time, and other indicators can be marshaled that suggest the polarization experienced in Brazil. With such weak parties, polarization in Brazil was manifested more clearly in terms of political realignments, particularly in Congress, that crossed party lines. It was also evident in the overtly political and electoral activities of nonparty groups. At the same time, political rhetoric became more ideological and strident.

As to the first of these, polarization was apparent in the internal fragmentation into more ideologically and programmatically defined factions of all

---

[10] In 1945, the combined vote for the left, including the PCB and the PTB, was 13 percent. The PCB was subsequently outlawed but collaborated electorally with the PTB.

[11] Using Schneider's (1965:67) slightly different figures that indicate a somewhat lower total for the PTB, one can calculate that in 1962 the three major parties, on their own and without entering coalitions, won seats as follows: PSD, 19 percent; PTB, 15 percent; UDN, 13 percent.

three of the major parties and, furthermore, in the ideological realignment of these factions into interparty groupings. Unfortunately, there is no good study of this crucial process (Souza 1976:141n). Nevertheless, the broad outlines can be sketched.

Significantly, the first party to develop a more ideological or policy-based faction was the PSD, the most "centrist" of the three major parties. In 1955, the Ala Moça was formed, primarily among those deputies who had been elected for the first time in 1954. The Ala Moça took positions that were more nationalist, socially progressive, and reformist (Schneider et al. 1965:37; Lamounier and Meneguello 1985:11). After the 1958 elections, the Ala Moça was largely supplanted when the more progressive freshman deputies provided the impetus for a new reformist grouping. This group, called the Invisibles, attracted and was sustained by the new, like-minded deputies elected in 1962 (Schneider et al. 1965:40). The progressive wing of the PSD came to be known as the Ala Jovem (Bastos 1981:115; Fleischer 1981:59).

Though this process began in the 1950s within the PSD, it accelerated in the 1960s, when other parties followed a similar pattern. The Bossa Nova was a renovation group formed within the UDN. For the most part it supported Quadros when the rest of the party turned against him, and after his resignation, the left wing of this faction cooperated with Goulart.[12] At the same time, a faction on the right in the PSD was formed and sided with the UDN in opposition to Quadros (Santos 1974:87). Also in 1960, factionalism within the PTB became much more explicit. Goulart, as minister of labor and later vice president during much of the 1950s, had long been the standard bearer of the labor wing of the PTB. After 1960, his brother-in-law Leonel Brizola emerged as a prominent leader of that faction, eventually becoming a major source of leftist pressure on Goulart. Other factions on the left emerged as well. Fernando Ferrari, a reformist party leader who clashed with Goulart, was expelled from the party and founded the Reform Labor Movement as a new party (Bastos 1981:114–16; Fleischer 1981:50). The remaining more radical deputies formed the Grupo Compacto, under the leadership of Almino Afonso, the leftist minister of labor under Goulart (Schneider et al. 1965:37, 39, 44).

The emergence of these factions became an even more significant development with their recombination into more coherent ideological and policy interparty groupings. On the left, the FPN (Nationalist Parliamentary Front), was formed in 1957, and from then on it was "on many issues . . . more important and effective than the parties" (Schneider et al. 1965:42). Among its leaders were Almino Afonso, Brizola, and other leading figures of the Grupo Compacto, which constituted its major base. The Ala Jovem of the PSD and the Bossa Nova of the UDN were also active in the FPN (Fleischer 1981:59; Bastos 1981:115). The ADP (Democratic Parliamentary Action) was the parliamentary bloc formed to oppose the FPN during the Goulart presidency. By

[12] Santos 1974:87; Fleischer 1981:59; Schneider et al. 1965:37.

1962 the ADP had organized in many state legislatures and municipal councils, and in addition it had established a network of Popular Democratic Action groups throughout the country (Dreifuss 1981:320; Schneider et al. 1965:37). In this way, polarization took place with the consolidation of two opposing parliamentary groupings and the decline of the PSD—and therefore of its ability to play a more pragmatic, brokerage role.

A parallel process of the consolidation of groups on the right and the left took place outside of Congress as well. On the left, as we shall see below, existing union confederations came increasingly under leftist and Communist influence, and the CGT was formed as a labor central that for the first time provided organizational ties and coordination among the various national confederations provided for in the Estado Novo labor legislation. Due in part to the limits the law placed on it in terms of its ability to play a role in the industrial relations arena, the CGT functioned more as a political pressure group. As a politically oriented group, it cooperated with the UNE, a radical student organization, as well as the FPN. In fact, these three groups, as well as other groups on the left, came together in the Popular Mobilization Front (FMP). Born of an ad hoc coalition that opposed the 1963 economic plan of Goulart and advocated a more radical program of "basic reforms," the FMP played a key role in a wide range of political issues.

The right also consolidated its organization. The CNI was a national organization of industrialists. More than the CNI itself, its state affiliates played a direct role in political and electoral issues. More important on a national level were IBAD and IPES, which worked closely with the ADP (Dreifuss 1981:320). Both were political action groups sponsored by the Brazilian economic elite. Dreifuss has argued that together the coordinated activities of the IPES/IBAD/ADP "complex" represented a hegemonic attempt by the "organic elite." This "complex" financed candidates in the 1962 elections at all levels, wrote the electoral platforms of many of them, and coordinated opposition to Goulart in Congress, where it was influential among almost half the deputies (Dreifuss 1981:320–21). Though the IBAD was banned for running afoul of the Goulart government, the IPES, which continued to function, was an important player in the preparations for the 1964 coup (Schneider et al. 1965:39).

Corresponding to this organizational realignment and consolidation was an ideological escalation. While the left, on the whole, was not overtly Marxist, as was the Chilean left, the battle line was equally sharp and the ideological distance seemed just as great to the actors (Flynn 1978:230). As we shall see below, the left adopted a structuralist position that saw questions of economic growth and national industrialization, on the one hand, and redistribution, on the other, as two sides of the same coin. Accordingly, it proposed a program of "basic reforms." Though not very radical, it alarmed the right, to whom it raised the specter of fundamental change, subversion, and a syndicalist state, based either on a Communist or an equally unacceptable Peronist model. Especially in comparative terms and with the advantage of hindsight, not only does the program of the left seem rather moderate, but

Goulart himself tried during virtually the whole of his presidency to play a conciliatory role. Nevertheless, with issue after issue, the forces of polarization accelerated and the space to maneuver in the center collapsed.

In comparison with Chile, the Brazilian polarization was more brief, less deeply rooted, and embedded in a party system with a much-less-well-defined left and right. Yet precisely within this framework of Brazilian politics, it represented an important departure.

Opposition and Crises

The political heritage of state incorporation in Brazil and Chile, then, was a multiparty, polarizing regime. These regimes failed to establish hegemonic resources and conflict-limiting mechanisms with which to confront the economic and political challenges that were presented starting in the late 1950s. No multiclass integrative party was established as part of the incorporation project, and subsequent attempts were failures. In the absence of a party that bound and integrated the popular sectors and their interest associations to the state, popular sector groups were able to maintain or gain political autonomy and carve out an independent course of action, based on a radical program calling for structural economic and social change. In this way, the popular sectors, both urban and rural, far from providing the regime with a base of support, became key components in a process of political action and reaction. A dynamic of polarization undermined the government's base of support, and in the ensuing political deadlock important policy areas were immobilized, as the political center collapsed.

Although the Socialist Party in Chile and the PTB in Brazil were formed as populist parties, they did not function during the aftermath period as integrative parties along the lines of the PRI in Mexico or AD in Venezuela. The fact that the political center was largely attracted to parties other than the populist parties had two consequences. First, until the very end of the period under consideration, the populist parties were either out of power or, at most, very junior partners in coalition governments. Second, being less controlled by centrist tendencies, these parties were more likely to be more responsive to their working-class base and to move to the left ideologically and politically. Far from acting as instruments of control of the labor movement and peasantry, the populist parties gradually became vehicles of popular sector political expression.

In the post-aftermath period, after 1960 in Brazil and 1952 in Chile, even less control was exercised through these parties, which, along with the Communist parties, were the dominant force in the labor movement. The politicization and radicalization of urban and rural popular sectors accelerated, particularly under the impact of the Cuban Revolution. With the failure of the coalitional pattern of government, other attempts to create a political center were made in both countries. These subsequent attempts to form political parties or movements were incapable of checking polarization and providing a consensual middle ground for policy formation. In contrast to the hegemonic party systems of Mexico and Venezuela, these party systems became the vehicles of polarization. At the end of this period, with the failure of the center, the Socialist Party and the PTB came to power—not this time as junior partners in a coalition government, but in their own right, occupying the presidency[13] in coalition with (Chile) or with the support of (Brazil) the Communist parties. By this time, polarization and radicalization had gone far enough so that these parties, now much more clearly identified with the left (especially in the case of Chile), were unable to serve as instruments of control over the popular sectors. Instead, labor and peasant activation played an important role in propelling these parties to the left and even further polarizing politics. With the loss of political control of the center and the polarizing, centrifugal dynamics of the party system, the military intervened to overthrow the regime.

Political Parties: Centrist Failure and Policy Immobilism

Of the countries considered in the present analysis, Brazil and Chile were the farthest from forming multiclass, integrative party systems. In Mexico and Venezuela, where such party systems were most successfully established, the populist party emerged from the aftermath period with a broad governing coalition in place. As we shall see, the regimes in these two countries had the political resources to sustain themselves in the face of the challenges of new leftist parties and political movements in the 1950s and 1960s. The regimes in Brazil and Chile did not have the same political resources. They could not hold the center or prevent political polarization. This was the case in Chile, where strong ideological parties were central actors in the polarization process; it was also true in Brazil where the parties were weak, non-ideological, and particularly heterogeneous, and where the polarization took place in part through the regrouping of party factions and in part, as it did also in Chile, through political activity in other, nonparty arenas.

In these two countries, along with Uruguay, the left became a more formidable political force than in the other countries under consideration. The Communist parties were more successful in those two countries than in the others, as were other parties on the left. This is particularly clear in the case of Chile, where the Communist Party and the Socialist Party, which had become even more radical than the Communist Party, formed a strong electoral coalition on the Marxist left. But in a more mild form, it is also true of Brazil, where the Communist Party, although remaining illegal, amassed substantial influence within labor and peasant unions and cooperated with a radicalizing PTB.

The radicalization of the left was countered with a hardening line on the

[13] Vargas ran as a PTB candidate in 1950, but this formality cannot disguise the fact that the PTB was nevertheless a junior partner in his government.

right. The accelerating polarization eliminated any space in the political center, and political deadlock immobilized policy and spelled the failure of the centrist coalitions. This process of polarization and policy stalemate was the principal political legacy of incorporation in Brazil and Chile.

In the postaftermath period, new attempts were made to produce a political center different from the attempted "populist" coalition of parties that had failed and was discredited in the previous period. These new experiments to produce a political center also failed, as they were not able to check the polarization process or provide a basis for stable policy formation. In both countries, though in quite different ways, centrist parties ultimately lost control of the presidency to the left—an outcome that did not occur in the other countries under consideration here. Under these circumstances, polarization accelerated. Santos (1974:85) has described the situation in Brazil in terms that would also apply to Chile nearly a decade later: "The feeling of an impending confrontation between the radicals of right and left was already widespread by the beginning of 1964. Parliament seemed more like a battlefield than an arena for negotiation and compromise." In the end, the military intervened to overthrow the democratic regime and impose the political and policy domination of the right opposition by coercion.

NEW EXPERIMENTS IN THE CENTER

In 1960 in Brazil and in 1952 in Chile, the center or center-right parties that had dominated politics in the aftermath of incorporation, the PSD and the Radical Party respectively, lost the elections. During the next period, new attempts were made to produce a center that could hold power and find some stable support basis for governing. This stage of experiments in the center was very short in Brazil and quite prolonged in Chile. With the widespread discrediting of coalition politics that occurred in the aftermath of incorporation, the center was occupied by a new, nonideological and even antiparty, personalistic force under a charismatic leader, Jânio Quadros in Brazil and, in Chile, Carlos Ibáñez, who returned to power in 1952. In the case of Chile, another and very different centrist experiment subsequently took place as well: an ideological center represented by the Christian Democratic government. These attempts to form a new force or movement in the center failed. Far from being able to overcome the polarization that had begun during the aftermath period, the new experiments in the center instead fell victim to it. The result of the accelerating polarization, as politics became increasingly zero-sum, was policy vacillation due to the center's inability to find a stable coalition as a basis for consistent policy making. This section focuses on this succession of governments.

The Ibáñez Government (1952-58) in Chile.   In Chile, by the end of the Radical period in 1952, tremendous disaffection with party politics had developed, specifically with the pattern of shifting alliances, patronage, corruption, and political immobilism that had come to characterize the period. The fluid nature of the parties themselves indicated a failure to form an institutionalized party system. By the time of the 1952 elections, the Socialist Party had undergone a series of splits and a substantial loss of vote-getting ability, while the Radical Party had split in three. Furthermore, ten different parties held seats in Congress, and ten new parties were registered for the elections (Gil 1966:73; Drake 1978:293).

It was in this context of party disintegration and fragmentation that Ibáñez campaigned on an anti-party platform. The general disillusionment with party politics at the end of the coalition period in 1952 was sufficiently great that one observer, referring to Ibáñez, would later comment: "No one understands this man. Last time he was elected President and he turned into a dictator. Now he was elected to be a dictator and he has turned into a President" (Olavarría 1962, vol. 2:121–22).

The Ibáñez coalition was extremely heterogeneous, embracing the gamut from fascist to Marxist groups (Pike 1963:258–59; Cavarozzi 1975:220). Accordingly, it encompassed political factions that sought a political alliance with the right and those that, with variations, had a more populist orientation and sought to appeal to labor support. This heterogeneity, forged from a common anti–status quo sentiment, was debilitating when it came to policy formation, and Ibáñez was unable to secure any stable basis for governing. Cavarozzi (1975:221ff) has traced out the twists and turns as each of these factions was able to assert itself briefly, only to be replaced by the political ascendancy of another. During the course of this coalitional instability, Ibáñez made overtures to populists in the PAL and PSP, to Frei, to the Radicals, and to the right, but was unable to form a stable coalition. The seven separate and very distinct cabinets he formed and disbanded during the six years of his presidency, each reflecting the dominance of a different faction, attest to the ongoing pattern of coalitional shifts in the context of an underlying process of polarization that Ibáñez was unable to overcome or contain.

The Ibáñez period was correspondingly one of policy vacillation, as Ibáñez, like the Radicals before him, alternately looked to a populist and an accommodationist coalition. Policy with respect to organized labor reflected these shifts, being characterized at different times by his support of a new labor central, the CUT, which maintained independence from the government (and which Ibáñez would later denounce); by his unsuccessful attempt, inspired by Peronism, to establish a co-opted labor movement; and in 1956, by labor repression. Initially the government had a populist coloration. The cabinet included representatives of the progressive wings of both the PSP and Ibáñez's Agrarian Labor Party (PAL). Perhaps most important was the PSP's Almeyda as minister of labor. The PSP, and Almeyda specifically, sought to use participation in the government to promote labor organizing. While Almeyda was minister of labor, the government supported the creation of a unified labor central, and industrial conflicts that came before the labor boards tended to be settled in favor of labor.

This policy soon divided the Ibáñez coalition and provoked the hostility of industrial interests. Accordingly, Almeyda was dismissed and a new cabinet was formed, but one in which PSP and progressive PAL ministers held key posts. Continued opposition by the right to the economic policies led to the collapse of this cabinet as well and its replacement by one more oriented toward appeasing entrepreneurial groups (Cavarozzi 1975:255). Additional cabinet changes brought a further rapprochement with the right. This trend culminated in mid-1955 with a cabinet based on the Conservative and Liberal parties and with the adoption of an orthodox economic stabilization program, based on the recommendation of the famous Klein-Saks Mission of U.S. economic consultants.

This policy change, which elevated the political position of the right and technocrats in institutions like the Central Bank, had a correspondingly negative impact on labor. Not only was the economic cost high (in 1955 and 1956 wages and salary adjustments equalled only 50 percent and 80 percent respectively of the inflation rate), but labor repression was stepped up (Cavarozzi 1975:275, 302; Loveman 1979:295). Though this cabinet and its orthodox policy was the most durable of the Ibáñez presidency, it did not last long. By October 1957 yet another cabinet change was made, and by the end of his government the stabilization policy began to come apart.

The Ibáñez movement, then, as an attempt to create a new force in the political center, was unable to stem the tendencies set in motion during the Radical period. Instead, the process of polarization was renewed. From the beginning, Ibáñez was unable to retain the support of the PSP (one of the Socialist splinters), which had joined his coalition, and the more decisive move of Ibáñez to the right near the end of his government constituted an impetus for leftist unity. In 1955, the Socialists explicitly adopted a "Workers' Front" orientation to replace the collaborationist line and shortly thereafter achieved reunification. In reaction to the 1956 repression, the FRAP was formed as a unity party on the left (Bray 1961:119, Drake 1978:306). The final swing of Ibáñez back toward the left only strengthened it as he re-legalized the Communist Party and promulgated important electoral reforms (Drake 1978:306).

Once again, the center would not hold. In the 1958 presidential election, the center parties together remained the largest electoral force, but, in a state of complete disunity and organizational disarray, lost the election. Alone, no centrist party was a close contender for the presidency. The left was more united than ever, but the renegade candidacy of a former FRAP candidate deprived its presidential candidate, Salvador Allende, of the margin of victory. There followed an interim period in which the right, still strong and united, returned to power under the presidency of Jorge Alessandri, before a new movement would once again try to create a viable political force in the center.

The Quadros Government (1961) in Brazil.   The short presidency of Jânio Quadros in Brazil from January to August 1961 had much in common with the Ibáñez period in Chile. Like Ibáñez, Quadros was a charismatic politician with tremendous electoral appeal, who used these personal qualities to come to power as an "anti-politician" (Skidmore 1967:187), beating the PSD-PTB candidate overwhelmingly. Appealing to "voters who had come to view the whole party structure with contempt" (Skidmore 1967:190), Quadros, during the course of his campaign, criticized "the system," promised to clean political house by attacking corruption and inefficiency, and carefully avoided clear identification with any of the political parties. In his political past, Quadros had been associated with many parties and political tendencies. In 1959 he was initially endorsed as a candidate for the 1960 elections by a number of small parties and subsequently by the UDN, the rightist opposition party, which opportunistically endorsed him as a ticket to power. During the course of the campaign, however, he made it clear that he would be beholden to no party (Skidmore 1967:190).

Unclassifiable in traditional political terms, Quadros led a heterogeneous coalition, attracting not only middle-class and rightist support, but also popular support as he presented himself as a fighter for social justice, a reformer, and a friend of the people. As in the case of Ibáñez, it was a contradictory coalition that he had little prospect of satisfying.

Like the Ibáñez presidency, the Quadros period was one in which economic crisis, particularly inflation, was a central political problem, exacerbated by the polarization and political deadlock surrounding the policies that would address it. The two periods were similar also in that, given the heterogenicity of their coalitions and the inability to find a stable basis for governing, both presidents vacillated in their approach. Whereas Ibáñez began with a populist orientation and, after other intervening policies, at the end adopted orthodox stabilization policies approved by the IMF, Quadros went in the other direction, starting with and then abandoning an orthodox approach. The issue of following IMF guidelines in an anti-inflation policy had already become extraordinarily controversial and polarizing during the presidency of Kubitschek, who had felt forced to abandon this approach. Quadros was subject to the same set of constraints, arising from a political polarization that prevented the forging of a governing alliance and that immobilized policy.

The crisis provoked by Quadros's turn to an independent, "radical" foreign policy was the culmination of his inability to create a center that would hold and that would support a coherent policy orientation. Though the new line in foreign policy may have been consistent with a conservative economic policy oriented toward the promotion of manufactured exports and the development of appropriate markets (Flynn 1978:215–16), it nevertheless provoked much opposition on the right and provided the spark for an attack against him by Carlos Lacerda, the UDN leader, who, in the "crisis of hegemony" (Flynn 1978:208, 210–11) and political deadlock that had come to characterize postincorporation Brazil, had become the era's "destroyer of presidents" (Skidmore 1967:200). In the context of increasingly polarized and zero-sum politics, Quadros alienated almost all sectors during his brief presidency. These included traditional politicians and the government bureaucracy (smarting from his attack on "the system," governmental corruption, and inefficiency); industrialists and merchants (nervous about economic policy); labor and the left (opposed to the hardship imposed on the working class by the stabilization policies); the UDN politicians (upset by his independence, his wavering on economic stabilization, and his foreign policy); and the military (also opposed to his foreign policy) (Skidmore 1967:202).

Quadros then made a gross miscalculation. In what he intended to be a tactical move, he submitted his resignation, expecting it would ultimately be rejected and he would emerge in a stronger position. One element in this calculation was the fact that with his resignation, the presidency would be assumed by the vice president, João Goulart, a leader of the left-labor wing of the PTB, who, throughout his political career, had been seen as an unacceptable threat by the right—particularly by Lacerda—and the military. (In 1954 Lacerda had conducted a campaign favoring a coup that would deprive Kubitschek of the presidency, out of fear of Goulart as his vice president [see Skidmore 1967:149–54]). Yet, with support for Quadros evaporating in the Congress and amid divisions within the military over the tactical approach to the question of succession, the resignation was accepted and Goulart became the president of Brazil.

The Alessandri (1958–64) and Frei (1964–70) Governments in Chile.   In Chile, though not in Brazil, there was yet another attempt to create a political center based on a coalition that included a popular following. Having grown rapidly during the 1950s and early 1960s, the Christian Democratic Party's victory in 1964 marked the return to power of a centrist movement, following the rightist Alessandri government that succeeded the Ibáñez presidency.

Before discussing the Christian Democratic experience, a word might be added about the Alessandri period. The government of Alessandri, who was elected as the candidate of the Conservative and Liberal parties, is notable here for its failure to do much better than the various center tendencies that preceded and followed it in its attempt to find a political basis from which to pursue a consistent program, given the process of polarization.

A leading member of the Chilean bourgeoisie and a former president of one of its major interest associations, Alessandri's election ushered in a right-wing government based on laissez-faire principles. Yet the coalition that supported him was quite heterogeneous. With the electoral reforms that reduced the role of electoral clientelism and fraud in the countryside, the rural vote for the right could no longer be counted on to the same extent. Alessandri managed to put together a new rightist, urban coalition, based on white-collar workers, professionals, and small entrepreneurs. This heterogeneity, as well as opposition from the left, made the orthodox economic policies that he favored difficult to sustain (Cavarozzi 1975:333).

Another factor was present as well. Cavarozzi (1975:ch. 4) has argued that Alessandri staffed his administration with corporate representatives of the bourgeoisie, replacing and subordinating party politicians and technical staff. In this way, he alienated the political parties, particularly the Radical Party, which was so prominent among government bureaucrats, but also the Liberal and Conservative parties. At least equally important, according to Cavarozzi, is the outcome that in this way Alessandri also reduced the autonomy of the state and further politicized it. This process accelerated political polarization.

In this context Alessandri was incapable of sustaining his orthodox economic policies, and by the second half of his term he was forced to abandon them and reincorporate the party politicians into the government. Even with the dismantling of most of the initial policies, the right was unable to stem voter disapproval and defection, and it continued its downward slide in popular support in the 1963 municipal elections (Cavarozzi 1975:385; Stallings 1978:90–91). At the same time, as a result of the new policies, the industrial bourgeoisie began to withdraw its support (Cavarozzi 1975:388) as "the large industrial entrepreneurs, as well as the other bourgeois fractions, began to realize that parliamentarian practices and partisan politics were becoming less efficient mechanisms for the implementation of their interests" (Cavarozzi 1975:398).

In summary, the failure of "Alessandri's experiment" was twofold. On the one hand, it showed the incapacity of the bourgeoisie's more direct representatives to carry out a program of further capitalist development within the framework of democratic institutions while maintaining effective bourgeois support. On the other hand, his failure further weakened the political mechanisms which had helped to maintain the supremacy of the economically dominant classes, and consequently, Chile's political stability (Cavarozzi 1975:396).

The 1964 presidential elections took place amid an unusual degree of ideological fervor, as the growing socialist left, still united in the FRAP, had a credible possibility of winning. In the face of this threat, the right decided to make common cause with the quickly rising new force in the center, the Christian Democratic Party. With this backing, Eduardo Frei was elected president.

In striking contrast to the Ibáñez movement, the Christian Democratic Party placed great emphasis on both ideology and the organization of a support base. Ideologically, it advocated a reformist, communitarian third way, rejecting both Marxism and liberalism, both communism and unfettered capitalism. In this way it represented an explicit recognition of, and response to, the political polarization that was occurring in Chile. Rejecting class conflict, the party sought to achieve social justice through a vision of a harmonious society modeled on the family. Its centrist, reformist program emphasized industrial development, based on the expansion of the domestic market and hence compatible with the rise of real wages and with agrarian reform; it called for 50 percent Chilean participation in the copper industry, although this was presented as an alternative to the left's call for total nationalization; it also favored domestic industry, but at the same time that it extended a broad welcome to foreign capital.

From this reformist position, the party undertook to mobilize and organize a broad support base, particularly among those popular sectors not already organized. These were primarily the peasantry and the "marginalized" urban population: slum dwellers, the unemployed, and women. To this end the party sponsored the organization of many community groups, neighborhood associations, sports groups, mothers' councils, and peasant unions. It also drew a following among the working class, particularly among white-collar workers, and, after the 1957 reorganization, maintained a union department within the party structure that maintained and oversaw party-union relations.

Despite a clear, well-articulated ideology, the party represented a heterogeneous constituency that was much less clearly delineated and consistent—that was, indeed, contradictory. With a rightist pedigree emerging from the Falange faction of the Conservative Party, the party had moved in a reformist position based on popular mobilization. Accordingly, it was most firmly rooted in the middle classes and petty bourgeoisie, at the same time that it mobilized a support base among the peasantry, the "marginalized" urban population, and parts of the working class, though the party never sought nor enjoyed friendly or cooperative relations with either the leftist parties or the union movement. Its constituency also included elements of the bourgeoisie who saw reforms as a necessary component of modernization, as well as former Ibáñez supporters.

Though it represented the ideological center, the party was pulled to both the right and the left. It contained a radical minority that took positions close to labor and the Marxist left. Yet, with the rapid expansion of the party in the 1950s and 1960s, it began to back off from its reformist ideology, becoming a more pragmatic, catch-all party in which the conservative faction became more predominant (Fleet 1985:77–79). The heterogeneity of the coalition and the weight of the conservative faction was reinforced by the fact that Frei was beholden for his election in 1964 to the Conservative and Liberal parties, which supported his candidacy in order to prevent an Allende victory.

The vacillation in policy that resulted from the inability to find a stable center coalition is now a familiar story. The Frei presidency can be divided into three periods (Stallings 1978:97ff): a reform period from 1964 to 1966, but one that was sufficiently cautious to alienate proponents of reform without appeasing its opponents; 1967, in which the internal divisions and contradictions became explicit; and the abandonment of the "revolution in liberty" agenda in favor of a programmatic turn to the right.

The moderate and "balanced" program of reforms on which the Frei government embarked at the outset produced divisions within the party that were evident already by mid-1965, as the left wing of the party began to oppose "the slow pace of reform, the administration's 'catering' to private capital, and its hostility towards labor and the left" (Fleet 1985:97). This last was characterized by economic and wage policies that were seen as favoring capital over labor and by conflictual relations with the CUT, the formation of three alternative but ultimately unsuccessful labor confederations as rivals to the CUT (see below), and the attempt, also unsuccessful, to revise the labor code to allow for parallel unions. At the same time, entrepreneurial groups opposed many of the reforms that the government was pursuing, and by 1967 they began to withdraw support from the government (Fleet 1985:125).

Inconsistent policy implementation, which resulted from divisions within the party, had the effect of accelerating the polarization. For instance, while the Frei faction of the party adopted a cautious posture on land reform, members of other factions organized peasants and mobilized them to press their demands for land. The result was the alienation of both landlord and peasant support (Fleet 1985:99, 106) and the increased hostility and suspicion of right and left both within and outside of the party.

Unable to satisfy its diverse coalition, the party thus fell victim to the very polarization it had sought to overcome. By 1967 the intensification of internal contradictions meant a loss of support that was evident in the party's showing in the municipal elections of that year. "The Christian Democrats were thus victims of *el desgaste de poder* [the erosion of power] . . . the phenomenon whereby an incumbent administration loses its initially broad support not despite but because of its incumbency" (Fleet 1985:100).

The loss of support prompted a search for coalition partners. The left wing of the party renewed its commitment to reformist programs and advocated cooperation with the FRAP. Another budget crisis exacerbated the division, and a new forced-savings proposal of the government united the CUT and the white-collar confederation, the CEPCh, against the Frei program, leaving the PDC's unionists in a difficult position. Against this backdrop, polarization increased significantly starting in 1968 (Stallings 1978:115), and both left and right became more unified. The PDC labor section voted to abandon the rival labor confederation and reenter the CUT, which also absorbed the CEPCh. On the other side, employers' syndicates in agriculture and commerce were strengthened and solidarity talks began between the associations of landowners and industrialists, the SNA and SOFOFA (Stallings 1978:117–20). The end of the Christian Democratic period saw the beginnings of forms of direct action that were undertaken by popular sector groups, often outside the control of the CUT. These would intensify under Allende. Factories were taken over by workers and land was seized by peasants, while the SOFOFA president called for "drastic and violent actions" if necessary to defend the rights of private property (quoted in Stallings 1978:117–18). In this context, a large part of the left wing of the party withdrew in order to make common cause with the new coalition of the left, Unidad Popular.

Thus, by 1969, when the left bolted from the party, the level of political polarization had risen sharply, and protest, violence, and unrest became more common. "Clashes between protesters and police were daily occurrences. On the one hand, militant landowners organized and armed themselves to forcibly resist peasant seizures and duly authorized expropriations. On the other, the leftist MIR began sporadic urban and rural guerrilla operations" (Fleet 1985:112).

At the same time, preparations were made for another presidential election in which the PDC candidate would run against a candidate of the National Party, which represented a newly consolidated union of the former Conservative and Liberal parties, and a candidate of the Unidad Popular, which represented a newly consolidated union of leftist forces. The Christian Democratic experiment thus came to an end amid growing social tensions, political polarization, a hardening of ideological lines, and continued political deadlock and policy immobilism, punctuated by a menacing and foreboding, but unsuccessful, army uprising in October 1969. The following year, the Christian Democrats failed in their bid for reelection. It was in this context that Salvador Allende, the Marxist candidate of Unidad Popular, came to power.

THE PRESIDENCY SHIFTS TO THE LEFT

Prior to the presidencies of Goulart and Allende, then, politics in Brazil and Chile were characterized by the failure to establish a viable center, increasing polarization, and the failure of the government to establish a support base for pursuing consistent policies. These tendencies came to a head in 1961 in Brazil and 1970 in Chile, when the center or center-right lost control of the executive, leading to an escalation of political polarization, decisional paralysis, and policy immobilism that was finally resolved by military intervention.

In Chile, it was unambiguously clear that a leftist president had come to power with the election of Allende, the candidate of a Marxist coalition. It was less clear in Brazil, where Goulart represented the PTB, a nonideological party that had formally been in the governing coalition during most of the post-1945 period. Yet, Goulart belonged to the wing of the party that was identified with labor and that was undergoing a process of radicalization. There is no doubt that the perception of many social sectors in Brazil was that the left had come to power: Goulart did indeed provoke a wave of anti-communist sentiment and the fear of a Marxist dictatorship (Santos 1982:155–56).

Thus, it is insufficient to say that the leftist/labor threat in Brazil was "in fact" not very great—that the radical nationalist program was not very radical and that the potential for revolutionary action was indeed quite limited— although all that was true. The "fact" is indeed the perception that the threat was a real one, for it was the perception that affected action. Stepan has emphasized the atmosphere of crisis that characterized the Goulart government. That government began inauspiciously in the context of "near civil war" that accompanied the transfer of power from Quadros to Goulart and continued throughout his truncated presidency. Groups on both the right and the left felt that "Brazil was entering a revolutionary stage that called for a new political order" (Stepan 1978a:117). The interesting question is not whether Brazil was "really" facing a radical or revolutionary threat comparable to that in Chile, but rather the other comparative question of why the Brazilian political system was on so short a fuse compared to the Chilean political system. Both countries were experiencing processes of radicalization and polarization, but the relation between these two processes was different. The more tolerant Chilean system could withstand a much greater degree of radicalization before the process of polarization reached a breaking point for the competitive regime. In the more "trigger-happy" Brazilian regime, on the other hand, polarization "outran" radicalization relative to Chile. In any case, the strikes and confrontations of the period add up to a period of major crisis in Brazil.

The threat represented by Goulart and Allende can be seen in the apprehension with which the assumption of power by both men was greeted and in the attempts of the opposition to control and harness the new presidents: the weakening of the presidency in Brazil and the declaration of constitutional loyalty required of Allende in Chile. Both presidents came to power in precarious political positions amid political crises that questioned the continuation of the democratic regime. In both cases, the crises were temporarily resolved by a constitutional amendment that represented a compromise permitting Goulart and Allende to assume office. Goulart, for a decade the *bête noire* of the right, did not enjoy the legitimacy of having been elected, and the alarm the prospect of his presidency triggered was such that there was great uncertainty about whether or not a constitutional succession would be allowed, with substantial sentiment opposing the constitutional path. Amid intense political struggle, a compromise was finally reached within Congress, which passed a constitutional amendment adopting a parliamentary system, thus substantially weakening presidential power and changing the balance of power between the president and the Congress.

The situation was similar in Chile, where great uncertainty also existed over whether or not Allende would be allowed to assume the presidency, as the world expectantly watched this unusual experiment of a democratic election of a Marxist president. In Chile, too, it was the Congress that finally decided on the presidential succession. Though, unlike Goulart, Allende had the advantage of having received popular electoral support as a candidate for president, he had received a bare plurality of 36.2 percent of the vote, only 1.3 percent ahead of Alessandri. In the absence of an absolute majority, the constitution provided for the election to be thrown into the Congress, where the UP did not enjoy a majority. As in Brazil, the struggle was intense, and the impasse was resolved by a constitutional amendment intended to reach a compromise that would favor Allende's election. This was the Statute of Guarantees, which required Allende to sign a formal declaration of commitment to preserve the constitution and respect civil liberties, elections, and freedom of the press. The succession crisis finally resolved, Allende's position remained precarious. Not only was Allende a minority president who faced a Congress controlled by the opposition, but the UP, on which he ran, was a coalition of several distinct parties, from the non-Marxist PIR to Marxist groups advocating a mass insurrectional road to socialism (A. Valenzuela 1978:67–69).

All in all, the conditions under which Goulart and Allende assumed office represented a culmination of the polarizing, multiparty, nonhegemonic regimes that had come to characterize Brazil and Chile since the end of the incorporation period. During these two presidencies, polarization was no longer only a process that occurred because of the inability of the center to hold contradictory forces and movements together. Now a new element was present: with a leftist in the presidency, groups on the left (and right) actively pursued polarization as a political strategy. At the extreme left, there were groups that sought to heighten the contradictions and sharpen class antagonisms as prerequisites for revolution. Less extreme, however, was the tendency for some groups on the left to engage in what Erickson (1977:122, part 3) described as "dissensus politics." Anxious to take advantage of a unique and long-hoped-for opportunity under a reformist or leftist president, these groups sought to adopt a strategy that would exert pressure for the adoption of a left-reform or socialist program. Thus, their activities—including strikes, protests, land occupations, and (in Chile) factory seizures—were aimed at forcing the president's hand. Given his precarious political position, neither president could easily risk alienating a crucial component of his coalition. Fearing the pull of political compromise, these groups thus adopted policy positions, undertook actions, and sometimes presented *faits accomplis* (see, for example A. Valenzuela 1978:74) to prevent or break up compromise and cooperation with more centrist or conservative groups. In both countries, these actions contributed to the inability of the government to form a "centrist" consensus, though the ideological location of this center was distinct in the two countries. Dissensus politics, then, was a conscious policy of polarization aimed at limiting the president's options so that he would have no choice but to rely on these groups and adopt a leftist program. It was a strategy pursued by party activists, as well as by radical groups in the labor movement and in other spheres.

As a result of the tactics of the right as well as of the left, the formal institutional channels of policy-making and political compromise either broke down or were bypassed. Polarization on the right could be seen most explicitly in three arenas. The first was within Congress itself, where ideological antagonisms grew and resulted in decisional paralysis (see Santos 1974). The second was in the battle between Congress and the executive, for, though Congress was divided, it constituted the formal political arena in which the right had the most power, having lost control of the presidency. Thus, the power of the right in Congress was deployed against the executive, which was seen as having gone unacceptably far to the left. In Brazil, the opposition blocked the president's "attempts to implement reforms through the legislature, forcing the Executive to use presidential decrees which delayed his plans, involved him in long procedural battles, and created an atmosphere of deadlock in the Congress; beyond this, a climate of general ungovernability was created which stimulated the search and legitimation of extraconstitutional solutions" (Dreifuss 1981:320–21). The situation in Chile was similar. The third arena was pressure, put on both the president and the parliament, that came from outside formal electoral institutions. Increasingly, as this period proceeded, pressure groups on the right as well as the left felt they could not rely on the formal electoral institutions, but had to exert pressure to force the hand of decision-making organizations. These outside groups became more and more important as the Goulart and Allende governments wore on and the process of polarization accelerated.

Dissensus politics, then, accentuated the long-standing inability of the party in power to achieve compromise and to establish a stable basis for governing. The corollary was the intensified policy immobilism and decisional paralysis that has been well described in analyses of these periods in both countries. In the ensuing political and economic crisis, the middle class was pulled to the right and became active in antigovernment demonstrations, thereby providing a substantial base of support for an antidemocratic solution. With the formation of a broad coalition favoring a coup, the military intervened and overthrew the two governments, ousting Goulart in 1964 and Allende nearly a decade later in 1973.

Several concluding observations may be made. The UP government, like that of Goulart, stepped into and intensified a process of polarization and mobilization that it was unable to control. While accepting the argument of Valenzuela that the single-party strategy of Frei made accommodation in the center more difficult, the present analysis suggests that Frei too stepped into an already polarizing party system. The polarizing dynamic of the party system, it is argued, is an outcome of the pattern of state incorporation and the inability in the postincorporation period to establish a viable integrative party system, and this dynamic can be followed down through the presidency of Allende.

Similarly, the present analysis would emphasize the structural context of polarization and policy immobilism in Brazil. Some analysts, such as Stepan (1978a), have pointed to Goulart's deficient leadership in analyzing the collapse of his government. Whatever these deficiencies may have been, it is the present argument that polarization, as the outcome of a process that can be traced back to the nature of the incorporation period, was already well advanced by the time Goulart stepped into the presidency. In this context, the political space for a centrist coalition was fast disappearing. As Santos (1974:45) put it, "political 'maneuvering space' toward the end of the Goulart government had become fully occupied by the struggles, threats and counterthreats of the various factions, with little or no opportunity for the initiation of badly needed new policies."

At the same time that we point to the similarities between the Goulart and Allende periods, the obvious differences must be emphasized. First, whereas Allende was elected president, Goulart's assumption to the presidency seems more accidental and conjunctural, being less an outcome of the structure of politics and political processes. It certainly seems true, as Flynn (1978:219) has emphasized, that the resignation of Quadros was the result of a gross miscalculation on his part. Nor was there anything in the underlying structure of the political situation, however stalemated, or in the crisis of the moment, that made his resignation inevitable. Nevertheless, it must be remembered that the same structures of a multiparty, polarizing regime were responsible for the impasses and frustrations that led to Quadros's resignation. If he had not resigned, it is possible that the experiment in the center might have been sustained for longer, perhaps even beyond his presidency. Without engaging in too much counterfactual speculation, however, one might question the ability of centrist governments to continue indefinitely, for the PTB, which was undergoing a process of radicalization, was the fastest growing of Brazil's major parties (Skidmore 1967:214) and the only one of the three major parties that was increasing its share of seats in Congress.

Second, as mentioned, the degree to which the left came to power was clearly different in these two countries. Whereas Goulart was an undecided and wavering president with a populist background and under pressure from his constituency to adopt a program of basic reforms, Allende, with strong Marxist credentials, was firmly committed to a revolutionary program of change and was under pressure from his constituency—or a part of it—to reject the country's legal framework as an unacceptable constraint. "Pledged to eliminate the hacienda, nationalize foreign mining interests and expropriate the largest industrial and commercial enterprises, Allende symbolized the end of the existing system of property and the political regime which served as its foundation" (Loveman 1976b:263). Furthermore, whereas Goulart was immediately faced with immobilism and accomplished little in policy terms, Allende moved rapidly during his first year on the path to socialist transformation. In this he was backed by a much more mobilized and radicalized civil society, which had spoken in a clear voice through the ballot, in a way that had no counterpart in Brazil and which continued to put much more extensive pressure on him through land invasions and factory occupations. Yet, like its counterpart in Chile, the left in Brazil included a "negative" left that was more radical than the Communist Party, being less willing to collaborate and compromise, more skeptical of achieving its aims through the political process as it was constituted, and more open to nondemocratic and violent solutions. The right feared that this left would be able to play a critical role in forcing the hand of Goulart (Skidmore 1967:279–83). These groups included the pro-Chinese splinter party of the PCB and "Fidelista" or "Jacobin" groups, that included radical student, labor, and peasant organizations.

> Many frustrated democratic leftist reformers who had been proregime became antiregime and argued that reform could only come through massive pressure and plebiscitary democracy, or even revolution. . . . Leonel Brizola, spoke of the need to form "Grupos de Onze" (clandestine groups of eleven armed revolutionaries). Conservatives prepared to defend themselves by force. In the countryside, landowners armed themselves in preparation for civil war. In the cities, especially São Paulo, right-wing vigilante units proliferated. This sense that the regime was doomed and that Brazil was at the threshold of revolution dominated much of the political dialogue in the period from 1961 to 1964 (Stepan 1978a:117).

The point, then, is that Brazil and Chile experienced similar party and political dynamics, although these similar dynamics occurred in quite different "ideological space"—nearer the left in Chile and nearer the center in Brazil. From quite different locations on the ideological spectrum, indeed in countries representing quite different ranges on that spectrum, Goulart and Allende tried unsuccessfully to carve out some middle ground, as we shall see below. They represented the same pattern of a president caught in a rapidly polarizing situation, unable to find a stable basis from which to form policy and govern, though in Chile this political drama took place at a point on an ideological continuum and in a sociopolitical context substantially to the left of that in Brazil. In discussing these differences, it is important to reiterate that the argument of this book does not pretend to predict exactly similar patterns in Brazil and Chile—or within any pair of cases. Rather, the argument seeks to trace out parallel, but not identical, processes and regime dynamics within contexts that were dissimilar in many respects. This difference in context accounts for differences in regime outcomes other than the ones examined here, as well as for variations in the similar but not identical outcomes on which we focus. Despite the differences, the underlying political dynamics in Brazil and Chile were much more similar to each other than to those in the other six countries in this analysis.

The Politics of Stabilization

The general pattern of policy immobilism that resulted from political polarization and deadlock is particularly well illustrated in responses to the economic challenge presented by inflation. In contrast to the experience of a country like Mexico, neither Brazil nor Chile had the political resources to prevent or control inflation. Rather, these polarizing regimes experienced stalemate and policy immobilism with respect to stabilization policy. Indeed, Flynn (1978:207) has suggested that it was only through inflation and concessions on all sides that Brazilian presidents were able to hold together any sort of coalition, and in a similar vein Hirschman (1965:293) concluded from his study of Chile that inflation "can serve to head off revolution or be considered as an alternative to civil war." The weak governments of Brazil and Chile were unable to impose austerity measures or to arrive at any consistent approaches to stabilization. Various attempts at more orthodox economic policies were tried and abandoned. By the end, any approach seemed politically unworkable.

Brazil. The pre-1964 history of Brazil reveals a record of nearly constant unsuccessful attempts to implement stabilization programs under every president since Dutra. These occurred in 1953–54, 1955–56, 1958–59, 1961, and 1962–63. Stabilization policies typically adversely affect the economic interests of many groups in society and may be the object of widespread opposition. However, in Brazil it may be suggested that most important in preventing implementation was the opposition of labor and the more independent position from which it attempted to defend its class interests. (Skidmore 1977:179; Harding 1973:390–98). In the context of polarization and a lack of party incorporation and the unraveling of state control (see below), the various governments had little leverage over the labor movement and were unable to secure its cooperation. On the contrary, labor was able to exert political pressure on the government to prevent the implementation of a policy that would result in a decline in the purchasing power of wages. The labor movement was not strong enough, however, to win the adoption of an alternative policy to meet the economic problems. In each case, the stabilization effort was abandoned, and the government was immobilized, unable to act effectively in this policy area.

By 1950, inflation in Brazil reached double digits and two years later rose to over 20 percent, considered a high rate of inflation by the standards of that period. At the same time, the external accounts deficit skyrocketed (Skidmore 1977:150; Flynn 1978:164). In October 1953, Vargas inaugurated a new cabinet and with it an orthodox stabilization plan. The political climate of polarization was particularly inauspicious for the success of the plan. Just a few months before, the labor movement of São Paulo had mounted its most impressive strike, affecting hundreds of thousands of workers, and social tensions rose as both the middle sectors and army officers reacted to what they saw as militant trade unionism and "resentment against [working class] groups . . . who appeared to command, by means of their unions, greater bargaining power" (Flynn 1978:165). As we have seen, in an attempt to steer a middle ground, Vargas, in his major appointments and contradictory policies, managed to alienate virtually all groups. His appointment of Goulart as minister of labor and the 100 percent readjustment of the minimum wage spelled the end of the stabilization policy less than a year after it was initiated.

A subsequent stabilization attempt under Kubitschek in 1958–59 did not fare any better. Kubitschek was caught among the contradictory aims of promoting rapid industrialization and economic growth (which meant continued public spending and expansionary policies), establishing international credit worthiness (which meant adhesion to the austerity guidelines of the IMF), and maintaining the political coalition (which meant some defense of working-class purchasing power). The issue of following IMF guidelines in an anti-inflation policy became extraordinarily controversial. No social groups were willing to undergo the sacrifices and hardship of a stabilization program, and labor protest and wage demands escalated. As the government negotiated with the IMF, a radical nationalist position that was hostile to international capital developed, and the stabilization controversy soon expanded into a more general polarization over development strategy. In mid-1959, amid these sharpening ideological divisions and the upcoming presidential elections, Kubitschek dramatically broke off negotiations with the IMF and abandoned the stabilization program (Skidmore 1967:174–82; Flynn 1978:204–7).

It was against this background that Quadros had to confront the problem of stabilization. With an inflation rate now over 40 percent, his government was subject to the same set of constraints, arising from a political polarization that prevented the forging of a governing alliance and that immobilized policy. He initially pursued the neo-liberal stabilization policies advocated by the IMF, emphasizing the need for a balanced budget, foreign investment, and reform of the exchange rate system. The credit and wage squeeze and the rise of food and other prices that ensued provoked opposition. With the political costs of the anti-inflation policy becoming clear, Quadros, by March and April 1961, began to shift toward a more "developmentalist" policy orientation, thereby triggering the criticism and opposition of the UDN.

Finally, then, it fell to Goulart to attempt a stabilization policy in the face of an inflation now over 50 percent. As soon as his presidential powers were restored in 1963, he undertook a new stabilization program. Still trying to steer a course among the demands of economic growth, redistribution and reform, and foreign investors, the Goulart government adopted a non-orthodox plan that tried to balance all of these goals, including a program of structural reforms, with agrarian reform prominent among them. An attempt was made to forge an alliance or social pact among the three major parties in Congress as well as among Goulart, groups representing national capital, the trade unions, and the Communist Party, which had become a dominant influence within the unions. This pact, however, did not last, as the stabilization plan was opposed by both right and left. By midyear, the plan had collapsed and was abandoned in favor of a firmer commitment to basic reforms. In 1963 and 1964, inflation rose to over 80 percent, jumping far beyond the rate of the previous peak year of 1959 and standing out as a clear area of policy failure (Skidmore 1977:150).

Chile. The incapacity of Chilean governments in the area of stabilization policy is similar to that in Brazil. Though inflation had a long history in Chile, the modern phase of the problem started under Aguirre Cerda (1938–41). During the ensuing Radical years (1942–52) inflation averaged 18 percent annually, but there was no serious attempt to control it. The basic Keynesian, underconsumptionist orientation of the government was consistent with its emphasis on economic growth. Seen as the price of growth, inflation was dealt with by a policy of mitigating its effects, rather than by attempting to control it directly. Wage policies were adopted that kept white-collar workers ahead, though blue-collar workers fared less well (Hirschman 1965:245–51).

By the end of the Radical period, inflation for the first time "became an obvious and critical threat to social and political stability" (Hirschman 1965:252). In 1948–49, with the turn to the right of the González Videla government, Finance Minister Jorge Alessandri undertook the first serious stabilization policy, balancing the budget and announcing a wage and price freeze and the suspension of all indexing measures then in effect. The policy, however, was blocked by an eruption of labor protest, perhaps most importantly that of white-collar workers, who formed an important Radical constituency and whom the Radicals were therefore less willing to repress than blue-collar workers. "Thus, what started out as a serious and unprecedented attempt to bring inflation to a dead stop ended in complete failure and, in fact, resulted in a more massive injection of new inflationary pressures than if the attempt had never been made" (Hirschman 1965:254). This first experience with the politics of stabilization constituted a pattern that would be repeated throughout the next two decades.

It was against this background that Ibáñez took office for the second time. The first two years of his presidency were marked by repeated policy failures. His Socialist Finance Minister Herrera set about increasing taxes, but his policy of "let the powerful also pay" provoked opposition and prompted a reorganization of the cabinet. Finance ministers Pedregal and Prat followed in rapid succession with different versions of "shared sacrifices" approaches to stabilization. In the context of political polarization, congressional opposition, and strikes undertaken by a labor movement newly united in the CUT, both failed. "With class pitted against class and the executive branch against the legislative . . . this was no time for . . . austerity and shared sacrifices" (Hirschman 1965:265).

By 1955, inflation had reached the runaway stage, with prices nearly doubling in the single year. At this point, a stabilization program was temporarily imposed with the mediation of the Klein-Saks Mission, which was important not so much for its technical advice as for the political legitimacy it gave the policy. The inflation rate came down in 1956 and 1957, but this was not sustained. It rose again in 1958 at the end of the Ibáñez presidency in the context of ongoing opposition, poor economic performance, and new heated debate between structuralists and monetarists (Hirschman 1965:257, 272, 281ff).

During his first two years in office, Alessandri pursued an orthodox economic strategy that represented a continuation of the policies begun at the end of the Ibáñez term (Cavarozzi 1975:315; Stallings 1978:81). The hostility between labor and the government was seen not only in CUT opposition to the stabilization plan, but in Alessandri's labeling CUT protest a "call to sedition" (Stallings 1978:82). The tension increased in 1960 when the government proposed a 10 percent wage readjustment in the face of 38 percent rate of inflation the previous year. The CUT response was a 24-hour general strike, followed by a series of individual strikes aimed at ending the stabilization plan. Tensions grew, with labor protest and marches escalating and the government answering unruliness with police repression in which two workers were killed (Stallings 1978:82–83). With the left in opposition and the other parties feeling excluded by the technocratic staffing of the government, support for Alessandri was rapidly slipping, as seen in the opposition gains in the 1961 congressional elections. At the same time that Alessandri moved to more fully include the Radicals, as well as Liberals and Conservatives, he made concessions in wage policy that constituted a serious setback for the stabilization program (Stallings 1978:85).

The policy immobilism intensified in the face of a foreign exchange crisis and government inability to make a decision regarding devaluation. In 1962, with inflation increasing and a controversial wage policy under consideration, workers once again mounted a series of strikes and demonstrations, and once again they turned bloody, with police killing six and wounding many more. It soon became clear that "the stabilization program—and with it the entire government strategy—was at an end" (Stallings 1978:89–90).

With this history of failure behind them and with an ideological commitment that gave greater prominence to social reform than previous governments, the two other governments before 1973 took more moderate approaches to inflation. Indeed, there was substantial disagreement within both the Frei and Allende governments over the extent to which stabilization should be a policy priority (Stallings 1978:190). In the end, Frei adopted a plan that aimed at lowering inflation gradually. It depended on the cooperation of both capital and labor in accepting government guidelines with respect to wages, prices, and returns to capital. In addition, the government undertook a tax reform that targeted the wealthy and a forced savings plan aimed at workers. In reaction, the bourgeoisie mounted a publicity campaign and workers struck. At the same time division within the PDC grew and the left gained in power. Once again, in the face of polarization, the government had to retreat in its stabilization policy (Stallings 1978:105–13).

The Allende government placed much greater emphasis on its reform program and a structuralist approach to the problem of inflation. However, by mid-1972, as inflation rose, Allende and the moderate wing of the UP coalition, which thought it important to consolidate gains and to exercise caution so as not to provoke further opposition from the right, proposed to hold down wage increases and government spending in order to reduce an accelerating inflation. Despite opposition from the left wing of the UP coalition, an attempt was made to implement the Allende plan.

It was at this time, however, that political polarization reached a new height. On the left, the movement of factory seizures grew, and the occupations expanded to factories not scheduled to be removed from the Private Area and placed in the Social and Mixed Areas (see below). The right went on the offensive on a number of fronts: industrialists engaged in capital strike, not investing, lowering production, laying off workers, and abandoning their factories; new forms of cooperation between the PDC and the PN (the united Liberal and Conservative parties) were forged; and the National Front of the Private Sector (FRENAP) was sponsored by the industrialists' association as a new organization to coordinate the activities of the private sector from the large industrialists to the petty bourgeoisie and its *grêmios*. These activities culminated with the October 1972 strike led by the truck-owners' *grêmio* and the swift mobilization in response by the CUT. Under Allende, as under the previous presidents, the government lacked the political resources to hold together a coalition to support a viable stabilization program. In this context, no consistent economic policy making was possible (Stallings 1978:135–45).

Labor Movement

State incorporation had placed primary reliance on the state and on largely coercive mechanisms of control over the working class. In the absence of a populist party, the working class remained politically autonomous from control by a multiclass or centrist party and subsequently became an important factor in the growth of a political left. It has been argued by analysts such as Angell (1972:7) that this leftist political orientation of labor was at least in part a result of the characteristics that have been associated here with state incorporation. That is, state incorporation had severely constrained the labor movement and left unions very weak in the system of industrial relations. As a result of this weakness, the working-class struggle centered to a greater degree on the political arena rather than the industrial-relations arena. Given the constraints on union activities in relation to employers, the labor movement found it beneficial to seek results through the political process and alignments with political parties. The result was a politicized labor movement that gave important support to leftist political tendencies and contributed to the growth of the left and the polarization of the party system.

The increasing strength of the left and labor's leading role within the development of the left was given further impetus by the breakdown of certain aspects of labor control. With the introduction of competitive politics and the bidding for electoral support of the working class, some of the constraints on the labor movement began to break down—more quickly in Chile and more slowly in Brazil. Thus in Chile, the official union movement established by Ibáñez during the incorporation period, never very successful to begin with, began to establish its independence immediately after he fell from power. In Brazil, the official, co-opted *pelego* leadership also started to give way to more democratic leaders. Given the reaction of the government, this process occurred with many setbacks, but at least by the middle of the Goulart presidency, a radical current had emerged as dominant within the labor movement on the national level.[14]

In addition, in both countries strikes that were formally "illegal" under the labor code grew in frequency and were tolerated by the government. Finally, extralegal labor confederations were formed, giving labor a more unified national presence, which the labor code had sought to prevent. These confederations became important political actors in the polarizing dynamic that came to characterize these regimes.

By the end of the period, the importance of the labor movement in Chile became clear from the electoral victory of the Marxist coalition that put Allende in power. Though perhaps less obvious in the case of Brazil, "observers of pre-1964 Brazil generally agreed that the two social forces with the greatest impact upon the political process were labor and the military" (Erickson 1977:97).

Brazil.   In Brazil, political parties had no important role during the initial incorporation period. When party politics subsequently reemerged, the new parties did only a very partial job of mobilizing popular sector support for the government. As the potential populist party that would embrace both the popular sectors and political elites in control of the state, the PTB fell short

---

[14] Costa 1981:48; Delgado 1986:53; Harding 1973:597.

for at least three reasons. First, it was not an effective vehicle of popular sector mobilization. As we have seen, it was largely dependent on the Communist Party (which, as a proscribed party, chose to work through the PTB) for its labor activities and mobilization. Second, and in part because of the Communist role, the PTB, like the other parties in Brazil, developed a left wing that became increasingly radicalized and dominant within the party. Consequently, it was a poor instrument of control. Third, the inclusion of the PTB in the governing coalition during much of the postincorporation period was problematic at best.

From the very beginning, as we have seen, the PTB failed to become the dominant political force within organized labor, despite the role of the co-opted PTB union leadership. In fact, the PTB, which was the potential vehicle for mobilizing mass support, was geared more to bureaucrats in the vast Labor Ministry and Social Security Institutes and to the co-opted union leadership than it was to the working masses (Schmitter 1971:273–75). The founding of the PTB coincided with the (temporary) legalization of the Communist Party, which had substantial strength within organized labor, and also with the founding of the PSP, which went on to achieve substantial success among the working class in the industrial core of São Paulo. Furthermore, during the Dutra period, the PTB was not closely tied to Dutra's government. As a result, the state did not have a political base in the labor movement, and the Labor Ministry competed directly for control of organized labor with the Communist Party and with the PTB itself, which grew increasingly hostile to the ministry and the repressive policies it was adopting (Harding 1973:200).

Nevertheless, in the beginning of the aftermath period, the working class did lend substantial support to the PTB. In part this was in response to the social welfare measures that had been part of state incorporation and to the new overtures made by Vargas in the 1943–54 period. These included a rhetorical commitment to *trabalhismo* and Getulismo as a prolabor, personalistic, populist movement that identified Vargas with labor. Working-class support for the PTB was reinforced by the renewed illegality of the Communist Party. However, it must be borne in mind that this support was limited, and the PTB remained a weak co-optive instrument. Even in his second presidency, the most populist of the aftermath period, Vargas evoked some populist themes but was careful to avoid mobilizing labor and limiting his options by identifying exclusively with the PTB. He never completely overcame his initial orientation toward depoliticizing the popular sector—or at least he remained ambivalent about this, as he vacillated between appeals to the popular sectors and to groups on the right, never really using the PTB to mobilize popular support (Skidmore 1967:ch. 3; Wirth 1970:22–23). The PTB was backed by only a minority of organized labor, and as the labor movement became more politicized, especially from the mid-1950s on, many political groups, including not only the Communists but also Marxist groups to their left, competed for influence. With the lack of party incorporation, the PTB was not in a position to be used as a mechanism of political control or of the hegemonic leadership of unions. Based as it was on bureaucrats within the Labor Ministry, PTB cadres had little experience or know-how in forging ties with the rank-and-file. In fact, in many places the PTB was so weak that it had to depend on the (again illegal) Communist Party to carry out rank-and-file organization and mobilization on its behalf (Harding 1973:352, 451). Thus, though working-class functional organizations were tightly controlled, severely constrained, and dependent on the state, the working class remained *politically* more independent and was thus in a better position to join or organize more radical, class-based political movements or parties in the context of a relatively open multiparty system.

In this situation the PTB was incapable of delivering working-class support to the government in both the electoral and trade union arenas. In 1960, much of the labor movement supported Quadros instead of the PSD-PTB candidate. Although Goulart won the vice presidency, he lost in those areas with the greatest concentrations of labor and the most class-conscious workers, evidence that the PTB had declined as a vigorous force in labor, especially in the most industrialized areas (Harding 1973:482–83,451). According to Harding (1973:460), this working-class support for Quadros represented a move away from the "populism" offered by the PTB—based on favors, influence, and personal attention—to a more class-conscious orientation that responded to appeals based on anti-imperialism, on more thorough-going reforms that attacked privilege and promoted structural change, and on greater autonomy of unions from government control and oversight. Under Quadros, the labor minister was a Christian Democrat who, competing with Goulart for labor support, began to replace ministry ties to the PTB with those to the *renovadores* (Harding 1973:488–89). In this way, the victory of Quadros contributed to the realignment of the labor movement and constituted yet another blow to what little potential the PTB may have had as an instrument of hegemonic control.

Under Goulart, as the process of radicalization advanced, the divided PTB came to serve more as a vehicle for opposition than for political control from the center. Radical populists such as Leonel Brizola emerged as strong forces on the left within the PTB and often clashed bitterly with Goulart as they tried to force his hand. Thus, the PTB was hardly a hegemonic or integrative party. For most of the 1946 Republic it was not even, for all intents and purposes, a governing party, and when it finally occupied the presidency it was still incapable of providing hegemonic control. Whereas it had been founded as a party closely identified with the Labor Ministry and based on the *pelegos*, with the dual goals of channeling political support among the working class to Vargas and exercising control over labor, it soon changed its nature. With the infusion of new leadership not tied to the Estado Novo, it became more identified with the left and became a defender of the proletariat. Far from constituting a vehicle of support for the government, under the Goulart presidency the radical, anti-imperialist wing became dominant and the party was a constant source of pressure on him (Carone 1981:xvii–xviii). Correspondingly, the labor movement did not fall in line behind Goulart.

Rather, it became a potent force that he was forced to deal with on an equal footing.

With the PTB failing to function as an instrument of co-optive or hegemonic control, *pelego* control of the union movement, one of the pillars of the Estado Novo and its pattern of state incorporation, began to break down. We have seen that the breakdown of official unionism began immediately after the incorporation period, but met a major setback with the reimposition of coercive controls under Dutra. Yet further important advances were made through the 1950s, as labor became an increasingly powerful political actor, and these accelerated after 1960.

During the 1950s, the *pelegos* had largely been replaced at the local union level and were relegated to the federations and confederations. During this period, in the context of greater freedom to strike, the characteristics of the labor movement and the nature of its leadership began to change. As strikes were called as a response to rising inflation and the erosion of real wages, the rank and-file came to participate in union affairs more and more, exerting pressure on leaders. As leaders in turn became more responsive to the rank and-file, they became more independent of the Labor Ministry (Costa 1981:24–26).

This change began in the freer environment of the second Vargas government and intensified after his suicide. The Kubitschek period was one of ideological redefinition and realignment within the labor movement, with the emergence of a host of new movements on the left. During this period the "labor movement became an arena of sharp political and ideological struggle" (Harding 1973:331).

Throughout the 1950s, then, an intense struggle for control of the labor movement ensued, and within the decade, leadership largely passed from the *pelegos* to the left (Erickson 1977:104). After 1955, the Communists became dominant in the labor movements of São Paulo and Rio de Janeiro (Harding 1973:332). Furthermore, the left within labor was revitalized and reinvigorated after the splits that followed the de-Stalinization of the Communist Party, which had been pursuing a fairly conciliatory, nonrevolutionary position, working within the official framework and hoping to gain legalization. Many of the groups that split from the party were oriented to developing new currents within the labor movement. They were particularly concerned with promoting union autonomy from government and the revitalization of grassroots participation within unions. In 1956, the Independent Socialist League was formed and emphasized the importance of union autonomy. At the same time, divisions within the PCB broke into the open following the Twentieth Party Congress in the Soviet Union, and in 1957 the "renewal" faction left the party as the Renewal Current of the Brazilian Marxist Movement. Soon thereafter the MRS was founded as a renewal movement also dedicated to the rejection of Labor Ministry control and paternalism—including the syndical tax—and to democratic, mass-based unionism (Harding 1973:338–39). In the following year, 1958, the FNT was formed with a similar agenda but ideologically tied to social Christian doctrine (Chilcote 1974:68–69; Harding 1973:338–45).

In response to this activation on the left, the *pelegos* reorganized as an anti-communist group of *democráticos* (Harding 1973:330). Though they still constituted an important force within the labor movement, their position continued to wane in the face of dynamism on the left. After 1960, their influence even in the federations and confederations began to erode quite rapidly. In December 1961, following a power struggle, radicals took control of the CNTI, the largest and most powerful of the seven national confederations (Delgado 1986:52–53). With this victory, radicals controlled three of the confederations, including not only the CNTI but the strategically placed transport workers. Thus, though the labor movement remained split, the radicals came to control the majority of the confederations, including the most important ones.

With the decline in *pelego* control of the labor movement, a new factor was injected into Brazilian industrial relations and national politics. First, it meant a new dynamic in industrial relations that led to a great increase in strike activity. The dramatic increase in strikes and labor activation, particularly in 1953 and 1954, has already been mentioned. After a brief lull, the frequency of strikes again picked up, increasing, according to figures reported by L. M. Rodrigues (1981:542), from 31 in 1958 to almost six times that number in 1963.

Second, the relationship between the government and labor necessarily changed dramatically. The government could no longer rely simply on *pelego* support. It had no choice but to deal with and appeal to other, rival currents within labor to the extent that it wanted to attract labor support, an increasingly valuable commodity as the electoral regime wore on. During the Kubitschek presidency, Goulart, as vice president, attempted to promote labor unity, but failed to achieve it in light of this process of polarization and radicalization. The split that erupted into the open at the Third National Union Congress in August 1960 meant that an appeal to one current tended to alienate the other. At this Congress the anticommunist *pelegos*, with U.S. support, adopted such a hard-line and uncompromising position that Goulart thought he had no choice but to break with them. He thus emerged from the congress identified with and supported by the PTB-PCB faction (Harding 1973:440). Following this break, the *pelegos* refused to support actively the PSD-PTB coalition ticket in the 1960 presidential and vice presidential elections. Thus, on the one hand, not only did *pelego* influence decline, but to the extent it continued to exist, it ceased to be a reliable source of support for the government. Once again in 1961, the *pelegos* decided not to support Goulart in his succession struggle. On the other hand, though the leftists within the labor movement basically continued to support the government, they were increasingly autonomous from it (Vianna 1976:17, 19; Erickson 1977:62, 77). They resisted state control of unions, became more militant and combative in the sphere of industrial relations, and felt free to oppose government policy and make political demands backed by general strikes.

Under the new leadership, the government did not have a reliable mechanism of control over the labor movement, nor could the government count on labor's support.

Another aspect of the breakdown of official unionism was the formation of horizontal interunion organizations or labor centrals not provided for in the Estado Novo *enquadramento*, which remained the legal framework for labor. Again, these first attempts began immediately in the postincorporation period. In 1946 an effort to form a labor central was undertaken by the Communist Party, but it came to an abrupt halt when the party was banned. In the 1950s, a number of new organizations were formed on the state or regional level. Often these were formed in the course of strike activity and the attempt to coordinate mobilization across unions. The 1953 strike in São Paulo occasioned the formation of a unity pact among the four principal unions. During the minimum wage campaign of 1956, this pact became the basis for the PUI, which came to play an important role in labor matters. The year 1958 saw an explosion of activity. Statewide congresses were held in at least ten states (Telles 1981:64). Two organizations were formed in the two most important states, the CST, which replaced the PUI in São Paulo, and the CPOS in Guanabara (which included the city of Rio de Janeiro). In the same year, the *renovadores* formed the MRS, and the *democráticos* formed the MSD (J. A. Rodrigues 1968:163). In 1960, another radical group, the PUA, was formed in São Paulo as a result of a strike of railroad and maritime workers.

There were thus three major tendencies within the labor movement: the leftists linked to the Communist Party and the PTB, who were willing to work within the formal labor framework; the *renovadores*, who were not; and the *pelegos* or *democráticos*, who maintained close ties to the Labor Ministry. At least by 1960, the first of these, a coalition of Communists and radical nationalists, was dominant. In 1960–61 *renovadores* and *democráticos* united around the MSD, thus producing more of a bifurcation of the labor movement, with one current linked to the Communists opposing an anticommunist bloc (Costa 1981:27–33; Delgado 1986:36–37). With the competition among these different tendencies, unity in the labor movement for the moment remained elusive.

The situation, however, quickly changed. In 1962, after the victory of the left in the CNTI, the three national confederations that were then under leftist leadership began preparations to establish a labor central. Its formation was given a major impetus in July 1962, when labor groups organized the General Strike Command (CGG) to carry out a program of mass mobilization to support Goulart in the cabinet crisis, in which Congress opposed his choice of prime minister. The following month at the Fourth National Union Congress, the CGG was reorganized as the CGT (General Workers Command), which was to replace the ad hoc formation of coordinating committees around particular strikes or mobilizations with a permanently organized labor central (Delgado 1986:53–57, 187–90). The CGT did not embrace the entire labor movement, but it certainly did encompass the dominant part of it. The dissident groups for the most part were organized in the MSD—the anticommunist group of *democráticos*—which was supported by the right-wing IBAD, which represented Brazilian capital, as well as by North American groups. MSD influence was limited. Of the 338 unions of São Paulo, it could claim only 89 affiliates, and of the national confederations, it enjoyed the support of only one. Costa has further suggested that unionists in the MSD were often leaders who had been defeated in union elections (Costa 1981:32–34).

A concomitant of the breakdown of *pelego* control of the labor movement—and one that was enhanced by the formation of the new labor centrals—was labor's increasing politicization and its emergence as an important political actor. At least by the Kubitschek presidency, the radicals within the labor movement started to turn their attention to a broader range of issues, and the new citywide union organizations became "rallying-points for leftist-nationalist demands" (Harding 1973:482). During the last years of the Kubitschek presidency the labor movement "became increasingly politically conscious and politically sophisticated on such issues as nationalism, class consciousness, inflation and economic development" (Harding 1973:356). These changes in the labor movement were reflected in its internal dynamics, tendencies, and leadership, in its opposition to the government's stabilization program, and in survey data available for the period. Accordingly, a radical nationalist movement on the left grew hand in hand with the radicalization of the labor movement and its increased attention to more broadly political and basic economic issues, instead of a more narrow concern with issues of wages and labor relations. By September 1959, the Second National Union Conference adopted a series of anti-imperialist resolutions. By May 1961, when the PTB and PCB called labor leaders together for a national meeting, the three key issues were the defense of the Cuban Revolution and agrarian reform, as well as the more traditional labor issue of the removal of all restrictions on the right to strike (Harding 1973:364–69; 498).

Under Goulart the labor movement's broader political orientation became even more central. The Goulart government lurched from one crisis to another, starting with the initial question of Goulart's succession to the presidency and then the restoration of his full presidential powers, which had been abridged as part of the bargain permitting his succession. It included also a major crisis over Congress's rejection of Goulart's nominee for prime minister. In all these crises, the radical labor groups played a major role in support of the government. Indeed the political action, mass mobilizations, and strikes undertaken in these efforts were key in the outcome of each crisis. This activity had additional effects in stimulating labor coordination and the formation of labor centrals, as well as in radicalizing and enhancing the power of the labor movement as it flexed its muscles in this way (Delgado 1986:182–94).

Once the CGT was formed, labor played an even more central role in the growing radical nationalist movement. The CGT was perhaps more radical and politically oriented than might otherwise have been the case because of the boycott by the anticommunist labor groups of the congress at which it was founded. At that founding meeting, a program of structural reform and political changes was adopted. These included the right to strike, the revocation of the national security law, a 100 percent increase in the minimum salary, universal suffrage, bank reform, the limitation of profit remittances abroad, and agrarian reform (Harding 1973:560). Also adopted was the use of the general strike as the means to achieve goals and force Goulart to adopt them. Labor thus became a key actor in the campaign for "basic reforms," and the CGT was a central player at the heart of the political battles of the first half of the 1960s. Indeed, in many ways the CGT was more nearly a political organization than a labor union.[15]

Whereas labor played an important—even decisive—role in supporting Goulart with respect to issues concerning his constitutional powers as president, labor did not support him on substantive issues. Rather, given the radicalization that labor was undergoing, the CGT often opposed Goulart. The opposition was clearest with respect to Goulart's three-year development plan, which included an austerity/stabilization component that labor opposed. With labor leading the opposition, the plan was ultimately a failure. The oppositional role was also apparent in the campaign for "basic reforms," which became the core of the left's political agenda and which was spearheaded by labor (Erickson 1977:131–50). The program of "basic reforms" was an alternative to the three-year plan. That Goulart was ultimately forced to identify with and support it was a measure of his weakness and of his dependence on the CGT.

In the course of these activities, the labor movement accrued real political power and became a major political force on the national scene. Not only was labor able to exert enormous pressure around particular issues, but it became the indispensable ally of Goulart. Indeed, overturning again the original pattern of incorporation, labor became politically independent of the government and managed to reverse the traditional pattern of dependence, with Goulart more dependent on the support of labor than the CGT was on him. By the end he was following the lead of that labor central (Erickson 1977:ch. 6; Harding 1973:528, 584, 598).

As Goulart grew more dependent upon an increasingly autonomous CGT—particularly after the *pelegos*, who were losing strength in any case, had failed to mobilize on his behalf during the succession crisis—he tried to maneuver out of this situation. With the opposition mounted by the CGT to his three-year plan, Goulart tried to do an end run around the CGT by establishing a new labor central that would support him and free him from dependence on the CGT. The UST, which was founded in September 1962, was set up as a nonideological central that dedicated itself to labor issues and eschewed partisan politics (Erickson 1977:135). It was indicative of the situation that Goulart was in—the growing strength of the CGT, his weakness vis-à-vis the CGT, the lack of hegemonic resources at Goulart's disposal, the

[15] L. M. Rodrigues 1981:541, 547–48; Erickson 1977:110; Harding 1973:560.

radicalization and politicization of labor—that the UST venture was not successful. In the end, Goulart had no choice but to once again turn to the CGT as an indispensable ally.

In these various ways, the system of control established by state incorporation broke down. This change, which as we have seen began as early as 1943, accelerated during the postincorporation period. With the party a weak cooptive instrument, there was widespread ferment in the union movement as new groups and new alignments arose, calling for more radical, structural economic and social changes and championing independent unionism. With increasing popular sector demands and independence, the Brazilian elite could rely only on further state control—that is, on the means of control set up during the incorporation period: on control through the legal-regulative system, through the repression of independent groups, and through co-optation into the Labor Ministry and social security institutes. However, all three of these elements of state control began to break down under the competitive bidding for popular sector electoral support and the growing political clout of labor in a polarizing system. Key provisions of the Estado Novo labor law, still on the books with few revisions, were not enforced and others were under strong attack by organized labor. Repression became decreasingly feasible given the political context. After 1960, even much of the patronage of the Labor Ministry and the social security institutes, the main source of state co-optation of labor, was given over to independent leaders in an unsuccessful bid for their support (Erickson 1977:62–63).

By the early 1960s, then, the position of labor had changed dramatically. Throughout the 1950s changes had occurred within the labor movement, but government control was not significantly eroded (Benevides 1976:87–95). The very short period from 1960 to 1964, however, brought a sharp change as the more gradual developments of the 1950s came to a head, with the passage of leadership of the union movement to radical nationalists and the assertion of greater autonomy (Erickson 1977:62–64). The intensive strike activity and the political activation of labor of this period has led Erickson (1977:98) to identify it as one of the " 'periodic and sudden expansions in the size, strength, and activity of social movements' which Eric Hobsbawm defines as social 'explosions.' "

This is not to say that no controls over labor existed. Nor, despite the political independence and clout attained by labor, must one overstate its strength. Quite the contrary. Many provisions of the labor law were intact, and that law continued to shape the labor movement and constituted one of the bases for its fundamental weakness. The legal emphasis on the municipal level of organization meant a serious weakness at the plant level and hence weak ties between the leadership and the rank-and-file. As a result, the leadership relied on ties to the political system rather than to the grassroots as a source of their power (Erickson 1977:119-21; L. M. Rodrigues 1969:121). Clearly it was not powerful enough to prevent the coup or to determine the course of events before or after it.

The important point, however, is that in an ironic way the legacy of the most control-oriented pattern of labor incorporation was an important degree of political autonomy from governing, centrist parties, and this political independence played an important role in the process of polarization that came to characterize Brazil as soon as the authoritarian Estado Novo fell. Furthermore, with few links between the governing party and the unions, the government did not have the political resources with which to defeat the challenge of an increasingly assertive and radicalizing labor movement, a challenge that intensified in the wake of the Cuban Revolution. Indeed, far from having the political resources to secure the cooperation of the labor movement, the government faced quite the opposite situation as the labor movement's growing political clout in a weak, polarizing regime facilitated its success in dismantling at least some of the controls the state had established over it. As Ianni (1970:200) has said, "The truth is that the rule of the masses was gaining fast at a time when the political power of the bourgeoisie was weakening." In this context, labor and the left took positions and made demands they did not have the power to back up, and the right, in turn, viewed the left as an unacceptable threat. The outcome was the emergence of a substantial coalition favoring a military coup, aimed at installing a new regime capable of breaking the political deadlock and of establishing domination by the political right through coercion.

Chile. In the post-aftermath period beginning in Chile in 1952, the union movement witnessed a similar pattern of organizational consolidation and politicization. A new central, the CUT, was formed, and under its leadership labor initially withdrew from, but then reentered, the political arena. Even during the period of withdrawal, party ties to the labor movement remained strong, but it was only with the renewal of participation in the political arena that the labor movement resumed its more active role in electoral politics and defined broader political issues among its primary concerns.

During most of this period, of course, labor and the parties tied to it played an oppositional role vis-à-vis the government. Thus, labor developed quite a long history and substantial experience as an active participant in left-wing, oppositional politics. This was an important contrast with Brazil, where the postaftermath period (1960–64) was exceedingly short, and where, in any case, the parties with ties to labor did not so definitively reject collaboration with the government. Thus, even more than in the case of Brazil, the Chilean labor movement developed as both highly politicized and politically autonomous from the government, and as such it played a central role in the process of polarization that was such a prominent feature of the heritage of state incorporation.

One aspect of the labor movement's political role was its ability to constitute itself on a national level. A key feature of the Chilean labor law was the focusing of trade union activity at the plant level. This provision, which meant that collective bargaining took place at the plant level, promoted base level organization but weakened unions, since most plants were very small. Yet, though the law never envisioned an important role for labor organizations above the plant level, national confederations were formed to replace the disbanded FOCh of the pre-incorporation period. This occurred initially, as we have seen, with the formation of the CTCh in 1936.

By the end of the coalition governments of the aftermath period, however, the Chilean labor movement was in disarray. The unity that had been forged under the CTCh came unglued under the impact of splits and divisions within the Socialist Party and hostility between the Socialists and the Communists. This hostility intensified under the impact of cold war rivalries, which began during the presidency of González Videla and which were fueled in the labor arena by the pressure of rival international labor confederations, each making strong bids for Chilean affiliates.

The period 1946–53, then, was one of disintegration of the labor movement. The CTCh broke into two wings headed by Bernardo Ibáñez and Bernardo Araya respectively, and both wings lost strength and membership. The Ibáñez wing was adversely affected by political problems related to a change in political strategy to one advocating union autonomy from the government, a position Bernardo Ibáñez himself opposed. The Araya wing, in turn, was weakened by government repression, which soon resulted in the banning of the Communist Party with which that wing was affiliated. Under this pressure, labor unity gave way to a multiplicity of competing, ideologically oriented labor confederations with different international affiliates: CIOSL (affiliated with the CIO and European confederations); FSM (affiliated with Moscow); the anarcho-syndicalist MUNT; and the Socialist CRUS, formed by labor federations of the Bernardo Ibáñez wing of the CTCh (Barría 1971:34–35).

At the same time that labor unity among blue-collar workers was collapsing, the white-collar union movement was undergoing a process of restructuring and consolidation. In December 1948, the JUNECh was founded, bringing together private and public employees into a single confederation. With the blue-collar movement in disarray, it was largely under the initiative of the white-collar movement that a new labor unity was forged in 1953 with the formation of the CUT.

There were several reasons for the role of white-collar unions in this respect. In part it was a question of the political strategy of the Radical Party, which was closely tied to white-collar unions. Given the middle-class base of the Radical Party, the government was reluctant to repress the JUNECh, thus affording it a great advantage in its ability to play a leadership role within the labor movement (Barría 1971:26). Furthermore, the Radical Party, having lost power in 1952, looked to union groups as a base of support from which to carry on its opposition politics (Barría 1971:41, Angell 1972:216). In addition, economic conditions contributed to JUNECh initiatives. The inflation of the postwar years and the orthodox stabilization measures undertaken by Jorge Alessandri as minister of finance led to white-collar labor activation and the strikes of January 1950, that resulted in a new cabinet and abandonment of the economic policies. Strengthened by this result, the JUNECh turned to actively promoting a new labor central (Barría 1971:33).

By the end of the year, with the encouragement and help of the student federation, the National Committee against Price Increases was formed and achieved a temporary unification of the various major labor confederations then existing, both white- and blue-collar. The following two years, 1951–52, saw a series of attempts to achieve labor unity, but all were short lived. Finally, in February 1953 the CUT was founded, uniting the most important labor groups for the next twenty years, until it was disbanded by the military government in the mid-1970s.

During the centrist and rightist governments that came to power in the interim between the coalitional governments of the aftermath period and the election of Allende, the political role of the labor movement changed. Labor continued to maintain close ties to the parties, but it no longer collaborated with the government, forming instead part of the opposition. In addition, it initially refocused on workers' issues as it retreated from a larger political, collaborationist role. Over the period, however, and particularly under the impact of Frei's policies, it turned its attention to broader issues, becoming an important political force.

This new position of greater political autonomy from the government indeed opposition to, rather than collaboration with, the government—presented a challenge to the various governments, which were sometimes looking for an expanded base of support, but in any case were always anxious to at least neutralize and control labor politically. The successive governments tried many different approaches, but none was able to capture the labor movement or, in the end, prevent the strong polarizing dynamic that was under way.

During the aftermath period, as we have seen, the stillborn, largely apolitical union movement of the incorporation period under Carlos Ibáñez had quickly given way to a union movement closely tied to political parties and willing, even anxious, to participate in government coalitions. The CTCh itself was primarily a political entity that resulted from the Popular Front and coalitional policies of the Communist and Socialist parties. Accordingly, union demands were often subordinated to party interests. Adopting the view that the working class would gain from the developmentalist policies of the Popular Front, the CTCh joined the government, its members serving on various governmental agencies, including for example CORFO (Barría 1972:89). As Drake (1978:178–79) notes, most of the CTCh leaders were "politicians whose first loyalty was to their party, and in the 1930s the CTCh produced more gains for the Socialists and Communists than for its worker members." Organized labor, during this period, then, was substantially subordinated to the parties and their political/electoral goals of coalitional politics, often at the expense of labor. One of the most blatant examples of the contradiction was the parties' sacrifice of rural unionization in exchange for participation in the government. Party politics was also reflected, as we have seen, in the political splits that fractured the labor movement at the end of this period. The period, then, ended in failure, with the Communist and Socialist parties weakened and labor in disarray as the CTCh collapsed as a unified labor central.

The rejection of the failed pattern of collaboration and of the subordination of union interests to party-political interests began at the end of the coalition governments with the splits in the Socialist Party. It was given impetus by the new position of parties with working-class support in the opposition rather than in the governing coalition. Greater consensus around this new line was achieved after 1953, when the PSP, originally participating in the Ibáñez government, joined the opposition. Out of this ideological reorientation came a commitment to a "workers' front," which formed the basis for the formation of the FRAP, an electoral pact on the left, made up primarily of the Communist and Socialist parties along with the PSP, which, in the process of joining the other two, lost some of its prominent non-Marxists (Barría 1971:87). The new line was reinforced by the influence, on the one hand, of the anarcho-syndicalists and, on the other, of the white-collar unions, which also suddenly found themselves with ties to a party, the Radical Party, that was out of power.

The new CUT clearly embodied the new line. Its first president, Clotario Blest, whose background was in the white-collar union movement, had no affiliation to any of the major parties and led the central to a militantly antiparty position. He favored the mass insurrectional tactic of the general strike and rejected participation in the party-electoral sphere as the means to advance working-class interests (Falabella 1980:342). Though an alternative tendency unwilling to retreat from the political arena in this way continued to exist, the Blest line became dominant within the CUT. In its original Statement of Principles, the CUT declared its intention of working for the overthrow of capitalism "from a position above the parties" (Barría 1971:52–53).

The new line reinforced a situation confronted by Carlos Ibáñez that made his 1952–58 government different from those of the aftermath period. A coalition with parties attracting worker support had lent the previous governments some political leverage over labor. After the failure of the aftermath experience from the point of view of labor, Ibáñez was to inherit the same condition that he created during his first presidency: state incorporation had proceeded without the political mobilization of the working class, without the formation of a populist coalition, and without the formation of a multiclass integrative party. Now, with the brief exception of the PSP at the very beginning of his second presidency, parties appealing to both blue- and white-collar workers—the Socialists, Communists, and Radicals—were not part of the political coalition that Ibáñez brought to power, and the government had no party-political resource at its disposal for controlling labor.

The government's initial response was to attempt to create a loyal union movement on the Peronist model. In November 1952, progovernment federations were formed, the UNACh for white-collar workers and the UNT for blue-collar workers. As with the other imitations of Peronism, this one failed quickly (Bray 1961:48), with Ibáñez expressing the realization, in a personal letter to Perón, that conditions in Chile were quite different from those that Perón was concurrently facing in Argentina (cited in Bray 1961:176–81).

The failure of the proto-Peronist attempt gave greater impetus to the creation of the autonomous CUT. Ibáñez's initial cabinet included the PSP's Almeyda as minister of labor. With the collapse of the Peronist alternative, Ibáñez had little choice but to accede to the formation of the CUT, and apparently Almeyda may have facilitated this development. Once the direction of the new CUT became clearer, however, Ibáñez viewed it with greater suspicion and, under pressure from industrialists, dismissed Almeyda (Cavarozzi 1975:233–35). The next attempt to control labor was the replacement of Almeyda with Leandro Moreno G., an Ibáñez loyalist on the CUT directorate. In accordance with the apolitical orientation of its new constitution, the CUT expelled Moreno (Barría 1971:62).

Ibáñez's final attempt at establishing a form of political control was also thwarted by the autonomous Chilean labor movement and the CUT. In 1955, a labor office affiliated with ATLAS (the international Peronist confederation) was opened in Santiago in another move to create a Peronist union movement that would be loyal to the government. Protests from the CUT, however, led to the abandonment of this move as well (Bray 1961:79–80).

By the end of the Ibáñez government, then, an independent labor movement politically independent from the state had emerged. Its unified organizational expression was the CUT, which adopted an apolitical orientation that rejected collaboration with the government and which adopted the general strike strategy rather than participation in the electoral-political arena. Attempts by Ibáñez to assert control by forging political ties failed, leaving continued reliance on the labor law and on repression as the only mechanisms of control, which, indeed, were used.

During the Alessandri government from 1958 to 1964, the labor movement experienced another change in orientation: a shift from the antipolitical, general strike emphasis to a reentry into the political arena. The general strike tactic had proved a failure. In part this failure was due to divisions within the labor movement, as when state workers refused to support the plan for a general strike in September 1954, and when left-wing parties opposed the general strike called by the CUT in January 1956 and ordered their militants back to work (Barría 1971:68, 81–82). In part the failure also was a result of government repression. This was seen most dramatically with the general strikes of October 1954, called in response to an anti-inflationary policy based on wage compression, and of January 1956, similarly called in response to new proposals, based on the Klein-Saks mission's recommendations, for controlled wages and uncontrolled prices. In both cases the government met the general strike with a declaration of a state of siege and the arrest of CUT leaders—including Blest, who was imprisoned for 110 days in 1956 (Barría 1971:69–70, 81–82). Thus, the general strike tactic often failed to achieve substantive results and left the labor movement tremendously weakened by both internal recriminations and repression. The general strike tactic of the CUT, in the absence of political ties with the Congress, exposed the unions to the full force of government repression, leaving them "defeated and demoralized" (Falabella 1980:343).

At the same time that the general strike tactic was resulting in failure, political action became more attractive. The antiparty sentiment that had ushered in the Ibáñez government in 1952 was abating, and traditional parties rebounded in the 1957 congressional elections. On the left, the Socialist Party was reunified in 1957, and the repeal of the Law for the Defense of Democracy (LDD) in 1958 led to the relegalization of the Communist Party. Also, the reform of the electoral system in 1958 changed the rules of the electoral game in a way more favorable to labor. Furthermore, both the repeal of the LDD and the electoral reform were the result of a victory in that political game by the opposition parties and the CUT, thus underscoring the possibilities afforded by participation in the political arena. At least equally important was the success of the left parties, united in the FRAP, in the 1958 presidential elections. The near victory of Allende meant that the potential payoff in the electoral game jumped enormously.

In the first part of the Alessandri presidency, these tendencies continued. They culminated in a CUT leadership crisis in August 1961 in which the tactic of the general strike was decisively rejected and Blest resigned, charging that interests of the parties were being placed ahead of those of unions (Barría 1971:103–7). In his resignation speech Blest declared, "I believe in direct massive action; others in legalism and co-operation with the pseudo-democratic bourgeoisie. The CUT ought to be the leader and vanguard of the working class and not the simple plaything of events and circumstances, and what is worse, an instrument of organization alien to the Chilean labour movement" (quoted in Angell 1972:220).

During the Alessandri presidency, there was no room for any type of collaboration between the government and the labor movement. The parties to which labor was closely tied were clearly in the opposition, and Alessandri's initial emphasis on staffing his government with direct representatives of the bourgeoisie alienated even the parties on the right, not to mention those with a labor constituency. The political autonomy of labor from the state was reinforced by Alessandri's right-wing, laissez-faire policies that sought to have the state withdraw from any role in industrial relations and leave labor to confront capital directly (Cavarozzi 1975:356–61, 364).

The pattern of political independence of the labor movement from the government continued under Frei. Though, to a much greater extent than either Ibáñez or Alessandri, Frei sought to mobilize a mass support base for his government and to establish some form of political control over the labor movement, he did not succeed in establishing cooperative relations with labor. On the contrary, the entire Frei period was one of very conflictual government-labor relations.

The reasons for the failure to establish co-operative ties were both economic and political. Labor, for its part, showed no inclination to revert to a collaborationist strategy (Falabella 1980:344), particularly following the Cuban Revolution, which injected a more radicalized orientation into the labor movement and the left parties. The government, for its part, was pursuing an economic strategy of international opening in which there was little room for cooperation (Stallings 1978:163, 166; Cavarozzi and Petras 1974:533). Indeed, Frei pursued a policy of wage restraint (Angell 1972:198). Politically, in seeking a mass support base, the government looked to the peasantry and urban poor—still unorganized sectors—rather than organized blue-collar workers. While the PDC drew significant support among the organized labor movement, a great deal of this came from white-collar and public sector unions (Angell 1972:184–86). In fact, the Frei government, far from seeing the labor movement as an ally, sought to weaken and isolate it as a source of political competition and opposition to its economic program (Petras 1969:246ff; Angell 1972:202). The Frei government, then, did not seek the support or the cooperation of labor, but instead assumed a position of trying simultaneously to break, restructure, and circumvent it (Miquel 1979:25–29).

Several aspects of Frei's labor policy antagonized the labor movement. The first was the attempt to weaken the CUT and establish rival confederations. This policy began with a proposed reform of the labor code that would have allowed more than one union per plant and outlawed the closed shop. These provisions would have weakened existing unions and created the space for the Christian Democrats to establish parallel unions. When the resulting protest led to the abandonment of the proposed change, the government turned to the sponsoring of a rival confederation. In this endeavor its success was no greater than that of Ibáñez. Three separate confederations appeared in succession: the MUTCh, the CNT, and the UTRACh. None was able to attract much support and all proved short-lived.

The government also sought to circumvent the labor movement by separating it from policy formation at all levels. It was largely shut out of representation within the government, despite the fact that before assuming the presidency Frei had been an advocate of union participation on economic and social councils and agencies, arguing that "unions must have a decisive role in the organization of the economic mechanism" (quoted in Angell 1972:198). In addition, the government took initiatives in which it tried to concentrate in the hands of the executive policies in which labor traditionally played a key role. One important example was the constitutional reform of 1969–70, which strengthened the role of the president at the expense of the legislature, where labor and the left parties had influence. This change affected a number of areas including budgetary matters and salary readjustments. Ironically, this enhanced presidential power, which included the power to set minimum wages, did not go into effect until the next presidential term—that of Allende (Barría 1971:149–50; A. Valenzuela 1978:37).

Many substantive policies were also viewed as antithetical to the interests of labor. One of the more serious conflicts occurred in 1967 over the government's *chiribono* policy of wage adjustment, forced savings, and national investment. According to this plan, a 20 percent wage adjustment would be granted to wage earners, but 5 percent, to be withheld in a "Workers' Capitalization Fund" and used for national investments, would be issued in government bonds. The plan was vehemently attacked by organized labor, which argued that the savings, at the modest interest rate proposed, would be wiped out by inflation. Probably even more central to labor's opposition, however, was the restriction on the right to strike, which came part and parcel with the plan (Angell 1972:202–3; Stallings 1978:110–11).

Another element in the hostile relations between labor and the government was the latter's use of repression. The most blatant example occurred at the El Salvador mine in the first part of 1966. When workers at that mine struck over wages, copper workers throughout the North struck in sympathy. The government decreed emergency zones and declared the strike illegal, but the incident did not end until the government sent in the military and six miners were killed and many wounded (Barría 1971:130–31; Angell 1972:200). "Frei . . . accused the marxist parties of inciting the trouble; [but] whatever the rights and wrongs of the matter, Frei's defense of the troops increased the union's hostility to the government and provided a frequently brandished symbol of its alleged brutality and indifference to the labour movement" (Angell 1972:200). While that incident was the most notable, it was not unique. Particularly toward the end of the government with the turn to the right, repression increased as national police were called in to break up strikes (Stallings 1978:114).

The government attitude toward the CUT was expressed in strong rhetorical terms that exacerbated the mutual hostility. For instance, the government labeled the CUT's demand for a thirteenth month income raise a FRAP-inspired subterfuge and called the CUT a "decadent force" (Barría 1971:115–16). Again, when forced to abandon the *chiribono* scheme, an indignant Frei attacked labor leaders as irresponsible (Angell 1972:203).

Government policy toward labor had the effect of further radicalizing labor and impelling it, and the CUT in particular, to define broader issues as central to its interests. Each offensive of the government defined a set of issues and put labor in a defensive position from which it felt obliged to respond. For instance, Frei's attempt to revise the labor code led not only to CUT opposition, but also to the clarification of CUT's own program of change. Thus, the 1965 "struggle platform" of the CUT now included demands for job security, committees of the unemployed, union management of social security, the defense of syndical unity, and extended rights for peasant unions (Barría 1971:120–22). As part of the escalation of conflict surrounding the El Salvador mine strike, labor sought to win a better position for Chile and Chilean labor in the bill providing for the Chileanization of the copper industry. As conflict with the government was extended into other arenas, the CUT's "struggle platforms" reflected its concern with broader economic and political issues. A defensive CUT began to outline positions on inflation, tax policy, and agrarian reform. In response to the *chiribono* plan, the CUT presented an alternative that emphasized a national public works program that would reduce unemployment. In 1967, the CUT also adopted a resolution against "social conciliation" and adopted an anti-U.S. position on the war in Vietnam (Barría 1971:131, 139–41, 146).

In general, then, the Frei period was one of state-labor conflict in which many within the labor movement considered the government to be overtly antilabor (Stallings 1978:102). Frei did not even have the sympathy of the labor section of the Christian Democratic Party, which, having left the CUT in 1965, reentered the central three years later over his opposition. When the party split in 1969, most of the labor section remained loyal to the PDC, but it gradually came to adopt the perspective of the rebel MAPU faction (Angell 1972:182). As we have seen, even the white-collar workers of CEPCh joined the CUT during the Frei government. In the last year or two of the Christian Democratic government, then, relations with labor had deteriorated. Labor activation and protest reached a new threshold with the beginnings of factory seizures in cases of labor conflict (Stallings 1978:116). For all the reformist theory and communitarian rhetoric, the Christian Democrats in power did not achieve a cooperative relationship with labor, far less embrace labor within the party in any sort of hegemonic project. On the contrary, as we have seen, Frei stepped into a polarizing system, which defied his goal of depolarization; instead his government "aggravated polarization and worsened the deadlock" (A. Valenzuela 1978:37–38).

One moment of cooperation did occur at the very end of the Frei period, on the occasion of the *tacnazo* of October 1969, when the CUT mobilized support in favor of the government, which was then faced with a military uprising. As a result, the government, although still refusing to recognize the CUT legally, for the first time negotiated an accord with the labor central on wage adjustments. The accord followed the usual Frei policy of wage adjustments equal to the previous year's inflation rate, but it provided for about double that increase for the minimum wage and the family allowance for blue-collar workers (Stallings 1978:121, Barría 1971:151). The spirit of cooperation, however, was short lived. The following July the CUT called a general strike with the purpose of "defending the democratic electoral practice, denouncing coup and terrorist adventures, and obtaining solutions to urgent economic problems [and restraining the] escalation of repression and terror by the government and the Right" (cited in Stallings 1978:121; see also Barría 1971:154).

Quite obviously, state-labor relations changed dramatically with the election of Allende. Whereas the parties dominant among the working class and in the CUT had remained in opposition in the prior postaftermath governments, now they formed the governing coalition, and the working class became the main pillar of support for the government.

The advantages labor reaped under the Allende government were enormous. Falabella (1980:362) has suggested that the Popular Unity government considered virtually all of the CUT's historic platforms and demands and met most of them. CUT leaders entered the government and held ministerial positions (finance, labor, and public works, and, somewhat later, interior). They sat on major government planning bodies and economic organs, such as ODEPLAN and CORFO, and became key participants in policy making not only for labor issues but for the public sector more generally (Stallings 1978:127–28).

The CUT for the first time was given legal recognition, as were federations of state workers and other sectoral federations, which were granted the right to bargain collectively without special government decrees (Falabella 1980:361, 369–70). These provisions for legal recognition were contained in the first of a series of annual agreements the CUT negotiated with the government. These included wages as well as other labor matters. The 1971 agreement provided for a 66.7 percent increase in the minimum wage for 1971, almost double both the previous year's rate of inflation and the increase in the minimum salary for white-collar workers. The wage policy resulted in a redistribution that was favorable not only to blue-collar workers vis-à-vis white-collar workers, but also to labor vis-à-vis capital. In the same year the share of national income that went to wages rose from 55 percent to 66 percent (Falabella 1980:362). The accord also covered questions of redundancy, pensions and family benefits, and worker control of the social security institutes (Falabella 1980:369–70). Finally, it included worker participation in state-controlled factories.

There is no question of working-class support for the Allende government. In the electoral arena the UP coalition, and Allende's Socialist Party in particular, did very well in the 1971 municipal elections. Perhaps even more indicative was the massive mobilization to support Allende undertaken by workers in times of crisis. Most notable was the occasion of the general strike called by the right in October 1972. Starting out as a truckers' strike, it was quickly joined by retail merchants and professionals while SOFOFA called for factory lockouts (Stallings 1978:141). The organizational and mobilizational response by workers in support of Allende was impressive indeed. Groups of factories had previously organized *cordones industriales* for mobilization and collective action. Both the CUT and these *cordones*, as well as newly formed *comandos comunales* comprised of the *cordones* and other mass-based groups, went all out to provide transportation and services disrupted by the strike and to seize factories under lockout in order to keep the economy functioning.

Yet, despite this support, the dynamic of polarization in Chilean politics meant that parties in Allende's coalition could not be counted on to line up the working class behind government policy or to prevent the left, both within and outside of the UP coalition, from engaging in dissensus politics. As in Brazil, the left supported Allende's presidency and went all out to meet any challenge to his position, but a significant part of it was unwilling to support him on certain substantive policies or in his attempt to maintain a multiclass alliance and carve out some middle ground.

From the beginning, Allende attempted to base his peaceful transition to socialism on "a strategy of uniting all classes against the monopolists, the landed oligarchy, and the foreign capitalist sectors" (Spence 1978:140). Government policy outlined three areas of economic enterprises: the Private Area, the Social Area of state-owned firms run jointly by workers and state representatives, and the Mixed Area of joint state-private ownership. After the first year, inflation, economic bottlenecks, and political opposition began to mount. At this point the Allende UP faction turned to a new strategy that would make an accommodation with the capitalist sector. This line emphasized the "battle of production" and sought to limit the expropriation of firms into the Social Area (Spence 1978:146–48). The Communist Party and the Allende wing of the Socialist Party were sufficiently strong to carry the CUT in support of this consolidation line. The left wing of the Socialists and MAPU, along with MIR, rejected that line.

Accelerated by this political fragmentation of the UP coalition, popular mobilization escaped government control.[16] Most notable in the labor field was the spread of factory occupations that took place with the goal of provoking government intervention in a way that would put firms in the so-called Social or Mixed Areas, thereby nationalizing them and paving the way for worker participation. On one occasion, after the government refused to take over an occupied factory, other factories in the area united behind the demand. The outcome was not only the retreat of the government, which backed down and thus undermined its attempt to reassure the right, but also the formation of the first *cordón industrial*, a spontaneously formed, locally based geographic grouping of factories. The *cordones*, which often acted in concert, relied on tactics such as roadblocks and mass demonstrations and acted independently of the CUT and the government (Stallings 1978:137).

Another area in which control of the working class eluded the government was in wage demands. Though the government was able to come to annual agreements with the CUT on wage adjustments, these were commonly ignored in plant-level collective bargaining by union leaders, who were skeptical about the future course of inflation. Their rejection of the CUT-government guidelines was aggravated by the opportunistic policy of the PDC of making life difficult for the government by encouraging such wage demands (Stallings 1978:129; Landsberger and McDaniel 1976:508).

Peasant Mobilization

In addition to labor mobilization, peasant mobilization was also a feature of the political dynamic in Brazil and Chile in the 1950s and 1960s (and, for Chile, the early 1970s). As Loveman (1976b:239, 241) has argued for Chile and as could be also be said for Brazil, the democratic system as it existed was premised on the *hacendado* system and the political resources it gave the right. A threat to that system could constitute a fundamental challenge to the regime. Peasant mobilization was certainly important in sharpening the crisis as it was developing, intensifying the polarization, and creating an atmosphere of assault on private property and on the system as it was constituted. Nevertheless, peasant mobilization played perhaps a less central role than labor mobilization in overall political developments. Roxborough

[16] A. Valenzuela 1978:62; Stallings 1978:137; Landsberger and McDaniel 1976; Spence 1978:153ff.

et al. (1977:135) have argued that "although there were important developments in the agrarian sector, the fate of the Chilean revolution was determined primarily by the developing class struggle between the urban working
class and the bourgeoisie, and by the response of the armed forces to these
developments." This assessment of the impact of peasant mobilization was
even clearer in the case of Brazil, where there were some indications that by
the time of the coup in 1964, a more limited peasant mobilization may have
already peaked (Flynn 1978:258–59).

As we have seen, not only was there no mobilization of the peasantry as a
support group during the incorporation period, in contrast to the cases of Mexico and Venezuela, but the peasantry was not included in the new "corporative" arrangements that set up a system of legal union organizations for
urban labor. Instead, part of the implicit accommodationist bargain was the
maintenance of social relations in the countryside, and control of the peasantry continued to be exercised by the traditional system of clientelism and
a kind of electoral manipulation, known as the "herd vote" in Brazil (Flynn
1978:258), which perpetuated the rule of the local and regional elite. Unlike
Mexico and Venezuela, agrarian reform was not on the agenda until the
1960s when, with U.S. encouragement through the Alliance for Progress, it
became part of the arsenal of anticommunist weapons following the Cuban
Revolution.

During the aftermath period, rural mobilization occurred in both countries. In Brazil the Communist Party began an organizing campaign among
the peasantry between 1945 and 1947. It achieved substantial success, electing Communist representatives to municipal and state assemblies despite
the literacy requirement. In Chile, as we have seen, both the Communists
and Socialists made various attempts to organize among the peasantry during
the aftermath period of the 1930s and 1940s. In both countries, however,
these early organizations came to naught. In Brazil, the Communist Party
was soon outlawed and the movement collapsed. In Chile, the Communists
and Socialists entered into a series of agreements with the governing Radical
Party to forego rural organizing as the price of remaining in the coalition
government. By 1947 and 1948 laws were passed that denied the right to organize rural unions and outlawed the Communist Party.

In the mid- to late 1950s, rural organizing was resumed in both countries,
further stimulated in Chile by a 1958 electoral reform law that constituted
an initial attack on the electoral hold of the rural elite over the peasantry and
thus invited the organizing activities of other parties. In the 1960s, rural organizing escalated as a reaction to both the revolutionary and counterrevolutionary implications of the Cuban Revolution. Although in both countries
the governments themselves played a part in these organizing activities, they
did not have already in place a party with affiliated peasant organizations that
could be used as an instrument of co-optation, like those in Mexico and Venezuela. Instead, as with labor, the new rural organizations to some extent
were forces for the growth of radicalism within the governing parties (the

PTB in Brazil and the PDC and later the UP in Chile) and for political polarization more generally.

Brazil. Starting in the mid-1950s, many groups in Brazil were active in rural organizing: the Church, the Communist Party, other Marxist groups, important political leaders in the Northeast, and finally the Goulart government. Two of the most important groups were the peasant leagues of the Northeast and the rural unions led by the Communist Party.

The peasant leagues, under the leadership of Francisco Julião, emphasized the organization of those working the land under conditions of precarious tenure, for example, sharecroppers, tenant farmers, and squatters, as well as those who had lost land from the spread of large-scale commercial farming. Starting out with limited aims, such as the provision of agricultural inputs, they soon broadened their demands to include agrarian reform, the right to rural unionization, increased minimum wages, and the abolition of the literacy requirement for the suffrage (Moraes 1970:467–68; Flynn 1978:260ff).

Assessments of the peasant leagues differ among analysts. Some emphasize their moderate nature, pointing especially to certain qualities of Julião and characterizing him as a large landlord himself, who was an opportunist with his eye on national politics.[17] Others see the peasant leagues as potentially more radical. Julião traveled to the Soviet Union, China, and Cuba, and, according to Page (1972:92), he drew inspiration from the Cuban Revolution. In any case, in that year, the peasant leagues formed a committee expressing solidarity with the Cuban Revolution and promoting agrarian reform. In the following years, in a period of radicalization and mobilization for militant action, some leagues prepared for guerrilla warfare and several skirmishes took place.[18]

Consistent with its focus on working-class unionization, the emphasis of the Communist Party was on the organization of rural workers rather than peasant leagues. In 1957 the PCB formed the ULTAB, particularly among sugar and coffee workers, to press for collective bargaining and improved working conditions. The PCB was anxious to join forces with the peasant leagues, but Julião rejected its initiatives (Page 1972:82).

By the early 1960s, then, peasant mobilization and agitation had reached a new stage, and in the northeastern state of Pernambuco, where the peasant leagues were most active, the hegemony of the PSD had been broken and was replaced with a loose leftist coalition. To deal with the situation, the new government of Goulart became a participant in peasant organizing as well, hoping to control and co-opt the process. In 1961, Goulart called a National Peasants' Congress, in which the ULTAB participated and accepted a reformist line. Julião, advocating a more radical agrarian reform, refused to participate. The cooperation between the government and the ULTAB isolated the peasant leagues and weakened that movement, since the ULTAB unions were given the benefits of access and financial support, and, after the Rural

[17] Leeds 1964:192–93; Moraes 1970:470–71; Flynn 1978:261–64.
[18] Moraes 1970:484–84; Hewlett 1980:388; Page 1972:94.

Workers Law of 1963, the advantage of legal recognition (Page 1972:83, 158). The leagues then began to disintegrate, but unrest in the Northeast continued, and the new governor, Miguel Arraes, took up a new form of radical challenge, perpetuating the political polarization. Like Brizola, the PTB governor continued to pressure the Goulart government from the left. Even with the weakening of the leagues, the PTB was not an instrument through which Goulart could mobilize support in the Northeast, but rather was a vehicle through which polarization was expressed.

In November 1963, in what many see as a government attempt to undercut the ULTAB, the minister of labor sponsored the formation, by the ULTAB, the PTB, and other parties, of a new rural workers confederation, the CONTAG. The CONTAG cooperated with the government and supported its mild agrarian reform bill. But even this moderate proposal, which defended private property and set no maximum property limits, was controversial in the polarizing atmosphere of Brazil. "The right, especially those close to Lacerda, portrayed the demand for agrarian reform as the thin end of the wedge, the start of an attack on all private property" (Flynn 1978:267). It was defeated in Congress.

In the next months, the general process of polarization had advanced yet further, and agrarian reform remained an important issue. In March 1964, Goulart held a rally and championed a program of "basic reforms." These included nationalization of oil refineries, the enfranchisement of illiterates, legalization of the Communist Party, university reform, and constitutional reform. At the same time, Goulart announced the signing of a land reform decree. The reaction was immediate, and the crisis, compounded by a naval mutiny, reached the boiling point, to be resolved within days by a military coup.

Chile.   The Chilean peasantry, undergoing a much more extensive process of organization and mobilization over a longer period of time, played an even more important role in the process of political polarization. During the Alessandri government, electoral reforms had the effect of reducing the possibilities for fraud and expanding the electorate. These changes provided an incentive for the PDC and the FRAP parties to turn their attention to the peasantry and seek to expand their support in the countryside. Under the pressure of peasant organizing, party competition in the rural areas, and U.S. urging through the Alliance for Progress, the Alessandri government passed an agrarian reform bill in 1962, but little was done to implement it.

More dramatic changes were visible once the Christian Democrats took office. The PDC saw the still unorganized peasantry as one of its major constituencies and set about trying to attract rural support and develop a firm base of rural organizations. In the years before 1967, when the Frei government was able to pass its own agrarian reform law, it used and expanded the Alessandri law and instituted a number of legal and administrative innovations that had a significant impact on property relations and the formation of unions in rural Chile (Loveman 1976b:248–49). In 1967 two important laws were passed: a law that guaranteed the right of all rural workers to join unions and a new agrarian reform law that provided for the expropriation of holdings above a certain size, with exceptions for efficient producers.

Though the laws had a big impact on the Chilean countryside, important changes can be dated from the onset of the Frei presidency. Government agencies and Church and Marxist groups had all started to organize rural unions and submit labor petitions even before 1967. Membership in rural unions increased from under 1,700 in 1964, to over 10,000 in 1966, and to nearly 115,000 in 1970 (Loveman 1976:253; Stallings 1978:246). Rural strikes increased from 43 in 1964, to 457 in 1966, to 1,580 in 1970 (Loveman 1976b:251). Expropriations increased less dramatically over the 1965–70 period, but totaled over 1,300 properties and 3.4 million hectares that were distributed to about 35,000 peasants—though this was only about a third of the government's original goal (Loveman 1976b:259). By the end of the Frei government, about half of the peasantry had been organized in some form of class association, including unions, cooperatives, and organizations of reform recipients (Loveman 1976b:260). Finally, illegal occupations of land increased from eight in 1968 to 73 and 220 in the next two years respectively (Stallings 1978:115n).

There is little consensus on the interpretation of this massive change in rural organization and mobilization. The two opposing views are represented by Landsberger and McDaniel (1976), who argue that Chile was experiencing a process of "hypermobilization," and A. Valenzuela (1978:30), who argues that this revealed a process of controlled mobilization that occurred as a result of purposive government policy. Given the division within the PDC and the polarization it was experiencing, one can reasonably stake out a middle ground by suggesting that while much of the mobilization took place under the guidance of the PDC, this did not necessarily mean that it was controlled by the Frei government. In the context of polarization, the party was split and many of the workers in the agrarian reform agencies were in the left wing of the party, carrying out an agrarian policy sometimes in surprising independence from the Frei wing of the party.

The Popular Unity government of Allende was committed to the destruction of the hacienda system, and, working within the framework of the Frei law, it lowered the maximum size of holding exempted from reform. By the end of 1972, about 33 percent of agricultural production, 20 percent of the rural labor force, and half of the irrigated land was in the reform sector (Roxborough et al. 1977:137).

The Allende years saw a dramatic increase in strikes and land seizures. In the first 18 months of the new government, about 1,700 land seizures occurred, many of which were answered with vigilante attempts by landlords to regain control (Loveman 1976b:266). In general, these actions were not taken in opposition to the government, which earned much sympathy among the peasantry. More typically, they were an effort to push the government farther and faster than it wanted to go in speeding up the pace of expropriation, drawing attention to new areas for expropriation, and attempting to incorporate properties that were smaller than the legal maximum.

On top of these demands, the various forms of protest reflected a layer of partisan politics and ideological differences. The Socialists, MAPU, and the MIR were committed to the elimination of the agrarian bourgeoisie. Allende, by contrast, felt dependent on the rural bourgeoisie for its contribution to agricultural production. Accompanying these differences were differences in political tactics. Allende was committed to work within the legal framework and adopted a consolidation line of trying to cooperate with the center. The left rejected both of these and supported land occupations, illegal strikes, and confrontations involving attempts by Indian groups to recover their ancestral lands (Roxborough et al. 1977:143; Loveman 1976b:254).

"From the start, the government lost the initiative to its leftist critics and was forced to react to militant *campesino* movements" (Loveman 1976b:264). Furthermore, the mobilizations often involved not only specific demands, but also a redistribution of power and assumption of grassroots control over important areas of decision-making (Spence 1978:161). This, then, was another face of dissensus politics, which was part of the polarization process.

Thus, in the sphere of peasant politics as in other domains, both Brazil and Chile experienced polarization and failures of conflict-regulation. As noted throughout, the character and strength of social forces that underlay this polarization differed greatly between the two countries. At the same time, they shared an important commonality at the macro-political level that was a legacy of state incorporation: the *absence* of a majoritarian or near majoritarian party, that grew out of a populist coalition, and that served as a principal mechanism of political mediation. This commonality is crucial to understanding their experience in the heritage period. Contrasting patterns, in which such parties were established as a legacy of party incorporation, are the focus of the following sections.

MEXICO AND VENEZUELA: INTEGRATIVE PARTY SYSTEMS

The political legacy of party incorporation in Mexico and Venezuela presented a striking contrast to the legacy of state incorporation in Brazil and Chile. It was characterized by a party-political system that was integative, not polarizing; that was one-party dominant or two-party with centripetal tendencies, not multiparty with centrifugal tendencies; that institutionalized something approaching a "coalition of the whole," not fractionalized, unstable coalitions; and that embodied important conflict-limiting mechanisms permitting the formation of consistent policy with some gradual, pendular swings, not accelerating zero-sum conflict that led to policy vacillation and immobilism. It was characterized as well by the predominance of centrist, multiclass parties that politically incorporated the working class electorally within the governing coalition, rather than by the relegation of parties with substantial working-class support to a position of nearly permanent opposition; by relatively greater reliance on hegemonic rather than coercive control over the activities of the labor movement; and by a labor movement that provided an important base of support for the regime, rather than by the political autonomy of the working class from centrist, governing parties. The two sets of regimes had different political resources with which to confront political and economic challenges. Likewise, the popular sectors had different resources, opportunities, and constraints in their political struggle. The outcome in Mexico and Venezuela was a stable hegemonic regime that weathered the economic crises and political challenges that confronted Latin American countries from the late 1950s through the 1970s.

In both Mexico and Venezuela, radical populism accomplished the incorporation of the popular sectors as a support group for the state. The result of the changes in the aftermath of incorporation was a new governing coalition, which included the dominant economic sectors, at least in a programmatic way if not in terms of functional or formal representation within the party; which excluded the left; and which continued to include the popular sectors. However, the mechanisms used were quite different in the two countries.

In Mexico, the mechanism was the one-party dominant regime. The PRI had been able to prevent its own ouster from power in the wake of the intense polarization of the incorporation period. As a result it was able to muster sufficient state and political resources to maintain its hegemonic position and the broad coalition it embraced. AD, having been ousted from power, was in a much weaker position. Unable to establish a stable civilian regime through its extensive mobilization of support in the incorporation period, AD came to rely on the interparty pact. This formula of an interparty pact provided the means of forming a broad, inclusive coalition—not so much within the party, as in Mexico, but among the major parties.

Thus, while the PRI in Mexico moved to establish a semicompetitive one-party dominant party system, AD in Venezuela oversaw the reestablishment of a competitive multiparty regime, but one in which political conflict was limited through interparty pacts and coalitions. Both countries, then, emerged from the aftermath of incorporation with integrative party systems that embraced a broad coalition, with only marginal groups outside of the major parties. This was the party heritage of incorporation, though both systems, especially the Venezuelan, evolved somewhat through the 1970s.

Far from being a vehicle through which polarization occurred, the party systems of Mexico and Venezuela functioned as integrative mechanisms that avoided or minimized future polarization, afforded the state substantial legitimacy, and provided the basis for consistent policy formation. The party system enhanced the hegemony of the regime in at least three ways: it embodied a progressive ideology, it held the partisan loyalties of the popular sectors, and it bound the functional organizations of the popular sectors to a centrist state. Whereas labor unions in Brazil and Chile were tied to increasingly radical and class-oriented parties or party fractions that, until the governments of Goulart and Allende, were in a position of permanent opposition (or at most, a very subordinate partner in a formal, electoral coalition), in Mexico and Venezuela unions were closely tied to the governing parties. We have seen that in the aftermath of incorporation, the party put much emphasis on retaining its close ties to unions, and this party-union link remained an important part of the political heritage. In both countries, these labor-party ties afforded the state significant influence in union leadership selection and activities and hence in the management of labor-capital relations.

Just as these regimes, with their formal links to both urban and rural mass organizations, were able to contain the impact of emerging dissident labor groups, they similarly provided the political resources to deal with independent peasant groups. Both the PRI and AD continued to receive overwhelming support among rural voters. However, the rapid urbanization that occurred in both countries meant that both parties faced a potential challenge in attempting to maintain their overall level of mass support, since both parties did relatively less well in major urban areas and among the unorganized urban informal sector.

In Mexico and Venezuela, then, the heritage of party incorporation and its mobilization of the working class as a support group was the creation of an inclusionary centrist coalition that afforded those two countries a long period of hegemonic politics. Unlike Brazil and Chile, they enjoyed political stability and escaped the extended and harsh repression of military authoritarianism. Yet these advantages were not without costs in terms of the political autonomy of popular sector groups, the pace of reform, and the inability to pursue more redistributive policies.

Unlike the other countries analyzed in this book, with the exception of Colombia, in Mexico and Venezuela no military coup dramatically brought to a close the period discussed in this chapter. For present purposes, we will follow the analysis from the end of the aftermath through the 1970s—or more precisely, to the end of the López Portillo presidency in 1982 in Mexico and to the end of the Carlos Andrés Pérez presidency in 1978 in Venezuela.

Though the Mexican and Venezuelan regimes did not experience the sharp discontinuities of military intervention that abruptly overturned regimes elsewhere, the question nevertheless arises of whether the political patterns of hegemonic policies that will be described below were changing incrementally and particularly what might be the impact of the debt crisis and economic reorientations of the 1980s. This issue will be briefly addressed in the concluding chapter.

MEXICO

Mexico entered the 1950s with a one-party dominant regime that was better institutionalized than ever before. The radical populism of the incorporation period had won the loyalty of the popular sectors as a support group for the state. The aftermath of incorporation built on that foundation a new set of relationships between the state and civil society and transformed the intermediating political structures. The changes, embodied in the reorganization of the party into the PRI, altered the balance of power within the party by further subordinating the role of the popular sectors, particularly organized labor, which had been the most autonomous of the sectors. The changes in electoral law institutionalized the PRI's preeminent position and the one-party dominant system. The expulsion of the left provided greater ideological homogeneity within the party at the same time that the PRI was able to construct and maintain a coalition of the whole. If the argument could be made that the PRM as reorganized by Cárdenas was a coalition party, at least by the time of PRI's reorganization in 1946, if not before, it had become a "corporative" party—a mechanism of interest intermediation that was able to control its constituencies and provide a number of services for the state.

The heritage of incorporation and its aftermath in Mexico was a hegemonic party that incorporated the popular sectors and their unions and virtually monopolized the political arena, allowing at best only marginal and largely symbolic opposition. With the shift to the center to accommodate the dominant economic sectors, the nature of the alliance with the popular sectors changed. It became less one in which the organized popular sectors were a relatively autonomous alliance partner, whose support was bargained for and won with concessions, and more one in which they were deprived, for the most part, of a basis for autonomous action and retained as a co-opted support group providing legitimacy for the regime. Thus, the ultimate heritage of incorporation was a party that embraced a coalition of the whole and enjoyed a number of hegemonic resources: it embodied a progressive ideology, it held the partisan loyalties of the popular sectors, and it bound the functional organizations of the popular sectors to a conservative state.

During the period presently under discussion, that is from 1952 to 1982, the Mexican government had to address a number of issues and challenges that toppled governments elsewhere in Latin America. Though the Mexican party system experienced some changes in response to these challenges, it contained them, remained stable, and was characterized primarily by continuity.

Overview of the Party System

The hegemonic one-party dominant regime in Mexico was characterized by the overwhelming predominance of what can be called an official or state party. The party, after all, had not been formed either out of a parliamentary bloc or out of groups in civil society. Rather, it had been created by the Mexican executive (though, as we have seen, this was the informal executive power of Calles during the Maximato) as an instrument for the centralization of state power. From the time of its formation, then, and particularly after the changes of the 1940s, the party did not serve as a base of legislative power or as an organization for fighting competitive elections but rather as a source of services for an increasingly centralized state with a weak legislature: it was a mechanism of executive power, of interest intermediation for the state, and of plebiscitary legitimation.

The Dominant-Party System. Though the dominance of the official party had been a prominent feature of the Mexican political landscape since the party's inception in 1929, its fundamentally unchallenged position was not attained for nearly three decades. The 1934 election had gone quite smoothly, but crisis again surrounded the 1940 succession. Though steps were taken during the aftermath period to reduce political conflict through the further institutionalization of one-party dominance, this process of strengthening the government party and reducing political dissent was not completed until the following *sexenio*, from 1952 to 1958. Despite the changes in the electoral laws and the attempt to avert the opposition that crystallized around the elections of 1940, the presidential elections of 1946 and 1952 saw the greatest challenges mounted to the official candidate since the party was founded. However, during the time period considered here (to 1982), these were the last "seriously" contested elections, and the one-party regime became well institutionalized thereafter.

The 1952 elections took place amid widespread disaffection caused by Alemán's policies. In addition to the conservative turn of his presidency, which alienated more progressively oriented groups, economic problems and blatant corruption adversely affected the sympathies of other groups. Furthermore, Alemán governed in a very authoritarian manner, imposing his will and running "roughshod" over the party in matters such as the nominations for governorships, instead of engaging in the traditional political consultations and negotiations (Brandenburg 1964:103). On top of this, Alemán's attempt to impose a conservative successor over the opposition of other party leaders aggravated the sense of crisis and brought into the open splits within the "Revolutionary Family," with the clear emergence of Cardenist and Avila Camacho factions opposed to the Alemán faction.

Ruiz Cortines, a compromise candidate with few ties to any of the factions, emerged as agreeable to all sectors, but the oppposition generated by Alemán had not been overcome by the time of the 1952 elections. Opposing Ruiz Cortines was Henríquez Guzmán, an aspirant to the PRI nomination, who had been expelled from the party for premature campaigning. With a background as a member of the Cardenist faction but with subsequent turns to the right, Henríquez appealed to many of the disaffected. In the election, 16 percent of the voters rallied to his candidacy, a level of support for an opposition party equaled or surpassed only twice in postrevolutionary Mexican history, in 1924 before the party was founded and in 1946. With the small additional opposition vote cast for Lombardo of the PPS and for the PAN candidate, the vote for the PRI candidate reached its lowest ebb prior to 1982.

The 1952 elections were the last in the postaftermath period to 1982 in which the PRI confronted an unwanted electoral challenge. By the time of the 1958 elections, an economic upturn, a more even-handed performance by Ruiz Cortines, and a new electoral law further raising the requirements for party registration had all intervened to return the official party to a position of attracting 90 percent of the votes, despite an upsurge of rural unrest and land invasions and the onset of a period of vigorous labor protest during the campaign period.

The 1958 elections constituted something of an inflection point in the evolution of the Mexican one-party dominant system. Even more than in the vote tallies, the overwhelming victory of the official party was seen in the near disappearance of opposition candidates. The PAN as usual presented a candidate, but no other registered party did. Instead, the two other parties backed the PRI candidate. The only other opposition votes were those cast for candidates not formally registered, particularly a candidate of the Mexican Communist Party (Taylor 1960b:727). Having overcome its problem of consolidating electoral power, the PRI now faced another problem: that of keeping up the appearance of electoral competition in order to maintain democratic legitimacy. The government thus turned its attention to an electoral reform that was quite opposite the previous set of changes in the electoral law, in that it was intended to liberalize the requirements for party registration rather than raise them.

The problem of democratic legitimacy raised by the PRI's near electoral monopoly was intensified by the pressure to open the closed party system that came from the wave of protests and strikes of 1958–59. These had not been channeled through the party system, and they opposed the regime's authoritarian nature and further challenged its legitimacy. In 1963 the Mexican government adopted a new electoral law that for the first time increased the representation in the political system of the small opposition parties, by distributing "party deputy" seats to parties that could not win many in the single-member electoral districts. As we shall see, following the upheavals and protest that emanated from the 1968 student movement and led to the formation of many opposition groups and to a major challenge to the PRI's legitimacy, additional laws were passed in 1972–73 and 1977 that pushed the liberalizing reforms of 1963 further.

A significant feature of the Mexican one-party dominant system, then, was precisely that: it was a dominant-party system, not a one-party system. Manipulating both a revolutionary and democratic claim to legitimacy, the PRI became increasingly dependent on the existence of opposition parties to lend the aura of electoral competition, particularly as the former claim rang more hollow with the passage of time and with the party's more conservative orientation.

By the beginning of the 1950s, three minor parties provided minimal or nominal electoral competition. The conservative PAN (National Action Party) was the oldest of these. It was also the strongest and provided the most consistent competition and outspoken opposition. Nevertheless, it was a weak party incapable of winning more than just a handful of seats in the Chamber of Deputies and, in the period to 1982, never attracted more than about 15 or 16 percent of the vote. Nor did it win either a Senate seat or a gubernatorial race, though it denounced the use of electoral fraud and over the years disputed the results of three of the latter (González Casanova 1982:68–69; Levy and Székely 1983:70).

The other two parties resulted from splits in the PRI. The first, discussed above, was the PPS (Popular Socialist Party), formed by Lombardo at the end of the 1940s when, alienated by its turn to the right, he left the PRI. The Authentic Party of the Mexican Revolution (PARM) was organized in the early 1950s by retired army generals. These two parties have often been seen as forming the "official" left and right respectively. Ideologically quite close to the PRI, they quickly established or reestablished cooperative relations with the parent party. Kenneth Johnson (1978:149–50) has referred to the former as "little more than the left wing of the PRI" and the latter as "a conservative extension of the PRI." Ideologically, the PPS emphasis on a broad front in the service of anti-imperialism and on the reformist position advocating the development of state capitalism virtually mandated cooperation with the PRI. Advocating a more conservative position, the PARM nevertheless continued to accept the symbols and ideology of the Mexican Revolution and did not particularly distinguish itself ideologically from the PRI.

The PPS and the PARM could never muster even the limited level of support attracted to the PAN. In legislative elections they never garnered more than 3 or 4 percent of the vote, and in presidential and gubernatorial elections they almost always supported the PRI candidate. Only in 1952 did the PPS present a presidential candidate when Lombardo himself ran. In many ways, then, these parties could be considered electoral front parties rather than opposition parties.

The importance of these weak parties to the Mexican regime is underscored by the artificial means by which they were maintained and by the support they received from the state. These included public funds to support their activities (Levy and Székely 1983:76) and a bending of the electoral laws to ensure their presence on the political scene. The minimum membership requirements for registration were ignored to favor the PPS and the PARM, party deputyships in the federal Chamber were allotted out of proportion to what those two parties had gained on the basis of their vote, and all three parties were known to benefit from the official declaration of electoral victories, especially at the municipal level, that were not properly theirs—like the rest of the Mexican political system, electoral fraud was a complex institution. The Mexican regime clearly felt the necessity to maintain a weak opposition as a mechanism to sustain legitimation and to channel and limit political dissent (González Casanova 1982:67–69).

The Mexican Communist Party should also be mentioned, although it lost its registration at the end of the 1940s and did not regain it for virtually the entire period under discussion here, until 1978. The party suffered an enormous decline since its heyday in the Cárdenas years. It suffered under the impact of international Communist strategy during World War II, including the policy of semiliquidation of Communist parties in the middle 1940s; was rent by divisions that led to two episodes of purges and mass expulsions in 1943 and 1947; and had to withstand defections to Lombardo's new party. Internally autocratic, having lost its way ideologically, and split in two (the PCM and POCM), by 1960 the PCM had declined "to the point of vanishing" (Carr 1981a:13–20; 1985:9).

The Mexican regime that emerged in the postaftermath period with its dominant party and weak opposition parties embodied a broad and very diverse coalition that was constantly renewed through a kind of exchange process. The pattern of state bargaining that characterized Mexico has been referred to as "two carrots, then a stick."[19] Newell and Rubio (1984:121) have similarly identified three stages: first, a process of conciliation and accommodation of opposing interests; followed by political and material co-optation; and finally, as a last resort if all else failed, repression. This pattern of pervasive negotiation occurred both internally within the PRI and externally among the various parties.

Internally, the PRI embraced a very large coalition through its sectoral organizations, along with its geographically based electoral apparatus, party functionaries, and political bosses with their extensive clientele networks. In the inclusionary pattern of PRI politics, all of these interests had to be reconciled and, to the extent possible, accommodated in order to contain dissent. Co-optation was based on the expectation that political influence or material benefits would be forthcoming in return for at least limited support (Anderson and Cockroft 1972). The centrality to Mexican politics of negotiation and bargaining within the party was an important factor in preserving certain features of the one-party dominant regime and impeding the course of democratic opening and reform. Sectoral organizations, particularly labor, · state governors, and local and regional political bosses were especially resistant to even those reforms proposed by the party, lest a new political, electoral game replace the intraparty bargaining game at which they felt more confident of their strength (Middlebrook 1981a:18, 20).

For those groups that remained outside of the PRI, another form of PRI-dominated coalition of the whole was created. In these cases ever more inclusive structures or higher levels of organization were established to incorporate the independent groups. This occurred in the party arena as well as in the arena of labor and peasant unions, as we shall see below. In the party sphere, the political reforms were an inclusionary device that granted (minor) opposition parties more legislative seats than they were able to win elector-

[19] This phrase was suggested by Larissa Lomnitz and has also been cited in P. Smith (1979:57).

ally in majority districts. Like the Venezuelan system of proportional representation, these reforms served as a mechanism to create a coalition of the whole, not only within the party but among the parties, that is, within an integrative party system. They served as an inducement to bring opposition parties into the system, with all the attendant concerns that thereby came to compete for their attention. In addition to focusing their energies on opposition to the regime and government policies, these parties became players in that regime, thereby, in a minimal but nonetheless significant way, accepting it and devoting much of their activity to electoral and parliamentary tasks and responsibilities.

The one-party dominant regime of Mexico, then, maintained a coalition of the whole in which, primarily through negotiation and accommodation, most groups were included within the purview of the party, while room was made for groups that remained outside the party. Minor parties not only helped to legitimate the regime but also provided a state-regulated institu tional channel for opposition and dissent.

Hegemonic Resources. The PRI, as the dominant, multiclass integrative party, provided a number of important hegemonic resources with which to meet the challenges of the 1960s and 1970s. It maintained legitimacy through the mobilization of electoral support, through the manipulation of a revolutionary ideology, and through the close ties it had established with labor and peasant unions.

The success the PRI attained at the polls as measured as a percent of the total vote had already been made clear. The PRI's capacity to mobilize electoral support resulted in its monopolization not only of the presidency, with at least three-quarters of the vote, but also of the governorships and the Senate seats, with only one partial exception, in which a deal was struck with the PPS. Only in the Chamber of Deputies and at the municipal level did the PRI meet defeat by the opposition. The PRI enjoyed overwhelming electoral victory not only in the 1950s but right through the period of challenge and opposition in the 1960s and 1970s. Some of the PRI's victories at the polls were undoubtedly won with the use of electoral fraud. Nevertheless, it is widely agreed that even if free elections had been held, the PRI would have won overwhelmingly. This supposition seems borne out by the 1979 and 1982 elections, which, though not free from fraud, were relatively clean. In these elections the percentage vote for the PRI was indeed reduced, but the party still captured about 70 percent of the vote (Levy and Székely 1983:69–70; Middlebrook 1981a:28, 39).

In addition to mobilizing electoral support, the PRI played the role of propagandist for the regime through its manipulation of ideology. As Cockcroft (1972:258–62) has suggested, ideology was a crucial element in the regime's establishment and maintenance of supremacy. The dominant ideology was formally expressed in the 1917 constitution, which provided a number of ideological symbols that were readily available to Mexican political leaders. On this basis, the PRI monopolized the symbols of the revolution and thus embodied a set of social and moral values and a normative world view that had widespread acceptance throughout Mexican society and could serve to legitimate the actions of the state.

The PRI regularly articulated a position of social justice and reformism but did not elaborate a sophisticated, coherent ideology. It did, however, claim a pantheon of heroes and a collection of revolutionary myths and symbols, and these played an important role in attracting and binding mass allegiance. Results of survey analysis in Mexico City underscored the success of the PRI in generating mass support precisely by symbolic reassurances and appeals to the revolutionary myth (David 1976). In this sense, it was the genius of Mexican politics that the social revolution, which was defeated during the civil war, nonetheless became the most important national myth and source of legitimacy of every subsequent Mexican government, and that Emiliano Zapata and Pancho Villa, the leaders of the defeated opposition, became national heroes while their constituencies became the backbone of support of the Mexican regime. It is no small testimony to the ideological success of the Mexican political elite that they also sold the myth of the revolution to professional political observers of the country, so that even those who were critical spoke of the "betrayal" of the revolution or questioned the future of the "continuing" revolution. To assert that Mexico even experienced a successful popular revolution is, as Schattschneider (1942:48) said when describing a comparable legitimacy myth in the United States, a "humorous inversion of the truth, an invention of persuasive politicians who told the fable to the historians."

The manipulation of revolutionary symbols was an important resource for the Mexican regime. Precisely because these symbols may have been fictive, their formal statement could give political leaders greater latitude for using rhetoric that would appeal to the popular classes without posing a genuine threat to the political right. Thus, the revolutionary myth could function as an important integrative symbol in Mexico, quite unlike the role of ideology in Brazil and Chile, where ideological themes that might appeal to the working class, such as *trabalhismo* or Getulismo or Marxist ideologies, were sources of polarization rather than integration.

In addition, the revolutionary claim of the PRI—both its frequent rhetorical evocation of the revolution and of the goals of social justice and its claims to be the institutional embodiment of the Mexican Revolution—put the opposition in a very difficult position. From the right, the popularity of the revolution virtually demanded the rhetorical acceptance of the revolution and its goals on the part of any group seeking to attract widespread popular support. On the left, the PRI to a large degree already occupied that ideological space with its rhetoric of revolution, social justice, and even, to some extent, class struggle. On both sides of the political spectrum, therefore, little room was left for other parties to distinguish themselves significantly from the PRI.

Finally, the Mexican regime was characterized by direct organizational ties between the PRI and the popular sector unions of its mass constituencies. From the time of the sectoral reorganization of the official party in 1938,

these links to labor and peasant unions were formal and strong. They constituted a political resource that provided the regime with a vehicle for mobilizing support, controlling these constituencies, and achieving political stability.

At the most minimal level, party-union links mobilized support through
the collective membership in and identity of unions with the party. Beyond
that they were the vehicle through which the regime could reinforce its legitimacy by making a show of formal endorsements by labor and peasant
organizations and through which it could carry out political propaganda campaigns and organize mass demonstrations. The ability of labor organizations
to fill the central plaza of Mexico City with workers and of peasant organizations to load their members into trucks to attend a political rally became
well known.

Party-union links also were a vehicle of political control. As we shall see
below, in the case of Venezuela party-union links gave the party an often
decisive hand in the choice of union leaders. In Mexico, this party influence
was perhaps not quite so direct and institutionalized. However, the leadership of the CNC, the peasant confederation, was vulnerable to presidential
manipulation, and the confederation often experienced a leadership change
at the beginning of a new presidential term (L. Meyer 1976:1303). A number
of incidents also occurred in which labor leaders were imposed on unions by
government tactics, the "model" for which was, of course, the *charrazo* of
1948. Though such incidents took place, these impositions and episodes of
heavy-handedness were exceptions and represented the failure of "normal"
mechanisms of leadership control. These included leadership co-optation
that was available through union-party links. As members of the PRI, union
leaders were in a position to be recruited to party roles, up to and including
candidates for election to the federal legislature. With both appointive and
electoral positions (the latter in a one-party dominant regime being tantamount to appointive), the Mexican regime enjoyed extraordinary patronage
resources, estimated at about 43,000 positions to be filled as each new president assumed office.[20] This vast system of leadership co-optation, enhanced
by the distribution of material benefits other than political positions, was an
important instrument of control not only of the leadership, of course, but
through those leaders of the mass organizations and their grassroots base.

The party-union links meant that the political and electoral activities of
labor and peasant unions were channeled through the official party, where
demands could be contained. Combined with the electoral dominance of the
PRI and its continuing legitimacy among workers and peasants, these ties
further eliminated any space for opposition parties that could claim support
among the popular sectors and present the challenge of more radical policy
positions speaking on their behalf. Within the party, policy positions of the
mass organizations were moderated. The party had to triangulate among
three different and often contradictory goals: to support the state's develop-

[20] Brandenburg 1964:157; Purcell 1978:9–10; K. Johnson 1971:chap. 3.

ment model, to maintain the state-popular sector alliance as a main under-pinning of the legitimacy of the regime, and to mediate the conflicting claims and demands of diverse social sectors. With the formal representation of mass organizations within the party, the PRI was a crucible in which com-peting demands were subjected to negotiation before compromise positions emerged in the public political arena.

The mass organizations did have influence within the party, but they were not able to initiate policy through their membership in the PRI—the party was not an important vehicle for the formulation of demands and aggregation of interests in a political system characterized by centralism and presiden-tialism. Their role was limited to influencing policy and modifying decisions (L. Meyer 1976:1313, 1323). More successful in this regard was the CTM, the largest component of the labor sector, which in turn was organizationally the strongest party sector; less influence was enjoyed by the peasant sector, the weakest and most dependent of the sectors. The main source of leverage for labor, which could be used only infrequently and in extreme circumstances, was the ability to threaten to break the party-union links—to take the mass confederation out of PRI or otherwise threaten the state-labor alliance. More typically, however, negotiations proceeded within the framework of the al-liance, and the popular sector organizations were quite weak. We will return to this below.

Party links were also used to transmit signals about what was acceptable in terms of union bargaining positions and thus to set limits on demands by indicating what outcome the government would support. In collective bar-gaining over wages, for instance, most negotiations took place at the plant level, but there were constraints on this process. Increasingly the guidelines for wage determination came to be established at a more centralized level in which the government played a key role. In the first place, the government as a major employer itself set wage policy in its agreements with the FSTSE, the confederation of government workers. In addition, the government reached understandings and agreements with the CTM about wage policy (Zapata 1981:364). Individual unions thus came to know up to what point they could count on political support for their demands, and at what point they might encounter opposition, by both the state and the CTM. This infor-mation was important to unions, which generally speaking and with some notable exceptions were economically weak and dependent on finding allies in their collective bargaining. In return, of course, they had to bring demands that might be generated by the grassroots in line with the government posi-tion (Everett 1967:165).

Available wage data suggest the degree to which real gains for labor have, in the aggregate, been limited. The real urban minimum wage, having dropped to nearly half of the level of the Cárdenas period at its low point in 1946–47 during the aftermath period, began a slow process of recuperation, returning to the earlier peak only in the mid-1960s and then doubling again by the mid-1970s. It thus followed a pattern of slow growth from 1946–47 until the economy ran into trouble in the mid-1970s, after which the real urban minimum began another downward slide (Gregory 1986:200, table 7-1). Surveys of industrial firms reveal a similar pattern. These annual surveys are not representative (nor even completely consistent over time) but they include the "most important" and largest firms in their respective industries and by 1950s accounted for about a quarter of the total workers (Gregory 1986:221). Because of these characteristics, they were likely to be a better sample of unionized workers than of workers as a whole. According to the results reported by Bortz (1977:157), the 1939 real wage level in industry was attained again in 1968, and from that year to 1975 real wages showed a gain of only about a third. Gregory (1986:242, table 7-7) reports a smaller 1968–75 increase of only 23 percent. Real wages in industry have thus displayed extraordinarily modest improvements over the long run: an average of only 1 percent annually from 1939 to 1975 (Bortz 1977:134) or of only about 3 percent from 1960 to 1975 (Gregory 1986:260).

Control over the mass organizations was also enhanced by the pluralistic nature of party-union ties. These links were pluralistic in two ways. First, the mass organizations were never unified organizationally but were formally divided among the three organized sectors of the PRI, the Labor, Peasant, and Popular Sectors, the last of which included several important unions of government workers, including the massive teachers' union. This divide-and-rule strategy limited horizontal ties among peasant, labor, and public sector unions and hence constrained their capacity for concerted action. Secondly, the PRI admitted multiple peak associations as members of the party sectors, thus establishing links with several confederations. Though the CTM and CNC were by far the most important centrals among labor and the peasantry respectively, they were not the only centrals represented within the organized sectors of the PRI. With quite similar orientations, these confederations nevertheless competed with one another for grassroots membership. The government thus had a mechanism for playing one cooperative confederation off against another as well as for using an allied confederation as a bulwark against a dissident union.

Finally, the organizational links between the party and mass organizations provided a vehicle for dispensing favors and resources. While these were concessions that doled out benefits, they were also a means of control. They were typically used in order to maintain support among constituency groups when necessary to meet any challenges from independent, more militant organizations with a minimum of coercion. Quite apart from leadership co-optation, then, party-union and party-*ejido* links were a channel for organizational co-optation in which government affiliated mass organizations put dissident organizations at a serious disadvantage as the conduits for material and organizational benefits. The quid pro quo for these benefits was playing according to the rules of the game and maintaining the state-labor and state-peasant alliance on which the legitimacy of the state was based.

The PRI thus provided political, ideological, and organizational resources that allowed the state to maintain legitimacy, mobilize support, and control the organizations of the popular sectors. It is important to emphasize the nature of these mechanisms because they underline the fundamentally political character of state-labor and state-peasant relations mediated for the most part by a hegemonic party. Though coercion and repression were certainly not unknown, control was primarily political.

It has been argued here that state-labor relations were an outcome of the state-labor alliance formed during the period of incorporation and the reaction to the dynamics of that period that occurred in its aftermath, in which the balance of forces shifted further in favor of the state, in which the terms of discourse were limited with the expulsion of the left, and in which a reordered alliance was maintained. These changes in the aftermath did not occur without some resort to coercion. In many analyses of Mexico, this last point became overemphasized. What has often been said to have emerged was a *charro* model of state-controlled unionism based on coercion. Such a description, however, is not the whole picture, and it ignores the other foundations of what was a much more complex pattern of labor dynamics in Mexico. Specifically, it understates the fundamental need the Mexican state had to maintain the alliance with labor and the role and importance of the continuing exchanges between state and labor. Though altered, the initial populist bargain of support for concessions was not superseded; however, it was in continual need of renewal, and the hegemonic resources acquired during the populist period gave the state the flexibility to make and to withhold concessions as it deemed necessary.

The *charro* model is based on coercive mechanisms of state control over unions. It emphasizes the role of violence, corruption, and bossism, drawing attention to the perpetuation of a nondemocratic, co-opted, sometimes state-imposed union leadership that is not responsive to the grassroots but is dependent upon the state and in league with the state to control the working-class base and its demands in exchange for personal rewards. While each of these features has many empirical referents in Mexican unions, the picture as a whole is distorted and has been modified in recent analyses.

As a general description, the *charro* model is inaccurate in many points. In an exploratory survey of Mexican unions, Thompson and Roxborough (1982) found that, contrary to the pervasive autocratic image, Mexican unions displayed great diversity in terms of how internally democratic they were, as indicated by the frequency of competitive elections, the closeness of elections, and the rate of turnover of leaders. In another study, Roxborough (1984:26) found that union bureaucracies were often weak and the state had only a limited capacity to intervene in internal union affairs, although it did so in some very important and highly visible cases. Contrary to the *charro* model, the unions retained or were allowed considerable autonomy. In addition, the Thompson and Roxborough (1982) study found no correlation between how democratic a union was and how effective it was in securing benefits for its workers, bringing further into question the supposed advantages to the state of a nondemocratic union leadership in deflecting worker demands.

It is also worth noting that in the Thompson and Roxborough (1982) study the overall democratic scorecard of Mexican unions was not all that different from those of American and British unions. The data are tentative and problematic in many ways, but the findings nevertheless remind us that in thinking about Mexican unions, it may be more useful to compare them to other cases rather than to hold them up to some abstract model of union democracy.

Indeed, an equally relevant model of union democracy—or lack thereof— would surely be the Michels model predicting the formation of a self-perpetuating, bureaucratized leadership in any organization. As many analysts have suggested, this was an important dynamic in the development of a union bureaucracy in Mexico. To this extent, the union bureaucracy must not only be seen as a product of the political system in which the state explicitly sought to exert its control over the working class. Rather it must also be seen as a phenomenon internal to Mexican unionism itself, a product of the expansion of unions and their need for permanent and professional staffs and representatives (Woldenberg 1980:18–19).

The *charro* model also fails to recognize the essential dynamics of the Mexican hegemonic regime and the centrality of the use of hegemonic rather than coercive mechanisms of control for its maintenance—and hence the centrality of the state-labor alliance. In this regard, a key aspect of the functioning of the regime was not state capacity to buy off union leaders or otherwise to ensure their compliance as puppets of the regime that would do the bidding of the state, but the capacity of union leaders to represent their constituencies as well as to discipline them. In the Mexican regime, unions were a vehicle for support mobilization as well as control. Unions and union leaders played a very complicated game of intermediation between the state and the working class.

The point is not that *charrismo* did not exist in Mexican state-labor relations, for surely it did. Rather, it might be suggested that *charrismo*, as a model of discipline without representation and of coercion without support mobilization, in many ways represented a malfunction of the hegemonic pattern of Mexican state-labor relations. It could even be argued that the probability of some "failure rate" was fairly high, given the economic context, bureaucratic dynamics, and short-term political exigencies. Nevertheless, it may be important to remember the way in which for Mexico the dual dilemma of labor-state relations was constantly posed as a central dynamic of the regime. An overtly antilabor policy was antithetical to the nature of the hegemonic regime. Even the assertion of control over the working class through a co-opted leadership, which would be responsive to the state rather than to the workers and which would impose state policy over the working class, could be problematic if it undermined labor support on which the regime was dependent. Given the centrality of labor support, the logic of the regime favored credible working-class representatives as union leaders in order to maximize its hegemonic controls and minimize its resort to coercive controls.

The union leadership was also torn in two directions. As Woldenberg has argued, even a PRI-aligned union leadership required acceptance by the membership and legitimacy as the workers' agents. The leadership did not have an unlimited capacity to act in a manner opposed to the immediate interests of the workers. Thus, the common and logical position taken by the union bureaucracy was reformism (Woldenberg 1980:20). Aside from the Michelian perspective of leadership perpetuation and divergence from the interests of the mass base, cooperation with the state was attractive as a way to seek institutional access and gain influence and concessions, at the same time that precisely the opposite relationship—autonomy from the state—could be a source of union power and bargaining strength vis-à-vis the state.

State-labor relations were thus complex, embedded in a complex political regime. As many analysts now recognize, these relations were characterized by working-class representation as well as control through the union bureaucracy, and the mechanisms of control were primarily, though not exclusively, hegemonic rather than coercive, with the PRI playing an important role.[21] As Trejo Delarbre (1980a:130) has said, by the end of the period under discussion here, a union bureaucracy in alliance with the state had maintained its "hegemony" over the labor movement during a period of about four decades, a feat that is inconceivable on the basis of coercion alone—inconceivable without the capacity to perform a representative function.

All this is not to say, of course, that the features of unionism depicted in the *charro* model did not exist in Mexico. They did, and the government did have a number of direct controls over the working class and unions. It did sometimes intervene and resort to coercive mechanisms. The corrupt, autocratic, *charro* style of leadership did exist in some unions, even in some of the most important and visible ones. In addition, the government had the usual forms of direct control available through the labor law, such as the power to recognize unions, the power to declare strikes legal or illegal, and a deciding voice on conciliation and arbitration boards and on the resolution of leadership disputes. There is no question that these more coercive mechanisms also played a role in the government's success in achieving substantial class harmony, holding down both strikes and wages and minimizing the challenge of more militant, independent unions that sought a rupture in the party-labor alliance.

Yet the government had to be careful about these forms of control. The complex political negotiations that underlay the coalition of the whole that the Mexican regime embodied and had to constantly reproduce required that the government present itself as a conciliator between classes by maintaining the appearance of neutrality between labor and capital, and at the same time it required that the government maintain the state-labor alliance (Camacho 1976:502). The more general pattern of control and of state-labor relations, then, would have to be described as more multifaceted, embodying a form of unionism that had elements of representation *as well as* control—and in a certain dialectical sense, representation *qua* control. As this last

[21] Zapata 1981:363, 384; Trejo Delarbre 1980a:129–30; Woldenberg 1980:18–20.

point indicates, hegemonic and political controls were more pervasive and salient.

In Mexico, then, the integrative, hegemonic, one-party dominant system became an important conflict-limiting mechanism that avoided or minimized future polarization. The popular sectors were electorally, ideologically, and functionally incorporated into the dominant party, which helped to mediate the relationship between the state and the popular sectors. In all three arenas—electoral, symbolic, and organizational—the PRI provided the state with a number of important hegemonic resources. With these resources, the Mexican regime attained a level of stability that had completely eluded it through the first three decades of this century. Instead, as Meyer (1976:1322, 1352) has put it, the open conflict of groups succumbed to the stronger forces of the coordination and conciliation of interests and the control of mass organizations through the dominant party.

Unlike the cases of Brazil and Chile, the party system, far from being a vehicle through which polarization occurred, was an integrative mechanism and afforded the state substantial legitimacy. The Mexican state confronted the challenges of the late 1950s to the 1970s with political, organizational, and symbolic resources unavailable in those other two countries. With these resources, the Mexican state had a greater capacity to pursue anti-popular sector policies on a short-term basis and to contain and co-opt radical and independent movements. As we shall see below, the initial incorporation period did not tie the popular sectors to the state "once and for all." There followed regular attempts to establish autonomous political movements and functional organizations. The point is that the incorporation period and its aftermath formed the parameters of the ongoing struggle, giving the state important resources with which to co-opt such movements on a continuing basis and making opposition movements more difficult to mount.

Opposition and Crises of the late 1950s to 1982

Starting in the late 1950s, the Mexican regime faced a series of challenges that occurred in the context of a number of internal social processes: the ongoing struggle within the labor movement against state-allied unionism, the growth of the middle class as well as the private sector, agrarian stagnation and the proletarianization of the peasantry, and the rapid urbanization that swelled the barrio population and the informal sector of major cities. The challenges took the form of what was called labor and municipal insurgency,[22] land invasions in the countryside, student protest movements, some guerrilla activity (though a major guerrilla movement was never mounted), and a general process of politicization and the proliferation of opposition

[22] Municipal insurgency, which had a counterpart at the state level, involved the occupation of mayoral or gubernatorial residences to protest electoral fraud or governmental policy (González Casanova 1982:73).

movements and parties. Though such activity occurred throughout the two decades, two waves could be distinguished.

The first, during the 1960s, was the political radicalization that coincided with and was in part an outcome of the demonstration effect of the Cuban Revolution. The diffusion of Cuban revolutionary fervor occurred in many Latin American countries, and many of these experienced a concurrent economic crisis of inflation and balance of payments disequilibria during the 1960s. With the initiation of the "stabilizing development" model in the mid-1950s, however, Mexico maintained both price stability and consistent and quite high growth throughout the period.

The second wave, during the 1970s, was set off in 1968, a year of political tumult in many parts of the world, particularly in terms of student protest, which was at the core of the precipitating event in Mexico. The incident started as a clash between students from two secondary schools, but following the violent intervention of the police, the nature of the movement changed. Issues of army brutality, government repression, and the democratization of student associations became central and as the movement spread to students in other schools, including the National University and other private and public universities in Mexico City, and eventually to students throughout the country and to nonstudent groups, including teachers and some workers (see Hellman 1978:132ff). As Mexico prepared to host the international Olympic games, the protest movement threatened to undermine Mexico's international image. In a self-defeating response, the government, under the pressure of time, decided on an uncharacteristic use of repression, climaxing in the massacre of Tlatelolco, in which perhaps hundreds of people were killed.

The demands of the movement had focused on the government repression: the release of political prisoners, the abolition of special riot police, the resignation of the chief of police and his deputy, and the end of military occupation of all schools. Yet underlying the movement was a more basic critique of the Mexican system—both its political authoritarianism and the failure of the economic model of growth to solve the problems of the poor. Though the movement per se quickly lost momentum after the Tlatelolco massacre, these more underlying themes animated the opposition groups that proliferated in the following decade as a response to the failure of the regime to deal with protest through hegemonic rather than coercive mechanisms. Ultimately more important than any international reaction, then, was the domestic response to state violence on this scale and the need for the government to recoup its lost legitimacy particularly, among middle-class groups. The year 1968 marked the onset of a decade of opposition, protest, and political ferment. Indeed many analysts have viewed it as a watershed in Mexican history.

Unlike the protest movements of the 1960s, this second wave of political challenge did coincide with an economic crisis, one that was not entirely unrelated to it. The growing political disaffection led to a questioning of the basic nature of the regime and a heightened concern with the costs of the development model the government was pursuing. At the heart of the protest was a demand for social justice and equity and a raising of basic distributive and redistributive issues. In response to these pressures, President Echeverría (1970–76) abandoned the "stabilizing development" policies in order to increase social spending. The inflationary impact of this policy, which was not accompanied by higher taxes, was accelerated by world inflation in the context of the oil shocks. A global recession contributed to imbalances in the international accounts, and by the middle of the decade Mexico was faced with the prospect of devaluing the peso for the first time in 20 years (J. Thompson 1979:ch. 8).

During the 1960s and 1970s, then, the challenges that confronted Latin American regimes throughout the continent were also manifested in Mexico. In meeting these challenges, the Mexican state had available to it the hegemonic resources discussed above. These provided the state with the ability not only to contain and overcome the potential threat but also to avoid the policy immobilism characteristic of Brazil and Chile, for instance, and to make policy decisions —even unpopular ones—when they were deemed necessary.

In this regard, an important difference between Mexico (and Venezuela), on the one hand, and Brazil and Chile, on the other, was that in the former "political space" and "organizational or syndical space" was largely filled with cooperating mass organizations and an encompassing party so that the challenges of new opposition movements posed different problems. In Mexico, the state had to co-opt dissident factions as they broke away from the party or the major confederations. It had to maintain an alliance in the face of dissident movements, whereas in Brazil and pre-1970 Chile, no such alliance existed to begin with, and under those circumstances the task of containing the challenge was much more difficult. Furthermore, the Mexican government had in place mass organizations that could act as interlocutors between it and the mass base, thus facilitating a process of negotiation, conciliation, co-optation, and the isolation of dissident movements through selective distribution of resources and benefits.

These organizations also formed the basis of another feature by which the Mexican regime co-opted dissident movements: the creation of ever-higher levels of organization that included and incorporated the independent movements but that were dominated by the collaborating organizations. In the sphere of labor and peasant organizations, overarching layers of blocs and congresses were established to encompass competing and dissident confederations, groupings, and unions. In the sphere of party politics, this process had a parallel in the electoral reforms that granted greater representation— even overrepresentation—to (minor) opposition parties. In each of these arenas—party politics, labor unions, and peasant organizations—independent groups got concessions and organizational benefits in exchange for playing according to the rules of the game and thereby supporting the system. This organizational co-optation was accompanied by an extraordinarily extensive system of leadership co-optation.

As in the other countries, then, the 1960s and 1970s constituted a period of substantial challenge. Particularly after 1968 Mexico experienced political polarization and ferment, characterized by a radicalization and mobilization on the left and a growing discontent among the middle classes and private sector. Yet unlike Brazil and Chile, for instance, this challenge was largely contained, and the Mexican regime overcame the most direct and overt challenges to the system. That the system seemed to enter a new phase in 1988 does not diminish this contrast with Brazil and Chile, nor, indeed with Argentina, Peru, and Uruguay. Mexico avoided the kind of harsh, repressive military regime that came to power in those other countries and instead had the resources and flexibility to deal with this period of crisis and challenge within the framework of the existing civilian political system.

The Politics of Stabilization.   Unlike Brazil and Chile, the integrative, hegemonic regime in Mexico provided a basis for consistent policy formation. This point must not be overstated. As Purcell and Purcell (1980:194–95) have emphasized, the Mexican regime rested on as diverse and contradictory a coalition as those unsuccessfully attempted by the centrist politicians in Brazil and Chile. As the failure in those two countries indicates, it was no small achievement to keep such a coalition together. A delicate balancing act was often necessary, and the Mexican government must be seen in dynamic terms as always walking on this political tightrope. In another metaphor often invoked by observers of Mexico, the political pendulum—by which successive presidential terms tended to correspond to policy periods that swung from left to center to right and then back again to center, left, and so on—is a reflection of the need to address the diverse interests the regime had to accommodate. These gradual pendular swings, however, were very different from the desperate vacillation of policy decision-making in Brazil and Chile, and in general the Mexican government had the resources to pursue consistent policy. Specifically, the incorporation of the popular sectors gave the government the resources to pursue policies it deemed necessary to address economic challenges, despite the high costs of those policies to the popular sectors. By contrast, the government—in anything but the shortest run—did not have the resources to pursue policies strongly opposed by the private sector. The ability of the private sector to sabotage the implementation of Echeverría's attempted fiscal reform is an example.

Mexico's capacity for policy-making can be seen with regard to inflation, an issue that presented an economic challenge to most Latin American countries in the postwar years. Stabilization policies were political lightning rods in Brazil and Chile. In neither country was a civilian regime able to implement such a program, once it was finally adopted, or to achieve price stability. Instead, as we have seen, policy immobilism was characteristic, above all, over this issue. By contrast, Mexico successfully implemented two stabilization programs in the postaftermath period after 1952, thus illustrating the policy-making capacity of the integrative, hegemonic regime.

The high-investment rapid-growth policy of the Alemán presidency of 1946–52 had been accompanied by high rates of inflation and balance of payments disequilibria, which had taken the country into an inflation-devaluation cycle (J. Thompson 1979:72–77). The peso had been devalued in 1948 and 1952, and another devaluation was undertaken in 1954. Though it was very unpopular in many sectors, particularly in labor circles, the policy was nevertheless instituted with the cooperation of labor: a wage policy was negotiated that, along with other measures, was part of an economic package that ended the inflationary spiral. Thus began a period of "stabilizing development," in which the Mexican government achieved price stability for the next two decades. Thus, unlike countries such as Brazil and Chile, where governments in a weak political position were unable to impose austerity measures as all groups fought to maintain income shares, the Mexican government had the political resources to orchestrate a coalition for a policy to achieve price stability, a policy that was more beneficial to all in the long run but that imposed serious costs in the short run.

The 1954 devaluation demonstrates the policy-making framework of conciliation in which the president could negotiate the support of organized labor. Despite its initial opposition, López Mateos had managed to line up a reluctant labor movement behind the devaluation of April 1954. Particularly interesting was the less grudging support given by the CROC, a new labor confederation that claimed greater independence from the government but that in fact had enjoyed government support vis-à-vis the CTM. The May Plan of the following month settled on a 10 percent increase in wages to offset inflation. By the end of the month, however, it became apparent that this increase was far lower than the rate of inflaton, and both the CROM and the UGOCM of Lombardo rejected the wage policy. The CROC continued to support the president, but the CTM threatened to defect from the coalition. Under the pressure of grassroots demands and a challenge for leadership within the labor movement (see below), Fidel Velázquez of the CTM moved into the opposition, threatening a general strike and a return to "revolutionary unionism" in which the CTM would leave the PRI. Toward the end of June, the president undertook negotiations in which the government, employers, and labor worked out a modified interpretation of government wage policy that allowed a 24 percent wage increase (Everett 1967:126–28).

During the following months, labor protest and discontent was expressed, but the negotiated policy held. If the policy constituted a test of the labor leadership, of the labor movement structure, and of state-labor relations, that test was passed. In September a huge demonstration of workers was staged to support the government and renew the state-labor alliance. The stabilization policy was successfully implemented and was followed by a new economic model and a prolonged period of price stability (Pellicer and Reyna 1978:94–105).

Indeed, it was not until two decades later that Mexico again experienced inflation and was confronted with the need for a stabilization policy. In response to the legitimacy crisis sparked off by the 1968 student protest and repression and in the context of political ferment by opposition groups, the Echeverria government embarked on a program of "shared development," in which, compared to the model of "stabilizing development," greater emphasis was put on issues of distribution and social welfare. With increases in social spending and an even more dramatic growth in the budget for economic projects (Newell and Rubio 1984:136–37), public spending increased at the same time that attempts to raise taxes were effectively vetoed by the private sector. The resulting public sector deficit led to mounting inflation, deficits in the international accounts, and capital flight, producing by 1975 an economic crisis that was aggravated by international inflation and recession. By the end of 1976, the Mexican government reached an agreement with the IMF and embarked on a new three-year devaluation and stabilization program.

The outlines of negotiations and settlement with labor were similar to those of 1954. An agreement was reached with the labor movement granting a 20 percent emergency wage hike to compensate for the expected price increase. During the next two years, 1977–78, labor leaders accepted lower gains than the inflation rate. In reaction, strikes occurred at a fairly high level, but not as high as they had been at their peak in 1974. Furthermore, independent labor movements were not able to take advantage of this situation. However, by 1979, the final year of the program, this level of wage restraint was abandoned. The pattern in Mexico, then, was one in which, in exchange for symbolic and other nonwage concessions, a deal could be struck with labor on the assumption or implicit understanding that in the future material losses would be recuperated. Thus, for a period that would be unimaginable in most South American countries, the Mexican government had the political resources to pursue a negotiated incomes policy that held the line on wages, and the "old-guard labour leadership . . . effectively rescued this regime" (Whitehead 1980:854). The way in which, at least in the short run, symbolic payoffs could substitute for material gains and facilitate policies that imposed economic hardship was seen in the 1978 decision (hotly contested at the time) to formally redefine the PRI as a "workers' party."[23]

In Mexico, then, the political integration of labor gave the government substantial leeway to pursue unpopular policies, particularly in the short run. In this sense, the PRI, which was a main vehicle of labor mediation, was "a source of services which allow[ed] those in control of the state to make decisions and pursue policies" (Portes 1977:194). Whereas the party systems of Brazil and Chile polarized decision-making, the inclusionary, integrative system of Mexico gave the government important resources for short-run "political management" (Whitehead 1980) and facilitated policy formation and implementation, despite the existence of opposition.

Political Parties. In the party sphere, as we have seen, the presence of the PPS, the PARM, the PAN, and even the PCM failed to constitute a major challenge to the one-party dominant regime as Mexico emerged from the aftermath period. Quite the contrary, the existence of the first three of these parties could be said to have contributed to the smooth functioning of that

---

[23] *Latin American Political Report* 12, no. 32 (London) Aug. 18, 1978:255.

regime by providing a loyal opposition of weak parties that were not too divergent from the PRI ideologically and that gave the appearance of democratic electoral competition. Nor did the PCM present any real challenge: "By 1957 the PCM's feeble membership, organizational chaos, and leadership style had almost succeeded in destroying the party as a real political force" (Carr 1985:11). The Mexican regime was not, however, immune from the challenges of radicalization and the formation of new opposition parties in the 1960s and 1970s. The challenges of the 1960s were contained through the usual mechanisms and hegemonic resources available to the regime; the implications of a second round of political mobilization and opposition, that which occurred in the 1970s in the wake of the 1968 student movement, were still being worked out by the end of the period under consideration here.

In the 1960s, a political reorientation was stimulated by the Cuban Revolution, which provided the fragmented Mexican left with a new revolutionary model and stimulated renewed militancy, a new organizational drive, and a common focus of attention. At a pro-Cuban international conference held in March 1961, the Mexican delegation determined to unite in a National Liberation Movement (MLN), a form of left front organization that was being encouraged by the Soviet Union at the time. The following month, a diverse group of the Mexican left—including Lombardo and the PPS, the PCM, and Lázaro Cárdenas and his supporters—agreed on a common political position that denounced the PRI's betrayal of the Mexican Revolution and called for its revitalization in a program that included agrarian reform, autonomy of trade unions and peasant collectives (ejidos), Mexican control of natural resources, nationalization of certain industries, just division of national wealth, the freeing of political prisoners, solidarity with Cuba, and opposition to U.S. imperialism. In terms of tactics, the MLN followed the Cuban example and emphasized the role of the peasantry, advocating its organization into a militant, revolutionary force (Garza 1964:450, 454).

In 1963, a new electoral reform made it easier for parties to win seats in the Chamber of Deputies by allocating, through a type of proportional representation, additional seats for "party deputies" to minority parties able to capture at least 2.5 percent of the national vote. "The 1963 reform was intended to defuse accumulated sociopolitical discontent; it followed the repression of teachers' and railroad workers' strikes in 1958–1959 and sought to channel the internal political opposition sparked by the Cuban Revolution into established institutional channels" (Middlebrook 1981a:11). Responding to this incentive, the MLN formed the FEP as an electoral front to contest the elections. The FEP, however, failed to demonstrate enough support to even qualify for registration. Nevertheless, the FEP illegally entered a candidate and took the occasion of the campaign to attack the PRI and advocate political violence. After the election, its candidate was arrested, and both the MLN and the FEP petered out (K. Johnson 1971:116).

In the end, then, both the MLN and the FEP failed, for perhaps two reasons. First, given the PRI's overwhelming popular support, little room existed for the opposition to mobilize grassroots support. Second, the one-party dominant system, which incorporated the PPS as a loyal opposition party, intensified and perpetuated the fragmentation of the left, thereby contributing to its weakness. Less than a year after it was formed, Lombardo took his PPS out of the MLN, arguing the advantages of loyal opposition and support for the "national bourgeoisie and State capitalism as an anti-imperialistic formula" (cited in Garza 1964:452) and the inappropriateness of a mechanically borrowed Cuban model. The MLN, in turn, responded with ideological attacks on Lombardo's "peaceful transition to power through legal means" and championed forms of direct action and agitation (Garza 1964:452–53). Such splits were debilitating for the left. In the end, the diffusion of post-Castro radicalization never amounted to much in the Mexican hegemonic context.

As fallout from the 1968 events, a new round of political organizing and opposition occurred. The legitimacy of the regime was particularly threatened in this incident by the inability to hold the coalition together without resort to violent repression, rather than the more usual approach of handling dissent through more co-optive means. The response of Luis Echeverría, who became president in 1970, was once again to incorporate and channel dissident groups into a legally defined and delimited electoral arena. Partly under this impetus, but also as an expression of autonomous, oppositional ferment, a number of new parties were organized, primarily but not exclusively to oppose the PRI from the left.

Echeverría undertook to integrate dissident groups through substantive policies and a democratic opening to the left that would attract and co-opt them. These included a populist rhetoric that emphasized solidarity with the third world and championed social justice both internationally and domestically. These were backed up by policies that distributed material benefits to key groups: wage increases, price controls on basic commodities, expansion of student scholarships, and additional public investment and credit in rural areas, where land invasions were also tolerated to some extent. He also attempted a fiscal reform, but capitalists were successful in scuttling the initiative and preserving their low-tax position. Finally, he introduced greater press freedom and released some of the political prisoners from the 1968 student movement.

In addition to these measures, Echeverría introduced a series of electoral reforms. Motivated by the same need to handle dissidence as the 1963 reforms, these built on that earlier attempt to expand the participation and representation of minority parties. A 1972 reform lowered the minimum national vote required for a party to be awarded a party deputy from 2.5 to 1.5 percent of the total, while the maximum number of party deputies was increased from 20 to 25. Another reform the following year reduced the minimum membership required by a party for legal registration. Finally, in 1975 the PRI published a statement outlining the direction of future reforms. These were not acted upon during the Echeverría presidency, but their intellectual author, Jesús Reyes Heroles, was named minister of interior by the new president, López Portillo (1976–82), and was responsible for the reforms of 1977 (Middlebrook 1981a:13).

Also in the 1970s, new parties appeared on the scene, in a burst of organizational creativity and change. The political process on the left in this period, however, was one of fragmentation. In 1971 groups from the dissident railroad workers movement of 1958–59, the MLN, and the 1968 student movement combined to form the CNAC. The unity did not last long, however, and by 1976 the CNAC had splintered into several separate and competing parties. Of these, the three that would retain some electoral importance and organizational identity included the PMT (which had connections with some of the most important dissident groups in the labor movement), the PST (which grew close to Echeverría and the left of the PRI), and the PSR. In addition, the PPM split from the PPS after Lombardo's death. On the ideological ends of the spectrum, the PRT emerged as a Trotskyist party and the PDM was formed as the electoral arm of the organizational descendants of the *sinarquistas* on the right (Rodríguez Araujo 1982). Yet, for all this organizational activity in the party arena, none of these parties nor the Communist Party had enough support to register in time for the 1976 elections.

By the time the new president, López Portillo, took office in 1976, the urgency for further reform had become acute. The economy was in crisis, as was the political system, with the opposition to the general reformist tilt of the outgoing president aggravated by a set of highly visible and contentious expropriations in response to peasant land invasions in the last months of Echeverría's term. The right was alarmed, and none of the new parties had yet been channeled into the legal electoral arena; for despite the liberalized law, no additional parties had been able to meet the requirements for registration, no less to become eligible for party deputies. To make matters worse, from the point of view of the regime, far from encompassing more opposition parties, the 1976 presidential elections had not even had the usual advantage of minimal competition from the PAN: due to internal disputes, that party had not been able to nominate a presidential candidate and the facade of competitive democracy was brought down, as the PPS and the PARM, the only other nominal opposition parties, continued their habitual support of the PRI candidate.

High on the agenda of the new president, therefore, was renewed attention to the problem of electoral reform, which was enacted at the end of the first year of López Portillo's term. Again, the requirements for legal registration were substantially lowered, though, as Middlebrook (1981a:24) points out, they were not eliminated and the state retained important controls on the entry of parties in the electoral arena. The idea of party deputies was expanded by a more fundamental reform of the Chamber of Deputies, which was enlarged to 400, one-fourth of which would not be elected in majority districts like the others, but reserved for minority parties to be elected by proportional representation. Other measures aimed at reducing electoral fraud and expanding opposition party access to mass media.

It was important to the government to show some quick results by the

time of the 1979 mid-term elections. Specifically, it wanted at a minimum
to achieve the formal participation of the PCM, PDM, PST, and PMT, the
first two representing opposite ends of the ideological spectrum and the last
two representing different left-of-center coalitions. Furthermore, they were
the largest and most important of the unregistered parties (Middlebrook
1981a:17).

Whether to participate was energetically debated by the unregistered parties. They were presented with the same dilemma that we have discussed
with respect to labor. On the one hand were the potential advantages. Participation in the electoral arena presented an opportunity (1) to mobilize support, (2) to acquire a national forum in the campaign and, if successful, in the
Congress, and (3) possibly even to exert some influence on policy. But this
had to be balanced against the possibility of co-optation by participation in
the electoral arena and the compromise of substantive goals by the logic of
electoral mobilization. Despite differences in poltical outlook and orientation, almost all parties resolved this dilemma in favor of registration, with
the major exception of the PMT. Of the others, only the PCM, PDM, and
PST qualified for registration for the 1979 elections.

Not only did more parties participate, but, necessarily according to the
new rules, their representation in the Chamber of Deputies increased from
17.4 percent under the party deputy system still in effect in 1976 to 26 percent in 1979—just 1 percent more than the 25 percent reserved for the opposition in the proportional representation seats (representing a PAN victory
of 4 majority seats). In these elections, in which the incidence of electoral
fraud was apparently reduced, the PRI vote did decline—but to "only" 70
percent. In relatively clean elections, then, the popularity of the PRI remained strong (Levy and Székely 1983:68–70; Baer and Bailey 1985:5). Yet,
despite the continued overwhelming electoral dominance of the PRI, as a
result of the reforms, debate in the Chamber began to change, and opposition
parties began to have success in modifying policy (Middlebrook 1981a:51).

The conclusion of the López Portillo term of office in 1982 represents the
end of the period under discussion here. More recent developments in the
party system will be alluded to in the final chapter. The point to be made
here is that despite some significant changes in Mexico in the 1970s, a
marked contrast continued to exist between the Mexican experience and the
pattern of polarization and crisis in Brazil and Chile in the 1960s and 1970s.
In Brazil and Chile, those dynamics accelerated and led to policy immobilism and military coups. By contrast, in the Mexican party sphere, as in the
union sphere, any challenge that was mounted was contained and channeled
into approved structures. That difference, as well as the evolution of the
Mexican system within the context of political stability and continuity, cannot be understood without reference to the hegemonic resources available to
the Mexican regime.

Labor Movement. As we have seen, by the end of the aftermath period,
Mexico had a labor movement in which state-labor relations were mediated
by the official party and, typically, by the close, formal integration of unions

into the PRI. Though the stability of the Mexican regime—including the state-labor alliance put in place by the end of the aftermath period—has been emphasized in analyses of Mexican politics, underlying this stability was an organizational structure that was in flux and a series of attempts to replace the "officialist" unions under the leadership of a "labor bureaucracy" with labor organizations that were more autonomous and responsive to the grassroots. Challenges to this pattern of state-labor relations were almost continual in the subsequent period, reaching a peak in the 1970s. The widely recognized stability of the Mexican system must be understood in terms of the constant renegotiation of the labor-state alliance. Given the political resources afforded the Mexican regime, however, these challenges ultimately failed to transform the system dramatically in the period under consideration here—to 1982.

Three types of challenges emerged within the labor movement. The first was that presented by the CTM itself. Such a challenge occurred at the time of the 1954 devaluation with the threat of Fidel Velázquez to take the CTM out of the PRI. These challenges were rare and probably not much more than posturing: Fidel Velázquez and the CTM were best understood as stalwart allies of the government and loyal members of the PRI. Nevertheless, the incident does underscore the fact that the Mexican governing coalition was held together primarily by political negotiations, and there was a limit beyond which the government could no longer retain labor within the coalition. Two features of the context of these negotiations together reveal the complexity of Mexican politics. On the one hand, in the postincorporation period, the balance of forces shifted further against labor; on the other, this occurred in a context in which Fidel Velázquez has been called the second most powerful man in Mexico. Leader of the CTM and an indispensable source of legitimacy and support for the regime, as of 1982 he had retained that post for virtually four decades while a succession of the "most" powerful men in Mexican politics rotated in and out of the presidency every six years.

The second type of challenge consisted of the rejection of CTM leadership and the formation of rival confederations. Throughout Mexican history, labor unity had never been achieved despite the long-standing goal to form a single central. In addition to the CROM and the CGT, which predated the CTM, new confederations were formed both in the aftermath and postaftermath periods. This "pluralism" in the Mexican labor movement did not present much of a threat to the pattern of state-labor relations. Because of the advantages of access and the possible distribution of benefits that would ensue, virtually all of the confederations affiliated with the PRI. Instead of making the state-labor relation more difficult to manage, the multiplicity of confederations allowed the state to some extent to play one confederation off against another, though the CTM remained the dominant labor player. One technique in dealing with the multiplicity of confederations was state support of umbrella organizations that would coordinate their activities but not displace them.

By the end of the aftermath period, the labor movement was perhaps more divided than it had been since the revolution. Within the PRI were several confederations in addition to the CTM: not only the CROM and CGT but also the newer CPN, COCM, and CNT. Beyond that, divisions had produced a dissident group within the labor movement that rejected PRI affiliation, specifically, the national industrial federations that formed the CUT and the group of unions that Lombardo took with him and that were affiliated with his new party. In 1952, in the last months of the Alemán presidency and with the support of the government, a new confederation was formed by those that rejected CTM affiliation. The new CROC did, however, join the PRI and added an interesting new element in state-labor relations. Because it embraced the newer confederations within the PRI (CPN, COCM, and CNT), it has been suggested that the CROC facilitated state control of labor by allowing the state to deal and bargain with fewer confederations (Pellicer and Reyna 1978:74). The CROC was also effective in helping the government respond to the dissident unions that had left the PRI. When the CUT divided, one faction opted to join the CROC, and the CROC's new secretary general was recruited from the ranks of the CUT. The inclusion of the CUT within the CROC and its consequent return to the PRI isolated the rest of the dissident labor movement. Two years later, most of the remaining CUT faction formed the CRT, which joined the PRI, and the Lombardistas in the UGOCM were left alone and weakened.

Finally, the CROC performed another function that became particularly important under the next president, Ruiz Cortines: it was used by the new president as an ally to counterbalance the CTM. Ruiz Cortines, as we have seen, came to power amid the discrediting of the prior president, Alemán, whose administration was both conservative and corrupt. As a compromise candidate, Ruiz Cortines had to steer a middle course between the Alemán and Cárdenas factions, but in so doing he had to restore the balance between the formerly ascendant Alemanistas and the more aggrieved Cardenistas—that is, he had to dislodge the former from their favored position. With the purge of the left that had taken place under Alemán, the CTM leaned toward the Alemán faction. It has been suggested that Ruiz Cortines may have found competition and conflict within the labor movement particularly attractive as a way to limit the power of the CTM. This was so especially since the CTM opposed some of Ruiz Cortines's efforts to reorient policy toward a more balanced pattern of agricultural and industrial growth and away from the more exclusive emphasis on industrialization that had characterized the previous period (Scott 1964:103, 164, 208).

In response to this attempt to support a rival confederation, Fidel Velázquez immediately began planning a new initiative to consolidate the dominant position of the CTM. Camacho (1980:54–55) has suggested that the CTM's general strike threat in 1954 over wage policy (see above) was part of its response to the CROC. Based on the principle of union "independence," the CROC had been projecting a more reformist, "authentic," and anti-*charro* image, despite the government support it received. However, with the threat of a general strike, the CTM countered this challenge and reaped the advantage of appearing more militant, especially when the CROC supported the government in opposition to the strike threat. In another move, the CTM took steps to unite the labor movement under its leadership. In 1953 the Plan de Guadalajara laid the basis for a united central, and in 1955 the BUO was formed by the CTM, CROM, CGT, and several national industrial unions as a labor bloc to coordinate the activities of existing confederations, but not absorb them. The CROC, however, remained apart as a "dissident" confederation that rejected the CTM and the BUO. Nevertheless, the CTM had retained its position as the most important interlocutor between the state and labor (Camacho 1980:55).

A similar pattern was repeated at the beginning of the next presidential term. The transition between presidents saw a period of labor turmoil in protest of wages and rejection of unresponsive leadership (see below). Once again, then, a new dissident movement had emerged that rejected the existing labor movement structures, and once again the government needed a flexible response that would make room for those labor groups unwilling to join the CTM or the BUO. In 1960 the government of López Mateos supported the formation of a new umbrella organization, the CNT, that embraced the CROC, the electricians, and other labor groups that proclaimed the principle of independent unionism but that nevertheless affiliated with the PRI (Reyna and Miquet 1976:71–72). The final organizational cap was put in place in 1966, when the Labor Congress (CT) was formed as a united central to replace both the BUO and CNT. Promoted by the PRI with the approval of President Díaz Ordaz, the CT was dominated by the CTM, although like its predecessors it allowed its members a great deal of autonomy (Reyna and Miquet 1976:75; Camacho 1980:60).

The third type of challenge was the most significant. It consisted not only of a rejection of CTM leadership, but also of the pattern of "official" unionism put in place in many unions by the end of the aftermath period. From the beginning, industrial unions had tended to organize nationally and furthermore to withdraw from the CTM. It was primarily from among these national industrial unions, often but not exclusively independent of the CTM, that "insurgencies" took place against a co-opted and sometimes corrupt union leadership and movements for union autonomy from the government. This third type was the most serious confronted by the Mexican regime because as a type of more militant unionism it threatened to undermine the system of labor control, and as a type of autonomous unionism it threatened to undermine the state-labor alliance that was a pillar of the legitimacy of the Mexican regime.

The first major challenge to official unionism and the state-labor coalition occurred in 1958–59. The most important strikes took place among the telegraph workers, elementary and kindergarten teachers, railroad workers, and oil workers—all public workers organized in national unions. This wave of protest was a clear continuation of the struggles of the past and, in some cases, of the fight against the imposition of *charro* unionism of the 1940s. In each case wage demands led to a rejection of union leadership, which was seen as co-opted, unrepresentative, and unwilling to defend the interests of workers. In addition to bread-and-butter issues, then, a major element in these strikes was the rebellion against the co-opted leadership and the attempt to supplant it with a democratically elected, independent leadership.

These cases of labor dissidence illustrate the characteristic flexibility with which the Mexican regime typically responded to the challenges it faced. The government played a sophisticated game, granting a number of concessions, including wage increases and even a willingness to abide by union elections and allow the dissidents to assume leadership of the union. However, independent unionism was not allowed to go so far as to threaten the PRI-labor alliance. If these concessions failed to achieve labor peace, the government intervened and once again imposed a nondemocratic leadership.

The means by which the state put down the challenge to the state-labor alliance represented by the 1958–59 strike wave illustrates the mechanisms available for maintaining control in Mexico. In addition to substantive concessions, these means consisted of the political resources afforded the state by the hegemonic regime and the state-labor alliance it embodied. In the first instance, existing labor leaders within the local union or particular union section resisted the rise of a dissident leadership. At levels above them, the state found allies in labor leaders of the national union and then in leaders at the federation and confederation level. At the highest level, the BUO entered the conflict on the side of government to oppose the insurgency against the union bureaucracy. In June 1958, for instance, the dissidents among the telegraph workers, teachers, and other groups rejected the FSTSE (the confederation of government workers) of which their unions had all been a part, and attempted to create a rival confederation. In reaction, Fidel Velázquez threw the weight of the CTM behind the FSTSE and warned that he would mobilize the BUO "to crush any attempt at social disbandment against the regime" (quoted in Loyo Brambilas and Pozas Horcasitas 1975:40). Repression of the independent movements through the use of police or the arrest and jailing of leaders was resorted to, but only after leaders refused the terms of co-optation, which exchanged concessions for cooperation with the PRI. Even after the government reasserted its control, the wage demands of the dissident unions were often met.[24]

The decade following the 1958–59 strike movement was characterized by three developments. The first was a series of concessions made by the government to labor. From the point of view of the government, the coercion used in the resolution of the 1958–59 strikes was a sign of failure of the smooth functioning of a hegemonic regime. In the following decade the government undertook to reestablish better relations with labor and to renew the exchange of material benefits for support in order to keep labor in the coalition. The list of such government responses included an expansion of social security and of the system of retail outlets selling subsidized goods to

[24] Loyo Brambila and Pozas Horcasitas 1975; Everett 1967:53–56; Handelman 1976:271–79; Stevens 1974:chap. 4.

workers, the implementation of the profit-sharing provision of the 1917 constitution, and the creation of a number of agencies and banks to promote the availability of working-class housing. In addition, the federal labor law was revised and the role of tripartite commissions was expanded (Leon and Xelhuantzi López 1985:13–14).

The second development was the formation of the Labor Congress, as the next step in the pattern of incorporating dissident labor groups through the creation of ever broader umbrella organizations. As we have seen, the union bureaucracy had a parallel interest to that of the government in reestablishing control over the labor movement. To this end, the CT was created as an organization that did not carry the same political baggage as the CTM, even though the CTM remained the most influential component within it. On this basis the Labor Congress could appeal to and embrace the former CNT as well as BUO and other labor groups. Despite CTM dominance of the Labor Congress, it has been argued that with its formation the union bureaucracy not only consolidated its control but also achieved a greater degree of autonomy from the state (Leon and Xelhuantzi López 1985:15).

The third feature of the 1960s was the continuation of movements for union autonomy. Though challenges were not mounted on the same scale, workers in several unions met with some success, for instance, the unions of telegraph operators, petroleum workers, miners, radio station employees, and auto tire workers (Handelman 1979b.7). Nevertheless, the system was flexible enough to accommodate these rather isolated cases, and analysts such as Ilan Semo (1982:61) could declare that "en la década de 1960 el 'charrismo' hegemonizó indisputadamente."[25]

All this changed rather abruptly in the highly charged, politicized atmosphere following the events of 1968. The student movement and the shocking and unexpected brutality of its repression produced a process of politicization and radicalization. The proliferation of leftist organization in the party sphere had its counterpart in the labor sphere in a new wave of protest involving demands for union autonomy from the state and the PRI. In the following decade, particularly in the major sectors of the economy, there was an explosion of labor insurgency that was seen as representing a potential threat to the regime, especially given the other challenges to the legitimacy of the regime among the middle sectors, students, and private capital and given the possibilities of solidarity and coordination among different labor sectors. Unlike the cases of Brazil and pre-1970 Chile, where protest accelerated as part of a process of general political polarization, in Mexico, as had occurred earlier in the 1958–59 wave of protest, the alliance of the dominant part of the labor movement with the state through the PRI gave the government the political resources to control and limit these movements. The part of the labor movement allied to the government was a mechanism through which pressure could be exerted against the insurgent movements and

---

[25] "In the decade of the 1960s *charrismo* established undisputed hegemony" (authors' translation).

through which an alliance with labor could be maintained after repression was used if that became necessary. Indeed, by the end of the 1970s, this phase of labor protest had come to a halt.

In the late 1960s and early 1970s, workers in a number of unions successfully elected more militant leaders in sectors including autos and textiles (Handelman 1979b:7). The crest of the new wave of union dissidence, however, began in 1972, in a context made more urgent by the collapse of Mexico's model of economic development. Following three decades of an "economic miracle," a growing economic crisis was reflected in indicators of GNP growth, balance of payments, declining rates of investment, renewed inflation (which had been held in check since 1955), and pressure on real wages (Ayala et al. 1890:86–89). In this context labor protest erupted in unions both within and outside of the CTM. From mid-1973 to mid-1974, the number of labor conflicts submitted to conciliation and arbitration boards increased sixfold over the previous year, and the following year the number of strikes under federal jurisdiction doubled (Leon and Xelhuantzi López 1985:19–20). The most impressive movements were mounted by the auto workers, electricians, metallurgical workers, and telephone workers, as well as the university workers, where academics joined forces with blue- and white-collar workers.

The pattern of union insurgency was similar to that of 1958–59. Typically the movement within each union started with economic demands and broadened as the existing union leadership came to be seen as an obstacle. In this way, it came to take on the dimensions of rejecting the existing union structure and advocating a more militant, representative, democratic, and autonomous form of unionism. Though the movement thus took on a political coloration—and indeed had profound political implications—it was not political in its origins nor, with some exceptions, was it ideological or closely tied to opposition political parties, including the Mexican Communist Party, whose influence remained limited. To the extent the insurgent groups were political, in a narrow sense, they represented a diversity of views, and thus, as a whole, the independent union movement of the 1970s was politically heterogeneous.

This observation suggests another feature of the independent union movement: its fractionalization. Perhaps three groupings of independent unions are worth mentioning. The first was the MSR, founded in 1975 in the course of the insurgency movement among the electrical workers. Following a kind of *charrazo* in which the dissident leadership was expelled, the dissidents formed a number of organizations to mobilize support. Within the electrical workers union they formed the Tendencia Democrática, which was in some ways the most important single movement of the decade, promulgating a "Declaration of Guadalajara," which set the general agenda for independent unionism in Mexico (see Trejo Delarbre 1980a:140; Marván 1985:36–38). On an interunion level, the MSR was founded as a labor confederation that would constitute a socialist rival to the CTM (Handelman 1979b:8). The following year, the FNAP was organized as a political front that would coordinate worker, student, peasant, and popular movements. In 1976, however, the Tendencia Democrática was defeated: faced with widespread worker dismissals as a response to its strike activities, it disbanded. The FNAP had never amounted to much. The MSR remained, drawing support primarily from nuclear workers and sectors of university and electrical workers. It never, however, succeeded in becoming an important focus of union activity (See Handelman 1979b:9; Leal 1985:62).

Another organization that drew a lot of attention in the 1970s was the FAT, which was Christian Democratic in orientation. It attained influence in dynamic industrial sectors, such as automobiles, electronics, and mining and metallurgy. By the end of the decade it had about 30,000 members (Leal 1985:66–67). Finally, the UOI was the largest of the new groupings, claiming more than 250,000 members at its peak but having about 50,000 to 100,000 by about 1980 (Carr 1983:94; Leal 1985:85). It drew support from workers in automobile, chemical, and textile industries as well as in the transportation sector. Its orientation was one of "militantly antipolitical economism" (Carr 1983:95).

Compared to the 1958–59 strikes, the movement of the 1970s was characterized by its greater magnitude, both encompassing more sectors and lasting over a number of years. Furthermore, the movement of the 1970s presented a greater challenge with the possibility of coordinated action among different working-class sectors and solidarity movements with students and the new left parties, particularly in the context of more general political ferment and of the regime's more fragile legitimacy. Nevertheless, the wave of protest was overcome with the same combination of responses, in which the government relied on its legal powers to recognize unions (and to decline recognition) and declare the legality of strikes; on the presence of a labor bureaucracy through which it could funnel benefits to workers and recruit an alternative, cooperative leadership; and finally on coercive means when a more flexible response failed to secure cooperation.

By the end of the Echeverría government in 1976 the labor challenge to the regime had been overcome. The CTM was not dislodged from its dominant position, and the CT continued to encompass most of organized labor. In the mid-1970s three-quarters of the estimated CT members were affiliated with one of the "official" confederations. Of these, almost half, or nearly one and a half million workers, belonged to the CTM, representing a greater percentage than the data indicate for 1948, 1954, and 1960. Those labor organizations that rejected affiliation with the 4 million–strong CT represented a small percent of the labor movement. At the end of the decade the UOI numbered about 106,000, the FAT about 30,000, and another organization, the SOL, about 7,000. Adding the higher estimates available for three unaffiliated national industrial unions (SUNTU, the university workers; SNTTAM, the aircarft workers; SNTAS, aviation workers) brings the total number of independent workers to at most under 200,000 (Leal 1985:39–40, 67–68, 85; Aguilar Garcia 1985:205–9).

Emphasizing the "durability of officially-sanctioned unionism," Carr

(1983:92–93, 96) has seen the 1970s as "a history of the enormous resilience of the 'official' labor union leadership and an illustration of the difficulties facing independent unions . . . which would threaten the existing pattern of relations between the state and the labor bureaucracy." Yet, as he recognizes, the defeat did not represent a complete failure. Though the CT continued to be the dominant interlocutor of the labor movement, Leon and Xelhuantzi López (1985:26) have emphasized the way that organization was transformed by the dynamics within the labor movement and the way it came to put greater emphasis on consensus and representativeness instead of coercion and violence. With the defeat of the movement of the 1970s, the struggle was largely displaced to the transformation of existing organizations within established channels (Trejo Delarbre 1980a:151).

In Mexico, then, unions were under strong pressure to participate in a state-labor coalition. The economic weakness of most Mexican unions and their need to find allies in their collective bargaining made them particularly vulnerable to this kind of pressure (Everett 1967:165). Among the economically stronger unions, dissident movements emerged. In these cases, the government was flexible and willing to tolerate substantial independence, but only within the framework of sustaining the overall PRI-labor alliance (Handelman 1976:289). The result was a largely co-opted and yet pluralistic labor movement that tended to contribute to rather than oppose the legitimacy of the state.

Peasant Mobilization.   Independent movements also emerged among the peasantry, but with even less success. These movements arose around two issues. The first was the reaction against the reversal of Cardenist agrarian policies in the aftermath period. The distribution of land under the agrarian reform had been dramatically cut back, and the government had turned its attention from the collective *ejido* as a base of agricultural development and the recipient of government resources to large private holdings, for which constitutional amendments had been required. The second was the growing impoverishment of the countryside and the proletarianization of the peasantry, leading to an agrarian crisis that became apparent in 1965 and that by the mid-1970s caused Mexico to become a large importer of food grains.

The grievances among the peasantry included the demand for land—especially in view of the existence of large holdings above the legally permitted size, higher prices for crops, better access to markets, greater availability of credit and other inputs such as water, and employment and better wages for the landless. In addition they included the demand for independent organizations that would allow greater participation by the grassroots and be more responsive to the needs of the peasantry than the CNC.[26]

The first major dissident peasant confederation was the UGOCM, that stemmed from Lombardo's break with the CTM and the PRI in 1948. Its affiliates included the strongest independent peasant unions. In the late 1950s, the UGOCM carried out a series of land invasions, especially on land owned

[26] Warman 1980:118; Cornelius and Craig 1984:445; Montes de Oca 1977:53–54.

by foreigners. The example of the invasion of the Cananea Cattle Company demonstrates the Mexican pattern of responding to protest. The invasion was led by Jacinto López, the most important UGOCM peasant leader, who was first offered a bribe to buy his cooperation. When this cooperation was rejected and the invasion took place, Jacinto López was jailed. Upon his defeat, however, the land was expropriated and distributed to the peasants. Typically, it was the threat to the coalition, not the substantive concessions, that was ultimately intolerable.

In the 1960s, with Jacinto López out of jail, the UGOCM became "a very serious threat" (Montes de Oca 1977:55). Once again, the response of the government conformed to the Mexican model of handling dissent: resources were distributed and benefits were granted, but through the CNC, thus making that confederation, rather than dissident organizations, the channel for access and concessions. As a result, while the UGOCM initially maintained its agrarian militancy, it supported the candidacy of Díaz Ordaz in 1964 and found it helpful to cooperate with rather than oppose the PRI; indeed, following the elections for the Chamber of Deputies, Jacinto López became a Party Deputy of the PPS, a PRI "satellite" party (Anderson and Cockroft 1972:237–38). By the early 1970s, after the death of Jacinto López, the UGOCM was no longer the combative organization it had once been. Divided into two factions, one more radical than the other, both nevertheless joined the CONPA, the new umbrella organization (see below) (Montes de Oca 1977:55).

A similar pattern was followed by the CCI (Independent Peasants Central), founded in the early 1960s as the other major independent peasant confederation. In its characteristic fashion, the government responded to CCI demands flexibly and co-optively as well as by employing some coercion and repression. Under this pressure, the CCI, like the UGOCM, split over the question of the relationship it should adopt toward the PRI. The more moderate and larger faction cooperated with, and later joined, the PRI; the more radical dissidents remained in the opposition. In 1964, Danzós Palomino, the leader of the dissident CCI, ran as the presidential candidate of the FEP, the electoral front formed by the CCI with the MLN and the PCM. In subsequent years it suffered under the impact of harassment and the jailing of its leaders.

Parallel to developments in the labor arena, part of the response to the independent UGOCM and CCI was the formation in 1973 of the Permanent Agrarian Congress (CONPA) as a new umbrella organization embracing the CNC as well as the UGOCM and a faction of the CCI. It was the new vehicle through which Echeverría would both grant concessions and carry out his new agrarian policy, with its emphasis on the *ejido*, and also bring the activities of the dissident peasant organization back within a legal framework. This development was followed by the Pacto de Ocampo, in which the organizations decided to unite around the CNC (Montes de Oca 1977:60–61).

In addition to the emergence of independent peasant organizations, peasant land invasions took place throughout the country in the 1970s. The independent faction of the CCI was involved with some of them, but in general they were fragmented and organizationally uncoordinated. They aimed primarily at forcing the hand of the government in the stalled program of land distribution within the framework of the agrarian reform. In the first years of the decade, the CNC and the Department of Agriculture were inclined not to move against the invaders and even, on occasion, encouraged them, particularly when the land invaded was a traditional holding that the government viewed as an obstacle to development or whose owner it had no interest in protecting. Action was taken against the invasions only when they became widespread (Montes de Oca 1977:59).

The general policy response to the invasions of the 1970s was in line with the new "shared development" strategy by which the Echeverría government sought to reaffirm its bonds with the popular sectors. In the agrarian field, the government sought to distribute benefits to the peasantry and even to redistribute resources from the urban to the rural sector, especially in light of the developing crisis in food production. CONASUPO, the government purchasing agency, raised the support prices it paid for certain crops. Between 1972 and 1975 the price it paid for corn and wheat approximately doubled, while the inflation rate was about 50 percent. In the Plan of Rural Development, the government embarked on a new program of infrastructural investment. It also adopted a series of policies to extend to *ejidos* and small farms the use of key inputs already in use on large farms, such as improved seeds, irrigation, and fertilizer, and it expanded credit and extension services. Finally, the government extended education and health programs including social security in the rural areas (Sanders 1975:12).

The techniques of control, containing dissidence, and preserving the state alliance with the peasantry were thus essentially the same as those used for the labor sector. They centrally employed the resources afforded by the links between the PRI and the mass organizations in a process of negotiation and co-optation. In comparison with the state-labor relations, state-peasant relations displayed two variations. First, the organized peasantry and the CNC had always been more subordinated to the state than was the labor movement, and within the party the peasant sector never had the degree of autonomy of the labor sector. As a result, the CNC, as the organizational intermediary between the state and the peasantry, had a role more heavily weighted toward state control as opposed to mass representation, compared to that of the labor confederations. Second, repression was more widespread and has been called a "complement to negotiation and absorption" even though "by itself [it] could not explain the nature of the whole configuration nor its stability" (Warman 1980:118).

Guerrilla Movements.   During the 1970s, a number of guerrilla movements sprang up in Mexico. None, however, grew very large or had major lasting power (see K. Johnson 1978:156ff). Many of the urban and rural guerrilla groups were loosely related under the umbrella organization ACNR, which attempted to organize a political party, the Party of the Poor (PDLP), committed to abolition of capitalism through armed struggle and terrorist activities. During the Echeverría administration, a number of terrorist acts, including some rather spectacular assassinations and kidnappings, were carried out. Among these were the kidnappings of Jaime Castrejón Díaz, the rector of the University of Guerrero; of Rubén Figueroa, the federal senator and the PRI's candidate for governor of Guerrero; and of José Guadalupe Zuno, the father-in-law of Echeverría; as well as the assassination of industrialist Eugenio Garza Sada, a member of one of the oldest and most prominent families of the Monterrey entrepreneurial elite.

These activities were certainly impressive and were met with prompt responses that ranged from the imprisonment of leftist leaders on trumped up charges, the murder or assassination of others, and some military encounters. Compared to other countries in Latin America, however, the guerrilla movement remained limited. Indicative of the way in which the Mexican regime filled political space, leaving relatively little room for guerrilla organizations, were the rumors and interpretations that suggested that the creation of some of these groups—and even the kidnapping of Echeverría's father-in-law—was the responsibility of government or PRI officials. Guerrero was the site of the most extensive guerrilla activity. It is a state that over the years experienced a great deal of "endemic violence, both revolutionary, and more frequently, nonrevolutionary." Yet, it should also be remembered that even there no guerrilla group was able to build a mass movement (Hellman 1978:173–74).

Finally, though some of the groups were "authentic," in evaluating their significance it is important to keep in mind the phenomenon of what might be called mercenary terrorists. In reaction especially to the reform program with which Echeverría sought to reestablish the legitimacy of the Mexican regime following the events of 1968, groups of conservative capitalists "provided money to recruit, arm, and train paramilitary shock troops [and] . . . sponsored pseudo-guerrilla groups to carry out terrorist activities in the name of leftist causes" (Hellman 1978:160). There is evidence that this phenomenon began earlier and that these hired thugs even played a part in the violence and army intervention during the 1968 student movement. In the following years their role increased, with the "falcons," a paramilitary group apparently sponsored by the Monterrey capitalists and aided by government officials who were enemies of Echeverría, becoming particularly well known (Hellman 1978:160–61). All in all, the leftist guerrilla challenge was quite limited in Mexico, and in response to the political reform of 1977, much energy on the left was subsequently channeled into the electoral arena.

By 1982, then, the Mexican regime seemed to have met the party, labor, and peasant challenges of the previous two decades. Unlike regimes in many of other countries, it survived, but not unscathed. As events in the next few years would demonstrate, its decision-making capacity seemed impressively intact. However, its legitimacy was slipping, as many Mexicans increasingly saw the one-party dominant regime as authoritarian, unrepresentative, rigid, and obsolete. In response to the flagging legitimacy, sustained and further fueled by political and financial corruption, the electoral system was in a state of flux, and the elections of that year would be the first under the new reform. This was the situation when the debt crisis of 1982 sent the country reeling. Between the elections of 1982 and the inauguration of the new president, outgoing president López Portillo nationalized the banks in a dramatic reaction to the economic and political crisis. The move was extraordinarily popular and was greeted with a wave of nationalistic enthusiasm; however, it also incurred a level of hostility from the private sector that hearkened back to the time of Cárdenas. Thus, de la Madrid entered presidential office under the most inauspicious circumstances and with a big question mark concerning the debt crisis. The enormous pressure for a new round of austerity measures from international creditors, the IMF, and orthodox economists and policy-makers, along with the collapse of confidence in the system on the part of important components of the national business community, raised new questions about the survivability of the PRI as a party able to keep together a large, heterogeneous coalition based on material and symbolic payoffs. Yet the party had a history of successfully maneuvering through difficult times, and the general consensus seemed to be that the country was not in for more than incremental political change, largely directed by the government itself. The unanticipated opposition that erupted from within the PRI itself toward the end of the de la Madrid presidency will be considered in the following chapter.

VENEZUELA

As in Mexico, the heritage of Venezuela was a hegemonic, integrative party system. In Venezuela, rather than the semiauthoritarian one-party dominant regime of Mexico, this took the form of a multiparty, competitive democratic regime. Some analysts have seen Venezuela's enormous oil wealth and hence its resource base as essential in producing this outcome, while others (see D. Levine 1985) have argued that while oil wealth facilitated stable democracy and the party pact on which it is based, political factors were more important determinants. While the present argument is closer to the latter of these two perspectives in emphasizing the causal importance of the type of incorporation and its aftermath, it should be remembered that it is not so much the outcome of democracy per se that we are interested in here, as in the broader category of integrative hegemonic regimes with centripetal dynamics.

Venezuela's Second Republic began with the institutionalization of the Punto Fijo Pact and a carefully crafted coalition government built on a system of coparticipation, in which AD shared power with other parties. However, the system of coparticipation, which was instituted with the inauguration of the Betancourt government in the beginning of 1959, did not last long, and the breakdown of the coalition in the 1960s led to a reconfiguration of the party system. As the system evolved, AD and COPEI became more equal in strength and other parties lost electoral appeal. With the emergence of a two-party dominant system, the electoral competition between AD and COPEI became increasingly intense at the same time that they came to resemble each other more. Less and less differentiated, these two major centrist, multiclass parties were able to continue to cooperate on policy issues. They also cooperated in other spheres: they developed an understanding over the sharing of bureaucratic posts (Myers and Martz 1986:449) and cooperated to reinforce the two-party system and contain any challenge from a third party, particularly within the labor movement. The basic agreement on policy orientation of the two parties, the political cooperation between them, and the centrist pull of the party system are fundamental in understanding the "limited pluralism" (Myers and Martz 1986:466) that came to characterize Venezuelan democracy and the dynamics of its integrative two-party system. Incorporating the working class as well as the peasantry within the governing coalition, this system had the hegemonic resources to withstand the challenges of the 1960s and 1970s.

The contrast with the pattern in Brazil and Chile may be noted. Those two countries exhibited a pattern of complex electoral coalitions, but unsuccessful attempts to form governing coalitions, in the context of polarization. The Venezuelan pattern came to consist of just the opposite: the absence of electoral coalitions combined with the successful formation of governing coalitions. This occurred in the context not of polarization but, quite the contrary, of interparty cooperation.

Overview of the Party System

Evolution of the Pact: From Power-Sharing to Two-Party Competition.   The original agreements between the political parties, which were contained in the set of pacts and accords discussed in the previous chapter, can be thought of as containing three basic components: a regime-founding pact, a programmatic pact, and a coalitional pact. The regime-founding pact was a basic agreement among the political and economic elites to support the development of a liberal-democratic system within the framework of a capitalist economic order. Democratic, electoral institutions were established and proportional representation was adopted as the basis for maintaining an inclusionary form of pluralist participation both in government and in other institutions, such as labor unions. The programmatic pact represented an agreement on a particular mix of social and economic compromises among the political parties, their peasant and labor support groups, and the major traditional and economic elites, such as the military, the Church, and business. Finally, the coalitional pact represented a commitment to coparticipation or power-sharing in which all three parties to the pact—AD, COPEI, and URD—would participate in a coalition government regardless of the outcome of the election. This agreement to create a "coalition of the whole" involved the decision by AD leaders not to press their electoral advantage, but to ensure adequate representation to COPEI and URD within the government and the popular sector organizations.

While the regime-founding and programmatic pacts remained largely intact, there was a gradual evolution away from the original coalitional agreement and toward a competitive, two-party dominant system. Two stages in this evolution can be discerned. In the original agreement, which was maintained from 1958 to 1960, the three components of the pact were rigidly adhered to. In 1958, though AD won over 49 percent of the vote, the Betancourt administration followed the agreements of the pact of Punto Fijo and divided positions within the national administration evenly among the major parties in the pact. Betancourt's first cabinet was composed of three ministers from each of the parties as well as six independents. Within the legislature, the three parties moved quickly to pass legislation that formalized the programmatic aspects of the agreement, much of which was contained in the new Venezuelan constitution that went into effect in 1961. Finally, as we have seen, AD helped COPEI and URD establish themselves within the labor movement by accepting its own underrepresentation on union and federation boards to make room for COPEI and URD representatives.

The first stage in the evolution away from the original pact in some sense began in 1960 though its major features emerged around the dynamics of the 1963 elections at the end of the Betancourt government. This period, which lasted until 1968, was one in which the coalition of the whole began to disintegrate, due to both the withdrawal of parties from the coalition and defections within AD, though this latter, as we have seen, was really part of the expulsion of the left.

The splintering of AD itself began in April 1960 (see Chapter 6) when the party expelled its increasingly fractious Youth Federation, which eventually formed the MIR. Briefly joining the legislative opposition, the MIR soon abandoned the electoral arena and joined the Communist Party in leading the Fidelista guerrilla movement. The ARS defection and that group's decision to join the opposition cost the AD-COPEI coalition its majority in the Chamber of Deputies, where COPEI leader Rafael Caldera was deposed as president and replaced by an ARS member. The government coalition maintained its majority in the Senate but its control was shaky (Alexander 1964:83; Herman 1980:57). As a consequence, the last year of the first administration was characterized by legislative immobilism as the various parties and factions prepared for the 1963 presidential and legislative elections.

The most serious split within AD occurred in 1967 with the defection of the MEP. The cause of the split was the division among AD leaders in reaction to the electoral decline that the party suffered in 1963 following the ARS split. Though AD remained the largest party, its plurality was reduced to a third, so that it was more dependent than it had been on coalition partners. The new president, Leoni, reacted to AD's weakened position by forming a center-right coalition with the probusiness FND, as well as with the increasingly rightist URD, which had expelled its own left wing in 1964. He also moved to increase the role of private business in public policy decisions. The leadership of the party organization, however, favored rebuilding the "party's former rapport with and undisputed leadership of the popular classes to reverse the decline of the party" (Blank 1973:158). Led by Luis Prieto, this group consistently opposed the Leoni government. The conflict escalated as the two factions differed over AD's 1968 presidential candidate. After complex negotiations, the two factions agreed to a party primary in September 1967 to determine the party's candidate. Prieto apparently won a clear majority over Leoni and Betancourt's candidate, Gonzalo Barrios, but Betancourt, alleging fraud and irregularities on the part of Prieto's party machinery (Blank 1973:160), refused to accept the Prieto candidacy. The party officially split in October 1967, when the Prieto forces reorganized as the MEP (People's Electoral Movement).

While the first cause of the disintegration of the broad coalition that AD had been attempting to sustain since 1958 was fractionalization of AD itself, the second was the disaffection of the pacting parties. From 1960 to 1968, the Venezuelan political system was characterized by a series of fluid legislative coalitions as well as brief periods, usually prior to presidential elections, of legislative immobility. A governing coalition of all parties included in the pact was thus replaced by shifting coalitions dominated by AD but including various other parties. During this period, AD governed alternately with COPEI and URD.

The first break in the power-sharing pact occurred, as we have seen, in November 1960 when the URD withdrew from the coalition government. Relations between AD and URD, the second largest party, had been testy, and frequent cabinet crises occurred as URD jockeyed for position, fought for greater patronage, and differed with AD over policy issues (Alexander 1964:99). In the end, the URD withdrawal was largely due to the party's opposition to the government's hostile policy toward Castro's Cuba as well as to the belief that it could strengthen its chances for victory in the 1963 elections by dissociating itself from the ruling coalition (Martz 1966:331–32).

From 1960 to 1962, then, AD and COPEI alone formed a legislative coalition. The defection of MIR and the URD from the governing coalition forced AD and COPEI into closer cooperation. Over the next two years, AD and COPEI continued to rule through small majorities in the Senate and Chamber of Deputies. This cooperation between the two parties was so close that it was referred to as a "guanábana" after the fruit that is white on the inside (AD's party color) and green on the outside (COPEI's color). As a consequence of the close cooperation required by the coalition, both parties moved toward the center, coming closer together on a number of issues (Herman 1980:56–59).

In the face of the 1963 elections, however, the AD-COPEI coalition broke down. These elections saw a significant shift in the electoral fortunes of the three parties that originally established the pact and a growing fractionalization of the party system. This fractionalization was sped along by a demographic shift caused by a process of extraordinarily rapid urbanization during the 1930–70 period. The result was the emergence of a new urban popular sector without organizational ties to the incorporating party. This factor, in combination with the economic downturn of the late 1950s and early 1960s, created fertile ground for opposition to the governing parties that participated in the pact. For the 1963 elections, two new, largely urban parties were formed. Portrayed as antiparty or electoral protest parties, they developed out of urban dissatisfaction with the governing AD and COPEI. On the right, the IPFN, later renamed the National Democratic Front (FND), was led by a conservative intellectual, Arturo Uslar Prieti. On the left, the FDP (Popular Democratic Front) was led by Jorge Dáger, one of the founders of MIR who subsequently dropped out as that group shifted to armed insurrection (Blank 1973:174–76). These two parties polled 26 percent of the vote, cutting deeply into AD's support base. As a result, AD won the presidential elections but suffered a large decline in its vote, from 49 to 33 percent. At the same time, the 1963 elections saw the beginning of URD's decline as it fell from 31 to 18 percent. COPEI, on the other hand, saw its vote total increase from 15 to 20 percent (Silva Michelena and Sonntag 1970:73).

Seriously weakened and with only a plurality in the legislature, AD needed other parties to form a governing coalition. COPEI, having increased its strength, chose to form a "loyal opposition" and declined to renew the coalition government. After long negotiations, AD finally formed a new coalition government with the URD (which, having abandoned a brief flirtation with armed struggle, returned to the electoral arena) and the newly emerging FND (Fagan 1977:180). The new coalition began to unravel in 1966, however, when the FND withdrew, angered over its failure to influence oil and tax policies and dissatisfied over what it regarded as insufficient representation in the cabinet.

This first stage, then, was one of declining AD dominance and AD's growing inability to hold together a coalition of the whole. AD's decision to maintain the programmatic aspects of the pact, with its emphasis on nonconflictual, centrist compromise—that is, the process observed in the last chapter of the move to the center, the emphasis on conflict limitation, and the expulsion of the left—led to a serious loss in AD's own electoral strength. It culminated in the elections of 1968, in the context of the MEP defection. The MEP presented a much stiffer challenge to the AD leadership than that posed by MIR in 1960 or ARS in 1962. First, MEP controlled too much of the party's electoral and labor membership to be easily crushed. Second, it had more formidable organizational resources than previous splinters, such as the ARS (Blank 1973:161). The MEP defection, therefore, was a decisive blow to AD and provided COPEI's Caldera a narrow 29 to 28 percent victory over AD's Barrios in the 1968 presidential elections.[77] MEP polled 17 percent, effectively reducing what would have been AD's large electoral advantage. At the same time, the URD (12 percent), FDP (7 percent), and FND (4 percent) all lost ground (Silva Michelena and Sonntag 1979:73).

The 1968 presidential victory of COPEI initiated a transition to the subsequent stage in the evolution of the Venezuelan party system, which came to be characterized by three features. First, in that election AD and COPEI emerged as more nearly equal parties. AD lost its position of overwhelming dominance. Having won about three-quarters (74.4 percent) of the popular vote in 1947, it had emerged in 1958 with about half (49.2 percent), while subsequent defections of its left wing meant that its percent of the vote plummeted in 1968 before recuperating to a level of nearly half in 1973. COPEI's strength meanwhile was increasing, so that in 1968 not only was it the equal of AD for the first time, but its growing popularity led to a second feature of this next stage: the alternation of AD and COPEI in power.

Third, as AD lost its position of political dominance, the mechanisms of coparticipation, which had been premised on AD's dominance and willingness to share power, became a thing of the past. Instead, what emerged was a two-party competitive system that operated without a formal governing coalition between the parties but within the framework of substantial cooperation between them and the ongoing observance of the programmatic pact. In 1968, AD and COPEI agreed to a new "institutional pact" that stopped short of renewing a governing coalition but nevertheless extended the idea of cooperation and coparticipation. According to this pact, which lasted

[27] The effective standoff between the two parties may be further noted in the results for congressional seats. While COPEI barely eked out a victory in the presidential vote, AD took the edge in seats in the legislature: 66 to 59 in the Chamber of Deputies and 19 to 16 in the Senate (D. Levine 1978:97).

through the presidency of COPEI's Herrera Campíns, who was elected in 1978, the party winning the national presidency would name the president of the Senate while the other party would name the president of the Chamber of Deputies, and both parties together would jointly fill other important positions, such as supreme court seats and the national comptrollership (McCoy 1989:65, n. 19).

This institutional pact did not include the formation of a governing coalition. Despite its narrow victory in 1968, COPEI rejected a coalitional pact with AD and attempted to govern on its own. Over the next year and a half, as relations between the parties became increasingly strained, AD prevented the passage of COPEI-initiated legislation, while using its strength within the labor confederation to put pressure on the COPEI government. At the same time, AD control of the CTV as well as its electoral strength had been undermined by the MEP split. Both parties thus saw advantages in cooperation and entered into discussions concerning "areas of coincidence" (Tugwell 1975:106), finally reconstituting a working agreement between them. The outcome in early 1970 was an informal legislative coalition, which brought to an end the period of legislative immobility, and cooperation between the parties within the CTV. This outcome severely limited the success of the MEP, not only in the labor movement but consequently in the electoral sphere as well. Thus, a looser form of coalition was maintained within the framework of a competitive party system.

The 1973 elections constituted an additional step toward a two-party system. While the 1968 elections established the principle of party rotation in office, the greater equality of AD and COPEI, and a looser form of governing coalition, the 1973 elections established the unquestioned dominance of AD and COPEI. The earlier process of party fractionalization, which had seemed to be a prominent feature of the 1968 elections when a host of new parties had appeared, came to a halt. It was replaced by what in Venezuela was labeled a process of "polarization," but which is more accurately referred to as the monopolization of the electoral arena by the two parties (or, perhaps, a process of "bi-polarization"). Whereas in 1968 AD and COPEI together accounted for under 60 percent of the vote, in 1973 their combined total was over 85 percent and reached nearly 90 percent in subsequent presidential elections, with the level in congressional voting generally only 10 percent less. In 1973, then, in what some analysts consider a "realigning" election, "third parties" became a decidedly minor force in Venezuelan politics. From a period of shifting coalitions and minority governments, the Venezuelan political system evolved into a stable two-party dominant system.

Somewhat paradoxically, in the years following 1968, the system evolved both toward more openness and toward stronger two-partyism. In rejecting a formal alliance with AD, COPEI initially had to rely on transitory congressional alliances with smaller parties. In this context, an accommodation was sought with parties of the left, all of which, including the MIR, were legalized by the next electoral campaign (Martz 1980a:12). Parties of the right also benefited from the new atmosphere of openness, as represented by the CCN, which Pérez Jiménez had founded in 1968 and through which he had made a bid for popular support upon which to stage a political comeback.

Against this background and the fractionalization evident in the 1968 elections, the two major parties began a period of intense organizational effort in preparation for what many saw as the crucial 1973 presidential and legislative elections. They had at their disposal control of the state resources provided by rapidly expanding oil revenues, which gave AD and COPEI a significant advantage in competing for the support of the growing urban popular sectors. The return to economic prosperity in the mid-1960s and the oil bonanza of the 1970s helped AD and COPEI defeat the smaller personalist or antiparty electoral challenges. The degree of AD and COPEI success in the 1973 elections surprised many observers, but the electoral dominance of AD and COPEI and of the two-party system was indeed being consolidated. A prominent observer of Venezuelan elections and party politics has noted that the 1978 elections clearly demonstrated that "the era for antiparty electoral phenomena had passed. . . . A presidential aspirant in the late 1970s could not compete effectively on the basis of personality, style, and denunciations of the party system" (Martz 1980b:169). In Venezuela, the two-party system became self-reinforcing: as the strength of the two major parties increased, more and more Venezuelans perceived a presidential, and to a lesser extent a legislative, vote for one of the minority parties as wasted.

The dynamics of the two-party system in Venezuela followed another common pattern of such systems as well: the programmatic and ideological pull of the parties to the center. The tendency reinforced the ongoing observance of the programmatic pact as the party system evolved away from the formal coalitional pact of power-sharing. The Venezuelan political system evolved into a stable two-party system, but one that continued to operate within the confines of a narrow range of policy options. The consensus on a centrist program, first agreed to in the late 1950s, was reinforced by the political dynamics of a two-party system, which pulled the parties to the center. In this way, a kind of interparty coalition of the whole was sustained, with the overwhelming electoral dominance of two cooperating, programmatically similar, centrist parties.

Multiclass Integrative Party System.   As in Mexico, Venezuela developed a party system that was integrative and hegemonic, embracing a broad coalition. Unlike Brazil and Chile, with their intense polarization in the context of a party system with centrifugal dynamics, Venezuela, with its centrist, multiclass parties, evolved toward a competitive but centripetal two-party system. Despite the electoral competition then, the Venezuelan party system was not the vehicle through which political and ideological conflict took place. Rather it was the vehicle through which such political competition was contained.

This outcome of a hegemonic, integrative party system occurred because the breakdown of the formal pact of power-sharing and the evolution toward greater competitiveness were mediated by an important feature of the system: the electoral dominance of two converging, cooperating, centrist, multiclass parties that nevertheless were locked in intense electoral two-party competition. Though it is perhaps overstated to label Venezuela a "simulated one-party competitive" system, the term can be provocatively invoked in passing to emphasize the underlying programmatic agreement and cooperation between the two parties that dominated the Venezuelan political system while they simultaneously engaged in often fierce electoral competition. Indeed, the less provocative term, "el status" is more commonly used to evoke the same features of convergence and cooperation of two establishment parties which, as Martz (1977:110) put it, were two sides of the same coin. The result was a democracy characterized by limited pluralism.

Three points may be distinguished here. The first is the electoral dominance of the two major parties. The second is their convergence in terms of a centrist program and multiclass social base. The third is the centrality of party linkages to popular sector organizations, specifically to urban and rural unions. An important aspect of these linkages is not only that the two major parties each had such ties, but also that through a system of proportional representation, the governing coalition, which the two parties maintained in the context of greater electoral competitiveness, was replicated within these popular sector organizations and provided a firm basis for the institutionalization of union-state linkages regardless of which party controlled the government. We may consider each of these points in turn.

We have already seen the degree to which AD and COPEI together came to dominate the electoral arena. Myers's (1986:110–12, 127–28) label of the Venezuela party system as "two-and-a-sixth-plus" serves to emphasize additional characteristics. Only these two dominant parties were capable of winning the presidency. Other parties existed, but they were not contenders in the same sense. The "sixth" refers to the fraction of the combined vote that could be claimed by the set of parties on the left. Of these, the MAS emerged as the third largest party in presidential elections after 1973, but won just 5 to 6 percent of the vote. Finally, the "plus" refers to the even smaller share of votes garnered by right-wing and largely personalist parties.

Needless to say, two-party dominance of the electoral arena implied AD and COPEI dominance of government decision making. As Martz (1977:110), writing a few years after the 1973 election, could anticipate, "It does not take a wild stretch of the imagination to envisage Venezuela's immediate future as one in which the formulation and implementation of public policy will, in one way or another, be primarily the handiwork of COPEI and Acción Democrática." This control over policy, particularly in light of the convergence of the two parties and the ongoing programmatic pact, meant that Venezuela avoided the policy immobilism and vacillation that characterized Brazil and Chile. It should further be mentioned that AD and COPEI cooperated to maintain the two-party system by warding off threats to one of the parties. As we shall see below, this occurred very clearly in the case of the MEP challenge to AD's position within the CTV. In that instance, AD and COPEI cooperated to defeat MEP control and to restore AD's position of leadership within the CTV.

At the local level, two-party dominance was somewhat less pronounced. In municipal elections, the smaller parties, especially of the left, were able to mount successful challenges to the two parties. Far from being a destabilizing factor, however, the electoral success of opposition parties at the municipal level was an integrative mechanism, serving as an incentive to these parties to participate in the electoral system. This may be one reason why pressures on the left to turn to extralegal opposition were weaker in Venezuela than in Colombia, thus leaving the Venezuelan political system strengthened as a consequence.

The second point is the convergence of AD and COPEI in terms of both policy orientation and social base. Programmatically, the two parties converged on the center. The move of AD toward the right and the jettisoning of its left wing have already been described. What needs to be added here is the complementary move of COPEI to the center. When it was founded in 1946 during the Trienio, COPEI was a conservative party based on the support of entrepreneurs, the middle classes, and the Catholic Church (Yepes 1981:63). Indeed, this Social Christian Party represented a "response to the perceived leftist threat represented by AD. . . . The desire to protect the Church, the parochial educational system, and the family from the perceived onslaught of AD radicalism were all critical factors in [its] early political activity" (Handelman 1978c:5–6). In the post-1958 period, however, COPEI moved to the center of the political spectrum. This move was primarily a pragmatic response to the new electoral game that made mass popular support a critical political resource, although it also occurred in the context of the development of a left wing within the party. Like the Chilean Christian Democratic Party, this new non-Marxist, Christian left, which derived its ideological orientation from the Papal encyclicals concerned with social justice, promoted communitarianism as a limit to individualism and private ownership in order to promote social welfare. The presence of this left wing within COPEI made the party more ideologically diverse than AD and gave it an organic, moral, paternalistic ideological orientation based on notions of social harmony as opposed to the more pragmatic and economic orientation of AD, combined with analyses based on class conflict (Handelman 1978c:7–9). This difference in ideological orientation, however, did not reflect left-right differences. Indeed, in their analysis of Venezuelan parties, Martz and Harkins (1973:535–36) distinguished five ideological positions on a left-right spectrum, and not only did they put both AD and COPEI in the same center category in the post-1958 period, but among the ten or so major parties or tendencies considered, those two alone occupied that position.

As the two parties converged on the center of the political spectrum, the sectors, interests, and policy orientations they represented became increasingly difficult to distinguish. Both became multiclass parties with converging social bases of support. A survey taken before the 1978 elections showed broad support for both parties across all income categories, with AD stronger among the richest 4 percent and poorest third of the population (O'Connor

1980:59, 81). Earlier differences in education and region also diminished as distinguishing characteristics of the parties' respective support bases.

Finally, there were some sectoral differences, but both parties had close ties to all sectors. While AD predominated in the labor movement, COPEI also had an important presence and very actively sought the votes of workers. Though as a result of demographic change the peasantry had been declining as an important political and electoral factor, both parties counted this group among their support bases, though their strengths tended toward different geographical regions, with COPEI's influence concentrated in the Andean area. Just as COPEI made inroads in AD's traditional bases of strength, so AD drew close to the business sector. Both parties sought close ties with the private sector and provided places on their legislative lists for business representatives. As it became increasingly clear to the business elite that differences between the parties were narrow, the affinity between COPEI and the private sector began to erode. Indeed, it was an open secret that leaders of FEDECAMERAS favored AD in the 1968 and 1973 elections (J. Gil 1977:154; Handelman 1978c:8). After 1973, under President Carlos Andres Pérez, AD-business links became even closer.

Electorally, then, the Venezuelan party system came to be dominated by two, converging and cooperating, multiclass parties, which together attracted overwhelming majorities among all social classes, including the popular sectors. Indeed, the electoral support of the working class, both urban and rural, became such an important political resource in the Venezuelan electoral regime that it has been called "tantamount to political survival" for the parties, and even the business-oriented FND found it necessary to attract labor support and win seats on the CTV's executive committee (Boeckh 1972:236). The necessity to attract working-class votes produced an inclusionary regime in which the urban and rural working class became part of the party coalition and hence the governing coalition as well.

The inclusionary features of the party system were not limited to the electoral sphere. A main aspect consisted of the links parties developed with urban and rural popular sector organizations, specifically with labor organizations, which in Venezuela included both labor and peasant unions. This then is the third feature of the party system: the strong organizational ties all parties sought, and the major parties had, with unions. These organizational links, first forged during the incorporation period, afforded the parties the mechanisms of hegemonic control over the political, electoral, and sectoral activities and behavior of the working class.

The links between AD and the unions, the formal integration of labor within the party through its sectoral organization, and the dual roles of party-union leadership have been described above. These links were replicated in the case of the other major parties, which established similar sectoral organizations. Formally and legally, union affiliation with parties was prohibited. Nevertheless, through these links union leaders were always clearly identified with political parties. In 1958, in the interest of preserving labor unity and preventing the fractionalization of the labor movement along party lines, union leaders adopted proportional representation so that all parties would be represented within singular union structures. What emerged in Venezuela, then, was a labor movement in which individual leaders were clearly identified with parties but that, through proportional representation, accommodated close ties with all major parties. By the end of the aftermath period, with the exception of the CUTV, which emerged when the left was purged, the CTV was the unified labor central.

The distribution of party loyalties within the CTV congresses and within its executive committee reveals two things. First, it confirms the notion that all parties found it important to mobilize working-class support and to establish a presence within the organized labor movement. By 1964, the three major parties (not counting the ousted PCV) as well as the FND and FDP were represented in CTV Congresses, and, in the following years of party fractionalization, the new parties, as well as the readmitted PCV and MIR, were represented (McCoy 1985:150, 254). Second, the distribution demonstrates the overwhelming dominance within the organized labor movement of AD as a result of the support and control it had achieved during the incorporation period and the way it subsequently managed to retain that support, despite its conservatization. By the end of the aftermath period, with the manipula tions and machinations that accompanied the purge of the left, AD alone accounted for nearly three-quarters of the delegates to the CTV congresses. Following the low point with the MEP defection, AD regained just a bare majority, but given the programmatic and sometimes overtly political cooperation between AD and COPEI, it is worth noting that together "el status" came to account for three-quarters of the delegates (McCoy 1985:254). These same percentages were duplicated in the distribution of seats in the CTV Executive Committee (Lestienne 1981:27). We will return to these developments below.

Hegemonic Resources. The party heritage of incorporation and its aftermath, then, was a party system that was hegemonic and integrative, embodying a broad coalition from which few groups were excluded and maintaining strong organizational ties to the labor movement. It was "characterized by increased competitiveness among ideologically converging multiclass parties which use[d] proportional representation in their linked nongovernmental organizations" (Fagan 1977:184). This party system provided the state with a number of hegemonic resources. One of these was a particular form of party-mediated control over the labor movement, control which limited political conflict, ensured social peace, and facilitated decision making. In a similar analysis, Salamanca (1988:110) has pointed to 1936, 1945, and 1958 and the events around those dates as constituting key developmental moments in producing a particular form of state-labor relations characterized by a "sindicalismo de conciliación" based on social concertation or a social pact between labor and capital, on substantial state control over the labor movement, and on the major role of parties in mediating this control.

State control over the labor movement was achieved through the familiar features of labor law. These included the regulation of the use of the strike, as well as the state's power to declare the legality or illegality of all strikes, the role of the state in conciliation and arbitration, and state recognition of unions, the use and importance of which was already described for the period following the PCV-MIR split. Control was also achieved by the co-optation that attends state subsidy and financial dependence. It has been reported that the CTV received about 90 percent of its funds from government subsidies by 1961 and received additional funding from sources such as the Venezuelan parties and the American AFL-CIO, which had a long history of operating in Latin America with the purpose of opposing communist and leftist influence in the labor movement (Boeckh 1972:201; McCoy 1985:147). Another mechanism of state control was the exclusive representation the state sometimes extended to the CTV, thus excluding more left-leaning, oppositionist centrals. As we shall see in greater detail below, other confederations were formed and legally recognized by the state, and even received state subsidies, though quite clearly, because of its size as well as its political connections, the CTV received the lion's share of these. Within some state institutions, however, the CTV was in effect uniquely recognized as sole representative of the working class, without even any symbolic equality of treatment of other labor confederations. This occurred when the state established certain corporatist institutions and granted the CTV exclusive representation of labor on tripartite commissions. This monopolistic position was also reflected in the special treatment afforded the CTV in connection with the state-founded workers' bank (BTV) and workers' housing agency (CORACREVI) (McCoy 1985:246, 147–48).

Fundamentally, however, the means of control over the labor movement that were put in place by 1964 were mediated by the major parties. Party affiliation determined the use the state made of the powers and mechanisms of control that it possessed. It also determined the access to the ministry of labor that was afforded to different unions. This differential political influence and access strengthened unions affiliated with the major parties, enhancing their ability to reach more favorable settlements in labor disputes. It thus also increased their popularity and support vis-à-vis more oppositionist unions (McCoy 1985:217; Boeckh 1972:203–04).

After the restoration of civilian rule in 1958, the dual party-union roles resumed the importance they had enjoyed during the incorporation period. These renewed roles were particularly important within AD—the party that was clearly dominant both in the government and in the labor movement at the end of the aftermath period. Though influence flowed in both directions, the dominance of the party role soon became apparent. In the union sphere, the influence of the party was witnessed, for example, in the support of the CTV for Betancourt's austerity measures. Party dictates were particularly strong at the national level, weakening somewhat at lower levels, where union leaders called strikes that did not have the approval of the party. In these cases, however, disciplinary action was often forthcoming, as in the case of a mining strike after which AD expelled the leaders from the party (Boeckh 1972:243).

Within the party sphere, the organized working class was formally represented through the sectoral organization of the party. The AD labor bureaus were given "considerable autonomy from central party direction," and unlike the case for other sectors within the party, the central party organs never rejected any labor member though they had the authority to do so (Fagan 1974:146). Furthermore, according to an analysis carried out by Martz (1966:256), one-fifth of the 25 most prominent AD leaders came out of the labor movement. Thus, as in the case of the Mexican PRI, the position of labor in AD was quite special. Nevertheless, the influence of union leaders within the party was limited. Though union leaders held important party posts and were elected to Congress from 1958 on, a reform of the labor law was not forthcoming despite the presence of such a reform on the labor agenda (Boeckh 1972:253–54). In fact, when a change in the law was finally made in 1973, it further limited the right to strike, though some additional benefits related to retirement and dismissals were added in 1974–75 (McCoy 1989:52–53, 57–58). The dominance of the party over unions was explicitly elaborated in the early "Labor Thesis" of AD, which stated that while workers should be the "organized vanguard of the democratic revolution," it was the party's role to "inculcate . . . party doctrines, and teach [workers] the theory and tactics of the party" (cited in McCoy 1985:136).

Party-union links also created a largely self-perpetuating, bureaucratized union leadership substantially immune from rank-and-file control. The major mechanism through which this occurred was the unified list of candidates in union elections. From 1958 on, the CTV adopted the practice at all levels of having all parties represented in the union agree on a single slate of candidates, thus reducing elections to "acts of approval of a prearranged political deal" (Boeckh 1972:230). This procedure did avoid open partisan struggles within the unions, as originally intended, but also led to the establishment of an entrenched, self-perpetuating leadership insulated from the pressures of competitive elections and democratic selection by the mass base. In the 1970s the unified list became much less prevalent at lower levels (Boeckh 1972:230).

Leadership cooperation with the state and with a conciliatory pattern of industrial relations was also advanced by co-optation. The role of the parties in leadership selection was one factor. In addition, the parties and the state controlled the co-optive resources not only of support and subsidy but also of the offer of positions in both the party and the state, including state enterprises (Salamanca 1988:186).

Party mediation was also a central feature of the type of industrial relations that emerged in Venezuela out of the incorporation and aftermath periods. Labeling it "programmed bargaining," Fagan (1977:225) has described it as a type of political bargaining in which the outcome was more dependent on the party linkages of labor leaders than on economic action. Since in the post-1964 period AD was usually dominant in both the government and the labor movement, this form of party-mediated programmed bargaining primarily involved AD. In this pattern of bargaining, national labor policy was negotiated between union leaders in AD's labor bureaus and other party officials. It was thus primarily a form of bargaining that took place within the party rather than between labor and capital. When an AD president was in power, his approval of the final policy meant that the weight of the state was brought to bear on enforcing the labor terms agreed upon. There was thus little scope for agreements outside the terms of the negotiated framework: given the political connections of AD labor leaders to the Labor Ministry and to the government more generally, other leaders without such access and support could not hope to achieve more favorable collective contracts, and employers likewise knew ahead of time what position the government would defend. Labor-capital bargaining thus by and large took the form of acceptance of the results of prior negotiations within AD. In describing the importance of this party-mediated programmed bargaining between labor and capital, Fagan (1977:188) uses a quotation, drawn from a study of another country, to emphasize the "little space for maneuver within or outside the bargaining room." Interestingly, from the point of view of the comparative analysis of this book, the quotation is from an author describing the Mexican pattern of collective bargaining (Miller 1968:178). And like Mexico, the result in Venezuela was an industrial relations system in which the state managed to impose industrial peace and keep strikes to a minimum. The low level of strikes, particularly in the first decade following the return to civilian rule, was particularly notable (McCoy 1985:209, table 5.3). Furthermore, wage increases were maintained at modest levels. We have seen that in Mexico real industrial wages rose 23 to 33 percent, depending on the estimate, in the period 1968–1975. In the same period in Venezuela, real wages in manufacturing rose 19 percent, climbing a bit more until reaching a peak in 1979 of 26 percent over the 1968 level, and then drifting downward again for the next two years.[28]

Two sources of change in this pattern of collective bargaining have been suggested in the literature. First, the pattern has seemed applicable only when AD held governmental power, and twice so far since the pattern evolved, COPEI in fact captured the presidency. Most authors, for instance, seem to agree that a more combative labor movement emerged in 1969, in part as a political tactic used by AD to oppose the COPEI government. Unfortunately, good analyses of the pattern of collective bargaining during the COPEI governments are not available, but the following is suggested by a kind of structural logic, though empirical confirmation is necessary but lacking.

The important clue to what occurred may not be the brief change in the first year or so—when COPEI came to power for the first time and labor relations seemed to escape government control—of which so much has been made. More revealing may be an understanding of the political context and the nature of the reimposition of party-mediated state control over labor that occurred shortly thereafter. It is important to remember that this was the

[28] Calculated from McCoy (1989:51, table 3).

first time that AD lost control of the government, and more generally, according to the above analysis, it was a transition period in the evolution of the party system. Specifically, it was the point of greatest disintegration of the party pact, a transition when formal coalitions broke down and informal patterns of cooperation had not yet been worked out. Furthermore, AD, the dominant party that had been in a position to oversee the coalitional or cooperative nature of party politics, had also lost control of the CTV with the defection of the MEP. All of this, however, was about to change. In government, as we have seen, AD and COPEI were about to reestablish cooperative, though not formal coalitional, relations, and these would remain in place. Furthermore, as we shall see below, AD would soon regain its control of the CTV, and it would do this with the help and cooperation of COPEI. These new cooperative relations within the government and within the labor movement would seem essential in understanding both the quick demise of the brief period of greater labor militance at the beginning of the COPEI government in 1969 and the status of the existing pattern of collective bargaining in a more electorally competitive two-party system. Finally, it is important to remember that although the AD-dominant system was replaced by what is generally considered a two-party system—and indeed up to 1988 the two parties followed a pattern of perfect rotation in the presidency—that system nevertheless was not based on two equal parties. Instead, AD remained clearly dominant in the labor union sphere and even in the political-electoral sphere. When AD won the presidency, it generally captured about 10 percentage points more than COPEI; whenever COPEI won the presidency, it managed only to tie AD in the legislature. In other words, COPEI victories represented a close, fairly even distribution of the vote, whereas AD's victories were more decisive, representing its substantially greater strength. This continued dominance of AD, despite the high level of party competition and alternation in the presidency, resulted in the continuation of party cooperation within the unions. When COPEI rejected cooperation and attempted to win at a more competitive game, it met with failure.

Specifically, then, it may be suggested that programmed collective bargaining continued in Venezuela, but must be understood not simply as a state-union relationship mediated by AD but rather as one mediated by cooperating parties. In general this cooperation between AD and COPEI was based on the similarity between the two parties in terms of program and even social base, and as a result the parties engaged in only limited conflict. In the union sphere this cooperation took the form of an inclusionary, unitary labor movement with a multiparty leadership. This cooperation extended to power-sharing between AD and COPEI, as in the agreement discussed below in which AD ceded to COPEI the post of secretary-general of the CTV in exchange for its support.

It would appear to be the case, then, that although AD remained dominant in the unions and particularly in the CTV, the cooperation between AD and COPEI in both government and unions meant that state-union relations re-

mained fairly stable no matter which party held power. Both parties had sectoral organizations and through them maintained close, formal links to the
labor movement. Furthermore, both parties conducted their labor policy
within the context of their larger political orientation. While it is the competitive political context that is often emphasized, it is essential to bear in
mind the cooperative nature of Venezuelan political competition. Thus, it
would seem that while AD was much stronger within the labor movement
than COPEI, the cooperation between the parties in both union and state
spheres meant that labor acted as an integrative force and base of support for
governments formed by either party. The overall statistics on labor conflict
during the Caldera government support this perspective. Though some of the
early strikes were considered political and reflected AD's opposition to the
government, the renewal of the pact of party cooperation meant that the pattern of programmed bargaining was quickly reinstated and that the overall
increase in labor conflict is better understood as part of a longer-term trend
that was to continue through subsequent periods, including those of AD
rule.[29]

This last point, the increased labor conflict during the next presidential
term, brings us to the second source of potential breakdown in the pattern of
programmed bargaining. McCoy (1985:213ff, 300ff; 1989:50), for instance,
has suggested that starting in the mid- to late 1970s, Venezuelan labor became more independent and combative, as indicated by a rise in strikes. This
is said to be due to a new financial independence of the CTV, leftist gains in
some unions, and, more importantly perhaps, to a change in economic policy. Nevertheless, as McCoy (1985:388) recognized, a real change from past
patterns remained still in the realm of potentialities.

The heritage of working-class incorporation and its aftermath in Venezuela, then, was, despite some obvious differences, rather similar to that in
Mexico. An inclusionary union movement with marginalized dissident elements was created—one that contributed to industrial peace and policies of
class compromise and that afforded the government popular support that led
to an integrative and stable political system. Both Salamanca (1988:147) and
Boeckh (1972:317) have emphasized the role of the restrained Venezuelan labor movement as instruments of control, the former going so far as to call
them "transmission belts" and the latter referring to them as "bureaucratic
service organizations with little homogeneous demand input from mass
membership."

The peasant sector closely parallels the labor sector, with which it was
organizationally integrated. Like the CTV, of which it was a part, the peasant

[29] Fagan 1974:224; McCoy 1985:165–66, 205–6; Salamanca 1988:147. Of the various indicators of strike activity reported by McCoy (1989:48–49, Table 2)—legal and illegal
strikes, number of total workers and workers per stoppage, length of strike, and worker
hours lost—only the average length of strikes seems correlated to the position of AD in
government or in oppositions, and McCoy suggests that an alternate (or additional) explanation lies in the deteriorating economic situation in these two periods (McCoy 1989: 48–
49, Table 2, 47).

federation, the FCV, was characterized by the same type of party-union links. These could be seen in the fact, for instance, that the entire directorate of the FCV elected in 1962 was composed of party and labor-movement careerists rather than leaders with peasant backgrounds.

Through the intermediation of the FCV, the Venezuelan peasants became the "ideal clients"—who, like their Mexican counterparts, were perhaps the most loyal government supporters both in their electoral behavior and in their availability to be corralled into government trucks and buses and mobilized for demonstrations of government support when this was deemed necessary. The FCV was also the conduit for government policy implementation. "Rather than representing the peasantry before the . . . government bureaucratic apparatus administering agrarian reform, the FCV has been partially absorbed by this government apparatus" (Blank 1973:229–30).

The fate of the agrarian reform in Venezuela reflected these relationships and the control afforded the Venezuelan state. In 1960, when the new agrarian reform was adopted, it was estimated that about 300,000 peasant families needed land and were potential beneficiaries. By 1970, there were fewer than 120,000 recipients, over one-third of whom had actually abandoned their plots because of their unviability due to lack of credit, infrastructure, technical assistance, or poor soil. Furthermore, few recipients had received title to their plots, making their legal position precarious and hence increasing the risk associated with any potential investment. The trajectory of the government's commitment to agrarian reform can be seen in the fact that the budget of the agrarian reform agency (IAN) declined steadily in real terms after it was founded. By 1973, the government had, for all intents and purposes, abandoned its program of land redistribution (Handelman 1978b:4).

Another source of hegemonic dominance enjoyed by the party system was the widespread ideological commitment to democracy. As in Mexico, the official ideology in Venezuela was rather vague, with even fewer manipulable symbols, heroes, and villains (Pérez Jiménez, after all, reappeared in a legitimate, electoral guise in the post-1958 period). Nevertheless, the commitment to democracy quickly became widespread and deeply held. As Levine (1973:237) noted, the Pérez Jiménez dictatorship had a traumatic effect on Venezuela. In response, the major parties and organized sectors of Venezuelan society emphasized democracy, institutional stability, and the avoidance of conflict rather than "social revolution," and these idological referents were explicitly used. For instance, during the 1978 electoral campaign, documentaries were shown in movie theaters to emphasize these themes. The government also took out advertisements on television and other media, which presented a kind of lesson in Venezuelan history and ended with the slogan, "Democracy, the only path." News programs on government TV channels likewise left the viewer with the thought that "only in a democratic society is such a show possible" (Handelman 1978c:1). The spread of democratic norms can be seen in surveys in which Venezuelans registered very high levels of diffuse support for the regime. They indicated strong support for elections, the democratic parties, and the democratic regime, even when they indicated disenchantment with or disapproval of the various parties or the governments formed since 1958 (Baloyra 1977:50–51; Baloyra and Martz 1976:10–11). Just as the revolutionary mystique of the PRI served to dampen popular antagonisms to the government in Mexico, the strong support for democratic forms and elections performed an important integrative role in maintaining support of the Venezuelan regime, despite widespread skepticism about the parties and the government's policies. The effectiveness of the commitment to democracy in successfully meeting challenges to the regime can be seen in the failure of the strategies of armed struggle on the left and of putchist parties on the right.

In addition to its democratic component, the "official ideology," as it were, championed a commitment to reformism. Like the Mexican PRI, the establishment parties in Venezuela both sought to occupy left-of-center positions on the ideological spectrum. Though in some sense AD and COPEI competed to occupy the center-left, "decades of cooperation and controlled competition . . . have made each more comfortable with the other than with any militantly leftist organization" with which they might otherwise be tempted to form a coalition. Instead, the cooperation between AD and COPEI meant that together they "monopolize[d] political space on the democratic left" and from this position were successful in crowding out the left opposition, which, in addition, was particularly vulnerable to the success of AD's historic nationalist attack on the Communists and to the unpopularity of the guerrilla war with which much of the left was associated (Myers 1986:128–29).

The heritage in Venezuela, then, was an integrative, multiclass two-party system based on the electoral dominance of two, quite similar cooperating parties, which together embodied a coalition of the whole so that no major groups, including the urban working class and the organized peasantry, felt excluded. Whereas in Mexico the integrative coalition was achieved within a dominant party, in Venezuela it was achieved in the form of what evolved into an informal, but institutionalized pact between the two major parties that competed in elections. In both countries the parties that controlled the government were "popular" in that they maintained formal ties to the organized peasants and working class, from whom they received indispensable electoral support, at the same time that they maintained close informal ties to capital.

As a concluding comment about the Venezuelan party system, a word might be added about the role of proportional representation, which became a prominent feature in Venezuela. Much has been made in the literature on electoral systems of the differences between systems of proportional representation, which maximize representativeness and the participation of small groups or parties, and systems such as single-member constituencies, which to a greater extent distort representation in favor of large groups or parties. A common theme is that there is a trade-off, or a kind of contradiction, between representation and governability; or as Milnor put it: "The end product of pure representation is an elite able to disagree on almost anything"

(Milnor 1969:2; see also Lowi 1976:258). This assessment seems consistent with the experience of Chile and Brazil. What is interesting, of course, is that proportional representation in Venezuela seems to have functioned in exactly the opposite way, thus underlining Rae's (1967:137) note of caution that the effects of electoral systems must be explored empirically for each case.

To understand this outcome in Venezuela, it is important to remember that the system was introduced in reaction not only to the Pérez Jiménez dictatorship and its exclusionary regime but also to the Trienio, when AD incurred intense opposition in part because of its monopolization of power. In this context, proportional representation in the post-1958 period became the mechanism for achieving a broad interparty coalition. Proportional representation maximized the inclusion of small parties both in government and in important social or sectoral organizations such as the labor movement. This inclusionary feature was particularly significant at lower levels of governmental and union organization, and it imparted to opposition groups a stake in a system in which they participated. At the higher, national levels, the forces that produced two-party dominance were much stronger than any potential fragmenting, centrifugal forces that might have been produced by proportional representation. At this level, the integrative forces that impelled the system toward two similar, centrist parties derived from the politics of incorporation and its aftermath. They included the fact that AD, as the incorporating party, was a multiclass populist alliance that established the parameters of future political patterns. The existence in 1958 of a dominant, populist party with tight union links made it necessary for any challenger to make a bid for popular support and constitute itself on a similar multiclass basis. The integrative forces also included the dynamics that occurred in the aftermath period: the programmatic move to the center and the commitment to democracy, both of which came to be seen as preconditions for holding power. Thus the aggregation of group and sectoral interests took place at two complementary levels: both within the dominant parties and among the various ones. In this context, proportional representation increased governability and hegemonic control; it did not challenge it.

Opposition and Crises of the 1960s and 1970s

In Venezuela, the two major parties, each embracing a broad coalition, together dominated the electoral arena, the terms of ideological debate, and the party affiliations and loyalties within the organizations of the urban and rural working class. These traits constituted hegemonic resources that afforded the state legitimacy and stability in the face of the challenges of the 1960s and 1970s that toppled many regimes throughout the region. Increasingly the party system was a source of services for the state, which was effective in controlling the mass constituencies and in insulating decision making from pressures from civil society.

The Politics of Stabilization. The politics of stabilization in Venezuela were quite different from elsewhere. Through almost the entire period under consideration, Venezuela did not have a problem with inflation, although this record itself must in part be regarded as an outcome of the capacity of the political system in the policy arena. In addition, once inflationary pressures did emerge in the mid-1970s, they were to a great extent externally generated by the international inflation that followed the 1974 oil shock. The large external component of Venezuela's inflation combined with its own windfall profits from oil meant that it could take a different approach to the problem.

The most important period of economic crisis occurred right at the outset of the new regime—in fact, it occurred as the form of the regime was still being worked out at the end of the 1950s. Under Pérez Jiménez economic growth, led by oil exploitation but including the industrial sector as well, had been spectacular, averaging 9.4 percent annually and 5.7 percent per capita (Martz and Myers 1986:73). Despite the economic boom, however, by the end of the dictatorship Pérez Jiménez had depleted the treasury with public spending on a number of grandiose projects, including many white elephants, and Venezuela entered a period of economic recession.

As we have seen, during the interim government of Larrazábal (1958–59) an elaborate process of pact-making was going on among the parties. The Emergency Plan, which was agreed to by all the parties and which set the outlines for policy, emphasized wage subsidies and more public works. Though this policy, combined with a fall in oil prices, aggravated the economic situation, it also set the basis for cooperation on policy as it demonstrated the parties' commitment to reformism and redistribution. Cooperation was further exemplified by the Worker-Employer Accord in which the labor movement agreed to moderate demands and ensure labor peace (see previous chapter).

When Betancourt came to power in 1959, he had to confront the growing economic crisis but could do so against this background of cooperation. The commitment of his government and all the major parties to a reformist orientation, including full employment, trade union rights, and social welfare, was confirmed at the outset in the Minimum Program of government. With its close ties to the dominant part of the labor movement, the Betancourt government had the political resources it needed to pursue economic policies that it deemed necessary, even though they adversely affected labor. Specifically, during this period the government was able to get the CTV to continue its policy of industrial peace and to accede to two 10 percent cuts in government salaries, thus setting an important tone in overall wage policy. With this beginning, Venezuela, like Mexico, embarked on a period of economic development with monetary stability, which was quite distinct from the other countries considered here.

Inflationary pressures did begin to make themselves felt in the early 1970s. By the time Carlos Andrés Pérez took office in 1974, inflation, though low by international standards, was regarded as a serious problem. Faced with a stagnating economy and a flattening out of the previous pattern of rising real wages, the new Pérez government undertook an expansionary policy based on public-sector spending in both social welfare and investment activities. To confront the problem of inflation, the government instituted a 90-day price freeze and a wage reform package to defend and boost the purchasing power of workers. Inflation was given a further jolt in 1974 when OPEC raised oil prices. Though Venezuela enjoyed a corresponding increase in oil revenues, the resulting international inflation had its repercussions by affecting the price of imports. In response, Pérez did not try to adopt the austerity measures of stabilization, but instead introduced a number of programs to defend consumer purchasing power. These included price controls and subsidies on basic consumption goods, particularly food. Combined with labor reform, which regulated severance pay and the dismissal of workers without cause, and policies to boost employment, the approach of Pérez was in many ways similar to those of Echeverría, concurrently under way in Mexico. And as in Mexico, the increase in public spending led to increased foreign borrowing, despite the oil revenues, and a rising rate of inflation, which reached double digits in Caracas in 1975 (McCoy 1985:98, 305–12).

In 1976, policy switched gears, retreating from an emphasis on the defense of purchasing power, thereby also accommodating the opposition to those policies on the part of private capital, and adopting instead an orientation toward "growth *before* redistribution" (McCoy 1985:101). In 1979, under the new president Herrera Campins, the austerity program hesitantly begun by Pérez was intensified. This policy, however, emerged amid the growing international debt crisis and takes us beyond the period under consideration here.

In the period 1958–78, then, Venezuela did not have much experience with austerity or stabilization policies, and it is hard to reach firm conclusions about its policy-making capacity in this area. Nevertheless, it might be added that the Venezuelan regime did seem to have the resources to articulate a government coalition in a way that led to relatively stable policy making throughout the period. Based on the pacts of the late-1950s, a bi-partisan consensus on economic policy was maintained. That consensus consisted of a similar theoretical orientation toward nationalism, statism, developmentalism, and redistribution that would close the income gap and make the benefits of growth available to all groups in society (Martz and Myers 1986:74). In practice as well as in principle, there was sufficient agreement that no dramatic reorientations occurred when the parties rotated in office—although some swings in policy were evident, as they were also, of course, in the one-party dominant regime in Mexico. Nor did paralysis and immobilism affect economic decision making, as it did in Brazil and Chile. The Congress, a potentially important arena for policy making and the influence of social groups, was never very strong. Without strong standing committees, it was unable to initiate policy, although it was able to veto policy. Furthermore, under Pérez, economic decision making became even more firmly lodged in the executive and state bureaucracy. An administrative reform, changes in the planning process, and a new Organic Law passed by Congress gave Pérez unprecedented autonomy in economy policy (Kelley 1977:40–41; Hellinger 1984:54). In this way, the state substantially insulated decision making from party politics and achieved a policy-making capacity quite unlike the cases, for instance, of Brazil and Chile.

Guerrilla Movement.   Whereas Mexico, with its hegemonic system did not experience a significant guerrilla movement in opposition to the government, the Venezuelan regime was faced with a very substantial guerrilla movement that emerged shortly after the Cuban Revolution, which clearly inspired it. Despite its very recent founding, the Venezuelan government was able to overcome and discredit the guerrilla challenge. In addition to the hegemonic resources available to the government, it could also make use of the enormous oil revenues then flowing into the state. As Lombardi has said (1982:234–37), use of oil revenues for land reform and government-sponsored social programs played an important role in weakening the appeal of revolutionary groups (Lombardi 1982:236).

As we have seen, the onset of the aftermath in Venezuela coincided with the Cuban Revolution, which had a powerful demonstration effect throughout Latin America. For Venezuela, however, the Cuban Revolution occurred precisely at the time the left was being excluded from participation as a full partner in the new civilian political arrangements then being established. With the exclusion of the PCV from the Punto Fijo accords and the expulsion/defection of AD's left wing that occurred as that party moved to the center, a strategy of armed struggle was adopted by much of the left. In other words, in addition to the influence and example of the events in nearby Cuba, the exclusion of the left from the power-sharing pact led to its rejection of the regime-founding and programmatic pacts. Both the internal dynamic and international diffusion combined to produce what has been called the strongest Latin American guerrilla movement in the period immediately following the Cuban Revolution.[30]

Yet, if the hegemonic regime was not yet in place to preempt the emergence of a substantial guerrilla movement (indeed the very process of establishing the hegemonic regime even encouraged it), within a short time that regime overcame the armed challenge and did so largely through hegemonic resources, though repression was also employed. Particularly important in this regard were the ideological resources of the regime and the very widespread popular commitment to democracy. Even that part of the left which moved into opposition as a result of the rightward turn of the government— that is, the PCV, MIR, and also URD—was reluctant to abandon the democratic game and opt for armed struggle. The decision to adopt armed tactics and guerrilla warfare was taken in 1962 by the youth members of the MIR and PCV, who forced the hand of a reluctant party leadership unable to maintain party discipline. In late 1962, these student revolutionaries formed the FALN to coordinate guerrilla activity. The nonstudent leaders of the MIR and PCV were unable to control FALN policy. Indeed, while the FALN went

[30] *Latin American Political Report* 11, no. 10 (London) March 11, 1977:78.

in its own direction, the regular party leaders were going in quite another: attempting to regain legality in order to reenter the democratic game and participate in the December 1963 elections. Thus, at the same time that the FALN worked to prevent the elections and urged abstention, regular party leaders were more aware of the way in which armed struggle and the use of violence were made counterproductive by the popular commitment to democracy and the belief that reform and change were possible through the democratic process (Ellner 1980:8–9; Harding and Landau 1964:122–23). The ideological resources of the Venezuelan regime, then, severely limited the appeal of the armed left, isolating it politically.

Also important were the party-union linkages, which, along with the ideological factor, deprived the guerrillas of working-class support, even though the PCV and MIR, those parties leading the armed struggle, previously had substantial support within organized labor before adopting the new strategy. The formation of an opposition bloc by the MIR, PCV, and URD had produced a stand-off with the AD-COPEI coalition (Boeckh 1972:206). Yet, as we have seen, AD was able to use its links to the unions to regain its dominant position. Consequently, the parties participating in the guerrilla movement were unable to retain a large following among the trade unions In ad dition, there was much opposition within the labor movement to the attempt by the guerrillas to subordinate working-class economic demands to the armed struggle and to convert unions into "veritable appendages" of the guerrilla movement (including, for instance, the use of union locals as depots for the storage of arms). In addition, while the guerrillas operated underground, affiliated or sympathetic union leaders continued above ground, from which position they were the ones most vulnerable to arrest (Ellner 1980:20).

The organized strength of the parties also constituted a barrier to guerrilla success in the countryside. Initially pursuing socialist revolution through peasant revolt, the guerrillas "attacked the system at its strongest point" (Martz 1977:95): AD had placed great emphasis on organizing peasant unions ever since the 1930s, and peasants were a central part of AD's support base. It was rejection by the peasantry that prompted the reorientation of the guerrilla struggle to the urban areas.

The tactic of armed struggle, then, met with little support. The URD left the rapidly radicalizing opposition almost immediately. By 1965, with the guerrillas isolated politically, the PCV leadership, much of which was in jail, called for an abandonment of armed struggle. President Leoni allowed a Communist front organization to compete in the 1968 elections, and the following year President Caldera legalized both the PCV and the MIR and offered a broad amnesty. Most guerrilla fighters accepted the amnesty and abandoned the armed struggle in favor of participation in the electoral arena (Ellner 1980:21; McCoy 1985:143).

The integrative hegemonic regime, which organizationally linked the popular sectors to the multiclass parties and ideologically reinforced a commitment to democracy, thus provided the government with the resources to contain and defeat what might have been a substantial guerrilla threat. In subsequent years, what pockets of guerrilla activity remained were eliminated as militants opted to take advantage of an amnesty offered by President Herrera and to reenter the electoral arena.

Labor Movement. The heritage with respect to the labor movement was its affiliation with AD and more broadly with "el status," or the establishment parties. The participation of the labor movement in the dominant coalition meant first that the working class became an important source of popular support and hence of legitimacy for the state and, second that the government had available to it a mechanism through which it could exercise influence or control over the working class and maintain social peace.

This state-labor relationship, mediated by the "status" parties, and particularly by AD, met two kinds of challenges in the 1960s and 1970s: external and internal. The external challenges took the form of the creation of rival confederations that tried to present an alternative pattern of state-labor relations to that represented by the CTV. None of these, however, met with much success, given the resources available to the government.

The events leading to the formation of the CUTV in 1963 by the left opposition have been discussed in the previous chapter. Founded in the context of the adoption of armed struggle by the PCV and MIR, it was unable to transfer the support those groups had enjoyed within the CTV, given the unpopularity of the guerrilla movement within the labor movement. The URD, which had originally left the CTV along with the PCV and MIR, returned to the CTV when the armed struggle was adopted by the other parties, and it expelled from the party those dissenting from this decision (Ellner 1980:20). Even after the abandonment of the armed struggle, the CUTV was unable to expand its influence significantly or even to maintain the influence it had enjoyed among the petroleum workers. The defeat of the guerrilla movement meant that the CUTV ceased to represent much of an alternative to the CTV, whose orientation it came to resemble more closely and which, in any case, had the greater effectiveness that affiliation to the governing parties afforded (Lestienne 1981:13; McCoy 1985:249).

CODESA, a Catholic confederation that was legalized in 1964 but founded in 1958, represented a very different ideological orientation from that of the CUTV. It was formed with the goal of creating a confederation that was politically autonomous from political parties. This formally declared autonomy, however, was not preserved. Rather, CODESA was sympathetic to COPEI and even associated with the COPEI faction within the CTV. Indeed, on occasion it appeared to be an instrument available to COPEI when that party wanted to challenge the domination of AD within the labor movement (Lestienne 1981:14). Thus, CODESA preserved the link between the "status" parties and the labor movement even though it operated outside of the CTV.

The Catholic and left alternatives each spawned a more politically autonomous group. Precisely because of the failure of CODESA to pursue its stated goal of political autonomy, the CGT was founded in 1971 from a division within CODESA. On the left, a few large unions rejected the CUTV because of both its ineffectiveness and its party ties and consequent orientation toward national politics at the expense of attention to base organization (Lestienne 1981:14).

None of these groups rivaling the CTV was able to present any real challenge to it or to the state-labor relationship it embodied. They remained minor players in a game dominated by the CTV. While the CTV had a membership of over a million workers around 1980, the others combined had a total estimated membership of well under 170,000, with some estimates much lower than that (Lestienne 1981:12; McCoy 1985:249–50). This dominance, constantly reinforced by links to the major parties, gave the CTV the decisive advantage of access to and protection from the state, despite the fact that all confederations received state subsidies. Thus, though multiple confederations existed, for all practical purposes the CTV enjoyed a near monopoly of representation of organized labor (Salamanca 1988:182, 194).

The second challenge to state-labor relations in Venezuela was that mounted from within the CTV as dissident groups made bids to become influential and change the direction and orientation of that central. The first of these, the PCV-MIR bloc of the early 1960s, has already been discussed: the AD-COPEI coalition within the CTV forced the dissident bloc out of the con federation and thus gained an unprecedented level of control within the CTV. Other challenges soon followed. In 1967, the MEP was formed as a left splinter from AD. This challenge was the most serious and not only cost AD its majority in the CTV (as it did in the electoral sphere with the victory of COPEI's Caldera as President), but also threatened the majority status of the combined AD-COPEI coalition in the confederation. In the 1970s other groups on the left, the returning MIR and PCV as well as newer groups like the MAS and the Causa R also tried to take advantage of the formal pluralism within the CTV in order to attain a position of influence. Given the resources available to AD and the hegemony it and the AD-COPEI coalition enjoyed, none of these attempts was successful. AD put down the challenge from MEP and prevented the recurrence of any challenge on a similar scale. Once the MEP challenge was overcome, AD retained majority status within the CTV Congress and Executive Committee, and the coalition of AD and COPEI together dominated both with about three-quarters of the membership (Lestienne 1981:27; McCoy 1985:254).

The defection of the MEP illustrates the resources and techniques used to meet challenges within the CTV. The dissident faction within AD took with it not only a very substantial part of the labor movement but also the CTV president, José Navarro. As a result, AD actually lost control of the CTV. The response to this challenge included a variety of tactics. Initially, the government, still in AD hands, supported the party in its efforts to defeat MEP unionism and regain its position. One such example was the way in which, through political support and connections, AD was able to buy additional stock and beat MEP in the elections for control of the new Labor Bank. In another particularly blatant case, AD opposed a strike, supported by MEP, of Maracaibo municipal workers who were trying to force the city to fulfill the terms of a previously signed collective contract. Though the strikers enjoyed wide public sympathy, the AD governor broke the strike by force (Boeckh 1972:208–9).

Another tactic used by AD in the face of the MEP challenge was the postponement of union elections. New elections for the CTV congress and Executive Committee were postponed until AD was confident of its victory. This moment did not present itself until 1970, when a new informal coalition with COPEI was once again possible following its 1968 presidential victory and its abortive attempt to govern alone. Ultimately, then, AD was able to regain its position by turning to COPEI and renewing the coalition. In exchange for COPEI support and votes in the CTV congress of 1970, AD agreed to give the post of secretary-general of the CTV to COPEI, a position COPEI would not have been able to win on its own. In this way, AD, with COPEI support, not only regained the presidency and its leadership of the CTV, but also pevented the MEP, which had nearly as many delegates to the congress as AD, from holding the second leadership post. The AD-COPEI coalition within the CTV virtually became formalized and provided those two parties with the means to maintain dominance and meet challenges within the confederation. In 1970 the new elections were held, and the continuity of this arrangement is reflected in the fact that ten years later José Vargas of AD was elected to his third five-year term as president of the CTV and COPEI's Rafael León León was reelected as secretary-general. It may also be mentioned that the offer of cooperation extended to COPEI by AD also brought to an end an as-yet-unsuccessful strategy by COPEI to follow up its presidential victory with a push to gain control of the CTV (McCoy 1985:156–58, 253).

Dislodged from a position of credible threat, the MEP continued to exist as the third largest force within the CTV. However its position got weaker as its electoral strength dwindled. By 1980 it represented only 12 percent of the delegates to the Eighth CTV Congress. Furthermore, the degree to which it represented a leftist challenge may also be questioned. Lestienne (1981:29) has suggested that the MEP failed to develop a coherent alternate vision or policy and that its unions became as bureaucratized and corrupt as those of AD and COPEI.

The subsequent challenges to AD or AD-COPEI hegemony were not so great. They were mounted by various leftist parties that opposed the CTV orientation toward social concertation and conciliation as well as the corruption and lack of democracy within the confederation and its unions. These parties—most importantly the MIR and PCV (once they rejected armed struggle and returned to the CTV) and the more newly formed MAS—were divided and unable to pursue concerted action. Each represented quite a small segment of organized labor. Even together they were not able to gain much of a foothold within the confederation. By 1980 they could claim only 6 percent of the delegates to the CTV congress, 9 percent including the representation of URD. In addition to the disadvantages these factions within the labor movement faced compared to the advantages that accrued to AD and COPEI unions because of their links to the state, these unions faced the problems of preeminence of party-political over union considerations. Furthermore, MAS had the particular problem of being based in the middle class with only a weak orientation to the working class.

Finally, there developed within the CTV other class-oriented tendencies that operated primarily on the local level. Dedicated to mobilization at the grassroots, these groups, like those discussed above, presented an alternative, classist model to the conciliatory, bureaucratic model presented by AD-COPEI, but were not linked to political parties. They remained a minor phenomenon within organized labor, but one, the Causa R, gained some influence. The example of the Causa R is illustrative of the difficulties faced by all groups within the CTV that presented a challenge to AD or AD-COPEI hegemony.

The Causa R became particularly influential in the industrial states of the Guayana. In 1979, the left won a majority of seats in elections of the metal workers union, SUTISS, one of the strongest and largest in Venezuela. Of 10 leadership positions, Causa R won four, with four more going to other radical factions allied with Causa R, and AD and COPEI winning only one each. AD used the subsequent negotiations with the state owned steel mill, Sidor, as the opportunity to reinstate its position. Despite their success at the local union level, the Causa R and the other dissident unionists in SUTISS did not have any representation on Fetrametal, the CTV-affiliated industrial federation to which it belonged. The electoral system of one vote per union, regardless of size, was a mechanism that in this case, and others, functioned to restrict minority representation at higher levels of union organization (Salamanca 1988:184–85; Lestienne 1981:20). In the negotiations, Fetrametal submitted a parallel contract nearly identical to that which met an impasse on the bargaining table between SUTISS and Sidor. The resolution of the conflict came about when this contract was accepted and the CTV, through Fetrametal and the state federation, intervened in SUTISS and replaced its leaders with those representing only AD and COPEI (Blank 1984:188–89; McCoy 1985:258–60). This example sounds very much like the pattern observed in Mexico. Much more important than the terms of the contract was the control of the union. As in Mexico, when concessions were needed, they presented no problem; what was not negotiable was AD and COPEI dominance in the labor movement on which hegemony of the regime in part was based.

Peasant Mobilization. The challenge within the peasant movement closely paralleled that within the larger labor movement of which it was an integral part. We have already discussed the purge within the FCV in 1961–62 (see Chapter 6). Out of that experience came the practice by which AD and COPEI cooperated to produce a common, single slate for leadership elections within the FCV and state federations. This ongoing collaboration prevented any major challenges or defections from within the peasant movement. It was the basis for continuing links between the government and the FCV at all levels, for the support the peasantry lent the government, and for

the quiescence of the peasant movement, despite the slowing of agrarian reform.

The one brief period in which these cooperative relations threatened to
come apart began in mid-1964, mirroring the withdrawal of COPEI from the
coalition government of Leoni. Going its own way in the party-electoral
arena, COPEI founded a rival peasant federation, the MASC, though the
party also continued to participate in the FCV. At the same time, the URD
returned to the electoral sphere. These two developments led to new and
intense party competition within the peasant movement, which took the
form of the establishment of parallel unions and challenges to the legal
status of existing unions. This pattern of party competition, however, was
soon brought to a halt and replaced with a new form of cooperation. The
three parties cooperated to establish a new set of rules that would govern the
formation of unions and hence limit the phenomenon of parallel unionism.
They also set up Mixed Commissions, on which the three parties were represented, to pass on challenges of legality brought against a union (Powell
1971:187–88).

The 1966 conventions of the state peasant federations, described by Powell
(1971:201–2), demonstrate the kind of cooperative, conflict-limiting mechanisms that characterized the peasant movement and linked it to the cooperating parties. At these state conventions, two kinds of caucuses convened
simultaneously. The first was a party caucus that was held in the headquarters of the three parties and was attended by peasant delegates affiliated with
the respective parties as well as by national party leaders. On these occasions, decisions were made about issues and positions to be adopted. The
second was the interparty caucus of state federation leaders and national
party leaders, who met to constitute a single, joint slate for leadership positions of the state federation. These negotiations tended to produce a compromise slate that had the effect of overriding the effects of the majority rule
procedures of the state federation (according to which each union had a single vote) and of producing an outcome that more nearly reflected the proportional partisan affiliation of the peasantry.

Following the caucuses, a public session was convened. Open nominations
were entertained, but in the end the compromise slate was elected. Thus,
party cooperation was renewed within the peasant movement, even before it
was reestablished on the level of national government. Party competition
was subordinated to party cooperation, and together the cooperating parties,
in presenting a unified compromise list, also prevented any challenge from
dissident groups. As in the urban unions, strong organizational links between
the cooperating parties and the popular sector organizations provided a great
deal of control.

Political Parties.   As we have seen, given the geographic proximity to Cuba
and the similar timing of the fall of the dictatorships in the two countries,
Venezuela was hardly immune to the demonstration effect of the Cuban Revolution. As elsewhere, groups and parties on the left proliferated in this context. However, with the hegemonic resources that derived from the political

heritage of incorporation and its aftermath, the Venezuelan government defeated these challenges. The defeat of the guerrilla struggle was a more extreme example of the political weakness of the left more generally in an inclusionary party system that exerted a strong pull to the center and inhibited polarization. We have already discussed the party fragmentation that occurred in the mid-1960s and the way in which it gave way to a two-party dominant system by 1973. Subsequently, parties, primarily on the left, continued to proliferate and participate in the country's political and electoral life. However, unlike the growth of the political left in Chile and Brazil, which gained substantial influence in the political system, in Venezuela, as in Mexico, the left met with very limited success. Instead, the dominance of the two centrist, integrative, multiclass, cooperating parties remained intact.

In the 1970s a number of leftist parties made a bid for popular support. These included the older, more traditional parties, such as the PCV and the MIR, which rejoined the electoral arena once they abandoned the armed struggle but which never really recovered from that unpopular episode. It also included the MEP, whose strength was initially impressive when it first split from AD but quickly dissipated as a result of the concerted attack on it by AD and COPEI and the unpopularity of its attempts to make common cause with groups on the left (Blank 1984:79).

Also on the left were a number of newer parties. Most important among these was the MAS (Movement to Socialism), which was founded in 1971 as a splinter from the PCV, taking with it about 60 percent of the PCV, including many of its intellectuals and much of its youth wing (Blank 1984:75). The MAS identified with the Eurocommunist movement and showed some tendency toward a social democratic orientation that failed to present a major alternative to AD or COPEI. In the 1970s, its projects and proposals looked much like the reforms proposed by Carlos Andrés Pérez, which the party supported but which were not in the end carried out. The MAS maintained a position of much greater distance from private capital, advocating a planned economy, the nationalization of major firms, and greater taxation on capital, though it was careful to recognize the exigencies of dependent relations and tread rather lightly on foreign capital. It sought the support of the working class but did not consider itself a working-class party, placing emphasis as well on the urban poor and the middle class; it championed a number of reforms beneficial to workers, including a change in the labor codes to ease restrictions on the use of the strike, but it did not attract a large following among workers. Finally, the MAS was committed to democratic structures not only in its support for the democratic regime but internally within the MAS itself, as well as in the form of workers' control of enterprises (Handelman 1978c:12–14). The MAS quickly became the strongest force on the left and the third strongest party in Venezuela, with the decline of the MEP. Through the 1970s, however, its accomplishments were not overwhelming: in the elections of the decade the MAS won only 5 to 6 percent of the congressional vote—and, not surprisingly, even less of the presidential vote.

Much smaller were two other splinters from the PCV-MAS axis: the Communist Vanguard formed in 1974 and the New Alternative formed in 1980 as a left-center coalition. Other groups included the Socialist League and the Venezuelan Revolutionary Party, which had their origins in the guerrilla movement, the Revolutionary Action Group, and the EPA (The People Advance) (Blank 1984:82–84).

As is evident from this description, the proliferation of left parties represents not so much vitality on the left as a process of factionalism and splintering. Efforts were made to achieve unity, but they failed. At the same time, the left vote grew somewhat after 1973. Nevertheless, it remained very small at around 12 to 13 percent in congressional elections in the 1970s (Silva Michelena and Sonntag 1979:73). Its greatest success was achieved at the local level. In the municipal election of 1979, the combined vote for the left reached 18 percent of the total (O'Connor 1980:82–83).

This limited success of the left did more to enhance the legitimacy of the democratic regime than to challenge it. It reflected the broad consensus that was created around AD and COPEI, a consensus that cannot be understood apart from the political dynamics that have their origin in the incorporation and aftermath episodes. It was a consensus that produced a hegemonic regime with certain advantages, but also with costs.

> At first glance, the Venezuela story seems to have a happy ending. Institutions are legitimized and "everyone" is united behind the new system and its rules. . . . [However] in policy terms, this kind of accommodation has clear social costs: those groups which reject the incorporation of traditional sectors, and their conservative impact on policy formation, are defeated. Traditional oppositions are incorporated as the dominant party moves to the center. The center is strengthened. Who used to be left out? The traditional Right. Who is excluded from the new revised spectrum . . . ? The Left (Levine 1973:223–24).

URUGUAY AND COLOMBIA: ELECTORAL STABILITY AND SOCIAL CONFLICT

Although the traditional parties in both Uruguay and Colombia faced a significant electoral challenge during the 1970's, they largely dominated the electoral arena during the period analyzed in this chapter, which extends from 1942 to 1973 in Uruguay and from 1958 to 1986 in Colombia. In one sense this outcome was *not* a distinctive legacy of incorporation, in that it built on a much older tradition of two-party dominance. Yet this tradition was unquestionably renewed and reinforced by the experiences of the incorporation and aftermath periods. Indeed, any account of the successful "reproduction" of these long-standing two-party systems would have to focus closely on the dynamics of these two periods. A central issue of the subsequent heritage period was whether this ongoing electoral stability in fact constituted a form of electoral stasis that inhibited badly needed political innovation.

This electoral stability was accompanied by relatively high levels of social conflict. In contrast to other cases of party incorporation—and this *was* a distinctive legacy of how these party systems functioned during the incorporation period—in Uruguay and Colombia the parties that led the incorporation project had been relatively ineffective in building enduring ties with unions. Therefore, the union-party ties that in some countries provided a framework for establishing long-term political accommodation with labor were weak or nonexistent. Correspondingly, worker protest became an important issue in Colombian politics, notwithstanding the weakness of the Colombian labor movement. In Uruguay worker protest reached such a magnitude that it was a central factor in the regime crisis of the late 1960s and early 1970s and in the coup of 1973.

In the rural sector, the type of reorganization of political relationships found in the incorporation period in Mexico and Venezuela had not occurred, and traditional partisan ties had remained relatively untouched in rural areas. Whereas in Uruguay these relationships continued to be relatively stable, in Colombia the interaction of old partisan antagonisms with new models of guerrilla struggle produced nearly continuous rural insurgency.

This juxtaposition of an unusual degree—indeed, arguably an excessive degree—of electoral stability and severe social conflict contributed to political paralysis in both countries. States of siege became a principal mechanism of governance, and the militarization of the state was an important feature of these periods. In Uruguay this process culminated in the military coup of 1973, though interestingly the new military government initially retained the elected civilian president. Colombia, by contrast, although it experienced substantial militarization, retained an elected, civilian executive throughout these years.

URUGUAY

Overview of Party System

During most of the period from 1942 to 1973, the Colorados and Nationals (Blancos) were the predominant parties in Uruguay. The Colorados had stronger support in Montevideo, but both parties enjoyed important backing in the interior. The two parties were highly factionalized, and much of the dynamics of politics continued to revolve around struggles among factions within each party and around coalitions of factions drawn from both parties.

At the beginning of the heritage period, the Colorados—and specifically their Batlle wing—established a strong electoral position. The tradition of coparticipation was temporarily abandoned, largely because the Batlle Colorados did not need it to hold power. Yet in the 1950s, in part in response to a new split in the Colorados, coparticipation was restored and the Nationals regained an important position in the party system.

Notwithstanding the substantial dominance of the Colorados and Nationals, in the late 1960s and early 1970s politics became polarized in important spheres. These years saw a significant shift to the left in electoral allegiances, to the point that in the 1971 presidential election a left coalition, the Frente Amplio (Broad Front) won 18 percent of the vote. This vote placed the Front in a subordinate electoral position, but it was unprecedented for an electoral group outside of the two traditional parties to win this high a percentage.

Although workers in important measure continued to vote for the Colorados, union politics remained highly pluralistic and unions were affiliated with parties of the left. Relatedly, the 1960s and early 1970s brought intense labor conflict that was widely viewed as constituting a major political and economic crisis. Finally, these same years also saw the spectacular eruption of an urban guerrilla movement, the Tupamaros, whose dramatic exploits shook the established political system to its roots.

The impressive showing of the Frente Amplio, the labor conflict, and the rise of the Tupamaros triggered a powerful conservative reaction, producing a major polarization of Uruguayan politics. Yet this polarization occurred in a context in which the Colarados and the Nationals continued to play a predominate role in the electoral arena.

To understand party dynamics during this period, it is useful to explore the interaction between, on the one hand, the factional struggles within and between the parties; and on the other, three broad, interrelated issues of Uruguayan politics: the restoration and subsequent abolition of the collegiate executive; the pursuit of alternative development models, including the effort to revive the Batlle reform program and later the frustrating search for policies that would address Uruguay's severe economic stagnation; and finally the complex reactions and counterreactions to the growing polarization of the late 1960s and early 1970s.

The discussion of this interaction focuses on three phases. The first (1942–52) saw a return to power of the Batlle wing of the Colorado Party and the renewal of the earlier Batlle reforms based on a broad urban, multiclass coalition. This program was led by the majority Colorado faction, headed by Luis Batlle (List 15), a nephew of former President José Batlle y Ordóñez. During this period the National Party was in a marginal position.

The second phase (1952–66) witnessed a renewed experiment with a collegiate executive and a return to power-sharing between the parties. This phase was brought on by a split in the Colorado Party and an alliance between anti-List 15 Colorados and Nationals, who used the collegiate structure to block a continuation of the reform effort. These years saw the beginning of the long crisis of economic stagnation and the initial failed attempts by both Colorado and National governments to address the crisis.

The third phase (1966–73) brought paralysis and substantial polarization. It saw growing use of exceptional powers by the executive; increasing militarization of the state, as public authorities tried to suppress popular opposition; increasingly harsh economic measures to deal with the economic crisis; the emergence of the Tupamaros; and the successful unification of the country's left parties under the umbrella of the Frente Amplio. This phase ended in 1973 when the process of militarization of the state culminated in a coup.

Two major themes that emerge from an examination of these phases are, first, the capacity of the traditional parties, building on deep party loyalty and on their ability to manipulate voting procedures, to maintain substantial electoral stability; and, second, their incapacity to address major economic and social issues and thereby deal with the problem of social conflict.

The New Batlle Project, 1942–52. During the years immediately after the return to democracy in 1942, the Colorados dominated politics and redefined their programmatic and ideological stance in the direction of renewing the Batllista urban reform program. This period saw the extension of significant new social and labor legislation, including the creation in 1943 of tripartite Wage Councils with labor, industrial, and state representation; new benefits to workers, including longer paid vacations, an increased minimum wage, and dismissal pay; and the creation of an agency concerned with employment and unemployment.[31]

The presidency of Luis Batlle (1947–51) brought a successful redefinition of Batllismo and the emergence of policies geared toward the creation of labor-capital peace through building a coalition between industry and commerce, labor, and public sector workers, both blue collar and white collar. As D'Elia (1982:37) notes: "From the social point of view, industrial development translated into the growth and consolidation of the entrepreneurial sector as well as the working and middle classes, all of which, despite their differences and antagonisms, agreed on a policy in support of national

---

[31] Millot, Silva, and Silva 1973:144; H. Rodríguez 1965:39–40; Frega, Maronna, and Trochón 1984:31–35; Rial 1983:18; Cosse 1984:94–95.

industry." To build this coalition Batlle established an economic policy that gave local industry strong protection from foreign competition through multiple exchange rates and state subsidies, while effectively redistributing profits from the stock-raising sector to urban workers and food-producers. Under Batlle's project industry grew at an impressive rate and the standard of living rose rapidly in Montevideo. With high prices for stock-raising products in the foreign market, the rural cattle and wool producers acquiesced to Batlle's economic and social policies.[32] Industrialists, in exchange for strong protectionist measures and favorable tax policies, offered grudging support (Errandonea and Costabile 1969:124).

Batlle carried out the redistributive aspect of his program through direct and indirect means. First, he oversaw a considerable expansion of public employment and of the state sector in general (D'Elia 1982:33, 47–48; Finch 1981:218). Second, the state's mediation within the Wage Councils was consistently prolabor, insuring rising wages. It was even "alleged that his supporters encouraged strikes, illegal or not, in order to force the government bodies which control wage rates in a number of enterprises to approve raises" (Taylor 1954:397, n29). Finally, Batlle initiated policies that reduced the cost of living to all urban classes through the subsidy of food and essential products, paid for by export taxes on the rural stock producers (Lamas and Piotti 1981:224–25).

It is interesting to note the relationship between this reform project and the earlier reforms of José Batlle y Ordoñez at the beginning of the century. The earlier project was, as noted in Chapter 5, built to some degree on a vision of a *future* urban support coalition that would benefit from the reforms Batlle initiated. Indeed, Batlle had hoped these reforms would create the social actors to build this coalition. Now, decades later, these actors had grown greatly in importance, and a new reform project was constructed around their actual, rather than potential, existence.

The new Batlle project had considerable success. The purchasing power of urban workers grew rapidly, as did the industrial and commercial sectors, and workers generally supported Batlle and the Colorados at the polls (Millot, Silva, and Silva 1973:152). Yet, as in the past, the labor movement maintained its independence from the Colorados, despite some attempt by Batllistas to create more direct party-labor links (Sala and Landineli 1984:270–71).

However, Batlle's new project was weakened by a family struggle over who would inherit the mantle of Batllismo, a struggle that would contribute to the emergence of the next phase of Uruguayan politics. The family struggle involved growing competition between former President Batlle's son, César Batlle, and his nephew, Luis Batlle. The conflict led to a division in the party, which endured up to the 1973 coup. For the 1950 elections Luis Batlle supported the candidacy of longtime Batllista, Martínez Trueba, under his own List 15, and César Batlle and *El Día* promoted an opposing candidate under List 14. Though List 14 was slightly more conservative, and became more so

---

[32] Cosse 1984:94–95; D'Elia 1982:27–29; Finch 1981:177.

as it defined itself against Luis Batlle, the programmatic differences between the two groups were minimal, underlining the personalistic basis of the division (D'Elia 1982:58). Fortunately for the Colorados, the mechanism of the double simultaneous vote insured that the division would have no negative consequences for the Colorados' control over the executive. This provision in effect combined the primary election and the general election in a single vote. Under the provision, the winner of the election was the faction with the most votes within the party that overall won the most votes. In this manner, a party was not penalized for becoming highly factionalized.[33] Indeed, the division in one sense helped the Colorados at the polls, in that the energetically contested race between Lists 15 and 14 gave the Colorados overall a large victory, 53 to 31 percent, over the Nationals in 1950.

The New Colegiado, Erosion of the Batlle Reform Project, and Economic Stagnation, 1952–66. This second phase saw a defeat of the Batlle economic model and the revival of the National Party, within the framework of the restoration of the collegiate executive. The Martínez presidency (1951–54) began as a continuation of Luis Batlle's project, but soon Martínez announced his support for a constitutional reform to restore the collegiate system that was in place prior to the 1933 coup. Martínez's call was quickly picked up by Luis Batlle's rivals within the Colorado Party, and in particular by List 14, which saw the reform as a means to prevent Luis Batlle's reelection. At the same time Luis Alberto de Herrera, faced with the prospect of more years of the National's minority electoral status and exclusion from the executive, made another shift, this time in support of the very collegiate system he had opposed so vehemently before the Terra coup. In July 1951, Herrera and Martínez, enjoying List 14 and considerable List 15 support, agreed to a plebiscite on the proposal to restore the collegiate executive.[34]

The new system restored coparticipation. The nine-member National Council of Government was divided between the two traditional parties, with six positions going to the majority party and three to the minority party. The six majority party positions would also be shared, with four going to the majority faction and the other two majority positions divided according to proportional representation among the minority factions of the winning party. The three minority Council positions were divided by proportional representation among the factions of the minority party. Hence, the majority faction of the majority party would *not* hold a majority in the Council.

The change to the Council brought an end to Luis Batlle's hopes for reelection and insured that his faction of the Colorados would not control the executive, since they held just four of the nine positions on the new Council. This made it difficult to extend the Batlle program, since List 15 had to govern in coalition with more conservative factions. Very importantly, the Batlle faction to some degree lost control of the mediation of labor-capital relations.

---

[33] In addition, it was possible for the leading faction of the winning party to have a smaller percentage of the vote than the leading faction of the other party.

[34] Taylor 1960a:63; Zubillaga 1985b:62; D'Elia 1982:61–62.

One example was the Council decision, opposed by Luis Batlle, to call for a state of siege to deal with an important public sector strike in late 1952. Besides reflecting the diminished control over the state by List 15, the use of emergency powers to crush a strike began to change the tenor of state-labor relations, in some respects encouraging the independence of the labor movement (D'Elia 1982:62–65).

The 1954–58 period was a fateful one for the future of Uruguayan democracy. Luis Batlle's successful urban coalition—uniting the working class, the growing middle class, and the business elite—was built on an important premise: that a favorable world market for Uruguay's exports would continue. With high earnings, not only could Batlle continue to protect industry, but he could also maintain significant income redistribution policies, especially from rural export sectors to the urban working and middle classes. The economic basis for the Batllista project came unraveled in the mid-1950s as a crisis in the export sector, caused by falling world market prices, deepened (Real de Azúa 1971:185; 1964:107).

The problems of the export sector had important implications for the balance of power between the two parties. As long as prices were high, rural producers' opposition to the Batllista project was muted. But with falling prices, rural opposition to the urban-centered project of the Colorados began to grow, with rising criticism of the "artificiality of Uruguayan industrialization" (Zubillaga 1985b:44). A new organization emerged that successfully expressed this opposition, the Federal League of Rural Action (Liga Federal de Acción Ruralista). Led by Benito Nardone, the Ruralistas would play an important role in tipping the balance of power between the Colorados and Nationals. The Ruralistas initially emerged as a nonpartisan interest group representing the needs of the interior, especially of the growing middle and lower classes. Characterized as a "poujadist" movement (Graillot 1973b:489), the League's first entrance into electoral politics was in 1954, when Nardone asked his supporters to vote for both Colorado and National Party candidates sympathetic to their needs. With the growing economic crisis, however, Nardone began to establish stronger contacts with Herrera's faction of the Nationals. In 1958, the League's support for Nardone and the Nationals was crucial in giving the Nationals their first control of the executive in 93 years.[35]

The crisis in the export sector was almost immediately felt in other areas of Uruguay's economy as well. Between 1955 and 1957, industrial productivity and real wages began to fall, while unemployment began to climb. Consequently, the late 1950s saw a growing radicalization of the labor movement, which further increased when the new National Party government signed a letter of intent with the International Monetary Fund and initiated a period of austerity measures and crackdowns on illegal strikes. But despite the Nationals' shift away from Batlle's urban industrialization program toward policies more favorable to the rural sector, they were unable to reduce

[35] Zubillaga 1985b:44–47; D'Elia 1982:93; Jacob 1981a:91–110.

the state role in the economy. This was due in part to the constraints imposed by the Council, and also to the Nationals' own dependence on state patronage. In response to the former problem, the Herrera faction began to push for a new constitutional reform and a return to a presidential system.[36]

The failure of the Herrera-Ruralista coalition to impose its new rural strategy, as well as the deepening economic crisis, contributed to defeat in the 1962 elections, this time to its rival within the National Party, the UBD (Democratic Blanca Union) faction. This faction, built on the nucleus of the old Independent Nationals, rested primarily on urban middle-class support, with significant support from towns of the interior as well. With an economic policy that focused on a rejection of the austerity measures imposed by Herrera and a general concern with promoting rural economic development, the UBD was held together by opposition to corruption and immorality in government and its emphasis on the need to return to traditional values. The UBD's period as the majority in the Council was made increasingly difficult by the Colorados' certainty that they would win in 1966, given the narrow National victory in 1962, as well as by a genuine antagonism toward the successors of Herrera within the Ruralista faction. Herrera's death in 1959 caused a bitter struggle for control within the Nationals, making the UBD's period of government even more difficult.

The UBD sought to develop a neo-liberal approach based on treating political and socioeconomic problems, which were seen as growing out of the failure of the Batllista model, as technical issues that could be solved through careful planning. The creation of CIDE (Commission on Investment and Economic Development), a planning body closely associated with ideas of the Economic Commission for Latin America, led to an Economic and Social Development Plan that sought to rationalize production and achieve social peace. However, the UBD was unable to implement its plan, thus "demonstrating the divorce between economic planning and the political will to carry it out" (Zubillaga 1985b:55). By 1966, the National Party alternative was exhausted and the voters returned a very changed Colorado Party to power, this time within a new presidential system (D'Elia 1982:98–102; Finch 1981:239).

The period between 1958 and 1966 had seen significant changes in the Colorado party. The death of Luis Batlle in 1964 led to a succession struggle between the more conservative and moderate to left groups in the List 15 faction. The victory of Jorge Batlle, Luis Batlle's son, led to the exodus of the more moderate groups centered around Amílcar Vasconcellos and the formation of a rival list. Consequently, as the 1966 elections approached, the Colorados were more divided then ever, with both major factions having shifted significantly to the right.

Despite the evident failures of the Batllista, Ruralista, and technocratic

[36] Handelman 1981a:375; L. González 1976:89, 165; Sala and Landineli 1984:272; Jacob 1981a:124; Finch 1981:61, 86, 109–10; D'Elia 1982:81–82; Zubillaga 1985b:47–48; McDonald 1971:201.

strategies to deal with the continuing economic crisis, the 1966 electoral campaign hardly dealt with competing strategies to end the crisis, reflecting the traditional parties' conclusion that the reason for the inability to chart a successful course during the 1955–66 period was the existence of the Council and the concomitant weakness of the executive. Rather, debate revolved around the issue of a new plebiscite and constitutional reform that would end the second colegiado experiment and again return the country to a presidential system. The major parties finally agreed to a single reform proposal that was approved by 83 percent of voters in 1966 (Zubillaga 1985b:58; Ruddle and Gillette 1972:98). The reform not only unified the executive but also created new executive powers—such as the right of the president to restrict legislative spending, to demand immediate legislative consideration of urgent projects, and to limit the legislature's ability to create new state jobs. The reform also gave the executive greater control over the state's commercial and industrial sector by ending the traditional party's coparticipation on directorates, established in the 1952 constitution (Weinstein 1975:116; Zubillaga 1985b:59). The electorate was apparently convinced of the merits of the proposal, giving heavy support to the reform in the plebiscite but, at the same time, returning power to the Colorados. However, for the first time, List 14 triumphed over Jorge Batlle's badly weakened List 15.

Paralysis and Polarization, 1966–73. This third phase saw the return of the Colorados to power, the ongoing search for solutions to the economic crisis, and the complex political struggles triggered by growing polarization. Oscar Gestido (1966–67) began his presidency with an attempt to maintain UBD's relatively moderate economic project, rejecting any rapprochement with the IMF. Emphasizing "equitable austerity," Gestido argued that the urban working class had been paying the costs of stabilization, to the benefit of urban and rural capital. Gestido promised to encourage dialogue among all social groups and a distribution of the costs of stabilization. But the Colorados' narrow majority in the legislature required him to seek support from List 15, which strongly supported the IMF project and its austerity measures. Thus, Gestido's presidency was marked by a gradual shift toward the monetarist approach, supported by a growing number within his own faction and the List 15 faction (Zubillaga 1985b:68–70).

Gestido's death in late 1967 and the assumption of the presidency by Jorge Pacheco represented an end to the careful tightrope act between moderate and monetarist policies and a definitive shift to the latter. Pacheco moved quickly to implement an austerity program that, while increasing class tensions, was nevertheless successful in reducing inflation and the fiscal deficit. Beginning with wage and price freezes, which further affected the purchasing power of the working and middle classes, Pacheco also liberalized trade and foreign exchange policy. This period, coming as it did after the successful unification of the labor movement within the CNT (National Workers Central), saw a series of strikes and rising protest. Labor opposition to an agreement with the IMF was heightened even further by the decision of the Pacheco government to end the Wage Councils that had existed since the

1940s, in favor of a new arrangement that weighted the results heavily against labor.[37] To deal with growing labor protest and radicalization, Pacheco evoked emergency powers and initiated a state of siege that continued, almost uninterrupted, until the 1973 coup.

Pacheco's economic austerity program was successful. Inflation fell, and the industrial and export sectors began to recover, aided by falling wages and rising world market prices. But the austerity program had negative social consequences that became an increasingly serious problem for Pacheco, who had decided to seek reelection through a new constitutional reform and plebiscite. As a result, beginning in 1970 Pacheco began to shift away from austerity, increasing state employment and salaries for middle- and working-class sectors in an attempt to rebuild support for his candidacy in the 1971 elections.[38]

The year leading up to the 1971 elections was marked by growing polarization of the electorate. To the right was the Pacheco majority faction of the Colorado Party, as well as the Aguerrondo minority National faction, heir to the Herrera-Ruralistas. The Colorado List 15, now led by Jorge Batlle, had shifted to a center-right position, while the majority National faction, led by Wilson Ferreira, had staked out a center-left position. Finally, a new grouping on the left of the party spectrum was created by the successful formation of the Frente Amplio around the nucleus of the Communists' FIDEL coalition, Michelini's List 99, progressive lists from within traditional parties, the Christian Democrats, the Socialist Party, and other smaller left-wing groups (L. González 1976:163–64; 1984: fn 51).

A look at the class composition of the 1971 election results suggests that the vote for the left was somewhat stronger in the middle class than in the working class. Ures's analysis indicates that the different Colorado factions retained nearly a third of the vote of the working class (including the unemployed).[39] The working class vote for the two traditional parties combined came to slightly over 50 percent. Given the larger context of radicalization, this is a substantial share of the vote. By contrast, 43 percent of the upper middle class voted for the Frente, with the traditional parties retaining slightly over 40 percent of their vote.

The results of the election were contradictory, defeating Pacheco's reelection bid while electing his hand-picked successor, Juan Bordaberry. Besides the impressive 18 percent won by the Frente Amplio, a major consequence of the elections was that the Bordaberry government would face a very difficult period in the legislature, given that it held less than one-third of either chamber (Zubillaga 1985b:86).

Bordaberry's lack of a legislative majority resulted in a frantic attempt to build a majority coalition, finally achieved in 1972 but resting on shaky agreements. The opposition to Bordaberry in the legislature grew as both

[37] Handelman 1981a:382; Graillot 1973b:511–12; Gillespie 1982a:3–4.
[38] McDonald 1971:213; 1972:39–40; Finch 1981:242–44; Macadar and Barbato 1985:13–14; Rial 1984a:26; Sala and Landineli 1984:290; Rial 1984a:25–26; Gillespie 1982a:17.
[39] Ures 1972:14.

Bordaberry and the armed forces began to attack the legislature as immobilist and corrupt. The growing conflict among the military, the legislature, and the executive over the conduct of the war against the Tupamaros led to a series of crises in 1972 and the first half of June 1973 (E. Kaufman 1979:28–29; Vasconcellos 1973). The different branches of government became increasingly divided against one another at a time that the economy was once again entering into recession; as the left, especially the CTN, was becoming more and more radical in its demands; and as the military began to play an ever larger role in politics.

Opposition and Crises of the 1950s to 1970s

The regional climate created by new opposition movements in the late 1950s to the 1970s had a substantial impact on Uruguay, and the growing crisis within the party system and the state must be understood in that context. The Uruguayan situation was distinctive in that the crisis occurred in the setting of long-term economic stagnation, which was more extreme than in any other country considered in this book.

Party System.   Major developments in the party system included the defection to the left by some factions of both the Colorado and National parties, failed attempts in the 1960s to build a united left, and, prior to the 1971 presidential election, the emergence of the Frente Amplio. A number of new currents developed within the Colorado Party in the 1960s. These shifts had significant consequences for the party's identity, as well as for the new Frente Amplio. Here we will focus on two significant divisions within the Colorados: the creation of List 99 under the leadership of Zelmar Michelini and Renán Rodríguez, and the consequence of the struggle for leadership within List 15 between Jorge Batlle and Amílcar Vasconcellos, which Batlle ultimately won. The first suggests some of the consequences of deserting the Colorado *lema*, while the second suggests some conclusions about intraparty opposition.

In the early 1960s, an important realignment began within the Colorado Party. Until that period, the significant Colorado division was between List 14 and List 15, a division that emerged out of the struggle for leadership and control over the Batlle heritage. During the 1940s and 1950s, the non-Batllista wing of the party gradually disappeared. It was not until the emergence of List 99, in opposition to the growing conservatism of the two traditional Batllista lists, that strong ideological differences began to appear within the Colorado Party. List 99 brought together two important leaders of the traditional factions—Zelmar Michelini, previously of List 15 and leader of the Colorado bench in the Chamber of Representatives, and Renán Rodríguez, a longtime Batllista figure of List 14. List 99, composed of left and moderate elements and based primarily on urban support (Graillot 1973a:481), began with the vague promise to restore the original Batllismo. This list achieved a significant vote and important legislative representation in the 1962 elections. Its stated intention was to "revitalize the essential features of *coloradismo batllista*: a dynamic and populist liberal-progressivism" (Zubillaga 1985b:66).

List 99's attempt to build a consistent program and establish links with the labor movement was fatally weakened by its own division over the 1966 constitutional reform. Many List 99 leaders defected to another new list around the moderate Amílcar Vasconcellos. For List 99, the result of the division was immediately evident in the 1966 election, when this list suffered a decline to just 48,000 votes. Fearing further losses to Vasconcellos's moderate opposition, Michelini finally led List 99 out of the Colorado Party, together with a smaller and more progressive List 88, and into the Frente Amplio. This defection meant the end of any moderate left presence within the Colorado Party. Despite Michelini's move and the great success of the Frente Amplio, this defection was apparently not popular with many of his supporters, and his vote fell even lower, this time to just 31,000 votes. This was a familiar consequence of the desertion of traditional party factions to other movements (Gillespie 1982a:9; Zubillaga 1985b:67).

A second division, precipitated by Amílcar Vasconcellos, ended List 15's internal Colorado majority. Vasconcellos, who had carried out a spirited leadership struggle with Jorge Batlle, was defeated and defected from List 15 in 1965, forming his own List 315. Drawing additional support from List 99, from Renán Rodríguez, and from some figures within List 14, Vasconcellos wished to maintain or restore the Batllista vision of the 1940s in response to the growing conservatism of figures surrounding Jorge Batlle. In his first electoral contest, in 1966, Vasconcellos won 77,000 votes, giving the internal Colorado Party election to Gestido and Pacheco. Reacting to his defeat, Vasconcellos made the prophetic statement that "it was a victory for the Colorado party, but a defeat for Batllismo" (Zubillaga 1985b:68). A strong opponent of Pacheco's monetarist policies, Vasconcellos demanded a return to Gestido's aborted program of developmentalism with additional progressive changes in various aspects of the Uruguayan socioeconomic system (Graillot 1973b:515). Vasconcellos's problem was his difficulty in defining these "necessary" changes and in presenting himself and his faction as a realistic alternative, especially at a time that List 99, FIDEL, and the Frente Amplio, made much stronger and more coherent arguments. In 1971, the growing polarization of the electorate and the decline of the Vasconcellos faction's plausibility as a political force contributed to a significant reduction in his vote, to just 49,000. The end result of the Vasconcellos defection was to consolidate the conservatism of List 15 and List 14 while shifting the internal balance of power to the latter and thus contributing to the victory of Juan Bordaberry.

The conclusions that can be drawn from these two cases point to the importance in the 1960s of the party name, as well as the problem of moderate or moderate-left groups in competing in a setting of significant polarization. Thus, the traditional parties could count on the double simultaneous vote to reduce the importance of internal schisms (Graillot 1973b:516), while depending on the strength of traditional party attachments to prevent voter defection to lists that moved outside the parties. But these latter cases were unusual and, as Gillespie points out, "programmatic disputes within the two traditional parties only rarely caused factions to break away" (Gillespie 1982a:16). That two important breakaways occurred in 1971, the first since the unsuccessful attempt of the National Independent Party two decades earlier, may have marked the beginning of a more fundamental breakdown in the parties' control over internal splits. The 1973 coup made it impossible to tell whether, within the context of the 1970s, these would have been isolated defections or the beginning of a more general trend.

In any case, the only significant challenge to the traditional parties' hold on the electorate came not from within their own ranks, but from a coalition that had been gestating for over a decade but which, for a variety of reasons, was unable to come together until the creation of the Frente Amplio under the *lema* of the Christian Democratic Party (PDC) in 1971. To understand this development, it is useful to examine: (1) several early attempts to create electoral unity on the left; (2) the successful emergence of the Frente Amplio in the context of opposition to Pacheco's stabilization policies; (3) the consequences for the Uruguayan party system; and (4) the weak response of the traditional parties to this threat to their electoral hegemony.[40]

During the late 1940s and early 1950s, the electoral importance of both the Communist and the Socialist parties declined, reflecting the success of the Batllista project in attracting new electoral support. Meanwhile, the Civic Union continued to hold a conservative to moderate line, even though a growing progressive faction was developing, especially within its youth wing. Nontraditional party fortunes began to improve relative to the traditional parties in the late 1950s under the impact of the economic crisis, a rise in anti-U.S. feelings, and growing sympathy for the Cuban Revolution. Thus, for the 1962 elections, all three of these parties presented a new face to the Uruguayan electorate. The Communists, drawing on this growing sympathy, created their new party, FIDEL, which brought together a number of minor left-wing groups and progressive National and Colorado splinter groups. The Communists' goal of creating a full-fledged union of the left was defeated, however, by the decision of the Socialist Party to initiate its own unification attempt, this time under the name of Popular Union. During the 1950s a schism had developed within the Socialist Party, with one group upholding the traditional social democratic orientation of the party founded by Emilio Frugoni, while the other groups supported an increase in the party's attention to the needs of labor and labor unity. Frugoni, much against his will, was convinced to support the formation of the Popular Union, which brought together various elements: the youth movement of the Civic Union, which had been expelled for its refusal to sign an anti-Castro statement in 1961 (Zubillaga 1985b:73); an important faction centered around the moderate-to-left National leader of List 41, Enrique Erro, who headed the Popular Blanco Movement; and also several members of think tanks established by the Ru-

---

[40] The following section draws extensively on Zubillaga (1985b:71–80).

ralista movement. The 1961 schism within the Civic Union, which lost its youth wing to the Popular Union, was compounded by the loss of another progressive sector, which formed the Christian Democratic Movement. In reaction to these losses, and in an attempt to capitalize on the growing success in Europe and Latin America of the Christian Democratic parties, the Civic Union changed its name to the Christian Democratic Party (PDC). Despite the loss of some of its left wing, two important factions remained within the new PDC: one sought to maintain the confessional and conservative nature of the party, and the other sought to move the party to the left in support of radical social change.

The electoral support for these new movements was disappointing. The Popular Union saw a serious decline from 1958, losing nearly a quarter of its vote. The results for the new Christian Democratic Party were even more negative, and for the first time its vote total fell below that of the new Communist Party, FIDEL, which appeared to gain from the decline of these new parties. The effort to achieve unity suffered a setback as a consequence of these disastrous results for the Socialists and the Christian Democrats. Frugoni withdrew his group from the Popular Union, taking up once again the Socialist *lema*. Meanwhile, the Christian Democrats split in 1965 as the left-wing groups that had been expelled or departed prior to 1962 returned with the support of the progressive wing. This led to a permanent division within the Christian Democratic party as the traditional wing departed to reestablish the original Civic Union. Unable to achieve unity, the left entered the 1966 elections once again seriously divided. In the election, FIDEL substantially increased its vote, and the Christian Democrats also achieved a significant vote. By contrast, the Socialists, the Christian Civic Movement, and the Popular Union won little support.

These unsuccessful experiences at building front-style parties delayed the development of a united left, due not only to the failures of these attempts but to the growing evidence that the left could not achieve an effective opposition by uniting old ideological blocks with profoundly different social models (Zubillaga 1985b:76–77). Nevertheless, the increasing unity of the labor movement after the formation of the National Confederation of Workers (CNT) as the sole labor central, as well as growing opposition to the policies of the Pacheco government, played a crucial role in creating the political momentum that made it possible to overcome these earlier failures.

The early initiatives to create a new progressive front came from the Christian Democrats, first in 1968 and again in early 1970. Considerable skepticism within the left about the electoral possibilities of such a front was overcome by a group of nonparty figures who acted as a catalyst bringing together on 15 December 1970 the PDC, Erro's Popular Blanco Movement and Michelini's List 99. These more moderate elements within the Uruguayan left announced their desire to create "a broad front without exclusions," which would pursue progressive, electoral means for political change, a clear rejection of the Tupamaros' route of armed rebellion (Zubillaga 1985b:78). This push for unity was consolidated in early January 1971 with the decision of the Christian Democrats and List 99 to constitute a new movement, the People's Front. Over the next month a series of talks led to the formation on 5 February 1971 of the Frente Amplio. The Frente's diverse composition suggests how complex a coalition it was: the Christian Democrats; List 99 (ex-Colorado); the Popular Blanco Movement (ex-National); List 58 (ex-National); FIDEL; the Communists, Socialists, Popular Unity, and the Socialist Movement (Frugoni); and various progressive splinter groups. The subsequent creation of a party program was intended to avoid ideological divisions and, as a consequence, was relatively moderate (L. González 1984:4).

The Frente Amplio emerged as a response to a growing feeling that the political class and the traditional parties were exhausted as options for positive social change (de Sierra 1985:152–53). Yet the Frente faced serious problems, one of which was overcome by a legal stratagem, the others of which could not be solved so easily. The 1966 constitution, seeking to prevent popular front or interparty coalitions, restricted the application of the double simultaneous vote to "permanent" parties, defined as those with parliamentary representation in the session of the legislature prior to the election. However, the left managed to overcome this obstacle by establishing the Frente Amplio under the party name of the Christian Democrats, with the parties that made up the Frente functioning as *sublemas* under that party name (Weinstein 1975:124). The second problem, which would go unsolved, was how to build electorally on the left's control of organized labor and especially the CNT. The inability to break the traditional parties' hold on the electoral sympathies of workers limited the electoral support of the new Frente Amplio.

In the 1971 elections, the Frente Amplio challenged the long-standing tradition of a two-party system, achieving 18 percent of the national vote. In Montevideo they ran a close second to the Colorados, winning 30 percent of the vote. The traditional parties, relatively certain of their hold on Uruguay's electorate despite pre-election opinion polls that showed the Frente a close second to the Colorados, had failed to mount a united response to this challenge, due to internal fragmentation and personal rivalries. Rather, most of the traditional party factions had sought to prevent a loss of votes to the Frente by questioning its support of democracy. On the other hand, President Pacheco, worried about losing the votes of workers and state employees to the Frente, announced one month before the elections a general wage increase and interest-free loans for state workers (Graillot 1973b:515; Gillespie 1982a:9). This ploy apparently did not succeed. In sum, the traditional parties' response to the emergence of the Frente proved nearly as weak and ineffective as the response they would later make to the rapid growth of the military's involvement in the state and their own exclusion from Uruguayan politics in June 1973.

Labor Movement.   Three themes stand out in the development of the labor movement: the growing independence of unions from the Communist Party; labor's reaction to the growing economic crisis and the emergence of a new style of unionism, leading eventually to the successful unification of labor within the CNT; and labor's reaction to the growing repression of the Pacheco and Bordaberry governments and to the military takeover in June 1973.[41]

In 1942, within the framework of wartime collaboration on the left, the Montevideo labor movement had been successfully centralized within the Communist labor central, the UGT.[42] This new unity was a consequence of the struggle, led by the Communists, for Wage Councils and other labor benefits that were achieved under the Amézaga government in 1943. However, the labor movement soon became divided once more. The UGT suffered an almost immediate loss of strength due to the leadership's insistence that the important dock workers' and meatpackers' unions give up the use of the strike to avoid harming the Allied effort in World War II. This policy, added to the insistence by UGT leadership that member unions follow Communist Party doctrine, led to growing division.

Not only did the export sector unions defect, but as new unions developed under the impetus of the Batlle industrialization project, they resisted joining the UGT and created an increasingly autonomous union sector. Despite enormous gains in real wages and in the general standard of living of urban workers as a consequence of the Batllista policies, the labor movement maintained its independence from the traditional parties and from the Colorados in particular. This was due, in part, to the change to the colegiado form of government in 1952 and the inability of the Colorados to prevent the Council from reacting negatively to labor pressures. As a result, a growing contradiction between labor organization independence and the addition of the urban working and middle classes to the Batllista electoral coalition created a division in the loyalty of the working class. Though this became an obstacle to the emergence of a labor party, it was part of a dual labor movement strategy that began to develop during this period and became characteristic of labor in the 1950s and 1960s: direct action against management through strikes and demands, on the one hand, and indirect action through pressure on the Colorado-dominated legislature for favorable labor legislation, on the other.[43]

This strategy became more problematic with the advent of the economic crisis of the mid-1950s. The crisis had a serious impact on labor, with the collapse of many small-sized industrial firms, the removal of protection under the first National government (1959–63), an increase in unemployment from 3.7 percent in 1955 to 12.5 percent in 1963, and a decline in real wages of 15 percent in the private sector between 1958 and 1968 and of 10 percent in the public sector between 1961 and 1968. The advent of the National governments, with the concomitant end of Batlle's industrial policies, marked, therefore, a significant rupture in the relationship between unions and the

[41] This section draws extensively on the work of Sala and Landinelli (1984:251–329).

[42] Sala and Landineli 1984:265; Solari 1965, vol. 2:125–26; Finch 1981:60–61.

[43] Sala and Landineli 1984:268–69, 271; Rodríguez 1965:38–39, 51–52; Pintos 1960:344–46, 410–11; Finch 1981:60–61; D'Elia 1982:64–65; Errandonea and Costabile 1969:126–27; Gargiulo 1984:20–22; Rial 1983:24.

SHAPING THE POLITICAL ARENA

state that developed between 1942 and 1958. This period, characterized by significant labor reform, an average annual increase in real wages of 6 percent, and a significant increase in workers' standard of living, contrasted sharply with the period between 1959 and 1973. Although labor fought a relatively successful rear-guard action between 1959 and 1968—focusing on extending its presence to nonunionized sectors and attempting to defend its earlier gains, thereby maintaining most of its gains from the Batlle era—beginning in 1968 labor suffered serious reverses. As Zubillaga notes, the urban social accord began to break down, with the industrial sector actively attacking the state's "paternalist support" of labor, while the labor movement, for its part, increased its pressure on the government and the legislature through increasingly confrontational means. These changes in the status of labor's relation to the state were also to have a significant impact on the composition and structure of the labor movement.[44]

Labor's success during the Batlle era had a negative impact on its over-all unity. Growing dissent from the ideological line of the UGT, including the formation in 1951 of the anticommunist Uruguayan Union Confederation (CSU) (Pintos 1960:338), created a pluralistic labor movement during the 1950s. Political differences between various unions sabotaged attempts to work together, especially support-strikes and general strikes, but as long as the government was favorable in its overall labor policy, these differences could be overlooked. However, the economic crisis of the mid-1950s and the subsequent National governments provided a significant stimulus to unification of an increasingly defensive labor movement.[45]

The Communist Party was the first to make a serious bid in the 1960s for unification, dissolving the UGT in 1961 to form a temporary umbrella organization, the CUT (Central Unica de Trabajadores). This stance was the result of a significant policy change within the Communist Party which, recognizing the causes of the failure of the UGT, began to deal more flexibly with other unions. The 1950s had also seen an important change in overall union strategy, from one that emphasized achieving state power and destroying the bourgeoisie, to a more moderate strategy that took into account the consequences of strikes on the economic sector. This transition was encouraged by the rising level of unemployment brought on by the crisis. As a consequence, the labor movement, as it entered the 1960s, had seen the virtual disappearance of the anarcho-syndicalist trade unions and the CSU, which lost many member unions as its collaborationist and antistrike strategies were increasingly perceived as inadequate responses to the economic crisis and the antagonistic National governments. This change in the labor movement left two main sectors: the unions that were still grouped around

---

[44] Sala and Landineli 1984:275–76; Rodríguez 1965:79–81; Zubillaga 1985b:63; D'Elia 1982:85; Gargiulo 1984:24.

[45] H. Rodríguez 1965:81–82; Handelman 1981a:375; Sala and Landineli 1984:281; Finch 1981:61.

the UGT and the Communist Party; and those, especially of public sector workers, that emerged during the 1940s and 1950s.[46]

The growing importance of public sector workers, who depended on the very state that the Communist Party sought to overthrow, increased pressure for building the unity of the two sectors on a pragmatic defense of workers' economic and political rights. The Communists' willingness to adopt this stand was evident in the formation of the CUT. The CUT established as its primary goals the unification of the labor movement and the development of solutions to the country's economic crisis, solutions that would avoid the kind of policies being attempted by the National Party governments. Despite these positive overtones, the CSU refused to join the CUT, thus presenting a brief obstacle to unification but hastening its own demise, as many pro-unification unions began to withdraw. In 1964, after three years of dialogue, the CUT and several important unions created the CNT (National Workers Confederation) and over the next two years negotiations with the many independent trade unions were successfully carried out, leading to the acceptance in 1966 of the status of the CNT as the nation's main trade union organization. By 1966, not only had the CNT brought together the great majority of the country's trade unions, but it also had developed close organizational ties with a variety of progressive organizations.[47]

The new labor central proposed solutions to the country's economic problems that were progressive, but certainly not revolutionary. In the first general meeting of the CNT, the delegates supported a political and economic program that included a strong attack on the National government's economic and social policies; agrarian, budgetary, urban and educational reforms; promotion of industrialization; and nationalization of monopolies and foreign firms in key economic sectors (Sala and Landineli 1984:283–85; Cosse 1984:102). The CNT's program found little support within the traditional parties, but the emergence of the Frente Amplio gave electoral support to many of the central points of their program.

The period 1968–73 brought an important change in the relationship between labor and the state. For Pacheco, the primary source of the economic crisis lay in the continual demand for higher wages. Therefore, Pacheco's stabilization plan focused on antilabor measures such as a freeze on wages and an only partial freeze on prices, as well as the elimination of the Wage Councils through which labor had previously exercised considerable influence. The creation of the Council on Wages and Prices (COPRIN), which centralized wage decisions within an executive branch increasingly dominated by business, had immediate negative effects on labor and led to a period in which class conflict became endemic. Over 300 private sector strikes and 500 public sector strikes occurred between June and December of 1968 alone

[46] Rial 1983:23–24; Pintos 1960:412; Errandonea and Costabile 1969:128–29, 133–34; Cosse 1984:96; Rial 1983:25.

[47] Rodríguez 1965:66–70, 81, 83; Errandonea and Costabile 1969:145–46; Sala and Landineli 1984:281.

(Sala and Landinelli 1984:293). The government responded, first, with state of siege measures that limited the right to strike,[48] and later with direct repression, which included closing left-wing and prolabor newspapers as well as the arrest of hundreds of labor activists and leaders (Rial 1984b:26 and fn 28; Handelman 1981a:382–83).

The growing mobilization of labor unions and popular movements in opposition to the Pacheco government played a significant role in the gradual emergence of a united electoral option on the left, that is, the Frente Amplio. Nevertheless the division of allegiances of the urban working and middle classes between support for the CNT and their unions, on the one hand, and electoral support for the traditional parties, on the other, limited the possibilities of closer relations between the Frente Amplio and the CNT. As the political crisis grew sharper during the last two years of the Bordaberry government, the CNT took an increasingly confrontational stance toward Bordaberry. Making the elimination of COPRIN a primary demand, the CNT led a massive nationwide strike that effectively shut down the Uruguayan economy on 13 April 1972. The next day, the Tupamaros initiated their "final" offensive, and on April 15 Bordaberry received almost unanimous support from Congress in declaring a state of "internal war" (Sala and Landineli 1984:306–8). With the suspension of habeas corpus, the military began its own offensive against the Tupamaros. In this state of political crisis, the CNT began to equivocate in its position. In February 1973 the CNT announced its support for the military reform plan announced in Communiqués No. 4 and No. 7. Nevertheless, the subsequent weeks made clear the different positions of the military and the CNT, and the CNT moved to oppose the growing military role. When Bordaberry closed Congress on 27 June 1973, the CNT launched a national strike with support of the Frente Amplio and the National Party. The government responded by declaring the CNT illegal on June 30, breaking the general strike by forcibly ending the workplace seizures, inducting all public sector workers into the military, arresting hundreds of CNT leaders and activists, and repressing the huge July 9 demonstration called by the opponents of the military coup. Finally, on July 11, the strike ended and the CNT effectively ceased to exist. While the strike failed, the CNT had effectively undermined any claim to popular legitimacy that the Bordaberry-military regime might make.[49]

This discussion of the labor movement makes it clear that the relationship between the state and labor changed drastically from the highly favorable state role during the period of Batlle dominance, toward a more neutral state role during the period of National Party governance, and finally into a sharply antagonistic state-labor relationship during the 1968–73 period. This area of conflict is commonly seen as a crucial part of the set of crises that led up to the coup.

[48] Pacheco initiated the practice of threatening striking public sector workers with losing their jobs and being drafted into the army (Gillespie 1982a:8).

[49] Rial 1983:25; Kaufman 1979:38–40; Handelman 1981a:387; Sala and Landineli 1984: 317–19.

The Politics of Stabilization. The Uruguayan heritage period differs greatly from the other cases in the length of its economic crisis, which extended over nearly 20 years.[50] In response to the crisis that emerged in the mid-1950s, the various traditional party governments attempted several programs of economic stabilization of which only one, from 1968 to 1970, was successful, and only temporarily at that. According to Finch (1981:190): "The severe crisis in the rural sector provoked both supply and demand problems and exposed the fragility of the industrialization model. However, the realignment of economic policy was frustrated by the continued command of the state machinery by the political parties. It was not finally achieved until the advent of the military."

The initial stabilization effort, pursued by the National Party government of 1958–62, failed due in part to growing division within the party caused by Herrera's death in 1959, but also due to inappropriate policies. These policies involved a redistribution of income from the urban to the rural sector through devaluations, restriction of the money supply, and the ending of multiple exchange rates. While in line with the letter of intent signed with the IMF in 1960, the policies had a negative impact on industry without having a positive effect on stagnation in the livestock sector. The immediate consequences were the rapid growth of fiscal deficits, growing balance of payments problems, high unemployment and falling urban wages, high inflation, and the continued expansion of state employment. By 1962, the failure of this first attempt at stabilization was evident, and further efforts were put off in deference to the pressures of elections.[51]

With the defeat of the Herrara-Ruralista alliance, which had sought to carry out the stabilization program, and the fear that electoral defeat would be the only result of such economic policies, another serious attempt at a thorough stabilization program was not made until the Colorado Pacheco government in 1968. The National Party government, led by the UBD (1962–66) and the first year of the Gestido-Pacheco government (1967–68), saw economic policies marked "by a limited return to trade and exchange control practices and the absence . . . of any new policy initiatives" (Finch 1981:242). In fact, the 1966 elections were remarkable for their lack of any serious proposals to deal with economic problems, in part due to the parties' focus on the 1966 constitutional reform ending the colegiado. In fact, one might argue that this reform was the traditional parties' indirect response to the economic crisis.

It was only with the death of President Gestido and the assumption of the presidency by Pacheco that a second IMF-supported stabilization program was attempted. The Pacheco stabilization effort was based on a dual strategy. First, Pacheco carried out a massive devaluation of the Uruguayan peso and initiated a wage and price freeze in an attempt to control inflation, which

---

[50] This section draws extensively on Finch (1981:191–247).

[51] Weinstein 1975:114; Jacob 1981:124; Macadar and Barbato 1985:10–12; L. González 1976:165–66; Finch 1981:219, 227–29, 236–39; Gillespie 1982a:21; McDonald 1971:208.

had reached 180 percent in 1968—an extremely high rate in the context of the 1960s. Second, Pacheco began a systemic attack on the labor movement, including the abolition of the Wage Councils that had mediated between labor and capital since 1943. Pacheco replaced them with the COPRIN, which was dominated by the executive and by business. The response from labor was an unprecedented wave of strikes and public demonstrations that led Pacheco to declare a state of siege and use the police to repress labor.[52]

While the social consequences of Pacheco's stabilization policy were negative, the GDP grew an average of 5 percent a year in 1969 and 1970 and inflation fell sharply. Nevertheless, the reasons for its success lay less in the specific economic policies pursued by Pacheco, although devaluation stimulated export sector production, than in a fortuitous rise in the world market price for Uruguay's livestock products and in the growing confidence in business circles due in part to Pacheco's sharp repression of labor. This business support was strengthened by the growing tendency during Pacheco's government to name to cabinet positions business representatives who had no clear political ties, thus reducing the ability of the traditional parties to oppose his economic policies.[53]

Pacheco's success was short lived. First, while the state's fiscal deficits were sharply reduced during this period, state spending as a whole climbed, benefiting from the surge in export earnings. When world market prices fell again, fiscal deficits once more began to grow. The use of state resources to cover some of the effects of the resulting drop in real wages was expanded by Pacheco to include a number of election-time measures that greatly increased state spending.[54] These initiatives, together with the failure of the wage and price freezes to contain inflation, led to a return to high inflation in 1972, as Uruguay's GDP fell an average of 1 percent a year in 1971 and 1972. As a result, the stabilization attempt collapsed after the election, followed by another major devaluation, a large increase in inflation, and a decline in GDP (Gillespie 1982a:5–6; Finch 1981:244–45). Though Finch blames the failure of Pacheco's stabilization program on his return to "traditional political practices, especially inflated government expenditure, in anticipation of the 1971 elections" (Finch 1981:247), the failure may in part have been due to the perception that Pacheco's growing use of authoritarian methods to deal with social and labor protest was out of place in a liberal democratic polity. This reflects the high price paid for the government's lack of stable political links with organized labor.

In conclusion, the traditional parties were unable to develop and carry out a consistent stabilization program or to implement the reforms necessary to deal with the economic crisis. It is evident that such reforms might well

[52] Macadar and Barbato 1985:12–14; Finch 1981:242–43; Frega et al. 1984:35–36; Gillespie 1982a:3–4; Sala and Landineli 1984:290, 293.

[53] L. González 1976:165–66; Finch 1981:242–44; Macadar and Barbato 1985:13–14; Zubillaga 1985b:69–71.

[54] According to Graillot (1973b:470) in 1966 an estimated 30 percent of Uruguay's population received state aid in one form or another.

have required a radical change in the character of Uruguay's socioeconomic system. González addresses this issue when he argues that the growth of the state was economically inefficient, but politically efficient, through reducing conflict and increasing, or at least maintaining, party strength.[55] During this period, Uruguayan leaders did not succeed in moving beyond this trade-off, in part because social and political forces were too strong to allow them to do so, and also because they lacked the capacity for union-party-state mediation to win compromises among these forces.

Guerrilla Movement. Uruguay, unlike Colombia, had no significant history of guerrilla movements prior to the emergence in the 1960s of the National Liberation Movement, the Tupamaros.[56] The last civil war had taken place in 1904, and an attempt to revert to this type of revolt failed ignominiously in 1935 during the Terra dictatorship. Indeed, the Uruguayan political system had been characterized far more by civility than by violence. The Tupamaros' emergence within this context will be examined in terms of three components: (1) the origins of the movement during a period when significant groups within the left were strongly attracted by the model of the Cuban Revolution; (2) the ideology, strategy, and tactics utilized by the Tupamaros during their active period beginning approximately in 1968; and (3) their final defeat. We will evaluate the impact of the Tupamaros on the political system, especially the growing role of the armed forces in national politics.

The Tupamaros emerged out of the efforts in 1961 of a group of young socialist labor leaders to organize a union among poverty-stricken sugar workers in the north. These workers, under the impetus of the urban organizers, broadened their demands to include land expropriation and redistribution. Setting out on a 350-mile march to Montevideo, the workers and organizers were met by the police, and shootings and arrests ensued. Frustrated by the lack of legislative or executive response to their demands, the organizers subsequently formed the Tupamaros (Porzecanski 1973:5; Rial 1984b:26, fn 28; Kaufman 1979:34).

The Tupamaros, profoundly influenced by their experience in 1961, believed that the traditional parties could not provide the leadership needed to achieve progressive solutions to Uruguay's problems; only through violence could a new vision of Uruguayan society be achieved. From the early 1960s the Tupamaros began to build their organization, supply it with arms, and develop the tactics and programs that might bring them to power. The goal of their violence was to discredit the government's decision-making process while reducing the effectiveness of its coercive powers and its capacity to command loyalty and legitimacy (Porzecanski 1973:4–5, 13; Rial 1984b:27).

Although they began with some failed attempts at rural organization (Porzecanski 1973:15–17), the Tupamaros were aware of the strategic value of locating their movement within Montevideo, where virtually the entire state

[55] L. González 1976:156. See also Gillespie (1982a:24).
[56] This section draws extensively on Porzecanski (1973).

apparatus and nearly 50 percent of the national population were located. Building a rigidly compartmentalized organization, the Tupamaros adopted a strategy that emphasized: development of a parallel government; presentation of themselves as a legitimate alternative to the traditional parties; development of nonmilitary support groups within the popular sector, as well as the state bureaucracy, which would wield mass influence on their behalf; and creation of a climate of crisis that would precipitate the final seizure of power (Porzecanski 1973:17-24). As a first phase of implementing this strategy, the Tupamaros carried out a number of bank robberies and kidnappings between 1965 and 1968, keeping a low profile until they were strong enough to confront the state directly.

Beginning in 1968, the Tupamaros began to use the full range of their tactics, which included the theft of arms, spectacular prison breaks, interruption of television programs for propaganda purposes, exposure of corruption within the parties, kidnapping of well-known political figures, and Robin Hood-style robberies after which they distributed the proceeds in the poorer neighborhoods of Montevideo. Their actions were marked both by a good sense of political theater, using clever tactics to expose and criticize the defects of the Uruguayan political system, and by a strong commitment to a "teaching" role that was reflected in many of their actions and communications. The effectiveness of this role was reinforced by their minimal use of violence up to 1970.

Until 1970, the government sought to defeat the Tupamaros using conventional police methods. The failure of this approach, as well as growing opposition to it within the police and the military, led to a change in tactics in January 1970, as the soft-liners within the police were purged and the extensive torture and other more aggressive tactics were adopted (Porzecanski 1973:55–56). After a massive prison break in September 1971, the government charged the armed forces with defeating the Tupamaros. With the declaration of a state of internal war in April 1972, the "Armed Forces merged into a unified anti-Tupamaro command and were set free to pursue their counterinsurgency objectives without regard for judicial accountability or individual rights."[57]

The Tupamaros, upon returning to the offensive in April, were met with a coherent military strategy that had been developed during the unilateral cease-fire. Using systematic torture and gaining the advantage of extracting information from a high-level member of the Tupamaros, the military was able to break the compartmentalization of the Tupamaros that had thwarted police efforts (Porzecanski 1973:69). Between April and September of 1972, the military defeated the Tupamaros, jailing thousands of real or suspected members.

Although they were defeated, the Tupamaros had a major impact on the Uruguayan political system. By publicizing corruption within the highest reaches of the traditional parties, they discredited the country's political

---

[57] Porzecanski 1973:68. See also Weinstein (1975:117–18); Rial (1984b:26–27).

leadership. They also influenced the military. Through the thousands of hours that the military spent with captured Tupamaros and through the military's exposure to the information that the Tupamaros had unearthed, "the military leaders themselves became painfully aware of the defects of Uruguayan society" (from the *New York Times*, cited in Porzecanski 1973:73). This knowledge was used by the military in its subsequent efforts to delegitimate the parties and the legislature. Finally, the military, through undertaking the destruction of the Tupamaros, assumed a position of central importance within the Uruguayan political system.[58]

Military Role. Just as Uruguay had no significant 20th-century history of guerrilla movements prior to the emergence of the Tupamaros, it also had no experience with military rule. Terra's overthrow of the democratic government in 1933 was carried out with no military support, and between the 1940s and 1960s the military played a marginal role in politics. This changed under the impetus of the growing violence within Uruguayan society in the late 1960s and early 1970s. In this section we will explore the growing perception within the military in the late 1960s that both the government and the police were incapable of dealing with the Tupamaros; the effects on the armed forces of their "internal war" with the Tupamaros, including a growing perception of the country's political parties and institutions as corrupt and ineffective; and the development and execution of the military's strategy to discredit these institutions, and their systematic effort to broaden their role within the state, which culminated in serious crises in October 1972 and February and June 1973. We will conclude by noting the gradual escalation in the confrontation between the armed forces and the country's political institutions and the failure of the political parties to react effectively to the growing military role within the state.

The war with the Tupamaros had a major impact on the relationship between the military and national political institutions. The evidence of massive corruption within the parties, as well as a growing concern with the failure of the political system to deal with the nearly 20-year-long economic crisis, fed the conviction in the armed forces that the political parties were incapable of finding a solution to Uruguay's escalating crisis. The military's ability to rapidly defeat the Tupamaros after several years of government failures convinced it of its ability to deal more broadly with Uruguay's problems (Rial 1984b:34–35). Also, the military became accustomed to substantial freedom from legal constraints, and it moved gradually into a more predominant role within the state that culminated in the partial coup of 27 June 1973.

The military initiated three crises in civil-military relations involving charges of corruption and subversion against members of Congress (Kaufman 1979:27–29). As Kaufman ably demonstrates, the military sought to "split the political forces in Parliament," first through divisive tactics and later by forcing the legislature to respect the military's prerogatives (Kaufman

---

[58] Porzecanski 1973:73–74. See also Rial (1984b:27); Kaufman (1979:37–38).

1979:27–30). In October of 1972, the military accused Jorge Batlle, leader of the Colorado List 15, of corruption and demanded that the legislature repeal his electoral immunity and turn him over to the military courts. The Congress refused to do this, and the military arrested Batlle and kept him in prison for over a month (McDonald 1975:34–36). As McDonald (1975:36–37) points out, "the military waged a vigorous campaign from 1966 to 1974 against the nation's governmental structures, specifically the national police, the constitution . . . the Congress, and ultimately the presidency itself." The rather weak response of the Congress encouraged the military to take on the increasingly isolated Bordaberry in February 1973.

Specifically, the crisis of February 1973 developed out of the military's refusal to accept the president's appointment of a minister of defense whom the military felt did not support its mission of ending subversion and assuring "internal security for economic development" (Vasconcellos 1973:38–42). The crisis was deepened by strong attacks on the military and support for the executive from within the legislature, particularly by Vasconcellos, head of the Colorado List 315. Accusing Vasconcellos of aiding subversion, the military attempted to try him in a military court. This was never necessary, since Bordaberry caved in to military pressure. During this crisis the military released Communiqués No. 4 and No. 7, which contained a blueprint of changes the military wished to see carried out by the government (Vasconcellos 1973:44–50). These two military communiqués, with their "random listing of policy aims suggests that the communiqués were simply an expression of intent with no basis in a coherent and systematic analysis of national problems" (Finch 1981:249). What was most astonishing about these military proposals was their breadth, and the implication of growing military involvement in virtually every area of state activity (Vasconcellos 1973:44–50).

This perception was confirmed by the agreement between Bordaberry and the military on 12 February 1973, called the Boisso Lanza Pact after the air force base where the president and the armed forces met (Vasconcellos 1973:74). This pact represented a significant grant of state power to the military and established the basis for participation of the three branches of the military in politico-administrative activities (Zubillaga 1985b:87). Most important was the creation of CONASE (National Security Council), made up of executive and military representatives as "an instrument of action to carry out the program proposed by the military" (Vasconcellos 1973:57). CONASE was given power to look into corruption charges against several important congressmen. The pact also redefined the military role in the cabinet, ended the quotas for political appointments to state enterprises, redesigned military promotions, removed several persons the military saw as corrupt from the foreign service, and gave the military the right to enter into direct political debate with any legislator or politician who made statements detrimental to the honor of the armed forces. On 23 February, Bordaberry officially announced the formation of CONASE, which effectively gave the military the right to request public-sector documents and to call on public functionaries to answer questions. The secrecy of all CONASE activities and documents was guaranteed.

The executive's tendency to give way to the military demands encouraged the military to pursue an even greater role in politics. Over the next three months, the military extended its presence in the state, moving into what Rial (1984b:33) refers to as a "power-vacuum" created by the parties through their inability to confront the military. Its final attack on the legislature took place in June 1973, when the military demanded that the Frente Amplio congressman Erro be turned over to military justice for supporting the Tupamaros. The legislature rejected the military demand, and after days of charges and countercharges the military arrested Erro. As the legislature gathered to consider impeachment proceedings against President Bordaberry, he closed the legislature.

What emerges from this discussion is a growing escalation of military demands on the executive and legislative branches and the steady erosion of civilian control over politics. The inability of the parties to prevent this attack on the institutions of the political system was a significant indicator of their growing weakness. The military appears to have been able to focus attention on the deficiencies of the traditional political leadership, its corruption, immobilism, and failure to act decisively against subversion. The military succeeded in acting on its view of Uruguay's problem as one of order, rather than as a political and social problem, which was not a majority view in the general population at the time of the 1973 coup (Zubillaga 1985b:87–88; L. González 1976:166–67).

Also, as a number of authors have agreed, the coup resulted from the collapse of the prior political equilibrium and the inability of political actors to create a new dominant coalition that could deal with the economic crisis (Finch 1981:246; Rial 1984b:9–22, 39). At the same time, among those who supported the growing military role, there seems to have been a perception that the military was only an instrument, without autonomy, which could break the institutional log-jam after a brief period of military rule, and then return power to the traditional parties. Unlike the Colombian case, where Rojas's earlier attempt to maintain power was successfully thwarted by the traditional parties, Uruguay's traditional parties lacked the strength or will to confront the military. The military removed the traditional parties from politics with relative ease, and subsequently when Bordaberry became a liability, they removed him. The unique features of the 1973 coup lie in the role Bordaberry played, a role that disguised the nature of the Uruguayan dictatorship until his removal.

The 27 June 1973 "autogolpe" exhibited both similarities and contrasts to the Terra coup of 1933 in Uruguay. On the one hand, it was President Bordaberry who closed Congress and who remained head of state thereafter, just as Terra had done. However, the military played a decisive role behind him and removed him in June 1976 when it fitted its needs (L. González 1976:44). In fact, the coup was essentially military-directed and simply an intermediate step in the removal of all significant opposition to the armed forces' self-defined mission to end "subversion" and insure the "security of the development process."

Capacity for Conflict Regulation. The parallels and contrasts with Colombia place in sharp relief distinctive features of the Uruguayan experience. On the one hand, many factors in common with Colombia favored the ongoing stability of Uruguayan politics. The deeply embedded loyalties connected with the two-party system tied much of the Uruguayan electorate to political organizations and leaderships that jointly constituted a majority power bloc. In both countries, the manipulation of electoral and institutional mechanisms played a role in perpetuating this bloc, though the details of this manipulation differed. In Uruguay a crucial mechanism was the double simultaneous vote.

At the same time, contrasts were evident. Colombia was one of the countries that during the aftermath period saw a decisive conservatization of the party that led the incorporation project, a conservatization that was institutionalized in the post-1958 political structures. In Uruguay, the Colorados did not conservatize in the context of the restoration of a competitive regime in the early 1940s. As we saw in Chapter 6, they had a shared interest with Baldomir in retaining voters in the traditional parties, rather than allowing the reaction to the Terra period to stimulate an opening to the left within the electorate. Unlike what occurred in some other cases of party incorporation, the restoration of a democratic regime was premised on the *retention* of the left within the traditional parties, rather than on its *expulsion*. In this framework, the reformist agenda of Batllismo was fully renewed during the following years.

Thus, whereas in some other cases of party incorporation the aftermath period saw the creation of conflict-regulating mechanisms to enforce more conservative policy options, in Uruguay the concern was with reinforcing the traditional parties in a context in which more progressive policy agendas were acceptable. This outcome was of course juxtaposed with the Uruguayan tradition—partially shared with Colombia—of a pluralistic labor movement, which represented another area in which mechanisms of mediation and control common in other countries were absent. The combination of these factors left the two traditional parties in Uruguay—and hence the Uruguayan state—with less capacity to mediate labor conflict than was found in some of the other cases of party incorporation, most obviously Mexico and Venezuela.

During the period of prosperity this political pattern doubtless made it easier for Uruguay to renew the earlier progressive policies of Batlle. But with the prolonged economic slump, and given the deeply ingrained expectations and enormous sunk costs connected with the welfare state, this very same political pattern made it far more difficult to back away from earlier policies. This problem became a key to the growing crisis.[59]

---

[59] This argument, which is cast in comparative terms, is in part parallel to Real de Azua's classic analysis of Uruguay's reformist "impulse" and its "break"—*El impulso y su freno*

Thus, one explanation for the depth of the crisis, and for the contrasting regime outcome vis-à-vis Colombia, was the absence of these mechanisms of conflict-regulation that could facilitate the shift to the right in economic policy, a shift viewed by important sectors of the elite as a solution to the economic difficulties. A second major cause, as we have seen, was the high level of labor militancy. Handelman places central emphasis on this as a cause of the coup and reports that for industrialists, labor militancy—far more than the guerrilla threat—was the central issue of the crisis during the early 1970s (1981:378).

Third, the Tupamaros were of great importance. Handelman (1981a:386–87) usefully places their role in perspective with his emphasis on the greater importance of the labor "threat" on the eve of the coup. He also notes evidence that the dramatic escape of many Tupamaros from prison in 1971 may have been deliberately permitted by the government in order to sustain a sense of threat that would make it easier to justify the state of siege that helped enforce the repression of labor. Yet as we have seen, and as Handelman recognizes, the Tupamaros' dramatic assault on the military and on the legitimacy of civilian political institutions was a major long-term factor leading up to the coup.

Fourth, one must consider the impact of the Frente Amplio. Though the Frente did not represent the kind of spectacular threat posed by the guerrillas or labor radicalization, it also contributed to the general atmosphere of crisis, reflecting a partial, but definitely not complete, erosion of the hold of the traditional parties on the working class and other key sectors of the electorate. Together, these several factors precipitated the 1973 coup, which brought a far more radical departure from Uruguay's democratic tradition than that experienced in Uruguay's authoritarian period of the 1930s.

To conclude, we may review these same four factors from the perspective of assessing how they were shaped by Uruguay's incorporation experience. We are not concerned here with assessing the overall historical outcome of the incorporation period in Uruguay, but rather with accounting for specific contrasts with Colombia.

First, the absence of conflict-limiting mechanisms has been interpreted in part as a result of the mild conservative reaction to incorporation in Uruguay, and hence as a distinctive consequence of the way incorporation occurred within the Uruguayan context. Second, intense labor militancy was in important measure a concomitant of Uruguay's tradition of labor pluralism, which we have suggested is a more likely outcome of the type of incorporation Uruguay experienced. In a setting where patterns of socioeconomic development in Uruguay had been far more favorable for a strong labor movement than they were in Colombia, this pluralism further facilitated labor militancy. Third, in comparison with the guerrillas in Colombia, the

(1964). Real de Azua observes that Batllismo created a false image of, and expectations about, the state, an image that prevented attempts to move forward under the shadow of the economic crisis (Real de Azua 1964:107).

Tupamaros had a greater impact in part due to the profound stagnation and frustrations of the Uruguayan economy and political system over many years. The stagnation and frustrations certainly had some links with the incorporation experience, but they were obviously due to other factors as well. Fourth, in discussing the Frente Amplio it is important to note that Colombia also experienced important electoral opposition during these years, though it was not on the left, as in Uruguay. This contrasting outcome was connected with Uruguay's much deeper tradition of progressive politics. Although this tradition was very evident in the incorporation period, it is essential to recognize that it had earlier roots in the 19th century.

Thus, not surprisingly, these contrasts between Uruguay and Colombia must be understood both in light of the incorporation experience, and in light of other features of the two countries' development.

COLOMBIA

Overview of the Party System

During the years of the National Front (1958–74) and in the following period of more open party competition, the Liberals and Conservatives continued to dominate the Colombian party system. Despite challenges from within their own ranks, as well as from populist and left parties, the majority factions of the traditional parties were able to maintain the Front through its constitutional end-point in 1974 and emerged electorally unchallenged in the subsequent post-Front period.

The Front was successful from the standpoint of the traditional political elite in two other respects as well. First, during this period the state initiated important changes in economic policy more readily than some other Latin American countries, making it easier for the Colombian economy to achieve crucial economic adjustments in the 1960s and 1970s. Second, the Front governments were able to demobilize rural violence in the 1960s, though this early success became increasingly tenuous as guerrilla movements began to expand in the mid-1970s. Nevertheless, the level of rural violence receded significantly under the Front compared to the level of the 1950s.

However, though the parties were able to maintain their traditional multiclass and multisectoral bases of support, the Front period saw a decline in party identification, increased voter apathy, the emergence of an increasingly autonomous and powerful military role in politics, growing elite and middleclass perceptions of regime delegitimation, and a large floating segment of the voting population not tied to either party, especially in urban areas. Thus, although the National Front brought greater consolidation and unification of Colombia's ruling elite in comparison with the 1940s, the traditional parties began to lose their hold on the popular sector, leaving the way open for the potential emergence of competing, antiregime popular forces. Yet as of the mid-1980s, although these forces created growing problems for the governments in power, they were far from posing a challenge equivalent to that seen in the 1970s in the Southern Cone.

In the case of Colombia, the consolidation of what we have called an integrative party system was thus incomplete. The Liberals did maintain their majority status, and the two traditional parties did continue to dominate the electoral arena, yet they were less successful in maintaining party control over the labor movement and other popular sector groups. Likewise, as community and peasant associations organized by Front governments grew, they became increasingly difficult to control. The state's response included the introduction of reform, ideological exhortation, the use of traditional patronage, and repression, depending on the severity of the challenge (Bagley and Edel 1980). By the mid-1970s the connections between the traditional parties and their mass base were increasingly tenuous.

Maintaining Electoral Majorities. Although the terms of the National Front agreement restricted electoral participation to the Liberals and Conservatives, significant electoral opposition to the Front existed both within and outside the traditional parties,[60] for both programmatic and personalistic reasons. This opposition took three forms, expressing disaffection with the government, with the National Front, or with specific policies (Dix 1980:134–35). Though the majority Liberal and Conservative factions were able to maintain the Front, all three types of opposition presented serious challenges.

The Conservatives entered the period of the National Front still suffering from the division that had contributed to the emergence of Rojas Pinilla's military government. Both Ospina and Gómez had supported the Front plebiscite, yet their respective factions were in continual competition during the Front for control of the Conservative Party. As a result, except for brief periods of party unity, the faction that won the majority of Conservative seats would join the Liberal Party in forming a government, while the Conservative minority would go into opposition and would start preparing for the next round of elections. These two major wings of the Conservatives did not really disagree over fundamental policy issues or contrasting postures toward the Front, but rather were fighting for access to top governmental positions and for control of the Conservative Party (Dix 1980:134).

Though the antigovernment Conservatives presented some difficulties to the governing cluster of party factions, it was in fact the growth of anti-Front factions that presented the most important challenge to the continuation of the National Front coalition. From 1960 to 1966, the strongest challenge came from the rebel Liberal faction, the Liberal Revolutionary Movement (MRL), led by Alfonso López Michelsen. This faction received less then 20 percent of the Chamber vote at its peak in 1962, yet it was able, when combined with the antigovernment Conservative faction, to frustrate the government's legislative program by depriving it of the necessary two-thirds vote. With the decline of the MRL and its eventual reintegration with the "official" Liberal Party in 1967, Rojas Pinilla's movement called ANAPO (National Popular Alliance) emerged as the major opponent of the coalition government. ANAPO, which absorbed the left-wing faction of the MRL that was disenchanted with López's decision to rejoin the governing coalition, grew rapidly in the period up to the 1970 election and nearly toppled the Front.

Along with the emergence of ANAPO, the crucial element in the near defeat of the Front in the 1970 election was the emergence of strong opposition to the policies of the Front within the Conservative Party, under the leadership of dissident presidential candidates. Both the Liberal Party and the major factions of the Conservative Party had announced their support for Misael Pastrana Borrero as the official Front candidate in 1970. But two dis-

---

[60] Opposition groups were not excluded electorally, provided that they ran under the label of one of the two main parties. The terms of the Front guaranteed that in any given election, according to whether it was the Liberals' or the Conservatives' "turn," the leading vote-getter of that party would automatically become president.

sident factions within the Conservative Party, one led by Belisario Betancur, the other by Evaristo Sourdis, announced their own candidates for the presidency. Sourdis, from the Atlantic region, was supported by groups dissatisfied with the growing fiscal and administrative centralization under the Front, which had a negative impact on the Atlantic departments. Betancur, on the other hand, pushed for progressive reforms and appealed to Colombia's growing middle class. Since both the Atlantic region and the middle class had generally supported the Front governments, their disproportionate defection to these two opposition candidates, who won 20 percent of the vote, cut deeply into the Front support base and nearly led to the victory of Rojas Pinilla's ANAPO in 1970.

Although pro-Front forces maintained a majority in the legislature through the 1970 election, the terms of the Front required a two-thirds vote to pass all legislation. Consequently, except for the 1958–60 and 1964–66 periods, the Front governments did not have sufficient votes to carry out their legislative programs. They dealt with this problem through using the state of siege and through the 1968 constitutional amendment. Under Article 121 of the Colombian constitution, the president could declare a state of siege, giving him broad decree powers and expanding the powers of the military and the number of criminal offenses that could be tried in military rather than civilian courts. Remarkably, nearly 75 percent of the National Front period was conducted under a state of siege, and this mechanism was crucial to the success of the Front and allowed it to continue operating despite its loss of a two-thirds majority within the Congress (Leal Buitrago 1984:252; Hoskin 1980:111). At the same time, continuous use of what had previously been considered an exceptional executive power created serious legitimacy problems for the Front and growing criticism of the abuse of the state of siege provisions.

The political elite responded to these concerns with the 1968 constitutional reform, which addressed four central points. First, the two-thirds vote was abolished in favor of a simple majority. Second, the parity agreement for noncivil service bureaucratic posts was extended through 1978. After 1978 the majority party would grant the next largest party "equitable" representation. This agreement allowed the two traditional parties to continue their coalition, at least informally, well after the official end of the National Front. Third, open electoral competition was restored for municipal and departmental assemblies in 1970 and for all elections in 1974, allowing third parties to compete. Finally, the president's planning and budgetary powers vis-à-vis the Congress were greatly expanded (Kline 1980:72).

In the short run, the 1968 reforms did not solve the Front's problem. The strong showing of the opposition forces in the 1970 election for the first time cost the ruling coalition its majority within the legislature, so that even under the terms of the 1968 reform it could not, by itself, pass legislation. However, with the return to open electoral competition, the opposition groups were unable to maintain their electoral strength. ANAPO's share of the vote fell below 10 percent in the 1974 elections and it quickly faded as an electoral force.

After the end of the Front in 1974, the two traditional parties were essentially unchallenged in the electoral arena. That this should continue to be the case despite the growing evidence of popular sector disenchantment was perhaps the strongest indicator of the underlying strength of the two parties' hold on the electoral process.

Voter Apathy and Successive Attempts to Reengage the Electorate. Though the two traditional parties continued to dominate the electoral arena, one of the effects of the National Front was to erode traditional party loyalties within a growing segment of the electorate. Two manifestations of this trend, especially in the urban popular sector, were electoral abstention and an increased tendency for voters to base their electoral decisions on candidate appeal rather than on previous party loyalties. Nevertheless, the traditional parties remained strong enough to prevent the emergence of a credible alternative.

Within this overall pattern, these tendencies fluctuated over time. Turnout in the presidential elections of 1962 and 1966 dropped significantly compared with the first election of the National Front period in 1958. Whereas 50 percent of the voting-age population participated in the presidential election in 1958, this figure declined to 38 percent in 1962 and 34 percent in 1966. In congressional elections the decline was slightly greater, falling from 60 percent in 1958 to 31 percent in 1968. This trend created serious problems for the political elite in terms of perceived regime illegitimacy.[61]

Subsequently, turnout rose in 1970 in response to the entry into the campaign of Rojas and the two dissident Conservative candidates in the last presidential election to be held under the National Front agreement. What stands out in this election is that it was the first and only time in Colombian electoral history (as of the late-1980s) that the vote was class-based. Rojas was able to make a strong appeal to the urban popular sector, which, as Dix (1980:143) argued, had been left behind in the push for development under the National Front governments. This urban disaffection with the economic and social policies of the Front was combined with the support of some rural voters—especially from regions deeply affected by La Violencia—who were opposed to the Conservative coalition with the Liberal Party and to the Front candidate Pastrana's campaign promise to end Lleras Restrepo's land reform policies.

As dramatic as Rojas's challenge had been in 1970, the fragility of his support base and of ANAPO became evident with the return to open, competitive elections in 1974. The restoration of genuine electoral competition between the Liberals and Conservatives stimulated a high voter turnout and drew nearly 90 percent of the vote to these two parties, a restoration of their dominance that was maintained throughout the period analyzed in this sec-

[61] Talbot and McCamant 1972:56, Table 19; Ruddle and Gilette 1972:76; Losada 1980:90, 95; F. Leal 1984:153.

tion (Dix 1980:166). The Liberals also succeeded in regaining strong support in the urban popular sector due to López Michelsen's effort to remobilize their traditional urban base in the 1974 campaign (Leal Buitrago 1984:154). Building on his reputation from the 1960s as a reformer and opponent of the National Front, López appealed to sectors disenchanted with the Front's policies. By running a partisan, populist, and reform-oriented campaign, López was able to recapture and successfully mobilize the urban popular sector (Bagley 1984:145).

However, the Liberals' appeal to the popular sector in 1974 proved ephemeral. Once in office, the López administration was incapable of delivering on its campaign rhetoric, in part due to the economic recession that hit Colombia in 1974 and 1975. The economic policies pursued during López's government contributed to a rise in social protest in both the urban and rural sectors that continued to the early 1980s. The general strike of 1977 led to increased military pressure on the civilian administration to curtail rights of union organizers and other activists connected to the popular sector. Although the traditional parties continued to dominate most of the small rural municipalities, a growing peasant movement, centered primarily in the northern *latifundia* regions, initiated a number of land seizures and protest marches. Dissatisfaction with the traditional parties also led to the first attempt to form a national peasant party. However, factional infighting and an inability to compete with the traditional parties' patronage system led to a dismal showing by the new party, the National Democratic Popular Movement (MNDP), and its subsequent disbanding. Electoral participation again dropped in the 1978 congressional and presidential elections to 34 percent and 41 percent, respectively. Though the Liberal Party was able to maintain its majority, the narrowness of its victory—as well as the fact that Belisario Betancur, the Conservative candidate, had won a significant number of votes in traditionally Liberal urban areas—indicated that the Liberals' hold over the popular sector, and the traditional parties' hold over the electorate, was increasingly tenuous.[62]

The trend toward a more restrictive regime continued during the Turbay administration (1978–1982). In 1978 Turbay, through presidential decree, set up the repressive Security Statute, which greatly expanded the role of the military. Military security agencies arrested thousands of suspected "subversives," including large numbers of labor leaders and activists, and tried them in nonpublic military trials. This period saw widespread human rights abuses, and this sharp turn toward a harsher regime, combined with an austere stabilization policy, cost the Liberal Party considerable support in the 1982 elections (Hartlyn 1983:65–66, 83; Bagley 1984:145).

The Turbay administration's policies severely divided the Liberals, yet these policies were only part of the growing disaffection within Liberal ranks. Following the election of López Michelsen in 1974, the strength of the regional and primarily rural party machines had grown considerably. At the

[62] Bagley 1984:142; 1989:44–45; Ruhl 1978:34, 39–40.

same time both traditional parties had emphasized the development not of redistributive measures, but of particularistic, distributive policies meant to maintain the clientelistic, patronage-oriented bases of party support. Both parties had turned away from mobilizational, reformist politics in favor of a politics of distribution and control. A number of Liberal politicians and intellectuals who developed a strong critique of this approach coalesced around the former Liberal president, Carlos Lleras Restrepo, and his protégé, Luis Carlos Galán. In 1982, having failed to prevent the nomination of López, Galán launched an independent presidential campaign, hoping to tap the disaffection with the traditional parties.

While the Liberals were suffering an important division, Betancur was nominated to represent the Conservatives. Betancur based his appeal on a reformist platform that stressed building a base of support independent from the traditional parties by appealing directly to the popular sector. Betancur's emphasis on "national unity" had a great appeal to the middle sectors, while his reformist platform was well-received by urban popular sector. The Liberals, on the other hand, found their party divided between López Michelsen's candidacy, supported by party regulars and the rural machines, and that of Galán, who appealed primarily to urban voters. As a consequence of the Liberal division, Betancur was victorious, becoming only the second Conservative president in over half a century to win a competitive presidential election, and this only by a plurality. What made the Liberal defeat even more conclusive was Betancur's victory in Bogotá, a Liberal stronghold.

Much as occurred during the earlier López administration, Betancur also suffered from an inability to deliver on the promises of his campaign (Bagley 1984:147). He was elected in the middle of one of the most severe recessions in Latin American history. At a time of declining government resources, Betancur lacked the room to maneuver around the traditional party politicians, who depended on government revenues for patronage resources. He was thus unable to build a consensus for redistributive measures to benefit the popular sectors. At the same time, his effort to achieve social peace through a negotiated truce with the country's guerrilla movements also failed, due to military and civilian opposition to such agreements. The result was the continued deterioration of support for Betancur and an electoral victory of unprecedented magnitude for the technocratic Liberal Party presidential candidate, Virgilio Barco, in 1986.

In light of the above discussion, three points may be made about the relationship between the traditional parties and the electorate, with special reference to the popular sector. First, the noncompetitive National Front period was marked by growing electoral abstention of popular sector groups and their activation by an anti-Front candidate, Rojas Pinilla. Second, during the post-Front period both Liberal and Conservative candidates mobilized popular support by direct appeals and reformist platforms, but they proved incapable of delivering on their promises. As a result, abstention rates again rose and the vote of the part of the urban popular sector that did participate electorally was volatile. Finally, despite these trends, no credible alternative to the traditional parties emerged either from within the Liberal and Conservative parties or from the left.

Union-Party Links. Though the CTC and the UTC—with their historic connections with the Liberals and the Conservatives, respectively—both supported the original National Front plebiscite, relations between the labor confederations and the National Front government were increasingly strained during the early 1960s as the confederations regrouped and initiated numerous strikes. Given the nature of the Front coalition, neither party could use state resources, except for small financial subsidies, to provide partisan support for either labor confederation at the expense of the other (Bailey 1977:284). Further, given the larger goal of depoliticizing the Colombian population, it is not evident that either party wished to return to the period of closer party-union relations. Finally, after Uruguay, Colombia emerged from the incorporation period with the most pluralistic labor movement among the eight cases. The inability of the established labor centrals to draw on significant state support led to the growth of independent and leftist unions that took a more confrontational approach to the Front governments. In a sense, the period between 1958 and 1984 saw a reversal in the tendency of the labor movement to concentrate within one (and later two) confederations, a tendency that had characterized the incorporation and aftermath periods. The ability of unions to move in and out of the various labor confederations also indicated a considerable degree of union autonomy, an autonomy that came increasingly to characterize the relationship between the state and the majority of Colombia's labor unions.

As noted in the last chapter, in 1960 the Liberal Party, with Front support, had pressured the CTC leadership to purge unions with Communist Party affiliations at the CTC congress of that year. The fact that this congress was financed in large part by private enterprises, the Front government, and the U.S. embassy left the CTC open to charges of having sold out and greatly weakened the labor federation (Caicedo 1971:132). Despite this progovernment and promanagement reputation, CTC unions joined with their UTC counterparts in initiating a major strike wave between 1958 and 1963. Several of the country's largest industrial enterprises were organized or struck during this period and both confederations recovered from the reverses they suffered during the Gómez and Rojas administrations. In 1964 they were joined in the labor arena by a new confederation, the Union Confederation of Colombian Workers (CSTC), which brought together the unions expelled from the CTC as well as other unions organized by the Communist Party after the initiation of the Front. As a result, although the trade union movement was growing, it was also seriously divided as it moved into a period of considerable antagonism and conflict between the Front and the labor movement.

The first major break between the government and the labor movement occurred in early 1965. The trade union movement had expressed strong opposition to the new sales tax and the government's handling of the price support system. At the same time, the national confederations were pushing for reforms in the labor laws, especially with respect to public sector and agrarian workers. On January 14 the CTC and the UTC announced that unless the government addressed their demands, they would initiate a national strike. The way the crisis was resolved was a good indicator of the relationship between the trade union movement and the traditional parties at this point: the dispute was mediated through a carefully organized effort of producers' associations (Hartlyn 1981a:217). Thus, capital helped mediate between labor and the political system, in contrast to the perhaps more familiar pattern in which the political system mediates between labor and capital. In the end, private-sector intervention was successful in dealing with the conflict, and the Front government made a number of concessions to trade union demands. However, the government was unable to secure congressional approval for many of the reforms and was forced to resort to its state of siege powers and introduce some of the reforms through executive decree (F. González 1975:97).

What is interesting about this labor-state conflict, other than the role of producers' organizations, is that it was a high-water mark for union activism for several years and led the Front governments, especially that of Carlos Lleras Restrepo, to introduce a series of labor decrees that greatly limited the ability of the labor movement to strike. In 1966 an executive decree provided for compulsory arbitration after forty days of strike activity, while a 1968 law gave the minister of labor the right to propose binding arbitration at any time, even prior to a union's strike vote, if the strike was perceived as "gravely affecting the interests of the national economy." During the same period the government greatly expanded the definition of what constituted the public sector, thus increasing the number of workers and trade unions for whom any strike would be automatically declared illegal (Epstein 1981:11–12). Finally, the right of management to countersue to prevent a union from calling off a strike before the 40-day limit to avoid binding arbitration was introduced in 1967 and affirmed in 1970. The result, according to Epstein (1981:14), was that "while the legal right to strike has continued to the present, at least in Manufacturing, the 1966 and 1968 innovations clearly undermined it, resulting in a fall from a high of one hundred and eleven strikes in 1966 to a low of forty four in 1968."

One result of the increasingly tight state control over the union movement, and of the perceived willingness of the UTC and CTC to adhere to the new labor laws, was the rapid expansion of the CSTC, the founding of the Christian Democratic General Labor Confederation (CGT) in 1971, and the emergence of other more radical independent unions. The percentage of labor unions not represented by the traditional CTC and UTC confederations was growing and by 1974 had reached between 30 and 40 percent of the union movement, with even higher percentages in the more industrialized and populous departments. Though the UTC was still the largest (40 percent), the CTC (25 percent) was being rapidly overtaken by the CSTC (20 to 25 percent). González notes that between 1966 and 1975 a large part of the growth of the union movement occurred outside the CTC and UTC. This judgment is supported by Epstein (1981:15) who argues that one result of "both the new legal changes and the deterioration of real wages" was the relatively rapid growth of the more radical confederations and independent unions during the 1967–74 period, especially of the CSTC in comparison to the more traditional CTC and UTC. As Hartlyn noted, "by the end of the National Front period, organized labor was gradually becoming a somewhat more autonomous force, in spite of its limited size. The links between the traditional parties and the UTC and CTC had weakened, although along with the CGT they remained pro-regime. Yet, the growing strength of the CSTC and of independent labor federations marked the emergence of a more important nonelectoral opposition to the regime."[63]

This trend away from the traditional organized labor confederations continued into the mid-1980s. In 1984 the Labor Ministry carried out the first labor union census in nearly 40 years. The most surprising finding was that the four organized confederations—the CTC, UTC, CSTC, and CGT—represented a minority of the trade union movement. The more class-based, radical, and independent unions, primarily located in the growing public sector, represented about 51 percent of the movement. Meanwhile, the UTC and the CTC were still the largest confederations, with the CSTC a close third (*El Tiempo*:31 March 1986).

Although the growing weakness of party-union ties, as well as the increased use of state control over the labor movement, contributed to the growth of independent and more class-based trade unions and the decline of the older party-linked confederations, the long-term result was the ongoing weakness and division of the trade union movement. Attempts to unify labor consistently failed as the more radical sectors refused to take part in state-labor agreements. In 1968 the UTC, CTC, CSTC, CGT, and a few independent unions, mostly in the transportation sector, created the National Committee for United Action. Shortly afterwards, the CTC withdrew. Nevertheless, the government's decision to raise public transportation prices brought all four of the confederations together in a national strike. The strike was successful in forcing the government to back down and negotiate, yet the noncommunist left strongly criticized the CSTC's participation in the agreements and, according to Caicedo (1971:178–79), the fragile unity between the labor confederations was broken. Subsequent attempts to create a unified labor central failed due to divisions between and within the various confederations and "the combination of state concessions and repression proved to be an effective strategy for maintenance of government control over labor" (Bagley 1989:51). Nevertheless, the period between 1971 and 1986 saw continuing efforts toward labor unification and occasional agreements, such as the national strikes carried out between 1965 and 1985, which often brought together the major labor confederations with urban pro-

[63] Hartlyn 1988:187. See also Tenjo (1975:23, 25); G. González, 1975:87–88; Epstein 1981:15.

test groups to challenge government economic and social policies (Londoño 1986:123–36).

The Front period saw the promulgation of various laws that sought to establish nondiscretionary procedures for labor management relations, thereby giving the state and parties an indirect role in labor mediation. These laws established compulsory arbitration to limit the potential economic cost of strike activity, and reduced the areas in which legal strikes could occur by expanding the definition of the public sector to include such areas as finance, transportation and communication, and public utilities (Epstein 1981:11). At the same time, both Front and post-Front governments provided some access for the UTC and CTC to government policy-making, primarily on the boards of such decentralized state organizations as the Land Reform Institute (IN-CORA) and the Social Security Institute (ICSS), but the result was a growing perception among workers and analysts that these confederations had lost some of their independence and, consequently, their capacity to push their workers' demands (Bailey 1977:288; Bagley 1984:132).

The existence of large numbers of parallel labor organizations, while maintaining union autonomy and independence to a degree uncommon in most Latin American countries, weakened the labor movement. The governments dominated by the traditional parties saw little reason to organize and unify and thus strengthen the union movement. As Berry and Solaún (1980:451) comment, "Labor was too weak economically to sustain long strikes prior to new contracts, and the unions were threatened by high levels of unemployment." As a result, the major labor confederations were willing to accede to the new system of compulsory arbitration. At the same time, this fact, "coupled with the recurrent legitimacy problems facing governments and the regime itself, continued to favor a certain amount of courting of labor by government in the form of intervention in the labor market, not to expand labor organization (as earlier) but to 'adapt-neutralize' a force that was needed for system-maintenance" (Berry and Solaún 1980:451). The continued growth of the independent trade union movement, especially within the public sector, indicated that this policy was only partially successful.

Assessment. In contrast to Venezuela and Mexico, the Colombian party system established partially institutionalized multiclass agreement on the basic structures and agenda of national politics. The inability of the traditional parties to maintain their ties to the labor movement—or more precisely, given the nature of the Front accords, the parties' decision to deemphasize these ties—meant that the union movement was only partially integrated into the established party system. Much as occurred in Uruguay in the late 1960s and early 1970s, the result was the continued expansion of a radicalized, antiregime, and independent trade union sector at the expense of those confederations, like the UTC and CTC, that accepted the limitations imposed by the state on the use of strikes. However, given the greater underlying weakness of the Colombian labor movement, this radicalization had a far more limited impact than it did in Uruguay.

At the same time, the traditional parties were incapable of building strong, enduring ties, electoral or otherwise, with important parts of the urban popular sector, resulting in an increasingly apathetic and fluid electorate. The traditional parties, both during and after the Front, were demonstrably unsuccessful in creating new mechanisms of representation to link the parties to the urban marginal classes and the peasantry at a time when the old partisan identifications began to erode. Like the traditional parties in Uruguay, the Colombian parties continued to depend on clientelistic, patronage politics in a context of falling government revenues and an increasing public debt. Yet no credible alternative to the parties emerged. The left remained weak, and autonomous popular organizations organized from below failed to present a significant and lasting challenge to the front and post-Front governments.[64] As a result, the parties were able to act as if an institutionalized multiclass agreement on the role of the state existed, while at the same time ignoring the reality that their support base was increasingly tenuous and open to future challenge should a credible alternative emerge.

Opposition and Crises of the late 1950s to 1980s

During the three decades that followed the formation of the National Front in 1958, the Colombian elite faced a number of significant challenges. High levels of violence continued in the country's rural areas as a legacy of tensions created by the earlier Violencia. The success of the Cuban Revolution in 1959 provided a model to opponents of the regime, and periodic waves of popular discontent led to continuous eruptions of significant guerrilla movements over this entire period. The rapid expansion of capitalist agriculture, as well as the lack of popular participation in political decision-making, led to a number of important nonviolent opposition movements within the rural and urban sectors. At the same time, the Colombian elite faced a number of important decisions about the future direction of the economy. Early reform efforts pursued by the Front governments, especially those of the Alliance for Progress, were often limited in their effect. Decisions about the economic model the country should pursue, the role of the state in economic planning, and who should benefit from economic development all added to the political ferment of these years.

Yet during this period, what emerges most clearly is the relative paucity of popular or left challenges to the political control exercised by the two traditional parties. Rather, as Berry and Solaún (1980:452) note: "The more cred-

---

[64] Berry and Solaún 1980:443. See Bagley (1989:37–48) for an account of the decline of one of the most significant autonomous peasant organizations, ANUC-Sincelejo. He also discusses the continued fragmentation of the Colombian left and the consequences of this fragmentation. Bagley (1989:48) argues that the disintegration of such independent rural organizations at a time of "continued deterioration among some sectors of the traditional subsistence peasantry and colonists and rising lawlessness and rural violence provided fertile recruiting grounds for revolutionary guerrilla organizations operating in the Colombian countryside."

ible challenges to the National Front were not posed by working class or
peasant unrest, the student movement, or the small middle-class, student-
led bands of social revolutionaries. They came, rather, from within the regime itself, from the military and anti-Front electoral coalitions of varying
scope." This pattern of weak popular opposition continued into the 1980s.
What we will do now is try to explain precisely how the traditional parties
met this opposition by looking at electoral, labor, peasant, guerrilla, and military challenges to the traditional parties. We will illustrate the methods and
techniques by which the traditional parties maintained their position of electoral dominance during a period of decaying partisan attachments, perceived
normlessness, regime illegitimacy, and increasingly violent military and
guerrilla confrontations.

Party System.   Unlike Uruguay, where the left was able to establish an important electoral presence through the Frente Amplio, the left in Colombia
was incapable of posing any significant electoral challenge to the rule of the
two traditional parties, although some short-lived challenges did occur.

   Thus, the Front created the conditions that allowed the MRL and ANAPO
to grow and even flourish. These two movements were able to make use of
partisan (Liberal or Conservative) lists and run themselves as dissident factions within the traditional parties. The MRL presented a brief but significant challenge to the Front government. López Michelsen's decision to ally
with the Communists and his occasional use of revolutionary rhetoric troubled the political elite. Yet the MRL and López quickly moderated their tone
and broke with the Communists after their first important electoral success.
Disaffected leftists, who had originally seen López's MRL as a means to oppose the Front, broke with him after his decision in 1965 to rejoin the main
Liberal Party. Some entered the various guerrilla movements that had developed following the impetus of the Cuban Revolution, while others joined the
next significant opposition movement, ANAPO. ANAPO's ambiguous ideological program, a mixture of right-wing authoritarianism and left-populist
rhetoric, provided these leftists with a platform from which to attack the
regime. However, ANAPO's attempt, like the MRL's, to establish itself during the post-Front period as a third party, independent of the traditional parties, was a failure.

   Why, given the evident dissatisfaction with the Front and post-Front governments, have these third-party movements been unsuccessful? Part of the
answer lies in the control over the central state by the two traditional parties,
as well as the Front agreement that limited representation to members of the
Liberal and Conservative parties and the subsequent agreement (1968 constitutional reform) of the majority party to allocate positions "equitably" to
the second largest party. As a consequence, third-party movements were fro-
zen out of the decision-making process and have been unable to build local
bases of power capable of challenging the hold on national politics of the two
traditional parties. As Bagley (1984:131) noted, the effect of this arrangement
was the exclusion of "all but traditional party elites from serving in electoral
or bureaucratic posts. In effect, this restriction guaranteed that the Liberal

and Conservative parties would be in a position to block or filter out demands that did not correspond to the dominant interests within the system." One consequence of this exclusionary arrangement was the decision of many left-wing groups to opt for challenging the central state through violence. Parties of the left were unable to achieve even 5 percent of the national vote, and their few local successes have not been a sufficient incentive for them to participate within the electoral arena.

The explanation for the failure of third party movements, therefore, lies in part in the way the National Front functioned in the context of the highly centralized arrangement of Colombia's political institutions. The constitution of 1886 established a unitary form of government that maintained some of the trappings of the previous federalist regimes. However, while governors and mayors, departmental assemblies, and town councils continued to exist, they acted as representatives not of the municipalities and departments, but of the central government. The president appointed the departmental governors, while the governors appointed the municipal mayors. At the same time, departmental assemblies and town councils were not legislative bodies, as they often appeared to be, but rather administrative agencies beholden to the central government's directives and appointees. While city councils drafted their municipal budgets, these budgets had to be approved by departmental and national agencies. Town mayors could give guidance and suggestions to the city council, but they functioned primarily as administrators of departmental and national directives. At the departmental level, while assemblies also drafted budgets and allocated funds, their decisions were subject to review by higher officials. This arrangement of decision-making power made it difficult for new political movements to break into the system. Once the two dominant parties agreed to cooperate and once they ensured their control over the executive, the institutional arrangement ensured that they would have the capacity to control access to power.

The Betancur administration (1982–86) for the first time directly tackled this problem of the excessive foreclosing of political opportunities for new actors. The truce worked out by Betancur between the guerrillas and the government was only the first step in a larger attempt to open the political system to greater participation by nontraditional political groups and provide them with the incentives to lay down their arms and appeal for votes. While several groups, including the National Liberation Army (ELN) and the M-19 (a spin-off from ANAPO), dropped out of the truce talks, the largest guerrilla movement, the Communist-backed Revolutionary Armed Forces of Colombia (FARC), continued its rapprochement with the government and participated, with typically limited impact, in the 1986 congressional and presidential elections. At the heart of the reform process was the attempt to redefine the role of opposition groups and to expand political participation in general.[65] Apart from initiating the direct election of mayors, the Betancur administration was unsuccessful in carrying out this reform agenda. If subse-

[65] Kline 1985:66–67; Bagley 1989:58–60; Santamaria and Silva 1984:78–79.

quent governments were to pursue this agenda further, it is clear that the result would be the initiation of new, more potent challenges to their dominance and the possibility that the increase in regime legitimacy created by these reforms might be accompanied by a decrease in their control over the national political system.

Labor Movement. Much as the left had little success in the electoral arena, the trade union movement had only limited success in challenging the economic policies of the Front and post-Front governments. Organized labor's relative weakness, due both to its small size (about 10 percent of the economically active population)[66] and its division into four labor centrals and a myriad of independent unions, greatly limited its effectiveness. Indeed, given these factors, along with the unions' weak to nonexistent ties with the traditional parties, their dependence on the state for financial support, the legal restrictions that permitted only enterprise unions, and limitations on the right to strike, the Colombian labor movement was the weakest among the eight countries. Nevertheless, the trade union movement mounted a series of challenges in the 1960s and 1970s. Though most were failures, or led to only limited government compromises, the 1977 general strike was in the short-run a great success for its organizers, although it subsequently led to a major government crackdown on union officials during the Turbay administration (1978–82).

According to a number of scholars, the 1977 general strike "is of singular importance in the trajectory of the Colombian labor movement due to the realization of the most widespread urban protest carried out autonomously by the labor movement up to that point."[67] For the first time all the major labor confederations (the UTC, CTC, CSTC, and CGT) united to express their opposition to the continued unwillingness of the government to consider the demands of salaried workers and other popular groups. Fueled by growing dissatisfaction with the López Michelsen administration and the perception that López had not fulfilled his campaign pledge to the urban popular sector, the major labor confederations together with other popular sector organizations agreed to carry out a national strike. The united labor front was successful in generating popular support for the strike, but this support was not forthcoming from the traditional parties or the López government. High ranking party and government officials held a series of meetings with the UTC and CTC, pressuring them to break with the other confederations, but they refused. At the same time, the López government charged that the national strike was both illegal and "subversive." Despite the government's "aggressive and menacing tone" (Londoño 1986:125–26), the unions carried out the strike on September 14.

What happened that day is still controversial (M. Medina 1984:123–86). What is clear, however, is that the government's decision to confront striking workers with police and army units led to the death or injury of over 30

---

[66] *El Colombiano*: March 27, 1986.
[67] Londoño 1986:123; see also Medina (1984:chap. 8).

people. The results of the strike were ambiguous. On the one hand, the strike nearly paralyzed the country's economy. The government did agree to negotiate with the UTC and CTC, but the negotiations broke down, leading the government to unilaterally decree an increase in the minimum wage. Nevertheless, in terms of the major demands made by the unions and other popular groups "the strike had practically no effect" (Londoño 1986:127). However, it was followed by a growing combativeness on the part of labor, and the years 1977 to 1980 saw an unprecedented level of worker protest (Hartlyn 1988:188, Table 6–9).

The long-term consequences were even more dismal for the labor movement. Turbay's decision to implement the Security Statute led to a massive crackdown on union officials and organizers, including several cases of imprisonment, torture, and assassination. Subsequently, both the CTC and the UTC broke with the more radical unions and refused to join the 1981 and 1985 general strikes, which failed as a consequence. It was evident that when the major confederations were able and willing to act in concert, they could bring considerable pressure to bear on the government. Nevertheless, the governmment demonstrated that even under these conditions it could react harshly to the attempts of labor to use the general strike as a means of presenting its demands. When the CSTC chose to go ahead and initiate a general strike in 1985, the government responded by stripping it of its legal standing (*personería judírica*) for several months, while also freezing its bank accounts. Yet an underlying reason why the general strikes were unsuccessful was that the relatively small size of the labor movement, along with its highly pluralistic composition, left labor in a weak position to challenge the government.

The Front and post-Front governments thus used a number of different mechanisms to control or mediate the relationship between labor and the state. On the one hand, they provided concessions to labor confederations like the UTC and CTC, which took a generally cooperative stance vis-à-vis the government. On the other hand, they erected a set of labor laws that greatly restricted the freedom of action of labor unions through an emphasis on collective bargaining and by defining economically crucial industries as being in the public sector, thereby making strikes illegal. When these methods were unsuccessful, as in 1977, the government showed no hesitation to respond to illegal strikes with force. In the general strike of June 1985, even the reformist Betancur placed the military on high alert and filled the streets of major cities with tanks and troop carriers. This combination of co-optation, bureaucratic controls, and repression was successful through the mid-1980s in greatly reducing the ability of labor to successfully press its demands on the government, even though there was a significant increase in strikes during this period.

Economic Policy. Given the general weakness of popular sector and anti-government forces, Colombia's leaders did not face the kind of organized opposition other Latin American countries had to deal with in making economic policy. In this context, economic policy during this period tended to be relatively "middle of the road," to exhibit substantial continuity, and to have an increasingly technical character (Berry 1980:312). The 1968 constitutional reform, which gave the executive more control over the budget and greater authority over the planning agencies of the state, assured increased autonomy in policy-making.

Within this framework of substantial continuity, the Lleras Restrepo administration (1966–70) oversaw a significant shift in the Colombian economic model. Through 1967 the economic model had emphasized import-substitution and protection for Colombian industries. Lleras Restrepo's effort to redirect the model toward export-led growth was greatly aided by the increased state planning and coordination capacity noted above, which allowed him to take a series of initiatives, including the provision of effective subsidies for nontraditional exports, initiation of a floating exchange rate that stabilized expectations about export and import prices, and the successful carrying out of the transition without causing the major economic dislocations familiar from some other countries.[68] The new controls over the labor movement noted above also facilitated this transition.

A second reform under the Lleras Restrepo administration was the effort to impose order on the decentralized system of state institutions responsible for policy-making in different economic sectors. For years presidents had attempted to exercise some measure of control over these institutions, but the attempts tended to be blocked because these institutions were a source of party patronage and also because they tended to be captured by the peak business association of the relevant economic sector. By withdrawing financial support from recalcitrant agencies and centralizing economic policy-making authority, Lleras was able to streamline the state's planning functions and develop a more coherent long-term economic plan.[69]

From a comparative perspective, in carrying out major economic reforms such as these, Colombia succeeded in implementing under a civilian regime policy innovations that in other contexts appeared difficult to introduce under civilian auspices and were only implemented under military rule (Hirschman 1979:78–79; see also Skidmore 1977). Within the framework of its technocratic orientation, the Colombian state thus managed to tackle some of the difficult economic policy issues of this period.

Later governments built on the successes of the Lleras Restrepo administration, yet each of the subsequent administrations tended to pursue slightly different short-term economic goals. There was a growing tendency for each administration to select a "leading sector" and to focus the attention of state fiscal and monetary policy on improving its performance. The Pastrana administration (1970–74) moved to improve the construction sector, ending what had been Lleras Restrepo's emphasis on the rural sector. López Michelsen (1974–78) focused on basic infrastructure projects, and Betancur

---

[68] Thoumi 1980:337; Berry 1980:301 and fn. 53; see also Revéiz and Pérez (1986:273).
[69] J. Bailey 1977:286; Hartlyn 1988:126–31; Revéiz and Pérez 1986:272–73.

(1982–86) emphasized social reforms and the development of the country's oil and gas resources (Hartlyn 1988:132, 138, 200, 207–8).

Although Colombian economic development policy was relatively successful throughout this period, it was nonetheless characterized by a "series of gaps in the decision-making process" (Revéiz and Pérez 1986:265, 274). From 1970 to 1986 the unequal influence of economic elites over economic policy, the growing strength of regional politicians with their emphasis on regional over national developmental goals, and the growing privatization and technocratization of important economic decisions, have all reduced the role of popular sector organizations in determining economic policy. As a consequence, there has been a growing perception of "a certain vacuum regarding state legitimacy in its decision making" (Revéiz and Pérez 1986:276).

Though Colombia was one of the most successful of the eight cases in its economic policy of the period covered in this chapter, this success was not effectively extended to the poorer two-thirds of the population. The system of economic policy-making was primarily characterized by close negotiations between the state and economic elites, with little input from the popular sector and an increasing depoliticization of economic decision making (Cepeda and Mitchell 1980). Attempts, such as those of Lleras Restrepo and Betancur, to put a priority on redistributive measures failed due to the opposition of economic elites or to international recessions. More typically, policies responded to the needs of these elites—whether in industry, construction, or finance—or focused on large-scale efforts to upgrade public infrastructure and the exploitation of natural resources. The consequence was growing maldistribution of income (Berry and Urrutia 1976) and popular sector dissatisfaction with the traditional parties' handling of economic policy, leading to a significant increase in worker protest in both urban and rural areas (Bagley 1984:142).

Peasant Mobilization. During the Front the traditional parties generally shied away from creating new popular sector organizations. Two exceptions to this pattern were the formation of the ANUC (Asociación Nacional de Usuarios Campesinos) and the JAC (Communal Action Groups). The first, ANUC, was created by Lleras Restrepo in an attempt to build support for the agrarian reform program he had helped initiate during the administration of Lleras Camargo. The latter, JAC, is discussed below as part of the Front's strategy of coping with rural left-wing guerrilla movements. The evolution of these organizations, their growing autonomy from state control, and the eventual government reaction to this new independence provide a clear illustration of the difficulties faced by the traditional parties when they attempted to build their support base and deal with popular sector opposition.

The agrarian reform of 1961 was largely initiated from within the state, with little role of societal actors in demanding it (Berry and Solaún 1980:443). Given the lack of a support base, the reform was easily sabotaged by landowners, and the agencies intended to implement it were generally left unsupported during the subsequent Leon Valencia administration (1962–66). With the administration of Carlos Lleras Restrepo (1966–70), the architect of the reform, the agrarian reform agencies entered into their most active period, but were seriously hampered by lack of political support. Hoping to push the reform of the agricultural sector further, Lleras began to develop the peasant organization discussed above—ANUC—which would improve the delivery of services, provide a base of political support for the reform program, and serve as a personal base of support for Lleras. Legislation providing the legal basis for ANUC was passed in 1967, 1968, and 1969, and by June 1971, the new peasant organization had recruited approximately 1 million members in 496 government-recognized municipal groups (Berry 1980:299, 309; Bagley and Edel 1980:270–73).

With the Conservative administration of Misael Pastrana (1970–74) in power, however, relations between the government and ANUC organizers soured, and the ANUC organization became increasingly radicalized. Bagley and Edel point to four reasons for this radicalization. First, the political disruption of the transition from the Lleras to the Pastrana administrations weakened government control over the peasant organization. Second, Pastrana recognized the future threat to the Conservative Party of a large national organization tied to a Liberal party leader, especially with competitive elections scheduled for 1974. Pastrana therefore made a concerted effort to establish Conservative control over the organization, a move that alienated the national leadership of the ANUC. Third, Pastrana had made his opposition to the reform program clear during the 1970 presidential campaign and was opposed to its continuation. The shift in government priorities naturally weakened ANUC's relationship with various government agencies and further soured relations between the Pastrana government and ANUC. Finally, during the early 1970s the economic condition of the country's peasantry was steadily worsening, increasing the pressure on ANUC leadership to take a less conciliatory stance toward the Pastrana government's slowdown of the agrarian reform. In June 1971 the leaders announced its independence from the government and issued a strongly worded program demanding an expansion of land redistribution efforts and supporting peasant land invasions in the absence of government support (Bagley and Edel 1980:274–76; Bagley 1989).

The government's response to its loss of control over the peasant organization proceeded along a variety of tracks. The first move was the creation of an official, parallel ANUC organization that became known as ANUC-Armenia after the northern city in which this new government-sponsored entity held its first congress. Over the next year, government-ANUC confrontations continued, with an increase in the number of civil strikes and land invasions led by the rebel group. At the same time, the government initiated a strategy of bureaucratic noncooperation, legal harassment, and frequent jailings of rebel ANUC leaders, while some local landowners were apparently responsible for the assassinations of ANUC activists. In July 1972 the rebel group held its own congress in the city of Sincelejo (thus it is usually referred to as the Linea Sincelejo) and again rejected the government's agricultural policies and restated its opposition to the ANUC-Armenia group. The Sincelejo group was apparently successful in gaining control of ANUC-Armenia, but the membership fell drastically as the government cut funding to rebel municipal groups. Throughout 1972 the ANUC led a series of marches on departmental capitals but backed down from its plan to march on Bogotá when the Pastrana government threatened the organization with mass arrests. As Bagley and Edel (1980:280) note, "it is undeniable that ANUC had emerged as the most powerful and radical peasant organization in Colombia during the period of the *Frente Nacional.*" Nevertheless, lacking government support and access to state bureaucracies, the movement quickly faded as a significant source of opposition to the government. While it continued to lead marches—sometimes, as in the 1985 march on Cartagena, with the help of the Marxist FARC—its impact and size never again reached the levels achieved in the early 1970s (Bagley and Edel 1980:278–79; Bagley 1989:26–27).

Overall, the government's response to rural opposition was characterized by three basic strategies. First, the Front governments used its control over the state's administrative apparatus to punish or reward rural sector organizations, depending on their opposition to, or support for, government policies. Second, when the government could not bring recalcitrant groups to cooperate, it then developed parallel organizations that undercut the support bases of the opposition movements. It either set up competing organizations like the Linea Armenia group or developed new regional or local organizations that bypassed the existing groups. Finally, if these more peaceable methods failed, the government turned to threats or repression. The consequence was the continued failure of rural opposition movements and a growing perception, especially among the landless peasants, that the only alternative was to join guerrilla groups.

Guerrilla Movements. Guerrilla activity was a persistent feature of the heritage period in Colombia. In the early 1960s, as La Violencia wound down, a few of the guerrilla organizations previously identified with the two traditional parties refused to accept the government's amnesty. Some of these groups formed the Southern Guerrilla Bloc in 1964 under the leadership of the Communist Party, and this bloc became the FARC in mid-1966. The FARC thus grew out of the earlier partisan violence in the rural sector. Although FARC made use of revolutionary rhetoric and the model of the Cuban Revolution, in the early 1960s it seemed to concentrate more on the defense of the "independent republics" it had carved out in inaccessible areas in Colombia's mountainous terrain. With the fall of these "republics" to the military in 1964 and 1965, the Marxist guerrilla groups began to reorient their strategy toward more revolutionary goals, including the end of the National Front regime (Maullin 1973:14; Ruhl 1980:195).

This shift in FARC goals was preceded by the formation of the ELN (National Liberation Army), a revolutionary organization formed primarily by university students emulating the Cuban Revolution. However, the ELN found it difficult to generate support in peasant areas and was never successful either in establishing physical control of anything beyond extremely limited territory, or in achieving any kind of broader public support. In the first part of the 1970s, the military substantially defeated the ELN, leaving the group "more of a nuisance than a serious concern" (Ruhl 1980:196; see also Maullin 1973:21, 52).

With the election of 1970 and the narrow loss of Rojas Pinilla, a new guerrilla organization was formed by elements from the left wing of ANAPO convinced that the election had been rigged and that the traditional parties would never give up their control of the political system. This organization, the M-19 (April 19 Movement), was named after the date of the election and initiated a number of picturesque slaps at the Pastrana government, including the 1973 theft of Simón Bolívar's sword, a symbol of the nation's founding. At first viewed as a nuisance, M-19's decision to steal several thousand rifles from a military arsenal in January 1979 resulted in a massive military dragnet and the arrest of many of the group's leaders, as well as the recovery of most of the weapons. The M-19 followed up on this disaster with the seizure of the embassy of the Dominican Republic during a diplomatic social gathering in February 1980, taking several ambassadors hostage. The government responded by giving key M-19 guerrillas passage to Cuba. In the mid-1980s the group continued to operate and was involved in several violent seizures of small country towns. In 1985 it dropped out of the truce talks with the Betancur government and later stormed the Supreme Court building, taking dozens of hostages, including a number of the Supreme Court justices. The military refused to negotiate with the guerrillas and stormed the building, leaving most of the guerrillas and many of the Supreme Court justices dead (Bagley 1989:51–52, 62–64).

What this account demonstrates is that although the military was able to defeat the guerrillas militarily and though the guerrillas did not become a direct threat to the government, they were indeed difficult to eliminate. Though such organizations as the FARC showed a willingness to negotiate their reentry into Colombian politics, other guerrilla groups stepped up their attacks on the armed forces and police. In the process, the guerrillas created an indirect threat to the civilian government in that their continuing presence led to a greatly expanded role of the military.

Along with the military response to the guerrillas, the principal civilian political response in the early 1960s was the community action organizations, the JACs, discussed above. They were formed in 1958–59 as part of the government's program to end the partisan conflict and were thus initially geared toward pacification of areas overrun by La Violencia. These organizations were built around local representatives and provided financial support and technical assistance for community projects such as paving streets, sewer systems, and new schools. Through the mid-1960s the JACs were successful, not only helping end the violence but also in promoting economic development (Bagley and Edel 1980:262; Bagley 1989:9–18).

Though in many ways effective, these organizations, like the ANUC, began to escape from central government control and various local JACs began to form regional organizations to increase their ability to pressure the government. Lleras Restrepo responded by reorganizing the JACs and placing them under the jurisdiction of the National Council of Popular Integration, which would be responsible for overseeing all community development programs. Under the Pastrana administration (1970–74), government funding was carefully monitored, with moneys going only to those JACs that cooperated with the government or with local or regional politicians who put the organizations to partisan use during the 1974 elections. By 1975 the organizations' autonomy from central control was nearly gone (Bagley 1989:16–18; Bagley and Edel 1980:266–70). However, this loss of autonomy did not prevent them from being successful in limiting the impact of the left insurgent movements, even though they could not end the conditions that gave rise to the guerrillas in the first place.

The efforts by the civilian administrations during the Front and post-Front period to establish state-sponsored organizations that would guide and control the activities of peasants was motivated to a considerable extent by the threat posed by the left guerrilla movements. Yet these governments faced a constant dilemma. If peasants were to develop any strong interest and affinity toward these organizations, the organizations had to some degree to represent their interests. But political leaders were more concerned with supporting organizations that could be used to promote goals of the government or their own personal political goals. When the government's and the peasants' interests diverged, the government tended to rein in the newly created groups. However, by constraining these organizations, the government created new groups of angry, cynical peasants who were, as a consequence, more likely to support the very guerrilla groups that these organizations were originally intended to combat. After the difficulties of the 1960s and early 1970s with ANUC, the civilian governments turned increasingly to the military to find a solution to the problem of guerrilla opposition movements.

Military Role. The military played an important part in the Front's plan to pacify the countryside after the 1958 plebiscite. From 1958 to 1986 this role continued to grow, reaching its peak during the presidency of Turbay (1978–82). In the mid-1960s General Ruiz Novoa, the minister of defense, "argued that the army must not only destroy guerrillas, once they were raised in arms, but must also attack the social and economic causes as well as the historic political reasons for their existence" (Maullin 1973:68). Ruiz's argument for a "developmental role for the military" (Leal Buitrago 1984:210–11) was taken up under the rubric of Civic Action. Not only would the military fight guerrillas, but it would also build roads into previously inaccessible areas, thus creating government support, as well as providing government expertise for other regional and municipal developmental projects. Though Ruiz's ideas were generally accepted, his outspoken criticism of National Front policies, as well as his heavily reformist rhetoric, drew both military and civilian opposition. Ruiz was removed from his post in 1965 by President Guillermo Leon Valencia, a move that brought a surge of rumors of a coup. Leon Valencia was supported in this initiative by a growing group within the military concerned by the shift in guerrilla activity from local shakedowns to revolutionary activities. At the same time, they were concerned by Ruiz's stance, which placed the military in a politically sensitive role and which was creating substantial negative reactions among some factions in the Congress (Maullin 1973:71).

Though Ruiz's plan for a two-part military mission was never completely abandoned, after the mid-1960s a growing number of officers began to take a hard-nosed "law and order" approach that viewed the military's task in far narrower terms (Maullin 1973:73). This approach became doctrine over the next ten years, a process accompanied by the growth of strong ties among Colombian, Brazilian, and Argentine military officers and by the Colombian military's admiration for the national security doctrines followed by the authoritarian regimes in these other two countries (Leal Buitrago 1984).

The failure of the government to eradicate the guerrilla movements completely, as well as the growth of the military's technical and managerial expertise through the civic action programs, created the conditions for growing military autonomy. The military were perceived as the "political arbiters of the National Front" (Leal Buitrago 1984:231), or as "the defenders of an essentially closed political system in which power became an exclusive prerogative of traditional partisan interests."[70] The growing political role of the Colombian military, as well as the continuous rumors of coup plans that circulated when presidents exercised their constitutional prerogatives to remove military personnel from sensitive posts, led the military to seek further limits on the "interference" of the political parties in their handling of the nation's security and to promote military autonomy from civilian control (Berry and Solaún 1980:453; Leal Buitrago 1984:259). This growing military independence reached its peak during the presidency of Turbay between 1978 and 1982.

The violence of the 1977 general strike led to a hardening of the military position toward social groups that "disturbed public order" or "promoted subversion." The strike had begun on a small scale, but then turned into a virtual social explosion that the military had difficulty controlling. In Bogotá alone, the strike left 19 dead, many injured, and over 3,000 people detained. It had a major impact on the relationship between the military and the labor movement (Leal Buitrago 1984:261; M. Medina 1984:162–63). What was needed, according to the military, was an immediate declaration of a state of siege and emergency powers for the military. For the first time the military demanded unlimited freedom of action in exercising its coercive power (Leal Buitrago 1984:262). López, who had never been comfortable with the military, ignored this request, but his successor, Turbay, did not. In September 1978 Turbay issued the Security Statute, which greatly expanded the powers of the military, including the right to hold prisoners without charge or trial for a specified period of time and to charge and try them in military tribunals.

Within a few weeks, press accounts of disappearances and tortures began to appear. But it was the theft of thousands of rifles in January 1979 from a

---

[70] Maullin (1973:115).

military armory by the M-19 that led to a massive wave of indiscriminate detentions, trials, and torture. The military's response stunned large sectors of the middle and upper classes. Up to this point the M-19 had generally been perceived as just one more guerrilla group, if somewhat more quixotic. The military's apparent overreaction, however, did not lead to massive protest, but rather brought the public support of most of Colombia's major producer organizations, many of whom had been hard hit by the wave of kidnappings that occurred during the mid- to late 1970s. The military continued its attack on the left through 1981, supporting the creation of local death squads, the most infamous being MAS (Death to Kidnappers), which was formed by the Medellín drug cartel. Virtually all dissidents were repressed, from armed guerrillas to virtually any group that demanded a return to a more open political and electoral system (Leal Buitrago 1984:273–74, 267, and fn. 81).

By the end of 1981, the military announced that its campaign had been successful. One month before the inauguration of the new Conservative president, Belisario Betancur, in August 1982, Turbay ended the state of siege for the first time in six years, thereby annulling the Security Statute, which had been decreed under the state of siege (Leal Buitrago 1984:275). The Betancur presidency was marked by constant conflicts between the military and Betancur. While the military claimed that it had defeated the guerrilla insurgents, they had in fact only driven them further underground. The FARC still claimed some 6,000 members, and the military raised this estimate to 15,000 in 1985, perhaps to increase the perception of threat. The M-19 and the ELN, meanwhile, had renewed their attacks on the government.

Rather than unleash the military once again, Betancur took a radically different tack. Clearly, the repression of the Turbay administration had not solved the guerrilla problem. What was needed was a new approach that would provide the guerrilla movements the incentives to reenter the political arena and use ballots, not bullets, in their struggle with the government. Betancur initiated truce discussions with the major guerrilla groups in 1982 and declared a full amensty for those guerrillas who turned in their guns. He also launched a panoply of political, social, and economic reforms designed to convince the guerrillas that the democratic opening was a reality.

The military's reaction to Betancur's initiatives was generally negative. The amnesty had led to the release of hundreds of real or suspected subversives imprisoned by the military during the Turbay administration, making Bentancur's promises seem sincere. However, periodic assassinations of the released prisoners undermined the amnesty. The military, despite the presumed truce, either encouraged or initiated armed actions against guerrilla encampments, especially those of the M-19, further souring the mood of the guerrilla groups involved in negotiations with the Betancur government. The decision of the M-19 to break the truce and return to the mountains gave the military a free hand to continue their activities and greatly weakened the momentum built up behind the reform process. Whether the military's refusal to negotiate with the M-19 during the 1985 hostage seizure in the Palace of Justice indicated Betancur's capitulation to military demands, or simply the refusal of the military to back down, the Betancur administration ended with many of the issues still unresolved.

Parallels between the Turbay administration and the Bordaberry government in Uruguay were noted above. The capitulation of the political parties to military demands, the vast expansion in military authority and activity, the near suspension of civil rights, and the unprecedented use of torture and imprisonment of regime opponents had much in common with the Uruguayan military's repression of the Uruguayan left. What differentiates the two cases, however, was the fact that the Colombian military backed down before they had managed to eradicate the guerrilla insurgents and their sympathizers. In addition, they did not take power away from the civilian politicians. In contrast to Uruguay, despite the military's claims, the opposition in Colombia was not as threatening to the regime, nor was there apparently any group within the Colombian military that advocated the removal of the civilian politicians. Rather, what appears to have occurred was an effective division of labor between the military and the parties. The political parties tolerated a great expansion of the military's power to deal with antiregime forces, while retaining their power to run the government and the economy. Whether the Colombian military would be content with so restricted an arena in the future is open to question.

Capacity for Conflict Regulation. This review of the government's reaction to the opposition movements of the Front and post-Front period suggests that although they were clearly capable of containing conflict and regime opposition, their extensive use of the military made it equally clear that the Colombian political system was incapable of integrating these groups in a well-institutionalized way. Though the guerrilla movement was still not a threat to the traditional parties' control, it created growing anxiety as violence escalated and the role of the military increased. The cost of the parties' failure to integrate and represent peasants, organized labor, and other popular sector groups was the continued growth of attacks on the legitimacy of the regime. In this atmosphere, armed insurgents continued to wage war against the state and found it increasingly easy to find recruits. The escalation of violence and the subsequent expansion of the military's role in politics increased the number of groups within the middle and upper classes who might see a more harsh authoritarian solution as the only means to contain the violence and return order to the countryside. Betancur's democratic opening was a step in a new direction, but this step was viewed as a failure and abandoned by the next presidential administration.

On the other hand, a number of areas of stability and continuity were evident. First, the traditional parties continued to dominate the electoral arena. Second, labor and rural peasant sector organizations continued to be weak and disorganized, much as they were when the Front was initiated. Third, although the mid-1980s saw yet another increase in the level of rural violence, periodic ebbs in such violence had long been a feature of Colombian politics, so that this could be viewed as a cyclical phenomenon. Even with their increased size, the guerrilla movements did not become a major threat

to the continuation of the existing regime, and they generally limited themselves to takeovers of small, relatively undefended rural villages and towns.
Finally, the Colombian elite's capacity to "muddle through" political and
economic crises was once again demonstrated by the country's relatively
strong recovery from the Latin American recession of the early 1980s.

PERU AND ARGENTINA: POLITICAL STALEMATE

In Peru and Argentina, the period analyzed in this chapter is relatively short in comparison with the other countries. The initial conservative reaction to incorporation did not end until the second half of the 1950s, thereby initiating the heritage period. Yet Peru and Argentina saw the inauguration of military-authoritarian regimes in the second half of the 1960s, a transition that ended the experience of party politics analyzed here. The analysis thus focuses on the interval from 1956 to 1968 in Peru and from 1958 to 1966 in Argentina.

A central fact of Peruvian and Argentine politics in this period was the prohibition, imposed by the military, of full electoral participation of APRA and Peronism. This prohibition was the cornerstone of the "impossible game" in Argentina and the "difficult game" in Peru, introduced in the previous chapter. In the context of this prohibition, these two countries conspicuously failed to establish integrative party systems. Unlike Mexico and Venezuela, Peru and Argentina experienced ongoing stalemate, political crisis, and a failure to address basic policy issues of the day. On the other hand, in contrast to Brazil and Chile—which also experienced crises—the political crisis in Peru and Argentina prior to their respective coups in 1968 and 1966 did not involve the same dynamic of radicalization, polarization, and a substantial move to the left within the political system. This was due in important measure to the degree to which a major segment of the popular sector had been won away from the left during the incorporation period.

Because the evolving ban in Peru and Argentina played such an important role in this period, it receives central attention. The analysis reveals that in comparison with the ban on APRA in Peru, the dynamics of the ban on Peronism in Argentina were more complex, for two principal reasons. First, Argentina had more elections during this period than Peru, which lacked elected governors and had no municipal elections until 1963. Relatedly, in Argentina the issue of the ban came into play at all electoral levels, and hence arose in all of Argentina's numerous elections. In Peru, apart form 1956, the ban on APRA operated only at the level of presidential elections. Second, in a curious way the ban in Argentina actually helped Perón retain control over his movement, in that it aided him in preventing rivals from within the movement from challenging his power.

The impact of the ban on the two parties was also distinct. This period saw the further conservatization of a relatively cohesive APRA party, as it accommodated itself to partial access to power. By contrast, during this period Peronism, which was excluded from power, was ideologically diverse and fragmented. In part as a result of APRA's conservatism, by the end of the 1960s the party was losing its dominant position in the labor movement, whereas the Argentine labor movement, at the same time that it was ideologically heterogenous, remained largely Peronist.

Yet the larger political implications of the ban were in important respects similar in the two cases, for in both countries the ban played a central role in the political stalemate and regime crisis that led to the democratic breakdown in the second half of the 1960s. In addition, important steps in the evolution of this period of stalemate and crisis were parallel. As shown in the previous chapter, in both cases the president elected in the second half of the 1950s (Prado and Frondizi) came to power by making an electoral accord with the banned party. In Peru this accord produced a relatively stable governing coalition that lasted to the end of Prado's presidency in 1962. In Argentina, by contrast, such an ongoing accord was not permitted, and Frondizi's government was far less stable. Yet neither of these governments was successful in tackling many of the most urgent policy issues of the day, a matter of growing concern to various sectors, including the military. In Argentina this failure was in some respects directly attributable to the ban and to the political crises it produced. In Peru the failure was not as directly due to the ban, although the enforced conservatization of APRA, Prado's coalition partner, in conjunction with the ban was certainly an important part of the context in which the Prado government failed to address a broader policy agenda.

The presidencies of Prado and Frondizi were both ended by a coup in 1962, which served to block the electoral success of the banned party. Both countries saw interim governments that assumed only a caretaker, transitional role and held new elections in 1963,[71] which in both countries were won by a candidate (Belaúnde and Illia) who had a middle-class base and lacked a working-class constituency. The authority of both these weak middle-class governments was dramatically undermined by the intense opposition of the banned party and/or the labor movement.

Subsequently, confronted with the failure of these governments and the prospect of further elections in which the banned party seemed likely to make major gains, the military intervened once again, in Peru in 1968 and Argentina in 1966. This time, instead of brief transitional governments, the armed forces established long-term military rule intended to supersede the stalemated electoral system.

[71] For the purpose of our study, it is crucial that Argentina and Peru passed through these parallel steps in this analytic period, but simply a coincidence that these steps occurred in exactly the same years—i.e., 1962 and 1963.

Overview of the Party System

During the heritage period in Peru (1956–68), three major parties largely dominated the electoral arena: APRA, Acción Popular (Popular Action or AP), and Odría's UNO. APRA had middle-class leadership, a strong base in the labor movement, and important regional strength on the north coast and around modernized enclaves in the central highlands, but a relatively modest presence in most traditional areas of the highlands. During this period APRA captured about a third of the vote in the two presidential elections in which it was allowed to run and at least 40 percent of the seats in the congressional elections of the early 1960s, ranging up to 47 percent in the senatorial contest of 1962. Notwithstanding Haya's personal domination of the organization, APRA was a well-institutionalized and well-organized party.

Acción Popular which brought together the followers of Belaúnde, had strong support among newer middle-class and professional groups, virtually no role in the labor movement, major regional support in the south, and a growing role in the highlands. Acción Popular tended to capture around a third of the votes in presidential elections and a third of the seats in Congress. The support for Odría and his UNO (Odriísta National Union) was centered in Lima, particularly in the squatter settlements, and in the coastal departments to the extreme north and south, where under Odría's earlier government extensive public works spending, intended to consolidate the authority of the state near Peru's borders, had established a strong patronage base. Odría was from the central highlands and had close ties with the traditional elite of the highlands. He won about a quarter of the votes in the two presidential elections in the 1960s and 20 percent or less of the seats in Congress. In contrast to APRA, Acción Popular and UNO were both poorly institutionalized movements surrounding an individual leader.

Manuel Prado had also organized his political following into a party, the MDP (Pradista Democratic Movement). However, this party had an even more ephemeral organizational existence than Acción Popular and UNO, and it was important only during Prado's presidency as a reflection of his own political power. The small Christian Democratic Party was identified with the "new reformism" discussed in the previous chapter. On the left, the Communists never had a strong electoral position, though beginning in the late 1960s they regained the important role in the labor movement they had earlier enjoyed in the late 1920s and early 1930s. The Communists and other small left parties somewhat increased their electoral strength during the 1960s, winning 10 percent of the vote in an important by-election in Lima in 1967 (Neira 1973:415–460; Cotler 1978:374; Bourricaud 1970:290; Astiz 1969b:103–4).

The Ban on APRA. Within this party panorama, a central fact of politics was the evolving ban on APRA and the electoral alliances APRA entered into as a result of the ban. Since this ban was in part a legacy of the antagonisms of the incorporation period, the nature and consequences of the ban are of particular importance to our analysis.

Given the ban, APRA was pushed into a series of coalitions—with Prado's MDP, Odría's UNO, and Acción Popular—as a way of using its electoral strength in a context in which it could not assume the presidency. APRA's participation in these alliances pushed further the conservatization of the party already discussed in the previous chapter. In contrast to Mexico and Venezuela, where the conservatization of the party that led the incorporation project placed it in a strong coalitional position, located roughly in the center or center-reformist portion of the political spectrum, in Peru this conservatization took APRA further to the right. APRA could potentially play the role of bringing the labor movement into a broad multiclass coalition, thereby contributing to what we have called an integrative party system, and indeed it did so between 1956 and 1962 and from 1967 to 1968. However, APRA's capacity to play this role was increasingly undermined by the zigzags of the party's coalitional shifts during the 1950s and 1960s. In addition, APRA's obstruction of reform in the 1960s seriously undermined the legitimacy of the democratic regime.

Particularly because the ban played such an important role in this period, it is essential to recognize that both the nature of the ban and its consequences are complex. First of all, the ban took different forms, including preventing APRA from entering an election, canceling the results of the subsequent election in which APRA gained a plurality, and later using a coup in part to prevent an election from occurring in which an APRA coalition was virtually assured of victory. Second, the underlying goal of the ban changed, in that the traditional anti-Aprismo of the military, which opposed APRA's radicalism and violence, was partially supplanted by an anti-Aprismo that derived from a concern that an APRA government would fail to carry out needed reforms. Third, although APRA's conservative alliances in some respects undermined the party, in other respects the alliances were successful in policy terms and gave the party important new resources to maintain and strengthen at least some of its bases of support. Fourth, though the ban on APRA was an important feature of the period, it was not the only source of the problems of APRA or of Peruvian politics. For example, in contrast to PRI in Mexico or Acción Democrática in Venezuela, APRA was in a much weaker electoral position. The dynamics of APRA's alliances revolved in part around the issue of the ban, but the problem of dealing with this weaker electoral position also shaped the party's coalitional choices. On the other hand, there was a complex interaction among these factors, since this weaker electoral position was doubtless in part due to the long history of repression and prohibition of the APRA. Finally, the steps that led to the democratic breakdown of 1968 not surprisingly involved a complex interaction among the negative dynamics that resulted from the ban and a series of other problems.

This section provides a new assessment of the ban and of APRA's evolving alliances by attempting to sort out these several issues. The discussion focuses on three phases in the evolution of APRA's role: the party's alliances with the oligarchy between 1956 and 1962, the alliances with APRA's former archenemy Odría between 1962 and 1967, and the alliance with AP in 1967– 68. Figure 7.3 provides an overview of the phases covered in the analysis.

APRA's Alliances with the Oligarchy. APRA's initial alliance, beginning in 1956, was with Manuel Prado, a prominent member of the Peruvian oligarchy. This alliance with the right and its repercussions for APRA were discussed in the previous chapter, and will be reviewed only briefly here. APRA was still illegal at the time of the 1956 presidential and congressional elections and could not present a candidate for the presidency or an official party list for the Congress. After bargaining with different presidential contenders, APRA established its first alliance with Prado in 1956 in the electoral accord called the Pact of Monterrico. Aprista congressional candidates were allowed to run on independent lists in the 1956 election, and this Prado-APRA alliance won a majority in Congress and a strong plurality, though not an absolute majority, in the presidential election. APRA maintained an ongoing coalition with Prado—called the *convivencia*—until the end of his presidency.

During the 1956–62 Prado administration, APRA achieved important access to state resources, and particularly in the urban labor sector was quite successful in further consolidating its partisan position. The accord with Prado also produced a relatively stable period of government. Combining as it did a leading representative of capital (Prado) and the party that at the time was a dominant force in the labor movement (APRA), this alliance was able to play a strong role in labor-capital mediation. Indeed, Cotler (1978:339) argues that from the point of view of capital, APRA had become an indispensable intermediary in its relations with the popular sector. According to Pease (1977:29–30), APRA had replaced the military as the most important political ally of the economic elite. The elite, in turn, was apparently ready to defend its ally. For instance, under the 1962–63 military government, when reformist officers were considering an effort to weaken APRA's hold on the labor movement, Beltrán's newspaper *La Prensa* defended APRA trade unionism. The paper argued that while apolitical trade unionism would be preferable to the partisan unions found in Peru, given that the unions were politicized, APRA control of the unions was preferable to control by "communists or 'totalitarians' " (Bourricaud 1970:316).

As noted in Chapter 6, APRA's gains from this alliance—that is, its new access to state resources—came at high cost. APRA's conservatization isolated it from the major wave of "new reformism" that appeared in the 1950s and limited its capacity to court the new political constituencies emerging in this period. This failure made it difficult for the party to move beyond the roughly one-third of the electorate that it commanded in presidential elections.

An important component of APRA's accord with Prado was that APRA would be allowed to compete openly in the 1962 election and that Haya could run for president as the official candidate of the Prado administration. In this subsequent electoral alliance, called the Democratic Alliance, APRA enjoyed the support of Prado's outgoing government, of Pedro Beltrán, and of other leading conservatives. Several political leaders linked to Prado ran on APRA's congressional lists, thereby further identifying APRA with the incumbent government. The alliance was thus a continuation of the *convivencia*, except that Haya was now the presidential candidate. Both Beltrán and Manuel Cisneros Sánchez, who was president of Prado's party (the MDP) and had been Prado's first prime minister in 1956, had attempted to launch presidential campaigns of their own. Their conspicuous inability to mobilize popular support led them to give up their candidacies and turn instead to an alliance with APRA as a better vehicle for promoting conservative political aspirations. This coalition also had the visible support of the U.S. embassy.[72]

Because APRA maintained its conservative alliance in the 1962 election, in which it was allowed to run freely, one might conclude that the ban on the party was not the only explanation for its conservative alliances. In fact, other explanations have already been suggested. Yet even in this election, two constraints operated that were linked to the ban. First, APRA's alliance grew out of the commitments built into the earlier pact with Prado, and hence the alliance was indirectly a product of the ban. In addition, though the election itself was open to APRA, the military subsequently did not respect the results of the election and intervened to cancel them. Hence, the ban was ultimately still in effect, and the anticipation that this might be the case certainly played a role in actors' calculations prior to the electoral contest.

In the 1962 election, APRA's Democratic Alliance won an extremely narrow plurality, gaining 32.98 percent of the vote, as opposed to 32.12 percent for Belaúnde and 28.44 percent for Odría. APRA performed far more impressively in the vote for the national Congress, winning 47 percent of the seats in the Senate and 45 percent in the Chamber of Deputies (Sulmont 1977:194; Astiz 1969b:103). APRA's presidential vote fell just short of the one-third needed to win the presidency, and under the Peruvian constitution the selection of the president would therefore occur by a majority vote of the two houses of Congress. Attention therefore shifted to the problem of building a majority coalition in Congress that could elect a president.

Apart from the problem of building such a coalition, accusations of electoral fraud clouded the prospects for a smooth presidential succession. Even before the election, fears that the APRA-Prado alliance would seek to perpetuate itself in power through fraud led to a debate on this issue, and the weeks following the election saw a series of charges and countercharges. On June 28 the army issued a communiqué denouncing irregularities in seven departments. These departments were important centers of APRA strength, and if their votes were invalidated Belaúnde would emerge the winner. Belaúnde

---

[72] Jaquette 1971:113; A. Payne 1968:36–37; Neira 1973:436; Werlich 1978:268; Bourricaud 1970:286.

Figure 7.3 The Veto of APRA and APRA's Political Alliances, 1956–1968

Evolution of Veto against APRA	Alliance	Date	Coalition Partner	APRA's Goal	Outcome
Alliances with the "Oligarchy"					
Odría does not permit APRA to run openly in 1956 presidential and congressional election.	Pact of Monterrico and *convivencia*	1956–1962	Prado and MDP	Win congressional representation by running APRA candidates on independent lists; gain access to state resources (esp. via-à-vis labor sector) as junior partner in Prado's government.	Produces stable governing coalition. Yet high cost to APRA: seen as being in alliance with oligarchy; apparent conservatization inhibits APRA from becoming part of "new reformism," further discredits party among elements of military.
APRA allowed to run presidential and congressional candidates in 1962.	Alianza Democrática	1962	Prado and MDP	Contest 1962 presidential election.	APRA wins plurality in presidential and vice presidential election and a near majority in Congress.
Alliances with Odría					
In July 1962 military vetoes Haya's assumption of presidency. Veto based both on older anti-Aprismo and new military concern that APRA will not carry out reform.	First Pact with Odría	1962	Odría	Elect Odría president in runoff within Congress, with APRA a major coalition partner.	Alliance with Odría, who earlier had severely repressed APRA, enhances image that APRA is "selling out" and further discredits APRA in the reformist camp and on the left.

Second pact with Odría: la Coalición	1963–1967	Odría	Establish a strong majority coalition in Congress in order to become a major force vis-à-vis the Belaúnde government.	Opposition coalition undermines Belaúnde's reforms. Growing perception in military that APRA has become too conservative to govern Peru reinforces a new form of military veto of APRA.
1962 coup vetoes assumption of presidency by Odría in coalition with APRA, leaving a majority in opposition after Belaúnde wins presidency in 1963. Veto also inhibits APRA-AD alliance.				

Alliance with AP

Apro-Carlista Alliance: The *superconvivencia*	1967–1968	Conservative wing of AP, PDC, Ulloa	Take advantage of coalitional opportunity created by split of AP and PDC; undo damage caused by APRA's obstruction of Belaúnde between 1963 and 1967.	Many reforms are carried out, but delegitimation of civilian regime and of APRA has already gone too far.
APRA's obstruction of Belaúnde's reforms appears to increase likelihood of renewed veto of APRA in 1969 election.			[End of democratic period.]	
One goal of 1968 coup is to block electoral victory of Apro-Carlista alliance in 1969 presidential election.				

also seized on the theme of fraud, and his supporters suggested that the military should perhaps intervene to resolve the crisis. Belaúnde left Lima for his native city of Arequipa, where supporters dramatically erected barricades around the party headquarters as if to prepare for a confrontation over the electoral outcome (Bourricaud 1970:296–97; A. Payne 1968:45–46).

On 4 July 1962, before the vote in the Congress, Haya announced that Prado had just informed him that the military had vetoed Haya's election (Bourricaud 1970:298). This veto reflected both continuity and change in the military's posture. Víctor Villaneuva (1962:203) argues that opposition to APRA on the ground that it was perceived as a leftist party was still an important current in military thinking. Intense military antipathy toward Haya remained a fact of Peruvian political life, and as of the early 1960s "anti-*Aprista* indoctrination [was] still an integral part of every recruit's military training."[73] However, certain sectors in the military were strongly committed to reform in order to ensure the continuing development and stability of Peru, and they opposed Haya and favored Belaúnde out of a belief that Belaúnde was much more likely to carry out reform (Werlich 1978:273).

It is also possible that an implicit veto by the economic elite stood behind the military veto. Villaneuva argues that Prado and other members of the elite may have indirectly supported the veto of APRA. He suggests that the elite still viewed APRA as a dangerous political alternative and that Prado may have been playing a double game in which he appeared to support APRA, but also encouraged the armed forces to challenge the presumed electoral fraud. Prado thereby displaced the responsibility for opposing APRA onto the armed forces. A crucial piece of evidence presented by Villaneuva (1962:198–200) for this interpretation is the fact that the leaders identified with Prado who ran for Congress in the coalition with APRA were all figures of secondary importance within the Prado movement. The most prominent Prado supporters were not involved, suggesting that Prado had reason to suspect that their election would be invalidated and that he was perhaps even promoting this outcome.

Regardless of whether this thesis about the economic elite is correct, APRA faced a major dilemma. Though APRA had gained a near-majority position in Congress, even without the ban on Haya's presidency it would have been necessary to form an alliance with one of the other two major parties, since the minor parties did not hold enough seats to provide the basis of a majority coalition with APRA in the Congress. Hence, APRA's dilemma was not exclusively a consequence of the ban. Yet given the ban, APRA now had to bargain with the other two parties from a weaker position, with the goal of electing one of the other candidates to the presidency through a coalition that would ensure APRA a large role in the new government, taking advantage of the party's newly won strength in Congress and of the fact that the popular Aprista leader Manuel Seoane had won the first vice presidency

---

[73] A. Payne 1968:37, fn. 12; See also Werlich 1978:268.

(A. Payne 1968:47). There followed a period of complex bargaining among the three presidential contenders.

Haya initially offered to give his votes to Belaúnde in exchange for a role in the new government, but Belaúnde refused, convinced that his strong support from the military would ultimately assure him the presidency. Given Belaúnde's earlier role in the National Democratic Front between 1945 and 1948, it is hard to imagine that he was not also dubious about being a non-APRA president within a coalition in which APRA held such a strong position in Congress. A coalition of Belaúnde with Odría was likewise not a viable option. Apart from the lack of ideological affinity, such a coalition fell short of producing a majority in Congress (Werlich 1978:271–72; Cotler 1978:349).

APRA's Alliances with Odría. At this point APRA opted for the third alternative alliance and entered into its first accord with Odría,[74] in which Odría would become president, with strong APRA participation in his government. While this agreement had the merit of producing a congressional majority, Odría's announcement of this accord "stunned the public, especially the Aprista faithful" (Werlich 1978:272). Odría had violently repressed APRA during his own earlier government, had declared Haya a common criminal "unworthy of Peruvian citizenship" (Villanueva 1962:128), and had held Haya prisoner in the Colombian embassy in Lima for over five years. Hence, this was an astonishing further step in the evolution of APRA's alliances with the right. This alliance would also have led to the dubious outcome of giving the presidency to the candidate who had finished third in the election. Yet the accord met important concerns of APRA. It took advantage both of the party's strong position in Congress and, given Odría's age and poor health, of the fact that APRA would have held the first vice presidency and would therefore assume the presidency in the event of Odría's death.[75]

However, such outcomes were precluded by the next step in the military veto: the coup of 17 July 1962. The Odría-APRA alliance was unacceptable to the military, and the military intervention prevented Odría's assumption of the presidency and effectively canceled the results of the 1962 election. APRA's achievements of gaining a plurality in the presidential vote, of winning the vice presidency, and of establishing a near-majority position in Congress were thereby lost.

The reasons behind the military intervention involved essentially the same issues that underlay the veto of APRA, which had been announced two

[74] While this is sometimes referred to as the *superconvivencia*, we follow what we believe is the more common usage of applying this term to the Apro-Carlista alliance of 1967–68.

[75] Werlich 1978:272. Kuczynski suggests two other factors that may help explain this alliance. First, during the campaign Belaúnde had taken positions on agrarian reform and economic nationalism that were substantially to the left of either of the other two leading candidates, leaving them, by contrast, on more nearly common ideological ground—given the ongoing conservatization of APRA. Second, Haya and Odría were more nearly from the same political generation, "compared to the much more youthful and upstart organization put together by Belaúnde" (1977:41).

weeks earlier. However, in this instance more progressive military elements who saw the need for reform as a cornerstone of national stability and security not only opposed Haya, but now also the assumption of power by Odría, who was unlikely to carry out reform. Some genuine concern with electoral fraud was also involved, though it appears that while APRA and Prado may well have intended to commit fraud, they were probably prevented from doing so. Finally, fear of a sustained political crisis in the wake of the ambiguous electoral outcome was also a factor behind the coup.[76]

The military junta immediately announced new elections for June 1963 and held power as an interim government until the candidate selected in those elections was inaugurated. In contrast to the earlier Odría government of 1948–56, this junta did not repress APRA or prevent it from running in the coming elections (though there was some repression of the left), and the military regime came to be known as a *dictablanda*, or "soft dictatorship" (Bourricaud 1970:308).

In the new elections of 1963, the Christian Democrats, who had secured just under 3 percent of the vote in 1962, entered into an alliance with Acción Popular. Belaúnde was also supported by small parties of the left that were banned by the military government. Boosted by these and other factors, Belaúnde won the presidency with 39 percent of the vote, as against 34 percent for APRA and 26 percent for Odría. Belaúnde's coalition also performed well in the Senate and House, winning 45 percent and 36 percent of the seats, respectively. APRA again competed successfully in the congressional election, though with a slight decline, gaining roughly 40 percent of the seats in both chambers (Astiz 1969b:104).

APRA's relative position was thus slightly weakened. With the military in power, APRA no longer enjoyed the support of the incumbent government, and several congressional candidates identified with Prado, who in 1962 had run on the list of the APRA coalition, ran on separate lists in 1963. APRA's percentage of the presidential vote actually rose by a small amount, due to the reduced number of small parties in the 1963 contest, but APRA won a somewhat smaller percentage of seats in both legislative bodies. This relative continuity in the vote for APRA in relation to 1962 casts doubt on any argument that the party benefited significantly from electoral fraud in 1962 (Neira 1973:420; Astiz 1969b:103–04; Jaquette 1971:130).

APRA's second alliance with Odría occurred after the 1963 election, when the party entered into a legislative accord called "La Coalición." While participants in this accord at first maintained that they would cooperate only in the initial selection of parliamentary officers, in fact for four years they functioned as a powerful opposition bloc that commanded 61 percent of the seats in the Chamber of Deputies and 56 percent in the Senate (Astiz 1969b:104).

APRA's renewed alliance with Odría was certainly not inevitable, and after the 1963 election Belaúnde and APRA explored the possibility of forming a governing alliance. From many perspectives this would have been an attrac-

[76] Werlich 1978:273; Bourricaud 1970:307; A. Payne 1968:49.

tive alternative. It could have built on the older reformist tradition within APRA and would have commanded an overwhelming 80 percent of the seats in Congress. However, a disadvantage was that if Acción Popular entered this alliance it would lose essential support from the armed forces. This influence of the military's preferences on coalition formation was yet another facet of the military veto of APRA. The veto thus played a direct role as one of the factors that inhibited APRA from entering into a more progressive alliance, though partisan rivalry between Acción Popular and APRA also made this alliance difficult. In the event, a major opportunity for promoting reform was lost.

Instead, APRA continued its earlier accord with Odría, forming an opposition coalition that played an extremely destructive role under the Belaúnde administration (Cotler 1978:355–56). From their position in Congress, which under Peruvian law has considerable power vis-à-vis the executive, the opposition parties thoroughly sabotaged Belaúnde's reform program, and "APRA appeared to have sold its soul for the narrowest of partisan reasons" (Werlich 1978:281).

This obstruction by the opposition was particularly noteworthy because Belaúnde began his term with widespread popular support and high public expectations of reform. Indeed, his inauguration as president was greeted with a "euphoria previously unknown in Peruvian politics" (Cotler 1978:353). One symbol of Belaúnde's commitment to vigorous initiatives was the promise in his inaugural address to resolve within 90 days a long-standing dispute with the International Petroleum Company (IPC), a subsidiary of Standard Oil (Werlich 1978:292). The status of the IPC holdings in Peru was highly problematic under Peruvian law, and the company had long been an object of criticism among those concerned with Peru's tenuous national control of its own economy.

Unfortunately for Belaúnde, neither this specific promise concerning the IPC dispute nor these broader expectations were fulfilled. Using its power of parliamentary "interpellation," the APRA/UNO coalition undermined the functioning of the executive branch. The opposition forced Belaúnde to change ministers 178 times during his five-year government, the equivalent of having to change his cabinet three times per year. Belaúnde's principal initiatives in the rural sector were undermined. The opposition cut the budget of Cooperación Popular, a dynamic rural development program initiated by Belaúnde, claiming that the program was inciting peasant land seizures and insisting that the peasant mobilization should be energetically repressed. Belaúnde's agrarian reform bill was transformed in the Congress into an extremely complex and nearly inoperative measure under which virtually no land distribution took place. Two of the President's most important initiatives were thus blocked by the opposition, and the new government came to be perceived as powerless to deal with its opponents. Congressional initiatives on spending and taxation also created difficulties for the government. The congressional opposition spent funds generously on programs and projects of concern to its own constituencies and clienteles, but would not increase taxes to cover growing public expenditures, producing expanding budget deficits, inflation, and a growing sense of economic crisis (Cotler 1978:358–59; Jaquette 1971:150).

The reformist wing of Belaúnde's own party encouraged him to take countermeasures, such as the use of peasant mobilization as a means to pressure the Congress, or an *auto-golpe*[77] through which military support would be used to close the Congress, to be followed by a plebiscite on Belaúnde's program. However, Belaúnde resisted such steps, a posture that reinforced the growing sense of failure of presidential leadership (Cotler 1978:360–61).

At the same time that Belaúnde faced this internal opposition, he was also undermined externally by economic pressure from the United States, which sought to encourage Peru to soften its position in the dispute over the International Petroleum Company. However, in the face of U.S. pressure and the loss of reformist momentum of his administration, the IPC case proved tragically difficult to resolve—culminating in a scandal in 1968 over a settlement with the IPC that destroyed the credibility of Belaúnde's government and was the immediate determinant of the timing of the 1968 military coup, though not an underlying cause (Werlich 1978:298). At a more immediate level, this cutoff in foreign assistance further aggravated the imbalance in public expenditure and hence the economic difficulties of the Belaúnde administration.

APRA's Alliance with Acción Popular. APRA's final alliance came in 1967–68, when the party established an accord with the conservative wing of Acción Popular, known as the Carlistas,[78] thereby forming a new majority coalition in the Congress known as the Apro-Carlista alliance. The vigorous policy initiatives taken with the support of this alliance stood in marked contrast to the earlier paralysis of the Belaúnde administration.

The emergence of this new coalition was facilitated by two developments. First, by this time APRA had recognized that its successful obstruction of Belaúnde's program had discredited the democratic regime to a point that a coup was becoming likely. The party's obstruction had also deepened the antagonism toward APRA on the part of reformist elements within the military. The party therefore took steps to help deal with the economic crisis and overcome the political stalemate (Kuczynski 1977:226; Lynch 1980:171). Second, both Acción Popular and the Christian Democrats had split over disputes concerning the failure of Belaúnde's reform program, leaving the conservative wing of Acción Popular available for an alliance with APRA.

This new cooperation between APRA and Acción Popular had several components. In the period after a large devaluation of the Peruvian currency in September 1967, "the main factor in holding down the price rise was the great restraint exercised by APRA on the unions that it controlled" (Kuczynski 1977:185). Likewise, as early as October 1967, Belaúnde had begun consulting with Haya, as well as with Odría, about Peru's economic difficulties,

---

[77] A coup initiated by the incumbent government.
[78] Several key leaders of this wing were named Carlos—hence the name (Pease 1977:35).

and they agreed to a joint effort to seek solutions (Hilliker 1971:137). By February 1968 the APRA bloc in Congress was explicitly cooperating on economic policy with Belaúnde's new cabinet, headed by Ferrero.

This cooperation became even more extensive under the Hercelles cabinet from early June to just before the coup in early October 1968, which was formed with APRA's prior "advice and consent" (Kuczynski 1977:221). This further accord was based on a coalition of the conservative wing of Acción Popular (the Carlistas), the conservative wing of the Christian Democratic Party (which had now become the Christian Popular Party), and APRA. Odría was marginalized within this coalition and his party also split. Odría himself withdrew from cooperation with APRA, while other leading figures in his movement remained linked to the accord. This new coalition commanded a congressional majority (Pease 1977:35,38; Cotler 1978:379; Valderrama 1980:171).

This phase of the APRA–Acción Popular alliance brought together the financial, industrial, and agro export elite, encompassing private sector leaders with strong ties to foreign capital. It marginalized the traditional landowners of the highlands, which certainly contributed to Odría's withdrawal. The finance minister and leading figure within the cabinet was Manuel Ulloa, a prominent business leader with strong international connections who wished to promote the vigorous modernization of Peruvian capitalism. Ulloa supported a larger role of the state in the economy and promoted a type of economic nationalism that sought to differentiate carefully between areas of the economy where foreign capital should be strongly encouraged and those where national capital would be favored and protected.

Within the framework of this alliance, on 19 June Congress granted the executive branch special emergency powers for 60 days to stabilize and reactivate the economy. During this period the new cabinet issued roughly 300 decrees, which subsequently were ratified by Congress. Ulloa strengthened the tax system, imposed restrictions on the role of foreign capital in the banking system, attempted to encourage domestic capital formation, and expanded state control over the monetary system. His program included initiatives favoring greater regulation of the extractive sector, and he began to move toward a more effective agrarian reform. He renegotiated the foreign debt and attracted new foreign investment in mining—investment designed to produce constructive linkages with Peru's manufacturing sector. Ulloa's initiatives, and hence this new coalition that backed him, were widely viewed as a success. Jaquette suggests that APRA's cooperation with Ulloa, and also the agreement between APRA and the Ferrero cabinet of February 1968, increased business confidence in the political and economic situation in Peru.[79]

The success of this alliance and of Ulloa's program renewed APRA's hopes

[79] Jaquette 1971:177, 182–85. She derives this conclusion from an index of "confidence" in the economic and political situation based on fluctuations in the free market rate of the Peruvian currency, the sol. On this policy period, see also Jaquette (1971:176–77), Kuczynski (1977:226), Cotler (1978:378–79).

that the party would be able to compete freely in the 1969 election. These
hopes were further raised in May 1968 by a statement at a press conference
made by the minister of the army, a military officer. In response to a question
as to whether the armed forces would veto the appointment of a member of
a commission that was investigating military involvement in smuggling, the
minister replied that "the word 'veto' should be erased from the dictionary
of the armed forces" (*Caretas*, May 16–20, 1968:pp. 10–12a). APRA believed
that this signaled an end to the veto of the party, and there was an immediate
celebration at APRA headquarters. In June 1968, APRA once again nominated Haya to be its presidential candidate, though it seems likely that
APRA would have entered the election in coalition with AP, with Ulloa
heading the ticket. Given the divisions in all the other parties, this coalition
would certainly have won the 1969 presidential election, had it been held
(Werlich 1978:298; Jaquette 1971:181; Chullen 1980:149).

However, the delegitimation of the democratic regime and of APRA had
already gone too far, bringing the final step in the ban of APRA. Though the
coup of 3 October 1968 had several immediate and long-term causes (see below), this delegitimation and the military's concern with blocking APRA's
further access to power were central among them. As Werlich (1978:299) put
it, APRA's "sabotage of Belaúnde's reform program convinced the armed
forces of the complete cynicism and civic bankruptcy of the party. APRA, for
many officers, had demonstrated its unworthiness to rule the nation."

Assessment.   It is evident that elements of what we have called an integrative party system were present in Peru. First of all, much of the time APRA
was able to enter into majority coalitions. The 1956 alliance with Prado produced a strong plurality in the presidential vote and a majority in Congress,
a majority that remained stable throughout Prado's term of office. The
APRA-Odría alliance of 1962 commanded a strong congressional majority
and could easily have elected Odría to the presidency had it been allowed to
do so. In 1967–68 the APRA Acción Popular alliance controlled the presidency and a strong congressional majority, and had the 1969 election been
held, this alliance would probably have won an overwhelming majority.
Only in its 1962 coalition with Prado did APRA's alliance fail to win either
the required one-third of the presidential vote or a congressional majority
that could have elected the president in the legislature.

In addition, though APRA lost some ground in its relationship with the
popular sector, it retained a major working-class electoral base both in the
urban sector and in modernized enclaves, and at least until the mid-1960s
(see below) the CTP remained the dominant force in the labor movement.
APRA's alliances therefore provided the basis for direct mediation between
labor and capital, most conspicuously through APRA's links with figures
such as Prado and Beltrán, and subsequently through the party's cooperation
with Belaúnde in 1967 and the alliance with Ulloa in 1968. Thus, important
components of an integrative party system were present.

APRA's opponents rhetorically attacked the party's coalitions in terms
that are interesting from the comparative perspective of this book. In 1962,

leaders identified with the rival candidacy of Belaúnde "claimed that APRA and MDP leaders had in mind a plan to unite the country's plutocracy and popular-labor sectors in order to establish a kind of Mexican PRI-style government to perpetuate themselves in power" (A. Payne 1968:37). A book by Belaúnde published in 1963 claimed that an important Prado minister had "publicly stated that *pradismo* and *aprismo* would be able to rule Peru through a fifty-year *'convivencia'* " (cited in A. Payne 1968:37).

However, nothing resembling this outcome occurred, due principally to three interrelated problems: the military veto of APRA, the issue of APRA's electoral strength, and APRA's failure to address basic reform issues of the 1960s. These problems will be considered in turn.

One reason for APRA's failure was of course the veto. We have noted the evolving basis of the veto, from the earlier tradition of anti-Aprismo in the military to the newer currents of military reformism. Correspondingly, at first APRA was vetoed in part for being too radical, then the party conservatized to overcome the veto, and subsequently it was vetoed in part for being too conservative. Despite the veto, APRA did enter into two strong majority alliances during these years (with Prado and later with Belaúnde and Ulloa). However, in 1962 and 1968 these alliances were destroyed by military coups.

In assessing arguments about the veto, one may reasonably ask whether it was an unalterable "rule of the game," or whether the veto could have been overcome. There is substantial ground for thinking that in the 1962 election the political viability of APRA's Democratic Alliances could have been increased had APRA run a presidential candidate other than Haya. This would have addressed the problem of the strong enmity toward Haya himself within the armed forces, as well as increasing the party's appeal among voters who traditionally had misgivings about APRA and about Haya. Manuel Seoane, APRA's vice presidential candidate in 1962, ran well ahead of Haya, suggesting that this strategy might have been successful. Indeed, Seoane wanted to be the APRA presidential candidate in 1963, and when Haya ran again, Seoane refused to accept any other position on the APRA ticket (A. Payne 1968:37; Werlich 1978:268, 279). There apparently had also been some discussion of the possibility that if another APRA leader, Ramiro Priale, had been the candidate in 1962, the military would not have interfered in the election (*Caretas*, 22 February 1988).

However, replacing Haya as head of the ticket would have been difficult. Bourricaud (1970:288) argues that "throughout Prado's term of office . . . [the party] had reassured [its] followers with the prospect of the magic year in which Víctor Raúl would at last take over the Presidency," and if Haya had not run it would have appeared to the APRA rank and file as yet another setback for the party. Also, given the personal rivalry between Haya and Seoane, Haya's "firm monolithic control over the party" (Kuczynski 1977:31), and the degree to which for over three decades the party had served as the vehicle for the political career of its *jefe máximo*, such a choice was unlikely. Yet through such a choice APRA might well have been able to overcome the military veto and, given Seoane's popularity, might have won the presidency.

Though having an Aprista other than Haya head the APRA ticket had not been a viable alternative in 1963, APRA's participation in a multiparty coalition in which a non-Aprista headed the ticket did not appear to pose a similar problem for the party and had already occurred in 1936, 1945, and 1956. A similar coalition appeared likely for 1969, with Ulloa heading the ticket. However, given the scope of the larger political crisis of the second half of the 1960s, combined with remaining elements of anti-Aprismo in the military (see below), this became one of the alliances that was blocked by a coup.

Another obstacle to APRA's effort to become a more dominant political force was the party's level of electoral support in presidential elections. In the 1962 and 1963 contests, which provided a crucial test of the party's electoral strength, it won a third of the presidential vote. Hence, APRA was far from establishing the kind of dominance in the electoral arena enjoyed by PRI in Mexico. APRA's claim to being the party of the "national majorities," to "represent the masses," thus appeared to be undermined (Bourricaud 1970:271, 295).

How is one to explain this electoral failure? One interpretation views APRA's performance in the 1962 election as a setback in relation to 1945 and 1956, when the presidential candidates backed by APRA got a much stronger vote (Sulmont 1977:194; Neira 1973:420). It could be argued that in reaction to APRA's alliance with Prado, the party suffered an erosion of support. Along with the broader reaction to the 1956 *convivencia*, the economic stabilization program led by Beltrán from 1959 to 1961 and indirectly supported by APRA had, in particular, been exceedingly unpopular. Beltrán emerged as "one of the most disliked figures that Peruvian politics had produced in many years" (Pike 1967:299; see also Werlich 1978:260). APRA's partial identification with these policies can hardly have helped the party in 1962.

However, two cautionary observations must be made about APRA's electoral support. First, in 1945 and 1956 APRA was in a broad alliance headed by a prominent non-APRA candidate who drew a substantial non-APRA vote. Though in 1962 the party did have support from the Prado forces, in that year APRA was to a greater degree running on its own, and as noted above the leaders identified with Prado, who ran with APRA, were minor figures in the Prado movement. Hence, a more appropriate comparison is with 1931, the only prior presidential election when APRA ran by itself. North (1973:chap. 4) compares the electoral outcomes of the early 1960s with 1931 and finds substantial continuity in the core vote for the party over these three decades, encompassing the support of approximately one-third of the electorate. Therefore, APRA's alliances with conservative forces could be seen as being necessary in part because in regional and sectoral terms, APRA's own core support never extended far beyond its original constituencies. On the other hand, the party's somewhat narrow electoral base may in turn be seen in part as the result of many years of repression and banning of the party, which deprived it of opportunities to extend its own base. Hence, the analysis comes back to the issue of the ban.

From another perspective, it must be argued that APRA was not so electorally weak after all, in light of the party's strong performance in congressional, as opposed to presidential, contests. This discrepancy had various explanations. First, the military veto of APRA did not prevent the party from playing a strong role in Congress, so that a concern in the electorate with wasting votes on an APRA candidate who might not take office did not arise at that level. Relatedly, because Haya himself was the presidential candidate in 1962 and 1963, ambivalence and antipathies toward him affected the presidential vote, whereas they were less relevant for the congressional vote. This contrast highlights APRA's special problems at the presidential level. Finally, APRA was adept at forming alliances with local elites in different regions and at selecting candidates who had a strong appeal to regional electorates (McClintock 1981:69–70). Thus, the perception of APRA's modest electoral success was partially incorrect, and to the extent that the difference in presidential and congressional performance was due to the ban, this was yet another way in which the ban had adversely affected the party's fortunes.

A final problem underlying APRA's failure to become a more dominant political force concerned the way APRA's conservatization undermined the party's capacity to play a central role in addressing major policy problems of the day. This outcome was ironic, since this failure resulted from APRA's programmatic shift to the right, which was in part an adaptation at an earlier point to the military veto. This issue of policy failure and APRA's relationship to it will be explored in the next section.

Before proceeding with the analysis of opposition and crisis in the next section, it is appropriate to address a comparative implication of the issue of APRA's electoral strength and of the party's experience of entering coalitions as a rather subordinated, junior partner—especially under Prado, but also with Ulloa. These facts suggest a comparison with the subordinate role of populist parties in Brazil and Chile (the PTB and the Socialists) discussed in the aftermath chapter. These two parties both had a significant but not overwhelming electoral base, and during the aftermath period they played the frustrating role of entering electoral coalitions as a junior partner and ultimately receiving few payoffs for their participation. This experience helped trigger their later move to the left.

The experience of APRA, in fact, was quite different. Particularly if one looks at the congressional vote and not just the presidential vote, APRA was in a vastly stronger electoral position than these two parties, with its level of electoral support and representation in Congress ranging from a third up to nearly a half. In addition, though the operation of the partial ban placed APRA in a junior and in some ways humiliating position in its coalition with Prado, in exchange for its cooperation the party received invaluable payoffs that played a vital role in its institutional consolidation.

Opposition and Crises of the late 1950s and 1960s

As in Venezuela and Colombia, in both Peru and Argentina the restoration of a civilian regime in the second half of the 1950s came on the eve of the period of new opposition movements and crises discussed in the previous sections. These developments had a major impact in Peru.

In the political sphere, new political models of great salience to the Peruvian left, the labor movement, and the student movement were posed by the Cuban Revolution, by major changes in international communism brought by the 20th Party Congress and the Sino-Soviet split, and by the independence and national liberation movements in different parts of the Third World.[80] Obviously, the impact of these external models must be understood in the framework of the ongoing erosion within Peru of traditional social relations due to economic growth and rapid urbanization, as well as the internal evolution of demands for change and reform. Yet in this setting of ongoing internal change, international developments dramatically posed new alternatives for Peru's future.

In the economic sphere, the major new influx of U.S. investment in the 1950s and 1960s produced growing concern about the loss of national control of Peru's economy, and nationalism became an important theme in the press and in political discourse (Werlich 1978:263). Benchmarks in the evolution of this theme included the negative reaction to the decision of the Eisenhower administration earlier in the 1950s to award the Legion of Merit to President Odría, the hostile reception received by U.S. Vice President Nixon upon his visit in Lima in 1958, and the evolving debate over the problematic legal status of the International Petroleum Company. Two subsequent developments led to an understandable perception that the United States was using "financial blackmail" against the Peruvian government. First, as a result of the IPC dispute, the United States cut funding to Peru under the Alliance for Progress, thus denying funds to what potentially could have been a "showcase" reform government. Later, after the United States refused to sell new fighter aircraft to Peru in the interest of discouraging an arms race with Chile, and when Peru subsequently purchased fighters from France, the United States imposed a further embargo on loans to Peru (Werlich 1978:263, 294). The immediate crisis that toppled Belaúnde derived from the paralysis of his government in its efforts to deal with the IPC dispute in the face of these complex pressures and constraints.

Party System.   One of the spheres in which these evolving issues had a visible impact was the party system. The emergence of the new reformism in the mid-1950s and APRA's failure to become part of this movement was explored in the previous chapter. The late 1950s and 1960s brought significant, though not dramatic, polarization in the party system.

In the aftermath of Castro's victory in Cuba, the left opposition within APRA intensified. At the party congress in late 1959, a number of interme-

[80] Béjar 1969:47–49; Sulmont 1977:173–82; Bourricaud 1970:210, 222.

diate level progressive leaders within APRA, some of whom had visited Cuba that year, challenged the policy of cooperation with President Prado and were immediately expelled. They formed a movement initially called APRA Rebelde, which they renamed the Movement of the Revolutionary Left (MIR) in 1960 to identify themselves more explicitly with Castroism, thereby adopting the same name employed by the left dissidents from Venezuela's Acción Democrática. The leader of this group played a central role in the guerrilla insurgency of the mid-1960s.[81]

The rise of Castro likewise accelerated the erosion of APRA's role in the student movement. The party's strong political presence in universities had its roots in Haya's days as a student leader in the late 1910s, and APRA had for decades been a dominant force in student politics. While the APRA student movement initially supported Castro in 1958, it soon came to oppose him as he moved further to the left, thereby distancing itself from the thinking of many students for whom Castro and Cuba were coming to represent a political model of paramount importance. In 1960 APRA lost control of the Peruvian Student Federation, and by the time of the 1963 National Student Congress, APRA's position within the national student movement had been largely eclipsed (Hilliker 1971:88; Werlich 1978:268). Though APRA retained influence in some universities, a crucial arena for recruiting and training future political leaders was thus partially lost to the party.

The years of the Belaúnde administration (1963–68) saw some further movement to the left within the party system. While not remotely comparable to the polarization of Chile or Uruguay, within the Peruvian context it was a significant development. At the start of the Belaúnde period, APRA's alliance with Odría triggered a new round of defections from APRA to MIR and to other reformist parties. Ironically, the success of the APRA-Odría alliance in blocking the Belaúnde reforms also led to disillusionment on the part of members of Acción Popular with the prospects for reform within a democratic framework, and some of them also defected to the left (Cotler 1978:357, 361). These defections strengthened MIR and other groups on the left, which in 1963 and 1965 led episodes of guerrilla warfare that were also important steps in this process of polarization. However, as emphasized below, these guerrilla experiences were important more for their impact on national politics than for the actual scope of guerrilla activity.

In February 1967 both Acción Popular and the Christian Democrats split due to the frustration of the progressive wing of each party with the failure of reform under Belaúnde. The conservative wing of the Christian Democrats formed the Popular Christian Party, which continued to support the government, while the progressive wing, which retained the earlier party name, went into opposition and became more identified with the left. At the February 1967 party congress of Acción Popular, Belaúnde lost control of the party, which severely criticized his administration and elected a secretary general who had advocated far more vigorous reform and to whom Belaúnde

[81] Neira 1969:458; Sulmont 1977:186; Gott 1972:341–42.

was strongly opposed. Some increase in polarization was also reflected in a crucial by-election in the department of Lima in November 1967, two months after the devaluation of that year. This election served as a kind of plebiscite on the government, since this department contained nearly half of Peru's electorate. Not only did the APRA-UNO candidate defeat the government candidate, but the election produced what by Peruvian standards was a significant "protest" vote, with the left receiving 10 percent of the vote and 8 percent of the voters casting blank ballots (Astiz 1969b:127; Cotler 1978:373–74).

Yet the picture within the party system was not in any sense one of centrifugal polarization. The 1968 Apro-Carlista alliance represented a major, successful initiative located at what could be seen as the center-right, involving APRA—with its still important, though by now somewhat eroded, popular base (see below)—and the elites of the agro-export and manufacturing sector. This coalition marginalized the traditional agrarian elite and Odría, who might be thought of as the far right, leading Odría to withdraw from his alliance with APRA and pursue separately his more conservative orientation. Thus, the consolidation of this new center-right bloc that excluded the far right in a sense was a check on polarization, rather than an expression of it. Given the splits in Acción Popular and the Christian Democratic Party, the Apro-Carlista alliance would have been a likely victor in the presidential election scheduled for 1969. However, the delegitimation of the democratic system had already gone too far to be reversed by the emergence and apparent policy successes of this new alliance.

Labor Movement. Throughout the post-1956 period, APRA faced challenges in the labor sector, though with the help of its allies in the state, the party was able up to a point to defeat them. Nonetheless, in the final years of the Belaúnde administration, the labor movement saw the growth of the left of far greater scope than occurred in the electoral arena.

These changes occurred against the backdrop of rapid expansion of industry and the service sector and of high rates of union formation. This period saw major growth in the manufacture and assembly of consumer durables, including automobiles. By comparative standards this growth occurred on a small scale, given the size of the Peruvian market. Yet between 1955 and 1970 there was, for instance, a nearly fourfold increase in the number of factory workers in different branches of metal-working. Within the service sector, rapidly growing employment in banking and education would prove especially important for the labor movement. In comparison with the years of the Prado administration, the annual rate of recognition of new unions during 1962–68—encompassing roughly the 1962–63 military government and the Belaúnde administration—increased nearly threefold. The rate of recognition in manufacturing increased by a factor of more than 2.6, and that in banking and commerce more than threefold.[82]

[82] Calculated from Sulmont (1977:316–17); see also Sulmont (1977:309); (1985:72–74); and Werlich (1978:282).

The challenges to APRA's dominance within the labor movement were linked to the economic crises of this period, to the demonstration effect of the Cuban Revolution, and to APRA's shifting political coalitions. Given its access to state resources under Prado and its long-establihsed skill in labor organizing, between 1957 and 1961 APRA was able not only to hold its own in the labor sector, but to gain some ground vis-à-vis the left (J. Payne 1965:97). However, important currents of opposition were emerging.

In 1959, in the midst of the economic crisis and in the immediate aftermath of the Cuban Revolution, a Committee for Reorganization of the CTP (Comité de Reorganización de la CTP) was established within the APRA confederation by leaders of the bank, construction, and metal workers' unions in order to challenge the CTP leadership. The Trotskyite-linked Federation of Metallurgical Workers (FETIMP)—based in the relatively younger work force of this rapidly growing, and in part foreign-owned, sector—represented a particularly important current within this new movement. The metallurgical workers carried out several significant strikes in the early 1960s, and during a strike in 1964 initiated the first factory seizures in Peru, occupying at least 20 factories. In the Federation of Bank Workers (FEB), the Aprista leadership was displaced in 1958 by a new group with important Communist leadership. This sector also emerged as a particularly militant force within the labor movement and later became involved in an extended labor conflict in 1964. However, beginning with the arrests and other measures against the Peruvian left in late May of that year, and extending into 1965 with the more general crackdown on the left triggered by the emergence of guerrilla movements in the highlands, these new trade-union groups were for the time being defeated, and APRA succeeded in regaining control of the federations of both the Bank Workers and the Metallurgical Workers and FETIMP (Sulmont 1977:202–6).

Nevertheless, opposition to CTP dominance in the labor sector continued to grow. In 1965 the Communists established a new Committee for Trade Union Defense and Unification (CDUS) outside the CTP, and the economic crisis of 1967 brought a "decisive" step in the erosion of the CTP's position (Sulmont 1977:210). In the context of substantial inflation and a 35 percent devaluation of the currency (followed by a further decline of 10 percent), the government sought to stabilize the economy and granted a wage adjustment of only 10 percent in 1967. As noted above, at this point APRA was moving into an alliance with Belaúnde, reducing its latitude to oppose the stabilization program. This was likewise a coalitional turning point at the level of the party system, in that it was also the year in which both Acción Popular and the Christian Democrats split into more progressive and more conservative factions. In this context, the CTP initially rejected the limited wage increase, then reversed itself and accepted the increase, projecting an image of weakness and vacillation. The CDUS rejected the increase, thereby increasing its leverage among workers who believed the CTP had betrayed the labor movement. Building on this momentum, in 1968 the CDUS formed its own confederation, adopting the name of the confederation founded by Mariátegui in

1929 and identified with the Communist Party—the CGTP (General Confederation of Peruvian Workers) (Sulmont 1977:209–12).

The CGTP grew rapidly in the following years. In the post-1968 period, the new military government granted this confederation official recognition and provided it with important support, while APRA and the CTP lost all access to state resources and state support. Whereas in the first half of the 1960s the CTP encompassed at least three-quarters of the labor movement, by the mid-1970s this proportion had declined to less than a quarter, remaining at approximately that level as of the mid-1980s.[83]

In sum, the combination of the general change in the political climate, new political currents within the labor movement, and the vicissitudes of APRA's successive political coalitions created a situation in which, in the face of the economic crisis of 1967, APRA and the CTP found it increasingly difficult to maintain their credibility within the labor sector. The initial changes set in motion by this erosion of credibility were then strongly reinforced by the new political circumstances of the post-1968 period. In the process, APRA lost a major part of its trade-union base, which from the beginning of Haya de la Torre's movement in 1919 had been a cornerstone of Aprismo.

The Politics of Stabilization.   As in other countries, the politics of stabilization is a particularly important aspect of union-party mediation. These years saw two important efforts to stabilize the economy that have already received some attention above: the 1959–61 program of Beltrán and 1967–68 program at the end of the Belaúnde administration. Both programs raised important issues of labor-capital mediation, and in both cases APRA played a significant role in securing acquiescence to the programs. However, on the second occasion this was achieved at high cost to the party.

Beltrán's stabilization program of the late 1950s brought an important wave of strikes in the mining, oil, construction, factory, and bank sectors. Cotler stresses that APRA played a deliberately ambiguous role in this context. The party could not overtly oppose popular protest against the program, but it sought to control it so as to avoid a confrontation like that which occurred under Bustamante in the mid-1940s. While on the one hand APRA supported the stabilization effort, the party also tried to "protect its image with the popular sector by formally distancing itself from Beltrán and criticizing secondary aspects of the stabilization program" (Valderrama 1980:84; see also Cotler 1978:306).

APRA's approach is illustrated by the carefully executed and controlled one-day general strike carried out by the CTP in 1960 to protest the repression and worker deaths that followed a series of strikes in different parts of Peru—including the killing of workers on some of the most important sugar estates on the north coast, which were central to the APRA trade-union movement (Valderrama 1980:84). The strike was highly effective and

[83] J. Payne 1965:167; Kuczynski 1977:185, fn. 6; Stephens 1980:193–94; Sulmont 1985:210.

strongly expressed worker grievances, yet without threatening the Prado government. "The CTP made it clear that it was protesting not against the government but against the 'assassins at the service of imperialistic companies' " (J. Payne 1965:169—quotation cited from the CTP publication).

APRA thus effectively both channeled protest and also protected its credibility within the labor movement. Beltrán's program succeeded in dealing with the fiscal and balance of payments crisis, though this success was aided by a new expansion of primary product exports and must be understood within the narrowly monetarist framework of the program (Kuczynski 1977:42; Cotler 1978:306; Scheetz 1986:104–5).

As noted above, the 1967 program likewise posed important issues of party compromise and labor-capital mediation. With the beginning of APRA's cooperation with Belaúnde, the program had strong support at the level of party coalitions, both in its initial phase in 1967 and during the phase of Ulloa's leadership in 1968. Within the labor movement, given APRA's continuing control of the CTP, there was also strong support from important union leaders, who following the 1967 devaluation helped restrain pressure for wage increases and thereby contributed to the success of the program.

However, at the level of both party politics and trade union politics the supporters of this program were soon overtaken by events. APRA's coalition with Belaúnde and Ulloa was in some respects a constructive step after the party's earlier coalitional zigzags. Yet it was insufficient to reverse the larger process of delegitimation of the democratic regime during this period, and the accumulation of political antagonisms and policy failures of the 1960s would soon lead to events that took Peruvian politics in a very different direction after 1968. At the level of the labor movement, by contrast, the events connected with the program directly contributed to the erosion of APRA's position in the labor sector.

Peasant Mobilization. The accelerating disintegration of traditional social relations and growing peasant mobilization in the highlands was a major focus of attention for a broad spectrum of political actors in the 1950s and 1960s. Established elites saw these changes as threatening the stability of a major portion of the national territory. When more progressive sectors of the economic elite sought to promote agrarian reform in the highlands that would defuse the crisis in that region, new political cleavages emerged, as these policies were understandably opposed by the highland elite. For the new reformist parties, the highlands became a major new political constituency and agrarian reform a high priority. Finally, new political groups on the left, for whom the Chinese and Cuban revolutions were important models, saw the peasantry as having a central role in the first phase of the hoped-for revolution (Béjar 1969:49; Bourricaud 1970:222).

Though peasant mobilization and land seizures had already begun by the mid-1950s, the first episodes that really captured national attention occurred in the agricultural valley of La Convención in the southern highlands, where in 1958 the Trotskyite leader Hugo Blanco built upon an existing peasant movement and launched an extraordinarily successful campaign to organize agricultural unions. By 1962 these unions dominated the valley and had spread widely in the southern highlands. They were defeated only with the capture of Blanco in early 1963 and the application by the 1962–63 military government of extensive repression, combined with an agrarian reform within this region that distributed land and provided infrastructure and services.[84]

Belaúnde's many years of political campaigning in the highlands on the issue of agrarian reform had doubtless raised expectations of rural change, as well as expectations of leniency on the part of the Belaúnde government toward rural mobilization. Correspondingly, in mid- to late-1963, as Belaúnde assumed the presidency, Peru experienced an explosion of land seizures involving as many as 300,000 peasants throughout the highlands, constituting "one of the largest peasant movements in Latin American history" (Handelman 1975:121). Whereas earlier land seizures had generally involved the peaceful occupation of uncultivated zones, they now became more violent and included cultivated land. Interestingly, the national political left, which had been sharply repressed by the military government in early 1963, had little involvement in this wave of land seizures and thereby lost the opportunity to link itself with this massive popular mobilization. In late 1963, under pressure from the APRA-UNO coalition, President Belaúnde appointed a new minister of government who launched a major repression of the peasant mobilization (Béjar 1969:56–58; Handelman 1975:111–23).

These dramatic events had placed agrarian reform even more centrally on the national political agenda. Bourricaud (1970:325) points out that prior to 1956, any advocacy of agrarian reform had been a "badge of radicalism" identified with such grand figures of the Peruvian left as Mariátegui. With the increasingly frequent land seizures of the 1950s and President Prado's initiative at the beginning of his second presidency in 1956 to set up a commission to study agrarian reform, there was growing acceptance of the idea that some kind of land reform would have to occur, at least in the more traditional areas of the highlands (Bourricaud 1970:326). The initial agrarian reform implemented by the 1962–63 military government in La Convención valley underlined the military's support for wide-ranging reform.

What is remarkable, given the magnitude and urgency of the agrarian question and the broad consensus favoring agrarian reform, is that the APRA-UNO coalition successfully blocked meaningful land reform during the 1960s. This is certainly one of the reasons that APRA came to be perceived as hopelessly unable to help the country address the basic problems of the day. APRA likewise did not respond adequately to the opportunity to address the newly mobilized peasant sector as a potential new political constituency. While it did establish a national peasant organization in 1959 called FENCAP, this organization proved relatively ineffective in organizing and mobilizing peasants. Up to the period of the massive land invasions of 1962–63, FENCAP's program was minimal. After that point the FENCAP activities

[84] Neira 1973:460; Werlich 1978:263; Béjar 1969:56; Cotler 1978:330.

were expanded, but it adopted a trade-union approach parallel to that of the CTP, APRA's labor confederation, that gave it little leverage in the rapidly changing conditions of the highlands. Successfully penetrating the highlands required a new type of long-term organizational investment that APRA seemed incapable of making.[85]

Guerrilla Movements. Elements of the Peruvian left took seriously Fidel Castro's prediction that the Andes would become the Sierra Maestra[86] of South America and were doubtless further encouraged by guerrilla activities in Venezuela, Colombia, and Bolivia. As left groups continued to split away from Peru's traditional parties, a shift to tactics of insurgency was an important option. Yet the scope of actual guerrilla activity in Peru was limited. A brief guerrilla episode occurred in late 1963 when a small group of Peruvians who had received training in Cuba entered Peru through Bolivia, seeking to establish contact with the peasants in the Cuzco region who had earlier been mobilized by Hugo Blanco. The group was quickly destroyed by the police, but the death of one member of the group, a young Peruvian poet of upper-class origin named Javier Heraud, caused considerable shock at a national level. One of the guerrilla fronts later established in 1965 was named after him (Bourricaud 1970:222; Werlich 1978:277; Gott 1972:330–31).

In 1965 the MIR (formerly APRA Rebelde) and the National Liberation Army (ELN) established several small guerrilla fronts in the southern and central highlands and were initially more successful in sustaining themselves. Belaúnde's apparent lack of attention to the insurgency triggered extensive criticism from the congressional opposition and became yet another area in which his government appeared weak and indecisive. Yet within six months, a massive effort by army counterinsurgency forces had destroyed the movements (Werlich 1978:285–86; Cotler 1978:362–63). Though such subsequent developments as rumors that Ché Guevara was in the Peruvian highlands kept the issue of insurgency alive, there were no further guerrilla episodes in the 1960s. Notwithstanding the limited scope of the Peruvian insurgencies, they had an important impact on Peruvian politics, as we shall see below.

Military Role. The experience of suppressing the guerrilla insurgency, of dealing with the peasant movement of La Convención, and of observing the paralysis of Peruvian politics in the 1960s had a dramatic impact in military thinking. However, this impact must be seen in the framework of a longer-term evolution within the military. This evolution in part involved the changing attitudes toward APRA discussed above, from antipathy toward the party due to its radicalism and violence, to an anti-Aprismo found especially among younger officers that derived from frustration over the party's opposition to reform.

The concern with reform was rooted in the emergence within the Peruvian armed forces of what Stepan calls a "new professionalism" based on a strong

---

[85] Hilliker 1971:95–102; Handelman 1975:36n, 150; McClintock 1981:70, 280, 285.
[86] The mountains in Cuba where Castro's successful guerrilla movement began.

military concern with the interrelationship between internal security and national development. Such a concern may lead the military themselves to become actively involved in promoting national development, especially when—as in Peru—the civilian political system conspicuously fails to do so. This concern was already emerging within the Peruvian military in the second half of the 1950s, and the Cuban Revolution greatly accelerated the development of this position. The increasing importance of this orientation is reflected in the fact that by the mid-1960s, roughly half the articles in Peru's leading military journal addressed topics related to this new professionalism (Stepan 1978b:133; see more generally pp. 123–44).

The first major expression of this new orientation was the military government of 1962–63, discussed above. While the coup that brought this government to power derived in part from traditional anti-Aprismo, the military at this point was also centrally concerned with promoting change. The military government initiated a limited agrarian reform, as well as other reforms, and sought to ensure that they would be succeeded by a reform-oriented democratic government headed by Belaúnde.

The guerrilla episodes of the mid-1960s pushed this line of thinking further and had a particularly important radicalizing effect on the Intelligence Service, which had been directly involved in repressing the guerrillas. Military concern focused particularly on issues such as the agrarian question, the role of the state in labor-capital mediation, and the perceived threat to national sovereignty posed by the IPC dispute. The military increasingly believed that the democratic regime was incapable of taking needed initiatives in areas such as these, and began planning the implementation of such reforms through the militarization of the state (Stepan 1978b:135–40; Cotler 1978:363–65).

The Coup of 3 October 1968. The coup of 1968 had a series of more general and more proximate causes. At a more general level, it occurred against the backdrop of this changing self-definition of the military role and the military's preparation to carry out reform itself. As noted above, this involved the armed forces' concern with promoting fundamental economic and social reform as an indispensable prerequisite for national security, for preempting what they perceived as the growing radicalization of Peruvian society. This commitment had earlier led them to support Belaúnde in 1962–63. With APRA's successful efforts to undermine Belaúnde's program and the other failures of the Belaúnde administration, the armed forces began preparations to take matters into their own hands, and as early as February 1968 a coup was being prepared. While the Apro-Carlista alliance and the Ulloa economic program clearly was a step in a more constructive direction, the events of 1963–67 had so strongly reinforced military antipathy toward APRA and Haya that the likely victory of his new alliance in 1969 was completely unacceptable, and the coup that among other things blocked this victory became more and more likely (Cotler 1978:382; Werlich 1978:298–99).

The coup thus again reflected in part a veto of APRA, and again elements of both the "old" and the "new" version of the veto were present. The more senior officers and more traditional sectors of the armed forces still harbored antagonisms that dated from the days when APRA was perceived as a radical and violent party. Among the younger officers who played a central role in the coup, "APRA was contemptible for having sold out to the oligarchy in 1956" (Neira 1973:465), for its subsequent deals with the political right, and for its obstruction of reform under Belaúnde.

The immediate crisis that preceded the coup was a major political scandal over the terms of an agreement with the International Petroleum Company and the apparent disappearance of a crucial page of the agreement. Conflicts between Ulloa and the armed forces over the military budget appear also to have played a role as an immediate antecedent of the coup. However, while these events affected the timing of the coup, the underlying causes had been unfolding for some time. First of all, the IPC scandal came on top of a series of other failures and blunders by Belaúnde and his administration: his premature promise in 1963 to resolve the IPC dispute in 90 days, his inability or unwillingness to overcome the paralysis of his reform program, his foolish declaration shortly before his 1967 devaluation of the currency that a devaluation would be "treason," and the smuggling scandals of the latter part of his administration that directly involved figures close to the president. The IPC scandal was thus just another step in what was perceived as a longer-term pattern of failure and incompetence. The cumulative effect was an extraordinary sense of political "comedy," and of cynicism and incredulity regarding the government and Peruvian democracy, that had devastating consequences for the legitimacy of the regime (Werlich 1978:292; Cotler 1978:372, 381).

Capacity for Conflict Regulation. The review of these different policy areas provides further insights into the partial successes and ultimate failure to establish anything resembling an integrative party system in Peru. APRA held its own in the electoral arena, but conspicuously failed to build on its earlier reform program to respond to the broad spectrum of new political constituencies emerging in the 1950s and 1960s. The party was ultimately unable to deal with powerful new currents in the labor movement and likewise failed to respond to the massive changes occurring in the highlands. It was able to achieve a balancing act with the 1959 stabilization program that allowed it to support the program while sustaining its links with its labor base. However, by the time of the 1967 program, the political parameters had changed to such a degree that it became difficult to do this. While this second stabilization program was in important respects a success—due in part to APRA's role—the events surrounding this program proved to be a turning point in the erosion of APRA's position in the labor sector.

More broadly, APRA's move to the right and the position of opposition into which it was pushed from 1963 to 1967 made it an enemy rather than an exponent of reforms that appeared necessary to address major national problems, such as the agrarian question and the IPC case. The failure of these reforms occurred precisely at the time when the military became even more urgently concerned with seeing them implemented, further exacerbating military opposition to the existing civilian regime.

The combination of APRA's coalitional zigzags and these policy failures had created by the end of Belaúnde administration what Pease (1977:15–16) has called one of the most profound crises of governmental legitimacy that Peru had seen in some time. Though Przeworski (1986:51–52) has usefully argued that loss of legitimacy may have little consequence for regime change if a viable regime alternative is not available, in this case the military was quite ready to provide a regime alternative.

ARGENTINA

Overview of the Party System

The major electoral actors in Argentina during the heritage period were the Peronists, the People's Radical Civic Union (UCRP), and the Intransigent Radical Civic Union (UCRI).[87] Peronism's bastion of support was the urban working class, but it also drew considerable backing from the lower and middle classes in rural and semirural areas. Peronism was poorly institutionalized as a party, and whatever unity Peronism enjoyed in the post-1955 period depended not so much on a shared organizational framework or a common set of goals as on the exaltation of Perón and his perceived historical role.

Within the framework of this disunity and of the complex effects of the ban on Peronism, three major components may be identified. The first consisted of Perón himself and the traditional Peronist leadership, mostly former Peronist legislators, governors, party officials, or cabinet members from the 1946–55 period. These "orthodox" Peronists proclaimed personal loyalty to Perón, lacked independent power resources, and were largely pawns in a game controlled in important measure by Perón.

Second, the Peronist-dominated trade unions were the main organizational base of the movement, and Peronism's campaign finances and organizational capacity were largely in the hands of Peronist union leaders. The most important figure in the conservative wing of the labor movement was Augusto Vandor of the metalworkers' union, who by 1963 was mounting an increasingly explicit challenge to Perón's control of the day-to-day affairs of Peronism, including in the electoral sphere. As noted in Chapter 6, a wing of the labor movement located more nearly on the left received substantial encouragement from Perón as part of his effort to play different factions off of one another.

The third sector of Peronism was the neo-Peronist parties, whose leaders claimed continuity with the Peronist tradition but generally did not submit to Perón's personal direction. The neo-Peronists frequently found themselves exempt from electoral restrictions that applied to Perón and the orthodox Peronist politicians and were strongest in the less developed interior provinces, where electoral outcomes were of least concern to anti-Peronist military and civilian elites.

In the six major elections between 1957 and 1965, the Peronists generally won between 20 and 36 percent of the vote, divided according to the election in question between blank (protest) ballots, votes for *neo*-Peronist parties, and votes for small *non*-Peronist parties for which the Peronists voted in conjunction with an electoral alliance. Perón's coalition with the UCRI in 1958 produced a substantially larger vote. The level of the Peronist vote for most

[87] For useful descriptions of the party system, see Graillot (1973a) and Snow (1979:chap. 2).

of this period was thus well below that received either earlier (in the relatively free election of 1946) or later (in the elections of 1973). It appears the ban played a central role in preventing the Peronists from building the broader coalitions that made possible these stronger performances. The ban may also have discouraged voters from wasting their votes on Peronist candidates.

The two wings of the Radical Party both had primarily middle-class leadership and backing, but the UCRP was somewhat stronger in the more developed provinces, whereas the UCRI had a slight advantage in the less developed provinces of the interior. The UCRI, led initially by Arturo Frondizi, generally secured roughly 20 to 25 percent of the vote between 1957 and 1962. This party declined after it split prior to the 1963 elections. The UCRP, which received some 20 to 30 percent of the vote, proved more durable and later, prior to the 1973 elections, changed its name back to the Radical Civic Union (UCR). The two elected presidents during the years analyzed in this chapter both came from the Radicals: Frondizi of the UCRI and Illia of the UCRP. The ramifications of the ban on Peronism produced for these two leaders extremely dubious electoral mandates, and much of the politics of this period revolved around the crises of their governments, which must be understood in part in light of the ban.

Completing the party panorama was a host of minor actors, including three Socialist parties, a Communist party, numerous conservative parties whose labels differed from election to election and according to the province in which they operated, the Christian Democrats, the Progressive Democrats, the Popular Conservatives, and several smaller parties. These parties jointly won from 20 to 30 percent of the vote in each of the six major elections of the 1957–65 period.

The Ban on Peronism.   In Argentina, as in Peru, the electoral ban on the party that had led the incorporation project constituted a major axis around which party politics revolved during the heritage period. This ban was again in important measure a legacy of political and social antagonisms generated—or at least greatly intensified—during the incorporation period.

In three successive steps, the operation of the bans in Argentina and Peru was similar. In both countries the ban was in effect for the first presidential election of the heritage period (1958 and 1956, respectively); a coup canceled an important electoral victory by the populist party in 1962 in both countries; and a subsequent coup (in 1966 and 1968, respectively) had the consequence of canceling elections in which the populist party would probably have had further electoral victories.

In general, however, the ban was more severe in Argentina. In Peru, once the 1956 election had taken place, APRA was allowed to function fully as a party. APRA ran in all subsequent elections, and Haya de la Torre was permitted to return to Peru and to run for president, though in 1962 the military coup canceled the results of the presidential election in which he won a plurality. By contrast, in Argentina Peronism was illegal for much of the heritage period, Perón was not allowed to return to Argentina, and successive elections brought a long series of proscriptions directed against different Peronist groups. Yet the severity of the ban on Peronism decreased between 1957 and 1966, with the exception of an increase in restrictiveness prior to the 1963 election.

A final point of comparison of the bans suggests both similarities and differences. In both countries the organized labor movement affiliated with the populist party was able to function normally for most (Argentina) or all (Peru) of the heritage period. In Peru, the APRA party and party apparatus was also functioning normally, so this did not create an unusual situation. In Argentina, by contrast, where the ban both directly and indirectly inhibited the reestablishment of the authority and organization of the Peronist party, this created a dynamic in which the organized labor movement, rather than the party, became the strongest organizational locus of Peronism. This became a central feature of a dual political system in Argentina (Cavarozzi 1986:144) in which the sphere of legal parties and the sphere of the "organized sectors" of society—for example, business and labor, operated separately. Actors in the first sphere had little capacity to mediate conflicts in the other sphere.

The Disunity and Weak Organization of Peronism. This distinctive role of the union movement within Peronism points to a broader theme that is crucial for our analysis: the lack of unity and weak organization of Peronism. These attributes had several explanations, some connected with the ban and some involving longer-term factors. As argued in Chapter 5 and as emphasized by Little (1973b), Cavarozzi (1986:146), and McGuire (1989:chap. 2), prior to 1955 Perón failed to build a strong party organization that could provide a framework for the unity of the movement. This failure constitutes a base line against which the subsequent disunity of Peronism must be evaluated. In addition, as we saw in Chapter 3, since the beginning of the century the Argentine labor movement had been the most militant in the region, and with the rise of Perón in 1943 it was in organizational terms the strongest component of Peronism, which was in fact constructed "on top of" the labor movement. Hence, it is not surprising that the union wing of Peronism would reemerge in a strong and independent role in the late 1950s, especially after the experience of the repression under Aramburu and the Peronist resistance discussed in Chapter 6.

Other explanatory factors connected to the proscription of Peronism either reinforced this disunity or blocked efforts to overcome it. First of all, the ongoing exclusion of Peronism directly inhibited the development of party organization after 1955 (Cavarozzi 1986:147). In addition it had an indirect impact. Perón was banned from the country and unable to return to any kind of normal role either in Argentine politics or within his own party. He therefore had a strong incentive to sow divisions within Peronism, to perpetuate its organizational weakness, and to undermine rival centers of power within the movement as a means of maintaining whatever control he still enjoyed.[88]

[88] Baily 1965:358; Cavarozzi 1986:146–47; James 1988:176. For an alternative view of these patterns, see McGuire (1989:chap. 1).

Perón's destructive role in part paralleled that of Haya de la Torre in Peru—that is, the role of a personalistic, charismatic leader of a populist movement who was unwilling to give up his own power in the larger interest of the movement. In Peru, this problem occurred in the early 1960s when, if Haya had stepped aside and allowed Seoane to run, APRA might well have gained the presidency. In Argentina, with Perón in forced exile, this problem took the more extreme form of his systematic attempts to undermine powerful opponents within Peronism. This was, of course, something he had previously done while president. However, as president he had been the overwhelming center of authority within the movement. After 1955, the movement lacked such a center of authority, and Perón's efforts to undermine other leaders helped ensure that one was not established.

Finally, in addition to the role of the ban in encouraging this behavior on the part of Perón, the ban also reinforced the labor movement's already strong and potentially independent role because of the ban's much more limited application to the unions. The trade union sector of Peronism grew in strength at the same time that other spheres of party organization were stymied.

To reiterate, although the disunity and weak organization of Peronism had longer-term causes, the ban both aggrevated these features of the movement and frustrated efforts to overcome them. The impact of the ban was in part mediated through its consequences for the internal dynamics of Peronism, and the ban must be analyzed in these terms.

Peronism's Evolving Tactics.   Notwithstanding the evident disunity of Peronism, it can nonetheless be said that the movement did have an overall goal during this period, which paralleled that of APRA in Peru. Leaders of Peronism repeatedly sought to establish—through a coalition or potentially by themselves—the basic components of what we have called an integrative party system, in which Peronism would constitute or be part of a majority block in the electoral arena, located roughly at the center of the political spectrum, to which the labor movement would be linked politically. In Peru, APRA's basic tactic was to pursue this goal by forming coalitions with parties or leaders who were not banned. In Argentina, in the context of a ban that was more comprehensive and was applied differentially against Perón, orthodox Peronist politicians, and neo-Peronist parties, four different tactics were employed: (1) blank ballots were used to protest the ban; (2) Peronists entered coalitions to support candidates of other parties that were allowed to contest elections; (3) they participated in elections through neo-Peronist parties, which were led either by traditional Peronist politicians, often in the interior provinces, or by Peronist trade-unionists; and (4) they attempted to overcome the ban through reestablishing a Peronist party directly headed by Perón. The evolution of these alternative tactics obviously interacted with choices not only of the military, as they continually modified the ban on Peronism, but also of the non-Peronist parties. In particular, during the 1957–62 period the tactics of Frondizi's UCRI were a crucial element in the overall political equation.

The following discussion explores the interaction between these alternative options and the evolving crisis of Argentine politics that led up to the military coup of 1966. The discussion is in many respects parallel to O'Donnell's (1973:chap. 4) analysis of the "impossible game" discussed in the last chapter, but the focus is more centrally on the frustrated efforts by leaders within Peronism to create something resembling an integrative party system.

Elections of 1957 and 1958: Blank Ballots and the Coalitional Option. These two elections were discussed in the previous chapter and will be referred to only briefly here. The Constituent Assembly election of 1957 was held to select delegates to replace the Peronist Constitution of 1949. Peronists were banned and chose to follow the strategy of casting blank ballots, which gained a slight plurality. Subsequently, when delegates of Frondizi's party, the UCRI, walked out of the assembly to demonstrate their opposition to its anti-Peronist orientation, the assembly lost its quorum and was unable to conduct any business beyond adopting one constitutional change. Thus, the results of this first electoral round were delegitimated and disrupted both by the ban on Peronism and by partisan competition within the assembly that was heavily influenced by an attempt by the UCRI, exploiting the coalitional opportunity posed by the ban, to cultivate Peronist votes (Potash 1980:259–60).

The presidential election of 1958 saw the first attempt to overcome this impasse through a coalition between Peronism and a non-Peronist party. Perón made a pact with Frondizi, in which Frondizi promised to legalize Peronism and extend a variety of policy benefits to Peronism and to the popular sector once he was in office. With Peronist backing, Frondizi won a strong plurality in the presidential election and a decisive legislative majority. However, a series of factors soon undermined this coalition: a continuing military veto on the restoration of Perón or the Peronist party; military opposition to policies favorable to the labor movement; a shift in Frondizi's own policy preferences away from the nationalist and populist platform on which he had campaigned; the exigencies of an economic crisis that created great pressure to implement an economic stabilization plan; and Frondizi's own ambivalence about legalizing Peronism, because this would reduce his chances of winning Peronists over to his own party. The result was a rapid unraveling of the Frondizi-Peronist alliance and the eruption of a major episode of worker protest in 1958–59, intended in important measure as a direct political assault on the government.

Electoral Alternatives under Frondizi, 1958–62: The Peronist Party Option, Blank Ballots, and Neo-Peronism. The failure of the coalition with Frondizi pushed the Peronists into an unsuccessful search for alternative modes of electoral participation, and during the Frondizi period they tried to reestablish a Peronist party, then returned to blank ballots, and finally revived the coalitional strategy. The first of these alternatives was initiated in mid-1959, when orthodox Peronist leaders within Argentina attempted to constitute a new Peronist party through which Perón, in collaboration with the new party's leadership, could once again play a direct role in Argentine politics. To get around the ban on using party labels based on the names of individuals, the new organization would be called the Justicialist Party. However, whereas the Frondizi government and the military officers on whom its survival depended were willing to tolerate the neo-Peronist parties, they were opposed to any scheme that would restore to Perón himself a role in Argentine politics. In October 1959, Frondizi signed a decree banning the Justicialist Party on the grounds that it violated the 1956 Party Statute, both because it had selected for the party name the official name of the earlier Perón administration, and because it was directly answerable to Perón (Potash 1959:521; Ranis 1965:85).

Given the ban on the Justicialist Party, in 1960 the Peronists again adopted the strategy of blank ballots in the first nationwide election after Frondizi's inauguration. Most of the neo-Peronist parties, including the Popular Union, followed the Peronist leadership and refrained from presenting candidates. As in the constituent assembly election of 1957, the blank ballots gained a plurality of the vote (Show 1979:28).

The blank ballot strategy was successful in demonstrating the underlying strength of the Peronists. However, it was increasingly challenged by party activists, especially after the victories of various UCRI candidates in traditionally Peronist provinces of the interior in 1961. These results, when combined with the victory of a Socialist candidate in a by-election in the federal capital, apparently with support from Peronist voters, added to the fears that the long-term result of this strategy would be the gradual defection of Peronist voters to other parties. As a consequence, Peronist activists pushed for the creation of neo-Peronist parties and, where such parties were banned, they supported parties that could pose a viable electoral challenge to the UCRI.[89]

Although Perón supported the neo-Peronist strategy, the upcoming 1962 elections presented severe dilemmas, not only for the future of the party but for Perón's own leadership of the movement. On the one hand, the creation of neo-Peronist parties posed the possibility of increased fractionalization at a time when polls showed that electoral victory depended on the unity of Peronism. On the other hand, the successful unification of Peronism posed two serious issues. First, the proscription of Perón's own participation meant that other Peronists would lead the electoral effort, creating the possibility of major challenges to his role as head of the movement. Second, too big an electoral victory would almost certainly lead to a coup, an outcome more to be feared than electoral defeat. In the face of these conflicting pressures, Perón adopted an increasingly ambiguous position toward electoral participation in the 1962 elections and initiated a series of maneuvers to protect and strengthen his hold on the movement (Potash 1980:356).

The greatest challenge to Perón's continued supremacy came from Augusto Vandor, leader of the metalworkers' union who had come to promi-

[89] Guardo 1963:292–93; James 1979:251, 259; Potash 1980:328.

nence after the failure of the 1959 general strike. Vandor headed a strong, well-organized segment of the Peronist movement, controlling the strategic Buenos Aires and federal capital branches of the neo-Peronist Popular Union Party (Lamadrid 1986:26). Vandor supported the candidacy of the Peronist leader Andrés Framini for governor of Buenos Aires, and a victory of this ticket would give the Popular Union access to considerable patronage and greatly enhance Vandor's claims to leadership.

Faced with this threat, Perón first indicated his preference for a return to the blank ballot strategy, playing on the fears of a possible coup held by some Peronist activists. But Vandor and members of the Peronist labor grouping, the "62," convinced Perón that a return to the old strategy could be disastrous for the Peronist movement. Perón's second move was his surprising decision that he himself would be candidate for vice governor of Buenos Aires and that he would lead the Popular Union lists in the federal capital in the contests for the National Assembly. Perón may have believed this step would lead to the proscription of all Popular Union candidates. In the event, the military reacted quickly and did veto Perón's candidacy. However, they left the rest of the Popular Union's candidates free to run. Having exhausted other options, Perón was forced to endorse the Popular Union lists and thus supported the neo-Peronist alternative (Potash 1980:355–56).

President Frondizi, for his part, was also seeking to gain maximum advantage from existing—or potential—electoral arrangements. The proscription of the Justicialist Party in 1959 should be understood in part in this light. It was common knowledge that the decree banning the party was signed under military pressure. At the same time, the ban was convenient from Frondizi's point of view, given his goal of absorbing the Peronist electorate into a new "integrationist" movement. The appearance that the ban derived from military pressure allowed Frondizi to pursue this goal at the same time that he championed the goal of reinstating a more competitive electoral regime.

The electoral results between 1959 and 1961 did not permit a clear assessment of the relative strength of the UCRI and the Peronist movement, and hence of Frondizi's success in winning over the Peronist vote. However, Kvaternik (1987:37) suggests that the results of the 1961 contest, in which the UCRI won several provinces, led to hopes that the UCRI could defeat the Peronists. Subsequently, the 1962 elections became a crucial test of this strategy. Although early polls showed that the UCRI held a slim advantage in Buenos Aires, the large number of undecided voters convinced Frondizi that the Peronists would probably win the province, thus dealing a major political blow to the UCRI and, at worst, leading to a coup (Pandolfi 1968:137). As a result, Frondizi sought military support for a proscription of Peronist candidates. Both of the principal factions of the military, the *gorilas* and the *legalistas*, refused to intercede, the former because they saw a Peronist victory as a ready-made excuse for a coup, the latter because they did not wish to strain military unity through further involvement in politics (Potash 1980:357–58). Frondizi was thus unable to cite military pressure as a reason for banning the Peronists, and he was also reluctant to antagonize Peronist voters any more than he already had, since this interfered with the UCRI's goals of winning over part of the Peronist electorate. Hence, the government decided to allow the neo-Peronist option to play itself out and took the risk of allowing various neo-Peronist parties to present candidates in 1962.[90]

The results were substantially what Frondizi, Perón, and the more cautious Peronist activists expected. Framini, who had received strong support from the "62" and headed a ticket dominated by the Peronist left, was victorious in Buenos Aries, receiving 37 percent of the vote, well ahead of his nearest rival from the UCRI. Nationwide, the Popular Union received nearly 17 percent of the vote and other Peronist parties roughly 15 percent, for a combined total of nearly 32 percent (Snow 1979:28).

This electoral outcome triggered an immediate military alert and the beginning of an extended debate among top officers over the appropriate response. Under military pressure, Frondizi ordered military interventors to take power in the provinces where Peronists had won. Within a week and a half, after Frondizi refused to respond to military pressure to resign, he was removed by the armed forces. He was replaced by José María Guido, president of the Senate, who was next in the line of succession because Frondizi's initial vice president had not been replaced after his resignation in 1958. Despite the formal continuation of civilian rule, the government was dominated by the military during Guido's year and a half in office.[91] Thus, the first major effort by Peronism to reenter the electoral arena ended in failure and in an interim military government.

The Guido Period, 1962–63: New Electoral Restrictions and a Failed Electoral Front.   The 1962 coup had important consequences for the party system and for the leadership struggle within the Peronist movement. In response to the Peronist victory, new restrictions were placed on electoral participation, which reflected conflicts within the military. The *legalista* faction of the armed forces, which was opposed both to Peronism and to military government, successfully arranged a quick return to full civilian rule. However, it was necessary to make some concession to the *gorila* faction, which saw Peronism as a possible precursor of Communism and thus favored a military dictatorship that would expunge all traces of Peronism from Argentine politics. Consequently, a new statute was adopted that greatly restricted the types of parties and candidates that could participate electorally.[92]

These new restrictions accentuated a tendency, already growing within the movement, for Peronist politicians to distance themselves from Perón's lead-

---

[90] It should be noted that other analysts cast a slightly different interpretation on Frondizi's role at this juncture. Wynia portrays Frondizi's decision as a gamble that he could defeat the Peronists (1978:107). Rock claims that it was the military that tried to force Frondizi to proscribe the neo-Peronist parties and that the UCRI's victory in three gubernatorial elections in 1961 convinced Frondizi that his party could actually defeat the Peronists (Rock 1985:342). Whichever of these interpretations is correct, however, has no effect on the central arguments of this chapter.

[91] Kvaternik 1987:58–63; Potash 1980:361ff.; Liewen 1964:10–11, 18–19.

[92] Rouquié 1982:213; Kvaternik 1987:84–88; Snow 1965:18.

ership. Neo-Peronist politicians began to consolidate their hold on several interior provinces, while Vandor continued to gain national prominence. Vandor's rise came primarily at the expense of textile workers' leader Andrés Framini, who as head of the country's second largest industrial union commanded considerable power and prestige within the "62."

In the face of Vandor's growing power, Perón threw his support behind Framini, who among the prominent Peronists of the day (and certainly among the unionists) was the least inclined to distance himself from Perón. Framini began to push this organization toward the left, advocating such controversial policies as worker control of production, nationalization of basic industries, and land reform through noncompensated expropriation. Since Perón had never proposed such policies during his own tenure in office, one might conclude that his support of Framini at this point was strongly influenced by his desire to contain Vandor and to restrain the growing independence of Peronism from his own leadership.[93]

Despite the efforts of Vandor and other neo-Peronist unionists and politicians to portray the Peronist movement as more centrist and restrained, the *gorila* fraction within the military reacted negatively to the court's ruling in 1962 that the Popular Union met the requirements of the new Political Party Statute. After a subsequent rebellion by the navy *gorilas* was suppressed by the *legalistas*, their complaints were heeded and new restrictions on participation were imposed. The penalties for Peronist propagandizing were increased, and the government issued a decree formalizing a previously implicit understanding that the Popular Union would not be allowed to submit nominations for executive office, but only for national deputies, provincial legislators, municipal councilors, and school board members. The government's April 1963 decree also barred the UCRI from running a presidential candidate, reflecting the military's distrust of Frondizi in light of his earlier collaboration with Peronism.[94]

The banning of Popular Union candidacies at the executive level gave Perón a new opportunity to consolidate his hold over Peronism. Ever since Guido had taken office, the Popular Union, the UCRI, and several smaller parties had been discussing the formation of an electoral front that would support a single slate of candidates. The military had generally supported such an effort as a means of integrating Perón's following into the party system and reducing his control over the movement, and apparently this military would approve such a front as long as the presidential candidate was not a Peronist and did not belong to the Frondizi wing of the UCRI (Kvaternik 1978:421–22).

A leading candidate for the front nomination was Oscar Alende, the head of the UCRI's National Committee and governor of Buenos Aires from 1958 to 1962. But Alende's bid was undercut by Perón's surprising decision to back

[93] Ducatenzeiler 1980:111–12; Lamadrid 1986:77–85; Calello and Parcero 1984, vol. 1:55–56.
[94] Kvaternik 1987:122–25; Snow 1965:20; Halperín Donghi 1983:136; O'Donnell 1973:187–88.

the candidacy of Vicente Solano Lima, head of the tiny Popular Conservative Party. Perón's backing of a relative nonentity with little popular support—of a conservative businessman with no relationship with the union movement just one year after his apparent shift to the left—strongly indicates that his choice was shaped by his desire to place a man in power personally beholden to him, thus protecting his leadership role.

However, this electoral front was also banned. The government, under military pressure, extended the prohibition of Peronist candidates for executive positions to those who had any connection with the Popular Union. This meant the end of Solano Lima's candidacy, given his close link to Popular Union politicians. Although the military's decision was a serious defeat for the front, the decision was by no means a defeat for Perón. The ban allowed Perón to return to the blank ballot strategy, this time with the support of the "62" and prominent leaders of the Popular Union.[95]

With the banning of Peronist participation, of Frondizi's wing of the UCRI, and of the front, the 1963 presidential elections were fought out between the remaining parties—the most important of which was the UCRP, the other wing of the Radical Party, led by Arturo Illia. Illia was victorious, winning the presidency with only 25 percent of the vote (Cantón, 1968a, vol. 1:236–38) and thereby inaugurating a difficult period in which the president himself had a weak mandate and the legislature was dominated by opposition parties that had been banned from contesting the presidency.

The Illia Period: Further Evolution and Failure of the Neo-Peronist Option. Due to Illia's weak electoral mandate, he began his presidency in many respects in a vulnerable political position. Ironically, his government was marred both by confrontations with the labor movement and by skepticism within the military and civilian elite over his apparent vacillation in dealing with Peronism. He also faced crises over economic policy and the widespread perception that he was not an effective leader. He was referred to as the "turtle" because of his slow response to political challenges.

Nonetheless, the beginning of the Illia administration offered some promise that the stalemate and confrontation of the previous years could be overcome. Illia campaigned for the presidency advocating an approach to development policy that emphasized nationalism and economic expansion. In contrast to Frondizi, Illia held to his campaign commitments regarding economic policy, reversing the foreign oil concessions granted by Frondizi and initially granting wage increases favorable to labor (Rock 1985:345). Illia's economic policies were thus more compatible than those of Frondizi with a conciliatory posture toward Peronism.

In fact, these economic policies were accompanied by a major effort at accommodation with Peronism, and Illia believed, along with the *legalista* faction of the military, which was now dominant, that the ban on Peronism had become a major obstacle to political stability in Argentina. Illia's strategy toward Peronism was twofold. First, he hoped that the opportunity for nor-

[95] McGuire 1989:chap. 3; Kvaternik 1987:125–29; James 1979:296; Rowe 1964:17n.

mal electoral participation would encourage the Peronists to abondon the massive use of strikes and other disruptive tactics, leading them instead to work within the existing political framework. Second, he tried to weaken the Peronists politically and to convince workers that his own UCRP was a more effective vehicle for achieving their political aspirations (Whitaker 1965:16–17; Baily 1965:357; 1966:303).

Developments within Peronism also seemed favorable to an accommodation. Vandor had won out over Framini, who was identified with the Peronist left. Vandor set out to build a labor-based Peronist party independent of Perón, thereby placing Perón in the role of the figurehead of the movement and consolidating his own control not only over the union wing but also the political branch of Peronism. Vandor was careful to avoid the radical political rhetoric employed by Framini and was willing to accept the conditions laid down in the 1965 Statute of Political Parties. Though Vandor was an expert at the dramatic use of strikes, by this time he had also established excellent relations with industrial management and maintained active contacts within the military (Rouquié 1982:236). These developments appeared to increase further the likelihood of reintegrating Peronism through a neo-Peronist strategy in which the union movement would play a central role.

In May and June of 1964 Vandor orchestrated a Plan de Lucha (battle plan), a massive wave of strikes and factory occupations to protest Illia's economic policies, his failure to eliminate all restrictions on Peronism, and his attempt to divide the movement. Though in the long-run this labor action significantly increased elite perception of a serious threat to the existing order, in the short run it represented a major step forward in Vandor's rise to power within Peronism.

In December 1964, an additional development further strengthened Vandor's position: an unsuccessful attempt by Perón to return to Argentina. After elaborate preparations, which were strongly supported by Peronist leaders within Argentina, Perón flew from Madrid to Rio de Janeiro, where the Brazilian authorities, in response to a request from the Argentine government, removed him from the plane, which was scheduled to continue to Buenos Aires. The Brazilians later placed Perón on the return flight to Spain. This clumsy incident served to dramatize a crucial aspect of the proscription of Peronism,—that is, Perón's exclusion from the country—and to increase the plausibility of Vandor's approach of developing a political party based on Peronism without Perón.[96]

Earlier, in July 1964, Vandor had won full control of Peronism and revived the Justicialist Party, with Perón as its titular head, in the expectation that the party would be able to compete in the 1965 election. Both Illia and "growing public sentiment" (Whitaker 1965:19) favored this outcome, and three developments appeared to make it less risky for sectors skeptical about

[96] Whitaker 1965:18; Page 1983:380–89; Rouquié 1982:237–38. Whether Vandor deliberately orchestrated Perón's failed return to Argentina in order to strengthen his own position, or whether the goals of relevant actors were more complex and confused than this, is unclear. See Rouquié (1982:237), as opposed to Page (1983:384).

Peronism. First, the Peronists could not win the kind of victory they achieved in 1962, both because no governorships were at stake and because of a new system of proportional representation. Second, there was a perception that the Peronists' strength had declined due to internal conflict. Finally, it was hoped that an upswing in the economy would reduce the Peronists' appeal (Whitaker 1965:17–19).

In the March 1965 election, the neo-Peronist party associated with Vandor, the Popular Union, along with the provincial neo-Peronist parties, won an impressive 36 percent of the vote, as opposed to 29 percent for Illia's UCRP, giving them a substantial delegation in the national legislature and hence a major new role in that body. As always, a Peronist victory raised the issue among anti-Peronist officers of possible military interference in the elections, but this did not occur, and the Peronists who won were allowed to assume office (Baily 1965:357; Rouquié 1982:239).

On one level, these events appeared to favor the further consolidation of political stability in Argentina. The March 1965 elections established neo-Peronists as the main opposition force, and the main body of the Peronist unions now moderated their strike behavior, attempting to avoid any acts that would be perceived as subversive. It was now at least possible that if the Peronists maintained their political moderation and their distance from Perón, they might have the opportunity to make major further gains in the 1967 elections for governors. Thus, up to this point, Illia's approach to dealing with Peronism appeared to be more successful than any during the previous decade (Baily 1965:356–59; Page 1983:390–91).

However, a major new complication presented itself. The unity of Peronism and Vandor's increasing dominance within the movement represented a challenge to Perón's control. To counter this challenge, Perón sent his third wife, Isabel Martínez, first to Paraguay in May of 1965 and then to Buenos Aires. Isabel successfully galvanized the opposition to Vandor, leading to a split in the main Peronist union organization, the "62," and also among the Peronists in the legislature (Page 1983:391–93; Rouquié 1982:240).

The confrontation between Perón and Vandor culminated in a decisive "test" (Rouquié 1982:240) in an election for the governor of the province of Mendoza in April 1966. Vandor had backed a neo-Peronist candidate, and two days before the election Perón conveyed a recorded message that ordered his followers to vote for a different neo-Peronist candidate. Though the two Peronist candidates lost to a conservative rival, Perón's candidate gained over 100,000 votes, to just over 60,000 for Vandor's candidate. Thus, in an open electoral competition, it was demonstrated that Perón himself, even under these slightly irregular circumstances, could command mass support. The election discredited Vandor's role of promoting Peronism without Perón, and Vandor abandoned his effort to lead the political wing of Peronism (Page 1983:392; Rouquié 1982:240; James 1988:186).

Though for the time being Vandorismo continued to have a strong presence in the national Congress, a major opportunity for integrating Peronism on a more stable basis into the political system had been lost. It seemed that at least the *legalista* faction in the armed forces favored Vandor's version of Peronism, and—as noted above—there was some possibility that if the Vandoristas had continued their political moderation, the military would have permitted them to run in the 1967 elections. But the viability of Vandor's effort to create a coherent, relatively unified version of Peronism in which Perón did not play a direct role had now been seriously challenged. As a consequence, the approach of the 1967 elections would raise complex and unpredictable issues for the military of dealing with Peronist candidates and with Perón's own role in the elections, issues that could be threateningly divisive for the armed forces. The prospect that Peronism would approach the 1967 elections newly unified around Perón himself made those elections far more threatening and also tended to discredit Illia for having tolerated these political initiatives of Perón and Isabel (Halperín Donghi 1983:150–51).

Vandor's political initiatives now took quite a different direction. Vandor had well-established contacts within the armed forces, and at this point he entered into negotiations with the military in order to limit the negative impact of a possible coup on his power in the union movement (Page 1983:391; Rouquié 1982:236, 240). This turn of events meant that both the *legalista* and other, more adamantly anti-Peronist sectors of the military now had some interest in a coup. At the same time that *legalista* officers were negotiating with Vandor about the details of post-coup labor policy, anti-Peronist officers also favored a coup as a means to avoid a Peronist victory in the 1967 elections (Rouquié 1982:247).

If the election in Mendoza had discredited Vandor's political initiatives, subsequent events further eroded Illia's position as he wrestled with the issue of Peronism, which was the central problem of his administration (Rouquié 1982:235). Hoping to take advantage of the major split in Peronism, Illia decreed new regulations for unions that were highly unfavorable to the existing union leaders. However, Illia misjudged the union leaders' ability to retaliate. Using their strength in the Chamber of Deputies, the Vandoristas delayed Illia's budget—thereby seriously disrupting the financial basis of the government—and circulated a petition in the Congress calling for Illia's impeachment. Illia also miscalculated his ability to win over Peronist voters to his UCRP, and the Peronists were victorious in a series of provincial elections. In an election in May 1966 in the Province of Catamarca, Illia's UCRP was sufficiently confident of victory that they passed a law giving the party with the first plurality 60 percent of the legislative seats. When the Peronists won a plurality with 45 percent of the vote, they gained control of the provincial government (Baily 1966:303–4). Illia's initially successful policies toward Peronism now seemed to have been thoroughly derailed.

As we shall see below, the Illia government did not end in a dramatic crisis like that of the final weeks of the Belaúnde government in Peru. Yet this ironic failure to resolve the Peronist question, along with the further conflicts between Peronism and the government, added further to the cumulative sense of crisis, failure, and stalemate.

Assessment. In many respects, the evolution of Peru and Argentina during these years exhibits remarkable parallels. In the first election following military rule at the start of the heritage period (1956 and 1958), APRA and Peronism were banned, and each entered into a coalition with the candidate of another party who lacked a working class base, thereby electing a new president (Prado and Frondizi) with a strong plurality in the presidential vote and a clear legislative majority. Though this president was far more successful in Peru in establishing a coherent direction for public policy, by the end of both presidencies there was a widespread sense of frustration—very crucially within the military—over a pressing agenda of unaddressed policy issues. In Argentina this failure was, in part, directly attributable to the ban, and in Peru the ban at least indirectly contributed to this outcome.

In the context of this frustration, in 1962 these populist parties won important electoral victories in both countries, and these victories were soon canceled by military coups. Following roughly a year of interim military rule, both militaries called new elections in 1963. At this point, in part as a consequence of the ban, a weak, middle-class president came to power who lacked a working-class electoral base and who was confronted with major congressional opposition from the populist party, which during his presidential period came to occupy a strong position in the legislature. This produced further stalemate and widespread perception that the political system was not functioning properly, pointing to the possibility of a coup that would introduce an entirely new political system.

Yet prior to this coup, the party system in both countries had a chance to "redeem" itself. In Peru this involved the "Apro-Carlista" alliance of 1968 between APRA and Acción Popular, led by Ulloa, which initiated a period of remarkable policy innovation that overcame many of the earlier policy failures. This alliance had the merit of presenting an APRA ticket for the 1969 elections that would not be headed by Haya de la Torre, in contrast to the presidential elections of 1962 and 1963. In Argentina it involved the trade-union-led variant of neo-Peronism, headed by Vandor, which provided a channel of Peronist political participation that had the dual merit of being independent of Perón and of being led by Vandor, who was well-respected within important segments of the economic and military elite.

Many differences between Peru and Argentina are also evident, one of the most important being a major contrast in the behavior of the leaders of the two populist parties in this final phase of "redemption." Haya, who in the early 1960s had probably cost his party the presidency by refusing to allow another candidate to head APRA's ticket, acquiesced to the leadership of Ulloa. In a sense this was easier for him to do, since he was allowed to be in Peru, was an active participant in day-to-day politics, and would probably have held substantial power under a coalition government. However, by this time the negative repercussions of the earlier stalemate had gone too far to avert a coup. In Argentina, by contrast, Perón was still banned from the country, and the failure of his attempt to return in late 1964 had dramatically underlined his exclusion. For Perón, the cost of Vandor's success in terms of the loss of his own power was probably far greater than the cost of Ulloa's success for Haya, leading to Perón's decision to undermine Vandor's political movement. The ban in Argentina thus had a mischievous effect on Perón's behavior.

Another major contrast between Argentina and Peru is the difference in the evolution of the parties, which was initially explored in the aftermath chapter. In Peru, APRA followed a pattern of conservatization that went further than in most other cases of party incorporation, as the party sought acceptance within the established political system. Yet APRA was placed in the contradictory position of giving up important parts of its program in order to gain access to power, while never achieving sufficient access to power to give it adequate control of state resources to maintain and reinforce the new definition of the party. In this as well as other senses, APRA was caught in the damned-if-you-do, damned-if-you-don't predicament in which it both compromised its program and later lost much of its trade-union base.

In Argentina, an opposite dynamic prevailed. Peronism's access to power was even more partial, and there was less need or opportunity to carry out a comprehensive homogenization and conservatization of the movement as a price for gaining such access. At certain points, greater moderation appeared in some segments of Peronism—as in the political party phase of Vandorism in the mid-1960s—but there was no comprehensive conservatization like that in Peru. In addition, whatever control Perón managed to maintain over his movement was achieved not primarily by excluding opponents, but by encouraging diversity and by playing Peronism's factions off against one another.

We may conclude this assessment by returning to the larger question of Argentina's potential for forming an integrative party system during this period and the reasons it failed to do so. As in Peru, the possibility of establishing such a system was present. The Peronists won majorities in free elections in the 1940s and the 1970s, and in the period considered here they potentially could either have commanded an electoral majority on their own,[97] or could have established one through a coalition. Further, the bulk of the Peronist labor movement was located roughly at the center of the political spectrum, another basic component of an integrative party system. Yet the ban on Peronism proved to be an obstacle to both of the routes through which Peronism might have taken advantage of its potential majority status. A principal direct expression of the ban was the military's repeated initiatives to block Peronism's coalitional option, and a major indirect effect was to give Perón a strong incentive to undermine the trade-union variant of the neo-Peronist option. Both of these outcomes helped to block the construction of an integrative party system.

[97] It seems likely that contesting elections under the shadow of the ban contributed to holding the Peronist vote to closer to one-third during this period.

Opposition and Crises of the Late 1950s and 1960s

In the 1940s and 1950s, Argentine politics had already experienced a sustained polarization between Peronism and anti-Peronism. Beginning with the end of the 1950s, the international political climate in the region—including very centrally the Cuban revolution—added a new dimension to this polarization and to the military reaction it triggered. Substantial interest in and support for Cuba was found among Argentine students, intellectuals, and workers, and the Cuban model was made perhaps even more salient by the fact that Che Guevara was Argentine. Guevara appeared to have a direct link with the effort to establish a guerrilla insurgency in Argentina. The Argentine military saw the Cuban model and the enthusiasm for it within Argentina as a grave threat to national security, and the question of the diplomatic and political relations with Cuba of the Argentine government became a highly charged political issue.[98]

Economic change also contributed to political tensions. Within the regional framework of important increases in the entry of foreign investment and transnational corporations into the Latin American economies, Argentina received a substantial amount of such investment, and a large number of TNC subsidiaries were established in the late 1950s and early 1960s (Kaufman 1979:222). Given the Argentine political setting, in which a highly politicized labor movement was well situated to express nationalist opposition to such economic changes, this added yet another dimension to the polarization of Argentine politics.

Party System.   To an even greater extent than in Peru, the political transformations during this period that were perceived as threatening by established elites did *not* include a radicalization in the party system. A major fragmentation of parties occurred, and nearly 70 opposition parties competed in the 1963 and 1965 elections. Yet no significant move to the left took place within the major parties, and parties of the left remained small. Although left-oriented Peronists did win some key posts in the 1962 election (which was annulled), in the next couple of years the growing dominance of the Vandoristas meant that the moderate wing of Peronism held electoral sway.

Instead, the crisis at the level of party politics centrally involved the numerous complications that arose from the ongoing electoral ban on Peronism, which as we have seen played a central role in producing the extremely weak and ambiguous electoral mandates for the two constitutionally elected presidents during this period, Frondizi and Illia. This outcome was particularly dramatic in the case of Illia, a minor, provincial politician who until shortly before the election was not thought to have any chance of winning and who gained the presidency with only a quarter of the national vote. These weak governments were dramatically incapable of dealing with issues

---

[98] Potash 1980:335, 338ff.; Rock 1985:340; O'Donnell 1973:72; Kohl and Litt 1974:323n.

such as labor militancy and economic policy, and by the mid-1960s the party system had been thoroughly discredited.

Labor Movement. Whereas the crisis in the party system and at the level of successive presidential administrations involved an ongoing stalemate and inability to take decisive action, the perceived crisis posed by the labor movement involved precisely its remarkable capacity for collective action. This capacity had been a basic feature of Argentine politics since the beginning of the century. Hence, the occurrence of major waves of strikes during these years was in no way, by itself, distinctive. The labor movement remained predominantly Peronist, and the Communists only controlled a few unions (Snow 1979:91). Thus, the major opening to the left in the labor sector that occurred in Peru did not take place in Argentina during this period.

What was distinctive during the period beginning in the late 1950s—and which contributed greatly to the growing sense of crisis—was the form and intensity of worker mobilization. In the late 1950s and early 1960s, in addition to conventional strikes, street demonstrations, and militant declarations of worker demands, the unions in Argentina increasingly resorted to factory occupations, in a number of instances taking as hostages executives of the companies they occupied. Under the unions' Battle Plan of May to June 1964, the country was divided into eight zones, which were systematically paralyzed during successive 24-hour periods by work stoppages and factory seizures. The CGT estimated the number of workplace occupations during those two months at approximately 11,000 and the number of workers involved at over 3 million. These figures have been shown to be seriously overestimated, yet even the Argentine government puts the number of workplace occupations at 2,361 (McGuire 1989:204–8). In addition to this major episode of overt worker mobilization, the 1962 Huerta Grande program of the "62"—though it represented the proclaimed program of just one wing of this labor group—also presented a threatening picture of union radicalization in its call for nationalization of key sectors of the economy, including the banks, expropriation of large agricultural holdings without compensation, repudiation of the foreign debt, and worker control of production (O'Donnell 1988:44, 47–48; Snow 1979:94; Munck et al. 1987:158).

On one level, these actions and declarations must be seen as part of a game of political opposition, involving a systematic attempt to discredit the government and precipitate a coup, and in that sense the apparent leftism of the labor movement was simply a tactic. However, according to O'Donnell, three features caused these actions to be perceived as a more fundamental threat: the remarkable scope of coordinated mobilization involved in this massive takeover of Argentina's industrial sector, which represented a dramatic assault on the control of these enterprises; the evident enthusiasm of the workers in going beyond the dictates of the national leadership, as in the taking of hostages and in instances when the workers kept the occupied factories in production; and the possibility that, at some point in the future, this capacity for collective action might be employed in pursuit of political goals far more threatening than the destabilization of the Frondizi or Illia governments. As a result, these labor actions contributed greatly to the perception that Argentina was not simply suffering from the crisis of a particular presidential administration or regime, but instead was moving toward a far more profound crisis of "social domination" that threatened capitalist control of the work place and of the economy (O'Donnell 1988:48–51).

Politics of Stabilization. As we saw in Chapter 6, the ban on Peronism and Frondizi's precarious coalitional relationship with the Peronist movement left Frondizi in a poor position to win labor's acquiescence to the severe austerity program he imposed. The fact that this program was accompanied by a substantial denationalization of the economy only intensified the opposition of this nationalistic labor movement. In Peru in the same year, APRA went along with what was also in a sense a politically "embarrassing" stabilization effort, receiving ongoing organizational and institutional payoffs in exchange for its cooperation. Though Frondizi tried to provide some benefits to the labor movement, he was prohibited from delivering sufficient payoffs to win its cooperation. In particular, he could not pay off its top leadership—specifically Perón—and was thus unable to establish a political exchange at that level to secure cooperation with the program. Frondizi's austerity program of 1958–59 was a dramatic failure and triggered a wave of worker protest, and his policies of industrial development that began in 1959, though they met with some initial success, likewise generated major confrontations with the labor movement, massive strikes, and high inflation (Rock 1985:338–41).

In contrast to Frondizi's central preoccupation with economic stabilization and austerity measures, Illia's policies emphasized economic nationalism and an effort to stimulate economic growth. He did not work with the International Monetary Fund, as had Frondizi, but instead was oriented more toward the contrasting policy recommendations of the Economic Commission for Latin America. Nonetheless, Illia faced parallel problems of enforcing basic economic policies and wage policies in the face of intense union militancy, and in early 1966 he was forced to abandon wage controls when confronted with a new round of strikes. The failure of these economic policies contributed to the growing perception that Illia was an ineffective president and that the unions represented an obstacle to economic development.[99]

Peasant Mobilization and Guerrilla Movements. As noted earlier, Argentina did not have an a extensive peasantry. The agricultural production of importance to the national economy was based on non-labor-intensive forms of production, involved wage labor, and was located in the modern sector. Within this modern agricultural sector, the sugar industry did experience an important wave of worker militancy in the mid-1960s (Waisman 1982:115–18), but this was not part of a larger pattern of rural mobilization. Hence, the type of massive peasant mobilization that occurred in Peru in the 1960s was absent in Argentina.

Beginning in the late 1960s Argentina would experience major urban and

---

[99] Wynia 1978:112–15; Mallon and Sourrouille 1975:29; O'Donnell 1988:45.

rural guerrilla movements. Yet the period considered in this chapter saw only small-scale episodes of guerrilla activity.[100] In 1959 the Uturuncos (Quechua for *tigermen*) established a base in a mountainous area of Tucumán province, and in 1963 the People's Guerrilla Army (EGP) appeared in a mountainous region of Salta province. Members of these groups were generally of urban and student origin and were inspired in important degree by the victory of the Cuban revolution, in addition to having some ties with Peronism. The EGP received funds and arms from Cuba, and three members of the group had earlier fought in the Cuban Sierra Maestra. Both of these insurgencies were quickly defeated.[101]

In their immediate threat to internal security, these guerrilla episodes were of little importance. Yet the larger conservative reaction to them must be seen in light of the perceived threat posed by the considerable appeal of the Cuban Revolution in Argentina among the youth, among students, in some sectors of Peronism, and among some minor political parties that were not at all revolutionary, yet strongly identified themselves with Castro. The Communist Party energetically supported Castro and would give its electoral support to any party or leader publicly favoring Cuba (Rouquié 1982:183). Against this backdrop, and given the strong reaction of civilian and military conservatives to anything that even ambiguously suggested an outside subversive threat (see Rouquié 1982: 183–84), it seems likely that these brief guerrilla episodes further contributed to the military's growing concern about internal security.

Military Role. The military had entered this period overwhelmingly concerned with—and divided by—the question of what to do about Peronism. The armed forces were themselves greatly concerned with this issue, and they also functioned as the channel through which groups outside the military expressed their anti-Peronism (O'Donnell 1973:156–57). In the mid-1950s the most dramatic expressions of divisions within the military over Peronism were General Aramburu's coup against General Lonardi in late 1955, which brought a shift from mild to harsh anti-Peronism; and the failed pro-Peronist military rebellion against Aramburu in mid-1956, which triggered the execution of leaders of the revolt, including a retired general. Later, the armed forces' preoccupation with policy toward Peronism was reflected in the pervasive military involvement in influencing, pressuring, and threatening the Frondizi government, which produced over 30 civil-military crises and threatened coups during the Frondizi period (Rouquié 1982:155).

The Cuban Revolution, along with the continent-wide concern with internal security and the growing "new professionalism" within the military, had a major impact on the Argentine armed forces and modified this preoccupation with Peronism in two directions. First, the military's continuous in-

---

[100] As noted above, under Aramburu the Peronist Resistance produced numerous incidents of violence in urban areas, but these tended to involve sabotage and disruptive bombings, rather than the far more threatening assassinations and kidnappings carried out by urban guerrillas beginning in the late 1960s. The Peronist Resistance had ended by 1960.

[101] Kohl and Litt 1974:323; Hodges 1976:40–41, 142–43; Rock 1985:353.

volvement in the political sphere, plus a long string of civil-military and in-
tramilitary crises produced by this involvement, seriously disrupted the
military hierarchy, precipitating many forced early retirements of officers
and weakening the military as an institution. The *legalista* faction of the
military, which was identified with the concerns of the new professionalism,
sought to end this close involvement in day-to-day politics. During the interim Guido government of 1962–63, after a series of military confrontations
with their opponents within the armed forces, the *gorilas*, the *legalistas* became the dominant current of military thinking. Whereas the *gorilas* opposed having elections at all in 1963, the *legalistas* supported the elections,
avoided close interference in the resulting Illia government, and tolerated
greater Peronist electoral participation. In the short run, they adopted a posture of being "above politics" (O'Donnell 1973:157–59). Thus, one consequence of the new professionalism, in the short run, was that the military
gave civilian politicians a further opportunity to solve the nation's problems
on their own. At this level, there is a strong parallel to Peru, where the new
professional current among the officers led to strong support in the early to
mid-1960s for giving Belaúnde a chance to carry out reform under a civilian,
electoral regime.

The second consequence of the new focus on internal security was very
different from that in Peru, where new professional officers came to oppose
APRA for its excessive conservatism. In Argentina, by contrast, a major concern developed within the military that Peronism would become a source of
internal subversion. For many elements within the military, the intense an-
ticommunism of the 1960s became intertwined with anti-Peronism, and Peronism and communism were seen as "complementary (or successive) forms
of the same totalitarianism" (Rouquié 1982:156). In fact, the political orientations of Peronists during these years were diverse, including the moderating role increasingly played by Vandor and the radicalism of the Huerta
Grande program. In addition, a major goal for most Peronists in carrying out
massive labor mobilizations under Frondizi and Illia was to discredit the government, not to promote revolution. Yet as noted above, conservative sectors
both within and outside the military saw in this capacity for mobilization a
tremendous threat, should the goals of Peronism change.

Coup of 1966.   In analyzing the coup, it is essential to underline a concomitant of the point just noted above: in comparison with the situation prior to
the coups of the 1960s and 1970s in Brazil, Uruguay, and Chile, the immediate crisis prior to the Argentine coup of 1966 was more limited. Although
it was widely believed that Argentina was in the midst of a serious, long-
term crisis, elites did not perceive a strong, immediate threat (O'Donnell
1973:102–3; 1975:36ff.; Rouquié 1982:248). Beginning in 1964 the prospect
of a coup was widely discussed, and preparations for the coup had begun
nearly a year before it occurred. A dispute between Illia and the future military president General Onganía did occur in late 1965, leading to Onganía's
resignation and perhaps affecting the preparation of the coup, but there were

no special triggering conditions in the period prior to the event, such as the crisis over the oil contract in Peru in 1968 (Rouquié 1982:234, 244, 248).

On the other hand, O'Donnell suggests that the immediate timing of the coup was strongly influenced by the general elections to be held in 1967. *Legalista* officers were divided as to whether Peronism should be permitted to run. It was important that the coup should occur sufficiently close to the elections for military officers to recognize the serious risk of a dangerous split within the armed forces on this issue, but not so close to the elections as to permit the campaigning to begin. This timing would make military cohesion more likely, at the same time minimizing civilian opposition to the coup (O'Donnell 1973:162–63).

A crucial, longer-term issue underlying the coup was the evolving posture of the *legalista* faction of the military. In 1962–63 this faction had sought to maintain a position "above politics," out of a conviction that repeated attempts to influence both the government and electoral outcomes—particularly with reference to the treatment of the Peronists—had dangerously divided and weakened the military. Yet although the military had in one sense pulled back from politics, O'Donnell suggests that there was a threshold of long-term crisis above which the military would launch an intervention far more ambitious and comprehensive—and based on much greater military unity. In the mid-1960s, this threshold was reached (O'Donnell 1973:154–65).

Capacity for Conflict Regulation. It is appropriate, before summarizing the impact of the ban on Peronism in limiting Argentina's capacity for conflict-regulation, to place the ban in perspective. Obviously, the underlying problem was the presence of deep antagonisms in Argentine politics and society. Chapter 4 argued that these antagonisms, along with the failure to develop institutions to mediate them, had already surfaced in the first two decades of the 20th century and contributed to the crises of the late 1910s that led to a long postponement of the incorporation period. This delay in turn caused incorporation to occur in a way that reinforced these antagonisms, further deepening the dilemmas of conciliation and later contributing to the emergence of the ban, as a new attempt at conflict regulation. Thus, the ban on Peronism was at the same time not only a *cause* of the political failures of the 1950s and 1960s, but also a *consequence* of longer-term failures of political mediation. The ban was an intervening variable and should be understood as such.

Within this framework, the ban in Argentina (and in Peru) may be viewed comparatively in relation to the mechanisms of conflict regulation established in most cases of party incorporation to avoid a recurrence of the polarization earlier stimulated by the incorporation period. In Mexico these mechanisms consisted of the accommodations reached within the dominant party, and in Venezuela and Colombia they entailed the elaborate compromises forged during the regime transitions of the late 1950s and sustained in the political practice of subsequent decades. In Argentina (and Peru), by contrast, the most important mechanism intended to avert a resurgence of the earlier polarization was the ban on the populist party, enforced in the case of Argentina through the coups of 1962 and 1966, through numerous threatened coups, and through frequent military interference in policy-making. Yet, as we have seen, this military attempt at conflict regulation was unsuccessful and in fact created further dramatic conflict: within the military, in the sphere of civil-military relations, within Peronism, and among the major parties. This form of conflict regulation directly and indirectly contributed to a highly unstable dynamic of politics and ultimately to the regime breakdown of 1966.

To anticipate a theme explored in the conclusion, these observations point to major contrasts in the stability of the heritage of incorporation. In some countries, most obviously Mexico and Venezuela, the heritage was a robust set of institutions that persisted for many decades. In Argentina, as in Peru, the heritage was unstable and soon self-destructed.

Part V

SUMMATION

8

Conclusion: Shaping the Political Arena

THE OBSERVER even casually acquainted with 20th-century Latin American history will not be surprised by the suggestion that the labor movement and state-labor relations have played an important role in the region's development. Likewise, it is a familiar observation that the evolution of state-labor relations has seen both major episodes of state domination of the labor movement and also dramatic instances of labor mobilization by actors within the state, and that these experiences have had important ramifications for the larger evolution of national politics. It is more novel to construct a model of political change and regime dynamics in Latin America that builds upon an analysis of the dialectical interplay between labor control and labor mobilization. This book has developed such a model. Obviously, the argument is not that labor politics and state-labor relations can, by themselves, explain broader patterns of change. Rather, the focus on these issues provides an optic through which a larger panorama of change can be assessed and, in part, explained.

The book has examined a crucial historical transition, referred to as the initial incorporation period, which brought the first sustained and at least partially successful attempt by the state to legitimate and shape an institutionalized labor movement. These initiatives were accompanied by a broader set of social and economic reforms and an important period of state-building. Labor policy during this period placed varying degrees of emphasis on the control of the labor movement and the mobilization of labor support, and these variations had a profound impact on the subsequent evolution of politics, playing a central role in shaping the national political arena in later decades.

The incorporation periods and their impact have been analyzed within what was called the critical juncture framework, which suggests that political change cannot be seen only as an incremental process. Rather, it also entails periods of dramatic reorientation—such as the incorporation periods—that commonly occur in distinct ways in different countries, leaving contrasting historical legacies.

The Historical Argument

The book explores a series of analytically comparable, but chronologically divergent, periods that emerged sequentially in each country: the period of the "oligarchic state," the incorporation period, and the aftermath and heritage of incorporation. The centerpiece of the historical argument is the comparison of incorporation periods. We first distinguish between cases of state incorporation and party incorporation. In state incorporation, which characterized Brazil and Chile, the principal agency of the incorporation project was the legal and bureaucratic apparatus of the state, and the primary concern was with depoliticizing the working class and exercising control over its sectoral organizations. In the authoritarian context within which state incorporation occurred, few channels of labor expression or political bargaining existed. Some benefits to labor were paternalistically extended through a new state-controlled union structure, which, particularly in Brazil, became an agency for the distribution of state social welfare programs. At the same time, (pre)existing independent and leftist unions were repressed. In party incorporation, by contrast, along with the state's role, a political party or political movement which later became a party was also crucial. Major concessions were extended to labor in the attempt to win its political support, and typically, though not always, the left within the labor movement was tolerated or co-opted, rather than repressed. Three subtypes of party incorporation were distinguished, based on the distinct forms of party-led mobilization, thus yielding four types of incorporation periods (see Figure 8.1).

In Uruguay and Colombia, party incorporation entailed the electoral mobilization of workers in the framework of two-party competition between traditional parties that dated from the 19th century. With the concern of the incorporating party to attract electoral support of the working class, substantial policy concessions were made. However, in contrast to other types of party incorporation, the construction of union-party links was either a marginal aspect of the incorporation project (Colombia) or did not occur at all (Uruguay). The labor populism of Peru and Argentina saw extensive electoral mobilization of labor by a newer, populist party that also constructed union-party links as a central feature of the incorporation project. Major concessions were granted to labor in exchange for its more extensive electoral support and organizational affiliation. Finally, the radical populism of Mexico and Venezuela was similar, except that the electoral and organizational incorporation of the working class in the modern sector was accompanied by a parallel incorporation of the peasantry. Therefore, in addition to the concessions granted to labor, the incorporating government also made concessions to the peasantry, particularly a commitment to agrarian reform, which raised the possibility of a more comprehensive restructuring of property relations.

Explaining Different Types of Incorporation.   The earlier part of the analysis sought to show how, after the turn of the century, different types of incorporation emerged out of the period of the oligarchic state. The project of labor incorporation arose from two goals on the part of elites acting through the state. The first, which responded to rising worker protest, was to regularize and institutionalize channels for the resolution of labor-capital conflict and to control the radicalization of the working class. Labor issues and demands had become too disruptive and the inefficiency and unworkability of the coercive approach of repression was increasingly recognized by leaders

Figure 8.1 Transformation of the Oligarchic State and the Incorporation Period

	Chile and Brazil	Uruguay and Colombia	Peru and Argentina	Mexico and Venezuela
	To 1920 / To 1930	To 1903 / To 1930	To 1919 / To 1916	To 1910 / To 1935
End of Period of Oligarchic State	Oligarchy in an unusually strong political position.	Presence of elements of oligarchy in both parties and tradition of interparty alliances that will later provide a basis for blocking mobilization stimulated by party competition.	Oligarchy in many respects strong, but a crucial "flaw" in its political position.	Least strong political position of oligarchy, disintegrating control of social relations in rural sector.
			Aborted Incorp. Periods 1919–20 / 1916–19 Timid incorporation efforts aborted in face of collision between intense labor mobilization and strong conservative reaction. Oligarchic control restored in 1930s.	
Incorporation period	1920–31 / 1930–45	1903–16 / 1930–45	1939–48 / 1943–55	1917–40 / 1935–48
	State incorporation: Depoliticization and control	*Party Incorporation: Electoral mobilization by traditional party*	*Party incorporation: Labor populism*	*Party incorporation: Radical populism*
	Depoliticization. Paternalistic benefits. Left repressed.	Electoral mobilization only. Substantial or major concessions to labor. Left tolerated.	Electoral and organizational mobilization. Major concessions to labor. Left co-opted or repressed.	Electoral and organizational mobilization. Encompasses rural sector. Major concessions to labor. Left cooperates.

within both the oligarchy and the middle sectors. The second goal was to
transform the laissez-faire oligarchic state, in which the middle sectors were
politically subordinate, and to create a more activist state that would assume
new social responsibilities. The character of the accommodation or confrontation between the reform project and the oligarchic state helped shape the
politics of incorporation. In cases of confrontation, reformers tended to promote labor mobilization as a political resource in the conflict.

The scope of labor mobilization and hence the type of incorporation project that emerged can therefore be understood in part in terms of an inverse
relation between the political strength of the oligarchy toward the end of this
prior period and the degree to which this option of mobilization was pursued
in the incorporation period. This relationship captures the dynamics of six
of the cases and brings into sharp focus the factors that led the other two
countries, Peru and Argentina, to deviate from the pattern.

The inverse relationship is most evident in the contrast between Brazil and
Chile, on the one hand, and Mexico and Venezuela, on the other. In Brazil
and Chile, the strong political position of the oligarchy provided the framework for accommodationist relations between it and the rising middle sectors and hence for a control-oriented incorporation period. In Mexico and
Venezuela, a disruption of clientelistic relations in the countryside meant a
relative erosion of oligarchic strength, which created an opportunity for the
wide-ranging urban and rural mobilization that accompanied incorporation.

Colombia and Uruguay may in certain respects be seen as intermediate
cases within this inverse relationship, to be understood in light of the special
character of their well-institutionalized, two-party systems. In both countries the oligarchy was not united in a single political bloc. Rather, it was
split between the two parties, which in many periods confronted each other
not only in intense electoral competition, but in armed conflict. The dynamic of deeply ingrained two-party competition created a major incentive
for the electoral mobilization of workers, thus disposing these countries toward more mobilizational incorporation periods. At the same time, a long
tradition of interparty alliances created the potential for building a strong,
bipartisan, antireformist coalition that could reunite elements of the oligarchy and limit the scope of incorporation. Thus, although an important electoral mobilization occurred in the incorporation periods, this antireform alliance blocked more elaborate efforts at support mobilization such as the
creation of strong organizational links between unions and the party. In sum,
the political split in the elite—which represented a greater degree of oligarchic weakness than was found in Brazil and Chile—made mobilization more
likely, yet the tradition of interparty alliances provided a basis for limiting
this mobilization.

Peru and Argentina deviate from this inverse relationship. In both cases
the oligarchy was in many spheres powerful on the eve of the reform period,
yet its power suffered from a crucial "flaw." In Argentina, the oligarchy's
lack of a major electoral base in a peasantry placed it in a difficult position
in periods of free electoral competition. In Peru, an interaction between di-

visions within the elite[1] and a level of labor protest that was unusually intense, given Peru's relatively low level of development, resulted in two episodes of dramatic loss of control of the political system by the oligarchy, in 1912–13 and 1918–20. Both episodes were followed by the repression of labor protest, and control of the political system was restored.

In this context of flawed political strength of the oligarchy, reform movements emerged in the 1910s in both Argentina (the Radicals) and Peru (Leguía) that undertook important policy initiatives, but that also suffered from what was ultimately a decisive subordination to oligarchic interests. As a result, in both cases a labor incorporation project was contemplated, but due in part to oligarchic opposition, it was aborted and postponed. The reform projects ultimately failed, and overt oligarchic domination was reestablished in the 1930s.

When the incorporation period finally did occur in Peru and Argentina in the 1940s, it took a highly mobilizational form, due in part to the ongoing political frustrations resulting from the long delay and to an international political climate in the 1940s supportive of popular mobilization. Yet as of that decade, these two countries were still characterized by the persistence of an oligarchy that remained a powerful political, economic, and social force. The political "collision" between this oligarchy and the goals of the incorporation project would have important consequences for the subsequent legacy of incorporation.

It is noteworthy that this account of the emergence of different types of incorporation seems to go further toward explaining the degree and form of mobilization initiated from above during the incorporation project than another obvious factor: the prior scope of worker organization and protest, which we will again refer to for the sake of convenience as the "strength" of the labor movement.[2] A relevant hypothesis might be that strong labor movements would "push" the leaders of the incorporation project to initiate more extensive mobilization.

Yet arraying the cases in terms of the scope of mobilization initiated from above during the incorporation period—from Brazil and Chile with little or no mobilization, to Uruguay and Colombia, to Peru and Argentina, to Mexico and Venezuela[3] (see Table 5.1)—one finds no clear pattern. Of the two cases with the lowest levels of mobilization by the state, Chile had a strong labor movement, whereas the strength of the Brazilian labor movement was substantial but much more limited. Of the two cases with the highest levels of mobilization by the state, Mexico had one of the strongest labor move-

---

[1] In contrast to Uruguay and Colombia, where the divisions were more predominantly political, these divisions in Peru involved deep social and economic cleavages.

[2] See discussion in Chapter 3.

[3] It could be pointed out that the final two pairs—Peru and Argentina, and Mexico and Venezuela—are similar in the scope of mobilization in the modern sector (see Table 5.1) and should therefore be viewed as "tied" on this variable for the purpose of the present discussion. However, in this case as well there seems to be no consistent patterning in relation to early labor movement strength.

ments, whereas Venezuela had one of the weakest as of the start of incorporation. With regard to the third pair, Argentina had the strongest labor movement in the region, whereas the scope of early labor movement development
in Peru was far more modest. One interesting regularity that does stand out
is the early emergence of the incorporation periods in Uruguay and Colombia
in relation to the development of their labor movements. Yet we argued in
Chapter 4 that this was not due to the characteristics of the labor movement,
so much as to the way the dynamics of intra-elite and interparty competition
pushed party leaders at an earlier point to make a political overture to labor.
Hence, no systematic relationship between labor movement strength and
type of incorporation period emerges, although at many points the strength
of the labor movement was an important issue in the analysis.

The Legacy of Incorporation.   Against the backdrop of the emergence of
different types of incorporation projects, the central concern of the book has
been with tracing their consequences through subsequent periods (see Figure
8.2). To understand the heritage of state incorporation, it is useful to consider
the generalization that in Latin America, labor movements tend to become
politicized, and if, as under state incorporation, this politicization is not promoted by the state during the incorporation period, it tends to occur later
from within society in a way that may readily escape state control. This occurred dramatically in the 1930s in Chile and began to occur in Brazil after
1945. This radicalization was a principal legacy of the failure to fill political
space that was a basic characteristic of state incorporation.

   In the cases of party incorporation, the heritage derived in important measure from the playing out, during the aftermath period, of the opposition and
polarization generated by incorporation. The events of the aftermath constituted, in the language of Chapter 1, the "mechanisms of production" of the
legacy. One can summarize these events in terms of a "modal" pattern of
change followed by most of the countries. The conservative reaction to incorporation generally culminated in a coup[4] which instituted an authoritarian period that brought a more intense form of the conservative reaction.
Later, when a more competitive regime was eventually restored, in most
cases[5] the party that had led the incorporation period underwent a process of
conservatization in its program and policy goals. This conservatization reflected the terms under which it was believed that the party could either
retain power (Mexico), maintain a newly constructed civilian regime (Venezuela and Colombia), or be readmitted to the political game (Peru, and to a
much lesser extent Argentina).[6]

   This conservatization had several components. One involved the imposi-

   [4] Mexico had a strong conservative reaction but avoided a coup.
   [5] In Uruguay this transition was carried out in a way intended to channel the electorate
into the two traditional parties and away from the left, but a conservatization of the Colorado Party did not occur at this time.
   [6] In Argentina, conservatization under these terms might be said to have occurred in the
period of Vandor's leadership in the mid-1960s, but it was not an overall characteristic of
the aftermath or heritage period.

tion of a substantial limitation on working-class demand-making,[7] though the party made a systematic effort to retain its political ties with the working class and/or the labor movement. Another was the introduction of mechanisms to limit political conflict and ensure that the polarization earlier triggered by incorporation would not be repeated. In Mexico, this mechanism took the form of strengthening the one-party dominant system; in Venezuela and Colombia, it took the form of the party pact. In Peru and Argentina, where the oligarchy remained strong and labor mobilization had been so extensive, the residue of antagonisms from the incorporation period was intense, inhibiting the regulation of conflict through the cooperation of the political parties. Under these conditions the military attempted to limit conflict through the veto of the full participation of the populist party—enforced by coups if necessary. Among the cases of party incorporation, only in Uruguay did no conservatization take place at this point.

The party heritage of incorporation was summarized in terms of three dimensions: whether there was a majority bloc in the electoral arena located roughly at the center of the political spectrum, whether the union movement was organizationally linked to parties of the center, and whether the union movement was usually in the governing coalition. These three outcomes were in important measure a result of the dynamics of the incorporation and aftermath periods. The incorporation period was the critical juncture in which the working class was or was not electorally mobilized by and organizationally linked to a reformist party, which thereby gained the potential capacity to form a majority bloc. Where neither of these occurred (the cases of state incorporation), attempts to form a majority bloc based on labor mobilization during the aftermath period failed. Where one or both of these occurred (the cases of party incorporation), the important question was whether in the aftermath period the polarization and opposition that resulted from the labor mobilization was worked out in a way that the potential to form an effective centrist majority bloc was realized. Different combinations of these three dimensions led to distinct regime dynamics, with Brazil and Chile emerging as what we characterized as multiparty, polarizing systems; Mexico and Venezuela as hegemonic, integrative party systems; Uruguay and Colombia as cases of electoral stability and social conflict; and Peru and Argentina as instances of political stalemate.

Thus, in Brazil and Chile, in the context of state incorporation, the absence of labor mobilization through a multiclass, populist party during the incorporation period contributed to a legacy of a highly fractionalized party system and the affiliation of labor to parties that were either out of power or were formally "in," but were junior partners in governing coalitions. With the government having few or no political ties to the labor movement, and hence lacking means of hegemonic control, the labor movement, assigned to a position of virtually permanent opposition, underwent a process of radicalization, as did the non-communist parties with which it was affiliated. In

---

[7] Again, Uruguay is an exception.

Figure 8.2 Incorporation and Its Legacy

	Chile and Brazil	Uruguay and Colombia	Peru and Argentina	Mexico and Venezuela
	State Incorporation	Party Incorporation	Party Incorporation	Party Incorporation
	Chile 1920–31 / Brazil 1930–45	Uruguay 1903–16 / Colombia 1930–45	Peru 1939–48 / Argentina 1943–55	Mexico 1917–40 / Venezuela 1935–48
Incorporation	*Depoliticization and Control*	*Electoral Mobilization by Traditional Party*	*Labor Populism*	*Radical Populism*
	Depoliticization. Paternalistic benefits. Left repressed.	Electoral mobilization only. Substantial or major concessions to labor. Left tolerated.	Electoral and organizational mobilization. Major concessions to labor. Left co-opted or repressed.	Electoral and organizational mobilization. Encompasses rural sector. Major concessions to labor. Left cooperates.
	→	→	→	→
	1931–52 / 1945–60	1916–45 / 1945–60	1948–60 / 1955–60	1940–52 / 1948–63
Aftermath[a]	*Aborted Populism*	*Reinforcing traditional Two-Party Systems*	*"Difficult" and "Impossible" Games*	*Transformation of Majority Coalition*
	Failure of "belated" populist attempt to create a multiclass center. Labor affiliated with radical or radicalizing opposition parties.	Regime transition reinforces electoral role of traditional parties. Workers vote for these parties, but unions either completely or increasingly affiliated with left.	Populist party banned. Labor either in opposition or forced into subordinate role in coalitions.	Populist party retains or regains power and moves toward center, reconstituting a conservative "coalition of the whole," including labor.
	→	→	→	→

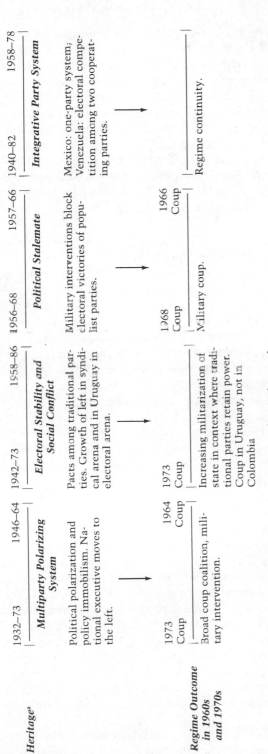

Heritage[a]

1932–73   1946–64

Multiparty Polarizing System

Political polarization and policy immobilism. National executive moves to the left.

1942–73   1958–86

Electoral Stability and Social Conflict

Pacts among traditional parties. Growth of left in syndical arena and in Uruguay in electoral arena.

1956–68   1957–66

Political Stalemate

Military interventions block electoral victories of populist parties.

1940–82   1958–78

Integrative Party System

Mexico: one-party system; Venezuela: electoral competition among two cooperating parties.

Regime Outcome in 1960s and 1970s

1973 Coup   1964 Coup

Broad coup coalition, military intervention.

1973 Coup

Increasing militarization of state in context where traditional parties retain power. Coup in Uruguay, not in Colombia

1968 Coup   1966 Coup

Military coup.

Regime continuity.

[a] As noted in Chapter 7, the heritage period overlaps with the aftermath period.

addition to these parties, the labor movement also had close ties to the communist parties. During the 1960s and 1970s, when new opposition movements, polarization, and political crisis were experienced throughout Latin America, this legacy played a central role in the process of radicalization that occurred in both countries, though the radicalization in Brazil took place on a more limited scale. The growing strength of the left culminated in its actual or apparent victory: in Chile, an electoral front of Marxist parties won the presidential election in 1970; and in a different way the turn of events in Brazil also moved the presidency to the left after 1961. As polarization and decisional paralysis proceeded in both countries, a broad coup coalition formed and the military intervened, establishing an extended period of military rule and attempting to eliminate the political system that was the heritage of incorporation.

If Brazil and Chile were "negative" on all three dimensions, Mexico and Venezuela were just the opposite, "positive" on all three. In those countries, the party that led the incorporation period mobilized both labor and peasant support and was able to establish electoral dominance. By the end of the aftermath, a conservatization of the populist party allowed for the formation of broad coalitions based on the incorporating party, either alone (Mexico) or in cooperation with other parties (Venezuela). Maintaining close ties with the labor movement, this party provided the state with legitimacy and offered the government important political resources with which to respond to the opposition movements and crises of the 1960s and 1970s.

Colombia and Uruguay were intermediate cases, differing from Mexico and Venezuela largely due to the absence of strong organizational links between the labor movement and the incorporating party. In the heritage periods in both countries, the vote of the working class in important measure remained tied to the traditional parties, but labor confederations were much less closely linked to these parties, and both countries experienced a significant increase in labor militancy. In the face of worker and guerrilla challenges during the period of polarization and crisis in the 1960s and 1970s, Uruguay and Colombia experienced social conflict and substantial militarization of the state, even though the traditional parties did not lose control of the electoral arena, although the left did grow significantly in Uruguay. In Uruguay this militarization of the state went further, to the point that it culminated in the coup of 1973. Factors that help account for this divergence between the two countries, within the framework of many commonalities, include the greater labor radicalization in Uruguay; the more dramatic impact of the guerrilla insurgency on national institutions; the unsettling effect of the left's growing electoral strength; the long-term decline of the export sector, which undermined the economic base for the Uruguayan state's heavy commitment to welfare spending; and the much greater difficulty of the Uruguayan government in shifting economic models to address the economic decline.

Finally, Peru and Argentina were similar to Mexico and Venezuela on the three dimensions with one exception: the labor movement was not in the governing coalition. A central feature of the heritage of incorporation was the ban on an electorally strong populist party that was thereby relegated to an opposition role for much (Peru) or all (Argentina) of the later 1950s and 1960s. This ban reflected a legacy of antipathy between populist and antipopulist forces that had no counterpart in the other six countries. Anti-*Peronismo* and anti-*Aprismo* were fundamental points of reference in political life, and populist/antipopulist antagonisms encompassed not only a political dimension, but also reflected profound cultural antagonisms. These antagonisms and this ban played a central role in the distinctive pattern of political stalemate in the 1950s and 1960s. This stalemate was one of the principal conditions that led to the coups of 1968 (Peru) and 1966 (Argentina), coups that—unlike the "veto" coups of the early 1960s in these two countries—inaugurated long-term military rule through which the military sought to supersede the stalemated party system.

To conclude, if one considers the implications of the failure to fill political space in the state incorporation experiences of Chile and Brazil, the scope of mobilization in the different types of party incorporation, and the contrasting ways in which the conservative reaction to party incorporation was accommodated, one can order a large body of information concerning the political history of these countries.

Erosion of the Heritage?

The analysis has traced out the heritage of incorporation to one of two end points. In five of the countries (Brazil, Chile, Uruguay, Peru, and Argentina), the political dynamic that derived from incorporation inhibited the establishment of stable patterns and ultimately resulted in a military coup that appeared to bring this political dynamic to an abrupt end. In the other countries (Mexico, Venezuela, and Colombia), the legacy was a more stable pattern that endured, with no dramatic end point. For the first five cases the analysis extended to this coup, whereas for the other three it extended to approximately 1980. The question of what happened beyond these periods then arises: how long did the heritage of incorporation persist? Though no clear answer could be given as of the late 1980s, a few comments can be made.

Among the five countries where coups overturned the civilian regimes and interrupted established patterns of party politics, Brazil and Chile experienced the longest periods of military rule and elaborate attempts by the military to impose new political structures. In both countries, the political project of the military was to purge the left, rid the country of the prior political system, and establish new institutions that would prevent the recurrence of the old political dynamics of radicalization, polarization, and decisional paralysis. In both cases, the military oversaw a long and complex period of constitution-mongering and electoral engineering in an attempt to create a new civilian political arena restricted to actors it considered acceptable. In both cases, too, this effort failed.

In Brazil, by the end of the 1980s the transition from a military to a democratic regime was completed, with the new constitution and direct presidential elections at the end of 1989 capping a long process that included the earlier introduction of elections at other levels and, in 1985, the restoration of civilian rule with the inauguration of President Sarney. The Brazilian military had gone through contortions of institutional experimentation, attempting to find a solution first in a two-party system and then in a multiparty system. Yet what immediately emerged, as the military stepped down and a strong bandwagon effect produced tremendous support for the opposition, was on the surface a one-party dominant system based on the PMDB, which won about 70 percent of the presidential vote in the electoral college in late 1984, combined with splintering and fractionalization in the rest of the party system. However, just as in the 1946–64 Republic, when one could conclude little about regime dynamics from the formal existence of a three-party system, so in the post-military period after 1985 the image of a single large party was deceiving. Indeed, after the long interruption by military rule and the great effort of the military government to design and control the new political regime, what was striking was the apparent reappearance of some of the old dynamics.

Hidden under the dominant-party facade was an emerging pattern of fractionalization that became more marked as the Sarney government wore on. Internally, the PMDB could not hold its diverse factions together, as witnessed for example by the defection from the party of what became the PSDB. Even more striking was the level of fractionalization that became explicit in the 1989 elections: no fewer than 24 presidential candidates initially threw their hats into the ring and the two who made it to the final runoff election represented parties that jointly held less than 5 percent of the congressional seats.[8]

As this pattern indicates, parties in Brazil continued to be fragmented and weak. Indeed, unlike the case of Chile, the post-military parties in Brazil were largely new. Nevertheless, the potential for a restoration of a polarizing dynamic seemed evident. Interparty (or interfactional) groupings along more ideological or programmatic lines reappeared. This pattern was especially evident in the blocs that formed in the Constituent Assembly of 1987–88 (Bruneau 1989). In addition, on the right the private sector resumed an active role in political and electoral affairs through its organization, FIESP. At the same time the labor movement seemed to be in a similar coalitional position to that in the pre-1964 period, that is to say, in a position of substantial political autonomy. As in the pre-1964 period, unions had some connection with the PMDB and other center-left parties, but these links did not provide the kinds of mechanisms for labor conciliation and class compromise found in cases such as Mexico and Venezuela. A new element, however, was the PT (Work-

[8] *New York Times*, Nov. 20, 1989.

ers' Party), which was founded on the basis of the workers' movement that erupted in the late 1970s. The PT achieved unanticipated electoral success in municipal elections at the end of 1988, and it emerged as the second-place winner in the initial round of the 1989 presidential contest.[9] The potential for renewed polarization could be seen in the collapse of the PMDB as a broad centrist coalition representing a viable electoral force and its replacement by forces more clearly identified with the right and left. Indeed, the runoff elections pitted a free market candidate Fernando Collor de Mello, the ultimate victor, against Luis Inácio da Silva (Lula), leader of the strike movement of the late 1970s and founder of the PT.

A further word might be added about the reactivation of the Brazilian labor movement, which began with the São Paulo strikes of the late 1970s and continued through the civilian regime with the formation of two new labor centrals, the CUT and the CGT, and with protest against economic stabilization policies. To many analysts—who focused on the high level of state control over the union movement introduced during the Vargas government of the 1930s and early 1940s and on the subsequent retention of that legal framework through the military period labor reactivation in the 1970s strike movement came as a surprise. The socioeconomic change Brazil had experienced during the military period was typically invoked as an explanation. That is, with the economic "miracle" and sustained high rates of growth, the military regime oversaw a process of industrial expansion and the formation of a larger, more skilled labor force, working and living in concentrated areas of industrial production. This "new" working class was often seen as providing the basis for the labor activation that began in the late 1970s.

Although these socioeconomic changes were undeniably part of the explanation, the labor activism of the 1970s and 1980s was no surprise from the standpoint of the present analysis, which places more emphasis on the dynamics set in motion by the incorporation experience, particularly on two aspects of its evolving legacy: the relative political autonomy of the labor movement from governing centrist parties and the consequent polarizing dynamic, which was most apparent whenever controls were relaxed—that is, in the mid-1940s and in the last years before the 1964 coup. The reemergence of these tendencies with the return to an open regime is an outcome that might be anticipated from the perspective of the present analysis.

Finally, immobilism in important areas of policy seemed to be reemerging, most dramatically in sharp vacillations of economic policy, suggesting yet another aspect of continuity with the heritage of incorporation in Brazil. Even the military regime, as it was preparing its exit, was unable to implement a stabilization policy over any sustained period, in part because of the political pressure that accompanied the regime opening. The vacillation of

[9] The third runner-up, with nearly the same level of electoral support as Lula, was a familiar figure on the populist left, Leonel Brizola.

the civilian government beginning in 1985 in confronting the stabilization and debt issues was reminiscent of post-1950 Brazil.

In Chile, the transition to a democratic regime was just occurring with the December 1989 elections, the first since the coup of 1973. Having been masterful in his capacity to dominate the political arena during 15 years of military rule, General Pinochet miscalculated on the last step of his carefully laid out plans and, at the end of 1988, lost the plebiscite that would have paved the way for introducing a civilian regime under his own presidential tutelage. With this defeat, support for the proregime forces began to hemorrhage. The ability of opposition groups to work together for the "No" campaign in the plebiscite provided the basis for ongoing cooperation and the formation of a single opposition list for the 1989 elections. Thus, as in Brazil, a strong electoral pole of opposition was created. The Christian Democratic Party was the anchor of the new 17-party Concertation of Parties for Democracy (CPD) and provided its presidential candidate, Patricio Aylwin, who decisively won the election.

Yet, despite the emergence of a majority electoral bloc, the reappearance of a polarizing dynamic could certainly not be ruled out. The unity within the CPD could well be fragile. As Pinochet's power dissipated, constitutional amendments, ratified in a July 1989 plebiscite, were forced upon him, and these included a provision backing off from the ban on Marxist parties. Because of the short interval to the December elections, this change did not have much of an impact on those elections, but it had clear implications for the future. Also, on the right, some consolidation had been achieved with the cooperation of forces representing the political (RN) and economic (UDI) right, though a host of pro-Pinochet parties were not included in this major challenge to the CPD. In short, by the end of 1989 a great multiplicity of parties continued to exist in Chile—and often the same pre-1973 parties. For the moment, they had solidified around two major electoral fronts, though it was impossible to predict that these political blocs would endure, rather than fractionalize, as occurred in Brazil. In addition, the prospect of renewed political polarization could certainly not be discounted. The CPD was committed to an economic policy that would not represent a major departure from that of the final years of the Pinochet period, raising the possibility of a perpetuation of economic hardships that could produce a strong resurgence of new forms of opposition politics.

Mexico and Venezuela did not undergo the sharp regime discontinuities introduced in Brazil and Chile by military coup. Yet behind the relative continuity of regimes in Mexico and Venezuela, one must inquire about underlying changes. Rapid urbanization and social change had important consequences for both of the parties that earlier led the incorporation project. In the context of urbanization, the declining demographic and political importance of peasants cut into a major pillar of support for both the PRI and AD, at the same time that these parties, traditionally dependent on mobilization through sectoral organizations, were unable to win much support within the swelling urban informal sector. With the economic crisis of the 1980s, the government was constrained in its ability to offer material payoffs to sustain the coalition. Indeed, the austerity and stabilization policies prompted by the debt crisis, as well as a more general turn to economic restructuring, took a heavy toll on growth, employment, and real wages. In both countries, land reform virtually ground to a halt, and there was some evidence of the emergence of a new, incipient, more combative unionism, though this remained difficult to assess.

Venezuela seemed in a better position than Mexico to absorb these pressures for change, since during the postincorporation period Venezuela made the transition to an electoral basis of legitimacy and moved to a competitive system, thereby opening a channel for expressing opposition and discontent by "throwing the bums out." Somewhat paradoxically, however, in the 1980s, the regular alternation of the two parties in the presidency was interrupted. In 1984 AD's Carlos Andrés Pérez was succeeded in the presidency by fellow party member Jaime Lusinchi, and five years later Pérez returned to the presidency. Nevertheless, cooperation between AD and COPEI remained a significant feature of the Venezuelan regime, and the ongoing need for this cooperation was evident in the failure of AD to win a majority in either house of Congress in the 1988 election.

In Mexico, the PRI's capacity to cope initially seemed impressive. Following the onset of the debt crisis in 1982, the government instituted an orthodox economic shock treatment and began to reorient the economy along liberal lines. Furthermore, with some variations, it sustained these policies and particularly the economic restructuring during the entire presidency of de la Madrid, from 1982 to 1988. The result was the first presidential term since the revolution showing no economic growth, a general drop in the standard of living, and a dramatic decline in real wages. Moreover, this occurred with relatively little protest or mobilization of popular sector opposition; and though the conservative PAN was able to present a greater challenge in the midterm elections of 1985, the parties of the left were not very successful in capitalizing on this situation. As 1988 opened, the government engineered a social pact between labor and capital that once again seemed to confirm the capacity of the PRI to negotiate and bargain with major social groups.

In the July 1988 elections, however, discontent burst forth in the dramatic success of Cuauhtémoc Cárdenas, son of the former president, who broke with the PRI to stand as an opposition candidate on a reformist platform of democratization, nationalism, and a policy reorientation that would address the forgotten issues of social justice and equitable development. Even if one accepts the official results, rather than Cárdenas's claim of victory in the three-way race with the PRI and the PAN, the PRI was reduced to just half of the votes, an outcome that seemed to mark the initiation of a new era.

At a time when past patterns of negotiation and conciliation in Mexico were limited by the constraints of economic policy and when symbolic assurances were wearing thin as policy moved to the right, a potential opposition victory appeared to undermine the hegemonic regime in a way that did not seem to be the case for Venezuela. Strong pressures emerged within

Mexico to hold genuinely competitive elections. Social sectors and opposition groups on both the right and the left, which had not been centrally included in the PRI's system of negotiations, demanded political liberalization and democratization with increasing vehemence. Reformist factions within the PRI had earlier wanted to democratize the party internally, and Cárdenas represented only the most recent, though certainly the most important, of these. Even the PRI faction associated with President Carlos Salinas de Gortari sensed that a transition from negotiation and clientelism to electoral support would be more consonant with a liberalization of the economy in which the market was left free to impose hardship. Yet the transition was difficult, being opposed by groups that benefited from the old system, and it was not clear to what extent the Salinas forces could politically afford to let go of the traditional patterns of support, particularly with the continuing vitality of the Cardenist opposition.

Though the future was unpredictable, at the end of 1989 it was possible to contemplate perhaps three scenarios, which differed with respect to the success of Cárdenas's PRD. The first focused on the capacity of the PRI, using a variety of political and coercive resources including blatant electoral fraud along with repressive measures that targeted PRD activists, to defeat the Cárdenas challenge and remain a majority party, if no longer a dominant party in the same sense. In this scenario, the PAN would be the major but limited opposition force, substantially cooperating with the PRI over largely shared economic policy. This strategy seemed to be that of the new Salinas government inaugurated at the end of 1988 (R. Collier forthcoming). In the second, the PRI would not be successful in this strategy in the medium to long run. Instead, the newly formed PRD of the Cárdenas forces would remain a viable and more institutionalized challenger, and the PRI and PRD would compete openly as two more evenly matched parties, with the PAN in a more secondary role. In this case, broader cooperation between the PRI and the PAN to meet the PRD challenge seemed a strong possibility. Indeed, such cooperation was evident in the politics of the new electoral law. In this two-and-a-half party system, a dynamic of convergence would likely come into play. It would seem probable that the PRI, in order to compete with the PRD, would have no choice but to moderate its economic policy in order to attract the support of its traditional mass constituencies. For its part, the PRD in many ways, aside from its commitment to competitive democracy, represented the same nationalist, reformist rhetorical/ideological space historically occupied by the PRI, though abandoned by it in the 1980s. Aside from its rhetoric, its program was moderate and pragmatic, explicitly recognizing economic constraints and the new economic realities, to which the PRI program was responding. However, for the PRD, the new realities meant that a simple return to old formulae was not possible. In the third and least likely scenario for Mexico, a massive defection from the PRI would accrue to the PRD. The result, in some sense, would be the replacement of the PRI with the PRD as a kind of resurrected and renamed PRM (the populist party of the 1930s incorporation period), a dominant, progressive party, but probably without the same kind of formal linkages to the labor movement, though with its support.

Among the four pairs of countries, Uruguay and Colombia constituted the only pair in which one country had a coup and the other did not. In Uruguay, despite the efforts of the military during more than a decade of harsh authoritarian rule to eliminate or subdue actors they deemed responsible for the earlier crisis, with the transition to democracy in the mid-1980s the earlier characteristics of the party system were quickly restored: the strong electoral position of the Colorados and the Nationals, a significant role for the electoral left, and a pluralistic labor movement affiliated with the left.

Indeed, as of the 1980s, the electoral left in Uruguay became more important. The left coalition, the Frente Amplio, increased its vote between the 1971 and 1984 elections from 18 to 21 percent. Subsequently in 1989, despite the defection of a cluster of small parties from the Frente, it gained roughly 20 percent of the seats in both chambers of the legislature, and, together with the parties that had split from the coalition, won around 30 percent of the seats in the lower chamber. The Frente also won the municipal election in Montevideo with 34 percent of the vote. This was a significant outcome, because Montevideo contained roughly half the country's population and because this victory gave the Frente the post of mayor in the capital city.

This showing might be taken to suggest a potential process of polarization, yet such an assessment should be evaluated with caution. It could be argued that even in the polarized context of the early 1970s, the Uruguayan electoral left had been more moderate than that, for instance, in Chile. Relatedly, with regard to the electoral outcome of 1984, it is noteworthy that the title of Rial's (1986) analysis of the 1984 election referred to it as a "Triumph of the Center." These considerations, plus the deflation of developmental expectations in the profoundly changed political climate of the 1980s, made the immediate potential for polarization limited. Further, given Uruguay's reasonable economic performance, some of the gravest aspects of the earlier economic crisis seemed to have been superseded. Nonetheless, with an important left in the electoral arena and a labor movement strongly linked to the left, the possibility of a renewed political crisis could be substantial in a context that presented an opportunity for polarization.

As of the late 1980s, Colombia had experienced four decades of regime continuity. The two traditional parties continued to perpetuate their strong electoral dominance, though with a modest change in interparty relations in the fact that, after 1986, President Virgilio Barco of the Liberal Party ended the tradition of coparticipation with the Conservatives, opening the possibility of more vigorous two-party competition.

However, notwithstanding this step, which could potentially lead to greater competitiveness, a central issue remained unaddressed: the stability of the two-party system was so extreme as to produce a strong delegitimation of the regime, with low voting rates, extensive violence on the right, the continuing guerrilla insurgency on the left, and widespread frustration with the existing order. In the early to mid-1980s President Betancur had launched a democratic opening, introducing the election of mayors at the municipal level for the first time and providing a channel through which the insurrectional left could enter the electoral arena. As of the end of the 1980s, the consequences of this new sphere of electoral competition were still hard to assess. Yet it was clear that the initiative had not created significant new space for political opposition. The electoral incorporation of the left was unsuccessful, due both to the failure to sustain a cease-fire with important insurgent groups and to the systematic assassination of leftist politicians by right-wing death squads. These assassinations were part of a larger pattern of harassment and killing of leaders of virtually any progressive political group that sought to mount serious opposition to the government, with the result that the political space for a legitimate opposition was very limited indeed. This harassment and killing seriously debilitated the labor movement, whose weakness at this point was dramatically reflected in the failed general strike of late 1988.

The drug trade, though it may have given the economy a considerable boost, posed an enormous political problem, as the government tried unsuccessfully to deal with the drug lords, who fought back with impressive resources. The already-high level of violence and killing that derived from drug trafficking escalated into a sustained assault on the system of justice through the assassination of judges, police officers, and a minister of justice, and also through attacks on journalists and newspapers that reported news on drug issues or supported the government's campaign against the drug lords. In 1989, the crisis further escalated with the spectacular confrontation between the government and the narcotics cartel, following the cartel's assassination of the leading presidential candidate, Luis Carlos Galán. This confrontation threatened the authority of the state and raised questions about the ability of the government to maintain basic policies, such as effectively prosecuting criminals, that were essential to dealing with the narcotics trade.

Thus, although the established two-party system did not seem immediately threatened, Colombia faced multiple crises, including especially the political and legal crisis posed by the drug trade and the crisis of legitimacy due to the relentless assaults on the normal functioning of virtually any form of political opposition. Yet, despite the depth of these crises, it was not clear that drastic change was imminent. Hartlyn (1988:235) argues that "the Colombian political process has confounded pessimists and disappointed optimists. If the recent past is the best indicator of the immediate future, then the process of . . . political re-accommodation will be drawn-out, resisted, and uneven."

In Peru and Argentina the obvious point to make was that the "centerpiece" of the analysis of the heritage period—the ban on APRA and Peronism—no longer existed. In Argentina, the post-1966 military government, which had self-confidently launched its project to eliminate the pre-1966 political system, collapsed in the face of massive social protest, and in 1973, after a decisive electoral victory, Perón was allowed to assume the presidency. An evaluation of the experiment in Peronist rule from 1973 to 1976 could potentially be used as a comparison case to explore the "counterfactual" question of what a Peronist government would have been like, had it been allowed in the 1950s or 1960s. Yet three complications during the 1973 to 1976 period made the situation so distinctive that such an exercise is dubious: Juan Perón's death in 1974; the political incompetence of his wife Isabel Martínez de Perón, who succeeded him in the presidency; and the extreme polarization of Argentine politics at that time, including a major urban insurgency and exceptionally high levels of violence and killing on both the left and the right. This insurgency and violence occurred in the second phase of regional radicalization discussed in Chapter 7. It therefore posed a far greater challenge than in most of the other countries or in Argentina in the 1960s.

Following this failed experiment in reintegrating Peronism into the political system, the military government, which ousted the Peronists in 1976, launched its infamous "dirty war" against the "subversives" and initiated a neoconservative economic project that—in conjunction with the heavily overvalued exchange rate and the emerging debt crisis—produced an economic disaster. Discredited by the scope of repression and by the economic difficulties, the armed forces made things worse through military adventurism in the debacle of the Falklands/Malvinas war with Great Britain, which they lost dramatically.

In the 1983 election that followed the precipitous collapse of the military regime, the Radicals[10] won with the help of various factors, including their candidate's close identification with the human rights movement that had emerged out of the military repression and also a poor choice of candidates by the Peronists. However, the Peronists became well established as the second party in a competitive two-party system, and in 1989 they won the presidency with the election of Carlos Saúl Menem. As noted above, following the period of the ban on Peronism, the Peronists had previously assumed the presidency in 1973. However, at that point their assumption of power was permitted as a desperate attempt to find a solution to the extraordinary crisis of Argentine politics. In 1989, the Peronists' succession to the presidency was, by comparison, a routine transfer of power. In fact, remarkably, 1989 was the first time in Argentine history that a president who came to office through a fully free election was replaced by a president of a different party who also came to office through a fully free election.

Notwithstanding these important steps toward institutionalizing a competitive regime, among the four countries with newly established civilian regimes in place by 1989, Argentina was the most actively threatened by military rebellions, with repeated crises revolving around the prosecution of officers in connection with their role in the earlier military repression. Later in his term, President Alfonsín sought to mitigate these crises by limiting the scope of prosecutions, and shortly after coming to office in 1989, President Menem granted a broader amnesty that played an important role in al-

[10] After the decline of the UCRI in the 1960s, the UCRP adopted the old party name.

leviating military tension. The severe economic crisis and the emergence of new forms of social protest over food prices posed ongoing threats, but by the standard of 20th-century Argentine history the country had entered a period of at least some stability at the level of regime and of governmental transitions, having achieved a competitive two-party system.

In Peru, the post-1968 military government had assumed power with an ambitious agenda for restructuring the political system. To a greater extent than in the other cases of military rule, the military's efforts not only failed, but backfired. Seeking to undermine APRA, the military government first supported the Communist Party within the labor movement and later created its own labor confederation and also an organization for social mobilization called SINAMOS, which decisively raised, and then dramatically frustrated, expectations in the popular sector. These initiatives had the effect of pushing much further the process of labor radicalization that had begun in the late 1960s. By the end of the 1970s, APRA largely lost its ties with organized labor, which came to be affiliated primarily with the left. Peru also developed an important electoral left, which, as in Uruguay, was a significant force above all in the national capital, where a leftist mayor was also elected. In comparing APRA's loss of the labor movement and of popular sector support with Peronism's ongoing strength in that sector, one sees a further legacy of APRA's conservatization in the 1950s and 1960s.

During the transition in Peru to a civilian regime in the late 1970s, the ban on APRA was superseded and the party was allowed to play a full role in the Constituent Assembly of 1979 and in the general elections of 1980. Haya de la Torre died in 1979, exactly 60 years after he launched his political career in the worker-student protests of the late 1910s, yet without ever achieving his dream of becoming president of Peru. Belaúnde regained the presidency in 1980, in part due to a poor choice of candidates by APRA.[11] However, in the next presidential election APRA finally won under the leadership of Alan García. This might seem to be a major step toward establishing a competitive two-party system, as in Argentina. Yet Belaúnde and his party, AP, were so discredited in 1985 after his presidential term that the party's vote plummeted in the election of that year. What seemed instead to be emerging was a multiparty system with a substantial left; APRA, whose policies and political posture range from the center-left to the center-right; and a variety of smaller center-right to conservative parties.

One of the major questions about Alan García's presidency beginning in

---

[11] This represents again a partial parallel with the Argentine election of 1983 (see above), in both cases involving candidates from the more "unsavory" wing of these parties that had gone through so many years of underground struggle and that had developed sectors oriented toward thuggery and political violence. In Argentina this involved the candidate for the second most important public office in the country, the governor of the province of Buenos Aires, who was a leader from the trade-union wing of Peronism and who proved to be a major liability to the party in an open electoral contest. In Peru, the presidential candidate of 1980 had a background in the *búfalo* wing of the party (which had earlier promoted the use of thugs in APRA's "security" operations).

1985 was whether he would use APRA's renewed access to state resources in an effort to win back party control of the labor movement. Interestingly, he did not. Whereas APRA's historic appeal to the working class had been to the labor movement in the formal sector, García deemphasized this traditional tie and focused on a broader appeal oriented more centrally toward Peru's massive informal sector.

At the beginning of his presidential term, García was perceived by many to have gotten his administration off to a good start. Yet throughout his years in office, he was bedeviled by grave problems: Peru's severe economic difficulties; the Sendero Luminoso insurgency, which departed from the tradition of Latin American guerrilla movements in its extreme use of terror and which, as of 1989, was proving to be increasingly powerful; the distortion of social and economic relations through the growing prevalence of drug trafficking; the growing corruption of the police and the ineffectiveness of the legal system and the prison system; and dramatically rising levels of social violence. García also committed a series of policy blunders including a poorly executed nationalization of Peruvian banks, which produced a confrontation with the banking sector that the president dramatically lost. At the end of his term, García was fully as discredited as Belaúnde had been in 1985.

Thus, the changes in Peru had three crucial components. First, as in Argentina, the ban on the populist party was no longer a fact of politics. Second, as in Uruguay, a substantial new electoral left had emerged. Third, in contrast to Peronism's ongoing dominant role in the Argentine labor movement, APRA largely lost its position in the Peruvian labor movement, and in a new socioeconomic context, in which the formal sector was declining and the informal sector appeared to be of rising importance, APRA did not seek to regain this old constituency. Finally, among the eight countries, Peru—along with Colombia—was experiencing the most grave social and economic crisis, accompanied by severe delegitimation of the state and deterioration of the functioning of state institutions. With these transformations, Peruvian politics was probably the most changed in relation to earlier periods of all the eight cases.

The overall patterns of continuity and change among the full set of countries are summarized in Figure 8.3. This figure replicates Figure 7.2 from the heritage chapter, locating the countries in terms of three dimensions: whether there was a centrist majority bloc in the electoral arena, whether the union movement was organizationally linked to a party or parties of the center, and whether the union movement was usually in the governing coalition. In Figure 8.3, the corners of the cube, which represent alternative "poles" in terms of different combinations of the three variables, are numbered to facilitate identification of different trajectories of change.

As the 1980s closed, it seemed possible that both Brazil and Chile would remain at (or return to) Pole 7. In both, the antigovernment forces at the end of the military regime initially came together in impressive unity. In Brazil, that unity fell apart and a fractionalized and potentially polarizing regime

Figure 8.3 Framework for Analyzing Trajectories of Change

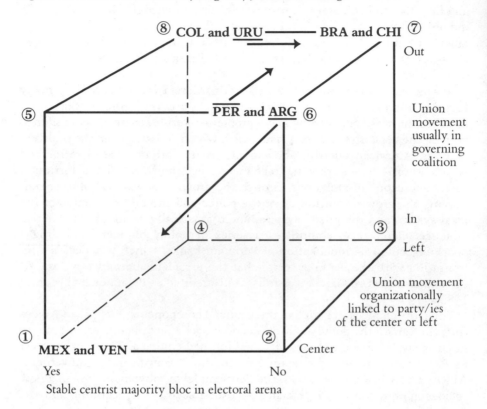

Stable centrist majority bloc in electoral arena

seemed to be reemerging. Chile was, in a sense, a step behind Brazil in regime evolution. Elections in the final days of the decade would bring about the return to civilian rule. In connection with that transition, as in Brazil, substantial consolidation of opposition forces occurred, forming the basis of a new government. The stability of this electoral front would be an important issue of the next period. A further element affecting the potential for renewed polarization in both countries was the international reorientation of Communist movements and the crisis of Marxism in Eastern Europe and the Soviet Union. Accompanying these developments was a greater consensus favoring market mechanisms, reinforced by the constraints of the debt crisis and IMF conditionality.

Venezuela seemed likely to remain near Pole 1, showing little movement on any of the dimensions. With the left unable to capitalize significantly on discontent over economic policy, a change toward fragmentation seemed unlikely. A potential source of change was the discontent over economic stabilization policy, which dealt harshly with those who could least afford it. President Pérez quickly followed his inauguration in 1989 with a "shock" program of economic adjustment and stabilization. This was immediately greeted, in February 1989, with widespread rioting in which 300 to 500 lives were lost. In addition, relations between labor and the government grew increasingly tense, as wages dropped about 50 percent during 1989, according to CTV calculations.[12] Nevertheless, despite a potential tendency toward a more combative labor movement, one could find no clear indication of a loosening of AD-labor ties. In the case of such a change in the labor sector, movement would be toward Pole 8, with greater social conflict and perhaps a strengthening of AD-COPEI cooperation.

The direction of change in Mexico was harder to discern. The growing importance of PAN and the dramatic appearance of the Cárdenist movement pointed to the end of the one-party hegemonic system, a fundamental change, the significance of which should not be underestimated. Yet, none of the three scenarios sketched above represented a movement away from Pole 1. One way or another, it seemed likely that if a greater degree of competitiveness was introduced into the regime, movement would be toward a pattern more similar to that in Venezuela. That is, to the extent one party dominance was undermined, what might emerge was a "one-and-a-half" or "two-and-a-half" party system with centripetal dynamics, a more open regime with greater electoral competition among parties that tended toward programmatic convergence.

In Uruguay, the regime transition of 1985 largely restored the prior political system, with the two traditional parties still in a strong role and, as of 1989, in control of the presidency. The left sustained, and even strengthened substantially, its position in relation to the early 1970s in a pattern that might be approaching that of a three-party system. Uruguay thus showed potential for movement toward Pole 7, though as noted above, in the political climate of the late 1980s, and given the political moderation of the Uruguayan electoral left, even before the 1973 coup, polarization hardly seemed imminent. In Colombia the overwhelming dominance of the two traditional parties had persisted without interruption since 1958, and the electoral arena remained largely closed to the left. Thus Colombia seemed more likely to stay at Pole 8, although as of the end of the 1980s the severity of the confrontation with the drug lords raised many questions about the future of the Colombian political system.

The major innovation in the post-military regimes of Peru and Argentina was the end of the ban on the populist party.[13] In the first election in the 1980s in both countries, the populist party (APRA and Peronism) lost, so these parties did not immediately assume power. Nevertheless, the populist party remained a strong electoral contender, as witnessed by its subsequent victory in both countries. In the framework of this commonality, the two countries were changing in different directions. In Peru, APRA lost its close ties to the labor movement. Subsequently, a strong electoral left emerged in the 1970s, drawing major support from labor. The possibility thus emerged

[12] *Latin American Weekly Report*, Nov. 16, 1989.

[13] This ban had been briefly removed in 1973 in Argentina but then reimposed by the 1976 coup.

that Peru might be moving toward Pole 7. In Argentina, on the other hand, Peronism maintained its close ties to the labor movement and no strong electoral force emerged on the left. Argentina therefore had the potential for movement toward Pole 1 and some form of integrative two-party system. It was this possibility that gave efforts at concertation and social pact formation in Argentina a special analytic importance from the standpoint of this study. It is noteworthy that Peru and Argentina were the only pair in which both countries were moving in new directions. In this sense, the heritage of incorporation was least stable in these two cases. Indeed, this makes sense, since a principal feature of the heritage was the ban in APRA and Peronism. With this ban eliminated, politics changed.

The Role of Social and Economic Explanations

This book has presented an argument centered on the long-term legacy of political contrasts among the incorporation periods. It has explored the political dynamics through which this legacy was perpetuated, and, in the previous section, the political dynamics that would be entailed in the potential erosion of the legacy. Despite this emphasis on political dynamics, it is not our position that socioeconomic factors are unimportant as determinants of politics, but rather that for outcomes of broad regime type and regime dynamics, which are of interest here, their impact is not continuous, but rather occurs in crucial episodes of reorientation and institutional founding.

Given this model, it is worth returning to the question: what is the impact of socioeconomic change and which socioeconomic changes triggered the critical juncture of the incorporation periods on which we have focused? The literature on Latin American development has presented numerous arguments about the varied ways in which socioeconomic change has shaped the political sphere, focusing on such transformations as the emergence of the new export economies beginning in the latter half of the 19th century, the economic disruption that occurred in the context both of the world depression and the two world wars, the internationalization of these economies beginning in the 1950s, and the distinct phases of import-substituting industrialization that have accompanied these other transformations. Many scholars have pointed to the links between the phases of import substitution commonly seen as linked with the depression, on the one hand, and the emergence of such political phenomena as the incorporation periods and populism, on the other.[14]

A basic conclusion of the analysis is that the connection between many of these economic changes and the specific political transitions and regime outcomes we analyze is not as direct as some of the literature would seem to suggest. With reference to the relative timing of the initial incorporation period and the phases of import substitution that began with the depression, it

---

[14] For an overview of some of this literature, see D. Collier (1979:chap. 1).

is evident that the incorporation period sometimes came earlier, sometimes coincided with these economic transitions, and sometimes came later. There was no regular pattern. These major economic changes were a significant part of the context in which such political transformations occurred and at certain points played a conjunctural role in influencing the incorporation periods, but their causal importance has at times been overstated.

If one wished to single out a major economic and social transformation that did appear crucial in setting into motion the processes of political change that are the focus of this book, it would be the earlier period of export expansion, which began in the latter part of the 19th century and extended into the first decades of the 20th century. As we saw, this period of growth stimulated not only massive urban and commercial development, but also significant expansion in manufacturing that occurred well before the industrialization often identified in the literature with the period during and after the depression.[15] This earlier era of growth brought into being the actors and processes of change that were central to the political transformations analyzed here. These included the export oligarchies themselves and the middle sectors which, at times in alliance with dissident elements of the oligarchy, initiated the major reform efforts of the first decades of the century. This earlier period of growth also created the economic and demographic base in the commercial, manufacturing, enclave, and transportation sectors for the emergence of new labor movements, whose increasing capacity for collective organization and intense social protest was a principal stimulus for the reform periods and the incorporation projects that began to emerge in country after country.

This is not to say that an event such as the depression was not extremely important. Indeed, our analysis revealed that it did have a significant impact. The crisis of the depression contributed to the fall of Ibáñez in Chile and cut short his state incorporation project, with the result that the opportunity to implement his policies was far more limited than that enjoyed by Vargas in Brazil. The crisis of the depression contributed to discrediting the Conservative government in Colombia and facilitated the Liberals' rise to power in 1930, which launched the incorporation period. In Uruguay, the shock of the depression helped stimulate the polarization that led to the coup of 1933. In Peru and Argentina, the economic crisis contributed to the fall of the Leguía and Yrigoyen governments in 1930—both of which had earlier made an unsuccessful attempt to launch an incorporation project. Thus, the depression did have an impact. Yet it appears to have been a marginal factor rather than a central factor in explaining the key outcome in this analysis: why different countries were set onto distinct trajectories of change during the incorporation periods.

These observations about the depression may be applied more generally to the impact of a series of other external events, political as well as economic,

[15] With reference to the early employment effects of this manufacturing growth, see Table 3.3.

that successively influenced these cases. In the Overview, we referred to these events, such as World War I, the Russian Revolution, the depression, World War II, the onset of the cold war, economic internationalization, and the Cuban Revolution, as a kind of transnational historical grid through which these countries passed and which was the source of a sequence of cross-sectional influences that cut across the longitudinal trajectory within each case encompassing the incorporation, aftermath, and heritage periods. As with the depression, these other influences also had an important impact, at times reinforcing the patterns associated with internal dynamics of change and at times producing variations but not, within the decades considered here, superseding these internal patterns.

We have just argued, however, that the transnational development that did have a fundamental, founding influence was the enormous expansion of world trade beginning in the second half of the 19th century, which triggered the export growth that in turn set in motion the processes of change that have been the focus of this book. In addition to this highly visible impact of economic change, the other area in which we found a clear relationship between socioeconomic and political change was in the emergence of the labor movements analyzed in Chapter 3. We observed a close connection between the political outcome—the scope of worker organization and protest—and social and economic change, which had created the economic and demographic base for labor movements. However, as noted earlier in the present chapter, the scope of organization and protest did not, in turn, seem to have a systematic impact on the type of incorporation period that emerged in each country. Once again, to explain the different types of incorporation it appears more fruitful to go back to the broader transformations in social and political structure that derived from the period of export-led growth—as well as to political institutions with roots further back in the 19th century.

Thus, the impact of socioeconomic change on politics is sometimes unambiguous, direct, and relatively unmediated; sometimes unambiguous, yet indirect and mediated through other variables; and sometimes ambiguous and at most indirect. The task is to distinguish which of these alternatives pertains for the particular political outcomes one wishes to explain.

The pattern of links between socioeconomic change and politics that best summarizes our analysis is one in which a major economic and social transformation (such as this earlier period of export-led growth) sets into motion processes of political change (such as the incorporation period and its legacy), which later achieve a certain margin of autonomy in relation to the socioeconomic context. Thus, though the emergence of distinct types of incorporation reflected prior socioeconomic and political differences among countries, the subsequent dynamics derived to a significant extent from the political logic of incorporation itself.

Figure 8.4, adapted from Figure 1.1 in the first chapter, diagrammatically highlights the socioeconomic context of the critical juncture of the incorporation period, which in turn produced the partially autonomous legacy that has been the focus of this book. Against this base line, we may now return

Figure 8.4 The Socioeconomic Context of Critical Junctures

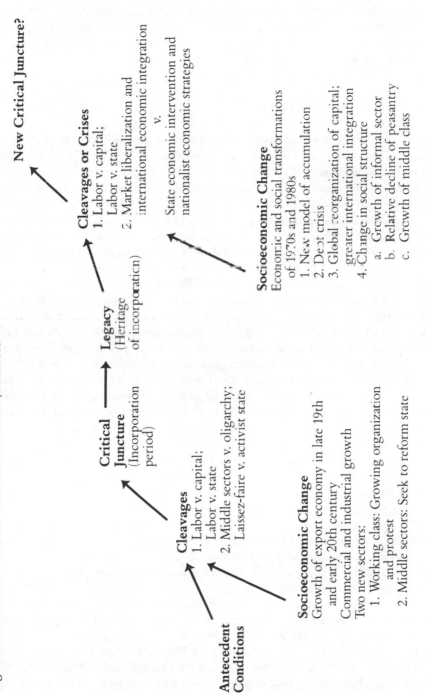

**Antecedent
Conditions**

Socioeconomic Change
Growth of export economy in late 19th
and early 20th century
Commercial and industrial growth
Two new sectors:
1. Working class: Growing organization
   and protest
2. Middle sectors: Seek to reform state

Cleavages
1. Labor v. capital;
   Labor v. state
2. Middle sectors v. oligarchy;
   Laissez-faire v. activist state

**Critical
Juncture**
(Incorporation
period)

Legacy
(Heritage
of incorporation)

Cleavages or Crises
1. Labor v. capital;
   Labor v. state
2. Market liberalization and
   international economic integration
   v.
   State economic intervention and
   nationalist economic strategies

Socioeconomic Change
Economic and social transformations
of 1970s and 1980s
1. New model of accumulation
2. Debt crisis
3. Global reorganization of capital;
   greater international integration
4. Change in social structure
   a. Growth of informal sector
   b. Relative decline of peasantry
   c. Growth of middle class

New Critical Juncture?

to the question of the erosion of the legacy and ask whether or not, in the context of changes such as the internationalization of production, the debt crisis, and economic liberalization, the period of the late 1980s was possibly producing a new critical juncture.

A New Critical Juncture?

In discussing the possibility that the heritage of incorporation may erode, we noted elements of political continuity and change. However, a broader question must be posed. The critical juncture of the incorporation periods emerged under specific historical conditions of economic and social change, and these conditions made certain political coalitions possible. As of the 1980s, when many of these conditions seemed to be changing, one might ask whether these changes would trigger a new critical juncture, based on the founding of quite different coalitional patterns and regime dynamics.

Evidence of economic transformations that might constitute the basis for a new critical juncture was not hard to find. It could be observed in many areas, both international and domestic. Indeed, the international factors by themselves seemed important enough to suggest the possibility of fundamental change. At the most general level, the period of the 1970s and 1980s was one of a major reorganization of capital on a global scale. Several elements were involved, and these suggested the emergence of a post-postwar order. Central among these were the decline of U.S. hegemony and the final reconstruction of Japan and Europe as economic competitors; the growing importance of world trade and the closer integration of national economies with the global economy; the rise of the NICs as low-cost producers and suppliers of industrial goods; and the adoption of new kinds of global production and marketing strategies by multinational corporations. Accompanying the new internationalization of production and economic interdependence was a strong downward pressure on wages throughout the world and a retreat from Keynesian economics and class compromise between capital and labor. Keynesianism was replaced by a new hegemony of economic orthodoxy, liberalism, and free market ideologies, the effects of which were seen in countries as diverse as the laissez-faire United States, the welfare state of Great Britain, and, most dramatically, the command economies of the communist world, as well as Latin America.

In addition to these global trends, other, often related factors specifically affected Latin American countries. Most obvious was the staggering debt burden that erupted into a full-fledged crisis in 1982. Subsequently, policies to confront the debt crisis, influenced by IMF conditionality, produced low or at times even negative economic growth, net capital outflows, unemployment, and plummeting real wages. Equally familiar were changing patterns of industrialization and the introduction of new models of accumulation, specifically the shift from inward-oriented growth to new industrial production for export. In addition, within Latin American countries over the several decades since the incorporation period, social structure had been trans-formed. The most obvious changes were the growth of the middle class, the strengthening of the private sector, and rapid urbanization, involving a de-clining peasantry and a growing urban informal sector.

Indeed, some of these same socioeconomic factors were advanced as prin-cipal explanations of the coups of the 1960s and 1970s and of the more subtle regime changes in countries that did not have coups. Specifically, O'Donnell (1973, 1979, 1982) sought an explanation for those coups and the new forms of bureaucratic-authoritarian regimes they instituted in factors such as the internationalization of the Latin American economies, changing patterns of industrialization, and the impact of a newly emerging technocratic class. Likewise, it has been suggested (McCoy 1985) that in Venezuela, a country with no coup, a similar change in the model of accumulation led to more subtle changes in state-labor relations. The 1989 riots in reaction to the debt-induced austerity package were illustrative of the potential acceleration of social protest. With reference to Mexico, even before the dramatic results of the 1988 election, many of the changes listed above were evoked in explain-ing the PRI's declining hegemony and the possible unraveling of the one-party system. In Peru, APRA's efforts at support mobilization under Alan García, that focused more on the informal sector and unorganized workers than on the organized labor movement, suggested that the stagnation of the formal sector and the dynamism of the informal sector could produce impor-tant changes in politics.[16]

By the end of the 1980s, it was not possible to establish unambiguously either the erosion of the prior legacy or the presence of a new critical junc-ture. Nevertheless, some initial observations can be made.

First, many of the changes noted above seemed to undermine populist co-alitions and put pressure on labor and wages—especially the relatively pro-tected wages of unionized workers—in a way that could contribute to the erosion of past patterns. Furthermore, in the conjuncture of the late 1980s, change seemed so widespread and thorough-going on a global scale and so multifaceted within Latin America that it appeared likely that a new critical juncture might be imminent. Nevertheless, as mentioned, the causal impact even of convulsive changes such as the world depression of the 1930s may have been less important than is sometimes supposed for the *specific kinds* of political alignments or regime outcomes considered here. Thus, caution was necessary in proclaiming the emergence of a new critical juncture that would produce a major regime reorientation.

Second, even if a new critical juncture was emerging, the timing of the political reorientation would not necessarily be concurrent in all countries. The incorporation periods earlier in this century were strung out over nearly

[16] As indicated in Chapter 6, in the 1940s and 1950s President Odría of Peru also made a major appeal to an important part of the informal sector—the squatter settlements. How-ever, because he was at the time repressing APRA and the APRA-dominated labor move-ment, he was in a less good position to cultivate organized labor. In the 1980s, by contrast, APRA might reasonably have tried to regain control of organized labor.

five decades, and the timing of a new critical juncture might similarly vary, although increasing economic integration and the growing impact of international factors as well as the acceleration of technological change might condense the timing.

Third, even if a similar crisis or cleavage produced the critical juncture in each country, a similar political outcome could not be assumed. The argument about the earlier periods of initial incorporation is that different countries confronted the given cleavages in a variety of ways, in part depending on antecedent conditions. The new conditions represented by a new critical juncture in the 1980s and beyond could well produce a common set of constraints or parameters limiting the political structures that appeared, but different countries would confront the situation differently.

Finally, it follows that if a new critical juncture was emerging, the political structures and dynamics described in the course of this book would doubtless continue to be important antecedent causal factors, conditioning the distinctive response of each country.

Appendix

Heads of State since 1900

Argentina

1898–1904	Julio Argentino Roca
1904–1906	Manuel Quintana
1906–1910	José Figueroa Alcorta
1910–1913	Roque Sáenz Peña
1913–1916	Victorino de la Plaza
1916–1922	Hipólito Yrigoyen
1922–1928	Marcelo Torcuato de Alvear
1928–1930	Hipólito Yrigoyen
1930–1932	José Félix Uriburu
1932–1938	Agustín P. Justo
1938–1940	Roberto M. Ortiz
1940–1943	Ramón S. Castillo
1943	Arturo Rawson
1943–1944	Pedro P. Ramírez
1944–1946	Edelmiro J. Farrell
1946–1955	Juan Domingo Perón
1955	Eduardo Lonardi
1955–1958	Pedro Eugenio Aramburu
1958–1962	Arturo Frondizi
1962–1963	José María Guido
1963–1966	Arturo Illia
1966–1970	Juan Carlos Onganía
1970–1971	Roberto Marcelo Levingston
1971–1973	Alejandro A. Lanusse
1973	Héctor Cámpora
1973	Raúl Lastiri
1973–1974	Juan Domingo Perón
1974–1976	María Estela (Isabel) Martínez de Perón
1976–1981	Jorge Rafael Videla
1981	Roberto Viola
1981–1982	Leopoldo Fortunato Galtieri
1982–1983	Reynaldo Benito Antonio Bignone
1983–1989	Raúl Ricardo Alfonsin
1989–	Carlos Saúl Menem

Brazil

1898–1902	Manuel Ferraz de Campos Sales
1902–1906	Francisco de Paula Rodrigues Alves
1906–1909	Afonso Augusto Moreira Pena
1909	Nilo Peçanha
1910–1914	Hermes da Fonseca
1914–1918	Venceslau Brás Pereira Gomes
1918–1919	Delfim Moreira da Costa Ribeiro

1919–1922   Epitácio da Silva Pessôa
1922–1926   Artur da Silva Bernardes
1926–1930   Washington Luís Pereira de Sousa
1930–1945   Getúlio Dornelles Vargas
1945–1946   José Linhares
1946–1951   Eurico Gaspar Dutra
1951–1954   Getúlio Dornelles Vargas
1954–1955   João Café Filho
1955   Carlos Coimbra da Luz
1955–1956   Nereu Ramos
1956–1961   Juscelino Kubitschek de Oliveria
1961   Jânio da Silva Quadros
1961–1964   João B. M. Goulart
1964–1967   Humberto de Alencar Castello Branco
1967–1969   Artur da Costa e Silva
1969   Augusto Hamann Rademaker Gruenewald
1969–1974   Emílio Garrastazú Médici
1974–1979   Ernesto Geisel
1979–1985   João Baptista de Oliveira Figueiredo
1985–1990   José Sarney
1990–   Fernando Collor de Mello

Chile

1896–1901   Federico Errázuriz
1901–1905   Germán Riesco Errázuriz
1905–1906   Rafael Rayas
1906–1910   Pedro Montt
1910   Elías Fernández Albano
1910–1911   Emiliano Figueroa
1911–1915   Ramón Barros Luco
1915–1920   José Luis Sanfuentes
1920   Luis Barros Borgoño
1920–1924   Arturo Alessandri Palma
1924–1925   Luis Altamirano
1925   Carlos Ibáñez del Campo
1925   Arturo Alessandri Palma
1925   Luis Barros Borgoño
1925–1927   Emiliano Figueroa Larraín
1927–1931   Carlos Ibáñez del Campo
1931   Pedro Opazo Letelier
1931   Juan Esteban Montero Rodríguez
1931   Manuel Trucco Franzani
1931–1932   Juan Esteban Montero Rodríguez
1932   Arturo Puga
1932   Marmaduque Grove
1932   Carlos Dávila Espinoza
1932   Bartolomé Blanche Espejo
1932   Abraham Oyanedel
1932–1938   Arturo Alessandri Palma
1938–1941   Pedro Aguirre Cerda

1941–1942   Geronimo Méndez Arancibia
1942–1946   Juan Antonio Ríos Morales
1946   Alfredo Duhalde Vásquez
1946   Juan A. Irabarren
1946–1952   Gabriel González Videla
1952–1958   Carlos Ibáñez del Campo
1958–1964   Jorge Alessandri Rodríguez
1964–1970   Eduardo Frei Montalva
1970–1973   Salvador Allende Gossens
1973–1990   Augusto Pinochet Ugarte
1990–   Patricio Aylwin

Colombia

1898–1900   Manuel Antonio Sanclemente
1900–1904   José Manuel Marroquín
1904–1909   Rafael Reyes Prieto
1909   Jorge Holguín
1909–1910   Ramón González Valencia
1910–1914   Carlos E. Restrepo
1914–1918   José Vincente Concha
1918–1921   Marco Fidel Súarez
1921–1922   Jorge Holguín
1922–1926   Pedro Nel Ospina
1926–1930   Miguel Abadía Méndez
1930–1934   Enrique Olaya Herrera
1934–1938   Alfonso López Pumarejo
1938–1942   Eduardo Santos
1942–1945   Alfonso López Pumarejo
1945–1946   Alberto Lleras Camargo
1946–1950   Mariano Ospina Pérez
1950–1951   Laureano Gómez Castro
1951–1953   Roberto Urdaneta Arbeláez
1953–1957   Gustavo Rojas Pinilla
1957–1958   Gabriel París
1958–1962   Alberto Lleras Camargo
1962–1966   Guillermo León Valencia
1966–1970   Carlos Lleras Restrepo
1970–1974   Misael Pastrana Borrero
1974–1978   Alfonso López Michelsen
1978–1982   Julio César Turbay Ayala
1982–1986   Belisario Betancur
1986–1990   Virgilio Barco Vargas
1990–   César Gaviria Trujillo

Mexico

1884–1911   Porfirio Díaz (previously president from
               1876–1880)
1911   Francisco León de la Barra
1911–1913   Francisco Madero
1913–1914   Victoriano Huerta

1915–1920	Venustiano Carranza
1920	Adolfo de la Huerta
1920–1924	Alvaro Obregón
1924–1928	Plutarco Elías Calles
1928–1930	Emilio Portes Gil
1930–1932	Pascual Ortiz Rubio
1932–1934	Abelardo Rodríguez
1934–1940	Lázaro Cárdenas
1940–1946	Manuel Avila Camacho
1946–1952	Miguel Alemán
1952–1958	Adolfo Ruiz Cortines
1958–1964	Adolfo López Mateos
1964–1970	Gustavo Díaz Ordaz
1970–1976	Luis Echeverría Alvarez
1976–1982	José López Portillo
1982–1988	Miguel de la Madrid Hurtado
1988–	Carlos Salinas de Gortari

Peru

1899–1903	Eduardo López de Romaña
1903–1904	Manuel Candamo
1904	Serapio Calderón
1904–1908	José Pardo y Barreda
1908–1912	Augusto B. Leguía
1912–1914	Guillermo E. Billinghurst
1914–1915	Oscar R. Benavides
1915–1919	José Pardo y Barreda
1919–1930	Augusto B. Leguía
1930	Manuel Ponce
1930–1931	Luis M. Sánchez Cerro
1931	Ricardo Leoncio Elías
1931	Gustavo A. Jiménez
1931	David Sámanez Ocampo
1931–1933	Luis M. Sánchez Cerro
1933–1939	Oscar R. Benavides
1939–1945	Manuel Prado y Ugarteche
1945–1948	José Luis Bustamante i Rivero
1948	Zenón Noriega
1948–1950	Manuel A. Odría
1950	Zenón Noriega
1950–1956	Manuel A. Odría
1956–1962	Manuel Prado y Ugarteche
1962–1963	Ricardo Pérez Godoy
1963	Nicolás Lindley López
1963–1968	Fernando Belaúnde Terry
1968–1975	Juan Velasco Alvarado
1975–1980	Francisco Morales Bermúdez
1980–1985	Fernando Belaúnde Terry
1985–1990	Alan García Pérez
1990–	Alberto Fujimori

Uruguay

1897–1903	Juan Lindolfo Cuestas
1903–1907	José Batlle y Ordóñez
1907–1911	Claudio Williman
1911–1915	José Batlle Ordóñez
1915–1919	Feliciano Viera
1919–1923	Baltasar Brum
1923–1927	José Serrato
1927–1931	Juan Campisteguy
1931–1938	Gabriel Terra
1938–1943	Alfredo Baldomir
1943–1947	Juan José de Amézaga
1947	Tomás Berreta
1947–1948	Luis Batlle y Berres
1948	César Mayo Gutiérrez
1948–1951	Luis Batlle Berres
1951–1952	Andrés Martínez Trueba
1952–1967	Second Colegiado
1967	Oscar Daniel Gestido
1967–1972	Jorge Pacheco Areco
1972–1976	Juan María Bordaberry
1976–1981	Aparicio Méndez
1981–1985	Gregorio Alvarez
1985–1990	Julio María Sanguinetti
1990–	Luis Alberto Lacalle

Venezuela

1899–1908	Cipriano Castro
1908–1915	Juan Vicente Gómez
1915–1922	Victorino Márquez Bustillos
1922–1929	Juan Vicente Gómez
1929–1931	Juan Bautista Pérez
1931–1935	Juan Vicente Gómez
1935–1941	Eleazar López Contreras
1941–1945	Isaias Medina Angarita
1945–1948	Rómulo Betancourt
1948	Rómulo Gallegos
1948–1950	Carlos Delgado Chalbaud
1950–1952	Germán Suárez Flamerich
1952–1958	Marcos Pérez Jiménez
1958–1959	Wolfgang Larrazabál Ugueto
1959–1964	Rómulo Betancourt
1964–1969	Raúl Leoni
1969–1974	Rafael Caldera López
1974–1979	Carlos Andrés Pérez
1979–1984	Luis Herrera Campíns
1984–1989	Jaime Lusinchi
1989–	Carlos Andrés Pérez

Glossary

ACCOMMODATIONIST ALLIANCE. An alliance between middle-sector political leadership and more traditional, agrarian elites. This term is used in analyzing the incorporation and aftermath periods and is contrasted with the coalitional alternative of a populist alliance.

AFTERMATH. The period immediately following initial incorporation. Within the framework in which the incorporation period is viewed as a critical juncture, the aftermath is the first phase of the legacy of incorporation. See also heritage.

ANTECEDENT POLITICAL SYSTEM. In the discussion of critical junctures, this is the prior political period that is the "base line" against which the (presumably different) legacy of the critical juncture is compared.

BOURGEOISIE. Owners and high-level managers of enterprises in the urban commercial, financial, and industrial sector, as well as in the modern enclave sector. The relation between the terms bourgeoisie and oligarchy is discussed under oligarchy below.

CENTER, POLITICAL. A middle position between fundamental political alternatives. This may involve a middle position with reference to a left-right ideological spectrum, to alternative choices about political regimes, or to other basic political issues. The "center" is a relative term that must be understood in relation to the spectrum of alternatives within a given national context. Very crucially, during the aftermath period in the cases of party incorporation, the center represents a compromise between the often-radical reforms of the incorporation period and the policies of the conservative reaction to incorporation.

COMPETITIVE REGIME. Applied to civilian regimes under which there is at least substantial electoral competition, although they may not be fully democratic. This term covers a range of cases from post-1958 Venezuela to pre-1973 Chile. See also democratic regime and semicompetitive regime.

CONSTRAINTS. See corporatism.

CORPORATISM. A pattern of relationships between the state and interest groups based on state *structuring* of representation that produces a system of officially sanctioned, noncompetitive, compulsory interest associations; state *subsidy* of these associations; and state imposed *constraints* on leadership, demand-making, and internal governance. In this book, the discussion of corporatism focuses specifically on unions. Structuring and subsidy together constitute *inducements*. While both inducements and constraints are viewed as instruments of control, inducements are double edged as they bestow certain advantages. Crucial periods in the evolution of state-labor are viewed in terms of a strategic interaction involving the varied application and consequences of inducements and constraints in the context of the dual dilemma. While the Latin American cases considered here predominantly involve variants of "state corporatism," this definition could also be applied in contexts of societal corporatism (see Chapter 2), in which case the constraints would be limited, and state structuring and subsidy would in important measure serve to ratify patterns of interest politics that had initially been forged outside the state (Collier and Collier 1979:978–79).

CRITICAL JUNCTURE. A period of significant change, which typically occurs in distinct ways in different countries (or in other units of analysis), and which is hypothesized to produce distinct legacies. Criteria for identifying a critical juncture are discussed in Chapter 1.

DEMOCRATIC REGIME. Used in the sense of Dahl's term "polyarchy," which he defines as a regime that allows extensive political participation and is broadly open to public contestation (1971:7–8). Our usage is thus restricted to *political* democracy. Questions of economic and social democracy are discussed in terms of such themes and labels as equity and welfare. See also competitive regime and semicompetitive regime.

DUAL DILEMMA. The choices on the part of both the state and labor about the type of state-labor relations to pursue. Each alternative presents both advantages and pitfalls. On the side of the state, this choice is between the option of controlling the labor movement and seeking to mobilize labor support; on the side of the labor movement it is between cooperating with the state and resisting such cooperation in order to maintain greater autonomy, as well as the choice between entering or abstaining from the sphere of partisan politics.

ELITE. Relatively small groups or strata that exert great influence, authority, and power of decision. We refer to owners and managers of large enterprises as the "economic elite," and to the leaders of the initial incorporation period as the "incorporating elite." We also refer to the "state elite," in the sense of leaders at the pinnacle of the state, and to the "political elite," in the sense of the principal political leaders. There is a long debate over the merits of the term "elite," as opposed to an expression such as the "dominant class" (or classes), which is common in Latin American political analysis. We have generally opted for the expression "elite," although the term "dominant classes" is also sometimes used. In some cases, union leaders have reached positions of substantial power over economic policy and resources. However, we do not include them when we employ this term.

ENCLAVE. An isolated area of modernized production or extraction in the agricultural, mining, or petroleum sector.

GOVERNMENT. The head of state and the immediate political leadership that surrounds the head of state. In this sense one speaks of the "Perón government" with the same meaning as the Perón administration. This usage contrasts with that in some fields of political analysis, including the field of American politics (see Sartori 1984:20), where the term is used in a way more similar to our usage of state.

HEGEMONY. The capacity to rule through consent and mediation, rather than coercion. "Hegemonic resources" refers to the political resources—institutional, ideological, and symbolic—that facilitate this type of rule. This usage derives from Gramsci.

HERITAGE. The political system and political dynamics that are the legacy of the incorporation period. The heritage encompasses most of what we refer to as the aftermath, with the exception of the periods of conservative military rule that follow party incorporation in some countries (see introduction to Chapter 7). The issue of the end of the heritage is addressed in Chapter 8.

INCORPORATION. See initial incorporation.

INDUCEMENTS. See corporatism.

INITIAL INCORPORATION OF THE LABOR MOVEMENT. The first sustained and at least partially successful attempt by the state to legitimate and shape an institutionalized labor movement. For the sake of brevity, we often refer to the "incorporation period" and to the "legacy of incorporation." The components of the definition of initial incorporation are understood as follows:

1. "First sustained and at least partially successful" means that these state policies are maintained for more than a brief period, such as just a few months; that they actually affect a substantial portion of the labor movement, and not just a few unions; and that this is the first such policy episode in the particular country.

2. The definition refers to the "state" (in the sense of the bureaucratic and legal institutions of the public sector and the incumbents of those institutions) rather than the government (in the sense of the head of state and the immediate political leadership that surrounds the head of state). Though in general the incorporation periods were initiated by the government in this sense, the important commonality that we focus on is the way and degree to which, as a result of these policies, the state more broadly comes to regulate or oversee unions and industrial relations.

3. "Legitimate and shape" refers to state support and approval of the existence of unions as organizations, along with an effort to influence the role of the labor movement either in the economic system, involving an attempt to institutionalize a system of labor and industrial relations; and/or in the political system, involving alternatively an attempt to depoliticize the labor movement or to win its loyalty to a political party or political movement. Often, though not always, these two dimensions of incorporation occur simultaneously, and the different combinations in which they occur is one of the central concerns of this study.

A central argument of the book is that initial incorporation occurs in relatively well defined policy periods, which we frequently refer to as the "incorporation period." These periods emerge as part of a larger program of political and economic reform, and in five of the eight countries, the onset of the incorporation period coincides with the onset of what we call the "reform period," whereas in the other three there is at least a moderate delay in the incorporation period (see Table 0.1 in the Overview).

Four important issues that arise in analyzing the incorporation period may be noted here.

1. *Incremental Change.* Most countries experience long-term, incremental growth of the state role in labor relations and the labor movement, constituting an ongoing "ratchet effect" in spheres such as that of labor legislation (Webb

1975:6). The incremental character of this process raises the problem of identifying the period that meets the criterion of being the "first sustained and at least partially successful attempt." This task is further complicated by contrasts among countries in the timing of the incorporation periods. Not surprisingly, countries in which these periods occur later—as in Peru and Argentina—have a more extensive history of prior incremental initiatives. This more extensive prior history can and does lead to debates among country specialists about the degree to which the incorporation period itself represents a major disjuncture, and these debates must be examined with great care.

2. *Phases of the incorporation period.* Not surprisingly, the overall policy period that fits the above definition may fall into two or more phases. Most countries had a first phase of the incorporation period—led by what we call "conservative modernizers"—characterized by cautious or ambivalent initiatives toward the labor movement and/or attempts at reform that were initially blocked. This is followed by a more extensive and ambitious phase of incorporation. These phases are discussed extensively in Chapter 5 and are summarized in Figure 5.1.

In some countries the incorporation period is interrupted by a hiatus of several years, yet given the larger political context it seems reasonable to treat the period both before and after the hiatus as part of the incorporation period. For instance, in Colombia the incorporation period includes not only the main phase of López's Revolución en Marcha (i.e., his first administration, 1934–38), but also his second administration (1942–45), which was an important period of progressive labor policy. While the Santos administration (1938–42) clearly represented a pause in terms of labor reforms, it seems reasonable to treat it as one step within the larger incorporation period. In Mexico, the relationship between the 1920s, the "Maximato" (1928–34), and the Cárdenas period was interpreted in the same manner.

3. *Transition versus Outcome.* The incorporation periods, as analyzed here, are viewed primarily as *transitions*, rather than as *outcomes*, and the attributes in terms of which any one country is classified in the typology of incorporation periods may not characterize that country in the heritage period. For instance, the type of transition referred to as party incorporation may or may not result in the long run in a labor movement strongly tied to the party or movement that launched the incorporation period. Correspondingly, when we refer to a country as a case of party—or state—incorporation, we are referring to this earlier transition, and not to the longer-term legacy.

4. *Relation to other definitions of "incorporated," "incorporating," and "incorporation."* The definition of the initial incorporation period is thus grounded in specific issues of this particular historical transition and is distinct from at least three equally valid usages of related forms of this term: (a) The term *incorporated* is sometimes used in the analysis of subsequent historical periods to describe situations in which a major part of the union movement (and/or the working class or the lower classes more broadly) is linked in a stable, well-institutionalized manner to the political system. In some cases this usage is intended to mean that organized labor is "in" the governing coalition, albeit in a subordinate position, or is at least a serious contender among claimants for the benefits of state policy. Examples of this usage are found in Purcell (1975:chap. 1) and Davis and Coleman (1986). Alternatively, the stress may be on the co-optation and control of labor, typically within a corporative frame-

work. The relationship between the different types of initial incorporation periods analyzed in this book and the outcome of a union movement that is incorporated in this sense is complex, as we show in Chapters 7 and 8. (b) The term *incorporating* is sometimes used in the sense of O'Donnell's definition of an "incorporating political system" which "purposely seeks to activate the popular sector and to allow it some voice in national politics—or that, without deliberate efforts at either exclusion or incorporation, adapts itself to the existing levels of political activation and the given set of political actors" (1973:55). Such a definition could apply both to the historical period analyzed here and to some subsequent periods. (c) Subsequent incorporation periods that also involve a major new attempt to legitimate and shape the labor movement obviously occur in some countries, as in the post-1968 period in Peru. These episodes, while very important, are not the initial incorporation period, involving the first such attempt, and hence do not fit the present definition.

INTEGRATIVE PARTY SYSTEM. A party system in which there is a majority bloc in the electoral arena located roughly at the center of the political spectrum, and in which the labor movement is organizationally linked to this majority bloc and is usually part of the governing coalition. The majority bloc may involve the electoral dominance of a single party; or of two centrist parties that are either linked by stable ties of cooperation, or that compete actively, but in a context of centrifugal competition. The analysis of the heritage of incorporation in Chapter 7 contrasts the integrative party system with three other types: stalemated party systems, systems characterized by electoral stability and social conflict, and multiparty polarizing systems (see the introduction to Chapter 7). In addition to serving as a description of two cases (Mexico and Venezuela), the concept of an integrative party system is used in the analysis as a "polar type," with which the other kinds of party systems are compared.

LABOR MOVEMENT. The organizations and collective action of wage earners in the modern sector, which have the purpose of promoting shared occupational goals. Also referred to as labor or the union movement.

LABOR POPULISM. A subtype of party incorporation, found in Peru and Argentina, involving the extensive mobilization of labor in the modern sector by a political party or movement that in the Latin American usage is conventionally called populist. See also populism, populist party, radical populism.

LEGACY. The sequence of political events, relationships, and dynamics of change hypothesized to be the outcome of a critical juncture. In this book the legacy is divided into two periods, the aftermath and the heritage.

MIDDLE SECTOR. Members of a broad range of occupational groups that stand between the working class and the economic elite. This expression was introduced by John J. Johnson (1958) to avoid what seemed to be the overly restrictive implications of speaking of the middle "class." In the text, the expression "middle class" is also on occasion used in this narrower sense.

MODERN SECTOR. The economy of the urban sector, as well as of rural agricultural production and mineral or oil extraction, that is characterized by the application of technology that yields relatively high levels of productivity. O'Donnell (1973:Chap. 1) discusses the problem of identifying a threshold in terms of relevant indicators that could serve as a point of demarcation between the modern and traditional sector. See also traditional sector.

OLIGARCHIC STATE. A characterization of the state during roughly the late 19th and early 20th century, when in most of these countries the state imposed relative political stability that greatly facilitated massive export growth and the emergence of new, more dynamic sectors of the "oligarchy," or export elite. With reference to economic and social policy, these were characteristically laissez-faire states that made significant use of the concession of important spheres of economic activity to the private sector (often to foreign capital) as a means of creating basic infrastructure that helped promote economic growth.

The adjective "oligarchic" also refers to the tight control over the political process reflected in such practices as a narrow franchise, widespread electoral fraud, or in certain cases dictatorial rule, which were a common characteristic of politics in this period. These attributes could therefore be seen as aspects of an "oligarchic regime," and a broader label such as "oligarchic political system" might appropriately be applied to this period. However, following common usage in the literature (e.g., Ianni 1975), the expression "oligarchic state" is retained here.

OLIGARCHY. This term is used here primarily with reference to the late 19th century and the first decades of the 20th century to refer to national and regional (i.e., subnational) economic elites, primarily the landed elite and the elites in the mineral/extractive sector. The relative importance of these different sectors within the oligarchy varies greatly among countries. To the extent that enterprises in these sectors are foreign owned, the foreign corporations themselves as they exist abroad are not part of the oligarchy, but the leading managers of these firms who are actors within the national context are. The oligarchy is identified both in terms of its control of these sectors of the economy and in terms of its attributes as an elite social and cultural network identified with the leading "40 families" (the number varies), membership in a leading club or clubs, and so on. For a sophisticated effort to identify members of an oligarchy or "aristocracy" in Argentina, see Smith (1974a:appendix A).

In the literature on this earlier period, the assessment of whether the emerging elites of the commercial, financial, industrial, and enclave sectors are viewed as part of this oligarchy, as opposed to representing a bourgeoisie, depends on the degree to which these new elites differentiate themselves from the established oligarchy in economic, political, and cultural terms. Particularly to the extent that the same individuals or families are involved in both "oligarchic" and "bourgeois" pursuits, such differentiation is a matter of degree, and it is difficult to establish precise criteria of demarcation. Although a full empirical assessment of the degree of differentiation for all eight cases over the period covered in this book would be an enormous task, we make some tentative observations about this differentiation at specific points in time.

In discussions of certain later points, such as the post-1930 period in Peru and Argentina, the return to political power of elements of the same political leadership that had earlier been described as oligarchic is often referred to as a restoration of oligarchic rule, and we follow this usage. In discussions of still more recent periods, the literature sometimes uses the term oligarchic to refer more loosely to governments that are not responsive to popular demands and are oriented toward elite economic interests. This final usage is not adopted in this book. (For a discussion of criteria relevant for applying the term in this sense, see J. Payne 1968.) The usage adopted here is of course distinct from Robert Michels' "iron law of oligarchy," to which reference is made in Chapter 2.

ORGANIZED LABOR. The collectivity of occupational associations (alternatively called interest associations, representative associations, or, adapting from Schmitter [1977], "intermediative" associations) of wage earners of the working class and middle sector within the modern sector, thus including the modernized agricultural and extractive sector as well as the urban sector. The scope of this definition corresponds to the common pattern of aggregation of workers associations in these countries, in that agricultural workers in modern enclaves or the modern rural sector typically belong to the national organized labor movement. With this last exception, unions of rural workers are not included. The expression *organized labor* is used interchangeably with *organized labor movement*, *trade union movement*, and *union movement*. The choice to restrict ourselves to one of these expressions would have been preferable in terms of consistency, but was stylistically unappealing, since the expression thus chosen would have been used with such frequency in the text. The alternative of using an abbreviation throughout—as in O'Donnell's use of "BA" for the "bureaucratic-authoritarian state" (1975, 1979, 1982)—did not seem appropriate. We hope that this glossary will establish adequate criteria of consistency.

ORGANIZED LABOR MOVEMENT. See organized labor. Used interchangeably with organized labor, trade union movement, and union movement.

ORGANIZED PEASANTRY. The collectivity of occupational associations of peasants.

PARTY. See political party.

PARTY INCORPORATION. A type of initial incorporation in which the incorporating elite seeks to mobilize labor support for a political party—or a political movement that later becomes a party—as a fundamental aspect of the incorporation project. A more complete though less convenient label for this set of cases would thus be party/movement incorporation. Within the framework of our definition of initial incorporation, the state is by definition involved in the incorporation project, but the political dynamics are so different where a party also played a strong role as to justify this distinct label. See also state incorporation.

PEASANTS. Small-scale cultivators, who may have any one of a number of alternative relationships to the land they till, including private or collective ownership, tenancy, sharecropping, or a feudal relationship of exchange.

POLITICAL PARTY. A political group that presents candidates in elections to public office; or a political group that would do so but is unable to, either because it is proscribed or because elections are not held. This is an adaptation of Sartori's (1976:64) "minimal definition." Since the banning of parties and the failure to hold elections are recurring events in Latin America, the second component of the definition is essential.

POPULAR SECTOR. The urban and rural lower classes, including the lower middle class. From the perspective of the present analysis, the inclusion of segments of the lower middle class in this category is crucial because it is often part of the organized labor movement.

POPULISM. A political movement characterized by mass support from the urban working class and/or peasantry; a strong element of mobilization from above; a central role of leadership from the middle sector or elite, typically of a personalistic and/or charismatic character; and an anti–status-quo, nationalist ideology and program. This definition draws heavily on the widely cited discussion of di Tella, and also on Drake (1978:chap. 1). Whereas analyses of some other parts of the world use the term populism to refer to movements with a strong agrarian and grassroots character, the Latin American literature has placed central emphasis on the working class in the modern sector and on mobilization from above. In the present book, it is essential to note that the initial incorporation periods do not necessarily involve populism. In Mexico, Venezuela, Peru, and Argentina they do. In Uruguay and Colombia, the role of a traditional political party in leading the incorporation period, along with other factors, makes them at most marginally populist. In Brazil and Chile, the control-oriented incorporation periods are not populist, though in the aftermath of incorporation leaders associated with the incorporation periods subsequently seek to form populist parties. See also labor populism, radical populism, and populist party.

POPULIST ALLIANCE. An alliance between middle-sector political leadership and important elements of the popular sector. This term is used in analyzing the initial incorporation period and the aftermath period and is contrasted with the coalitional alternative of an accommodationist alliance.

POPULIST PARTY. A political party that possesses attributes associated with populism as defined above, including mass support from the urban working class and/or peasantry; a strong element of mobilization from above; a central role of leadership from the middle sector or elite, commonly of a personalistic and/or charismatic character; and an anti–status-quo, nationalist ideology and program. Important populist parties considered in this study are the revolutionary party in Mexico, Acción Democrática in Venezuela, APRA in Peru, Peronism in Argentina, the PTB in Brazil, and (as Drake 1978 insists) the Socialist Party in Chile, at least up to the 1950s. The term populist would typically not be applied to communist parties, which to a greater degree are characterized by more impersonal, institutionalized norms of hierarchy that include an important international dimension.

RADICAL POPULISM. A subtype of party incorporation, found in Mexico and Venezuela, in which the extensive mobilization of labor in the modern sector is accompanied by agrarian reform and peasant mobilization. This mobilization is carried out by a party or movement that in the Latin American literature is conventionally called populist. The adjective *radical* is intended to refer to the more comprehensive assault on preexisting property relations entailed in this type of incorporation period. See also populism, labor populism.

REFORM PERIOD. This expression is used at a number of points as an abbreviated way of referring to the period of reform in the first decades of this century that we call the transformation of the oligarchic state. In five of the eight countries, the onset of the reform period coincides with the onset of the incorporation period (see Figure 0.1 in the Overview).

REGIME. The formal and informal structure of state and governmental roles and processes. The regime includes the method of selection of the government and of representative assemblies (election, coup, decision within the military, etc.), formal and informal mechanisms of representation, and patterns of repression. The regime is typically distinguished from the particular incumbents who occupy state and governmental roles, the political coalition that supports these incumbents, and the public policies they adopt (except of course policies that define or transform the regime itself).

SEMICOMPETITIVE REGIME. Applied to civilian regimes under which severe restrictions on electoral competition make the label competitive or democratic regime inappropriate, as in Colombia during the post-1958 National Front period, Peru after 1956, and Argentina after 1958. See also competitive regime and democratic regime.

STATE. This concept is used in the Latin American literature both to refer more concretely to the bureaucratic and legal institutions of the public sector and the incumbents of those institutions, and more analytically to refer to a larger set of political relationships or a larger "pact of domination." This book adopts the former usage, which is understood to encompass the government, in the narrow sense of the head of state and the immediate political leadership that surrounds the head of state, as well as the public bureaucracy, legislature, judiciary, public and semipublic corporations, legal system, armed forces, and the incumbents of these institutions.

STATE ELITE. The cluster of top political leaders at the pinnacle of the state. Commonly, this term has the same meaning as the government. This expression is extensively used by Stepan (1978b), and is occasionally employed here.

STATE INCORPORATION. An initial incorporation period in which the incorporating elite was at most marginally concerned with cultivating labor support and for whom the principal concern was with controlling the labor movement through a system of bureaucratic and legal restrictions imposed by the state. See also party incorporation.

STATE-LABOR RELATIONS. As a means of avoiding excessive repetition of a long phrase, this expression is sometimes used to refer to the relationship between the state and the organized labor movement. To avoid confusion, in the text we use the labels *workers* or the *working class*, rather than *labor*, when we wish to refer to individual workers, to workers as an occupational category, or to unorganized as well as organized workers.

STRENGTH OF THE LABOR MOVEMENT. The capacity of the labor movement to achieve its goals through collective action. As noted in Chapter 3, in the earlier period considered in this analysis, before the emergence of institutionalized patterns of state-labor relations, the initial scope of labor organizing and protest can be taken as a partial basis for assessing the strength of the labor movement. In later periods, when labor movements more routinely extract concessions from employers and/or the state in exchange for restraining labor protest, such an indicator is less satisfactory.

TRADE UNION. See union.

TRADE UNION MOVEMENT. See organized labor. Used interchangeably with *organized labor* and *organized labor movement*, and *union movement*.

TRADITIONAL SECTOR. That portion of the rural sector not characterized by the application of technology that yields relatively high levels of productivity. See also modern sector.

TRANSFORMATION OF THE OLIGARCHIC STATE. The period of political reform and state-building that occurred in the first decades of the 20th century. This expression is used to encompass both cases of dramatic political reorientation, such as the Mexican Revolution, and cases of more modest reform that occurred in the context of the continuing political strength of elements of the oligarchy, as in Argentina. See reform period.

UNION. An occupational association of wage-earners in the modern sector, encompassing members of the working class and middle class in both the urban sector and the modernized rural sector. Used interchangeably with *trade union*. See also organized labor.

UNION MOVEMENT. See organized labor. Used interchangeably with *organized labor*, *organized labor movement*, and *trade union movement*.

WORKERS. Organized and unorganized manual wage laborers in the modern sector, including both the urban sector and the modernized rural sector. See also peasants.

WORKING CLASS. Organized and unorganized manual wage labor in the modern sector, including both the urban sector and the enclave sector. See also peasants.

Abbreviations

AD	Acción Democrática (Venezuela)
ADP	Ação Democrática Parlamentar (Brazil)
AFL-CIO	American Confederation of Labor-Congress of Industrial Organizations (U.S.)
ANAPO	Alianza Nacional Popular (Colombia)
ANCAP	Administración Nacional de Combustibles, Alcohol, y Portland (Uruguay)
ANL	Aliança Nacional Libertadora (Brazil)
ANUC	Asociación Nacional de Usuarios Campesinos (Colombia)
AOAN	Asamblea Obrera de Alimentación Nacional (Chile)
AP	Acción Popular (Peru)
APRA	Alianza Popular Revolucionaria Americana (Peru)
ARN	Alianza Revolucionaria Nacional (Mexico)
ARS	(AD splinter group) (Venezuela)
ATLAS	Agrupación de Trabajadores Latinoamericanos Sindicalistas
BND	Bloque Nacional Democrática (Venezuela)
BNDE	Banco Nacional de Desenvolvimento Econômico (Brazil)
BUO	Bloque de Unidad Obrera (Mexico)
CCI	Central Campesina Independiente (Mexico)
CEPCh	Confederación de Empleados del Sector Privado (Chile)
CGE	Confederación General Económica (Argentina)
CGG	Comando Geral de Greve (Brazil)
CGOCM	Confederación General de Obreros y Campesinos de Mexico (Mexico)
CGT	Central Geral dos Trabalhadores (Brazil)
CGT	Comando Geral dos Trabalhadores (Brazil)
CGT	Confederación General del Trabajo (Argentina)
CGT	Confederación General de Trabajadores (Colombia)
CGT	Confederación General de Trabajadores (Mexico)
CGTP	Confederación General de Trabajadores del Peru (Peru)
CIT	Confederación Interamericana de Trabajadores (Venezuela)
CNAC	Comité Nacional de Auscultación y Coordinación (Mexico)
CNC	Confederación Nacional Campesina (Mexico)
CNI	Confederação Nacional da Indústria (Brazil)
CNIT	Cámara Nacional de la Industria de la Transformación (also called CANACINTRA) (Mexico)
CNOP	Confederación Nacional de Organizaciones Populares (Mexico)
CNS	Confederación Nacional de Sindicatos Chilenos (Chile)
CNT	Cámara Nacional de Trabajo (Mexico)
CNT	Central Nacional de Trabajadores (Chile)
CNT	Confederación Nacional de Trabajadores (Argentina)
CNT	Confederación Nacional de Trabajadores (Uruguay)
CNT	Confederación Nacional de Trabajadores (Venezuela)

CNTI	Confederação Nacional dos Trabalhadores da Indústria (Brazil)
COB	Confederação Operária Brasileira (Brazil)
COCM	Confederación Obrera y Campesina de México (Mexico)
CODESA	Confederación de Sindicatos Autónomos de Venezuela (Venezuela)
CON	Confederación Obrera Nacional (Mexico)
CONASE	Consejo Nacional de Seguridad (Uruguay), later called COSENA
CONASUPO	Compañía Nacional de Subsistencias Populares (Mexico)
CONPA	Congreso Permanento Agrario (Mexico)
CONTAG	Confederação Nacional de Trabalhadores da Agricultura (Brazil)
COPARMEX	Confederación Patronal de la República Mexicana (Mexico)
COPEI	Comité de Organización Política Electoral Independiente
COPRIN	Consejo de Precios e Ingresos (Uruguay)
CORFO	Corporación de Fomento (Chile)
COSENA	Consejo de Seguridad Nacional (earlier called CONASE) (Uruguay)
CPD	Concertación de Partidos por la Democracia (Chile)
CPN	Confederación Proletaria Nacional (Mexico)
CPOS	Comissão Permanente das Organizações Sindicais (Brazil)
CRAC	Confederación Republicana de Acción Cívica de Obreros y Empleados (Chile)
CROC	Confederación Revolucionaria de Obreros y Campesinos (Mexico)
CROM	Confederación Regional Obrera Mexicana (Mexico)
CRUS	Comité Relacionador de Unidad Sindical (Chile)
CST	Conselho Sindical dos Trabalhadores (Brazil)
CSTC	Confederación Sindical de Trabajadores de Colombia (Colombia)
CT	Congreso del Trabajo (Mexico)
CTAL	Confederación de Trabajadores de América Latina
CTB	Confederação dos Trabalhadores do Brazil (Brazil)
CTC	Central de Trabajadores de Colombia (Colombia)
CTCh	Confederación de Trabajadores de Chile (Chile)
CTM	Confederación de Trabajadores de Mexico (Mexico)
CTP	Confederación de Trabajadores del Peru (Peru)
CTV	Confederación de Trabajadores de Venezuela (Venezuela)
CUT	Central Única dos Trabalhadores (Brazil)
CUT	Central Unica de Trabajadores (Uruguay)
CUT	Confederación Unificada de Trabajadores (Chile)
CUTV	Central Unica de Trabajadores de Venezuela (Venezuela)
EGP	Ejército Guerillero del Pueblo (Argentina)
ELN	Ejército de Liberación Nacional (Colombia)
EPA	El Pueblo Avanza (Venezuela)
FALN	Fuerzas Armadas de Liberación Nacional (Venezuela)
FARC	Fuerzas Armadas Revolucionarias de Colombia (Colombia)
FAT	Frente Auténtico del Trabajo (Mexico)

FATRE	Federación Argentina de Trabajadores Rurales y Estibadores (Argentina)
FCV	Federación Campesina de Venezuela (Venezuela)
FDN	Frente Democrático Nacional (Peru)
FDP	Frente Democrático Popular (Venezuela)
FEDECAMARAS	Federación Venezolana de Cámaras y Asociaciones de Comercio y Producción (Venezuela)
FEDENAL	Federación Nacional del Transporte (Colombia)
FEI	Frente Electoral Independiente (Venezuela)
FENCAP	Federación Nacional de Campesinos del Perú (Peru)
FEP	Frente Electoral Popular (Mexico)
FIDEL	Frente Izquierda de Liberación (Uruguay)
FIESP	Federação das Indústrias do Estado de São Paulo (Brazil)
FMP	Frente de Mobilização Popular (Brazil)
FNAP	Frente Nacional Acción Popular (Mexico)
FND	Frente Nacional Democrático (Venezuela)
FNT	Frente Nacional do Trabalho (Brazil)
FOCh	Federación Obrera de Chile (Chile)
FOIC	Federación Obrera de la Industria de la Carne (Argentina)
FORA	Federación Obrera Radical Alberdi (Argentina)
FORA	Federación Obrera Regional Argentina (Argentina)
FORCh	Federación Obrera Regional de Chile (Chile)
FORU	Federación Obrera Regional del Uruguay (Uruguay)
FOTIA	Federación Obrera de Trabajadores de la Industria Azucarera (Argentina)
FPN	Frente Parlamentar Nacionalista (Brazil)
FRAP	Frente de Acción Popular (Chile)
FRENAP	Frente Nacional del Area Privada (Chile)
FSODF	Federación de Sindicatos Obreros del Distrito Federal (Mexico)
FSTDF	Federación Sindical de Trabajadores del Distrito Federal (Mexico)
FSTSE	Federación de Sindicatos de Trabajadores al Servicio del Estado (Mexico)
GAR	Grupo de Acción Revolucionaria (Venezuela)
GATT	General Agreement on Tariffs and Trade
GCO	Gran Central Obrero (Argentina)
GOU	Grupo de Oficiales Unidos (Argentina)
IAPI	Instituto Argentino para la Promoción del Intercambio (Argentina)
IBAD	Instituto Brasileiro de Ação Democrática (Brazil)
IMF	International Monetary Fund
IPES	Instituto de Pesquisas e Estudos Sociais (Brazil)
IPFN	Independientes para un Frente Nacional (Venezuela)
IWW	International Workers of the World
JAC	Junta de Acción Comunal (Colombia)
JUNECh	Junta Nacional de Empleados de Chile (Chile)
M-19	Movimiento del 19 de Abril (Colombia)
MAPU	Movimiento para Acción Popular Unitario (Chile)
MAS	Movimiento al Socialismo (Venezuela)

MAS	Muerte a los Secuestradores (Colombia)
MASC	Movimiento Agrario Social-Cristiano (Venezuela)
MDP	Movimiento Democrático Pradista (Peru)
MEP	Movimiento Electoral del Pueblo (Venezuela)
MIR	Movimiento de Izquierda Revolucionaria (Venezuela)
MLN	Movimiento de Liberación Nacional (Mexico)
MNDP	Movimiento Nacional Democrático Popular (Colombia)
MNPT	Movimento Nacional Popular Trabalhista (Brazil)
MOSIT	Movimiento Sindical Independiente de Trabajadores (Venezuela)
MRL	Movimiento Revolucionario Liberal (Colombia)
MRS	Movimento Renovador Sindical (Brazil)
MSD	Movimiento Sindical Democrático (Brazil)
MSR	Movimiento Sindical Revolucionario (Mexico)
MUNT	Movimiento Unitario Nacional de Trabajadores (Chile)
MUT	Movimiento Unificador dos Trabalhadores (Brazil)
MUTCh	Movimiento Unitario de Trabajadores de Chile (Chile)
ORVE	Organización Venezolana (Venezuela)
PAL	Partido Agrario Laborista (Chile)
PAN	Partido de Acción Nacional (Mexico)
PARM	Partido Auténtico de la Revolución Mexicana (Mexico)
PCB	Partido Comunista Brasileiro
PCC	Partido Comunista Colombiano
PCCh	Partido Comunista Chileno
PCM	Partido Comunista Mexicano
PCP	Partido Comunista Peruano
PCV	Partido Comunista de Venezuela (Venezuela)
PCVU	Partido Comunista Venezolano Unitario (Venezuela)
PDC	Partido Demócrata Cristiano (Chile)
PDM	Partido Demócrata Mexicano (Mexico)
PDN	Partido Democrático Nacional (Venezuela)
PIR	Partido de Izquierda Radical (Chile)
PLC	Partido Liberal Constitutionalista (Mexico)
PLM	Partido Laborista Mexicano (Mexico)
PLM	Partido Liberal Mexicano (Mexico)
PMDB	Partido do Movimento Democrático Brasileiro (Brazil)
PMT	Partido Mexicano de Trabajadores (Mexico)
PN	Partido Nacional (Chile)
PNA	Partido Nacional Agrarista (Mexico)
PNC	Partido Nacional Cooperatista (Mexico)
PNR	Partido Nacional Revolucionario (Mexico)
POCM	Partido Obrero Campesino de México (Mexico)
POS	Partido Obrero Socialista (Chile)
PPM	Partido del Pueblo Mexicano (Mexico)
PP	See PPS
PPS	Partido Popular Socialista (formerly the Partido Popular) (Mexico)
PRD	Partido Revolucionario Democrático (Mexico)
PRI	Partido Revolucionario Institucional (Mexico)
PRM	Partido de la Revolución Mexicana (Mexico)

PRP	Partido Republicano Progresista (Venezuela)
PRP	Partido Revolucionario Proletario (Black Communists) (Venezuela)
PRT	Partido Revolucionario de los Trabajadores (Mexico)
PS	Partido Socialista (Chile)
PSA	Partido Socialista Auténtico (Chile)
PSD	Partido Social Democrático (Brazil)
PSDB	Partido Social Democrático Brasileiro (Brazil)
PSP	Partido Socialista Popular (Chile)
PSP	Partido Social Progressista (Brazil)
PSR	Partido Socialista Revolucionario (Colombia)
PSR	Partido Socialista Revolucionario (Mexico)
PST	Partido Socialista de los Trabajadores (Mexico)
PSU	Partido Socialista Uruguayo (Uruguay)
PT	Partido dos Trabalhadores (Brazil)
PTB	Partido Trabalhista Brasileiro (Brazil)
PUA	Pacto de Unidade e Ação (Brazil)
PUI	Pacto de Unidade Intersindical (Brazil)
RN	Renovación Nacional (Chile)
SENDAS	Secretariado Nacional de Asistencia Social (Colombia)
SINAMOS	Sistema Nacional de Apoyo a la Mobilización Social (Peru)
SME	Sindicato Mexicano de Electricistas (Mexico)
SNA	Sociedad Nacional de Agricultura (Chile)
SNTAS	Sindicato Nacional de Trabajadores de Aviación y Similares (Mexico)
SNTTAM	Sindicatos Nacional de Técnicos y Trabajadores de Aeronaves de México (Mexico)
SOFOFA	Sociedad de Fomento Fabril (Chile)
SOL	Sindicato de Obreros Libres (Mexico)
SRA	Sociedad Rural Argentina (Argentina)
SUNTU	Sindicato Unico Nacional de Trabajadores Universitarios (Mexico)
SUTISS	Sindicato Unificado de Trabajadores de la Industria del Sector Siderúrgico (Venezuela)
UBD	Unión Blanca Democrática (Uruguay)
UCR	Unión Cívica Radical (Argentina)
UCRI	Unión Cívica Radical Intransigente (Argentina)
UCRP	Unión Cívica Radical del Pueblo (Argentina)
UDI	Unión Demócrata Independiente (Chile)
UDN	União Democrática Nacional (Brazil)
UECh	Unión de Empleados de Chile (Chile)
UGOCM	Unión General de Obreros y Campesinos de Mexico (Mexico)
UGT	Unión General de Trabajadores (Uruguay)
UIA	Unión Industrial Argentina (Argentina)
ULTAB	União de Lavradores e Trabalhadores Agrícolos do Brasil (Brazil)
UNACh	Unión Nacional de Asalariados de Chile (Chile)
UNE	União Nacional dos Estudantes (Brazil)
UNIR	Unión Nacional Izquierdista Revolucionaria (Colombia)
UNO	Unión Nacional Odriísta (Peru)

UNR	Unión Nacional Republicana (Venezuela)
UNSP	National Union of Public Servants (Brazil)
UNT	Unión Nacional de Trabajadores (Chile)
UOI	Unidad Obrero Independiente (Mexico)
UP	Unidad Popular (Chile)
URD	Unión Republicana Democrática (Venezuela)
USP	Unión Socialista Popular (Chile)
USRACh	Unión Social Republicana de Asalariados (Chile)
UST	União Sindical dos Trabalhadores (Brazil)
UTC	Unión de Trabajadores de Colombia (Colombia)
UTRACh	Unión de Trabajadores de Chile (Chile)
WFTU	World Federation of Trade Unions (Chile)

Bibliography

Abad de Santillan, Diego. 1971. *La F.O.R.A.: Ideología y trayectoria del movimiento obrero revolucionario en la Argentina*. 2d ed. Buenos Aires: Editorial Proyección.

Adams, Michael Paul. 1984. "The *Partido Aprista Peruano* and the Limitations of Peruvian Democratization: A Case Study." Honors thesis, Department of Government, Harvard University.

Aguiar, César A. 1984. "La doble escena: Clivajes sociales y subsistencia electoral." In Charles Gillespie, Louis Goodman, Juan Rial, and Peter Winn, eds., *Uruguay y la democracia*. Vol. 1. Montevideo: Ediciones de la Banda Oriental.

Aguilar García, Francisco Javier. 1980. "Las organizaciones obreras en el sector automotriz mexicano, 1965–1976." In *Memorias del encuentro sobre historia del movimiento obrero*. Vol. 3. Puebla, Mexico: Universidad Autónoma de Puebla.

Aguilar García, Javier. 1985. "Los sindicatos nacionales." In Pablo Gonzalez Casanova, Samuel León, and Ignacio Marva, eds., *Organización y sindicalismo*. Vol. 3 of *El obrero mexicano*. Mexico City: Siglo XXI.

Alba, Víctor. 1968. *Politics and the Labor Movement in Latin America*. Stanford: Stanford University Press.

Alexander, Robert J. 1950. "Labor Relations in Chile." Doctoral diss., Department of Political Science, Columbia University.

————. 1951. *The Perón Era*. New York: Columbia University Press.

————. 1957. *Communism in Latin America*. New Brunswick, N.J.: Rutgers University Press.

————. 1962a. *Labor Relations in Argentina, Brazil, and Chile*. New York: McGraw-Hill.

————. 1962b. *Prophets of the Revolution: Profiles of Latin American Leaders*. New York: Macmillan.

————. 1964. *The Venezuelan Democratic Revolution*. New Brunswick, N.J.: Rutgers University Press.

————. 1965. *Organized Labor in Latin America*. New York: Free Press.

————. 1977. *Arturo Alessandri: A Biography*. Ann Arbor: University Microfilms International.

————. 1979. *Juan Domingo Perón: A History*. Boulder, Colo.: Westview.

————. 1982. *Rómulo Betancourt and the Transformation of Venezuela*. New Brunswick, N.J.: Transaction Books.

————. 1983. "A Historical Perspective on the Contemporary Labor Movement in Latin America." Paper presented at the meetings of the Latin American Studies Association, Mexico City.

Alfonso, Pedro H. 1970. *Sindicalismo y revolución en el Uruguay*. Montevideo: Ediciones del Nuevo Mundo.

Allende, Alfredo E. 1963. *Historia de una gran ley*. Buenos Aires: Ediciones Arayú.

Almond, Gabriel A., Scott Flanagan, and Robert Mundt, eds. 1973. *Crisis, Choice, and Change*. Boston: Little, Brown.

Alonso, Antonio. 1972. *El movimiento ferrocarrilero en México, 1958–1959.* Mexico City: Ediciones Era.

Althusser, Louis. 1969. *For Marx.* London: Penguin Press.

―――. 1971. *Lenin and Philosophy and Other Essays.* New York: Monthly Review Press.

Ames, Barry. 1987. *Political Survival: Politicians and Public Policy in Latin America.* Berkeley and Los Angeles: University of California Press.

Anderson, Bo, and James D. Cockcroft. 1972. "Control and Co-optation in Mexican Politics." In James Cockcroft, et al., eds., *Dependence and Underdevelopment: Latin America's Political Economy.* Garden City, N.J.: Doubleday and Company.

Anderson, Charles W. 1967. *Politics and Economic Change in Latin America.* Princeton, N.J.: Van Nostrand.

Anderson, Rodney D. 1974. "Mexican Workers and the Politics of Revolution, 1906–1911." *Hispanic American Historical Review* 54, no. 1 (February), pp. 94–113.

―――. 1976. *Outcasts in Their Own Land: Mexican Industrial Workers, 1906–1911.* DeKalb: Northern Illinois University Press.

Angell, Alan. 1972. *Politics and the Labour Movement in Chile.* New York: Oxford University Press.

―――. 1980. "Peruvian Labour and the Military Government since 1968." University of London, Institute of Latin American Studies, working paper no. 3.

Anguiano Orozco, Arturo. 1975. *El estado y la política obrera del cardenismo.* Mexico City: Ediciones Era.

Araiza, José Luis. 1964. *Historia del movimiento obrero mexicano,* Vols. 1–4. Mexico City: Editorial Cuauhtemoc.

Arceneaux, William. 1969. *The Venezuelan Experience: 1958 and the Patriotic Junta.* Doctoral diss., Louisiana State University and Agricultural and Mechanical College.

Archila, Mauricio. 1984. "De la revolución social a la conciliación? Algunas hipótesis sobre la transformación de la clase obrera colombiana (1919–1935)." *Anuario Colombiano de historia social y de la cultura* (ACHSC), no. 12, pp. 51–102.

Arroio, Raymundo. 1980. "Notas metodológicas para el estudio del sector industrial en México." In *Memorias del encuentro sobre historia del movimiento obrero.* Vol. 1. Puebla, Mexico: Universidad Autónoma de Puebla.

Ashby, Joe C. 1967. *Organized Labor and the Mexican Revolution under Lázaro Cárdenas.* Chapel Hill: University of North Carolina Press.

Astiz, Carlos. 1969a. "The Argentine Armed Forces: Their Role and Political Involvement." *Western Political Quarterly* 22, no. 4 (December), pp. 862–78.

―――. 1969b. *Pressure Groups and Power Elites in Peruvian Politics.* Ithaca, N.Y.: Cornell University Press.

Auguste, Michael Hector. 1980. "Metodología para el estudio de la huelga." In *Memorias del encuentro sobre historia del movimiento obrero.* Vol. 1. Puebla, Mexico: Universidad Autónoma de Puebla.

Ayala, José, José Blanco, Rolando Cordera, Guillermo Knockenbauer, and Armando Labra. 1980. "La crisis económica: Evolución y perspectivas." In Pablo González Casanova y Enrique Florescano, eds., *México, hoy.* Mexico City: Siglo XXI.

Ayres, Robert L. 1973. "Political History, Institutional Structure, and Prospects for Socialism in Chile." *Comparative Politics* 5, no. 4 (July), pp. 497–522.

Baer, Delal, and John Bailey. 1985. "Mexico's 1985 Midterm Elections: A Preliminary Assessment." *LASA Forum* 16, no. 3 (Fall).

Baer, Werner. 1965. *Industrialization and Economic Development in Brazil.* Homewood, Ill.: Economic Growth Center, Yale University.

————. 1979. *The Brazilian Economy: Its Growth and Development.* Colombus, Ohio: Grid.

Bagley, Bruce Michael. 1984. "National Front and Economic Development." In Robert Wesson, ed., *Politics, Policies, and Economic Development in Latin America.* Stanford: Hoover Institution Press.

————. 1989. *The State and the Peasantry in Contemporary Colombia.* Allegheny College, Monograph Series on Contemporary Latin American and Caribbean Affairs, no. 6.

Bagley, Bruce, and Matthew Edel. 1980. "Popular Mobilization Programs of the National Front: Cooptation and Radicalization." In Albert Berry, Ronald G. Hellman, and Mauricio Solaún, eds., *Politics of Compromise: Coalition Government in Colombia.* New Brunswick, N.J.: Transaction Books.

Bailey, David C. 1974. *¡Viva Cristo Rey! The Cristero Rebellion and the Church-State Conflict in Mexico.* Austin and London: University of Texas Press.

————. 1979. "Obregón: Mexico's Accommodating President." In George Wolfskill and Douglas W. Richmond, eds., *Essays on the Mexican Revolution: Revisionist Views of the Leaders.* Austin: University of Texas Press.

Bailey, John. 1975. "Bureaucratic Politics and Social Security Policy in Colombia." Paper adapted from a longer paper, "Policymaking in Colombian Decentralized Agencies: Presidential Control Versus Agency Autonomy," presented at the annual meeting of the American Political Science Association, San Francisco, September.

————. 1977. "Pluralist and Corporatist Dimensions of Interest Representation in Colombia." In James M. Malloy, ed., *Authoritarianism and Corporatism in Latin America.* Pittsburgh: University of Pittsburgh Press.

Baily, Samuel J. 1965. "Argentina: Reconciliation with the Peronists." *Current History* 49, no. 292 (December), pp. 356–60, 368–69.

————. 1966. "Argentina: Search for Consensus." *Current History* 51, no. 303 (November), pp. 301–6.

————. 1967. *Labor, Nationalism, and Politics in Argentina.* New Brunswick, N.J.: Rutgers University Press.

Balbi, Carmen Rosa. 1980. *El Partido Comunista y el APRA en la crisis revolucionaria de los años treinta.* Lima: G. Herrera Editores.

Balbis, Jorge. 1984. "Los resultados en cifras: 1958–1982." *Cuadernos* 31, no. 3, pp. 101–13.

Baloyra, Enrique A. 1977. "Public Attitudes toward the Democratic Regime." In John D. Martz and David J. Myers, eds., *Venezuela: The Democratic Experience.* New York: Praeger.

Baloyra, Enrique A., and John D. Martz. 1976. "Classical Participation in Venezuela: Campaigning and Voting in 1973." Paper presented at the Seminar on the Faces of Participation in Latin America: A New Look at Citizen Action in Society, San Antonio.

Bambirra, Vania. 1974. *El capitalismo dependiente latinoamericano.* Mexico City: Siglo XXI.

Bandeira, Moniz. 1978. *O governo João Goulart: As lutas sociais no Brasil*. 4th ed. Rio de Janeiro: Editora Civilização Brasileira.

———. 1979. *Brizola e o trabalhismo*. Rio de Janeiro: Editora Civilização Brasileira.

Baretta, Silvio R. Duncan, and John Markoff. 1981. "Democracy, Authoritarianism, Deadlock: The Political Role of the Brazilian Military, 1930–1964." Unpublished paper, Department of Sociology, University of Pittsburgh.

Barrán, José P. and Benjamín Nahum. 1978. *Historia rural del Uruguay moderno*. Vol. 7 of *Agricultura, crédito y transporte bajo Batlle 1905–1914*. Montevideo.

———. 1979. *El Uruguay del novecientos*. Vol. 1 of *Batlle, los estancieros y el imperio británico*. Montevideo: Ediciones de la Banda Oriental.

———. 1981. *Un diálogo difícil, 1903–1910*. Vol. 2 of *Batlle, los estancieros y el imperio británico*. Montevideo: Ediciones de la Banda Oriental.

———. 1982. *El nacimiento del batllismo*. Vol. 3 of *Batlle, los estancieros y el imperio británico*. Montevideo: Ediciones de la Banda Oriental.

———. 1983. *Las primeras reformas, 1911–1913*. Vol. 4 of *Batlle, los estancieros y el imperio británico*. Montevideo: Ediciones de la Banda Oriental.

———. 1984. *La reacción imperial-conservadora, 1911–1913*. Vol. 5 of *Batlle, los estancieros y el imperio británico*. Montevideo: Ediciones de la Banda Oriental.

———. 1985. *Crisis y radicalización, 1913–1916*. Vol. 6 of *Batlle, los estancieros y el imperio británico*. Montevideo: Ediciones de la Banda Oriental.

Barrera, Manuel. 1971. "Perspectiva histórica de la huelga obrera en Chile." *Cuadernos de la Realidad Nacional*, no. 9 (September), pp. 119–55.

Barría, Jorge S. 1971. *Historia de la CUT*. Santiago: Ediciones Prensa Latinoamericana.

———. 1972. *El movimiento obrero en Chile: Síntesis históricosocial*. Santiago: Ediciones de la Universidad Técnica del Estado.

Barton, Alan H., and Paul F. Lazarsfeld. 1969. "Some Functions of Qualitative Analysis in Social Research." In George J. McCall and J. L. Simmons, eds., *Issues in Participant Observation*. Reading, Mass.: Addison-Wesley.

Basadre, Jorge. 1963. *Historia de la República del Perú*. Vols. 7 and 8. Lima: Ediciones Historia.

———. 1968. *Historia de la República del Perú*. Vol. 13. Lima: Editorial Universitaria.

Basáñez, Miguel. 1981. *La lucha por la hegemonía en México. 1968–1980*. Mexico City: Siglo XXI.

Bastos, Suely. 1981. "A cisão do MTR com o PTB." In David V. Fleischer, ed., *Os partidos políticos no Brasil*, vol. 1. Brasília: Editora Universidade de Brasília.

Basurto, Jorge. 1983. *En el régimen de Luís Echeverría*. Vol. 14 of *La clase obrera en la historia de México*. Mexico City: Siglo XXI.

———. 1984. *Del avilacamachismo al alemanismo, 1940–1952*. Vol. 11 of *La clase obrera en la historia de México*. Mexico City: Siglo XXI.

Bauer, Arnold J. 1975. *Chilean Rural Society from the Spanish Conquest to 1930*. Cambridge: Cambridge University Press.

Bazán, Lucia. 1980. "El sindicato independiente de Nissan Mexicana." In *Memorias del encuentro sobre historia del movimiento obrero*. Vol. 3. Puebla, Mexico: Universidad Autónoma de Puebla.

Beezley, William H. 1979. "Madero: The 'Unknown' President and His Political Failure to Organize Rural Mexico." In George Wolfskill and Douglas W. Richmond, eds., *Essays on the Mexican Revolution: Revisionist Views of the Leaders*. Austin: University of Texas Press.

Béjar, Héctor. 1969. *Peru 1965: Notes on a Guerrilla Experience*. New York: Monthly Review Press.

Bendix, Reinhard. 1964. *Nation-Building and Citizenship: Studies of Our Changing Social Order*. New York: John Wiley and Sons.

Benevides, María Victória de Mesquita. 1976. *O governo Kubitschek: Desenvolvimento econômico e estabilidade política, 1956–1961*. Rio de Janeiro: Paz e Terra.

———. 1981. "A União Democrática Nacional." In David V. Fleischer, ed., *Os partidos políticos no Brasil*. Brasília: Editora Universidade de Brasília.

Berenson, William Mark. 1975. "Group Politics in Uruguay: The Development, Political Activity, and Effectiveness of Uruguayan Trade Associations." Doctoral diss., Department of Political Science, Vanderbilt University.

Bergquist, Charles W. 1981. "Exports, Labor, and the Left: An Essay on Twentieth-Century Chilean History." Latin American Program, Wilson Center, working paper no. 97.

———. 1986. *Labor in Latin America: Comparative Essays on Chile, Argentina, Venezuela, and Colombia*. Stanford: Stanford University Press.

Bergsman, Joel. 1970. *Brazil: Industrialization and Trade Policies*. New York: Oxford University Press.

———. 1980. "Income Distribution and Poverty in Mexico." World Bank staff working paper no. 395, July.

Bernardo, Antonio Carlos. 1982. *Tutela e autonomia sindical: Brasil, 1930–1945*. São Paulo: DIFEL.

Bernstein, Marvin D. 1964. *The Mexican Mining Industry, 1890–1950*. Albany: State University of New York Press.

Berry, R. Albert. 1980. "The National Front and Colombia's Economic Development." In R. Albert Berry, Ronald G. Hellman, and Mauricio Solaún, eds., *Politics of Compromise: Coalition Government in Colombia*. New Brunswick, N.J.: Transaction Books.

Berry, R. Albert, Ronald G. Hellman, and Mauricio Solaún, eds. 1980. *Politics of Compromise: Coalition Government in Colombia*. New Brunswick, N.J.: Transaction Books.

Berry, R. Albert, and Mauricio Solaún. 1980. "Notes Toward an Interpretation of the National Front." In R. Albert Berry, Ronald G. Hellman, and Mauricio Solaún, eds., *Politics of Compromise: Coalition Government in Colombia*. New Brunswick, N.J.: Transaction Books.

Berry, R. Albert, and Miguel Urrutia. 1976. *Income Distribution in Colombia*. New Haven: Yale University Press.

Besserer, Francisco, Daniel González, and Laura Pérez Rosales. 1980. "El conflicto de la Caridad." In *Memorias del encuentro sobre historia del movimiento obrero*. Vol. 3. Puebla, Mexico: Universidad Autónoma de Puebla.

Betancourt, Rómulo. 1979. *Venezuela: Oil and Politics*. Boston: Houghton-Mifflin.

Biles, Robert E. 1975. "Patronage Politics: Electoral Behavior in Uruguay." Doctoral diss., Department of Political Science, Johns Hopkins University.

Binder, Leonard, et al. 1971. *Crises and Sequences in Political Development*. Princeton: Princeton University Press.

Bisio, Raúl H., and Floreal H. Forni. 1976. "Economía de enclave y satelización del mercado de trabajo rural: El caso de los trabajadores con empleo precario en un ingenio azucarero del noroeste argentino." *Desarrollo Económico* 16, no. 62 (April–June), pp. 3–56.

Blanchard, Peter. 1982. *The Origins of the Peruvian Labor Movement, 1883–1919.* Pittsburgh: University of Pittsburgh Press.

Blank, David Eugene. 1973. *Politics in Venezuela.* Boston: Little, Brown.

———. 1980. "The Regional Dimension of Venezuelan Politics." In Howard R. Penniman, ed., *Venezuela at the Polls: The National Elections of 1978.* Washington, D.C.: American Enterprise Institute for Public Policy Research.

———. 1984. *Venezuela: Politics in a Petroleum Republic.* New York: Praeger.

Blanksten, George I. 1953. *Peron's Argentina.* Chicago: University of Chicago Press.

Bodenheimer, Susanne J. 1971. "The Ideology of Developmentalism: The American Paradigm-Surrogate for Latin American Studies." Sage Professional Papers in Comparative Politics 2, no. 01–015. Beverly Hills, Calif.: Sage.

Boeckh, Andreas. 1972. "Organized Labor and Government under Conditions of Economic Scarcity: The Case of Venezuela." Doctoral diss., Department of Political Science, University of Florida.

Bond, Robert D., ed. 1977. *Contemporary Venezuela and Its Role in International Affairs.* New York: New York University Press.

Bonilla, Frank. 1962. "Rural Reform in Brazil." *Descent* 9, no. 4 (Autumn).

Borón, Atilio A. 1970. "Movilización política y crisis económica en Chile, 1920–1950." *Aportes* (April).

———. 1971. "Movilización política y crisis política en Chile." *Aportes,* no. 20 (April), pp. 41–69.

———. 1975. "Notas sobre las raíces histórico-estructurales de la movilización política en Chile." *Foro Internacional* 16 (July–September), pp. 64–121.

———. 1976. "The Formation and Crisis of the Liberal State in Argentina, 1880–1930." Doctoral diss., Department of Political Science, Harvard University.

Bortz, Jeffrey. 1977. "El salario obrero en el Distrito Federal, 1937–1975." *Investigación Económica* 36, no. 4 (October–December), pp. 129–70.

———. 1980. "Problemas de la medición de la afiliación sindical." *A: Revista de Ciencias Sociales y Humanidades* 1, no. 1, Universidad Autónoma Metropolitana de Azcapotzalco, (September–December), pp. 29–66.

Bossert, Thomas John. 1977. "Dependency and the Disintegration of the State: Lessons from Allende's Chile." Paper presented at the Annual Meeting of the American Political Science Association, Washington, D.C.

Botana, Natalio R. 1975. "La reforma política de 1912." In Gímenez Zapiola, Marcos, ed., *El régimen oligárquico: Materiales para el estudio de la realidad argentina (hasta 1930).* Vol. 1. Buenos Aires: Amorrortu Editores.

Bourricaud, François. 1964. "Lima en la vida política peruana." *América Latina* 7, no. 4, Río de Janeiro (October–December), pp. 89–95.

———. 1970. *Power and Society in Contemporary Peru.* New York: Praeger.

Boyer, Richard E., and Keith A. Davies. 1973. *Urbanization in 19th Century Latin America: Statistics and Sources.* Supplement to the Statistical Abstract of Latin America. Los Angeles: Latin American Center, University of California.

Brady, David. 1988. *Critical Elections and Congressional Policy-Making.* Stanford: Stanford University Press.

Brandenburg, Frank. 1964. *The Making of Modern Mexico*. Englewood Cliffs, N.J.: Prentice-Hall.

Brasil de Lima, Olavo. 1981. "O sistema partidário brasileiro, 1945–1962." In David V. Fleischer, ed., *Os partidos políticos no Brasil*. Brasília: Editora Universidade de Brasília.

———. 1983. *Tradução de Gustavo F.G. Aronwick: Os partidos políticos brasileiros—a experiência federal e regional: 1945–1964*. Rio de Janeiro: Edições Graal.

Braun, Herbert. 1985. *The Assassination of Gaitán: Public Life and Urban Violence in Colombia*. Madison: University of Wisconsin Press.

Bray, Donald William. 1961. "Chilean Politics during the Second Ibañez Government, 1952–58." Doctoral diss., Hispanic American Studies, Stanford University.

———. 1964. "Chile: The Dark Side of Stability." *Studies on the Left* 4, no. 4 (Fall), pp. 85–96.

———. 1967. "Peronism in Chile." *Hispanic American Historical Review* 48, no. 1 (February), pp. 38–49.

Brewer-Carías, Allan-Randolph. 1975. *Cambio político y reforma del estado en Venezuela*. Madrid: Editorial Tecnos.

Brown, James Chilton. 1979. "Consolidation of the Mexican Revolution under Calles, 1924–28: Politics, Modernization, and the Roots of the Revolutionary National Party." Doctoral diss., University of New Mexico.

Brown, Jonathan C. 1979. *A Socio-Economic History of Argentina, 1776–1860*. Cambridge: Cambridge University Press.

Brown, Lyle C. 1964. "General Lázaro Cárdenas and Mexican Presidential Politics, 1933–1940: A Study in the Acquisition and Manipulation of Political Power." Doctoral diss., Department of Political Science, University of Texas.

Bruneau, Thomas C. 1989. "The Brazilian Experience in Formulating its New Constitution, 1987–1988." Mimeo, Naval Postgraduate School, Monterey, California.

Bruneau, Thomas C., and Philippe Faucher, eds. 1981. *Authoritarian Capitalism: Brazil's Contemporary Economic Development*. Boulder, Colo.: Westview.

Bureau of National Affairs. 1973. *Primer of Labor Relations: A Guide to Employer-Employee Conduct*. Washington, D.C.: Bureau of National Affairs.

Burford, Camile Nick. 1971. "A Biography of Luis N. Morones, Mexican Labor and Political Leader." Doctoral diss., Department of History, Louisiana State University and Agricultural and Mechanical College.

Burga, Manuel, and Alberto Flores Galindo. 1979. *Apogeo y crisis de la república aristocrática: Oligarquía, Aprismo y comunismo en el Perú, 1895–1932*. Lima: Rikchay.

Burggraff, Winfield J. 1971. "The Military Origins of Venezuela's 1945 Revolution." *Caribbean Studies* 11, no. 3 (October), pp. 35–54.

———. 1972. *The Venezuelan Armed Forces in Politics, 1933–1959*. Columbia: University of Missouri Press.

Burnham, Walter Dean. 1965. "The Changing Shape of the American Political Universe." *American Political Science Review* 59, no. 1 (March), pp. 7–28.

———. 1970. *Critical Elections and the Mainsprings of American Politics*. New York: W. W. Norton.

———. 1974. "Theory and Voting Research: Some Reflections on Converse's

'Change in the American Electorate.' " *American Political Science Review* 68, no. 3 (September), pp. 1002–23.

Burns, E. Bradford. 1976. "A *State of Siege* that Never Was." *Journal of Latin American Lore* 2, no. 2, pp. 257–63.

Bustamante i Rivero, Jose Luis. 1949. *Tres años de lucha por la democracia en el Perú*. Buenos Aires: Bartolomé U. Chiesino.

Butler, David J. 1969. "Charisma, Migration and Elite Coalescence: An Interpretation of Peronism." *Comparative Politics* 1, no. 3 (April), pp. 423–39.

Caetano, Gerardo. 1983a. *La agonía del reformismo*. Vols. 1 and 2. Serie Investigaciones, no. 37–38. Centro Latinoamericano de Economía Humana, Montevideo.

———. 1983b. "Las fuerzas conservadoras en el camino de la dictadura: El golpe de estado de Terra." *CLAEH*, no. 28 (October–December), pp. 41–89.

———. 1985. "Los caminos políticos de la reacción conservadora (1916–1933)." In Jorge Balbis et al., eds., *El primer Batllismo: Cinco enfoques polémicos*. Montevideo: CLAEH.

Caetano, Gerardo, and Jose Pedro Rilla. 1985. "El sistema de partidos: Raices y permanencias." In Gerardo Caetano, et al., eds., *De la tradición a la crisis: Pasado y presente de nuestro sistema de partidos*. Montevideo: CLAEH.

Caicedo, Edgar. 1971. *Historia de las luchas sindicales en Colombia*. Bogotá: Ediciones C.E.I.S.

Calello, Osvaldo, and Daniel Parcero. 1984. *De Vandor a Ubaldini*. Vol. 1. Buenos Aires: Centro Editor de América Latina.

Camacho, Manuel. 1976. "Control sobre el movimiento obrero en México." *Foro Internacional* 16, no. 4 (April–June), pp. 496–525.

———. 1980. *El futuro inmediato*. Vol. 15 of *La clase obrera en la historia de México*. Mexico: Siglo XXI.

Camou, María M. 1986. "El nacional-socialismo en Uruguay, 1933–1938." In *Cuadernos del CLAEH*, no. 38, pp. 67–83.

Camp, Roderic. 1976. "The 1929 Presidential Campaign and Political Leadership in Mexico." Paper presented at the annual meeting of the Latin American Studies Association, Atlanta.

Campa, Valentín. 1978. *Mi testimonio*. Mexico: Fondo de Cultura Popular.

Campbell, Donald T. 1975. " 'Degrees of Freedom' and the Case Study." *Comparative Political Studies* 8, no. 2, (July), pp. 178–93.

Campello de Souza, Maria do. 1981. "Evolução e crise do sistema partidário." In David V. Fleischer, ed., *Os partidos políticos no Brasil*. Brasília: Editora Universidade de Brasília.

Canak, William L. 1981. "National Development in Colombia: Accumulation, Crisis, and the State." Doctoral diss., Department of Sociology, University of Wisconsin, Madison.

Cantón, Darío. 1966. *El parlamento argentino en épocas de cambio: 1890, 1916, y 1946*. Buenos Aires: Editorial del Instituto.

———. 1968a. *Materiales para el estudio de la sociología política en la Argentina*. 2 vols. Buenos Aires: Instituto Torcuato Di Tella.

———. 1968b. "Military Intervention in Argentina: 1900–1966." Instituto Torcuato di Tella, Centro de Investigaciones Sociales, Documento de Trabajo no. 39.

———. 1973. *Elecciones y partidos pólíticos en la Argentina: Historia, interpretación, y balance, 1910–1966*. Buenos Aires: Siglo XXI.

Caravedo Molinari, Baltazar. 1976. *Burguesía e industria en el Perú, 1933–1945.* Lima: Instituto de Estudios Peruanos.

————. 1978. *Desarrollo desigual y lucha política en el Perú, 1948–1956.* Lima: Instituto de Estudios Peruanos.

Cardoso, Fernando Henrique. 1979. "On the Characterization of Authoritarian Regimes in Latin America." In David Collier, ed., *The New Authoritarianism in Latin America.* Princeton: Princeton University Press.

Cardoso, Fernando Henrique, and Enzo Faletto. 1969. *Dependencia y desarrollo en América Latina.* Mexico City: Siglo XXI.

————. 1979. *Dependency and Development in Latin America.* Expanded and emended version of 1969 Spanish edition. Berkeley and Los Angeles: University of California Press.

Cardoso, Oscar R., and Rodolfo Audi. 1982. *Sindicalismo: El poder y la crisis.* Buenos Aires: Editorial de Belgrano.

Carone, Edgard. 1973. *A Segunda República, 1930–1937.* São Paulo: DIFEL.

————. 1980. *A Quarta República, 1945–1964.* São Paulo: DIFEL.

————. 1981. *Movimento operário no Brasil, 1945–1964.* São Paulo: DIFEL.

Carr, Barry. 1972. "Organised Labour and the Mexican Revolution, 1915–1928." Latin American Centre Occasional Papers II, St. Antony's College, Oxford University.

————. 1976. *El movimiento obrero y la política en México, 1910–1929.* Mexico City: Secretaría de Educación Pública.

————. 1981a. "The Development of Communism and Marxism in Mexico: A Historiographical Essay." Paper presented at the Sixth Conference of Mexican and United States Historians, Chicago.

————. 1981b. "Los orígenes del Partido Comunista Mexicano." *Nexos* 4, no. 40 (April), pp. 37–47.

————. 1983. "The Mexican Economic Debacle and the Labor Movement: A New Era or More of the Same?" In Donald L. Wyman, ed., *Mexico's Economic Crisis: Challenges and Opportunities,* Monograph Series, 12. La Jolla: Center for U.S.-Mexican Studies, University of California, San Diego.

————. 1985. *Mexican Communism, 1968–1983: Eurocommunism in the Americas?* Research Report Series, 42. San Diego: Center for U.S.-Mexican Studies.

Carri, Roberto. 1967. *Sindicatos y poder en la Argentina.* Buenos Aires: Editorial Sudestada.

Carril, Bonifacio del. 1959. *Crónica interna de la revolución libertadora.* Buenos Aires: Emecé Editores.

Castillo, Fernando, et al. 1975. *Liberalismo y socialismo: Problemas de la transición: El caso chileno.* Madrid: Tucar Ediciones.

Cavarozzi, Marcelo J. 1975. "The Government and the Industrial Bourgeoisie in Chile: 1938–1964." Doctoral diss., Department of Political Science, University of California, Berkeley.

Cavarozzi, Marcelo. 1979a. *Consolidación del sindicalismo peronista y emergencia de la fórmula política argentina durante el gobierno frondizista.* Estudios CEDES, vol. 2, no. 7/8. Buenos Aires: Centro de Estudios de Estado y Sociedad.

————. 1979b. *Sindicatos y política en Argentina 1955–1958.* Estudios CEDES. Buenos Aires: Centro de Estudios de Estado y Sociedad.

————. 1979c. "Unions and Politics in Argentina, 1955–1962." Latin American program working paper no. 63, Wilson Center, Washington, D.C.

————. 1980. "Crisis política y golpes militares en Argentina: 1966 y 1976." Paper prepared for the conference on Prospects for Democracy: Transitions from Authoritarian Rule in Latin America and Latin Europe, The Wilson Center, Washington, D.C.

———. 1982. "Argentina at the Crossroads: Pathways and Obstacles to Democratization in the Present Political Conjuncture." Latin American program working paper no. 115, Wilson Center, Washington, D.C.

———. 1983. *Autoritarismo y democracia (1955–1983)*. Buenos Aires: Centro Editor de América Latina.

———. 1984. "El sistema de partidos y el parlamento en la Argentina contemporánea: Obstáculos recurrentes y oportunidades para la estabilización de la democracia." Paper presented at the planning meeting for "The Role of Political Parties in the Democratic Opening in the Southern Cone," Wilson Center, Washington, D.C., April.

———. 1986. "Peronism and Radicalism: Argentina's Transitions in Perspective." In Paul Drake and Eduardo Silva, eds., *Elections and Democratization in Latin America, 1980–1985*. San Diego: Center for Iberian and Latin American Studies, Center for U.S.-Mexican Studies, and Institute of the Americas, University of California, San Diego.

Cavarozzi, Marcelo J., and James F. Petras. 1974. "Chile." In Ronald Chilcote and Joel Edelstein, eds., *Latin America: The Struggle with Dependency and Beyond*. Cambridge, Mass.: Schenkman.

Cavarozzi, Marcelo J., Lilliana de Riz, and Jorge Feldman. 1985. "El contexto y los dilemas de la concertación en la Argentina actual." Paper presented at the workshop on "Labor in Contemporary Latin America: An Agenda for Research," Kellogg Institute for International Studies, University of Notre Dame.

Cepeda Ulloa, Fernando, and Christopher Mitchell. 1980. "The Trend Towards Technocracy: The World Bank and the International Labor Organization in Colombian Politics." In R. Albert Berry, Ronald G. Hellman, and Mauricio Solaún, eds., *Politics of Compromise: Coalition Government in Colombia*. New Brunswick, N.J.: Transaction Books.

Cerquería, Silas. 1973. "Brazil." In Richard Gott, ed., *Guide to the Political Parties of South America*. Middlesex, England: Penguin Books.

Cerruti, Mario. 1980. "Desarrollo capitalista y fuerza de trabajo en Monterrey, 1890–1910." In *Memorias del encuentro sobre historia del movimiento obrero*. Vol. 1. Puebla, Mexico: Universidad Autónoma de Puebla.

Chacon, Vamireh. 1981. *História dos partídos brasileiros: Discurso e práxis dos seus programas*. Brasília: Editora Universidade de Brasília.

Chalmers, Douglas A. 1972. "Parties and Society in Latin America." *Studies in Comparative International Development* 7, no. 2 (1972), pp. 102–30.

———. 1977. "The Politicized State in Latin America." In James M. Malloy, ed., *Authoritarianism and Corporatism in Latin America*. Pittsburgh: University of Pittsburgh Press.

Chaplin, David. 1967. *The Peruvian Industrial Labor Force*. Princeton: Princeton University Press.

Chen, Chi-Yi. 1969. *Economía social del trabajo: Caso de Venezuela*. Caracas: Librería Editorial Salesiana.

Chilcote, Ronald H. 1974. *The Brazilian Communist Party: Conflict and Integration, 1922–1972*. New York: Oxford University Press.

Chu, David S. C. 1972. "The Great Depression and Industrialization in Latin

America: Response to Relative Price Incentives in Argentina and Colombia, 1930–1945." Doctoral diss., Department of Economics, Yale University.

Chullén, Jorge. 1980. "El APRA frente al régimen de Belaúnde: Oposición conservadora y superconvivencia." In Mariano Valderrama et al., eds., El APRA: Un camino de esperanzas y frustraciones. Lima: El Gallo Rojo.

CIE-DAP (Centro de Investigaciones Económicas, Universidad de Antioquia/Departmento Administrativo de Planeación, Gobierno de Antioquia). 1973. La estructura económica del Departamento de Antioquia. Medellín.

Ciria, Alberto. 1968. Partidos y poder en la Argentina moderna. Buenos Aires: Editorial Jorge Alvarez.

———. 1972. "Peronism and Political Structures, 1945–1955." In Alberto Ciria et al., eds., New Perspectives on Modern Argentina. Bloomington: Latin American Studies, Indiana University.

———. 1974. Parties and Power in Modern Argentina. Albany: State University of New York Press.

———. 1977. "Cardenismo and Peronismo: A Needed Comparison." Paper prepared for the joint national meeting of LASA and ASA, Houston, November 2–5.

———. 1983. Política y cultura popular: La Argentina peronista 1946–1955. Buenos Aires: Ediciones de la Flor.

Clark, Marjorie Ruth. 1973. Organized Labor in Mexico. Chapel Hill: University of North Carolina Press.

Cleaves, Peter S. 1981. "Mexican Politics: An End to Crisis?" Latin American Research Review 16, no. 2, pp. 191–202.

Cline, Howard F. 1963. Mexico: Revolution to Evolution, 1940–1960. New York: Oxford University Press.

———. 1969. The United States and Mexico. New York: Atheneum.

Cockcroft, James D. 1963. Venezuela's Fidelistas: Two Generations. Stanford: Stanford University Press.

———. 1972. "Coercion and Ideology in Mexican Politics." In James D. Cockcroft, Andre Gunder Frank, and Dale L. Johnson, eds., Dependence and Underdevelopment: Latin America's Political Economy. New York: Anchor Books.

———. 1974. "Mexico." In Ronald Chilcote and Joel Edelstein, eds., Latin America: The Struggle with Dependency and Beyond. Cambridge, Mass.: Schenkman.

———. 1974. Precursores intelectuales de la revolución mexicana. Mexico City: Siglo XXI.

Colegio de México. 1965. Estadísticas económicas del Porfiriato: Fuerza de trabajo y actividad económica por sectores. Mexico City: Colegio de México.

Coleman, Kenneth M. 1975. "The Capital City Electorate and Mexico's Acción Nacional: Some Survey Evidence on Conventional Hypotheses." Social Science Quarterly 56, no. 3 (December), pp. 502–9.

———. 1976. "Diffuse Support in Mexico: The Potential for Crisis." Sage Professional Papers, Comparative Politics Series 5, no. 01–057.

Coleman, Kenneth M., and Charles L. Davis. 1978. "Some Structural Determinants of Working Class Politicization: Political Regimes, Degree of Union Incorporation and Strategic Location of Unions." Research proposal, Department of Political Science, University of Kentucky.

Collier, David. 1976. Squatters and Oligarchs: Authoritarian Rule and Policy Change in Peru. Baltimore: Johns Hopkins University Press.

Collier, David. 1978. "Industrial Modernization and Political Change: A Latin American Perspective." *World Politics* 30, no. 4 (July), pp. 593–614.

Collier, David, ed. 1979. *The New Authoritarianism in Latin America*. Princeton: Princeton University Press.

Collier, David, and Ruth Berins Collier. 1977. "Who Does What, to Whom, and How: Toward a Comparative Analysis of Latin American Corporatism." In James M. Malloy, ed., *Authoritarianism and Corporatism in Latin America*. Pittsburgh: University of Pittsburgh Press.

Collier, Ruth Berins. 1982. "Popular Sector Incorporation and Political Supremacy: Regime Evolution in Brazil and Mexico." In Sylvia Ann Hewlett and Richard S. Weinert, eds., *Brazil and Mexico: Patterns in Late Development*. Philadelphia: Institute for the Study of Human Issues.

Collier, Ruth Berins. Forthcoming. *The Contradictory Alliance: State-Labor Relations and Regime Change in Mexico*. Institute of International Studies, University of California, Berkeley.

Collier, Ruth Berins, and David Collier. 1979. "Inducements versus Constraints: Disaggregating Corporatism." *The American Political Science Review* 73, no. 4 (December), pp. 967–86.

Colque, Víctor. 1977. "Historia del movimiento obrero en Arequipa." M.A. thesis, Department of Sociology, Pontificia Universidad Católica del Perú.

Communist Party of Chile. n.d. *Ricardo Fonseca: Combatiente ejemplar*. Santiago: Ediciones 21 de Julio.

Concheiro Bórquez, Luciano, Alejandro Rosado, and Ilán Semo G. 1980. "El nuevo sindicalismo en la zona industrial Vallejo." In *Memorias del encuentro sobre historia del movimiento obrero*. Vol. 3. Puebla, Mexico: Universidad Autónoma de Puebla.

Conniff, Michael L. 1981. *Urban Politics in Brazil: The Rise of Populism, 1925–1945*. Pittsburgh: University of Pittsburgh Press.

———. 1982. "Introduction: Toward a Comparative Definition of Populism." In Conniff, ed., *Latin American Populism in Comparative Perspective*. Albuquerque: University of New Mexico.

Conniff, Michael L., et al. 1971. "Brazil." In Richard M. Morse et al., eds., *The Urban Development of Latin America, 1750–1920*. Stanford: Center for Latin American Studies, Stanford University.

Contreras, Ariel José. 1977. *México 1940: Industrialización y crisis política*. Mexico City: Siglo XXI.

Converse, Philip E. 1972. "Change in the American Electorate." In Angus Campbell and Philip E. Converse, eds., *The Human Meaning of Social Change*. New York: Russell Sage Foundation.

———. 1974. "Comment on Burnham's 'Theory and Voting Research.' " *American Political Science Review* 68, no. 3 (September), pp. 1024–27.

Cordero, Salvador, and Silvia Gómez-Tagle. 1980. "Estado y trabajadores de las empresas estatales en México." In *Memorias del encuentro sobre historia del movimiento obrero*. Vol. 3. Puebla, Mexico: Universidad Autónoma de Puebla.

Córdova, Arnaldo. 1972. *La formación del poder político en México*. Mexico City: Ediciones Era.

———. 1973. *La ideología de la revolución mexicana: La formación del nuevo régimen*. Mexico City: Ediciones Era.

———. 1974. *La política de masas del cardenismo*. Mexico City: Ediciones Era.

———. 1976. "La transformación del PNR en PRM: El triunfo del corporativismo en México." In James W. Wilkie, Michael C. Meyer, and Edna Monzón de Wilkie, eds., *Contemporary Mexico: Papers of the IVth International Congress of Mexican History,* Latin American Studies Series, vol. 29. Los Angeles: UCLA, Latin American Center.

————. 1977. "Los orígenes del Estado en América Latina." *Cuadernos Políticos* 14, no. 4 (October–December), pp. 23–43.

————. 1979. *La política de masas y el futuro de la izquierda en México.* Mexico City: Ediciones Era.

————. 1981. *En una época de crisis (1928–1934).* Vol. 9 of Pablo González Casanova, ed., *La clase obrera en la historia de México.* Mexico City: Siglo XXI.

Cornelius, Wayne A. 1973. "Nation Building, Participation, and Distribution: The Politics of Social Reform under Cárdenas." In Gabriel Almond et al., eds., *Crisis, Choice, and Change: Historical Studies of Political Development.* Boston: Little, Brown.

————. 1986. "Political Liberalization and the 1985 Elections in Mexico." In Paul W. Drake and Eduardo Silva, eds., *Elections and Democratization in Latin America, 1980–85.* San Diego: Center for Iberian and Latin American Studies, Center for U.S.-Mexican Studies, and Institute of the Americas, University of California.

Cornelius, Wayne A., and Ann L. Craig. 1984. "Politics in Mexico." In Gabriel A. Almond and G. Bingham Powell, eds., *Comparative Politics Today.* Boston: Little, Brown.

Corradi, Juan. 1974. "Argentina." In Ronald Chilcote and Joel Edelstein, eds., *Latin America: The Struggle with Dependency and Beyond.* Cambridge, Mass.: Schenkman.

Corradi, Juan Eugenio. 1977. "Between Corporatism and Insurgency: The Sources of Ambivalence in Peronist Ideology." In Morris J. Blackman and Ronald G. Hellman, eds., *Terms of Conflict: Ideology in Latin American Politics.* Philadelphia: Institute for the Study of Human Issues.

————. 1978. "The Politics of Silence: Discourse, Text, and Social Conflict in South America." *Radical History Review* 18, no. 1 (Fall 1978), pp. 38–57.

————. 1984. "The Culture of Fear in Civil Society: The Argentine Case." Paper prepared for the Conference on Argentina held at the University of California, San Diego.

————. 1985. *The Fitful Republic: Economy, Society and Politics in Argentina.* Boulder, Colo.: Westview.

Cosse, Gustavo. 1984. "Notas acerca de la clase obrera, la democracia y el autoritarismo en el caso uruguayo." In Charles Gillespie, Louis Goodman, Juan Rial, and Peter Winn, eds., *Uruguay y la democracia.* Vol. 1. Montevideo: Ediciones de la Banda Oriental.

Costa, Sergio Amad. 1981. *C.G.T. e as lutas sindicais brasileiras (1960–64).* São Paulo: Grêmio Politécnico.

Cotler, Julio. 1978. *Clases, estado, y nación en el Perú.* Lima: Instituto de Estudios Peruanos.

————. 1979. "La crisis política (1930–1968)." In Luis Guillermo Lumbreras, et al., *Nueva historia general del Perú.* Lima: Mosca Azul Editores.

————. 1980. *Democracia e integración nacional.* Lima: Instituto de Estudios Peruanos.

Croes, Hemmy. 1973. *El movimiento obrero venezolano: Elementos para su historia.* Caracas: Ediciones Movimiento Obrero.

Cúneo, Dardo. 1967. *Comportamiento y crisis de la clase empresaria*. Buenos Aires: Pleamar.

Cusack, David. 1970. "The Politics of Chilean Private Enterprise under Christian Democracy." Doctoral diss., Graduate School of International Studies, University of Denver.

————. 1974. "Confrontation Politics and the Disintegration of Chilean Democracy." *Viertel Jahres Berichte*, no. 58 (December), pp. 581–600.

D'Abate, Juan Carlos. 1983. "Trade Unions and Peronism." In Frederick Turner and José Enrique Miguens, eds., *Juan Perón and the Reshaping of Argentina*. Pittsburgh: University of Pittsburgh Press.

Dahl, Robert A. 1971. *Polyarchy: Participation and Opposition*. New Haven: Yale University Press.

David, Paul A. 1985. "Clio and the Economics of QWERTY." *American Economic Review* 75, no. 2 (May), pp. 332–37.

————. 1987. "Some New Standards for the Economics of Standardization in the Information Age." In Partha Dasgupta and Paul Stoneman, eds., *Economic Policy and Technological Performance*. Cambridge: Cambridge University Press.

Davies, Thomas M. 1971. "The *Indigenismo* of the Peruvian Aprista Party: A Reinterpretation." *Hispanic American Historical Review* 51, no. 4 (November), pp. 626–45.

Davis, Charles L. 1976. "The Mobilization of Public Support for an Authoritarian Regime: The Case of the Lower Class in Mexico City." *American Journal of Political Science* 20, no. 4 (November), pp. 653–70.

Davis, Charles L., and Kenneth M. Coleman. 1986. "Labor and the State: Union Incorporation and Working-Class Politicization in Latin America." *Comparative Political Studies* 18, no. 4 (January), pp. 395–417.

Davis, Stanley, and Louis Wolf Goodman, eds. 1972. *Workers and Managers in Latin America*. Lexington, Mass.: D. C. Heath and Company.

de Ferrari, Francisco. 1955. "Batlle y la legislación del trabajo." In *Batlle: Su vida y su obra*. Montevideo: Editorial Acción.

D'Elia, Germán. 1982. *El Uruguay neo-batllista, 1946–1958*. Montevideo: Ediciones de la Banda Oriental.

De Ipola, Emilio. 1989. "Ruptura y continuidad: Claves parciales para un balance de las interpretaciones del peronismo." *Desarrollo Económico* 29, no. 115 (October–December), pp. 331–59.

de Riz, Liliana. 1970. "Ejército y política en Uruguay." In Facultad de Derecho y Ciencias Sociales, Instituto de Ciencias Sociales, ed., *Uruguay: Poder, ideología y clases sociales*. Vol. 1 of *Cuadernos de ciencias sociales*. Montevideo: Instituto de Ciencias Sociales.

de Sierra, Gerónimo. 1985. "La izquierda de la transición." In Charles Gillespie, Louis Goodman, Juan Rial, and Peter Winn, eds., *Uruguay y la democracia*. Vol. 2. Montevideo: Ediciones de la Banda Oriental.

Dean, Warren. 1969. *The Industrialization of São Paulo, 1880–1945*. Austin: University of Texas Press.

Deas, Malcolm. 1971. "Coalition in Colombia." *Current History* 60, no. 354 (February), pp. 90–118.

————. 1973. "Colombian Aprils." *Current History* 64, no. 378 (February), pp. 77–88.

Del Barco, Ricardo. 1983. *El régimen peronista, 1946–1955*. Buenos Aires: Editorial de Belgrano.

Del Campo, Hugo. 1983. *Sindicalismo y peronismo: Los comienzos de un vínculo perdurable*. Buenos Aires: Consejo Latinoamericano de Ciencias Sociales.

del Huerto Amarilla, María. 1984. "Participación política de las fuerzas armadas." In Charles Gillespie, Louis Goodman, Juan Rial, and Peter Winn, eds., *Uruguay y la democracia*. Vol. 1. Montevideo: Ediciones de la Banda Oriental.

Delgado, Lucilia de Almeida Neves. 1986. *O comando geral dos trabalhadores no Brasil, 1961–1964*. Petrópolis: Vozes.

Delpar, Helen Victoria. 1967. "The Liberal Party of Colombia, 1863–1903." Doctoral diss., Department of History, Columbia University.

DeShazo, Peter. 1983. *Urban Workers and Labor Unions in Chile: 1902–1927*. Madison: University of Wisconsin Press.

Dias, Everado. 1962. *História das lutas sociais no Brasil*. São Paulo: Editora Edaglit.

Díaz Alejandro, Carlos F. 1970. *Essays on the Economic History of the Argentine Republic*. New Haven: Yale University Press.

Díaz Ramírez, Manuel. 1974. *Apuntes sobre el movimiento obrero y campesino de México, 1844–1880*. Mexico City: Ediciones de Cultura Popular.

Dietz, Henry A. 1980. "The IMF from the Bottom Up: Social Impacts of Stabilization Policies in Lima, Peru." Paper prepared for the national meeting of the Latin American Studies Association, Bloomington, Indiana.

———. 1983. "Urban Electoral Behavior: An Examination of Three Elections in Lima, Peru." Paper prepared for the annual meeting of the American Political Science Association, Chicago.

Di Tella, Guido, and Manuel Zymelman. 1967. *Las etapas del desarrollo económico argentino*. Buenos Aires: Editorial Universitario de Buenos Aires.

Di Tella, Torcuato S. 1965. "Populism and Reform in Latin America." In Claudio Véliz, ed., *Obstacles to Change in Latin America*. New York: Oxford University Press.

———. 1968. "The Working Class in Politics." In Claudio Véliz, ed., *Latin America and the Caribbean—A Handbook*. New York: Praeger.

Dix, Robert H. 1967. *Colombia: The Political Dimension of Change*. New Haven: Yale University Press.

———. 1980a. "Political Oppositions under the National Front." In R. Albert Berry, Ronald G. Hellman, and Mauricio Solaún, eds., *Politics of Compromise: Coalition Government in Colombia*. New Brunswick, N.J.: Transaction Books.

———. 1980b. "Consociational Democracy: The Case of Colombia." *Comparative Politics* 12, no. 3 (April), pp. 303–19.

Domínguez, Jorge I. 1980. *Insurrection and Loyalty: The Breakdown of the Spanish-American Empire*. Cambridge: Harvard University Press.

Domínguez, Nelson. 1977. *Conversaciones con Juan J. Taccone*. Buenos Aires: Colihue/Hachette.

Donnelly, Vernon Charles. 1975. "Juan Vicente Gómez and the Venezuelan Worker." Doctoral diss., Department of History, University of Maryland.

Donoso, Ricardo. 1952–1954. *Alessandri, agitador y demoledor: Cincuenta años de história política de Chile*. 2 vols. Mexico City: Fondo de Cultura Económica.

Dooner, Patricio. 1984. *Cambios sociales y conflicto político: El conflicto político nacional durante el gobierno de Eduardo Frei (1964–1970)*. Santiago, Chile: Corporación de Promoción Universitaria.

Dorfman, Adolfo. 1970. *Historia de la industria argentina*. 2d ed. Buenos Aires: Solar/Hachette. (1st ed. 1942).

Dos Santos, Theotonio. 1974. "Brazil: The Origins of a Crisis." In Ronald Chilcote and Joel Edelstein, eds., *Latin America: The Struggle with Dependency and Beyond*. Cambridge, Mass.: Schenkman.

Downs, Anthony. 1957. *An Economic Theory of Democracy*. New York: Harper & Row.

Doyon, Louise M. 1975. "El crecimiento sindical bajo el peronismo." *Desarrollo Económico* 15, no. 57 (April–June), pp. 151–61.

———. 1977. "Conflictos obreros durante el régimen peronista (1946–1955)." *Desarrollo Económico* 17, no. 67 (October–December), pp. 437–73.

———. 1978. "Organized Labour and Perón (1943–1955): A Study in the Conflictual Dynamics of the Peronist Movement." Doctoral diss., Department of Political Economy, University of Toronto.

———. 1984. "La organización del movimiento sindical peronista 1946–1955." *Desarrollo Económico* 24, no. 94 (July–September), pp. 203–34.

Drake, Paul W. 1978. *Socialism and Populism in Chile, 1932–52*. Urbana: University of Illinois Press.

Dreifuss, René Armand. 1981. *1964: A conquista do estado: Ação política, poder e golpe de classe*. Petrópolis: Vozes.

Ducatenzeiler, Graciela. 1980. *Syndicats et politique en Argentine (1955–1973)*. Montreal: Les Presses de L'Université de Montréal.

Dulles, John W. F. 1961. *Yesterday in Mexico: A Chronicle of the Revolution, 1919–1936*. Austin: University of Texas Press.

———. 1970. *Unrest in Brazil: Political-Military Crises 1955–1964*. Austin and London: University of Texas Press.

———. 1973. *Anarchists and Communists in Brazil, 1900–1935*. Austin: University of Texas Press.

Durand, Francisco. n.d. "Notas sobre el problema de la burguesía en el Perú." *Debates en Sociología*. No. 7, Departamento de Ciencias Sociales, Catholic University of Peru.

Durand Ponce, Víctor Manuel. 1980. "Notas sobre las relaciones entre estructura y coyuntura para el análisis de la clase obrera mexicana, 1944–1952." In *Memorias del encuentro sobre historia del movimiento obrero*. Puebla, Mexico: Universidad Autónoma de Puebla.

Eakin, Marshall C. 1978. "Determining the Population in the Largest City of Each Latin American Country, 1900–1970." In James W. Wilkie and Peter Reich, eds., *Statistical Abstract of Latin America*. Vol. 19, pp. 400–403. Los Angeles: Latin American Center, University of California.

Eckstein, Susan, and Peter Evans. 1978. "Revolution as Cataclysm and Coup: Political Transformation and Economic Development in Mexico and Brazil." *Comparative Studies in Sociology* 1, pp. 129–55.

Economic Commission for Latin America (ECLA). 1965. "Structural Changes in Employment within the Context of Latin America's Economic Development." *Economic Bulletin for Latin America* 10, no. 2 (October), pp. 163–87.

———. 1966. *The Process of Industrialization in Latin America: Statistical Annex*. Santiago: United Nations.

Ellner, Steve. 1979. "Acción Democrática–Partido Comunista de Venezuela: Rivalry on the Venezuelan Left and in Organized Labor, 1936–1948." Doctoral diss., Department of History, University of New Mexico.

————. 1980. "Political Party Dynamics in Venezuela and the Outbreak of Guerrilla Warfare." *South American Economic Affairs* 34, no. 2 (Fall), pp. 3–24.

Epstein, Edward C. 1975. "Politicization and Income Distribution in Argentina: The Case of the Peronist Worker." *Economic Development and Cultural Change* 23, no. 4 (July), pp. 615–31.

————. 1981. "The Weakness of the Colombian Labor Movement." Paper prepared for the meetings of the Southwest Labor Studies Association, Albuquerque, N.M., May.

Erickson, Kenneth P. 1977. *The Brazilian Corporative State and Working Class Politics.* Berkeley and Los Angeles: University of California Press.

Erickson, Kenneth P., and Patrick V. Peppe. 1976. "Dependent Capitalist Development, U.S. Foreign Policy, and the Repression of the Working Class in Chile and Brazil." *Latin American Perspectives* 3, no. 1 (Winter), pp. 19–44.

Erickson, Kenneth P., Patrick V. Peppe, and Hobart A. Spalding, Jr. 1974. "Research on the Urban Working Class and Organized Labor in Argentina, Brazil, and Chile: What is Left to be Done?" *Latin American Research Review* 9, no. 2, pp. 115–42.

Errandonea, Alfredo, and Daniel Costabile. 1969. *Sindicato y sociedad en el Uruguay.* Montevideo: Biblioteca de Cultura Universitaria.

Estrada Urroz, Rosalina. 1980. "El poder de compra en la clase obrera de Puebla en 1940–1960." In *Memorias del encuentro sobre historia del movimiento obrero.* Vol. 1. Puebla, Mexico: Universidad Autónoma de Puebla.

Everett, Michael D. 1967. "The Role of the Mexican Trade Unions, 1950–1963." Doctoral diss., Department of Economics, Washington University.

Fabregat, Julio T. 1948. *Elecciones uruguayas.* Vol. 1. Montevideo: República Oriental del Uruguay, Cámara de Senadores.

Fagan, Stuart Irwin. 1974. "The Venezuelan Labor Movement: A Study in Political Unionism." Doctoral diss., Department of Political Science, University of California, Berkeley.

————. 1977. "Unionism and Democracy." In John D. Martz and David J. Myers, eds., *Venezuela: The Democratic Experience.* New York: Praeger.

Falabella, Gonzalo. 1980. "Labour under Authoritarian Regimes: The Chilean Union Movement, 1973–1979." Doctoral diss., Department of Development Studies, University of Sussex.

Falcoff, Mark. 1976. "The Uruguay that Never Was: A Historian Looks at Costa-Gavras's *State of Siege.*" *Journal of Latin American Lore* 2, no. 2, pp. 239–56.

Faraone, Roque. 1965. *El Uruguay en que vivimos: 1900–1965.* Montevideo: Editorial Arca. (New edition 1968).

Fausto, Boris. 1970. *A revolução de 1930.* São Paulo: Editora Brasiliense.

————. 1977. *Trabalho e conflito social (1890–1920).* Rio de Janeiro and São Paulo: DIFEL.

Favre, Henri. 1969. "El desarrollo y las formas del poder oligárquico en el Perú." In François Bourricaud, et al., eds., *La oligarquía en el Perú.* Lima: Moncloa-Campodonico.

Fayt, Carlos S. 1967. *La naturaleza del peronismo.* Buenos Aires: Viracocha S. A.

Ferns, H. S. 1973. *The Argentine Republic.* New York: Barnes and Noble.

Ferrer, Aldo. 1967. *The Argentine Economy.* Translated by Marjory M. Urquidi.

Berkeley and Los Angeles: University of California Press. (First published in Spanish as *La economía argentina: Las etapas de su desarrollo y problemas actuales*. Mexico City: Fondo de Cultura Económica, 1963.)

Ffrench-Davis, Ricardo. 1973. *Políticas económicas en Chile 1952–1970*. Santiago: CEPLAN, Ediciones Nueva Universidad.

Filho, Evaristo de Moraes. 1952. *O problema do sindicato único no Brasil (seus fundamentos sociológicos)*. São Paulo: Editora Alfa-Omega.

Fillol, Tomás Roberto. 1961. *Social Factors in Economic Development: The Argentine Case*. Cambridge: MIT Press.

Finch, M. H. J. 1971. "Three Perspectives on the Crisis in Uruguay." *Journal of Latin American Studies* 3 (November), pp. 169–90.

———. 1981. *A Political Economy of Uruguay since 1870*. London and Basingstoke: Macmillan.

———. 1985. "El régimen militar y la clase dominante en Uruguay." In Charles Gillespie, Louis Goodman, Juan Rial, and Peter Winn, eds., *Uruguay y la democracia*. Vol. 2. Montevideo: Ediciones de la Banda Oriental.

Fishlow, Albert. 1973. "Some Reflections on Post-1964 Brazilian Economic Policy." In Alfred Stepan, ed., *Authoritarian Brazil: Origins, Policies, and Future*. New Haven: Yale University Press.

Fitzgibbon, Russell H. 1954. *Uruguay: Portrait of a Democracy*. New Brunswick, N.J.: Rutgers University Press.

Flanagan, Scott C. 1973. "Models and Methods of Analysis." In Gabriel Almond et al., eds., *Crisis, Choice, and Change: Historical Studies of Political Development*. Boston: Little, Brown.

Fleet, Michael H. 1973. "Chile's Democratic Road to Socialism." *Western Political Quarterly* 26, no. 4 (December), pp. 766–86.

———. 1985. *The Rise and Fall of Chilean Christian Democracy*. Princeton: Princeton University Press.

Fleischer, David V. 1981. "Dimensões do recrutamento partidário." In Fleischer, ed., *Os partidos políticos no Brasil*. Brasília: Editora Universidade de Brasília.

Fleischer, David V., ed. 1981. *Os partidos políticos no Brasil*. Brasília: Editora Universidade de Brasília.

Flichman, Guillermo. 1977. *La rente del suelo y el desarrollo agrario argentino*. Mexico City: Siglo XXI.

Fluharty, Vernon Lee. 1957. *Dance of the Millions*. Pittsburgh: University of Pittsburgh Press.

Flynn, Peter. 1978. *Brazil: A Political Analysis*. Boulder, Colo.: Westview.

Fodor, Jorge. 1975. "Perón's Policies for Exports: Dogmatism or Common Sense?" In David Rock, ed., *Argentina in the 20th Century*. Pittsburgh: University of Pittsburgh Press.

Forman, Shepard. 1972. "Disunity and Discontent: A Study of Peasant Political Movements in Brazil." In Ronald H. Chilcote, ed., *Protest and Resistance in Angola and Brazil: Comparative Studies*. Berkeley: University of California Press.

Fraser, Nicholas, and Marysa Navarro. 1980. *Eva Perón*. New York: W. W. Norton & Company.

Frega, Ana, Mónica Maronna, and Yvette Trochón. 1984. "Los consejos de salarios como experiencia de concertación." Paper presented at the conference on "Concertation and Democracy." Montevideo, Aug. 14–17.

———. 1985. " 'Frente Popular' y 'Concertación Democrática': Los partidos de izquierda ante la dictadura terrista." In *Cuadernos del CLAEH*, no. 34, pp. 49–62.

———. 1987. *Baldomir y la restauración democrática: 1938–1946*. Montevideo: Ediciones de la Banda Oriental.

French, John D. 1985. "Industrial Workers and the Origin of Populist Politics in the ABC Region of Greater São Paulo, Brazil, 1900–1950." Doctoral diss., Yale University.

———. 1988. "Workers and the Rise of Adhemarista Populism in São Paulo, Brazil 1945–1947." *Hispanic American Historical Review* 68, no. 1, pp. 1–43.

———. 1989. "Industrial Workers and the Birth of the Populist Republic in Brazil, 1945–1946." *Latin American Perspectives* 16, no. 4 (Fall), pp. 5–27.

Fuentes Díaz, Vicente. 1959. "Desarrollo y evolución del movimiento obrero a partir de 1929." *Revista de Ciencias Políticas y Sociales* 5, no. 17 (July–September), pp. 325–48.

Furtado, Celso. 1976. *Economic Development of Latin America*. 2d ed. New York: Cambridge University Press. (1st ed., 1970).

Furtak, Robert K. 1974. *El partido de la revolución y la estabilidad política en México*. Serie Estudios 35. Mexico City: UNAM.

Galicia, S., et al. 1980. "Estudio de la relación de bienes salarios y su impacto en las condiciones sociales de vida de los trabajadores de Talleres Rice." In *Memorias del encuentro sobre historia del movimiento obrero*. Vol. 1. Puebla, Mexico: Universidad Autónoma de Puebla.

Gallo, Ezequiel, and Silvia Sigal. 1963. "La formación de los partidos políticos contemporáneos—La Unión Cívica Radical (1890–1916)." *Desarrollo Económico* 3, no. 1–2 (April–September), pp. 173–230.

Gallo, Ricardo. 1983. *Balbín, Frondizi y la división del radicalismo (1956–1958)*. Buenos Aires: Editorial de Belgrano.

Gamson, William A. 1968. *Power and Discontent*. Homewood, Ill.: Dorsey.

Garcés, Joan E. 1976. *Allende y la experiencia chilena: Las armas de la política*. Barcelona: Ariel.

García, César R. 1983. *Historia de los grupos y partidos políticos de la República Argentina desde 1810 a 1983*. Buenos Aires: Saint Claire Editores.

Gargiulo, Martín. 1984. "Movimiento sindical y estabilidad democráta." *CLAEH*, no. 30 (April–June), pp. 17–38.

Garretón, Manuel A. 1976. "Una perspectiva para el análisis de los aspectos ideológico-políticos del período 1970–1973 en Chile." Documento de trabajo, Facultad Latinoamericana de Ciencias Sociales, Santiago.

———. 1983. *El proceso político chileno*. Santiago: Facultad Latinoamericana de Ciencias Sociales.

Garretón, Manuel A., and Tomás Moulian. 1977. "Procesos y bloques políticos en la crisis chilena, 1970–1973." Documento de trabajo, Facultad Latinoamericana de Ciencias Sociales.

Garrett, Gary R. 1973. "The Oncenio of Augusto B. Leguía: Middle Sector Government and Leadership in Peru, 1919–1930." Doctoral diss., Department of History, University of New Mexico.

Garrido, Luis Javier. 1984. *El partido de la revolución institucionalizada: La formación del nuevo estado en México, 1928–1945*. Mexico City: Siglo XXI.

Garza, David T. 1964. "Factionalism in the Mexican Left: The Frustration of the MLN." *Western Political Quarterly* 17, no. 3 (September), pp. 447–60.

Gaudio, Ricardo, and Jorge Pilone. 1976. "Estado y relaciones obrero-patronales en los orígenes de la negociación colectiva en Argentina." Estudios Sociales no. 5, Centro de Estudios de Estado y Sociedad, Buenos Aires.

――――. 1983. "El desarrollo de la negociación colectiva durante la etapa de modernización industrial en la Argentina, 1935–1943." Desarrollo Económico 23, no. 90 (July–September), pp. 255–87.

――――. 1984. "Estado y relaciones laborales en el período previo al surgimiento del peronismo, 1935–1943." Desarrollo Económico 24, no. 94 (July–September), pp. 235–73.

Gazzera, Miguel. 1970. "Nosotros: Los dirigentes." In Miguel Gazzera and Norberto Ceresole, eds., Peronismo: Autocrítica y perspectivas. Buenos Aires: Editorial Descartes.

George, Alexander L., and Timothy J. McKeown. 1985. "Case Studies and Theories of Organizational Decision Making." Advances in Information Processing in Organizations. Vol. 2. Santa Barbara, Calif.: JAI Press.

Germani, Gino. 1955. La estructura social de la Argentina: Análisis estadístico. Buenos Aires: Editorial Raigal.

――――. 1965. Política y sociedad en una época de transición: De la sociedad tradicional a la sociedad de masas. Buenos Aires: Editorial Paidos.

――――. 1973. "El surgimiento del peronismo: El rol de los obreros y de los migrantes internos." Desarrollo Económico 13, no. 51 (October–December), pp. 435–88.

Gerschenkron, Alexander. 1962. Economic Backwardness in Historical Perspective. Cambridge: Harvard University Press.

――――. 1968. "On the Concept of Continuity in History." In Gerschenkron, ed., Continuity in History and Other Essays. Cambridge: Harvard University Press.

Gibson, William M. 1948. The Constitutions of Colombia. Durham, N.C.: Duke University Press.

Gil, Federico G. 1962. Genesis and Modernization of Political Parties in Chile. Gainesville: University of Florida Press.

――――. 1966. The Political System of Chile. Boston: Houghton Mifflin.

Gil, Federico G., and Charles J. Parrish. 1965. The Presidential Election of September 4, 1964. Part 1, An Analysis. Institute for the Comparative Study of Political Systems. Washington, D.C.: Operations and Policy Research.

Gil, Federico G., et al., eds. 1979. Chile at the Turning Point: Lessons of the Socialist Years, 1970–1973. Philadelphia: Institute for the Study of Human Issues.

Gil, José Antonio. 1977. "Entrepreneurs and Regime Consolidation." In John D. Martz and David J. Myers, eds., Venezuela: The Democratic Experience. New York: Praeger.

Gilhodes, Pierre. 1973. "Colombia." In Richard Gott, ed., Guide to the Political Parties of South America. Middlesex, England: Penguin Books.

Gillespie, Charles G. 1982a. "The Breakdown of Democracy in Uruguay: Alternative Political Models." Paper prepared for the 12th World Congress of the International Political Science Association, Rio de Janeiro.

――――. 1982b. "Regime Instability and Partisan Endurance: Authoritarianism and Opposition in Uruguay." Paper prepared for the 12th World Congress of the International Political Science Association, Rio de Janeiro.

――――. 1982c. "Report on the Planning Meeting on 'Redemocratization in Latin

America'." Woodrow Wilson Center Latin American Program, Washington, D.C.

———. n.d. "Activists and Floating Voters: The Unheeded Lessons of Uruguay's 1982 Primaries." Department of Political Science, Yale University.

Gillespie, Charles G., Louis Goodman, Juan Rial and Peter Winn, eds. 1984. *Uruguay y la democracia.* 2 vols. Montevideo: Ediciones del la Banda Oriental.

Glade, William P., and Charles W. Anderson. 1963. *The Political Economy of Mexico.* Madison: University of Wisconsin Press.

Gleick, James. 1987. *Chaos.* New York: Viking.

Godio, Julio. 1980. *El movimiento obrero venezolano, 1850–1944.* Vol. 1. Caracas: Editorial Ateneo de Caracas.

———. 1982. *El movimiento obrero venezolano, 1945–1980.* Vol 2. Caracas: Editorial Ateneo de Caracas.

———. 1985. *La caída de Perón.* 2 Vols. Buenos Aires: Centro Editor de América Latina.

Goldar, Ernesto. 1985. *John William Cooke y el peronismo revolucionario.* Buenos Aires: Centro Editor de América Latina.

Gómez, Rosendo A. 1947. "Intervention in Argentina: 1860–1930." *Inter-American Economic Affairs* 1, no 3 (December), pp. 55–73.

González, Fernán E. 1975. "Pasado y presente del sindicalismo colombiano." *Controversia,* no. 35–36. Bogotá: Centro de Investigaciones y Acción Social.

———. 1982. "Caudillismo y regionalismo en el siglo XIX latinoamericano." Centro de Investigación y Educación Popular, Documentos Ocasionales no. 4, November.

González, Luis E. 1976. "La transformación del sistema política uruguayo." Masters thesis, Departamento de Ciencias Sociales, Fundación Bariloche, Bariloche, Argentina.

———. 1982. "Uruguay 1980–81: Una apertura inesperada." Paper prepared for the Tenth National Meeting of the Latin American Studies Association, Washington, D.C.

———. 1983a. "Uruguay 1980–1981: An Unexpected Opening." *Latin American Research Review* 18, no. 3, pp. 63–76.

———. 1983b. "The Legitimation Problems of Bureaucratic-Authoritarian Regimes: The Cases of Chile and Uruguay." Montevideo: CIESU.

———. 1984. "Political Parties and Redemocratization in Uruguay." Washington, D.C.: Wilson Center Working Paper, no. 163, August.

———. 1985. "Transición y partidos en Chile y Uruguay." Montevideo: Centro de Informaciones y Estudios del Uruguay.

González Casanova, Pablo. 1970. *Democracy in Mexico.* New York: Oxford University Press.

———. 1980. *La clase obrera en la historia de México: en el primer gobierno constitucional (1917–1920).* Mexico: Siglo XXI.

———. 1982. *El estado y los partidos políticos en México.* Mexico City: Ediciones Era.

González Videla, Gabriel. 1975. *Memorias.* Santiago: Gabriela Mistral.

Goodman, Louis Wolf. 1972. "Worker Dependence in a Labor Surplus Economy." In Stanley M. Davis and Louis Wolf Goodman, eds., *Workers and Managers in Latin America.* Lexington, Mass.: D. C. Heath and Company.

———. 1973. "Paternal Triangles: Workers, Managers, and Politicians in the Politics of Latin American Industrialization." Paper presented at the World Congress of the International Political Science Association, Montreal.

————. Forthcoming. *Perspectives on Democratization in South America*. Latin American Program, Wilson Center, Washington, D.C.

Goodsell, Charles T. 1975. "That Confounding Revolution in Peru." *Current History* 68, no. 401 (January), pp. 20–23.

Gott, Richard. 1972. *Guerrilla Movements in Latin America*. New York: Anchor Books.

————. 1973a. Part Four: "Disaster in Peru." In Gott, *Rural Guerrillas in Latin America*. Middlesex, England: Penguin Books.

————. 1973b. Part Three: Colombia. In Gott, *Rural Guerrillas in Latin America*. Middlesex, England: Penguin Books.

Gourevitch, Peter Alexis. 1986. *Politics in Hard Times: Comparative Responses to Crises*. Ithaca: Cornell University Press.

Graceras, Ulíses F. 1977. "Inter-Generational Cleavages and Political Behavior: A Study of the 1971 Presidential Election in Uruguay." Doctoral diss., Department of Sociology, Michigan State University.

Graham, Douglas H. 1982. "Mexican and Brazilian Economic Development: Legacies, Patterns, and Performances." In Sylvia Ann Hewlett and Richard S. Weinert, eds., *Brazil and Mexico: Patterns in Late Development*. Philadelphia: Institute for the Study of Human Issues.

Graillot, Hélène. 1973a. "Argentina." In Richard Gott, ed., *Guide to the Political Parties of South America*. Middlesex, England: Penguin Books.

————. 1973b. "Uruguay." In Richard Gott, ed., *Guide to the Political Parties of South America*. Middlesex, England: Penguin Books.

Gramsci, Antonio. 1971. *Selections from the Prison Notebooks*. Translated by Quintin Hoare and Geoffrey Nowell Smith. New York: International Publishers.

Granovetter, Mark. 1978. "Threshold Models of Collective Behavior." *American Journal of Sociology* 83, no. 6 (May), 1420–43.

Gregory, Peter. 1986. *The Myth of Market Failure: Employment and the Labor Market in Mexico*. Baltimore: Johns Hopkins University Press.

Grew, Raymond. 1978. *Crises of Political Development in Europe and the United States*. Princeton: Princeton University Press.

Gruening, Ernest. 1928. *Mexico and its Heritage*. New York and London: Century.

Guadarrama, Rocío. 1981. *Los sindicatos y la política en México: La CROM, 1918–1928*. Mexico: Ediciones Era.

Guardo, Ricardo C. 1963. *Horas difíciles: 1955 Septiembre 1962*. Buenos Aires: Ediciones Ricardo C. Guardo.

Guzmán Campos, German. 1968. *La violencia en Colombia: Parte descriptiva*. Cali: Ediciones Progreso.

HAR. See *Hispanic American Report*.

Habermas, Jürgen. 1975. *Legitimation Crisis*. Boston: Beacon Press.

Hall, Linda B. 1981. *Alvaro Obregón: Power and Revolution in Mexico, 1911–1920*. College Station: Texas A & M University Press.

Halperín Donghi, Tulio. 1969. *Historia contemporánea de América Latina*. Madrid: Alianza Editorial.

————. 1975. "Algunas observaciones sobre Germani, el surgimiento del peronismo y los migrantes internos." *Desarrollo Económico* 14, no. 56 (January–March), pp. 765–79.

———. 1983. *Argentina: La democracia de masas*. Buenos Aires: Editorial Paídos.

Hamilton, Nora. 1978. "Mexico: The Limits of State Autonomy," Doctoral diss., Department of Sociology, University of Wisconsin, Madison.

———. 1982. *The Limits of State Autonomy: Post-Revolutionary Mexico*. Princeton: Princeton University Press.

Hammergren, Linn A. 1977. "Corporatism in Latin American Politics: A Reexamination of the Unique Tradition." *Comparative Politics* 9, no. 4 (July 1977), pp. 443–62.

Handelman, Howard. 1975. *Struggle in the Andes: Peasant Political Mobilization in Peru*. Austin: University of Texas Press.

———. 1976. "The Politics of Labor Protest in Mexico." *Journal of Inter-American Studies and World Affairs* 18, no. 3 (August), pp. 267–94.

———. 1977. "Oligarchy and Democracy in Two Mexican Labor Unions: A Test of Representation Theory." *Industrial and Labor Relations Review* (January), pp. 205–18.

———. 1978a. "Military Authoritarianism and Political Change in Uruguay." American Universities Field Staff Reports, South America Series no. 26.

———. 1978b. "Scarcity Amidst Plenty: Food Problems in Oil-Rich Venezuela." American Universities Field Staff Reports, South America Series no. 42.

———. 1978c. "Venezuela's Political Party System on the Eve of National Elections." American Universities Field Staff Reports, South America Series no. 44.

———. 1978d. "The Making of a Venezuelan President: 1978." American Universities Field Staff Reports, South America Series no. 45.

———. 1979a. "Economic Policy and Elite Pressures in Uruguay." American Universities Field Staff Reports, South America Series no. 27.

———. 1979b. "Organized Labor in Mexico: Oligarchy and Dissent." American Universities Field Staff Reports, North America Series no. 18.

———. 1981a. "Labor-Industrial Conflict and the Collapse of Uruguayan Democracy." *Journal of Inter-American Studies and World Affairs* 23, no. 4 (November), pp. 371–94.

———. 1981b. "Politics and Plebiscites: The Case of Uruguay." Latin American Program working paper no. 89, Wilson Center, Washington, D.C.

———. n.d. "Prelude to the 1984 Uruguayan Elections: The Military Regime's Legitimacy Crisis and the 1980 Constitutional Plebiscite." Department of Political Science, University of Wisconsin, Milwaukee.

Hansen, Roger D. 1974. *The Politics of Mexican Development*. Baltimore: Johns Hopkins University Press.

Hanson, James A. 1977. "Cycles of Economic Growth and Structural Change since 1950." In John D. Martz and David J. Myers, eds., *Venezuela: The Democratic Experience*. New York: Praeger.

Hanson, Simon. 1938. *Utopia in Uruguay: Chapters in the Economic History of Uruguay*. New York: Oxford University Press.

Harding, Timothy. 1973. "The Political History of Organized Labor in Brazil." Doctoral diss., Hispanic-American Studies, Stanford University.

Harding, Timothy F., and Saul Landau. 1964. "Terrorism, Guerrilla Warfare and the Democratic Left in Venezuela." *Studies on the Left* 4, no. 4 (Fall), pp. 118–28.

Haring, Clarence H. 1931. "Chilean Politics, 1920–1928." *Hispanic American Historical Review* 11, no. 1 (February), pp. 1–26.

Harker, Mary Margaret. 1937. "The Organization of Labor in Mexico since 1910." Doctoral diss., Department of History, University of Southern California.

Harsanyi, John C. 1960. "Explanation and Comparative Dynamics in Social Sciences." *Behavioral Science*, no. 5 (April), pp. 136–45.

Hart, John Mason. 1978. *Anarchism and the Mexican Working Class, 1860–1931.* Austin: University of Texas Press.

Hartlyn, Jonathan. 1981a. "Consociational Politics in Colombia: Confrontation and Accommodation in Comparative Perspective." Doctoral diss., Department of Political Science, Yale University.

———. 1981b. "Interest Groups and Political Conflict in Colombia: A Retrospective and Prospective View." Department of Political Science, Vanderbilt University.

———. 1982. "The Impact of a Country's Pre-Industrial Structure and the International System on Political Regime Type: A Case Study of Colombia." Paper prepared for the 23rd Annual International Studies Association Convention, Cincinnati, Ohio, March.

———. 1983. "Colombia: Old Problems, New Opportunities." *Current History* 82 (February), pp. 62–65, 83–84.

———. 1984a. "The Impact of Patterns of Industrialization and of Popular Sector Incorporation on Political Regime Type: A Case Study of Colombia." *Studies in Comparative International Development* 19, no. 1 (Spring), pp. 29–59.

———. 1984b. "Military Governments and the Transition to Civilian Rule: The Colombian Experience of 1957–1958." *Journal of Inter-American Studies and World Affairs* 26, no. 2 (May), pp. 245–81.

———. 1988. *The Politics of Coalition Rule in Colombia.* Cambridge: Cambridge University Press.

Hartz, Louis. 1964. *The Founding of New Societies: Studies in the History of the United States, Latin America, South Africa, Canada, and Australia.* New York: Harcourt, Brace, and World.

Haya de la Torre, Víctor Raúl. 1976. *Obras completas.* 7 vols. Lima: Editorial Juan Mejía Baca.

Hayes, James Riley. 1951. "The Mexican Labor Movement, 1931–1951." M.A. thesis, University of California, Berkeley.

Hellinger, Daniel. 1979. "Class and Politics in Venezuela: Prologue to a Theory of Representative Democracy in Dependent Nations." St. Olaf College, Northfield, Minn.

———. 1984. "Populism and Nationalism in Venezuela: New Perspectives on Acción Democrática." *Latin American Perspectives* 11, no. 4 (Fall), pp. 33–59.

Hellman, Judith Adler. 1978. *Mexico in Crisis.* New York: Holmes and Meier.

———. 1980. "Social Control in Mexico." *Comparative Politics* 12, no. 2 (January), pp. 225–42.

Henderson, Peter. 1981. *Félix Díaz, the Porfirians, and the Mexican Revolution.* Lincoln: University of Nebraska Press.

Herbold, Carl F. 1971. "Peru." In Richard M. Morse et al., eds., *The Urban Development of Latin America, 1750–1920.* Stanford: Center for Latin American Studies, Stanford University.

———. 1973. "Developments in the Peruvian Administrative System, 1919–1939: Modern and Traditional Qualities of Government under Authoritarian Regimes." Doctoral diss., Department of Political Science, Yale University.

Herman, Donald. 1980. *Christian Democracy in Venezuela.* Chapel Hill: University of North Carolina Press.

Hernández Chávez, Alicia. 1979. *Historia de la Revolución Méxicana, 1934–1940: La mecánica cardenista*. Vol. 16. Mexico City: El Colegio de México.

Hewlett, Sylvia A. 1980. *The Cruel Dilemmas of Development: Twentieth-Century Brazil*. New York: Basic Books.

Hexter, J. H. 1979. *On Historians*. Cambridge: Harvard University Press.

Hilliker, Grant. 1971. *The Politics of Reform in Peru: The Aprista and other Mass Parties of Latin America*. Baltimore: Johns Hopkins University Press.

Hirschman, Albert O. 1965. *Journeys toward Progress: Studies of Economic Policy-Making in Latin America*. New York: Anchor Books.

———. 1977. *The Passions and the Interests: Political Arguments for Capitalism before its Triumph*. Princeton: Princeton University Press.

———. 1979. "The Turn to Authoritarianism in Latin America and the Search for its Economic Determinants." In David Collier, ed., *The New Authoritarianism in Latin America*. Princeton: Princeton University Press.

Hispanic American Report (HAR). Stanford: Stanford University 1955–1964.

Hodges, Donald C. 1976. *Argentina, 1943–1976: The National Revolution and Resistance*. Albuquerque: University of New Mexico Press.

Horcasitas, Juan Molinar. n.d. "The Mexican Electoral System: Continuity by Change." Mimeo, Universidad Nacional Autónoma de México.

Horgan, Terrence B. 1983. "The Liberals Come to Power in Colombia, por Debajo de la Ruana: A Study of the Enrique Olaya Herrera Administration, 1930–1934." Doctoral diss., Department of History, Vanderbilt University.

Horowitz, Irving Louis. 1964. *Revolution in Brazil*. New York: E. P. Dutton.

Horowitz, Joel. 1979. "Adaptation and Change in the Argentine Labor Movement, 1930–1943: A Study of Five Unions." Doctoral diss., Department of History, University of California, Berkeley.

———. 1983. "The Impact of Pre-1943 Labor Union Traditions on Peronism." *Journal of Latin American Studies* 15, no. 1 (May), pp. 101–16.

———. 1984. "Ideologias sindicales y políticas estatales en la Argentina, 1930–1943." *Desarrollo Económico* 24, no. 94 (July–September), pp. 275–96.

———. 1990. *Argentine Unions, the State, and the Rise of Perón, 1930–1945*. Institute of International Studies, University of California, Berkeley.

Hoskin, Gary. 1980. "The Impact of the National Front on Congressional Behavior: The Attempted Restoration of El País Político." In R. Albert Berry, Ronald G. Hellman, and Mauricio Solaún, eds., *Politics of Compromise: Coalition Government in Colombia*. New Brunswick, N.J.: Transaction Books.

———. 1983. "The Colombian Political Party System: The 1982 Reaffirmation and Reorientation." Paper prepared for the 11th International Congress of the Latin American Studies Association, Mexico City.

Huizer, Gerrit. 1970. *La lucha campesina en México*. Mexico City: C.I.D.A.

———. 1972. *The Revolutionary Potential of Peasants in Latin America*. Lexington, Mass.: Lexington Books.

———. 1973. *Peasant Rebellion in Latin America: The Origins, Forms of Expression, and Potential of Latin American Peasant Unrest*. Harmondsworth: Penguin Books.

Humphrey, John. 1982. *Capitalist Control and Workers' Struggle in the Brazilian Auto Industry*. Princeton: Princeton University Press.

Hunter, John M. 1966. "A Testing Ground in Colombia." *Current History* 51, no. 303 (November), pp. 8–14.

Huntington, Samuel P. 1968. *Political Order in Changing Societies*. New Haven: Yale University Press.

ILO. See International Labor Office.

Ianni, Octavio. 1970. *Crisis in Brazil*. New York: Columbia University Press. See also Portuguese edition.

———. 1975. *La formación del estado populista en América Latina*. Mexico City: Ediciones Era.

Imaz, José Luis de. 1970. *Los que mandan (Those Who Rule)*. Albany: State University of New York Press.

Informes Laborales. Buenos Aires: Documentación e Información Laboral, 1963–1966.

Institute for the Comparative Study of Political Systems. 1963. *The Chilean Presidential Election of September 4, 1964*. Part 1. Washington, D.C.: Operations and Policy Research.

———. 1965. *The Chilean Presidential Election of September 4, 1964*. Part 2. Washington, D.C.: Operations and Policy Research.

International Labour Office (ILO). 1930. *Freedom of Association*. Vol. 5. Studies and Reports, series A, no. 32. Geneva: International Labour Office.

———. 1950. *Freedom of Association and Conditions of Work in Venezuela*. Studies and Reports, new series no. 21. Geneva: International Labour Office.

Iscaro, Rubens. 1973. *Historia del movimiento sindical*. Vol. 2, *El movimiento sindical argentino*. Buenos Aires: Editorial Fundamento.

Jacob, Raúl. 1981a. *Breve historia de la industria en Uruguay*. Montevideo: Fundacíon de Cultura Universitaria.

———. 1981b. *Benito Nardone: El ruralismo hacia el poder (1945–1958)*. Montevideo: Ediciones de la Banda Oriental.

———. 1983. *El Uruguay de Terra, 1931–1938: Una crónica del terrismo*. Montevideo: Ediciones de la Banda Oriental.

Jaguaribe, Hélio. 1965. "The Dynamics of Brazilian Nationalism." In Claudio Véliz, ed., *Obstacles to Change in Latin America*. New York: Oxford University Press.

———. 1968. *Economic and Political Development: A Theoretical Approach and a Brazilian Case Study*. Cambridge: Harvard University Press.

James, Daniel. 1976. "The Peronist Left, 1955–1975." *Journal of Latin American Studies* 8, no. 2 (November), pp. 273–96.

———. 1978. "Power and Politics in Peronist Trade Unions." *Journal of Inter-American Studies and World Affairs* 20, no. 1 (February), pp. 3–36.

———. 1979. "Unions and Politics: The Development of Peronist Trade Unionism, 1955–1966." Doctoral diss., Department of History, University of London.

———. 1981. "Rationalisation and Working Class Response: The Context and Limits of Factory Floor Activity in Argentina." *Journal of Latin American Studies* 13, no. 2 (November), pp. 375–402.

———. 1988. *Resistance and Integration: Peronism and the Argentine Working Class, 1946–1976*. Cambridge: Cambridge University Press.

Jaquette, Jane S. 1971. "The Politics of Development in Peru." Latin American Studies Program, Dissertation Series no. 33, Cornell University.

Jobet, Julio César. 1955. *Ensayo crítico de desarrollo económico-social de Chile*. Santiago: Editorial Universitario.

Johnson, Dale L. 1968. "Industrialization, Social Mobility, and Class Formation in Chile." *Studies in Comparative International Development* 3, no. 7, pp. 127–51.

————. 1969. "The National and Progressive Bourgeoisie in Chile." *Studies in Comparative International Development* 4, no. 4.

————. 1973. *The Chilean Road to Socialism.* New York: Anchor Books.

Johnson, John J. 1958. *Political Change in Latin America: The Emergence of the Middle Sectors.* Stanford: Stanford University Press.

Johnson, Kenneth F. 1971. *Mexican Democracy: A Critical Review.* Revised ed. Boston: Allyn and Bacon, Inc.

————. 1975. "Guerrilla Politics in Argentina." *Conflict Studies*, no. 63 (October), pp. 1–21.

————. 1978. *Mexican Democracy: A Critical Review.* New York: Praeger.

Jordan, David C. 1972. "Argentina's Bureaucratic Oligarchies." *Current History* 62, no. 366 (February), pp. 70–115.

Joxe, Alain. 1970. *Las fuerzas armadas en el sistema político chileno.* Santiago: Editorial Universitaria.

Jurema, Abelardo de Araujo. 1979. *Juscelino & Jango: PSD & PTB.* Rio de Janciro. Editora Artenova.

Kahil, Raouf. 1973. *Inflation and Economic Development in Brazil, 1946–1963.* Oxford: Clarendon Press.

Karl, Terry Lynn. 1981. "The Political Economy of Petrodollars in Venezuela." Doctoral diss., Department of Political Science, Stanford University.

————. 1986. "Petroleum and Political Pacts: The Transition to Democracy in Venezuela." In Guillermo O'Donnell et al., eds., *Transitions from Authoritarian Rule: Latin America.* Baltimore: Johns Hopkins University Press.

Karlsson, Weine. 1975. *Manufacturing in Venezuela.* Stockholm: Almquist and Wiksell International.

Karno, Howard Laurence. 1970. "Augusto B. Leguía: The Oligarchy and the Modernization of Peru, 1870–1930." Doctoral diss., Department of History, University of California, Los Angeles.

Katz, Friedrich. 1974. "Labor Conditions on Haciendas in Porfirian Mexico: Some Trends and Tendencies." *Hispanic American Historical Review* 54, no. 1 (February), pp. 1–47.

Katzenstein, Peter J. 1985. *Small States in World Markets: Industrial Policy in Europe.* Ithaca: Cornell University Press.

Katznelson, Ira, and Aristide R. Zolberg. 1986. *Working Class Formation: Nineteenth-Century Patterns in Western Europe and the United States.* Princeton: Princeton University Press.

Kaufman, Edy. 1979. *Uruguay in Transition: From Civilian to Military Rule.* New Brunswick, N.J.: Transaction Books.

Kaufman, Robert R. 1967. "The Chilean Political Right and Agrarian Reform: Resistance and Moderation." Institute for the Comparative Study of Political Systems, Washington, D.C.

————. 1972. *The Politics of Land Reform in Chile, 1950–1970: Public Policy, Political Institutions and Social Change.* Cambridge: Harvard University Press.

————. 1976. "Transitions to Stable Authoritarian-Corporate Regimes: The Chilean Case." Sage Professional Papers, Comparative Politics Series 1, no. 01–060.

————. 1977a. "Corporatism, Clientelism, and Partisan Conflict: A Study of Seven Countries." In James M. Malloy, ed., *Authoritarianism and Corporatism in Latin America.* Pittsburgh: University of Pittsburgh Press.

Kaufman, Robert R. 1977b. "Mexico and Latin American Authoritarianism." In José Luis Reyna and Richard S. Weinert, eds., *Authoritarianism in Mexico*. Philadelphia: Institute for the Study of Human Issues.

———. 1979. "Industrial Change and Authoritarian Rule in Latin America: A Concrete Review of the Bureaucratic-Authoritarian Model." In David Collier, ed., *The New Authoritarianism in Latin America*. Princeton: Princeton University Press.

———. 1986. "Liberalization and Democratization in South America: Perspectives from the 1970s." In Guillermo O'Donnell, Philippe C. Schmitter, and Laurence Whitehead, eds., *Transitions from Authoritarian Rule: Comparative Perspectives*. Baltimore: Johns Hopkins University Press.

Keesing, Donald B. 1969. "Structural Change Early in Development: Mexico's Changing Industrial and Occupational Structure from 1895 to 1950." *Journal of Economic History* 24, no. 4, pp. 716–38.

———. 1977. "Employment and Lack of Employment in Mexico, 1900–1970." In James W. Wilkie and Kenneth Ruddle, eds., *Quantitative Latin American Studies: Methods and Findings*. Statistical Abstract of Latin America, Supplement 6. Los Angeles: Latin American Center, University of California.

Kelley, R. Lynn. 1977. "Venezuelan Constitutional Forms and Realities." In John D. Martz and David J. Myers, eds., *Venezuela: The Democratic Experience*. New York: Praeger.

Kenworthy, Eldon. 1970. "The Formation of the Peronist Coalition." Doctoral diss., Department of Political Science, Yale University.

———. 1972. "Did the 'New Industrialists' Play a Significant Role in the Formation of Perón's Coalition, 1943–1946?" In Alberto Ciría et al., eds., *New Perspectives on Modern Argentina*. Bloomington: Latin American Studies, Indiana University.

———. 1973. "The Function of the Little Known Case in Theory Formation or What Peronism Wasn't." *Comparative Politics* 6, no. 1 (October), pp. 17–46.

———. 1975. "Interpretaciones ortodoxas y revisionistas del apoyo inicial del peronismo." *Desarrollo Económico* 14, no. 56 (January–March), pp. 749–63.

Kerr, Clark, et al. 1960. *Industrialism and Industrial Man*. Cambridge: Harvard University Press. Reprint. New York: Oxford University Press, 1964.

Key, V. O., Jr. 1955. "A Theory of Critical Elections." *Journal of Politics* 17, no. 1 (February), pp. 3–18.

King, Timothy. 1970. *Mexico: Industrialization and Trade Policies since 1940*. New York: Oxford University Press.

Kirby, John. 1973. "Venezuela's Land Reform: Progress and Change." *Journal of Inter-American Studies and World Affairs* 15, no. 2, pp. 205–20.

Klarén, Peter F. 1973. *Modernization, Dislocation, and Aprismo*. Austin: University of Texas Press.

Kline, Harvey F. 1980. "The National Front: Historical Perspective and Overview." In R. Albert Berry, Ronald G. Hellmen, and Mauricio Solaún, eds., *Politics of Compromise: Coalition Government in Colombia*. New Brunswick, N.J.: Transaction Books.

———. 1985. "New Directions in Colombia." In *Current History* 84 (February, 1985), pp. 65–68, 83.

Knight, Alan. 1986. *The Mexican Revolution*. 2 vols. Cambridge: Cambridge University Press.

Kohl, James, and John Litt. 1974. "Urban Guerrilla Warfare: Uruguay." In Kohl and Litt, eds., *Urban Guerrilla Warfare in Latin America*. Cambridge: MIT Press.

Krasner, Stephen D. 1982. "Punctuated Equilibrium: An Approach to the Evolution of State-Society Relations." Department of Political Science, Stanford University.

———. 1983. "Regimes and the Limits of Realism." In Krasner, ed., *International Regimes*. Ithaca: Cornell University Press.

———. 1984. "Approaches to the State: Alternative Conceptions and Historical Dynamics." *Comparative Politics* 16, no. 2 (January), pp. 223–46.

———. 1988. "Sovereignty: An Institutional Perspective." *Comparative Political Studies* 21, no. 1 (April), pp. 66–94.

Krauze, Enrique, Jean Meyer, and Cayetano Reyes. 1977. *La reconstrucción económica*. Vol. 10 in *Historia de la revolución mexicana*. Mexico City: El Colegio de México.

Kuczynski, Pedro-Pablo. 1977. *Peruvian Democracy under Economic Stress: An Account of the Belaúnde Administration, 1963–1968*. Princeton: Princeton University Press.

Kvaternik, Eugenio. 1978. "Sobre partidos y democracia en la Argentina entre 1955 y 1966." *Desarrollo Económico* 18, no. 71 (October–December), pp. 409–31.

———. 1987. *Crisis sin salvataje: La crisis político-militar de 1962–63*. Buenos Aires: Ediciones de Ides.

Labarthe, Maria de la Cruz. 1980. "La industria del calzado en León." In *Memorias del encuentro sobre historia del movimiento obrero*. Vol. 1. Puebla, Mexico: Universidad Autónoma de Puebla.

Laclau, Ernesto. 1977. *Politics and Ideology in Marxist Theory*. London: Verso Editions.

Lafertte, Elias. 1961. *Vida de un comunista*. Santiago: Horizonte.

Lamadrid, Alejandro. 1986. "Sindicatos y política: El gobierno Guido." Centro de Estudios de Estado y Sociedad (CEDES), Buenos Aires.

Lamas, Mario Daniel, and Diosma E. Piotti de Lamas. 1981. *Historia de la industria en el Uruguay: 1730–1980*. Montevideo: Cámara de Industrias del Uruguay.

Lamounier, Bolivar, and Rachel Meneguello. 1985. "Political Parties and Democratic Consolidation: The Brazilian Case." Working Papers, no. 165. Wilson Center, Latin American Program, Washington, D.C., May.

Landsberger, Henry A. 1978. "Working Class Revolutionary Consciousness: Chile 1970–1973, Germany 1918–1923." Paper presented at the Workshop on Urban Working Class Culture and Social Protest in Latin America. Woodrow Wilson International Center for Scholars, Washington, D.C.

Landsberger, Henry A., and Tim McDaniel. 1976. "Hypermobilization in Chile, 1970–1973." *World Politics* 28, no. 4 (July), pp. 502–41.

Lange, Peter. 1984. "Unions, Workers and Wage Regulation: The Rational Bases of Consent." In John H. Goldthorpe, ed., *Order and Conflict in Contemporary Capitalism*. Oxford: Clarendon Press.

Lasswell, Harold D., and Abraham Kaplan. 1950. *Power and Society: A Framework for Political Inquiry*. New Haven: Yale University Press.

Latin American Political Report (London).

Leal, Juan Felipe. 1976. *México: Estado, burocracia, y sindicatos*. Mexico City: Ediciones 'El Caballito'.

Leal, Juan Felipe. 1985. "Las estructuras sindicales." In Pablo González Casanova, Samuel León, and Ignacio Marván, eds., *Organización y sindicalismo*. Vol. 3 of *El obrero mexicano*. Mexico City: Siglo XXI.

Leal, Juan Felipe, and José Woldenberg. 1976. "El sindicalismo mexicano: Aspectos organizativos." *Cuadernos Políticos*, no. 7 (January–March), pp. 35–53.

Leal Buitrago, Francisco. 1984. *Estado y política en Colombia*. Bogotá: Siglo XXI.

Leeds, Anthony. 1964. "Brazil: The Myth of Francisco Julião." In Joseph Maier and Richard Weatherhead, eds., *Politics of Change in Latin America*. New York: Praeger.

Leff, Nathaniel. 1968. *Economic Policy Making and Development in Brazil, 1947–1964*. New York: Wiley Press.

———. 1982. *Underdevelopment and Development in Brazil: Economic Structure and Change, 1822–1947*. Vol. 1. London: Allen and Unwin.

León, Samuel. 1980. "Estado y movimiento obrero." In *Memorias del encuentro sobre historia del movimiento obrero*. Vol. 1. Puebla, Mexico: Universidad Autónoma de Puebla.

León, Samuel, and Maria Xelhuantzi López. 1985. "Los obreros, las burocracias sindicales y la política del gobierno." *La política y la cultura*. Vol. 5 of *El obrero mexicano*. Mexico City: Siglo XXI.

Lestienne, Bernard. 1981. *El sindicalismo venezolano*. Caracas: Centro Gumilla.

Levenstein, Harvey A. 1966. "The U.S. Labor Movement and Mexico, 1910–1951." Doctoral diss., University of Wisconsin.

Levine, Daniel H. 1973. *Conflict and Political Change in Venezuela*. Princeton: Princeton University Press.

———. 1978. "Venezuela since 1958: The Consolidation of Democratic Politics." In Juan J. Linz and Alfred Stepan, eds., *The Breakdown of Democracy: Latin America*. Baltimore: Johns Hopkins University Press.

———. 1985. "On the Nature, Sources, and Future Prospects of Democracy in Venezuela." Paper prepared for a Conference on Democracy in Developing Nations at the Hoover Institution, Stanford, California, December.

Levine, Robert M. 1970. *The Vargas Regime: The Critical Years, 1934–38*. New York: Columbia University Press.

———. 1980. "Perspectives on the Mid-Vargas Years, 1934–37." *Journal of Inter-American Studies and World Affairs* 22, no. 1 (February), pp. 57–80.

Levy, Daniel C., and Gabriel Székely. 1983. *Mexico: Paradoxes of Stability and Change*. Boulder, Colo.: Westview.

Lewis, Paul H. 1973. "The Durability of Personalist Followings: The Vargas and Peronist Cases." *Polity* 5, no. 3 (Spring), pp. 401–14.

Lieberson, Stanley. 1985. *Making it Count: The Impoverishment of Social Research and Theory*. Berkeley and Los Angeles: University of California Press.

Lieuwen, Edwin. 1957. *Petroleum in Venezuela: A History*. Publications in History. Vol. 47. Berkeley: University of California.

———. 1961. *Arms and Politics in Latin America*. New York: Praeger.

———. 1964. *Generals versus Presidents: Neo-Militarism in Latin America*. New York: Praeger.

———. 1965. *Venezuela*. 2d ed. London and New York: Oxford University Press.

———. 1967. *Petroleum in Venezuela*. New York: Russell & Russell.

Lindahl, Goran. 1962. *Uruguay's New Path: A Study in Politics during the First Colegiado*. Stockholm: Library and Institute of Ibero-American Studies.

Lininger, Andrew C. 1968. "Información sobre sindicatos del área de Lima-Callao." Centro de Investigaciones Sociales por Muestro, Lima, Peru.

Linz, Juan J., and Alfred Stepan. 1978. *The Breakdown of Democratic Regimes.* Baltimore: Johns Hopkins University Press.

Lipset, Seymour Martin. 1983. "Radicalism or Reformism: The Source of Working-Class Politics." *American Political Science Review* 77, no. 1 (March), pp. 1–18.

Lipset, Seymour Martin, and Stein Rokkan. 1967. "Cleavage Structures, Party Systems, and Voter Alignments: An Introduction." In Lipset and Rokkan, eds., *Party Systems and Voter Alignments: Cross-National Perspectives.* New York: Free Press.

Little, Walter. 1973a. "Electoral Aspects of Peronism, 1946–54." *Journal of Inter-American Studies and World Affairs* 15, no. 3 (August), pp. 267–84.

———. 1973b. "Party and State in Peronist Argentina, 1945–55." *Hispanic American Historical Review* 53, no. 4 (November), pp. 644–62.

———. 1975. "The Popular Origins of Peronism." In David Rock, ed., *Argentina in the Twentieth Century.* Pittsburgh: University of Pittsburgh Press.

———. 1979. "La organización obrera y el estado peronista, 1943–1955." *Desarrollo Económico* 19, no. 75 (October–December), pp. 331–76.

Llanos, Miguel. 1983. "Uruguayan Trade Unions: Where They Have Been and Where They Are Going." Department of Political Science, University of California, Berkeley.

Llorente, Ignacio. 1980. "La composición social del movimiento peronista hacia 1954." In Manuel Mora y Araujo and Ignacio Llorente, eds., *El voto peronista: Ensayos de sociología electoral argentina.* Buenos Aires: Editorial Sudamericana.

Lombardi, John V. 1977. "The Patterns of Venezuela's Past." In John D. Martz and David J. Myers, eds., *Venezuela: The Democratic Experience.* New York: Praeger.

———. 1982. *Venezuela: The Search For Order, The Dream of Progress.* New York: Oxford University Press.

Lombardo, Adriana. 1980. "Relaciones entre sindicatos, partidos y el Estado." In *Memorias del encuentro sobre historia del movimiento obrero.* Vol. 3. Puebla, Mexico: Universidad Autónoma de Puebla.

Londoño Botero, Rocio. 1986. "La estructura sindical colombiana en la década del 70." In Hernando Gómez, Rocio Londoño, and Guillermo Perry, eds., *Sindicalismo y política económica.* Bogotá: CEREC, 1986.

Looney, Robert E. 1975. *Income Distribution Policies and Economic Growth in Semi-Industrialized Countries: A Comparative Study of Iran, Mexico, Brazil and South Korea.* New York: Praeger.

Lopez-Alves, Fernando. 1985. "Urban Guerrillas and the Rise of Bureaucratic Authoritarianism in Uruguay, 1959–1972." Paper prepared for the annual meeting of the American Political Science Association, New Orleans.

López Aparicio, Alfonso. 1952. *El movimiento obrero en México: Antecedentes, desarrollo y tendencias.* Mexico City: Editorial Jus.

Losada, Rodrigo. 1980. "Electoral Participation." In R. Albert Berry, Ronald G. Hellman, and Mauricio Solaún, eds., *Politics of Compromise: Coalition Government in Colombia.* New Brunswick, N.J.: Transaction Books.

Losada, Rodrigo, and Miles Williams. 1970. "El voto presidencial en Bogotá." In

Boletín Mensual de Estadística. Bogotá: Departamento Administrativo Nacional de Estadística, no. 229 (August), pp. xv–xvii.

Love, Joseph L. 1970. "Political Participation in Brazil, 1881–1969." *Luso-Brazilian Review* 7, no. 2 (December), pp. 3–24.

Loveman, Brian. 1976a. *Struggle in the Countryside: Politics and Rural Labor in Chile, 1919–1973.* Bloomington: Indiana University Press.

———. 1976b. "The Transformation of the Chilean Countryside." In Arturo Valenzuela and J. Samuel Valenzuela, eds., *Chile: Politics and Society.* New Brunswick, N.J.: Transaction Books.

———. 1979. *Chile: The Legacy of Hispanic Capitalism.* New York: Oxford University Press.

Lowenthal, Abraham F. 1980. "Dateline Peru: A Sagging Revolution." *Foreign Policy,* no. 38 (Spring), pp. 182–90.

———. 1982. "Colombia 1982: Some Quick Impressions." Latin American Program, Wilson Center, Washington, D.C.

———. 1983. "The Peruvian Experiment Reconsidered." In Cynthia McClintock and Abraham F. Lowenthal, *The Peruvian Experiment Reconsidered.* Princeton: Princeton University Press.

Lowi, Theodore J. 1976. *American Government: Incomplete Conquest.* Hinsdale, Ill.: Dreyden Press.

Loyo Brambila, Aurora. 1975. "El marco socio-económico de la crisis política de 1958–1959 en México." *Revista Mexicana de Sociología* 37, no. 2 (April–June), pp. 349–62.

Loyo Brambila, Aurora, and Ricardo Pozas Horcasitas. 1975. "Notes on the Mechanisms of Control Exercised by the Mexican State over the Organized Sector of the Working Class. A Case Study: The Political Crisis of 1958." Institute of Social Research, National University of Mexico, April.

Loyola Díaz, Rafael. 1984. *La crisis Obregón-Calles y el estado mexicano.* 2d ed. Mexico City: Siglo XXI.

Luebbert, Gregory M. 1986. "Origins of Modern Capitalist Polities and Labor Markets in Western Europe." Paper presented at the Fifth International Conference of Europeanists of the Council for European Studies, Washington, D.C.

———. 1987. "Social Foundations of Political Order in Interwar Europe." *World Politics* 39, no. 4 (July), pp. 449–78.

Luna, Félix. 1969. *El 45: Crónica de un año decisivo.* Buenos Aires: Editorial Jorge Alvarez.

———. 1972. *Argentina, de Perón a Lanusse (1943–1973).* Buenos Aires: Editorial Planeta.

———. 1983. *Golpes militares y salidas electorales.* Buenos Aires: Editorial Sudamericana.

Luna Marez, Patricia. 1980. "Situación económica y social de los trabajadores textiles en el estado de Veracruz, 1920–1935." In *Memorias del encuentro sobre historia del movimiento obrero.* Vol. 3. Puebla, Mexico: Universidad Autónomo de Puebla.

Luparia, Carlos H. 1973. *El grito de la tierra: Reforma agraria y sindicalismo.* Buenos Aires: Ediciones La Bastilla.

Lynch, Nicolas. 1980. "El APRA y la dictadura militar (1968–1978)." In Mariano Valderrama, et al., eds., *El APRA: Un camino de esperanzas y frustraciones.* Lima: Ediciones El Gallo Rojo.

McClintock, Cynthia. 1981. *Peasant Cooperatives and Political Change in Peru.* Princeton: Princeton University Press.

————. 1984. "Why Peasants Rebel: The Case of Peru's Sendero Luminoso." *World Politics* 37, no. 1 (October), pp. 48–84.

McClintock, Cynthia, and Abraham F. Lowenthal. 1983. *The Peruvian Experiment Reconsidered.* Princeton: Princeton University Press.

McCoy, Jennifer Lynn. 1985. "Democratic Dependent Development and State-Labor Relations in Venezuela." Doctoral diss., Department of Political Science, University of Minnesota.

————. 1989. "Labor and the State as a Party-Mediated Democracy: Institutional Change in Venezuela." *Latin American Research Review* 24, no. 2, pp. 35–67.

McDonald, Ronald H. 1971. *Party Systems and Elections in Latin America.* Chicago: Markham.

————. 1972. "Electoral Politics and Uruguayan Political Decay." *Inter-American Economic Affairs* 26, no. 1 (Summer), pp. 25–46.

———— 1975. "The Rise of Military Politics in Uruguay." *Inter-American Economic Affairs* 28, no. 4 (Spring), pp. 25–44.

————. 1978. "Party Factions and Modernization: A Comparative Analysis of Colombia and Uruguay." In Frank P. Belloni and Dennis C. Beller, eds., *Faction Politics.* Santa Barbara, Calif.: ABC Clio.

————. 1982. "The Struggle for Normalcy in Uruguay." *Current History* 81, no. 472 (February), pp. 69–86.

McGreevey, William Paul. 1971. *An Economic History of Colombia.* Cambridge: Cambridge University Press.

McGuire, James W. 1984. "Argentina, 1880–1930: Economic Aspects of Oligarchic Rule." Unpublished paper, Department of Political Science, University of California, Berkeley.

————. 1989. "Peronism Without Perón: Unions and Party Politics in Argentina, 1955–1966." Doctoral diss., Department of Political Science, University of California, Berkeley.

Macadar, Luis, and Celia Barbato de Silva. 1985. "Fracasos y expectativas de la economía uruguaya." In Charles Gillespie, Louis Goodman, Juan Rial, and Peter Winn, eds., *Uruguay y la democracia.* Vol. 2. Montevideo: Ediciones de la Banda Oriental.

Macadar, Luis, Nicolas Reig, and José Enrique Santías. 1971. "Una economía latinoamericana." In Luis Benvenuto et al., eds., *Uruguay, hoy.* Buenos Aires: Siglo Veintiuno Argentina Editores.

Macías, José Luís. 1980. "Principales efectos de la formación sindical." In *Memorias del encuentro sobre historia del movimiento obrero.* Vol. 3. Puebla, Mexico: Universidad Autónoma de Puebla.

Magallanes, Manuel Vicente. 1973. *Los partidos políticos en la evolución histórica venezolana.* Madrid: Editorial Mediterraneo.

Maingot, Anthony Peter. 1967. "Colombia: Civil-Military Relations in a Political Culture of Conflict." Doctoral diss., University of Florida.

Mainwaring, Scott. 1975. "The State, Political Crisis, and Regime Breakdown: Peronism, 1952–1955." Master's thesis, Department of Political Science, Yale University.

————. 1986. "The State and the Industrial Bourgeoisie in Perón's Argentina,

1945–55." *Studies in Comparative International Development* 21, no. 3 (Fall), pp. 3–31.

Mallon, Richard D., and Juan V. Sourrouille. 1975. *Economic Policy-Making in a Conflict Society: The Argentine Case.* Cambridge: Harvard University Press.

Malpica, Carlos. 1968. *Los dueños del Perú.* 3d ed. Lima: Ediciones Ensayos Sociales.

Mamalakis, Markos J. 1976. *The Growth and Structure of the Chilean Economy: From Independence to Allende.* New Haven: Yale University Press.

———. 1978. *Historical Statistics of Chile.* Westport, Conn.: Greenwood Press.

Mamalakis, Markos J., and Clark W. Reynolds. 1965. *Essays on the Chilean Economy.* Homewood, Ill.: Irwin.

Manigat, Leslie F. 1973. "Venezuela." In Richard Gott, ed., *Guide to the Political Parties of South America.* Middlesex, England: Penguin Books.

Maram, Sheldon L. 1977. "Labor and the Left in Brazil, 1890–1921: A Movement Aborted." *Hispanic American Historical Review* 57, no. 2 (May), pp. 254–72.

———. 1972. "Anarchists, Immigrants, and the Brazilian Labor Movement, 1890–1920." Doctoral diss., Department of History, University of California, Santa Barbara.

March, James G., and Johan P. Olsen. 1984. "The New Institutionalism: Organizational Factors in Political Life." *American Political Science Review* 78 (April), pp. 734–47.

———. 1989. *Rediscovering Institutions: The Organizational Basis of Politics.* New York: Free Press.

Marotta, Sebastian. 1960, 1961, 1970. *El movimiento sindical argentino, su génesis y desarrollo.* 3 vols. Buenos Aires: Ediciones 'Lacio.'

Marshall, Alfred. 1916. *Principles of Economics: An Introductory Volume.* London: Macmillan.

Marshall, T. H. 1950. *Citizenship and Social Class.* Cambridge: Cambridge University Press.

Martínez Ces, Ricardo. 1962. *El Uruguay Batllista.* Montevideo: Ediciones de la Banda Oriental.

Martínez de la Torre, Ricardo. 1947, 1948, 1949. *Apuntes para una interpretación marxista de historia social del Perú.* 3 Vols. Lima: Empresa Editora Peruana.

Martínez López, Nelson. 1966. *Las organizaciones de los trabajadores y el conflicto industrial.* Montevideo: Colombino Hnos.

Martínez Moreno, Carlos. 1971. "Crepúsculo en Arcadia: La institucionalidad y su derrumbe a la Uruguaya." In Luis Benvenuto et al., eds., *Uruguay, Hoy.* Buenos Aires: Siglo XXI.

Martins, Luciano. 1975. *Nação e Corporação Multinacional.* Rio de Janeiro: Paz e Terra.

Martz, John D. 1962. *Colombia: A Contemporary Political Survey.* Chapel Hill: University of North Carolina Press.

———. 1963. "The Growth and Democratization of the Venezuelan Labor Movement." *Inter-American Economic Affairs* 17 (Fall), pp. 3–18.

———. 1964. "Venezuela's 'Generation of 28': The Genesis of Political Democracy." *Journal of Inter-American Studies* 6, no. 1 (October), pp. 17–32.

———. 1966. *Acción Democrática: Evolution of a Modern Political Party in Venezuela.* Princeton: Princeton University Press.

———. 1977. "The Party System: Toward Institutionalization." In John D. Martz and David J. Myers, eds., *Venezuela: The Democratic Experience*. New York: Praeger.

————. 1980a. "The Evolution of Democratic Politics in Venezuela." In Howard R. Penniman, ed., *Venezuela at the Polls: The National Election of 1978*. Washington, D.C.: American Enterprise Institute.

————. 1980b. "The Minor Parties." In Howard R. Penniman, ed., *Venezuela at the Polls: The National Election of 1978*. Washington, D.C: American Enterprise Institute.

————. 1986. "Petroleum: The National and International Perspectives." In John D. Martz and David J. Myers, eds., *Venezuela: The Democratic Experience*. New York: Praeger.

Martz, John D., and Enrique Baloyra. 1976. *Electoral Mobilization and Public Opinion: The Venezuelan Election of 1973*. Chapel Hill: University of North Carolina Press.

Martz, John D., and Peter B. Harkins. 1973. "Urban Electoral Behavior in Latin America: The Case of Metropolitan Caracas, 1958–1968." *Comparative Politics* 5, no. 4 (July), pp. 523–49.

Martz, John D., and David J. Myers. 1977. "Venezuelan Democracy and the Future." In John D. Martz and David J. Myers, eds., *Venezuela: The Democratic Experience*. New York: Praeger.

————. 1986. "The Politics of Economic Development." In John D. Martz and David J. Myers, eds., *Venezuela: The Democratic Experience*. New York: Praeger.

Martz, John D., and David J. Myers, eds. 1977. *Venezuela: The Democratic Experience*. New York: Praeger.

Marván, Ignacio. 1985. "El proyecto nacional de las organizaciones obreras." *La política y la cultura*. Vol. 5 of *El obrero mexicano*. Mexico City: Siglo XXI.

Mata, Milton da, and Edmar L. Bacha. 1973. *Empresa e salários na indústria de transformação, 1949–1969*. Rio de Janeiro: Pesquisa e Planejamento Econômico.

Matsushita, Hiroschi. 1983. *Movimiento obrero argentino 1930–45: Sus proyecciones en los orígenes del peronismo*. Buenos Aires: Ediciones Siglo Veinte.

Maullin, Richard. 1973. *Soldiers, Guerrillas, and Politics in Colombia*. Lexington, Mass.: Lexington Books.

Medhurst, Kenneth N. 1984. *The Church and Labour in Colombia*. Manchester: Manchester University Press.

Medín, Tzvi. 1972. *Ideología y praxis política de Lázaro Cárdenas*. Mexico City: Siglo XXI.

————. 1982. *El minimato presidencial: Historia política del maximato (1928–1935)*. Mexico City: Ediciones Era.

Medina, Luis. 1978a. *Evolución electoral en el México contemporáneo*. Mexico City: Comisión Federal Electoral.

————. 1978b. *Del cardenismo al avilacamachismo*. Vol. 18 of *Historia de la revolución méxicana*. Mexico City: Colegio de México.

————. 1979. *Civilismo y modernización del autoritarianismo*. Vol. 20 of *Historia de la revolución méxicana: 1940–1952*. Mexico City: Colegio de México.

Medina, Medofilo. 1984. *La protesta urbana en Colombia en el siglo veinte*. Bogotá: Ediciones Aurora.

Melman, Richard M. 1978. "Populist Mass Mobilization in Latin America:

ANAPO." Doctoral diss., Department of Political Science, Columbia University.

Mendes de Almeida, Angela, and Michael Lowy. 1976. "Union Structure and Labor Organizations in Contemporary Brazil." *Latin American Perspectives* 3, no. 1 (Winter), pp. 98–119.

Mericle, Kenneth S. 1977. "Corporatist Control of the Working Class: The Case of Post-1964 Authoritarian Brazil." In James M. Malloy, ed., *Authoritarianism and Corporatism in Latin America*. Pittsburgh: University of Pittsburgh Press.

Merkx, Gilbert W. 1968. "Political and Economic Change in Argentina from 1870 to 1966." Doctoral diss., Department of Sociology, Yale University.

———. 1969. "Sectoral Clashes and Political Change: The Argentine Experience." *Latin American Research Review* 4, no. 3 (Fall), pp. 89–114.

Merrick, Thomas W., and Douglas W. Graham. 1979. *Population and Economic Development in Brazil: 1800 to the Present*. Baltimore: Johns Hopkins University Press.

Mesa-Lago, Carmelo. 1978. *Social Security in Latin America: Pressure Groups, Stratification, and Inequality*. Pittsburgh: University of Pittsburgh Press.

Meyer, Jean, et al. 1977. *Estado y sociedad con Calles*. Vol. 10 of *Historia de la revolución mexicana, 1924–1928*. Mexico City: Colegio de México.

Meyer, Lorenzo. 1976. "La encrucijada." In Daniel Cosío Villegas, ed., *Historia general de México*. Vol. 2. Mexico City: Colegio de México.

———. 1977a. "El primer tramo del camino." In Meyer, *Historia general de méxico*. Vol. 4. Mexico City: Colegio de México.

———. 1977b. "Historical Roots of the Authoritarian State in Mexico." In José Luis Reyna and Richard S. Wienert, eds., *Authoritarianism in Mexico*. Philadelphia: Institute for the Study of Human Issues.

———. 1977c. *La crisis en el sistema político mexicano, 1928–1977*. Mexico City: Colegio de México.

———. 1978. *El conflicto social de los gobiernos del maximato*. Vol. 13 of *Historia de la revolución méxicana, 1928–1934*. Mexico City: Colegio de México.

Meyer, Lorenzo, et al. 1978. *Los inicios de la institucionalización*. Vol. 12 of *Historia de la revolución méxicana, 1928–1934*. Mexico City: Colegio de México.

Meyer, Michael C., and William L. Sherman. 1979. *The Course of Mexican History*. New York: Oxford University Press.

Michaels, Albert L. 1966. "Mexican Politics and Nationalism from Calles to Cárdenas." Doctoral diss., Department of History, University of Pennsylvania.

———. 1970. "The Crisis of Cardenismo." *Journal of Latin American Studies* 2, no. 1 (May), pp. 51–79.

Michels, Robert. 1959. *Political Parties: A Sociological Study of the Oligarchical Tendencies of Modern Democracy*. New York: Dover Publications. (Originally published in 1915.)

Middlebrook, Kevin J. 1977. "State Structure and Labor Participation in Mexico." Paper presented at the annual meeting of the Latin American Studies Association, Houston.

———. 1981a. "Political Change and Political Reform in an Authoritarian Regime: The Case of Mexico." Working paper no. 103, Latin America Program of the Woodrow Wilson International Center for Scholars, Smithsonian Institute, Washington, D.C.

———. 1981b. "The Political Economy of Mexican Organized Labor, 1940–1978." Doctoral diss., Department of Political Science, Harvard University.

Mill, John Stuart. 1974. "Of the Four Methods of Experimental Inquiry." In Mill, *A System of Logic*. Toronto: University of Toronto Press. (Originally published in 1843.)

Miller, Richard U. 1966. "The Role of Labor Organizations in a Developing Country: The Case of Mexico." Doctoral diss., New York State School of Industrial and Labor Relations, Cornell University.

———. 1968. "Labor Legislation and Mexican Industrial Relations." *Industrial Relations* 7, no. 2 (February), 171–82.

Millon, Robert Paul. 1966. *Mexican Marxist—Vicente Lombardo Toledano*. Chapel Hill: University of North Carolina Press.

Millot, Julio, Carlos Silva, and Lindor Silva. 1973. *El desarrollo industrial del Uruguay: De la crisis de 1929 a la posguerra*. Montevideo: Universidad de la República, Departamento de Publicaciones.

Milnor, A. J. 1969. *Elections and Political Stability*. Boston: Little, Brown.

Ministerio de Trabajo y Seguridad Social. 1961, 1966. *Conflictos del trabajo*. República de Argentina, Ministerio de Trabajo y Seguridad Social, Dirección General de Estudios e Investigaciones, Departamento de Estadísticas Sociales.

Miquel, Janine. 1979. *Proceso de gestión y desarrollo histórico del movimiento laboral chileno*. Paper no. 16, Institute of Latin American Studies: Stockholm.

Moisés, José Alvaro. 1977. "Theoretical and Historical Notes on the Strike of the Three Hundred Thousand, São Paulo, 1953." *Latin American Research Unit Studies* 2, no. 1 (October), pp. 3–20.

———. 1978. "Brazil: New Questions on 'The Strike of the 300 Thousand' in São Paulo, 1953." Paper presented at the Workshop on Urban Working Class Culture and Social Protest in Latin America. Woodrow Wilson International Center for Scholars, Washington, D.C.

Molina, Gerardo. 1974. *Las ideas liberales en Colombia, 1915–1934*. Vol. 2. Bogotá: Ediciones Tercer Mundo.

———. 1977. *Las ideas liberales en Colombia: De 1935 a la iniciación del Frente Nacional*. Vol. 3. Bogotá: Ediciones Tercer Mundo.

Molinas Horcasitas, Juan. n.d. "The Electoral System: Continuity by Change." Mimeo. Mexico City: UNAM.

Molloy, Peter A. 1984. "The National Front and Authoritarianism: Emergence and Evolution of the Colombian Political Regime." Center for Latin American Studies, University of California, Berkeley, December.

Monteón, Michael. 1982. *Chile in the Nitrate Era: The Evolution of Economic Dependence, 1880–1930*. Madison: University of Wisconsin Press.

Montero M., René. 1952. *La verdad sobre Ibáñez*. Santiago: Zig-Zag.

Montes de Oca, Rosa Elena. 1977. "The State and the Peasants." In José Luis Reyna and Richard S. Weinert, eds., *Authoritarianism in Mexico*. Philadelphia: Institute for the Study of Human Issues.

Moore, Barrington, Jr. 1966. *Social Origins of Dictatorship and Democracy: Lord and Peasant in the Making of the Modern World*. Boston: Beacon Press.

Moraes, Clodomir Santos de. 1970. "Peasant Leagues in Brazil." In Rodolfo Stavenhagen, ed., *Agrarian Problems and Peasant Movements in Latin America*. New York: Anchor Books.

Moran, Theodore H. 1974. *Multinational Corporations and the Politics of Dependence: Copper in Chile*. Princeton: Princeton University Press.

Morris, James O. 1966. *Elites, Intellectuals, and Consensus: A Study of the Social Question and the Industrial Relations System in Chile*. Ithaca: New York State School of Industrial and Labor Relations, Cornell University.

————. 1967. "Consensus, Ideology, and Labor Relations." *Journal of Inter-American Studies* 7, no. 3 (July), pp. 301–15.

Morris, James O., and Roberto Oyaneder. 1962. *Afiliación y finanzas sindicales en Chile, 1932–1959*. Santiago: Departamento de Relaciones Laborales, Instituto de Organización y Administración (INSORA).

Morse, Richard M., et al., eds. 1971. *The Urban Development of Latin America, 1750–1920*. Stanford: Center for Latin American Studies, Stanford University.

Mosk, Sanford A. 1950. *Industrial Revolution in Mexico*. Berkeley and Los Angeles: University of California Press.

Moss, Robert. 1972. "The Tupamaros: Masters of the Game." In Moss, *Urban Guerrillas: The New Face of Political Violence*. London: Temple Smith.

Moya Obeso, Alberto. 1978. "Sindicalismo aprista y sindicalismo clasista en el Perú, 1920–1956." Lima: Centro de Investigaciones Socio-Económicas del Norte, Pontificia Universidad Católica del Perú.

Munck, Ronaldo. 1981. "The Labor Movement and the Crisis of the Dictatorship in Brazil." In Thomas C. Bruneau and Philippe Faucher, eds., *Authoritarian Capitalism: Brazil's Contemporary Economic Development*. Boulder, Colo.: Westview.

Munck, Ronaldo, with Ricardo Falcón and Bernardo Galitelli. 1987. *Argentina: From Anarchism to Peronism: Workers, Unions and Politics, 1855–1985*. London: Zed Books.

Murmis, Miguel, and Juan Carlos Portantiero. 1971. *Estudios sobre los orígenes del peronismo*. Vol. 1. Buenos Aires: Siglo XXI.

Myers, Daniel J. 1979. "Venezuelan Party System Evolution: Implications of the 1978 Presidential Elections." Paper presented at the annual meeting of the Latin American Studies Association, Pittsburgh.

Myers, David J. 1980a. "The Acción Democrática Campaign." In Howard R. Penniman, ed., *Venezuela at the Polls: The National Elections of 1978*. Washington: American Enterprise Institute.

————. 1980b. "The Elections and the Evolution of Venezuela's Party System." In Howard R. Penniman, ed., *Venezuela at the Polls: The National Election of 1978*. Washington: American Enterprise Institute.

————. 1986. "The Venezuelan Party System: Regime Maintenance under Stress." In John D. Martz and David J. Myers, eds., *Venezuela: The Democratic Experience*. New York: Praeger.

Myers, David J., and John D. Martz. 1986. "The Venezuelan Democracy: Performance and Prospects." In John D. Martz and David J. Myers, eds., *Venezuela: The Democratic Experience*. New York: Praeger.

Nagel, Ernest. 1979. "Patterns of Scientific Explanation." In Nagel, *The Structure of Science: Problems in the Logic of Scientific Explanation*. New York: Harcourt, Brace and World.

Nahum, Benjamín. 1975. *1905–1929: La época batllista*. Montevideo: Ediciones de la Banda Oriental.

Narancio, Edmundo M. 1955. "Panorámico histórico del Uruguay." In Jorge Batlle et al., eds., *Batlle: Su vida, su obra*. Montevideo: Editorial Acción.

Navarro, Marysa. 1982. "Evita's Charismatic Leadership." In Michael L. Conniff, ed., *Latin American Populism in Comparative Perspective*. Albuquerque: New Mexico Press.

—. 1983. "Evita and Peronism." In Frederick Turner and José Enrique Miguens, eds., *Juan Perón and the Reshaping of Argentina*. Pittsburgh: University of Pittsburgh Press.

Neira, Hugo. 1973. "Peru." In Richard Gott, ed., *Guide to the Political Parties of South America*. Middlesex, England: Penguin Books.

Newell, Roberto, and Luis Rubio F. 1984. *Mexico's Dilemma: The Political Origins of Economic Crisis*. Boulder, Colo.: Westview.

Noriega, Francisco. 1980. "El movimiento del sindicato de telefonistas de la República Mexicana, 1976–1977." In *Memorias del encuentro sobre historia del movimiento obrero*. Vol. 3. Puebla, Mexico: Universidad Autónoma de Puebla.

North, Liisa. 1966. *Civil-Military Relations in Argentina, Chile, and Peru*. Berkeley: Institute of International Studies, University of California.

—. 1973. "The Origins and Development of the Peruvian Aprista Party." Doctoral diss., Department of Political Science, University of California, Berkeley.

—. 1976. "The Military in Chilean Politics." *Studies in Comparative International Development* 11, no. 1 (Spring), pp. 73–106.

North, Liisa, and David Raby. 1977. "The Dynamic of Revolution and Counterrevolution: Mexico under Cárdenas, 1934–1940." *Latin American Research Unit Studies* 2, no. 1 (October).

Nunes, Edson de Oliveira, and Barbara Geddes. 1987. "Dilemmas of State-led Modernization in Brazil." In John D. Wirth, Edson de Oliveira Nunes, and Thomas E. Bogenschild, eds., *State and Society in Brazil: Continuity and Change*. Boulder, Colo.: Westview.

Nunn, Frederick M. 1967. "Military Rule in Chile: The Revolutions of September 5, 1924 and January 23, 1925." *Hispanic American Historical Review* 47, no. 1 (February), pp. 1–21.

—. 1970. *Chilean Politics, 1920–1931: The Honorable Mission of the Armed Forces*. Albuquerque: University of New Mexico Press.

—. 1975. "New Thoughts on Military Intervention in Latin American Politics: The Chilean Case, 1973." *Journal of Latin American Studies* 7, no. 2 (November), pp. 271–304.

O'Connor, James. 1973. *The Fiscal Crisis of the State*. New York: St. Martin's Press.

O'Connor, Robert E. 1980. "The Electorate." In Howard R. Penniman, ed., *Venezuela at the Polls: The National Elections of 1978*. Washington, D.C.: American Enterprise Institute.

Oddone, Jacinto. 1949. *Gremialismo proletario argentino*. Buenos Aires: Editorial La Vanguardia.

O'Donnell, Guillermo A. 1973. *Modernization and Bureaucratic-Authoritarianism: Studies in South American Politics*. Politics of Modernization Series, no. 9. Institute of International Studies, University of California, Berkeley.

—. 1975. "Reflexiones sobre las tendencias generales de cambio en el estado burocrático-autoritario." Documento CEDES/GE CLASCO/no. 1, Centro de Estudios de Estado y Sociedad, Buenos Aires.

—. 1977. "Corporatism and the Question of the State." In James M. Malloy, ed., *Authoritarianism and Corporatism in Latin America*. Pittsburgh: University of Pittsburgh Press.

————. 1978. "State and Alliances in Argentina, 1956–1976." *Journal of Development Studies* 15, no. 1 (October), pp. 3–33.

————. 1979. "Tensions in the Bureaucratic-Authoritarian State and the Question of Democracy." In David Collier, ed., *The New Authoritarianism in Latin America*. Princeton: Princeton University Press.

————. 1982. *El estado burocrático-autoritario, 1966–1973: triunfos, derrotas, y crisis*. Buenos Aires: Editorial de Belgrano.

————. 1984. "¿Y a mí, que me importa?" Notre Dame: University of Notre Dame, Helen Kellogg Institute working paper.

————. 1988. *Bureaucratic-Authoritarianism: Argentina, 1966–1973, in Comparative Perspective*. Berkeley and Los Angeles: University of California Press. (English edition of O'Donnell 1982.)

O'Donnell, Guillermo A., Philippe C. Schmitter, and Laurence Whitehead, eds. 1986. *Transitions from Authoritarian Rule in Latin America and Southern Europe*. Baltimore: Johns Hopkins University Press.

Offe, Claus. 1985. "Two Logics of Collective Action." In Offe, *Disorganized Capitalism*. Cambridge: MIT Press.

Ogliastri, Enrique. 1983. "Liberales conservadores versus conservadores liberales: Faccionalismos trenzados en la estructura de poder en Colombia." Centro de Asuntos Internacionales, Harvard University.

Ohassen de López, Francie R. 1977. *Lombardo Toledano y el movimiento obrero mexicano, 1917–1940*. Mexico City: Editores Extemporáneos.

Olavarría Bravo, Arturo. 1962. *Chile entre dos Alessandri*. Vols. 1–4. Santiago: Editorial Nascimento.

Oliveira Vianna, Francisco de. 1977. *A economia da dependência imperfeita*. Rio de Janeiro: Edições Graal.

Olson, Mancur. 1968. *The Logic of Collective Action: Public Goods and the Theory of Groups*. New York: Schocken Books.

Oquist, Paul H. 1980. *Violence, Conflict and Politics in Colombia*. New York: Academic Press.

Ortega Aguirre, Maximino. 1980. "La asamblea del Congreso del Trabajo y el sindicalismo universitario." In *Memorias del encuentro sobre historia del movimiento obrero*. Vol. 3. Puebla, Mexico: Universidad Autónoma de Puebla.

O'Shaughnessy, Laura. 1977. "Opposition in an Authoritarian Regime: The Incorporation and Institutionalization of the Mexican National Action Party." Doctoral diss., Department of Political Science, Indiana University.

Otto, Erwin Stephen. 1980. "La asamblea del Congreso del Trabajo, algunas consideraciones con respecto a la estructura del movimiento obrero mexicano y su relación con el Estado." In *Memorias del encuentro sobre historia del movimiento obrero*. Vol. 3. Puebla, Mexico: Universidad Autónoma de Puebla.

Oved, Iaacov. 1978. *El anarquismo y el movimiento obrero en Argentina*. Mexico City: Siglo XXI.

Padgett, L. Vincent. 1966. *The Mexican Political System*. Boston: Houghton Mifflin.

Page, Joseph A. 1972. *The Revolution That Never Was: Northeast Brazil 1955–1964*. New York: Grossman.

————. 1983. *Perón: A Biography*. New York: Random House.

Palermo, Vicente. 1986. "Democracia interna en los partidos: Las elecciones partidarias de 1983 en el radicalismo y el justicialismo porteños." Centro de Estudios de Estado y Sociedad (CEDES), Buenos Aires.

Panaia, Marta, Ricardo Lesser, and Pedro Skupch. 1973. *Estudios sobre los orígenes del peronismo.* Vol. 2. Buenos Aires: Siglo XXI.

Pandolfi, Rodolfo. 1968. *Frondizi por él mismo.* Buenos Aires: Editorial Galerna.

Paoli B., Francisco J., et al. 1980. *Estado y clase obrera en México.* Special edition of *A: Revista de Ciencias Sociales y Humanidades* 1, no. 1, Universidad Autónoma Metropolitana de Azcapotzalco (September-December).

Pareja Pflucker, Piedad. 1980. *Aprismo y sindicalismo en el Perú.* Lima: Ediciones Rikchay.

París de Oddone, M. Blanca, et al. 1969. *Cronología comparada de la historia del Uruguay, 1830–1945.* Montevideo: Universidad de la República, Departamento de Publicaciones.

Paso, Leonardo. 1983. *Historia de los partidos políticos en la Argentina (1900–1930).* Buenos Aires: Ediciones Directa.

Payne, Arnold. 1968. *The Peruvian Coup d'Etat of 1962: The Overthrow of Manuel Prado.* Washington, D.C.: Institute for the Comparative Study of Political Systems.

Payne, James L. 1965. *Labor and Politics in Peru.* New Haven: Yale University Press.

———. 1968. "The Oligarchy Muddle." *World Politics* 20, no. 3 (April), pp. 439–53.

Pease García, Henry. 1977. *El ocaso del poder oligárquico: Lucha política en la escena oficial, 1968–1975.* Lima: DESCO.

Pécaut, Daniel. 1973. *Política y sindicalismo en Colombia.* Medellín: Ediciones La Carreta.

———. 1987. *Orden y violencia: Colombia 1930–1954.* Vol. 1. Bogotá: Siglo XXI.

Pellicer de Brody, Olga, and José Luis Reyna. 1978. *El afranzamiento de la estabilidad política.* Vol. 22 of *Historia de la revolución mexicana, 1952–1960.* Mexico City: Colegio de México.

Peña, Milciades. 1971. *Masas, caudillos y élites: La dependencia argentina de Yrigoyen a Perón.* Buenos Aires: Ediciones Fichas.

Pendergast, L. O. 1937. "Growing Pains of Mexican Labor." *The Nation* 144, no. 24 (June), pp. 671–74.

Pendle, George. 1963. *Uruguay.* London: Oxford University Press.

Peppe, Patrick V. 1971. "Working Class Politics in Chile." Doctoral diss., Department of Political Science, Columbia University.

Peralta Ramos, Mónica. 1972. *Etapas de acumulación y alianzas de clase en la Argentina (1930–1970).* Buenos Aires: Siglo XXI.

Pereira, Luiz Carlos Bresser. 1965. *Trabalho e desenvolvimento no Brasil.* São Paulo: Difusão Européia do Livro.

Perón, Juan D. 1983. *Correspondencia.* Vol. 1. Buenos Aires: Corregidor.

Peterson, Phyllis Jane. 1962. "Brazilian Political Parties: Formation, Organization, and Leadership, 1945–59." Doctoral diss., Department of Political Science, University of Michigan.

———. 1970. "Coalition Formation in Local Elections in the State of São Paulo, Brazil." In Sven Groennings, E. W. Kelley, Michael Leiserson, eds., *The Study of Coalition Behavior: Theoretical Perspectives and Cases from Four Continents.* New York: Holt, Rinehart and Winston.

Petras, James F. 1969. *Politics and Social Forces in Chilean Development*. Berkeley and Los Angeles: University of California Press.

————. 1970. *Politics and Social Structure in Latin America*. New York: Monthly Review Press.

Petras, James F., et al. 1977. *The Nationalization of Venezuelan Oil*. New York: Praeger.

Pike, Frederick B. 1963. *Chile and the United States, 1800–1962*. Notre Dame: Notre Dame University Press.

————. 1967. *The Modern History of Peru*. New York: Praeger.

————. 1986. *The Politics of the Miraculous in Peru: Haya de la Torre and the Spiritualist Tradition*. Lincoln: University of Nebraska Press.

Pike, Frederick, and Donald Bray. 1960. "A Vista of Catastrophe: The Future of U.S.-Chilean Relations." *Review of Politics* 22 (July), pp. 393–418.

Pinheiro, Paulo Sérgio. 1977. "O proletariado industrial na primeira república." In Boris Fausto, ed., *História geral da civilização brasileira*. Vol. 3, part 2, *O Brasil republicano: Sociedade e instituções* (1889–1930). Rio de Janeiro and São Paulo: DIFEL.

Pinto Lagarrigue, Fernando. 1972. *Crónica política del siglo XX*. Santiago: Editorial ORBE.

Pintos, Francisco R. 1939. *Batlle y el proceso histórico del Uruguay*. Montevideo: Claudio Garcia & Cia. Editores.

————. 1960. *Historia del movimiento obrero del Uruguay*. Montevideo: Editorial 'Gaceta de Cultura.'

Pla, Alberto J., et al. 1982. *Clase obrera, partidos y sindicatos en Venezuela, 1936–1950*. Caracas: Ediciones Centauro.

Poblete Troncoso, Moisés. 1945. *El movimiento de asociación profesional en Chile*. Jornadas, no. 29. Mexico City: Colegio de México, Centro de Estudios Sociales.

————. 1946. *Movimiento obrero latinoamericano*. Mexico City: Fondo de Cultura Económica.

Poblete Troncoso, Moisés, and Ben G. Burnett. 1960. *The Rise of the Latin American Labor Movement*. New York: Bookman.

Pont, Elena Susana. 1984. *Partido Laborista: Estado y sindicatos*. Buenos Aires: Centro Editor de América Latina.

Ponte Durand, Victor Manuel. 1979. *México: La formación de un país dependeniente*. Mexico City: UNAM.

Pontones, Eduardo. 1976. "La migración en México." In James W. Wilkie et al., eds., *Contemporary Mexico: Papers of the IV International Congress of Mexican History*. Berkeley and Los Angeles: University of California Press.

Portes, Alejandro. 1977. "Legislatures under Authoritarian Regimes: The Case of Mexico." *Journal of Political and Military Sociology* 5, no. 2 (Fall), pp. 185–201.

————.1983. "The Informal Sector." *Review* 7, no. 1 (Summer 1983), pp. 151–74.

Portes, Alejandro, and John Walton. 1975. *Urban Latin America: The Political Condition from Above and Below*. Austin: University of Texas Press.

Portocarrero Maisch, Gonzalo. 1983. *De Bustamante a Odría: El fracaso del Frente Democrático Nacional, 1945–1950*. Lima: Mosca Azul Editores.

Porzecanski, Arturo. 1973. *Uruguay's Tupamaros: The Urban Guerrilla*. New York: Praeger.

————. 1974. "Uruguay's Continuing Dilemma." *Current History* 66, no. 389 (January), pp. 28–39.

Potash, Robert A. 1959. "Argentine Political Parties: 1957–1958." *Journal of Inter-American Studies* 1, no. 4 (October). pp. 515–24.

————. 1969. *The Army and Politics in Argentina, 1928–1945: Yrigoyen to Perón.* Stanford: Stanford University Press.

————. 1980. *The Army and Politics in Argentina, 1945–1962.* Stanford: Stanford University Press.

————. 1984. *Perón y el G.O.U.* Buenos Aires: Editorial Sudamericana.

Potter, Anne L. 1981. "The Failure of Democracy in Argentina, 1916–1930: An Institutional Perspective." *Journal of Latin American Studies* 13, no. 1 (May), pp. 83–109.

Poulantzas, Nicos. 1969. "The Problem of the Capitalist State." *New Left Review*, no. 58, pp. 67–78.

Powell, John Duncan. 1971. *Political Mobilization of the Venezuelan Peasant* Cambridge: Harvard University Press.

Powers, James Carl. 1979. "The Dynamics of Colombian Two-Party Democracy: An Historical Analysis." Doctoral diss., Washington State University.

Pozas Horcasitas, Ricardo. 1981. "La consolidación del nuevo orden institucional en México (1929–1940)." In Pablo González Casanova, ed., *América Latina: Historia de medio siglo.* Mexico City: Siglo XXI.

Prieto, Ramón. 1977. *Treinta años de vida argentina: 1945–1975.* Buenos Aires: Editorial Sudamericana.

Primera Plana. Buenos Aires, 1964.

Przeworski, Adam. 1986. "Some Problems in the Study of the Transition to Democracy." In Guillermo O'Donnell, Philippe C. Schmitter, and Laurence Whitehead, eds., *Transitions from Authoritarian Rule: Comparative Perspectives.* Baltimore: Johns Hopkins University Press.

————. 1987. "Methods of Cross-National Research, 1970–1983: An Overview." In Meinolf Dierkes, Hans N. Weiler, and Ariane Berthoin Antal, eds., *Comparative Policy Research: Learning from Experience.* Aldershot, England: Gower.

Przeworski, Adam, and Henry Teune. 1970. *The Logic of Comparative Social Inquiry.* New York: John Wiley and Sons.

Przeworski, Adam, and Michael Wallerstein. 1982. "The Structure of Class Conflict in Democratic Capitalist Societies." *American Political Science Review* 76, no. 2 (June), pp. 215–38.

Purcell, Susan Kaufman. 1973. "Decision-Making in an Authoritarian Regime: Theoretical Implications from a Mexican Case Study." *World Politics* 26, no. 1 (October), pp. 28–54.

————. 1975. *The Mexican Profit-Sharing Decision: Politics in an Authoritarian Regime.* Berkeley and Los Angeles: University of California Press.

————. 1978. "Clientelism and Development in Mexico." Paper presented at a conference on Political Clientelism, Patronage and Development, Bellagio, Italy.

Purcell, Susan Kaufman, and John F. H. Purcell. 1980. "State and Society in Mexico: Must a Stable Polity be Institutionalized?" *World Politics* 32, no. 2 (January), pp. 194–227.

Quintero, Rodolfo. 1964. "Sindicalismo y cambio social en Venezuela." *Edición Especial del Boletín Bibliográfico de la Facultad de Economía.* Caracas: La Universidad de Venezuela.

Quirk, Robert E. 1970. *The Mexican Revolution: 1914–1915.* New York: Norton Library.

———. 1973. *The Mexican Revolution and the Catholic Church, 1910–1929.* Bloomington: Indiana University Press.

Rae, Douglas W. 1967. *The Political Consequences of Electoral Laws.* New Haven: Yale University Press.

Ragin, Charles C. 1987. *The Comparative Method: Moving Beyond Qualitative and Quantitative Strategies.* Berkeley and Los Angeles: University of California Press.

Rama, Angel. 1971. "La generación crítica, 1939–1969." In Luis Benvenuto et al., eds., *Uruguay, hoy.* Buenos Aires: Siglo XXI.

Rama, Carlos M. 1955. "Batlle y el movimiento obrero y social." In Jorge Batlle et al., eds., *Batlle: Su vida, su obra.* Montevideo: Editorial Acción.

———. 1957. *Ensayo de la sociología uruguaya.* Montevideo: Editorial Medina.

———. 1972. *Historia social del pueblo uruguaya.* Montevideo: Editorial Comunidad del Sur.

Randall, Laura. 1978. *An Economic History of Argentina in the Twentieth Century.* New York: Columbia University Press.

Rangel, Domingo Alberto. 1966. *La revolución de las fantasías.* Caracas: Ediciones OFIDI.

Ranis, Peter J. 1965. "Parties, Politics and Peronism: A Study of Post-Perón Argentine Political Development." Doctoral diss., Department of Political Science, New York University.

Real de Azúa, Carlos. 1964. *El impulso y su freno: Tres décadas de batllismo.* Montevideo: Ediciones de la Banda Oriental.

———. 1971. "Política, poder y partidos en el Uruguay de hoy." In Luis Benvenuto et al., eds., *Uruguay, hoy.* Buenos Aires: Siglo XXI.

Reinhardt, Nola. 1986. "The Consolidation of the Import-Export Economy in Nineteenth-Century Colombia: A Political-Economic Analysis." *Latin American Perspectives* 13, no. 1 (Winter), pp. 75–98.

Remmer, Karen L. 1977. "The Timing, Pace, and Sequence of Political Change in Chile, 1891–1925." *Hispanic American Historical Review* 57, no. 2 (May), pp. 205–30.

———. 1984. *Party Competition in Argentina and Chile: Political Recruitment and Public Policy, 1890–1930.* Lincoln: University of Nebraska Press.

———. 1985. "Redemocratization and the Impact of Authoritarian Rule." *Comparative Politics* 17, no. 3 (April), pp. 253–75.

Rennie, Ysabel. 1945. *The Argentine Republic.* New York: Macmillan.

Revéiz, Edgar, and María José Pérez. 1986. "Colombia: Moderate Economic Growth, Political Stability, and Social Welfare." In Jonathan Hartlyn and Samuel A. Morley, eds., *Latin American Political Economy: Financial Crisis and Political Change.* Boulder, Colo.: Westview.

Reyes, Cipriano. 1946. *Qué es el laborismo.* Buenos Aires: Ediciones R.A.

Reyna, José Luis. 1977. "Redefining the Established Authoritarian Regime." In José Luis Reyna and Richard Weinert, eds., *Authoritarianism in Mexico.* Philadelphia: Institute for the Study of Human Issues.

———. 1979. "El movimiento obrero en una situación de crisis: México, 1976–1978." *Foro Internacional* 19, no. 3.

Reyna, José Luis, and Marcelo Miquet. 1976. "Introducción a la historia de las organizaciones obreras en México: 1912–1966." In José Luis Reyna et al., eds., *Tres estudios sobre el movimiento obrero en México*. Mexico City: Colegio de México.

Reyna, José Luis, and Raúl Trejo Delarbre. 1981. *De Adolfo Ruiz Cortines a Adolfo López Mateos, 1952–1964*. Vol. 12 of *La clase obrera en la historia de México*. Mexico City: Siglo XXI.

Reyna, José Luis, et al., eds. 1976. *Tres estudios sobre el movimiento obrero en México*. Mexico City: Colegio de México.

Reyna Muñoz, Manuel. 1980. "Sindicatos ideológicos, sindicatos unitarios." In *Memorias del encuentro sobre historia del movimiento obrero*. Vol. 3. Puebla, Mexico: Universidad Autónoma de Puebla.

Reyna, Manuel, Laura Palomares, and Guadalupe Córtez. 1972. "El control del movimiento obrero como una necesidad del estado de México (1917–1936)." *Revista Mexicana de Sociología* 34, no. 3–4 (October–December), pp. 785–813.

Reynolds, Clark W. 1965. "Development Problems of an Export Economy: The Case of Chile and Copper." In Markos J. Mamalakis and Clark Reynolds, eds., *Essays on the Chilean Economy*. Homewood, Ill.: Irwin.

———. 1970. *The Mexican Economy: Twentieth-Century Structure and Growth*. New Haven: Yale University Press.

Rial, Juan. 1983. "Breve sinopsis de la evolución del movimiento sindical en Uruguay." Mimeo. Montevideo: CIESU.

———. 1984a. *Partidos políticos, democracia y autoritarismo*. Vol. 1. Montevideo: CIESU.

———. 1984b. *Partidos políticos, democracia y autoritarismo*. Vol. 2. Montevideo: CIESU.

———. 1985. "Emilio Frugoni." Mimeo. Montevideo: CIESU.

———. 1986. "The Uruguayan Elections of 1984: Triumph of the Center." In Paul W. Drake and Eduardo Silva, eds., *Elections and Democratization in Latin America, 1980–85*. Center for Iberian and Latin American Studies, Center for U.S.-Mexican Studies, and Institute of the Americas, University of California, San Diego.

Richmond, Douglas W. 1979. "Carranza: The Authoritarian Populist as National President." In George Wolfskill and Douglas W. Richmond, eds., *Essays on the Mexican Revolution: Revisionist Views of the Leaders*. Austin: University of Texas Press.

Rivera Castro, José. 1983. *En la presidencia de Plutarco Elías Calles, 1924–1928*. Vol. 8. of *La clase obrera en la historia de México*. Mexico City: Siglo XXI.

Rivera Marín, Guadalupe. 1955. "Los conflictos de trabajo en México, 1937–1950." *Trimestre Económico* 22, no. 2 (April–June), pp. 181–208.

Rock, David. 1975a. *Politics in Argentina, 1890–1930: The Rise and Fall of Radicalism*. London and New York: Cambridge University Press.

———. 1975b. "Radical Populism and the Conservative Elite, 1912–1930." In David Rock, ed., *Argentina in the Twentieth Century*. Pittsburgh: University of Pittsburgh Press.

———. 1985. *Argentina, 1516–1982: From the Spanish Colonization to the Falklands War*. Berkeley and Los Angeles: University of California Press.

Rodrigues, José Albertino. 1968. *Sindicato e desenvolvimento no Brasil*. São Paulo: Difusão Européia do Livro.

Rodrigues, Leôncio Martins. 1966. *Conflito industrial e sindicalismo no Brasil.* São Paulo: Difusão Européia do Livro.

———. 1969. *La clase obrera en el Brasil.* Buenos Aires: Centro Editor de América Latina.

———. 1981. "Sindicalismo e classe operária (1930–1964)." In Boris Fausto, ed., *História geral da civilização brasileira.* Vol 3, part 2. O Brasie republicano: Sociedade e política (1930–1964). São Paulo: DIFEL.

Rodríguez, Héctor. 1965. *Nuestros sindicatos, 1865–1965.* Montevideo: Ediciones Uruguay.

Rodríguez Araujo, Octavio. 1982. *La reforma política y los partidos en México.* Mexico: Siglo XXI.

Rodríguez Lamas, Daniel. 1984. *La presidencia de Frondizi.* Buenos Aires: Centro Editor de América Latina.

———. 1985. *La revolución libertadora.* Buenos Aires: Centro Editor de América Latina.

Roett, Riordan. 1978. *Brazil: Politics in a Patrimonial Society.* Revised ed. New York: Praeger.

Rojas Sandoval, Javier. 1980. "Los sindicatos blancos de Monterrey: Modelo patronal de organización sindical." In *Memorias del encuentro sobre historia del movimiento obrero.* Vol. 3. Puelba, Mexico: Universidad Autónoma de Puebla.

Rokkan, Stein. 1970. *Citizens, Elections, and Parties.* New York: David McKay.

Romero, José Luis. 1963. *A History of Argentine Political Thought.* Stanford: Stanford University Press.

Rosenzweig, Fernando. 1965. "El desarrollo económico de México de 1877 a 1911." *Trimestre Económico* 32, no. 3–4 (July–December), pp. 405–54.

Rotondaro, Rubén. 1971. *Realidad y cambio en el sindicalismo.* Buenos Aires: Editorial Pleamar.

Rouquié, Alain. 1982. *Poder militar y sociedad política en la Argentina.* Vol. 2. *1943–1973.* Buenos Aires: Emecé Editores.

Rowe, James W. 1964. *The Argentine Elections of 1963: An Analysis.* Washington, D.C.: Institute for the Comparative Study of Political Systems.

Roxborough, Ian. 1981. "The Analysis of Labor Movements in Latin America: Typologies and Theories." *Bulletin of Latin American Research* 1, no. 1 (October), pp. 81–95.

———. 1984. *Unions and Politics in Mexico: The Case of the Auto Industry.* Cambridge: Cambridge University Press.

———. 1986. "The Mexican Charrazo of 1948: Latin American Labor from World War to Cold War." Working paper no. 77, Helen Kellogg Institute for International Studies, University of Notre Dame, August.

Roxborough, Ian, and Ilian Bizberg. 1983. "Union Locals in Mexico: The 'New Unionism' in Steel and Automobiles." *Journal of Latin American Studies* 15, part 1 (May), pp. 117–35.

Roxborough, Ian, Philip O'Brien, and Jackie Roddick. 1977. *Chile: The State and Revolution.* New York: Holmes and Meier.

Ruddle, Kenneth, and Philip Gillette, eds. 1972. *Latin American Political Statistics.* Supplement to *The Statistical Abstract of Latin America.* Los Angeles: Latin American Center, University of California.

Ruhl, J. Mark. 1978. "Party System In Crisis? An Analysis of Colombia's 1978 Elections." *Inter-American Economic Affairs* 32, no. 3 (Winter), pp. 29–43.

———. 1980. "The Military." In R. Albert Berry, Ronald G. Hellman, and Mauricio Solaún, eds., *Politics of Compromise: Coalition Government in Colombia*. New Brunswick, N.J.: Transaction Books.

———. 1981. "Civil-Military Relations in Colombia: A Societal Explanation." *Journal of Interamerican Studies and World Affairs* 23, no. 2 (May), pp. 123–46.

Ruiz, Ramón Eduardo. 1976. *Labor and the Ambivalent Revolutionaries: Mexico, 1911–1923*. Baltimore: Johns Hopkins University Press.

———. 1980. *The Great Rebellion: Mexico, 1905–1924*. New York: W. W. Norton & Company.

Rusk, Jerrold G. 1974. "Comment: The American Electoral Universe: Speculation and Evidence." *American Political Science Review* 68, no. 3 (September), pp. 1028–49.

Russell, Philip. 1977. *Mexico in Transition*. Austin: Colorado River Press.

Sala de Touron, Lucía, and Jorge E. Landineli. 1984. "50 años del movimiento obrero uruguayo." In Pablo González Casanova, ed., *Historia del movimiento obrero en América Latina*. Vol 4. Bogotá: Siglo XXI.

Salamanca, Luis. 1988. "La incorporación de la Confederación de Trabajadores de Venezuela al sistema político venezolano, 1958–1980." Universidad Central de Venezuela.

Saldívar, Américo. 1982. "Una década de crisis y luchas (1969–1978)." In Enrique Semo, ed., *México: Un pueblo en la historia*. Vol. 4. Mexico City: Nueva Imagen.

Sánchez, Gonzalo. 1976. *1929: Los "Bolcheviques del Líbano."* Bogotá: Ediciones El Mohan.

Sánchez, Pedro. 1983. *La presidencia de Illia*. Buenos Aires: Centro Editor de América Latina.

Sánchez Díaz, Sergio Guadalupe. 1980. "Sobre la unidad obrera independiente." In *Memorias del encuentro sobre historia del movimieto obrero*. Vol. 3. Puebla, Mexico: Universidad Autónoma de Puebla.

Sanders, Thomas G. 1975. "Mexico in 1975." *American University Field Staff Reports*, North America Series, vol. 3, no. 4.

Santamaría S., Ricardo, and Gabriel Silva Lujan. 1984. *Proceso político en Colombia: Del Frente Nacional a la apertura democrática*. Bogotá: Fondo Editorial CEREC.

Santistevan, Jorge, with Angel Delgado. 1980. *La huelga en el Perú: Historia y derecho*. Lima: Centro de Estudios de Derecho y Sociedad.

Santos, Wanderley Guilherme dos. 1974. "The Calculus of Conflict: Impasse in Brazilian Politics and the Crisis of 1964." Doctoral diss., Department of Political Science, Stanford University.

———. 1979. *Cidadania e justiça*. Rio de Janeiro: Editora Campus.

———. 1982. "Autoritarismo e Após: Convergências e Divergências entre Brasil e Chile." *Dados* 25, no. 2, pp. 151–63.

Saragoza, Alex. 1988. *The Monterrey Elite and the Mexican State, 1880–1940*. Austin: University of Texas Press.

Sartori, Giovanni. 1970. "Concept Misformation in Comparative Politics." *American Political Science Review* 64, no. 4 (December), pp. 1033–53.

Sartori, Giovanni. 1976. *Parties and Party Systems: A Framework For Analysis*. Cambridge: Cambridge University Press.

———. 1984. "Guidelines for Concept Analysis." In Sartori, ed., *Social Science Concepts: A Systematic Analysis*. Beverly Hills, Calif.: Sage.

Schattschneider, E. E. 1942. *Party Government*. New York: Holt, Rinehart and Winston.

———. 1960. *The Semi-Sovereign People: A Realist's View of American Democracy*. New York: Holt, Rinehart and Winston.

Scheetz, Thomas. 1986. *Peru and the International Monetary Fund*. Pittsburgh: University of Pittsburgh Press.

Schelling, Thomas. 1978. *Micromotives and Macrobehavior*. New York: Norton.

Schmitter, Philippe C. 1971. *Interest Conflict and Political Change in Brazil*. Stanford: Stanford University Press.

———. 1972. "Paths to Political Development in Latin America." In Douglas A. Chalmers, ed., *Changing Latin America: New Interpretations of its Politics and Society*. New York: Academy of Political Science, Columbia University.

———. 1974. "Still the Century of Corporatism?" *Review of Politics* 36, no. 1 (January), pp. 85–131.

———. 1979. "Modes of Interest Intermediation and Models of Societal Change in Western Europe." In Philippe C. Schmitter and Gerhard Lehmbruch, eds., *Trends toward Corporatist Intermediation*. Beverly Hills, Calif.: Sage.

———. 1981. "Interest Intermediation and Regime Governability in Contemporary Western Europe and North America." In Suzanne Berger, ed., *Organizing Interests in Western Europe: Pluralism, Corporatism and the Transformation of Politics*. Cambridge: Cambridge University Press.

Schneider, Ronald M. 1971. *The Political System of Brazil: Emergence of a 'Modernizing' Authoritarian Regime, 1964–1970*. New York: Columbia University Press.

Schneider, Ronald M., et al. 1965. *Brazil Election Factbook*. No. 2, Washington, D.C.: Institute for the Comparative Study of Political Systems.

Schoultz, Lars. 1972. "Urbanization and Changing Voting Patterns: Colombia, 1946–1970." *Political Science Quarterly* 87, no. 1 (March), pp. 22–45.

———. 1977. "The Socioeconomic Determinants of Popular-Authoritarian Electoral Behavior: The Case of Peronism." *American Political Science Review* 71, no. 4 (December), pp. 1423–46.

Schuyler, George Warren. 1976. "Political Change in Venezuela: The Origins of Acción Democrática 1936–1945." Doctoral diss., Department of History, Stanford University.

Schvarzer, Jorge. 1980. "La industria argentina: Un cuarto de siglo." *El país de los argentinos: Primera historia integral*. Buenos Aires: Centro Editor de América Latina.

Scobie, James R. 1969. *Revolution on the Pampas: A Social History of Argentine Wheat*. Austin: University of Texas Press.

Scott, Robert E. 1964. *Mexican Government in Transition*. Urbana: University of Illinois Press.

Scully, Timothy R. Forthcoming. *Rethinking the Center: Cleavages, Critical Junctures, and Party Evolution in Chile*. Stanford: Stanford University Press.

Sebreli, Juan José. 1984. *Los deseos imaginarios del peronismo*. Buenos Aires: Legasa.

Seeley, George P., Jr. 1950. "Venezuelan Labor Legislation." Bachelor's essay, Princeton University.

Selznick, Philip. 1957. *Leadership in Administration: A Sociological Interpretation*. New York: Harper & Row.

Semo, Enrique. 1978. *Historia mexicana: Economía y lucha de clases.* Mexico City: Ediciones Era.

Semo, Ilán. 1982. "El ocaso de los mitos (1958–1968)." In Enrique Semo, ed., *México: Un pueblo en la historia.* Vol. 4. Mexico City: Nueva Imagen.

Senén González, Santiago. 1971. *El sindicalismo después de Perón.* Buenos Aires: Editorial Galerna.

Senén González, Santiago, and Juan Carlos Torre. 1969. *Ejército y sindicatos: Los sesenta días de Lonardi.* Buenos Aires: Editorial Galerna.

Shapiro, Samuel. 1969. "Uruguay: A Bankrupt Welfare State." *Current History* 56, no. 329 (January), pp. 36–51.

———. 1972. "Uruguay's Lost Paradise." *Current History* 62, no. 366 (February), pp. 98–103.

Shapira, Yoram. 1977. "Mexico: The Impact of the 1968 Student Protest on Echeverría's Reformism." *Journal of Inter-American Studies and World Affairs* 19, no. 4 (November), pp. 557–80.

Sharpless, Richard E. 1978. *Gaitán of Colombia: A Political Biography.* Pittsburgh: University of Pittsburgh Press.

Shulgovski, Anatol. 1968. *México en la encrucijada de su historia: La lucha liberadora y antiimperialista del pueblo mexicano en los años treinta y la alternativa de México ante el camino de su desarrollo.* Mexico: Fondo de Cultura Popular.

Sigal, Silvia, and Juan Carlos Torre. 1979. "Una reflexión en torno a los movimientos laborales en América Latina." In Rubén Kaztman and José Luis Reyna, eds., *Fuerza de trabajo y movimientos laborales en América Latina.* Mexico City: Colegio de México.

Silva Michelena, José A., 1971. *The Illusion of Democracy in Dependent Nations.* Cambridge: MIT Press.

Silva Michelena, José A., and Heinz Rudolf Sonntag. 1979. *El proceso electoral de 1978: Su perspectiva histórica estructural.* Caracas: Editorial Ateneo de Caracas.

Silverman, Bertram. 1967. "Labor and Left-Fascism: A Case Study of Peronist Labor Policy." Doctoral diss., Department of Political Science, Columbia University.

Silvert, Kalman H. 1965. *Chile Yesterday and Today.* New York: Holt, Rinehart, and Winston.

Silvert, Kalman, and Gino Germani. 1961. "Politics, Social Structure, and Military Intervention in Latin America." *European Journal of Sociology* 2, no. 1, pp. 62–81.

Simão, Azis. 1981. *Sindicato e Estado.* São Paulo: Editora Atica.

Singer, Morris. 1969. *Growth, Equality, and the Mexican Experience.* Austin: University of Texas Press.

Skidmore, Thomas E. 1967. *Politics in Brazil, 1930–1964.* New York: Oxford University Press.

———. 1975, 1976. "The Historiography of Brazil, 1889–1964." Parts 1 and 2. *Hispanic American Historical Review* 55 and 56, nos. 4 and 1 (November and February), pp. 716–48 and 81–109.

Skidmore, Thomas E. 1977. "The Politics of Economic Stabilization in Postwar Latin America." In James M. Malloy, ed., *Authoritarianism and Corporatism in Latin America.* Pittsburgh: University of Pittsburgh Press.

———. 1979a. "Workers and Soldiers: Urban Labor Movements and Elite Responses in Twentieth-Century Latin America." In Virginia Bernhard, ed., *Elites, Masses, and Modernization in Latin America, 1850–1930.* Austin: University of Texas Press.

———. 1979b. "The Politics of Economic Stabilization in Latin America: Notes toward a Complete Analysis of Selected Cases in Argentina, Brazil, Chile and Mexico." Latin America Program working papers no. 43, Woodrow Wilson International Center for Scholars.

Skidmore, Thomas E., and Peter H. Smith. 1984. *Modern Latin America.* New York: Oxford University Press.

Skocpol, Theda, and Margaret Somers. 1980. "The Uses of Comparative History in Macrosocial Inquiry." *Comparative Studies in Society and History* 22, no. 2 (April), pp. 174–97.

Smith, Donald Lee. 1974. "Pre-PRI: The Mexican Government Party, 1929–1946." Doctoral diss., Department of Philosophy, Texas Christian University.

Smith, Peter H. 1972. "The Social Bases of Peronism." *Hispanic American Historical Review* 52, no. 1 (February), pp. 55–73.

———. 1974a. *Argentina and the Failure of Democracy: Conflict among Political Elites, 1904–1955.* Madison: University of Wisconsin Press.

———. 1974b. "Las elecciones argentinas de 1946 y las inferencias ecológicas." *Desarrollo Económico* 13 (July–September), pp. 385–98.

———. 1978. "The Breakdown of Democracy in Argentina, 1916–1930." In Juan J. Linz and Alfred Stepan, eds., *The Breakdown of Democratic Regimes: Latin America.* Baltimore: Johns Hopkins University Press.

———. 1979. *Labyrinths of Power: Political Recruitment in Twentieth Century Mexico.* Princeton: Princeton University Press.

Smulovitz, Catalina. 1986. "El sistema de partidos en la Argentina: Modelo para armar." *Desarrollo Económico* 26, no. 101, pp. 143–47.

Snow, Peter G. 1965. *Argentine Radicalism: The History and Doctrine of the Radical Civic Union.* Iowa City: University of Iowa Press.

———. 1979. *Political Forces in Argentina.* Revised edition. Boston: Allyn and Bacon.

Soares, Glaucio Ary Dillon. 1973. *Sociedade e política no Brasil (Desenvolvimento, classe e política durante a Segunda República).* São Paulo: Difusão Européia do Livro.

———. 1981. "A formação dos partidos nacionais." In David V. Fleischer, ed., *Os partidos políticos no Brasil.* Brasília: Editora Universidade de Brasília.

Sofer, Eugene F. 1980. "Recent Trends in Latin American Historiography." *Latin American Research Review* 15, no. 1, pp. 167–76.

Solari, Aldo. 1965. *Estudios sobre la sociedad uruguaya.* 2 vols. Montevideo: Editorial Arca.

———. 1967. *El desarrollo social del Uruguay.* Montevideo: Editorial Alfa.

Solari, Aldo, et al. 1966. *Uruguay en cifras.* Montevideo: Universidad de la República, Departamento de Publicaciones.

Solaún, Mauricio. 1980. "Colombian Politics: Historical Characteristics and Problems." In R. Albert Berry, Ronald G. Hellmen, and Mauricio Solaún, eds., *Politics of Compromise: Coalition Government in Colombia.* New Brunswick, N.J.: Transaction Books.

Solberg, Carl M. 1970. *Immigration and Nationalism: Argentina and Chile, 1890–1914.* Austin: University of Texas Press.

———. 1979. *Oil and Nationalism in Argentina.* Stanford: Stanford University Press.

Souza, Maria do Carmo Carvalho Campello de. 1976. *Estado e partidos políticos no Brasil, 1930–1964*. São Paulo: Alfa-Omega.

Spalding, Hobart A. 1965. "Aspects of Change in Argentina, 1890–1914." Doctoral diss., Department of History, University of California, Berkeley.

————. 1970. *La clase trabajadora argentina: Documentos para su historia, 1890–1912*. Buenos Aires: Editorial Galerna.

————. 1972. "The Parameters of Labor in Hispanic America." *Science and Society* 36, no. 2 (Summer), pp. 202–16.

————. 1977. *Organized Labor in Latin America: Historical Case Studies of Workers in Dependent Societies*. New York: Harper & Row.

Spence, Jack. 1978. "Class Mobilization and Conflict in Allende's Chile: A Review Essay." *Politics and Society* 8, no. 2, pp. 131–64.

Stabb, Martin S. 1967. *In Quest of Identity: Patterns in the Spanish American Essay of Ideas, 1890–1960*. Chapel Hill: University of North Carolina Press.

Stallings, Barbara. 1978. *Class Conflict and Economic Development in Chile, 1958–1973*. Stanford: Stanford University Press.

Stein, Steven. 1980. *Populism and the Politics of Social Control: The Emergence of the Masses in Peru*. Madison: University of Wisconsin Press.

Stepan, Alfred. 1971. *The Military in Politics: Changing Patterns in Brazil*. Princeton: Princeton University Press

————. 1978a. "Political Leadership and Regime Breakdown: Brazil." In Juan J. Linz and Alfred Stepan, eds., *The Breakdown of Democratic Regimes*. Baltimore: Johns Hopkins University Press.

————. 1978b. *The State and Society: Peru in Comparative Perspective*. Princeton: Princeton University Press.

————. 1988. *Rethinking Military Politics: Brazil and the Southern Cone*. Princeton: Princeton University Press.

Stepan, Alfred, ed. 1973. *Authoritarian Brazil: Origins, Policies, and Future*. New Haven: Yale University Press.

Stephens, Evelyne H. 1980. *The Politics of Workers' Participation: The Peruvian Approach in Comparative Perspective*. New York: Academic Press.

Stephens, John D. 1986. "Democratic Transition and Breakdown in Europe, 1870–1939: A Test of the Moore Thesis." Paper presented at the annual meeting of the American Sociological Association.

Stevens, Evelyn P. 1974. *Protest and Response in Mexico*. Cambridge: MIT Press.

————. 1975. "Protest Movements in an Authoritarian Regime: The Mexican Case." *Comparative Politics* 7, no. 3 (April), pp. 361–82.

————. 1977. "Mexico's PRI: The Institutionalization of Corporatism?" In James M. Malloy, ed., *Authoritarianism and Corporatism in Latin America*. Pittsburgh: University of Pittsburgh Press.

Stevenson, John R. 1942. *The Chilean Popular Front*. Westport, Conn.: Greenwood Press.

Stinchcombe, Arthur L. 1968. *Constructing Social Theories*. New York: Harcourt, Brace and World.

Story, Dale. 1978. "Industrialization and Political Change: The Political Role of Industrial Entrepreneurs in Five Latin American Countries." Doctoral diss., Department of Political Science, Indiana University.

Sulmont, Denis. 1975. *El movimiento obrero en el Perú, 1900–1956*. Lima: Pontificia Universidad Católica del Perú, Fondo Editorial.

————. 1977. *Historia del movimiento obrero en el Perú (de 1890 a 1977)*. Lima: Editorial Tarea.

Sulmont, Denis. 1985. *El movimiento obrero peruano (1890–1980)*. 5th ed. Lima: Tarea.

Szulc, Tad. 1959. *Twilight of the Tyrants*. New York: Henry Holt and Company.

Talbot Campos, Judith, and John F. McCamant. 1971. "Colombia política 1971." In *Boletín Mensual de Estadística*. Bogotá: Departamento Administrativo Nacional de Estadística, no. 242 (September).

———. 1972. *Cleavage Shift in Colombia: Analysis of the 1970 Elections*. Beverly Hills, Calif.: Sage.

Tamarin, David. 1977. "The Argentine Labor Movement in an Age of Transition, 1930–1945." Doctoral diss., Department of History, University of Washington.

———. 1985. *The Argentine Labor Movement, 1930–1945: A Study in the Origins of Peronism*. Albuquerque: University of New Mexico Press.

Tannenbaum, Frank. 1966. *Peace by Revolution: Mexico after 1910*. New York: Columbia University Press.

Taylor, Philip B., Jr. 1952. "The Uruguayan Coup d'Etat of 1933." *Hispanic American Historical Review* 32, no. 3 (August), pp. 301–20.

———. 1954. "Interparty Co-operation and Uruguay's 1952 Constitution." *Western Political Quarterly* 7 (September), pp. 391–400.

———. 1960a. *Government and Politics of Uruguay*. New Orleans: Tulane University Press.

———. 1960b. "The Mexican Elections of 1958: Affirmation of Authoritarianism?" *Western Political Quarterly* 13, no. 4 (December), pp. 722–44.

———. 1966. "Democracy for Venezuela?" *Current History* 51, no. 303 (November), pp. 284–90, 310.

———. 1967. "Progress in Venezuela." *Current History* 53, no. 315 (November), pp. 270–74, 308.

Telles, Jover. 1981. *O movimento sindical no Brasil*. São Paulo: Livraria Editora Ciências Humanas.

Tenjo, Jaime. 1975. "Aspectos cuantitativos del movimiento sindical colombiano." *Cuadernos Colombianos* 2, no. 5, pp. 1–40.

Therborn, Goran. 1979. "The Travail of Latin American Democracy." *New Left Review*, no. 113–14 (January–April), pp. 71–109.

Thompson, John K. 1979. *Inflation, Financial Markets, and Economic Development: The Experience of Mexico*. Greenwich, Conn.: JAI Press.

Thompson, Mark Elliot. 1966. "The Development of Unionism among Mexican Electrical Workers." Doctoral diss., New York State School of Industrial and Labor Relations, Cornell University.

Thompson, Mark, and Ian Roxborough. 1982. "Union Elections and Democracy in Mexico: A Comparative Perspective." *British Journal of Industrial Relations* 20, no. 2 (July), pp. 201–17.

Thorp, Rosemary, and Geoffrey Bertram. 1974. "Foreign Investment and Industrial Development: A Case Study of Peru 1890–1940." Paper presented at the Symposium on Foreign Investment and External Finance in Latin America, Cambridge, England.

———. 1978. *Peru, 1890–1977: Growth and Policy in an Open Economy*. New York: Columbia University Press.

Thoumi, Francisco E. 1980. "Industrial Development Policies during the National Front Years." In R. Albert Berry, Ronald G. Hellman, and Mauricio Solaún, eds., *Politics of Compromise: Coalition Government in Colombia*. New Brunswick, N.J.: Transaction Books.

Tirado, Thomas Charles. 1977. "Alfonso López Pumarejo: His Contributions to Reconciliation in Colombian Politics." Doctoral diss., Department of History, Temple University.

Tirado Mejía, Alvaro. 1981. *Aspectos políticos del primer gobierno de Alfonso López Pumarejo: 1934–1938*. Bogotá: Procultura.

Toledo, Caio Navarro de. 1982. *O governo Goulart e o golpe de 64*. São Paulo: Editora Brasiliense.

Tornquist, Ernesto & Co. 1919. *Economic Development of the Argentine Republic in the Last Fifty Years*. Buenos Aires: Ernesto Tornquist & Co.

Torre, Juan Carlos. 1976. "La CGT y el 17 de Octubre de 1945." *Todo es Historia*, no. 107 (March), pp. 71–105.

———. 1980a. "La cuestión del poder sindical y el orden político en la Argentina." *Criterio* 53, no. 1843 (September 11), pp. 528–33.

———. 1980b. "Sindicatos y trabajadores en la Argentina: 1955–1976." El país de los argentinos: Primera historia integral. Centro Editor de América Latina.

———. 1989. "Interpretando (una vez más) los orígenes del peronismo." *Desarrollo Económico* 28, no. 112 (January–March), pp. 526–48.

Torres, Cristina. 1985. "Las fuerzas armadas uruguayas en la transición hacia la democracia." In Charles Gillespie et al., eds., *Uruguay y la democracia*. Vol. 2. Montevideo: Ediciones de la Banda Oriental.

Torres Giraldo, Ignacio. 1973a. *Los inconformes: Historia de la rebeldía de las masas en Colombia*. Vol. 2. Bogotá: Editorial Margen Izquierdo.

———. 1973b. *Los inconformes: Historia de la rebeldía de las masas en Colombia*. Vol. 4. Bogotá: Editorial Margen Izquierdo.

———. 1973c. *La cuestión sindical en Colombia*. Bogotá: Letras del Pueblo.

Trejo Delarbre, Raúl. 1976. "The Mexican Labor Movement: 1917–1975." *Latin American Perspectives* 3, no. 1 (Winter), pp. 133–53.

———. 1980a. "El movimiento obrero: Situación y perspectivas." In Pablo González Casanova and Enrique Florescano, eds., *México, hoy*. Mexico City: Siglo XXI.

———. 1980b. "Notas sobre la insurgencia obrera y la burocracia sindical." In *Memorias del encuentro sobre historia del movimiento obrero*. Vol. 3. Puebla, Mexico: Universidad Autónoma de Puebla.

Trotsky, Leon. 1968. *Marxism and the Trade Unions*. London: Socialist Labour League.

Tugwell, Franklin. 1975. *The Politics of Oil in Venezuela*. Stanford: Stanford University Press.

Turiansky, Wladimir. 1973. *El movimiento obrero uruguayo*. Montevideo: Ediciones Pueblos Unidos.

Tyler, William G. 1981. *The Brazilian Industrial Economy*. Lexington, Mass.: Lexington Books.

Ures, Jorge. 1972. "La relacíon clase-voto en Montevideo en las elecciones del 28 de noviembre de 1971." *Revista Uruguaya de Ciencias Sociales* 1, no. 1 (April–June), pp. 7–14.

Urrutia, Miguel. 1969a. *The Development of the Colombian Labor Movement*. New Haven: Yale University Press.

———. 1969b. *Historia del sindicalismo en Colombia*. Bogotá: Ediciones Universidad de Los Andes.

Urzua Valenzuela, Germán. 1979. *Diccionario político-institucional de Chile*. Santiago: Editorial Chile.

Valderrama, Mariano. 1980. "La evolución ideológica del APRA: 1924–1962." In Valderrama et al., eds., *El APRA. Un camino de esperanzas y frustraciones*. Lima: Ediciones El Gallo Rojo.

Valenzuela, Arturo. 1978. *The Breakdown of Democratic Regimes: Chile*. Baltimore: Johns Hopkins University Press.

————. 1985. "Origins and Characteristics of the Chilean Party System: A Proposal for a Parliamentary Form of Government." Working paper, Latin American Program, Wilson Center, Washington, D.C.

Valenzuela, J. Samuel. 1976. "The Chilean Labor Movement: The Institutionalization of Conflict." In Arturo Valenzuela and J. Samuel Valenzuela, eds., *Chile: Politics and Society*. New Brunswick, N.J.: Transaction Books.

————. 1979. "Labor Movement Formation and Politics: The Chilean and French Cases in Comparative Perspective, 1850–1950." Doctoral diss., Department of Sociology, Columbia University.

————. 1983. "Movimientos obreros y sistemas políticos: Un análisis conceptual y tipológico." *Desarrollo Económico* 23, no. 91 (October–December), pp. 339–68.

Vanger, Milton. 1963. *José Batlle y Ordóñez of Uruguay: The Creator of His Times, 1902–1907*. Cambridge: Harvard University Press.

————. 1980. *The Model Country: José Batlle y Ordóñez of Uruguay*. Waltham, Mass.: Brandeis University Press.

Vasconcellos, Amilcar. 1973. *Febrero amargo*. La Paz, Uruguay: Vanguardia.

Verba. Sidney. 1971. "Sequences and Development." In Leonard Binder et al., eds., *Crises and Sequences in Political Development*. Princeton: Princeton University Press.

Vernon Raymond. 1964. *Public Policy and Private Enterprise in Mexico*. Cambridge: Harvard University Press.

————. 1965. *The Dilemma of Mexico's Development: The Roles of the Private and Public Sectors*. Cambridge: Harvard University Press.

Vianna, Luiz J. Werneck. 1976. *Liberalismo e sindicato no Brasil*. Rio de Janeiro: Editoria Paz e Terra.

Victor, Mario. 1965. *Cinco anos que abalaram o Brasil (de Jânio Quadros ao Marechal Castelo Branco)*. Rio de Janeiro: Editora Civilização Brasileira.

Villalobos R., Sergio, et al. 1976. *Historia de Chile*. Vol 4. Santiago: Editorial Universitaria.

Villanueva, Javier. 1975. "Economic Development." In Mark Falcoff and Ronald Dolkart, eds., *Prologue to Perón: Argentina in Depression and War, 1930–1943*. Berkeley and Los Angeles: University of California Press.

Villanueva, Víctor. 1962. *El militarismo en el Perú*. Lima: Empresa Gráfica T. Scheuch.

————. 1977. "The Petty-Bourgeois Ideology of the Peruvian Aprista Party." *Latin American Perspectives* 4, no. 3 (Summer), pp. 57–76.

Villarreal, René. 1977. "The Policy of Import-Substituting Industrialization, 1929–1975." In José Luis Reyna and Richard S. Weinert, eds., *Authoritarianism in Mexico*. Philadelphia: Institute for the Study of Human Issues.

Vitale, Luis. 1962. *Historia del movimiento obrero*. Santiago: Editorial Por.

Waisman, Carlos H. 1982. *Modernization and the Working Class: The Politics of Legitimacy*. Austin: University of Texas Press.

———. 1987. *Reversal of Development in Argentina: Postwar Counterrevolutionary Policies and Their Structural Consequences*. Princeton: Princeton University Press.

Walker, David. 1981. "Porfirian Labor Politics: Working Class Organizations in Mexico City and Porfirio Díaz, 1876–1902." *Americas* (January), pp. 257–89.

Walsh, Rodolfo. 1985. *¿Quién mató a Rosendo?* Buenos Aires: Ediciones de la Flor.

Walter, Richard J. 1968. *Student Politics in Argentina: The University Reform and its Effects, 1918–1964*. New York: Basic Books.

———. 1977. *The Socialist Party of Argentina, 1890–1930*. Latin American Monographs, no. 42. Austin: Institute of Latin American Studies, University of Texas, Austin.

Ward, Michael D. 1978. *The Political Economy of Distribution: Equality vs. Inequality*. New York: Elsevier.

Warman, Arturo. 1980. "El problema del campo." In Pablo González Casanova and Enrique Florescano, eds., *México, hoy*. Mexico City: Siglo XXI.

Washington Office on Latin America. 1981. "Uruguay: The Plebiscite and Beyond." Washington Office on Latin America, Occasional paper no. 1, Washington, D.C., March.

Watkins, Holland Dempsey. 1968. "Plutarco Elías Calles: El Jefe Máximo of Mexico." Doctoral diss., Texas Technological College.

Weaver, Frederick Stirton. 1980. *Class, State, and Industrial Structure: The Historical Process of South American Industrial Growth*. Westport, Conn.: Greenwood Press.

Webb, Richard C. 1975. "Wage Policy and Income Distribution in Developing Countries." Paper prepared for the Princeton University-Brookings Institution Project on Income Distribution in Less Developed Countries.

Weber, Max. 1968. *Economy and Society*. Berkeley and Los Angeles: University of California Press.

Weffort, Francisco C. 1970. "State and Mass in Brazil." In Irving Louis Horowitz, ed., *Masses in Latin America*. New York: Oxford University Press.

———. 1980. *O populismo na política brasileira*. Rio de Janeiro: Editora Paz e Terra.

Weil, Felix. 1944. *Argentine Riddle*. New York: John Day Co.

Weinstein, Martin. 1975. *Uruguay: The Politics of Failure*. Westport, Conn.: Greenwood Press.

Wellhofer, E. Spencer. 1974. "The Mobilization of the Periphery: Perón's 1946 Triumph." *Comparative Political Studies* 7, no. 2 (July), pp. 239–51.

———. 1977. "Peronism in Argentina: The Social Base of the First Regime, 1946–1955." *Journal of Developing Areas* 11, no. 3 (April), pp. 335–56.

Werlich, David. 1978. *Peru: A Short History*. Carbondale: Southern Illinois University Press.

Wesson, Robert, and David V. Fleischer. 1983. *Brazil in Transition*. New York: Praeger.

Whitaker, Arthur P. 1964a. *Argentina*. Englewood Cliffs, N.J.: Prentice-Hall.

———. 1964b. "Argentina: A Fragmented Society." *Current History* 46, no. 269 (January), pp. 15–18, 51–52.

———. 1965. "Argentina: Struggle for Recovery." *Current History* 48, no. 281 (January), pp. 16–20, 51–52.

Whitaker, Arthur P. 1976. *The United States and the Southern Cone: Argentina, Chile, and Uruguay*. Cambridge: Harvard University Press.

Whitehead, Laurence. 1980. "Mexico from Bust to Boom: A Political Evaluation of the 1976–1979 Stabilization Programme." *World Development* 8, no. 11 (November), pp. 843–64.

Wiarda, Howard J. 1969. "The Brazilian Catholic Labor Movement: The Dilemmas of National Development." Labor Relations and Research Center, University of Massachusetts.

———. 1976. "The Corporative Origins of the Iberian and Latin American Labor Relations Systems." Labor Relations and Research Center Paper, University of Massachusetts.

———. 1978. "Corporative Origins of the Iberian and Latin American Labor Relations Systems." *Studies in Comparative International Development* 13, no. 1 (Spring), pp. 3–37.

Wilde, Alexander W. 1978. "Conversations among Gentlemen: Oligarchical Democracy in Colombia." In Juan J. Linz and Alfred Stepan, eds., *The Breakdown of Democratic Regimes: Latin America*. Baltimore: Johns Hopkins University Press.

Wilkie, James W. 1970. *The Mexican Revolution*. Berkeley and Los Angeles: University of California Press.

———. 1974. "Statistics and National Policy." In *Statistical Abstract of Latin America*. Supplement 3. Los Angeles: Latin American Center, University of California.

Wilkie, James W., and Stephen Haber. 1983. *Statistical Abstract of Latin America*. Vol. 22. Los Angeles: Latin American Center, University of California.

Wilson, James Q. 1973. *Political Organizations*. New York: Basic Books.

Winn, Peter. 1976. "British Informal Empire in Uruguay in the Nineteenth Century." *Past and Present*, no. 73 (November), pp. 100–26.

———. 1986. *Weavers of Revolution: The Yarur Workers and Chile's Road to Socialism*. New York: Oxford University Press.

Wirth, John D. 1964. "Tenentismo in the Brazilian Revolution of 1930." *Hispanic American Historical Review* 44, no. 2 (May), pp. 161–79.

———. 1970. *The Politics of Brazilian Development, 1930–1954*. Stanford: Stanford University Press.

———. 1977. *Minas Gerais in the Brazilian Federation, 1889–1937*. Stanford: Stanford University Press.

Woldemberg M., José. 1980. "Notas sobre la burocracia sindical en México." *A: Revista de Ciencias Sociales y Humanidades* 1, no. 1, Universidad Autónoma Metropolitana de Azcapotzalco (September–December), pp. 16–28.

Wolfskill, George, and Douglas W. Richmond, eds. 1979. *Essays on the Mexican Revolution: Revisionist Views of the Leaders*. Austin: University of Texas Press.

Womack, John, Jr. 1978. "The Mexican Economy during the Revolution, 1910–1920: Historiography and Analysis." *Marxist Perspectives* 1, no. 4 (Winter), pp. 80–123.

Wynia, Gary W. 1978. *Argentina in the Postwar Era: Politics and Economic Policy Making in a Divided Society*. Albuquerque: University of New Mexico Press.

———. 1984. *The Politics of Latin American Development*. 2d ed. Cambridge: Cambridge University Press.

Yepes, José Antonio Gil. 1981. *The Challenge of Venezuelan Democracy*. New Brunswick, N.J.: Transaction Books.

Yepes del Castillo, Ernesto. 1980. "El desarrollo peruano en las primeras décadas del siglo XX." In L. G. Lumbreras et al., eds., *Nueva historia general del Perú*. Lima: Mosca Azul Editores.

Yoast, Richard A. 1975. "The Development of Argentine Anarchism: A Socio-Ideological Analysis." Doctoral diss., Department of Political Science, University of Wisconsin.

Zamosc, Leon. 1986. *The Agrarian Question and the Peasant Movement in Colombia: Struggles of the National Peasant Association 1967–1981*. Cambridge: Cambridge University Press.

Zapata, Francisco. 1979a. "Las organizaciones sindicales." In Rubén Kaztman and José Luis Reyna, eds., *Fuerza de trabajo y movimientos laborales en América Latina*. Mexico City: Colegio de México.

———. 1979b. "Las relaciones entre la Junta Militar y los trabajadores chilenos: 1973–1978." *Foro Internacional* 20, no. 2 (October–December), pp. 191–219.

———. 1981. "Mexico." In Albert A. Blum, ed., *International Handbook of Industrial Relations: Contemporary Developments and Research*. Westport, Conn.: Greenwood Press.

Zermeño, Sergio. 1982. "De Echeverría a de la Madrid: Las clases altas y el estado mexicano en la batalla por la hegemonía." Working paper No. 118, Latin American Program, the Wilson Center, Washington, D.C.

Zubillaga, Carlos. 1983. "El batllismo: Una experiencia populista." *Publicación del Centro Latinoamericano de Economía Humana*, no. 27 (July–September), pp. 27–57.

———. 1985a. "Los desafíos de la historia sindical: Algunos problemas teóricos y metodológicos." *Cuadernos* 33, no. 1, pp. 59–71. Montevideo: CLAEH.

———. 1985b. "Los partidos políticos ante la crisis, 1958–1983." In Gerardo Caetano, José Pedro Rilla, Pablo Mieres, and Carlos Zubillaga, eds., *De la tradición a la crisis: Pasado y presente de nuestro sistema de partidos*. Montevideo: CLAEH.

Zschock, Dieter K. 1977. "Inequality in Colombia." *Current History* 72, no. 424 (February), pp. 68–86.

Index of Countries by Analytic Period ──────────

ARGENTINA

BRAZIL

CHILE

COLUMBIA

MEXICO

PERU

URUGUAY

VENEZUELA

General Index _____

874

SHAPING THE POLITICAL ARENA

PSU (Partido Socialista Uruguayo), 277–78, 444–48, 647, 650–52
PT (Partido dos Trabalhadores) (Brazil), 756–757
PTB (Partido Trabalhista Brasileiro) (Brazil), 355, 360–61, 363–67, 369–74, 378, 381–82, 385–89, 391–92, 401–2, 514–16, 523–27, 532, 536, 540, 546–55, 568
PUA (Pacto de Unidade e Agao) (Brazil), 551
PUI (Pacto de Unidade Intersindical) (Brazil), 381, 551

Quadros, Jânio da Silva, 388, 509, 515, 524, 528, 530–32, 536, 539–40, 542–43, 548
Queremista movement (Brazil), 369
Quijada, Ramón, 435

Radical Party (Argentina), 134–35, 137–38, 140–41, 146–49, 154, 340, 344, 488–90, 722. *See also* UCRP and UCRI
Radical Party (Chile), 362, 364, 377–80, 383–85, 391, 519–20, 522, 528–30, 532, 543–45, 558
Radical populism: defined, 16, 165; in Mexican incorporation period, 196–250; in Venezuelan incorporation period, 196–201, 251–70. *See also* Labor populism
Ramirez, Pedro R., 332
Recabarren, Luis Emilio, 74, 112, 180, 193
Red Battalions (Mexico), 123, 205, 211–13
Red International of Labor Unions, 180
Renewal Current of Brazilian Marxist Movement, 549
Renovadores (Brazil), 387–88
Republican Party (Brazil), 108
Rerum Novarum, 101–2, 189–90
Restrepo, Carlos E., 290
Revolución en Marcha (Revolution on the March), 289, 291–92, 464
Revolutionary Action Group (Venezuela), 638
"Revolutionary Family" (Mexico), 575
Revolutionary Government Council (Venezuela), 256
Revolutionary myth, Mexican political system and, 580–81
Revolution of 1930 (Brazil), 102, 173–75
Reyes, Cipriano, 345
Ríos Morales, Juan Antonio, 378, 385, 389–90
Roca, Julio Argentino, 131, 135
Rodríguez, Abelardo, 225, 409
Rodríguez, Renán, 648
Rojas, María Eugenia, 460–61, 463

Rojas Pinilla, Gustavo, 359, 438–39, 459–61, 471, 486, 668–73, 686
Roman Catholic Church: in Argentina, 334, 347–48; in Brazil, 567–68; in Chile, 189–90, 569; in Colombia, 86, 301–3, 303n.55, 307, 311, 457–60; in Mexico, 114, 222–23, 247; in Peru, 321; reform period and, 101, 134; in Uruguay, 287; in Venezuela, 426–29
Romualdi, Serafino, 261–62, 264–65
Roosevelt, Franklin D., 321
Ross, Gustavo, 368
Ruiz Cortines, Adolfo, 575–76, 598
Rural Federation (Uruguay), 286–88, 441, 443
Rural sector. *See* Agrarian reform; Peasantry
Rural-urban migration, 69–70
Rural Workers Law (Brazil), 567–68
Russian Revolution, 19–20, 62, 71, 90, 101–2, 146

Sabroso Montoya, Arturo, 318, 322–23, 470, 480–81
Sáenz, Aarón, 210
Sáenz Peña, Roque, 135
Salinas de Gortari, Carlos, 760
Sánchez Cerro, Luis M., 149–52
San Marcos University (Peru), 137
Santa Anna (Antonio López), 114
Santos, Eduardo, 289, 293–94, 295n.45, 298, 300–305
Santos Salas, José, 182
São Paulo revolt (1932) (Brazil), 170
Saravia, Aparicio, 273–74, 284
Sarney, José, 756
Segmented labor market, 64n.5
"Semana Trágica" (Argentina), 147–48
Semicompetitive regime, 789
SENDAS (Secretariado Nacional de Asistencia Social) (Colombia), 460
Sendero Luminoso (Peru), 765
Seoane, Manuel, 700–701, 724
SINAMOS (Sistema Nacional de Apoyo a la Mobilización Social) (Peru), 764
Sinarquismo (Mexico), 245, 247, 411, 418, 595
Sino-Soviet split, 710
"62 Organizations" (Argentina), 491–92, 494–96, 725–28, 730
SNA (Sociedad Nacional de Agricultura) (Chile), 368, 383–84, 535
SNTAS (Sindicato Nacional de Trabajadores de Aviación y Similares) (Mexico), 603